The Consumer Credit and Sales
Legal Practice Series

FEDERAL DECEPTION LAW

FTC and CFPB Rules, RICO, False Claims Act, Debt Relief, TCPA, Telemarketing, and Parallel State Statutes

Second Edition

www.nclc.org/library

See *page vii* for details.

Jonathan Sheldon
Carolyn L. Carter

Contributing Authors: Andrew Pizor, Elizabeth De Armond, Jeffrey Thorn

National Consumer Law Center®

7 Winthrop Square, 4th Floor   Boston, MA 02110   www.nclc.org/library

About NCLC®

The National Consumer Law Center®, a nonprofit corporation founded in 1969, assists consumers, advocates, and public policy makers nationwide who use the powerful and complex tools of consumer law to ensure justice and fair treatment for all, particularly those whose poverty renders them powerless to demand accountability from the economic marketplace. For more information, go to www.nclc.org.

Ordering NCLC Publications

Order online at www.nclc.org/library, or contact Publications Department, National Consumer Law Center, 7 Winthrop Square, 4th Floor, Boston, MA 02110, (617) 542-9595, FAX: (617) 542-8028, e-mail: publications@nclc.org.

Training, Conferences, and Webinars

NCLC participates in numerous national, regional, and local consumer law trainings. Its annual fall conference is a forum for consumer rights attorneys from legal services programs, private practice, government, and nonprofit organizations to share insights into common problems and explore novel and tested approaches that promote consumer justice in the marketplace. Contact NCLC for more information or see our website. NCLC offers free webinars and views of past webinars. Go to www.nclc.org/webinars.html for more information.

Case Consulting

Case analysis, consulting and co-counseling for lawyers representing vulnerable consumers are among NCLC's important activities. Administration on Aging funds allow us to provide free consulting to legal services advocates representing elderly consumers on many types of cases. Massachusetts Legal Assistance Corporation funds permit case assistance to advocates representing low-income Massachusetts consumers. Other funding may allow NCLC to provide very brief consultations to other advocates without charge. See our website for more information at www.nclc.org.

Charitable Donations and Cy Pres Awards

NCLC's work depends in part on the support of private donors. Tax-deductible donations should be made payable to National Consumer Law Center, Inc. For more information, contact Gerald Tuckman of NCLC's Development Office at (617) 542-8010 or gtuckman@nclc.org. NCLC has also received generous court-approved cy pres awards arising from consumer class actions to advance the interests of class members. For more information, contact Rich Dubois (rdubois@nclc.org) or Gerald Tuckman (gtuckman@nclc.org) at (617) 542-8010.

Comments and Corrections

Write to the above address to the attention of the Editorial Department or e-mail consumerlaw@nclc.org.

About This Volume

This is the Second Edition of *Federal Deception Law*. Discard prior editions and supplements.

Cite This Volume As

National Consumer Law Center, Federal Deception Law (2d ed. 2016), *updated at* www.nclc.org/library.

Attention

This publication is designed to provide authoritative information concerning the subject matter covered. Always use the most current edition, check online for updates, and use other sources for more recent developments or for special rules for individual jurisdictions. This publication cannot substitute for the independent judgment and skills of an attorney or other professional. Non-attorneys are cautioned against using these materials to conduct a lawsuit without advice from an attorney and are cautioned against engaging in the unauthorized practice of law.

ISBN: 978-1-60248-164-0 (this volume)
ISBN: 978-0-943116-10-5 (Series)

Library of Congress Control Number: 2015959824

About the Authors

Jonathan Sheldon, co-author, is an NCLC staff attorney writing on deceptive practices, leasing, automobile issues, warranty law, and other consumer law topics since 1976. From 1973 to 1976 he was a staff attorney with the Bureau of Consumer Protection, Federal Trade Commission. His publications include *Unfair and Deceptive Acts and Practices*, *Consumer Warranty Law*, *Automobile Fraud*, *Consumer Credit Regulation*, and *Collection Actions*. He is a contributing author to a number of other NCLC publications.

Carolyn L. Carter, co-author, is NCLC's director of advocacy and was formerly co-director of Legal Services, Inc., in Gettysburg, Pennsylvania and director of the Law Reform Office of the Cleveland Legal Aid Society. She is the editor of *Pennsylvania Consumer Law*, editor of the first edition of *Ohio Consumer Law*, co-author of NCLC's *Automobile Fraud*, *Collection Actions*, *Consumer Credit Regulation*, *Mortgage Lending*, *Repossessions*, *Unfair and Deceptive Acts and Practices*, and contributing author to other NCLC publications. She was the 1992 recipient of the Vern Countryman Consumer Law Award.

Andrew G. Pizor, contributing author, is a staff attorney in NCLC's Washington office and a co-author of *Consumer Credit Regulation* and *Mortgage Lending* and a contributing author to *Truth in Lending* and to *Foreclosures and Mortgage Servicing*. He was formerly an attorney at the Connecticut Fair Housing Center, Consumer Law Group L.L.C., and Legal Services Corp. of Delaware, where he worked on housing and consumer protection issues, focusing on defending foreclosures and fighting predatory lending.

Elizabeth De Armond, contributing author, is on the faculty of Chicago-Kent College of Law, where she directs the legal research and writing program and focuses on consumer law and privacy issues. She is a contributing author *Fair Credit Reporting* and *Consumer Warranty Law*. Previously, she was in private practice in Texas and a clerk for the Hon. Cornelia Kennedy of the United States Court of Appeals for the Sixth Circuit. She is a member of the Illinois, Massachusetts, and Texas bars.

Jeffrey Thorn, contributing author, is a private attorney in Boston, Massachusetts whose practice focuses on consumer protection and class action litigation. He is an author or co-author for multiple Massachusetts continuing legal education chapters and also teaches legal writing at the Boston University School of Law.

Acknowledgments

We especially want to thank Daniel A. Edelman of the Chicago firm of Edelman, Combs, Latturner & Goodwin, L.L.C. for his extensive contributions concerning the Telephone Consumer Protection Act and to Thomas Grande of the Grande Law Office in Honolulu for writing the Federal False Claims Act chapter for the First Edition. Thanks also to Robert M. Bramson and Daniel E. Birkhaeuser of the California firm of Bramson, Plutzik, Mahler, and Birkhaeuser for writing the anti-trust section; Stephen H. Ring, an attorney in Gaithersburg, Maryland, for his contributions to the section on spam email; Emily Green Caplan for the state false claims act appendix, and Mary Kingsley for extensive research for a number of the chapters and appendices. Kurt Terwilliger, Allen Agnitti, Michael Denham, Jasmine Gomez, and Lucy Colby also made important substantive contributions.

We also want to thank Dorothy Tan for editorial supervision; Janice Binder and Emilio Englade for editorial assistance; Shannon Halbrook for organizing the companion materials; Allen Agnitti for assistance with cite checking; Mary McLean for indexing; Scribe for typesetting and composition services; and iFactory and Codearium for designing and implementing the website for the online version of this treatise.

What Your Library Should Contain

Subscriptions are available for individual titles or for the complete 20-title set.

NCLC no longer releases print supplements. Subscription to a print edition includes <u>online access</u> to the complete text, fully integrating all prior supplements and new updates, plus offers additional pleadings, primary sources and practice tools.

> **Online subscriptions without a print edition are available.** Go to www.nclc.org/library for more information on subscription options and about each title—including a title's table of contents, about the authors, and index. Go to page vii, *infra*, for login instructions and more about the online resource.

The Consumer Credit and Sales Legal Practice Series

DEBTOR RIGHTS

Consumer Bankruptcy Law and Practice (10th ed. 2012), updated online (two volumes): the definitive personal bankruptcy manual, from the initial interview to final discharge, including consumer rights when a company files for bankruptcy.

Fair Debt Collection (8th ed. 2014), updated online (two volumes): the basic reference covering the Fair Debt Collection Practices Act and common law, state statutory, and other federal debt collection protections.

Foreclosures and Mortgage Servicing (5th ed. 2014), updated online: examines RESPA, CFPB rules, and other requirements placed on mortgage loan servicers, details loan modification and mediation programs, and covers every aspect of foreclosure defense.

Repossessions (8th ed. 2013), updated online: a unique guide to seizures of motor vehicles, manufactured homes, and household goods, including statutory liens, leases and rent-to-own.

Student Loan Law (5th ed. 2015), updated online: loan deferments, discharges, consolidations and repayment plans; tax intercepts, wage garnishment, and offset of Social Security benefits; private loans, and school abuses.

Access to Utility Service (5th ed. 2011), updated online: regulated and unregulated utilities, telecommunications, terminations, billing errors, low-income payment plans, subsidized housing, LIHEAP, and weatherization.

CREDIT AND BANKING

Truth in Lending (9th ed. 2015), updated online (two volumes): <u>all</u> aspects of TILA, the Consumer Leasing Act, the Fair Credit Billing Act, the Home Ownership and Equity Protection Act (HOEPA), and the Credit CARD Act.

Fair Credit Reporting (8th ed. 2013), updated online: cleaning up blemished credit records, suing reporting agencies and creditors for inaccurate reports, identity theft, credit scoring, privacy issues, and the Credit Repair Organizations Act.

Mortgage Lending (2d ed. 2014), updated online: regulation (and federal preemption) of the origination and the terms of mortgage loans, including ability to pay, steering, appraisals, loan brokers, insurance, adjustable rates, reverse mortgages, and claims against failed banks.

Consumer Credit Regulation (2d ed. 2015), updated online: federal and state regulation (and federal preemption) concerning credit cards, payday loans, automobile finance, title pawns, rent-to-own, installment loans, and other non-mortgage lending.

Consumer Banking and Payments Law (5th ed. 2013), updated online: checks and telechecks; EFT; money orders and remittances; debit, payroll, and other prepaid cards; E-Sign; and electronic transfers of benefit payments.

Credit Discrimination (6th ed. 2013), updated online: the Equal Credit Opportunity Act, Fair Housing Act, Civil Rights Acts, and state credit discrimination statutes.

National Consumer Law Center • **(617) 542-9595** • **FAX (617) 542-8028** • **publications@nclc.org**
Order online at www.nclc.org/library

CONSUMER LITIGATION

Collection Actions (3d ed. 2014), updated online: defenses to collection lawsuits for credit card, medical, and other consumer debt, setting aside default judgments, and limitations on a collector's post-judgment remedies.

Consumer Arbitration Agreements (7th ed. 2015), updated online: numerous ways to challenge the enforceability of an arbitration requirement.

Consumer Class Actions (8th ed. 2013), updated online: step-by-step approach to all aspects of class litigation, with numerous sample class pleadings, and state-by-state analysis of class action rules.

Consumer Law Pleadings (online only): over 2000 notable pleadings from all types of consumer cases, ready to paste into a word processor.

DECEPTION AND WARRANTIES

Unfair and Deceptive Acts and Practices (8th ed. 2012), updated online: covering all aspects of a deceptive practices case in every state, with citations to tens of thousands of state UDAP and FTC cases.

Automobile Fraud (5th ed. 2015), updated online: title law, "yo-yo" sales, odometer tampering, lemon laundering, sale of wrecked cars, undisclosed prior use, and prior damage to new cars.

Consumer Warranty Law (5th ed. 2015), updated online: new and used car lemon laws, the Magnuson-Moss Warranty Act, UCC Article 2, manufactured home and new home warranty laws, and other state statutes.

Federal Deception Law (2d ed. 2016), updated online: FTC Holder and Telemarketing Sales Rules, other FTC and CFPB rules, TCPA, limits on unwanted calls and texts, junk faxes and spam, RICO, the False Claims Act, and regulation of debt relief services.

Other NCLC Titles

Foreclosure Prevention Counseling (3d ed. 2013 with website): loan modifications and workouts for Fannie Mae, Freddie Mac, subprime, FHA-insured, VA, and Rural Housing Service loans, plus dealing with servicers and foreclosure defense and mediation.

Bankruptcy Basics (2d ed. 2013 with website): A Step-by-Step Guide for Pro Bono Attorneys, General Practitioners, and Legal Services Offices: how to file your first bankruptcy case.

Instant Evidence: A Quick Guide to Federal Evidence and Objections (2d ed. 2013): objections by rule number and common objections and motions—all in 21 pages! Spiral-bound to lay flat, and laminated to allow use with a dry-erase pen.

The Practice of Consumer Law (2d ed. with CD-Rom): how to get started in a private or legal services consumer practice, with sample pleadings and practice pointers for even experienced attorneys.

NCLC Guide to Surviving Debt (2016 ed.): Everything a paralegal, new attorney, or client needs to know about home foreclosures and mortgage modifications, debt collectors, managing credit card debt, whether to refinance, credit card problems, evictions, repossessions, credit reporting, utility terminations, student loans, budgeting, and bankruptcy.

NCLC Guide to the Rights of Utility Consumers (1st ed.): consumer rights concerning utility services: shut-off protections, rights to restore terminated service, bill payment options, weatherization tips, and rights to government assistance.

NCLC Guide to Consumer Rights for Domestic Violence Survivors (1st ed.): practical advice to help survivors get back on their feet financially and safely establish their economic independence.

National Consumer Law Center • (617) 542-9595 • FAX (617) 542-8028 • publications@nclc.org
Order online at www.nclc.org/library

ONLINE VERSION OF THIS TREATISE

Active subscribers to this treatise have free access to its online version at *www.nclc.org/library* for as long as the subscription remains active. The online versions of all twenty NCLC treatises are found at this site, comprising the "NCLC Digital Library."

Subscribers will find online the full text of this print edition, including the chapters, appendices, and index. Periodic updates to this print edition will also be found online, fully integrated into the online text. In addition, the online version includes sample pleadings and discovery, the full text of primary sources, and practice tools not found in the print edition.

The online site allows users to:

- View the site with full functionality on desktop computers, tablets, and smartphones.
- Highlight material added or updated since this print edition.
- Download, print, email, bookmark, or copy/paste material from the text.
- Download additional companion material, including sample pleadings, hard-to-find primary sources, and unique practice tools.
- Quickly search this treatise, across all 20 treatises, or any combination of treatises—even without a subscription.
- Search any combination of chapters, appendices, pleadings, primary sources, or practice tools.
- Pinpoint the exact pleading needed using the "advanced pleadings search," which enables searches by pleading type, subject, or legal claims.
- Rapidly navigate through the treatise using a detailed table of contents, index, bookmarks, and a "recently viewed" list.
- Link from references in the text to other of the treatise's subsections, to subsections in other NCLC treatises, to pleadings, primary sources, and other companion material, and to external web addresses.

HOW TO LOG IN TO THE ONLINE VERSION OF THIS TREATISE

The online versions of this and other NCLC treatises are found at *www.nclc.org/library*.

Subscribers have already created a user name and password. The same user name and password is used for all your NCLC subscriptions. A link on the login page helps those who have forgotten their user name and/ or password. Any subscribers who have not set up log-in information can contact NCLC at publications@nclc.org or (617) 542-9595 for assistance.

Access without a user name or password: Organizations subscribing to the complete 20-title set, for an additional charge, can opt for "IP access," allowing anyone at one location to log onto the site without a user name or password. Law school libraries with IP access may obtain a license allowing remote access for law students and certain others. Contact NCLC Publications for more information. Even those who had IP access to our old companion websites of pleadings and primary sources must still contact NCLC to set up IP access to the NCLC Digital Library.

Additional user names: Any user, for a small additional charge, can obtain additional user names to allow others in an organization to access existing subscriptions. Again, contact NCLC Publications for details.

Contact NCLC Publications at (617) 542-9595 or publications@nclc.org with any further questions. Or visit www.nclc.org/library for more information.

National Consumer Law Center • (617) 542-9595 • FAX (617) 542-8028 • publications@nclc.org
Order online at www.nclc.org/library

Summary Contents

Contents

Chapter 6 — Unwanted Calls and Texts, Junk Faxes, and Spam

Chapter 1 First Considerations

1.1 Introduction to This Treatise

1.1.1 Print and Online Versions

Federal Deception Law is available in both a print and an online version. Print revisions are released every few years. The online version is updated more frequently, as developments require, with all changes integrated into the text.

The online version allows pinpoint searches of the book, provides easy navigation between subsections, and contains active links to external websites and other sections in the book and other NCLC treatises. Material in the online version can be copied and pasted, downloaded, printed, or emailed. Clicking on "highlight updates" in the online version at the top of the screen will highlight online additions to the treatise since release of the print book. This option also shows, in curly brackets at the beginning of each online footnote, the corresponding footnote number in the print book.

Subscription options are available as either online-only or print and online. Subscribers to print and online subscriptions receive, as part of their subscription price and at no additional charge, any revised print edition that is released during their subscription period. For more information, go to www.nclc.org/library.

1.1.2 The Treatise's Subject Matter

Federal Deception Law is a unique NCLC treatise. While other NCLC publications generally focus on one substantive area, this title examines a large number of federal (and parallel state) requirements and remedies that apply to many marketplace transactions. Examples are the federal and state RICO statutes that apply broadly to any form of consumer transaction and the federal False Claims Act that also provides strong remedies as long as the government is also victimized by a practice.

Federal Trade Commission (FTC) rules and other federal requirements analyzed typically apply broadly to different types of sales transactions. Rules regulate telephone marketing, telemarketing fraud, mail order sales, door-to-door sales, unordered merchandise, creditor liability for seller-related claims, and the like. The new Consumer Financial Protection Bureau (CFPB) has not yet enacted similar rules but, when it does, future updates to this treatise will cover those rules. For now, the treatise examines the CFPB's authority, guidance documents, and enforcement actions.

1.2 Relation to NCLC's *Unfair and Deceptive Acts and Practices*

Federal Deception Law is a companion treatise to NCLC's *Unfair and Deceptive Acts and Practices*. As the amount of UDAP precedent proliferates, it was deemed more manageable for readers in 2012 to split *Unfair and Deceptive Acts and Practices* into two separate treatises. *Unfair and Deceptive Acts and Practices* now focuses on practices that are unfair or deceptive and on private and state attorney general UDAP litigation to challenge those practices. *Federal Deception Law* concentrates on federal and state statutes and regulations that, while often related to UDAP litigation, establish distinct requirements and remedies.

Thus, moved from *Unfair and Deceptive Acts and Practices* to *Federal Deception Law* are discussions of all FTC and CFPB rules (including the FTC "Holder" Rule), the federal and state RICO sections, the federal False Claims Act section, sections on telemarketing fraud, sections on the Telephone Consumer Protection Act's regulation of inconvenient phone calls and junk faxes, federal regulation of spam, regulation of unordered merchandise, plain English statutes, and disclosure language requirements when sales are conducted in other languages. Additionally, related statutory and regulatory material found prior to 2012 in the appendices of *Unfair and Deceptive Acts and Practices* have also been moved to the appendices of *Federal Deception Law*, including the FTC rules, telemarketing statutes and regulations, and federal and state RICO statutes.

Nevertheless, *Federal Deception Law* and *Unfair and Deceptive Acts and Practices* are companion treatises, and it is recommended that practitioners use both titles. Many of the federal and state requirements set out in this treatise do not have a direct private remedy, and a state UDAP claim is often the best approach to remedy violations of these requirements. Conversely, in challenging a practice as unfair or deceptive, it is often helpful to refer to FTC rules and other federal and state standards examined in this treatise.

In addition, in some cases in which an FTC rule or other federal standards regulate a category of marketplace conduct, this treatise (and not *Unfair and Deceptive Acts and Practices*) includes a discussion of state and FTC UDAP case law defining unfair and deceptive acts relating to that same conduct. Thus for certain types of transactions, *Unfair and Deceptive Acts and Practices* refers the reader to this title.

1.3 Topics Covered by Other NCLC Treatises

This treatise and *Unfair and Deceptive Acts and Practices* set out consumer remedies for broad forms of marketplace conduct, in particular the sales aspects of consumer transactions. Other NCLC titles focus on credit and collection of credit obligations. *Truth in Lending, Credit Discrimination, Consumer Credit Regulation*, and *Mortgage Lending* deal with the origination of credit. *Fair Debt Collection, Collection*

Actions, Foreclosures and Mortgage Servicing, Repossessions, and *Consumer Bankruptcy Law and Practice* focus on the collection of credit obligations. *Fair Credit Reporting* deals with the reporting of credit obligations, and *Student Loan Law* and *Access to Utility* law focus on both the origination and collection of specialized types of credit. *Consumer Banking and Payments Law* details consumer payments other than via credit.

There are two important exceptions to the general rule that this treatise and *Unfair and Deceptive Acts and Practices* cover NCLC's treatment of sales transactions. *Automobile Fraud*, not this treatise, details federal and state laws regulating motor vehicle odometers, lemon laundering, title branding, yo-yo sales, sublease scams, wreck and flood damage, prior use, grey market origin, and bad title or other negative vehicle history. *Consumer Warranty Law* analyzes consumer rights after a sale when the goods or services—including new and used motor vehicles, manufactured homes, home improvement services, and the like—are defective.

Importantly, this treatise does not consider limits on consumer litigation derived from mandatory arbitration clauses found in consumer contracts. Tactics to avoid such arbitration requirements are set out in NCLC's *Consumer Arbitration Agreements*. In addition, consumer class actions raise specialized issues, which are detailed in NCLC's *Consumer Class Actions*. Finally, the online version of this treatise includes a number of consumer law pleadings that practitioners can use as samples, but *Consumer Law Pleadings* provides over 2000 pleadings covering scores of subject areas and stages of a litigation, and these pleadings can be copied and pasted into a word processing program.

More information on NCLC treatises is available at www.nclc.org/library, including detailed tables of contents, indexes, and a quick reference to the complete twenty-volume series.

1.4 Organization of This Treatise

1.4.1 The Chapters

This chapter provides background information on this treatise. Chapter 2, *infra*, examines eight of the most important Federal Trade Commission (FTC) trade regulation rules and also considers the scope of FTC rules, the rulemaking process, government and private remedies for rule violations, and parallel state statutes. Chapter 2 also lists FTC rules and guides not considered in the chapter and refers readers to where such other rules and guides are analyzed.

Chapter 3, *infra*, considers rulemaking by the Consumer Financial Protection Bureau (CFPB). Rules that have been transferred to the CFPB (under the "enumerated statutes") are examined in other NCLC treatises. The chapter instead focuses on CFPB authority to issue rules preventing unfair, deceptive, and abusive practices (UDAAP) rules that require disclosure and rules that regulate the information creditors must provide to consumers. Since the CFPB to date has not enacted any such rules, the chapter is limited to a discussion of the CFPB authority in these areas, including guidance documents, enforcement actions, the potential scope of CFPB UDAAP rules, and remedies to enforce CFPB rules.

Chapter 4, *infra*, analyzes in great detail a ninth FTC trade regulation rule and perhaps the most important FTC rule—the Rule Concerning Preservation of Consumer Claims and Defenses, also known as the Holder Rule. The rule requires a notice to be placed in credit agreements providing that the consumer can raise against the holders of their credit agreements all claims and defenses that the consumer can raise against the seller. The chapter examines the operation of the rule, consumer rights if the notice is not placed in the credit agreement, and also state statutes similar to the Holder Rule.

Chapter 5, *infra*, considers portions of another FTC rule, the Telemarketing Sales Rule, and parallel state statutes. The chapter focuses on those portions of the rule and state law that do far more than just regulate inconvenient calls to consumers—they also provide important substantive rights preventing merchant fraud, even when the consumer initiates a call.

Chapter 6, *infra*, focuses on the Telephone Consumer Protection Act and other federal laws that limit inconvenient calls, junk faxes, and email spam. Chapter 6 considers the Telephone Consumer Protection Act and Federal Communications Commission regulation of unwanted calls and junk faxes, federal statutes and regulations affecting email spam, and the portions of the Telemarketing and Consumer Fraud and Abuse Prevention Act and the FTC Telemarketing Sales Rule that deal with unwanted telemarketing phone calls.

Chapter 7, *infra*, provides a detailed analysis with extensive case law interpreting the federal RICO statute, with an emphasis on issues of relevance to a consumer case. Chapter 8, *infra*, then considers state RICO statutes and also state civil theft statutes. Chapter 9, *infra*, covers important private remedies available under the federal False Claims Act when the government is also a victim of fraud and also describes state false claims acts.

Chapter 10, *infra*, in a departure from other chapters in this treatise, focuses on federal and state regulation of one particular industry. Some of the worst abuses targeting consumers today are engaged in by debt relief service agencies, including certain credit counseling agencies offering debt management plans, and by many debt settlement, debt negotiation, and debt elimination companies.

Finally, Chapter 11, *infra*, briefly sets out other forms of federal and state regulation of broad applicability to consumer transactions. It examines the utility of federal and state antitrust statutes to consumer transactions. It then considers federal and state regulation of transactions that provide (and bill) consumers for unordered merchandise. Other sections examine state plain English statutes and federal and state requirements for non-English disclosures when a transaction is not conducted in English. The chapter then turns to an analysis of the 2010 Restore Online Shoppers' Confidence Act, which provides protections against two types of Internet sales: negative option sales and sales by an unrelated merchant that are solicited as a consumer is completing a transaction with an original merchant. The chapter now also covers the federal

Computer Fraud and Abuse Act, which prohibits unauthorized access to a computer and related practices.

1.4.2 The Appendices

The appendices are generally organized in the same order as the chapters to which they relate. FTC rulemaking legislation and nine FTC trade regulation rules (organized by their Code of Federal Regulations number) are found in Appendix A, *infra*. CFPB rulemaking authority and remedies are found in Appendix B, *infra*, and relevant CFPB rules will also be included in this appendix when enacted.

Appendix C, *infra*, contains federal statutes and rules relating to telemarketing fraud, inconvenient calls, junk faxes, and spam. This includes the Telemarketing and Consumer Fraud and Abuse Prevention Act and, enacted pursuant to that Act's authority, the FTC Telemarketing Sales Act. Also included are the Telephone Consumer Protection Act and Federal Communications Commission rules under that Act, as well as the federal CAN-SPAM Act and FTC rules under that Act. Appendix D, *infra*, summarizes state telemarketing fraud statutes.

Infra, Appendix E reprints the federal RICO statute; Appendix F summarizes state RICO statutes; Appendix G reprints the federal False Claims Act; Appendix H summarizes state false claims acts; and Appendix I summarizes state statutes relating to debt relief and credit counseling. Appendix J, *infra*, reprints a federal statute concerning delivery of unordered merchandise. Appendix K, *infra*, contains the Restore Online Shoppers' Confidence Act, and Appendix L, *infra*, reprints the Federal Computer Fraud Abuse Act.

1.4.3 Pleadings and Primary Sources

The online version of this treatise also includes pleadings, discovery, and primary sources that can easily be downloaded, emailed, and cut and pasted into documents. They are listed at the bottom of the table of contents found in the left pane and are fully searchable. Search filters allow users to search across only pleadings or only primary sources. Searching for pleadings is recommended using the Advanced Pleadings Search tool, found above the Search box.

The primary sources include FTC interpretations relating to FTC rules, selected items from the regulatory history of key FTC rules, FTC guides, federal and state rulings regarding telemarketing and unwanted calls and faxes, and other agency materials. The pleadings and discovery include sample complaints, discovery requests, class action documents, orders, and settlements. Most pleadings are available in Microsoft Word format. Over 2000 additional pleadings are available online in NCLC's *Consumer Law Pleadings*.

1.4.4 Unreported Cases

This treatise cites to unreported decisions and other material as available at www.nclc.org/unreported. All such

decisions and material are provided in alphabetical order in portable document format (PDF). For possible inclusion at this site, readers are encouraged to submit similar material to publications@nclc.org for NCLC's consideration.

A limited number of the older cases and other materials in this book are cited with Clearinghouse numbers. These were submitted to and stored by the National Clearinghouse for Legal Services (now the Sargent Shriver National Center on Poverty Law, at www.povertylaw.org) and are not stored at NCLC. So that NCLC can make them more easily available to the public, we would appreciate readers forwarding to us copies of any of these cases that are obtained from the Shriver Center or from the court or another source (since some of this material is presently unavailable from the Shriver Center).[1] We will post these cases on a website that provides access to the general public.

1.5 What Is "UDAP"?

The term "UDAP" appears frequently in this treatise (and even more frequently in the companion title, *Unfair and Deceptive Acts and Practices*). All fifty states, the District of Columbia, Puerto Rico, Guam, and the Virgin Islands have enacted at least one statute with broad applicability to most consumer transactions, aimed at preventing consumer deception and abuse in the marketplace.[2] Many of these statutes are patterned after the language found in section 5(a)(1) of the Federal Trade Commission (FTC) Act,[3] which prohibits "unfair or deceptive acts or practices." The term "UDAP" is an acronym for this prohibition. UDAP is distinguishable from UDAAP, which describes the Consumer Financial Protection Bureau's new authority to challenge unfair, deceptive, and abusive practices, examined in Chapter 3, *infra*.

"UDAP" will be used in this treatise somewhat imprecisely to refer to all state consumer statutes of general applicability, whether the legislation proscribes unfair, unconscionable, deceptive, misleading, or even simply fraudulent practices. This terminological convenience is necessitated by the lack of any other common name for such statutes. These statutes are referred to in different states as consumer protection acts, consumer sales acts, unfair trade practices acts, deceptive and unfair trade practices acts, deceptive consumer sales acts, deceptive trade practices acts, and consumer fraud acts. In addition, commentators often call these statutes "Little FTC Acts," although this name is only precise for those statutes that parallel the FTC Act and prohibit "unfair methods of competition and unfair or deceptive acts or practices."

Most UDAP statutes were enacted in the ten-year span between the mid-1960s and the mid-1970s, but significant

---

1 Please mail such cases to NCLC, UDAP Editor, 7 Winthrop Sq., Boston, MA 02110; fax them to (617) 542-8028 to the attention of "UDAP editor"; or email them to publications@nclc.org, with "Attention: UDAP Editor" in the subject line.

2 *See* National Consumer Law Center, Unfair and Deceptive Acts and Practices Appx. A (8th ed. 2012), *updated at* www.nclc.org/library.

3 15 U.S.C. § 45(a)(1).

amendments and even some new statutes have been enacted since that period. There continues to be legislative activity in this area.

UDAP statutes apply to most consumer transactions and provide a flexible and practical consumer remedy for many abuses. These statutes are particularly important because, while the Federal Trade Commission Act is often viewed as sharply limiting the doctrine of *caveat emptor*,[4] the Act provides only FTC enforcement and not state or private enforcement.[5] State UDAP statutes, by incorporating the FTC Act concepts of deception and unfairness and by providing significant state and private remedies, allow for widespread redress of marketplace misconduct and abuse of consumers.

Legislatures and courts have been careful to guarantee that UDAP statutes are broad and flexible and can apply to creative, new forms of abusive business schemes in almost all types of consumer transactions. Even when UDAP statutes enumerate specifically prohibited practices, most statutes also prohibit other unfair, unconscionable, and/or deceptive practices in more general terms. UDAP statutes typically do not require proof of the seller's fraudulent intent or knowledge. In some cases, consumer reliance, damage, or even actual deception is not a prerequisite to a UDAP action. Thus a UDAP claim is a far easier cause of action to prove than common law fraud.

All UDAP statutes authorize private damage actions. In order to encourage private litigation and deter merchant misconduct, many provide such special private remedies as attorney fees for prevailing consumers and punitive, treble, or minimum damage awards. UDAP statutes often provide a practical remedial approach for consumer complaints as well as counterclaims and defenses to collection actions.

The breadth of UDAP statutes and their avoidance of overly precise definitions of prohibited practices are their unique strengths. NCLC's *Unfair and Deceptive Acts and Practices* describes a large body of Federal Trade Commission interpretations and cases, state regulations, and tens of thousands of state UDAP case decisions that can provide clear guidance in initiating most UDAP claims.

But it is when a specific abusive practice has not been previously prohibited by statute or common law that a UDAP statute should be most relied upon. Where a practice does not fall precisely under a debt collection act, state or federal credit legislation, warranty law, or other statutes, UDAP statutes can provide an all-purpose remedy. Almost any abusive business practice aimed at consumers is at least arguably a UDAP violation, unless the trade practice clearly falls outside the scope of the statute. For far more detail on all aspects of UDAP law, see NCLC's *Unfair and Deceptive Acts and Practices*.

---

4 Legal historians point out that *caveat emptor*, or "let the buyer beware," is not an ancient doctrine. Medieval economic concepts included a "just price" and "a sound price warranting a sound commodity." The prices of many goods and services were fixed, allowing courts to examine contracts for their fairness independently of the terms agreed upon. However, emerging nineteenth-century commercial notions of markets, speculation, and business bargains gradually ended notions of contractual fairness apart from the original intent of the bargaining parties. Notions of the sanctity of contracts and *caveat emptor* thus only reached full development in the nineteenth century. At about the same time, the common law action of "Trespass on the Case in the Nature of Deceit" that applied even to negligent misrepresentations was replaced by common law actions for deceit or fraud that required the defendant's knowledge of the falsity and intent to deceive. *See, e.g.*, Horwitz, *The Historical Foundation of Modern Contract Law*, 87 Harv. L. Rev. 917 (1974).

5 *See* § 2.2.4.1, *infra*.

Chapter 2 FTC Trade Regulation Rules

2.1 Overview

2.1.1 Introduction

The Federal Trade Commission (FTC) has broad authority under the FTC Act to prohibit unfair or deceptive acts and practices in trade or commerce and to enact trade regulation rules that define and prevent such practices.[1] The FTC has issued sixteen such trade regulation rules, and many of them establish important standards and requirements for sellers, creditors, and others.

This chapter focuses on eight FTC trade regulation rules of special relevance to consumer law:

- The Credit Practices Rule
- The Used Car Rule
- The Rule Concerning Door-to-Door and Off-Premises Sales
- Mail or Telephone Order Merchandise Rule
- The Negative Option Rule
- The Franchise Rule
- The Business Opportunity Rule
- The Funeral Rule

A ninth and most important FTC rule, the Trade Regulation Rule Concerning the Preservation of Consumers' Claims and Defenses (Holder Rule), is treated in its own chapter, Chapter 4, *infra*. The seven other trade regulation rules, listed at § 2.1.2, *infra*, are not covered in this treatise.

The FTC has also issued other rules not pursuant to the FTC Act but under other statutes. These other rules are *not* treated in this chapter, but the most important of these are examined either in other NCLC treatises or in other chapters of this treatise.[2]

The FTC also issues industry guides, providing guidance to companies as to which specific practices the FTC considers unfair or deceptive. The guides do not establish new requirements nor are there special remedies for guide violations other than the normal remedies for any unfair or deceptive practice.[3] Because of this, guides have similar precedential value as FTC and court decisions under the FTC Act as to what practices are unfair or deceptive. Consequently, as with FTC case law, these guides are treated in the NCLC treatise, *Unfair and Deceptive Acts and Practices*.[4] FTC guides are simply listed at § 2.10, *infra*, with an indication as to which guides are discussed in *Unfair and Deceptive Acts and Practices*.

2.1.2 Rules Not Covered in This Chapter

The FTC has issued over fifty rules, and this chapter only considers eight trade regulation rules. This subsection lists the FTC rules *not* covered in this chapter but indicates where additional information on these other rules is to be found.

NCLC's *Fair Credit Reporting* examines the nine FTC rules interpreting the Fair Credit Reporting Act.[5] NCLC's *Consumer Warranty Law* examines four rules interpreting the Magnuson Moss Warranty Act.[6] NCLC's *Fair Debt Collection* details a former FTC rule, now republished by the CFPB, that prescribes procedures for states to apply for exemptions from the Fair Debt Collection Practices Act.[7] NCLC treatises do not cover the FTC's three rules under the Hart-Scott-Rodino Anti-Trust Improvements Act[8] or the four rules under the Fair Packaging and Labeling Act.[9]

This chapter also does not consider seventeen FTC rules under other specific acts of Congress.[10] One of these seventeen rules, the FTC Telemarketing Sales Rule,[11] is examined in some detail in Chapters 5 and 6, *infra*. Another, the CAN-SPAM Rule,[12] is covered in § 6.10, *infra*. The Rule concerning pay-per-call or 900-numbers[13] is considered in NCLC's *Access to Utility Services*. The other fourteen rules under specific acts of Congress, such as fur products labeling, labeling standards for recycled oil, and rules under the Hobby Protection Act are not considered in any NCLC treatise.

Eight of the FTC's sixteen trade regulation rules are examined in this chapter. A ninth rule, the Preservation of Consumers' Claims and Defenses (Holder Rule), is considered in its own chapter, Chapter 4, *infra*. The remaining seven trade regulation rules are not covered in any NCLC treatise. These seven are:

- Unfair and Deceptive Advertising and Labeling of Cigarettes in Relation to the Health Hazards of Smoking;[14]
- Deceptive Advertising As to the Sizes of Viewable Pictures Shown by Television Receiving Sets.[15]
- Care Labeling of Textile Wearing Apparel and Certain Piece Goods;[16]
- Retail Food Advertising;[17]

---

1 *See* § 2.2.1, *infra*.
2 *See* § 2.1.2, *infra*.
3 *See* § 2.10, *infra*.
4 National Consumer Law Center, Unfair and Deceptive Acts and Practices (8th ed. 2012), *updated at* www.nclc.org/library.

5 *See* 16 C.F.R. §§ 602–698. The FTC promulgated fifteen rules, but six have been transferred to the Consumer Financial Protection Bureau. These six rules are also considered in NCLC's treatise, Fair Credit Reporting (8th ed. 2013), *updated at* www.nclc.org/library
6 *See* 16 C.F.R. §§ 700–703.
7 12 C.F.R. pt. 1006 (former 16 C.F.R. pt. 901).
8 16 C.F.R. §§ 801–803.
9 16 C.F.R. §§ 500–503.
10 16 C.F.R. §§ 300–322. At one point there were nineteen, but two have been transferred to the CFPB.
11 16 C.F.R. pt. 310.
12 16 C.F.R. pt. 316.
13 16 C.F.R. pt. 308.
14 16 C.F.R. pt. 408.
15 16 C.F.R. pt. 410.
16 16 C.F.R. pt. 423.
17 16 C.F.R. pt. 424.

- Power Output Claims for Amplifiers Utilized in Home Entertainment Products;[18]
- Ophthalmic Practice Rules;[19] and
- Labeling and Advertising of Home Insulation.[20]

In addition, the Mortgage Advertising Rule,[21] formerly an FTC rule but now a CFPB rule, is discussed in National Consumer Law Center, *Unfair and Deceptive Acts and Practices*.[22]

2.2 FTC Trade Regulation Rulemaking

2.2.1 *The Nature of Trade Regulation Rules*

Trade regulation rules (TRRs) "define with specificity acts and practices which are unfair or deceptive acts or practices. . . . Rules under this subparagraph may include requirements prescribed for the purpose of preventing such acts or practices."[23] Trade regulation rules not only enumerate practices that are unfair or deceptive but add requirements to prevent such practices—for example, three-day cooling-off periods, required disclosures, and notices placed in contracts that alter substantive rights.

Since the 1970s, the FTC has not been very active in enacting TRRs. In part this is because the statutory procedure to promulgate a TRR is quite resource-intensive and lengthy, much more so than notice and comment rulemaking. Informal hearings are conducted by hearing officers, who issue recommended decisions based upon the evidence.[24] The hearings include oral testimony and even cross-examination by group representatives, with a verbatim transcript.[25] The FTC's final rule must also include a statement of basis and purpose meeting certain statutory standards.[26] Appeal rights are provided.[27]

The Dodd-Frank Act has given the FTC streamlined authority to write rules preventing unfair or deceptive practices by motor vehicle dealers, who were excluded from the CFPB's authority.[28] The FTC is authorized to use rulemaking under the Administrative Procedure Act rather than the more cumbersome procedures required of other FTC Trade Regulation Rules. The FTC has not yet exercised this streamlined authority.

2.2.2 *Scope*

The FTC can enact TRRs with respect to unfair and deceptive practices "in or affecting commerce."[29] This is a broad standard applying to almost any commercial activity. Nevertheless, there are a number of statutory exemptions to the FTC's authority and thus to the scope of its TRRs. The FTC has no authority over banks, savings associations, and credit unions[30]—rulemaking concerning unfair and deceptive and abusive practices by these entities now resides with the CFPB.[31] Also exempt from FTC rulemaking are common carriers and air carriers.[32]

The McCarran-Ferguson Act provides that state statutes prohibiting unfair and deceptive acts and practices in insurance transactions strip the FTC of jurisdiction over such practices, so FTC TRRs do not apply to insurance.[33] In addition, while the FTC has jurisdiction over corporations, that is a defined term including most forms of ownership as long as a company carries on "business for its own profit or that of its members."[34] Thus FTC rules do not apply to purely governmental entities or to truly nonprofit entities. Of course, FTC TRRs may still apply to a for-profit entity associated with a governmental entity or a for-profit company masquerading as a nonprofit.

2.2.3 *Substantive Scope of FTC Rulemaking*

The FTC Act gives the FTC authority to adopt rules defining unfair or deceptive acts or practices in or affecting interstate commerce.[35] In order to declare an act unfair, the FTC must find that it causes or is likely to cause substantial injury to consumers that is not reasonably avoidable by consumers themselves and not outweighed by countervailing benefits to consumers or to competition.[36] The Act provides that the FTC may consider established public policies as evidence of unfairness, but public policy considerations may not serve as a primary basis for such a determination.[37]

The FTC Act does not define deception, but the FTC and the courts have interpreted this concept in detail over the years. Neither intent nor knowledge of a statement's falsity is necessary.[38] The defendant's good faith is not a defense, nor is its cessation of the practice at the time of suit.[39] Actual deception is unnecessary as long as the practice is likely to deceive its consumers.[40] While the deception must be material, the FTC

---

18   16 C.F.R. pt. 432.
19   16 C.F.R. pt. 456.
20   16 C.F.R. pt. 460.
21   12 C.F.R. pt. 1014.
22   National Consumer Law Center, Unfair and Deceptive Acts and Practices § 6.6.2 (8th ed. 2012), *updated at* www.nclc.org/library.
23   15 U.S.C. § 57a(a)(1)(B).
24   15 U.S.C. § 57a(b), (c).
25   15 U.S.C. § 57a(c).
26   15 U.S.C. § 57a(d).
27   15 U.S.C. § 57a(e).
28   12 U.S.C. § 5519(d).
29   15 U.S.C. § 57a(a)(1)(B).

30   15 U.S.C. § 45(a)(2).
31   *See* §§ 3.7, 3.9, 3.10, *infra*.
32   15 U.S.C. § 45(a)(2).
33   15 U.S.C. § 1012.
34   15 U.S.C. §§ 44, 45(a)(2).
35   15 U.S.C. §§ 45, 57a(a)(1).
36   15 U.S.C. § 45(n). *See* National Consumer Law Center, Unfair and Deceptive Acts and Practices § 4.3 (8th ed. 2012), *updated at* www.nclc.org/library.
37   15 U.S.C. § 45(n).
38   *See* National Consumer Law Center, Unfair and Deceptive Acts and Practices §§ 4.2.4.1, 4.2.5.1 (8th ed. 2012), *updated at* www.nclc.org/library.
39   National Consumer Law Center, Unfair and Deceptive Acts and Practices §§ 4.2.6, 4.2.7 (8th ed. 2012), *updated at* www.nclc.org/library.
40   National Consumer Law Center, Unfair and Deceptive Acts and Practices §§ 4.2.9, 4.2.11 (8th ed. 2012), *updated at* www.nclc.org/library.

can infer materiality, and proof of reliance by consumers is not required.[41]

In determining whether a statement is deceptive, the FTC looks at its overall net impression, not just the specific explicit claim.[42] Representations are deceptive if necessary qualifications are not made, if material facts are not disclosed, or if disclosures or qualifications are too inconspicuous.[43]

2.2.4 Private Remedies

2.2.4.1 No FTC Act Private Right of Action for FTC Rule Violations

There is no private right of action under the FTC Act to challenge unfair or deceptive practices or trade regulation rules (TRR) violations.[44] Private litigants have attempted to bring individual enforcement actions under the FTC Act, but judicial precedent, with only a few exceptions, indicates that there is no implied private right of action under the FTC Act.[45]

In 1978 the FTC attempted to carve out an exception to the line of cases that find no private right of action under the FTC Act. It explicitly stated in the statement of basis and purpose to its Franchise Rule that there is a private right of action at least to enforce the FTC Franchise Rule.[46] Nevertheless, courts have

consistently held that it is for Congress and the courts, not the FTC, to decide if there is a private right of action under an FTC rule, and, since there is no evidence that Congress changed its mind, the FTC statement of basis and purpose should be given no effect.[47] When it announced amendments to this rule in 2007, the FTC retreated from this position and stated that there is no private cause of action under the rule.[48]

2.2.4.2 FTC Rule Violation As a State UDAP Violation

Even though the FTC Act itself does not provide a private right of action, an FTC TRR defining unfair or deceptive practices provides guidance in interpreting unfair or deceptive state UDAP statutes, and state UDAP statutes provide strong private remedies. Therefore, violations of an FTC TRR should lead to a private state UDAP challenge of the same practices. An individual cannot bring a claim specifically founded upon a violation of the FTC Act, but the individual may bring a claim based on a violation of the state UDAP statute and then argue that the court should be guided in its determination of whether a practice violates the state statute by the fact that the practice violates the FTC TRR.

Most state UDAP statutes are modeled after the FTC Act, and, because of this "parentage," most state UDAP statutes declare that "it is the intent of the legislature that in construing . . . this Act the courts will be guided by the interpretations given by the Federal Trade Commission and the federal courts to Section 5(a)(1) of the Federal Trade Commission Act (15 U.S.C. 45(a)(1))."[49] An FTC rule is one such interpretation. In states with this statutory provision, courts show great deference to FTC guidelines when interpreting the state UDAP statute.[50]

Even when the UDAP statute does not expressly refer to the precedential value of FTC decisions, courts often show great deference to FTC actions.[51] Courts find a legislative intent that FTC decisions be used to interpret state UDAP acts based upon the similarity of the federal and state statutes and the fact that UDAP statutes are patterned after the FTC Act.[52] What better guidance as to what is unfair and deceptive under a state UDAP statute than an FTC rule specifying unfair and deceptive practices?

An FTC TRR violation should be a per se UDAP violation even when a practice that is not unfair or deceptive in

---

41 National Consumer Law Center, Unfair and Deceptive Acts and Practices § 4.2.12 (8th ed. 2012), *updated at* www.nclc.org/library.

42 National Consumer Law Center, Unfair and Deceptive Acts and Practices § 4.2.13 (8th ed. 2012), *updated at* www.nclc.org/library.

43 National Consumer Law Center, Unfair and Deceptive Acts and Practices § 4.2.14.2 (8th ed. 2012), *updated at* www.nclc.org/library.

44 *See* § 2.2.5, *infra*.

45 Baum v. Great W. Cities, Inc., 703 F.2d 1197 (10th Cir. 1983); Dreisbach v. Murphy, 658 F.2d 720 (9th Cir. 1981); Fulton v. Hecht, 580 F.2d 1243 (5th Cir. 1978); Alfred Dunhill Ltd. v. Interstate Cigar Co., 499 F.2d 232 (2d Cir. 1974); Holloway v. Bristol-Myers Corp., 485 F.2d 986 (D.C. Cir. 1973); Carlson v. Coca Cola Co., 483 F.2d 279 (9th Cir. 1973); Ingraham v. Planet Beach Franchising Corp., 2009 WL 909567 (E.D. La. Apr. 1, 2009); Haun v. Don Mealy Imports, Inc., 285 F. Supp. 2d 1297 (M.D. Fla. 2003); Morales v. Walker Motors Sales, Inc., 162 F. Supp. 2d 786 (S.D. Ohio 2000) (no private cause of action to enforce FTC Holder Rule); Tacker v. Wilson, 830 F. Supp. 422 (W.D. Tenn. 1993); Dash v. Wayne, 700 F. Supp. 1056 (D. Haw. 1988); Days Inn of Am. Franchising, Inc. v. Windham, 699 F. Supp. 1581 (N.D. Ga. 1988); Waldo v. North Am. Van Lines, Inc., 669 F. Supp. 722 (W.D. Pa. 1987); Freedman v. Meldy's, Inc., 587 F. Supp. 658 (E.D. Pa. 1984); First Phone Co. of New England v. New England Tel. & Tel. Co., 1981 U.S. Dist. LEXIS 11538 (D. Mass. Mar. 31, 1981); Greenberg v. Michigan Optometric Ass'n Inc., 483 F. Supp. 142 (E.D. Mich. 1980); Meyer v. Bell & Howell Co., 453 F. Supp. 801 (D. Mo. 1978), *appeal dismissed*, 584 F.2d 291 (8th Cir. 1978); Summey v. Ford Motor Credit Co., 449 F. Supp. 132 (D.S.C. 1976), *aff'd without op.*, 573 F.2d 1306 (4th Cir. 1978); Dill v. Barnett Funeral Home, 83 P.3d 1270 (Kan. Ct. App. 2004) (table, text at 2004 WL 292124) (no private cause of action to enforce funeral industry regulation); Culbreth v. Lawrence J. Miller, Inc., 477 A.2d 491 (Pa. Super. Ct. 1984); SCI Tex. Funeral Services, Inc. v. Hijar, 214 S.W.3d 148 (Tex. App. 2007) (no private cause of action for violation of FTC funeral rule). *But see* Guernsey v. Rich Plan of the Midwest, 408 F. Supp. 582 (N.D. Ind. 1976); Donnelly v. Mustang Pools, Inc., 374 N.Y.S.2d 967 (N.Y. Sup. Ct. 1975).

46 43 Fed. Reg. 59,614 (Feb. 10, 1978). The rule is examined at § 2.8.2, *infra*.

47 Federal Trade Comm'n v. Davis, 5 Trade Reg. Rptr. (CCH) ¶ 22,741 (D. Nev. Oct. 17, 1989); Days Inn of Am. Franchising, Inc. v. Windham, 699 F. Supp. 1581 (N.D. Ga. 1988); Mon-Shore Mgmt., Inc. v. Family Media, 1985 U.S. Dist. LEXIS 12407 (S.D.N.Y. Dec. 23, 1985); Freedman v. Meldy's, Inc., 587 F. Supp. 658 (E.D. Pa. 1984); Chelson v. Oregonian Publ'g Co., 1981 U.S. Dist. LEXIS 12488 (D. Or. Mar. 4, 1981).

48 *See* § 2.8.2, *infra*.

49 *See* National Consumer Law Center, Unfair and Deceptive Acts and Practices Appx. A (8th ed. 2012), *updated at* www.nclc.org/library ("Precedential Value of FTC Interpretations").

50 *See* National Consumer Law Center, Unfair and Deceptive Acts and Practices § 3.4.5 (8th ed. 2012), *updated at* www.nclc.org/library.

51 *Id.*

52 *Id.*

its own right violates a requirement meant to prevent unfair or deceptive practices. Many courts find that violation of a state or federal statute meant to protect the public is a per se UDAP violation,[53] and that approach should apply to a FTC rule as well.[54]

Precedent finding a specific TRR violation to be a per se UDAP violation is set out in the sections, *infra*, examining each particular rule. This subsection lays out some general principles.

First, a violation of an FTC rule, even one not defining unfair or deceptive practices, should be treated as an unfair practice. The predominant definition of an unfair practice is that it:

- Causes substantial consumer injury;
- Is not outweighed by countervailing benefits to consumers or competition; and
- Could not be reasonably avoided by consumers.[55]

Under this definition, a violation of an FTC rule should be unfair when the statutory violation causes consumer injury. There is no countervailing benefit to consumers or to competition to have companies violate the federal requirement. Consumers are not reasonably expected to avoid law violations.

Some courts interpreting unfairness under state UDAP statutes do not use this unfairness definition but use the old FTC "*S&H*" standard for determining when a practice is unfair.[56] Under this standard the following criteria are used to determine if a practice is unfair:

- Whether the practice offends public policy. Is it within at least the penumbra of some common law, statutory, or other established concept of unfairness?

- Whether the practice is immoral, unethical, oppressive, or unscrupulous.
- Whether the practice causes substantial injury to the consumer.

FTC rule violations are unfair under these criteria, as they are not only within the penumbra of a statutory concept of unfairness (the FTC Act's concept of unfairness) but directly offend the public policy that is embodied in the rule violated.

In states whose UDAP statute only prohibits deceptive practices, consumers are in a different position in arguing that the TRR violation is actionable under the state UDAP statute. Consumers can claim that it is deceptive for a seller to fail to disclose that its conduct violates the FTC rule.[57] In addition, it can be argued that a seller who violates an FTC rule has misrepresented its own legal rights or has confused the consumer as to the consumer's legal rights.[58] Furthermore, by entering into a transaction, the seller makes an implicit or explicit representation that its conduct is legal, which is deceptive if in fact it is violating the law.[59]

When arguing that a rule violation is a per se UDAP violation or an automatic deceptive practice, to be safe, consumer litigants should also argue that the conduct that caused the FTC rule violation is unfair or deceptive in its own right. This mitigates any danger that the court may find that the conduct does not violate the rule or that a rule violation is not a per se UDAP violation.

One problem with seeking private remedies under a state UDAP statute is that the scope of an FTC rule and that of the state UDAP statute may not be the same. For example, a few state UDAP statutes do not apply to credit or to business opportunities or practices regulated by a state agency, raising issues as to UDAP enforcement of the FTC Credit Practices Rule, the FTC Business Opportunities Rule, or the FTC Funeral Rule. When an FTC rule violation is outside the coverage of a state UDAP statute, the violation cannot be remedied by the state UDAP statute.

On the other hand, sometimes the scope of the state UDAP statute is broader than that of the FTC Act, so the state UDAP statute can challenge businesses, such as banks, that are not within the scope of the FTC's authority. In that case, an FTC rule may still be useful precedent for a state UDAP action against the bank even though the FTC itself cannot sue the bank for the rule violation.

2.2.5 FTC Remedies

The FTC may institute a civil action in federal court for TRR violations[60] seeking consumer redress, including rescission or reformation of contracts, refund of money or return of property, damages, and public notification of the rule violation,

---

53 *See* National Consumer Law Center, Unfair and Deceptive Acts and Practices § 3.2 (8th ed. 2012), *updated at* www.nclc.org/library.

54 *See* Brown v. Cincyautos, Inc., 2009 WL 88736 (S.D. Ohio Jan. 12, 2009) (failure to include in buyers' guide all contact information required by FTC rule is per se UDAP; bona fide error not defense to liability but relevant to damages); Tirado v. Ofstein, 2008 WL 902506 (Conn. Super. Ct. Mar. 14, 2008) (violation of used car rule that results in ascertainable loss is CUTPA violation); North Haven Funeral Home, Inc. v. Sortito, 1995 WL 630996 (Conn. Super. Ct. Oct. 19, 1995) (furnishing funeral goods and services before providing accurate written information as to the cost for each specific item, in violation of FTC rule, is UDAP violation); Swiss v. Williams, 445 A.2d 486 (N.J. Dist. Ct. 1982) (finding of UDAP violation buttressed by reference to federal legislation and FTC Cooling Off Period Rule regulating the same subject matter and designating the conduct as unfair and deceptive); Eastern Roofing & Aluminum Co. v. Brock, 320 S.E.2d 22 (N.C. Ct. App. 1984); Iron & Glass Bank v. Franz, 9 Pa. D. & C.3d 419 (Pa. Ct. Com. Pl. Allegheny Cnty. 1978). *See also* Anderson v. DaimlerChrysler Corp., 2005 WL 3891034 (Ohio Ct. Com. Pl. Nov. 23, 2005) (unpublished) (consent order; seller's failure to include FTC Holder Notice in financing contract is UDAP violation). *See generally* National Consumer Law Center, Unfair and Deceptive Acts and Practices §§ 3.2.7.3.6, 3.4.5.1, 3.4.5.6 (8th ed. 2012), *updated at* www.nclc.org/library.

55 *See* National Consumer Law Center, Unfair and Deceptive Acts and Practices § 4.3.2 (8th ed. 2012), *updated at* www.nclc.org/library.

56 *See* National Consumer Law Center, Unfair and Deceptive Acts and Practices § 4.3.3.3 (8th ed. 2012), *updated at* www.nclc.org/library.

57 *See* National Consumer Law Center, Unfair and Deceptive Acts and Practices § 3.2.7.4.2 (8th ed. 2012), *updated at* www.nclc.org/library.

58 *Id.*

59 *Id.*

60 15 U.S.C. § 57b(a)(1).

but not for punitive damages.[61] There is a three-year statute of limitations.[62]

In addition, when there is actual knowledge or knowledge is fairly implied on the basis of objective circumstances that the act is unfair or deceptive and prohibited by a rule, the FTC can seek in federal court civil penalties of not more than $10,000 per violation.[63] When there is a continuing failure to comply with a TRR, each day is treated as a separate violation.[64] Factors in determining the size of the penalty include the degree of culpability, similar prior conduct, ability to pay, and the effect on ability to continue in business.[65] The FTC can also issue administrative cease and desist orders.[66]

2.2.6 CFPB Remedies

The Consumer Financial Protection Bureau (CFPB) has authority to take action to prevent a person covered by the CFPB's authority from committing an unfair or deceptive or abusive act or practice (UDAAP).[67] This CFPB authority and CFPB remedies to enforce this authority are examined in Chapter 3, *infra*.

Since the CFPB's definitions of deception and unfairness are the same as the FTC's, it would appear clear that the CFPB can enforce any FTC TRR violation through its UDAAP authority as to persons covered by the CFPB. The scope of CFPB authority generally includes creditors, debt collectors, and others related to consumer financial services. Only certain FTC TRRs relate to such parties; other TRRs instead focus only on merchants engaged in sales transactions outside the CFPB's authority.[68]

2.3 The FTC Credit Practices Rule

2.3.1 General Overview

An important precedent dealing with unfair remedies used by creditors when enforcing consumer credit contracts is the FTC's trade regulation rule concerning credit practices[69] (hereafter "the Credit Practices Rule"). This rule has been upheld by the District of Columbia Circuit.[70]

The prohibitions under the Credit Practices Rule apply to lenders and retail installment sellers who extend credit to consumers.[71] Lease-purchase contracts are included as long as the consumer is obligated to pay a specified amount and is permitted to become the owner of the property for little or no additional consideration.[72] The Credit Practices Rule also covers creditors such as physicians and contractors who use deferred payment plans.[73] The rule does not, however, cover nonprofit organizations[74] or a city that administers a housing rehabilitation grant program.[75]

The Credit Practices Rule overrides inconsistent provisions of state law.[76] However, several states have been granted exemptions from the rule.[77]

The Credit Practices Rule prohibits the following six practices:

- Confessions of judgment, *cognovits*, and other waivers of the right to notice and opportunity to be heard in the event of suit;
- Waiver of exemptions from execution on personal or real property, such as waiver of a homestead exemption, unless the waiver applies only to property that is the subject of a security interest granted in that credit transaction;
- Most irrevocable wage assignments;
- Non-purchase money security interests in certain household goods;
- Pyramiding late charges by assessing more than one delinquency charge for one late payment (pyramiding late charges for a *missed* payment is not prohibited); and
- Failure to provide co-signers with a specified warning indicating the potential obligations of a co-signer.

These prohibitions are discussed individually at §§ 2.3.4 through 2.3.10, *infra*.

The best sources for understanding the FTC's Credit Practices Rule are the FTC's statement of basis and purpose

---

61 15 U.S.C. § 57b(b).

62 15 U.S.C. § 57b(d).

63 15 U.S.C. § 45(*l*).

64 15 U.S.C. § 45(m)(1)(C).

65 *Id.*

66 15 U.S.C. § 45(b).

67 12 U.S.C. § 5531(a).

68 *Id.*

69 16 C.F.R. § 444 (effective Mar. 1, 1985). The FTC's Statement of Basis and Purpose is found at 49 Fed. Reg. 7789 (Mar. 1, 1984), *available online as companion material to this treatise.*

   After reviewing the regulation as required by the Regulatory Flexibility Act, the FTC concluded in 1995 that revisions to the rule were not warranted. 60 Fed. Reg. 24,805 (May 10, 1995).

70 American Fin. Services Ass'n v. Federal Trade Comm'n, 767 F.2d 957 (D.C. Cir. 1985).

71 16 C.F.R. § 444.1.

   The prohibition against pyramiding of late charges applies to collection of these extensions of credit. *See* 16 C.F.R. § 444.4.

72 16 C.F.R. § 444.1(b). *See* Green, FTC Informal Staff Opinion Letter (Mar. 16, 1985) (rule covers lease-purchase contracts when consumer is obligated to pay specified amount and is permitted to become owner of property for little or no additional consideration).

73 Martin, FTC Informal Staff Opinion Letter (July 16, 1987); Shevin, FTC Informal Staff Opinion Letter (Apr. 30, 1986).

74 Marwil, FTC Informal Staff Opinion Letter (May 17, 1985); Lush, FTC Informal Staff Opinion Letter (Mar. 8, 1985).

75 Balaban, FTC Informal Staff Opinion Letter (Nov. 26 1985).

76 Free Bridge Auto Sales v. Fitzgerald, 48 Va. Cir. 1 (Va. Cir. Ct. 1999).

77 The Board and the FTC have granted exemptions to California, New York, and Wisconsin. 53 Fed. Reg. 29,233 (Aug. 3, 1988) (Board exemption for California); 53 Fed. Reg. 19,893 (June 1, 1988) (FTC exemption for California); 52 Fed. Reg. 2398 (Jan. 22, 1987) (Board exemption for New York); 51 Fed. Reg. 41,763 (Nov. 19, 1986) (Board exemption for Wisconsin); 51 Fed. Reg. 28,328 (Aug. 7, 1986) (FTC exemption for New York); 51 Fed. Reg. 24,304 (July 3, 1986) (FTC exemption for Wisconsin).

   The Office of Thrift Supervision (OTS) granted an exemption to Wisconsin. 51 Fed. Reg. 45,879 (Dec. 23, 1986).

   The National Credit Union Administration (NCUA) never granted any exemptions.

for the rule[78] and, to a lesser extent, the informal FTC staff opinion letters on the rule. All of these documents are available online as companion material to this treatise.[79]

2.3.2 Similar FRB, OTS, and NCUA Rules for Banks

The FTC rule applies to finance companies, retailers, and other creditors within the FTC's jurisdiction but does not apply to most banks. Nevertheless, after the FTC promulgated its rule, the National Credit Union Administration (NCUA),[80] the Office of Thrift Supervision (OTS), and the Federal Reserve Board (FRB) adopted analogous rules for credit unions, savings and loan institutions,[81] and all other banks,[82] respectively.

Effective July 21, 2011, OTS authority was transferred to the Office of the Comptroller of the Currency (OCC). There was no change at that time in the OTS regulation, but the OCC did not include the OTS version of the rule when it republished the regulations applicable to federal savings and loan associations.[83]

In the meantime, the 2010 Dodd-Frank Act repealed the rulemaking authority under which the FRB, OTS, and NCUA rules had been promulgated, transferring that rulemaking authority to the CFPB.[84] In late 2014, the OCC, the FRB, and the NCUA repealed or proposed to repeal their rules and replace them with a guidance[85] jointly adopted with the CFPB.[86] Consumer groups urged the CFPB to replace the repealed rule with another rule rather than a guidance. The matter remained unresolved as of late 2014.

While the rules enacted by the OCC, the FRB, and the NCUA closely tracked the FTC rule, there were a number of differences.[87] The most important difference was that the FRB, OTS (now OCC), and NCUA rules only prohibited banks and

credit unions from entering into credit agreements containing or enforcing the prohibited creditor remedies. The FRB, OTS, and NCUA rules did not prohibit a bank or credit union from purchasing consumer credit agreements containing the prohibited terms as long as the financial entity did not enforce the prohibited creditor remedy.

In 1985, the FRB staff issued guidelines containing important material for interpreting the FRB rule.[88] These guidelines apply only to a bank's compliance with the FRB rule and not to the compliance of finance companies, retailers, and others with a similar FTC rule.

2.3.3 FTC Staff Letters As Precedent

FTC staff letters interpret the Credit Practices Rule very narrowly. For example, while the Credit Practices Rule restricts security interests in "household goods,"[89] the FTC staff has tried to limit the number of items treated as "household goods," excluding such common household items as books, encyclopedias, rugs, luggage, and children's car seats. This seems at variance with the intent of the FTC's statement of basis and purpose for the rule, which states that security interests in household goods are unfair because "[d]ebtors lose property which is of great value to them and little value to the creditor . . . . Although creditors are entitled to payment, such security interests offer little economic return to creditors at great cost to the debtor."[90]

While the FTC informal staff opinion letters often seem overly restrictive and are not binding on courts or the FTC itself, it is important for practitioners to be familiar with these letters. While a party can argue that the letter is wrong if necessary, courts are likely to give the letter an initial presumption of validity. The following six subsections summarize these FTC letters as they apply to the specific provisions of the Credit Practices Rule. The letters are also available online as companion material to this treatise.

2.3.4 Confession of Judgment Provision

The Credit Practices Rule prohibits confessions of judgment, *cognivits*, and other waivers of the right to notice and opportunity to be heard in the event of suit.[91] There is an exception for executory process in Louisiana.[92] These protections cannot be waived by the consumer.[93]

This prohibition bars the use of a clause waiving the right to a hearing before the creditor gets a repossession order from

78 49 Fed. Reg. 7740 (Mar. 1, 1984).

79 Available online as companion material to this treatise at Primary Sources>FTC Trade Regulation Rules>Credit Practices Rule>FTC Interpretation Letters.

80 *See* 12 C.F.R. § 706.

81 12 C.F.R. § 535.

82 12 C.F.R. §§ 227.12–227.16.

83 49 Fed. Reg. 48,950 (Aug. 9, 2011).

84 Dodd-Frank Wall Street Reform and Consumer Protection Act, Pub. L. No. 111-203, § 1092, 124 Stat. 1376 (July 21, 2010) (amending 15 U.S.C. § 57a(f)).

85 Fed. Reserve Bd., Interagency Guidance Regarding Unfair or Deceptive Credit Practices (Aug. 22, 2014), *available at* www.federal-reserve.gov.

86 *Id. See also* 79 Fed. Reg. 51,115 (Aug. 27, 2014) (FRB proposal to repeal its rule).

87 While the FTC rule is silent on its applicability to real estate loans, the FRB and OTS rules do not apply to credit extended for the purchase of real property. The FRB and OTS rules, however, do apply to credit extended to improve a home or to purchase a manufactured home deemed to be personalty under state law. The NCUA, OTS, and FRB rules also give the creditor the added option of including the co-signer notice in the contract, and not just in a separate document, and of modifying the notice in some respects. In addition, the definition of "co-signer" and "household goods" have been clarified and limited. The FRB and OTS rules do not prohibit certain types of *cognivits*,

and the FRB Rule allows refinancing of purchase money loans without losing their purchase money characterization.

88 50 Fed. Reg. 47,036 (Nov. 14, 1985), *as updated at* 51 Fed. Reg. 39,646 (Oct. 30, 1986) *and at* 53 Fed. Reg. 29,225 (Aug. 3, 1988).

89 *See* § 2.3.7, *infra*.

90 49 Fed. Reg. 7763 (Mar. 1, 1984).

91 16 C.F.R. § 444.2(a). *See also* 16 C.F.R. § 429.1(d) (prohibiting confessions of judgment clauses or waivers of rights in door-to-door sales contracts).

92 16 C.F.R. § 444.2(a).

93 Kienzl, FTC Informal Staff Opinion Letter (Sept. 26, 1985).

a magistrate.[94] It applies to instruments executed after a consumer defaults as well as to notes and contracts signed at the time of the transaction.[95]

Informal FTC staff opinion letters distinguish between judicial proceedings and self-help creditor remedies. For example, the rule does not prohibit a "power of sale" clause that allows a creditor, upon default, to exercise a self-help right to take possession of property and sell it,[96] nor does it prohibit waiver of notice of default.[97] A court has ruled that a confession of judgment provision did not violate the Pennsylvania UDAP statute, even if it would violate the FTC rule,[98] but the Pennsylvania UDAP statute has since been amended to make it clear that confession of judgment clauses are violations.[99]

2.3.5 Waiver of Exemption Clauses

The Credit Practices Rule prohibits contract clauses that waive or limit exemptions from attachment, execution, or other process on the debtor's real or personal property.[100] The prohibition applies not only to property owned by the consumer but also to property held by or "due" to the consumer, thus covering wages or other debts owed to the consumer.[101] There is an exception for property subject to a security interest executed in connection with the transaction.[102]

2.3.6 Wage Assignments

The Credit Practices Rule prohibits wage assignments,[103] with certain exceptions. The FTC found that "consumers suffer substantial injury when wage assignments are used as a collection device."[104] The FTC found that:

- Wage assignment, unlike garnishment, occurs without the procedural safeguards of a hearing and an opportunity to assert defenses or counterclaims. The use of wage assignments causes interference with employment relationships, pressure from threats to file wage assignments with employers, and disruption of family finances.
- Employers are hostile to wage assignments, and loss of employment for the debtor is possible.
- Wage assignments also cause serious consumer injury when used as a threat to obtain payment. The pressure from these threats may cause consumers to abandon legitimate defenses to prevent the creditors from contacting the employers.
- Wage assignments also cause disruption of a family's finances and make it difficult for the debtor to purchase necessities. This disruption can result in costly refinancing or the impossibility of discharging other obligations in a timely fashion.[105]

The rule contains three exceptions to the prohibition of wage assignments. First, there is an exception for wage assignments that are, by their terms, revocable at the will of the debtor.[106] According to informal FTC staff opinion letters, a creditor may require that revocation of a wage assignment be in writing.[107] However, the creditor cannot place any time limit on the debtor's right to revoke a wage assignment.[108] Thus, limiting the right to revoke to the first ten days violates the rule,[109] as does a requirement that the revocation be done a specified number of days before it is given effect.[110]

The condition that, to fall within the exception for revocable wage assignments, the assignment must be revocable "by its terms"[111] is particularly important. If the wage assignment does not explicitly say that it is revocable, a consumer will have no way to know of his or her right to revoke it. Wage assignments that do not have this explicit condition violate the rule.[112]

Mandatory irrevocable[113] wage assignments are allowed in the context of payroll deduction plans of the sort used in

---

94 Curlee, FTC Informal Staff Opinion Letter (May 9, 1985); Torkildson, FTC Informal Staff Opinion Letter (Apr. 17, 1985).

95 Raver, FTC Informal Staff Opinion Letter (Jan. 22, 1986). *But cf.* Piche v. Clark County Collection Serv., L.L.C., 119 Fed. Appx. 104 (9th Cir. 2004) (unpublished) (collection agency not bound by FTC Credit Practices Rule because it is not a lender or retail installment seller; opinion does not state whether debt arose from a covered transaction).

96 Leverick, FTC Informal Staff Opinion Letter (Mar. 29, 1985) (Arizona "deed of trust" procedure); Witzel, FTC Informal Staff Opinion Letter (Mar. 22, 1985).

97 Clancy, FTC Informal Staff Opinion Letter (Dec. 14, 1988).

98 Zhang v. Southeastern Fin. Grp., Inc., 980 F. Supp. 787 (E.D. Pa. 1997).

99 73 Pa. Stat. § 201-2(4)(xviii). *See* Commonwealth *ex rel.* Fisher v. Percudani, 825 A.2d 743 (Pa. Commw. Ct. 2003) (refusing to dismiss claim that contractual liquidated damages clause was prohibited confession of judgment clause).

100 16 C.F.R. § 444.2(a)(2). *See* United States v. Action Loan Co., 5 Trade Reg. Rep. (CCH) ¶ 24,793 (W.D. Ky. Aug. 24, 2000) (proposed consent decree against company that used waiver of exemption clause).

101 Free Bridge Auto Sales v. Fitzgerald, 48 Va. Cir. 1 (Va. Cir. Ct. 1999).

102 16 C.F.R. § 444.2(a)(4).

103 16 C.F.R. § 444.2(a)(3)(i).

104 Fed. Trade Comm'n, Statement of Basis and Purpose, 49 Fed. Reg. 7789, 7757 (Mar. 1, 1984) (footnote omitted), *available online as companion material to this treatise.*

105 *Id.* at 7757, 7758 (footnotes omitted).

106 16 C.F.R. § 444.2(a)(3)(i); F.T.C. v. LoanPointe, L.L.C., 525 Fed. Appx. 696 (10th Cir. 2013) (affirming order requiring disgorgement of interest creditor received through wage garnishment that was based on wage assignments; defendants conceded that language of wage assignment, "I agree to have my wages garnished to pay any delinquent amount on this loan," violated credit practices rule).

107 Miller, FTC Informal Staff Opinion Letter (Apr. 17, 1985); Torkildson, FTC Informal Staff Opinion Letter (Apr. 17, 1985); F.T.C. v. Payday Fin., L.L.C., 989 F. Supp. 2d 799 (D.S.D. 2013) (not violation to require opt-outs within first ten days to be written and thereafter to be by phone).

108 Wilson, FTC Informal Staff Opinion Letter (July 29, 1986).

109 F.T.C. v. Payday Fin., L.L.C., 989 F. Supp. 2d 799 (D.S.D. 2013) (opt-out provision limited to ten days violates credit practices rule).

110 Wilson, FTC Informal Staff Opinion Letter (July 29, 1986); Torkildson, FTC Informal Staff Opinion Letter (Apr. 17, 1985).

111 16 C.F.R. § 444.2(a)(3)(i).

112 Fed. Trade Comm'n, Statement of Basis and Purpose, 49 Fed. Reg. 7789, 7760 (Mar. 1, 1984) ("To fit within this exception the wage assignment must be revocable by its terms; therefore the wage assignment must include language that establishes revocability"; also noting in footnote that hiding or obfuscating revocability disclosures may itself be an unfair or deceptive practice under the FTC Act), *available as online companion material to this treatise.*

113 Wilson, FTC Informal Staff Opinion Letter (July 29, 1986) ("a payroll deduction plan need not be revocable at the will of the debtor"); Klewin, FTC Informal Staff Opinion Letter (June 26, 1986) ("It is the

credit union loans.[114] Only part of the debtor's paycheck may be taken.[115] The payroll deduction plan must "commenc[e] at the time of the transaction" and must be "a method of making each payment,"[116] rather than a collection device utilized after default.[117]

The final other exception allows assignment of wages that the consumer has already earned at the time of the credit extension.[118]

Wage assignments that predated the Credit Practices Rule were not invalidated by it.[119] An employer does not violate the rule by complying with a wage assignment, regardless of its legality under the rule.[120]

The lending laws of many states also restrict wage assignments.[121]

2.3.7 Household Goods Security Interests

The Credit Practices Rule prohibits non-purchase money and non-possessory security interests in household goods.[122]

The rule defines household goods as clothing, furniture, appliances, one radio, one television, linens, china, crockery, kitchenware, and personal effects, including wedding rings.[123] The FTC staff considers "personal effects" to be limited to items that an individual would ordinarily carry about on his or her person and possessions of a uniquely personal nature, such as family photographs, personal papers, or a Bible.[124] When the FTC rule is unclear, state law will determine whether an item is considered furniture or an appliance.[125]

The FTC staff has indicated that the following items fall within the rule's definition of "household goods":

- Sewing machines;[126]
- Vacuum cleaners;[127]
- Telephones and answering machines;[128]
- Air conditioners;[129]
- Household pets;[130]
- Freezers;[131]
- Floor polishers;[132]
- Patio furniture;[133]
- Ovens, including microwave ovens;[134]
- Dishwashers;[135] and
- Fans, clocks, lamps, toasters, and electric can openers.[136]

Duplicate items are protected by the Credit Practices Rule, except that only one television and one radio are protected.[137]

The definition of "household goods" in the Credit Practices Rule excludes works of art, items acquired as antiques, jewelry (except wedding rings), and electronic entertainment equipment (except one television and one radio).[138] In addition, the FTC staff has indicated that the following items would not fall within the definition of "household goods":

FTC staff's view that the foregoing exemption means that the Rule would not prohibit any payroll deduction plan, including the 'mandatory irrevocable' one you described in your letter").

114 16 C.F.R. § 444.2(a)(3)(ii); Wilson, FTC Informal Staff Opinion Letter (July 29, 1986); Klewin, FTC Informal Staff Opinion Letter (June 26, 1986); Parker, FTC Informal Staff Opinion Letter (Mar. 29, 1985).

115 Kelley, FTC Informal Staff Opinion Letter (June 17, 1987) ("[a]n assignment of all of the consumer's wages to a creditor is not a wage 'deduction' as described in the Rule," even when creditor takes only monthly installment due and then gives balance to consumer). *But cf.* Parker, FTC Informal Staff Opinion Letter (Mar. 29, 1985); Kaswell, FTC Informal Staff Opinion Letter (Mar. 20, 1985) (assignment of entire final paycheck to credit union does not violate rule).

116 16 C.F.R. § 444.2(a)(3)(ii).

117 Wilson, FTC Informal Staff Opinion Letter (July 29, 1986) (a payroll deduction plan must commence at time of the transaction, "rather than subsequently in connection with consumer default or delinquency"). *See also* Kaswell, FTC Informal Staff Opinion Letter (Mar. 20, 1985) (approving provision of payroll deduction plan on the assumption that it was a means by which a borrower makes payments on an outstanding loan balance, "not a collection device utilized after default").

118 16 C.F.R. § 444.2(a)(3)(iii). *See* Scott, FTC Informal Staff Opinion Letter (Mar. 1, 1985).

119 Treaster, FTC Informal Staff Opinion Letter (Apr. 15 1985).

120 McCarthy, FTC Informal Staff Opinion Letter (Jan. 27, 1986); Patterson, FTC Informal Staff Opinion Letter (June 20, 1985).

121 *See* Fed. Trade Comm'n, Statement of Basis and Purpose, 49 Fed. Reg. 7789, 7756 (Mar. 1, 1984) (listing state provisions in effect as of 1984), *available online as companion material to this treatise*; National Consumer Law Center, Consumer Credit Regulation Appxs. D, E (2d ed. 2015), *updated at* www.nclc.org/library (summarizing wage assignment restrictions and other provisions of state installment loan and open-end credit laws).

122 16 C.F.R. § 444.2(a)(4). *See* Federal Trade Comm'n v. Stewart Fin. Co., 5 Trade Reg. Rep. (CCH) ¶ 15,499 (Oct. 28, 2003) (preliminary injunction); Federal Trade Comm'n v. Stewart Fin. Co., No. 103CV-2648, 5 Trade Reg. Rep. (CCH) ¶ 15,477 (N.D. Ga. Sept. 4, 2003) (complaint alleging that subprime lender took household goods as collateral in violation of Credit Practices Rule); Consent Decree, United States v. West Capital Fin. Services Corp., F.T.C. File No. 922 3306 (S.D. Cal. June 15, 1994) (creditor allegedly took non-purchase-money security interest in household goods; relief includes restitution of all filing fees and related finance charges concerning household goods collateral).

123 16 C.F.R. § 444.1(i).

124 Scott, FTC Informal Staff Opinion Letter (Aug. 8, 1985); Scott, FTC Informal Staff Opinion Letter (Mar. 1, 1985); Chamness, FTC Informal Staff Opinion Letter (Feb. 11, 1985); Dyer, FTC Informal Staff Opinion Letter (May 1, 1984). *See also In re* Branch, 368 B.R. 80 (Bankr. D. Colo. 2006) (vehicle is not a "personal effect," nor is it a "household good" under Louisiana law).

125 Dyer, FTC Informal Staff Opinion Letter (May 1, 1984).

126 Scott, FTC Informal Staff Opinion Letter (Aug. 8, 1985).

127 Letter from the Sec'y of the Fed. Trade Comm'n to the Honorable Wendell Ford, Clearinghouse No. 49,972 (Mar. 8, 1994); Scott, FTC Informal Staff Opinion Letter (Aug. 8, 1985).

128 *But see* Mewhinney, FTC Informal Staff Opinion Letter (Feb. 16, 1989) (Letter 2).

129 Scott, FTC Informal Staff Opinion Letter (Aug. 8, 1985).

130 Scott, FTC Informal Staff Opinion Letter (Mar. 1, 1985).

131 Scott, FTC Informal Staff Opinion Letter (Aug. 8, 1985).

132 *Id.*

133 *Id.*

134 Letter from the Sec'y of the Fed. Trade Comm'n to the Honorable Wendell Ford, Clearinghouse No. 49,972 (Mar. 8, 1994); Mewhinney, FTC Informal Staff Opinion Letter (Feb. 16, 1989) (Letter 2); Chamness, FTC Informal Staff Opinion Letter (Feb. 11, 1985).

135 Chamness, FTC Informal Staff Opinion Letter (Feb. 11, 1985).

136 Letter from the Sec'y of the Fed. Trade Comm'n to the Honorable Wendell Ford, Clearinghouse No. 49,972 (Mar. 8, 1994).

137 16 C.F.R. § 444.1(i); Chamness, FTC Informal Staff Opinion Letter (Feb. 11, 1985).

138 16 C.F.R. § 444.1(i).

- Bicycles;[139]
- Typewriters;[140]
- Power tools;[141]
- A butane tank;[142]
- Livestock;[143]
- Barbecue grills;[144]
- Luggage;[145]
- Carpets and rugs;[146]
- A hot tub;[147]
- Fireplace equipment;[148]
- A child's car seat;[149]
- Firearms;[150]
- Camping and sports equipment;[151]
- Hunting and fishing equipment;[152]
- Cameras;[153]
- Musical instruments;[154]
- Home computers and computer equipment;[155]
- Lawn equipment;[156]
- Mechanic and carpenter tools;[157]
- Boats;[158]

- Snowmobiles;[159]
- Stamp and coin collections;[160]
- Stereo equipment;[161]
- Bank deposits;[162]
- Credit insurance proceeds;[163]
- Tape players;[164] and
- VCRs.[165]

The FTC staff has also issued an opinion that a security interest in "fixtures" is permissible even if it includes items that might be considered household goods if they were not attached to the real property.[166]

As mentioned earlier, many of these staff exclusions from the definition of household goods seem at variance with the full FTC opinion in its statement of basis and purpose for the Credit Practices Rule.[167] Consumer attorneys should not view these staff opinions as binding on the courts but must be aware that creditors may use these letters as justification for their practices.

A creditor that lists a security interest in household goods violates the Credit Practices Rule even if a clause in the contract says that the security interest does not apply to non-purchase money consumer loans.[168] The clause might not be clear to all consumers, thus leading them to believe that the creditor has the power to repossess their household goods.

A purchase-money security interest in household goods may be retained when the credit transaction is consolidated or refinanced, even by a new creditor,[169] as long as the new creditor makes a reasonably prudent business judgment that the original transaction complied with the Credit Practices Rule.[170] This is true regardless of the number of times the transaction is consolidated or refinanced.[171] A blanket security interest in household goods that was taken before the rule's effective date may not, however, be retained if the transaction is refinanced or renewed after the effective date.[172] A cross-collateralization clause that applies a purchase-money security interest in household goods to other extensions of credit does not violate the Credit Practices Rule if it is limited to

139 Mewhinney, FTC Informal Staff Opinion Letter (Feb. 16, 1989) (Letter 2); Chamness, FTC Informal Staff Opinion Letter (Feb. 11, 1985); Scott, FTC Informal Staff Opinion Letter (Mar. 1, 1985).

140 Chamness, FTC Informal Staff Opinion Letter (Feb. 11, 1985); Geary, FTC Informal Staff Opinion Letter (Mar. 22, 1985); Scott, FTC Informal Staff Opinion Letter (Mar. 1, 1985).

141 Mewhinney, FTC Informal Staff Opinion Letter (Feb. 16, 1989) (Letter 2); Chamness, FTC Informal Staff Opinion Letter (Feb. 11, 1985); Scott, FTC Informal Staff Opinion Letter (Mar. 1, 1985).

142 Scott, FTC Informal Staff Opinion Letter (Aug. 8, 1985).

143 *Id.*

144 *Id.*

145 *Id.*

146 Scott, FTC Informal Staff Opinion Letter (Aug. 8, 1985); Scott, FTC Informal Staff Opinion Letter (Mar. 1, 1985).

147 Scott, FTC Informal Staff Opinion Letter (Aug. 8, 1985).

148 *Id.*

149 *Id.*

150 Mewhinney, FTC Informal Staff Opinion Letter (Feb. 16, 1989) (Letter 2); Geary, FTC Informal Staff Opinion Letter (Mar. 22, 1985); Scott, FTC Informal Staff Opinion Letter (Mar. 1, 1985).

151 Mewhinney, FTC Informal Staff Opinion Letter (Feb. 16, 1989) (Letter 2); Scott, FTC Informal Staff Opinion Letter (Aug. 8, 1985); Scott, FTC Informal Staff Opinion Letter (Mar. 1, 1985).

152 Geary, FTC Informal Staff Opinion Letter (Mar. 22, 1985); Scott, FTC Informal Staff Opinion Letter (Mar. 1, 1985); Chamness, FTC Informal Staff Opinion Letter (Feb. 11, 1985).

153 Mewhinney, FTC Informal Staff Opinion Letter (Feb. 16, 1989) (Letter 2); Geary, FTC Informal Staff Opinion Letter (Mar. 22, 1985); Scott, FTC Informal Staff Opinion Letter (Mar. 1, 1985).

154 Mewhinney, FTC Informal Staff Opinion Letter (Feb. 16, 1989) (Letter 2); Geary, FTC Informal Staff Opinion Letter (Mar. 22, 1985); Scott, FTC Informal Staff Opinion Letter (Mar. 1, 1985); Chamness, FTC Informal Staff Opinion Letter (Feb. 11, 1985).

155 Geary, FTC Informal Staff Opinion Letter (Mar. 22, 1985); Scott, FTC Informal Staff Opinion Letter (Mar. 1, 1985).

156 Mewhinney, FTC Informal Staff Opinion Letter (Feb. 16, 1989) (Letter 1); Mewhinney, FTC Informal Staff Opinion Letter (Feb. 16, 1989) (Letter 2); Scott, FTC Informal Staff Opinion Letter (Mar. 1, 1985).

157 Scott, FTC Informal Staff Opinion Letter (Mar. 1, 1985).

158 Scott, FTC Informal Staff Opinion Letter (Mar. 1, 1985).

159 *Id.*

160 Geary, FTC Informal Staff Opinion Letter (Mar. 22, 1985); Scott, FTC Informal Staff Opinion Letter (Mar. 1, 1985).

161 Scott, FTC Informal Staff Opinion Letter (Mar. 1, 1985).

162 Bucchi, FTC Informal Staff Opinion Letter (June 21, 1985).

163 *Id.*

164 Mewhinney, FTC Informal Staff Opinion Letter (Feb. 16, 1989) (Letter 2).

165 *Id.*

166 Hazlett, FTC Informal Staff Opinion Letter (Apr. 16, 1985).

167 *See* § 2.3.3, *supra.*

168 Henry, FTC Informal Staff Opinion Letter (Sept. 27, 1988).

169 Lax, FTC Informal Staff Opinion Letter (Mar. 6, 1987); Wilkinson, FTC Informal Staff Opinion Letter (June 28, 1985); Chamness, FTC Informal Staff Opinion Letter (June 28, 1985); Feldman, FTC Informal Staff Opinion Letter (Feb. 20, 1985).

170 Chamness, FTC Informal Staff Opinion Letter (June 28, 1985).

171 *Id.*

172 Wilkinson, FTC Informal Staff Opinion Letter (June 28, 1985); Chamness, FTC Informal Staff Opinion Letter (June 28, 1985) (security interest may be retained in post-rule refinancing only if original transaction was a purchase money extension of credit).

refinancings or consolidations of the original purchase money transaction.[173] But presumably the converse is also true: a cross-collateralization clause that is not limited to refinancings or consolidations does violate the rule.

The prohibition of non-purchase money security interests in household goods under the Credit Practices Rule is discussed in more detail in the NCLC treatise, *Repossessions*.[174]

2.3.8   *Pyramiding Late Charges*

The Credit Practices Rule prohibits pyramiding by assessing more than one delinquency charge for one late payment (pyramiding late charges for a *missed* payment is not prohibited).[175] This prohibition does not, according to the FTC staff, affect a creditor's choice of accounting methods, as long as the method chosen does not result in the assessment of late charges when the only delinquency is attributable to late charges assessed on earlier installments.[176] The Credit Practices Rule does not prevent a creditor from assessing a late charge for each month that an installment remains unpaid.[177] Nor does the rule dictate to which month a late payment should be applied—the month when it was due or the month in which it was actually paid.[178]

2.3.9   *Co-Signer Warning Notice*

The rule requires a notice to co-signers, warning them of their potential obligations.[179] The notice must be in the form prescribed by the FTC.[180] However, references to creditor remedies that are not allowed under the laws of a particular state may be deleted in order to make the notice accurate.[181] The creditor may add a summary identifying information such as the date, account number, name, address, and loan amount[182]

as well as a signature line.[183] The creditor can also print the notice on its letterhead[184] but should not include any other statements[185] or information about such matters as the creditor's insurance or its national affiliations.[186]

The Credit Practices Rule is not violated by including both a Spanish and an English version[187] or both a state law version and the FTC version of the notice on the same sheet.[188] Creditors may also modify the notice by substituting a word such as "buyer" for "borrower" if necessary to make the notice an accurate reflection of the underlying transaction.[189] The type size and style of the notice should be clear and conspicuous.[190]

A person who signs to be liable on someone else's consumer credit contract but who does not receive compensation is a co-signer under the Credit Practices Rule even if he or she is described as a "buyer" in the contract documents.[191] However, a person who is to be the co-owner of the property purchased or is to share in its use, or is entitled to receive the proceeds of a loan, is not a co-signer.[192] Nonetheless, if a person's signature

---

173   Lax, FTC Informal Staff Opinion Letter (Mar. 6, 1987); Torkildson, FTC Informal Staff Opinion Letter (July 1, 1985); Torkildson, FTC Informal Staff Opinion Letter (Apr. 17, 1985).

174   National Consumer Law Center, Repossessions (8th ed. 2013), *updated at* www.nclc.org/library.

175   16 C.F.R. § 444.4.

176   O'Connell, FTC Informal Staff Opinion Letter (May 31, 1985); Caspo, FTC Informal Staff Opinion Letter (Dec. 21, 1984).

177   Bucchi, FTC Informal Staff Opinion Letter (June 21, 1985); Caspo, FTC Informal Staff Opinion Letter (Dec. 21, 1984).

178   Caspo, FTC Informal Staff Opinion Letter (Dec. 21, 1984).

179   16 C.F.R. § 444.3.
        The FTC has exempted New York contracts from the co-signer disclosure because state law offers similar or greater protections. *See* 51 Fed. Reg. 28,328 (Aug. 7, 1986). *See also* Royal Furniture Co., 93 F.T.C. 422 (1979) (consent order) (failure to disclose rights and obligations to co-signers).

180   Moore, FTC Informal Staff Opinion Letter (Mar. 1, 1985).

181   Lozoff, FTC Informal Staff Opinion Letter (May 22, 1986); LaBarfera, FTC Informal Staff Opinion Letter (Nov. 19, 1985); Gwynne, FTC Informal Staff Opinion Letter (Sept. 17, 1985); Gwynne, FTC Informal Staff Opinion Letter (July 12, 1985); Kaswell, FTC Informal Staff Opinion Letter (Mar. 20, 1985); Lozoff, FTC Informal Staff Opinion Letter (Mar. 6, 1985); Kinsler, FTC Informal Staff Opinion Letter (Mar. 1, 1985); Scott, FTC Informal Staff Opinion Letter (Mar. 1, 1985).

182   Topoluk, FTC Informal Staff Opinion Letter (Mar. 10, 1986); Dayton, FTC Informal Staff Opinion Letter (Nov. 18, 1985); Gwynne, FTC

Informal Staff Opinion Letter (July 12, 1985); Colello, FTC Informal Staff Opinion Letter (July 1, 1985); Kaswell, FTC Informal Staff Opinion Letter (Mar. 20, 1985); Miller, FTC Informal Staff Opinion Letter (Feb. 25, 1985); Dyer, FTC Informal Staff Opinion Letter (May 1, 1984).

183   Gwynne, FTC Informal Staff Opinion Letter (July 12, 1985); Colello, FTC Informal Staff Opinion Letter (July 1, 1985); Miller, FTC Informal Staff Opinion Letter (Feb. 25, 1985); Meegan, FTC Informal Staff Opinion Letter (Feb. 19, 1985); Caspo, FTC Informal Staff Opinion Letter (Dec. 21, 1984); Feldman, FTC Informal Staff Opinion Letter (July 24, 1984); Dyer, FTC Informal Staff Opinion Letter (May 1, 1984).

184   Colello, FTC Informal Staff Opinion Letter (July 1, 1985); Miller, FTC Informal Staff Opinion Letter (Feb. 25, 1985); Meegan, FTC Informal Staff Opinion Letter (Feb. 19, 1985); Caspo, FTC Informal Staff Opinion Letter (Dec. 21, 1984); Feldman, FTC Informal Staff Opinion Letter (July 24, 1984).

185   Weise, FTC Informal Staff Opinion Letter (Apr. 26, 1985). *But see* Harter, FTC Informal Staff Opinion Letter (June 12, 1987) (statement that creditor is required to give the notice under certain circumstances is allowed).

186   Meegan, FTC Informal Staff Opinion Letter (Feb. 19, 1985).

187   Waterman, FTC Informal Staff Opinion Letter (Apr. 18, 1985).

188   Harter, FTC Informal Staff Opinion Letter (June 12, 1987); Topoluk, FTC Informal Staff Opinion Letter (Mar. 10, 1986); Caspo, FTC Informal Staff Opinion Letter (Dec. 21, 1984).

189   Feldman, FTC Informal Staff Opinion Letter (July 24, 1984).

190   Caspo, FTC Informal Staff Opinion Letter (Dec. 21, 1984).

191   Mintz, FTC Informal Staff Opinion Letter (Dec. 9, 1986); 16 C.F.R. § 444.1(k) (definition of "co-signer"). *See* Qualkenbush v. Harris Trust & Sav. Bank, 219 F. Supp. 2d 935 (N.D. Ill. 2002); Lee v. Nationwide Cassel, L.P., 660 N.E.2d 94 (Ill. App. Ct. 1995) (seller may violate UDAP statute by listing co-signer as co-buyer, contrary to state law), *rev'd in part on other grounds*, 675 N.E.2d 599 (Ill. 1996).

192   Riley, FTC Informal Staff Opinion Letter (July 10, 1985); Stodard, FTC Informal Staff Opinion Letter (July 10, 1985); Norskog, FTC Informal Staff Opinion Letter (June 11, 1985); Witzel, FTC Informal Staff Opinion Letter (Mar. 22, 1985); Caspo, FTC Informal Staff Opinion Letter (Dec. 21, 1984) (co-owner of real estate that is to be improved through credit transaction is a buyer, not a co-signer, even if he or she does not reside there). *See also* Rudolph, FTC Informal Staff Opinion Letter (May 19, 1985) (person who is already obligated on a debt, and then finds another person to buy the property and sign the note, is not a co-signer).

is obtained after the initial applicant is told that the signature of another person is necessary, that person is a co-signer even if his or her name is also placed on the title documents.[193] A person who merely provides collateral for an extension of credit without becoming obligated on the underlying debt is not considered a co-signer.[194]

In seeking to establish that a person shown as a co-buyer or sole buyer is actually a co-signer, it is helpful to subpoena the dealer's file at the earliest possible moment. Usually it will have a credit application signed by the real principal buyer. The attorney should also check both persons' credit records to see if and when the dealer checked their credit reports. The dealer probably checked the real buyer's credit report first, and the co-signer's only later, after telling the real buyer that a co-signer was necessary.

A creditor does not violate the Credit Practices Rule by providing the notice to persons involved in the transaction who may not technically be "co-signers," as long as there is no deception.[195]

2.3.10 Private Remedies for Credit Practices Rule Violations

There is generally no private right of action under the FTC Act for a violation of an FTC trade regulation rule.[196] It seems clear, however, that a consumer can challenge a violation of the FTC Credit Practices Rule under the almost forty state UDAP statutes that prohibit "unfair" and/or "unconscionable" practices.[197] The rule is an official FTC ruling that use of certain creditor remedies is an "unfair" trade practice. This FTC ruling guides courts in interpreting what is unfair under a state UDAP statute. Moreover, it may be a per se state UDAP violation to violate an FTC rule.[198]

Even in states where the UDAP statute prohibits only "deceptive" practices, it is deceptive for a creditor to violate the Credit Practices Rule because including illegal provisions in a credit agreement misrepresents the consumer's legal

rights.[199] It is certainly deceptive for a creditor to make false threats that it will utilize remedies that are now outlawed.

Since a contract term prohibited by the Credit Practices Rule is unlawful, creditors have no right to enforce that term.[200] A consumer can therefore base a defense on a violation of the rule or can bring an affirmative suit to declare a contract provision unenforceable.

The federal Truth in Lending Act (TILA) may provide another remedy whereby a creditor takes a security interest in violation of the Credit Practices Rule. The TILA requires disclosure of the security interest, and disclosure of an invalid and unenforceable security interest may entitle the consumer to an award of statutory damages and attorney fees.[201]

2.3.11 Attempts to Circumvent FTC Credit Practices Rule

Some creditors seek to circumvent the FTC Credit Practices Rule. It is unfair and deceptive to try to evade the rule by taking a prohibited security interest in household goods but then disclaiming the security interest in another part of the contract.[202]

Some lenders—particularly installment lenders and certain lenders that market themselves as payday lending alternatives—closely analyze FTC staff opinion letters to determine what types of collateral are not prohibited by the ban in the Credit Practices Rule on "household goods" collateral. These creditors take non-purchase-money security interests in second televisions and radios and in such items as lawn equipment, tools, stereos, VCRs, cameras, typewriters, firearms, bicycles, and musical instruments. The creditor

---

193 Fed. Trade Comm'n, Regulatory Flexibility Act Review of Trade Regulation Rule Concerning Credit Practices, 60 Fed. Reg. 24,805, 24,806 (May 10, 1995).

194 Witzel, FTC Informal Staff Opinion Letter (Mar. 22, 1985); Lynott, FTC Informal Staff Opinion Letter (Feb. 22, 1985).

195 Miller, FTC Informal Staff Opinion Letter (Feb. 25, 1985).

196 See § 2.2.4.1, *supra*.

197 See National Consumer Law Center, Unfair and Deceptive Acts and Practices §§ 4.3, 4.4, Appx. A (8th ed. 2012), *updated at* www.nclc.org/library. *Cf.* Provident Fin. Co. v. Rowe, 399 S.E.2d 368 (N.C. Ct. App. 1991) (reversing dismissal of claim that creditor violated UDAP statute by taking non-possessory, non-purchase money security interest in household goods in violation of credit practices rule). *But see* Zhang v. Southeastern Fin. Grp., Inc., 980 F. Supp. 787 (E.D. Pa. 1997) (violation of FTC rule prohibiting confession of judgment provisions did not violate Pennsylvania UDAP statute; Pennsylvania courts "routinely" uphold and enforce confessed judgments in connection with consumer transactions). *But cf.* Ken-Mar Fin. v. Harvey, 368 S.E.2d 646 (N.C. Ct. App. 1988) (violation of FTC Credit Practices Rule not UDAP violation because it was not in effect at time contract was entered into).

198 See § 2.2.4.2, *supra*.

199 See Iron & Glass Bank v. Franz, 9 Pa. D. & C.3d 419 (Pa. Ct. Com. Pl. Allegheny Cnty. 1978). See also People v. McKale, 602 P.2d 731 (Cal. 1979); Orlando v. Finance One, 369 S.E.2d 882 (W. Va. 1988). See generally National Consumer Law Center, Unfair and Deceptive Acts and Practices §§ 3.2.7.4.2, 5.6.8 (8th ed. 2012), *updated at* www.nclc.org/library.

200 W. Va. Code § 46A-2-104(a) (providing that no person shall be held liable as co-signer or charged with personal liability for payment in consumer credit sale, lease, or loan, unless creditor gave notice of potential liability); In re Raymond, 103 B.R. 846 (Bankr. W.D. Ky. 1989) (security interest unenforceable); Boyer v. ITT Fin. Services (In re Boyer), 63 B.R. 153 (Bankr. E.D. Mo. 1986) (security interest unenforceable); Free Bridge Auto Sales v. Fitzgerald, 48 Va. Cir. 1 (Va. Cir. Ct. 1999) (waiver of exemptions unenforceable). See also Consent Decree, United States v. Action Loan Co., No. 3:00CV-511-H (W.D. Ky. Aug. 24, 2000) (nullifying waivers of exemptions and extinguishing security interests in household goods that violated Credit Practices Rule), *available at* www.ftc.gov.

201 National Consumer Law Center, Truth in Lending § 5.8.4 (9th ed. 2015), *updated at* www.nclc.org/library. *But see* Szumny v. American Gen. Fin., 246 F.3d 1065 (7th Cir. 2001) (bona fide attempt to describe a security interest in household goods is not TILA violation even if security interest might be invalid under Credit Practices Rule).

202 FTC Informal Staff Letter of Sandra Wilmore to the Legal Aid Soc'y of Northwest N. Carolina (Sept. 27, 1988). See also Orlando v. Finance One, 369 S.E.2d 882 (W. Va. 1988) (waiver of exemption rights contrary to state law is deceptive even though contract clause made it inapplicable to these transactions).

then sells highly-profitable credit property insurance on these items.

The value of these items is often exaggerated in the collateral inventory, thus increasing premium costs. In some states, such an exaggerated evaluation may also be used to avoid state legislation prohibiting security interests in items under a specified value. Also closely examine whether the creditor is selling duplicate coverage for items already covered by the debtor's own household insurance policy.

Creditors may use a preprinted form listing the types of collateral falling outside the Credit Practices Rule's definition of "household goods" and then just check appropriate items. For example, a creditor might check "jewelry," "stereo," and "tools." But a valid security agreement must identify collateral with particularity so a sheriff or other party knows precisely what property to seize.[203] It is unlikely that checking boxes on a preprinted form will suffice. Consequently, the security interest would be invalid, attempts or threats to enforce the interest would be actionable, and disclosure of the interest may be deceptive or violate the Truth in Lending Act's disclosure requirements.

2.4 Used Car Rule

2.4.1 The Rule's Scope

The FTC's trade regulation rule on the sale of used motor vehicles (hereafter "the Used Car Rule")[204] applies to motor vehicles, defined as any motorized vehicle other than a motorcycle, with a gross vehicle weight rating under 8500 pounds, a curb weight less than 6000 pounds, and a frontal area less than forty-six square feet.[205] The Used Car Rule applies to any used vehicle, defined as a vehicle driven more than the limited use necessary in moving or road testing a new vehicle prior to delivery to a consumer.[206] Since this definition applies even to vehicles for which the title has never been transferred to a retail purchaser, the Used Car Rule applies to demonstrators, executive vehicles, and any other car with even minimal mileage already registered on the odometer.[207]

The obligations under the Used Car Rule apply to any dealer (defined as a business that sells five or more used vehicles in the prior twelve months).[208] It does not, however, apply to a bank or financial institution, a business selling a used vehicle to an employee of that business, or a lessor selling a leased vehicle to the lessee.[209] The rule protects a wide class of consumers, including those who buy a car for business purposes.[210]

The Used Car Rule generally applies whenever a dealer *offers* a used vehicle for sale. Thus even if a vehicle is eventually leased, and not sold, to a consumer, the dealer still must comply with most rule provisions when it first offers the vehicle to the public for sale.

The Used Car Rule is discussed in more detail in NCLC's *Consumer Warranty Law*.[211]

2.4.2 Rule Requirements

The Used Car Rule has three main requirements:

- A window sticker must be affixed to the vehicle, containing specified information;
- A copy of the window sticker must be provided to the consumer, the information from that sticker must be incorporated into the sales agreement, and no statements can be made to the consumer contradicting information on the sticker;
- A series of misrepresentations are prohibited, and certain warranty information must be disclosed.

The window sticker must be exactly as set out in the rule, reprinted at Appendix A.11, *infra*, with the same wording, heading, punctuation, type styles, sizes, and format indicated.[212] The sticker must be displayed prominently on a location on the vehicle such that the sticker is readily readable on both sides. While it can be taken down during a test drive, it must be returned as soon as the test drive is over.[213]

---

203   National Consumer Law Center, Repossessions § 3.2.7 (8th ed. 2013), *updated at* www.nclc.org/library.

204   16 C.F.R. § 455, *reprinted at* Appx. A.11, *infra. See also* Staff Compliance Guidelines, 53 Fed. Reg. 17,658 (May 17, 1988).

     This is not the same rule that was promulgated on August 18, 1981. *See* 46 Fed. Reg. 41328 (1981).

     In May, 1982, Congress vetoed the 1981 rule, but the congressional veto was overturned on constitutional grounds. Consumers Union v. Federal Trade Comm'n, 691 F.2d 575 (D.C. Cir. 1982), *aff'd*, U.S. Senate v. Federal Trade Comm'n *and* U.S. House of Representatives v. Federal Trade Comm'n, 463 U.S. 1216 (1983).

     The FTC then reconsidered the 1981 rule and finally adopted a more limited rule by deleting the "known defects" requirement of the 1981 rule. Consequently, while the 1985 rule requires certain dealer disclosures, it does not require dealers to disclose known defects in the cars they are selling. In 1994, as part of its periodic review under the Regulatory Flexibility Act, the FTC solicited comments on whether changes were warranted to the Used Car Rule. After reviewing the rule, the FTC concluded that it was working and achieving its objectives at minimal cost to dealers. The FTC retained the rule, with several non-substantive amendments. 60 Fed. Reg. 62,195 (Dec. 5, 1995).

     In 2008, the Commission began a review of the rule, but as yet has taken no final action. *See* 73 Fed. Reg. 42,285 (July 21, 2008) (calling for comments on the rule). *See also* Comments of Consumer Action, Consumers for Auto Reliability & Safety, Consumer Fed'n of Am., Consumer Fed'n of Cal., National Consumer Law Center on behalf of its low income clients, U.S. Pub. Interest Research Grp., and the Watsonville Law Ctr., Re: Request for Public Comments, Used Car Rule Regulatory Review, Matter No. P087604, *available at* www.docplayer.net.

205   16 C.F.R. § 455.1(d)(1).

206   16 C.F.R. § 455.1(d)(2).

207   *See also* Regulatory Flexibility Act and Periodic Review of Used Motor Vehicle Trade Regulation Rule, 60 Fed. Reg. 62,195, 62,197 (Dec. 5, 1995) (re-affirming that demonstrators are covered even if original certificate of origin has never been transferred).

208   16 C.F.R. § 455.1(d)(3).

209   16 C.F.R. § 455.1(d)(3).

210   16 C.F.R. § 455.1(d)(4).

211   National Consumer Law Center, Consumer Warranty Law Ch. 15 (5th ed. 2015), *updated at* www.nclc.org/library.

212   16 C.F.R. § 455.2(a)(2).

213   16 C.F.R. § 455.2(a)(1).

When a sale is conducted in Spanish, the window sticker and the contract language disclosures must be available in both Spanish and English.[214] The Spanish version of the window sticker is also reprinted in the Used Car Rule.

The dealer must check the box describing the type of warranty being offered—no warranty, full warranty, or limited warranty—and whether the dealer pays only a percentage of labor and parts. Systems covered and the duration of each warranty must be listed. The dealer must also indicate, by checking a box, if a service contract is available.[215]

The window sticker (sometimes called the Buyer's Guide) must be amended if negotiations alter the warranty coverage,[216] must be given to the consumer upon sale,[217] and must be incorporated by reference into the contract, overriding any contrary provisions in the contract.[218]

For example, if a service contract is sold after the initial accepted offer, and the car can no longer be sold "as is,"[219] the dealer must amend the Buyer's Guide to delete the "as is" disclosure. Moreover, the sales agreement must be changed so that it also does not state that the car is sold "as is." Sometimes, after selling a service contract, the dealer will stamp the sales agreement with language overriding the "as is" disclaimer, but elsewhere in the same contract will be language stating that the vehicle is sold "as is." Not only is this inadequate, but the Buyer's Guide must be amended as well.

Similarly, state law may prohibit disclaimers of implied warranties or create certain minimum standards as to a used car warranty.[220] In that case, the dealer cannot check the "as is" box on the Buyer's Guide, and nothing in the contract should indicate the sale is "as is."

The Used Car Rule also specifies that it is deceptive for a used car dealer to:

- Misrepresent the mechanical condition of a used vehicle;
- Misrepresent the terms of any warranty offered in connection with the sale of a used vehicle; or
- Represent that a used vehicle is sold with a warranty when the vehicle is sold without a warranty.[221]

The Used Car Rule also makes it an unfair practice for any used car dealer to:

- Fail to disclose, prior to sale, that a used vehicle is sold without any warranty; or
- Fail to make available, prior to sale, the terms of any written warranty offered in connection with the sale of a used vehicle.[222]

2.4.3 Common Rule Violations

FTC enforcement of the Used Car Rule has found widespread violations.[223] Consumer attorneys thus should be alert for potential violations of the FTC Used Car Rule and should ensure that dealers:

- Post a *completed* guide on their cars and leave them there except during test drives;[224]
- Replace the Buyer's Guide after its removal for a test drive;
- Follow the type, size, production, capitalization, color, and wording requirements, with no extraneous information included;
- Complete the Buyer's Guide properly, particularly in checking the correct warranty disclosure boxes; an implied-warranty-only box should be included in the form and checked where appropriate, particularly in states not allowing the waiver of implied warranties;
- Make sure the warranty disclosed on the guide matches the warranty provided for in the written agreement;
- Use the Spanish-language Buyer's Guide when required;
- Include the required language in the contract;
- Give the buyer the Buyer's Guide or a copy of it; and
- If a service contract is sold, the service contract box must be checked, as well as either the warranty box or the implied warranty box.

2.4.4 Remedies for Rule Violations

Violations of the Used Car Rule violate the FTC Act, and the FTC has brought enforcement actions for Used Car Rule violations.[225] As with any FTC rule, there is no private right of

---

214 16 C.F.R. § 455.5.
215 16 C.F.R. § 455.2.
216 16 C.F.R. § 455.2(b)(2).
217 16 C.F.R. § 455.3(a).
218 16 C.F.R. § 455.3(b).
219 The Magnuson-Moss Warranty Act prohibits disclaimers of implied warranties when a service contract is sold in conjunction with the goods.
220 *See* National Consumer Law Center, Consumer Warranty Law Ch. 15 (5th ed. 2015), *updated at* www.nclc.org/library.
221 16 C.F.R. § 455.1.
222 *Id.*

223 *See* § 2.4.4, *infra.*
224 *See* Buskirk v. Harrell, 2000 Ohio App. LEXIS 3100 (Ohio Ct. App. June 28, 2000) (giving credence, in consumer's case alleging dealer failed to provide a window sticker, to consumer's photographs of dealer's lot that show cars without window stickers). *But cf.* Lester v. Wow Car co., 83 U.C.C. Rep. Serv. 2d 830 (S.D. Ohio 2014) (fact that buyer did not see used-car guide on vehicle when he test-drove it does not establish rule violation, as it is to be removed for test drives; seller testified as to its practice of checking each car daily to make sure guide was displayed), *aff'd*, 601 Fed. Appx. 399 (6th Cir. 2015); Conte v. Sonic-Plymouth Cadillac, Inc., 2008 WL 783632 (E.D. Mich. Mar. 20, 2008) (failure to post window sticker not a violation when car never displayed on lot; dealer special-ordered vehicle from wholesaler at request of consumer seeking a Bentley).
225 *See, e.g.,* Federal Trade Comm'n v. Abernathy Motor Co., 2015 WL 3750455 (E.D. Ark. June 4, 2015) (stipulation for permanent injunction and civil penalty); United States v. Middleton, 1995 WL 314540 (N.D. Ill. May 19, 1995) (summary judgment); United States v. American Sys., Inc., 5 Trade Reg. Rep. (CCH) ¶ 23,389 (M.D. Fla. 1993); United States v. Payless Auto Sales, Inc., 5 Trade Reg. Rep. (CCH) ¶ 23,371 (E.D. Va. 1993) (consent decree); Federal Trade Comm'n v. Americlean Ltd., 5 Trade Reg. Rep. (CCH) ¶ 23,369 (E.D. Va. 1993) (consent decree); United States v. TJ Motors, Inc. 5 Trade Reg. Rep. (CCH) ¶ 23,294 (N.D. Ill. 1992) (consent decree); United States v. Liberty Motors, Inc., 5 Trade Reg. Rep. (CCH) ¶ 23,275 (E.D. Va. 1992) (consent decree); United States v. Car City, Inc., 5 Trade Reg. Rep. (CCH) ¶ 23,274 (S.D. Iowa 1992) (consent decree); Federal Trade Comm'n v. Tom's Motors, Inc., 5 Trade Reg. Rep. (CCH) ¶ 23,255 (D.N.M. 1992) (consent decree); Federal Trade

action under the FTC Act for rule violations.[226] Nevertheless, a rule violation should be actionable under a state UDAP statute, since an FTC rule should guide courts in interpreting state UDAP statutes.[227] In addition, failure to provide the information required by the Used Car Rule may amount to negligent misrepresentation.[228] Since the FTC Used Car Rule was in part promulgated under the federal Magnuson-Moss Act,[229] a good

argument can be made that it is a Magnuson-Moss Act violation to violate the Used Car Rule.[230]

2.4.5 When Buyer's Guide Warranty Disclosure Conflicts with Warranty Provided in the Sales Agreement

The Used Car Rule states clearly that the dealer may not make any statements, oral or written, that contradict the disclosures in the Buyer's Guide. The dealer can negotiate the warranty coverage so that the final sale has different terms than those first disclosed on the Buyer's Guide. However, in such a case, the final warranty terms have to be identified in the contract of sale and summarized on the copy of the Buyer's Guide that is provided to the consumer.[231]

Consequently, if the Buyer's Guide provided to the consumer indicates that any implied or express warranties are given with the sale, then the sales agreement cannot identify the transaction as "as is" or without warranties. The same is true if the agreement provides for warranties but the guide discloses the sale as "as is." These sales agreement provisions would directly contradict the disclosures in the Buyer's Guide. This rule violation should also be a state UDAP violation.[232]

The same should be true if the contract is silent on warranties and the Buyer's Guide states the sale is "as is." Silence means that implied warranties are not disclaimed. If the contract provides for implied warranties, this is inconsistent with a Buyer's Guide that states the sale is "as is."

2.4.6 FTC Used Car Rule Does Not Insulate Sellers from UDAP Liability

Seller compliance with the FTC Used Car Rule does not insulate the seller from UDAP liability. For example, although the FTC considered and rejected a rule requirement that dealers disclose known defects, compliance with the rule does not prevent a state UDAP action alleging the dealer failed to disclose known defects.[233]

Comm'n v. Montoya, 5 Trade Reg. Rep. (CCH) ¶ 23,254 (D.N.M. 1992) (consent decree); United States v. McNevin Cadillac, 5 Trade Reg. Rep. (CCH) ¶ 23,246 (N.D. Cal. 1992) (consent decree); Federal Trade Comm'n v. Quality Motor Co., 5 Trade Reg. Rep. (CCH) ¶ 23,229 (W.D. Okla. 1992) (consent decree); Federal Trade Comm'n v. M.A.S.H. Motors, Inc., 5 Trade Reg. Rep. (CCH) ¶ 23,226 (D. Okla. 1992) (consent decree); United States v. Hern Oldsmobile-GMC Truck, Inc., 5 Trade Reg. Rep. (CCH) ¶ 23,220 (N.D. Ohio 1992) (consent judgment); Federal Trade Comm'n v. John Michael Auto Sales, Inc., 5 Trade Reg. Rep. (CCH) ¶ 23,216 (D. Md. 1992) (consent decree); United States v. Ghoregan, 5 Trade Reg. Rep. (CCH) ¶ 23,170 (W.D. Okla. 1992) (consent order); United States v. Credit Car Connection, 5 Trade Reg. Rep. (CCH) ¶ 23,148 (M.D. Fla. 1992) (consent order).

226 *See* § 2.2.4.1, *supra.*

227 Brown v. Cincyautos, Inc., 2009 WL 88736 (S.D. Ohio Jan. 12, 2009) (failure to include in Buyer's Guide all contact information required by FTC rule is per se UDAP violation; bona fide error not defense to liability but relevant to damages), *later decision at* 2009 WL 2912136 (S.D. Ohio Sept. 8, 2009) (whether seller's procedures to avoid window sticker disclosure violations satisfies Ohio UDAP statute's bona fide error defense is fact question); Martinez v. Rick Case Cars, Inc., 278 F. Supp. 3d 1371 (S.D. Fla. 2003); Tirado v. Ofstein, 2008 WL 902506 (Conn. Super. Ct. Mar. 14, 2008) (violation of Used Car Rule that results in ascertainable loss is CUTPA violation); Barnes v. Holliday, 1990 WL 269884 (Conn. Super. Ct. June 6, 1990) (failure to comply with FTC Used Car Rule was a violation of Connecticut UDAP statute); Milton v. Riverside Auto Exch. (Ohio Ct. Com. Pl. Montgomery Cnty. Aug. 27, 1991), *available at* www.nclc.org/unreported (UDAP statute allows rescission of used car sale when seller did not post Buyer's Guide); § 2.3.3.2, *supra. See also* Buskirk v. Harrell, 2000 WL 943782, at *5 (Ohio Ct. App. June 28, 2000) (failure to post Buyer's Guide in violation of FTC Used Car Rule is violation of Ohio UDAP statute, which requires court to give weight to FTC orders and rules); Rubin v. Gallery Auto Sales, 1997 WL 1068459 (Ohio Ct. Com. Pl. June 9, 1997) (failure to display Buyer's Guide and to fill it in properly are UDAP violations); Consumer Protection Division Enforcement Statements Concerning Motor Vehicle Advertising & Sales Practices, Iowa Dep't of Transp., Dealer Operating Manual VII-2, Clearinghouse No. 49,156. *Cf.* Cummins v. Dave Fillmore Car Co., 1987 WL 19186 (Ohio Ct. App. Oct. 27, 1987) (omission of statement that information on Buyer's Guide was part of contract was UDAP violation, but no actual damages shown and buyer not entitled to rescission). *But see In re* Lake Auto, Inc., 1989 Minn. App. LEXIS 178 (Minn. Ct. App. Feb. 10, 1989) (unpublished) (failure to post Buyer's Guide not state UDAP violation); Shumaker v. Hamilton Chevrolet, Inc., 920 N.E.2d 1023 (Ohio Ct. App. 2009) (technical violation of FTC Used Car Rule, here omission of contact information from back of buyers guide, not a per se UDAP). *But cf.* Lester v. Wow Car co., 83 U.C.C. Rep. Serv. 2d 830 (S.D. Ohio 2014) (technical violation of Used Car Rule is not UDAP violation), *aff'd*, 601 Fed. Appx. 399 (6th Cir. 2015).

228 Moore v. It's All Good Auto Sales, Inc., 907 F. Supp. 2d 915, 929 (W.D. Tenn. 2012).

229 *See* 15 U.S.C. § 2309(b); 16 C.F.R. § 455 (Authority). *See also* National Consumer Law Center, Consumer Warranty Law Ch. 2 (5th ed. 2015),

updated at www.nclc.org/library (discussion of Magnuson-Moss Warranty Act).

230 *See* Currier v. Spencer, 772 S.W.2d 309 (Ark. 1989) (upholding trial court's award of Magnuson-Moss attorney fees for violation of FTC Used Car Rule); Nassar v. Wiz Leasing, Inc., 2013 WL 4734851 (Conn. Super. Ct. Aug. 12, 2013) (violation of Used Car Rule is actionable as Magnuson-Moss violation).

231 16 C.F.R. § 455.4; Schultz v. Burton-Moore Ford, Inc., 2008 WL 5111897 (E.D. Mich. Dec. 2, 2008) (fact issue whether warranty information adequately disclosed; neither box checked but "nearly illegible" note on Buyer's Guide indicated manufacturer's warranty only, and title application disclosed that seller disclaimed warranties).

232 Lawhorn v. Joseph Toyota, Inc., 750 N.E.2d 610 (Ohio Ct. App. 2001).

233 Hinds v. Paul's Auto Werkstatt, Inc., 810 P.2d 874 (Or. Ct. App. 1991). *Accord* Totz v. Continental DuPage Acura, 602 N.E.2d 1374 (Ill. App. Ct. 1992).

2.5 Door-to-Door and Off-Premises Sales

2.5.1 The FTC Cooling-Off Period Rule Described

Door-to-door sales have a history of high-pressure tactics, deception and other systematic consumer abuse.[234] A three-day cooling-off period is a remedy designed to meet these problems by giving consumers an opportunity to reevaluate their purchase decisions away from the salesperson's hard sell. The remedy also lessens sellers' incentive to use high-pressure sales tactics because, when consumers cancel high-pressure sales, sellers are left with no profit for their investment of time and energy.

The FTC has promulgated a trade regulation rule concerning a cooling-off period for door-to-door sales (hereafter "the Cooling-Off Period Rule").[235] The rule is reprinted at Appendix A.4, *infra*. The online companion material to this treatise includes not only the rule itself but also the FTC's statement of basis and purpose when it adopted the rule. The online companion material to this treatise also includes three advisory opinion letters issued by the FTC.

The Cooling-Off Period Rule gives the consumer the right to cancel a home-solicitation transaction, requires that certain information and forms be given to the consumer at the time of the transaction, and provides rights, duties, and responsibilities of merchants, consumers, and other parties involved in such transactions. The rule applies not just to door-to-door transactions but other off-premises transactions, such as sales events in motels or other temporary locations.

It is important to be familiar with all aspects of this rule. While many door-to-door sellers comply with the rule's basic requirements, sellers often neglect to comply with several less well-known requirements. For sales covered by the Cooling-Off Period Rule, the seller must provide the consumer with a fully completed copy of the sales contract,[236] attach to that contract two copies of a written notice of cancellation,[237] and orally inform the consumer of his or her cancellation rights at the time the contract is signed.[238] In immediate proximity to the space reserved in the contract for the buyer's signature must be a statement of the buyer's right to cancel.[239] Both the contract and the notice of cancellation must be in the same language (for example, Spanish) as the oral sales presentation.[240]

Note that two copies of the notice of cancellation must be attached to the contract. Sellers may get into trouble by failing to include the second of these two notices.[241] The seller has several options as to how to provide two copies of the notice, as long as one copy can be easily returned to the seller. One copy may be in the contract and one copy in a separate form, or the seller can give the consumer two copies of the contract with the form integrated into each copy. But when one copy of the form is returned, the consumer must be able to retain a completed copy of both the form and the contract. The contract itself must also notify consumers where to find these forms (for example, back of the contract, in a separate form).[242]

The Cooling-Off Period Rule requires that the right to cancel be disclosed on "the contract" or receipt.[243] Under Ohio's similar statute, the disclosure must appear on the contract between the particular seller and the consumer, not on a contract with a different entity for a related transaction.[244] A California decision interpreting similar language in its statute held that a contract was formed when consumers signed a clause accepting a home improvement contractor's "Labor Estimate," authorizing him to begin work, and stating that payment would be made upon completion.[245] The fact that the

---

234 *See* International Soc'y for Krishna Consciousness v. Lee, 505 U.S. 672, 112 S. Ct. 2701, 2722, 120 L. Ed. 2d 541 (1992) (Kennedy, J., concurring).

235 16 C.F.R. § 429, *reprinted at* Appx. A.4, *infra*.

The rule was adopted by 37 Fed. Reg. 22,933 (Oct. 26, 1972). The effective date of June 7, 1974, was set by 38 Fed. Reg. 33,766 (Dec. 7, 1973). The rule was amended by 38 Fed. Reg. 30,105 (Nov. 1, 1973) (revising language of notice of right to cancel), 38 Fed. Reg. 31,828 (Nov. 19, 1973) (correcting a misstatement in previous *Federal Register* notice), and 53 Fed. Reg. 45,455 (Nov. 10, 1988) (creating exemption for sellers of arts and crafts and for automobiles sold at temporary locations and allowing minor variations in wording of notice of right to cancel).

In 1995, after requesting public comment and reviewing the rule, the FTC continued the rule in effect with minor changes. 60 Fed. Reg. 54,180 (Oct. 20, 1995).

In 2009, the FTC initiated another review of the rule. 74 Fed. Reg. 18170 (Apr. 21, 2009) (requesting public comment), 74 Fed. Reg. 36972 (July 27, 2009) (extending comment period). *See* Comments of the National Consumer Law Center, Consumers for Auto Reliability & Safety, Consumer Fed'n of Am., and Consumers Union Regarding Cooling-Off Rule Regulatory Review (Sept. 25, 2009), *available at* www.nclc.org. The FTC concluded its review and issued amendments to the rule in early 2015. 80 Fed. Reg. 1329 (Jan. 9, 2015). Its only substantive revision was to limit the rule to sales of $130 or more (formerly $25 or more).

236 16 C.F.R. § 429.1(a). *See* Paramount Builders, Inc. v. Commonwealth, 530 S.E.2d 142 (Va. 2000) (ruling on civil investigative order; failure to give copies violates state cooling-off statute). *Cf.* Consolidated Tex. Fin. v. Shearer, 739 S.W.2d 477 (Tex. App. 1987) (upholding verdict in favor of homeowners under Texas home solicitation sales law when one of violations was failure to provide copy of contract).

237 16 C.F.R. § 429.1(b); United States v. Mission Plans, Inc., 5 Trade Reg. Rep. (CCH) ¶ 23,660 (S.D. Tex. Sept. 2, 1994) (consent decree requiring pre-need funeral plan seller to give notice of right to cancel and cancellation forms). *See also* United States v. Dixie Readers' Serv., Inc., 3 Trade Reg. Rep. (CCH) ¶ 22,306 (S.D. Miss. Nov. 14, 1985) (consent order).

238 16 C.F.R. § 429.1(e).

239 16 C.F.R. § 429.1(a).

240 16 C.F.R. § 429.1(a), (b).

241 Eastern Roofing & Aluminum Co. v. Brock, 320 S.E.2d 22 (N.C. Ct. App. 1984). *See also* Op. Mich. Att'y Gen. No. 5792, 1980 WL 113944 (Oct. 1, 1980) (notice on reverse side of contract does not comply with Michigan law).

242 16 C.F.R. § 429.1(a).

243 16 C.F.R. § 429.1(a).

244 Equicredit Corp. v. Jackson, 2004 WL 2726115 (Ohio Ct. App. Nov. 24, 2005) (unpublished) (rejecting mortgage broker's argument that appearance of notice on consumer's contract with home improvement company was sufficient).

245 Handyman Connection of Sacramento, Inc. v. Sands, 20 Cal. Rptr. 3d 727, 737–38 (Cal. Ct. App. 2004).

consumer also signed a document titled "Contract" a month later when the contractor began work made no difference.

While the Cooling-Off Period Rule, as originally drafted, required sellers to include the exact notice language mandated by the rule, it now allows sellers to shorten the mandated notice language by omitting certain language that does not apply to a particular transaction.[246] For example, the seller can delete language relating to trade-ins when there is no trade-in, language relating to negotiable instruments when there is no negotiable instrument, or language about property delivered before expiration of the three-day period.[247] This actually increases the likelihood of rule violations. Thus be aware that a seller may copy another seller's notice, not realizing that the latter has properly deleted language that is not applicable to the latter's own notice but which is applicable to the copier of the notice and must be included in the copier's notice.

The Cooling-Off Period Rule also specifies that the seller may not misrepresent the buyer's right to cancel[248] nor include in the contract any waiver of rights created by the rule.[249] It is no defense that the seller offers a better cancellation policy than the FTC rule; the seller must disclose and comply with its own stated policy and also with the FTC rule.[250]

The seller cannot assign or sell the consumer's note for five business days[251] and must make a full refund of all payments and cancel all indebtedness within ten business days of receipt of a buyer's cancellation notice.[252] Obviously, it is improper for a seller to backdate the contract and cancellation notice to thwart the consumer's three-day cancellation right.[253]

2.5.2 Interrelation of FTC Rule with State Law

Every state has enacted a three-day cooling-off period law analogous to the FTC rule.[254] Such statutes are constitutional

even though they single out door-to-door sales for special treatment.[255]

Some of these statutes reiterate the FTC rule almost exactly or state that compliance with the FTC rule automatically satisfies the requirements of the state law. But other state cooling-off statutes set out requirements different than those specified in the FTC rule. The North Dakota cooling-off statute, for example, provides those over sixty-five years of age with a fifteen-day cooling-off period or a right to return the product within thirty days if the consumer is not satisfied with it.[256] Most of the differences between the state rules and the FTC rule are relatively minor, so interpretations of one are relevant to the other.

Compliance with the FTC rule does not exempt a seller from complying with state laws regulating door-to-door sales, except to the extent that the state law is directly inconsistent with the FTC rule. A state law that applies to more transactions than the FTC rule is not inconsistent and is not preempted.[257] A state law is directly inconsistent with the FTC rule and is preempted by the FTC rule when it provides the consumer a right to cancel which is weaker than that provided by the FTC rule or permits the imposition of any cancellation fee or penalty on the buyer.[258] State law is also preempted if it does

---

246 16 C.F.R. § 429.1(b).

247 *See* 53 Fed. Reg. 45,455 (Nov. 10, 1988) (giving these examples).

248 16 C.F.R. § 429.1(f).

249 16 C.F.R. § 429.1(d). *See also* Tee Pee Fence & Railing Corp. v. Olah, 544 N.Y.S.2d 112 (N.Y. Civ. Ct. 1989) (waiver of right to cancel is void even though on a separate sheet of paper); Paramount Builders, Inc. v. Commonwealth, 530 S.E.2d 142 (Va. 2000) (ruling on civil investigative order; having consumer sign waiver of right to cancel as condition of getting a discount violates state cooling-off statute even though waiver is void).

250 State v. Sears Roebuck & Co., Clearinghouse No. 40,629 (Me. Super. Ct. Aug. 1985).

251 16 C.F.R. § 429.1(h).

252 16 C.F.R. § 429.1(g), (i). *See also* United States v. Dixie Readers' Serv., Inc., 3 Trade Reg. Rep. (CCH) ¶ 22,306 (S.D. Miss. Nov. 14, 1985) (consent order).

253 Consolidated Tex. Fin. v. Shearer, 739 S.W.2d 477 (Tex. App. 1987).

254 Ala. Code §§ 5-19-1(8), 5-19-12; Alaska Stat. §§ 45.02.350 (door-to-door sales; five-day period), 45.63.030 (telephonic solicitations; seven-day period); Ariz. Rev. Stat. Ann. §§ 44-5001 to 44-5008; Ark. Code Ann. §§ 4-89-101 to 4-89-110; Cal. Civ. Code §§ 1689.5 to 1689.14 (West); Colo. Rev. Stat. §§ 5-3-401 to 5-3-405; Conn. Gen. Stat. §§ 42-134a to 42-143; Del. Code Ann. tit. 6, §§ 4401 to 4407; D.C. Code § 28-3811; Fla. Stat. §§ 501.021 to 501.055; Ga. Code Ann. § 10-1-6; Haw. Rev. Stat. §§ 481C-1 to 481C-6; Idaho Code Ann. §§

28-43-401 to 28-43-405; 815 Ill. Comp. Stat. Ann. § 505/2B; Ind. Code §§ 24-4.5-2-501 to 24-4.5-2-502, §§ 24-5-10-1 to 24-5-10-18; Iowa Code §§ 555A.1 to 555A.6; Kan. Stat. Ann. § 50-640; Ky. Rev. Stat. Ann. §§ 367.410 to 367.460 (West); La. Rev. Stat. Ann. §§ 9:3538 to 9:3541.1; Me. Rev. Stat. tit. 32, §§ 4661 to 4670, tit. 9-A, §§ 3-501 to 3-507; Md. Code Ann., Com. Law §§ 14-301 to 14-306 (West); Mass. Gen. Laws Ann. ch. 93, § 48; Mich. Comp. Laws §§ 445.111 to 445.117; Minn. Stat. §§ 325G.06 to 325G.11; Miss. Code Ann. §§ 75-66-1 to 75-66-11; Mo. Rev. Stat. §§ 407.700 to 407.725; Mont. Code Ann. §§ 30-14-501 to 30-14-508; Neb. Rev. Stat. §§ 69-1601 to 69-1607; Nev. Rev. Stat. §§ 598.140 to 598.280, 598.2801; N.H. Rev. Stat. Ann. §§ 361-B:1 to 361-B:3; N.J. Stat. Ann. §§ 17:16C-61.1 to 17:16C-61.9 (West); N.J. Stat. Ann. §§ 17:16C-95 to 17:16C-103 (West) (door-to-door home repair sales); N.M. Stat. Ann. § 57-12-21; N.Y. Pers. Prop. Law §§ 425 to 431 (McKinney); N.C. Gen. Stat. §§ 25A-38 to 25A-42; N.D. Cent. Code §§ 51-18-01 to 51-18-09; Ohio Rev. Code Ann. §§ 1345.21 to 1345.28 (West); Okla. Stat. tit. 14A, §§ 2-501 to 2-505; Or. Rev. Stat. §§ 83.710 to 83.750; 73 Pa. Stat. Ann. § 201-7 (West); R.I. Gen. Laws §§ 6-28-1 to 6-28-8; S.C. Code Ann. §§ 37-2-501 to 37-2-506; S.D. Codified Laws Ann. §§ 37-24-5.1 to 37-24-5.7; Tenn. Code Ann. §§ 47-18-701 to 47-18-708; Tex. Bus. & Com. Code Ann. §§ 601.001 to 601.205 (West); Utah Code Ann. §§ 70C-5-101 to 70C-1-105 (West); Vt. Stat. Ann. tit. 9, §§ 2451a, 2454; Va. Code Ann. §§ 59.1-21.1 to 59.1-21.7:1; Wash. Rev. Code §§ 63.14.040, 63.14.120, 63.14.150, 63.14.154; W. Va. Code §§ 46A-1-102(22), 46A-2-132 to 46A-2-135; Wis. Stat. §§ 423.201 to 423.205; Wyo. Stat. §§ 40-12-104, 40-14-251 to 40-14-255.

255 State v. Direct Sellers Ass'n, 494 P.2d 361 (Ariz. 1972).

256 N.D. Cent. Code §§ 51-18-02, 51-18-04.

257 *See* 80 Fed. Reg. 1329, 1331 (Jan. 9, 2015).

258 16 C.F.R. § 429.2(b), *reprinted at* Appx. A.4, *infra*; United Consumer Fin. Services Co. v. Carbo, 982 A.2d 7 (N.J. Super. Ct. App. Div. 2009) (FTC rule preempts New Jersey home solicitation sales statute's provision of slightly shorter cancellation period, its more onerous method of cancellation (certified mail), and its requirement to use a non-bold small typeface, but not the requirement that notice explain certain rights and identify product and price or the requirement that buyer be given copy in English and in language of the transaction).

not require that the seller give the buyer notice of his or her right to cancel the transaction in substantially the same form and manner provided for in the FTC rule.[259] But if there is no conflict, the seller will have to comply with both the FTC rule and state law.[260]

The FTC has issued an advisory opinion clarifying the issue of preemption of state cooling-off statutes.[261] A seller can be required to give two incompatible cooling-off-period notices—one mandated by the FTC rule and one by state law "as long as any language in the state or municipal notice directly inconsistent with the rule is stricken."[262] The FTC gave two examples:

> Since the Commission's rule gives the consumer a unilateral right to cancel a transaction within three days, without penalty or fee, language in a state notice misinforming the buyer of the existence of a penalty or fee (i.e., "If you cancel, the seller may keep all or part of your cash down payment") is directly inconsistent with the rule and, if included in the sales contract or receipt, must be stricken. Moreover, since the buyer's right to cancel transactions covered by the rule is not limited to agreements solicited at or near the buyer's residence, does not require the buyer to furnish any reason for cancellation, and may be exercised by mail or delivery of any written notice or telegram, any language to the contrary in a state notice is similarly directly inconsistent with the rule.[263]

The FTC has issued another advisory opinion that the cooling-off notice provided for in the Uniform Consumer Credit Code (UCCC) misinforms buyers as to their rights under the FTC rule and conflicts with the FTC notice because the FTC rule's coverage is broader than that of the UCCC, and the UCCC notice implies that the buyer must state a specific reason for canceling the transaction.[264]

2.5.3 Interrelation of FTC Rule and State Law with Truth in Lending Rescission

Another source of consumer cancellation rights is the rescission notice required by the Truth in Lending Act when a creditor takes a non-purchase-money security interest in the debtor's home.[265] The FTC rule explicitly states that it does not apply in situations in which the TILA rescission notice

is required.[266] In fact, mistakenly disclosing a right to cancel under the FTC rule or state law may violate the Truth in Lending Act by obscuring or contradicting the notice of the TILA rescission right.[267]

While the FTC rule does not apply when TILA rescission rights are applicable, state cooling-off statutes *do* apply, unless the statute has a similar explicit exception[268] or is inconsistent with the TILA requirements.[269] For example, a federal court has ruled that Mississippi's state cooling-off law is not inconsistent with the TILA even though the state law places extra requirements on the creditor and that, consequently, the creditor must comply with both statutes.[270] Giving the consumer the Truth in Lending Act rescission notice does not constitute substantial compliance with a state law requirement that the consumer be given a notice of cancellation.[271]

2.5.4 Scope of the FTC Rule

2.5.4.1 Sales Outside the Home Are Also Covered

The Cooling-Off Period Rule applies to the sale, lease, or rental of consumer goods or services primarily for personal, family, or household purposes.[272] For the rule to apply, the sale need not be consummated in the buyer's home. The definition of "door-to-door sale" extends to all sales in which "the seller or his representative personally solicits the sale, including those in response to or following an invitation by the buyer, and the buyer's agreement or offer to purchase is made at a place other than the place of business of the seller."[273]

---

259 16 C.F.R. § 429.2(b).

260 *See* United Consumer Fin. Services Co. v. Carbo, 982 A.2d 7 (N.J. Super. Ct. App. Div. 2009) (requiring compliance with various provisions of state law that provided greater protections to consumers and did not conflict with FTC rule); Bruntaeger v. Zeller, 515 A.2d 123 (Vt. 1986).

261 FTC Advisory Opinion, 85 F.T.C. 1215 (May 20, 1975), *available online as companion material to this treatise.*

262 *Id.*

263 *Id.*

264 FTC Advisory Opinion, 87 F.T.C. 1444 (1976), *available online as companion material to this treatise.*

265 15 U.S.C. § 1635(a).

266 16 C.F.R. § 429.0(a)(2). *See also* Letter No. 1054, Consumer Cred. Guide (CCH) ¶ 31,378 (June 1, 1976).

267 *See* Williams v. Empire Funding Corp., 109 F. Supp. 2d 352 (E.D. Pa. 2000).

268 *See, e.g.,* Hanlin v. Ohio Builders & Remodelers, Inc., 196 F. Supp. 2d 572 (S.D. Ohio 2001) (state home solicitation sales act does not give right to cancel contract with home improvement lender since TILA provides right to rescind).

269 *See* 12 C.F.R. § 1026.28. *See also* Reynolds v. D&N Bank, 792 F. Supp. 1035 (E.D. Mich. 1992).

270 Cole v. Lovett, 672 F. Supp. 947 (S.D. Miss. 1987). *See also* Reynolds v. D&N Bank, 792 F. Supp. 1035 (E.D. Mich. 1992).

271 Gross v. Bildex, Inc., 647 N.E.2d 573 (Ohio Mun. Ct. 1994); Hines v. Thermal-Gard of Ohio, Inc., 546 N.E.2d 487 (Ohio Mun. Ct. 1988).

272 16 C.F.R. § 429.0(a), (b). *Cf.* Moore v. R.Z. Sims Chevrolet-Subaru, Inc., 738 P.2d 852 (Kan. 1987) (state cooling-off statute does not apply when truck not intended for personal, family, or household purpose); Reagan Nat'l Adver. v. Lakeway 620 Partners, 2001 Tex. App. LEXIS 4375 (Tex. App. June 29, 2001) (unpublished) (Texas statute only applies to consumer transactions, and successor to consumer's interest cannot sue as consumer).

273 16 C.F.R. § 429.0(a). *See* Louis Luskin & Sons, Inc. v. Samovitz, 212 Cal. Rptr. 612 (Cal. Ct. App. 1985) (state statute applies to contract entered into a vacant house owned by buyers); State *ex rel.* Abrams v. Kase, Clearinghouse No. 43,079 (N.Y. Sup. Ct. 1986). *See also* Bruntaeger v. Zeller, 515 A.2d 123 (Vt. 1986) (sale in hotel room is within state cooling-off statute). *Cf.* Reusch v. Roob, 610 N.W.2d 168 (Wis. Ct. App. 2000) (sale at one of seller's two places of business not covered by state cooling-off statute).

The rule lists sales "at facilities rented on a temporary or short-term basis, such as hotel or motel rooms, convention centers, fairgrounds and restaurants, or sales at the buyer's workplace or in dormitory lounges" as examples of sales to which the rule applies.[274] A company that persuades a sales prospect to set up and invite neighbors to an in-home sales meeting is also covered by the rule.[275]

Sellers of automobiles, vans, trucks or other motor vehicles at auctions, tent sales, or other temporary places of business are specifically exempted from the rule, as long as the seller is a seller of vehicles with a permanent place of business.[276] This provision, which was added to the rule in 1995, expands an exemption the FTC adopted in 1988[277] in that it exempts sellers of all motor vehicles rather than just automobiles. The provision also exempts "curbstone" sales as long as the seller has a permanent place of business.[278] Sales of arts and crafts at fairs and similar places are also exempt.[279]

2.5.4.2 Effect of Prior Negotiations, Seller Being Invited to the Home

If the sale is made in the consumer's home following prior negotiations at the seller's place of business, the rule does not apply.[280] The theory is that, "while such sales are actually consummated in the home, the attributes of the typical door-to-door sale are not present—the consumer has not been duped or otherwise deceived as to the nature of the sales call."[281] In order for this exception to apply, the seller's place of business where the prior negotiations occurred must be a retail business establishment at a fixed permanent location where the goods are exhibited or the services are offered for sale on a continuing basis.[282] Some state statutes have this same exception.[283]

Merely exchanging contact information at the seller's place of business is insufficient.[284]

The Cooling-Off Period Rule does not apply when the consumers go to the seller's place of business and commit themselves there to the sale, even though the seller later visits their home to determine what materials will be needed and to calculate a firm price.[285] Likewise, when a loan transaction takes place at the creditor's place of business, and subsequently an appraiser visits the consumer's home, a state statute similar to the FTC rule is inapplicable.[286] The contact in the home must involve personal solicitation.[287]

---

274 16 C.F.R. § 429.0(a). *See* 60 Fed. Reg. 54,180 (Oct. 20, 1995) (discussing reasons for adding these examples to the rule); 53 Fed. Reg. 45,455, 45,458 (Nov. 10, 1988); FTC Advisory Opinion to "est, an educational corporation" (July 14, 1976) (this FTC advisory opinion is one of the letters available online as companion material to this treatise); Holloway, FTC Informal Staff Opinion Letter (May 11, 1990), Clearinghouse No. 45,909 (photo session and sale of prints in hotel room). *See also* Federal Trade Comm'n v. Screen Test USA, 5 Consumer Cred. Guide (CCH) ¶ 24,699 (E.D. Va. Aug. 31, 1999) (consent decree) (hotel room sales).

275 United States v. Sanders, 5 Trade Reg. Rep. (CCH) ¶ 24,742 (D. Md. Apr. 2, 2000) (consent order).

276 16 C.F.R. § 429.3(a).

277 53 Fed. Reg. 45,455 (Nov. 10, 1988).

278 *See* 60 Fed. Reg. 54,180, 54,183 (Oct. 20, 1995).

279 16 C.F.R. § 429.3(b).
      This exemption, added to the rule in 1995, codifies an exemption adopted by the FTC in 1988. 53 Fed. Reg. 45,455 (Nov. 10, 1988).

280 16 C.F.R. § 429.0(a)(1).

281 Statement of Basis and Purpose, 37 Fed. Reg. 22,946 (Oct. 26, 1972). *See* Moore v. R.Z. Sims Chevrolet-Subaru, Inc., 738 P.2d 852 (Kan. 1987) (state statute inapplicable when consumer signed contract in home only after her husband negotiated it at dealership). *But cf. In re* Bayless, 326 B.R. 411 (Bankr. E.D. Mich. 2005) (applying state home solicitation sales law when initial contact with seller, but not negotiations, occurred in store).

282 16 C.F.R. § 429.0(a)(1).

283 *See, e.g.,* Altek Envtl. Serv. Co. v. Harris, 2009 WL 1145233 (Ohio Ct. App. Apr. 27, 2009) (unpublished) (applying this exception); Knight v.

Colazzo, 2008 WL 5244640 (Ohio Ct. App. Dec. 17, 2008) (unpublished) (denying exemption; no showing that home improvement contractor's home office was open to public or that goods were displayed there); Carpet One Mentor, Inc. v. Bridge, 2007 WL 1731728 (Ohio Ct. App. June 15, 2007) (exception applies under state statute; final agreement made pursuant to prior negotiations in the course of buyers' visits to seller's retail establishment); Equicredit Corp. v. Jackson, 2004 WL 2726115 (Ohio Ct. App. Nov. 24, 2005) (unpublished) (exemption does not apply unless mortgage broker proves it had fixed business location where services were offered); Kamposek v. Johnson, 2005 WL 238152 (Ohio Ct. App. Jan. 28, 2005) (unpublished) (home office probably insufficient); Gallagher v. O'Connor, 2003 WL 22220337 (Ohio Ct. App. Sept. 26, 2003) (unpublished) (exemption did not apply when seller's home office did not have separate entrance, phone lines, or showroom and was not made known to public); Bratka v. Smiley, 2003 WL 1065603 (Ohio Ct. App. Mar. 11, 2003) (unpublished) (finding exception applicable); New Phila. Inc. v. Sagrilla, 2002 WL 1467771 (Ohio Ct. App. June 26, 2002) (unpublished) (exemption does not have to be pleaded as an affirmative defense but does not apply unless seller displays or offers goods for sale at fixed location); Patterson v. Stockert, 2000 Ohio App. LEXIS 6004 (Ohio Ct. App. Dec. 13, 2000); Chegan v. AAAA Cont'l Heating, 1999 Ohio App. LEXIS 5572 (Ohio Ct. App. Nov. 24, 1999) (finding that transaction fell within exception); Zolg v. Yeager, 701 N.E.2d 723 (Ohio Ct. App. 1997); Clemens v. Duwel, 654 N.E.2d 171 (Ohio Ct. App. 1995) (comparable state law exception did not apply because home improvement contractor's home, where he maintained his office, was not a retail business establishment); Cook v. Stevens, 541 N.E.2d 628 (Ohio Ct. App. 1988) (home improvement sale initiated by buyer not excluded under Ohio statute when seller did not have a fixed business location at which the goods and services were exhibited or offered); Teeters Constr. v. Dort, 869 N.E.2d 756 (Ohio Mun. Ct. 2006) (exception does not apply); Hines v. Thermal-Gard of Ohio, Inc., 546 N.E.2d 487 (Ohio Mun. Ct. 1988) (same). *See also* Teeters Constr. v. Dort, 869 N.E.2d 756 (Ohio Mun. Ct. 2006) (exception does not apply).

284 *In re* Bayless, 326 B.R. 411 (Bankr. E.D. Mich. 2005) (interpreting comparable language of state law).

285 Cooper v. Crow, 574 So. 2d 438 (La. Ct. App. 1991) (interpreting FTC rule). *Cf.* Aluminum Shake Roofing v. Hirayasu, 131 P.3d 1230 (Haw. 2006) (state statute does not apply when homeowners approached business and requested home visit to discuss suitability and cost of copper roof).

286 Saler v. Hurvitz, 84 B.R. 45 (Bankr. E.D. Pa. 1988) (state home solicitation sales law inapplicable). *See also In re* Lewis, 290 B.R. 541 (Bankr. E.D. Pa. 2003) (single contact, which debtor initiated by calling mortgage broker from home, did not bring brokerage contract within state door-to-door sales provision). *But see* Christopher v. First Mut. Corp., 2008 WL 1815300 (E.D. Pa. Apr. 22, 2008) (taking under advisement the issue of whether conducting loan closing in borrower's home was sufficient to bring transaction within state home solicitation sales law).

287 Meeker v. Medi-Chari, L.L.C., 2012 WL 7037561 (Ill. App. Ct. June 18, 2014) (construing demonstration and fitting of wheelchair in consumer's home at her request not to be a solicitation under FTC rule or Arizona home solicitation sales law).

2.5.4.3 Buyer-Initiated Visits to Home to Repair Personal Property

The FTC rule does not include a general exception for buyer-initiated contracts. However, it has a narrower exception. The Cooling-Off Period Rule, like many state rules,[288] does not apply if the buyer initiates the contact and asks the seller to visit the buyer's home for the purpose of repairing personal property.[289] But if, in the course of that visit, the repairman sells the buyer additional goods (other than necessary replacement parts) or additional services, that additional sale must comply with the rule. Similarly, after a product is sold in a store, the rule should apply to subsequent in-home solicitations to sell a maintenance agreement on that product.[290] Sales based on a referral by neighbors are considered seller-initiated.[291]

2.5.4.4 Emergency Exception

There is also an emergency exception to the FTC's Cooling-Off Period Rule. For this to apply, the buyer must provide a statement in the buyer's handwriting describing the emergency and expressly waiving the three-day cancellation right.[292] A

seller must comply strictly with the requirements of the emergency exception, and courts will scrutinize alleged emergency waivers closely.[293] A seller cannot claim an emergency waiver when it did not start work until after the three-day cancellation period had passed.[294] Some state home solicitation sale laws contain similar exceptions.[295]

2.5.4.5 Mail and Telephone Sales

Transactions conducted and consummated entirely by mail or telephone and without other contact between the buyer and seller prior to delivery of goods or services are explicitly excluded from coverage under the Cooling-Off Period Rule.[296] If there is other contact with the buyer, however, this exception does not apply.[297] Note that state telemarketing laws may provide buyers the right to cancel a telephone sale, even though the FTC rule does not.[298]

2.5.4.6 Leases, Rent-to-Own Transactions, Transactions Under $130

The FTC's Cooling-Off Period Rule explicitly applies to leases and rentals of consumer goods.[299] The rule's statement of basis and purpose explains that the rule was redrafted to make it clear that leases were covered so that door-to-door sellers could not escape the rule by leasing their goods instead of selling them.[300] The rule may thus provide an often overlooked way to challenge "rent-to-own" appliance transactions, particularly if the original order was not taken at the seller's place of business or if the contract was consummated in the buyer's home (even if an order was taken over the telephone).

The Cooling-Off Period Rule exempts sales under $130.[301] Prior to March 13, 2015 (the effective date of the FTC's 2015 amendments to the rule), the amount was $25.[302] Rent-to-own companies may argue that this exclusion for small sales also covers "rent-to-own" terminable leases when the initial deposit and weekly or monthly payments do not exceed $130 (formerly $25). In other words, there is an issue of whether the $130 minimum applies to each monthly or weekly lease payment or to

---

288 *See* Brown v. Jacob, 476 N.W.2d 156 (Mich. 1990) (contract signed in home after buyer called seller's place of business and began negotiations over phone not covered), *rev'g* 454 N.W.2d 226 (Mich. Ct. App. 1990); Wenger v. Cardo Windows, Inc., 2009 WL 649458 (N.J. Super. Ct. App. Div. Mar. 16, 2009) (fact issue whether "repair or maintenance" exception applies when consumers responded to advertisement by inviting seller to home to demonstrate replacement windows), *appeal granted, summarily remanded*, 992 A.2d 791 (N.J. 2010), *on remand*, 2012 WL 280254 (N.J. Super. Ct. App. Div., Feb. 1, 2012) (affirming certification of class); Altek Envtl. Serv. Co. v. Harris, 2009 WL 1145233 (Ohio Ct. App. Apr. 27, 2009) (unpublished) (applying exception to buyer-initiated home repair without noting that exception is limited to personal property); Bratka v. Smiley, 2003 WL 1065603 (Ohio Ct. App. Mar. 11, 2003) (unpublished) (finding exception applicable); Papp v. J&W Roofing & Gen. Contracting, 1999 Ohio App. LEXIS 6042 (Ohio Ct. App. Dec. 17, 1999) (exception for repair of personal property under identical state statutory language applies to contract to replace roof). *But cf. In re* Bayless, 326 B.R. 411 (Bankr. E.D. Mich. 2005) (home improvement contract covered; although initial contact was made in hardware store, actual solicitation was made at residence); Williams v. Schroyer, 2000 Ohio App. LEXIS 5798 (Ohio Ct. App. Dec. 13, 2000) (home repair transaction covered when buyer called seller but then further negotiations took place at home).

289 16 C.F.R. § 429.0(a)(5); Wenger v. Cardo Windows, Inc., 2009 WL 649458 (N.J. Super. Ct. App. Div. Mar. 16, 2009) (fact issue as to repair or maintenance exception; question whether, when consumers invited salesman to demonstrate windows, they had already decided to purchase).

290 State v. Sears Roebuck & Co., Clearinghouse No. 40,629 (Me. Super. Ct. 1985).

291 Cole v. Lovett, 672 F. Supp. 947 (S.D. Miss. 1987) (state home solicitation sales law covers seller's solicitation of buyer at buyer's home after referral by neighbor).

292 16 C.F.R. § 429.0(a)(3), *reprinted at* Appx. A.4, *infra*. *See* Smaldino v. Larsick, 630 N.E.2d 408 (Ohio Ct. App. 1993) (even in undisputed emergency, cooling-off period applies unless buyer signs statement under comparable provision of state law). *See also* McClure v. Kline Roofing Siding & Insulation, Inc., 35 Pa. D. & C.3d 1 (Pa. Ct. Com. Pl. Lancaster Cnty. 1985) (seller's responsibility, not consumer's, to obtain written waiver in emergency situations under state home solicitation sales law).

---

293 Tee Pee Fence & Railing Corp. v. Olah, 544 N.Y.S.2d 112 (N.Y. Civ. Ct. 1989).

294 *Id.*

295 *See* Paul Davis Restoration v. Karaman, 2005 WL 1846988 (Ohio Ct. App. Aug. 24, 2005) (unpublished) (applying state home solicitation law's emergency exception to water mitigation work that was necessitated by flooding of home); Kamposek v. Johnson, 2005 WL 238152 (Ohio Ct. App. Jan. 28, 2005) (state home solicitation law's exception does not apply when remodeling could have waited until after three-day period); Smaldino v. Larsick, 630 N.E.2d 408 (Ohio Ct. App. 1993) (applying state home solicitation law's emergency exception to installation of new furnace in winter).

296 16 C.F.R. § 429.0(a)(4).

297 *Id.*; Smaldino v. Larsick, 630 N.E.2d 408 (Ohio Ct. App. 1993) (construing comparable language of state cooling-off period law).

298 *See* § 5.9.2, Appx. D, *infra*.

299 16 C.F.R. § 429.0(a), (b).

300 37 Fed. Reg. 22,945 (Oct. 26, 1972).

301 16 C.F.R. § 429.0(a).

302 *See* 80 Fed. Reg. 1329 (Jan. 9, 2015).

the total amount of payments. But the purpose of the rule's exemption for sales under $130 is not to exclude such things as appliance leases but only "sales by milkmen, laundrymen, and other route salesmen who customarily make sales which would otherwise fall within the scope of the Rule. . . ."[303] The rule also defines purchase price as "the total price paid or *to be paid* for the consumer goods."[304] The rule's $130 minimum also applies to the total of multiple contracts to ensure "that the rule would apply to transactions in which the seller writes up a number of invoices or contracts none of which show a price of [$25, but now $130] or more, but when taken together the total price exceeds that amount."[305] In light of these limitations, it is unlikely that a rent-to-own contract would be construed to fall below the $130 threshold when the total of payments to acquire ownership exceeds $130, even if each weekly payment is less than that amount.

2.5.4.7　Sales of Real Property, Home Improvements, Securities, and Insurance

The Cooling-Off Period Rule explicitly exempts the sale or rental of real property, the sale of insurance, and the sale of securities.[306] However, the rule may apply to transactions in which a consumer engages a real estate broker to sell the consumer's home or to rent and manage the consumer's residence during a temporary period of absence.[307] The rule should also apply to mortgage brokers, since they are selling a service, not selling or renting the real estate.[308]

The exclusion for the sale or rental of real property has no effect on the coverage of home improvement transactions. The FTC has explicitly stated that transactions "such as the sale of driveway resurfacing, aluminum siding, roofing materials or treatment, landscaping, or repairs to the home or to other real property" are not excluded from the rule.[309]

2.5.4.8　Transactions Subject to Truth in Lending Rescission

The FTC rule exempts transactions in which the consumer is afforded the right of rescission under the Truth in Lending Act (TILA).[310] Accordingly, since the TILA affords the consumer the right to rescind non-purchase-money credit secured

by the borrower's principal dwelling,[311] the FTC's rule does not apply to these transactions.[312]

2.5.4.9　What Sellers Are Covered

The Cooling-Off Period Rule covers sellers who are "engaged in the door-to-door sale of consumer goods or services."[313] On its face, this language does not require that the seller be regularly engaged in that type of transaction, so occasional door-to-door sales by a seller who usually sells from a regular business location should be covered. The Hawaii Supreme Court, interpreting similar language, agrees.[314] But Montana interprets its differently-worded cooling-off statute to apply only to sellers who are regularly engaged in door-to-door sales.[315]

2.5.5　Scope of State Laws

2.5.5.1　Overview

If a sale is outside the scope of the Cooling-Off Period Rule but covered by state law, the seller must still comply with the state law. If the FTC rule, but not the state statute, applies to a sale, the seller must comply with the FTC rule. If both the FTC rule and state law apply, the seller must comply with both to the extent that the state law does not conflict with the FTC rule.[316]

The fact that the buyer may be a sophisticated consumer who initiated contact with the seller and who conducted lengthy negotiations over the purchase of a very expensive product does not make a state cooling-off law inapplicable.[317] State cooling-off laws apply whether or not the consumer appears to need special protection.[318] But a home improvement contract that was worked out because of the parties' prior personal relationship was not covered by the Pennsylvania cooling-off statute even though it was signed in the buyer's home.[319]

State home improvement laws generally protect buyers only, so a person who signs a contract in his or her home to sell something does not have the right to cancel it.[320] Nonetheless, a

---

303　Statement of Basis and Purpose, 37 Fed. Reg. 22,945 (Oct. 26, 1972).

304　16 C.F.R. § 429.0(e).

305　Statement of Basis and Purpose, 37 Fed. Reg. 22,945 (Oct. 26, 1972). *Cf.* Holloway, FTC Informal Staff Opinion Letter, Clearinghouse No. 45,909 (May 11, 1990) (test is whether two charges involve two separate transactions).

306　16 C.F.R. § 429.0(a)(6).

307　Statement of Basis and Purpose, 37 Fed. Reg. 22,948 (Oct. 26, 1972).

308　*See* Equicredit Corp. v. Jackson, 2004 WL 2726115 (Ohio Ct. App. Nov. 24, 2005) (unpublished) (interpreting similar state law); Bank of N.Y. v. Kaiser, 2003 WL 23335972 (Ohio Ct. Com. Pl. Aug. 16, 2003) (interpreting similar state law).

309　Statement of Basis and Purpose, 37 Fed. Reg. 22,947 (Oct. 26, 1972). *See also* § 2.5.5, *infra.*

310　16 C.F.R. § 429.0(a)(2).

311　15 U.S.C. § 1635. *See* National Consumer Law Center, Truth in Lending Ch. 10 (9th ed. 2015), *updated at* www.nclc.org/library.

312　*See* Argent Mortg. Co. v. Ciemins, 2008 WL 4949848 (Ohio Ct. App. Nov. 20, 2008) (unpublished) (interpreting comparable provision of state law).

313　16 C.F.R. § 429.0(c). *See also* 16 C.F.R. § 429.0(a) (broadly defining "door-to-door sale" to cover any off-premises sale).

314　Aluminum Shake Roofing v. Hirayasu, 131 P.3d 1230 (Haw. 2006) (applying state home solicitation sales law).

315　Bradley v. North Country Auto & Marine, 999 P.2d 308 (Mont. 2000) (applying state home solicitation sales law).

316　*See* § 2.5.2, *supra.*

317　Burke v. Yingling, 666 A.2d 288 (Pa. Super. Ct. 1995).

318　*Id. But cf.* Smith v. Nat'l W. Life Ins. Co., 2010 WL 1904041 (M.D. Pa. Mar. 22, 2010) (magistrate decision) (holding state door-to-door sales statute inapplicable on policy grounds to sale of annuity when seller provided a period of twenty days from delivery to cancel, in part on the theory that twenty days from delivery is more helpful to consumer than three days from date of contract), *adopted by* 2010 WL 1904040 (M.D. Pa. May 11, 2010).

319　Lou Botti Constr. v. Harbulak, 760 A.2d 896 (Pa. Super. Ct. 2000).

320　DeFazio v. Gregory, 836 A.2d 935 (Pa. Super. Ct. 2003).

consumer who conveyed her home to a fraudulent foreclosure "rescuer" was not a seller but a buyer of the rescuer's services.[321] A homeowner is a buyer covered by Ohio's statute even if the homeowner's insurance company pays for the services that are sold.[322]

When a transaction has connections to more than one state, the court must decide which state's law to apply. In one case, a court applied the California home solicitation sales law when an heir-finder hired by the attorney for an estate in Texas entered into a contract with the heir in the heir's California home.[323] In another case, a federal court in Illinois concluded at the summary judgment stage that New York law could be applied when the seller was a New York corporation, the purchased good was in New York during the negotiations, and the buyer visited New York to view the good.[324]

A claim under a state home solicitation sales law is a statutory claim, not one based on contract.[325]

2.5.5.2 Coverage That Is Broader Than the FTC Rule

In a number of states, the cooling-off legislation covers an even wider range of consumer transactions than the FTC rule. For example, some states exclude only sales under $10 or $15 instead of the FTC's cap of $25 (increased to $130 as of March 13, 2015). Some state cooling-off statutes apply to seller-initiated telephone sales, either by explicit statutory definition[326] or by judicial interpretation.[327] For statutes that cover

telephone sales, it is the location where the call is received, not where it originates, that is decisive.[328]

Unlike the FTC rule, the Texas state cooling-off statute explicitly applies to purchases of realty except when the purchaser is represented by a licensed attorney or when the transaction is negotiated by a licensed real estate broker.[329] Ohio's statute implies that some sales or rentals of real property are covered, since it excludes sales and rentals by licensed real estate brokers or salespersons.[330] Mortgage brokers are covered since the statute includes sellers of services.[331]

Several states, while excluding the sale of insurance, do include the services of an insurance adjuster within the scope of the home solicitation statute.[332] Unlike the FTC rule, the Pennsylvania statute does not have special exemptions for any types of transactions and is applicable to all buyer-initiated sales.[333]

Like the FTC's rule,[334] California's law has an exception for emergencies, but the exception is narrower in that it must relate to repairs or services that are necessary for the immediate protection of persons or real or personal property.[335] The buyer's personal desire to start home improvement work right away did not meet this standard, nor did the fact that the house had exposed particleboard that could be damaged if the homeowners walked on it over the long term.[336]

2.5.5.3 Narrower Coverage Than the FTC Rule

Of course, state cooling-off legislation may have a narrower coverage than the FTC rule. Some states exclude certain categories of sellers completely.[337] In addition, state laws patterned after the cooling-off period created by the Uniform Consumer Credit Code may apply only to credit sales.

Some state statutes require that "the seller or his representative personally solicit the sale." This has been interpreted

---

321 Fowler v. Rauso (*In re* Fowler), 425 B.R. 157, 188–90 (Bankr. E.D. Pa. 2010).

322 White v. Allstate Ins. Co., 2008 WL 152120 (Ohio Ct. App. Jan. 17, 2008) (unpublished).

323 *In re* Estate of Rhymer, 969 S.W.2d 126 (Tex. App. 1998) ("very nature of home solicitation statutes argues strongly in favor of applying the law of the state where the solicitation occurred").

324 Pritzker v. Krishna Gallery of Asian Arts Inc., 1996 U.S. Dist. LEXIS 14398 (N.D. Ill. Sept. 30, 1996).

325 Fowler v. Rauso (*In re* Fowler), 425 B.R. 157, 190–91 (Bankr. E.D. Pa. 2010) (Pennsylvania rule that breach-of-contract claims cannot be recast as tort claims is inapplicable to claim under home solicitation sales act, since it is a statutory claim).

326 Alaska Stat. § 45.02.350; Ark. Code Ann. § 4-89-102(4)(B); Fla. Stat. § 501.021(1); La. Rev. Stat. Ann. § 9:3516(20); Me. Rev. Stat. tit. 32, § 4662; Mich. Comp. Laws § 445.111(a); Mont. Code Ann. § 30-14-502(2); N.D. Cent. Code § 51-18-01; Or. Rev. Stat. §§ 83.710(4), 83.715 (telephone solicitation sale provision apply only to periodicals, magazines, and other reading material except for newspapers); 73 Pa. Stat. Ann. § 201-7 (West); Va. Code Ann. § 59.1-21.2(A); Vt. Stat. Ann. tit. 9, § 2451a(d); Wash. Rev. Code § 63.14.154(1)(a) (commercial telephone solicitation); Wis. Stat. § 423.201; Wyo. Stat. Ann. § 40-12-104; State v. Sears Roebuck & Co., Clearinghouse No. 40,629 (Me. Super. Ct. 1985). *See also* State v. Roob, 671 N.W.2d 717 (Wis. Ct. App. 2003) (table, text at 2003 WL 22137896) (interpreting Wis. Admin. Code ATCP § 127.01 to cover sale that was solicited by telephone call to buyer's home and fax to her job). *But cf.* Yarney v. Wells Fargo Bank, 2010 WL 3663182 (W.D. Va. Sept. 15, 2010) (state home solicitation sales law does not apply to sale conducted by telephone and mail when consumer initiated the call in which she agreed to accept seller's offer).

327 People v. Toomey, 203 Cal. Rptr. 642 (Cal. Ct. App. 1984) (telephone solicitations initiated from seller's offices are included within statute's scope when contract was made at buyer's home); Hollywood

Decorators, Inc. v. Lancet, 118 Misc. 2d 1096 (N.Y. Sup. Ct. 1983) (statute applies when seller advertised by radio, buyer telephoned seller, and seller met with buyer at his home and executed contract); Brown v. Martinelli, 419 N.E.2d 1081 (Ohio 1981) (Ohio's home solicitation sales act includes telephone contacts initiated by the seller). *But see* United Consumers Club v. Griffin, 619 N.E.2d 489 (Ohio Ct. App. 1993) (sale initiated by seller's call to consumer's home not covered when contract signed at seller's fixed, permanent retail establishment).

328 State v. Roob, 671 N.W.2d 717 (Wis. Ct. App. 2003) (table, text at 2003 WL 22137896).

329 Tex. Bus. & Com. Code Ann. § 601.002(b)(4) (West). *See* McDaniel v. Pettigrew, 536 S.W.2d 611 (Tex. 1976).

330 Ohio Rev. Code Ann. § 1345.21(F)(1) (West).

331 Equicredit Corp. v. Jackson, 2004 WL 2726115 (Ohio Ct. App. Nov. 24, 2005) (unpublished); Bank of N.Y. v. Kaiser, 2003 WL 23335972 (Ohio Ct. Com. Pl. Aug. 16, 2003).

332 Williams v. Kapilow & Son, Inc., 164 Cal. Rptr. 176 (Cal. Ct. App. 1980); Culbreth v. Lawrence J. Miller, Inc., 477 A.2d 491 (Pa. Super. Ct. 1984).

333 Burke v. Yingling, 666 A.2d 288 (Pa. Super. Ct. 1995).

334 16 C.F.R. § 429.0(a)(3). *See* § 2.5.4.4, *supra*.

335 Cal. Civ. Code § 1689.13 (West).

336 Handyman Connection of Sacramento, Inc. v. Sands, 20 Cal. Rptr. 3d 727, 738–39 (Cal. Ct. App. 2004).

337 *See, e.g.*, Ohio Rev. Code Ann. § 1345.21(F)(5) (West) (excluding goods or services sold by licensed motor vehicle dealers).

to require an affirmative act on the part of the seller and no prior contact between the seller and buyer.[338] Other courts do not look to see whether the transaction was initiated by the seller or the buyer but only consider whether the contract was made at the buyer's home.[339] Some state statutes, like the

FTC rule, exempt buyer-initiated sales if the seller maintains a business establishment in the state at a fixed location where the goods and services are offered or exhibited for sale.[340] The seller has the burden of proving that it falls within this exception.[341]

The Hawaii Supreme Court has held that the protections of the home solicitation sales law are not automatically suspended because the buyer initiated contact with the vendor.[342] However, the court construed the language—"unless the context or subject matter otherwise requires"—to allow the trial court to exempt a transaction when the consumers approached the vendor, requested a home visit, and visited the company's warehouse at least once prior to the start of work.

A Minnesota decision holds that the statutory exemption for sales of real property means that a contract to rebuild a garage is excluded.[343] The decision fails to note that the language of its exemption is substantively identical to that in the FTC rule, which the FTC has interpreted to apply to home improvement contracts.[344]

2.5.5.4   Level of In-Home Contact Required Under State Statutes

State statutes vary in the level of in-home contact with the consumer that is required. The Illinois statute at one time granted a right to cancel any sale that occurred "as a result of or in connection with a salesman's direct contact with or call on the consumer at his residence." An Illinois appellate court interpreted this language to cover a membership campground sale that was initiated by a written solicitation mailed to the consumer's home.[345] The court distinguished between advertisements aimed at the general public, which would not constitute "contact" under the statute, and these solicitations, which were personally addressed to selected individuals and asked them to take specific steps. While the Illinois statute was subsequently amended to require the seller to be physically

---

338   All Am. Pools, Inc. v. Lato, 569 A.2d 562 (Conn. App. Ct. 1990) (Connecticut statute applies only when "seller or his representative personally solicits the sale"; transaction not covered by state cooling-off law when buyer initiated contact at seller's place of business); Op. Att'y Gen. No. 077-32, 1977 WL 26545 (Fla. Mar. 28, 1977) (telephone solicitation sale is not home solicitation sale because central to definition of home solicitation is personal contact between seller and buyer) (citing Op. Att'y Gen. No. 075-31 (Fla. Feb. 14, 1975) (if sale is result of a request for specific goods or services by purchaser rather than as result of personal persuasion or inducement on the part of seller, it is not subject to right-to-cancel provision)); Meeker v. Medi-Chair, L.L.C., 2012 WL 7037561 (Ill. App. Ct. June 18, 2012) (unpublished) (construing Arizona's statute, which applies only when seller "personally solicits the sale," not to apply when consumer initiated contact with seller and asked seller to come to her home to demonstrate product); State v. Stereo Importers, Inc., 114 Misc. 2d 864 (N.Y. Sup. Ct. 1982) (home solicitation sales act does not apply when buyer initiates contact and seller has fixed place of business in the state where goods are offered for sale); Tambur's Inc. v. Hiltner, 379 N.E.2d 231 (Ohio Ct. App. 1977) (home solicitation sales act requires that "seller or a person acting for him engages in a personal solicitation of the sale at a residence of the buyer"; transaction not subject to statute when buyer initiates contact by calling seller, invites seller to residence for purpose of submitting estimate, and subsequently signs agreement for repair services); Ferachi v. Cady, 2009 WL 1506899 (Tex. App. May 28, 2009) (former version of statute not applicable when seller did not solicit transaction); Langston v. Brewer, 649 S.W.2d 827 (Tex. App. 1983) (former version of home solicitation sales act applies when merchant personally solicits sale at place other than place of business; does not apply when parties were involved in prior transaction, buyer contacted seller with regard to furnishing services, and after negotiations a contract was entered into at home of buyer; current version, Tex. Bus. & Com. Code Ann. §§ 601.002 (West), also requires "personal solicitation"). *See also* Sanford v. Nat'l Ass'n for the Self-Employed, Inc., 640 F. Supp. 2d 82 (D. Me. 2009) (statute applies when merchandise is sold or contracted to be sold "without the consumer soliciting the initial contact or sale"; statute inapplicable when buyer contacted one company and was sold items by a related company); Clemens v. Duwel, 654 N.E.2d 171 (Ohio Ct. App. 1995) (statute requires that "seller or a person acting for him engages in a personal solicitation of the sale at a residence of the buyer, including solicitations in response to or following an invitation by the buyer"; seller did not fall within exception for some buyer-initiated sales because room in seller's residence did not constitute business establishment at fixed location in state); R. Bauer & Sons Roofing & Siding, Inc. v. Kinderman, 613 N.E.2d 1083 (Ohio Ct. App. 1992) (Ohio statute's exclusion for buyer initiated contact when seller has fixed locations that exhibit the goods or services is satisfied when consumer contacts seller and seller has sample of home improvement products at its store). *But cf.* Aluminum Shake Roofing, Inc. v. Hirayasu, 131 P.3d 1230 (Haw. 2006) (statute requires "sale of goods or services solicited in person and signed by the buyer at a place other than the seller's business address"; refusing to establish blanket exception for all buyer-initiated transactions; proper inquiry must focus on "presence of coercive pressure"). *See generally* Julie Khoury Robie, Ohio Consumer Law § 3.6 (2012 13th ed.) (further discussion of the Ohio Home Solicitation Sales Act and *Tambur's*).

339   Weatherall Aluminum Products Co. v. Scott, 139 Cal. Rptr. 329 (Cal. Ct. App. 1977) (contract entered into a buyer's home fell within purview of statute even though buyer initiated negotiations by telephoning seller and expressing an interest in his product). *Cf.* Hollywood

Decorators, Inc. v. Lancet, 118 Misc. 2d 1096 (N.Y. Sup. Ct. 1983) (contract for interior decoration solicited by means of radio advertisement and negotiated at a subsequent meeting between the parties at buyer's home is subject to the statute even when buyer first contacted seller by telephone); Von Lehn v. Astor Art Galleries, 86 Misc. 2d 1, 11–12 (N.Y. Sup. Ct. 1976) (sale is subject to state home solicitation sales act when seller solicited buyers in their home and there were no prior negotiations at a business establishment); Op. of Va. Att'y Gen. William Broaddus to the Honorable George Heilig, Jr., Member, House of Delegates, Clearinghouse No. 40,630 (Jan. 29, 1985) ("prior negotiations" exception does not apply to brief telephone conversation nor to prior dealings between the parties concerning a different product).

340   *See* § 2.5.4.2, *supra.*

341   New Phila, Inc. v. Sagrilla, 2002 WL 1467771 (Ohio Ct. App. June 26, 2002) (exemption need not be pleaded in defendant's answer as affirmative defense, but party seeking to assert the exemption has burden of proving it); Teeters Constr. v. Dort, 869 N.E.2d 756 (Ohio Mun. Ct. 2006).

342   Aluminum Shake Roofing v. Hirayasu, 131 P.3d 1230 (Haw. 2006).

343   Busch v. Model Corp., 708 N.W.2d 546 (Minn. Ct. App. 2006).

344   *See* § 2.5.4.7, *supra.*

345   Warren v. Borger, 539 N.E.2d 1284 (Ill. App. Ct. 1989).

present at the buyer's residence,[346] the decision is still persuasive precedent for interpretation of other states' statutes.

Similarly, while the Pennsylvania statute only applies to contacts or calls at the buyer's residence,[347] its coverage goes beyond sales that are consummated at the consumer's home. The statute also covers sales that are finalized outside the home, as long as there was sufficient initial contact at the buyer's home.[348] For example, a court refused to dismiss a claim under the Pennsylvania statute when the sales presentation was at the seller's place of business and the only in-home contact was that the seller wrote and telephoned the consumers at their home.[349] Pennsylvania's statute also makes it clear that it covers sales that are made in connection with a contact or call upon the buyer either in person or by telephone.[350] It applies when the buyer invited the seller to her home after receiving a "door opener" mailing and a series of calls from the seller soliciting her business.[351]

On the other hand, New York's statute has been interpreted to apply only when the contract is actually signed in the consumer's home.[352] Michigan's statute likewise requires that the agreement to purchase be given in the home.[353] The same court also held that an order given by telephone fell outside of the statute when it occurred as part of the parties' ongoing relationship, not in response to a call or visit to the home.[354] Another court held that there was no solicitation, and therefore the statute was inapplicable, when a contractor was dispatched by the homeowners' insurance company to secure their home after a fire and was then hired by them to do repair work without having solicited them.[355] Ohio's law requires that the buyer be personally solicited at a residence but, if the buyer has more than one residence, the transaction is covered if the solicitation occurs at any of them.[356]

2.5.5.5 Particular Interpretations of State Law Scope Provisions

Coverage of home improvement contracts has been an issue under Ohio's Home Solicitation Sales Act. An older Ohio case[357] held that home improvement transactions are not covered by its statute. Newer cases, citing the interpretation of the FTC rule, the prevalence of "flim-flam artists" in the home improvement business, and the unlikelihood that the legislature would have intended to exclude these transactions, overwhelmingly find that they are covered.[358] The Maryland Supreme Court, interpreting a virtually identical statute and relying on the FTC's statement of the basis and purpose for its rule, finds that home improvement transactions are covered.[359]

The Kansas door-to-door sales statute applies to sales conducted in any location that is not the seller's place of business, whether or not it is the consumer's home.[360] Since the statute is not restricted to consumer goods and applies to sole proprietors as well as individuals, it allowed a restaurant owner to cancel a contract for a jukebox entered into in the restaurant.[361]

A Massachusetts court, relying merely on the "spirit" of its home-solicitation sales statute, held that subsequent negotiations can remove a transaction from the scope of the state rule. It held that, if a buyer asks the seller to visit the buyer's home and then enters into "a course of negotiation and an exchange of drafts" of the contract, the rule is no longer necessary to protect the buyer from undue pressure.[362] Other courts have been more willing to follow the statutory language.[363]

---

346 *See* 815 Ill. Comp. Stat. § 505/2B, *as amended by* Illinois Laws 86-898 § 2 (effective Jan. 1, 1990).

347 73 Pa. Stat. Ann. § 201-7(a) (West). *Cf.* St. Hill v. Tribeca Lending Corp., 403 Fed. Appx. 717 (3d Cir. 2010) (unpublished) (no right to cancel when borrower signed papers for business loan in her home office).

348 Staub v. Outdoor World Corp., 70 Lanc. 412, Clearinghouse No. 45,940 (Pa. Ct. Com. Pl. Lancaster Cnty. 1987). *But cf.* Lewis v. Delta Funding Corp. (*In re* Lewis), 290 B.R. 541 (Bankr. E.D. Pa. 2003) (single call by buyer from her home to seller insufficient).

349 Staub v. Outdoor World Corp., 70 Lanc. 412, Clearinghouse No. 45,940 (Pa. Ct. Com. Pl. Lancaster Cnty. 1987).

350 73 Pa. Stat. Ann. § 201-7(a) (West).

351 Fowler v. Rauso (*In re* Fowler), 425 B.R. 157, 191 (Bankr. E.D. Pa. 2010).

352 Niemiec v. Kellmark Corp., 581 N.Y.S.2d 569 (N.Y. City Ct. 1992).

353 Patrick v. U.S. Tangible Inv. Corp., 595 N.W.2d 162 (Mich. Ct. App. 1999) (also finding statute inapplicable because buyer sought out seller in hopes of enhancing investments). *See also In re* Bayless, 326 B.R. 411 (Bankr. E.D. Pa. 2005) (Mich. statute applies when initial contact made at hardware store, but sales pitch or solicitation was made at home).

354 Patrick v. U.S. Tangible Inv. Corp., 595 N.W.2d 162, 166 (Mich. Ct. App. 1999).

355 Luckoski v. Allstate Ins. Co., 5 N.E.3d 73 (Ohio Ct. App. 2013).

356 White v. Allstate Ins. Co., 2008 WL 152120 (Ohio Ct. App. Jan. 17, 2008) (unpublished) (Home Solicitation Sales Act covered sale when buyer was solicited at home he owned and planned to move into).

357 Tambur's, Inc. v. Hiltner, 379 N.E.2d 231 (Ohio Ct. App. 1977).

358 Garber v. STS Concrete Co., 991 N.E.2d 1225 (Ohio Ct. App. 2013); Knight v. Colazzo, 2008 WL 5244640 (Ohio Ct. App. Dec. 17, 2008) (unpublished); Camardo v. Reeder, 2002 WL 1349083 (Ohio Ct. App. June 20, 2002) (unpublished); Rusk Indus. v. Alexander, 2002 Ohio App. LEXIS 2137 (Ohio Ct. App. May 3, 2002); Papp v. J&W Roofing & Gen. Contracting, 1999 Ohio App. LEXIS 6042 (Ohio Ct. App. Dec. 17, 1999); Rosenfield v. Tombragel, 1996 WL 741988 (Ohio Ct. App. Dec. 31, 1996); R. Bauer & Sons Roofing & Siding, Inc. v. Kinderman, 613 N.E.2d 1083 (Ohio Ct. App. 1992) *and cases cited therein*; Gross v. Bildex, Inc., 647 N.E.2d 573 (Ohio Mun. Ct. 1994); Hines v. Thermal-Gard of Ohio, Inc., 546 N.E.2d 487 (Ohio Mun. Ct. 1988). *See also* Himes v. Smith, 2012 WL 171112 (Ohio Ct. App. Jan. 17, 2012) (applying home solicitation sales act to home improvement contractor); Clemens v. Duwel, 654 N.E.2d 171 (Ohio Ct. App. 1995) (applying cooling-off statute to home improvement contract without discussion of *Tambur's*).

359 Crystal v. West & Callahan, 614 A.2d 560 (Md. 1992). *Accord* Domestic Bank v. Johnson (*In re* Johnson), 239 B.R. 255 (Bankr. D.R.I. 1999) (when contract is signed in home, door-to-door solicitation of home improvement work is covered by home solicitation sales act).

360 Kan. Stat. Ann. § 50-640.

361 Dealers Leasing, Inc. v. Allen, 994 P.2d 651 (Kan. Ct. App. 1999).

362 Donaher v. Porcaro, 715 N.E.2d 464 (Mass. App. Ct. 1999).

363 *See, e.g.*, Burke v. Yingling, 666 A.2d 288 (Pa. Super. Ct. 1995).

2.5.6   *Consumers' Rights Under FTC Rule, State Statutes*

2.5.6.1   Mechanics of Three-Day Cancellation Right

A consumer may cancel a covered home-solicitation sale under the FTC rule and the typical state statute without penalty or obligation within three business days[364] from the day on which the contract was signed. Cancellation may be available even if rescission would not be available under the state UDAP statute.[365] To cancel the transaction, the consumer must mail or deliver either a signed and dated copy of the "Notice of Cancellation" or any other written notice of intent to cancel. The consumer may also cancel the transaction by telegram.[366] Merely stopping payment on a check may be insufficient to serve as cancellation, however.[367] Ohio decisions hold that, when the statute specifies that the cancellation notice must be sent to the seller's address stated in the contract, cancellation cannot be accomplished through a pleading served on the seller's attorney.[368] However, other courts may find that the attorney is the seller's agent for delivery of notices.

If the consumer cancels, the seller must return any payments made and any property traded in within ten days after receiving the cancellation notice.[369] The consumer then must either make available to the seller any goods delivered under the contract or comply with the instructions of the seller regarding the return shipment of the goods at the seller's risk and expense.[370] If the seller does not pick up the goods within twenty days of the cancellation notice, the goods become the property of the buyer without further obligation.[371] If the buyer fails to make the goods available to the seller, or fails to return the goods after agreeing to do so, the buyer remains liable for performance of all obligations under the contract.[372]

2.5.6.2   No Recovery for Services Performed Prior to Cancellation

The FTC interprets the cancellation right strictly against the seller, even when the seller has already performed the contracted-for services before the cancellation period has expired. In non-emergency situations, the seller bears the full risk of cancellation if it elects to perform before the three days have expired.[373] If the buyer exercises his or her cancellation right under the FTC rule or a state statute, the buyer does not have to pay a penalty and is not liable on the basis of *quantum meruit* for services performed.[374]

---

364   *See* Flodman v. Robinson, 864 N.W.2d 716 (Neb. Ct. App. 2015) (Sunday is not a business day, so notice was defective under state home solicitation sales law when it listed a Sunday as deadline for cancelling; even though statute does not require deadline date to be listed, if seller lists it, it must be accurate; as a result, consumer may cancel by any means, so oral cancellation within three-day period was effective).

365   Kamposek v. Johnson, 2005 WL 238152 (Ohio Ct. App. Jan. 28, 2005) (unpublished) (state UDAP statute allows rescission only before any substantial change in condition of the subject of transaction, while home solicitation sales act does not contain this proviso). *But see* Williams v. Schroyer, 2000 Ohio App. LEXIS 5798 (Ohio Ct. App. Dec. 13, 2000) (importing requirement from different statute that consumer cancel within reasonable time after discovering grounds).

366   16 C.F.R. § 429.1(b); Gulf Indus., Inc. v. Hahn, 750 P.2d 911 (Ariz. Ct. App. 1988) (buyer or buyer's agent placing notice into possession of seller, without intervention of a third party, is notice given "in person" within meaning of state cooling-off statute). *See also* American Buyer's Club, Inc. v. Shaffer, 361 N.E.2d 1380 (Ill. App. Ct. 1970) (oral or other notice reasonably calculated to inform seller is adequate under Illinois law). *But see* State v. Columbus Kirby Co., 37 Ohio Misc. 106 (Ohio Ct. Com. Pl. Franklin Cnty. 1974) (holding hand-delivered notice to cancel ineffective when statute required certified mail).

367   Williams v. Schroyer, 2000 Ohio App. LEXIS 5798 (Ohio Ct. App. Dec. 13, 2000).

368   Camardo v. Reeder, 2002 WL 1349083 (Ohio Ct. App. June 20, 2002) (unpublished); Teeters Constr. v. Dort, 869 N.E.2d 756 (Ohio Mun. Ct. 2006).

369   16 C.F.R. § 429.1(g).

370   16 C.F.R. § 429.1(b).

371   16 C.F.R. § 429.1(b). *See also* Cole v. Lovett, 672 F. Supp. 947 (S.D. Miss. 1987); Domestic Bank v. Johnson (*In re* Johnson), 239 B.R. 255 (Bankr. D.R.I. 1999) (goods become property of buyer if seller does not return money and demand return of goods).

372   16 C.F.R. § 429.1(b).

373   Garber v. STS Concrete Co., 991 N.E.2d 1225 (Ohio Ct. App. 2013) (applying state home solicitation sales act); Kamposek v. Johnson, 2005 WL 238152 (Ohio Ct. App. Jan. 28, 2005) (unpublished) (applying state home solicitation sales act); Teeters Constr. v. Dort, 869 N.E.2d 756, 776 (Ohio Mun. Ct. 2006) (applying state home solicitation sales law).

374   Statement of Basis and Purpose, 37 Fed Reg. 22,947 (Oct. 26, 1972). *See also* Cole v. Lovett, 672 F. Supp. 947 (S.D. Miss. 1987); Louis Luskin & Sons, Inc. v. Samovitz, 212 Cal. Rptr. 612 (Cal. Ct. App. 1985) (no *quantum merit* recovery); Brown v. Jacob, 454 N.W.2d 226 (Mich. Ct. App. 1990) (Mich. Comp. Laws § 445.115(2) explicitly states seller not entitled to compensation for work before cancellation), *rev'd on other grounds*, 476 N.W.2d 156 (Mich. 1991) (holding statute inapplicable); Kamposek v. Johnson, 2005 WL 238152 (Ohio Ct. App. Jan. 28, 2005) (unpublished); Patterson v. Stockert, 2000 Ohio App. LEXIS 6004 (Ohio Ct. App. Dec. 13, 2000); Papp v. J&W Roofing & Gen. Contracting, 1999 Ohio App. LEXIS 6042 (Ohio Ct. App. Dec. 17, 1999) (risk is on contractor who begins performance during cancellation period); Clemens v. Duwel, 654 N.E.2d 171 (Ohio Ct. App. 1995) (seller who does home improvement work before giving notice of right to cancel cannot recover value of goods or services, and buyer need not return goods that have already been installed in the home); R. Bauer & Sons Roofing & Siding, Inc. v. Kinderman, 613 N.E.2d 1083 (Ohio Ct. App. 1992) (home improvement contractor who begins performance prior to giving notice of right to cancel assumes the risk); Teeters Constr. v. Dort, 869 N.E.2d 756 (Ohio Mun. Ct. 2006) (when seller fails to comply with cooling-off statute, contract is void and seller cannot recover for the work); Gross v. Bildex, Inc., 647 N.E.2d 573 (Ohio Mun. Ct. 1994) (builder cannot complain of injustice when it began work before giving a notice of the right to cancel); Hines v. Thermal-Gard of Ohio, Inc., 546 N.E.2d 487 (Ohio Mun. Ct. 1988) (seller who installed windows before giving notice of cancellation cannot recover them after consumer cancels); American Quality Roofing, Inc. v. Ipock, 730 S.W.2d 470 (Tex. App. 1987) (failure to offer cancellation right apparently complete defense to action to collect on services rendered). *Cf.* Udi v. Rosenbaum, 2011 WL 5831769 (Cal. Ct. App. Nov. 21, 2011) (unpublished) (holding that trial court has discretion to award *quantum meruit* relief, but upholding trial court's refusal to do so); Barrett Builders v. Miller, 576 A.2d 455 (Conn. 1990) (contractor could not recover in quasi contract for work performed when home improvement contract did not comply with

Thus, if a home improvement contractor performs work on a house and the consumer properly cancels, the consumer owes nothing, although the contractor can take back any materials supplied. When the materials are already attached to the house, the consumer's attorney should argue that the materials should only be removed when the contractor can provide adequate assurance the house will be returned to its original condition.[375] In any event, it may be a UDAP violation for a seller to systematically perform services during the three-day period if this is used as a method of frustrating consumers' cancellation rights.[376]

2.5.6.3 Continuing Right to Cancel If Notice Is Defective

Another issue is whether the cooling-off period begins to run after a defective notice of the right to cancel. State cooling-off statutes have been interpreted as providing consumers with a continuing right to cancel when the seller has not provided the consumer with proper notice of the consumer's right to cancel, for example by providing a blank cancellation notice, failing to explain the consumer's cancellation right orally, failing to attach the notice of cancellation to the contract, or failing to set forth a required statement of the buyer's right to cancel on the

front of the contract.[377] The Illinois cooling-off statute provides

---

statutory requirement that written contract contain the entire agreement of the parties); Scibek v. Longette, 770 A.2d 1242 (N.J. Super. Ct. App. Div. 2001) (repair shop that violated UDAP rule requiring estimates and authorizations could not recover for work). *But see In re* Bayless, 326 B.R. 411 (Bankr. E.D. Mich. 2005) (requiring consumers to pay fair value of home improvements, which on these facts is the contract price, as a condition of retaining the goods, when consumers had enjoyed improvements for ten years before canceling and were satisfied with the work); Pelletier v. Johnson, 937 P.2d 668 (Ariz. Ct. App. 1996) (allowing *quantum meruit* recovery to builder when buyer knew of right to cancel and was not harmed by omission of contract language required by statute); Kidd v. Greenspan Co., 2003 WL 356870 (Cal. Ct. App. Feb. 19, 2003) (unpublished) (possibility of *quantum meruit* recovery defeats class certification); Beley v. Ventura County Mun. Court, 160 Cal. Rptr. 508 (Cal. Ct. App. 1979) (contractor was entitled to recover on *quantum meruit* for reasonable value of improvements); Precision Builders & Restoration Specialties, Inc. v. Shea, 1995 Mass. App. Div. 103 (Mass. Dist. Ct. 1995) (contractor's *quantum meruit* claim against homeowners who canceled renovation claim was not barred by cooling-off statute). *But cf.* Hurlbert v. Cottier, 372 N.E.2d 734 (Ill. App. Ct. 1978) (consumer could rescind a contract for siding already installed but had to tender the siding's reasonable value if it could not be returned "in its original condition"); White v. Allstate Ins. Co., 2009 WL 3649739 (Ohio Ct. App. Nov. 5, 2009) (unpublished) (refusing to require home improvement contractor to make refund when work was satisfactory and consumer waited six years after completion before seeking to cancel); Laymance v. Vaughn, 857 S.W.2d 36 (Tenn. Ct. App. 1993) (state statute specifies that seller entitled to fair market value of services performed prior to cancellation).

375 Family Constr. v. District of Columbia Dep't of Consumer & Regulatory Affairs, 484 A.2d 250 (D.C. 1984).

376 State *ex rel.* Corbin v. United Energy Corp. of Am., 725 P.2d 752 (Ariz. Ct. App. 1986). *See also* Op. Ky. Att'y Gen. No. 92-41, 1992 WL 540962 (Mar. 17, 1992) (seller's performance of work in order to discourage buyer from exercising cancellation rights may be an unfair trade practice).

377 Tellado v. Indymac Mortg. Services, 2011 WL 3495990, at *5–6 (E.D. Pa. Aug. 8, 2011), *rev'd on other grounds*, 707 F.3d 275 (3d Cir. 2013) (holding that district court lacked subject matter jurisdiction); Reynolds v. D&N Bank, 792 F. Supp. 1035 (E.D. Mich. 1992) (state cooling-off statute explicitly gives continuous right to cancel); Cole v. Lovett, 672 F. Supp. 947 (S.D. Miss. Feb. 2, 1987) (purchasers who had not received statutorily required notice of right to cancel properly and timely exercised their right to cancel by letter two years after contract signed), *aff'd without op.*, 833 F.2d 1008 (5th Cir. 1987); Fowler v. Rauso (*In re* Fowler), 425 B.R. 157, 191–92 (Bankr. E.D. Pa. 2010); Domestic Bank v. Johnson (*In re* Johnson), 239 B.R. 255 (Bankr. D.R.I. 1999) (when contract does not conform to statute, buyer's right to cancel is not time-limited); Williams v. Kapilow & Son Inc., 164 Cal. Rptr. 176 (Cal. Ct. App. 1980) (consumer had cause of action for rescission when contract contained no notice of his right to cancel); Beley v. Ventura County Mun. Court, 160 Cal. Rptr. 508 (Cal. Ct. App. 1979); Pinnacle Energy v. Price, 2001 Del. C.P. LEXIS 28 (Del. Ct. Com. Pl. New Castle Cnty. Mar. 21, 2001) (allowing continuing right to cancel when seller did not print cancellation notice in conspicuous different ink color and cancellation form was not attached to contract; even if cancellation within reasonable time was a requirement, consumer met this criterion); Warren v. Borger, 539 N.E.2d 1284 (Ill. App. Ct. 1989) (when seller gave buyers no notice of right to cancel, buyers had continuing right to cancel); Brown v. Jacob, 454 N.W.2d 226 (Mich. Ct. App. 1990) (statute gives continuing right to cancel when no cancellation notice provided to consumer), *rev'd on other grounds*, 476 N.W.2d 156 (Mich. 1991); Swiss v. Williams, 445 A.2d 486 (N.J. Dist. Ct. 1982) (three-day notification period for rescission does not begin until buyer receives a receipt with information about rescission rights); Community Nat'l Bank & Trust Co. v. McClammy, 525 N.Y.S.2d 629 (N.Y. App. Div. 1988); State *ex rel.* Abrams v. Kase, Clearinghouse No. 43,079 (N.Y. Sup. Ct. 1986); Hollywood Decorators, Inc. v. Lancet, 118 Misc. 2d 1096 (N.Y. Sup. Ct. 1983) (buyer's time to cancel did not begin to run until seller's compliance with the act); Vom Lehn v. Astor Art Galleries, 86 Misc. 2d 1 (N.Y. Sup. Ct. 1976) (to gain benefit of three-day time limitation, seller was required to furnish buyers with perforated card specifically advising them of their right to cancel sale within three-day period); Rossi v. 21st Century Concepts, Inc., 618 N.Y.S.2d 182 (N.Y. Yonkers City Ct. 1994) (seller's failure to fill in name, address, date of transaction, and last day to cancel on notice gives consumer continuing right to cancel); Knight v. Colazzo, 2008 WL 5244640 (Ohio Ct. App. Dec. 17, 2008) (unpublished); Camardo v. Reeder, 2002 WL 1349083 (Ohio Ct. App. June 20, 2002) (unpublished); Patterson v. Stockert, 2000 Ohio App. LEXIS 6004 (Ohio Ct. App. Dec. 13, 2000) (does not begin to run when seller did not give notice of right to cancel); Papp v. J&W Roofing & Gen. Contracting, 1999 Ohio App. LEXIS 6042 (Ohio Ct. App. Dec. 17, 1999); Clemens v. Duwel, 654 N.E.2d 171 (Ohio Ct. App. 1995); Teeters Constr. v. Dort, 869 N.E.2d 756 (Ohio Mun. Ct. 2006) (failure to print cancellation notice in boldface ten-point type, to provide separate cancellation form, or to disclose cancellation deadline and address); Gross v. Bildex, Inc., 647 N.E.2d 573 (Ohio Mun. Ct. 1994) (consumer's right to cancel never expired when seller gave consumer a notice of the Truth in Lending rescission right rather than a notice of right to cancel under Home Solicitation Sales Act); Hines v. Thermal-Gard of Ohio, Inc., 546 N.E.2d 487 (Ohio Mun. Ct. 1988); American Quality Roofing, Inc. v. Ipock, 730 S.W.2d 470 (Tex. App. 1987) (failure to give notice gives consumer complete defense to seller's collection action); De La Fuente v. Home Sav. Ass'n, 669 S.W.2d 137 (Tex. App. 1984) (sellers violated home solicitation sales act by assigning note to third party on same day it was executed, giving buyer cause of action for rescission); Gramatan Home Investors Corp. v. Starling, 470 A.2d 1157 (Vt. 1983). *See also* Blacker v. Crapo, 964 A.2d 1241 (Conn. App. Ct. 2009); New England Custom Concrete, L.L.C. v. Carbone, 927 A.2d 333 (Conn. App. Ct. 2007) (when contractor was not in substantial compliance with statute

Federal Deception Law

the consumer with actual damages and "other relief," and this has been held to include a right to rescind when no cooling-off notice was provided.[378]

A laches argument will be unavailing when the consumer was not informed of the right to cancel.[379] If the seller has performed before giving a proper notice of the right to cancel, the consumer has the right to cancel even if the goods or services can no longer be returned, as the seller acted at its own risk.[380]

2.5.6.4 Other Consumer Protections

The FTC rule includes several other protections for the buyer aside from the right to cancel. It prohibits confession of judgment clauses or waivers of rights in door-to-door sales contracts[381] and prohibits sale or assignment of the note or contract to a third party prior to midnight of the fifth business day following the sale.[382] Many state laws impose these or additional requirements, such as particular disclosures.[383]

---

with respect to cancellation notice and other requirements, homeowners were not obligated to pay balance of contract); Crystal v. West & Callahan, Inc., 614 A.2d 560 (Md. 1992) (when seller fails to give required disclosures, right to cancel continues for a reasonable length of time, since Maryland's statute deleted provision that it runs until notice is given); RAB Performance Recoveries, L.L.C. v. George, 16 A.3d 406 (N.J. Super. Ct. App. Div. 2011); Oxford Fin. Cos. v. Velez, 807 S.W.2d 460 (Tex. App. 1991); Consolidated Tex. Fin. v. Shearer, 739 S.W.2d 477 (Tex. App. 1987) (defective notice allows consumer to cancel foreclosure sale when seller enforced statutory lien on consumer's home); Letter from Va. Att'y Gen. Mary Terry to Judge J.R. Zepkin, Clearinghouse No. 44,810 (Feb. 24, 1989) (failure to include required contract term, such as cancellation right, makes contract void and unenforceable). *But see* ADT Sec. Services, Inc. v. Swenson, 276 F.R.D. 278, 299–300 (D. Minn. 2011) (noting that there is no time limit on cancellation when seller provides insufficient notice of right to cancel, but finding cancellation unavailable when error is misstatement of cancellation deadline and consumer accepted benefits of the contract); Wright Bros. Builders, Inc. v. Dowling, 720 A.2d 235 (Conn. 1998) (strict, but not perfect and ritualistic, compliance is required; failure to include second copy of cancellation notice and to fill in transaction date and cancellation date did not give buyer continuing right to cancel); Ochocinska v. Nat'l Fire Adjustment Co., 577 N.Y.S.2d 998 (N.Y. App. Div. 1991) (error in specifying last day to cancel, when there was no consumer reliance, does not create continuing right to cancel).

378 Guess v. Brophy, 517 N.E.2d 693 (Ill. App. Ct. 1987).

379 Domestic Bank v. Johnson (*In re* Johnson), 239 B.R. 255 (Bankr. D.R.I. 1999). *But cf.* Williams v. Schroyer, 2000 Ohio App. LEXIS 5798 (Ohio Ct. App. Dec. 13, 2000) (importing requirement from different statute that consumer cancel within reasonable time after discovering grounds).

380 *See* § 2.5.6.2, *supra*.

381 16 C.F.R. § 429.1(d).

382 16 C.F.R. § 429.1(h).

383 Fowler v. Rauso (*In re* Fowler), 425 B.R. 157, 192 (Bankr. E.D. Pa. 2010) (seller violated Pennsylvania home solicitation sales provision by telling buyer she had no right to cancel); Rossi v. 21st Century Concepts, Inc., 618 N.Y.S.2d 182 (N.Y. Yonkers City Ct. 1994). *Cf.* Rusk Indus. v. Alexander, 2002 Ohio App. LEXIS 2137 (Ohio Ct. App. May 3, 2002) (nondisclosures violated home solicitation sales act but caused no damage so were not UDAP violations).

2.5.7 Consumer Remedies Under Cooling-Off Rule, State Statutes

There is no direct right to bring a private damage action for violation of the Cooling-Off Period Rule.[384] Of course, if the seller includes the cancellation notice in the contract, the consumer should be able to enforce this contract right. Otherwise, the consumer should argue that a violation of the FTC rule is a per se UDAP violation.[385] In fact, several states have enacted UDAP regulations that reiterate the FTC rule,[386] so that a violation of the rule in these states is clearly a per se UDAP violation.

State cooling-off statutes often provide an explicit private remedy, either in the statute itself[387] or by stating that a violation is an automatic UDAP violation.[388] Equitable relief may be available if necessary to undo the transaction.[389] Even when a violation of the cooling-off statute is not explicitly defined as a violation of the state UDAP statute, a strong argument can still be made that a violation of that statute is a per se UDAP violation.[390] When the state cooling-off statute allows a private action for cancellation and states that a violation is a UDAP violation, the consumer may be required to elect one remedy or the other.[391]

---

384 *See, e.g.*, Smith v. Gutter Covers of Maryland & Virginia, 2005 WL 3276280 (D.D.C. Aug. 4, 2005) (remanding case to state court; accepting consumers' concession that there is no private cause of action to enforce FTC rule). *See generally* § 2.2.4.1, *supra*.

385 *See* §§ 2.2.4.2, *supra. See also* Eastern Roofing & Aluminum Co. v. Brock, 320 S.E.2d 22 (N.C. Ct. App. 1984). *But see* State *ex rel.* Miller v. Santa Rosa Sales & Mktg., Inc., 475 N.W.2d 210 (Iowa 1991) (attorney general cannot utilize UDAP remedies when cooling-off statute provides attorney general with different remedial scheme; statute has now been amended to correct this defect); Laymance v. Vaughn, 857 S.W.2d 36 (Tenn. Ct. App. 1992).

386 *See* Ga. Comp. R. & Regs. 122-3-.01 (cooling-off period for door-to-door sales); Idaho Admin. Code r. 04.02.01.170 (same).

387 *See* Levitan Sons v. Francis, 88 Misc. 2d 125 (N.Y. Sup. Ct. 1976); Vom Lehn v. Astor Art Galleries, 86 Misc. 2d 1 (N.Y. Sup. Ct. 1976); De La Fuente v. Home Sav. Ass'n, 669 S.W.2d 137 (Tex. App. 1984).

388 *See, e.g.*, Gross v. Bildex, Inc., 647 N.E.2d 573 (Ohio Mun. Ct. 1994) (failure to provide notice of cancellation, commencing performance prematurely, and failure to return deposit violated UDAP statute; treble damages awarded); Hines v. Thermal-Gard of Ohio, Inc., 546 N.E.2d 487 (Ohio Mun. Ct. 1988) (commencing performance before giving notice of cancellation was a violation of state cooling-off statute and, therefore, violated state UDAP statute as well); Culbreth v. Lawrence J. Miller, Inc., 447 A.2d 491 (Pa. Super. Ct. 1984).

389 *See, e.g.*, Fowler v. Rauso (*In re* Fowler), 425 B.R. 157 (Bankr. E.D. Pa. 2010) (consumer is entitled to equitable relief to restore home to her that foreclosure rescuer acquired).

390 *See* Rossi v. 21st Century Concepts, Inc., 618 N.Y.S.2d 182 (N.Y. Yonkers City Ct. 1994); Laymance v. Vaughn, 857 S.W.2d 36 (Tenn. Ct. App. 1993); Bruntaeger v. Zeller, 515 A.2d 123 (Vt. 1986). *See generally* § 2.2.4.2, *supra*.

391 White v. Allstate Ins. Co., 2009 WL 3649739 (Ohio Ct. App. Nov. 5, 2009) (unpublished) (consumer who chooses to cancel under home solicitation sales act cannot recover UDAP damages); Clemens v. Duwel, 654 N.E.2d 171 (Ohio Ct. App. 1995). *See also* Garber v. STS Concrete Co., 991 N.E.2d 1225 (Ohio Ct. App. 2013) (consumer who cancels under home solicitation sales act cannot also recover UDAP treble damages or attorney fees). *Cf.* McGill v. Image Scapes, L.L.C., 2010 WL 5288975 (Ohio Ct. App. Dec. 20, 2010) (buyer may opt for

---

Other possible theories for enforcing the right to cancel are that the right to cancel is an express or implied contract term; that the absence of the notice of the right to cancel makes the contract illegal and unenforceable;[392] or that the consumer should be allowed to invoke the equitable remedy of cancellation. If the contract is subject to the FTC Holder Rule, an assignee is liable for cancellation to the same extent as the original contracting party, with monetary liability capped at the amount the consumer has paid.[393] An officer of a company who participates personally in the company's violation of the statute may be individually liable.[394]

2.6 Mail, Internet, or Telephone Order Merchandise Rule

2.6.1 The FTC Rule

The FTC's Mail or Telephone Order Merchandise Rule[395] requires that sellers of merchandise by mail, Internet, or telephone have a reasonable basis to expect to be able to deliver the merchandise within the time specified in their advertising or within thirty days if no time is specified.[396] The rule requires that all merchandise ordered by telephone, Internet, or mail be delivered within thirty days, unless the merchant at the time of sale provided for a longer delivery time or unless the buyer later opts to wait a longer period instead of receiving a full refund.[397] (The rule allows the thirty-day period to be extended to fifty days when the order is accompanied by a request for an extension of credit from the merchant to pay for the merchandise.[398])

If this deadline cannot be met, the seller, as soon as it becomes aware of that fact, must give the consumer the option of canceling the order and receiving a full refund or consenting to a delay. Posting information about the order on the seller's website is insufficient; the seller must contact the customer directly.[399] The rule includes requirements if the consumer agrees to a revised delivery date but then the seller fails to meet that new deadline.[400] If the consumer opts for a refund, it must be paid within either seven working days or one billing cycle, depending on the manner of payment.[401]

The initial thirty-day delivery period begins to run from the buyer's order date.[402] The seller cannot extend the delivery deadline by counting the thirty days as running from a later date when the seller actually charges the buyer's credit card.[403]

The merchant does not comply with the rule by sending only part of what was ordered within thirty days. For example, if software is bundled with a computer, the merchant violates the Mail or Telephone Order Merchandise Rule by not shipping the software with the computer and not offering consumers the option of either consenting to a delay in shipping or canceling the order and receiving a full refund.[404] Charging a cancellation fee is a violation because it is inconsistent with the requirement of a full refund.[405]

As originally promulgated, the rule applied only to merchandise ordered by mail. In 1993 the FTC amended the rule, effective March 1, 1994, to apply to merchandise ordered by telephone as well.[406] That version applied to merchandise ordered through the Internet, although it left some ambiguity about Internet sales when the consumer accessed the

---

cancellation if complaint seeks cancellation and damages in the alternative); Rosenfield v. Tombragel, 1996 WL 741988 (Ohio Ct. App. Dec. 31, 1996) (by filing suit for UDAP damages before sending cancellation letter, buyer elected damages remedy).

392 Baird v. Oldfield, 728 N.W.2d 223 (Iowa Ct. App. 2006) (table, text at 2006 WL 3615053) (contract is void, but consumer has no private cause of action for refund); Teeters Constr. v. Dort, 869 N.E.2d 756 (Ohio Mun. Ct. 2006).

393 Cole v. Lovett, 672 F. Supp. 947 (S.D. Miss. 1987), *aff'd without op.*, 833 F.2d 1008 (5th Cir. 1987). *See generally* §§ 4.2, 4.3, *infra*.

394 Garber v. STS Concrete Co., 991 N.E.2d 1225 (Ohio Ct. App. 2013). *See also* National Consumer Law Center, Unfair and Deceptive Acts and Practices § 10.3.2 (8th ed. 2012), *updated at* www.nclc.org/library.

395 16 C.F.R. § 435, *reprinted at* Appx. A.6, *infra*. *See* United States v. DelMonte Corp., 3 Trade Reg. Rep. (CCH) ¶ 22,307 (N.D. Cal. Nov. 18, 1985) (consent order) (upholding FTC's authority to issue the rule).
    In 2007 the FTC began a review of the rule. 72 Fed. Reg. 51,728 (Sept. 11, 2007). In 2011 it announced that it had determined to retain it. 76 Fed. Reg. 60,715 (Sept. 30, 2011). On the same day, it proposed amendments to the rule and asked for comment on them. 76 Fed. Reg. 60,765 (Sept. 30, 2011). In 2014 it adopted amendments to the rule. 79 Fed. Reg. 55,615 (Sept. 17, 2014).

396 16 C.F.R. § 435.2(a)(1); Federal Trade Comm'n v. Thompson, 2003 WL 23220597 (N.D. Ill. Aug. 13, 2003) (stipulated final judgment and permanent injunction prohibiting Internet sales company from violating mail order rule). *See also* Federal Trade Comm'n v. Staples, Inc., 5 Trade Reg. Rep. (CCH) ¶ 15411 (D. Mass. May 22, 2003) (proposed consent decree) (website claimed one-day delivery but did not disclose limitations); Federal Trade Comm'n v. Computers by Us, Inc., 5 Trade Reg. Rep. (CCH) ¶ 15148 (D. Md. Aug. 30, 2001) (web-based auction); *In re* Market Dev. Corp., 95 F.T.C. 100 (1980); *In re* Jay Norris Inc., 91 F.T.C. 751 (1978); *In re* Nursery Barn, 92 F.T.C. 924 (1978) (consent order); *In re* Wards Co., 86 F.T.C. 938 (1975) (consent order); *In re* Baltimore Stereo Wholesalers, 86 F.T.C. 930 (1975) (consent order); *In re* Auslander Decorator Furniture, 83 F.T.C. 1542 (1973).

397 16 C.F.R. § 435.2(b)(2).

398 16 C.F.R. § 435.2(a)(1)(ii).

399 United States v. Pet Express, Inc., 5 Trade Reg. Rep. (CCH) ¶ 15,185 (E.D. Va. Dec. 10, 2001) (proposed consent decree).

400 16 C.F.R. § 435.2(b)(2).

401 16 C.F.R. § 435.1(b) (definition of "prompt payment"). *See also* 79 Fed. Reg. 55,615 (Sept. 17, 2014) (explanation of this provision).

402 16 C.F.R. § 435.2(b)(1).

403 Fed. Trade Comm'n, A Business Guide to the Federal Trade Commission's Mail or Telephone Order Merchandise Rule (Sept. 2011), *available at* http://business.ftc.gov (time period begins to run when seller receives properly completed order, regardless of when seller posts or deposits payment); Fed. Trade Comm'n, Supplementary Information for Amended Mail Order Rule, 58 Fed. Reg. 49,096, 49,113–114 (Sept. 21, 1993).

404 Federal Trade Comm'n v. Dell Computer Corp., 5 Trade Reg. Rep. (CCH) ¶ 24,411 (W.D. Tex. 1998) (proposed consent decree).

405 United States v. Dynamic Wheels & Tires, Inc., 5 Trade Reg. Rep. (CCH) ¶ 15,308 (C.D. Cal. Sept. 30, 2002) (proposed consent decree against company that charged "restocking fee"); Federal Trade Comm'n v. Charles Smith, 5 Trade Reg. Rep. (CCH) ¶ 15,194 (C.D. Cal. Dec. 20, 2001) (proposed consent decree).

406 58 Fed. Reg. 49,096 (Sept. 21, 1993), *amending* 16 C.F.R. § 435 (effective Mar. 1, 1994), *reprinted at* Appx. A.6, *infra*.

Internet through something other than a telephone line.[407] Effective December 8, 2014, the rule was amended to include all Internet orders of merchandise.[408] The rule does not apply to face-to-face transactions in which a seller's representative merely received product or inventory information through the Internet, as in such a transaction the buyer is not ordering the merchandise via the Internet.[409] However, it does apply whenever a consumer places an order via the Internet, even if the consumer is standing in the seller's place of business and using a smartphone to do so.[410]

While there is little that the FTC rule can do about a fly-by-night operation that takes telephone orders and disappears, the rule does give consumers a specific time frame within which to follow up a seller's failure to respond. If, within thirty days of a telephone order, the consumer neither receives the ordered merchandise nor receives some communication offering a full refund, there has been a violation. The thirty-day period begins to run from the buyer's order date. This should also be an early warning of a possible scam and an indication that the merchandise may never be delivered. At that point, if not before, the consumer should actively pursue the matter with the proper authorities before the seller goes out of business. It may also not be too late for the consumer to withhold payment of a credit card bill for the purchase.[411] Violation of the rule, or a comparable state regulation, can also be the basis for a UDAP claim.[412]

2.6.2 State Mail and Telephone Order Laws and Regulations

The FTC rule does not preempt state laws that provide greater protections to consumers.[413] Two states have incorporated the FTC rule into their UDAP regulations.[414] A California statute tracks the federal rule but explicitly applies to services as well as goods.[415] Other state UDAP regulations are similar but slightly weaker, for example by giving sellers six weeks instead of thirty days to make delivery or by giving sellers the

additional option of delivering substitute goods of equivalent or superior value.[416]

Still other state UDAP regulations require mail-order sellers to disclose in all materials their legal name and address.[417] It has been found deceptive for sellers to fail to disclose that not all items are kept in stock,[418] to misrepresent that parcels are insured against loss,[419] and to misrepresent that refunds or exchanges will be processed promptly.[420]

2.7 Negative Option Rule

Negative option plans—a book-of-the-month club is a common example—require plan participants to make affirmative and timely rejection of a sale offer. Silence is treated as a binding contract. The FTC rule concerning use of negative option plans requires sellers to disclose plan terms, including the negative option, minimum purchase requirements, cancellation rights, postage charges, and refusal rights.[421] Membership must be canceled upon request when minimum obligations have been met.[422]

The seller must also give the consumer written notice of the nature of the goods before their arrival, including a form allowing the consumer to refuse the selection. The FTC has indicated that notification by e-mail may suffice if the seller gives the consumer clear notice, before enrolling in the plan, about how notices will be sent.[423] In addition, the federal E-Sign statute[424] requires the seller to make specific disclosures prior to obtaining the consumer's consent to receive

---

407   *See* 79 Fed. Reg. 55,615 (Sept. 17, 2014) (describing history of the rule); Fed. Trade Comm'n, Dot Com Disclosure § 14(A)(2) (2000) (providing guidance on how online sellers should comply with rule). *See also* Federal Trade Comm'n v. Bargains & Deals Magazine, 5 Trade Reg. Rep. (CCH) ¶ 15,162 (W.D. Wash. Oct. 11, 2001) (complaint filed and TRO issued to enforce mail order rule for Internet sale).

408   79 Fed. Reg. 55,615 (Sept. 17, 2014). *See also* 75 Fed. Reg. 60765 (Sept. 20, 2011) (proposing amendments to the rule).

409   79 Fed. Reg. 55,615 (Sept. 17, 2014).

410   *Id.*

411   *See* National Consumer Law Center, Truth in Lending § 7.11 (9th ed. 2015), *updated at* www.nclc.org/library.

412   *See* § 2.2.4.2, *supra.*

413   16 C.F.R. § 453.3(b).

414   Ga. Comp. R. & Regs. 122-2.01 (time of delivery or performance, mail order sales); Idaho Admin. Code § 04.02.01.141 (same).

415   Cal. Bus. & Prof. Code § 17538 (West). *See* Delong v. TaxMasters, Inc., 2011 WL 3715251 (C.D. Cal. Aug. 24, 2011) (refusing to dismiss claim that tax relief service provider violated statute by accepting funds, failing to provide services within thirty days, and denying requests for refunds); People v. Columbia Research Grp., 139 Cal. Rptr. 517 (Cal. Ct. App. 1977) (vacation certificates are consumer goods or services and do not fall within any exemption to state mail order merchandise statute).

416   N.J. Admin. Code § 13:45A-1.1 (deceptive mail order practices) (allows six weeks); Ohio Admin. Code 109:4-3-09, (failure to deliver/substitution of goods or services) (allows eight weeks); Utah Admin. Code r. 152-11-8 (failure to deliver/substitution of goods); 06-031-010 Vt. Code R. § 105 (substitution of products/failure to deliver). *See also* McWhorter v. Elsea, Inc., 2007 WL 1101249 (S.D. Ohio Apr. 11, 2007) (Ohio courts strictly construe eight-week delivery rule; summary judgment for plaintiff); Knoth v. Prime Time Mktg. Mgmt., Inc., 2006 WL 3114273 (Ohio Ct. App. Oct. 27, 2006) (violation of delivery rule actionable even when membership organization gave written notice that it could not ensure timely delivery and members attempted to cancel order after eight weeks).

417   Idaho Admin. Code r. 04.02.01.163 (mail order and catalog sales); N.J. Admin. Code § 13:45A-1.1 (deceptive mail order practices).

418   *In re* U.S. Gen. Supply Co., 80 F.T.C. 857 (1972) (consent order).

419   Jay Norris Inc., 91 F.T.C. 751 (1978).

420   *Id.*

421   16 C.F.R. pt. 425.

In 1998 the FTC completed a periodic review of the Negative Option Plan Rule, retaining it in its existing form with minor technical changes. 63 Fed. Reg. 44,555 (Aug. 20, 1998). *See* 62 Fed. Reg. 15,135 (Mar. 31, 1997).

In 2014, the FTC completed another review of the rule. The FTC determined to retain the rule without change. It also noted that abusive negative option sales remain a continuing problem and indicated that it may address them as part of its review of the Telemarketing Sales Rule. 79 Fed. Reg. 44,271 (July 31, 2014).

422   16 C.F.R. § 425.1(b)(4).

423   Fed. Trade Comm'n, Dot Com Disclosures § IV(A)(2) (2000).

424   15 U.S.C. §§ 700115 U.S.C. § 7001–7006. *See* National Consumer Law Center, Consumer Banking and Payments Law Ch. 11 (5th ed. 2013), *updated at* www.nclc.org/library (detailed discussion of this statute).

electronic notification.[425] E-Sign also requires the consumer to either give or confirm consent electronically, in a manner that "reasonably demonstrates" that the consumer can access information in the electronic form that the seller will use.[426]

The FTC has ruled that it is deceptive to misrepresent that the buyer can reject each product upon receipt or that after cancellation the consumer will not receive anything.[427] Obscure disclosures and restrictions designed to impede consumers from cancelling violate the FTC Act.[428] The FTC's telemarketing rule has additional restrictions and requirements for negative option plans sold through telemarketing.[429] Georgia,[430] Idaho,[431] Missouri,[432] New York,[433] Oregon,[434] Utah,[435] and Wisconsin[436] have their own negative option UDAP regulations, specifying disclosures required in such plans. Some states require automatic renewal or continuous service plans to include certain consumer protections.[437]

The Restore Online Shoppers' Confidence Act requires disclosures and other protections for certain negative option sales over the Internet.[438] The Federal Cable Television Consumer Protection and Competition Act prohibits negative option billing for cable TV services.[439]

2.8 Franchise and Business Opportunity Rules

2.8.1 Overview and History of the FTC Franchising and Business Opportunity Rules

According to a 2004 FTC survey, over a two-year period almost half a million U.S. adults purchased business opportunities involving false earnings claims or false promises of assistance.[440] Recognizing the level of fraud in this area, the FTC has adopted two trade regulation rules: the Franchising Rule, which sets disclosure requirements and prohibitions concerning franchising,[441] and the Business Opportunity Rule.[442]

As originally adopted in 1978,[443] the Franchising Rule applied to both franchises (in which the franchisee sells goods or services that are associated with the franchisor's trademark) and certain non-franchise business opportunities. However, its coverage of non-franchise business opportunities was quite limited. It applied only if the purchaser was required to make a payment of at least $500 (now $540) within the first six months,[444] only if the seller promised to help the buyer secure locations or accounts, and only if the opportunity involved selling goods or services directly to end-users other than the seller.[445] This final requirement excluded the typical work-at-home scheme.

By 2007, the FTC had decided that non-franchise business opportunities were so different from franchises that they should be governed by a separate rule with simpler disclosure requirements.[446] As a first step toward developing two separate regimes, the FTC split the original franchise rule into two parts. One rule governed only franchises,[447] and the other governed only non-franchise opportunities.[448] However, the substantive provisions—detailed disclosures plus prohibitions of several types of misrepresentations—of the two rules were identical.

Effective March 1, 2012, the FTC adopted a revised, separate rule for non-franchise business opportunities.[449] The new rule expands coverage, streamlines disclosure requirements, and prohibits a long list of misrepresentations and deceptive acts. This new Business Opportunity Rule applies to opportunities that are more likely to be marketed to ordinary consumers, as compared to the more complicated arrangements governed by the Franchising Rule.

The following subsections first examine the Franchising Rule and then the 2012 Business Opportunity Rule. The section concludes with a discussion of other sources of authority, such as state franchise laws, the FTC Act's general prohibition of unfair and deceptive acts and practices, and state UDAP statutes. The FTC rules do not preempt state laws that offer equal or greater protections, except to the extent of any inconsistency with the FTC rules.[450] Thus, for example, state laws

---

425 15 U.S.C. § 7001(c)(1)(B), (C). *See* National Consumer Law Center, Consumer Banking and Payments Law Ch. 11 (5th ed. 2013), *updated at* www.nclc.org/library (further discussion of E-Sign).

426 15 U.S.C. § 7001(c)(1)(C)(ii).

427 Grolier, Inc., 91 F.T.C. 315 (1978), *vacated on other grounds*, 615 F.2d 1215 (9th Cir. 1980); Marshall Cavandish Corp., 86 F.T.C. 86 (1975) (consent order); Greystone Corp., 86 F.T.C. 94 (1975) (consent order); Crowell-Collier & Macmillan, Inc., 82 F.T.C. 1292 (1973) (consent order).

428 Fed. Trade Comm'n v. Grant Connect, L.L.C., 827 F Supp. 2d 1199, 1228 (D. Nev. 2011), *aff'd in part, rev'd in part on other grounds*, 763 F.3d 1094 (9th Cir. 2014).

429 *See* §§ 5.3.4, 5.4.4.3, *infra*.

430 Ga. Comp. R. & Regs. 122-4-.01 (adopting FTC rule by reference).

431 Idaho Admin. Code r. 04.02.01.020(34).

432 Mo. Code Regs. Ann. tit. 15, § 60-8.060.

433 N.Y. Comp. Codes R. & Regs. tit. 16, § 890.93 (cable TV).

434 Or. Admin. R. 137-020-0300.

435 Utah Admin. Code R152-11-12.

436 Wis. Admin. Code ATCP § 123.06 (electronic communication services).

437 *See, e.g.*, Cal. Bus. & Prof. Code §§ 17601 to 17606 (West); N.Y. Gen. Obligation Law §§ 5-901 to 5-903 (McKinney). *See also* Ovitz v. Bloomberg, L.P., 967 N.E.2d 1170 (N.Y. 2012) (noting vendor's concession that automatic renewal clause was unenforceable).

438 *See* § 11.5, *infra*.

439 47 U.S.C. § 543(f). *See* National Consumer Law Center, Unfair and Deceptive Acts and Practices § 2.5.6 (8th ed. 2012), *updated at* www.nclc.org/library.

440 Fed. Trade Comm'n, Consumer Fraud in the United Sates: An FTC Survey 30 (Aug. 2004).

441 16 C.F.R. pt. 436.

442 16 C.F.R. pt. 437.

443 43 Fed. Reg. 59,614 (Dec. 21, 1978).

444 *See* 16 C.F.R. §§ 436.1(s), 436.8(a)(1) (provisions of current Franchising Rule).

445 76 Fed. Reg. 76,816, 76,817 (Dec. 8, 2011).

446 72 Fed. Reg. 15,444 (Mar. 30, 2007).

447 16 C.F.R. pt. 436.

448 16 C.F.R. pt. 437.

449 76 Fed. Reg. 76,816 (Dec. 8, 2011).

450 16 C.F.R. §§ 436.10(b) (Franchising Rule), 437.9(b) (Business Opportunity Rule). *See* H.R.R. Zimmerman v. Tecumseh Products Co., 2001 WL 184982 (N.D. Ill. Feb. 22, 2001).

can regulate the substantive terms of franchise contracts. Sellers cannot mix in state-required disclosures with the ones required by the FTC's Business Opportunity Rule, however.[451]

2.8.2   The FTC's Franchising Rule

The FTC's Franchising Rule requires detailed disclosures and prohibits a list of unfair or deceptive acts by sellers of franchises that fall within its scope.[452] The FTC has brought many enforcement proceedings under it.[453]

The Franchising Rule includes a very specific definition of the franchises to which it applies.[454] A covered franchise is one in which the franchisee obtains the right to operate a business that is identified or associated with the franchisor's trademark or involves offering, selling, or distributing trademarked goods, services, or commodities.[455] The franchisor must have authority to exert significant control over or provide significant assistance to the franchisee.[456] The franchisee must make a payment of at least $540 that is required by the terms of the contract or by practical necessity (excluding payments for reasonable amounts of inventory at bona fide wholesale prices).[457] There are several exceptions to the definition, including one for large sophisticated franchise purchasers.[458]

The Franchising Rule requires franchisors to give prospective franchisees a detailed disclosure statement containing information on the franchise operation, including the franchisor's business experience, balance sheet, and recurring fees.[459]

The nature of the involvement of public figures in a franchise must be disclosed.[460] The franchisor must also have substantiation for income and profit claims and must inform prospects that these are only estimates.[461]

On March 30, 2007, the FTC announced significant amendments to the rule, effective July 1, 2007.[462] Franchisors had the option of continuing to comply with the old rule until July 1, 2008.[463] The changes largely streamline the rule and account for the use of electronic disclosures. Additionally, the FTC revised many of its required disclosures to be consistent with the Uniform Franchise Offering Circulating (UFOC) Guidelines adopted by the North American Securities Administrators Association. Previously, the FTC allowed compliance with the UFOC instead of the FTC's rule.[464] The new FTC rule, however, requires some disclosures beyond those included in the UFOC Guidelines.[465]

One interesting note about the FTC Franchising Rule is that, when it adopted the rule in 1978, the FTC stated that it believed there was a private right of action for the violation of the FTC rule:

> The Commission believes that the courts should and will hold that any person injured by a violation of the rule has a private right of action against the violator under the Federal Trade Commission Act, as amended, and the rule. Such a private right of action is necessary to protect those meant to benefit from the rule. The FTC also finds this consistent with the legislative intent of the Congress in enacting the Federal Trade Commission Act, as amended, and is necessary to the FTC's enforcement scheme.[466]

Nevertheless, federal district courts have consistently rejected this view, holding that it is for Congress and the courts to make this decision, not the FTC, and that there is

---

451   16 C.F.R. § 437.9(b).

452   16 C.F.R. pt. 436.

453   *See, e.g.,* Federal Trade Comm'n v. Network Services Depot, Inc., 617 F.3d 1127 (9th Cir. 2010) (Ponzi-type scheme; sale of locations for nonexistent or non-functional Internet kiosks; payments to early investors from sums received from later purchasers); Federal Trade Comm'n v. Essex Mktg. Grp., 2008 WL 2704918 (E.D.N.Y. July 8, 2008) (sale of vending machine locations; misleading income projections; failure to provide required disclosures).

 Many other examples of FTC enforcement proceedings may be found on the FTC's website, www.ftc.gov.

454   *See* United States v. Lasseter, 2005 WL 1638735 (M.D. Tenn. June 30, 2005) (business opportunity was franchise within meaning of rule when there was a unique trade name, seller provided significant assistance, and cost of becoming a licensee was more than $500); Mercy Health Sys. v. Metropolitan Partners Realty L.L.C., 2005 WL 957722 (Pa. Ct. Com. Pl. Phila. Cnty. Mar. 6, 2005) (rule did not apply to relationship between health care provider and realty company that rented it space and allowed it to use a trademark).

455   16 C.F.R. § 436.1(h)(1).

456   16 C.F.R. § 436.1(h)(2).

457   16 C.F.R. §§ 436.1(h)(3), 436.8(a)(1).

458   16 C.F.R. § 436.8(a)(5), (6). *See* 58 Fed. Reg. 15,444, 15,448 (Mar. 30, 2007).

459   16 C.F.R. §§ 436.2, 436.5. *See* Federal Trade Comm'n v. Accent Mktg., Inc., 2002 WL 31257708 (S.D. Ala. July 1, 2002) (issuing preliminary injunction against company that failed to make required disclosures). *See also* Federal Trade Comm'n v. Holiday Enterprises, Inc., 2008 WL 953358 (N.D. Ga. Feb. 5, 2008); Federal Trade Comm'n v. Netfran Dev. Corp., 508 F. Supp. 2d 1194 (S.D. Fla. 2007) (permanent injunction against companies that violated disclosure requirements); Federal Trade Comm'n v. Transnet Wireless Corp., 506 F. Supp. 2d 1247 (S.D. Fla. 2007) (franchise disclosure documents provided by Internet kiosk

companies were deficient according to rule). *But cf.* Rich Food Services, Inc. v. Rich Plan Corp., 98 Fed. Appx. 206 (4th Cir. 2004) (disclosure requirements do not apply when franchise agreement is renewed or extended without interruption or material change); Red Roof Inns, Inc. v. Murat Holdings, L.L.C., 223 S.W.3d 676, 690 (Tex. App. 2007) (disclosure requirements do not apply to current franchisees).

460   16 C.F.R. § 436.5.

461   *See* Federal Trade Comm'n v. Tashman, 318 F.3d 1273 (11th Cir. 2003) (ordering entry of judgment for FTC when promoter had no basis for sales estimates); Federal Trade Comm'n v. Transnet Wireless Corp., 506 F. Supp. 2d 1247 (S.D. Fla. 2007) (franchise disclosure documents failed to include or provide a reasonable basis for earnings claims made to prospective purchasers); United States v. Vend Direct, Inc., 2007 WL 2176205 (D. Colo. May 11, 2007) (material misrepresentations concerning anticipated income when defendants repeatedly misled purchasers by providing estimated earnings and so-called testimonials without supporting documentation), *adopted by* 2007 WL 3407357 (D. Colo. Nov. 13, 2007).

462   72 Fed. Reg. 15,444 (Mar. 30, 2007). *See also* Gerald C. Wells & Dennis E. Wieczorek, *A Road Map to the New FTC Franchise Rule*, 27 Franchise L.J. (Fall 2007).

463   72 Fed. Reg. 15,444 (Mar. 30, 2007).

464   58 Fed. Reg. 69,224 (Dec. 30, 1993).

465   72 Fed. Reg. 15,444, 15,448–49 (Mar. 30, 2007).

466   43 Fed. Reg. 59,614 (Feb. 10, 1978).

no congressional intent underlying the FTC position.[467] The FTC's announcement of the 2007 amendments to the rule include a statement that there is no private right of action to enforce the Franchising Rule.[468] UDAP,[469] contract, fraud, and other common law claims[470] therefore provide the most likely vehicles for private enforcement of the FTC rule.

2.8.3 The FTC's Business Opportunity Rule

2.8.3.1 Introduction

The Business Opportunity Rule[471] is an outgrowth of the FTC's Franchising Rule. The FTC's Franchising Rule originally covered certain non-franchise business opportunities. In 2007, the FTC decided to confine the Franchising Rule to sales of franchises that were associated with trademarks and met certain other criteria. It adopted an interim Business Opportunity Rule that applied to certain non-franchise business opportunities but imposed the same substantive requirements as the Franchising Rule.[472] In 2012, it revised and finalized the Business Opportunity Rule. The revised rule, discussed in the next two subsections, is significantly different from the Franchising Rule.

2.8.3.2 Scope

The revised Business Opportunity Rule applies to any commercial arrangement in which the seller solicits a prospective buyer to enter into a new business, the buyer makes a required payment (excluding voluntary purchases of reasonable amounts of inventory at bona fide wholesale prices for resale),[473] and the seller promises assistance in the form of providing locations (for example, for display racks), outlets, accounts, or customers, or buying the goods or services the buyer makes.[474] Sales to which the Franchising Rule applies are exempt.[475]

Compared to the interim Business Opportunity Rule that the FTC adopted in 2007, the revised rule significantly expands coverage by:

- Eliminating the requirement that the buyer's payment be at least $500; and
- Covering non-franchise business opportunities even if they involve selling goods or services to the seller of the business opportunity rather than to end-users.

The result is that the 2012 rule, like the 2007 rule, continues to cover such business opportunities as vending machine opportunities but does so regardless of the amount the buyer is required to pay. The rule also now covers work-at-home schemes such as medical billing and envelope stuffing. The FTC noted that these types of business opportunities are fraught with unfair and deceptive practices, such as false earnings claims.[476]

However, at the same time as it broadened the rule in these ways, the FTC took pains to draft the rule to exclude what it considered legitimate multi-level marketing programs. It acknowledged that some of these programs are pyramid schemes, but the FTC was unable to devise meaningful disclosures that would help consumers identify them. Instead, the FTC intends to address fraud in multi-level marketing programs through enforcement actions.[477]

2.8.3.3 Substantive Requirements

The FTC's substantive approach to the non-franchise business opportunities governed by its 2012 rule combines streamlined disclosures with prohibitions of various types of deception.

The FTC determined that non-franchise business opportunity contracts are usually less complicated than franchise arrangements and that the extensive disclosures required for franchises would more likely obscure than illuminate the key facts that non-franchise business opportunity purchasers

---

467 Meissner v. BF Labs Inc., 2014 WL 2558203 (D. Kan. June 6, 2014); Yogo Factory Franchising, Inc. v. Ying, 2014 WL 1783146 (D.N.J. May 5, 2014); Robinson v. Wingate Inns Int'l Inc., 2013 WL 6860723 (D.N.J. Dec. 20, 2013); United Consumers Club, Inc. v. Bledsoe, 441 F. Supp. 2d 967, 987 (N.D. Ind. 2006), *as amended by* 2006 WL 2361818 (N.D. Ind. Aug. 14, 2006); G&R Moojestic Treats, Inc. v. Maggiemoo's Int'l, Inc., 2004 WL 1110423 (S.D.N.Y. May 19, 2004); Federal Trade Comm'n v. Davis, 5 Trade Reg. Rep. (CCH) ¶ 22,741 (D. Nev. Oct. 17, 1989); Days Inn of Am. Franchising, Inc. v. Windham, 699 F. Supp. 1581 (N.D. Ga. 1988); Freedman v. Meldy's, Inc., 587 F. Supp. 658 (E.D. Pa. 1984). *See also* Holiday Hospitality Franchising, Inc. v. 174 W. St. Corp., 2006 WL 2466819 (N.D. Ga. Aug. 22, 2006). *See generally* § 2.2.4.1, *supra*.

468 72 Fed. Reg. 15,444, 15,478 (Mar. 30, 2007).

469 *See* § 2.2.4.2, *supra*; National Consumer Law Center, Unfair and Deceptive Acts and Practices § 3.2.7.3.6 (8th ed. 2012), *updated at* www.nclc.org/library (decisions allowing UDAP claims based on franchise rule violations). *See also* Legacy Academy v. Mamilove, L.L.C., 761 S.E.2d 880, 2014 WL 3557617, at *9 (Ga. Ct. App. July 16, 2014) (claim for violation of franchise rule can be asserted as violation of Georgia statute allowing cause of action for breach of a duty imposed by a law that does not provide its own private cause of action).

470 *See, e.g.*, Bans Pasta, L.L.C. v. Mirko Franchising, L.L.C., 2014 WL 637762 (W.D. Va. Feb. 12, 2014) (allowing plaintiff to proceed with negligence per se claim based on violation of FTC Franchise Rule; plaintiff must show that the rule dictates a standard of conduct or care, and that (1) plaintiff falls within class of persons the statute was intended to protect; (2) the harm complained of was same harm the statute was intended to guard against; and (3) violation of the statute proximately caused plaintiff's injury.).

471 16 C.F.R. pt. 437.

472 *See* § 2.8.2, *supra*.

473 16 C.F.R. § 437.1(p).

474 16 C.F.R. § 437.1(c). *But cf.* United States v. Zaken Corp., 2013 WL 3983400 (C.D. Cal. July 31, 2013) (denying preliminary injunction under broadened version of Business Opportunity Rule; agreeing with seller of home business plan kit that it does not offer new business opportunity or buyback provisions, or provide outlets and customers).

475 16 C.F.R. § 437.8 (exempting sales of franchises as defined by the Franchising Rule, except those that meet the definition of "franchise" but are not governed by the rule because the buyer's payment falls under the $500 threshold or the franchise agreement is reached without any written document describing any term or aspect of the relationship).

476 76 Fed. Reg. 76,816, 76,821 (Dec. 8, 2011).

477 76 Fed. Reg. 76,816, 76,822 (Dec. 8, 2011).

need to know. Accordingly, the Business Opportunity Rule requires a simple, standardized, one-page disclosure of just five items:[478]

- The seller's identifying information;[479]
- Whether the seller is making a claim about earnings—if so, the seller must attach an earnings statement with prescribed information[480] and must make written substantiation of all the claims available to the buyer upon request;[481]
- Whether the seller, its affiliates, any prior business of the seller, or any of the seller's key personnel have been the subject of any civil or criminal action for misrepresentation, fraud, securities law violations, or unfair or deceptive practices within the past ten years—if so, the seller must attach a list;[482]
- Whether the seller offers a refund or a right to cancel the purchase of the business opportunity—if so, the seller must attach a statement listing all the material conditions;[483]
- A list, with contact information, of everyone who purchased the business opportunity within the last three years (or, if there are more than ten purchasers, the ten located nearest to the prospective purchaser's location).[484] To deter the use of shills, the seller must also disclose any payments made to any of these purchasers and any personal relationships with them.[485]

This disclosure must be in the language in which the transaction is conducted.[486] It must use exactly the language prescribed by the rule[487] and cannot include any extraneous information.[488]

Complementing the disclosure requirement is a series of prohibitions, including:

- Making unsubstantiated earnings claims to buyers or in the media;[489]
- Requiring a buyer to disclaim reliance on the disclosures;[490]
- Misrepresenting potential earnings,[491] the assistance the seller will provide,[492] the cost, performance, efficacy, nature,

or central characteristics of the business opportunity,[493] any endorsements or affiliations,[494] or the seller's cancellation policy;[495]

- Claiming that the law prohibits the seller from releasing information about earnings or other buyers;[496]
- Failing to provide a refund when the buyer has satisfied the disclosed conditions;[497] and
- Misrepresenting a business opportunity as an employment opportunity.[498]

2.8.4 Other FTC, State UDAP Precedent

Some states have business opportunity laws or UDAP rules that specify certain unfair practices in the sale of franchises or business opportunities.[499] Some business opportunities may also be considered securities that will be governed by the state's securities law.[500] A state's regulation of business opportunities within its borders does not violate the Commerce Clause even though the franchise may make sales in other states.[501]

In other states, unfair practices will be determined under the more general standards of the state's UDAP statute, taking the prohibitions of the FTC rule into account. Most UDAP statutes cover franchise and business opportunity schemes.[502] As long as there are no questions about UDAP coverage, it should be a per se UDAP violation to violate the FTC rule.[503]

---

478 16 C.F.R. § 437.3.
479 16 C.F.R. § 237.3(a)(1).
480 16 C.F.R. §§ 437.3(a)(2), 437.4(a)(4).
481 16 C.F.R. §§ 437.4(a)(3), 437.6(f).
482 16 C.F.R. § 437.3(a)(3)(ii).
483 16 C.F.R. § 437.3(a)(4).
484 16 C.F.R. § 437.3(a)(5).
485 16 C.F.R. § 437.6(r). *See also* 16 C.F.R. § 437.6(q) (prohibiting referral of potential buyers to fictitious purchasers).
486 16 C.F.R. § 437.5.
487 16 C.F.R. § 437.3(a).
488 16 C.F.R. § 437.6(c).
489 16 C.F.R. § 437.4(a), (b).
490 16 C.F.R. § 437.6(a).
491 16 C.F.R. § 437.6(d). *See also* 16 C.F.R. § 437.6(g) (misrepresentation of timing of payments).
492 16 C.F.R. § 437.6(i). *See also* 16 C.F.R. § 437.6(j) (misrepresentation of likelihood that seller will find locations, outlets, accounts, or customers for the purchaser).

493 16 C.F.R. § 437.6(h). *See also* 16 C.F.R. § 437.6(n), (o) (misrepresentations regarding territorial exclusivity).
494 16 C.F.R. § 437.6(p).
495 16 C.F.R. § 437.6(k).
496 16 C.F.R. § 437.6(e).
497 16 C.F.R. § 437.6(*l*).
498 16 C.F.R. § 437.6(m).
499 *See, e.g.,* Ga. Code Ann. §§ 10-1-410 to 10-1-417; Haw. Rev. Stat. ch. 482E; 940 Code Mass. Reg. § 3.11; Md. Code Ann., Bus. Reg. §§ 14-101 to 14-305 (West); Ohio Rev. Code Ann. §§ 1334.01 to 1334.99 (West); Utah Admin. Code R152-11-11(B) (franchises, distributorships, referral sales). *See* §§ 2.8.2, 2.8.3, *supra. See also* 7-Eleven v. Spear, 2011 WL 2516579 (N.D. Ill. June 23, 2011) (Illinois UDAP statute's franchise disclosure requirements are coextensive with FTC rule); People v. iMergent, Inc., 87 Cal. Rptr. 3d 844 (Cal Ct. App. 2009) (preliminary injunction that prohibited home-based Internet business promoter from conducting any business in the state without complying with state business opportunity law was within trial court's very broad discretion); League v. U.S. Postmatic, Inc., 508 S.E.2d 210 (Ga. Ct. App. 1998) (violation of Georgia business opportunity statute is per se UDAP violation); Julie Khoury Robie, Ohio Consumer Law Ch. 8 (2012–13 ed.) (analysis of Ohio's law).
500 *See, e.g.,* State *ex rel.* Miller v. Pace, 677 N.W.2d 761 (Iowa 2004); State v. Justin, 779 N.Y.S.2d 717 (N.Y. Sup. Ct. 2003).
501 H.R.R. Zimmerman v. Tecumseh Products Co., 2001 WL 184982 (N.D. Ill. Feb. 22, 2001).
502 National Consumer Law Center, Unfair and Deceptive Acts and Practices §§ 2.2.9.2, 2.2.9.4 (8th ed. 2012), *updated at* www.nclc.org/library.
503 Nieman v. DryClean U.S.A. Franchise Co., 178 F.3d 1126 (11th Cir. 1999) (violation is per se violation of Florida UDAP statute, but Franchise Rule did not apply here); Aurigemma v. Arco Petroleum Products Co., 734 F. Supp. 1025 (D. Conn. 1990) (violation of FTC Franchise rule is per se violation of Connecticut's UDAP statute); Final Cut, L.L.C. v. Sharkey, 2009 WL 415527 (Conn. Super. Ct. Jan. 14,

In addition, whether or not either of the FTC rules applies, the FTC can base charges against franchisors and sellers of non-franchise business opportunities on its general authority to prohibit unfair and deceptive acts.[504]

FTC[505] and state[506] decisions hold that it is deceptive to misrepresent the prospective profits or earnings of a business opportunity or franchise. Thus it is deceptive to: represent that a substantial number of distributors have made or can make the profits advertised when only a few have made that high a profit;[507] claim earnings that far exceed the earnings normally received;[508] or make representations with only limited knowledge of actual profits received.[509] Earnings figures, even those attributed to a specific distributor, unaccompanied by limiting or explanatory language, imply that a substantial number of distributors will earn the figure indicated.[510]

2009) (violation of franchising rule, here incomplete and inaccurate financial information in offering statement, is per se UDAP violation); Honey Dew Associates, Inc. v. Creighton Muscato Enterprises, Inc., 903 N.E.2d 239 (Mass. App. Ct. 2009) (violation of franchising rule is per se UDAP violation; footnote 13 explains interaction of FTC Act and rules, Massachusetts UDAP statute and rules); Morgan v. Air Brook Limousine, Inc., 510 A.2d 1197 (N.J. Super. Ct. Ch. Div. 1986); Texas Cookie Co. v. Hendricks & Peralta, 747 S.W.2d 873 (Tex. App. 1988) (deceptive to fail to disclose information required by FTC Franchise Rule). *Cf.* Lui Ciro, Inc. v. Ciro, Inc., 895 F. Supp. 1365, 1387–88 (D. Haw. 1995) (state franchise law states that violation is a UDAP violation, but plaintiffs must still show that they meet UDAP statute's standing requirements; these non-consumers can bring UDAP claim for unfair competition based on violation of franchise statute, but only consumers can bring UDAP claim for deception). *But cf.* Englert, Inc. v. LeafGuard, U.S.A., Inc., 2009 WL 5031309 (D.S.C. Dec. 14, 2009) (open question whether violation of FTC franchise rule is per se UDAP violation); Leblanc v. Belt Ctr., Inc., 509 So. 2d 134 (La. Ct. App. 1987) (failure to make disclosures required by Franchise Rule not UDAP violation when buyer proved no damage resulting from non-disclosure and seller's misrepresentations related to matters that rule did not require to be disclosed).

504 *See, e.g.,* Federal Trade Comm'n v. Tashman, 318 F.3d 1273 (11th Cir. 2003) (baseless sales estimates violated FTC Act). *See also* United States v. Vend Direct, Inc., 2007 WL 2176205 (D. Colo. May 11, 2007), *adopted by* 2007 WL 3407357 (D. Colo. Nov. 13, 2007); Federal Trade Comm'n v. Transnet Wireless Corp., 506 F. Supp. 2d 1247 (S.D. Fla. 2007).

505 The following are among the many FTC cases on this topic: United States v. Zaken Corp., 57 F. Supp. 3d 1233 (C.D. Cal. 2014) (summary judgment and permanent injunction; guarantee of commission payments in work-at-home scheme); Federal Trade Comm'n v. Essex Mktg. Grp., 2008 WL 2704918 (E.D.N.Y. July 8, 2008) (sale of vending machine locations; misleading income projections; failure to provide required disclosures); Federal Trade Comm'n v. End70 Corp., 2003 WL 21770837 (N.D. Tex. July 31, 2003) (preliminary injunction); Federal Trade Comm'n v. Accent Mktg., Inc., 2002 WL 31257708 (S.D. Ala. July 1, 2002); Federal Trade Comm'n v. Data Med. Capital, Inc., 5 Trade Reg. Rep. (CCH) ¶ 15,129 (C.D. Cal. July 6, 2001) (work-at-home scheme); Federal Trade Comm'n v. Five Star Auto Club, Inc., 97 F. Supp. 2d 502 (S.D.N.Y. 2000) ($2.9 million restitution order); Federal Trade Comm'n v. Patriot Alcohol Testers, 798 F. Supp. 851 (D. Mass. 1992) (coin-operated blood alcohol testing device); Akers v. Bonifasi, 629 F. Supp. 1212 (M.D. Tenn. 1985); National Dynamics Corp., 82 F.T.C. 488 (1973), *remanded in part*, 492 F.2d 1333 (2d Cir. 1974), *on remand*, 85 F.T.C. 391, 1052 (1975); Universal Credit Acceptance Corp., 82 F.T.C. 570 (1973), *rev'd in part sub nom.* Heater v. Federal Trade Comm'n, 503 F.2d 321 (9th Cir. 1974); Universal Electronics Corp., 78 F.T.C. 265 (1971); Windsor Distrib. Co., 77 F.T.C. 204 (1970) *aff'd*, 431 F.2d 443 (3d Cir. 1971); Waltham Watch Co., 60 F.T.C. 1692 (1962), *aff'd*, 318 F.2d 28 (7th Cir. 1963). *See also* Federal Trade Comm'n v. Freecom Communications, Inc., 401 F.3d 1192 (10th Cir. 2005) ("colorable" claim that success stories and earnings claims for small vending machines were deceptive); United States v. Vend Direct, Inc., 2007 WL 2176205 (D. Colo. May 11, 2007), *adopted by* 2007 WL 3407357 (D. Colo. Nov. 13, 2007).

506 Colorado Coffee Bean, L.L.C. v. Peaberry Coffee, Inc., 251 P.3d 9 (Colo. App. 2010) (limiting language added to earnings figures in offering circular was sufficient to comply with FTC rule but did not provide safe harbor from state common law or UDAP claims); Abbo

v. Wireless Toyz Franchise, L.L.C., 2014 WL 1978185 (Mich. Ct. App. May 13, 2014) (failure to disclose discounts for customers to purchase phones and chargebacks against commissions upon premature cancellation of service contracts); La Notte, Inc. v. New Way Gourmet, Inc., 350 S.E.2d 889 (N.C. Ct. App. 1986); Rendon v. Sanchez, 737 S.W.2d 122 (Tex. App. 1987); Staley v. Terns Serv. Co., 595 S.W.2d 882 (Tex. Civ. App. 1980); Woo v. Great Southwestern Acceptance Co., 565 S.W.2d 290 (Tex. Civ. App. 1978). *See also* Final Cut, L.L.C. v. Sharkey, 2009 WL 415527 (Conn. Super. Ct. Jan. 14, 2009) (incomplete and inaccurate financial information in offering statement is per se UDAP violation).

507 United States v. Zaken, 57 F. Supp. 3d 1233 (C.D. Cal. 2014) (contrary to representations as to average commission check, fewer than 1% of over 100,000 consumers earned any income); Bailey Employment Sys., Inc. v. Hahn, 545 F. Supp. 62 (D. Conn. 1982); Nat'l Dynamics Corp., 82 F.T.C. 488 (1973), *remanded in part*, 492 F.2d 1333 (2d Cir. 1974), *on remand*, 85 F.T.C. 391, 1052 (1975); Woo v. Great Southwestern Acceptance Co., 565 S.W.2d 290 (Tex. Civ. App. 1978).

508 *See, e.g.,* Coraud, L.L.C. v. Kidville Franchise Co., 2015 WL 3651423 (S.D.N.Y. June 12, 2015) (motion to dismiss; projected profit of $44,000 but first year loss of $168,000); F.T.C. v. Minuteman Press, 53 F. Supp. 2d 248 (E.D.N.Y. 1998); Nat'l Dynamics Corp., 82 F.T.C. 488 (F.T.C. 1973), *remanded in part*, 492 F.2d 1333 (2d Cir. 1974), *on remand*, 85 F.T.C. 391, 1052 (F.T.C. 1975); Windsor Distrib. Co., 77 F.T.C. 204 (F.T.C. 1970), *aff'd*, 431 F.2d 443 (3d Cir. 1971); Von Schroder Mfg. Co., 33 F.T.C. 58 (F.T.C. 1941). *See also* United States v. Vend Direct, Inc., 2007 WL 2176205 (D. Colo. May 11, 2007), *adopted by* 2007 WL 3407357 (D. Colo. Nov. 13, 2007); Kugler v. Koscot Interplanetary, Inc., 293 A.2d 682 (N.J. Super. Ct. Ch. Div. 1972). *Cf.* KC Leisure, Inc. v. Haber, 972 So.2d 1069 (Fla. Dist. Ct. App. 2008) (motion to dismiss; speculative spreadsheets of anticipated costs and revenues).

In addition, FTC enforcement actions regarding false earnings claims for business opportunities may be found on the FTC's website, www.ftc.gov.

509 United States v. Turnkey Vending, 5 Trade Reg. Rep. (CCH) ¶ 15,475, No. CV-1:02-cv-75-ST (D. Utah June 27, 2003) (stipulated permanent injunction against marketer of business opportunity who made earnings claims without reasonable basis); Commonwealth v. Mirror World, Inc., No. 4058 June Term 1973, Clearinghouse No. 26,022 (Pa. Ct. Com. Pl. Phila. Cnty. Dec. 31, 1978); Kugler v. Koscot Interplanetary, Inc., 293 A.2d 682 (N.J. Super. Ct. Ch. Div. 1972); Von Schroder Mfg. Co., 33 F.T.C. 58 (1941). *See also* 940 Mass. Code Regs. 3.11 (private employment agencies and business schemes) (specifying data on which earnings claims must be based).

510 Colorado Coffee Bean, L.L.C. v. Peaberry Coffee, Inc., 251 P.3d 9 (Colo. App. 2010) (limiting language added to earnings figures in offering circular was sufficient to comply with FTC rule but did not provide safe harbor from state common law or UDAP claims); Nat'l Dynamics Corp., 82 F.T.C. 488 (1973), *remanded in part*, 492 F.2d 1333 (2d Cir. 1974), *on remand*, 85 F.T.C. 391, 1052 (1975). *See also* 940 Mass. Code Regs. 3.11 (private employment agencies and business schemes) (requiring limiting language).

Franchise operators may not misrepresent the profitability[511] or risk[512] of a franchise location.

Misrepresentations concerning business arrangements, the goods to be distributed, operations, termination provisions, and benefits of a business opportunity are also deceptive.[513] Franchisors cannot misrepresent that the franchise is guaranteed to remain active for years.[514] Franchisors may not exaggerate the assistance they will offer the franchisee in reselling the franchise and equipment, in advertising, and in training and other management assistance.[515]

Franchise operations may not be advertised in help-wanted sections.[516] Using shills as references is deceptive.[517]

Equally deceptive are business opportunity offers to recruit other distributors or sell products when the market at the time of the offer is already saturated with such distributors.[518] The same exclusive territory may not be assigned to two franchisees, and franchise agents may not assign territories without proper authority.[519] The franchisor must also determine the ability of the prospective franchisee to run the business opportunity and may not falsely represent that no special ability is needed to be a success.[520]

It is deceptive to represent that a franchisor is more selective than it actually is in choosing franchisees.[521] Also deceptive is a franchisor's failure to provide all promised aspects of the franchise package to franchisees,[522] to fail to disclose the attrition rate of franchisees,[523] or to fail to disclose lawsuits by

---

511 Utah Admin. Code r. 152-11-11 (franchises, distributorships, referral sales); United States v. C.D. Control Tech., Inc., 3 Trade Reg. Rep. (CCH) ¶ 22,267 (E.D.N.Y. 1985) (preliminary injunction); Cope Enterprises Ltd., 87 F.T.C. 129 (1976) (consent order); Consolidated Int'l Tool & Oil, Inc., 86 F.T.C. 947 (1975) (consent order); Multi-State Distrib., Inc., 80 F.T.C. 754 (1972) (consent order); Universal Electronics Corp., 78 F.T.C. 265 (1971); International Sales Co., 79 F.T.C. 159 (1971) (consent order); Youngstown Spectrum Corp., 75 F.T.C. 457 (1969) (consent order).

512 *In re* Consolidated Chem. Corp., 84 F.T.C. 379 (1974) (consent order); *In re* Universal Credit Acceptance Corp. et al., 82 F.T.C. 570 (1973), *rev'd in part sub nom.* Heater v. Federal Trade Comm'n, 503 F.2d 321 (9th Cir. 1974); Mercury Electronics, Inc., 74 F.T.C. 548 (1968) (consent order). *See also* United States v. Vaughan, 2001 U.S. Dist. LEXIS 20084 (D. Kan. Oct. 18, 2001) (denying motion to dismiss contempt charges against defendant who misrepresented franchise failure rate); State *ex rel.* Miller v. Pace, 677 N.W.2d 761 (Iowa 2004) (misrepresentation and nondisclosure of investment's risk).

513 Utah Admin. Code r. 152-11-11(B) (franchises, distributorships, referral sales); Federal Trade Comm'n v. Richard J. Scott, 2002 WL 32151636 (D. Cal. Oct. 3, 2002) (consent decree against sellers who marketed spam lists as business opportunity); Salkeld v. V.R. Bus. Brokers, 548 N.E.2d 1151 (Ill. App. Ct. 1989); State *ex rel.* Ashcroft v. Marketing Unlimited, 613 S.W.2d 440 (Mo. Ct. App. 1981); Potere, Inc. v. Nat'l Realty Serv., 667 S.W.2d 252 (Tex. App. 1984); Anhold v. Daniels, 614 P.2d 184 (Wash. 1980); Federal Trade Comm'n v. Davis, 5 Trade Reg. Rep. (CCH) ¶ 22,741 (D. Nev. Oct. 17, 1989) (consent order); *In re* Consolidated Chem. Corp., Inc., et al., 84 F.T.C. 379 (1974) (consent order); *In re* Redi-Brew Corp. et al., 83 F.T.C. 1347 (1974) (consent order); *In re* Universal Credit Acceptance Corp. et al., 82 F.T.C. 570 (1973), *rev'd in part sub nom.* Heater v. Federal Trade Comm'n, 503 F.2d 321 (9th Cir. 1974); Universal Electronics Corp., 78 F.T.C. 265 (1971); *In re* Windsor Distrib. Co. et al., 77 F.T.C. 204 (1970), *aff'd*, 431 F.2d 443 (3d Cir. 1971); *In re* Waltham Watch Co. et al., 60 F.T.C. 1692 (1962), *aff'd*, 318 F.2d 28 (7th Cir. 1963); *In re* Washington Mushroom Indus., Inc., et al., 53 F.T.C. 368 (1956); Von Schroder Mfg. Co., 33 F.T.C. 58 (1941). *See also* Binder v. Medicine Shoppe Int'l, 2010 WL 2854308 (E.D. Mich. July 20, 2010) (when offering circular stated incorrectly that Michigan law forbade distant-forum arbitration, arbitration clause is enforceable, but venue must be Michigan). *But see* Andre v. SellState Realty Sys., Inc., 2010 WL 3259415 (M.D. Fla. July 30, 2010) (offering circular silent as to jury waiver contained in other documents for sale of real estate franchise; omission did not violate FTC rule, and waiver was enforceable).

514 *In re* Universal Credit Acceptance Corp. et al., 82 F.T.C. 570 (1973), *rev'd in part sub nom.* Heater v. Federal Trade Comm'n, 503 F.2d 321 (9th Cir. 1974).

515 Utah Admin. Code r. 152-11-11(B)(5) (franchises, distributorships, referral sales); Salkeld v. V.R. Bus. Brokers, 548 N.E.2d 1151 (Ill. App. Ct. 1989); Staley v. Terns Serv. Co., 595 S.W.2d 882 (Tex. Civ. App. 1980); Federal Trade Comm'n v. Nat'l Bus. Consultants, 5 Trade Reg. Rep. (CCH) ¶ 22,816 (E.D. La. 1990) (permanent injunction); *In re* Universal Credit Acceptance Corp. et al., 82 F.T.C. 570 (1973), *rev'd in part sub nom.* Heater v. Federal Trade Comm'n, 503 F.2d 321 (9th Cir.

1974); *In re* Universal Electronics Corp. et al., 78 F.T.C. 265 (1971); *In re* Windsor Distrib. Co. et al., 77 F.T.C. 204 (1970), *aff'd*, 431 F.2d 443 (3d Cir. 1971).

516 *In re* Windsor Distrib. Co. et al., 77 F.T.C. 204 (1970), *aff'd*, 431 F.2d 443 (3d Cir. 1971); North Am. Mktg. Sys., Inc., 5 Trade Reg. Rep. (CCH) ¶ 15,111 (May 18, 2001) (proposed consent decree against franchise seller that placed newspaper ads that appeared to be from individuals selling established local vending routes).

517 Consent Decree, Federal Trade Comm'n v. Inspired Ventures, Inc., No. 02-CV-21760 (S.D. Fla. Feb. 24, 2004) (consent decree against marketer of bogus vending machine business opportunity; defendants directed consumers to shills as references); Federal Trade Comm'n v. Universal Greeting Card Corp., 5 Trade Reg. Rep. (CCH) ¶ 15,350 (M.D. Fla. Jan. 5, 2003) (proposed consent decree); Federal Trade Comm'n v. Affiliated Vendors Ass'n, Inc., 5 Trade Reg. Rep. (CCH) ¶ 15,282 (N.D. Tex. July 25, 2002) (proposed consent decree against sham BBB-type organization); Federal Trade Comm'n v. International Computer Concepts, Inc., 5 Trade Reg. Rep. (CCH) ¶ 23,927 (N.D. Ohio 1995) (permanent injunction). *See also* 16 C.F.R. § 437.6(q), (r) (prohibiting use of shills in sale of non-franchise business opportunities).

518 Utah Admin. Code r. 152-11-11(B)(3) (franchises, distributorships, referral sales); Federal Trade Comm'n v. Network Services Depot, Inc., 617 F.3d 1127 (9th Cir. 2010) (Ponzi-type scheme; sale of locations for non-existent or non-functional Internet kiosks; payments to early investors from sums received from later purchasers); Federal Trade Comm'n v. Cruz, 2008 WL 5277735 (D. P.R. Dec. 18, 2008) (enjoining deceptive marketing of work-at-home opportunity; purchasers were provided with materials instructing them on how to recruit others); *In re* Holiday Magic, Inc. et al., 84 F.T.C. 748 (1974).

519 Utah Admin. Code r. 152-11-11(B)(10) (franchises, distributorships, referral sales); Federal Trade Comm'n v. Stephen I. Tashman, 5 Trade Reg. Rep. (CCH) ¶ 24,511 (S.D. Fla. 1998) (TRO); Federal Trade Comm'n v. Nat'l Bus. Consultants, 5 Trade Reg. Rep. (CCH) ¶ 22,816 (E.D. La. 1990) (permanent injunction); United States v. C.D. Control Tech., Inc., 3 Trade Reg. Rep. (CCH) ¶ 22,267 (E.D.N.Y. 1985) (preliminary injunction). *See also In re* Universal Credit Acceptance Corp. et al., 82 F.T.C. 570 (1973), *rev'd in part sub. nom.* Heater v. Federal Trade Comm'n, 503 F.2d 321 (9th Cir. 1974); *In re* Universal Electronics Corp. et al., 78 F.T.C. 265 (1971).

520 Woo v. Great Southwestern Acceptance Co., 565 S.W.2d 290 (Tex. Civ. App. 1978); *In re* International Mktg. Corp. et al., 82 F.T.C. 1074 (1973) (consent order).

521 *In re* Meredith Corp., 101 F.T.C. 390 (1983) (consent order).

522 State *ex rel.* Ashcroft v. Marketing Unlimited, 613 S.W.2d 440 (Mo. Ct. App. 1981).

523 Aurigemma v. Arco Petroleum Products Co., 734 F. Supp. 1025 (D. Conn. 1990) (failure to disclose potential loss of franchise due to lease

or judgments in favor of the franchisees for fraud or UDAP violations.[524]

A franchise or investment operation that involves recruiting additional investors may run afoul of the state's pyramid sales law.[525] Since business opportunities are often marketed by telephone, the FTC's Telemarketing Sales Rule or state telemarketing laws may provide additional remedies.[526]

2.9 Funeral Rule

2.9.1 The FTC Rule

Funeral and burial services are often high-priced packages purchased by bereaved relatives of the deceased under time pressures allowing little reflection. Religious, racial, or ethnic preferences may create virtual local monopolies of services.

Because of this market power, consumer vulnerability, and the prevalence of deception, the FTC has enacted a Funeral Industry Practices Trade Regulation Rule (hereafter "the Funeral Rule").[527] In 1994, the FTC amended the rule,[528] concluding a lengthy review.[529] The amended rule made a number of minor changes and clarifications and also added a ban on fees for "handling" caskets purchased from third parties.[530] In 1998, the FTC began another review of the rule,[531] but it closed the review in 2008 without making any changes in the rule.[532]

The Funeral Rule requires funeral homes to offer itemized price information and to reveal prices over the telephone.[533] The rule also prohibits misrepresentations and specifies disclosures concerning the need or legal requirements for embalming, a casket for cremation purposes, or an outer burial container.

Also prohibited are misrepresentations about cemetery requirements and about the preservative or protective value of funeral goods. Funeral homes must disclose if they make a profit on cash-advance items[534] and may not condition a funeral sale on the purchase of a casket or other items.[535] With a limited exception for subsequent approval of embalming already performed, a funeral home may not embalm a body without a family member's prior authorization unless state law requires embalming.[536]

The Fourth Circuit rejected all challenges to the original rule in *Harry and Bryant Company v. Federal Trade Commission*,[537] holding that the rulemaking proceeding did not deny due process rights and the rule was within the FTC's statutory authority and supported by substantial evidence. The remedy of itemized price lists did not exceed the FTC power under the FTC Improvements Act, and the rule did not violate First Amendment rights of commercial free speech. In 1994, the Third Circuit upheld the newly added ban on casket-handling fees, finding that it was supported by substantial evidence and was not arbitrary or capricious.[538]

The FTC staff has issued staff compliance guidelines covering the rule. These guidelines do not represent the views of, and are not binding on, the FTC. The first set of guidelines explains staff views on who must comply with the rule, the type of representations that are prohibited, what price disclosures must be made, when disclosures are clear, when the purchase of one good is improperly conditioned on the purchase of another,

---

termination violates UDAP statute); Bailey Employment Sys., Inc. v. Hahn, 545 F. Supp. 62 (D. Conn. 1982).

524 Bailey Employment Sys., Inc. v. Hahn, 545 F. Supp. 62 (D. Conn. 1982).

525 *See* Giarratano v. Midas Muffler, 630 N.Y.S.2d 656 (N.Y. Yonkers City Ct. 1995); National Consumer Law Center, Unfair and Deceptive Acts and Practices § 9.6.3 (8th ed. 2012), *updated at* www.nclc.org/library.

526 *See* Federal Trade Comm'n v. Stefanchik, 559 F.3d 924 (9th Cir. 2009); Federal Trade Comm'n v. John Beck Amazing Profits, L.L.C., 865 F. Supp. 2d 1052 (C.D. Cal. 2012) (finding violation of telemarketing rule; infomercials falsely claimed that training materials would enable average consumers to earn substantial sums with little effort in real estate dealings or Internet business). *See generally* Ch. 5, *infra*.

527 16 C.F.R. § 453, *reprinted at* Appx. A.10, *infra*.

528 59 Fed. Reg. 1592 (Jan. 11, 1994).

529 *See* Notice of Proposed Rulemaking, 53 Fed. Reg. 19,864 (May 31, 1988). On July 30, 1990, the FTC published for comment a final staff report and the recommended decision of the presiding officer. *See* 55 Fed. Reg. 30,925 (July 30, 1990).

530 16 C.F.R. § 453.4(b)(ii) (listing the services for which a funeral home may charge, without including casket handling). *See* St. Joseph Abbey v. Castille, 712 F.3d 215, 219 (5th Cir. 2013) (explaining history and rationale of ban on casket handling fees).

531 63 Fed. Reg. 62,740 (Nov. 8, 1998).

532 73 Fed. Reg. 13,740 (Mar. 14, 2008).

533 *See* Olson v. State Mortuary & Cemetery Bd., 216 P.3d 325 (Or. Ct. App. 2009) (requirement to provide price list is mandatory, not a safe harbor). *But cf.* Durant-Baker v. Secor Funeral Home, 2010 WL 3488243 (Ohio Ct. App. Sept. 3, 2010) (unpublished) (not UDAP violation to fail to provide price list when funeral home did not even have a price list for the oversized casket decedent needed).

534 16 C.F.R. § 453.3(f). *See* Funeral Consumer Alliance, Inc. v. Federal Trade Comm'n, 481 F.3d 860 (D.C. Cir. 2007) (dismissing challenge to FTC advisory letter; court lacks jurisdiction over petition for review because the 2005 letter was not a substantive amendment to the rule); FTC Advisory Letter to the Honorable Dan Flynn, Tex. State Representative (July 7, 2005), *available at* www.ftc.gov (clarifying that cash advance rule applies "only to those items that the funeral provider represents expressly to be 'cash advance items' or represents by implication to be procured on behalf of a particular customer and provided to that customer at the same price the funeral provider paid for them" and that "the corrective disclosure about cash advance items . . . is unnecessary when the funeral provider does not mislead the customer through either express representations that the item is a 'cash advance item' (or alternative formulations), or implied representations that the customer is paying more for an item than the amount the funeral provider paid for it"). *Cf.* Baudino v. SCI Cal. Funeral Services, Inc., 87 Cal. Rptr. 3d 147 (Cal. Ct. App. 2008) (not all goods or services provided by vendors are "cash advance" items; no need to disclose mark-up on embalming and transportation purchased from vendor that sold only to funeral homes; no misrepresentation that these services were being provided at cost).

535 16 C.F.R. § 453.4.

536 *Cf.* Dill v. Barnett Funeral Home, 83 P.3d 1270 (Kan. Ct. App. 2004) (table, text at 2004 WL 292124) (when Kansas law required body to be embalmed because of delayed burial, FTC rule allows funeral home to charge for embalming even though it had not received consent from family).

537 726 F.2d 993 (4th Cir. 1982). *See also* Federal Trade Comm'n v. Hughes, 710 F. Supp. 1524 (N.D. Tex. 1989).

538 Pennsylvania Funeral Directors Ass'n v. Federal Trade Comm'n, 41 F.3d 81 (3d Cir. 1994).

and when services are charged to the consumer without prior approval.[539] The second set of guidelines deals with the rule's state exemption provisions.[540] The FTC's 1978 staff report is also useful background for understanding the FTC rule.[541]

FTC surveys of consumers show widespread violations of the rule by funeral parlors, and the FTC has brought a number of enforcement actions for rule violations.[542] Other decisions have prohibited misrepresenting the durability of burial vaults and tombstones,[543] misrepresenting synthetic tombstones as granite or marble,[544] and deceptive pricing practices.[545]

The FTC and an industry trade association have developed the Funeral Rule Offenders Program, which requires funeral providers who have violated the rule to make voluntary payments to the U.S. Treasury in an amount slightly less than the FTC would seek in an enforcement action and to participate in a training and competency testing program. The FTC identifies non-complying providers through test shopping.[546]

The FTC's rule on door-to-door and off-premises sales[547] may also apply to some funeral contracts. "Pre-need" contracts are often sold in the consumer's home, thus mandating the right to cancel under the FTC rule and possibly state door-to-door-sales laws as well.[548]

There is no private right of action for violation of the FTC rule.[549] However, it may be enforceable as a violation of the state UDAP statute[550] or a state funeral services law.[551]

2.9.2 *State Claims*

UDAP statutes typically prohibit misrepresenting the standard, quality, or composition of goods and thus will apply when a funeral supplier substitutes inferior products.[552] Some states have enacted special consumer protection statutes about funeral homes and cemetery sales. The Oklahoma UDAP statute specifically prohibits failure to perform cemetery services that are promised in the contract.[553] Many states also have funeral director licensing laws, some of which include consumer protections. In some states, however, the portions of a licensing statute that required casket sellers to have funeral director licenses have been struck down on due process and equal protection grounds.[554] The courts found that the licensing requirements merely perpetuated a monopoly and allowed the maintenance of higher prices.

In any case involving deceptive funeral practices, the consumer should stress the particularly vulnerable conditions under which the sale was made.[555] In some states, consumer litigants dealing with burial space misrepresentations may face scope issues as to whether the sale of a burial space is the sale of "goods or services" within the scope of the statute. One court has said it is not.[556] In contrast, the Oklahoma UDAP statute's coverage of these transactions is clearly demonstrated by its inclusion of specific prohibitions relating to cemetery services.[557]

2.10 FTC Guides

The FTC has issued a number of industry guides. Trade regulation rules are distinguished from guides in that the TRRs often create disclosure requirements or other bright line requirements to prevent unfair and deceptive practices. Guides generally just list practices that are likely to be found unfair and deceptive. In addition, while violation of a trade regulation rule leads to special remedies as provided for in the statute, this is not the case with violation of a guide.[558]

The FTC has stated the following concerning its guides:

Industry guides are administrative interpretations of laws administered by the Commission for the guidance of the public in conducting its affairs in conformity with legal requirements. They provide the basis for voluntary and

---

539   50 Fed. Reg. 28,062 (July 9, 1985).

540   50 Fed. Reg. 12,521 (Mar. 29, 1985).
      The application by the state of Texas for an exemption from the rule was denied. *See* 56 Fed. Reg. 28,829 (June 25, 1991).
      New York also applied for an exemption, but there is not a record of any decision by the FTC. *See* 57 Fed. Reg. 34,532 (Aug. 5, 1992); 56 Fed. Reg. 11,381 (Mar. 18, 1991).

541   Clearinghouse No. 31,044 (June, 1978).

542   *See, e.g.*, Missouri Bd. of Embalmers & Funeral Directors, Analysis of Agreement Containing Consent Order to Aid Public Comment, 72 Fed. Reg. 12,615 (Mar. 16, 2007) (proposed consent agreement).
      Many other FTC actions and consent orders for violation of the funeral rule may be found on the FTC's website, www.ftc.gov.

543   United States v. Wilbert, Inc., 5 Trade Reg. Rep. (CCH) ¶ 22,849 (N.D. Ill. 1990) (consent decree); Batesville Casket Co., 111 F.T.C. 112 (1988) (consent order); Egyptian Vault Co., 59 F.T.C. 1349 (1961) (consent order); Asa L. Wooten, 31 F.T.C. 508 (1940).

544   *In re* Roy Burnsed, 30 F.T.C. 436 (1940).

545   Olive v. Graceland Sales Corp., 293 A.2d 658 (N.J. 1972); *In re* Service Corp. Int'l, 88 F.T.C. 530 (1976) (consent order) (agreement that major chain would not misrepresent price it pays for third-party services or the quality and legal requirement for purchasing caskets and would disclose availability of immediate cremation service).

546   Press Release, Fed. Trade Comm'n, Undercover Inspections of Funeral Homes in Six States Prompt Compliance with Funeral Rule Disclosure Requirements (May 5, 2015), *available at* www.ftc.gov.

547   16 C.F.R. § 429. *See* § 2.5, *supra*.

548   United States v. Mission Plans, Inc., 5 Trade Reg. Rep. (CCH) ¶ 23,660 (S.D. Tex. Sept. 2, 1994) (consent decree requiring pre-need funeral contract seller to give notice of right to cancel).

549   SCI Texas Funeral Services, Inc. v. Hijar, 214 S.W.3d 148 (Tex. App. 2007). *See generally* § 2.2.4.1, *supra*.

550   *See* § 2.2.4.2, *supra*.

551   *See* Olson v. State Mortuary & Cemetery Bd., 216 P.3d 325 (Or. Ct. App. 2009) (upholding Oregon statute's incorporation of FTC funeral rule in its form at the time of the statute's enactment).

552   *See, e.g.*, Baynes v. George E. Mason Funeral Home, Inc., 2011 WL 2181469 (W.D. Pa. June 2, 2011) (substitution of steel casket for promised bronze casket is UDAP violation).

553   Okla. Stat. tit. 15, § 753(21).

554   Craigmiles v. Giles, 312 F.3d 220 (6th Cir. 2002); Casket Royale, Inc. v. Mississippi, 124 F. Supp. 2d 434 (S.D. Miss. 2000). *See* St. Joseph Abbey v. Castille, 712 F.3d 215 (5th Cir. 2013). *But see* Powers v. Harris, 379 F.3d 1208 (10th Cir. 2004). *But cf.* Brown v. Hovatter, 561 F.3d 357 (4th Cir. 2009) (upholding Maryland's requirement that funeral homes be owned by licensed individuals, not corporations).

555   *See, e.g.*, Baynes v. George E. Mason Funeral Home, Inc., 2011 WL 2181469 (W.D. Pa. June 2, 2011).

556   Hutchings v. Valhalla Cemetery, 622 S.W.2d 296 (Mo. Ct. App. 1981).

557   Okla. Stat. Ann. tit. 15, § 753(21).

558   *See* § 2.2.5, *supra*.

simultaneous abandonment of unlawful practices by members of industry. Failure to comply with the guides may result in corrective action by the commission under applicable statutory provisions. Guides may relate to a practice common to many industries or to specific practices of a particular industry.[559]

FTC guides are not considered in this volume, although certain guides are examined in NCLC's *Unfair and Deceptive Acts and Practices*,[560] as indicated below. A list of FTC guides follows:

- Guides for the Nursery Industry, 16 C.F.R. pt. 18
- Guides for the Rebuilt, Reconditioned, and Other Used Automobile Parts Industry, 16 C.F.R. pt. 20
- Guides for the Jewelry, Precious Metals, and Pewter Industries, 16 C.F.R. pt. 23
- Guides for the Select Leather and Imitation Leather Products, 16 C.F.R. pt. 24
- Guides Against Deceptive Pricing, 16 C.F.R. pt. 233[561]

- Guides Against Bait Advertising, 16 C.F.R. pt. 238[562]
- Guides for the Advertising of Warranties and Guarantees, 16 C.F.R. pt. 233[563]
- Guides for Advertising Allowances and Other Merchandising Payments and Services, 16 C.F.R. pt. 240
- Guides Concerning Use of the Word "Free" and Similar Representations, 16 C.F.R. pt. 251[564]
- Guides for Private Vocational and Distance Education Schools, 16 C.F.R. pt. 254[565]
- Guides Concerning Use of Endorsements and Testimonials in Advertising, 16 C.F.R. pt. 255[566]
- Guides Concerning Fuel Economy Advertising for New Automobiles, 16 C.F.R. pt. 259
- Guides for the Use of Environmental Marketing Claims, 16 C.F.R. pt. 260

---

559   16 C.F.R. pt. 17.

560   National Consumer Law Center, Unfair and Deceptive Acts and Practices (8th ed. 2012), *updated at* www.nclc.org/library.

561   *See* National Consumer Law Center, Unfair and Deceptive Acts and Practices § 5.3.3 (8th ed. 2012), *updated at* www.nclc.org/library.

562   *See* National Consumer Law Center, Unfair and Deceptive Acts and Practices § 5.3.1 (8th ed. 2012), *updated at* www.nclc.org/library.

563   *See* National Consumer Law Center, Unfair and Deceptive Acts and Practices § 5.6.7.3 (8th ed. 2012), *updated at* www.nclc.org/library.

564   *See* National Consumer Law Center, Unfair and Deceptive Acts and Practices § 5.3.4 (8th ed. 2012), *updated at* www.nclc.org/library.

565   *See* National Consumer Law Center, Unfair and Deceptive Acts and Practices § 10.1.7.2 (8th ed. 2012), *updated at* www.nclc.org/library.

566   *See* National Consumer Law Center, Unfair and Deceptive Acts and Practices § 5.4.8.3 (8th ed. 2012), *updated at* www.nclc.org/library.

Chapter 3 Consumer Financial Protection Bureau Rules and Guidance

3.1 Introduction

3.1.1 The Consumer Financial Protection Bureau

Effective on July 21, 2011,[1] the Dodd-Frank Wall Street Reform and Consumer Protection Act (Dodd-Frank Act)[2] created a new Consumer Financial Protection Bureau (CFPB), with authority to issue extensive new regulations and otherwise dramatically change lending practices. Title X of the Dodd-Frank Act contains the CFPB's authority, and Title X may be cited as the Consumer Financial Protection Act of 2010[3] and is referred to in this chapter as "the Act."

The CFPB is part of the Federal Reserve Board (FRB), but the Act guarantees the CFPB's independence. The FRB funds the CFPB, but the FRB has no control over the amount or allocation of the budget. The CFPB's budget is set by the CFPB's director, up to a cap adjusted each year, and for FY 2015 is about $619 million. By comparison, the Federal Trade Commission's 2015 budget was $290 million. The CFPB's director is appointed by the president.

The CFPB is given rule-writing authority for almost all the major consumer financial protection statutes—called the "enumerated statutes."[4] A new Financial Stability Oversight Council (with representatives from eight federal agencies and one state appointee) has authority to veto the CFPB rules by a two-thirds vote. To veto a rule, the council must find that the rule "would put the safety and soundness of the United States banking system or the stability of the financial system of the United States at risk."[5]

The CFPB's authority has been upheld as constitutional by at least two federal courts. The courts dismissed challenges that restrictions on the removal of the CFPB director violated the president's constitutional powers of removal and that legislation mandating *Chevron* deference did not impermissibly limit judicial oversight.[6]

3.1.2 CFPB Rules and Guidance Covered in This Chapter

The CFPB has extensive rule-writing authority concerning consumer financial services. This chapter is limited to three new types of rules (and related guidance) that the CFPB may issue outside of the regulations under specific consumer protection statutes: rules prohibiting unfair, deceptive, or abusive acts or practices,[7] rules requiring certain disclosures,[8] and rules providing for consumers' rights to obtain certain information.[9] With the exception of the combined TILA/RESPA disclosure form, examined in detail in another NCLC treatise,[10] the CFPB has not issued any rules in these three areas.

Nevertheless, the CFPB issues guidance to providers about specific areas that raise concerns with regard to unfair, deceptive, or abusive acts or practices (UDAAP).[11] The CFPB also publishes a supervision and examination manual, covering UDAAP and other issues, which also provides insight into practices that could violate the UDAAP standard.[12]

The Act transfers to the CFPB authority to issue many other regulations that were previously issued by the Federal Reserve Board, the Department of Housing and Urban Development, or other federal agencies, interpreting what are called the "enumerated statutes." Rules interpreting enumerated statutes will not be treated in this chapter, as they are analyzed in other NCLC treatises:

- Regulation B on equal credit opportunity and Regulation C on home mortgage disclosure are examined in *Credit Discrimination*.
- Regulation D on alternative mortgage parity, Regulations G and H on the SAFE Mortgage Licensing Act, and parts of Regulation X on RESPA are examined in *Mortgage Lending*.
- Regulation E on electronic fund transfers (also now covering remittances) and Regulation DD on truth in savings are covered in *Consumer Banking and Payments Law*.
- Regulation F on fair debt collection is treated in *Fair Debt Collection*.
- Regulations M on consumer leasing and Regulation Z on truth in lending are analyzed in *Truth in Lending*.

---

1 The Dodd-Frank Act made the new agency effective on the "designated transfer date." 75 Fed. Reg. 57,252 (Sept. 20, 2010) set the designated transfer date as July 21, 2011. The Department of Treasury retained certain authority to issue rules until July 21, 2011.

2 Pub. L. No. 111-203, 124 Stat. 1376 (July 21, 2010).

3 Pub. L. No. 111-203, tit. X, § 1001, 124 Stat. 1376 (July 21, 2010).

4 12 U.S.C. §§ 5481(12), 5512.

5 12 U.S.C. § 5513. A decision by the council to veto a rule—but not a decision to refrain from a veto—is reviewable by the courts.

6 Consumer Fin. Prot. Bureau v. ITT Educ. Services, Inc., 2015 WL 1013508 (S.D. Ind. Mar. 6, 2015); Consumer Fin. Prot. Bureau v. Morgan Drexen, Inc., 60 F. Supp. 3d 1082 (C.D. Cal. 2014). *But cf.* State Nat'l Bank of Big Spring v. Lew, 795 F.3d 48 (D.C. Cir. 2015) (bank had standing and issue was ripe to challenge CFPB's constitutionality when grounds underlying challenge were that the CFPB was headed by a single person, its authority was overly broad, and the director was improperly appointed).

7 *See* § 3.2, *infra.*

8 *See* § 3.5, *infra.*

9 *See* § 3.6, *infra.*

10 *See* National Consumer Law Center, Truth in Lending Ch. 5 (9th ed. 2015), *updated at* www.nclc.org/library.

11 *See* § 3.3, *infra.*

12 *See* Consumer Fin. Prot. Bureau, Supervision and Examination Manual, at UDAAP 1–10 (Oct. 2012) (Version 2), *available at* www .consumerfinance.gov *and online as companion material to this treatise.*

- Regulation N on mortgage acts and practices is summarized in *Unfair and Deceptive Acts and Practices.*
- Regulation O on mortgage assistance relief practices and parts of Regulation X on RESPA are covered in *Foreclosures and Mortgage Servicing.*
- Regulation V on fair credit reporting is treated in *Fair Credit Reporting.*

In addition, the CFPB, having released in March 2015 its study of arbitration agreements,[13] now has authority to issue rules concerning mandatory binding arbitration provisions in consumer credit agreements.[14] That authority is discussed in NCLC's *Consumer Arbitration Agreements* treatise and will not be considered here.

3.2 UDAAP Standards

3.2.1 General

The Act authorizes the CFPB to take action against any entity under its jurisdiction that engages in an unfair, deceptive, or abusive act or practice in connection with any transaction with a consumer for a consumer financial product or service or the offering of such a product or service.[15] The Act also authorizes the CFPB to write rules and issue guidance to prevent unfair, deceptive, or abusive acts or practices in connection with a broad array of consumer financial products and services.[16] To date the CFPB has issued no rules under its UDAAP authority. The CFPB has, however, issued some guidance documents and an examination manual that touch on UDAAP issues.[17]

This section discusses UDAAP standards generally—the standards for deception, unfairness, and abusive practices, and how those standards relate to each other. Succeeding sections consider specific guidance and other CFPB announcements concerning these UDAAP standards.

3.2.2 Deception

The Act does not include a definition of "deception," but the FTC[18] and a large body of decisions have interpreted the deception standard under the Federal Trade Commission Act (FTC Act) and state UDAP.[19] The CFPB's *Supervision and Examination Manual* utilizes these preexisting deception standards to provide guidance on deception, including examples of deceptive practices.

The manual states that the representation, omission, act, or practice must mislead or must be likely to mislead the consumer. Implied claims can be deceptive. Omission of information can be deceptive. Written disclosures cannot cure oral misrepresentations. Disclosures must be prominent enough to notice, the format must be easy to understand, the information must be placed in a location that consumers can be expected to notice, and qualifiers must be in close proximity to claims they qualify.[20]

The manual also states that the representation, omission, act, or practice must be considered from the perspective of a reasonable consumer. When representations target a particular audience, the communication must be based upon the point of view of a reasonable member of that group. It is enough if a significant minority of the group is misled. If a representation has two meanings and one is false, the representation is misleading.[21]

The manual provides that representations, omissions, or practices must be material to be deceptive. Presumed material is information about the product's or service's central characteristics, such as costs, benefits, or restrictions on use or availability. Express claims regarding a financial product are presumed material. Implied claims are presumed material if the institution intended to make the claim. Omissions are presumed material if the institution should have known that the consumer needed the omitted information.[22]

The supervision and examination manual provides examples of deceptive practices:

- Inadequate disclosure of material lease terms in television advertising;
- Misrepresentation about loan terms.[23]

Similarly, a federal court has found that the CFPB's deception standard could reach situations where a firm's litigation practices misled consumers acting reasonably in the circumstances that a lawyer had reviewed the consumer's file and determined that it validly merited collection litigation against the consumer.[24]

3.2.3 Unfairness

The statutory definition of "unfair" incorporates the definition found in the FTC Act:

(A) the act or practice causes or is likely to cause substantial injury to consumers which is not reasonably avoidable by consumers; and

(B) such substantial injury is not outweighed by countervailing benefits to consumers or to competition.[25]

---

13 Consumer Fin. Prot. Bureau, Arbitration Study (Mar. 2015), *available at* http://files.consumerfinance.gov.

14 12 U.S.C. § 5518.

15 12 U.S.C. § 5531(a).

16 12 U.S.C. § 5531(b).

17 *See* §§ 3.3, 3.4, *infra.*

18 *See In re* Cliffdale Associates, Inc., 103 F.T.C. 110 (1984) (including, in an appendix, an analysis of the meaning of deception).

19 *See generally* National Consumer Law Center, Unfair and Deceptive Acts and Practices § 4.2 (8th ed. 2012), *updated at* www.nclc.org/library.

20 Consumer Fin. Prot. Bureau, Supervision and Examination Manual, UDAAP 5-6 (Oct. 2012), *available at* www.consumerfinance.gov *and online as companion material to this treatise.*

21 *Id.* at UDAAP 6.

22 *Id.* at UDAAP 6-7.

23 *Id.* at UDAAP 7-8.

24 Consumer Fin. Prot. Bureau v. Frederick J. Hanna & Associates, P.C., 2015 WL 4282252 (N.D. Ga. July 15, 2015).

25 12 U.S.C. § 5531(c)(1). *See also* National Consumer Law Center, Unfair and Deceptive Acts and Practices § 4.3.2.1 (8th ed. 2012), *updated at* www.nclc.org/library. *Cf.* 15 U.S.C. § 45(n).

This is the same standard as applicable not only under the FTC Act but also under many state UDAP statutes, and the meaning and interpretation of this standard is discussed in detail at NCLC's *Unfair and Deceptive Acts and Practices*.[26] The Act provides that the CFPB may consider established public policies in determining whether an act or practice is unfair, but public policy cannot be the primary basis for a determination.[27] The CFPB's *Supervision and Examination Manual* provides several examples of unfair practices:

- Refusing to release the lien after a consumer makes a final payment on a mortgage;
- Dishonoring credit card convenience checks without notice;
- Processing payments for companies engaged in fraudulent activities.[28]

Just as the FTC's unfairness standard has withstood challenges that it is unconstitutionally vague,[29] a federal court has upheld the CFPB's use of "unfairness" as not unconstitutionally vague.[30]

3.2.4 Abusive Practices

3.2.4.1 General Standard

The Act's grant of authority over abusive acts and practices has no counterpart in the FTC Act or in state UDAP statutes. To find an act is abusive, the CFPB must find that it:

(1) Materially interferes with a consumer's ability to understand a term or condition of a consumer financial product or service; or

(2) Takes unreasonable advantage of—

   (A) A consumer's lack of understanding of the material risks, costs, or conditions of the product or service;

   (B) A consumer's inability to protect his or her own interests when selecting or using a product or service; or

   (C) The consumer's reliance on a covered person.[31]

A federal court has found that the Congressional intent was to create a more flexible, expansive standard than unfairness or deception.[32] At the same time, this standard has withstood challenges that it is unconstitutionally vague.[33]

3.2.4.2 Application of the Abusive Standard

While the CFPB has not issued any rules interpreting the abusive standard, it has touched on the standard in at least one guidance bulletin and utilized the abusive standard in a number of enforcement actions.

The guidance bulletin deals with certain offers of credit cards with promotional APRs without clearly disclosing that acceptance of the offer may lead to the consumer losing the grace period to make payments on new credit card purchases.[34] The guidance finds a promotion abusive if it is so complex and difficult for consumers to understand that, depending on the circumstances, a card issuer may take unreasonable advantage of consumers by not fully explaining the offer's conditions and may exploit consumers' lack of understanding in order to impose additional costs. The way in which this offer operates runs so counter to consumer expectations that, if not sufficiently clarified, it can be abusive.

The CFPB's first enforcement action under the "abusive" standard illustrates the breadth and usefulness of the standard. The CFPB in 2013 alleged that a debt settlement organization engaged in abusive practices by signing up and charging fees to vulnerable consumers who the defendants knew had inadequate income to complete the debt relief programs.[35] As a result, consumers spent their last savings on fees for services from which they would not benefit.

The CFPB's complaint alleged that the defendant's acts took unreasonable advantage of consumers' lack of understanding of how long it would take the defendant to settle their debts, and of consumers' reasonable reliance on the defendant to enroll them in a debt settlement program that they could complete. The CFPB's rationale could be applied to other unaffordable transactions such as payday loans and to other sales of goods or services of little value, from which consumers were unlikely to benefit.

In 2014, the CFPB also brought a court action relying on the abusive standard against CashCall for extending credit in violation of state licensing and usury laws. Consumers were generally unaware that CashCall's violation of those laws made their loans void or otherwise limited the consumer's obligation to repay. CashCall nevertheless sought the full loan balance from the consumers, thus taking unreasonable advantage of consumers' lack of understanding about the impact of the applicable state laws on their rights.[36]

A 2014 CFPB federal court complaint was brought against ITT, a for-profit school for its lending conduct, relying in large

---

26 National Consumer Law Center, Unfair and Deceptive Acts and Practices § 4.3.2 (8th ed. 2012), *updated at* www.nclc.org/library.

27 12 U.S.C. § 5531(c)(2).

28 Consumer Fin. Prot. Bureau, Supervision and Examination Manual, UDAAP 3-4 (Oct. 2012), *available at* www.consumerfinance.gov *and online as companion material to this treatise.*

29 National Consumer Law Center, Unfair and Deceptive Acts and Practices § 11.9.3 (8th ed. 2012), *updated at* www.nclc.org/library.

30 Consumer Fin. Prot. Bureau v. ITT Educ. Services, Inc., 2015 WL 1013508 (S.D. Ind. Mar. 6, 2015).

31 12 U.S.C. § 5531(d).

32 Consumer Fin. Prot. Bureau v. ITT Educ. Services, Inc., 2015 WL 1013508 (S.D. Ind. Mar. 6, 2015).

33 Consumer Fin. Prot. Bureau v. ITT Educ. Services, Inc., 2015 WL 1013508 (S.D. Ind. Mar. 6, 2015).

34 Bulletin 2014-02, Marketing of Credit Card Promotional APR Offers (Sept. 3, 2014), described at § 3.3.5, *infra*.

35 Complaint, Consumer Fin. Prot. Bureau v. Am. Debt Settlement Solutions, Inc. (S.D. Fla. May 30, 2013), *available at* www.consumerfinance.gov. *See also* Stipulated Final Judgment and Order, Consumer Fin. Prot. Bureau v. Am. Debt Settlement Solutions, Inc. (S.D. Fla. June 7, 2013), *available at* www.consumerfinance.gov.

36 *See* Complaint, Consumer Fin. Prot. Bureau v. CashCall, Inc. (D. Mass. Mar. 21, 2014), *available at* www.nclc.org/unreported.

part on the abusive standard.[37] ITT took advantage of students by giving them little choice but to take out high-priced private loans with ITT because ITT's initial loans to those students had to be repaid before the course was completed, and ITT knew that would be impossible. The students were thus left with the choice of taking out a new loan from the school or not completing the course, in which case the partial course credits would not be transferable to another school.

The CFPB also considered abusive the school encouraging its students to rely on the school's financial aid staff to act in the students' interests when financial aid employees were actually paid like a sales staff. Instead of acting in the students' interests, the school took unreasonable advantage of the students' reliance in order to use aggressive repackaging tactics, including threatening students with expulsion and pushing students into expensive high-risk loans that the school knew were likely to default.

The federal court rejected all grounds in ITT's motion to dismiss that related to the abusive standard. It found that ITT's practices could be found abusive where ITT took unreasonable advantage of students who could not protect their own interests and who had reasonably relied upon the school. [38] Taking unreasonable advantage of the students' reasonable reliance on the school could be found where the students believed the school was acting in their interests and school employees represented themselves as financial aid staff.[39]

The court adopted a broad definition of when a practice takes "unreasonable advantage," finding that there need not be proof of a monetary benefit to the school, as long as there is advantage to the school.[40] The court also found that taking advantage of the student's inability to protect their interests did not require proof that the students were incapable of acting, but only that the school was in an excessively stronger position than the students.[41]

The state of Illinois also has brought a similar case against a for-profit school relying on its authority under the Consumer Financial Protection Act to challenge abusive practices. The federal court in the case similarly found that a school's financing practices can be found to be abusive within the meaning of the statute when the complaint alleges the school targeted unsophisticated students, characterized salespeople as admission representatives, used aggressive sales techniques, and knew that most students would not be able to repay their loans.[42]

The CFPB also relied on the abusive standard in a 2014 case against ACE Cash Express that produced an administrative consent order. The CFPB had concluded that ACE Cash Express collectors created and leveraged an artificial sense of urgency to induce delinquent borrowers with a demonstrated inability to repay their existing loans to take out a new ACE loan with accompanying fees.[43] The CFPB found that ACE Cash Express took unreasonable advantage of the consumers' inability to protect their interests and thus engaged in abusive practices.

In 2015, the CFPB brought an enforcement action against an internet payday lender, where the complaint included allegations of abusive practices.[44] The CFPB alleged that the payday loans were void and uncollectible in a number of states, and that it was thus material that such consumers were not obligated to pay on the loans. The lender materially interfered with consumer's ability to understand that fact, and then, by collecting on the loans, took unreasonable advantage of consumer's lack of understanding that the loans were unenforceable by repeatedly asserting that state law did not apply to the loan agreements.

3.2.5 Distinguishing Deception, Unfairness, and Abusive Practices

Deception, unfairness, and abusive practices are separate concepts, and practices can violate any one of these standards without violating the others. Unfairness does not rely on bad conduct by the creditor or a consumer being misled, but instead involves a balancing of interests between a practice's injury to the consumer that cannot be avoided and the benefits to competition. If the benefits to competition are outweighed, then the practice is unfair even if the creditor is acting in good faith.

Thus a practice can be unfair even if the practice is not deceptive or abusive, as long as there is consumer injury. But the consumer injury must be balanced against the practice's benefits to competition and the consumer's ability to avoid the practice. For example, if the consumer injury outweighs the benefits and the consumer cannot avoid the practice, then a credit term may be unfair even if it is clearly disclosed to the consumer and the consumer understands the term. But even if a term is deceptive or abusive, it is not unfair if the consumer could reasonably avoid the term or there are significant benefits to competition outweighing the injury.

Deceptive and abusive practices, on the other hand, are standards that do not involve a balancing of interests between the consumer and creditor. Instead, misleading a consumer, interfering with a consumer's understanding, or taking unreasonable advantage of a consumer is enough in itself to find a violation, even if a practice provides strong benefits to competition and even if the consumer could avoid the practice. Congress has announced that there is no place in the credit marketplace for deception, taking unreasonable advantage of consumers, or interfering with a consumer's ability to

---

37 Complaint, Consumer Fin. Prot. Bureau v. ITT Educ. Services, Inc. (S.D. Ind. Feb. 26, 2014), *available at* www.nclc.org/unreported.

38 Consumer Fin. Prot. Bureau v. ITT Educ. Services, Inc., 2015 WL 1013508 (S.D. Ind. Mar. 6, 2015).

39 *Id.*

40 *Id.*

41 *Id.*

42 People v. Alta Colleges, Inc. (N.D. Ill. Sept. 4 2014), *available at* www .nclc.org/unreported.

43 Consent Order, *In re* ACE Cash Express (Consumer Fin. Prot. Bureau July 8, 2014), *available at* www.nclc.org/unreported.

44 Consumer Fin. Prot. Bureau v. NDG Fin. Corp. (S.D.N.Y. July 31, 2015) (complaint), *available at* www.nclc.org/unreported.

understand. These standards of conduct trump any counter-vailing benefits for the practice.

"Deceptive" and "abusive" are also distinct concepts. A practice can be abusive even when the consumer is not deceived. Taking unfair advantage is sufficient even if no misrepresentation is present. For example, price gouging in an emergency might be considered abusive even if the seller is transparent about why the price is so high. On the other hand, a practice can be deceptive even if there is no intent to deceive and even if the seller is acting in good faith, such that the practice is deceptive even if not abusive.

3.3 CFPB's UDAAP Guidance Bulletins

3.3.1 General

While the CFPB has not to date issued UDAAP rules, it has issued a limited number of guidance bulletins dealing with UDAAP.[45] Guidance bulletins tend to be less specific than rules and address concerns about problematic practices without specifically identifying those practices as violations of the Act. Guidance documents are also generally addressed only to institutions that the CFPB supervises.

Nonetheless, guidance documents can be useful to identify acts or practices that the CFPB believes are potential UDAAP violations or at least raise UDAAP concerns. There is no private right of action for violations of standards set out in a guidance bulletin, but such bulletins can still be helpful for private litigants. Guidance documents can bolster arguments that practices should be considered a violation of state UDAP statutes or to counter arguments that a state law claim is pre-empted by federal banking regulations.[46]

While the CFPB has issued a significant number of guidance bulletins, most do not deal with UDAAP issues. To date, the CFPB has issued four guidance documents that touch on UDAAP issues:

> (1) Prohibition of unfair, deceptive, or abusive acts or practices in the collection of consumer debts.
> (2) Harmful practices by mortgage servicers in dealing with military homeowners who have received a permanent change of station.
> (3) Deceptive marketing and sales of credit card add-on practices, and
> (4) A specialized form of credit card promotion that often leads to consumer confusion.

3.3.2 Collection of Consumer Debts

In 2013, the CFPB issued a bulletin on collection of consumer debts.[47] After describing general standards as to unfair, deceptive or abusive practices, the bulletin provides a non-exhaustive list of ten examples of conduct related to the collection of consumer debts that could constitute an unfair, deceptive, or abusive practice:

- Collecting debts, interest, fees, or charges not authorized by the agreement or permitted by law;
- Failing to timely post payments and then charging late fees;
- Taking property without the legal right to do so;
- Revealing the consumer debt to the consumer's employer or co-workers;
- Misrepresenting the character, amount or legal status of a debt;
- Misrepresenting that a communication is from the government or an entity affiliated with the government;
- Misrepresenting whether information will be reported to a reporting agency;
- Misrepresenting that a debt will be forgiven if a settlement offer is accepted;
- Threatening actions that are not intended or when the person does not have authorization to pursue, including false threats of lawsuits, arrest, prosecution, or imprisonment.

Note that many of these practices are also clearly prohibited by the Fair Debt Collection Practices Act.[48]

3.3.3 Mortgage Servicing for Military Homeowners Ordered to Relocate

The CFPB together with the banking agencies has issued guidance on mortgage servicing practices arising when dealing with military homeowners who have received Permanent Change of Station orders. The guidance directs servicers to ensure that employees are adequately trained to avoid misleading or harmful practices. The guidance raises concerns about practices including:

- Failure to provide clear information about assistance options;
- Asking homeowners to waive their legal rights under the Servicemembers Civil Relief Act or other laws;
- Advising homeowners to skip payments;
- Failing to provide information on the status of requests;
- Failing to communicate the servicer's decision.

3.3.4 Marketing and Sales of Credit Card Add-On Products

The CFPB has addressed troubling practices in connection with products like debt protection, identity theft protection,

---

45 The CFPB's guidance documents can be found at www.consumerfinance.gov.

46 If federal and state law both prohibit or discourage the same conduct, then it will be harder for a bank to argue that the state law significantly interferes with a bank power, the new standard for bank preemption. *See* National Consumer Law Center, Mortgage Lending § 5.5 (2d ed. 2014), *updated at* www.nclc.org/library.

47 Prohibition of Unfair, Deceptive, or Abusive Acts or Practices in the Collection of Consumer Debts, CFPB Bulletin 2013-07 (July 13, 2013).

48 *See* National Consumer Law Center, Fair Debt Collection (8th ed. 2014), *updated at* www.nclc.org/library.

credit score tracking, and other products that are supplementary to the credit provided by a credit card.[49] The guidance is primarily addressed under the CFPB's authority to prevent deceptive practices, but it also cites the CFPB's Truth in Lending Act (TILA) and Equal Credit Opportunity Act (ECOA) authority.

The guidance specifically addresses concerns about deceptive marketing and sales practices, failure to adequately disclose important terms and conditions, failure to obtain the consumer's knowing consent to enroll in or pay for programs, and inadequate handling of cancellation requests. In addition to advising directly against deceptive practices, the guidance notes that employee incentive or compensation programs, as well as scripts and manuals used by telemarketing and customer service centers, should be designed to avoid deceptive practices or incentives to provide inaccurate or misleading information. For example, telemarketers should be instructed on the number of times they are permitted to rebut the consumer's request for more information or to decline the product.

3.3.5 *Marketing of Credit Card Promotional Offers*

The CFPB has issued a bulletin informing credit card issuers of the risk of engaging in deceptive or abusive practices in connection with certain offers of promotional APRs on particular transactions.[50] These offers provide zero or low interest rates for balance transfers or other advances without clearly disclosing to consumers that acceptance of the offer may lead to the consumer losing the grace period to make payments on new purchases.

That is, most card issuers do not assess finance charges if a consumer, starting with a zero balance, makes payment in full on all purchases prior to the due date. But accepting, for example, a low promotional rate on a balance transfer will mean that all future purchases will result in a finance charge even if paid in full before the due date, at least until the balance transfer obligation is paid off.

The CFPB is concerned that such offers may be deceptive to consumers. There is also a potential for Truth in Lending Act violations if the terms are not disclosed properly. Significantly, the CFPB also pointed out why such practices may be abusive. The promotions are so complex and difficult for consumers to understand that, depending on the circumstances, a card issuer may take unreasonable advantage of consumers by not fully explaining the offer's conditions and may exploit consumers' lack of understanding in order to impose additional costs. The way in which such offers operate runs so counter to consumer expectations that, if not sufficiently clarified, they can be abusive.

3.4 CFPB Supervision and Examination Manual

The CFPB has issued a supervision and examination manual that outlines UDAAP issues for CFPB supervisors who are examining a bank or nonbank under CFPB supervision.[51] The manual gives examples of practices that other federal agencies have found to be unfair or deceptive. The manual emphasizes that "the perspective of a reasonable consumer" is one of the tests for deceptiveness and thus directs examiners to go beyond disclosure documents and look at consumer complaints, Internet complaint forums, and other sources that indicate that consumers are being misled.[52]

The examination procedures list a number of documents examiners should review, a list that may be a useful starting place for discovery.[53] The manual also describes several areas where examiners should delve deeper and engage in transaction testing. Examiners are directed to determine whether:

- Credit is not underwritten for ability to repay;
- Profitability depends significantly on penalty or other back-end fees;
- A product has high rates of repricing or other changes in terms;
- Complex features make it difficult for consumers to understand the costs, risks, or potential for harm;
- Penalties are imposed for terminating use of a product;
- Fees or other costs are imposed to obtain information about an account;
- The product is targeted to particular populations without appropriate tailoring to ensure understanding.[54]

This list should be viewed as a list of practices that have a high likelihood of UDAAP violations.

The supervision and examination manual also discusses issues that should be examined to determine if there are UDAAP violations in particular areas, including:

- Marketing and disclosures;
- Availability of terms or services as advertised;
- Availability of actual credit;
- Employees and third parties who interact with consumers;
- Servicing and collections.[55]

3.5 Disclosure Rules

The CFPB has authority to prescribe rules to ensure that the features of consumer financial products are fully, accurately, and effectively disclosed so that consumers understand the costs, benefits, and risks associated with the product.[56] The

---

49 CFPB Bulletin 2012-06, Marketing of Credit Card Add-on Products (July 18, 2012), *available at* www.consumerfinance.gov *and online as companion material to this treatise.*

50 Bulletin 2014-02, Marketing of Credit Card Promotional APR Offers (Sept. 3, 2014).

51 *See* Consumer Fin. Prot. Bureau, Supervision and Examination Manual (Oct. 2012) (version 20, *available at* www.consumerfinance .gov *and online as companion material to this treatise.*

52 *Id.* at UDAAP 9.

53 *Id.* at Procedures 1 (Version 2).

54 *Id.* at Procedures 4 (Version 2).

55 *Id.* at Procedures 4-7 (Version 2).

56 12 U.S.C. 5532(a).

CFPB is authorized to issue model disclosure forms that may be used by creditors and that will then provide a safe harbor for the creditor.[57] Additionally, the CFPB may permit creditors to experiment with trial disclosures, also under a safe harbor.[58] To date the only rule issued under this authority was also issued under other Congressional authority in the combined Truth in Lending Act and Real Estate Settlement Procedures Act.

The CFPB is specifically mandated to propose model disclosures that combine disclosures for mortgage loans under the TILA/RESPA rule into a single integrated disclosure.[59] The CFPB finalized the forms and the accompanying regulations on December 31, 2013,[60] and the new regime was effective on October 3, 2015.[61] This rule is examined in both NCLC's *Truth in Lending* and *Mortgage Lending* treatises.[62]

3.6 Right to Information Rules

The Act requires that creditors, upon request, must supply consumers with certain information about the credit product or service purchased.[63] The CFPB is mandated to prescribe standards applicable to the development and use of standardized formats for information to be made available to consumers. The CFPB has not issued any rules to date under this authority.

3.7 Persons and Transactions Covered by CFPB Rulemaking

CFPB rulemaking authority concerning UDAAP, disclosures, and right to information relate to "covered persons" and "consumer financial products and services." A consumer financial product or service is a financial product or service offered or provided for use by consumers primarily for personal, family, or household purposes.[64] A financial product or service means one of a number of listed activities (with certain exceptions):

- Extending credit and servicing loans;
- Extending or brokering leases;
- Providing real estate settlement services;
- Engaging in deposit-taking or funding custodial activities;
- Selling, issuing, or providing stored value cards or payment instruments;
- Check cashing, check collection, or check guaranty services;
- Providing payments or other financial data processing products or services;
- Providing financial advisory services;

- Collecting, maintaining, or providing consumer report information or other account information;
- Debt collection;
- Other products or services that are a subterfuge to evade the statutory scope;
- Products or services permissible for a bank or financial holding company to offer that will impact consumers.[65]

A covered person is anyone offering or providing a financial product or service, and anyone controlling, controlled by, or under common control with such a person who acts as a service provider for such a person.[66] In addition, a covered person includes any entity that engages in the provision of a financial product even if this does not constitute the entity's principal business—for example, a school making loans to students.[67] A covered person is also someone who provides credit counseling to a consumer or provides a service related to a financial product.[68]

As a result, the CFPB has rule-writing authority over virtually everyone in the financial services area, including banks, credit unions, mortgage lenders, credit bureaus, auto finance companies, debt collectors, student lenders, and payday lenders. Nevertheless, there are limits to the CFPB's authority and a number of exemptions.

Most dealers of automobiles, motorcycles, boats, recreational vehicles, and motor homes are exempt and stay under FTC authority.[69] The FTC instead has been given streamlined authority to write rules preventing unfair or deceptive practices by auto dealers exempted from the CFPB's jurisdiction[70] and retains enforcement power over these dealers. If the FTC does issue such rules, they will be included in Chapter 2, *supra*.

The CFPB cannot enforce any new rules against attorneys for conduct that constitutes the practice of law and occurs exclusively within the scope of the attorney-client relationship with a consumer.[71] The CFPB has the authority to issue rules applicable to attorneys who offer or provide "consumer financial products or services."[72] This term is defined to include not just extensions of credit but also credit counseling, debt management, debt settlement, loan modification, foreclosure

---

57 12 U.S.C. § 5532(b), (d).
58 12 U.S.C. § 5532(e).
59 12 U.S.C. § 5532(f).
60 78 Fed. Reg. 79,730 (Dec. 31, 2013).
61 80 Fed. Reg. 43,911 (July 24, 2015).
62 National Consumer Law Center, Truth in Lending (9th ed. 2015), *updated at* www.nclc.org/library; National Consumer Law Center, Mortgage Lending (2d ed. 2014), *updated at* www.nclc.org/library.
63 12 U.S.C. § 5533(a).
64 12 U.S.C. § 5481(5).

65 12 U.S.C. § 5481(15).
66 12 U.S.C. § 5481(6). *See also* §§ 5481(1), (26).
67 Consumer Fin. Prot. Bureau v. ITT Educ. Services, Inc., 2015 WL 1013508 (S.D. Ind. Mar. 6, 2015).
68 *Id.*
69 12 U.S.C. § 5519.
   The exemption for motor vehicle dealers does not extend to dealers that retain financing or sell or assign financing to a related entity, such as many buy-here, pay-here dealers. *See* 12 U.S.C. § 5519(b)(2).
   However, such dealers are likely exempt through the merchant exception, discussed below, if they are a small business.
70 The FTC generally must follow the lengthy and cumbersome "Magnuson-Moss" procedures when writing rules, but for motor vehicle dealers it now can use the more streamlined Administrative Procedure Act process. For rules affecting dealers under the TILA and other enumerated statutes, authority is retained at the FRB.
71 12 U.S.C. § 5517(e)(2).
72 12 U.S.C. §§ 5481(6) (definition of "covered person"), 5481(15) (definition of "financial product or service"), 5517(e) (exception or practice of law), 5531 (general authority to adopt UDAAP rules for "covered persons").

avoidance, and debt collection.[73] It can enforce rules against attorneys if the consumer is not the attorney's client.

The CFPB does not have authority over the purely sales aspect of a non-financial product,[74] including the sale of manufactured homes and modular homes.[75] Certain credit from "merchants, retailers or sellers" is also exempt from the CFPB's coverage (but not from its authority under the enumerated statutes such as TILA). To be exempt under this "merchant" exception, the credit must be offered by the merchant directly, for its own non-financial good or service; must not be assigned or conveyed; cannot exceed the market value of the good or service or be used as an evasion; and must be offered by a merchant who does not regularly extend credit subject to a finance charge, unless the merchant is a small business or does not significantly engage in offering consumer financial products or services.[76]

The CFPB also lacks authority over insurers,[77] including credit insurers, but it has authority over lenders who offer or sell such insurance. Less clear is whether it has rulemaking authority over rent-to-own transactions.[78] Exempt from the CFPB's rulemaking authority are real estate brokerage activities,[79] accountants and tax preparers,[80] employee benefit and compensation plans,[81] persons regulated by the state securities commissioner,[82] the Commodities Futures Trading Commission[83] or the Farm Credit Administration,[84] and solicitations for tax-exempt charities.[85]

Irrespective of the exemptions noted above, the CFPB also has authority to challenge any person who knowingly or recklessly provides substantial assistance to a covered person or service provider when that covered person or service provider engages in a UDAAP violation.[86] Thus in one case a federal court allowed the CFPB to proceed against a payment processor—and intermediaries between the payment processor and a fraudulent merchant—because those entities could be found to be reckless and to have provided substantial assistance.[87]

3.8 No Direct Private Enforcement of CFPB Rules

There is no direct private right under the Act to take action for a UDAAP violation or for a violation of a UDAAP, disclosure, or right-to-information rule—that is, there is no private right of action under the rules and guidance examined in this chapter. On the other hand, there are private rights of action for violations of many of the regulations enacted under the "enumerated statutes" examined in other NCLC treatises, such as regulations interpreting the TILA, RESPA, and Fair Credit Reporting Act.

Even though there may not be a direct private action under the Consumer Financial Protection Act, state law theories may provide a basis for private rights of action for violations of the CFPB's UDAAP, disclosure, and right-to-information rules. CFPB rule violations should be state UDAP violations, with state UDAP statutes providing a private right of action, often including attorney fees, actual damages, and statutory, punitive, or multiple damages.[88]

When the CFPB specifies that a rule prohibition is unfair or deceptive, this is powerful precedent for a court to find the same practice unfair or deceptive under a state UDAP statute. Similarly, when the CFPB defines a practice as abusive, courts may find this excellent precedent for ruling the practice unconscionable under those state UDAP statutes that prohibit unconscionable practices—the statutory definition of "abusive" is similar to a number of state UDAP statutes' definition of "unconscionable."[89]

Violation of a CFPB rule should also bolster a private unfairness challenge under a state UDAP statute, whether the rule is intended to prevent deception, unfairness, or abuse or seeks to foster disclosure or uphold the consumer's right to information. A practice is unfair if it causes substantial injury that consumers cannot reasonably avoid, when such injury is not outweighed by countervailing benefits to consumers or to competition.[90] There can hardly be a benefit to consumers or competition for a creditor to engage in a practice violating a federal rule. In addition, the failure to disclose that a transaction is in violation of a federal rule may be considered a failure to disclose a material term and thus may be a deceptive practice in violation of a state UDAP statute.[91]

The Consumer Financial Protection Act also makes it unlawful "to offer or provide to a consumer any financial product or service not in conformity with Federal consumer financial law."[92] "Not in conformity with Federal consumer financial law" includes violation of a UDAAP or other CFPB

---

73 12 U.S.C. § 5481(15)(A)(viii), (x). *See* Consumer Fin. Prot. Bureau v. Frederick J. Hanna & Associates, P.C., 2015 WL 4282252 (N.D. Ga. July 15, 2015) (attorney collecting debt is covered).

74 12 U.S.C. § 5517(a).

75 12 U.S.C. § 5517(c).

76 12 U.S.C. § 5517(a).

77 12 U.S.C. § 5517(f), (m).

78 Rent-to-own transactions may not fall within the definition of leases subject to the CFPB's jurisdiction, 12 U.S.C. § 5481(15)(A)(2), though the CFPB does have jurisdiction if rent-to-own is considered credit. Notably, the Act defines the term "credit" at 12 U.S.C. § 5481(7) more broadly than the TILA definition at 15 U.S.C. § 1602(e). In addition, the TILA's restrictive definition of "creditor" (15 U.S.C. § 1602(f)) is not found in the Consumer Financial Protection Act.

79 12 U.S.C. § 5517(b).

80 12 U.S.C. § 5517(d).

81 12 U.S.C. § 5517(g).

82 12 U.S.C. § 5517(h).

83 12 U.S.C. § 5517(j).

84 12 U.S.C. § 5517(k).

85 12 U.S.C. § 5517(*l*).

86 12 U.S.C. § 5536(a)(3).

87 Consumer Fin. Prot. Bureau v. Universal Debt & Payment Solutions, L.L.C. (N.D. Ga. Sept. 1, 2015), *available at* www.nclc.org/unreported.

88 *See generally* National Consumer Law Center, Unfair and Deceptive Acts and Practices § 3.2 (8th ed. 2012), *updated at* www.nclc.org/library.

89 *See* National Consumer Law Center, Unfair and Deceptive Acts and Practices § 4.4 (8th ed. 2012), *updated at* www.nclc.org/library.

90 National Consumer Law Center, Unfair and Deceptive Acts and Practices § 4.3.2 (8th ed. 2012), *updated at* www.nclc.org/library.

91 National Consumer Law Center, Unfair and Deceptive Acts and Practices § 3.2.7.4.2 (8th ed. 2012), *updated at* www.nclc.org/library.

92 12 U.S.C. § 5536(a).

rule. Illegality is generally a defense to a contract,[93] and consumers may be able to assert this defense to void or enjoin enforcement of non-conforming agreements. Compliance with CFPB rules may also be part of the implied covenant of good faith and fair dealing.

3.9 Federal Enforcement of CFPB Rules

The CFPB has authority to enforce its rules over banks and credit unions with $10 billion or more in assets (and all of their subsidiaries).[94] Banking regulators have enforcement power over smaller institutions.[95]

Subject to the exemptions for vehicle dealers, some merchant credit, and other exemptions discussed at § 3.7, *supra*, the CFPB has enforcement authority over the following nonbanks:

- The mortgage industry (including brokers, lenders, and servicers);
- Private student lenders;
- Payday lenders;
- The "larger participants in a market for other consumer financial products or services";[96]
- Any other person the CFPB determines to "be engaging, or have engaged, in conduct that poses risks to consumers."[97]

The Act provides that the CFPB can stop rule violations through cease and desist orders and temporary orders to cease and desist.[98] Alternatively, the CFPB can seek a federal court order for a civil penalty or all other appropriate legal and equitable relief, including a permanent or temporary injunction.[99] More specifically, the CFPB can seek rescission or reformation of contracts; refunds of money or return of real property; restitution; disgorgement of unjust enrichment; damages or other monetary relief; costs of public notification

of the violation; limits on a person's activities; and civil penalties that can increase up to $5000 a day for any violation, $25,000 a day for reckless violations, and $1 million a day for knowing violations.[100] Punitive damages are not authorized, but the CFPB can recover costs.[101]

In addition, a CFPB rule violation can be enforced by the FTC against entities within the FTC's jurisdiction. The FTC can seek the same remedies for a CFPB rule violation as it can for a violation of an FTC rule.[102]

3.10 State Enforcement of CFPB Rules

State attorneys general and regulators[103] may enforce CFPB rules against any actor in their state, including national banks and federal savings associations.[104] Even absent a specific rule, states can also enforce the general UDAAP prohibition against nonbanks or state-chartered entities.[105] Actions can be brought in state or federal court, and the state can seek any of the remedies provided by the CFPB-enabling legislation.[106]

3.11 CFPB Rules' Relationship to State Law

CFPB rules do not preempt state law, except to the extent that the state law is inconsistent with the CFPB rule and then only to the extent of the inconsistency.[107] The Consumer Financial Protection Act specifies that state law is not inconsistent with a CFPB rule if it provides greater consumer protection than the CFPB rule.[108]

---

93 *See, e.g.,* Rugemer v. Rhea, 957 P.2d 184, 187 n.1 (Or. Ct. App. 1998) ("Illegal contracts may be rescinded by the party not at fault").

94 12 U.S.C. § 5515(a), (c).

95 12 U.S.C. § 5516.

96 *See* 12 C.F.R. § 1090 (defining the larger participants concerning consumer reporting).

97 12 U.S.C. § 5514(a)(1).

98 12 U.S.C. § 5563(b), (c).

99 12 U.S.C. § 5564(a).

100 12 U.S.C. § 5565.

101 12 U.S.C. § 5565(a)(3), (b).

102 12 U.S.C. § 5581(b)(5)(C).

103 *See* Lawsky v. Condor Capital Corp. (S.D.N.Y. Apr. 23, 2014) (complaint brought by New York superintendent of financial services), *available at* www.nclc.org/unreported.

104 12 U.S.C. § 5552(a). *See also* People v. Alta Colls., Inc. (N.D. Ill. Sept. 4 2014), *available at* www.nclc.org/unreported.

105 *See, e.g.,* Complaint, State v. CMK Investments, Inc. (Ill Cir. Ct. Mar. 18, 2014), *available at* www.nclc.org/unreported.

106 12 U.S.C. § 5552(a)(1).

107 12 U.S.C. § 5551(a)(1).

108 12 U.S.C. § 5551(a)(2).

Chapter 4 The FTC Holder Rule and State Law Counterparts

4.1 Overview

4.1.1 Importance of the FTC Holder Rule

The FTC's rule, Preservation of Consumers' Claims and Defenses,[1] is commonly called the "FTC Holder Rule," although a more accurate (and possibly more appealing) name for it is the Preservation of Claims Rule. In keeping with common usage, this chapter uses the term "FTC Holder Rule" to describe the rule and "FTC Holder Notice" to describe the notice that the rule requires.

The FTC Holder Rule allows consumers to raise seller-related claims and defenses against the holders of the consumer's credit obligation. This rule has four important practical effects.

First, the seller may be judgment proof, such that consumers would be left without a remedy if they had to pay the holder of the note and then try to recover all or some of this amount from the original seller. As the West Virginia Supreme Court stated, in construing a state law which incorporated the FTC Holder Rule, without such a rule a financial institution could "run in effect a 'laundry' for 'fly-by-night' retailers."[2] Without the rule, consumers would owe on the credit obligation even though they cannot recover from the fraudulent seller.

Second, even if the seller is solvent, it is usually impractical to expect a consumer to defend a collection action and simultaneously bring an affirmative suit against the seller. The collection suit may be resolved years before the affirmative suit, and it is often not feasible for a consumer to bring an affirmative action for the small amount of money at stake. By far the most practical action for the consumer is to defend the collection action by raising in that case against the collecting creditor the consumer's claims and defenses against the seller.

Third, making related creditors liable for the acts of the original seller serves the additional goal of establishing a market-based incentive for creditors to inquire into the merchants for whom they finance sales and to refuse to deal with those merchants whose conduct would subject the creditor to potential claims and defenses.[3] Forcing the market to police itself reduces unfair and deceptive practices.

Fourth, the related creditor is in a much better position than the consumer to recover money from the seller. "Consumers are not in a position to police the market, exert leverage over sellers, or vindicate their legal rights in cases of clear abuse. . . . Redress via the legal system is seldom a viable alternative for consumers when problems occur."[4] On the other hand, "[a]s a practical matter, the creditor is always in a better position than the buyer to return seller misconduct costs to sellers, the guilty party."[5]

The FTC emphasized in its statement of basis and purpose for the Holder rule that the holder is in an excellent position to recover money from the seller: the holder "has recourse to contractual devices which render the routine return of seller misconduct costs to sellers relatively cheap and automatic . . . The creditor may also look to a 'reserve' or 'recourse' arrangement or account with the seller for reimbursement."[6]

4.1.2 FTC Holder Rule Versus Other Theories of Lender Liability

4.1.2.1 Credit-Sale Obligations Assigned to Creditor

A common form of credit is an installment contract, in which a seller sells goods or services on credit and then assigns the contract to a financing entity. The seller itself is named as the original payee of the installment contract. An example is an installment sale of a car in which a Toyota dealer assigns the obligation to Toyota Motor Credit.

If the seller assigns an installment sales contract to the creditor, the general rule is that the creditor stands in the shoes

---

1 16 C.F.R. pt. 433, *reproduced at* Appx. A.5.1, *infra*. The procedures and substance of the FTC Holder Rule resisted challenge in United States v. Hertz Corp., 1981-1 Trade Cases ¶ 64,023 (S.D. Fla. 1981).

   In 1988 the FTC initiated a review of the rule to determine the rule's cost to small entities, as a first step toward consideration if the rule should be amended or repealed. *See* 53 Fed. Reg. 44,456 (Nov. 3, 1988).

   The FTC in 1992 announced that the rule will not be amended or repealed pursuant to this review. *See* 57 Fed. Reg. 28,814 (June 29, 1992).

2 State *ex rel.* McGraw v. Scott Runyan Pontiac-Buick, Inc., 461 S.E.2d 516, 526 (W. Va. 1995). *Accord* State *ex rel.* Easley v. Rich Food Services, Inc., 535 S.E.2d 84 (N.C. Ct. App. 2000). *See also* Green Tree Acceptance, Inc. v. Pirtle, 1999 WL 33740367 (E.D. Mich. Mar. 1, 1999) (purpose of rule is to reallocate cost of seller misconduct to creditor); Mitchell v. Church, 2006 WL 2194738 (Del. Super. Ct. July 31, 2006) (unpublished) (purpose is to prevent loan companies from enforcing purchase money loans without reference to the underlying transaction); Scott v. Mayflower Home Improvement Corp., 831 A.2d 564, 569 (N.J. Super. Ct. Law Div. 2001).

3 Bryant v. Mortg. Capital Res. Corp., 197 F. Supp. 2d 1357, 1364 n.23 (N.D. Ga. 2002).

4 Fed. Trade Comm'n, Statement of Basis and Purpose, Trade Regulation Rule Concerning the Preservation of Consumers' Claims and Defenses, 40 Fed. Reg. 53,523 (Nov. 18, 1975), *available online as companion material to this treatise.*

5 *Id. See also* Rollins v. Drive-1 of Norfolk, Inc., 2006 WL 2519516 (E.D. Va. Aug. 29, 2006) (policy rationale is that "financing companies are in a much better position to evaluate the risks of dealing with certain sellers than are individual consumers, and therefore are better suited to bear the risk that a given seller will have engaged in wrongful business practices").

6 Fed. Trade Comm'n, Statement of Basis and Purpose, Trade Regulation Rule Concerning the Preservation of Consumers' Claims and Defenses, 40 Fed. Reg. 53,523 (Nov. 18, 1975), *available online as companion material to this treatise.*

of the seller and is subject to seller-related *defenses*[7] (although not affirmative claims).[8] Even if the assignee has done nothing wrong, it is liable derivatively for the acts of its assignor (or the acts of its assignor's assignor). The assignment makes the assignee liable for all defenses the consumer can raise against the assignor.

The UCC creates an exception to this rule that formerly affected many consumer contracts. U.C.C. § 9-403 (formerly numbered § 9-206) allows contracts to contain a clause by which the buyer waives any defenses (with some exceptions) that the general rule might make available against the assignee.[9] However, many states prohibit waiver of defense clauses in at least some types of transactions.[10] More importantly, the FTC Holder Rule effectively has ended waiver of defense clauses in consumer contracts because it explicitly provides the contrary. As a result, such waivers are rarely used today.

The holder-in-due-course defense, although similar to that provided by a waiver of defense clause, has no application to installment sales contracts. The reason is that an installment sales agreement typically contains undertakings in addition to the promise to pay money, so it does not meet the UCC definition of "negotiable instrument." Article 3 of the UCC, which creates the holder-in-due-course doctrine, applies only to negotiable instruments. If there were any doubt about an assignee acquiring the rights of a holder in due course in a credit-sale obligation, the FTC Holder Rule defeats any such status for any transaction within the rule's scope.[11] More on the holder-in-due-course doctrine is found in another NCLC treatise.[12]

The FTC Rule makes any holder subject to the consumer's claims and defenses against the seller. It subjects the holder, as a matter of contract law, to the consumer's claims and defenses.[13] The holder of such a note cannot evade this rule by claiming to be enforcing a security interest rather than claiming under the note.[14]

The rule allows the consumer to raise all seller-related claims and defenses. This includes claims the consumer has against the seller, not only as they relate to the sale process or the quality or performance of the goods or services sold but also to the seller's conduct in providing the credit. What the rule does not cover is the consumer's claims against an assignee for an assignee's conduct.

The FTC Rule, unlike the basic common law rule about assignees, allows the consumer to raise against the assignee not only consumer-related defenses but also consumer-related claims. This allows the consumer to initiate the action or to bring counterclaims to a collection action and recover affirmatively over and beyond what remains owing on the obligation. The rule, though, caps the consumer's recovery to the amount paid on the installment contract plus the remaining balance.[15]

Because of this cap, consumers might also consider other grounds to find the assignee liable when the consumer's damage exceeds the cap amount. Assignees are liable for their own direct misconduct in addition to their derivative liability under the Holder rule, and this direct liability is not capped.[16] The holder's misconduct is not limited to the holder's direct dealings with the consumer and can include such state law theories as aiding and abetting, furnishing the means of deception, civil conspiracy, and joint enterprise.[17] The holder can also be liable for the seller's conduct if the seller is the holder's agent, as long as the agent has actual or apparent authority for its actions.[18]

4.1.2.2 Seller-Related Claims in Seller-Arranged Loans

In a second way of extending credit, the sale of goods is financed by a loan that a third-party lender makes directly to the consumer, without the seller being the originating creditor. The seller may arrange the direct loan, and the loan proceeds may even go directly from the lender to the seller, but the seller is not listed on the loan obligation as the original creditor. When financing is set up in this manner, the consumer's debt is owed to the lender from the outset.

Prior to the FTC Holder Rule, these third-party lenders and their assignees claimed insulation from the consumer's claims and defenses against the seller, but not because they were holders in due course. Instead, such third-party creditors claimed they loaned money directly to the consumer and were not responsible for how the consumer spent the proceeds. They

---

7   U.C.C. § 9-404(a); Nat'l City Bank v. Columbian Mut. Life Ins. Co., 282 F.3d 407 (6th Cir. 2002); Meyers v. Postal Fin. Co., 287 N.W.2d 614 (Minn. 1979); First of Am. Bank v. Thompson, 552 N.W.2d 516 (Mich. Ct. App. 1996); Delacy Investments, Inc. v. Thurman, 693 N.W.2d 479 (Minn. Ct. App. 2005) (assignee of real estate agent's commissions from realty company acquires them subject to setoffs that arise from the commission agreement); Arnold v. Ford Motor Co., 566 P.2d 98 (N.M. 1977); Capital City Fin. Grp., Inc. v. MAC Constr. Inc., 2002 WL 2016332 (Ohio Ct. App. Aug. 28, 2002) (unpublished); Etter v. Industrial Valley Bank & Trust Co., 515 A.2d 6, 9 (Pa. Super. Ct. 1986); Rosemond v. Campbell, 343 S.E.2d 641, 645 (S.C. Ct. App. 1986); DaimlerChrysler Services N. Am., L.L.C. v. Ouimette, 830 A.2d 38 (Vt. 2003) (assignee of credit sale contract stands in shoes of seller); 9 Corbin, Corbin on Contracts §§ 892 (interim ed. 2002); 29 Lord, Williston on Contracts §§ 74.47, 74.49 (4th ed. 2003); Farnsworth, Farnsworth on Contracts § 11.8 (2d ed. 1998); Restatement (Second) of Contracts § 336 (1981).

8   Novartis Animal Health US, Inc. v. Earle Palmer Brown, L.L.C., 424 F. Supp. 2d 1358 (N.D. Ga. 2006); Meyers v. Postal Fin. Co., 287 N.W.2d 614 (Minn. 1979).

9   U.C.C. § 9-403 (former § 9-206). *See* Compressors Plus, Inc. v. Service Tech de Mexico, S.A., 54 U.C.C. Rep. Serv. 2d 50 (N.D. Tex. 2004) (documents in commercial transaction did not constitute waiver-of-defense clause even when construed together); Rosemond v. Campbell, 343 S.E.2d 641, 645 (S.C. Ct. App. 1986).

10 *See* § 4.5, *infra*.

11 *See* U.C.C. § 3-106(d); U.C.C. § 3-106 cmt. 3. *See also* Mitchell v. Church, 2006 WL 2194738 (Del. Super. Ct. July 31, 2006).

12 *See* National Consumer Law Center, Mortgage Lending § 10.7 (2d ed. 2014), *updated at* www.nclc.org/library.

13 *See* § 4.2.1, *infra*.

14 *See* § 4.3.3, *infra*.

15 *See* § 4.3.4, *infra*.

16 *See* Mitchell v. Church, 2006 WL 2194738 (Del. Super. Ct. July 31, 2006).

17 *See* National Consumer Law Center, Unfair and Deceptive Acts and Practices § 11.4 (8th ed. 2012), *updated at* www.nclc.org/library.

18 National Consumer Law Center, Unfair and Deceptive Acts and Practices § 11.2.3 (8th ed. 2012), *updated at* www.nclc.org/library.

are not assignees of the seller and thus do not step into the shoes of the seller.

The FTC Holder Rule again offers consumers in this situation their best remedy. The rule requires sellers to arrange for the FTC Holder Notice to be present in all notes when the seller refers consumers to the lender or is affiliated with the lender by common control or contract or by any formal or informal business arrangement, understanding, course of dealing, or procedure.[19] The FTC Holder Rule language in the note states that the holder is subject to all claims and defenses the consumer has against the related seller, up to the amount of the loan. But if the consumer arranges the loan on his or her own, without the seller referring the consumer to the lender or otherwise having a business relationship with the lender, the FTC Holder Rule does not apply.

If the Holder rule applies, it caps the consumer's recovery at the amount the consumer paid plus the remainder of the loan. If the consumer's damages exceed this cap, the consumer will have to find a basis for recovery against the holder in addition to the Holder rule. Lenders are liable for their own direct misconduct in addition to their derivative liability under the Holder rule, and this direct liability is not capped.[20] The holder's misconduct is not limited to the holder's direct dealings with the consumer and can include its collusion with the seller under such state law theories as aiding and abetting, furnishing the means of deception, civil conspiracy, and joint enterprise.[21] The lender can also be liable for the seller's conduct if the seller is the lender's agent, as long as the agent has actual or apparent authority for its actions.[22]

4.1.2.3 Raising Seller-Related Claims Against the Credit Card Issuer

The FTC Holder Rule does not apply if the consumer pays by credit card, so the FTC Rule cannot provide the basis for consumers to raise against their credit card issuers' claims that consumers have against their sellers. Nevertheless, other federal law, part of the Truth in Lending Act, does provide such a right. This right is examined in another NCLC treatise, *Truth in Lending*.[23]

4.1.2.4 Loan-Related Claims in Direct Loans

Often the consumer will obtain credit not from a seller but from a lender. The consumer may have claims against the lender that arise from the nature of the loan origination or the terms of the loan. Examples might include payday loans, home equity loans, loans to purchase a home, or auto title loans. If the lender assigns the loan, the consumer may wish to raise against the assignee claims and defenses the consumer has against the originating lender.

The FTC Holder Rule does not apply to this type of transaction because the rule relates only to *seller*-related claims and defenses, not claims against a lender. If the seller extended the credit for the sale, the consumer can raise claims based on the seller's sales and credit-related actions against an assignee of the credit contract. But, if a lender extended the credit, and then assigns the loan note, the FTC Holder Rule does not give the consumer the right to raise lender-related claims against the assignee. If the consumer has claims or defenses arising from the creation of the loan obligation, such as misrepresentation of credit terms or unfair creditor remedies, some other theory must apply to raise these against the lender's assignee.

In general, assignees step into the shoes of the assignor, and the consumer can raise against the assignee any assignor-related defense (but not affirmative claims).[24] An exception to this is if the assignee becomes, or acquires the rights of, a holder in due course. This issue is of special import in mortgage loans when loan brokers and loan originators engage in improper conduct but the mortgage loan is then assigned to third parties or even securitized. Ways to defeat the holder-in-due-course status, particularly in the context of mortgage loans, are found in another NCLC's treatise.[25]

In addition, the assignee is liable for its own direct misconduct in addition to its derivative liability as an assignee. The assignee's misconduct is not limited to the assignee's direct dealings with the consumer and can include its collusion with the original lender under such state law theories as aiding and abetting, furnishing the means of deception, civil conspiracy, and joint enterprise.[26] The assignee can also be liable for the originating lender's conduct if the originating lender is the assignee's agent, as long as the agent has actual or apparent authority for its actions.[27]

4.1.2.5 Raising Seller-Related Claims in Lease Transactions

Some courts find that the FTC Holder Rule does not apply to leases,[28] and leases as a practical matter never include the FTC Holder Notice. Other theories may still be available to raise seller-related defenses against the holder of a lease.

Most consumer leases today are originated by the dealer in the leased goods, so the lease holder is an assignee of the dealer and steps into the shoes of the dealer, making it liable for dealer-related defenses. A lease may seek to waive the

---

19 16 C.F.R. § 433.1(d), (g), *reprinted at* Appx. A.5.1, *infra*.

20 *See* Mitchell v. Church, 2006 WL 2194738 (Del. Super. Ct. July 31, 2006).

21 *See* National Consumer Law Center, Unfair and Deceptive Acts and Practices § 11.4 (8th ed. 2012), *updated at* www.nclc.org/library.

22 National Consumer Law Center, Unfair and Deceptive Acts and Practices § 11.2.3 (8th ed. 2012), *updated at* www.nclc.org/library.

23 National Consumer Law Center, Truth in Lending § 7.11 (9th ed. 2015), *updated at* www.nclc.org/library.

24 *See* § 4.1.2.1, *supra*.

25 National Consumer Law Center, Mortgage Lending § 10.7 (2d ed. 2014), *updated at* www.nclc.org/library.

26 *See, e.g.*, Cazares v. Pacific Shore Funding, 2006 WL 149106 (C.D. Cal. Jan. 3, 2006) (assignee that actively participated in original lender's acts and dictated loan terms may be liable under state UDAP statute). *See also* National Consumer Law Center, Unfair and Deceptive Acts and Practices § 11.4 (8th ed. 2012 and Supp.).

27 National Consumer Law Center, Unfair and Deceptive Acts and Practices § 11.2.3 (8th ed. 2012), *updated at* www.nclc.org/library.

28 § 4.2.2.4, *infra*.

consumer's right to raise dealer-related defenses to the lease, but this waiver may violate a state statute[29] or otherwise be found unenforceable under state law.

State "holder" statutes may also apply to leases and make the lease holder liable for dealer-related defenses and may even make the lease holder liable for dealer-related affirmative claims.[30] Certain state holder statutes may also make the lease holder liable for dealer-related practices when the dealer merely refers the consumer to a lessor and the lessor is not the dealer's assignee.[31]

The lease holder is also liable for its own direct misconduct in addition to its derivative liability for the acts of the dealer. The lease holder's misconduct is not limited to its direct dealings with the consumer and can include its collusion with the dealer under such state law theories as aiding and abetting, furnishing the means of deception, civil conspiracy, and joint enterprise.[32] The lease holder can also be liable for the dealer's conduct if the dealer is the lease holder's agent, as long as the agent has actual or apparent authority for its actions.[33]

4.1.2.6   Stopping Check, Debit Card, or Other Payments As a Response to the Seller's Misconduct

The consumer's ability to stop payment in response to seller misconduct is significantly different when the consumer uses a check, debit card, or other payment device instead of obtaining credit to make the purchase. The FTC Holder Rule does not apply because there is no credit. As a practical matter, it is almost impossible to stop payment on many of today's payment devices.

Debit card or other electronic transfer payments are typically withdrawn from the consumer's bank account before a stop payment can be initiated. There is also no opportunity to stop payment by money orders, stored value and other prepaid cards, or similar devices.

A consumer can ask their bank to stop payment on his or her check if the consumer acts quickly, but the consumer has no recourse against the bank if the check is cashed and the amount withdrawn from the consumer's account. The check is a negotiable instrument, and the bank is a holder in due course. As such, the consumer may have difficulty bringing seller-related defenses to the bank's collection on the check.[34]

If the consumer has preauthorized a series of periodic electronic funds transfers from the consumer's bank account, the consumer can stop payment for future transfers. The consumer

notifies the consumer's bank at least three business days before the next scheduled transfer.[35]

Consumer rights to stop payment and other rights as to checks, debit cards, prepaid cards, money orders, electronic transfers, and similar payment devices are covered in another NCLC treatise, *Consumer Banking and Payments Law.*[36]

4.2   Scope of the FTC Holder Rule

4.2.1   *Operational Scope of the Holder Notice*

The FTC Holder Rule is unique in that the scope of the rule is somewhat different from the scope of the rule's operational effect. The rule operates by a notice placed in consumer credit agreements whereby, as a matter of the contract itself,[37] the parties agree that the consumer can raise seller-related claims and defenses against the holder of the note or contract. As such, the *effect* of the rule is directly felt by *any* agreement that includes the FTC Holder Notice.

Even if a transaction is beyond the scope of the FTC rule, such that there is no requirement that the notice be inserted, if the credit agreement contains the FTC Holder Notice, as a matter of contract, the holder is subject to seller-related claims and defenses.[38] The very terms of the contract govern the relationship between the parties.[39] Even if the FTC notice was not required to be inserted, it is given full effect if it is inserted.[40]

---

29   *See* § 4.5, *infra.*

30   § 4.5, *infra.*

31   § 4.5, *infra.*

32   *See, e.g.,* Cazares v. Pacific Shore Funding, 2006 WL 149106 (C.D. Cal. Jan. 3, 2006) (assignee that actively participated in original lender's acts and dictated loan terms may be liable under state UDAP statute). *See also* National Consumer Law Center, Unfair and Deceptive Acts and Practices § 11.4 (8th ed. 2012), *updated at* www.nclc.org/library.

33   National Consumer Law Center, Unfair and Deceptive Acts and Practices § 11.2.3 (8th ed. 2012 and Supp.).

34   *See* First Nat'l Bank, Conway Springs v. Jones, 839 P.2d 535 (Kan. Ct. App. 1992).

35   *See* 12 C.F.R. § 1005.10(c).

36   National Consumer Law Center, Consumer Banking and Payments Law (5th ed. 2013), *updated at* www.nclc.org/library.

37   Thomas v. Ford Motor Credit Co., 429 A.2d 277 (Md. Ct. Spec. App. 1981); Hempstead Bank v. Babcock, 453 N.Y.S.2d 557 (N.Y. Sup. Ct. 1982); Hiney v. Ford Motor Co., 1978 WL 215386 (Ohio Ct. App. Sept. 27, 1978), *as amended by* 1978 WL 215386 (Ohio Ct. App. Sept. 27, 1978) (regardless of whether the holder language is required by the FTC, it is part of contract and bank is therefore liable); De La Fuente v. Home Sav. Ass'n, 669 S.W.2d 137 (Tex. App. 1984). *See also* Peel v. Credit Acceptance Corp., 408 S.W.3d 191 (Mo. Ct. App. 2013). *But cf.* Whittington v. Patriot Homes, Inc., 2006 WL 2524143 (W.D. La. Aug. 30, 2006) (FTC Holder Notice not enforceable as contract term when contract stated that the notice applied if a box was checked and lender signed next to the box; since neither action was taken, notice was not enforceable).

38   Mariscal v. Aqua Supreme, 2009 WL 5216920 (N.D. Cal. Dec. 30, 2009); Gray v. Atlantic Permanent Sav. & Loan Ass'n, Inc., 49 B.R. 540 (Bankr. E.D. Va. 1985); Music Acceptance Corp. v. Lofing, 39 Cal. Rptr. 2d 159 (Cal. Ct. App. 1995); Mitchell v. Church, 2006 WL 2194738 (Del. Super. Ct. July 31, 2006); Boden v. Atlantic Fed. Sav. & Loan Ass'n, 396 So. 2d 827 (Fla. Dist. Ct. App. 1981); Jefferson Bank & Trust Co. v. Stamiatiou, 384 So. 2d 388 (La. 1980). *Cf.* International Harvester Credit Corp. v. Hill, 496 F. Supp. 329 (M.D. Tenn. 1979) (when form contract explicitly limits FTC Holder Rule language's applicability to consumer transactions, not business transactions, the notice is not effective as to a business transaction).

39   Turner v. CIT Grp./Sales Fin., Inc., 154 Fed. Appx. 2 (9th Cir. 2005); Mariscal v. Aqua Supreme, 2009 WL 5216920 (N.D. Cal. Dec. 30, 2009); Kish v. Van Note, 692 S.W.2d 463 (Tex. 1985). *See also In re* Armor, 1999 U.S. Dist. LEXIS 5885 (E.D.N.C. Mar. 15, 1999), *aff'd without op.,* 232 F.3d 887 (4th Cir. 2000); Jackson v. CIT Grp./Sales Fin. Inc., 630 So. 2d 368 (Ala. 1994); Maxwell v. Fidelity Fin. Services, Inc., 907 P.2d 51 (Ariz. 1995); BCS Fin. Corp. v. Sorbo, 444 S.E.2d 85 (Ga. Ct. App. 1994).

40   Turner v. CIT Grp./Sales Fin., Inc., 154 Fed. Appx. 2 (9th Cir. 2005).

There is no requirement that the Holder notice appear at any particular place in the loan documents,[41] so the consumer's attorney must carefully review all portions of all the documents for the notice. In open-end plans, the notice may be in the master credit agreement, in one or more monthly statements, or even in charge slips.[42]

Creditors cannot avoid the FTC Holder Rule by stating in credit agreements that holders are subject to claims and defenses *if* the rule applies to the transaction but that holders are not subject to such claims if the rule is found not to apply. The rule does not allow for such deviation from the proscribed language—the rule requires that the agreement contain the exact language contained in the rule. So altering the language is a rule violation and contrary to the FTC policies in enacting the rule.[43] If the rule's exact language is used, but the document contains language limiting the effect of the Holder notice, the limiting language is likely unenforceable, and the consumer instead can enforce his or her rights pursuant to the Holder notice.[44] On the other hand, even if an agreement is within the scope of the FTC Holder Rule, and the FTC notice is required to be inserted in the agreement, this may not happen. Then the rule does not work as intended. Another section details a consumer's remedies and ability to raise seller-related claims and defenses if the notice is required to be, but is not, in the contract.[45]

4.2.2 Legal Scope of the Rule

4.2.2.1 Relevance of the Rule's Legal Scope

As described in § 4.2.1, *supra*, the rule's operational scope is often different than its legal scope. If the FTC notice is found in the contract, then that notice is effective, as a matter of contract law, even if the transaction is outside the rule's legal scope. Legal scope of the rule is important because the FTC can enforce rule violations and because there are a number of theories to create lender liability if the FTC notice is required to be inserted into the credit agreement but it is not.[46] In other words, the consumer has a potential claim against the lender if the transaction is *either* within the rule's operational scope (the FTC notice is in fact included) or within the rule's legal scope (the FTC notice is required to be included).

4.2.2.2 Sales Transactions Covered

The FTC rule requires a notice to be inserted in credit agreements whenever the seller finances a sale or a creditor has a relationship with the seller and that creditor finances the sale. The rule applies broadly to "any sale or lease of goods or services to consumers in or affecting commerce."[47] The rule applies equally to the sale of services, such as home improvement contracting, vocational training, employment counseling, and health spa membership, as it does to the sale of tangibles.[48]

"Consumer" is defined as "a natural person who seeks or acquires goods or services for personal, family, or household use."[49] As such, the rule applies to virtually every type of consumer sales transaction. But the rule does not apply to the purchase of equipment for agricultural production, the purchase of securities, or purchases made by an organization.[50]

4.2.2.3 Application to Mortgage Loans

Importantly, the rule does not apply to the sale of real estate because real estate is not a good or service. As a result, the rule does not require the notice to be placed into mortgages or other loans to *purchase* real estate.[51] Nevertheless, when a transaction involves the sale of goods or services, the rule applies even when a home is taken as *security* for the loan.[52] A home improvement contract is an important example of a sale of goods and services to which the rule applies even if a home is taken as security for the loan.[53]

An important application of the FTC Holder Rule is illustrated when shoddy or non-existent home improvement work leads to the consumer refusing to make payments, which then leads to an assignee lender trying to foreclose. In this situation, the rule requires that a notice be inserted in the note stating

---

41 Fed. Trade Comm'n, Staff Guidelines, 41 Fed. Reg. 20,026 (May 14, 1976) (placement of the notice), *available online as companion material to this treatise*.

42 *Id.*

43 Federal Trade Commission Advisory Letter by Eric Rubin, Assistant Director for Compliance, FTC Bureau of Consumer Protection (Sept. 17, 1976).

44 *See* § 4.3.13, *infra*.

45 *See* § 4.4, *infra*.

46 *See* § 4.4, *infra*.

47 16 C.F.R. § 433.2, *reprinted at* Appx. A.5.1, *infra*.

48 Statement of Basis and Purpose for the Federal Trade Commission Rule Concerning the Preservation of Consumers' Claims and Defenses, 40 Fed. Reg. 53,524 (Nov. 18, 1975), *available online as companion material to this treatise*; Fed. Trade Comm'n, Staff Guidelines, 41 Fed. Reg. 20,024 (May 14, 1976) (affected transactions), *available online as companion material to this treatise*.

49 16 C.F.R. § 433.1(b), *reprinted at* Appx. A.5.1, *infra*. *See* Drew v. Chrysler Corp., 596 F. Supp. 1371 (W.D. Mo. 1984) (adopting objective test for determining whether goods were acquired for consumer purposes).

50 Fed. Trade Comm'n, Staff Guidelines, 41 Fed. Reg. 20,024 (May 14, 1976) (affected transactions), *available online as companion material to this treatise*.

51 Murphy v. Federal Deposit Ins. Corp., 408 Fed. Appx. 609 (3d Cir. 2010); Singleton v. Wells Fargo Home Mortg., 2012 WL 7345 (W.D. Mo. May 9, 2012); Kucheynik v. Mortg. Elec. Registration Sys., Inc., 2010 WL 5174540 (W.D. Wash. Dec. 15, 2010); Araki v. Bank of Am., 2010 WL 525970 (D. Haw. Dec. 14, 2010); Woodsbey v. Easy Mortg. (*In re* Woodsbey), 375 B.R. 145 (W.D. Pa. 2007); Hancock v. Homeq Servicing Corp., 2007 WL 1238746 (D.D.C. Apr. 27, 2007), *aff'd*, 526 F.3d 785 (D.C. Cir. 2008); Johnson v. Long Beach Mortg. Loan Trust 2001-4, 451 F. Supp. 2d 16 (D.D.C. 2006); *In re* Carmichael, 443 B.R. 698 (Bankr. E.D. Pa. 2011); Reagoso v. Mortg. Elec. Registration Sys., Inc. (*In re* Reagoso), 2007 WL 1655376 (Bankr. E.D. Pa. June 6, 2007); Citimortgage, Inc. v. Hoge, 962 N.E.2d 327 (Ohio Ct. App. 2011).

52 *See* Fed. Trade Comm'n, Staff Guidelines, 41 Fed. Reg. 20,024 (May 14, 1976) (affected transactions), *available online as companion material to this treatise*.

53 *Id.*

that the consumer's claims against the home improvement contractor can be raised against the foreclosing assignee.[54]

Of course, for the rule to apply, the seller must still originate the loan or have a business relationship with the originating lender. Thus a home improvement loan from a local credit union unrelated to the contractor is not within the rule's coverage. The typical home mortgage to purchase a home is similarly outside the rule's scope, not only because the purchase is not of a good or service but also because the mortgagee is usually (but not always) unrelated to the home seller. Moreover, a consumer will often want to raise loan-related claims against an assignee of a home mortgage, but the FTC Rule only provides for raising "seller"-related claims and defenses, so does not apply to claims against an originating lender that is not also a seller. The liability of holders of a mortgage loan for loan-related defenses is examined in another NCLC treatise, *Mortgage Lending.*[55]

4.2.2.4   Coverage of Leases

It is unclear whether the FTC Holder Rule applies to leases. While the rule explicitly indicates that it applies to a "sale or lease," other aspects of the rule require the lease to involve a "consumer credit contract."[56] "Consumer credit contract" is a defined term that refers to the Truth in Lending Act definition of a finance charge and a credit sale. The rule clearly applies to a transaction structured as a lease but falls within the Truth in Lending Act's definition of a credit transaction.[57] What is unclear is whether the rule applies to leases not within that definition.[58]

4.2.2.5   Covered Sellers

The rule places certain obligations on "sellers," defined as those in the ordinary course of business who sell or lease goods or services to consumers.[59] Since the rule only applies to sellers who sell in the ordinary course of their business, isolated sales by individuals are not covered.

Moreover, the rule only applies when a seller is within the scope of the FTC Act. This requires some explanation why it is the FTC Act's scope as to sellers, not creditors that is critical. The rule does not require creditors to place the Holder notice in their contracts. Nor does the rule place any obligations on assignees of a credit agreement. Instead, the rule requires that sellers place the notice in their credit sale contracts and that they arrange for the notice's inclusion when a loan is made by a related third-party lender.[60] Then, as a matter of contract law, the notice is binding on all subsequent holders because the notice is a term of the credit agreement.

The FTC Holder Rule applies when the seller is within the scope of the FTC Act, even if the assignee or related lender is not within that scope. Even if the seller is not within that scope, if the notice is found in the contract or note, as a matter of contract law the Holder notice is still effective.

Public entities and truly nonprofit corporations are not within the scope of the FTC Act,[61] and the FTC Holder Rule does not obligate these entities as *sellers* to arrange for the notice to be placed in consumer credit agreements. For example, the FTC Holder Rule does not apply to loans involving a community college.

When a public entity is the holder, another issue that may arise is whether the governmental entity is immune from suit because of sovereign immunity, even though the FTC Holder Notice is in the loan documents. When a governmental entity's loan documents include the FTC Holder Notice, this would appear to waive any claim of sovereign immunity as to claims against it based on the seller's conduct. But one court found that inclusion of the Holder notice did not waive sovereign immunity for a Texas municipality because, at least in Texas, sovereign immunity can only be waived by statute or legislative resolution.[62]

Other entities outside the scope of the FTC Act include banks, savings and loans, federal credit unions, and common carriers and air carriers subject to federal regulation.[63] The McCarran-Ferguson Act also prohibits FTC regulation of insurance when state law otherwise regulates the practice. It is possible that certain state regulation of unfair insurance practices would oust insurance transactions from the scope of the FTC Holder Rule.

4.2.2.6   Rule Applies to Financed Sale and Purchase Money Loans

The rule requires the FTC Holder Notice to be placed in any instrument evidencing a debt arising from a "financed sale" or

---

54 *See, e.g.,* Antuna v. Nescor, Inc., 2002 WL 725490 (Conn. Super. Ct. Apr. 1, 2002); Citifinancial Mortg. Co. v. Freeman, 2006 WL 1029321 (N.J. Super. Ch. Ct. Apr. 13, 2006); Green Tree Consumer Discount Co. v. Newton, 909 A.2d 811 (Pa. Super. Ct. 2006).

55 National Consumer Law Center, Mortgage Lending § 10.7 (2d ed. 2014), *updated at* www.nclc.org/library.

56 16 C.F.R. § 433.2(a), (b), *reprinted at* Appx. A.5.1, *infra.*

57 For example, the rule refers to Truth in Lending's definition of a credit sale, which refers to certain nominal leases as credit sales when the consumer pays a sum equivalent to the value of the goods or services and has the option to become the owner for nominal consideration. 12 C.F.R. § 1026.2(16) [§ 226.2(16)].

58 *See* Marchionna v. Ford Motor Co., 1995 U.S. Dist. LEXIS 11408 (N.D. Ill. Aug. 9, 1995) (rule does not apply to pure lease); Bescos v. Bank of Am., 129 Cal. Rptr. 2d 423 (Cal. Ct. App. 2003) (same); LaChappelle v. Toyota Motor Credit Corp., 126 Cal. Rptr. 2d (Cal. Ct. App. 2002) (same); Jarvis v. South Oak Dodge, 747 N.E.2d 383 (Ill. App. Ct. 2000) (same), *rev'd on other grounds,* 773 N.E.2d 641 (Ill. 2002); Fifth Third Bank v. Roberts, 55 U.C.C. Rep. Serv. 2d 378 (Ohio Ct. App. 2004) (same). *Cf.* Ford Motor Credit Co. v. Jones, 2009 WL 1912626 (Ohio Ct. App. July 2, 2009) (when FTC notice not found in lease, no derivative liability).

59 16 C.F.R. § 433.1(j), *reprinted at* Appx. A.5.1, *infra.*

60 The commission in 1979 tentatively adopted an amendment that would have allowed FTC enforcement of the rule against assignees and lenders but the commission never officially promulgated this amendment. After nine years of inaction, the FTC killed the amendment on the grounds that there was no evidence that the practice of creditors cutting off consumer defenses was prevalent. 53 Fed. Reg. 44,457 (Nov. 3, 1988).

61 15 U.S.C. § 44 (definition of "corporation").

62 Schoffstall v. City of Corpus Christi, 2014 WL 4249801 (Tex. App. Aug. 25, 2014).

63 15 U.S.C. § 45(a)(2).

a "purchase money loan."[64] A financed sale is the typical credit sale when the seller acts as the initial creditor.

The term "purchase money loan" is a defined term. The basic concept is that if a creditor is related in some fashion with the seller and makes a loan to the consumer to purchase goods or services from the seller, the FTC Holder Rule applies as if the financing came directly from the seller. Sellers cannot avoid the rule by arranging with third parties to finance a sales transaction.

For a credit transaction to be a "purchase money loan," the transaction must meet four preconditions. First, there must be a cash advance received by the consumer in return for a finance charge within the meaning of the Truth in Lending Act. Since the Truth in Lending Act's definition of finance charge is very broad, this should apply to virtually all credit transactions.

Second, the cash advance must be applied in whole or *substantial* part to a purchase of goods or services from the seller. A loan is still covered even if some part is kept by the consumer or goes to pay another debt, as long as a substantial part goes to purchase the goods or services from the seller.[65] The rule should thus apply to the refinancing of a note as long as a substantial part of the total proceeds can be traced back to the original sale. For example, when a seller offered initial financing, and then arranged permanent financing that paid off the original note owed the seller, this is covered by the FTC rule.[66]

Third, the seller must be related to the creditor, either by referring consumers to the creditor or by being affiliated with the creditor by common control, contract, or business arrangement.[67] This is an expansive definition.[68] The rule makes clear that the seller need not refer the particular consumer to the creditor as long as the seller refers consumers to the creditor. Moreover, "contract" and "business arrangement" are both defined terms that cover any formal or informal agreement between the creditor and seller, be it written or oral, or even an informal course of dealing, procedure, or arrangement.[69]

In short, the rule applies to any third-party loan transaction used to purchase goods or services when the seller and creditor have virtually *any* form of a relationship with each other. A referral relationship may exist between dealer and creditor when a car dealership refers consumers to an insurance agent and when the insurance agent then refers consumers to a creditor.[70]

Fourth, the rule only applies when the related creditor fits the rule's definition of "creditor." A creditor is a person who in the ordinary course of business makes purchase money loans or finances the sale of goods or services to consumers.[71] There is one important exception to this definition of creditor: the rule does not apply to a creditor who in the particular transaction at issue is acting as a credit card issuer.[72] A separate federal law analyzed in NCLC's *Truth in Lending* establishes consumer rights to raise seller-related claims and defenses against credit card issuers.[73]

While the rule's definition of creditor does not include credit card issuers, it does not exempt credit card issuers from the definition of "*seller*." Sellers that have their own "house" credit cards must still comply with the rule. Moreover, the rule applies to seller-provided open-end credit.[74] The rule will typically not apply to open-end credit provided by a lender because the consumer usually will use the money to purchase goods or services from various sellers not related to the lender.[75]

4.2.2.7 Does the Rule Apply to Loans with an Amount Financed Exceeding a Dollar Threshold?

An issue arises as to whether the FTC Holder Rule applies to loans when the amount financed is exempt from the Truth in Lending Act (TILA) because the loan exceeds a dollar threshold. Staff guidelines from 1976 on the rule state that terms used in the rule—financing a sale and purchase money loan—expressly refer to the TILA and its Regulation Z and "thus incorporate the limitations contained in these laws."[76] The guidelines then reach the conclusion that "a purchase involving an expenditure of more than [the then] $25,000 is not affected by the Rule."[77]

The staff's 1976 view is flawed in its totality. The FTC Holder Rule defines "financing a sale" as extending credit in connection with a credit sale "within the meaning of the Truth in Lending Act and Regulation Z."[78] The TILA and Regulation Z define a credit sale as any sale in which the seller is a creditor. The TILA and Regulation Z also define creditor and credit.[79] None of these definitions mentions a dollar limit.

The rule also defines "purchase money loan" as one involving a finance charge "within the meaning of the Truth in Lending

---

64 16 C.F.R. §§ 433.1(i), 433.2, *reprinted at* Appx. A.5.1, *infra*.

65 Fed. Trade Comm'n, Staff Guidelines, 41 Fed. Reg. 20,025 (May 14, 1976) (purchase money loans), *available online as companion material to this treatise*.

66 Associates Home Equity Services, Inc. v. Troup, 778 A.2d 529 (N.J. Super. Ct. App. Div. 2001). *But see* Whittington v. Patriot Homes, Inc., 2008 WL 1736821 (W.D. La. Apr. 11, 2008).

67 16 C.F.R. § 433.1(d), *reprinted at* Appx. A.5.1, *infra*.

68 *See* Associates Home Equity Services, Inc. v. Troup, 778 A.2d 529 (N.J. Super. Ct. App. Div. 2001).

69 16 C.F.R. § 433.1(f), (g), *reprinted at* Appx. A.5.1, *infra*. *See also* Iowa Attorney General Informal Opinion Letter (May 22, 2001) (informal referral agreement qualifies), *available online as companion material to this treatise*.

70 Brown v. LaSalle Northwest Nat'l Bank, 820 F. Supp. 1078 (N.D. Ill. 1993).

71 16 C.F.R. § 433.1(c), *reprinted at* Appx. A.5.1, *infra*.

72 *Id.*

73 *See* National Consumer Law Center, Truth in Lending § 7.11 (8th ed. 2015), *updated at* www.nclc.org/library.

74 Fed. Trade Comm'n, Staff Guidelines, 41 Fed. Reg. 20,024 (May 14, 1976) (financing a sale), *available online as companion material to this treatise*.

75 Fed. Trade Comm'n, Staff Guidelines, 41 Fed. Reg. 20,025 (May 14, 1976) (purchase money loans), *available online as companion material to this treatise*.

76 Fed. Trade Comm'n, Staff Guidelines, 41 Fed. Reg. 20,022 (May 14, 1976), *available online as companion material to this treatise*.

77 *Id.*

78 16 C.F.R. § 433.1(e).

79 15 U.S.C. § 1602(e), (f), (g); 12 C.F.R. § 1026.2(a)(14), (16), (17) [§ 226.2(a)(14), (16), (17)].

Act and Regulation Z."[80] Finance charge is defined in Regulation Z as the cost of consumer credit as a dollar amount. Again, neither Regulation Z's definitions of consumer, consumer credit, or finance charge in any way refer to a dollar limit.[81]

Instead, the TILA has a separate section that exempts certain transactions from the scope of the Act. One of these exemptions applies to certain transactions presently with an amount financed over $54,600.[82] This amount is increased annually for inflation.[83] This exemption in no way refers to finance charges or the term "credit sale."[84] The exemption does not state that transactions over $54,600 are not credit sales or do not have finance charges. It simply states that the TILA requirements are not applicable to that form of credit.

Why the TILA excludes large transactions in an exemption section and not in the definition of finance charge and credit sale is obvious. Clearly a credit sale over $54,600 still involves a seller who is a creditor. A loan over $54,600 still has a finance charge. In fact, it has a larger finance charge, on average, than a smaller loan. Transactions over $54,600 thus should still be covered by the FTC Holder Rule, to the extent to which they have finance charges or are credit sales within the TILA's definitions.

There is no indication that the FTC, in adopting the FTC Holder Rule, was seeking to make the scope of that rule exactly the same as the scope of the TILA. Instead, the FTC was only adopting definitions found in the TILA as a handy reference point so that they did not have to be defined again in the FTC rule.

A dollar exemption from the FTC Holder Rule has never been announced by the full Federal Trade Commission. The exemption is found neither in the rule nor in the lengthy Commission statement of basis and purpose for the rule. Instead, the exemption is found only in one 1976 staff interpretation.

Such staff statements are not binding on the commission and may not reflect the views of the commission. The statements are certainly not binding on a court. A court should not give credence to a staff statement so patently incorrect as not to even accurately track the TILA's exemption language,[85] nor which

fails to explain how an exemption from TILA's scope has any relevance as to how credit sale and finance charge are defined in the TILA.

4.2.2.8 Implications If Rule Does Not Apply to Loans Exempted from Truth in Lending

As the prior subsection indicates, there is no merit in the argument that the Holder rule applies only to loans under a dollar threshold. Moreover, when the Holder language is actually placed in credit documents for a loan exceeding the dollar threshold, the scope of the FTC Holder Rule becomes irrelevant. The credit agreement as a matter of contract law states that the holder is subject to all seller-related claims, whether or not the FTC Holder Rule applies to the transaction.[86]

In addition, the TILA's current $54,600 exemption only applies to certain transactions and not others, so the FTC Holder Rule clearly applies to transactions not covered by that TILA exemption. An important example is that the TILA (and thus any conceivable Holder rule) exemption does not apply to credit that is secured by real property or by personal property expected to be used as the consumer's principal dwelling, even when the amount financed exceeds the dollar threshold.[87] Many home improvement loans are secured by real property and thus are within the scope of the Holder rule irrespective of any argument about a dollar threshold. The same is the case with loans taking a manufactured home or motor home as security, when the home is expected to be the consumer's principal dwelling.[88] These loans are not within the TILA exemption and thus clearly not exempt from the FTC rule.

The TILA dollar threshold also does not apply to private educational loans.[89] Consequently, there is no argument that the Holder rule only applies to private educational loans under a certain dollar amount.

Finally, the TILA exemption applies to loans whose *amount financed* exceeds $54,600. For example, if a consumer expends $63,000 on a motor vehicle, the amount financed may still be under $54,600 if more than $8,400 in down payments, trade-ins, and rebates are involved.

4.2.2.9 Student Loans

Public and truly nonprofit schools fall outside the FTC's jurisdiction and are not covered by the FTC Holder Rule.[90] Thus the FTC Notice is not required to be included in student loans for attendance at such schools.

On the one hand, there is no question that for-profit schools such as proprietary trade schools are covered by the rule when they extend credit themselves or refer the consumer to a lender who extends a private loan. Despite the existence of a number of different federal student loan programs, a growing

---

80 16 C.F.R. § 433.1(d).

81 12 C.F.R. § 1026.2(a)(11) [§ 226.2(a)(11), (12)], 1026.4(a) [226.4(a)]. *See also* 15 U.S.C. § 1605(a).

82 *See* 79 Fed. Reg. 56,483 (Sept. 22, 2014) (increasing the exemption level effective January 1, 2015).

83 Effective July 21, 2011, the exemption applied only when the amount financed exceeded $50,000. *See* 15 U.S.C. § 1603(3). *See also* 76 Fed. Reg. 18,354 (Apr. 4, 2011).

   15 U.S.C. § 1603(3) also provides that the $50,000 amount is adjusted annually for inflation. In 2012, the exemption threshold was raised to $51,800. 76 Fed. Reg. 35,722 (June 20, 2011). In 2013, the threshold was raised to $53,000. 77 Fed. Reg. 69,736 (Nov. 21 2012). In 2013, the threshold was raised to $53,000. 77 Fed. Reg. 69,736 (Nov. 21 2012). In 2014, the threshold was raised to $53,500. *See* 78 Fed. Reg. 70,194 (Nov. 25, 2013).

84 15 U.S.C. § 1603(3); 12 C.F.R. § 1026.2(a)(14), (16), (17) [§ 226.2(a)(14), (16), (17)].

85 The staff statement is clearly unaware that the TILA's $25,000 exemption does not apply to certain types of transactions and only applies to the amount financed, not to the "expenditure."

86 *See* § 4.2.1, *supra*.

87 15 U.S.C. § 1603(3); 12 C.F.R. § 1026.3(b) [§ 226.3(b)].

88 15 U.S.C. § 1603(3); 12 C.F.R. § 1026.3(b) [§ 226.3(b)].

89 National Consumer Law Center, Truth in Lending § 2.4.4 (9th ed. 2015), *updated at* www.nclc.org/library.

90 *See* § 4.2.2.5, *supra*.

number of student loans are private loans to which the FTC rule applies, as it does to other private loan involving a covered seller.

On the other hand, more complex issues arise when a for-profit school arranges a federally-backed loan, either a Federal Family Education Loan (backed by a state guaranty agency and eventually by the United States) or a Federal Direct Loan (directly made by the United States). Federal law as to the student's ability to raise school-related claims in this area involves the interplay of the FTC Holder Rule and various Department of Education regulations and pronouncements that have varied over time. This topic is discussed in detail in another NCLC treatise, *Student Loan Law*.[91]

4.3 Operation of the FTC Holder Rule

4.3.1 Seller-Related Claims Covered by the Rule

The holder of a credit agreement containing the Holder notice is liable for all seller-related "claims or defenses connected with the transaction."[92] As a result, consumers may not only raise seller-related *defenses* against creditors but also may bring *affirmative claims* against the creditor relating to the seller.[93]

The FTC rule does not limit or define what claims can be brought against the seller and hence the holder. The consumer can bring *all* claims against the holder that are available against the seller under state and other applicable law, including those relating to the advertising, oral claims, sale, warranties, insurance, service contracts, financing, collection, servicing of warranty, and anything else connected with the transaction.[94] Even though the notice mentions claims against the seller, these are not limited to claims relating to the seller's sale of a good or service but include any claims against the seller, including the seller's extension of credit and collection on the debt.

On the other hand, these claims are limited to claims the consumer has against the seller, not those against the seller's assignee or the direct lender arranged by the seller.[95] For example, if a car dealer refers the consumer to the bank and the loan is directly with the bank, the FTC Holder Notice does not allow the consumer to raise bank-related claims against the bank's assignee. But, if the loan is originated by the car dealer and assigned to the bank, then a holder is subject to the consumer's claims against the car dealer— not just for the dealer's sales practices but its financing practices as well.

Holders are liable for the consumer's claims against the seller, but not for seller-related claims based on an entirely separate transaction with the seller that does not involve the creditor—that is, "the holder's obligations are limited to those arising from the transaction which he finances."[96] For example,

---

91 National Consumer Law Center, Student Loan Law (5th ed. 2015), *updated at* www.nclc.org/library.

92 16 C.F.R. § 433.2, *reprinted at* Appx. A.5.1, *infra. See also* Scaffidi v. United Nissan, 425 F. Supp. 2d 1172 (D. Nev. 2005) (holder has no derivative liability when buyer's claims against seller lack merit), *later op. at* 2005 WL 3940287 (D. Nev. Sept. 28, 2005) (similar holding).

93 *See* § 4.3.4, *infra.*

94 Fed. Trade Comm'n, Staff Guidelines, 41 Fed. Reg. 20,024 (May 14, 1976), *available online as companion material to this treatise*; Turner v. CIT Grp./Sales Fin., Inc., 154 Fed. Appx. 2 (9th Cir. 2005) (fraud and failure of consideration claims); Barrett v. Brian Bemis Auto World, 408 F. Supp. 2d 539, 547 (N.D. Ill. 2005) ("any valid claims"); Alvizo v. Metro Ford Sales & Serv., Inc., 2001 U.S. Dist. LEXIS 21777 (N.D. Ill. Dec. 28, 2001) (holder liable for dealer's conversion of personal property in car after buyer returned it); Javorsky v. Freedom Driving Aids, Inc., 2001 U.S. Dist. LEXIS 14078 (N.D. Ill. Aug. 29, 2001); Morales v. Walker Motors Sales, Inc., 162 F. Supp. 2d 786 (S.D. Ohio 2000) (because of FTC Holder Rule, holder steps into shoes of seller); Gaddy v. Galarza Motor Sport L.T.D., 2000 U.S. Dist. LEXIS 13881 (N.D. Ill. Sept. 18, 2000) (warranty claims); Armstrong v. Edelson, 718 F. Supp. 1372 (N.D. Ill. 1989) (FTC Holder Rule applies to claims for fraud, not just contract claims); Cole v. Lovett, 672 F. Supp. 947 (S.D. Miss. 1987) (state home solicitation sales act claims), *aff'd without op.*, 833 F.2d 1008 (5th Cir. 1987); Gill v. Fidelity Fin. Services, Inc., 631 So. 2d 913 (Ala. 1993); Lafferty v. Wells Fargo Bank, 153 Cal. Rptr. 3d 240 (Cal. Ct. App. 2013); Condor Capital Corp. v. Michaud, 2000 Conn. Super. LEXIS 1894 (July 25, 2000) (RISA and UCC claims);

Ford Motor Credit Co. v. Britton, 1996 Conn. Super. LEXIS 504 (Feb. 23, 1996) (used car lemon law claims); Mitchell v. Church, 2006 WL 2194738 (Del. Super. Ct. July 31, 2006) (unpublished) (creditor steps into seller's shoes); Felde v. Chrysler Credit Corp., 580 N.E.2d 191 (Ill. App. Ct. 1991) (warranty breach); First Homestead Fed. Sav. & Loan v. Boudreaux, 450 So. 2d 995 (La. Ct. App. 1984) (buyer can assert contractual arbitration requirement against assignee); GMAC v. Johnson, 426 So. 2d 691 (La. Ct. App. 1982) (warranty claims); Aillet v. Century Fin. Co., 391 So. 2d 895 (La. Ct. App. 1980) (nonperformance of seller's obligations grounds for return of amounts paid); First of Am. Bank v. Thompson, 552 N.W.2d 516, 520 (Mich. Ct. App. 1996) (by virtue of FTC Holder Notice, assignee steps into shoes of seller and is subject to all claims and defenses as seller would have been, including statute of limitations); Jerry v. Second Nat'l Bank, 527 N.W.2d 788 (Mich. Ct. App. 1994) (applying provision of Michigan law nearly identical to FTC Holder Rule and finding that buyer's claims and defenses arose out of the transaction); Green Tree Consumer Discount Co. v. Newton, 909 A.2d 811 (Pa. Super. Ct. 2006) (claims of substandard home improvement work and fraud); Alduridi v. Community Trust Bank, 1999 Tenn. App. LEXIS 718 (Tenn. Ct. App. Oct. 26, 1999) (consumer can raise against assignee claims against the dealer relating to the dealer's failure to pay off consumer's obligations on trade-in vehicles; this is not a separate transaction from the consumer's purchase of new vehicles from the dealer). *Cf.* Provident Bank v. Barnhart, 445 N.E.2d 746 (Ohio Ct. App. 1982) (issue of fact whether claim connected with the credit transaction). *But cf.* Primus Auto Fin. Serv. v. Brown, 840 N.E.2d 254 (Ohio Ct. App. 2005) (claims against assignee are barred when res judicata bars assertion of that claim against seller); Ford Motor Credit Co. v. Dunsmore, 542 A.2d 1033 (Pa. Super. Ct. 1988) (when consumer has no cause of action against seller, consumer cannot use the FTC Holder Rule to bring action against seller's assignee).

95 Epps v. JPMorgan Chase Bank, N.A., 2010 WL 4809130 (D. Md. Nov. 19, 2010), *rev'd on other grounds*, 675 F.3d 315 (4th Cir. 2012) (reversing decision that federal banking law preempted consumer's claims).

96 Fed. Trade Comm'n, Staff Guidelines, 41 Fed. Reg. 20,024 (May 14, 1976), *available online as companion material to this treatise. But see* Jerry v. Second Nat'l Bank, 527 N.W.2d 788 (Mich. Ct. App. 1994) (applying provision of Michigan law nearly identical to FTC Holder Rule and finding that buyer's claims and defenses arose out of the transaction); Marine Midland Bank, N.A. v. Vivlamore, 185 A.D. 2d 506 (N.Y. App. Div. 1992); Alduridi v. Community Trust Bank, 1999 Tenn. App. LEXIS 718 (Tenn. Ct. App. Oct. 26, 1999) (consumer can raise assignee claims against the dealer relating to the dealer's failure

if a consumer purchases two cars from a dealer, an assignee of only one of those sales is not liable for seller-related claims concerning the other sale.[97]

A holder is subject to the seller's violation of a statute even if the statute does not apply directly to the holder.[98] For example, even if a UDAP statute exempts banks, a bank can be derivatively liable under the Holder notice for the consumer's UDAP claims against a car dealer, when the dealer is within the UDAP statute's scope.

As long as the creditor's liability is below the maximum cap under the FTC rule, the creditor should be liable for the consumer's claims against the seller, even if those claims involve consequential damages or prejudgment interest,[99] and even attorney fees and statutory, treble, and punitive damages.[100]

4.3.2 Consumer's Claims Can Offset Remainder Due on the Note

Since the FTC Holder Rule limits the consumer's recovery from the creditor for seller-related claims to the "amounts paid by the debtor hereunder,"[101] sometimes there is confusion as to whether the consumer can also offset the remainder due on the note. The FTC Holder Rule statement that "recovery hereunder by the debtor shall not exceed amounts paid by the debtor hereunder" does *not* mean that the consumer can *only* get back payments already made on the loan. It means the consumer can get back these payments *plus* cancel all remaining indebtedness under the note.

According to the FTC, the consumer can "sue to liquidate the unpaid balance owed to the creditor and to recover the amounts paid under the contract."[102] "The consumer may assert, by way of claim or defense, a right not to pay all or part of the outstanding balance owed the creditor under the contract; but the consumer will not be entitled to receive from the creditor an affirmative recovery which exceeds the amounts of money the consumer had paid in."[103] In other words, the consumer can obtain a declaration that all or part of the remaining

loan balance is unenforceable, if the consumer's claims and defenses merit such relief.[104] Likewise, if the consumer has the right under applicable law to withhold payment from the seller, the consumer may withhold payment from the assignee.[105]

In an unfortunate use of language, Ohio's highest court has stated that the consumer could offset against the amount due the amount the consumer paid on the loan and not the amount of the consumer's damage.[106] In that case, the two amounts were identical, and the court's mistaken language had no impact on the consumer's rights. But the language is clearly wrong and may cause confusion for other courts, particularly those in Ohio.

If taken literally, this language in the Ohio case would mean that if a consumer has not yet paid the lender anything, then the consumer has no rights under the FTC Holder Notice to offset the amount due by the consumer's damages. This is clearly not the FTC's intent nor interpretation, as described above. If it were, then the FTC Holder Notice would actually give the consumer less rights than are available under the UCC and common law, when an assignee is subject to all defenses that can be raised against the assignor.

4.3.3 Effect on Security Interest

In the typical consumer transaction, the entity that financed the sale will have a security interest in the items purchased and possibly other property as well. If the consumer has claims or defenses that offset the entire debt, then there is no longer any obligation for the collateral to secure. In this event, the secured party has a duty under UCC Article 9 to document that the security interest has terminated.[107] Likewise, if the consumer's claims reduce the amount of the debt, the collateral secures only the reduced obligation, and the creditor must file a termination statement once the consumer pays the reduced amount.

---

to pay off consumer's obligations on trade-in vehicles; this is not a separate transaction from the consumer's purchase of new vehicles from the dealer).

97 *Cf.* Mercer v. Tumbleson Auto. Grp., 2013 WL 827716 (Ill. App. Ct. Mar. 5, 2013) (consumer cannot use right to sue lender for first-seller-related claims in order to sue the lender for second-seller-related claims).

98 Reagans v. Mountainhigh Coachworks, Inc., 881 N.E.2d 245 (Ohio 2008); Pratt v. North Dixie Manufactured Hous., Ltd., 2003 WL 21040658 (Ohio Ct. App. May 9, 2003); Nations Credit v. Pheanis, 656 N.E.2d 998 (Ohio Ct. App. 1995); Milchen v. Bob Morris Pontiac-GMC Truck, 680 N.E.2d 698 (Ohio Ct. App. 1996).

99 Houser v. Diamond Corp., 125 Wash. App. 1009 (Wash Ct. App. 2005) (text, table at 2005 WL 94452).

100 *See* §§ 4.3.5, 4.3.6, *infra*.

101 16 C.F.R. § 433.2, *reprinted at* Appx. A.5.1, *infra*.

102 Fed. Trade Comm'n, Staff Guidelines, 41 Fed. Reg. 20,023 (May 14, 1976), *available online as companion material to this treatise*.

103 *Id. See also* Letter from Fed. Trade Comm'n to Jonathan Sheldon & Carolyn Carter, National Consumer Law Center (May 3, 2012), *reprinted at* Appx. A.5.2, *infra*.

104 Ellis v. Gen. Motors Acceptance Corp., 160 F.3d 703, 709 (11th Cir. 1998) (Holder Notice gives buyer right to withhold payment if car is a lemon); Ransom v. Rohr-Gurnee Volkswagen, Inc., 2001 U.S. Dist. LEXIS 17363 (N.D. Ill. Oct. 22, 2001) (FTC Holder Notice gives buyer the right to withhold payment if a car is a lemon); Mount v. LaSalle Bank Lake View, 926 F. Supp. 759 (N.D. Ill. 1996); Music Acceptance Corp. v. Lofing, 39 Cal. Rptr. 2d 159 (Cal. Ct. App. 1995); Tinker v. DeMaria Porsche Audi, Inc., 459 So. 2d 487 (Fla. Dist. Ct. App. 1984); Jackson v. South Holland Dodge, Inc., 755 N.E.2d 462 (Ill. 2001) (FTC Holder Notice gives buyer right to withhold payment if car is a lemon); Ford Motor Credit Co. v. Morgan, 536 N.E.2d 587 (Mass. 1989); Perez v. Briercroft Serv. Corp., 809 S.W.2d 216 (Tex. 1991); Home Sav. Ass'n v. Guerra, 733 S.W.2d 134 (Tex. 1987); Reliance Mortg. Co. v. Hill-Shields, 2001 Tex. App. LEXIS 140 (Tex. App. Jan. 10, 2001); Oxford Fin. Cos. v. Velez, 807 S.W.2d 460 (Tex. App. 1991); Green Tree Acceptance, Inc. v. Pierce, 768 S.W.2d 416 (Tex. App. 1989); Alvarez v. Union Mortg. Co., 747 S.W.2d 484 (Tex. App. 1988). *See also* Tinker v. DeMaria Porsche Audi, Inc., 459 So. 2d 487 (Fla. Dist. Ct. App. 1984); Shelter Am. Corp. v. Edwards, 1987 Tex. App. LEXIS 7954 (July 30, 1987). *Cf.* Briercroft Serv. Corp. v. De Los Santos, 776 S.W.2d 198 (Tex. App. 1988).

105 FTC Advisory Op., 89 F.T.C. 675 (Apr. 6, 1977).

106 Reagans v. Mountainhigh Coachworks, Inc., 881 N.E.2d 245 (Ohio 2008).

107 U.C.C. § 9-513.

The consumer also has the right to deduct damages for breach of contract from the payments owing on the debt.[108]

Some courts have had difficulty with the analysis in the situation when the consumer revokes acceptance of the goods. Under UCC Article 2, after revoking acceptance and canceling the sale, the consumer no longer owes any part of the purchase price to the seller.[109] Further, Article 2 gives the consumer a security interest in the goods until the seller refunds the purchase price and reimburses the consumer for the expenses reasonably incurred in inspecting, receiving, transporting, caring for, and holding the goods.[110]

Properly analyzed, the FTC Holder Rule places the assignee or related lender in exactly the same shoes as the seller: because of the revocation of acceptance and cancellation of the sale, the consumer's obligation to pay for the goods is cancelled, so there is no obligation for the collateral to secure.[111] Since the assignee or related lender is subject to the same revocation claims as the dealer, the consumer owes no money and cannot be in default. As the FTC stated in a formal opinion letter soon after the FTC Holder Rule was adopted: "if the consumer, under applicable law, is entitled to withhold payments from the seller, he may, pursuant to the notice, withhold payment from the holder."[112] The consumer has the right to retain possession of the collateral until any payments and expenses are refunded.

While courts accept this analysis,[113] some Illinois courts have confused the issue with an analysis of UCC Article 9's rules regarding the priority among competing security interests.[114] This approach is wrong, because after revocation both the obligation and the creditor's security interest cease to exist, so the only security interest is the consumer's.

The factor that may have troubled the Illinois courts was that the consumer's revocation of acceptance was unilateral, neither accepted by the seller or creditor nor approved by a court. But the UCC also gives creditors self-help remedies such as repossession, so the existence of a self-help remedy for consumers as against the holder is perfectly consistent with the UCC's approach. Creditors unhappy with the consumer's revocation can always challenge it in court. Nonetheless, courts are more likely to accept the effect of the FTC Holder Rule on the creditor's security interest if the consumer is seeking or has obtained a court ruling upholding the claim or defense against the creditor.

4.3.4 Recovery of Amounts Already Paid
4.3.4.1 General

In addition to canceling under the FTC Holder Rule all or part of the remaining indebtedness, the consumer can seek an affirmative cash recovery.[115] In practice, in individual cases, the consumer's claim is usually applied first to reduce the indebtedness the consumer owes the holder. If the consumer's claim exceeds this amount, then the consumer can recover the difference affirmatively from the holder.[116]

The rule limits the consumer's affirmative recovery to the amount the consumer has already "paid in."[117] In other words, the consumer's maximum recovery under the rule is cancellation of all remaining indebtedness plus an affirmative recovery of the amount already paid in on the debt.

---

108 U.C.C. § 2-717. *See* National Consumer Law Center, Consumer Warranty Law § 8.5 (5th ed. 2015), *updated at* www.nclc.org/library.

109 U.C.C. § 2-711.

110 U.C.C. § 2-711(3).

111 *See* Third Nat'l Bank v. Imperial Auto Auction, 1989 WL 128488 (Tenn. Ct. App. Oct. 24, 1989).

112 Advisory Opinion, 89 F.T.C. 675, 1977 FTC LEXIS 233 (Apr. 6, 1977). *Accord* Ellis v. GMAC, 160 F.3d 703, 709 (11th Cir. 1998) (FTC Holder Notice "affirms the right of buyers to withhold payment from sellers *or* assignees, if the cars they purchase turn out to be lemons"); Ransom v. Rohr-Gurnee Volkswagen, Inc., 2001 U.S. Dist. LEXIS 17363 (N.D. Ill. Oct. 22, 2001); Jackson v. South Holland Dodge, 755 N.E.2d 462 (Ill. 2001) (erroneously confining affirmative actions against assignees to those when seller's breach is so substantial that rescission is warranted, but confirming the right to withhold payment from the assignee if a car is a lemon).

113 Ford Motor Credit Co. v. Caiazzo, 564 A.2d 931 (Pa. Super. Ct. 1989); Third Nat'l Bank v. Imperial Auto Auction, 1989 WL 128488 (Tenn. Ct. App. Oct. 24, 1989). *See also* Jackson v. South Holland Dodge, Inc., 755 N.E.2d 462 (Ill. 2001).

114 Ambre v. Joe Madden Ford, 881 F. Supp. 1182 (N.D. Ill. 1995); Valentino v. Glendale Nissan, Inc., 740 N.E.2d 538 (Ill. App. Ct. 2000).

115 Wales v. Ariz. RV Centers, L.L.C., 2015 WL 137260 (E.D. La. Jan. 9, 2015); Diaz v. Paragon Motors of Woodside, Inc., 424 F. Supp. 2d 519, 544 (E.D.N.Y. 2006) ("any claim which could be asserted against Paragon may be asserted against Americredit"); Gonzalez v. Old Kent Mortg. Co., 2000 WL 1469313 (E.D. Pa. Sept. 21, 2000); Boggess v. Lewis Raines Motors, Inc., 20 F. Supp. 2d 979 (S.D. W. Va. 1998) (allowing used-car buyer to assert claims against assignee arising from seller's misrepresentation of car's mileage); Maberry v. Said, 911 F. Supp. 1393 (D. Kan. 1995); Cole v. Lovett, 672 F. Supp. 947 (S.D. Miss. 1987) (FTC Holder Notice makes assignee liable for homeowner's claim under home solicitation sales law against contractor), *aff'd without op.*, 833 F.2d 1008 (5th Cir. 1987); Eachen v. Scott Hous. Sys., Inc., 630 F. Supp. 162 (M.D. Ala. 1986); Tinker v. De Maria Porsche Audi, Inc., 459 So. 2d 487 (Fla. Dist. Ct. App. 1984); Bennett v. D.L. Claborn Buick, Inc., 414 S.E.2d 12 (Ga. Ct. App. 1991); Taylor v. Trans Acceptance Corp., 641 N.E.2d 907 (Ill. App. Ct. 1994) (consumer can assert fraud claims against assignee); Ross v. Thousand Adventures of Iowa, Inc., 723 N.W.2d 449 (Iowa Ct. App. 2006) (text, table at 2006 WL 1896288, at *6) (rule "clearly preserves all of a borrower's causes of action and defenses such that they can be asserted against an assignee just as they could be asserted against the original party to the contract," but assignee does not step into shoes of assignor for purposes of long-arm jurisdiction analysis); Thomas v. Ford Motor Credit Co., 429 A.2d 277 (Md. Ct. Spec. App. 1981); Ford Motor Credit Co. v. Morgan, 536 N.E.2d 587 (Mass. 1989); Scott v. Mayflower Home Improvement Corp., 831 A.2d 564 (N.J. Super. Ct. App. Div. 2001); Hempstead Bank v. Babcock, 453 N.Y.S.2d 557 (N.Y. Sup. Ct. 1982); Letter from Fed. Trade Comm'n to Jonathan Sheldon & Carolyn Carter, National Consumer Law Center (May 3, 2012), *reprinted at* Appx. A.5.2, *infra*. *See also* Rosemond v. Campbell, 343 S.E.2d 641, 645 (S.C. Ct. App. 1986) (state law that requires same contract language as FTC Holder Rule subjects assignee to affirmative claims, not just defenses).

116 Hanes v. Darar, 722 S.E.2d 211 (table) (recover only amount paid in, not all amounts claimed). *Cf.* Schauer v. GMAC, 819 So. 2d 809 (Fla. Dist. Ct. App. 2002) (no affirmative recovery when did not allege claim exceeded amount still owed the creditor).

117 *See also* Resolution Trust Corp. v. Cook, 840 S.W.2d 42 (Tex. App. 1992); Oxford Fin. Cos. v. Velez, 807 S.W.2d 460 (Tex. App. 1991).

In calculating the amounts paid in, add both the amounts the consumer paid to the note holder and any amount paid to a prior holder of the note. The fact that a holder never received any money from the consumer is no defense to a judgment against that holder for amounts paid to other holders.[118] The FTC has made clear that the holder is in much better position than the consumer, through use of reserve and recourse arrangements, to easily recover any amounts owed from the holder's assignor.[119] While the holder can easily recover that amount paid to a prior holder, it may be practically impossible for the consumer to do so.

When a credit sales contract is assigned to a creditor, the amount paid in by the consumer includes all deposits and trade-ins the consumer has given to the seller.[120] The consumer can thus recover affirmatively all periodic payments and late charges paid either to the seller or an assignee and also the total amount of the consumer's down payment and the value of the trade-in. In determining the value of the trade-in, utilize the amount stated in the contract, even if the holder argues that this valuation was inflated.[121] After all, this is the value the parties agreed to after negotiation.

The amount paid in on a direct loan is calculated differently. This is the amount paid to the originating lender and all subsequent assignees. Since in this type of loan, the trade-in and down payments go to the dealer, and not the originating lender, these amounts given to the *seller* are *not* amounts paid to the creditor.

For example, in a credit sale, if a consumer makes a $1000 down payment and trades in a car for a $3000 credit and then purchases a $10,000 car, the amount financed will be $6000. Assume $15,000 in damages. The consumer, in an action against the seller's assignee, can seek a maximum of: (1) cancellation of the remaining indebtedness on the $6000 loan;

plus (2) an affirmative recovery of monthly installment payments already paid to the dealer or assignee; *plus* (3) the $4000 trade-in and down payment. If this were a direct loan from a related creditor, the remainder of the $6000 loan would be canceled and amounts paid the creditor could be returned, but the consumer could not recover the $4000 trade-in and down payment.

A creditor's maximum liability should also include the price which the creditor realizes when it sells collateral after repossession. This sale price reduces the size of the indebtedness and, in effect, is a payment on the loan. It should be treated as "an amount paid hereunder," and the creditor's maximum liability should include this amount.[122]

4.3.4.2   Recovering from a Prior Holder

In some cases, the consumer will want to bring into an action the prior holder and seek to recover from this intermediary holder for the seller's misconduct. There is little case law in this area, but the decisions that do exist hold that the consumer can bring seller-related claims against intermediate holders.[123]

4.3.4.3   Is Recovery of Amount Paid Only Available When Consumer Could Rescind the Sale?

4.3.4.3.1   Courts that get it wrong

Although the FTC rule clearly states that consumers can recover on their claims all amounts the consumer has already paid, a number of courts have found otherwise.[124] These courts

---

118 Green Tree Acceptance, Inc. v. Pirtle, 1999 WL 33740367 (E.D. Mich. Mar. 1, 1999) (buyer may recover down payment from assignee even though assignee did not receive it); *In re* Four Star Fin. Services, Inc., 444 B.R. 428 (Bankr. C.D. Cal. 2011), *vacated on other grounds*, 469 B.R. 30 (C.D. Cal. 2012) (addressing question of priority that claim should be given in bankruptcy case); Alduridi v. Community Trust Bank, 1999 Tenn. App. LEXIS 718 (Tenn. Ct. App. Oct. 26, 1999) (creditor, not the consumer should bear the risk of recovering payments made to the dealer); Resolution Trust Corp. v. Cook, 840 S.W.2d 42 (Tex. App. 1992).

119 *See* § 4.1.1, *supra.*

120 Green Tree Acceptance, Inc. v. Pirtle, 1999 WL 33740367 (E.D. Mich. Mar. 1, 1999); Maberry v. Said, 911 F. Supp. 1393 (D. Kan. 1995); Featherlite Credit Corp. v. Caride, 2000 Del. Super. LEXIS 206 (Del. Super. Ct. May 30, 2000); Credit Acceptance Corp. v. Banks, 1999 Ohio App. LEXIS 6058 (Ohio Ct. App. Dec. 16, 1999); Credit Acceptance Corp. v. Smith, 1997 WL 823562 (Ohio Mun. Ct. of Vandalia July 31, 1997); Fed. Trade Comm'n, Staff Guidelines, 41 Fed. Reg. 20,023 (May 14, 1976), *available online as companion material to this treatise. But see* Gen. Motors Acceptance Corp. v. Grady, 501 N.E.2d 68 (Ohio Ct. App. 1985) (without discussion, court grants judgment against assignee only in amount of monthly payment, not in amount of down payment; consumer had requested judgment only in this amount).

121 Featherlite Credit Corp. v. Caride, 2000 Del. Super. LEXIS 206 (Del. Super. Ct. May 30, 2000).

122 Alduridi v. Community Trust Bank, 1999 Tenn. App. LEXIS 718 (Tenn. Ct. App. Oct. 26, 1999). *See also* BCS Fin. Corp. v. Sorbo, 444 S.E.2d 85 (Ga. Ct. App. 1994). *But cf.* Oxford Fin. Cos. v. Velez, 807 S.W.2d 460 (Tex. App. 1991) (proceeds of foreclosure sale not recoverable when court voids the foreclosure sale).

123 *In re* Barker, 306 B.R. 339, 350–351 (Bankr. E.D. Cal. 2004) (assignor's repurchase of debt does not relieve assignee of liability); Associates Home Equity Services, Inc. v. Troup, 778 A.2d 529 (N.J. Super. Ct. App. Div. 2001); Resolution Trust Corp. v. Cook, 840 S.W.2d 42 (Tex. App. 1992).

124 Dufour v. Be L.L.C., 2010 WL 2560409 (N.D. Cal. June 22, 2010); Phillips v. Lithia Motors, Inc., 2006 WL 1113608, at *18 (D. Or. Apr. 27, 2006); Costa v. Mauro Chevrolet, Inc., 390 F. Supp. 2d 720, 736–737 (N.D. Ill. 2005); Comer v. Person Auto Sales, Inc., 368 F. Supp. 2d 478 (M.D.N.C. 2005) (magistrate judge); Herrara v. North & Kimball Grp., Inc., 2002 U.S. Dist. LEXIS 2640 (N.D. Ill. Feb. 15, 2002) (also seeming to indicate that forgery of contract is insufficient to warrant rescission); Crews v. Altavista Motors, Inc., 65 F. Supp. 4 388 (W.D. Va. 1999); Boggess v. Lewis Raines Motors, Inc., 20 F. Supp. 2d 979 (S.D. W. Va. 1998); Taylor v. Bob O'Connor Ford, Inc., 1998 U.S. Dist. LEXIS 5095 (N.D. Ill. Apr. 10, 1998); Mount v. LaSalle Bank Lake View, 926 F. Supp. 759 (N.D. Ill. 1996); *In re* Hillsborough Holdings Corp., 146 B.R. 1015 (Bankr. M.D. Fla. 1992); Mardis v. Ford Motor Credit Co., 642 So. 2d 701 (Ala. 1994); Bellik v. Bank of Am., 869 N.E.2d 1179 (Ill. App. Ct. 2007); Felde v. Chrysler Credit Corp., 580 N.E.2d 191 (Ill. App. Ct. 1991); Ford Motor Credit Co. v. Morgan, 536 N.E.2d 587 (Mass. 1989). *See also* Barrett v. Brian Bemis Auto World, 408 F. Supp. 2d 539 (N.D. Ill. 2005) (citing other Illinois decision that consumer must be entitled to rescission but finding that this consumer met this standard); Dees v. Bob

acknowledge that consumers in a collection action can raise defenses cancelling the remainder of the amount due and that they can sue affirmatively both to cancel the amount due and (at least in certain situations) to recover affirmatively. But these courts hold that consumers can only sue to recover the amount already paid when the consumer could rescind the sale or the goods or services have little or no value.

These courts reach this strange result based on a misinterpretation of two statements by the FTC in the rule's statement of basis and purpose, to the effect that a consumer will obtain a positive recovery from the creditor only when the consumer rescinds or has received little or nothing of value.[125] These cases misconstrue these quotations as setting up a *legal* requirement that the consumer can recover affirmatively against a creditor only if the claim is for rescission or when the product has little or no value.

Instead, the quotations simply make the obvious *practical* point that consumers will only recover affirmatively when their claims are serious enough to exceed the remainder of the debt owed.[126] For example, the FTC staff at the time stated: "The vast majority of cases, in the staff's opinion, will involve a limited right of set-off against the unpaid balance. Most sellers do not do business in a way that creates a right to rescission or significant consequential damages."[127]

The FTC is observing that consumers cannot receive an affirmative recovery until their claims are so large that the claims first wipe out the remainder of the debt. Then the claims can be used to obtain a positive recovery, capped by the amount the consumer has already paid on the loan.

4.3.4.3.2 Full Federal Trade Commission clarifies that these courts are wrong

In 2012, in response to a request for an advisory opinion, the full commission stated:

Thus the Commission affirms the plain language of the Holder Rule and the intent of the Rule as discussed in the entire SBP [Statement of Basis and Purpose]. Specifically, the Rule places no limits on a consumer's right to an affirmative recovery other than the limiting recovery to a refund of monies paid under the contract. Further, the Rule does not limit affirmative recovery only to those circumstances in which rescission is warranted or when the goods or services sold to the consumer are worthless.[128]

Courts must give great weight not only to this FTC interpretation of its own rule, but even more so to its interpretation of its own *Statement of Basis and Purpose*—who better to determine what was meant by a statement than the entity that said it.[129]

This opinion from the full commission re-affirms a 1999 FTC staff interpretation that also explicitly stated that courts limiting affirmative recovery incorrectly interpret the FTC rule and the FTC's language from the statement of basis and purpose.[130] The FTC letter, like the 2012 opinion from the full commission, stated that the FTC's statement of basis and purpose was merely making the practical point that an affirmative recovery requires a consumer claim large enough to first fully satisfy the remainder due on the debt before the consumer is entitled to a positive recovery. The FTC Staff Letter states that "the provision is quite clear. The consumer may recover his or her down payment (all deposits and trade-ins given to the seller) and all installment payments made pursuant to the contract, but no more. There are no other limitations on the creditor/assignee's liability under the required contract language."

The Holder rule itself indicates that holders are subject to *all* claims and in no way limits such claims to those for rescission or those for which the product has no value.[131]

> Moreover, to allow affirmative recovery only when a product has little or no value or when the claim is for "rescission" is too vague a standard to be administered. The FTC rule provides no guidance because there was no intent by the FTC to make this distinction.

This distinction also lacks any rational basis for its different treatment of consumers with identical claims. It makes no sense to allow one consumer to recover for the claim by deducting its amount from the amount due on the contract but to prevent affirmative recovery for the identical claim because

---

O'Connor Ford, Inc., 1995 WL 441629 (N.D. Ill. July 20, 1995) (agreeing with view that affirmative recovery is available only if consumer could rescind, but here consumer's allegations would justify rescission). *Cf.* Rollins v. Drive-1 of Norfolk, Inc., 2006 WL 2519516 (E.D. Va. Aug. 29, 2006) (although FTC commentary stated that affirmative relief is only available when rescission and restitution are justified, "the plain meaning of the FTC Holder Rule cannot be ignored"; plaintiff may be entitled to affirmative relief if she proves that car with malfunctioning odometer was worth significantly less than price she paid for it), *later op. at* 2007 WL 602089 (E.D. Va. Feb. 21, 2007) (granting creditor's motion for summary judgment; reduction in car's value not significant enough to allow affirmative relief against creditor).

125 *See* 40 Fed. Reg. 53,524, 53,527 (Nov. 18, 1975).

126 *See* Lozada v. Dale Baker Oldsmobile, 91 F. Supp. 2d 1087 (W.D. Mich. 2000); Beemus v. Interstate Nat'l Dealer Services, Inc., 823 A.2d 979 (Pa. Super. Ct. 2003); Oxford Fin. Cos. v. Velez, 807 S.W.2d 460 (Tex. App. 1991); M. Greenfield & N. Ross, *Limits on a Consumer's Ability to Assert Claims and Defenses Under the FTC's Holder in Due Course Rule*, 46 Bus. Law. 1135 (May 1991).

127 Fed. Trade Comm'n, Staff Guidelines, 41 Fed. Reg. 20,024 (May 14, 1976), *available online as companion material to this treatise.*

128 Letter from Fed. Trade Comm'n to Jonathan Sheldon and Carolyn Carter, National Consumer Law Center (May 3, 2012), *reprinted at* Appx. A.5.2, *infra.*

129 *See* Ford Motor Credit Co. v. Milhollin, 444 U.S. 555 (1980) (courts should show deference to FRB interpretations of Truth in Lending); Lozada v. Dale Baker Oldsmobile, 91 F. Supp. 2d 1087, 1096 (W.D. Mich. 2000) (citing Medine letter as part of analysis rejecting *Morgan*).

130 Letter from David Medine, Assoc. Director, Div. of Financial Practices, to Jonathan Sheldon, National Consumer Law Center (Sept. 25, 1999), *available online as companion material to this treatise.*

131 *See* Lozada v. Dale Baker Oldsmobile, 91 F. Supp. 2d 1087, 1094 (W.D. Mich. 2000); Simpson v. Anthony Auto Sales, Inc., 32 F. Supp. 2d 405 (W.D. La. 1998); Beemus v. Interstate Nat'l Dealer Services, Inc., 823 A.2d 979 (Pa. Super. Ct. 2003) (language of rule is unambiguous, so no need to refer to statement of basis and purpose); Oxford Fin. Cos. v. Velez, 807 S.W.2d 460 (Tex. App. 1991).

a second consumer has already paid off almost all or all of the debt.[132]

4.3.4.3.3 Courts that get it right

A combination of the 1999 FTC staff letter and a growing understanding among courts of the issues involved has produced an impressive array of cases that reject limits on affirmative recovery (other than those explicit in the rule).[133] It is hoped that the 2012 opinion from the full commission will result in future decisions ruling correctly on this issue.

4.3.4.3.4 Consumer tactics if a court still gets it wrong

There are a number of tactics that a consumer should pursue if a court ignores the 2012 full commission opinion and limits the consumer's affirmative recovery to cases in which the consumer could rescind the contract or in which the goods or services are worthless. The consumer should point out that the cases only require, for the consumer to recover affirmatively, that rescission be an available remedy in the facts of the case, not that the consumer must in fact have exercised the right to rescind the transaction.[134] If the court adopts this approach, then it is often easy for the consumer to show that the transaction could have been rescinded based on the seller's misrepresentation or because of substantial defects in the goods leading to revocation of acceptance. For example, one court found that fraudulent misrepresentation of odometer mileage is sufficient to justify rescission and restitution. Thus, the consumers could recover affirmatively from the holder.[135]

Another approach, if a court insists on ignoring the 2012 FTC opinion, is to bring a claim under a state statute that makes lenders derivatively liable for a related seller's misconduct.[136] The FTC has explicitly stated that state law is preserved when it would provide a greater consumer recovery against a lender than is provided for by the FTC Holder Rule.[137] If a court were to determine that the state law provides for an affirmative consumer recovery, then that should be allowed despite any contrary interpretation the court might have under the FTC rule.

4.3.4.4 Is Recovery of Amounts Paid Available Only When Otherwise Permitted By State Law?

In *LaBarre v. Credit Acceptance Corp.*,[138] the Eighth Circuit seriously misinterpreted the operation of the FTC Holder Rule. It held that Minnesota law should decide when consumers under the FTC Holder Rule can raise seller-related claims against assignees. Relying on a Minnesota statute that limits a consumer to raising defenses, not claims, against an assignee, the court came to the conclusion that the FTC Holder Rule does not allow affirmative recovery for cases brought in Minnesota. This conclusion by the Eighth Circuit is clearly wrong, as explained in detail at § 4.3.11.2, *infra*. State law limits what state law claims the consumer can bring against the seller, not which valid seller-related claims can be brought under the federal Holder rule against the obligation's holder. Since its issuance in 1999, *LaBarre* has not been followed by any court, nor should it be.[139]

4.3.5 Are Attorney Fees Limited by the Cap?

There is significant consensus that a consumer's recovery against a creditor for seller-related claims can include attorney

---

132 For a similar critique of *Morgan*, see M. Greenfield & N. Ross, Limits on a Consumer's Ability to Assert Claims and Defenses Under the FTC's Holder in Due Course Rule, 46 Bus. Law. 1135 (May 1991).

133 Gonzalez v. Old Kent Mortg. Co., 2000 WL 1469313 (E.D. Pa. Sept. 21, 2000); Lozada v. Dale Baker Oldsmobile, 91 F. Supp. 2d 1087 (W.D. Mich. 2000) (citing FTC staff letter); Riggs v. Anthony Auto Sales, Inc., 32 F. Supp. 2d 411 (W.D. La. 1998); Simpson v. Anthony Auto Sales, Inc., 32 F. Supp. 2d 405 (W.D. La. 1998); Maberry v. Said, 911 F. Supp. 1393 (D. Kan. 1995) (FTC Holder Rule permits affirmative claims); Lafferty v. Wells Fargo Bank, 153 Cal. Rptr. 3d 240 (Cal. Ct. App. 2013); Scott v. Mayflower Home Improvement Corp., 831 A.2d 564 (N.J. Super. Ct. Law Div. 2001); Jaramillo v. Gonzales, 50 P.3d 554 (N.M. Ct. App. 2002) (purchaser of manufactured home is not required to show that home had little or no value in order to recover affirmatively); Beemus v. Interstate Nat'l Dealer Services, Inc., 823 A.2d 979 (Pa. Super. Ct. 2003) (citing FTC staff letter); Homziak v. Gen. Elec. Capital Warranty Corp., Clearinghouse No. 54,551 (Pa. Ct. Com. Pl. May 21, 2001); Resolution Trust Corp. v. Cook, 840 S.W.2d 42 (Tex. App. 1992); Oxford Fin. Cos. v. Velez, 807 S.W.2d 460 (Tex. App. 1991); M. Greenfield & N. Ross, *Limits on a Consumer's Ability to Assert Claims and Defenses Under the FTC's Holder in Due Course Rule*, 46 Bus. Law. 1135 (May 1991). *See also* State *ex rel.* Stenberg v. Consumers' Choice Foods, 755 N.W.2d 583 (Neb. 2008) (state can recover from the lender $96,000 paid to seller). *Cf.* Reagans v. Mountainhigh Coachworks, Inc., 881 N.E.2d 245 (Ohio 2008) (seeming to assume that the consumer could receive a positive recovery); Shelter Am. Corp. v. Edwards, 1987 Tex. App. LEXIS 7954 (July 30, 1987) (allowing consumer recovery when *Morgan* reasoning would deny affirmative recovery).

134 Eromon v. Grand Auto Sales, Inc., 333 F. Supp. 2d 702 (N.D. Ill. 2004) (claim may be asserted against assignee if consumer would have been unlikely to enter into contract in absence of dealer's wrongdoing); Reavley v. Toyota Motor Sales U.S. Corp., 2001 WL 127662, at *4 (N.D. Ill. Feb. 14, 2001) (express claim of rescission is not required as long as breach was so substantial as to justify rescission). *See also* Boggess v. Lewis Raines Motors, Inc., 20 F. Supp. 2d 979 (S.D. W. Va. 1998); M. Greenfield & N. Ross, *Limits on a Consumer's Ability to Assert Claims and Defenses Under the FTC's Holder in Due Course Rule*, 46 Bus. Law. 1135 (May 1991).

135 Boggess v. Lewis Raines Motors, Inc., 20 F. Supp. 2d 979 (S.D. W. Va. 1998). *Accord* Barrett v. Brian Bemis Auto World, 408 F. Supp. 2d 539 (N.D. Ill. 2005); Eromon v. Grand Auto Sales, Inc., 333 F. Supp. 2d 702 (N.D. Ill. 2004). *See also* Alarcon v. Fireside Bank, 2010 WL 769690 (Cal. Ct. App. Mar. 8, 2010); Dees v. Bob O'Connor Ford, Inc., 1995 WL 441629 (N.D. Ill. July 20, 1995) (car's serious transmission and brake problems, making it unsafe to drive, and sale of it as new when it had previously been sold would justify rescission, so claims can be asserted against assignee). *But see* Rollins v. Drive-1 of Norfolk, Inc., 2007 WL 602089 (E.D. Va. Feb. 21, 2007) (when no evidence that transaction could be rescinded and when only evidence of loss of value indicated about 20% loss, not sufficient to show purchase was worthless).

136 Such state statutes are examined at § 4.5, *infra*.

137 *See* § 4.3.11, *infra*.

138 175 F.3d 640 (8th Cir. 1999).

139 *See* § 4.3.11.2, *infra*.

fees.[140] Ohio UDAP attorney fees are an exception to this rule, based on the fact that UDAP fees are available in Ohio only in the court's discretion and only against sellers who intentionally violate the statute.[141]

In jurisdictions other than Ohio, the issue is not whether attorney fees can be awarded but whether they can be awarded in excess of the FTC Holder Rule's cap. For example, if a consumer's affirmative recovery is capped under the Holder rule at $3000, and the consumer has over $3000 in actual damages, can the consumer also recover attorney fees over and above the $3000 if the consumer's seller-related claims authorize fees for a prevailing consumer? A number of courts have found that the creditor's liability for the consumer's attorney fees should not be capped by the creditor's maximum liability for seller-related claims.[142] In the above example, the consumer would recover affirmatively $3000 in damages and also recover from the holder the consumer's reasonable attorney fees.

The consumer's right to recover the fees incurred in enforcing the creditor's liability is based on the UDAP statute, not on the Holder notice, so it is not a "recovery hereunder" that is subject to the cap. In other words, the creditor's liability for fees is not a derivative liability but is based on its own actions in refusing to resolve the consumer's claim. Attorney fees are not awarded because of the seller's conduct but because of the creditor's conduct. It is the creditor who is refusing to settle the claim and who insists on litigating the issues. Even if the creditor's UDAP liability is based on the seller's misdeeds, its liability for attorney fees is based on its own actions in litigating the claim.[143]

The purpose of attorney fees is to encourage settlement, make it economically feasible for consumers to bring small claims and to discourage sellers and creditors from using their superior legal resources to wear down the consumer. All of these purposes would be thwarted if attorney fees were lumped in with the recovery on the merits and capped at the amount of the creditor's maximum liability.[144]

The argument for recovery of attorney fees above the cap is even stronger in those states, such as California, that treat fees as costs, incidental to a judgment, not as part of damages. Since the fees are in the nature of costs, they should be awarded separately from the issue of how much in damages can be provided under the cap.

Of course, if state law or the contract provides an independent basis to recover attorney fees from the holder other than prevailing upon a seller-related claim, then the FTC Holder Rule cap does not apply to such a recovery.[145] For example, in a number of states, if a credit agreement provides attorney fees for the creditor, state law requires that such fees be available to the consumer as well. There is no cap on such fees. Such attorney fees are not based on a statute relating to the seller's misconduct, or otherwise related to the FTC Holder Rule. Instead, the fees are squarely based on the fact that the contract provides that creditor can recover attorney fees and state law requires that a prevailing consumer recover attorney fees if a prevailing creditor is so entitled.

4.3.6 Multiple or Punitive Damages

To the extent that treble or punitive damages are based on the seller's willful misconduct, most courts find that the holder should be liable for those damages, but the holder's maximum liability for those damages is capped under the FTC rule.[146]

---

140 *See* Diaz v. Paragon Motors of Woodside, Inc., 2008 WL 2004001 (E.D.N.Y. May 7, 2008); Diaz v. Paragon Motors of Woodside, Inc. 2007 WL 2903920 (E.D.N.Y. Oct. 1, 2007); Riggs v. Anthony Auto Sales, Inc., 32 F. Supp. 2d 411 (W.D. La. 1998); Simpson v. Anthony Auto Sales, Inc., 32 F. Supp. 2d 405 (W.D. La. 1998); *In re* Stewart, 93 B.R. 878 (Bankr. E.D. Pa. 1988); State v. Consumer's Choice Foods, Inc., 755 N.W.2d 583 (Neb. 2008); Scott v. Mayflower Home Improvement Corp., 831 A.2d 564 (N.J. Super. Ct. Law Div. 2001); Alduridi v. Community Trust Bank, 1999 Tenn. App. LEXIS 718 (Tenn. Ct. App. Oct. 26, 1999); Patton v. McHone, 1993 Tenn. App. LEXIS 212 (Tenn. Ct. App. 1993); Home Sav. Ass'n v. Guerra, 733 S.W.2d 134 (Tex. 1987); Kish v. Van Note, 692 S.W.2d 463 (Tex. 1985); Reliance Mortg. Co. v. Hill-Shields, 2001 Tex. App. LEXIS 140 (Tex. App. Jan. 10, 2001); Oxford Fin. Cos. v. Velez, 807 S.W.2d 460 (Tex. App. 1991).

141 Reagans v. Mountainhigh Coach Works, Inc., 881 N.E.2d 245 (Ohio 2008).

142 *In re* Stewart, 93 B.R. 878 (Bankr. E.D. Pa. 1988); Home Sav. Ass'n v. Guerra, 733 S.W.2d 134 (Tex. 1987); Kish v. Van Note, 692 S.W.2d 463 (Tex. 1985); Reliance Mortg. Co. v. Hill-Shields, 2001 Tex. App. LEXIS 140 (Tex. App. Jan. 10, 2001); Oxford Fin. Cos. v. Velez, 807 S.W.2d 460 (Tex. App. 1991); Briercroft Serv. Corp. v. Perez, 820 S.W.2d 813 (Tex. App. 1990), *aff'd in relevant part, rev'd in part on other grounds*, 809 S.W.2d 216 (Tex. 1991); Green Tree Acceptance, Inc. v. Pierce, 768 S.W.2d 416 (Tex. App. 1989). *See also* Diaz v. Paragon Motors of Woodside, Inc., 2008 WL 2004001 (E.D.N.Y. May 7, 2008) (awarding attorney fees far in excess of the cap, but without discussion of a cap); Diaz v. Paragon Motors of Woodside, Inc. 2007 WL 2903920 (E.D.N.Y. Oct. 1, 2007) (same). *But see* Griffor v. Airport Chevrolet, Inc., 2009 WL 151696 (D. Or. Jan. 22, 2009); Riggs v. Anthony Auto Sales, Inc., 32 F. Supp. 2d 411 (W.D. La. 1998); Simpson v. Anthony Auto Sales, Inc., 32 F. Supp. 2d 405 (W.D. La. 1998); Scott v. Mayflower Home Improvement Corp., 831 A.2d 564 (N.J. Super. Ct. Law Div. 2001) (plaintiffs may not recover attorney fees in excess of amounts they paid); Alduridi v. Community Trust Bank, 1999 Tenn. App. LEXIS 718 (Tenn. Ct. App. Oct. 26, 1999); Patton v. McHone, 1993 Tenn. App. LEXIS 212 (Tenn. Ct. App. 1993). *But cf.* State *ex rel.* Stenberg v. Consumers' Choice Foods, 755 N.W.2d 583 (Neb. 2008) (when statute made attorney fees discretionary, and action was brought by the state attorney general, trial court did not abuse discretion in refusing to award fees against lender in excess of the cap).

143 *But see* Alduridi v. Community Trust Bank, 1999 Tenn. App. LEXIS 718 (Tenn. Ct. App. Oct. 26, 1999) (holding that fees awarded in whole or in part for claims based on the seller's misconduct are subject to the cap).

144 *See, e.g.,* Alarcon v. Fireside Bank, 2010 WL 769690 (Cal. Ct. App. Mar. 8, 2010) (finding no limit under a state law theory).

145 *See, e.g.,* Alarcon v. Fireside Bank, 2010 WL 769690 (Cal. Ct. App. Mar. 8, 2010) (awarding fees in excess of cap under state law). *See* National Consumer Law Center, Collection Actions § 13.1 (3d ed. 2014), *updated at* www.nclc.org/library (summary of such state law).

146 Simpson v. Anthony Auto Sales, Inc., 32 F. Supp. 2d 405 (W.D. La. 1998); Music Acceptance Corp. v. Lofing, 39 Cal. Rptr. 2d 159 (Cal. Ct. App. 1995); Scott v. Mayflower Home Improvement Corp., 831 A.2d 564 (N.J. Super. Ct. Law Div. 2001) (treble damages barred if they would push recovery over cap); Briercroft Serv. Corp. v. Perez, 820 S.W.2d 813 (Tex. App. 1990), *rev'd in part on other grounds*, 809

The fact that the holder did not authorize the willful conduct is irrelevant, because what is at issue is the holder's liability for all claims the consumer has against the seller, up to the cap.

Ohio's highest court, on the other hand, has ruled that a creditor is not derivatively liable for treble damages, based upon its interpretation of the purpose of treble damages under Ohio's UDAP statute.[147] The court finds the damages are awarded to deter seller misconduct, and they are punitive in nature. As such, the court found the lender liable only for the consumer's actual damages claim against the seller and not for multiple damages, even if those could be kept under the cap.[148]

In certain states, a holder might be liable for treble damages in excess of the cap. To the extent treble damages are awarded because the *creditor* has not engaged in a good faith attempt at settlement of seller-related claims,[149] such multiple damages should not be capped for the same reasons that attorney fees should not be capped.

4.3.7   No Limit on Creditor's Liability for Own Conduct

The FTC rule sets out a creditor's liability for the acts of the seller. The creditor is additionally liable for its own conduct,[150] or its own participation in another's misconduct.[151] The lender can even be independently liable for its own conduct in misleading the consumer as to the consumer's right to raise seller-related claims against the lender.[152] There are no limits under the FTC Holder Rule to the creditor's liability for its own conduct, and the amount of that liability is then added above and beyond its maximum derivative liability for the seller's conduct.[153]

Some creditors argue that their liability for their own misconduct is limited to the FTC Holder Rule limits. They argue that as a contract term, the consumer has waived any right to recovery beyond the "amounts paid by the debtor hereunder." What these arguments miss is that the provision states that recovery "hereunder" is so limited. But recovery on an independent theory clearly is not. The purpose of the FTC rule is to protect consumers, not to protect creditors. "The words 'recovery hereunder' . . . refer specifically to a recovery under the Notice. If a larger affirmative recovery is available against a creditor as a matter of state law, the consumer would retain this right."[154]

4.3.8   Impact of Federal Statutes Limiting Creditor's Derivative Liability

4.3.8.1   TILA Limits on Assignee Liability

The Truth in Lending Act (TILA) explicitly limits an assignee's TILA liability to those TILA violations apparent on the face of the documents. An assignee with no direct liability under the TILA arguably might still be liable pursuant to the FTC Holder Notice for the *assignor's* TILA liability. Most courts reject this argument when the TILA violation was not apparent on the face of the documents.[155]

In fact, Illinois courts and one New Jersey court have developed a unique and highly suspect doctrine as to the relationship of the TILA, state law, and UDAP claims.[156] The TILA's assignee liability provision does not just trump

---

S.W.2d 216 (Tex. 1991); Houser v. Diamond Corp., 125 Wash. App. 1009 (Wash. Ct. App. 2005) (text, table at 2005 WL 94452).

147   Reagans v. Mountainhigh Coachworks, Inc., 881 N.E.2d 245 (Ohio 2008). *See also* Hardeman v. Wheels, Inc., 565 N.E.2d 849 (Ohio Ct. App. 1988) (punitive and treble damages and attorney fees cannot be set off against amount owed on debt when assignee is not subject to state UDAP statute). For a critique of *Hardeman*, see M. Greenfield & N. Ross, *Limits on a Consumer's Ability to Assert Claims and Defenses Under the FTC's Holder in Due Course Rule*, 46 Bus. Law. 1135 (May 1991).

148   Reagans v. Mountainhigh Coachworks, Inc., 881 N.E.2d 245 (Ohio 2008).

149   *See* § 4.3.14, *infra.*

150   *See* National Consumer Law Center, Unfair and Deceptive Acts and Practices Ch. 6 (8th ed. 2012), *updated at* www.nclc.org/library (analysis of UDAP violations related to credit).

151   *See* National Consumer Law Center, Unfair and Deceptive Acts and Practices § 11.4 (8th ed. 2012), *updated at* www.nclc.org/library (analysis of UDAP violations related to credit).

152   *See* § 4.3.14, *infra.*

153   *See* Eremon v. Grand Auto Sales, Inc., 333 F. Supp. 2d 702 (N.D. Ill. 2004) (if creditor actually participated in deceptive scheme, FTC Holder Rule cap is inapplicable); Tidwell v. Crown Truck Sales & Salvage Inc., No. CV 2005-090937 (Ariz. Super. Ct., Maricopa Cnty. Feb. 14, 2008), *available at* www.nclc.org/unreported (FTC Holder Rule does not limit creditor's liability for its own conduct); Briercroft Serv. Corp. v. Perez, 820 S.W.2d 813 (Tex. App. 1990) (recognizing that independent wrongful conduct could be basis for recovery beyond amount paid to creditor), *rev'd in part on other grounds*, 809 S.W.2d

216 (Tex. 1991). *See also* McCann v. Delta Outsource Grp., Inc., 2013 WL 1490924 (M.D. Pa. Mar. 19, 2013). *Cf.* Resolution Trust Corp. v. Cook, 840 S.W.2d 42 (Tex. App. 1992).

154   Fed. Trade Comm'n, Staff Guidelines, 41 Fed. Reg. 20,023 (May 14, 1976) (mechanism of the rule), *available online as companion material to this treatise. See also* Tidwell v. Crown Truck Sales & Salvage Inc., CV 2005-090937 (Ariz. Super. Ct. Maricopa Cnty. Feb. 14, 2008), *available at* www.nclc.org/unreported.

155   Murphy v. Federal Deposit Ins. Corp., 408 Fed. Appx. 609 (3d Cir. 2010); Ramadan v. Chase Manhattan Corp., 229 F.3d 194 (3d Cir. 2000); Green v. Levis Motors, Inc., 179 F.3d 286 (5th Cir. 1999); Ellis v. GMAC, 160 F.3d 703 (11th Cir. 1998); Taylor v. Quality Hyundai, Inc., 150 F.3d 689 (7th Cir. 1998); Walker v. Wallace Auto Sales, Inc., 155 F.3d 927 (7th Cir. 1998); Carmen v. Metrocities Mortg. Corp., 2009 WL 1416038 (D.N.J. May 18, 2009); Jordan v. Chrysler Credit Corp., 73 F. Supp. 2d 469 (D.N.J. Nov. 12, 1999); Mayfield v. Gen. Elec. Capital Corp., 1999 U.S. Dist. LEXIS 4048 (S.D.N.Y. Mar. 31, 1999); Kinzel v. Southview Chevrolet Co., 892 F. Supp. 1211 (D. Minn. 1995). *Contra* Cox v. First Nat'l Bank of Cincinnati, 633 F. Supp. 236 (S.D. Ohio 1986); *In re* Stewart, 93 B.R. 878 (Bankr. E.D. Pa. 1988). *See generally* National Consumer Law Center, Truth in Lending § 12.3 (9th ed. 2015), *updated at* www.nclc.org/library.

156   Eromon v. Grand Auto Sales, Inc., 333 F. Supp. 2d 702 (N.D. Ill. 2004); Jenkins v. Mercantile Mortg. Co., 231 F. Supp. 2d 737 (N.D. Ill. 2002); Jarvis v. South Oak Dodge, Inc., 773 N.E.2d 641 (Ill. 2002); Jackson v. South Holland Dodge, 755 N.E.2d 462 (Ill. 2001); Psensky v. American Honda Fin. Corp., 875 A.2d 290 (N.J. Super. Ct. App. Div. 2005). *See also* Costa v. Mauro Chevrolet, Inc., 390 F. Supp. 2d 720, 734–735 (N.D. Ill. 2005); Alexiou v. Brad Benson Mitsubishi, 127 F. Supp. 2d 557 (D.N.J. 2000) (interpreting a New Jersey statute on assignee liability, not the FTC Holder Rule). *Cf.* Phillips v. Lithia Motors, Inc., 2006 WL 1113608, at *17–18 (D. Or. Apr. 27, 2006) (TILA assignee

the FTC Holder Notice as to the consumer's ability to raise TILA claims against the assignee. It also trumps the consumer's ability to raise TILA-related state law claims against the assignee. This is consistent with other unique rulings from Illinois courts about the TILA preempting related state law claims.[157]

Even the Illinois courts and the one New Jersey court do not apply the same logic to other types of state claims unrelated to credit agreement disclosures, so the TILA's assignee liability provision does not preempt the FTC Holder Notice for claims such as fraudulent repairs, shoddy or incomplete work, misrepresentations as to the nature of a service, sale of lemon cars, odometer misrepresentations, or any other claim not related to credit disclosures.[158] Moreover, most courts reject the Illinois approach,[159] so the reach of the Holder rule is only limited to instances in which the consumer is bringing seller-related TILA claims against the holder.

Of course, the TILA's assignee liability provision trumps the FTC Holder Notice only when the TILA violation is not apparent on the face of the document. If it is apparent, the assignee should be liable under both the TILA and the Holder notice, since there is no conflict between the FTC Rule and the TILA.[160] Similarly, the holder is certainly liable for its own misconduct; there is no TILA protection against an assignee that directly participates in the fraud.[161]

4.3.8.2 ECOA limits on Assignee Liability

While not found in the Equal Credit Opportunity Act (ECOA) itself, Regulation B implementing the Act limits the definition of creditor under the ECOA. The regulation specifies "a person is not a creditor regarding any violation of the Act or this regulation committed by another creditor unless the person knew or had reasonable notice of the act, policy or practice that constituted the violation before becoming involved in the credit transaction."[162]

This language should be irrelevant to the question of whether an assignee is derivatively liable for the acts of its assignor. The language just states that the assignee is not defined as a creditor for purposes of the ECOA and thus does not have affirmative obligations under the ECOA and is not exposed to direct liability under the ECOA. There can still be derivative liability for its assignor's ECOA violations. One case, though, finds the FTC Holder Rule not to apply to an ECOA claim, although in that case the plaintiff did not dispute this interpretation.[163]

4.3.8.3 Relation to the Magnuson-Moss Warranty Act

The federal Magnuson-Moss Warranty Act states that for purposes of civil liability under that Act, "only the warrantor actually making a written affirmation of fact, promise, or undertaking shall be deemed to have created a written warranty, and any rights arising thereunder may be enforced under this section only against such warrantor and no other person."[164] The question arises whether a claim under the Magnuson-Moss Warranty Act can be brought against an assignee of the warrantor, based on the FTC Holder language, or whether the above-quoted language restricts the consumer's ability to bring such a claim against anyone other than the warrantor.

Note what the above-quoted language does *not* say. Since by its very terms it is limited to written warranties, a consumer can certainly bring against an assignee a Magnuson-Moss Warranty Act claim that is not based on the enforcement of a written warranty. Examples of claims not based on a written warranty are claims for breach of an implied warranty, for breach of a service contract, for violation of various Magnuson-Moss disclosure requirements, or for violation of various substantive Magnuson-Moss Act restrictions, such as those dealing with tie-ins.[165] Warranty claims that are not based on the Magnuson-Moss Act are also not affected by this language.

The only issue is whether a claim based on a written warranty can be brought against the warrantor's assignee, based on the FTC Holder Notice. Two courts have suggested that the Magnuson-Moss language trumps the FTC Holder Notice.[166]

liability provision overrides FTC Holder Rule in "area regulated by TILA"; exact nature of claims not specified).

157 *See* National Consumer Law Center, Unfair and Deceptive Acts and Practices § 2.2.1.5.3 (8th ed. 2012), *updated at* www.nclc.org/library.

158 Eromon v. Grand Auto Sales, Inc., 333 F. Supp. 2d 702 (N.D. Ill. 2004); Psensky v. American Honda Fin. Corp., 875 A.2d 290 (N.J. Super. Ct. App. Div. 2005).

159 Green v. Levis Motors, Inc., 179 F.3d 286, 296 (5th Cir. 1999) (TILA "limits assignee liability on only one set of claims (i.e., the specified TILA claims")); Taylor v. Quality Hyundai, Inc., 150 F.3d 689, 693 (7th Cir. 1998) (TILA assignee liability rule "limits only certain TILA claims"); Irby-Greene v. M.O.R., Inc., 79 F. Supp. 2d 630, 633 (E.D. Va. 2000); *In re* Four Star Fin. Services, Inc., 444 B.R. 428 (Bankr. C.D. Cal. 2011), *vacated on other grounds*, 469 B.R. 30 (C.D. Cal. 2012) (addressing question of priority that claim should be given in bankruptcy case); Ramirez v. Nat'l Coop. Bank (NCB), 91 A.D. 3d 204 (N.Y. App. Div. 2011). *See also* Scott v. Mayflower Home Improvement Corp., 831 A.2d 564 (N.J. Super. Ct. Law Div. 2001), *overruled by* Psensky v. American Honda Fin. Corp., 875 A.2d 290 (N.J. Super. Ct. App. Div. 2005).

160 Eromon v. Grand Auto Sales, Inc., 333 F. Supp. 2d 702 (N.D. Ill. 2004). When a disclosure violation is apparent on the face of a credit agreement is detailed at National Consumer Law Center, Truth in Lending § 12.3.2 (9th ed. 2015), *updated at* www.nclc.org/library.

161 Psensky v. American Honda Fin. Corp., 875 A.2d 290 (N.J. Super. Ct. App. Div. 2005).

162 12 C.F.R. § 202.2(*l*).

163 Coleman v. GMAC, 196 F.R.D. 315 (M.D. Tenn. 2000), *vacated, remanded, on other grounds* 296 F.3d 443 (6th Cir. 2002) (class certification erroneous because predominance of common questions not shown).

164 15 U.S.C. § 2310(f).

165 *See* National Consumer Law Center, Consumer Warranty Law Ch. 2 (5th ed. 2015), *updated at* www.nclc.org/library.

166 Owens v. Tranex Credit Corp. (S.D. Ind. 1998), *available at* www.nclc.org/unreported; Patton v. McHone, 1993 Tenn. App. LEXIS 212, 40 U.C.C. Rep. Serv. 2d 299 (Tenn. Ct. App. 1993) (declining to make assignee subject to buyer's affirmative Magnuson-Moss claims, based on erroneous interpretation of FTC Holder Rule and on view that Magnuson-Moss does not impose obligation on party who

In one of these cases, the court based its ruling on similar case law relating to the relationship of the FTC Holder Rule to the TILA's limitation on assignee liability.[167] But the TILA specifically restricts assignee derivative liability, while the Magnuson-Moss Warranty Act limitation applies broadly to third-party direct liability and does not even mention the issue of derivative liability. It thus leaves open the issue of whether the legislative intent was to limit third parties' direct liability only or also their derivative liability.

The better view is that Congress only meant that third parties have no *direct* liability for breaches of the warrantor's written warranty. For example, a dealer is not liable if a manufacturer's written warranty is breached. But a third party can have derivative liability if that party has agreed by contract to be subject to claims the consumer can bring against the written warrantor.

4.3.9 Liability of Holders of Securitized Debt

An important current topic is the consumer's ability to raise claims and defenses under the FTC notice relating to securitized debt. A large number of consumer obligations are aggregated into pools, which are typically assigned to a trust. The trustee is then the legal owner of the obligation. Securities backed by this pool of obligations are then issued and sold by investment bankers to investors.[168]

The original lender or dealer may remain involved as the servicer of the obligation, dealing with the consumer, collecting payments, and initiating collection actions. When the seller or loan originator is the servicer, the consumer may be unaware that the obligation has been assigned.

The Holder notice applies to securitized transactions the same way it does to ordinary transactions. If the trustee is the holder of the note or contract, the trustee is liable for all claims and defenses that the consumer would have against the original seller or lender, up to the limit set by the FTC Holder Rule. However, investors who buy the securities backed by the obligations are probably not subject to the FTC Holder Rule, because they are not holding the notes.[169]

4.3.10 Liability of FDIC or Subsequent Holders

When a federally insured bank or savings and loan is taken over by the Federal Deposit Insurance Corporation, the consumer obligations held by the institution transfer to the federal agency as receiver. To promote the goals of confidence and stability in the banking system and efficiency in the trade of notes and other financial instruments, Congress and the courts have given the FDIC unique powers to enforce such instruments.

When the FDIC collects on the obligation, it often will claim complete insulation from all claims and defenses relating to it. Of even more significance, subsequent purchasers may claim that these defenses transfer with the obligation to the benefit of the subsequent purchaser. For example, a bank that purchases an insolvent bank's loan obligations from the FDIC may also claim insulation from all claims and defenses the consumer had against the seller related to the now insolvent bank.

The consumer's ability to raise defenses against the FDIC can be an issue both when the FTC Holder Notice is included in the credit obligation and when it is not. This subsection briefly considers the first situation, but this area is covered in far more detail in NCLC's *Mortgage Lending*.[170]

Three separate but overlapping doctrines may insulate the FDIC from debtor defenses in a given case. One is federal common law starting with the Supreme Court's 1942 decision in *D'Oench, Duhme and Company v. Federal Deposit Ins. Corp.*,[171] that the maker of the note could not raise an unrecorded side agreement as a defense on the note after the note was acquired by the FDIC. The second source of FDIC protection is 12 U.S.C. § 1823(e), which provides that no agreement that tends to diminish the FDIC's interest in an asset such as a note or other obligation acquired from a failed bank shall be valid against the FDIC unless the agreement is in writing and was properly signed, approved, and recorded by the bank. The third doctrine is a common law "super" holder-in-due-course status that goes beyond the scope of section 1823(e) and *D'Oench*.[172]

D'Oench and related doctrines should have minimal impact on sale-related consumer transactions that include the FTC Holder Rule Notice. If the FTC Holder Rule Notice is in a note or installment contract, it would appear that the FDIC cannot avoid the impact of that notice. The notice is in writing and is incorporated into the note or contract itself, and the federal agency and subsequent purchasers have adequate notice of that limitation on the obligation. Further, the inclusion of the Holder notice means that there cannot be a holder in due course of the note,[173] thus avoiding the "super holder-in-due-course" doctrine. Most *D'Oench, Duhme* litigation has dealt

---

did not make the warranty). *See also* Dufour v. Be L.L.C., 2010 WL 2560409 (N.D. Cal. June 22, 2010). *Cf.* Gaddy v. Galarza Motor Sport L.T.D., 2000 U.S. Dist. LEXIS 13881 (N.D. Ill. Sept. 18, 2000) (finding that assignee was not liable because it did not meet definition of "supplier" and did not make a warranty; also denying motion to dismiss a separate count that sought to impose liability against assignee based on Holder Notice, but not saying whether this count included a Magnuson-Moss claim).

167 Dufour v. Be L.L.C., 2010 WL 2560409 (N.D. Cal. June 22, 2010); Owens v. Tranex Credit Corp. (S.D. Ind. 1998), *available at* www.nclc .org/unreported. *See* § 4.3.8.1, *supra*.

168 *See* National Consumer Law Center, Mortgage Lending (2d ed. 2014), *updated at* www.nclc.org/library.

169 *See* Ross v. Thousand Adventures, 675 N.W.2d 812 (Iowa 2004) (FTC Holder Rule does not apply to bank that bought participation interest in pool of obligations held by a different bank).

170 National Consumer Law Center, Mortgage Lending Ch. 11 (2d ed. 2014), *updated at* www.nclc.org/library.

171 315 U.S. 447 (1942).

172 *See* National Consumer Law Center, Mortgage Lending Ch. 11 (2d ed. 2014), *updated at* www.nclc.org/library.

173 U.C.C. § 3-106(d).

with large commercial transactions, so there is little case law on the effect of the FTC Holder Rule Notice.[174]

Another question is whether a consumer can bring affirmative claims and counterclaims when the consumer has not first filed a timely administrative claim with the FDIC after receiving notice of a bank's insolvency.[175] Many courts have held that an administrative claim is not a precondition to raising defenses, even affirmative defenses such as those that might be based on seller misconduct.[176] It is unclear whether an administrative claim with the FDIC is required before bringing an action against the FDIC's subsequent assignee.[177] However, regardless of the effect of the FDIC administrative claims process, there must be a substantive basis to hold the assignee liable. When an assignee bank purchases the obligations of a failed bank, defenses probably travel with the note, but typically the purchase and assumption agreement provides that the FDIC retains the failed bank's liabilities.[178]

4.3.11 Relation of FTC Rule to State Law

4.3.11.1 FTC Rule Overrides Only Less Protective State Laws

Virtually all states have statutes that subject creditors in at least some circumstances to claims or defenses that the consumer could assert against the seller.[179] These statutes should be consulted whenever there is an issue of a creditor's derivative liability for acts or omissions of the seller.

Some of these state holder laws are broader than the FTC Holder Rule, covering more types of transactions[180] or making

the holder liable even if the Holder notice is omitted.[181] Even if the state law does no more than the FTC Holder Rule, a court may be more willing to enforce FTC Holder Rule liability if state law dictates the same result. The existence of the state law may deter the court from falling into an erroneous interpretation of the FTC Holder Rule.

The FTC Holder Notice states that the consumer's "recovery hereunder" is limited—that is, recovery pursuant to the FTC rule is limited to certain amounts. The FTC rule does not limit a larger recovery under a different state or federal law. A consumer can recover more than that allowed under the FTC rule if state or federal law so allows.[182] "The words 'recovery hereunder' . . . refer specifically to a recovery under the Notice. If a larger affirmative recovery is available against a creditor as a matter of state law, the consumer would retain this right."[183]

Conversely, state laws are typically more restrictive than the FTC rule. The state statute may impose a lower cap on the consumer's relief than the FTC Holder Rule, may be limited only to certain claims and defenses, or require the consumer to notify the creditor of particular claims and defenses within a specific period of time after the creditor sends the consumer a notice.

More restrictive state law does not limit the application of the FTC rule. For example, Alabama law allows consumers to raise seller-related *defenses* against assignees but not to raise those claims affirmatively. Alabama consumers nevertheless can use the FTC Holder Rule to bring affirmative claims against assignees.[184] Michigan consumers can recover from an assignee a down payment paid to the seller, even when the Michigan holder law would not allow such a recovery.[185] Consumers can recover under the FTC Holder Rule even if they could not recover under state law.

4.3.11.2 The *LaBarre* Court's Misinterpretation

Notwithstanding the language of the FTC Holder Rule and the FTC's multiple unequivocal statements that the Holder

---

174 *See* Leavings v. Mills, 175 S.W.3d 301, 312 n.9 (Tex. App. 2004) (FDIC and RTC take notes free only of terms or agreements that are not apparent from the face of the document, so FTC Holder Notice preserved claims even if current holder acquired note from one of those agencies); Resolution Trust Corp. v. Cook, 840 S.W.2d 42 (Tex. App. 1992) (declining to apply *D'Oench* and section 1823(e) to claims based on original lender's torts; FTC Holder Rule notice allows affirmative recovery against Resolution Trust Corp.). *But cf.* Smania v. Mundaca Inv. Corp., 629 So. 2d 242 (Fla. Dist. Ct. App. 1993) (FTC Holder Rule notice on note is insufficient to prevent bar of claims that could have been asserted against seller since those claims are based on a different document). *See generally* National Consumer Law Center, Mortgage Lending § 11.10 (2d ed. 2014), *updated at* www.nclc.org/library.

175 *See* National Consumer Law Center, Mortgage Lending § 11.3 (2d ed. 2014), *updated at* www.nclc.org/library.

176 National Consumer Law Center, Mortgage Lending § 11.3.5 (2d ed. 2014), *updated at* www.nclc.org/library.

177 National Consumer Law Center, Mortgage Lending § 11.3.9 (2d ed. 2014), *updated at* www.nclc.org/library.

178 National Consumer Law Center, Mortgage Lending § 11.3.9.2 (2d ed. 2014), *updated at* www.nclc.org/library.

179 *See* § 4.5, *infra*.

180 *See, e.g.*, § 4.5, *infra* (leases). *See also* Johnson v. Long Beach Mortg. Loan Trust 2001-4, 451 F. Supp. 2d 16 (D.D.C. 2006) (the District of Columbia statute apparently applies to real estate financing that would not otherwise be covered by the FTC rule); Blanco v. Keybank USA, N.A., 2005 WL 4135013 (N.D. Ohio Sept. 30, 2005) (state holder law applies even if FTC Holder Rule does not), *vacated on other grounds*, 2005 WL 5789023 (N.D. Ohio Dec. 28, 2005); Mich. Comp. Laws Ann. § 492.114a(b) (holder of installment sale contract is subject to all

buyer's claims and defenses arising out of the transaction, apparently including claims against the manufacturer). *Cf.* Chrysler Fin. Co. v. Flynn, 88 S.W.3d 142 (Mo. Ct. App. 2002) (seeming to assume this interpretation of the Missouri statute).

181 *See* § 4.5, *infra*.

182 *See, e.g.*, McCoy v. Southern Energy Homes, Inc., 2012 WL 1409533 (S.D. W. Va. Apr. 23, 2012) (consumer obtained affirmative recovery under state law when court—in error—ruled that could not recover affirmatively under the FTC Rule).

183 Fed. Trade Comm'n, Staff Guidelines, 41 Fed. Reg. 20,023 (May 14, 1976) (mechanism of the rule), *available online as companion material to this treatise. See also* F.T.C. Staff Advisory Letter, Diercks (Oct. 12, 1976), *summarized at* [1974–1980 Transfer Binder] Consumer Cred. Guide (CCH) ¶ 98,284; Resolution Trust Corp. v. Cook, 840 S.W.2d 42 (Tex. App. 1992).

184 Eachen v. Scott Hous. Sys., Inc., 630 F. Supp. 162 (M.D. Ala. 1986). *See also* De La Fuente v. Home Sav. Ass'n, 669 S.W.2d 137 (Tex. App. 1984); Hernandez v. Forbes Chevrolet Co., 680 S.W.2d 75 (Tex. App. 1984).

185 Green Tree Acceptance, Inc. v. Pirtle, 1999 WL 33740367 (E.D. Mich. Mar. 1, 1999).

rule is not limited by state holder law restrictions, the Eighth Circuit ruled to the contrary in *LaBarre v. Credit Acceptance Corp.*[186] The court held that state law should be used to determine what claims can be brought under the FTC Holder Rule, against assignees and related lenders. In that case, Minnesota law (and thus, it said, the FTC Holder Rule) was interpreted as allowing a consumer to raise seller-related claims only as a *defense* to the assignee's collection action and not in an affirmative action.

The decision is patently absurd. It would mean that the FTC Holder Rule, enacted because state law was not adequate, would have only the same reach as preexisting state law. What the Eighth Circuit got wrong is that the FTC stated applicable state law determines whether a seller is liable for certain conduct, not whether an assignee is liable when state law provides that the seller is liable.[187] *All* seller-related claims that are allowed by applicable law also can be brought against the assignee. Indeed, the Official Comment to UCC Article 3 clearly expresses this interpretation: "The effect of the FTC legend is to make the rights of a holder or transferee subject to *claims or defenses* that the issuer could assert *against the original payee* of the note."[188]

The *LaBarre* decision would not only mean that the FTC Holder Rule is a nullity (providing no greater rights than already provided by state law), but it is a deceptive nullity, because the notice mandated by the FTC Holder Rule clearly informs consumers they can bring *all* claims and defenses against the assignee, while *LaBarre* rules they cannot. The FTC itself in the statement of basis and purpose for the rule indicates the consumer can "maintain an affirmative action"[189]

and explicitly rejected a creditor proposal that the consumer only be able to use the FTC Holder Rule defensively.[190]

The Eighth Circuit ruling relied not on the commission's statement but on an FTC staff interpretation and, even then, misinterpreted that interpretation. The staff interpretation cited by the Eighth Circuit in fact states the opposite of what it is cited for—applicable law controls what is a claim against the *seller*, not which seller-related claims can be brought against an assignee. To underscore this, the staff interpretation contains three examples of controlling applicable law, and all three relate to whether the claim could be brought against the seller, not whether valid seller-related claims can be brought against an assignee.[191] The very next paragraph in the staff interpretation states that the consumer can bring affirmatively *all* claims against the lender that could be brought against the seller.[192]

Clearly then, the Eighth Circuit's interpretation is wrong and should not be adopted by any courts. *LaBarre*'s misinterpretation of the FTC Holder Rule has rarely if ever been followed since 1999. One 1999 decision, *Pescia v. Auburn Ford-Lincoln Mercury*,[193] cites *LaBarre* in a seemingly favorable way but also makes favorable reference to another decision[194] that took the opposite approach. *Pescia* required the plaintiff to show independent state law grounds for asserting her claims against the creditor but suggests that this ruling is based on the manner in which the plaintiff framed her complaint[195] rather than on an interpretation of the FTC Holder Rule. Another decision explicitly rejects *LaBarre*.[196] Other courts have implicitly rejected the *LaBarre* position by recognizing that state law is relevant only to whether there is a claim against the seller, not whether the consumer can raise that seller-related claim against a holder.[197]

---

186 175 F.3d 640 (8th Cir. 1999). *See also* Pescia v. Auburn Ford-Lincoln Mercury, 68 F. Supp. 2d 1269 (M.D. Ala. 1999) (construing FTC Holder Notice to nullify holder-in-due-course status, but holding that there still must be independent state grounds for holder's liability), *aff'd without op. sub nom.* Pescia v. Ford Motor Credit Corp., 2001 WL 1711051 (11th Cir. Dec. 17, 2001).

187 Fed. Trade Comm'n, Statement of Basis and Purpose for the Trade Regulation Rule Concerning Preservation of Consumers' Claims and Defenses, 40 Fed. Reg. 53,524 (Nov. 18, 1975), *available online as companion material to this treatise. See also* Letter from Christopher Keller, Fed. Trade Comm'n to Jonathan Sheldon (May 13, 1999), *available online as companion material to this treatise* (citing sections in the FTC's statement of basis and purpose showing the commission's intent).

188 Official Comment 3 to U.C.C. § 3-106 (emphasis added). *See* World Wide Tracers, Inc. v. Metropolitan Prot., Inc., 384 N.W.2d 442, 447 (Minn. 1986) (illustrating the weight the Minnesota Supreme Court gives to the U.C.C. Official Comments).

189 Fed. Trade Comm'n, Statement of Basis and Purpose for the Trade Regulation Rule Concerning Preservation of Consumers' Claims and Defenses, 40 Fed. Reg. 53,524 (Nov. 18, 1975), *available online as companion material to this treatise. See also* Letter from Christopher Keller, Fed. Trade Comm'n to Jonathan Sheldon (May 13, 1999), *available online as companion material to this treatise* (citing sections in the FTC's *Statement of Basis and Purpose* showing the commission's intent as to affirmative claims against holders).

190 FTC, Statement of Basis and Purpose, 40 Fed. Reg. 53,524, 53,526, 53,527 (Nov. 18, 1975), *available online as companion material to this treatise. See also* Letter from Christopher Keller, Fed. Trade Comm'n to Jonathan Sheldon (May 13, 1999), *available online as companion material to this treatise*.

191 Fed. Trade Comm'n, Staff Guidelines, 41 Fed. Reg. 20,024 (May 14, 1976), *available online as companion material to this treatise.*

192 *Id.*

193 68 F. Supp. 2d 1269 (M.D. Ala. 1999), *aff'd without op. sub nom.* Pescia v. Ford Motor Credit Corp., 2001 WL 1711051 (11th Cir. Dec. 17, 2001). *See also* Brooks v. O'Connor Chevrolet, Inc., 2003 WL 22427795 (N.D. Ill. Oct. 23, 2003) (not citing *LaBarre* but erroneously concluding that assignee's derivative UDAP liability is subject to same limits as would apply to liability for its own acts).

194 Eachen v. Scott Hous. Sys., Inc., 630 F. Supp. 162 (M.D. Ala. 1986) (inclusion of FTC Holder Rule in contract means that consumer can assert seller-related claims affirmatively against creditor, even though Alabama law made creditor liable only for defensive claims).

195 Pescia v. Auburn Ford-Lincoln Mercury, 68 F. Supp. 2d 1269, 1282 (M.D. Ala. 1999) (the FTC Holder Rule "creates a federal right but that federal right has not been invoked in this case"), *aff'd without op. sub nom.* Pescia v. Ford Motor Credit Corp., 2001 WL 1711051 (11th Cir. Dec. 17, 2001).

196 Alduridi v. Community Trust Bank, 1999 Tenn. App. LEXIS 718 (Tenn. Ct. App. Oct. 26, 1999).

197 *See, e.g.,* Eachen v. Scott Hous. Sys., Inc., 630 F. Supp. 162 (M.D. Ala. 1986); Thomas v. Ford Motor Credit Co., 429 A.2d 277 (Md. Ct. Spec. App. 1981); Credit Acceptance Corp. v. Banks, 1999 Ohio App. LEXIS 6058 (Ohio Ct. App. Dec. 16, 1999); Beemus v. Interstate Nat'l

4.3.12 Does the FTC Holder Rule Create Federal Jurisdiction?

A lender may attempt to remove a state law case to federal court (or the consumer may try to bring an action in federal court) based on the fact that the consumer's case relies in part on the FTC Holder Notice, which is required by a federal rule. But the consumer's claim is not based upon federal law but upon a state law contract claim derived from the language of the credit agreement that contains the FTC Holder Notice. As such, the FTC Holder Notice does not create federal jurisdiction.[198] As long as the seller-related claims being asserted are state law claims, then the FTC rule cannot create an independent basis for federal jurisdiction.[199] If there is any doubt about this, the consumer can bring the claim against the holder based upon a state law similar to the FTC Rule, if such a statute exists in the jurisdiction.[200]

4.3.13 Consumer's Waiver of Claims Against the Holder

Consumers sometimes sign documents indicating the work purchased with the loan proceeds has been completed and performed satisfactorily. Holders argue that they can rely on this statement and are not liable under the Holder notice for consumer claims against the seller inconsistent with this statement. Nevertheless, at a minimum, this statement should be no more binding on the consumer in an action against the holder as it would in the consumer's action against the seller. Courts should not give much credence to such a statement, particularly when it is part of boilerplate language the consumer is asked to sign.[201]

In fact, the waiver should be less binding when the Holder notice is included.[202] A federal court in *Heastie v. Community*

Bank[203] has found it to be a state UDAP violation for a creditor simultaneously to include in its loan agreements the FTC Holder Notice and a statement indicating that the creditor "does not guarantee the material or workmanship or inspect the work performed" by the seller. The two statements in the loan agreement directly contradict each other.

There is no private right of action under the FTC Act for violation of the FTC Holder Rule, and, as the *Heastie* court noted, the FTC rule does not even require lenders to insert the notice; only sellers have this obligation. Nevertheless, the *Heastie* court found that, since the state UDAP statute was not limited by the rule's scope, the creditor's inclusion in its loan agreement of a provision contradicting the FTC Holder Notice was a UDAP violation. The *Heastie* court found the UDAP violation even though there was no evidence the creditor intended to use the waiver provision to insulate itself from liability for the seller's conduct; the mere inclusion of the provision was enough.

A Missouri middle-level appellate court has mistakenly thought that it was the FTC position that a provision in a contract conflicting with the FTC Holder Notice negates the notice, and the lender would thus not be subject to the FTC notice.[204] In fact, in the FTC language the court quoted, the FTC was indicating that it would be a rule violation to insert both the FTC notice and the conflicting language in the same document because it would tend to negate the meaning of the Holder notice for the consumer.[205]

The FTC never indicated that a court confronted with such conflicting provisions should negate the legal effect of the FTC notice. In fact, it would almost certainly be the FTC's opinion that the FTC notice would negate the other language. Straight rules of contract construction should construe the ambiguous provisions against the drafter. No courts have ever followed this Missouri decision.

In any event, consumers faced with a waiver of rights under the FTC Holder Rule can allege that it is a state UDAP violation for a creditor to accept a consumer note containing such conflicting language. The consumer in the Missouri case never alleged such a state UDAP violation, so the court did not reach the issue.[206]

Finally, a number of state holder statutes explicitly provide that their provisions cannot be waived.[207]

4.3.14 Holder's Refusal to Accept Liability Under FTC Holder Rule as an Independent UDAP Violation

It is common for holders to inform consumers that the holder is not subject to the consumer's claims and defenses against the seller, even when the FTC Holder Notice is in the loan documents. Instead, the holder tells the consumer to take

---

Dealer Services, Inc. (Pa. Ct. Com. Pl. Feb. 8, 2002) (citing *LaBarre* but nonetheless applying the correct rule), *available at* www.nclc.org/unreported, *aff'd on other grounds*, 823 A.2d 979 (Pa. Super. Ct. 2003); Homziak v. Gen. Elec. Capital Warranty Corp., Clearinghouse No. 54,551 (Pa. Ct. Com. Pl. May 21, 2001) (citing *LaBarre* but nonetheless applying the correct rule); Hernandez v. Forbes Chevrolet Co., 680 S.W.2d 75 (Tex. App. 1984); De La Fuente v. Home Sav. Ass'n, 669 S.W.2d 137 (Tex. App. 1984).

198 *See* Medina v. Performance Auto. Grp., Inc., 841 F. Supp. 2d 1121 (E.D. Cal. 2012); Berry v. Suzuki of Plymouth Meeting, 2011 WL 2670083 (E. D. Pa. July 7, 2011); Trego v. Germain Ford of Columbus, 2009 WL 2913962 (S.D. Ohio Sept. 8, 2009); Friddle v. Gibson, 2008 WL 2704982 (D.S.C. July 9, 2008); Macey v. Gibson, 2008 WL 2704977 (D.S.C. July 9, 2008); McKeown v. Gibson, 2008 WL 2704985 (D.S.C. July 9, 2008); Mathis v. Gibson, 2008 WL 2330537 (D.S.C. June 3, 2008); Ohio *ex rel.* Dann v. Citibank, 2008 WL 1990363 (S.D. Ohio May 1, 2008); State v. Britlee, Inc., 2007 WL 3231819 (M.D. Tenn. Oct. 30, 2007); Glovier v. Barton Homes, L.L.C., 452 F. Supp. 2d 657 (W.D. La. 2006).

199 *See* Medina v. Performance Auto. Grp., Inc., 841 F. Supp. 2d 1121 (E.D. Cal. 2012); Mathis v. Gibson, 2008 WL 2330537 (D.S.C. June 3, 2008).

200 *See* Medina v. Performance Auto. Grp., Inc., 841 F. Supp. 2d 1121 (E.D. Cal. 2012). State statutes are described at § 4.5, *infra*.

201 *See* Alvarez v. Union Mortg. Co., 747 S.W.2d 484 (Tex. App. 1988). *See also* Mahaffey v. Investor's Nat'l Sec. Co., 747 P.2d 890 (Nev. 1987).

202 Hernandez v. Forbes Chevrolet Co., 680 S.W.2d 75 (Tex. App. 1984); Hinojosa v. Castellow Chevrolet Oldsmobile, 678 S.W.2d 707 (Tex. App. 1984).

203 727 F. Supp. 1133 (N.D. Ill. 1989).

204 Blackmon v. Hindrew, 824 S.W.2d 85 (Mo. Ct. App. 1992).

205 Fed. Trade Comm'n, Staff Guidelines, 41 Fed. Reg. 20,023 (May 14, 1976), *available online as companion material to this treatise.*

206 Blackmon v. Hindrew, 824 S.W.2d 85 (Mo. Ct. App. 1992).

207 *See, e.g.*, N.C. Gen. Stat. § 25A-25.

up the dispute with the seller but that the consumer must continue to pay the lender.

These representations by the holder mislead the consumer as to the status of the obligation and as to the consumer's legal rights.[208] As such, the holder's own conduct is a UDAP violation, and the holder is liable for that conduct over and above any derivative liability it has for the seller's conduct.[209] The holder's liability for its own conduct thus subjects itself to all applicable UDAP remedies, including attorney fees or multiple damages. Because the liability is for its own conduct and is not derivative of the seller's conduct, the Holder rule's cap on damages does not apply.

It may be possible to develop evidence that the defendant follows a pattern or practice of repudiating its obligations under the FTC Holder Rule.[210] Discovery on this issue could include questions such as:

- Whether the defendant has ever been a defendant in any similar claim in which the FTC Holder clause was asserted as a basis for a claim or defense against the defendants;
- The defendant's procedure for collecting debts and investigating consumers' claims when the consumer has asserted a claim or defense similar to the plaintiff's;
- The defendant's procedure for collecting debts and investigating consumers' claims when the consumer has asserted claims or defenses based on the FTC Holder clause; and
- Whether it is the defendant's procedure to insist that the consumer must pay regardless of any claim the consumer may have against the seller.

4.4 Theories of Recovery When FTC Holder Notice Is Improperly Omitted

4.4.1 General

A major problem with the FTC Holder Rule is that, if sellers violate the rule by failing to include or arrange for the prescribed notice in the credit contract, the consumer's rights to raise seller-related claims and defenses against creditors are muddied. If the notice is not placed in the consumer contract, then the consumer has no direct *contractual* right to raise seller-related defenses against the creditor.[211] Nor can the consumer directly claim a violation of the FTC rule, because only the FTC can directly enforce the FTC Holder Rule.[212] The

FTC Holder Rule does not provide a private right of action.[213]

There should be little doubt that the *seller's* violation of the FTC rule (by its failure to arrange for the Holder notice to be included in the loan documents) is a state UDAP violation. In some states, this may even directly violate a state UDAP regulation.[214] But this UDAP claim against the *seller* rarely is of value to the consumer, since the whole point of the Holder notice is that the consumer does not wish to bring a claim against the seller, but wishes instead to raise seller-related defenses to a *creditor's* collection action. Nevertheless, a UDAP injunctive or class action claim against a seller for systematically violating the FTC Holder Rule may prevent fraud and protect future consumers.[215]

The remainder of this section details theories a consumer can use to press seller-related claims against a creditor under the FTC Holder Rule *even if* the seller has not placed the FTC Holder Notice in the contract.

4.4.2 UCC Makes the Absent Holder Notice an Implied Contract Term

4.4.2.1 UCC Article 9 Requires Notice to Be Implied Into the Contract

UCC Article 9, adopted by all fifty states, makes an omitted Holder notice part of a credit-sale agreement as a matter of law, allowing the consumer to utilize the Holder notice as if it were included.[216] Article 9 states that an assignee of a contract without

---

208 *See* National Consumer Law Center, Unfair and Deceptive Acts and Practices § 5.6.8 (8th ed. 2012), *updated at* www.nclc.org/library.

209 *See* Jaramillo v. Gonzales, 50 P.3d 554 (N.M. Ct. App. 2002) (failure to concede liability under FTC Holder Rule is UDAP violation).

210 *See* National Consumer Law Center, Unfair and Deceptive Acts and Practices § 11.8.1.2 (8th ed. 2012), *updated at* www.nclc.org/library.

211 *See, e.g.,* Whittington v. Patriot Homes, Inc., 2006 WL 2524143 (W.D. La. Aug. 30, 2006).

212 United States v. Hollis, 2008 WL 4179474 (W.D. Tex. Sept. 7, 2008); Hancock v. Homeq Servicing Corp., 2007 WL 1238746 (D.D.C. Apr. 27, 2007), *aff'd on other grounds*, 526 F.3d 785 (D.C. Cir. 2008); Williams v. Nat'l Sch. of Health Tech., 836 F. Supp. 273 (E.D. Pa. 1993); Armstrong v. Accrediting Council for Continuing Educ. &

Training, Inc., 832 F. Supp. 419 (D.D.C. 1993); Jackson v. Culinary Sch. of Wash., 788 F. Supp. 1233 (D.D.C. 1992), *aff'd in part, rev'd and remanded in part on other grounds*, 27 F.3d 573 (D.C. Cir. 1994) (on de novo review, reversing district court's decision to issue declaratory judgment on state law issues), *vacated*, 515 U.S. 1139 (1995) (appellate court should have used abuse of discretion standard to review district court's decision to issue declaratory judgment on state law issues), *on remand*, 59 F.3d 254 (D.C. Cir. 1995) (remanding for district court to exercise its discretion about whether to issue declaratory judgment on state law issues); Vietnam Veterans of Am. v. Guerdon Indus., Inc., 644 F. Supp. 951 (D. Del. 1986); Capital Bank & Trust Co. v. Lacey, 393 So. 2d 668 (La. 1980). *See also* Blackmon v. Hindrew, 824 S.W.2d 85 (Mo. Ct. App. 1992).

213 *See* § 2.2.4.1, *supra*.

214 Georgia Office of Consumer Affairs Regulations, Ga. Comp. R. & Regs. Rule 122-5-.01 (state incorporates FTC Holder Rule as state UDAP regulation so that any violation of FTC Holder Rule is automatic Georgia UDAP violation); Massachusetts Consumer Protection Regulations, 940 Mass. Code Regs. § 3.07, Advertising or Offering to Sell on an "Easy Credit" Basis.

215 *Cf.* Federal Trade Comm'n v. Med Resorts Int'l, Inc., 5 Trade Reg. Rep. (CCH) ¶ 15,174 (N.D. Ill. Nov. 1, 2001) (proposed consent decree against seller of travel club memberships that did not include Holder Notice in contract).

216 U.C.C. §§ 9-403(d), 9-404(d). *See also* Official Comment 5, U.C.C. § 9-403; *In re* Barker, 306 B.R. 339, 350 (Bankr. E.D. Cal. 2004). *But cf.* Whittington v. Patriot Homes, Inc., 65 U.C.C. Rep. Serv. 2d 488 (W.D. La. 2008) (not implying Holder Notice, when court appears to be unaware of the UCC requirement).

These provisions were adopted as part of Revised Article 9, which was effective in most states July 1, 2001. The provisions apply enforcement of the consumer's rights after this effective date, even if the contract

the required notice is subject to a consumer account debtor's claims and defenses to the same extent as if the contract had contained the notice.[217] Neither the assignor nor the assignee can seek a waiver from the consumer avoiding this result.[218]

This Article 9 provision applies to any credit sales agreement assigned to a creditor. It does not apply to direct loans, even seller-referred purchase money loans that must include the Holder notice.[219] The Article 9 provision subjects *assignees* to claims the consumer could assert against the original *obligee* (the assignor).[220] This Article 9 provision only applies to assigned loans, so it does not allow for the assertion of seller-related claims when the credit was a direct loan from the lender to the consumer. In a direct loan, the seller is not the original obligee but the payee of the loan proceeds. In addition, the Article 9 provision does not apply to negotiable instruments, and many direct loans do involve negotiable instruments.[221]

Article 9 implies into the contract any holder notice required not only by federal but also by state law. Of special note, certain state holder laws clearly cover leases.[222] Article 9's rule implying holder notices into contracts applies to "account debtors,"[223] a term that includes anyone liable under a property lease.[224] Consequently, if state law requires a holder notice be included in a lease, but the notice is not present, then Article 9 will imply its insertion. On the other hand, if neither state nor federal law require a notice as to a creditor being subject to claims and defenses, then the UCC does not create this requirement.

4.4.2.2 Revised Article 3 Requires the Holder Notice to Be Implied in Negotiable Instruments

Filling the gap left by Article 9 for direct loans, Revised Article 3 states that the FTC Holder Notice shall be implied into any promissory note whenever that notice should have been inserted into the note.[225] Revised Article 3 was adopted in 2002 by the National Conference of Commissioners on Uniform State Laws and the American Law Institute, but the Article 3 FTC Holder provision has only been signed into law in ten jurisdictions.[226]

Revised Article 3 states that the consumer may assert against the holder all claims and defenses that would have been available against the "payee" if the note included the FTC Holder Notice.[227] A payee is the person who receives the funds from the loan, that is, the seller. But this provision does not apply in the forty-one states that have not adopted this provision.[228]

4.4.2.3 Case Law Implying the Notice into the Contract Without the Aid of the UCC

Even before enactment of the Article 9 and 3 provisions discussed at §§ 4.4.2.1 and 4.4.2.2, *supra*, a number of courts had implied the Holder notice into an agreement when it is required to be placed.[229] This precedent is particularly important in the case of negotiable instruments when the protection offered by Article 9 does not apply, and particularly in cases in which Revised Article 3 has not been adopted in a state.

A New Jersey appellate court has found that "it is inconceivable to us that [the holders] may evade the remedial reach of the FTC Holder Rule simply because of that omission."[230] The appellate court found support for reading into the contract the FTC Holder language in that the "law is a silent factor in every contract" and "equity looks to substance rather than form." In that case, the seller had a business arrangement with the lender, but the Holder notice was not found in the lender's direct loan with the consumer.

---

was created before that date. U.C.C. § 9-702; *In re* Barker, 306 B.R. 339, 350 (Bankr. E.D. Cal. 2004) (applying Revised Article 9's FTC Holder Notice rule to pre-revision transaction).

217 U.C.C. §§ 9-403(d), 9-404(d).

218 *In re* Barker, 306 B.R. 339 (Bankr. E.D. Cal. 2004).

219 *See* §§ 4.1.2.1, 4.1.2.2, *supra* (difference between purchase money loans and assignment of installment contracts as ways of financing purchases).

220 U.C.C. § 9-403(d), (d)(2).

221 *See* U.C.C. § 9-102(a)(3) (definition of "account debtor"); Official Comment 5(h), U.C.C. § 9-102; Official Comment 5, U.C.C. § 9-404.

222 *See* § 4.5, *infra*.

223 Rev. U.C.C. § 9-404(a).

224 Rev. U.C.C. § 9-102(a)(3) (definition of "account debtor"), (2) (definition of "account").

225 Rev. U.C.C. § 3-305(e).

226 *See* Ark. Code Ann. § 4-3-305; D.C. Code § 28-3-305(e); Ind. Code § 26-1-3.1-3-305(e); Mich. Comp. Laws § 440.3305(5) (effective April 10, 2014); Minn. Stat. § 336.3-305(e); Miss Code Ann. § 75-3-305(e); N.M. Stat. Ann. § 55-3-305(e); Okla. Stat. tit. 12A § 3-305(e); S.C. Code

§ 36-3-305; Tex. Bus. & Com. Code § 3.305 (West). *See also* Rylander v. Motor City, Inc., 259 P.3d 748 (Kan. Ct. App. 2011) (table) (not adopted in Kansas, so does not apply).

Revised Article 3 has also been adopted by two states without the FTC Holder protections. *See* Ky. Rev. Stat. Ann. § 355.3-305 (West); Nev. Rev. Stat. § 104.3305.

227 Rev. U.C.C. § 3-305(e)(2).

228 Rylander v. Motor City, Inc., 259 P.3d 748 (Kan. Ct. App. 2011) (table).

229 Gonzalez v. Old Kent Mortg. Co., 2000 WL 1469313 (E.D. Pa. Sept. 21, 2000); Anderson v. Central States Waterproofing (Minn. Dist. Ct. Hennepin Cnty. 1982), *available at* www.nclc.org/unreported; Associates Home Equity Services, Inc. v. Troup, 778 A.2d 529 (N.J. Super. Ct. App. Div. 2001). *See also* Xerographic Supplies Corp. v. Hertz Commercial Leasing Corp., 386 So. 2d 299 (Fla. Dist. Ct. App. 1980) (appellate court does not reach trial court's holding that FTC Holder Notice must be implied into contract). *But see* Abel v. KeyBank USA, NA, 2003 WL 26132935 (N.D. Ohio Sept. 24, 2003); Vietnam Veterans of Am., Inc. v. Guerdon Industries, 644 F. Supp. 951 (D. Del. 1986) (declining to read absent FTC Holder Notice into contract); Crisomia v. Parkway Mortg., Inc., 2001 Bankr. LEXIS 1469 (Bankr. E.D. Pa. Aug. 21, 2001); Rylander v. Motor City, Inc., 259 P.3d 748 (Kan. Ct. App. 2011) (table); Hayner v. Old Kent Bank, 2002 Mich. App. LEXIS 190 (Mich. Ct. App. Feb. 12, 2002) (FTC Holder Rule places no duty upon lender who accepted contract without Holder Notice); Pratt v. North Dixie Manufactured Hous., Ltd., 2003 WL 21040658 (Ohio Ct. App. May 9, 2003) (unpublished) (finding no basis for holder liability when assigned contract did not include FTC Holder Notice).

230 Associates Home Equity Services, Inc. v. Troup, 778 A.2d 529 (N.J. Super. Ct. App. Div. 2001). *See also* Citifinancial Mortg. Co. v. Freeman, 2006 WL 1029321 (N.J. Super. Ch. Ct. Apr. 13, 2006); Vultaggio v. Afzali, 2005 WL 2936900 (Ohio Ct. App. Nov. 7, 2005) (citing *Associates Home Equity Services, Inc.*, for the proposition that assignees cannot evade liability simply by omitting language, but finding in the instant transaction holder language was not required).

This approach, though, has not been successful in arguing that students should be able to raise school-related defenses to collection actions for federally-backed student loans.[231] In large part, this is because federally-backed student loans are regulated by the Department of Education; students' ability to raise such defenses is now generally found in federal regulations and directives.[232]

4.4.3 State Holder Statutes

Another approach to being able to raise claims or defenses against a holder when the holder notice is omitted is to bring a claim under a similar *state* statute. These state statutes are examined at § 4.5, *infra*, and it can be seen that there are extensive differences from state to state. In some jurisdictions, the statute offers greater consumer protection than is provided by the Holder notice, particularly when the state law provides derivative liability even when the notice of such liability is not placed in the agreement. On the other hand, in other states the statute does little more than prohibit waivers of the consumer's ability to raise defenses against the seller's assignee.

4.4.4 Omission of Holder Notice As the Holder's UDAP Violation

4.4.4.1 General

For both assigned installment sales contract and related direct loans, a creditor's attempt to enforce a note without the Holder notice should be a state UDAP violation. Even though the FTC Holder Rule requires only the *seller* to arrange for

the inclusion of the notice in the note or contract, the holder engages in an independent UDAP violation for its effort to deny the consumer rights provided by federal law. The consumer's damages equal the value of the consumer's claims or defenses that could have been raised against the creditor if the FTC Holder Notice had been included in the note.

4.4.4.2 Holder's Actions As a Deceptive Practice

When a creditor's promissory note violates the FTC Holder Rule, the creditor is engaging in a deceptive practice. As one court has put it, the creditor engages in "fraudulent conduct which creates a likelihood of confusion or misunderstanding" since the "FTC Regulation preserving defenses serves to eliminate confusion and misunderstanding created through an artificial bifurcation of a transaction by an installment seller in an effort to insulate the duty to pay from the duty to perform."[233]

---

231 Keams v. Tempe Technical Inst., Inc., 993 F. Supp. 714 (D. Ariz. 1997); Bartels v. Alabama Commercial College, 918 F. Supp. 1565 (S.D. Ga. 1995), *aff'd in part, rev'd in part, and remanded without op.*, 189 F.3d 483 (11th Cir. 1999); Armstrong v. Accrediting Council for Continuing Educ. & Training, Inc., 832 F. Supp. 419 (D.D.C. 1993), *vacated and remanded*, 84 F.3d 1452 (D.C. Cir. 1996) (table, text available at 1996 U.S. App. LEXIS 12241) (remanding for further consideration of whether to exercise jurisdiction over state claims), *on remand*, 950 F. Supp. 1 (D.D.C. 1996) (maintaining jurisdiction of pendent claims and finding case appropriate for declaratory relief), *on further remand*, 980 F. Supp. 53 (D.D.C. 1997) (determining that California law controls and inviting plaintiff to amend complaint to assert claims and defenses under California consumer protection laws), *aff'd*, 168 F.3d 1362 (D.C. Cir. 1999) (affirming district court's dismissal of claims); Spinner v. Chesapeake Bus. Inst. of Virginia, Clearinghouse No. 49,131A (E.D. Va. Feb. 5, 1993); Jackson v. Culinary Sch. of Washington, 788 F. Supp. 1233 (D.D.C. 1992), *aff'd in part, rev'd and remanded in part*, 27 F.3d 573 (D.C. Cir. 1994) (on de novo review, reversing district court's decision to issue declaratory judgment on state law issues), *vacated*, 515 U.S. 1139 (1995) (appellate court should have used abuse of discretion standard to review district court's decision to issue declaratory judgment on state law issues), *on remand*, 59 F.3d 254 (D.C. Cir. 1995) (remanding for district court to exercise its discretion about whether to issue declaratory judgment on state law issues); Hernandez v. Alexander, 1992 U.S. Dist. LEXIS 21930 (D. Nev. May 18, 1992); Shorter v. Alexander (N.D. Ga. Dec. 8, 1992), *available at* www.nclc.org/unreported.

232 *See* National Consumer Law Center, Student Loan Law Ch. 13 (5th ed. 2015), *updated at* www.nclc.org/library.

233 Iron & Glass Bank v. Franz, 9 Pa. D. & C.3d 419 (Pa. Ct. Com. Pl. Allegheny Cnty. 1978). *See also* Keams v. Tempe Technical Inst., Inc. (D. Ariz. Oct. 19, 1995), *available at* www.nclc.org/unreported; Brown v. LaSalle Northwest Nat'l Bank, 820 F. Supp. 1078 (N.D. Ill. 1993) (complaint survives motion to dismiss); Spinner v. Chesapeake Bus. Inst. of Virginia, Clearinghouse No. 49,131A (E.D. Va. Feb. 5, 1993) (practice may involve constructive fraud); Jackson v. Culinary Sch. of Washington, 788 F. Supp. 1233 (D.D.C. 1992) (complaint survives motion to dismiss), *later dismissed on summary judgment on other grounds*, 811 F. Supp. 714 (D.D.C. 1993) (finding insufficient facts to find UDAP liability), *aff'd in part, rev'd and remanded in part on other grounds*, 27 F.3d 573 (D.C. Cir. 1994) (on de novo review, reversing district court's decision to issue declaratory judgment on state law issues), *vacated*, 515 U.S. 1139 (1995) (appellate court should have used abuse of discretion standard to review district court's decision to issue declaratory judgment on state law issues), *on remand*, 59 F.3d 254 (D.C. Cir. 1995) (remanding for district court to exercise its discretion about whether to issue declaratory judgment on state law issues); Shorter v. Alexander (N.D. Ga. Dec. 8, 1992), *available at* www.nclc.org/unreported; Heastie v. Community Bank, 727 F. Supp. 1133 (N.D. Ill. 1989) (creditor liable under state UDAP statute for unfair practices in regard to FTC Holder Rule; creditor included a written notice in the contract in part contradicting the FTC Holder Notice). *But see* Kilgore v. Keybank, N.A., 712 F. Supp. 2d 939 (N.D. Cal. 2010), *vacated on other grounds*, 673 F.3d 947 (9th Cir. 2012); Williams v. Nat'l Sch. of Health Tech., 836 F. Supp. 273 (E.D. Pa. 1993) (only original seller, not seller's assignee, is liable for failure to include the FTC notice in the promissory note; decision ignores fact that if this UDAP violation is a defense against the lender, it is also a defense against the assignee); Capital Bank & Trust Co. v. Lacey, 393 So. 2d 668 (La. 1981) (only seller, not assignee, commits unfair act by failing to include Holder Notice in contract; assignee claimed transactions was commercial rather than consumer); Hayner v. Old Kent Bank, 2002 WL 227016 (Mich. App. Ct. Feb. 12, 2002) (unpublished) (no UDAP violation because FTC Holder Rule does not create a duty on the bank to place language in agreement, only on the seller); Nashville Elec. Serv. v. Stone, 1998 Tenn. App. LEXIS 474 (Tenn. Ct. App. July, 15, 1998) (only seller, not lender from which seller arranged loan, is liable for failure to include Holder Notice in loan documents). *Cf.* Brown v. Student Loan Xpress, Inc., 2012 WL 1029467 (W.D. Ky. Mar. 26, 2012) (finding no Kentucky UDAP violation because no Kentucky precedent on point); Morales v. Walker Motors Sales, Inc., 162 F. Supp. 2d 786 (S.D. Ohio 2000) (failure to use type size specified by FTC Holder Rule not material, so not a UDAP violation).

It is also a material nondisclosure for the creditor to fail to inform the consumer that the creditor's loan documents violate federal law. A court thus let a case proceed when RICO and UDAP claims were brought against a creditor who failed to include the FTC Holder Notice in its documents. The omission was alleged to be mail fraud, wire fraud, and deception, particularly in that the creditor covered up its relationship to the seller and supplied the documents violating the FTC rule.[234]

Even apart from the FTC rule violation, the very practice of insulating closely connected creditors from seller-related claims is a deceptive trade practice. FTC case law decided before the enactment of the FTC Holder Rule holds as deceptive the use of holder-in-due-course status in consumer transactions.[235]

A creditor also violates the state UDAP statute by supplying other forms for the consumer to sign, such as completion certificates, that contain language sidestepping the FTC Holder Rule by absolving the creditor of responsibility for some or all of the seller's liability.[236] This is the case even though the FTC rule only applies to the seller, placing no responsibility on the creditor to ensure that the notice is inserted in the credit agreement.

To the extent a creditor aids and abets the seller's scheme to avoid its responsibilities under the FTC Holder Rule, the creditor can be found directly liable under a UDAP statute for its conduct in furtherance of the fraud.[237] For example, does the creditor draft form loan documents knowing that in most cases the notes will violate the FTC Holder Rule? Does the lender participate in some subterfuge attempting to show the two are not related?

When a creditor's participation in violating the FTC Holder Rule is deceptive, the practice may also involve mail or wire fraud and thus lead to a RICO violation.[238] A failure to disclose can be enough to trigger mail fraud.[239]

4.4.4.3 Holder's Actions As a Violation of State UDAP Regulations

Massachusetts UDAP regulations also indicate that creditors violate the state UDAP statute if they fail to comply with standards similar to the FTC Holder Notice. These standards are that lenders are subject to all defenses if they are related to the seller, they prepared the loan documents, they supplied the loan forms, the seller recommended the creditor and the creditor financed at least two consumer loans related to the seller in the calendar year, or the creditor issued a credit card used in the transaction.[240]

Wisconsin UDAP regulations are similar in that it is unfair and deceptive for assignees of home improvement contracts to take those contracts unless they are subject to the consumer's *claims* and defenses against the assignor.[241] (Normally, assignees are just subject to the consumer's defenses against the assignor.)

The situation in Georgia is slightly different because Georgia has enacted as a state UDAP regulation the exact wording of the FTC Holder Rule.[242] As a result, any violation of the FTC Holder Rule automatically violates the Georgia regulation and thus the Georgia UDAP statute. Similarly, a creditor using a promissory note failing to comply with Georgia UDAP regulations should violate the Georgia UDAP statute.

Idaho UDAP regulations prohibit a "seller" from receiving a contract without the Holder notice, and the regulations define "seller" as anyone engaged in trade or commerce.[243] Thus a lender should be engaged in a per se UDAP violation in Idaho if the notice is not in the note.

4.4.4.4 Holder's Actions As an Unfair Practice

The creditor's use of a contract violating the FTC Holder Rule fits neatly into the FTC's definition of an unfair practice. There is substantial consumer injury and the consumer could not reasonably avoid the practice. Nor can there be any countervailing business justification for a lender to engage in loan practices that involve a violation of a federal regulation.[244]

Perhaps the best place to start in arguing that a lender engages in an unfair practice by so insulating itself is the statement of basis and purpose for the FTC Holder Rule:

> The Commission believes that relief under Section five of the FTC Act is appropriate when sellers or creditors impose adhesive contracts upon consumers, when such contracts contain terms which injure consumers, and when consumer injury is not off-set by a reasonable measure of value received in return. In this connection, the Commission's authority to examine and prohibit unfair practices in or

---

234 Brown v. LaSalle Northwest Nat'l Bank, 820 F. Supp. 1078 (N.D. Ill. 1993).

235 All-State Indus. of N. Carolina, Inc. v. Federal Trade Comm'n, 423 F.2d 423 (4th Cir. 1970); Certified Bldg. Products, Inc., 83 F.T.C. 1004 (1973); *In re* Southern States Distrib. Co., 83 F.T.C. 1125 (1973).

236 Heastie v. Community Bank, 727 F. Supp. 1133 (N.D. Ill. 1989). *See* § 4.3.13, *supra.*

237 *See* National Consumer Law Center, Unfair and Deceptive Acts and Practices § 10.4 (8th ed. 2012), *updated at* www.nclc.org/library.

238 Brown v. LaSalle Northwest Nat'l Bank, 820 F. Supp. 1078 (N.D. Ill. 1993).

239 *Id. See also* § 7.3.2.2, *infra.*

240 Massachusetts Consumer Protection Regulations, 940 Mass. Code Regs. § 3.07, Advertising or Offering to Sell on an "Easy Credit" Basis.

241 Wisconsin Dep't of Agriculture, Trade & Consumer Protection Rules, Wis. Admin. Code ATCP § 110.06, Home Improvement Trade Practices. *See* Jackson v. DeWitt, 592 N.W.2d 262 (Wis. 1999) (home improvement UDAP regulation that subjected assignee to buyer's claims and defenses trumped more general statute that limited assignee's liability to amount still owing on date consumer gave notice of claim).

242 Georgia Office of Consumer Affairs Regulations, Ga. Comp. R. & Regs. 122-5-.01.

243 Idaho Consumer Protection Regulations, Idaho Admin. Code r. 04.02.01.020(44), 04.02.01.210.

244 *See* National Consumer Law Center, Unfair and Deceptive Acts and Practices § 4.3.2 (8th ed. 2012), *updated at* www.nclc.org/library (further discussion of the FTC unfairness definition). *See also* Kilgore v. Keybank, N.A., 712 F. Supp. 2d 939 (N.D. Cal. 2010) (while unfairness claim was stated, this state law claim was preempted as to a UDAP claim against a national bank), *vacated on other grounds*, 673 F.3d 947 (9th Cir. 2012).

affecting commerce in the manner of a commercial equity court is appropriately applied to this problem. Where one party to a transaction enjoys substantial advantages with respect to the consumers with whom he deals, it is appropriate for the Commission to conduct an inquiry to determine whether the dominant party is using an overabundance of market power, or commercial advantage, in an inequitable manner.

We have conducted the contemplated inquiry in this case. We have reached a determination that it constitutes an unfair and deceptive practice to use contractual boilerplate to separate a buyer's duty to pay from a seller's duty to perform. We are persuaded that this bifurcation of duties with its attendant externalization of costs injures both consumers and the market. We know of no substantial benefits which may be received by consumers in return for the valuable legal rights they are compelled to relinquish. We can imagine no reasonable measure of value which could justify requiring consumers to assume all risk of seller misconduct, particularly when creditors who profit from consumer sales have access to superior information combined with the means and capacity to deal with seller misconduct costs expeditiously and economically.

Our findings with respect to the use of vendor related loans to separate a consumer's duty to pay from his seller's duty to perform are detailed in Chapter IV. We are of the view that the use of direct loan agreements is no less adhesive than the use of installment sales contracts which incorporate waivers or promissory notes. We have received substantial evidence that sellers work cooperatively with lenders to foreclose consumer equities, and that such cooperation involves high-pressure sales tactics and deceptive and misleading statements. We have received substantial evidence that this rule would be seriously weakened by a failure to address the vendor related loan problem. We are therefore persuaded that the reasoning appearing above in this chapter applies with equal force to direct loan financing, and that our rule must apply to "purchase money" loan transactions.[245]

Courts have recognized unfairness as a valid way to challenge the non-inclusion of the Holder notice[246] while not always ruling for the consumer in any specific case, particularly in federal student loan cases in which the Department of Education had approved of the loan notes.[247]

4.4.4.5 Are the Creditor's Actions Within the UDAP Statute's Scope?

When the FTC Holder Notice is included in a contract or promissory note, the consumer can raise a seller-related UDAP claim against the creditor even if the creditor is not within the scope of the UDAP statute.[248] All that is required is that both the seller and the challenged practice are within the scope of the UDAP statute. But when a consumer is bringing a UDAP claim directly against the creditor for using a contract or note failing to contain the Holder notice, both the creditor and the creditor's alleged violation must be within the scope of the UDAP statute.

A number of UDAP statutes exclude credit from their scope or exempt banks or financial institutions,[249] so that those institutions are not liable under the UDAP statute for the omission of the Holder notice from the note.[250] In a Virginia student loan case, the court seized on the argument that the student loan note was authorized by the government so that the practice was exempted from the UDAP statute under that statute's exclusion for practices authorized by federal laws or regulations.[251] A New Jersey court held that claims under New Jersey's consumer fraud statute relating to omission of the FTC Holder Notice from student loan documents were preempted by the federal Higher Education Act.[252] However, claims under a New

---

to a UDAP claim against a national bank), *vacated on other grounds* 673 F.3d 947 (9th Cir. 2012); Jackson v. Culinary Sch. of Wash., 811 F. Supp. 714 (D.D.C. 1993) (no evidence that a contract without the Holder Notice was unconscionable when consumer offered no evidence that contract unreasonably favored creditor), *aff'd in part on other grounds, vacated and remanded in part on other grounds*, 27 F.3d 573 (D.C. Cir. 1994) (finding, on de novo review, that district court should have refused to issue declaratory judgment on state law issues), *vacated and remanded*, 115 S. Ct. 2573 (1995) (circuit court should have used abuse of discretion standard, not de novo review, in determining whether district court should have ruled on state law issues), *on remand*, 59 F.3d 255 (D.C. Cir. 1995) (remanding for district court to exercise its discretion about whether to issue declaratory judgment on state law issues). *See also* Armstrong v. Accrediting Council for Continuing Educ. & Training, Inc., 832 F. Supp. 419 (D.D.C. 1993) (not unconscionable when United States had approved the student loan note), *vacated and remanded*, 84 F.3d 1452 (D.C. Cir. 1996) (table, text available at 1996 U.S. App. LEXIS 12241) (remanding for further consideration of whether to exercise jurisdiction over state claims), *on remand*, 950 F. Supp. 1 (D.D.C. 1996) (maintaining jurisdiction of pendent claims and finding case appropriate for declaratory relief), *on further remand*, 980 F. Supp. 53 (D.D.C. 1997) (determining that California law controls and inviting plaintiff to amend complaint to assert claims and defenses under California consumer protection laws), *aff'd*, 168 F.3d 1362 (D.C. Cir. 1999) (affirming district court's dismissal of claims).

248 § 4.3.1, *supra*.

249 *See* United States v. Ornecipe (S.D. Fla. 1995), *available at* www.nclc .org/unreported; Armand v. Secretary of Educ. (S.D. Fla. July 19, 1995), *available at* www.nclc.org/unreported. *See also* National Consumer Law Center, Unfair and Deceptive Acts and Practices §§ 2.2.1, 2.3.3 (8th ed. 2012), *updated at* www.nclc.org/library.

250 *See* Whittington v. Patriot Homes, Inc., 65 U.C.C. Rep. Serv. 2d 488 (W.D. La. 2008).

251 Spinner v. Chesapeake Bus. Inst. of Va., Clearinghouse No. 49,131A (E.D. Va. Feb. 5, 1993).

252 Morgan v. Markerdowne Corp., 976 F. Supp. 301 (D.N.J. 1997).

---

245 Statement of Basis and Purpose for the Federal Trade Commission Rule Concerning the Preservation of Consumers' Claims and Defenses, 40 Fed. Reg. 53,524 (Nov. 18, 1975), *available online as companion material to this treatise*.

246 Kilgore v. Keybank, N.A., 712 F. Supp. 2d 939 (N.D. Cal. 2010) (while unfairness claim was stated, this state law claim was preempted as to a UDAP claim against a national bank), *vacated on other grounds*, 673 F.3d 947 (9th Cir. 2012); Spinner v. Chesapeake Bus. Inst. of Va., Clearinghouse No. 49,131A (E.D. Va. Feb. 5, 1993); Jackson v. Culinary Sch. of Washington, 788 F. Supp. 1233 (D.D.C. 1992).

247 Kilgore v. Keybank, N.A., 712 F. Supp. 2d 939 (N.D. Cal. 2010) (while unfairness claim was stated, this state law claim was preempted as

Jersey state law similar to the FTC Holder Rule were not so barred.[253]

In another case the consumer brought a UDAP action under the District of Columbia statute, alleging a violation of a specific UDAP provision prohibiting the sale of consumer goods in a condition or manner not consistent with that warranted by requirement of federal laws. The court dismissed the claim because the contract dealt with trade school *services*, and the court found that the particular UDAP provision only applied to goods, not services.[254]

4.4.5 Aiding and Abetting Seller's Omission of Holder Notice

Aiding and abetting may be an appropriate challenge to a lender's participation with the seller in a scheme to avoid the FTC Holder Rule requirement. For example, in California, aiding and abetting involves a party knowing that another's conduct is improper and providing substantial assistance or encouragement to that other party.[255] In a California federal case, students alleged a claim for aiding and abetting when a bank was a sophisticated player well aware of the FTC Holder Rule requirement and consciously sought to avoid it. The bank knew a school was systematically violating the FTC Holder Rule but that, if the notice was included in the note, the bank would not be able to sell the loans on the secondary market. It was alleged the bank had specific knowledge of the violation because the bank reviewed and approved exemplars of the notes.[256]

As for substantial assistance, the consumers alleged that the bank was the school's preferred lender and that the bank's personnel helped create, review, approve, and ratify the school's representations to the students concerning the loan

documents and also the loan documents themselves. Funding the loans was also substantial assistance.[257] In this case, however, the bank was a national bank, and the trial court held that under old preemption standards, since altered, the National Bank Act preempted the state law theory of aiding and abetting as it was applied to a national bank.[258] Moreover, the case was vacated on appeal because the Ninth Circuit found that the case should instead have been sent to arbitration pursuant to an arbitration clause.[259]

4.4.6 Do State Law Theories for Omitted Holder Notice Apply to National Banks and Federal Savings Associations?

This section lists four state law theories to find a holder liable for claims and defenses, despite the absence of the Holder notice—theories under the UCC, state UDAP, state holder statutes, and state common law aiding and abetting precedent. When claims or defenses are asserted against a national bank or federal savings association, the depository is likely to respond that state law is preempted by the National Bank Act (NBA) (for national banks), the Home Owners' Loan Act (HOLA) (for federal savings associations), and Office of the Comptroller of Currency (OCC) regulations that define the scope of preemption for both types of federal depositories.

This federal preemption only applies to these entities. It does not apply to state-chartered banks or savings associations or to non-depositories, because these entities are not federally regulated. In addition, it does not apply to subsidiaries, affiliates, or agents of national banks or federal savings associations.[260]

Preemption should also not apply to situations in which the bank or federal savings association is an assignee of the seller. The UCC provides that the seller's note should be treated as if the Holder notice were included.[261] Before the note is assigned to the bank, it already is interpreted as including the holder notice. An assignment of a credit obligation cannot change the terms of the loan—the assignee has no greater rights than the assignor. Selling a note to a national bank does not change the loan terms.

In addition, the OCC has stated that federal regulation of national banks does not preempt the application of the UCC[262] or state contract law.[263] This means that claims based on Articles 3 and 9 implying the notice into the credit obligation are not preempted.

---

253 *Id.*
254 Jackson v. Culinary Sch. of Wash., 811 F. Supp. 714 (D.D.C. 1993), *aff'd in part on other grounds, vacated and remanded in part on other grounds*, 27 F.3d 573 (D.C. Cir. 1994) (finding, on de novo review, that district court should have refused to issue declaratory judgment on state law issues), *vacated and remanded*, 115 S. Ct. 2573 (1995) (circuit court should have used abuse of discretion standard, not de novo review, in determining whether district court should have ruled on state law issues), *on remand*, 59 F.3d 255 (D.C. Cir. 1995) (remanding for district court to exercise its discretion about whether to issue declaratory judgment on state law issues). *See also* Armstrong v. Accrediting Council for Continuing Educ. & Training, Inc., 832 F. Supp. 419 (D.D.C. 1993) (not unconscionable when United States had approved the student loan note), *vacated and remanded*, 84 F.3d 1452 (D.C. Cir. 1996) (table, text available at 1996 U.S. App. LEXIS 12241) (remanding for further consideration of whether to exercise jurisdiction over state claims), *on remand*, 950 F. Supp. 1 (D.D.C. 1996) (maintaining jurisdiction of pendent claims and finding case appropriate for declaratory relief), *on further remand*, 980 F. Supp. 53 (D.D.C. 1997) (determining that California law controls and inviting plaintiff to amend complaint to assert claims and defenses under California consumer protection laws), *aff'd*, 168 F.3d 1362 (D.C. Cir. 1999) (affirming district court's dismissal of claims).
255 Kilgore v. Keybank, N.A., 712 F. Supp. 2d 939 (N.D. Cal. 2010), *vacated on other grounds*, 673 F.3d 947 (9th Cir. 2012).
256 *Id.*

---

257 *Id.*
258 *Id. See* § 4.4.6, *infra* (discussing current standards of federal preemption as to national banks).
259 Kilgore v. Keybank, N.A., 673 F.3d 947 (9th Cir. 2012).
260 Until federal legislation enacted on July 21, 2010—12 U.S.C. §§ 25b(b) (2), (e), (h)(2)—operating subsidiaries of national banks could avail themselves of the same preemption standards as their parents. Waters v. Wachovia Bank, N.A., 550 US 1 (2007).
261 *See* § 4.4.2, *supra.*
262 O.C.C. Interpretive Letter No. 1005 (June 10, 2004).
263 *See* 12 C.F.R. § 34.4(b)(1).

In states that have not enacted this Article 3 provision, when a national bank or federal savings association originates a loan that fails to include the FTC Holder Notice, the question becomes whether the provisions of a state holder statute, state UDAP statute, or state aiding and abetting theory are preempted by federal regulation of depositories. According to a federal statute, the state law is preempted only if it prevents or significantly interferes with the exercise of the federal depository's powers.[264]

Based on this statutory standard, there should be no preemption of state law claims that parallel federal requirements.[265] A state holder statute paralleling the FTC Holder Rule should not be preempted. Thus this should be a valid basis to find a national bank liable for seller-related claims and defenses if a state's holder statute directly creates such substantive liability instead of creating it by requiring the insertion in the note of a notice to that effect.

Aiding and abetting is a state tort claim, and an OCC regulation carves out tort claims as an area that is not preempted.[266] As a result, a claim that a national bank is aiding and abetting a seller in engaging in a UDAP violation should not be preempted.[267]

State UDAP statutes should also not be preempted. The substantive core of the typical state UDAP statute—a prohibition of unfair or deceptive acts or practices—parallels similar prohibitions in the FTC Act, the Consumer Financial Protection Act, and OCC regulations applicable to banks.[268] It is hard to see how a UDAP statute could interfere with a bank's legitimate activities if federal law already prohibits the same acts. Indeed, the FTC Act has been interpreted as prohibiting a related lender's ability to cut off seller-related claims and defenses.[269] However, courts have held that UDAP claims are preempted when they attempt to impose substantive limits on loan terms.[270] One court preempted a UDAP claim that sought to hold a bank liable for accepting a note that did not include the Holder notice, on the ground that the Holder rule did not apply directly to the bank.[271] But it is hard to see how state law is infringing on the powers of a national bank when federal law requires that holders be subject to claims and defenses. There surely can be no federal policy to make banks immune

from fraud claims against their related sellers when the banks are participating in that fraudulent scheme. This does not have to do with the terms of credit but with the bank's active participation in a scheme to circumvent federal law.

Many decisions finding state laws preempted were decided under the preemption standards that were in effect prior to the effective date of the Dodd-Frank Act, enacted in 2010.[272] That Act significantly narrowed the grounds for preemption, and thus many of the earlier decisions are entitled to little weight.

4.5 State "Holder" Statutes

Virtually every state has enacted state "holder" laws.[273] These laws though vary dramatically from state to state. One

---

264 12 U.S.C. § 25b(b).

265 *See* First Nat'l Bank in St. Louis v. Missouri, 263 U.S. 640 (1924). *See generally* National Consumer Law Center, Mortgage Lending § 5.5 (2d ed. 2014), *updated at* www.nclc.org/library.

266 12 C.F.R. § 34.4(b)(2). *See generally* National Consumer Law Center, Mortgage Lending § 5.8.4.3 (2d ed. 2014), *updated at* www.nclc.org/library.

267 *But see* Kilgore v. Keybank, N.A., 712 F. Supp. 2d 939 (N.D. Cal. 2010), *vacated on other grounds* 673 F.3d 947 (9th Cir. 2012).

268 *See* National Consumer Law Center, Mortgage Lending § 5.8.4.9 (2d ed. 2014), *updated at* www.nclc.org/library.

269 *See* § 4.4.4.3, *supra*.

270 *See* National Consumer Law Center, Mortgage Lending § 5.8.4.9 (2d ed. 2014), *updated at* www.nclc.org/library.

271 *See* Kilgore v. Keybank, N.A., 712 F. Supp. 2d 939, 953–958 (N.D. Cal. 2010) (finding UDAP claims that were asserted against national bank based on Holder rule to be preempted), *vacated on other grounds*, 673 F.3d 947 (9th Cir. 2012).

272 *See* National Consumer Law Center, Mortgage Lending § 5.3 (2d ed. 2014), *updated at* www.nclc.org/library.

273 *ALABAMA*: Ala. Code §§ 5-19-5, 5-19-8 (applicable to consumer credit sales).

ALASKA: Alaska Stat. § 45.50.541 (contracts for sale or lease of consumer goods or services on credit).

ARIZONA: Ariz. Stat. §§ 44-145 (writings evidencing the obligation of a natural person as buyer, lessee, or borrower in connection with purchase or lease of goods or services), 45-5005 (home solicitation sales).

CALIFORNIA: Cal. Civ. Code §§ 1747.90 (credit cards), 1804.1, 1804.2 (retail installment contracts), 1810.7 (retail installment accounts), 2982.5 (motor vehicle loans), 2986.10 (motor vehicle leases) (West).

COLORADO: Colo. Rev. Stat. § 5-3-303 (consumer credit sales and leases).

CONNECTICUT: Conn. Gen. Stat. §§ 42-411(b) (consumer leases), 52-572g (credit transactions covering consumer goods or services, other than credit card transactions). *See* Tirado v. Ofstein, 2008 WL 902506 (Conn. Super. Ct. Mar. 14, 2008) (applying Conn. Gen. Stat. § 52-572g to hold consumer not liable to assignee of retail installment contract).

DELAWARE: Del. Code tit. 6, §§ 4311, 4312 (retail installment sales), 4342 (retail installment accounts).

DISTRICT OF COLUMBIA: D.C. Code §§ 28-3807, 28-3808 (consumer credit sales), 28-3809 (direct installment loan to purchase goods or services). *See* Carroll v. Fremont Inv. & Loan, 636 F. Supp. 2d 41, 56 (D.D.C. 2009) (D.C. Code § 28-3808 only preserves defenses and setoffs and is limited to consumer credit, defined as transactions when amount financed does not exceed $25,000); Johnson v. Long Beach Mortg. Loan Trust 2001-4, 451 F. Supp. 2d 16 (D.D.C. 2006) (D.C. Code § 28-3808 only preserves defenses and setoff claims, not affirmative claims; § 28-3809 does not apply to assignee of lender but does make original lender liable for mortgage broker's acts). *See also* Hancock v. Homeq Servicing Corp., 2007 WL 1238746 (D.D.C. Apr. 27, 2007) (statute not applicable to transactions over $25,000 or to loans secured by real estate), *aff'd on other grounds*, 526 F.3d 785 (D.C. Cir. 2008); Johnson v. Long Beach Mortg. Loan Trust 2001-4, 451 F. Supp. 2d 16 (D.D.C. 2006) (D.C. Code § 28-3808 only provides for defenses and not affirmative claims against lender; § 28-3809 does not apply to assignment but allows certain affirmative claims against a direct lender). *Cf.* Hancock v. Homeq Servicing Corp., 2007 WL 1238746 (D.D.C. Apr. 27, 2007) (D.C. Code § 28-3808 does not allow affirmative damage recovery, only defensive use or cancellation of transaction; does not cover consumer sales over $25,000 or real-estate-related loans).

FLORIDA: Fla. Stat. § 520.74 (home improvement contracts).

GEORGIA: Ga. Code Ann. §§ 10-1-9 (retail installment contracts), 10-1-33 (motor vehicle sales financing). *See also* Ga. Comp. R. & Regs. 122-5-.01 (Georgia's UDAP rule adopting FTC Holder Rule).

HAWAII: Haw. Rev. Stat. § 476-19 (credit sales).

IDAHO: Idaho Code § 28-43-306 (no negotiable instruments in credit sales).

significant aspect of many of these laws is that they are not dependent on a notice being placed in a note—consumers can

---

ILLINOIS: 815 Ill. Comp. Stat. §§ 405/17, 405/18 (retail installment contracts), 375/16, 375/17 (motor vehicle retail installment sales), 636/70 (consumer leases).

IOWA: Iowa Code §§ 537.3307, 537.3404 (consumer credit sales and leases), 537.3403 (credit cards), 537.3405 (loans for property or services).

KANSAS: Kan. Stat. Ann. §§ 16a-3-307, 16a-3-404 (consumer credit sales and leases), 16a-3-403 (credit cards), 16a-3-405 (loans for goods or services).

MAINE: Me. Rev. Stat. Ann. tit. 9-A, §§ 3-307, 3-403 (consumer credit sales and leases), 3-404 (loans for goods or services), 3-405 (consumer leases).

MARYLAND: Md. Code, Com. Law §§ 12-309 (loans to buy consumer goods or services), 12-628 (promissory notes in installment sales) (West).

MASSACHUSETTS: Mass. Gen. Laws Ann. ch. 255, §§ 12C (promissory notes in credit sales of goods), 12F (consumer loan transactions connected to consumer sale or lease transactions), ch. 255B, § 19A (motor vehicle retail installment contracts), ch. 255D, §§ 10(6), 25A (retail installment sale agreements). *See also* 940 Mass. Code Regs. § 3.07 (certain sellers).

MICHIGAN: Mich. Comp. Laws Ann. §§ 445.865 (retail installment contracts), 445.1207 (home improvement contracts), 492.114a (motor vehicle installment sale contracts). *See* Cannoy v. Interstate Builders, Inc., 2003 WL 133063 (Mich. Ct. App. Jan. 3, 2003) (language of state law limits recovery to amount paid to specific holder, not to amount paid on the debt to all holders); Jerry v. Second Nat'l Bank, 527 N.W.2d 788 (Mich. Ct. App. 1994) (finding assignee of retail installment contract liable for buyer's claims and defenses under Michigan statute similar to FTC Holder Rule); Koscielny v. Ford Motor Co., 2006 WL 1726486 (Mich. Cir. Ct. June 21, 2006) (assignee is subject to same claims that consumer could bring against manufacturer and dealer).

MINNESOTA: Minn. Stat. Ann. § 325G.16 (consumer credit sales).

MISSISSIPPI: Miss. Code Ann. § 63-19-41 (motor vehicle retail installment contracts).

MISSOURI: Mo. Rev. Stat. Ann. §§ 408.405 (purchase or lease of consumer goods or services), 408.410 (exclusion for certain loans and credit card transactions). *See* Boulds v. Chase Auto Fin. Corp., 266 S.W.3d 847 (Mo. Ct. App. 2008) (limitations placed on assertion of defenses and setoffs to creditor's claim by Mo. Rev. Stat. Ann. § 408.405 do not apply to UDAP suit that is not based on that statute).

NEVADA: Nev. Rev. Stat. § 97.275 (retail installment contracts and retail charge agreements). *Cf.* Scaffidi v. United Nissan, 425 F. Supp. 2d 1172 (D. Nev. 2005) (holder has no derivative liability when buyer's claims against seller lack merit), *later op. at* 2005 WL 3940287 (D. Nev. Sept. 28, 2005) (similar holding).

NEW HAMPSHIRE: N.H. Rev. Stat. §§ 320:21-a, 320:21-b (consumer credit sales and leases by hawker or peddler).

NEW JERSEY: N.J. Stat. Ann. §§ 17:16C-38.1, 17:16C-38.2 (retail installment contracts), 17:16C-64.1, 17:16C-64.2 (home repair contracts) (West).

NEW MEXICO: N.M. Stat. Ann. §§ 56-1-5, 56-1-7 (retail installment contracts and retail charge agreements).

NEW YORK: N.Y. Pers. Prop. Law §§ 302(9) (motor vehicle retail installment contracts), 403 (retail installment contracts), 413 (retail installment credit agreements); N.Y. Gen. Bus. Law § 253 (interlocking loans) (McKinney).

NORTH CAROLINA: N.C. Gen. Stat. § 25A-25 (consumer credit sales). *See* State *ex rel.* Easley v. Rich Food Services, Inc., 535 S.E.2d 84 (N.C. Ct. App. 2000) (attorney general can obtain cancellation of contracts and restitution from finance company based on FTC Holder Notice required by state statute).

OHIO: Ohio Rev. Code Ann. §§ 1317.031, 1317.032 (West) (purchase money loan installment notes and retail installment contracts in connection with consumer transactions). *See* Blanco v. Keybank USA, N.A., 2005 WL 4135013 (N.D. Ohio Sept. 30, 2005) (disagreeing with

Abel; state holder law applies to student loan made by national bank and is not preempted by National Bank Act), *vacated on other grounds*, 2005 WL 5789023 (N.D. Ohio Dec. 28, 2005). *But see* Abel v. Keybank USA, 313 F. Supp. 2d 720 (N.D. Ohio 2004) (Ohio Rev. Code Ann. § 1317.032 conflicts with and is therefore preempted by National Bank Act; failing to consider that the state statute is no greater impingement on the autonomy of national banks than is already imposed by the FTC Holder Rule).

OKLAHOMA: Okla. Stat. Ann. tit. 14-A, §§ 2-403, 2-404 (consumer credit sales and leases).

OREGON: Or. Rev. Stat. §§ 83.650 (retail installment contracts for motor vehicles and manufactured homes), 83.820 (contracts for sale or lease of motor vehicles or consumer goods or services on credit), 83.860 (interlocking loans).

PENNSYLVANIA: 12 Pa. Cons. Stat. Ann. §§ 6201 to 6275 (motor vehicle installment sale contracts), 6301 to 6355 (retail installment sales except motor vehicles), Pa. Stat. Ann. tit. 73, § 500-207 (home improvement contracts).

PUERTO RICO: P.R. Laws Ann. tit. 10, §§ 748, 749 (retail installment contracts).

RHODE ISLAND: R.I. Gen. Laws Ann. §§ 6-27-5 (promissory notes in retail contracts for goods or services; certain loans), 6-28-6 (home solicitation sales). *See also* R. I. Gen. Laws Ann. § 6-28.1-3 (liability of third parties for certain unfair home improvement loans to elders).

SOUTH CAROLINA: S.C. Code §§ 37-2-403, 37-2-404 (consumer credit sales and leases), 37-3-410 (interlocking loans), 37-3-411 (credit cards). *See* Rosemond v. Campbell, 343 S.E.2d 641, 645 (S.C. Ct. App. 1986) (state holder law allows consumer to assert affirmative claim, not just defense, against seller).

SOUTH DAKOTA: S.D. Codified Laws Ann. §§ 57A-3A-102–57A-3A-107 (contracts for sale or lease of consumer goods or services on credit).

TEXAS: Tex. Fin. Code §§ 345.304 (retail installment transactions) (West); Tex. Fin. Code § 348.412 (motor vehicle installment sales) (West).

UTAH: Utah Code §§ 70C-2-204, 70C-2-205 (West) (consumer credit sales).

VERMONT: Vt. Stat. Ann. tit. 9, § 2455 (consumer contracts), tit. 8, § 14303 (bank credit cards).

WASHINGTON: Wash. Rev. Code Ann. § 63.14.020 (retail installment contracts). *See also* Wash. Rev. Code Ann. § 63.14.145 (contract retains its character after assignment).

WEST VIRGINIA: W. Va. Code §§ 46A-2-101 (consumer credit sales and leases), 46A-2-102 (instruments, contracts, and other writings evidencing obligations arising from consumer credit sales and leases), 46A-2-103 (claims and defenses of borrowers, arising from consumer sales, with respect to consumer loans), 46A-2-103a (consumer finance leases and sale-leaseback agreements). *See* McCoy v. Southern Energy Homes, Inc., 2012 WL 1409533 (S.D. W.Va. Apr. 23, 2012) (can obtain affirmative recovery under state law even when court (incorrectly) assumed could not under FTC Rule); Chrysler Credit Corp. v. Copley, 428 S.E.2d 313 (W. Va. 1989) (assignee of note in consumer transaction takes it subject to consumer's claims and defenses regardless of whether assignee is holder in due course; consumer can assert defects in vehicle as defense to assignee's suit for balance due); McGraw v. Scott Runyan Pontiac-Buick, Inc., 461 S.E.2d 516 (W. Va. 1995) (under West Virginia law, assignee takes note subject to all rights of the consumer).

WISCONSIN: Wis. Stat. Ann. §§ 422.406 (consumer credit sales and leases and interlocking loans), 422.407 (certain consumer credit transactions), 422.408 (interlocking consumer loans); Wis. Admin. Code ATCP § 110.06 (home improvement contracts). *See also* Jackson v. DeWitt, 592 N.W.2d 262 (Wis. Ct. App. 1999) (Wis. Admin. Code applies even when installment sales agreement is not a negotiable instrument).

WYOMING: Wyo. Stat. §§ 40-14-237, 40-14-238 (consumer credit sales and consumer leases).

raise defenses and in some cases affirmative claims as a matter of the state's substantive law. This right is not just based on a contractual right derived from a notice included in the note and is not dependent on the seller or lender's insertion of the FTC Holder Notice into the note or contract.[274]

Consequently, state holder statutes with this feature are useful when a credit obligation fails to include the Holder notice. Article 9 in effect in every state already implies the FTC holder notice into assigned credit sales agreements without the FTC Notice; these state statutes are particularly useful if they apply to direct loans from related lenders in states where UCC Article 3 has not been amended to imply such liability. But for such state statutes to be useful in this regard, they must apply to related loans and not just to assigned credit sales.

About a third of the states have holder laws that allow a consumer to bring affirmative claims even when there is a direct loan that omits the FTC Holder Notice, as long as the seller is connected with lender in some way.[275] These statutes usually include a definition of the special relationship between the lender and seller that triggers this liability. Typically, it is enough if the seller gets a referral fee, the seller participates in the preparation of the loan documents, the loan is conditioned on a purchase from the seller, or the lender had knowledge of complaints against the seller. The state holder statute may require the consumer to first make a good faith effort to obtain satisfaction from the seller.

State holder statutes can also be useful when they apply to credit not covered by the FTC Holder Rule or at least when a court is willing to interpret the state statute in ways broader than it is willing to interpret the FTC Rule. An important example is leases. The FTC Rule's applicability to leases is unclear at best, while certain state holder statutes clearly apply to leases.[276] For example the Connecticut statute allows consumers to raise dealer-related claims and defenses against the lease holder.[277] Other state statutes may merely prohibit waivers of the consumer's rights to bring defenses against an assignee. But if these statutes apply to leases, they can overcome the most common way in which lease holders seek to evade liability for the conduct of their assignors—through waiver of defense clauses.

---

274   *See In re* Paradise Palms Vacation Club, 41 B.R. 916 (D. Haw. 1984) (interpreting Washington RISA); Wash. Rev. Code § 63.14.020; Gogola v. First South Sav. & Loan of Pittsburgh, 1990 WL 312777 (Pa. Ct. Com. Pl. Dec. 10, 1990).

275   Ariz. Rev. Stat. Ann. § 44-145; Cal. Civ. Code § 2982.5(d)(4) (West) (motor vehicle sales only); Conn. Gen. Stat. § 52-572g (allowing defenses to be raised when "in connection with a credit transaction covering consumer goods"; unclear whether this would apply to direct loans in connection with sale, or only to credit sales); D.C. Code Ann. § 28-3809; Iowa Code Ann. § 537.3405; Kan. Stat. Ann. §§ 16a-3-403, 16a-3-405; Me. Rev. Stat. Ann. tit. 9-A, §§ 3-404, 3-405 (interlocking loans and leases); Md. Com. Law Code Ann. § 12-309 (West); Mass. Gen. Laws Ann. ch. 255, § 12F; Massachusetts Consumer Protection Regulations, 940 Mass. Code Regs. § 3.07, Advertising or Offering to Sell on an "Easy Credit" Basis; Mo. Rev. Stat. §§ 408.400–408.410, 408.250; N.Y. Gen. Bus. Law § 253 (McKinney); N.C. Gen. Stat. § 25A-1 (exempting "bona fide direct loan transactions" from RISA; this language may not exempt lenders referred by seller); Ohio Rev. Code Ann. §§ 1317.01, 1317.031 (West) (preserving defenses as to purchase money loans); Or. Rev. Stat. §§ 83.850, 83.860; 12 Pa. Cons. Stat. Ann. §§ 6302, 6325 (West); R.I. Gen. Laws § 6-27-5 (requiring holder-type notice on contract with lender to which seller regularly refers buyers); S.C. Code Ann. § 37-3-410; Vt. Stat. Ann. tit. 9, § 2455 (unclear whether applies to direct loans or just credit-sales); W. Va. Code § 46A-2-103; Wis. Stat. Ann. § 422.408. *See also* Gonzalez v. Old Kent Mortg. Co., 2000 WL 1469313 (E.D. Pa. Sept. 21, 2000) (loan not a direct loan when consumer asked contractor to obtain financing and contractor contacted lender, even though eventual loan was for both the construction and other things such as debt consolidation); Heastie v. Community Bank, 727 F. Supp. 1133 (N.D. Ill. 1989) (UDAP violation when related lender included provision in contract which sought to disclaim any responsibility for seller's work); Drew v. Chrysler Credit Corp., 596 F. Supp. 1371 (W.D. Mo. 1984) (interpreting Missouri statute); *In re* Brown, 134 B.R. 134 (Bankr. E.D. Pa. 1991) (loan was covered by home improvement finance act when contractor agreed to arrange financing, drove consumer to lender's office, and stood by while she signed papers); Hernandez v. Atlantic Fin. Co., 164 Cal. Rptr. 279 (Cal. Ct. App. 1980) ("direct loan" exception to MVRISA narrowly construed to cover only financing arranged independently by buyer); Credit Fin. Co. v. Stevens, 558 P.2d 122 (Kan. 1976) (Kansas holder statute did not apply to lender who had no relationship with the seller, when loan was not conditioned upon the consumer purchasing goods from a particular seller); Halloran v. North Plaza State Bank, 844 P.2d 764 (Kan. Ct. App. 1993) (Kansas holder statute did not apply to loan

taken out to pay taxes, as it was not for the purpose of enabling a consumer to buy or lease from a particular seller); Roosevelt Fed. Sav. & Loan Ass'n v. Crider, 722 S.W.2d 325 (Mo. Ct. App. 1986) (exterior siding is a "consumer good," therefore home improvement loan fell within state holder statute); Collins v. Horizon Hous., Inc., 519 S.E.2d 534 (N.C. Ct. App. 1999) (RISA did not impose liability on bank which financed purchase of defective manufactured home, when borrowers directly approached bank; implication is that result might be different if seller and lender had business relationship); Turner v. Citywide Home Improvement, Inc., 2000 Ohio App. LEXIS 904 (Mar. 10, 2000) (state holder law allows debtor to raise seller-related claims against direct lender when loan meets statutory definition of "purchase money loan"); Bennett v. Reliable Credit Ass'n, Inc., 865 P.2d 496 (Or. Ct. App. 1993); State *ex rel.* McGraw v. Scott Runyan Pontiac-Buick, Inc., 461 S.E.2d 516 (W. Va. 1995) (West Virginia law allows attorney general to recover illegal charges from assignees even if they are free of wrongdoing); Gramatan Home Investors Corp. v. Starling, 470 A.2d 1157 (Vt. 1983) (allowing siding purchaser to assert failure of consideration defense against note's assignee); Randolph Nat'l Bank v. Vail, 308 A.2d 588 (Vt. 1973) (state holder statute did not apply to note given as security for a preexisting obligation); Jackson v. DeWitt, 592 N.W.2d 262 (Wis. 1999) (home improvement UDAP regulation which subjected assignee to buyer's claims and defenses trumped more general statute that limited assignee's liability to amount still owing on date consumer gave notice of claim). *Cf.* Beaudreau v. Chrysler Credit Corp., 1979 WL 195988 (R.I. Super. Ct. Feb. 13, 1979). *But see* Armstrong v. Accrediting Council for Continuing Educ. and Training, Inc., 168 F.3d 1362 (D.C. Cir. 1999) (D.C. statute preempted when applied to federally-guaranteed student loans); Alexiou v. Brad Benson Mitsubishi, 127 F. Supp. 2d 557 (D.N.J. 2000) (taking the absurd position that the New Jersey holder statute is preempted by the limitations on assignee liability in the Truth in Lending Act, even as to state claims; taking extraordinary position that Congress, when it limited assignee liability for TILA violations, intended to immunize assignees from all state law consumer protection violations); Butz v. Society Nat'l Bank, 83 B.R. 459 (S.D. Ohio 1987) (RISA does not apply if consumer goes to lender, borrows money for car, and gives lender a security interest).

276   *See, e.g.,* Conn. Gen. Stat. §§ 42-411(b).

277   *Id.*

Another example of an area wherein state statutes may be stronger than the FTC Rule is when the consumer has a claim against the manufacturer but not the dealer. Under the FTC Holder Rule, the holder is not subject to manufacturer-related claims but may have such liability under a state statute.[278] Similarly, the District of Columbia statute apparently applies to real estate financing that would not otherwise be covered by the FTC rule.[279] A federal court mistakenly ruled that consumers could not obtain affirmative recoveries under the FTC Rule but allowed such a recovery under a West Virginia holder statute.[280] When the consumer has more rights under state law than the FTC Holder Rule, the FTC Holder Rule does not preempt such rights.[281]

Of course, sometimes a state holder statute may not be as protective as the FTC Holder Rule. For example, some state statutes may have a lower maximum recovery than the FTC rule.[282] In that case, the FTC Rule prevails, not the state statute.[283]

Often state statutes parallel to a federal claim are useful if the consumer seeks to keep the case out of federal court. But the FTC Holder Rule does not create federal court jurisdiction,[284] so this is not an advantage of a state holder statute. Nevertheless, use of the state statute is insurance against a court incorrectly ruling in this area that the FTC Rule creates federal court jurisdiction.

---

278 *See, e.g.*, Mich. Comp. Laws Ann. § 492.114a(b) (holder of installment sale contract is subject to all buyer's claims and defenses arising out of the transaction, with recovery capped at amount paid to holder). *Cf.* Chrysler Fin. Co. v. Flynn, 88 S.W.3d 142 (Mo. Ct. App. 2002) (seeming to assume this interpretation of the Missouri statute).

279 Johnson v. Long Beach Mortg. Loan Trust 2001-4, 451 F. Supp. 2d 16 (D.D.C. 2006).

280 McCoy v. Southern Energy Homes, Inc., 2012 WL 1409533 (S.D. W.Va. Apr. 23, 2012).

281 *See* § 4.3.11.1, *supra.*

282 Wis. Stat. Ann. § 422.408. *See, e.g.*, Kan. Stat. Ann. § 16a-3-404 (cap is amount owing at time assignee has notice of the claims or defenses).

283 *See* § 4.3.11.1, *supra.*

284 *See* § 4.3.12, *supra.*

Chapter 5   Telemarketing Fraud: The FTC Rule and State Counterparts

5.1   Introduction

5.1.1   Topics Covered in This Chapter

The FTC Telemarketing Sales Rule[1] ("the Rule") offers far greater protections than just against unwanted or fraudulent telemarketing calls. For example, it offers important protections to consumers in the following areas even when it is not the seller who initiates the transaction by telephone but the consumer who calls the seller in response to an advertisement or direct solicitation by mail, email, or fax:

- Advance fee loans
- Debt relief services
- Credit repair
- Credit card protection products
- Offers to recover losses from past telemarketing fraud
- Certain investment and business opportunity offers and
- Prize promotions

This chapter focuses on the areas listed above and also on the Rule's more general provisions as to telemarketing fraud. The Rule's application to debt relief services is examined at Chapter 10, *infra*. Chapter 6, *infra*, examines aspects of the Rule relating to unwanted phone calls, including do-not-call lists, caller ID blocking, calls at inconvenient times, and abandoned calls.[2] This chapter concludes with a discussion of state telemarketing fraud statutes and a listing of several tips for consumers to avoid telemarketing fraud.

In 2013, the FTC proposed to strengthen the rule in several ways. Highlights include:

- Barring sellers and telemarketers from accepting several types of payment mechanisms such as remotely created checks that facilitate fraud;
- Expanding the scope of the advance fee ban on "recovery" services, currently limited to recovery of losses incurred in prior telemarketing transactions;
- Specifying that the recording of a consumer's "express verifiable consent" must include a description of the goods or services being purchased;
- Making it clear that a seller or telemarketer bears the burden of demonstrating that it has an existing business relationship with a person on the do-not-call list or has obtained an express written agreement to call that person; and

- Clarifying that the business-to-business exemption extends only to calls to induce the business to make a purchase or contribution, not to induce purchases or contributions from individuals employed by the business.[3]

As of late 2015, the FTC had not yet acted on these proposals. In 2014, the FTC also undertook a general review of the rule.[4] The rule is still under review as of 2015.[5]

5.1.2   Authority for FTC Telemarketing Sales Rule

Unlike the FTC rules examined in Chapter 2, *supra*, the authority for the FTC Telemarketing Sales Rule is not the Federal Trade Commission Act ("FTC Act") but the Telemarketing and Consumer Fraud and Abuse Prevention Act (TCFAPA).[6] The Telemarketing and Consumer Fraud and Abuse Prevention Act sets out only broad guidelines and requires the FTC to issue regulations prohibiting deceptive and abusive telemarketing acts and practices.[7] The statute sets forth only a few requirements for the substance of the FTC Telemarketing Sales Rule, specifying that the Rule restrict late-night and early-morning calls, require disclosures, and prohibit coercive calls and those that abuse the consumer's right to privacy.[8] Federal, state, and private remedies for violations of the Rule are set out in the statute.[9]

With certain exceptions, the statute also calls for the Securities Exchange Commission to either adopt a rule similar to the FTC Rule or require national securities exchanges or registered securities associations to promulgate similar rules.[10] A number of such rules have been adopted for telemarketing in the securities industry,[11] but those rules will not be treated in this chapter.

5.2   Scope of the FTC Telemarketing Sales Rule

5.2.1   General Coverage

The scope of the FTC Telemarketing Sales Rule is unusually complex. While the general scope is straightforward,

---

1   16 C.F.R. § 310, *reprinted at* Appx. C.1.2, *infra*. The *Federal Register* notices announcing the original rule, 60 Fed. Reg. 43842 (Aug. 23, 1995), and the 2003 amendments to it, 68 Fed. Reg. 4580 (Jan. 29, 2003), including the FTC's lengthy and detailed statements of basis and purpose, as well as related Federal Register notices at Primary Sources>Telemarketing, Junk Faxes>FTC Telemarketing Sales Rule are available online as companion material to this treatise.

2   *See* §§ 6.3–6.6, *infra*.

3   78 Fed. Reg. 41,200 (July 9, 2013).

4   79 Fed. Reg. 46,732 (Aug. 11, 2014).

5   80 Fed. Reg. 5713 (Feb. 3, 2015).

6   15 U.S.C. §§ 6101 to 6108, *reprinted at* Appx. C.1.1, *infra. But cf.* North River Ins. Co. v. Guarantee Trust Life Ins. Co., 2014 WL 1493951 (Ill. App. Ct. Apr. 14, 2014) (proposing that there is a "plausible argument to be made that violations of the TSR are in fact violations of the FTC Act, though in an indirect way").

7   15 U.S.C. § 6102.

8   15 U.S.C. § 6102(a).

9   *See* § 5.6, *infra*.

10   15 U.S.C. § 6102(d).

11   *See* 60 Fed. Reg. 31527 (June 15, 1995) (NASD); 60 Fed. Reg. 31337 (June 7, 1995) (NYSE).

exemptions apply to certain provisions or transactions but not to others. Many of the exemptions also are quite broad, drastically altering the scope of the FTC Rule as it applies to most provisions and transactions.

With few exceptions, the Rule applies to "sellers," "telemarketers," "customers," and "donors." A telemarketer is any person who, in connection with telemarketing, initiates or *receives* telephone calls to or from a customer or donor.[12] Telemarketing "means a plan, program, or campaign conducted to induce the purchase of goods or services, or a charitable contribution, by use of one or more telephones, and which involves more than one interstate telephone call."[13]

A seller is defined as "any person who, in connection with a telemarketing transaction, provides, offers to provide, or arranges for others to provide goods or services to the customer in exchange for consideration."[14] Thus, the FTC Rule reaches not just the telemarketers themselves but also entities who hire telemarketers to sell their goods or services.[15]

A customer is defined as any person who is or may be required to pay for goods or services offered through telemarketing.[16] Unlike many consumer protection statutes, the Rule's protections apply not just to consumers but to anyone paying for goods or services, thus eliminating any ambiguity concerning the Rule's application to investments, business opportunities, and sales of office supplies. Similarly, the Rule defines "donor" as any person solicited to make a charitable contribution.[17]

The general rule that the Rule covers sales when either the customer or the telemarketer initiates the phone call is swallowed up by many exemptions discussed at § 5.2.2, *infra*. In fact, the exemptions eliminate most, but not all, customer-initiated calls from the Rule's scope. Nevertheless, for transactions in which the Rule still applies to customer-initiated calls, the Rule has a broader applicability than is often realized.

5.2.2 Partial Exemption for Customer Initiated Calls

While the Rule's general coverage includes telephone sales whether initiated by the telemarketer or the customer, there are four major exceptions that eliminate most (but not all) customer-initiated calls from the Rule's scope. First, the Rule does not apply when the customer initiates a call that is not in response to any form of solicitation by the seller or telemarketer.[18] For example, the customer may call a seller after the customer's friend recommends the seller.

However, this exemption does not apply to "upselling."[19] Upselling is when the consumer initiates the call and the seller seeks to solicit the purchase of additional goods or services other than those that the customer is calling about.[20] An upsell is a solicitation for goods or services that follows an initial transaction of any sort in a single telephone call.[21] For example, an upsell occurs if a customer calls a company for technical support and, in the course of the call, the company solicits the customer to buy a new product or service. Or the customer may call a seller in response to an advertisement for one item and, in the course of the call, the seller tries to sell a different product. It is also an upsell if a telemarketer calls a consumer, makes a sale, and then starts another sales pitch or transfers the consumer to a different seller who makes a new sales pitch.[22]

Second, the Rule exempts sales that occur when the customer responds to a mailed catalog and initiates the call.[23] For this exception to apply, the catalog must describe the goods offered for sale, include multiple pages, and have been issued at least annually.[24] In addition, the exception applies only if the entity sending the catalog never solicits customers by telephone and only takes catalog orders without soliciting further orders except for items included in the same or a substantially similar catalog.[25]

Third, the Rule does not apply when the customer initiates a call in response to the seller's advertisement in any medium other than a direct mail solicitation.[26] For example, the Rule does not apply when the customer sees an advertisement on

---

12 16 C.F.R. § 310.2(cc).

13 16 C.F.R. § 310.2(dd). *See* United States v. DISH Network, L.L.C., 75 F. Supp. 3d 942, 1003 (C.D. Ill. 2014) (intrastate calls are covered by the TSR if they were part of a telemarketing campaign that meets the TSR's definition; "FTC's jurisdiction under the TSR extends to calls to wireless numbers."), *vacated in part on other grounds,* 80 F. Supp. 3d 917 (C.D. Ill. 2015); Fed. Trade Comm'n v. Centro Natural Corp., 2014 WL 7525697 (S.D. Fla. Dec. 10, 2014) (finding that the FTC Act and the TSR apply to telemarketers calling consumers in the U.S., regardless of the location or citizenship of the telemarketers); US v. FMFG, Inc., 2006 WL 2639366 (D. Nev. Sept. 13, 2006); Ward v. Kantar Operations, 705 S.E.2d 413 (N.C. Ct. App. 2011) (legitimate survey company that did not seek to sell anything or solicit charitable donations is not engaged in telemarketing).

14 16 C.F.R. § 310.2(aa). *See* Fed. Trade Comm'n v. Stefanchik, 559 F.3d 924 (9th Cir. 2009) (explaining that, under 16 C.F.R. § 310.2(z), Telemarketing Sales Rule applies to "any seller," defined as "any person who, in connection with a telemarketing transaction, provides, offers to provide, or arranges for others to provide goods or services to the customer in exchange for consideration").

15 *See, e.g.,* Fed. Trade Comm'n v. Stefanchik, 559 F.3d 924, 930 (9th Cir. 2009) (individual and his company liable under telemarketing rule when they arranged for telemarketer to promote sales, retained authority to review and approve all marketing materials, and decided what products would be sold); United States v. DISH Network, L.L.C., 2011 WL 98951 (C.D. Ill. Jan. 10, 2011) (key issue is whether seller of satellite television services caused telemarketing violations by its network of dealers), *later op. at* 754 F. Supp. 2d 1004 (C.D. Ill. 2011) (claim stated; giving weight to seller's failure to effectively monitor telemarketing by dealers).

16 16 C.F.R. § 310.2(*l*).

17 *Id.* § 310.2(n).

18 16 C.F.R. § 310.6(b)(4).

19 *Id.*

20 *Id.* § 310.2(ee).

21 16 C.F.R. § 310.2(ee). *See* 68 Fed. Reg. 4580, 4656 (Jan. 29, 2003).

22 68 Fed. Reg. 4580, 4596, 4597 (Jan. 29, 2003).

23 16 C.F.R. § 310.2(dd). *Cf.* Distributel, Inc. v. State, 933 P.2d 1137 (Alaska 1997) (similar language in Alaska telemarketing law does not exclude sales made when seller called consumer after having sent a catalog).

24 16 C.F.R. § 310.2(dd).

25 *Id.*

26 16 C.F.R. § 310.6(b)(5). Direct mail solicitations are covered by a different exemption, discussed in § 5.2.3, *infra*.

television, radio, a billboard, or the Internet and initiates a call to the seller. Nevertheless, there are a number of exceptions to this exemption. The Rule still applies to any upselling in the customer-initiated call.[27] The Rule also still applies to customer-initiated calls in response to advertisements relating to the following transactions:

- Investment opportunities
- Debt relief services
- Business opportunities other than business arrangements covered by the Franchise Rule or the Business Opportunity Rule[28]
- Credit card protection plans
- Credit repair
- Recovering funds lost to a telemarketing scam
- Advance fee loans[29]

Fourth, the Rule does not apply when the customer initiates the call after responding to a direct mail solicitation directed to a specific address or person, via mail, email, or fax, as long as the direct mail solicitation clearly and truthfully discloses the item's cost, restrictions on purchase, refund policy, and terms of any negative option.[30] The Rule still applies if such disclosures are not made or if the customer-initiated call involves upselling.[31]

In addition, the exemption does not apply to customer-initiated calls in response to direct mail solicitations relating to the seven forms of transactions listed immediately above.[32] The exception is also inapplicable to customer-initiated phone calls in response to a direct mail solicitation involving a prize promotion scheme.[33]

5.2.3 Exemptions That Apply Even to Telemarketer-Initiated Calls

5.2.3.1 Transactions Not Completed Until After Face-to-Face Meeting

No matter who initiates the call, the Rule does not apply to any transaction when the sale or charitable donation is not completed and payment is not required until after a face-to-face presentation.[34] But even these transactions must still comply with the FTC Telemarketing Sales Rule provisions relating to unwanted phone calls, calls at inconvenient times, and calls using threats or foul language (discussed at §§ 6.3–6.6, *infra*) and to the provision addressing billing information being submitted for payment without the customer's consent.[35]

5.2.3.2 Transactions Covered by Other FTC Rules

No matter who initiates the call, most of the Rule provisions do not apply to pay-per-call services subject to the FTC's 900 Number Rule or to transactions subject to the FTC's Franchise and Business Opportunity Rules.[36] But these transactions must still comply with provisions in the FTC Telemarketing Sales Rule relating to unwanted phone calls, calls at inconvenient times, and calls using threats or foul language, discussed at §§ 6.3–6.6, *infra*. These transactions must also comply with the Rule's provision dealing with billing information being submitted for payment without the customer's consent.[37]

5.2.3.3 Business-to-Business Exception

There is a business-to-business exemption for telephone calls between a telemarketer and any business,[38] but this exemption does not apply to calls made to induce retail sales of non-durable office and cleaning supplies.[39] However, if calls intended for businesses reach consumers, the Rule applies.[40]

5.2.3.4 General Limits to the FTC's Jurisdiction

Due to general limitations on the FTC's jurisdiction, the FTC Telemarketing Sales Rule does not apply to banks, federal credit unions, federal savings and loans, common carriers, and regulated insurers.[41] However, a federal court found that

---

27 16 C.F.R. § 310.6(b)(5).

28 *See* §§ 2.8.2, 2.8.3, *supra* (discussing these two rules).

29 16 C.F.R. § 310.6(b)(5). All these transactions are examined at § 5.5, *infra*.

30 16 C.F.R. § 310.6(b)(6).

31 *Id.*

32 *Id.*

33 *Id. See* § 5.5.7, *infra*.

34 16 C.F.R. § 310.6(b)(3).

35 16 C.F.R. § 310.6(b) (3) (referencing sections 310.4(a)(1), (a)(7), (b), (c)).

36 16 C.F.R. § 310.6(b)(1), (2). The 900 Number Rule is discussed at National Consumer Law Center, Access to Utility Service § 11.6.5.6 (5th ed. 2011), *updated at* www.nclc.org/library, the Business Opportunity Rule at § 2.8.3, *supra*, and the Franchise Rule at § 2.8.2, *supra*.

37 16 C.F.R. § 310.6(b)(1), (2), (3) (referencing §§ 310.4(a)(1), (a)(7), (b), (c)).

38 16 C.F.R. § 310.6(b)(7). *See* Cellco P'ship v. Wilcrest Health Care Mgmt. Inc., 2012 WL 1638056 (D.N.J. May 8, 2012) (operator of cellular phone equipment embedded in consumers' vehicles cannot assert claim against telemarketer for calls that were received by its system—causing it to incur charges—but were not answered by consumers, as these calls must be treated as business-to-business calls).

39 16 C.F.R. § 310.6(b)(7). *See* Fed. Trade Comm'n v. Inc21.com Corp., 745 F. Supp. 2d 975, 1006–1007 (N.D. Cal. 2010) (rule inapplicable to telemarketing campaign selling Internet yellow pages except to the extent calls reached non-business customers, but calls to businesses are subject to FTC Act's prohibition against unfairness and deception), *aff'd mem.*, 2012 WL 1065534 (9th Cir. Mar. 30, 2012); Fed. Trade Comm'n v. Corporate Supplies, Inc., 5 Trade Reg. Rep. (CCH) ¶ 24,884 (N.D. Ga. Mar. 5, 2001) (stipulated final judgment barring telemarketer from future sales of office supplies).

40 Fed. Trade Comm'n v. Inc21.com Corp., 745 F. Supp. 2d 975, 1007 (N.D. Cal. 2010), *aff'd mem.*, 2012 WL 1065534 (9th Cir. Mar. 30, 2012); Fed. Trade Comm'n v. Publishers Bus. Services, Inc., 821 F. Supp. 2d 1205 (D. Nev. 2010) (defendant magazine sales business that solicited consumers at their workplace is not exempt; it would be absurd to protect consumers at home but not at work).

41 68 Fed. Reg. 4580, 4581 n.19 (Jan. 29, 2003); Fed. Trade Comm'n, Complying with the Telemarketing Sales Rule 7 (Apr. 1996). *See* Clark v. Avatar Techs. PHL, Inc., 2014 WL 309079 (S.D. Tex. Jan. 28, 2014) (TSR does not apply to telecommunications common carriers because the FTC lacks jurisdiction). *But cf.* Fed. Trade Comm'n v. AT&T

the FTC has authority to enforce the Telemarketing Sales Rule against a subsidiary of a national bank.[42] Furthermore, the Rule covers non-bank entities that conduct telemarketing on behalf of banks.[43] The same principle applies to other exempt entities such as common carriers: they are exempt if they do their own telemarketing, but the Rule covers non-exempt entities that they hire.[44]

The FTC Act only applies to acts by a company organized to carry on business for profit or for the profit of their members.[45] As such, the Rule does not apply to true nonprofit enterprises but does apply to sham nonprofits. Thus the Rule does not apply to charities doing the telemarketing themselves.

Nevertheless, the Telemarketing and Consumer Fraud and Abuse Prevention Act explicitly includes within its scope and that of the Telemarketing Sales Rule charitable fund-raising conducted by for-profit telemarketers for or on behalf of charitable organizations.[46] The Telemarketing Sales Rule includes telemarketing conducted to induce a charitable contribution[47] while at the same time reiterates that nonprofit organizations themselves fall outside its jurisdiction.[48] One part of the Rule—governing the national do-not-call list—does not apply to telemarketers who solicit charitable donations,[49] but these telemarketers are subject to the requirement of a company-specific do-not-call list.[50] The Fourth Circuit has held that

these amendments to the Rule are constitutional and within the FTC's statutory authority.[51]

5.2.4 No Coverage for Online Fraud

The FTC's Telemarketing Sales Rule requires use of the telephone and does not apply to purely Internet-based sales. Thus, even when a consumer is directly solicited by an email,[52] the Rule does not apply, since a telephone call is not involved. However, the Rule does apply to certain transactions, listed in § 5.2.2, *supra*, in which the seller sends the consumer an email or advertises on the Internet and the consumer responds by telephone.[53]

Of course, even though the Telemarketing Sales Rule does not apply to purely online transactions, online fraud is actionable under state UDAP statutes and other theories. The FTC has taken a number of actions against online fraud under its authority to prohibit unfair and deceptive acts and practices.[54] For example, the FTC has brought a number of cases against businesses that billed consumers' credit cards for "free" website services or for unauthorized purchases, often obtaining credit card information by asking for a credit card number to verify that the user is over eighteen.[55] Courts have also allowed

---

Mobility, L.L.C., 87 F. Supp. 3d 1087 (N.D. Cal. 2015) (common carriers are only exempt if they are actually engaging in common-carrier activity; FTC may regulate a common carrier's non-common carriage activities); Navarro v. Sears Life Ins. Co., 2008 WL 3863451 (E.D. Cal. Aug. 18, 2008) (applying rule to telemarketing sale of insurance; McCarran-Ferguson Act does not prevent application of rule).

42 Minn. *ex rel.* Hatch v. Fleet Mortg. Corp., 181 F. Supp. 2d 995 (D. Minn. 2001).

43 68 Fed. Reg. 4580, 4586, 4587 (Jan. 29, 2003).

44 *Id.*

45 15 U.S.C. § 44.

46 Uniting and Strengthening America by Providing Appropriate Tools Required to Intercept and Obstruct Terrorism Act of 2001, Pub. L. No. 107-56, 115 Stat. 272 (Oct. 25, 2001) (amending 15 U.S.C. § 6102(a)(2)(3)). *See* 68 Fed. Reg. 4585, 4586 (Jan. 29, 2003) (discussion of ambiguities in scope of these amendments); United States v. Corps. For Character, L.C., ___ F. Supp. 3d ___, 2015 WL 4577051 (D. Utah Mar. 31, 2015) (granting summary judgment for TSR violations against corporation that provided telemarketing services to nonprofits); Broadcast Team, Inc. v. Fed. Trade Comm'n, 429 F. Supp. 2d 1292 (M.D. Fla. 2006) (FTC telemarketing rule covers for-profit entity that made prerecorded solicitations of contributions for charity even though it framed its contract as a lease of its equipment to the charity).

47 16 C.F.R. § 310.2(dd). "Charitable contribution" is defined at 16 C.F.R. § 310.2(f).

48 68 Fed. Reg. 4580, 4585, 4586 (Jan. 29, 2003).

49 16 C.F.R. § 310.6(a).

50 68 Fed. Reg. 4580, 4629 (Jan. 29, 2003). *See* Nat'l Federation of the Blind v. Fed. Trade Comm'n, 420 F.3d 331 (4th Cir. 2005) (application of company-specific do-not-call list to for-profit charitable solicitors is constitutional and within FTC's authority). *Cf.* Nat'l Coalition of Prayer, Inc. v. Carter, 455 F.3d 783 (7th Cir. 2006) (upholding state's application of do-not-call list to professional charitable solicitors); Fraternal Order of Police v. Stenehjem, 431 F.3d 591 (8th Cir. 2005) (state's prohibition of calls by outside charitable solicitors to persons registered on state do-not-call list is constitutional). *See generally*

§§ 6.5, 6.5.1 *infra* (more detailed discussion of company-specific do-not-call rule and its application to solicitors for charities).

51 Nat'l Fed'n of the Blind v. Fed. Trade Comm'n, 420 F.3d 331 (4th Cir. 2005). *See also* Fed. Trade Comm'n v. Corps. For Character, L.C., ___ F. Sup. 3d ___, 2015 WL 4577051(D. Utah Mar. 31, 2015) (First Amendment does not require that the FTC assert fraud when regulating charitable donations).

52 *See* 60 Fed. Reg. 30411 (June 8, 1995) (statement of basis and purpose for FTC's telemarketing rule at the proposal stage). *See also* 800-JR Cigar, Inc. v. GoTo.com, Inc., 437 F. Supp. 2d 273 (D.N.J. 2006).

53 *See* § 5.2.2, *supra*.

54 *See* Fed. Trade Comm'n v. Cyberspace.com, 453 F.3d 1196 (9th Cir. 2006) (online purchases of pornography disguised as phone calls to Madagascar; deceptive if phone bill format and hardline collection misled line subscribers who had not made or authorized the purchase that they must pay for pornography or lose phone service); Fed. Trade Comm'n v. Health Formulas, L.L.C., 2015 WL 2130504 (D. Nev. May 6, 2015) (issuing preliminary injunction against a network of corporations who engaged in deceptive online sales, including inadequate disclosures of terms and conditions, cancellation and refund policies, and cost of product); Fed. Trade Comm'n v. Zuccarini, 2002 WL 1378421 (E.D. Pa. Apr. 9, 2002) (entering permanent injunction against individual who redirected consumers from their intended destinations to his own web pages and then obstructed them from exiting those pages); Fed. Trade Comm'n v. Verity Int'l, Ltd., 194 F. Supp. 2d 270 (S.D.N.Y. 2002) (issuing preliminary injunction in scheme that purportedly routed Internet access through Madagascar and billed for international call), *final judgment aff'd in relevant part, rev'd in part on other grounds*, 443 F.3d 48 (2d Cir. 2006) (affirming finding that practices were deceptive but vacating and remanding monetary award due to errors in calculation); Letter from Fed. Trade Comm'n to Roy Ellyatt, Int'l Telemedia Assoc. (Sept. 29, 1999) *available at* www.ftc.gov (proposed disclaimer screens before consumers accessed toll-billed entertainment program are most likely inadequate to withstand challenge under section 5 of the FTC Act).

55 *See, e.g.*, Fed. Trade Comm'n v. Crescent Publ'g Grp., Inc., 129 F. Supp. 2d 311 (S.D.N.Y. 2001) (adult website offered free tour but did not clearly disclose when tour became not free and in fact crafted disclosure to

consumers to proceed with UDAP claims when the format, font, and sequence of web pages obscured the cost of an item presented as free.[56]

5.3 The Rule's General Requirements and Prohibitions

5.3.1 General

The FTC Telemarketing Sales Rule has a number of provisions that apply generally to any type of telemarketer- or seller-initiated phone solicitations. As will be discussed in this section, some of these require disclosures or prohibit misrepresentations concerning the nature of the sale. Other general provisions deal with inconvenient calls by telemarketers, such as automated dialing, calls at inconvenient times, and other unwanted calls. These provisions are examined at §§ 6.3–6.6, *infra*. While the general provisions discussed in this section apply to all seller- or telemarketer-initiated calls, they also apply to customer-initiated calls under certain circumstances, including upselling,[57] and a number of specific types of transactions examined in § 5.2.2, *supra*.

The general provisions relate both to required disclosures and prohibited misrepresentations and often limit their requirement by the use of the word "material," as in a requirement that material restrictions be disclosed or that material aspects of a refund policy not be misrepresented. The Rule defines "material" as likely to affect a person's choice of or conduct regarding goods, services, or charitable contributions.[58]

5.3.2 Required Disclosures

The FTC Telemarketing Sales Rule requires disclosures at two stages of a telemarketing transaction: at the outset of the call and before the consumer agrees to pay. In either case, the disclosures must be clear and conspicuous and truthful.[59]

The disclosures at the outset of the call are required for outgoing telemarketing calls and upsells. In any outgoing call to induce the purchase of goods or services, the telemarketer must make prompt oral disclosure regarding the identity of the seller, that the purpose of the call is to sell goods or services, and regarding the nature of the goods or services.[60]

These disclosures must also be made at the initiation of an upsell[61] if any of the information differs from that disclosed in the initial transaction.[62]

Callers seeking charitable donations must make prompt oral disclosure of the identity of the charitable organization on behalf of which the call is made and that the purpose of the call is to solicit a charitable donation.[63]

In response to suggestions to clarify that prompt disclosure means "at the onset of a call," the FTC stated that no clarification was necessary because prompt means "at once or without delay, and before any substantive information about a prize, product or service is conveyed to the consumer."[64]

The Rule also requires a number of disclosures that a seller or telemarketer must make before a consumer consents to pay for goods or services offered:[65]

- The cost of the purchase and quantity of the items purchased;[66]
- All material restrictions and conditions on the purchase;[67] and

---

deceive consumers about charges; seller processed credit card charges through VISA in Guatemala in order to evade VISA's chargeback monitoring program); Fed. Trade Comm'n v. J.K. Publications, Inc., 99 F. Supp. 2d 1176 (C.D. Cal. 2001). *See generally* § 5.4, *infra* (restrictions on unauthorized billing by telemarketers).

56 Keithly v. Intelius Inc., 764 F. Supp. 2d 1257 (W.D. Wash. 2011), *amended on reconsideration by* 2011 WL 2790471 (W.D. Wash. May 17, 2011) (withdrawing ruling that only Washington residents can bring suit under state UDAP statute). *See generally* National Consumer Law Center, Unfair and Deceptive Acts and Practices § 4.2, 14.3.9 (8th ed. 2012), *updated at* www.nclc.org/library (disclosures in online transactions).

57 *See* § 5.2.2, *supra*.

58 16 C.F.R. § 310.2(r).

59 16 C.F.R. §§ 310.3(a)(1), 310.4(d), (e).

60 16 C.F.R. § 310.4(d). *See* Fed. Trade Comm'n v. Corps. For Character, L.C., ___ F. Supp. 3d ___, 2015 WL 4577051(D. Utah Mar. 31, 2015)

(telemarketers did not sufficiently identify sellers by failing to give a registered trade name and by calling "on behalf of producers" but not disclosing who producers were); Fed. Trade Comm'n v. Tax Club, Inc., 994 F. Supp. 2d 461 (S.D.N.Y. 2014) (defendant purchased consumer leads from other businesses and then telemarketers identified themselves as calling "on behalf of" the company that sold them the lead). The FCC rule, 47 C.F.R. § 64.1200(d)(4), also requires disclosure of the identity of the company on whose behalf the call is placed.

61 *See* Fed. Trade Comm'n v. Tax Club, Inc., 994 F. Supp. 2d 461 (S.D.N.Y. 2014) (telemarketer failed to disclose purpose to sell by disguising upsell calls as fulfillment calls); § 5.2.2, *supra* (definition of upsell).

62 16 C.F.R. § 310.4(d). *See* 68 Fed. Reg. 4580, 4648 (Jan. 29, 2003) (noting addition of words "or internal or external upsell" in prefatory language of section 310.4(d)).

63 16 U.S.C. § 6102(a)(3)(D); 16 C.F.R. § 310.4(e). *See* Nat'l Fed'n of the Blind v. Fed. Trade Comm'n, 420 F.3d 331, 343 (4th Cir. 2005) (rule is constitutional and within FTC's authority).

64 67 Fed. Reg. 4502, 4526–4527 (Jan. 30, 2002). *Accord* 68 Fed. Reg. 4580, 4648 (Jan. 29, 2003).

65 16 C.F.R. § 310.3(a)(1). *See* Fed. Trade Comm'n v. Medical Billers Network, Inc., 543 F. Supp. 2d 283, 317–318 (S.D.N.Y. 2008) (disclosure must be made before consumer provides credit card information, even if creditor processes the charge later).

When a courier is used to pick up the customer's payment, the disclosures must be made before the courier is sent. *See* 16 C.F.R. § 310.3(a)(1) n.1.

66 16 C.F.R. § 310.3(a)(1)(i). *See, e.g.*, Fed. Trade Comm'n v. Oks, 2007 WL 3307009 (N.D. Ill. Nov. 2, 2007) (debiting consumer's accounts without disclosing total cost of products was violation). *See also* Fed. Trade Comm'n v. Bay Area Bus. Council, Inc., 423 F.3d 627 (7th Cir. 2005) (telemarketers violated prohibition by debiting consumer accounts more than they disclosed and delivering application that required additional fee instead of the promised credit card).

67 16 C.F.R. § 310.3(a)(1)(ii). *See also In re* Nat'l Credit Mgmt. Grp., 21 F. Supp. 2d 424 (D.N.J. 1998) (issuing injunction against telemarketer who disclosed only initial fee for marketed program without disclosing the total costs); New York v. Financial Services Network, 930 F. Supp. 865 (W.D.N.Y. 1996) (issuing preliminary injunction against telemarketer who revealed limitations on credit cards only after consumers paid fee); People *ex rel.* Spitzer v. Telehublink Corp., 756 N.Y.S.2d 285 (N.Y. App. Div. 2003) (affirming permanent injunction and restitution order against telemarketer that did not disclose that credit card could only be used to buy items from seller's catalog).

- Disclosure of a no-refund policy, if applicable, and all terms and conditions of any refund policy that is disclosed.[68]

With respect to the cost disclosures, although the FTC states that the best practice is to disclose the total of payments whenever possible, the telemarketer need only disclose the number of installment payments and the amount of each payment.[69] For offers of consumer credit products subject to the Truth in Lending Act (TILA), 15 U.S.C. § 1601–1666j, and Regulation Z, 12 C.F.R. § 226, compliance with the disclosure requirements under the TILA and Regulation Z constitutes compliance with the Rule's cost disclosure requirements.[70] Illegality of the goods or services offered is a material restriction that must be disclosed.[71]

5.3.3 Prohibited Misrepresentations

The FTC Telemarketing Sales Rule prohibits telemarketers from making any false or misleading statements to induce any person to pay for goods and services.[72] In evaluating alleged violations of this prohibition, a federal court looked beyond the seller's claim that its statements were literally true and granted a preliminary injunction against advertisements that were designed to foster the impression that the seller was actually offering a credit card when consumers only received information on an investment offer.[73]

The Rule also prohibits telemarketers from making, directly or by implication, a number of more specific misrepresentations:

- The total cost and quantity of goods or services;[74]
- Material restrictions, limitations or conditions to purchase, receive, or use the goods or services;[75]
- Any material aspect of the performance, efficacy, nature, or central characteristics of the goods or services;[76]

---

68 16 C.F.R. § 310.3(a)(1)(iii). *See* Fed. Trade Comm'n v. Health Formulas, L.L.C., 2015 WL 2130504 (D. Nev. May 6, 2015) (defendants failed to disclose that each upsell product must be cancelled separately or the contact information to cancel each product); Fed. Trade Comm'n v. Ivy Capital, Inc., 2013 WL 1224613 (D. Nev. Mar. 26, 2013) (sellers of Internet business products failed to disclose their strict three-day refund policy), *aff'd in relevant part, vacated in part on other grounds*, ___ Fed. Appx. ___, 2015 WL 5781664 (9th Cir. Oct. 5, 2015).

69 68 Fed. Reg. 4580, 4599, 4600 (Jan. 29, 2003).

70 16 C.F.R. § 310.3 n.2.

71 68 Fed. Reg. 4580, 4600 (Jan. 29, 2003); Fed. Trade Comm'n v. World Media Brokers, 415 F.3d 758 (7th Cir. 2005).

72 16 C.F.R. § 310.3(a)(4). *See* Fed. Trade Comm'n v. Stefanchik, 559 F.3d 924, 929–930 (9th Cir. 2009) (seller of work-at-home scheme is liable for telemarketer's misrepresentations regarding earning potential and availability of coaches, which violated the Telemarketing Sales Rule); Fed. Trade Comm'n v. Instant Response Sys., L.L.C., 2015 WL 1650914 (E.D.N.Y. Apr. 14, 2015) (granting summary judgment and permanent injunction against defendant who cold-called elderly consumers and falsely stated that call was in response to a request for medical alert services); Fed. Trade Comm'n v. Inbound Call Experts, L.L.C., 2014 WL 8105107 (S.D. Fla. Dec. 23, 2014) (issuing preliminary injunction against defendant who used a scripted sales pitch to convince consumers that their computers required repair); Fed. Trade Comm'n v. Resort Solution Trust, Inc., 2013 WL 6668712 (M.D. Fla. Dec. 18, 2013) (defendants falsely represented that they could sell consumer's timeshare quickly and for a specified price); Fed. Trade Comm'n v. Loewen, 2013 WL 5816420 (W.D. Wash. Oct. 29, 2013) (defendants misrepresented that they had found a buyer for consumer's vehicle and would put consumer in contact with buyer for a fee); Fed. Trade Comm'n v. Vacation Prop. Services, 2012 WL 1854251 (M.D. Fla. May 21, 2012) (misrepresentations about availability of buyer for consumers' timeshares); Fed. Trade Comm'n v. Affiliate Strategies, Inc., 849 F. Supp. 2d 1085 (D. Kan. 2011) (defendant grossly exaggerated its ability to assist individuals in obtaining government grants), *later op. at* 2011 WL 3300097 (D. Kan. Aug. 1, 2011) (enjoining various defendants from violating FTC Act, Telemarketing Sales Rule, and various state statutes); Fed. Trade Comm'n v. 1st Guarantee Mortg. Co., 2011 WL 1233207 (S.D. Fla. Mar. 30, 2011) (misrepresentations about ability to obtain loan modifications or improve credit scores; acceptance of advance payment in violation of the Telemarketing Sales Rule); Fed. Trade Comm'n v. Washington Data Res., 2011 WL 1118581 (M.D. Fla. Mar. 25, 2011) (denying defendants' motion for summary judgment; law firm misrepresented foreclosure rescue services as "government bailout"); Fed. Trade Comm'n v. U.S.

Mortg. Funding, Inc., 2011 WL 810790 (S.D. Fla. Mar. 1, 2011) (granting preliminary injunction against company that misrepresented ability to obtain loan modifications or stop foreclosures, falsely claimed to be affiliated with consumers' lenders, took advance fees, produced no results, and refused refunds); Fed. Trade Comm'n v. JPM Accelerated Services, Inc., 2011 WL 679938 (M.D. Fla. Jan. 25, 2011) (magistrate recommendation) (robocalls falsely promising dramatic reductions in credit card interest rates), *adopted by* 2011 WL 675400 (M.D. Fla. Feb. 16, 2011); Fed. Trade Comm'n v. Publishers Bus. Services, Inc., 821 F. Supp. 2d 1205 (D. Nev. 2010) (seller violated FTC Act and Telemarketing Sales Rule by misrepresenting that cancellation was not possible and by sending deceptive collection letters from fictitious legal department). *See also* Fed. Trade Comm'n v. Bay Area Bus. Council, 423 F.3d 627 (7th Cir. 2005) (affirming judgment against individual and corporate defendants who led consumers to believe they would receive a major credit card but delivered a card that could only be used as a stored value card); Fed. Trade Comm'n v. World Media Brokers, Inc., 415 F.3d 758 (7th Cir. 2005) (telemarketer's misrepresentation of legality of sale of foreign lottery tickets); Fed. Trade Comm'n v. Consumer Alliance, Inc., 2003 WL 22287364 (N.D. Ill. Sept. 30, 2003) (misrepresentation and unauthorized billing in sale of credit card protection and advance fee credit cards); People *ex rel.* Spitzer v. Telehublink Corp., 756 N.Y.S.2d 285 (N.Y. App. Div. 2003) (affirming permanent injunction and restitution order against telemarketer that promised major credit card but delivered card for purchasing items from seller's catalog). *But see* Fed. Trade Comm'n v. Corps. For Character, L.C., ___ F. Supp. 3d ___, 2015 WL 4577051(D. Utah Mar. 31, 2015) (FTC is not required to prove consumers relied on misleading statements, but it must prove the statements were made; sample call scripts were insufficient to prove misleading statements contained therein were actually made to consumers).

73 New York v. Fin. Services Network, 930 F. Supp. 865 (W.D.N.Y. 1996).

74 16 C.F.R. § 310.3(a)(2)(i). *See* Fed. Trade Comm'n v. E.M.A. Nationwide, Inc., 2013 WL 4545143 (N.D. Ohio Aug. 27, 2013) (defendant failed to include additional fees when disclosing cost to consumers), *aff'd*, 767 F.3d 611 (6th Cir. 2014).

75 16 C.F.R. § 310.3(a)(2)(ii). *See* Fed. Trade Comm'n v. Medical Billers Network, Inc., 543 F. Supp. 2d 283, 315 (S.D.N.Y. 2008) (seller of work-at-home medical billing program violated rule by failing to disclose additional fee necessary to connect to medical billing clearinghouse); People *ex rel.* Spitzer v. Telehublink Corp., 756 N.Y.S.2d 285 (N.Y. App. Div. 2003) (affirming permanent injunction and restitution order against telemarketer that did not disclose that credit card could only be used to buy items from seller's catalog).

76 16 C.F.R. § 310.3(a)(2)(iii). *See* Fed. Trade Comm'n v. Chapman, 714 F.3d 1211 (10th Cir. 2013) (sellers of grant-related materials misrepresented consumers' actual likelihood of obtaining grants); Fed. Trade Comm'n v. USA Fin., L.L.C., 415 Fed. Appx. 970 (11th Cir. 2011) (misrepresented credit card as general use card); Fed. Trade Comm'n v. Stefanchik, 559 F.3d 924, 929–930 (9th Cir. 2009) (seller

- Any material aspects of the seller's refund, cancellation, exchange, or repurchase policies;[77] or
- A seller's or telemarketer's affiliation with or endorsement by any government or third-party organization.[78]

5.3.4 Negative Option Features

The FTC Telemarketing Sales Rule also specifies general disclosures and misrepresentations that apply to sales with a

negative option feature. A negative option feature is any provision under which the customer's silence or failure to take an affirmative action to reject goods or services or to cancel the agreement is interpreted by the seller as an acceptance of the offer.[79] An example is a plan in which the consumer receives periodic announcements of selections that are sent automatically and billed to the consumer unless the consumer tells the company not to send the item.[80] The FTC also has a separate rule governing negative option plans in general.[81]

Whenever an offer includes a negative option feature, the Rule requires disclosure of all its material terms and conditions before the customer pays.[82] The disclosure must include the fact that the consumer's account will be charged unless the consumer takes an affirmative action to avoid the charge; the dates that charges will be submitted for payment; and the specific steps the consumer must take to avoid the charges.[83] Disclosing that the consumer will get a thirty-day free trial membership does not satisfy the requirement to disclose that the consumer must take affirmative action at the end of the thirty-day period to avoid being charged.[84] The Rule also prohibits misrepresentation regarding any material aspect of a negative option feature, including the existence of the feature, the date the charge will be submitted for payment, and the steps the customer must take to avoid the charge.[85]

Additional restrictions are applicable to one type of negative option feature—"free-to-pay conversion" sales in which the consumer has a free trial for a period of time but then is charged unless he or she takes some affirmative step to reject the sale. These are discussed at §§ 5.4.3 and 5.4.4.3, *infra*.

5.4 Restrictions on Billing and Payments
5.4.1 Introduction

The FTC Telemarketing Sales Rule has a number of restrictions on a telemarketer or seller's ability to charge a customer's credit card, bank account, telephone bill, or mortgage statement for goods, services, or donations. The Rule restricts the

---

of work-at-home scheme is liable for telemarketer's misrepresentations about earning potential and availability of coaches); Fed. Trade Comm'n v. Bay Area Bus. Council, 423 F.3d 627 (7th Cir. 2005) (affirming judgment against individual and corporate defendants who led consumers to believe they would receive a major credit card but delivered a card that could only be used as a stored value card); Fed. Trade Comm'n v. E.M.A. Nationwide, Inc., 2013 WL 4545143 (N.D. Ohio Aug. 27, 2013) (telemarketers convinced consumers to sign debt consolidation contracts but then failed to provide the promised debt relief assistance)), *aff'd*, 767 F.3d 611 (6th Cir. 2014); Fed. Trade Comm'n v. Ivy Capital, Inc., 2013 WL 1224613 (D. Nev. Mar. 26, 2013) (telemarketers of an Internet business coaching program misrepresented consumers' earning potential), *aff'd in relevant part, vacated in part on other grounds*, ___ Fed. Appx. ___, 2015 WL 5781664 (9th Cir. Oct. 5, 2015); Fed. Trade Comm'n v. Washington Data Res., 856 F. Supp. 2d 1247 (M.D. Fla. 2012), *aff'd*, 704 F.3d 1323 (11th Cir. 2013) (telemarketers violated rule by leading consumers to believe that paying the fee would make loan modification almost certain, when actual success rate was between 19% and 48%, and by misrepresenting involvement of attorney); Fed. Trade Comm'n v. Affiliate Strategies, Inc., 849 F. Supp. 2d 1085 (D. Kan. 2011) (telemarketer misrepresented success rate).

77 16 C.F.R. § 310.3(a)(2)(iv). *See* Fed. Trade Comm'n v. Loewen, 2013 WL 5816420 (W.D. Wash. Oct. 29, 2013) (consumers were often unable to obtain refunds even after they had paid an additional insurance fee to guarantee a refund of their original fee); Fed. Trade Comm'n v. Ivy Capital, Inc., 2013 WL 1224613 (D. Nev. Mar. 26, 2013) (telemarketers of an Internet business coaching program misrepresented aspects of their refund policy by failing to provide refunds even to those consumers who requested refunds within the three-day refund window), *aff'd in relevant part, vacated in part on other grounds*, ___ Fed. Appx. ___, 2015 WL 5781664 (9th Cir. Oct. 5, 2015); Fed. Trade Comm'n v. Vacation Prop. Services, 2012 WL 1854251 (M.D. Fla. May 21, 2012).

78 16 C.F.R. § 310.3(a)(2)(vii). *See also* Fed. Trade Comm'n v. World Media Brokers, 415 F.3d 758 (7th Cir. 2005) (misrepresentation that sale of foreign lottery packages was legal; one website displayed the FTC's official seal); Fed. Trade Comm'n v. Washington Data Res., 2011 WL 1118581 (M.D. Fla. Mar. 25, 2011) (misrepresenting law firm's foreclosure rescue services as "government bailout"); Fed. Trade Comm'n v. U.S. Mortg. Funding, Inc., 2011 WL 810790 (S.D. Fla. Mar. 1, 2011) (foreclosure rescue company falsely claimed affiliation with consumers' lenders); Fed. Trade Comm'n v. JPM Accelerated Services, Inc., 2011 WL 679938 (M.D. Fla. Jan. 25, 2011) (magistrate's recommendation) (false promise of refunds by company that took advance payment for attempts, almost invariably unsuccessful, to reduce credit card interest rates), *adopted by* 2011 WL 675400 (M.D. Fla. Feb. 16, 2011); Fed. Trade Comm'n v. Mallett, 818 F. Supp. 2d 142 (D.D.C. 2011) (websites advertising debt, tax, and mortgage relief used addresses including "gov" or the acronyms of federal agencies; Fed. Trade Comm'n v. 1263523 Ontario, Inc., 205 F. Supp. 2d 205 (S.D.N.Y. 2002) (entering permanent injunction against advance fee credit card telemarketer that misrepresented its refund policy); Fed. Trade Comm'n v. Growth Plus Int'l Mktg., Inc., 2001 U.S. Dist. LEXIS 1215 (N.D. Ill. Jan. 9, 2001) (granting preliminary injunction against defendants who misrepresented legality of selling Canadian lottery tickets in the United States, their authorization by the Canadian government to sell these tickets, and the chances of winning).

79 16 C.F.R. § 310.2(u). *See* 68 Fed. Reg. 4580, 4594 (Jan. 29, 2003) (explanation of definition). *See also* Fed. Trade Comm'n v. Health Formulas, L.L.C., 2015 WL 2130504, 16 (D. Nev. May 6, 2015) ("recurring payment plans, in which customers are automatically enrolled and through which they are charged if they do nothing, constitute negative option features"); Fed. Trade Comm'n v. John Beck Amazing Profits, L.L.C., 865 F. Supp. 2d 1052 (C.D. Cal. 2012), *later op. at* 888 F. Supp. 2d 1006 (C.D. Cal. 2012) (permanently enjoining sellers from telemarketing).

80 *See* 68 Fed. Reg. 4580, 4594 (Jan. 29, 2003).

81 16 C.F.R. pt. 425, *reprinted at* Appx. A.3, *infra*. The rule is discussed at § 2.7, *supra*.

82 16 C.F.R. § 310.3(a)(1)(vii). *See* Fed. Trade Comm'n v. John Beck Amazing Profits, L.L.C., 865 F. Supp. 2d 1052 (C.D. Cal. 2012), *later op. at* 888 F. Supp. 2d 1006 (C.D. Cal. 2012) (permanently enjoining sellers from telemarketing).

83 16 C.F.R. § 310.3(a)(1)(vii).

84 Fed. Trade Comm'n v. John Beck Amazing Profits, L.L.C., 865 F. Supp. 2d 1052 (C.D. Cal. 2012), *later op. at* 888 F. Supp. 2d 1006 (C.D. Cal. 2012) (permanently enjoining sellers from telemarketing).

85 16 C.F.R. § 310.3(a)(2)(ix).

Federal Deception Law

use of billing information, defined as any data that enables any person to access a customer's or donor's account, such as a credit card, checking, savings, share or similar account, utility bill, mortgage loan account, or debit card.[86]

Restrictions on billing information address two related problems. First, the customer may provide account information while *not* authorizing payment, but the telemarketer uses that account information to process a payment. The other problem is when the telemarketer already has acquired the customer's account information before the call and processes payment without the customer's authorization.[87]

As with the Rule in general, the restrictions apply to telemarketer- or seller-initiated calls and also to certain customer-initiated calls.[88] The Rule includes protections that apply to all forms of payment, including credit cards and debit cards, and these protections are analyzed at § 5.4.3, *infra*. In addition, the Rule includes special protections, analyzed at § 5.4.4, *infra*, for payment methods other than credit cards and debit cards.

5.4.2 Limits on Obtaining or Disclosing Unencrypted Account Information

One way to limit misuse of preacquired account information is to make it more difficult for telemarketers to obtain the account information. The FTC Telemarketing Sales Rule prohibits a telemarketer or seller from disclosing or receiving for consideration unencrypted account numbers for use in telemarketing.[89] This prohibition is consistent with the Gramm-Leach-Bliley Act,[90] under which financial institutions and third parties with which they do business may provide consumer account information for marketing purposes to other third parties only in encrypted form.[91] The effect of the Telemarketing Sales Rule is to expand this limitation beyond financial institutions to telemarketers and sellers.

5.4.3 Limits for All Payment Methods, Including Credit Cards and Debit Cards

The Rule includes several protections against unauthorized charges that apply to all payment methods, including credit cards and debit cards. When customers themselves provide the telemarketer or seller with their account information, the Rule prohibits this information from being submitted for payment without the express informed consent of the customer or donor.[92] The customer must consent to the use of the identified account to make that charge.[93]

The customer or donor must affirmatively and unambiguously articulate consent in order for it to be express.[94] Neither silence nor an ambiguous response constitutes consent.[95] Customers or donors must have received all required material disclosures under the Rule in order for the consent to be informed.[96]

Additional provisions apply when the telemarketer or seller has obtained the customer's credit or debit card information before making the call, or what is known as "preacquired account information." The seller or telemarketer must identify the account to be charged and obtain express consent from the consumer to be charged for the goods or services using that account number.[97] A federal court has upheld the Rule's restrictions on pre-acquired account telemarketing even though the restrictions in the final rule are broader than those in the proposed rule.[98]

A second provision adds further requirements for telemarketing transactions involving preacquired account information that also have a "free-to-pay conversion feature." A free-to-pay conversion means a transaction in which the customer receives a good or service for free for an initial period and incurs an obligation to pay after that for the good or service if the customer does not affirmatively cancel.[99] In such a transaction, the telemarketer or seller must obtain from the customer the last four digits of the account number (even if the seller or telemarketer already has it), obtain from the customer an express consent to be charged using that account, and make and maintain an audio recording of the entire telemarketing transaction.[100]

For credit cards and debit cards, the consumer has additional protections under the Truth in Lending Act[101] or the

---

86 16 C.F.R. § 310.2(c).

87 *See* Fed. Trade Comm'n v. J.K. Publications, Inc., 99 F. Supp. 2d 1176 (C.D. Cal. 2000) (non-telemarketing case in which the defendant purchased unencrypted lists of consumer account numbers and used the numbers to charge consumers' accounts without authorization); Faillace v. Columbus Bank & Trust Co., 605 S.E.2d 450 (Ga. Ct. App. 2004) (state RICO judgment in favor of bank against telemarketer that used preacquired account information to charge consumers' credit cards without their consent).

88 *See* § 5.2.2, *supra*.

89 16 C.F.R. § 310.4(a)(6). *See* 68 Fed. Reg. 4580, 4615, 4616 (Jan. 29, 2003).

90 15 U.S.C. §§ 6801–6810. The FTC's Privacy Rule, 16 C.F.R. pt. 313, as mandated by the Gramm-Leach-Bliley Act, prohibits financial institutions from disclosing customer account numbers or other similar forms of access to non-affiliated third parties for use in marketing (including telemarketing).

91 *See* 68 Fed. Reg. 4580, 4616 (Jan. 29, 2003).

92 16 C.F.R. § 310.4(a)(7).

93 *Id.*

94 68 Fed. Reg. 4580, 4620 (Jan. 29, 2003).

95 *Id.*

96 *Id.*

97 16 C.F.R. § 310.4(a)(7)(ii).

98 U.S. Sec. v. Fed. Trade Comm'n, 282 F. Supp. 2d 1285 (W.D. Okla. 2003), *aff'd on other grounds*, 358 F.3d 1228 (10th Cir. 2004) (upholding do-not-call rule).

99 16 C.F.R. § 310.2(p); 68 Fed. Reg. 4580, 4594 (Jan. 29, 2003). *Cf.* Minnesota *ex rel*. Hatch v. Fleet Mortg. Corp., 158 F. Supp. 2d 962 (D. Minn. 2001), *motion to dismiss denied*, 181 F. Supp. 2d 995 (D. Minn. 2001) (promoting "free trial period" while obscuring fact that monthly charges will be assessed unless consumer cancels is deceptive).

100 16 C.F.R. § 310.4(a)(7)(i). *See* 68 Fed. Reg. 4580, 4621 (Jan. 29, 2003); Fed. Trade Comm'n v. Inc21.com Corp., 745 F. Supp. 2d 975, 1008 (N.D. Cal. 2010) (finding violation when seller used consumers' telephone numbers to place charges on their telephone bills after "free" trial period without recording entire call), *aff'd mem.*, 2012 WL 1065534 (9th Cir. Mar. 30, 2012).

101 *See* National Consumer Law Center, Truth in Lending § 4.3 (9th ed. 2015), *updated at* www.nclc.org/library.

Electronic Fund Transfer Act,[102] both of which limit a customer's liability for unauthorized charges. Those statutes limit the customer's liability to the financial institution while the Telemarketing Sales Rule prohibits the telemarketer or seller from making the unauthorized charge.

5.4.4 Limits on Check, Electronic Funds Transfer, Telephone Bill, and Other Payment Methods

5.4.4.1 Introduction

Additional protections apply when payment is made using a check, an electronic funds transfer, an electronic check conversion, the customer's phone bill, mortgage statement, or any method other than a credit card governed by the Truth in Lending Act or a debit card governed by the Electronic Fund Transfer Act. There are two reasons for these additional protections. The Truth in Lending Act and Electronic Fund Transfer Act protections for unauthorized charges do not apply to check payments and charges that are added to the customer's phone bill. In addition, when a customer provides a credit card or debit card number, there is some expectation that the number may be used to charge the customer. Consumers are less likely to realize that payment can be processed based only on bank account information or a telephone number—many customers assume that this information cannot generate a charge without the customer's signature.[103]

Thus even when the customer provides the account information during the telemarketing transaction, additional Rule protections apply for any form of payment other than credit or debit cards. The key requirement is that the seller or telemarketer must obtain the consumer's "express verifiable authorization" to submit the billing information.[104] The customer or donor's express written, signed authorization meets this requirement.[105] A signature includes an electronic or digital signature if such a signature is considered valid under applicable federal law or state contract law.[106] The other ways by which a seller or telemarketer can meet this requirement are discussed in the next subsection.

5.4.4.2 Requirements for Payments Not Including a Written Signature

Absent a signature, additional FTC Telemarketing Sales Rule requirements apply to any form of payment other than credit or debit cards. These requirements apply to demand drafts or "telechecks" when the telemarketer generates an unsigned check drawn on the consumer's bank account and presents it to a bank for payment or requests an electronic funds transfer from the customer's bank. A similar form of payment occurs when the telemarketer or seller generates an unsigned check using the customer's bank account information and then uses that check as a source document to initiate an electronic funds transfer from the consumer's bank account. This is called an electronic check conversion or ECC. Another form of covered payment occurs when the telemarketer adds a charge to the customer's phone bill or mortgage statement.[107] These requirements apply not only to telemarketer-initiated calls but also to certain customer-initiated calls, as set out in § 5.2.2, *supra.*

To obtain payment without the customer's signature, the telemarketer must obtain the customer's express verifiable authorization by one of two methods. The first is to obtain oral authorization that is audio-recorded and available upon request to the customer or the customer's bank. The recording must include not only the customer's consent but also the number of payments, the dates the items will be submitted for payment, the amount of the payments, the customer's name, detailed information about the account, the customer's telephone number, and the date of the customer's oral authorization.[108] Not surprisingly, fraudulent telemarketers have sought to manipulate and evade this requirement.[109]

---

102 *See* National Consumer Law Center, *Consumer Banking and Payments Law* Ch. 5 (5th ed. 2013), *updated at* www.nclc.org/library.

103 *See* Fed. Trade Comm'n, Final Amended Rule, 68 Fed. Reg. 4580, 4605 (Jan. 29, 2003).

104 16 C.F.R. § 310.3(a)(3).

105 16 C.F.R. § 310.3(a)(3)(i).

106 16 C.F.R. § 310.3 n.5.

107 *See Lawn v. Enhanced Serv. Billing, Inc.*, 2010 WL 2773377 (E.D. Pa. July 13, 2010) (voluntary payment doctrine did not bar UDAP claim alleging addition of unauthorized charges to phone bill; fact question whether payment was truly voluntary when name of bill aggregator was buried on page five of six-page bill and name of seller did not appear); *Fed. Trade Comm'n v. Inc21.com Corp.*, 745 F. Supp. 2d 975 (N.D. Cal. 2010) (describing role of billing aggregator and how telemarketer added unauthorized charges to local telephone bills), *aff'd mem.*, 2012 WL 1065534 (9th Cir. Mar. 30, 2012); *Minnesota ex rel. Hatch v. Fleet Mortg. Corp.*, 158 F. Supp. 2d 962 (D. Minn. 2001), *motion to dismiss denied*, 181 F. Supp. 2d 995 (D. Minn. 2001) (refusing to dismiss claim that mortgage company violated various state laws by providing telemarketing firm with customer account information to sell membership programs for discount services such as car repair and health care, the cost of which was added to consumers' monthly mortgage statements). *See also Fed. Trade Comm'n v. Verity Int'l, Ltd.*, 443 F.3d 48 (2d Cir. 2006) (affirming decision holding billing services liable under FTC Act for surreptitiously capturing phone numbers of users who visited pornography websites and cramming charges onto their telephone bills); *Fed. Trade Comm'n v. RJB Telecom, Inc.*, 5 Trade Reg. Rep. (CCH) ¶ 15155 (D. Ariz. Sept. 26, 2001) (proposed consent decree against adult website company that billed phone bills without authorization). *See generally* National Consumer Law Center, *Consumer Banking and Payments Law* § 3.13 (5th ed. 2013), *updated at* www.nclc.org/library.

108 16 C.F.R. § 310.3(a)(3)(ii).

109 *See Fed. Trade Comm'n v. NHS Systems, Inc.*, 936 F. Supp. 2d 520, 2013 WL 1285424 (E.D. Pa. Mar. 28, 2013) (defendants violated Telemarketing Sales Rule by using inauthentic or altered recordings to authorize debits from consumers' accounts); *Inc21.com v. Flora*, 2008 WL 5130415 (N.D. Cal. Dec. 5, 2008) (describing scheme by which telemarketers doctored audiotapes to insert digitized and recorded responses to verification questions as if consumers were answering them), *later op. at Fed. Trade Comm'n v. Inc21.com Corp.*, 745 F. Supp. 2d 975 (N.D. Cal. 2010) (describing methods of falsification in detail; granting permanent injunction and ordering restitution), *aff'd mem.*, 2012 WL 1065534 (9th Cir. Mar. 30, 2012); *Fed. Trade Comm'n v. City W. Advantage, Inc.*, 2008 WL 2844696, at *3–4 (D. Nev. July 22,

The other option used to obtain the customer's express verifiable consent is to provide the customer with written confirmation of the transaction, identified in a clear and conspicuous manner as such on the outside of the envelope and sent using first class mail prior to submission of payment, that includes the same information required in the oral recording and the procedures by which the customer can obtain a refund if the confirmation is inaccurate.[110] Telemarketers must be prepared to offer proof of these authorizations, and written confirmations must contain all of the information required by the Rule.[111]

5.4.4.3 Additional Requirement When Payment Involves Preacquired Account Information and Free-to-Pay Conversion

There are additional requirements if the seller or telemarketer acquires the customer's account information prior to a telemarketing call that involves a free-to-pay conversion, as defined at § 5.4.3, *supra*. In that case, even if the seller or telemarketer obtains the customer's signature, it must still maintain an audio recording of the complete transaction.[112] In addition, mailing a written confirmation of the transaction to the consumer cannot serve as express verifiable authorization for the billing:[113] the seller or telemarketer must obtain the consumer's signature or record detailed oral authorization[114] and must record the entire transaction.

5.5 Special Regulation of Certain Transactions

5.5.1 Advance Fee Loans

The FTC Telemarketing Sales Rule prohibits telemarketers or sellers from requesting or seeking payment of any fee in advance of obtaining a loan or other credit extension when the seller or telemarketer has guaranteed or represented a high likelihood of success in obtaining or arranging a loan.[115] For example, a creditor violated this Rule provision by offering a credit card upon payment of a $200 advance fee.[116] A telemarketer that advertised pre-approved credit could not escape the prohibition against advance payment by arguing that it did not actually issue credit itself or by characterizing its charges as "membership fees" for its investment and credit application services rather than as fees for credit.[117]

The prohibition on advance fees applies not only to seller- or telemarketer-initiated calls, or attempts to upsell during a customer-initiated call, but also to customer-initiated calls in response to the seller's advertising or direct solicitations.[118] All the other Rule provisions, including limits on billing and payments, required disclosures, and prohibited misrepresentations,[119] also apply to customer-initiated calls regarding advance fee loans.

5.5.2 Credit Repair

The FTC Telemarketing Sales Rule limits when a telemarketer or seller can seek payment for credit repair, defined as goods or services represented to remove derogatory information from, or improve, a person's credit history, credit record, or credit rating.[120] The Rule applies to anyone soliciting such services, including attorneys.[121]

The telemarketer or seller cannot request or receive payment until the time frame has expired in which the credit repair agency has represented that all goods or services will be provided *and* the agency has provided a consumer report

---

credit but instead only distributed worthless general information regarding credit violated the Telemarketing Sales Rule); Fed. Trade Comm'n v. Consumer Alliance, Inc., 2003 WL 22287364 (N.D. Ill. Sept. 30, 2003); Fed. Trade Comm'n v. Bay Area Bus. Council, Inc., 2003 WL 1220245 (N.D. Ill. Mar. 14, 2003) (denying motion to dismiss); Fed. Trade Comm'n v. 1263523 Ontario, Inc., 205 F. Supp. 2d 205 (S.D.N.Y. 2002) (granting permanent injunction against advance fee credit card telemarketer); *In re* Nat'l Credit Mgmt. Grp., 21 F. Supp. 2d 424 (D.N.J. 1998) (offer of a pre-approved credit card promises a high likelihood of success in obtaining credit, therefore telemarketer's requesting and receiving funds in advance of delivering services violated rule); New York v. Financial Services Network, 930 F. Supp. 865 (W.D.N.Y. 1996) (granting preliminary injunction against advance fee credit telemarketer); People *ex rel.* Spitzer v. Telehublink Corp., 756 N.Y.S.2d 285 (N.Y. App. Div. 2003).

Innumerable other actions by the FTC and the states against telemarketers for violating this rule may be found on the FTC's website, www .ftc.gov.

116 Fed. Trade Comm'n v. USA Fin., L.L.C., 415 Fed. Appx. 970 (11th Cir. 2011) (misrepresented credit card as general use card).

117 New York v. Financial Services Network, 930 F. Supp. 865 (W.D.N.Y. 1996).

118 *See* Fed. Trade Comm'n v. Lalonde, 545 Fed. Appx. 825 (11th Cir. 2013) (per curiam) (TSR applies to consumer-initiated calls in response to advertisements of loan acquisition services); § 5.2.2, *supra*.

119 *See* §§ 5.3, 5.4, *supra*.

120 16 C.F.R. § 310.4(a)(2).

121 Tennessee v. Lexington Law Firms, 1997 U.S. Dist. LEXIS 7403, 1997-1 Trade Cas. (CCH) ¶ 71,8201 (M.D. Tenn. May 14, 1997) (rejecting arguments that application to attorneys was unconstitutional and beyond scope of statute).

2008) (describing telemarketers' statements that, to receive free gift, consumer had to answer "yes" to verification questions about other products but would not be charged for them).

110 16 C.F.R. § 310.3(a)(3)(iii).

111 *In re* Nat'l Credit Mgmt. Grp., 21 F. Supp. 2d 424 (D.N.J. 1998) (finding telemarketer of credit monitoring and credit card services violated rule by debiting consumers' accounts without proper authorization; accepting customer certifications that oral authorization was not given when company could not provide tape-recorded verification; written confirmations that did not confirm the date of the oral authorization or inform consumers of how to obtain a refund were insufficient to comply with the Rule).

112 16 C.F.R. § 310.4(a)(7)(i).

113 16 C.F.R. § 310.3(a)(3)(iii).

114 16 C.F.R. § 310.3(a)(3)(i), (ii).

115 16 C.F.R. § 310.4(a)(4). *See* Fed. Trade Comm'n v. Oks, 2007 WL 3307009 (N.D. Ill. Nov. 2, 2007) (holding that telemarketers' advance fee credit card scheme violated the Telemarketing Sales Rule); Fed. Trade Comm'n v. Pacific First Benefit, L.L.C., 472 F. Supp. 2d 974 (N.D. Ill. 2007) (telemarketer that promised to improve consumers'

demonstrating that the promised results have been achieved.[122] The report must be issued more than six months after the results were achieved.[123] This means that a credit repair service cannot seek payment until well over six months after the customer agrees to the service.

The prohibition on credit repair payments applies not only to seller- or telemarketer-initiated calls, or attempts to upsell during a customer-initiated call, but also to customer-initiated calls in response to the seller's advertising or direct solicitations.[124] All other Rule provisions, including limits on billing and payments, required disclosures and prohibited misrepresentations,[125] apply as well to customer-initiated calls in response to credit repair advertisements or direct solicitations.

Credit repair services that accept advance fees also run afoul of the federal Credit Repair Organizations Act (CROA).[126] The CROA prohibits advance payment, although it does not require the credit repair organization to wait six months after providing the consumer an improved credit report. It also requires a three-day right to cancel and prohibits various deceptions. CROA applies even when the consumer's contact with a credit repair agency is not in response to advertising or a direct solicitation.

Unlike the FTC Telemarketing Sales Rule, the CROA explicitly grants consumers a private cause of action regardless of the amount of damage.[127] The credit repair provisions of the FTC Telemarketing Sales Rule remain enforceable despite the subsequent passage of the CROA.[128] Many states have credit repair statutes, often with broader coverage that includes loan brokers as well as credit repair organizations, and these statutes usually also provide for a private cause of action.[129]

5.5.3 Offers to Recover Amounts Lost Through Past Telemarketing Fraud

The FTC Telemarketing Sales Rule has a special provision when a person offers to recover or otherwise assist an individual in the return of the individual's money lost in a previous telemarketing transaction.[130] These "recovery rooms" are a particularly pernicious form of what is called "reloading," that is, soliciting people who have demonstrated their vulnerability by succumbing to previous telemarketing pitches.[131] The

operator promises, for an advance fee, to obtain for victims refunds or the prizes or goods that were never delivered.[132]

The Rule prohibits a seller or telemarketer from requesting or receiving payment for such services until seven business days after the money or item is delivered to the customer.[133] The provision does not apply when a licensed attorney provides the assistance. But the prohibition applies not only to seller- or telemarketer-initiated calls, or attempts to upsell during a customer-initiated call, but also to customer-initiated calls in response to the seller's advertising or direct solicitations.[134] All other Rule provisions, including limits on billing and payments, required disclosures, and prohibited misrepresentations, also apply not only to telemarketer-initiated calls but also to customer-initiated calls in response to advertising or direct solicitations concerning such offers.[135]

5.5.4 Debt Relief Services

The FTC Telemarketing Sales Rule contains extensive provisions relating to debt relief services, defined as any program represented to negotiate, settle, or alter payment terms of debt between an individual and unsecured creditors or debt collectors.[136] The provisions apply both to seller- or telemarketer-initiated calls and to customer-initiated calls in response to advertising or a direct solicitation.[137] The Rule provisions and other law regulating debt relief services are examined at Chapter 10, *infra*.

5.5.5 Credit Card Protection Products

Unscrupulous sellers and telemarketers often misrepresent that they are affiliated with the credit card issuer and that, without a credit card protection plan, the consumer has unlimited liability for the unauthorized use of his or her credit

---

122 16 C.F.R. § 310.4(a)(2).

123 *Id. See* Fed. Trade Comm'n v. 1st Guarantee Mortg. Co., 2011 WL 1233207 (S.D. Fla. Mar. 30, 2011) (telemarketers violated rule by obtaining advance fee for attempts, generally unsuccessful, to improve credit scores or obtain loan modifications).

124 *See* § 5.2.2, *supra*.

125 *See* §§ 5.3, 5.4, *supra*.

126 15 U.S.C. § 1679b(b).

127 15 U.S.C. § 1679g. *See* National Consumer Law Center, Fair Credit Reporting Ch. 15 (8th ed. 2013), *updated at* www.nclc.org/library.

128 Tennessee v. Lexington Law Firms, 1997 U.S. Dist. LEXIS 7403, 1997-1 Trade Cas. (CCH) ¶ 71,820 (M.D. Tenn. May 14, 1997).

129 *See* National Consumer Law Center, Fair Credit Reporting Ch. 15 (8th ed. 2013), *updated at* www.nclc.org/library.

130 16 C.F.R. § 310.4(a)(3).

131 *See* 60 Fed. Reg. 8318 (Feb. 14, 1995) (describing reloading); United States v. Johnson, 297 F.3d 845 (9th Cir. 2002) (affirming wire fraud,

mail fraud, and money laundering convictions for telemarketing scheme that included reloading and targeting of older consumers); United States v. Ciccone, 219 F.3d 1078 (9th Cir. 2000) (affirming wire fraud conviction of reloader); United States v. Jackson, 95 F.3d 500 (7th Cir. 1996) (discussing vulnerability of those who have been victimized once).

132 The FTC's rule implementing the Telemarketing and Consumer Fraud and Abuse Prevention Act originally proposed to ban telemarketers from selling their customer lists when they were under a federal court order for telemarketing fraud. 60 Fed. Reg. 8320, 8332 (Feb. 14, 1995).

The FTC deleted this prohibition in its revised proposal, 60 Fed. Reg. 30420 (June 8, 1995), and it did not appear in the final rule or in the rule as amended in 2003. The final rule prohibits "recovery rooms" from receiving payment prior to restoring the money or property to the consumer. *See* 16 C.F.R. § 310.4(a)(3).

133 16 C.F.R. § 310.4(a)(3). *See also* United States v. Business Recovery Services, L.L.C., 2011 WL 1456837 (D. Ariz. Apr. 15, 2011) (granting preliminary injunction against telemarketer who took advance payment for recovery kits).

134 *See* § 5.2.2, *supra*.

135 *See* § 5.2.2, *supra*.

136 16 C.F.R. § 310.2(m).

137 *See* § 5.2.2, *supra*.

card.[138] In fact, federal law limits such liability to no more than $50 in most situations.[139]

The Telemarketing Sales Rule states that, in any sale of goods or services represented to protect, insure, or otherwise limit a customer's liability for unauthorized use of the customer's credit card, the seller or telemarketer must disclose the federal limits of such liability (that is, $50 in most situations).[140] The Rule also prohibits any misrepresentation that a customer needs to purchase goods or services to obtain the protection provided by federal law.[141]

These provisions apply not only to seller- or telemarketer-initiated calls, or attempts to upsell during a customer-initiated call, but also to customer-initiated calls in response to the seller's advertising or direct solicitations concerning credit protection products.[142] The same is the case with all other Rule provisions, including limits on billing and payments and the Rule's required disclosures and prohibited misrepresentations. Of special note are the Rule's provisions on billing and payments, particularly for free-to-pay conversions,[143] since these services are often charged to consumers' credit cards without the consumer's knowledge, often on a free-to-pay basis.

5.5.6 *Investment and Business Opportunity Sales*

The FTC Telemarketing Sales Rule prohibits a telemarketer or seller from misrepresenting any material aspect of an investment opportunity, including risk, liquidity, earnings potential, or profitability.[144] The legislative history indicates that investments covered by the Rule include intangible investments such as oil and gas leases, franchise agreements, and license rights.[145] This provision, as well as the other protections offered by the Rule, apply both to seller- or telemarketer-initiated calls and also to customer-initiated calls in response to an advertisement or direct solicitation.

Nonetheless, neither the specific prohibition against misrepresentations regarding investment opportunities nor most of the Rule's general provisions apply to business opportunities covered by the Franchise Rule or Business Opportunity Rule.[146] Those sales are covered only by the Telemarketing Sales Rule's prohibition of profane or foul language, threats, and intimidation; billing without express informed consent; unwanted calls; and calls at inconvenient hours.[147]

The FTC Telemarketing Sales Rule may be particularly relevant to investment and business opportunity transactions covered by the Rule, because the amount lost in such schemes could exceed $50,000, which is the minimum amount of actual damage required before a private right of action in federal court becomes applicable under the Rule. Private remedies under the Telemarketing and Consumer Fraud and Abuse Prevention Act can then become applicable not just to seller- or telemarketer-initiated calls but also to customer-initiated calls in response to advertisements or direct solicitations regarding investments or business opportunities.

5.5.7 *Prize Promotions*

The FTC Telemarketing Sales Rule includes special provisions relating to prize promotions. A prize promotion is defined as a sweepstakes or other game of chance or a representation that a person has won, been selected to receive, or may be eligible to receive a prize.[148] A prize is anything offered or given or purportedly offered or given to a person by chance.[149] The Rule requires the seller and telemarketer to keep a record for twenty-four months of the name and last known address of each prize recipient and the prize awarded for prizes represented as having a value of $25 or more.[150]

The Rule has a number of disclosure requirements for prize promotions. Before the customer consents to make any payment, the seller or telemarketer must disclose truthfully, in a clear and conspicuous manner:

- The odds of winning or, if the odds cannot be calculated in advance, the factors used in calculating the odds;
- That no purchase or payment is necessary to win a prize or participate in a prize promotion and that any purchase or payment will not increase the person's chance of winning;
- That there is a non-purchase, no-payment option and instructions on how to use that option or an address or local or toll-free telephone number from which this information can be obtained; and
- All material costs or conditions to receive the prize.[151]

The Rule also prohibits misrepresenting any material aspect of the promotion, including odds of receiving the prize, the nature or value of the prize, or that a purchase or payment is required to win a prize.[152] Similarly, the Rule prohibits any telemarketer soliciting charitable donations to misrepresent any material aspect of a prize promotion, including the odds of winning, the nature or value of the prize, or that a charitable contribution is required to win or to participate

---

138 *See* Fed. Trade Comm'n v. Consumer Alliance, Inc., 2003 WL 22287364 (N.D. Ill. Sept. 30, 2003) (finding deception). Innumerable FTC actions against credit card protection marketers may be found on the FTC's website, www.ftc.gov.

139 15 U.S.C. § 1643.

140 16 C.F.R. § 310.3(a)(1)(vi).

141 16 C.F.R. § 310.3(a)(2)(viii).

142 *See* § 5.2.2, *supra*.

143 *See* § 5.4, *supra*.

144 16 C.F.R. § 310.3(a)(2)(vi).

145 H. Rep. No. 103-20, 4 U.S. Code Congressional and Administrative News 1636 (103d Cong. 2d Sess. 1994).

146 *See* § 5.2.2, *supra*.

147 16 C.F.R. § 226.4(a)(1), (7), (b), (c).

148 16 C.F.R. § 310.2(z).

149 *Id.* § 310.2(y).

150 *Id.* § 310.5(2).

151 16 C.F.R. § 310.3(a)(1)(iv), (v).

Since telemarketers must disclose that no purchase or payment is required to win a prize or participate in a prize promotion, the FTC explained that the costs that must be disclosed are any incidental costs other than a purchase or payment. *See* 68 Fed. Reg. 4580, 4601 (Jan. 29, 2003).

152 16 C.F.R. § 310.3(a)(2)(v).

in the prize promotion.[153] All of these requirements are in addition to the standard disclosures required at the outset of the call.[154]

While none of the provisions described above apply to customer-initiated calls in response to an advertisement, they—and indeed all the provisions of the Rule—do apply to customer-initiated calls in response to a prize-promotion direct solicitation, such as a solicitation using the mail, fax, or e-mail.[155] Of course, all Rule provisions apply as well to seller- or telemarketer-initiated calls and to upsells. In a redundant provision that only applies to telemarketer-initiated calls and upsells, the Rule requires disclosure concerning prize promotions of essentially the same items as described in the bulleted list above.[156]

5.5.8 Charitable Contributions

The FTC Telemarketing Sales Rule has a number of provisions applicable to telemarketer-initiated calls soliciting charitable contributions from donors. These provisions do not apply to customer-initiated calls[157] or to calls made by a bona fide charity.[158] "Charitable contribution" is defined as any donation or gift of money or other thing of value,[159] and "donor" is defined as any person solicited to make a charitable contribution.[160]

The Rule prohibits telemarketers who are soliciting for charitable contributions from making any misrepresentations about the following:[161]

- The nature, purpose, or mission of any entity on behalf of which the charitable contribution is being requested;
- That any charitable contribution is tax deductible in whole or in part;
- The purpose for which the charitable contribution will be used;[162]
- The amount that goes to the charitable organization or program after administrative costs are deducted;
- Material aspects of prize promotions, including that a charitable contribution is required to win a prize; or
- Affiliation, endorsements, or sponsorship by any person or government.[163]

The Rule also requires the telemarketer to disclose truthfully, promptly, and in a clear and conspicuous manner the charitable organization's identity and that the purpose of the call is to solicit a charitable contribution.[164]

5.6 Remedies

5.6.1 Private Remedies

5.6.1.1 Remedies Under the Telemarketing and Consumer Fraud and Abuse Prevention Act

FTC Telemarketing Sales Rule violations can be remedied privately as set out in the Telemarketing and Consumer Fraud and Abuse Prevention Act.[165] The statute provides that any person adversely affected by any pattern or practice of telemarketing which violates the FTC Telemarketing Sales Rule may bring an action in federal court if the amount in controversy exceeds $50,000 in actual damages for each person adversely affected by such telemarketing.[166]

This provision requires that each consumer, or a member of a class, bringing an action have $50,000 in actual damages. The reference to actual damages excludes punitive damages,[167] and possibly attorney fees, from the computation of damages. On the other hand, the $50,000 in actual damages should include consequential damages, including damage to a consumer's credit worthiness (for example, having to pay a higher interest rate to obtain a mortgage), physical ailments as a result of the violation, and perhaps pain and suffering.[168] The Rule's private remedies are of particular relevance to cases involving investments or business opportunities, since these cases are the most likely to result in over $50,000 in actual damages.

The statute provides for a recovery of not only damages but also such further and other relief as the court may deem appropriate. The plaintiff can also enjoin the telemarketing or enforce compliance with the Rule.[169] The court may award to the prevailing party costs of suit and reasonable fees for attorneys and expert witnesses.[170] While this presents some risk that a plaintiff will have to pay the telemarketer's attorney fees and costs, the Supreme Court in a Civil Rights Act case has said that, when the court may issues fees to the prevailing party, a successful civil rights plaintiff should recover "in all but special circumstances" and that prevailing defendants

---

153 16 C.F.R. § 310.3(d)(5).
154 *See* § 5.3.2, *supra.*
155 *See* § 5.2.2, *supra.*
156 16 C.F.R. § 310.4(d)(4).
157 *See* § 5.2.2, *supra.*
158 *See* § 5.2.3.4, *supra.*
159 16 C.F.R. § 310.2(f).
160 16 C.F.R. § 310.2(n).
161 16 C.F.R. § 310.3(d). *See* 68 Fed. Reg. 4580, 4612, 4613 (Jan. 29, 2003) (discussing rationale and details).
162 The FTC interprets this prohibition to encompass misrepresentations that a charity or its services are local. 68 Fed. Reg. 4580, 4613 (Jan. 29, 2003). *See also* United States v. Corps. For Character, L.C., ___ F. Supp. 3d ___, 2015 WL 4577051 (D. Utah Mar. 31, 2015).
163 The FTC interprets this prohibition as extending to "sound-alikes," the use of a name similar or identical to that of a legitimate charity. 68 Fed. Reg. 4580, 4613 (Jan. 29, 2003).

164 16 C.F.R. § 310.4(e).
165 15 U.S.C. § 6101–6108.
166 15 U.S.C. § 6104(a).
      The legislative history indicates that federal courts will have exclusive jurisdiction and also that the $50,000 threshold applies to any action under the Act irrespective of which court the case is brought before. *See* 4 U.S. Code Congressional and Administrative News 1635 (103d Cong. 2d Sess. 1994).
167 *See* H. Rep. No. 103-20, 4 US Code Congressional and Administrative News 1635 (103d Cong. 2d Sess. 1994).
168 *See* Federal Aviation Admin. v. Cooper, 132 S. Ct. 1441 (2012) (discussing the meaning of actual damages as provided in federal statutes).
169 15 U.S.C. § 6104(a).
170 15 U.S.C. § 6104(d).

should recover only when the claim is frivolous, unreasonable, or without foundation.[171]

The statute provides for a three-year statute of limitations after discovery of the violation.[172] The private cause of action is available only if the plaintiff is adversely affected by a "pattern or practice" of telemarketing violations.[173] The heightened pleading requirements for allegations of fraud under Federal Rule of Civil Procedure 9(b) do not apply to claims made pursuant to the Rule.[174] Plaintiffs must notify the FTC of the action.[175] When feasible, this notice is to be given before suit is filed.[176]

5.6.1.2 Other Private Remedies for Rule Violations

Consumers can bring suit under their state UDAP statute for Telemarketing Sales Rule violations, since in most states a violation of an FTC rule will be treated as a per se UDAP violation.[177] In addition, a state's telemarketing law may

incorporate all or part of the federal law and provide a private cause of action.[178]

5.6.1.3 Private Remedies for Telemarketing Fraud Independent of Rule Violations

Of course, there are a number of private remedies for telemarketing fraud that are independent of the FTC Telemarketing Sales Rule. State telemarketing statutes examined at § 5.9, *infra*, typically provide a private right of action. Claims based on general UDAP standards and common law fraud may be available against entities involved in telemarketing fraud.[179] Advocates should also check their state's "door-to-door sales" law to see if it covers telephone solicitations. If it does, the consumer may be able to exercise a right to cancel even long after the date of the sale.[180] Some retail sales laws also include provisions regarding such matters as the need for written contracts in telephone sales.[181] If the fraud involved solicitations for phony charitable purposes, the state may have a charitable solicitations law that applies.

State and federal RICO statutes offer particularly promising approaches to telemarketing fraud.[182] Nearly all cases will

---

171 Christianburg Garment Co. v. Equal Emp't Opportunity Comm'n, 434 U.S. 412, 98 S. Ct. 694, 4 L. Ed. 2d 648 (1978).

172 15 U.S.C. § 6104(a). *See also* Navarro v. Sears Life Ins. Co., 2008 WL 3863451 (E.D. Cal. Aug. 18, 2008). *But see* United States v. DISH Network, L.L.C., 75 F. Supp. 3d 942 (C.D. Ill. 2014) (though TSR violations have a three-year limit, plaintiffs may seek remedies under the FTC Act such as civil penalties with a five-year limitation, and equitable relief, which has no statute of limitations), *vacated in part on other grounds,* 80 F. Supp. 3d 917 (C.D. Ill. 2015).

173 15 U.S.C. § 6104(a).

174 Fed. Trade Comm'n v. Consumer Health Benefits Ass'n, 2012 WL 1890242 (E.D.N.Y. May 23, 2012) (enhanced pleading standards not applicable, because Telephone Sales Rule covers much broader area than common law fraud). *See also* Fed. Trade Comm'n v. Tax Club, Inc., 994 F. Supp. 2d 461 (S.D.N.Y. 2014) (rejecting defendants' argument that heightened pleading is required); Fed. Trade Comm'n v. AFD Advisors, L.L.C., 2014 WL 274097 (N.D. Ill. Jan. 24, 2014) (heightened pleading standard not required because "neither fraud nor mistake is an element of deceptive conduct under the FTC Act and the TSR"); Fed. Trade Comm'n v. Sterling Precious Metals, L.L.C., 2013 WL 595713 (S.D. Fla. Feb. 15, 2013) (heightened pleading is not required for claims under FTC Act and "by extension the TSR" because, unlike a claim for fraud, the FTC is not required to prove "scienter, reliance, or injury to establish a § 5 violation"). *But see* Fed. Trade Comm'n v. ELH Consulting, L.L.C., 2013 WL 4759267 (D. Ariz. Sept. 4, 2013) (applying heightened pleading standard because allegations of deceptive acts and practices and making false representations "sound in fraud"); Tennessee v. Lexington Law Firms, 1997 U.S. Dist. LEXIS 7403, 1997-1 Trade Cas. (CCH) ¶ 71820 (M.D. Tenn. May 14, 1997).

175 15 U.S.C. § 6104(b); 16 C.F.R. § 310.7.

176 15 U.S.C. § 6104(b).

177 *See* Sharkey v. NAC Mktg. Co., L.L.C., 2012 WL 5967409 (N.D. Ill. Nov. 28, 2012) (violation of Telemarketing Sales Rule is sufficient to show unfairness in violation of the Illinois Consumer Fraud and Deceptive Practices Act); Fed. Trade Comm'n v. Info. Mgmt. Forum, Inc., 2013 WL 3323635 (M.D. Fla. June 28, 2013) (conduct considered to be an unfair or deceptive act or practice under § 5 of the FTC Act is an automatic violation of Florida UDAP statute). *But cf.* United States v. DISH Network, L.L.C., 2015 WL 682952 (C.D. Ill. Feb. 17, 2015) (California may not use its unfair competition law, which borrows the TSR, to get around TCFAPA's bar against states bringing TSR claims while there is an action pending on behalf of FTC for same violation). *See generally* National Consumer Law Center, Unfair and Deceptive

Acts and Practices §§ 3.2.6, 3.4.5 (8th ed. 2012), *updated at* www.nclc.org/library.

178 *See, e.g.,* Md. Code Ann., Com. Law §§ 14-3201, 14-3202 (West) (creating special statutory cause of action for $500 or actual damages, whichever is greater, plus attorney fees, for violation of Telemarketing and Consumer Fraud and Abuse Prevention Act, FTC telemarketing rule, or Telephone Consumer Protection Act; violations are also UDAP violations). *See* § 5.9, *infra.*

179 *See, e.g.,* Fed. Trade Comm'n v. Affiliate Strategies, Inc., 849 F. Supp. 2d 1085 (D. Kan. 2011) (discussing several states' UDAP standards); Lawn v. Enhanced Serv. Billing, Inc., 2010 WL 2773377 (E.D. Pa. July 13, 2010) (voluntary payment doctrine did not bar UDAP claim alleging addition of unauthorized charges to phone bill; fact question whether payment was truly voluntary when name of bill aggregator was buried on page five of six-page bill and name of seller did not appear); Fed. Trade Comm'n v. Think Achievement Corp., 144 F. Supp. 2d 993 (N.D. Ind. 2000) (applying FTC Act's general prohibition against deception to telemarketer), *later op. at* 144 F. Supp. 2d 1029 (N.D. Ind. 2000) (ordering disgorgement by non-wrongdoer who had possession of defendant's funds), *aff'd in part, rev'd in part on other grounds,* 312 F.3d 259 (7th Cir. 2002); Mercury Mktg. Techs. of Del., Inc. v. State *ex rel.* Beebe, 189 S.W.3d 414 (Ark. 2004) (affirming preliminary injunction under UDAP statute against telemarketer); State *ex rel.* Petro v. Pristine Secure Services, 2005 WL 3867419 (Ohio Ct. Com. Pl. July 5, 2005) (entering judgment under state UDAP statute against recovery room operator). *But cf.* Spivey v. Adaptive Mktg., L.L.C., 622 F.3d 816 (7th Cir. 2010) (holding that, when customer's credit card statement included the allegedly unauthorized charge, voluntary payment doctrine bars state contract and unjust enrichment claims based on telemarketing fraud).

180 *See* § 2.5.6, *supra.*

181 *See, e.g.,* La. Rev. Stat. Ann. § 45:831; Or. Rev. Stat. § 83.715.

182 *See, e.g.,* Reyes v. Zion First Nat'l Bank, 2012 WL 947139 (E.D. Pa. Mar. 21, 2012) (consumer stated RICO claim against payment processor that caused unauthorized withdrawal for fraudulent telemarketer and bank that held both consumer's and processor's accounts but not other banks involved in transaction; predicate offenses were money-laundering and use of unauthorized access device), *denial of class certification rev'd sub nom.* Reyes v. Netdeposit, ___ F.3d ___, 2015 WL 5131287 (3d Cir. Sept. 2, 2015); McClain v. Coverdell & Co., 272

involve federal wire fraud, making liability possible if the other requirements of the federal RICO statute can be satisfied.[183] A scheme to defraud may consist of failure to make disclosures required by the FTC's Telemarketing Sales Rule.[184]

Some state RICO statutes have less complex proof requirements than federal RICO, and many list federal wire fraud, or state offenses such as fraud, as predicate offenses.[185] Ohio's RICO statute lists operation of an unregistered credit services organization as a predicate offense, and the state supreme court upheld the conviction under this statute of an individual who telemarketed credit cards.[186] Interpreting the state RICO statute as a strict liability statute, the court held that no proof of culpable intent was required. While this decision relates to criminal rather than civil RICO liability, the principles should apply equally to civil cases.

5.6.2 State Remedies

State attorneys general and other state consumer protection authorities are authorized under the Telemarketing and Consumer Fraud and Abuse Prevention Act to file suit in federal court when there is a pattern or practice of violations of the FTC Telemarketing Sales Rule.[187] The statute authorizes them to seek an injunction to stop the telemarketing practice and to recover damages, restitution, or other compensation on behalf of the state's citizens.[188] The state should notify the FTC of the action.[189]

A state may rely on deceptive telemarketing acts and practices that took place outside the state in satisfying the statute's requirement of alleging a pattern or practice of telemarketing which violates the Rule.[190] The statute does not limit the time period within which the state can sue.[191]

5.6.3 Federal Remedies

The FTC and CFPB both have authority to enforce the Rule[192] with the same enforcement authorities that those agencies possess to enforce other rules.[193] For example, the FTC can seek a permanent injunction in federal court against a telemarketing practice,[194] even if the practice has already ceased.[195] The FTC can also seek monetary redress and, in one action, recovered $17 million dollars.[196] The CFPB enforces the Rule as if it were a UDAAP rule.[197]

F. Supp. 2d 631 (E.D. Mich. 2003) (refusing to dismiss federal RICO claims against telemarketer); Faillace v. Columbus Bank & Trust Co., 605 S.E.2d 450 (Ga. Ct. App. 2004) (upholding state RICO judgment against telemarketer in favor of bank that was duped into approving fraudulent charges to customers' credit cards).

183 *See, e.g.,* United States v. Manion, 339 F.3d 1153 (9th Cir. 2003) (affirming individual telemarketer's conviction for mail and wire fraud); United States v. Woods, 335 F.3d 993 (9th Cir. 2003) (affirming telemarketers' mail and wire fraud convictions); United States v. Ciccone, 219 F.3d 1078 (9th Cir. 2000) (affirming telemarketer's wire fraud conviction).

184 United States v. Woods, 335 F.3d 993, 1001 (9th Cir. 2003) (affirming telemarketers' mail and wire fraud convictions).

185 *See* Ch. 8, *infra.*

186 State v. Schlosser, 681 N.E.2d 911 (Ohio 1997).

187 15 U.S.C. § 6103(a), (f)(2).

188 15 U.S.C. § 6103(a). *See, e.g.,* Fed. Trade Comm'n v. Information Mgmt. Forum, Inc., 2013 WL 3323635 (M.D. Fla. June 28, 2013) (best practice to show state standing is to include in the complaint facts showing threat to the interests of state citizens; over 500 consumer complaints are sufficient to assume standing at motion to dismiss phase); Tennessee v. Lexington Law Firms, 1997 U.S. Dist. LEXIS 7403, 1997-1 Trade Cas. (CCH) ¶ 71,820 (M.D. Tenn. May 14, 1997) (seeking a permanent injunction and other equitable relief); New York v. Financial Services Network, 930 F. Supp. 865 (W.D.N.Y. 1996) (granting preliminary injunction in suit brought by New York and North Carolina). *See also* Iowa Code § 714.16 (authorizing Iowa attorney general to bring suit under the federal statute on behalf of Iowa residents).

189 15 U.S.C. § 6103(b); 16 C.F.R. § 310.7.

190 Tennessee v. Lexington Law Firms, 1997 U.S. Dist. LEXIS 7403, 1997-1 Trade Cas. (CCH) ¶ 71,820 (M.D. Tenn. May 14, 1997). *See also* Illinois v. Tri-Star Indus. Lighting, Inc., 2000 U.S. Dist. LEXIS 15376 (N.D. Ill. Oct. 5, 2000) (state can discover information about telemarketer's out-of-state sales because of its authority to protect legitimate in-state sellers from unlawful competition).

191 Illinois v. Tri-Star Indus. Lighting, Inc., 2000 U.S. Dist. LEXIS 14948 (N.D. Ill. Oct. 11, 2000).

192 15 U.S.C. §§ 6102(c), 6105. *See* Fed. Trade Comm'n v. Micom Corp., 1997 U.S. Dist. LEXIS 3404, 1997-1 Trade Cas. (CCH) ¶ 71,753 (S.D.N.Y. Mar. 12, 1997).

193 *See* §§ 2.2.5, 2.2.6, 3.9, *supra.*

194 15 U.S.C. § 53(b). *See, e.g.,* Fed. Trade Comm'n v. Lalonde, 545 Fed. Appx. 825 (11th Cir. 2013) (per curiam) (upholding permanent injunction banning defendant from telemarketing); Fed. Trade Comm'n v. USA Fin., L.L.C., 415 Fed. Appx. 970 (11th Cir. 2011); Fed. Trade Comm'n v. HES Merch. Services Co., 2015 WL 892394 (M.D. Fla. Feb. 11, 2015) (granting permanent injunction against individual, in spite of his age and poor health, because he did not recognize wrongfulness of his conduct and was likely to continue his business activities); Fed. Trade Comm'n v. Resort Solution Trust, Inc., 2013 WL 6668712 (M.D. Fla. Dec. 18, 2013) (ordering permanent injunction after default judgment); Fed. Trade Comm'n v. Loewen, 2013 WL 5816420 (W.D. Wash. Oct. 29, 2013) (granting permanent injunction against engaging in any future telemarketing or payment processing); Fed. Trade Comm'n v. John Beck Amazing Profits, L.L.C., 888 F. Supp. 2d 1006 (C.D. Cal. 2012) (finding that a broad permanent injunction from all telemarketing activity is warranted).

195 Fed. Trade Comm'n v. USA Fin., L.L.C., 415 Fed. Appx. 970 (11th Cir. 2011).

196 *Id. See also* Fed. Trade Comm'n v. Lalonde, 545 Fed. Appx. 825 (11th Cir. 2013) (per curiam) (court can freeze defendant's assets and appoint a receiver for potential disgorgement, and may even freeze assets of non-parties who were "in active concert or participation" with defendant); Fed. Trade Comm'n v. E.M.A. Nationwide, Inc., 2013 WL 4545143 (N.D. Ohio Aug. 27, 2013) ("Generally, the appropriate amount of restitution in consumer redress cases is the full purchase price of the product, less refunds paid."), *aff'd,* 767 F.3d 611 (6th Cir. 2014); Fed. Trade Comm'n v. Ivy Capital, Inc., 2013 WL 1224613 (D. Nev. Mar. 26, 2013) (finding defendants jointly and severally liable for over $130 million; amount was appropriate because FTC Act is "designed to protect consumers from economic injuries," so restitution may equal amount consumers lost rather than amount of defendant's profits), *aff'd in relevant part, vacated in part on other grounds,* ___ Fed. Appx. ___, 2015 WL 5781664 (9th Cir. Oct. 5, 2015).

197 15 U.S.C. § 6102(c). *See* Morgan Drexen, Inc., v. Consumer Fin. Prot. Bureau, 979 F. Supp. 2d 104 (D.D.C. 2013) (CFPB has authority to enforce Telemarketing and Consumer Fraud and Abuse Prevention Act and the TSR through administrative proceeding or civil action in district court, but only regarding consumer financial products and

FTC and CFPB actions for violations of the Telemarketing Sales Rule are generally subject to a three-year statute of limitations. There is no de minimis exception to the telemarketing rule.

5.7　Parties to Sue

5.7.1　The Telemarketer

Virtually all provisions of the Telemarketing Sales Rule apply to telemarketers, and they are thus liable for their rule violations. Both individuals and corporations can meet the definition of "telemarketer" and be liable for violating the FTC Telemarketing Sales Rule.[198] Individual officers or owners of a telemarketing company can also be found liable for their wrongful activities.[199]

It is true that it is often hard to sue and collect from a telemarketer that may have limited assets and be located anywhere in (or even out of) the country. On the other hand, some telemarketers have significant assets, and it may not be difficult to serve them and collect on a judgment. One trick for smaller telemarketers is to transfer assets to family members, but the FTC has had success in forcing these transferees to disgorge these assets.[200] In addition, the following subsections consider other parties that may be liable for the telemarketing violations. Another approach is to try to recover on a bond the seller may be required to purchase, pursuant to a state telemarketing law.

5.7.2　The Seller

Most provisions in the FTC Telemarketing Sales Rule apply not just to telemarketers but also to the seller. If a seller conducts its own telephone solicitations, it must comply with the Rule as to its phone solicitations. The Rule also applies in some contexts when the consumer initiates the call and contacts the seller. Then the seller must comply with all requirements as to disclosures and prohibited misrepresentations and forms of payment. Limits on when payment can be received for credit repair, advance fee loans, and other specific transactions

---

services), *aff'd*, 785 F.3d 684 (D.C. Cir. 2015). *See also* Consumer Fin. Prot. Bureau v. Morgan Drexen, 60 F. Supp. 3d 1082 (C.D. Cal. 2014) (CFPB's authority does not apply to attorneys unless they are offering or providing a consumer financial product or service; here, CFPB sufficiently alleges that defendant's debt resolution work is not part of practice of law).

198　Fed. Trade Comm'n v. Consumer Alliance, Inc., 2003 WL 22287364 (N.D. Ill. Sept. 30, 2003). *See also* Fed. Trade Comm'n v. Tax Club, Inc., 994 F. Supp. 2d 461 (S.D.N.Y. 2014) (complaint sufficiently alleged that corporate defendants functioned as a "common enterprise"; therefore, complaint need not specify which corporate defendants were responsible for which particular acts, as all are jointly and severally liable for acts of the others); Fed. Trade Comm'n v. E.M.A. Nationwide, Inc., 2013 WL 4545143 (N.D. Ohio Aug. 27, 2013) (applying "common enterprise" theory to find both corporate and individual defendants liable), *aff'd*, 767 F.3d 611 (6th Cir. 2014).

199　Fed. Trade Comm'n v. Lalonde, 545 Fed. Appx. 825 (11th Cir. 2013) (per curiam) (finding individual defendant, "acting through the corporate defendants," had violated the TSR); Fed. Trade Comm'n v. USA Fin., L.L.C., 415 Fed. Appx. 970 (11th Cir. 2011); Fed. Trade Comm'n v. Publishing Clearing House, Inc., 104 F.3d 1168 (9th Cir. 1997); Fed. Trade Comm'n v. HES Merchant Services Co., 2014 WL 6863506 (M.D. Fla. Nov. 18, 2014) (finding individual liability based on defendant's authority to cancel accounts and his strong influence in hiring and business practices); Fed. Trade Comm'n v. Loewen, 2013 WL 5816420 (W.D. Wash. Oct. 29, 2013) (finding individual owner had violated the TSR because he had knowledge of telemarketing scheme and authority to control deceptive practices, whether or not he actually exercised that control; his awareness of high chargeback rate is probative); Fed. Trade Comm'n v. Consumer Health Benefits Ass'n, 2012 WL 1890242 (E.D.N.Y. May 23, 2012) (must go beyond corporate titles and describe specific activity; individual liability sufficiently alleged here); Fed. Trade Comm'n v. Vacation Prop. Services, 2012 WL 1854251 (M.D. Fla. May 21, 2012) (fact issue as to individual defendant's knowledge and whether he tried to prevent telemarketers' violations); Fed. Trade Comm'n v. Washington Data Res., 856 F. Supp. 2d 1247 (M.D. Fla. 2012) (individual officers actively involved in deceptive telemarketing of foreclosure rescue services), *aff'd*, 704 F.3d 1323 (11th Cir. 2013); Fed. Trade Comm'n v. Ivy Capital, Inc., 2011 WL 2118626 (D. Nev. May 25, 2011) (individual defendants' participation in, or control of, phone calls to consumers on do-not-call list sufficiently alleged), *judgment on liability affirmed in relevant part, vacated in part on other grounds*, ___ Fed. Appx. ___, 2015 WL 5781664 (9th Cir. Oct. 5, 2015); Fed. Trade Comm'n v. 1st Guarantee Mortg. Co., 2011 WL 1233207 (S.D. Fla. Mar. 30, 2011) (granting summary judgment against owner who controlled company and against manager who personally made false statements to consumers, but finding genuine issue of fact

as to other corporate officer's knowledge of company's misconduct); Texas v. American Blast Fax, Inc., 164 F. Supp. 2d 892 (W.D. Tex. 2001) (officers of a company can also be held personally liable under the Telephone Consumer Protection Act if they actively engaged in the conduct that violated that Act or actively oversaw and directed such conduct). *See, e.g.*, Fed. Trade Comm'n v. Information Mgmt. Forum, Inc., 2013 WL 3323635 (M.D. Fla. June 28, 2013) (finding owner of corporation individually liable under the TSR and Florida's UDAP statute); Fed. Trade Comm'n v. Affiliate Strategies, Inc., 849 F. Supp. 2d 1085 (D. Kan. 2011) (finding president of telemarketing company personally liable under Kansas and Minnesota UDAP statutes). *See also* Fed. Trade Comm'n v. Consumer Health Benefits Ass'n, 2012 WL 1890242 (E.D.N.Y. May 23, 2012) (denying individual defendants' motions to dismiss; substantial assistance sufficiently alleged when FTC went beyond corporate titles and described specific activities causally connected with the violations). *See generally* National Consumer Law Center, Unfair and Deceptive Acts and Practices § 10.3.2 (8th ed. 2012), *updated at* www.nclc.org/library.

200　Fed. Trade Comm'n v. Tax Club, Inc., 994 F. Supp. 2d 461 (S.D.N.Y. 2014) (spouse who received over $6 million in transfers from consumer payment deposits could be named as a relief defendant for disgorgement purposes); Fed. Trade Comm'n v. Ivy Capital, Inc., 2013 WL 1224613 (D. Nev. Mar. 26, 2013) (finding that wife of defendant must disgorge $1.1 million in "ill-gotten gains" traceable to telemarketing scam), *reconsideration denied*, 2013 WL 3270534 (D. Nev. June 26, 2013) (refusing to reconsider liability and disgorgement findings), *aff'd in relevant part, vacated in part on other grounds*, ___ Fed. Appx. ___, 2015 WL 5781664 (9th Cir. Oct. 5, 2015) (holding that district court did not err in finding defendant's wife liable for disgorgement, but vacating disgorgement order under a double recovery theory); Fed. Trade Comm'n v. Think Achievement Corp., 144 F. Supp. 2d 993 (N.D. Ind. 2000) (telemarketer transferred large sums to wife a few days before FTC named him as defendant), *aff'd in part, rev'd in part on other grounds*, 312 F.3d 259 (7th Cir. 2002). *But cf.* McGregor v. Chierico, 206 F.3d 1378 (11th Cir. 2000) (reversing contempt order requiring fraudulent telemarketer's wife to forfeit joint assets when she was not guilty of contempt).

apply as much to the seller as to a telemarketer it hires. The Rule also has limits on collecting certain payments, and this can apply as much to a seller who collects payment as to its telemarketer who causes the billing information to be submitted for payment.

Even if a seller does not directly violate a Rule provision, it is a Rule violation for a seller to provide substantial assistance or support to any telemarketer when the seller knows or consciously avoids knowing that the telemarketer is violating the Rule.[201] That provision applies to "any person" who supports a seller or telemarketer, so it applies to a seller supporting a telemarketer.

5.7.3 Those Facilitating Credit Card Laundering

Legitimate merchants who want to be able to accept credit card payments from customers establish a merchant account with a financial institution that is a member of a credit card system such as VISA or Mastercard.[202] This financial institution is called the "merchant bank." When a customer pays the merchant by credit card, the merchant gives the charge slips to the merchant bank. The merchant bank then pays the amount of the charge, minus a fee, into the merchant's account and submits the charge slip through the credit card processing system to the customer's bank (the "issuing bank") for reimbursement. If, however, the customer returns the purchased item or disputes the charge, then the issuing bank re-credits the customer's account and gets a refund from the merchant bank, which then asks the merchant for a refund.

Because of the high rate of chargebacks and the fear that the telemarketer will not be around to pay refunds, banks do not like to let telemarketers open merchant accounts. Some banks prohibit telemarketers from directly depositing credit card transactions. These restrictions have led to the growth of credit card factoring services for telemarketers.

In credit card factoring, the telemarketer works out an agreement with a third party (the factoring merchant) to purchase or otherwise facilitate the telemarketer's credit card charges that have not yet been processed. The factoring merchant submits the transactions through its merchant account, often comingled with other transactions. The factoring merchant purchases the charges at a discount or charges a fee for this service. The

merchant bank may not be aware that charges for telemarketing transactions are being deposited in the account, although other signs such as a large number of chargebacks may become apparent to it.

The Telemarketing Sales Rule prohibits credit card factoring—called credit card laundering in the TSR—except as expressly permitted by the credit card system.[203] It is a violation for a telemarketer to obtain access to the credit card system through a business relationship or an affiliation with a merchant, unless such access is authorized under the terms of the merchant account and by the credit card system.[204] Both the factoring merchant[205] and the telemarketer[206] violate the Rule if the factoring merchant submits the telemarketer's charges for payment through its merchant account without authorization. The Rule prohibits anyone from soliciting or causing a merchant to violate this provision.[207] Misrepresenting the nature of the account to the merchant bank may also constitute bank fraud[208] and violate state criminal laws.[209]

5.7.4 Other Third Parties

Sellers using fraudulent telemarketers are often fly-by-night outfits that cannot be located or lack assets from which reimbursement to injured consumers can be exacted. Other times they may even be located out of the country. The ability to find third parties liable for Rule violations is often key if any amount is to be recovered.

The FTC's Telemarketing Sales Rule declares it a deceptive act for a person to provide substantial assistance to a telemarketer while knowing, or consciously avoiding knowledge, that the telemarketer is violating the Rule.[210] The FTC recognizes the following as examples of substantial assistance:

---

201   16 C.F.R. § 310.3(b). *See* Fed. Trade Comm'n v. Stefanchik, 559 F.3d 924, 930 (9th Cir. 2009); Fed. Trade Comm'n v. HES Merchant Services Co., 2014 WL 6863506, 7 (M.D. Fla. Nov. 18, 2014) (providing merchant accounts to TSR violators qualified as substantial assistance, as they were "essential to the success of the scheme"); United States v. DISH Network, L.L.C., 2011 WL 98951 (C.D. Ill. Jan. 10, 2011) (key issue is whether seller caused telemarketing violations by dealers), *later op. at* 754 F. Supp. 2d 1004 (C.D. Ill. 2011) (United States stated a claim; giving weight to seller's failure to effectively monitor telemarketing by its dealers).

202   This summary is based on United States v. Dabbs, 134 F.3d 1071 (11th Cir. 1998); Padilla v. State, 753 So. 2d 659 (Fla. Dist. Ct. App. 2000); and Fed. Trade Comm'n, Complying with the Telemarketing Sales Rule 22 (Apr. 1996).

203   16 C.F.R. § 310.3(c).

204   16 C.F.R. § 310.3(c)(3).

205   16 C.F.R. § 310.3(c)(1). *See, e.g.,* Padilla v. State, 753 So. 2d 659 (Fla. Dist. Ct. App. 2000) (both seller and factoring merchant would violate law if seller knows that merchant account is a subterfuge; not shown here); Stipulated Order for Permanent Injunction and Final Judgment, Fed. Trade Comm'n v. Woofter Inc. Corp., No. CV-97-0515 (D. Nev. 1999) (defendants allegedly assisted Canadian-based telemarketer in selling foreign lottery tickets and laundering credit cards); Complaint, Fed. Trade Comm'n v. Win USA Services, Ltd., 5 Trade Reg. Rep. (CCH) ¶ 24,530 (W.D. Wash. 1998) (international lottery scheme that targeted older consumers).

206   16 C.F.R. § 310.3(c)(2).

207   *Id.* § 310.3(c)(2).

208   United States v. Dabbs, 134 F.3d 1071 (11th Cir. 1998).

209   *See* Padilla v. State, 753 So. 2d 659 (Fla. Dist. Ct. App. 2000) (both seller and factoring merchant would violate law if seller knows that merchant account is a subterfuge; not shown here).

210   16 C.F.R. § 310.3(b). *See, e.g.,* Fed. Trade Comm'n v. Chapman, 714 F.3d 1211 (10th Cir. 2013) (author of grant-writing materials was in violation of the Telemarketing Sales Rule because she provided substantial assistance to the telemarketers and sellers of her materials and knew or consciously avoided knowing that her materials were being misrepresented to consumers); United States v. DISH Network, L.L.C., 75 F. Supp. 3d 942 (C.D. Ill. 2014) (question of fact whether defendant knew or consciously avoided knowing about co-defendant's TSR violations), *vacated in part,* 80 F. Supp. 3d 917 (C.D. Ill. 2015); Fed. Trade

- Providing lists of contacts to a seller or telemarketer that identify people who are over age fifty-five, have bad credit histories, or have been victimized previously by deceptive telemarketing or direct sales;[211]
- Processing payments, fulfilling orders, handling complaints, negotiating agreements with merchants, and providing other assistance to telemarketers;[212]
- Providing certificates for travel-related services to be used as a sales promotion device;
- Providing scripts, advertising, or other promotional material;[213] or
- Providing inflated appraisals or phony testimonials for goods or services sold through telemarketing.[214]

The FTC gives cleaning a telemarketer's office or delivering lunches to the telemarketer's premises as examples of activities that would not constitute substantial assistance.[215]

A lender that approves telemarketers' scripts allows them to use its name and benefits financially from the transactions can be held liable.[216] Companies that supply software for creditors to process and submit "demand drafts" may be liable under this provision if they do not take steps to ensure that the telemarketer complies with the requirements of the Rule for documenting the consumer's authorization.[217]

The FTC has proceeded against companies that assisted Canadian telemarketers in laundering credit card transactions,[218] performed customer service and shipped goods for a telemarketer,[219] and submitted telemarketers' charges to telephone companies to appear on consumers' telephone bills.[220] A court held that the principal of a group of companies that assisted Canadian telemarketers consciously avoided knowledge of their deceptive practices when he was substantially involved in managing and implementing the sales scheme and knew that buyers were returning the purchased items at an extraordinarily high rate.[221]

5.7.5　Third-Party Liability Outside the Rule

Even without this rule, companies that facilitate telemarketing fraud can be found liable under UDAP, fraud, aiding and abetting, and other legal theories.[222] Before the

---

Comm'n v. HES Merchant Services Co., 2014 WL 6863506 (M.D. Fla. Nov. 18, 2014) (finding individual liability based on owner's awareness of probable fraud and intentional avoidance of the truth); Fed. Trade Comm'n v. Affiliate Strategies, Inc., 714 F.3d 1211 (10th Cir. 2013) (writer of grant guide provided substantial assistance to fraudulent telemarketer of grant-finding services; drafted talking points for telemarketers, dealt with customer complaints, but never followed up to determine whether anyone actually received a grant). *See also* Fed. Trade Comm'n v. Consumer Health Benefits Ass'n, 2011 WL 3652248, at *10 (E.D.N.Y. Aug. 18, 2011) (individual who provides substantial assistance can be held liable for telemarketing rule violation even without meeting definition of "seller" or "telemarketer"); Fed. Trade Comm'n v. Global Mktg. Grp., Inc., 594 F. Supp. 2d 1281 (M.D. Fla. 2008) (United States-based principal, whose companies processed payments for Canadian advance-fee credit card telemarketers, fulfilled orders, handled complaints, negotiated agreements with merchants, and provided other assistance, is liable for telemarketers' fraud).

　　The FTC rejected law enforcement and consumer advocates' recommendations to change the "conscious avoidance" standard to a "knew or should have known" standard. It stated that the conscious avoidance standard was more appropriate "when liability to pay redress or civil penalties rests on another person's violation of the Rule." 68 Fed. Reg. 4580, 4612 (Jan. 29, 2003).

211 *See, e.g.*, Fed. Trade Comm'n v. Consumer Money Markets, Inc., 5 Trade Reg. Rep. (CCH) ¶ 24,796 (D. Nev. Sept. 6, 2000) (consent decree requiring list broker to disgorge $150,000); Fed. Trade Comm'n v. Marketing Response Grp., 5 Trade Reg. Rep. (CCH) ¶ 23,958 (M.D. Fla. 1996) (complaint against company that masterminded real estate telemarketing schemes by providing mailing lists, promotional mailings, and printing and mailing service).

212 Fed. Trade Comm'n v. Global Mktg. Grp., Inc., 594 F. Supp. 2d 1281 (M.D. Fla. 2008) (United States-based principal, whose companies processed payments for Canadian advance-fee credit card telemarketers, fulfilled orders, handled complaints, negotiated agreements with merchants, and provided other assistance, is liable for telemarketers' fraud).

213 Fed. Trade Comm'n, Statement of Basis and Purpose, 60 Fed. Reg. 43852 (Aug. 23, 1995). *See, e.g.*, Fed. Trade Comm'n v. Consumer Alliance, Inc., 2003 WL 22287364 (N.D. Ill. Sept. 30, 2003) (defendants who wrote telemarketers' scripts are liable).

214 Fed. Trade Comm'n, Statement of Basis and Purpose, 60 Fed. Reg. 43,852 (Aug. 23, 1995).

215 Fed. Trade Comm'n, Complying With the Telemarketing Sales Rule 21 (Apr. 1996).

216 Minnesota *ex rel.* Hatch v. Fleet Mortg. Corp., 158 F. Supp. 2d 962 (D. Minn. 2001).

217 Fed. Trade Comm'n, Complying with the Telemarketing Sales Rule at 21 (Apr. 1996). *See* Fed. Trade Comm'n v. Global Mktg. Grp., Inc., 594 F. Supp. 2d 1281 (M.D. Fla. 2008) (individual whose companies processed payments for deceptive telemarketers knew or consciously avoided knowing of telemarketers' misconduct); Fed. Trade Comm'n v. Cordeiro, 5 Trade Reg. Rep. (CCH) ¶ 24,870 (N.D. Cal. Feb. 5, 2001) (consent order against defendant who provided account debiting services to process demand drafts through U.S. banks for Canadian telemarketers; high rejection and return rates should have signaled that there were fundamental problems with telemarketer's business). *See also* Fed. Trade Comm'n v. First Am. Payment Processing, Inc., 5 Trade Reg. Rep. (CCH) ¶ 15550, No. CV 04-0074 PHX SRB (D. Ariz. Jan. 13, 2004) (complaint alleging that payment processors knowingly processed electronic payments for advance fee credit card telemarketers; complaint also alleges processor committed unfair practice by systematically breaching contractual promise to financial institutions to adhere to National Automated Clearing House Association rules against processing ACH transactions on behalf of outbound telemarketers making cold calls); Fed. Trade Comm'n v. Electronic Fin. Grp., Inc. (W.D. Tex. July 7, 2003), *available at* www.ftc.gov (complaint and TRO against company that processed electronic payments on behalf of telemarketers in violation of NACHA rules).

218 Consent Decree, Fed. Trade Comm'n v. Woofter Inv. Corp., 5 Trade Reg. Rep. (CCH) ¶ 24,437 (D. Nev. 1998).

219 Fed. Trade Comm'n v. Global Mktg. Grp., Inc., 594 F. Supp. 2d 1281 (M.D. Fla. 2008) (principal of companies that, *inter alia*, processed orders for Canadian telemarketers is liable).

220 Consent Decree, Fed. Trade Comm'n v. Hold Billing Services, 5 Trade Reg. Rep. (CCH) ¶ 24,659 (W.D. Tex. Oct. 6, 1999). *See also* United States v. Saferstein, 2008 WL 4925016 (E.D. Pa. Nov. 18, 2008) (criminal prosecution; describing how telephone billing aggregators cram charges onto bills); Fed. Trade Comm'n v. New Century Equity Holdings Corp., Inc., 5 Trade Reg. Rep. (CCH) ¶ 15139 (D.D.C. Aug. 1, 2001).

221 Fed. Trade Comm'n v. Global Mktg. Grp., Inc., 594 F. Supp. 2d 1281 (M.D. Fla. 2008).

222 Fed. Trade Comm'n v. Stefanchik, 559 F.3d 924 (9th Cir. 2009) (applying general FTC Act liability rules to hold central figure in scheme

Telemarketing Sales Rule was adopted, the FTC obtained an FTC consent order requiring a company to pay $9 million in consumer redress when it supplied the products that were sold, trained the telemarketers, and extended credit to the victims to buy the products.[223]

A credit card issuer may also be liable for telemarketing fraud if it continues to process a telemarketer's card charges even after it knew or should have known of the fraud.[224] In *Citicorp Credit Services, Inc.*,[225] the FTC claimed that Citicorp should have known of a fraud based on the large number of consumer complaints and a 25% chargeback rate that was about twenty times the industry average. ("Chargeback" is the rate at which the charge is removed from the consumer's account and charged back to the merchant.) While this was not a telemarketing case, it illustrates the types of evidence and arguments that may be effective. Any intermediary that processes or receives charges generated by a telemarketer should be liable under this standard if there is a high rate of chargebacks or other rejections.[226] In another case, a consumer stated a RICO claim against a payment processor[227] that caused unauthorized withdrawals for a fraudulent telemarketer and against the bank that held the processor's accounts.[228] Both the

bank and the payment processors were aware of the "staggering" percentage of these debits that could not be processed for reasons such as consumer complaints or insufficient funds.[229] The predicate offenses were money-laundering and use of an unauthorized access device.[230] The Third Circuit reversed the denial of class certification in this case.[231]

The FDIC has issued guidance warning banks about risks involved in establishing relationships with credit card processors that receive payments from telemarketers.[232] Banks that initiate transactions for payment processors should implement systems to monitor high rates of chargebacks and should regularly survey sources of consumer complaints that may be lodged with any party concerning the merchants.[233] Banks must implement procedures to avoid large numbers of returns and should outline thresholds for returns and actions to be taken if a merchant exceeds that threshold.[234]

There may also be an independent service organization (ISO)[235] involved in a telemarketing fraud. ISOs are entities that assist merchants in establishing relationships with bank card issuers. The FTC has obtained a consent order against an ISO for doing business with telemarketers when it should have known the telemarketers were deceiving consumers.[236]

5.8 Records That Telemarketers and Sellers Must Keep

The FTC Telemarketing Sales Rule requires both sellers and telemarketers to keep a number of different types of records relating to telemarketing activities for twenty-four months from when the record is produced. The telemarketer and seller can mutually agree on who retains which records so that neither has to keep all records.[237] The records often will prove useful in any private or public investigation of a telemarketing scheme.

Included among the records that must be kept are:

- All substantially different advertising, brochures, telemarketing scripts, and promotional materials;
- The name and last known address of each customer, the goods or services purchased, the date such goods or services

---

liable for acts of others who implemented it); Fed. Trade Comm'n v. Health Formulas, L.L.C., 2015 WL 2130504 (D. Nev. May 6, 2015) (granting a preliminary injunction against corporate telemarketing defendants and individuals); Fed. Trade Comm'n v. Global Mktg. Grp., Inc., 594 F. Supp. 2d 1281, 1288–1289 (M.D. Fla. 2008) (holding payment processor liable under general FTC Act unfairness standards).

223 Fed. Trade Comm'n v. Unimet Credit Corp., 5 Trade Reg. Rep. (CCH) ¶ 23,730 (C.D. Cal. Dec. 19, 1994).

224 *See, e.g.*, Reyes v. Zion First Nat'l Bank, 2012 WL 947139 (E.D. Pa. Mar. 21, 2012) (consumer stated RICO claim against payment processor that caused unauthorized withdrawal for fraudulent telemarketer and against bank that held both consumer's and processor's accounts, but not other banks involved in the transaction; predicate offenses were money-laundering and use of unauthorized access device), *denial of class certification rev'd sub nom.* Reyes v. Netdeposit, ___ F.3d ___, 2015 WL 5131287 (3d Cir. Sept. 2, 2015); Consent Decree, Fed. Trade Comm'n v. Electronic Clearinghouse, Inc., 5 Trade Reg. Rep. (CCH) ¶ 23,517 (D. Nev. Dec. 21, 1993); Consent Decree, Citicorp Credit Services, Inc., 5 Trade Reg. Rep. (CCH) ¶ 23,280 (F.T.C. Dkt. C-3413 1993). *See generally* National Consumer Law Center, Consumer Banking and Payments Law § 3.13.3 (5th ed. 2013), *updated at* www .nclc.org/library (federal enforcement actions against banks that facilitated telemarketing fraud).

225 Consent Order, 5 Trade Reg. Rep. (CCH) ¶ 23,280 (F.T.C. Dkt. C-3413 1993).

226 *See* Fed. Trade Comm'n v. Cordeiro, 5 Trade Reg. Rep. (CCH) ¶ 24,870 (N.D. Cal. Feb. 5, 2001). *See also* United States v. Payment Processing Ctr., L.L.C., 2006 WL 2990392 (E.D. Pa. Oct. 18, 2006) (refusing to dismiss suit against company that allegedly processed payments for fraudulent telemarketers). *Cf.* Fed. Trade Comm'n v. First Capital Consumer Membership Services, Inc., 206 F.R.D. 358 (W.D.N.Y. 2001) (denying credit card intermediary's motion to intervene in FTC suit against telemarketer).

227 *See* National Consumer Law Center, Consumer Banking and Payments Law § 5.3.1.3 (5th ed. 2013), *updated at* www.nclc.org/library for a discussion of payment processors.

228 Reyes v. Zion First Nat'l Bank, 2012 WL 947139 (E.D. Pa. Mar. 21, 2012), *denial of class certification rev'd sub nom.* Reyes v. Netdeposit, ___ F.3d ___, 2015 WL 5131287 (3d Cir. Sept. 2, 2015).

229 Reyes v. Netdeposit, ___ F.3d ___, 2015 WL 5131287, at *3 (3d Cir. Sept. 2, 2015).

230 *Id.*

231 Reyes v. Netdeposit, ___ F.3d ___, 2015 WL 5131287 (3d Cir. Sept. 2, 2015).

232 Payment Processor Relationships Revised Guidance, FIL-3-2012 (Jan. 1, 2012), *available online as companion material to this treatise.*

233 *Id.*

234 *Id.*

235 *See, e.g.*, Consent Decree, Fed. Trade Comm'n v. Electronic Clearinghouse, Inc., 5 Trade Reg. Rep. (CCH) ¶ 23,517 (D. Nev. Dec. 21, 1993) (example of an ISO dealing with telemarketers). *Cf.* Fed. Trade Comm'n v. Certified Merchant Services, Ltd., 5 Trade Reg. Rep. (CCH) ¶ 15,538, No. 4:02cv44 (E.D. Tex. Dec. 30, 2003) ($23.55 million settlement with ISO that falsely marketed its credit and debit-card merchant account services to small businesses).

236 *See* Consent Decree, Fed. Trade Comm'n v. Electronic Clearinghouse, Inc., 5 Trade Reg. Rep. (CCH) ¶ 23,517 (D. Nev. Dec. 21, 1993).

237 16 C.F.R. § 310.5(c).

were shipped or provided, and the amount paid for the goods or services;

- The name, fictitious name used, the last known home address and telephone number and the job title for all current and former employees directly involved in telephone sales; and

- All records of express informed consent or agreement required under the Rule.[238]

5.9 State Telemarketing Fraud Statutes

5.9.1 General

State telemarketing statutes are of special importance because they usually offer a private cause of action. These statutes are summarized in Appendix D, *infra*. The statutes typically require registration and bonding, disclosures, and submission of sales scripts and information about prizes to the state enforcement agency.

Also relevant may be state identity theft statutes. For example, in Arkansas, "[a] person commits financial identity fraud if, with the intent to unlawfully appropriate financial resources of another person to his or her own use . . . , and without the authorization of that person, he or she (A) [o]btains or records identifying information that would assist in accessing the financial resources of the other person; or (B) [a]ccesses or attempts to access the financial resources of the other person through the use of the identifying information." The Arkansas statute defines "identifying information" to include Social Security numbers, bank account numbers, credit and debit card numbers, digital signatures, and other identifiers.[239]

5.9.2 Right to Cancel

Many state telemarketing statutes give consumers the right to cancel the sale within a set time period.[240] Some states, like Alabama, accomplish the same purpose by requiring covered telephone sales to be confirmed by a signed written contract and prohibiting charges to the consumer's credit card until the signed contract is returned to the seller.[241] A few states, such as Virginia, have simply expanded upon a door-to-door sales law, which includes a right to cancel, to cover telephone

sales.[242] Even without special amendments, some state home solicitation sales laws may be phrased broadly enough to cover telemarketing.[243]

Idaho provides that minors can disaffirm telephone sales without liability and that parents are not liable for minors' purchases.[244] A number of states restrict or prohibit courier pickups of the consumer's payment.[245] Under Vermont's statute, any "telecheck" drawing on the consumer's bank account based on the consumer's oral approval must be accompanied by the consumer's authorization in writing.[246]

5.9.3 Scope of State Telemarketing Statutes

Coverage under state telemarketing statutes varies. Some, such as one of Indiana's two telemarketing statutes, target only a few types of telemarketing sales, such as prize promotions and sales of precious metals, gemstones, and oil and gas rights.[247] Many states that originally had narrow telemarketing statutes have broadened them in recent years or have adopted a second, broader statute.

More expansive statutes define telemarketing broadly and then list exceptions. Statutes that follow this pattern typically exclude sales that involve some face-to-face contact, sales to prior customers, sales by established businesses, catalog sales, and sales of specified items such as newspapers, magazines, cable TV service, and insurance.

Some state telemarketing statutes place responsibility not just on the telemarketers themselves but also on sellers who hire them.[248] Vermont's telemarketing statute also imposes

---

238 16 C.F.R. § 310.5(a).

239 Ark. Code Ann. § 5-37-227. *See generally* National Consumer Law Center, Fair Credit Reporting Ch. 9 (8th ed. 2013), *updated at* www .nclc.org/library.

240 *See, e.g.*, Ala. Code § 8-19A-14; Okla. Stat. tit. 15, § 775A.4; Utah Code Ann. § 13-26-5 (West); Wash. Rev. Code § 19.158.120.

241 Ala. Code § 8-19A-14. *See, e.g.*, Costley v. Service Prot. Advisors, L.L.C., 2013 WL 952237 (D. Md. Mar. 8, 2013) (fact question whether telemarketer hired by vehicle service contract provider was provider's agent, making provider liable for telemarketer's failure to obtain consumer's signature on contact and to disclose that payment was not required unless consumer signed); Fed. Trade Comm'n v. Affiliate Strategies, Inc., 849 F. Supp. 2d 1085 (D. Kan. 2011) (sale invalid if Kansas telemarketing statute's disclosure and confirmation requirements not strictly complied with; finding telemarketer liable for failing to send consumer information required by Kansas statute after reaching verbal agreement).

242 Va. Code Ann. § 59.1-21.2.

243 *See, e.g.*, Del. Code Ann. tit. 6, §§ 4401 to 4405 (door-to-door sales broadly defined in section 4403); Ind. Code § 24-4.5-2-501; Mich. Comp. Laws § 445.111; Minn. Stat. §§ 325G.06 to 325G.11 (home solicitation sale defined at § 325G.06); Mont. Code Ann. § 30-14-502 (includes telephone sales with few exceptions); Or. Rev. Stat. § 83.710 (extends state home solicitation sales law to seller-initiated telephone sales when there is no personal contact with buyer); 73 Pa. Stat. Ann., § 201-7(a) (West); Tenn. Code Ann. §§ 47-18-701 to 47-18-708 (home solicitation-credit sales); Wis. Stat. Ann. §§ 423.201 to 423.205 (consumer approval transactions, defined at section 423.201); Wyo. Stat. Ann. §§ 40-14-251 to 40-14-255 (home solicitation—credit sales only).

     Four other jurisdictions require that a door-to-door sale involve a solicitation at a residence, but their broad definitions may still cover telemarketing calls made to the home: D.C. Code § 28-3811; Mo. Rev. Stat. §§ 407.700 to 407.720 (home solicitation credit sales); N.C. Gen. Stat. §§ 25A-38 to 25A-42; and S.C. Code Ann. §§ 37-2-501 to 37-2-506.

244 Idaho Code Ann. § 48-1008.

245 Kan. Stat. Ann. § 50-670(e) (courier pick-up); Ky. Rev. Stat. Ann. § 367.46955(5), (6) (West) (courier pick-up; verifiable authorization); Me. Rev. Stat. Ann. tit. 32, § 14716 (transient seller may not use courier pick-up); Mich. Comp. Laws §§ 445.111c(d) (verifiable authorization), 445.112(1) (courier pick-up); Mo. Rev. Stat. § 407.1076 (8), (9) (verifiable authorization; courier pick-up); Vt. Stat. Ann. tit. 9, § 2464.

246 Vt. Stat. Ann. tit. 9, § 2464.

247 Ind. Code § 24-5-12-8. *See also* Cal. Bus. & Prof. Code § 17511.1 (West). Indiana's second telemarketing statute defines "telephone sales call" and "telephone solicitor" broadly and then lists exceptions. *See* Ind. Code §§ 24-4.7-1-1 to 24-4.7-5-6.

248 *See, e.g.*, Commonwealth v. Peoples Benefit Services, Inc., 895 A.2d 683, 691–692 (Pa. Commw. Ct. 2006).

liability upon a courier service or the telemarketer's financial institution that assists the telemarketer to violate the state telemarketing statute.

5.9.4 Federal Preemption and Constitutionality

The FTC Telemarketing Sales Rule does not preempt more restrictive state laws.[249] Only state laws that conflict with the Rule would be preempted.

State regulation of telephone solicitations does not violate the First Amendment[250] or equal protection and due process requirements.[251] States may regulate telemarketers who enter into transactions with consumers in the state through inbound calls, even if the telemarketer has no physical presence in the state.[252]

5.10 Tips to Prevent, Limit Fraud

5.10.1 Withholding Payment on Credit Card Bill for Fraudulent Telemarketing Sale

If the consumer used a credit card, federal law allows the consumer to refuse to pay for goods not delivered or delivered not as represented.[253] The credit card issuer is subject to all (except tort) claims and defenses arising out of the sale, up to the amount of credit still owing for the sale. The only preconditions to this right are that the consumer first make a good faith effort to resolve the matter with the telemarketer, the amount at stake must exceed $50, and the transaction must have occurred in the same state (or within 100 miles) of the cardholder's current address. Consumers should take the position that the telephone transaction occurred in the consumer's home state, since that is where the telemarketer initiated the sale. However, the consumer should not pay the disputed charge before invoking this right, as payment waives the right to assert the claims about the telemarketer's deceptive or fraudulent conduct against the card issuer.[254]

When the requirements for withholding payment have not been met, the consumer has the option of notifying the card issuer under the Fair Credit Billing Act (FCBA) of a billing error.[255] The Federal Reserve Board (FRB) has stated that the failure to provide purchased goods or services is a billing error.[256] The credit card issuer must then initiate an investigation and reverse the charge if warranted.

5.10.2 Reporting Telemarketing Fraud

A simple step that consumers can take if they suspect telemarketing fraud is to send an online report to the National Fraud Information Center.[257] This service was established by a coalition of groups, operated by the National Consumers League, that fights telephone fraud and supports victims of it.

The FTC maintains a database called Consumer Sentinel. The database is housed on a restricted-access secure website and provides national, international, federal, and local law enforcement agencies immediate access to Internet "cons," telemarketing scams, and other consumer fraud-related complaints. The database contains fraud complaints made to the FTC, the National Fraud Information Center, and other federal, state, and local law enforcement agencies and private organizations. The public website, www.ftc.gov/sentinel, contains consumer tips and information about fraud trends.[258]

Reporting telemarketing fraud to law enforcement authorities may be particularly useful for consumers who, having paid by check or cash, cannot withhold payment of a credit card bill. Reporting telemarketing fraud is also important so

---

249 Bluehippo Funding, L.L.C. v. McGraw, 609 F. Supp. 2d 576, 605 (S.D. W. Va. 2009); Nat'l Coal. of Prayer, Inc. v. Carter, 2005 WL 2253601, at *15–16 (S.D. Ind. Sept. 2, 2005), *aff'd on other grounds*, 455 F.3d 783 (7th Cir. 2006).

250 Nat'l Coal. of Prayer, Inc. v. Carter, 455 F.3d 783 (7th Cir. 2006) (upholding application of state do-not-call list to professional charitable solicitors); Fraternal Order of Police v. Stenehjem, 431 F.3d 591 (8th Cir. 2005) (upholding application of state do-not-call list to outside solicitors for charitable organizations; lower court's decision at 287 F. Supp. 2d 1023 (D.N.D. 2003), upholding these restrictions as to commercial telemarketers, was not appealed); Nat'l Fed. of the Blind v. Pryor, 258 F.3d 851 (8th Cir. 2001) (requirement that solicitor discontinue call upon request does not violate First Amendment even as applied to charitable solicitations); Spafford v. Echostar Communications Corp., 448 F. Supp. 2d 1220 (W.D. Wash. 2006) (Washington's ban on use of autodialing and announcing devices to deliver prerecorded commercial message does not violate First Amendment); Desnick v. Dep't of Prof'l Regulation, 665 N.E.2d 1346 (Ill. 1996). *See also* Fed. Trade Comm'n, Telemarketing Sales Rule, Final Rule, Statement of Basis and Purpose, 68 Fed. Reg. 4580, 4634–4637 (Jan. 29, 2003) (discussing First Amendment considerations in do-not-call lists for commercial and non-profit telemarketers); Minnesota *ex rel.* Humphrey v. Casino Mktg. Grp. Inc., 491 N.W.2d 882 (Minn. 1992) (lower court's temporary injunction under state automatic dialing-announcing devices statutes does not violate First Amendment or Minnesota Constitution); Erwin v. State, 908 P.2d 1367 (Nev. 1995) (generally upholding statute against First Amendment challenge but remanding case to determine if registration fees and bonding requirement are more onerous than necessary to cover administrative and enforcement costs of statute and to meet the statute's purposes).

251 Nat'l Fed'n of the Blind v. Pryor, 258 F.3d 851 (8th Cir. 2001) (equal protection); Erwin v. State, 908 P.2d 1367 (Nev. 1995).

252 Hovila v. Tween Brands, Inc., 2010 WL 1433417 (W.D. Wash. Apr. 7, 2010) (Washington's automatic dialing device statute applied to out-of-state telemarketer who called Washington consumer); Bluehippo Funding, L.L.C. v. McGraw, 609 F. Supp. 2d 576 (S.D. W. Va. 2009).

253 *See* 15 U.S.C. § 1666i; Reg. Z, 12 C.F.R. § 1026.12(c) [§ 226.12(c)]. *See also* National Consumer Law Center, Truth in Lending § 7.11 (9th ed. 2015), *updated at* www.nclc.org/library.

254 After payment, however, the claim could still be asserted as a billing error. National Consumer Law Center, Truth in Lending § 7.11 (9th ed. 2015), *updated at* www.nclc.org/library.

255 *See* 15 U.S.C. § 1666. *See also* National Consumer Law Center, Truth in Lending § 7.9 (9th ed. 2015), *updated at* www.nclc.org/library.

256 Reg. Z, 12 C.F.R. § 1026.13(a)(3) [§ 226.(a)(3)]; Official Staff Commentary, 12 C.F.R. pt. 1026 [pt. 226], Supp. I, § 1026.13(a)(3) [§ 226.(a)(3)].

257 The web address for online complaints is www.fraud.org.

258 *See* 5 Trade Reg. Rep. (CCH) ¶ 23,941 (D. Nev. 1995) (describing database).

that law enforcement authorities have information about the location and tactics of fraudulent telemarketers.

5.10.3 *Stopping Future Consumer Victimization*

Telemarketing fraud operators know that some of the best prospects for future sales are past victims, particularly older consumers. These individuals have shown a propensity to be duped by telephone pitches and are likely to be solicited again. For example, schemes offer (for a fee) to facilitate the delivery to the consumer of all those free prizes and gifts that were never delivered.[259] These operators often have all the trappings of a public agency or non-profit organization. One scheme, for example, called itself "Senior Citizens Against Telemarketing" and allegedly claimed a special relationship with the FTC and state attorneys general that helped it retrieve money for victims of telemarketing fraud.[260] To deter these kinds of "recovery room" fraud, some FTC orders prohibit the defendants from selling or transferring their customer lists.[261]

One way to reduce repeat fraud is to advise the consumer to register on the nationwide do-not-call list[262] and to warn the consumer of telemarketing schemes offering to recover past losses resulting from fraud. The consumer should also register on any statewide list, since the state do-not-call statute or rule may have a broader scope or better remedies. Registering on the nationwide do-not-call list will not protect the consumer from callers who solicit charitable contributions or from calls on behalf of companies that have an "established business relationship" with the consumer.[263] To stop these calls, the consumer should make a specific oral or written do-not-call request to each of them. These callers must then place the consumer on a company-specific do-not-call list.[264]

---

259 *See* § 5.5.3, *supra*.

260 Fed. Trade Comm'n v. USM Corp., 5 Trade Reg. Rep. (CCH) ¶ 23,862 (D. Nev. 1995) (complaint filed and TRO granted).

261 *See, e.g.*, Preliminary Injunction and Proposed Consent Order, Fed. Trade Comm'n v. United Wholesalers, Inc., 5 Trade Reg. Rep. (CCH) ¶

23,849 (S.D. Fla. 1995) (preliminary injunction), ¶ 23,965 (1996) (proposed consent order).

In the 2002 proposed amendments to the Telemarketing Sales Rule, the FTC stated that it would not adopt a blanket prohibition against the sale of "victim lists" in the Rule because "combating the practice of targeting vulnerable groups is a challenge best left to the discretion of law enforcement agencies who may seek injunctions and other penalties on a case-by-case basis in individual law enforcement actions." 67 Fed. Reg. 4525, 4526 (Jan. 30, 2002).

The FTC reiterated this position when it adopted the final amendment to the Rule. 68 Fed. Reg. 4580, 4653 (Jan. 29, 2003).

262 *See* § 6.5.2, *infra*.

263 *See* §§ 6.5.2.2, 6.5.2.3, *infra*.

264 *See* § 6.5.1, *infra*.

Chapter 6   Unwanted Calls and Texts, Junk Faxes, and Spam

6.1   Scope of This Chapter

This chapter examines federal and, to a lesser extent, state regulation of unwanted telephone and text message solicitations, junk faxes, and spam e-mail. It focuses on the two federal statutes that regulate telephone calls, text messages, and faxes—the Telemarketing and Consumer Fraud and Abuse Prevention Act (TCFAPA), under which the FTC adopted the Telemarketing Sales Rule, and the Telephone Consumer Protection Act (TCPA), which the Federal Communications Commission (FCC) administers. Both offer private causes of action to consumers.

The chapter starts with a summary of the substantive topics addressed by the FTC's Telemarketing Sales Rule and the TCPA and reviews their scope and validity.[1] It then examines the main applications of these laws:

- Section 6.3, *infra*, analyzes restrictions on autodialed and prerecorded calls to cell phones and other sensitive numbers;
- Section 6.4, *infra*, details restrictions on prerecorded calls (primarily telemarketing calls) to residential lines;
- Section 6.5, *infra*, addresses the FTC's and FCC's company-specific and nationwide do-not-call rules;
- Section 6.6, *infra*, summarizes other restrictions on unwanted calls: threats and harassment, disclosure requirements regarding the purpose of the call, restrictions on abandoned calls, calling-time requirements, caller ID blocking, and state statutes;
- Section 6.7, *infra*, analyzes the application to text messages of the restrictions on autodialed calls; and
- Section 6.8, *infra*, reviews limitations on junk faxes.
- Section 6.9, *infra*, then addresses general litigation issues under the TCPA: the availability of a private cause of action, TCPA remedies, standing, jurisdiction, class actions, who is liable, the statute of limitations, pleadings and discovery, the burden of proof, recovering from the defendant's insurance policy, and government enforcement.

Litigation issues that are specific to a particular prohibition are discussed in the section relating to that prohibition. Litigation to enforce the FTC's Telemarketing Sales Rule is briefly summarized in § 6.2.3, *infra*, but is addressed more fully in Chapter 5, *supra*.

The chapter concludes with a discussion of spam e-mail, which is regulated by a third federal statute, the CAN-SPAM Act. Litigation and remedies under that statute and other theories are considered in § 6.10, *infra*.

Between the TCPA and the TCFAPA, the TCPA has the most relevance to consumer litigation concerning unwanted calls, texts, and faxes. The TCFAPA does not apply to junk faxes, has less applicability to text messages, and provides a direct private right of action only when an individual's damages exceed $50,000. Its scope is also generally narrower than the TCPA.

Nevertheless, the TCFAPA remains of some importance. The FTC Telemarketing Sales Rule implements that statute, and it reaches certain telephone solicitations not covered by the TCPA and prohibits certain practices not covered by the TCPA. Of even more significance, the FTC Telemarketing Sales Rule also regulates the substance of sales transactions involving the telephone, including (but not limited to) sales relating to debt relief services, advance fee loans, credit repair, credit card protection products, offers to recover losses from past telemarketing fraud, investment and business opportunity offers, prize promotions, and charitable donations. The Telemarketing Sales Rule's regulation of the substance of these consumer transactions is treated in Chapter 5, *supra*.[2]

Chapter 5, *supra*, also examines in detail the scope of the FTC Telemarketing Sales Rule, government enforcement of the rule, and private remedies for rule violations—particularly through claims under a state UDAP statute. Remedies and litigation under the rule are only briefly treated in this chapter, as the primary treatment is found in Chapter 5, *supra*.

On the other hand, litigation and remedies under the TCPA are thoroughly treated in this chapter.[3] The TCPA provides a private right of action and significant consumer remedies for violations of its provisions relating to telephone calls, text messages to cell phones, and junk faxes. The TCPA is not examined in Chapter 5, *supra*, so the sole treatment of its remedies and litigation is found in § 6.2.4, *infra*.

6.2   Overview, Scope, and Validity of the FTC and TCPA

6.2.1   *FTC Telemarketing Sales Rule: Substantive Prohibitions, Comparison to TCPA*

The Telemarketing Sales Rule is the primary FTC-created protection against unwanted telephone calls. The FTC adopted this rule pursuant to a mandate in the Telemarketing and Consumer Fraud and Abuse Prevention Act (TCFAPA) to issue regulations prohibiting deceptive and abusive telemarketing acts and practices.[4] The Act sets forth only a few requirements for the substance of the FTC's rule, specifying

---

1   *See* § 6.2, *infra*.

2   One exception is that the rule's regulation of debt relief services is examined at § 10.5, *infra*.

3   *See* § 6.2.4, *infra*.

4   15 U.S.C. §§ 6101–6108, *reproduced at* Appx. C.1.1, *infra*.

that it restrict late-night and early-morning calls, require disclosures, and prohibit coercive calls and calls that abuse the consumer's right to privacy.[5]

The FTC's rule goes well beyond these mandated provisions.[6] It includes numerous prohibitions and preventive measures to deter deceptive and coercive telemarketing. These provisions are not discussed in this chapter but in Chapter 5, *supra*, and § 10.5, *infra*. With respect to unwanted calls, which are discussed in this chapter, it overlaps with the Telephone Consumer Protection Act (TCPA) in its prohibition of calls at inconvenient hours,[7] abandoned calls,[8] and caller ID blocking;[9] its requirement of company-specific do-not-call lists;[10] its nationwide do-not-call rule;[11] and its requirement that callers identify the entity on whose behalf they are calling.[12] It also includes a few provisions regarding threats, intimidation, the use of profane language, and harassment by repeat calls that are not duplicated in the TCPA.[13]

6.2.2   Scope of the FTC Rule: Comparison to the TCPA

In general, the coverage offered by the Telemarketing Sales Rule is narrower than that of the Federal Communications Commission (FCC) rule. The FTC rule requires that there be an interstate call,[14] while the FCC rule applies to interstate and intrastate calls.[15] Due to general limitations on the FTC's jurisdiction, the FTC Telemarketing Sales Rule does not apply to banks, federal credit unions, federal savings and loans, common carriers, and regulated insurers.[16] However, the sales rule applies to subsidiaries of national banks[17] and to non-bank entities that conduct telemarketing on behalf of banks.[18] The same principle applies to other exempt entities such as common carriers: they are exempt if they do their own telemarketing, but the rule covers non-exempt entities they hire.[19]

The Telemarketing Sales Rule covers telemarketing that is conducted to induce a charitable contribution.[20] However, the FTC Act applies only to acts by a company organized to carry on business for profit or for the profit of its members.[21] Accordingly, the Telemarketing Sales Rule does not apply to true nonprofit enterprises, including charities that are doing their own telemarketing, but does apply to sham nonprofits.[22] Most of its provisions also apply to for-profit telemarketers that solicit contributions from charities.[23] One part of the rule—the national do-not-call list—does not apply to telemarketers who solicit charitable donations,[24] but these telemarketers are subject to the requirement of a company-specific do-not-call list.[25] The Fourth Circuit has held that the application of the Telemarketing Sales Rule to telemarketers working for charities is constitutional and within the FTC's statutory authority.[26]

In contrast, many TCPA provisions do not apply to anyone making calls for a tax-exempt nonprofit.[27] Thus, in challenging telemarketers working for charities, the FTC Telemarketing Sales Rule is a more useful standard than the TCPA.

---

5   15 U.S.C. § 6102(a).

6   16 C.F.R. § 310, *as amended by* 68 Fed. Reg. 4580 (Jan. 29, 2003).

7   *See* § 6.6.4, *infra* (discussion of FTC and FCC restrictions on calling times).

8   *See* § 6.6.3, *infra* (discussion of FTC and FCC restrictions on abandoned calls).

9   *See* § 6.6.5, *infra* (discussion of FTC and FCC restrictions on caller ID blocking).

10 *See* § 6.5.1, *infra* (discussion of FTC and FCC company-specific do-not-call requirements).

11 *See* § 6.5.2, *infra* (discussion of FTC and FCC nationwide do-not-call rules).

12 *See* § 6.6.2, *infra*.

13 *See* § 6.6.1, *infra*.

14 16 C.F.R. § 310.2(dd). *Cf.* United States v. DISH Network, L.L.C., 75 F. Supp. 3d 942, 1003–1004 (C.D. Ill. 2014) (FTC do-not-call rule applies to intrastate calls as long as they are part of a telemarketing campaign that includes interstate calls), *vacated in part on other grounds,* 80 F. Supp. 3d 917 (C.D. Ill. 2015).

15 *See* §§ 6.2.1, 6.2.2, *infra*.

16 *See* § 5.2.3.4, *supra*. *But cf.* Fed. Trade Comm'n v. AT&T Mobility, L.L.C., 87 F. Supp. 3d 1087 (N.D. Cal. 2015) (common carriers are only exempted if they are actually engaging in common-carrier activity; FTC may regulate a common carrier's other activities); Navarro v. Sears Life Ins. Co., 2008 WL 3863451 (E.D. Cal. Aug. 18, 2008) (applying rule to telemarketing sale of insurance; McCarran-Ferguson Act does not prevent application of rule).

17 Minn. *ex rel.* Hatch v. Fleet Mortg. Corp., 181 F. Supp. 2d 995 (D. Minn. 2001) (FTC has authority to enforce Telemarketing Sales Rule against subsidiary of a national bank).

18 68 Fed. Reg. 4580, 4586-87 (Jan. 29, 2003).

19 *Id.*

20 16 C.F.R. § 310.2(f) (definition of "charitable contribution"), (dd) (definition of "telemarketing").

21 15 U.S.C. § 44.

22 68 Fed. Reg. 4580, 4585–4586 (Jan. 29, 2003).

23 Uniting and Strengthening America by Providing Appropriate Tools Required to Intercept and Obstruct Terrorism Act of 2001, Pub. L. No. 107-56, 115 Stat. 272 (Oct. 25, 2001) (amending 15 U.S.C. § 6102(a) (2)-(3)). *See* 68 Fed. Reg. 4580, 4585–4586 (Jan. 29, 2003) (discussing ambiguities in scope of these amendments); Broadcast Team, Inc. v. Fed. Trade Comm'n, 429 F. Supp. 2d 1292 (M.D. Fla. 2006) (FTC telemarketing rule covers for-profit entity that made prerecorded solicitations of contributions for charity even though it framed its contract as a lessee of its equipment to the charity).

24 16 C.F.R. § 310.6(a). *See* United States v. Corps. For Character, L.C., ___ F. Supp. 3d ___, 2015 WL 4577051 (D. Utah Mar. 31, 2015) (offering DVDs in exchange for a financial "donation" was a sale, not a solicitation of a contribution, so telemarketer was subject to nationwide do-not-call rule).

25 68 Fed. Reg. 4580, 4629 (Jan. 29, 2003). *See* Nat'l Fed'n of the Blind v. Fed. Trade Comm'n, 420 F.3d 331 (4th Cir. 2005) (application of company-specific do-not-call list to for-profit charitable solicitors is constitutional and within FTC's authority). *Cf.* Nat'l Coal. of Prayer, Inc. v. Carter, 455 F.3d 783 (7th Cir. 2006) (upholding state's application of do-not-call list to professional charitable solicitors); Fraternal Order of Police v. Stenehjem, 431 F.3d 591 (8th Cir. 2005) (state's prohibition of calls by outside charitable solicitors to persons registered on state do-not-call list is constitutional).

26 Nat'l Fed'n of the Blind v. Fed. Trade Comm'n, 420 F.3d 331 (4th Cir. 2005).

27 *See* § 6.2.4.2, *infra*.

6.2.3 Limited Private Enforcement of FTC Rule

Section 5.6.1, *supra*, analyzes private remedies for violations of the FTC Telemarketing Sales Rule. In brief, there is a direct private cause of action to enforce the rule only when the individual's damages exceed $50,000.[28] On the other hand, an FTC rule violation may be considered a state UDAP violation,[29] or the same conduct may violate a state telemarketing statute that has private remedies.[30] In addition, rule violations are enforceable by state attorneys general, the FTC, and other federal agencies.[31]

Litigation concerning the FTC Telemarketing Sales Rule is aided by a provision that a seller or telemarketer must keep records for two years of several items, including all authorizations or records of express informed consent or express agreement relating to provisions of the rule.[32] Several provisions of the rule allow calls only when there is such consent or agreement.

Under the FTC Telemarketing Sales Rule, both sellers and telemarketers must comply with most of the rule's provisions concerning unwanted calls.[33] In addition, it is a violation for any person to offer substantial assistance or support to any seller or telemarketer when that person knows or consciously avoids knowing that the seller or telemarketer is violating the provisions of the rule dealing with unwanted calls.[34]

By contrast, the TCPA provides a private cause of action for most violations, without requiring that the plaintiff allege any particular amount of damages (or any monetary damages at all). TCPA remedies and litigation are discussed in detail in this chapter.[35]

6.2.4 The Telephone Consumer Protection Act

6.2.4.1 Overview of TCPA Requirements

The Telephone Consumer Protection Act (TCPA)[36] and its implementing FCC rules[37] focus on abusive methods of contacting the consumer. The restrictions that are most important to consumers are:

- A prohibition against making autodialed or prerecorded calls to cell phones and other sensitive numbers without the prior express consent of the called party, applicable both to voice calls and text messages;[38]
- A prohibition against certain prerecorded calls (primarily telemarketing calls) to residential lines without prior express written consent;[39]
- A requirement that telemarketers maintain company-specific do-not-call lists, and refrain from calling consumers who ask that that particular caller stop calling;[40]
- A prohibition against telemarketing calls to consumers who place their names on the nationwide do-not-call list;[41]
- Disclosure requirements regarding the purpose of telemarketing calls;[42]
- Restrictions on abandoned calls[43] and calling times;[44]
- A prohibition against caller ID blocking;[45] and
- A prohibition against faxing unsolicited advertisements.[46]

The FCC has adopted a nationwide do-not-call rule pursuant to the statute. The nationwide and company-specific do-not-call rules adopted under the TCPA closely track similar provisions found in the FTC Telemarketing Sales Rule.[47] The TCPA's prohibition of prerecorded calls to residential lines also has a close analog in the FTC rule.[48] However, unlike the FTC rule, the TCPA also regulates junk faxes and robocalls to cell phones and has important application to text messages sent to cell phones.

When it enacted the TCPA, Congress made findings that automated calls and prerecorded messages are a "nuisance," an "invasion of privacy," and "when an emergency or medical assistance telephone line is seized, a risk to public safety."[49] Unwanted calls to cell phones are particularly abusive because the subscriber may have to pay for receiving each call, or the call may count against the number of minutes authorized each month under the subscriber's plan.[50]

---

28 *See* § 5.6.1.1, *supra*.
29 *See* § 5.6.1.2, *supra*.
30 *See* § 5.6.2, *supra*.
31 *See* §§ 5.6.2, 5.6.3, *supra*.
32 *See* 16 C.F.R. § 310.5(a).
33 *See* 16 C.F.R. § 310.4(b)(1).
34 16 C.F.R. § 310.3(b) (for anyone assisting in a violation of § 310.4 of the rule).
35 *See* §§ 6.3.5, 6.3.6 (litigation issues involving robocalls to cell phones), 6.4.5 (remedies for calls to residential lines), 6.5.3 (remedies for violation of do-not-call rule), 6.8.4 (junk fax litigation issues), 6.9 (general TCPA litigation issues), *infra*.
36 47 U.S.C. § 227, *reproduced at* Appx. C.2.1.2, *infra*. *See also* Kaufman v. ACS Sys., Inc., 2 Cal. Rptr. 3d 296 (Cal. Ct. App. 2003) (discussion of legislative history of TCPA). A good online resource on the statute can be found at www.tcpalaw.com.
37 47 C.F.R. § 64.1200. The FCC's report adopting the original version of this rule may be found at 7 F.C.C. Rcd. 8752 (F.C.C. Oct. 16, 1992). The FCC also set out its interpretation of the rule in a consumer information sheet, Telephone Solicitations, Autodialed and Artificial or Prerecorded Voice Message Telephone Calls, and the Use of Fax Machines, 8 F.C.C. Rcd. 480 (F.C.C. Jan. 11, 1993). The report adopting the 2003 amendments may be found at 2003 WL 21517853 (F.C.C. July 3, 2003).
38 *See* §§ 6.3, 6.7, *infra*.
39 *See* § 6.4, *infra*.
40 *See* §§ 6.5.1, 6.5.3, *infra*.
41 *See* §§ 6.5.2-6.5.3, *infra*.
42 *See* § 6.6.2.2, *infra*.
43 *See* § 6.6.3, *infra*.
44 *See* § 6.6.4, *infra*.
45 *See* § 6.6.5, *infra*.
46 *See* § 6.8, *infra*.
47 *See* §§ 6.2.1, 6.2.2, *supra*.
48 *See* § 6.4.1, *infra*.
49 Pub. L. 102–243, § 2, ¶¶ 5–6, 9–10, 13–14, 105 Stat. 2394 (1991). *See also* Statement of Sen. Warner, 137 Cong. Rec. S16206 (1991) (stating, in support of the TCPA: "Indeed the most important thing we have in this country is our freedom and our privacy, and this is clearly an invasion of that").
50 *See* Soppet v. Enhanced Recovery Co., L.L.C., 679 F.3d 637, 638–639 (7th Cir. 2012).

The TCPA is remedial legislation that is entitled to a liberal construction.[51]

6.2.4.2   TCPA Scope; Effect on State Laws

Since telephone lines are part of an aggregate interstate system even when used for intrastate calls, Congress has authority to regulate intrastate calls.[52] Accordingly, the TCPA covers both interstate and intrastate calls.[53] In this regard, the TCPA is broader than the FTC Telemarketing Sales Rule, which applies only to telemarketing campaigns that involve more than one interstate call.[54]

Calls by tax-exempt nonprofit organizations are excluded from the TCPA's definition of "telephone solicitation."[55] The FCC rule goes one step further and provides that a number of provisions also do not apply to calls *on behalf of* tax-exempt nonprofits,[56] with the result that much of the regulation does not apply to these for-profit solicitors.[57] Solicitors for tax-exempt nonprofit organizations must, however, comply with the FCC's company-specific do-not-call list rule, although the nonprofit organizations themselves need not.[58] The FTC Telemarketing Sales Rule more generally applies to companies working for nonprofits,[59] and that rule should be considered when the TCPA does not apply.

Each of the prohibitions in the TCPA has specific limitations. For example, the junk fax prohibition does not apply when the caller has an established business relationship with the called party.[60] Certain telemarketing restrictions apply only to calls to residential lines.[61] However, the prohibition against junk faxes applies to calls to business lines as well.[62]

The TCPA provides that it does not preempt state laws that impose more restrictive intrastate requirements on, or that prohibit, junk faxes, autodialers, artificial voice messages, or telephone solicitations.[63] The Seventh Circuit has given this language its plain meaning and held that it leaves states free to prohibit both intrastate and interstate artificial voice calls.[64]

6.2.4.3   Challenges to the TCPA and FCC Regulation

The TCPA has been repeatedly upheld against First Amendment and vagueness challenges.[65] The costs of receiving

51   Leyse v. Bank of Am., ___ F.3d ___, 2015 WL 5946456, at *8 (3d Cir. Oct. 14, 2015); Hossfeld v. Gov't Employees Ins. Co., 88 Supp. 3d 504, 509 (D. Md. 2015); Jemiola v. XYZ Corp., 802 N.E.2d 745 (Ohio Ct. Com. Pl. 2003). *See also* Hooters of Augusta, Inc. v. American Global Ins. Co., 272 F. Supp. 2d 1365, 1375–1376 (S.D. Ga. 2003) (TCPA is remedial statute), *aff'd on other grounds*, 157 Fed. Appx. 201 (11th Cir.2005); Standard Mut. Ins. Co. v. Lay, 989 N.E.2d 591 (Ill. 2013) ("The manifest purpose of the TCPA is remedial and not penal."); Terra Nova Ins. Co. v. Fray-Witzer, 869 N.E.2d 565, 575 (Mass. 2007) (TCPA is remedial statute). *But see* Sandusky Wellness Center, L.L.C. v. Medco Health Solutions, Inc., 788 F.3d 218, 224 (6th Cir. 2015) (stating that principle of liberal construction is either incomprehensible or superfluous).

52   Texas v. American Blast Fax, Inc., 121 F. Supp. 2d 1085 (W.D. Tex. 2000). *See also* Hilary B. Miller & Robert R. Biggerstaff, *Application of the Telephone Consumer Protection Act to Intrastate Telemarketing Calls and Faxes*, 52 Fed. Comm. L.J. 667, 686 (2000).

53   *See* Texas v. American Blast Fax, Inc., 121 F. Supp. 2d 1085 (W.D. Tex. 2000); Carnett's, Inc. v. Hammond, 610 S.E.2d 529, 530 (Ga. 2005); Hooters of Augusta, Inc. v. Nicholson, 537 S.E.2d 468 (Ga. Ct. App. 2000); Manufacturers Auto Leasing, Inc. v. Autoflex Leasing, Inc., 139 S.W.3d 342 (Tex. App. 2004); Chair King, Inc. v. GTE Mobilnet of Houston, Inc., 135 S.W.3d 365 (Tex. App. 2004) (covers intrastate faxes), *rev'd on other grounds*, 184 S.W.3d 707 (Tex. 2006); Omnibus Int'l v. AT&T, Inc., 111 S.W.3d 818 (Tex. App. 2003), *review granted, vacated and remanded by agreement*, 2004 Tex. LEXIS 11 (Jan. 12, 2004).

54   *See* §§ 6.2.1, 6.2.2, *supra*.

55   47 U.S.C. § 227(a)(4) (excluding calls from tax-exempt nonprofit organizations from definition of "telephone solicitation"); 47 C.F.R. § 64.1200(f)(14) (comparable definition in regulation; term "telephone solicitation" is used in section 64.1200(c), which restricts calling times and establishes the nationwide do-not-call list).

56   *See* 47 C.F.R. § 64.1200(a)(3)(iv) (restriction on recorded calls), (a)(7) (iv) (abandoned calls), (f)(14)(iii) (defining telephone solicitation as to exclude calls by or on behalf of nonprofits, thus excluding these calls from provisions dealing with inconvenient hours and the nationwide do-not-call registry).

57   *See* Charvat v. Telelytics, L.L.C., 2006 WL 2574019 (Ohio Ct. App. Aug. 31, 2006) (unpublished) (not beyond FCC's authority to exempt for-profit companies that solicit for nonprofits from nationwide do-not-call list rule).

58   47 C.F.R. § 64.1200(d)(7) (excluding only nonprofits and not those calling on behalf of nonprofits).

59   *See* §§ 6.2.1, 6.2.2, *supra*.

60   47 U.S.C. § 227(b)(1)(C)(i); 47 C.F.R. § 64.1200(a)(4)(ii)(C). *See also* 47 U.S.C. §§ 227(a)(2) (definition of "established business relationship" for purposes of junk fax prohibition); 47 C.F.R. § 64.1200(f)(5) (definition of "established business relationship" for purposes of junk fax prohibition). *See generally* § 6.4.3, *infra*.

61   47 C.F.R. § 64.1200(a)(3) (prerecorded calls), (c)(1) (hours between which calls cannot be made), (c)(2) (nationwide do-not-call rule), (d) (company -specific do-not-call rule). *See* Adamo v. AT&T, 2001 WL 1382757 (Ohio Ct. App. Nov. 8, 2001) (do-not-call list protections). *See also* §§ 6.4, 6.5.1–6.6.4, *infra*.

62   Grady v. Lenders Interactive Services, 2004 WL 1799178 (Ohio Ct. App. Aug. 12, 2004) (unpublished). *See generally* § 6.8.1, *infra*.

63   47 U.S.C. § 227(f). *See also* §§ 6.5.2.4, 6.5.2.5 (state do-not-call statutes), 6.6.6 (state autodialer statutes), 6.8.5 (state junk fax statutes), *infra*.

64   Patriotic Veterans, Inc. v. State of Ind., 736 F.3d 1041 (7th Cir. 2013). *See also* Hovila v. Tween Brands, Inc., 2010 WL 1433417 (W.D. Wash. Apr. 7, 2010) (TCPA does not preempt state law that prohibits all prerecorded calls to residential lines, without the TCPA's former exception for calls made pursuant to an established business relationship).

65   Gomez v. Campbell-Ewald Co., 768 F.3d 871 (9th Cir. 2014), *cert. granted*, 135 S. Ct. 2311 (2015); Physicians Healthsource, Inc. v. Stryker Sales Corp., 65 F. Supp. 3d 482, 497 (W.D. Mich. 2015); Centerline Equip. Corp. v. Banner Personnel Serv., Inc., 545 F. Supp. 2d 768 (N.D. Ill. 2008) (denial of motion to dismiss); Holtzman v. Caplice, 2008 WL 2168762 (N.D. Ill. May 23, 2008); State of Okla. *ex rel.* Edmondson v. Pope, 505 F. Supp. 2d 1098 (W.D. Okla. 2007) (requirement that party initiating a prerecorded or artificial voice call identify itself does not violate First Amendment even when call relates to political matters), *vacated on other grounds*, 516 F.3d 1214 (10th Cir. Feb. 26, 2008) (vacating decision because of failure to notify U.S. Attorney General of challenge to constitutionality of federal statute); Italia Foods, Inc. v. Marinov Enterprises, Inc., 2007 WL 4117626 (N.D. Ill. Nov. 16, 2007) (junk fax rule); Accounting Outsourcing, L.L.C. v. Verizon Wireless Personal Communications, L.P., 329 F. Supp. 2d 789, 805–818 (M.D. La. 2004); Harjoe v. Herz Fin., 108 S.W.3d 653 (Mo. 2003) (junk fax prohibition not unconstitutionally vague); Margulis v. P & M Consulting, Inc., 121 S.W.3d 246 (Mo. Ct. App. 2003) (prerecorded messages); Stefano & Associates v. Global Lending Grp., 2008 WL 186638 (Ohio Ct. App. Jan. 23, 2008) (unpublished) (junk

junk faxes, while small for individual consumers, are large enough in the aggregate to constitute a substantial government interest that justifies the statutory restrictions.[66] The TCPA also does not violate the Equal Protection Clause[67] or the Commerce Clause.[68]

The distinction the FCC made between commercial and non-commercial telephone solicitations in its do-not-call rule does not unconstitutionally restrict speech based on content.[69] The statutory damages available for violations of the TCPA do not violate the Eighth Amendment or the Due Process Clause of the Fifth Amendment.[70]

Review of FCC regulations is governed by the Administrative Orders Review Act or Hobbs Act.[71] Some courts, including the Sixth, Seventh, Eighth, and Eleventh Circuits, have held that FCC regulations are subject to direct review by the U.S. Court of Appeals for the District of Columbia Circuit for thirty days, after which they are incontestable, the only issue being whether they were violated.[72] Before seeking relief from the U.S. Court of Appeals, a party aggrieved by the FCC's final order must petition the FCC for reconsideration, also within thirty days.[73]

fax restrictions). *See* Phillip Randolph Enterprises, L.L.C. v. Rice Fields, 2007 WL 129052 (N.D. Ill. Jan. 11, 2007) (junk fax prohibition does not violate First Amendment). *See also* Missouri *ex rel.* Nixon v. Am. Blast Fax, Inc., 323 F.3d 649 (8th Cir. 2003) (junk fax prohibition); Destination Ventures, Ltd. v. Fed. Communications Comm'n, 46 F.3d 54 (9th Cir. 1995) (restriction on unsolicited fax transmissions directly advances substantial governmental interest in manner that is no more extensive than necessary); Moser v. Fed. Communications Comm'n, 46 F.3d 970 (9th Cir. 1995) (prerecorded message); Wreyford v. Citizens for Transp. Mobility, 957 F. Supp. 2d 1378 (N.D. Ga. 2013); In re Jiffy Lube Int'l, Inc., Text Spam Litig., 847 F. Supp. 2d 1253 (S.D. Cal. 2012); Pasco v. Protus IP Solutions, Inc., 826 F. Supp. 2d 825 (D. Md. 2011); Maryland v. Universal Elections, 787 F. Supp. 2d 408 (D. Md. 2011), *aff'd*, 729 F.3d 370 (4th Cir. 2013); Kramer v. Autobytel, 759 F. Supp. 2d 1165 (N.D. Cal. 2010) (prohibition on use of autodialer to send text messages to cell phones is not unconstitutionally vague); Phillip Randolph Enterprises, L.L.C. v. Rice Fields, 2007 WL 129052 (N.D. Ill. Jan. 11, 2007) (junk fax prohibition does not violate First Amendment); Spafford v. Echostar Communications Corp., 448 F. Supp. 2d 1220 (W.D. Wash. 2006) (Washington's ban on use of autodialing and announcing devices to deliver prerecorded commercial message does not violate First Amendment); Minn. *ex rel.* Hatch v. Sunbelt Communications & Mktg., 282 F. Supp. 2d 976 (D. Minn. 2002) (junk fax prohibition); Texas v. Am. Blast Fax, Inc., 121 F. Supp. 2d 1085 (W.D. Tex. 2000); Kenro, Inc. v. Fax Daily, Inc., 962 F. Supp. 1162 (S.D. Ind. 1997) (junk fax prohibition constitutional); Joffe v. Acacia Mortg. Corp., 121 P.3d 831 (Ariz. Ct. App. 2005) (upholding application of restriction on autodialed calls to send text messages to cell phones); Kaufman v. ACS Sys., Inc., 2 Cal. Rptr. 3d 296 (Cal. Ct. App. 2003) (junk fax prohibition does not violate First Amendment and is not void for vagueness); Covington & Burling v. Int'l Mktg. & Research, Inc., 2003 WL 21384825 (D.C. Super. Ct. Apr. 17, 2003) (junk fax prohibition does not violate First Amendment and is not void for vagueness); State *ex rel.* Humphrey v. Casino Mktg. Grp., Inc., 491 N.W.2d 882 (Minn. 1992) (upholding Minnesota's statutory restriction on automatic dialing announcement devices); Harjoe v. Herz Fin., 108 S.W.3d 653 (Mo. 2003) (junk fax prohibition does not violate First or Fourteenth Amendment and is not unconstitutionally vague); Rudgayzer & Gratt v. Enine, Inc., 779 N.Y.S.2d 882 (N.Y. App. Div. 2004) (junk fax prohibition does not violate First Amendment); Grady v. Lenders Interactive Services, 2004 WL 1799178 (Ohio Ct. App. Aug. 12, 2004) (unpublished); Jemiola v. XYZ Corp., 802 N.E.2d 745 (Ohio Ct. Com. Pl. 2003) (junk fax prohibition does not violate First or Fourteenth Amendment); Chair King, Inc. v. GTE Mobilnet of Houston, Inc., 135 S.W.3d 365 (Tex. App. 2004), *rev'd on other grounds*, 184 S.W.3d 707 (Tex. 2006). *But cf.* Cahaly v. Larosa, 796 F.3d 399 (4th Cir. 2015) (state statute prohibiting just political and consumer robocalls is content-based restriction on speech and not narrowly tailored to achieve its goals so is unconstitutional; suit by political consultant who was arrested for placing robocalls asking political survey questions). *See generally* § 6.3.1, *infra* (rejection of challenges to constitutionality of restrictions on calls to cell phones).

66 Centerline Equip. Corp. v. Banner Personnel Serv., Inc., 545 F. Supp. 2d 768 (N.D. Ill. 2008) (denial of motion to dismiss).

67 Texas v. American Blast Fax, Inc., 121 F. Supp. 2d 1085 (W.D. Tex. 2000); Chair King, Inc. v. GTE Mobilnet of Houston, Inc., 135 S.W.3d 365 (Tex. App. 2004), *rev'd on other grounds*, 184 S.W.3d 707 (Tex. 2006).

68 Levitt v. Fax.com, Inc., 857 A.2d 1089 (Md. 2004); Chair King, Inc. v. GTE Mobilnet of Houston, Inc., 135 S.W.3d 365 (Tex. App. 2004),

rev'd on other grounds, 184 S.W.3d 707 (Tex. 2006). *See also* Nat'l Notary Ass'n v. U.S. Notary, 2002 WL 1265555 (Cal. Ct. App. June 7, 2002) (unpublished) (Commerce Clause does not prevent nationwide injunction against junk faxer if it is tailored not to prohibit legal faxes and applies only when the enjoined activity has appropriate connection to forum state).

69 Mainstream Mktg. Services v. Fed. Trade Comm'n, 358 F.3d 1228 (10th Cir. 2004); Charvat v. Telelytics, L.L.C., 2006 WL 2574019 (Ohio Ct. App. Aug. 31, 2006) (unpublished) (not beyond FCC's authority to exempt for-profit companies that solicit for nonprofits from nationwide do-not-call list rule).

70 Holtzman v. Turza, 2011 WL 3876943 (N.D. Ill. Aug. 29, 2011); Holtzman v. Caplice, 2008 WL 2168762 (N.D. Ill. May 23, 2008); Sadowski v. Med1 Online, L.L.C., 2008 WL 489360 (N.D. Ill. Feb. 20, 2008); Centerline Equip. Corp. v. Banner Personnel Serv., Inc., 545 F. Supp. 2d 768 (N.D. Ill. 2008) (denial of motion to dismiss) (statutory penalty not wholly disproportioned to the offense, as recipients of junk faxes suffer additional unquantifiable costs such as loss of time; Due Process Clause does not require Congress to make illegal behavior affordable); Italia Foods, Inc. v. Marinov Enterprises, Inc., 2007 WL 4117626 (N.D. Ill. Nov. 16, 2007); Phillip Randolph Enterprises L.L.C. v. Rice Fields, 2007 WL 129052 (N.D. Ill. Jan. 11, 2007) ($500 minimum award per violation for junk fax does not violate Fifth Amendment as Due Process Clause does not obligate Congress to make illegal behavior affordable); Kenro, Inc. v. Fax Daily, Inc., 962 F. Supp. 1162, 1167 (S.D. Ind. 1997) (finding that "§ 227(b)(3)(B), which provides for a minimum penalty of $500 for each violation of the TCPA, does not violate the Due Process clause of the Fifth Amendment"); Pasco v. Protus IP Solutions, Inc., 826 F. Supp. 2d 825, 835 (D. Md. 2011) (quoting *Williams*, 251 U.S. at 67) ("the statutory penalties under the TCPA are not 'obviously unreasonable' and are not 'so severe and oppressive' as to violate due process").

71 28 U.S.C. § 2342(1); 47 U.S.C. § 402(a).

72 Murphy v. DCI Biologicals Orland, L.L.C., 797 F.3d 1302 (11th Cir. 2015) (FCC order interpreting prior express consent is incontestable under Hobbs Act); Imhoff Inv., L.L.C. v. Alfoccino, Inc., 792 F.3d 627, 637 (6th Cir. 2015); Mais v. Gulf Coast Collection Bureau, 768 F.3d 1110 (11th Cir. 2014); Nack v. Walburg, 715 F.3d 680 (8th Cir. 2013); CE Design, Ltd. v. Prism Bus. Media, Inc., 606 F.3d 443 (7th Cir. 2010); Toney v. Quality Resources, Inc., 75 F. Supp. 3d 727, 734 (N.D. Ill. 2014); Morse v. Allied Interstate, L.L.C., 65 F. Supp. 3d 407, 411–412 (M.D. Pa. 2014); Hartley-Culp v. Green Tree Servicing, L.L.C., 52 F. Supp. 3d 700 (M.D. Pa. 2014); Hudson v. Sharp Healthcare, 2014 WL 2892290 (S.D. Cal. June 25, 2014). *But see* Lusskin v. Seminole Comedy, Inc., 2013 WL 3147339 (S.D. Fla. June 19, 2013).

73 47 U.S.C. § 405(a). *See* Leyse v. Clear Channel Broad., Inc., 545 Fed. Appx. 444 (6th Cir. 2013).

Even if not incontestable, courts have held that the FCC's regulations are within its authority and entitled to *Chevron*[74] deference. Courts have also given deference to the FCC's interpretation of its rules,[75] sometimes under the somewhat less deferential *Skidmore*[76] standard.

6.3 Restrictions on Autodialed or Prerecorded Calls to Cell Phones, Other Sensitive Numbers

6.3.1 *Nature of the Prohibition*

The TCPA prohibits using an automatic telephone dialing system or an artificial or prerecorded voice to make any call to (1) an emergency telephone line, (2) a patient or guest room at a nursing home, hospital, or similar health facility, (3) a pager or cellular phone, or (4) any telephone service for which the called party is charged for the call.[77] The statute and regulations have been upheld against various constitutional challenges.[78]

The prohibitions on calling a cellular phone and any service for which the called party is charged for the call are alternative; a cellular consumer with an unlimited plan who is not charged for the call is protected.[79] Liability for making a prerecorded call falls on the entity that made the call, even if some other entity recorded the message that the caller delivered.[80] The Fifth Circuit has held that a caller is liable for making a prerecorded call only if the recording actually plays.[81]

In the absence of the called party's consent, the prohibition prevents any calls to cell phones that use a recorded or artificial voice. For example, many debt collection calls begin with a prerecorded message and so violate this provision if they are made to cell phones without consent.[82] But even if the only words are uttered by a live person, an autodialer cannot be used to initiate the call to the cell phone. As a practical matter, this prohibits virtually any telemarketing to cell phones.

When an autodialer is not used, the TCPA does not prevent live calls to a cell phone,[83] but subscribers can place their cellular telephone numbers on the national do-not-call list, which callers must honor.[84] Another section, *infra*, considers the applicability of this TCPA provision to text messages sent

---

74 Chevron v. Natural Res. Def. Council, Inc., 467 U.S. 837, 104 S. Ct. 2778, 81 L. Ed. 2d 694 (1984). *See* Satterfield v. Simon & Schuster, Inc., 569 F.3d 946, 953 (9th Cir. 2009) (giving *Chevron* deference to FCC determination that text messages are calls subject to robocall restrictions); Mainstream Mktg. Services v. Fed. Trade Comm'n, 358 F.3d 1228 (10th Cir. 2004) (affording *Chevron* deference to established business relationship exception to FCC's do-not-call rule); Portuguese-American Leadership Council of the U.S., Inc. v. Investors' Alert, Inc., 956 A.2d 671 (D.C. 2008) (FCC ruling on private right of action entitled to *Chevron* deference); Charvat v. Dispatch Consumer Services, 769 N.E.2d 829 (Ohio 2002) (requiring *Chevron* deference to FCC's definition of established business relationship in 47 U.S.C. § 227(a)(3)(B)); Charvat v. Telelytics, L.L.C., 2006 WL 2574019 (Ohio Ct. App. Aug. 31, 2006) (applying *Chevron* deference to FCC rule excepting nonprofits from certain TCPA requirements).

75 Murphy v. DCI Biologics Orland, L.L.C., 797 F.3d 1302 (11th Cir. 2015) (FCC order interpreting prior express consent is incontestable under Hobbs Act); Palm Beach Golf Center-Boca, Inc. v. John G. Sarris, D.D.S., P.A., 781 F.3d 1245, 1256–1257 (11th Cir. 2015) (applying *Chevron* deference and upholding FCC's interpretation of meaning of to "send" a junk fax); P & S Printing, L.L.C. v. Tubelite, Inc., 2015 WL 4425793 (D. Conn. July 17, 2015) (affording *Skidmore* deference to FCC rulings interpreting "unsolicited advertisement"); Zarichny v. Complete Payment Recovery Services, Inc., 80 F. Supp. 3d 610 (E.D. Pa. 2015) (FCC interpretations are entitled to *Skidmore* deference); Gomez v. Campbell-Ewald Co., 768 F.3d 871 (9th Cir. 2014) (affording *Chevron* deference to FCC's 2013 declaratory ruling about vicarious liability for telemarketing calls), *cert. granted*, 135 S. Ct. 2311 (2015); Margulis v. P & M Consulting, Inc., 121 S.W.3d 246 (Mo. Ct. App. 2003); Charvat v. Dispatch Consumer Services, 769 N.E.2d 829 (Ohio 2002); Omnibus Int'l v. AT&T, Inc., 111 S.W.3d 818 (Tex. App. 2003) (giving deference to interpretation at 8 F.C.C. Rcd. 480 (1993)), *review granted, remanded, by agreement* (Jan. 12, 2004). *Cf.* Sandusky Wellness Ctr., L.L.C. v. Medco Health Solutions, Inc., 788 F.3d 218 (6th Cir. 2015) (stating in dicta that it would not defer to FCC's interpretation when statute was unambiguous).

76 Skidmore v. Swift & Co., 323 U.S. 134, 65 S. Ct. 161, 89 L. Ed. 124 (1944).

77 47 U.S.C. § 227(b)(1)(A); 47 C.F.R. § 64.1200(a)(1). *See* Lary v. Flasch Bus. Consulting, 878 So. 2d 1158 (Ala. Civ. App. 2003) (reversing dismissal of claim that defendants used autodialer to call physician's emergency line).

78 *See, e.g.*, Sterk v. Path, Inc., 46 F. Supp. 3d 813, 816–821 (N.D. Ill. 2014) (rejecting overbreadth and vagueness arguments); De Los Santos

v. Millward Brown, Inc., 2014 WL 2938605 (S.D. Fla. June 30, 2014); Gruse v. Accuweather, Inc., 2013 WL 1858601 (N.D. Ill. Apr. 30, 2013); Pimental v. Google Inc., 2012 WL 691784 (N.D. Cal. Mar. 2, 2012); *In re* Jiffy Lube Int'l, Inc., Text Spam Litig., 847 F. Supp. 2d 1253 (S.D. Cal. 2012); Lozano v. Twentieth Century Fox Film Corp., 702 F. Supp. 2d 999 (N.D. Ill. 2010); Abbas v. Selling Source, L.L.C., 2009 WL 4884471 (N.D. Ill. Dec. 14, 2009); Joffe v. Acacia Mortg. Corp., 121 P.3d 831 (Ariz. Ct. App. 2006). *But cf.* Cahaly v. Larosa, 796 F.3d 399 (4th Cir. 2015) (state statute prohibiting just political and consumer robocalls is content-based restriction on speed and not narrowly tailored to achieve its goals, so is unconstitutional; suit by political consultant who was arrested for placing robocalls asking political survey questions). *See generally* § 6.2.4.3, *supra*.

79 Osorio v. State Farm Bank, 746 F.3d 1242, 1257 (11th Cir. 2014); Moore v. DISH Network, L.L.C., 57 F. Supp. 3d 639, 647–648 (N.D. W. Va. 2014); De Los Santos v. Millward Brown, Inc., 2014 WL 2938605 (S.D. Fla. June 30, 2014) (same); Diugosh v. Directbuy, Inc. of San Antonio, 2013 WL 5773043 (W.D. Tex. Oct. 24, 2013); Page v. Regions Bank, 917 F. Supp. 2d 1214 (N.D. Ala. 2012) (same); Agne v. Papa John's Int'l, Inc., 286 F.R.D. 559, 570 (W.D. Wash. 2012) (robodialed text messages to cell phones violate statute regardless of whether recipients were charged for the message); Smith v. Microsoft Corp., 2012 WL 2975712 (S.D. Cal. July 20, 2012); Buslepp v. Improv Miami, Inc., 2012 WL 1560408 (S.D. Fla. May 4, 2012) (plaintiff who uses a cell phone need not separately allege that he was charged for the call); Kane v. Nat'l Action Fin. Services, Inc., 2011 WL 6018403, at *8 (E.D. Mich. Nov. 7, 2011) (same); Abbas v. Selling Source, L.L.C., 2009 WL 4884471 (N.D. Ill. Dec. 14, 2009) (prohibition applies to calls to cell phones whether or not called party is charged for call).

80 Lardner v. Diversified Consultants Inc., 17 F. Supp. 3d 1215 (S.D. Fla. 2014).

81 Ybarra v. DISH Network, L.L.C., ___ F.3d ___, 2015 WL 6159755 (5th Cir. Oct. 20, 2015).

82 Lardner v. Diversified Consultants Inc., 17 F. Supp. 3d 1215 (S.D. Fla. 2014).

83 Boyd v. Gen. Revenue Corp., 5 F. Supp. 3d 940 (M.D. Tenn. 2013).

84 *In re* Rules and Regulations Implementing the Telephone Consumer Protection Act of 1991 ¶ 166, 18 F.C.C. 14014, 2003 WL 21517853 (F.C.C. July 3, 2003). *See* §§ 6.5.2, *infra* (FCC and FTC do-not-call rules).

---

to cell phones.[85] The Fair Debt Collection Practices Act[86] or the FTC Telemarketing Sales Rule[87] may also come into play when the debt collector makes a live call to a cell phone not using an automatic telephone dialing system.

Any artificial voice or prerecorded call, even if made with consent, must include disclosures.[88] In addition, those that include an advertisement or constitute telemarketing must have an opt-out mechanism even if made with consent.[89] These requirements are discussed in §§ 6.4.3 and 6.4.4, *infra*.

6.3.2 What Is an Autodialer?

The TCPA defines "automatic telephone dialing system" as equipment that has the capacity to store or produce telephone numbers to be called, using a random or sequential number generator, and to dial those numbers.[90] According to the FCC, the basic functions of an autodialer are to dial numbers without human intervention and to dial thousands of numbers in a short period of time.[91]

The FCC interprets the statutory definition to include predictive dialers, which do not generate the numbers to be dialed randomly but instead operate from a list of numbers fed into the device and use a complex formula designed to predict when a person will answer the phone.[92] The dispositive question is not whether a particular call was placed through random or sequential generation of telephone numbers but whether the system has the capacity to generate numbers in this way.[93] Many courts have agreed with this view and followed the FCC's interpretation.[94] Indeed, since the 2008 FCC

determination was not appealed within thirty days after it was issued, some courts hold that it is incontestable and no longer subject to attack.[95]

The FCC has made it clear that "the TCPA's use of 'capacity' does not exempt equipment that lacks the 'present ability' to dial randomly or sequentially."[96] Thus, hardware that can store or produce telephone numbers to be called using a random or sequential number generator is an autodialer even if software necessary to accomplish that functionality has not yet been installed.[97] Nor can callers evade the definition by

---

85 *See* § 6.7, *infra*.

86 *See* National Consumer Law Center, Fair Debt Collection (8th ed. 2014), *updated at* www.nclc.org/library.

87 *See* Ch. 5, *supra*.

88 47 C.F.R. § 64.1200(b)(1), (2) (applicable to "[a]ll artificial or prerecorded voice telephone messages").

89 47 C.F.R. § 64.1200(b)(3) ("In every case where the artificial or prerecorded voice telephone message includes or introduces an advertisement or constitutes telemarketing").

90 47 U.S.C. § 227(a)(1).

91 *In re* Rules & Regulations Implementing the Tel. Consumer Prot. Act of 1991 ¶ 17, CG Docket No. 02-278, No. 07-135, 2015 WL 4387780, ___ F.C.C. ___ (July 10, 2015).

92 *In re* Rules & Regulations Implementing the Tel. Consumer Prot. Act of 1991 ¶¶ 10–24, CG Docket No. 02-278, No. 07-135, 2015 WL 4387780, ___ F.C.C. ___ (July 10, 2015). *In re* Rules and Regulations Implementing the Telephone Consumer Protection Act of 1991 ¶¶ 131–34, 18 F.C.C. 14014, 2003 WL 21517853 (F.C.C. July 3, 2003). *But cf.* Marks v. Crunch San Diego, L.L.C., 55 F. Supp. 3d 1288 (S.D. Cal. 2014) (characterizing FCC interpretation as unauthorized and overbroad; third-party web-based platform for sending text messages to numbers inputted by several methods and then selected by sender is not an autodialer); Pollock v. Island Arbitration & Mediation Inc., 869 N.Y.S.2d 740 (N.Y. City Ct. 2008) (system that generates numbers from a list is not an autodialer).

93 *In re* Rules & Regulations Implementing the Tel. Consumer Prot. Act of 1991 ¶ 15, CG Docket No. 02-278, No. 07-135, 2015 WL 4387780, ___ F.C.C. ___ (July 10, 2015).

94 Dominguez v. Yahoo, Inc., ___ Fed. Appx. ___, 2015 WL 6405811 (3d Cir. Nov. 21, 2014) (device is an autodialer if it is part of a system that has the latent capacity to dial randomly or sequentially generated

numbers); Meyer v. Portfolio Recovery Associates, L.L.C., 707 F.3d 1036 (9th Cir. 2012); Satterfield v. Simon & Shuster, 569 F.3d 946 (9th Cir. 2009) (reversing grant of summary judgment to advertiser; fact question whether system had capacity to generate random or sequential numbers); King v. Time Warner Cable, ___ F. Supp. 3d ___, 2015 WL 4103689, at *4 (S.D.N.Y. July 7, 2015); Morse v. Allied Interstate, L.L.C., 65 F. Supp. 3d 407 (M.D. Pa. 2014) (predictive dialer meets definition); Moore v. DISH Network, 57 F. Supp. 3d 639 (N.D. W. Va. 2014) (predictive dialer is autodialer if it has capacity to be upgraded by software to store or generate numbers randomly or sequentially; human involvement in inputting the number is irrelevant); Sterk v. Path, Inc., 46 F. Supp. 3d 813, 816–821 (N.D. Ill. 2014); Davis v. Diversified Consultants, Inc., 36 F. Supp. 3d 217 (D. Mass. 2014) (LiveVox system is covered); Lardner v. Diversified Consultants Inc., 17 F. Supp. 3d 1215 (S.D. Fla. 2014) (FCC's interpretation is reasonable; LiveVox predictive dialing system is an autodialer); Hickey v. Voxernet, L.L.C., 887 F. Supp. 2d 1125, 1129–1130 (W.D. Wash. 2012) (predictive dialer is autodialer); Griffith v. Consumer Portfolio Services, Inc., 838 F. Supp. 2d 723 (N.D. Ill. 2011); Vance v. Bureau of Collection Recovery, L.L.C., 2011 WL 881550, at *6–7 (N.D. Ill. Mar. 11, 2011); Lozano v. Twentieth Century Fox Film Corp., 702 F. Supp. 2d 999, 1010–1011 (N.D. Ill. 2010); Kazemi v. Payless Shoesource, Inc., 2010 WL 963225 (N.D. Cal. Mar. 16, 2010); Rivas v. Receivables Performance Mgmt., 2009 U.S. Dist. LEXIS 129378, at *12 (S.D. Fla. Sept. 1, 2009); Hicks v. Client Services, Inc., 2008 WL 5479111, at *10 (S.D. Fla. Dec. 11, 2008). *But cf.* Gragg v. Orange Cab Co., Inc., 995 F. Supp. 2d 1189, 1191 (W.D. Wash. 2014) (automated dispatch system for taxicabs that sends an acknowledgment text message when a cab driver accepts the assignment. is not an autodialer because it "is capable of generating and sending dispatch notifications only in response to a driver's acceptance of an individual customer's request"); Ashland Hosp. Corp. v. Int'l Brotherhood of Elec. Workers Local 575, 708 F.3d 737 (6th Cir. 2013) (calls to hospital were not autodialed when union made robodialed calls to community residents and urged them to call hospital by pressing a certain key).

95 CE Design, Ltd. v. Prism Bus. Media, Inc., 606 F.3d 443 (7th Cir. 2010). *See also* Nack v. Walburg, 715 F.3d 680 (8th Cir. 2013) (Hobbs Act precludes court from invalidating junk fax regulations adopted by FCC under TCPA). *But cf.* Leyse v. Clear Channel Broad., Inc., 545 Fed. Appx. 444 (6th Cir. 2013) (holding that FCC determinations under TCPA are entitled only to *Chevron* deference).

96 *In re* Rules & Regulations Implementing the Tel. Consumer Prot. Act of 1991 ¶ 15, CG Docket No. 02-278, No. 07-135, 2015 WL 4387780, ___ F.C.C. ___ (July 10, 2015).

97 *Id.* at ¶¶ 16, 18–20; Moore v. DISH Network, 57 F. Supp. 3d 639 (N.D. W. Va. 2014) (predictive dialer is autodialer if it has capacity to be upgraded by software to store or generate numbers randomly or sequentially; human involvement in inputting number is irrelevant). *See also* Hunt v. 21st Mortg. Corp., 2014 WL 426275, at *5–6 (N.D. Ala. Feb. 4, 2014) (predictive dialer is autodialer if it could store or produce telephone numbers randomly or sequentially without substantial modification; fact question whether software could have easily been installed in this machine).

dividing ownership or pieces of dialing equipment that work in concert among multiple entities.[98]

The industry has responded by adopting "preview dialing," in which some degree of human intervention is required to authorize each call. In some cases, the person who will take the call if it is answered authorizes the call by illuminating or clicking on a number. There is some precedent for the proposition that this variant of "preview dialing" is covered.[99] In another form of preview dialing, the person who authorizes the call and the person who will take the call if it is answered are not the same. These devices should be considered autodialers, since such equipment necessarily functions as a predictive dialer and the "human intervention" is fictional and evasive. It is often necessary to retain an expert witness to establish that a particular dialing system meets the definition of an autodialer.

Manually dialed real-voice calls to cell phones are not prohibited,[100] but advocates should carefully investigate any claim that a call was manually dialed. In addition, even if the cell phone number was manually dialed, the call violates the TCPA if it uses an artificial or prerecorded voice for any part of the call.

The industry has repeatedly filed petitions with the FCC to narrow the definition of automated telephone dialing system, but the FCC has rejected them, most recently in July 2015.[101] As discussed in § 6.7, *infra*, text messages are treated in the same way as recorded and autodialed calls to cell phones.

6.3.3 Scope of the Prohibition

The TCPA prohibition on the use of autodialers and prerecorded messages to call cell phones and other sensitive numbers applies broadly. It is not limited to telemarketing calls; for example, informational calls[102] and debt collection calls[103] are covered. As the statute makes it unlawful to *make* an autodialed call to a cell phone without consent, a call is a violation even if it is answered only by an answering machine or not at all.[104] It is the placing of the call that is prohibited, even if the called party does not actually receive the call.[105]

The few exceptions to the prohibition are narrow. There is an exception for emergency calls.[106] There is also an exception when the call is made to a phone number that was a land line and was "ported" to a cell phone number within the last fifteen days, provided that the number is not on the general do-not-call list or the caller's company-specific do-not-call list.[107] In 2014, the FCC created an additional exemption, with certain conditions, for delivery notifications by carriers such as UPS attempting to deliver parcels.[108] In 2015, it adopted a limited exception for carriers that place collect calls to cell phones for prison inmates.[109]

On November 2, 2015, the statute was amended by an appropriations bill to exempt calls "made solely to collect a debt owed to or guaranteed by the United States."[110] The appropriations bill gives the FCC the authority to "restrict or limit the number and duration of calls made to a telephone number assigned to a cellular telephone service to collect a debt owed to or guaranteed by the United States,"[111] and an uncodified provision of the bill requires the FCC to adopt rules implementing these amendments within nine months after enactment.[112] In light of the mandated rules to implement the amendments, it appears that the amendments are not intended to be effective

---

98 *In re* Rules & Regulations Implementing the Tel. Consumer Prot. Act of 1991 ¶¶ 10, 23, 24, CG Docket No. 02-278, WC Docket No. 07-135, 2015 WL 4387780, ___ F.C.C. ___ (July 10, 2015).

99 Nelson v. Santander Consumer USA, Inc., 931 F. Supp. 2d 919, 930 (W.D. Wis. 2013), *vacated by stipulation*, 2013 WL 5377280 (W.D. Wis. June 7, 2013). *Cf.* Sherman v. Yahoo! Inc., 997 F. Supp. 2d 1129 (S.D. Cal. 2014) (fact question whether Yahoo! Messenger service involves an automated telephone dialing system). *But cf.* Luna v. Shac, L.L.C., ___ F. Supp. 3d ___, 2015 WL 4941781 (N.D. Cal. Aug. 19, 2015) (TCPA can apply to Internet-based calling systems, but not when human intervention is involved in drafting message, determining its timing, and clicking "send").

100 *See* § 6.3.1, *supra*.

101 *In re* Rules & Regulations Implementing the Tel. Consumer Prot. Act of 1991 ¶¶ 10–24, CG Docket No. 02-278, WC Docket No. 07-135, 2015 WL 4387780, ___ F.C.C. ___ (July 10, 2015).

102 *In re* Rules & Regulations Implementing the Tel. Consumer Prot. Act of 1991 ¶ 123, CG Docket No. 02-278, WC Docket No. 07-135, 2015 WL 4387780, ___ F.C.C. ___ (July 10, 2015).

103 Gager v. Dell Fin. Services, L.L.C., 727 F.3d 265 (3d Cir. 2013); Morse v. Allied Interstate, L.L.C., 65 F. Supp. 3d 407, 409 (M.D. Pa. 2014); Brown v. Hosto & Buchan, P.L.L.C., 748 F. Supp. 2d 847 (W.D. Tenn. 2010); Olney v. Progressive Cas. Ins. Co., 993 F. Supp. 2d 1220 (S.D. Cal. 2014); *In re* Rules and Regulations Implementing the Telephone Consumer Protection Act of 1991, Request of ACA International for Clarification and Declaratory Ruling ¶ 11, No. 02-278, FCC Release 07-232, 23 F.C.C. Rcd 559, 565, 2008 WL 65485, 43 Communications

Reg. (P & F) 877 (Jan. 4, 2008) (expressly rejecting argument that debt collection calls are not covered).

104 King v. Time Warner Cable, ___ F. Supp. 3d ___, 2015 WL 4103689, at *5 (S.D.N.Y. July 7, 2015); Castro v. Green Tree Servicing, L.L.C., 959 F. Supp. 2d 698, 720 (S.D.N.Y. 2013) ("[F]or purposes of Plaintiffs' TCPA claim, it is immaterial whether the Plaintiffs picked up all of Defendants' calls or whether several of the calls went unanswered."); Fillichio v. M.R.S. Associates, 2010 WL 4261442, at *3 (S.D. Fla. Oct. 19, 2010) (The TCPA "does not include [ ] a requirement . . . that the recipient of a call must answer the phone or somehow be aware of the call in order for there to be a violation"). *See also* Satterfield v. Simon & Schuster, Inc.,569 F.3d 946, 953–954 (9th Cir.2009) (holding that "to call" in the TCPA means "to communicate with or *try to get in communication with* a person by telephone").

105 First Nat'l Collection Bureau, Inc. v. Walker, 348 S.W.3d 329 (Tex. App. 2011).

106 47 U.S.C. § 227(b)(1)(A); 47 C.F.R. § 64.1200(a)(1). Some governmental units have "reverse 911" systems that can call or send a text message to all numbers in designated exchanges or areas to warn people of fires, police activity, road closings, and similar emergencies.

107 47 C.F.R. § 64.1200(a)(1)(iv).

108 Cargo Airline Ass'n Petition for Declaratory Ruling, 29 F.C.C. Rcd. 3432 (Mar. 27, 2014).

109 *In re* Rules & Regulations Implementing the Tel. Consumer Prot. Act of 1991 ¶¶ 43–46, CG Docket No. 02-278, WC Docket No. 07-135, 2015 WL 4387780, ___ F.C.C. ___ (July 10, 2015).

110 Pub. L. 114-74, § 301 (Nov. 2, 2015) (amending 47 U.S.C. § 227(b)(1)(A)(iii)).

111 *Id.* (amending 47 U.S.C. § 227(b)(2)(H)).

112 *Id.* ("Not later than 9 months after the date of enactment of this Act, the Federal Communications Commission, in consultation with the Department of Treasury, shall prescribe regulations to implement the amendments made by this section").

until rules are adopted. Online updates to this treatise will address developments regarding these amendments.

In addition, the statute authorizes the FCC to permit specific exemptions from the prohibition for calls that are not charged to the called party—called "free to end user calls."[113] Using this authority, in a 2015 declaratory ruling, the FCC allowed certain "free to end user" calls to be made by financial institutions and health care providers subject to very specific conditions:

- The calls can only be to the wireless telephone number provided by the customer;
- The calls must state the caller's name and contact information;
- For financial institutions, the calls must only be for limited purposes of (a) preventing fraudulent transactions or identify theft, (b) notifying of data security breaches, (c) preventing identity theft following a data breach, or (d) informing of a pending transfer;
- For health care providers, the calls must be limited to calls for which there is exigency and that have a healthcare treatment purpose, specifically: appointment and exam confirmations and reminders, wellness checkups, hospital re-registration instructions, pre-operative instructions, lab results, post-discharge follow-up intended to prevent readmission, prescription notifications, and home health care instructions;
- The calls or texts must be concise;
- No more than three messages per event over a three-day period are permitted;
- The calls or texts must include an immediately effective opt-out mechanism allowing the called party to stop all future calls of this type; and
- The "information provided in these exempted voice calls and texts must not be of such a personal nature that it would violate the privacy" of the person called if another person received the message.[114]

The most significant issue affecting the legality of autodialed or prerecorded calls to cell phones and other sensitive numbers is consent. The consent requirements differ depending on whether the call is a telemarketing call or for other purposes. The consent requirements are discussed in § 6.3.4, *infra*.

6.3.4 Exceptions for Calls Made with Consent

6.3.4.1 Prior Express Written Consent Is Required for Telemarketing Calls

The FCC regulation allows autodialed and prerecorded calls to cell phones only with the recipient's prior express written consent if the call constitutes telemarketing or introduces

an advertisement.[115] Prior express written consent is a defined term in the FCC regulations and means a signed agreement in writing clearly authorizing the seller to send solicitations using prerecorded voices to a designated phone number.[116] The signature requirement can be met by an electronic or digital signature if federal and state law allow.[117]

The writing must disclose that, by signing it, the consumer is agreeing to receive autodialed or prerecorded calls.[118] It must also disclose that agreeing to calls is not a precondition to purchasing any goods or services.[119] Consent to receive promotional material from a company's affiliates is not consent to receive calls from an unaffiliated third party to which the company sold the consumer's cell phone number.[120]

Until 2012, the exception for telemarketing calls did not require written consent, only express consent.[121] Under the old regime, the FCC had declared that the provision of a cell phone number to a creditor as part of a credit application or relationship constituted prior express consent to be contacted by the creditor or its debt collector via autodialed and prerecorded calls.[122] In any event, the definition of express *written* consent, described *supra*, now requires far more than mere provision of the cell phone number, so merely providing the number no longer authorizes telemarketing robocalls.

There are two exceptions to the current requirement of prior express written consent for autodialed or prerecorded

---

113 47 U.S.C. § 227(b)(2)(C).

114 *In re* Rules & Regulations Implementing the Tel. Consumer Prot. Act of 1991, ¶¶ 129–138 (financial institutions), ¶¶ 140–147 (health care providers), CG Docket No. 02-278, WC Docket No. 07-135, 2015 WL 4387780, ___ F.C.C. ___ (July 10, 2015).

115 47 C.F.R. § 64.1200(a)(2), *adopted by* 27 F.C.C. Rcd. 1830 (F.C.C.), 27 F.C.C.R. 1830, 55 Communications Reg. (P&F) 356, 2012 WL 507959 (Feb. 15, 2012). *See* Reardon v. Uber Technologies, Inc., ___ F. Supp. 3d ___, 2015 WL 4451209, at *3 (N.D. Cal. July 19, 2015) (unsolicited text messages to taxi drivers' cell phones, recruiting them to be Uber drivers, were not telemarketing or advertising because they did not promote a product or service); *In re* Rules & Regulations Implementing the Tel. Consumer Prot. Act of 1991 ¶ 104, CG Docket No. 02-278, WC Docket No. 07-135, 2015 WL 4387780, ___ F.C.C. ___ (July 10, 2015) (when consumer sends text message responding to an offer of a discount coupon, texting coupon in reply is not telemarketing). *See generally* § 6.8.2.1, *infra* (interpretation of "advertisement" for purposes of junk fax rule).

116 47 C.F.R. § 64.1200(f)(8).

117 47 C.F.R. § 64.1200(f)(8)(ii).

118 47 C.F.R. § 64.1200(f)(8)(i)(A).

119 47 C.F.R. § 64.1200(f)(8)(i)(B).

120 Satterfield v. Simon & Shuster, 569 F.3d 946, 955 (9th Cir. 2009).

121 *See* Zeidel v. YM LLC USA, 2015 WL 1910456, at *3 (N.D. Ill. Apr. 27, 2015) (fact question whether this consumer's provision of cell phone number might amount to consent to receive telemarketing text messages prior to effective date of requirement of written consent).

122 F.C.C. Declaratory Ruling, F.C.C. 07-232 ¶ 9 (Dec. 28, 2007), *summarized at* 73 Fed. Reg. 6041 (Feb. 1, 2008); *In re* Rules and Regulations Implementing the Telephone Consumer Protection Act of 1991, 23 F.C.C. Rcd. 559 (F.C.C. Jan. 4, 2008) (autodialed and prerecorded calls to wireless phone numbers are made with "prior express consent" when called party provides number in connection with existing debt). *Accord* Cavero v. Franklin Collection Services, Inc., 2012 WL 279448, at *3 (S.D. Fla. Jan. 31, 2012) (citing 23 F.C.C. Rcd. 559 (F.C.C. 2008)); Cunningham v. Credit Mgmt., L.P., 2010 WL 3791104, at *5 (N.D. Tex. Aug. 30, 2010). *But see* Leckler v. Cashcall, Inc., 554 F. Supp. 2d 1025 (N.D. Cal. 2008), *vacated on other grounds*, 2008 WL 5000528 (N.D. Cal. Nov. 21, 2008) (concluding that court lacked jurisdiction to review FCC interpretation). *See generally* § 6.3.4.2.3, *infra* (whether providing cell phone number amounts to express consent).

telemarketing calls to cell phones and other sensitive numbers. If the call is by or on behalf of a tax-exempt nonprofit, the caller's prior express consent is required, but the consent need not be written.[123] Second, calls that deliver health care messages by or on behalf of a covered entity or its business associate, as those terms are defined in the Health Insurance Portability and Accountability Act of 1996 (HIPAA), are exempt from this portion of the FCC's rule, so the called party's prior express consent need not be written.[124]

6.3.4.2 Prior Express Consent Is Required for Debt Collection and Other Non-Telemarketing Calls

6.3.4.2.1 *Prior oral or written consent is sufficient*

Autodialed or prerecorded calls other than telemarketing calls can be made to cell phones and other sensitive numbers with the called party's prior express consent. In contrast to telemarketing calls, however, the consent need not be written. The requirement that the called party's prior express consent be written, added to the regulation in 2012, applies only to telemarketing calls.[125] The FCC structured the regulation to provide that either written or oral consent is sufficient for autodialed or prerecorded debt collection calls to cell phones.[126]

6.3.4.2.2 *Methods of obtaining consent*

The caller must have obtained consent before the call is placed.[127] "Capturing" an incoming number[128] or obtaining it through skip-tracing[129] does not qualify. Nor does the fact that the caller has an existing business relationship with the called party create an exception to the prohibition if the debtor has not given prior express consent to receive calls.[130]

Consent may be given by an express provision in a contract.[131] However, a privacy policy posted on the caller's website, stating that the company and other organizations may call consumers for marketing purposes, is not a part of the contract in the absence of evidence that the consumer saw it and agreed to it.[132] Entering a phone number in an online application that the consumer decides not to complete or submit is also unlikely to amount to consent to receive calls at that number.[133]

The FCC has stated that consent may be given by the customary user even if that person is not the subscriber.[134] In addition, consent given to one seller may transfer to a third party contractor performing services for that seller.[135]

6.3.4.2.3 *Is mere provision of a cell phone number express consent to receive autodialed or prerecorded calls?*

A key question is whether mere provision of a cell phone number is express consent to receive autodialed or prerecorded calls to that number. In 2008, the FCC ruled:

> Because we find that autodialed and prerecorded message calls to wireless numbers provided by the called party in connection with an existing debt are made with the 'prior express consent' of the called party, we clarify that such calls are permissible. We conclude that the provision of a cell phone number to a creditor, *e.g.*, as part of a credit application, reasonably evidences prior express consent by the cell phone subscriber to be contacted at that number regarding the debt.[136]

The FCC's position is hard to justify, as it treats what at most might be implied consent as the "express consent"

---

123 47 C.F.R. § 64.1200(a)(2).

124 47 C.F.R. § 64.1200(a)(2). *See* Fed. Communications Comm'n, Public Notice, Consumer and Governmental Affairs Bureau Seeks Comment on Petition for Expedited Declaratory Ruling and Exemption from American Association of Health Care Administrative Management n.7 (Dec. 17, 2014), *available at* www.fcc.gov ("HIPAA-covered autodialed or prerecorded calls to a wireless number are exempt from the written consent requirement. See 47 C.F.R. § 64.1200(a)(2). These calls are still covered by the general consent requirement in 64.1200(a)(1).").

125 *In re* Rules & Regulations Implementing the Tel. Consumer Prot. Act of 1991, 27 F.C.C. Rcd. 1830, ¶ 28, 2012 WL 507959 (F.C.C. 2012). *See* § 6.3.4.1, *supra.*

126 47 C.F.R. § 64.1200(a)(2) (requiring express written consent for prerecorded or autodialed advertising and telemarketing calls to cell phones).

127 Meyer v. Portfolio Recovery Associates, L.L.C., 707 F.3d 1036, 1042 (9th Cir. 2012) (number need not be provided at time of application but must be provided before the call is placed). *Accord* Charvat v. Allstate Corp., 29 F. Supp. 3d 1147 (N.D. Ill. Mar. 5, 2014) ("prior" consent cannot be obtained during call).

128 Castro v. Green Tree Servicing, ___ F. Supp. 2d ___, 2013 WL 4105196 (S.D.N.Y. Aug. 14, 2013) (placing call from cell phone to creditor is not consent); *In re* Rules and Regulations Implementing the Telephone Consumer Protection Act of 1991, Request of ACA International for Clarification and Declaratory Ruling, 23 F.C.C.R. 559 n.34, 2008 WL 65485 (Jan. 4, 2008) ("The Commission also noted, however, that if a caller's number is 'captured' by a Caller ID or an ANI device without notice to the residential telephone subscriber, the caller cannot be considered to have given an invitation or permission to receive autodialer or prerecorded voice message calls.").

129 Meyer v. Portfolio Recovery Associates, L.L.C., 707 F.3d 1036, 1040 (9th Cir. 2012) (affirming preliminary injunction against autodialing cell phone numbers obtained through skip-tracing); Lardner v. Diversified Consultants Inc., 17 F. Supp. 3d 1215, 1224 (S.D. Fla. 2014).

130 Osorio v. State Farm Bank, 746 F.3d 1242 (11th Cir. 2014).

131 *See, e.g.*, King v. Time Warner Cable, ___ F. Supp. 3d ___, 2015 WL 4103689, at *5 (S.D.N.Y. July 7, 2015) (clause in cable company's terms of service agreement that it could call customer on the number provided, including autodialed or prerecorded calls, is consent to be mistakenly called for another customer's debt).

132 Toney v. Quality Resources, Inc., 75 F. Supp. 3d 727 (N.D. Ill. 2014).

133 Reardon v. Uber Technologies, Inc., ___ F. Supp. 3d ___, 2015 WL 4451209 (N.D. Cal. July 19, 2015) (denying motion to dismiss).

134 *In re* Rules & Regulations Implementing the Tel. Consumer Prot. Act of 1991 ¶ 75, CG Docket No. 02-278, WC Docket No. 07-135, 2015 WL 4387780, ___ F.C.C. ___ (July 10, 2015).

135 Toney v. Quality Resources, Inc., 75 F. Supp. 3d 727 (N.D. Ill. 2014).

136 Request of ACA International for Clarification and Declaratory Ruling ¶ 9, No. 02-278, FCC Release 07-232, 23 F.C.C. Rcd. 559, 565, 43 Comm. Reg. (P & F) 877, 2008 WL 65485 (Jan. 4, 2008). *Accord In re* Rules & Regulations Implementing the Tel. Consumer Prot. Act of 1991 ¶ 52, CG Docket No. 02-278, WC Docket No. 07-135, ___ F.C.C. ___, 2015 WL 4387780 (July 10, 2015) (reaffirming this position).

required by the statute.[137] Moreover, even if providing a number can be construed as consent to receive a call, it is hard to construe it as consent to receive autodialed or prerecorded calls.[138] Nonetheless, a number of courts have followed the FCC's ruling and held that provision of a cell phone number to a creditor is consent to be contacted by a debt collector regarding the debt.[139] As stated by one court, "the thrust of the FCC's Rulings is that a person need not specifically consent to be contacted using an autodialer or artificial or prerecorded voice. Rather, a person who knowingly provides his telephone number to a creditor in connection with a debt is agreeing to allow the creditor to contact him regarding his debt, regardless of the means."[140] The Eleventh Circuit applied this principle outside the debt collection context, holding that providing a cell phone number when donating blood was consent to receive text messages asking for more donations.[141] Another court held that furnishing a cell phone number to a credit reporting agency as part of a fraud alert authorizes potential creditors to use it to contact the consumer, because that is the purpose of a fraud alert.[142]

Even if providing a cell phone number can be construed as consent to receive certain robocalls, it should not be construed as consent to receive them on any and all topics. Thus, a second question should be whether, by providing a cell phone number, the consumer consented to the subject matter of the autodialed calls.[143] In 2012, the FCC stated:

> One commenter . . . appears to suggest that oral consent is sufficient to permit any autodialed or prerecorded calls to wireless numbers. It argues that its customers may orally provide their wireless phone number as a point of contact and therefore those customers expect *marketing* and service calls. We disagree. Consumers who provide a wireless phone number for a limited purpose—for service calls only—do not necessarily expect to receive telemarketing calls that go beyond the limited purpose for which oral consent regarding service calls may have been granted.[144]

---

137 *See* Reardon v. Uber Technologies, Inc., ___ F. Supp. 3d ___, 2015 WL 4451209, at *7 n.5 (N.D. Cal. July 19, 2015) (following FCC's interpretation, but disagreeing with it because providing a telephone number is at most implied rather than express consent); Zyburo v. NCSPlus, Inc., 44 F. Supp. 3d 500, 503 (S.D.N.Y. 2014) (patient's provision of telephone number to medical office in context wholly divorced from debt collection does "not appear to be tantamount to even implied consent to be robo-called by a third party about one's debt"); Lusskin v. Seminole Comedy, Inc., 2013 WL 3147339, at *3 (S.D. Fla. June 19, 2013) (concluding that FCC's order "deviates from the plain language of the statute"; providing cell phone number when buying a comedy show ticket was not consent to receive autodialed text messages promoting other shows when seller never told subscriber that it might send him autodialed text messages); Thrasher–Lyon v. CCS Commercial, 2012 WL 3835089, at *5 (N.D. Ill. Sept. 4, 2012) (treating FCC ruling as binding, but concluding that it goes beyond plain language of the TCPA, and refusing to apply it outside the context of a voluntary transaction giving rise to a debtor-creditor relationship). *See also* Mais v. Gulf Coast Collection Bureau, 944 F. Supp. 2d 1226, 1239 (S.D. Fla. 2013) ("The FCC's construction is inconsistent with the statute's plain language because it impermissibly amends the TCPA to provide an exception for 'prior express *or implied* consent' "), *rev'd*, 768 F.3d 1110 (11th Cir. 2014) (finding FCC's ruling incontestable under Hobbs Act). *But see* Hill v. Homeward Residential, Inc., 799 F.3d 544, 552 (6th Cir. 2015) (requirement that consumer consent specifically to receiving robocalls applies only to certain telemarketing calls; providing cell phone number to creditor is consent to receive robodialed collection robocalls even when it is silent about robodialing).

138 Thrasher–Lyon v. CCS Commercial, 2012 WL 3835089, at *3 (N.D. Ill. Sept. 4, 2012) (statute should be interpreted to require prior express consent to robocalls, not just to calls in general). *See also* Lusskin v. Seminole Comedy, Inc., 2013 WL 3147339, at *3 (S.D. Fla. June 19, 2013) (providing cell phone number insufficient when subscriber never gave express consent to be contacted through an autodialing system).

139 *See, e.g.*, Hill v. Homeward Residential, Inc., 799 F.3d 544 (6th Cir. 2015) (providing cell phone number to creditor, whether at the outset of transaction or later, is consent to receive collection robocalls); Mais v. Gulf Coast Collection Bureau, 768 F.3d 1110 (11th Cir. 2014) (finding FCC's ruling incontestable under Hobbs Act and holding that it applies to collection of medical debt, not just consumer credit; wife's provision of patient's cell phone number to hospital is sufficient consent); Johnson v. Credit Prot. Ass'n, L.P., 2012 WL 5875605 (S.D. Fla. Nov. 20, 2012) (providing cell phone number to creditor at outset of transaction is prior express consent); Conover v. Byl Collections Services, L.L.C., 2012 WL 4363740, at *6 (W.D.N.Y. Sept. 21, 2012) (providing cell phone number on credit application constitutes prior consent to be contacted at that number regarding debt).

140 Ranwick v. Texas Gila, L.L.C., 37 F. Supp. 3d 1053, 1058 (D. Minn. 2014). *Accord* Miller v. 3G Collect, L.L.C., 302 F.R.D. 333 (E.D. Pa.

2014); Hudson v. Sharp Healthcare, 2014 WL 2892290, at *6 (S.D. Cal. June 25, 2014).

141 Murphy v. DCI Biologicals Orland, L.L.C., 797 F.3d 1302 (11th Cir. 2015).

142 Greene v. DirecTV, Inc., 2010 WL 4628734 (N.D. Ill. Nov. 8, 2010).

143 *See, e.g.*, Zeidel v. YM LLC USA, 2015 WL 1910456 (N.D. Ill. Apr. 27, 2015) (provision of telephone number to sales clerk is not *carte blanche* to receive automated messages of any kind but is limited by facts surrounding consent); Toney v. Quality Resources, Inc., 75 F. Supp. 3d 727, 735–736, 739 (N.D. Ill. 2014) (providing cell number for an explicitly limited purpose—"Questions about your order"—is not consent to receive telemarketing calls about other products, including upselling calls made on pretext of confirming order); Zyburo v. NCSPlus, Inc., 44 F. Supp. 3d 500, 503 (S.D.N.Y. 2014) (patient's provision of telephone number to medical office in context wholly divorced from debt collection does "not appear to be tantamount to even implied consent to be robo-called by a third party about one's debt"); Kolinek v. Walgreen Co., 2014 WL 3056813, at *3 (N.D. Ill. July 7, 2014) (holding that plaintiff provided his phone number for identification purposes only and did not consent to receive phone calls, and that "turning over one's wireless number for the purpose of joining one particular private messaging group did not amount to consent for communications relating to something other than that particular group"). *See also* Nigro v. Mercantile Adjustment Bureau, L.L.C., 769 F.3d 804 (2d Cir. 2014) (man's provision of his cell phone number to utility company so that it could disconnect his deceased mother-in-law's service was not consent to receive calls about her unpaid bill because he did not provide phone number in connection with transaction created debt). *But cf.* Roberts v. Paypal, Inc., ___ Fed. Appx. ___, 2015 WL 6524840 (9th Cir. Oct. 29, 2015) (for pre-2012 call, to which FCC's 2012 and later orders did not apply, consent created by provision of cell phone number was not limited to problems regarding the transaction in question or to "normal business communications" when customer had not communicated that limitation).

144 *In re* Rules & Regulations Implementing the Tel. Consumer Prot. Act of 1991 ¶ 25, Report and Order, 27 F.C.C. Rcd. 1830, 1840, 2012 WL 507959 (Feb. 15, 2012) (emphasis in original).

The FCC reiterated this position in a 2015 declaratory ruling:

> By 'within the scope of consent given, and absent instructions to the contrary,' we mean that the call must be closely related to the purpose for which the telephone number was originally provided. For example, if a patient provided his phone number upon admission to a hospital for scheduled surgery, then calls pertaining to that surgery or follow-up procedures for that surgery would be closely related to the purpose for which the telephone number was originally provided.[145]

In a Second Circuit case, *Nigro v. Mercantile Adjustment Bureau, LLC*,[146] a utility company told a man that it needed his cell phone number in order to comply with his request that it disconnect his mother-in-law's utility service after she died. It then made 72 robocalls to his number to collect a $68 bill she owed. The court held that the man had not provided his number during the transaction that resulted in the debt owed. Instead, he provided the number long after the debt was incurred, and he was not in any way responsible for the debt. The court reversed the district court's holding that the man had consented to receive the calls by providing his cell phone number.

When there was a series of similar transactions such as visits to a medical provider, a court held that providing a cell number in connection with one is effective for later transactions.[147] The later calls need not be for the exact purpose for which the number is provided, as long as they "bear some relation to the product or service for which the number was provided."[148] On the other hand, the cell phone number may not be used for marketing[149] or collecting for[150] a different product or service.

6.3.4.3 Consent of the Called Party Is Required; Reassigned Numbers

The TCPA requires that the caller have the consent of the "called party" to make an autodialed or prerecorded call to a cell phone.[151] The FCC has specifically stated that the called party is not the intended recipient but the actual current subscriber or customary user.[152] Accordingly, consent must be given by the person who presently subscribes to or uses the cell phone.[153] Thus, a non-debtor who receives an autodialed or prerecorded collection call on a cell phone has standing to bring a TCPA claim.[154] For example, if a debt collector places automated calls to a cell number that has been reassigned to someone other than the debtor, consent given by the debtor is not effective.[155]

Under the FCC's 2015 omnibus ruling, a caller is permitted to make one wrong number call to a party who has not consented to be called after the number is reassigned, so long as the caller does not have actual knowledge of the reassignment.[156] Private vendors offer services to check whether a cell

---

145 *In re* Rules & Regulations Implementing the Tel. Consumer Prot. Act of 1991 ¶ 47 n.474, CG Docket No. 02-278, WC Docket No. 07-135, 2015 WL 4387780, ___ F.C.C. ___ (July 10, 2015). *But cf. id.* at § 52 (stating that, "[f]or non-telemarketing and non-advertising calls, express consent can be demonstrated by the called party giving prior express oral or written consent, or in the absence of instructions to the contrary, by giving his or her wireless number to the person initiating the autodialed or prerecorded call"; this more general statement, made in the context of a different question, should be viewed as shorthand summary of consent requirements, not a repudiation of more specific statement in ¶ 47).

146 Nigro v. Mercantile Adjustment Bureau, L.L.C., 769 F.3d 804 (2d Cir. 2014). *See also* Letter from FCC Gen. Counsel to Clerk, Second Cir. Ct. of Appeals, in Nigro v. Mercantile Adjustment Bureau, 2014 WL 2959062 (F.C.C. June 30, 2014) ("Although Nigro presumably consented to receive calls regarding the termination of service to the Thomas residence by providing his cell phone number to National Grid in connection with his request to terminate that service, under the ACA Order that consent did not extend to debt collection calls with respect to debts that did not arise 'during the transaction' in which Nigro provided his number").

147 Hudson v. Sharp Healthcare, 2014 WL 2892290 (S.D. Cal. June 25, 2014) (visit to hospital; "the Court is not persuaded by Plaintiff's argument that there was no prior express consent because her cellular telephone number 'autopopulated' " from prior visit).

148 *Id.*

149 Connelly v. Hilton Grant Vacations, L.L.C., 2012 WL 2129364 (S.D. Cal. June 11, 2012).

150 Moise v. Credit Control Services, Inc., 950 F. Supp. 2d 1251 (S.D. Fla. 2011) (giving cell phone number to doctor does not authorize autodialed

calls by collector for medical laboratory that performed tests ordered by doctor).

151 47 U.S.C. § 227(b)(1)(A).

152 *In re* Rules & Regulations Implementing the Tel. Consumer Prot. Act of 1991 ¶ 73, CG Docket No. 02-278, WC Docket No. 07-135, 2015 WL 4387780, ___ F.C.C. ___ (July 10, 2015) ("We find that the 'called party' is the subscriber, i.e., the consumer assigned the telephone number dialed and billed for the call, or the non-subscriber customary user of a telephone number included in a family or business calling plan. Both such individuals can give prior express consent to be called at that number. Thus, with the limited exception discussed below, calls to reassigned wireless numbers violate the TCPA when a previous subscriber, not the current subscriber or customary user, provided the prior express consent on which the call is based.")

153 Breslow v. Wells Fargo Bank, 755 F.3d 1265 (11th Cir. 2014); Osorio v. State Farm Bank, 746 F.3d 1242 (11th Cir. 2014); Soppet v. Enhanced Recovery Co., L.L.C., 679 F.3d 637 (7th Cir. 2012); Moore v. DISH Network L.L.C., 57 F. Supp. 3d 639, 648–650 (N.D. W. Va. 2014) (any person or entity can bring claim, and "called party" does not refer solely to intended recipient); Zyburo v. NCSPlus, Inc., 44 F. Supp. 3d 500, 504 (S.D.N.Y. 2014); Olney v. Progressive Cas. Ins. Co., 993 F. Supp. 2d 1220 (S.D. Cal. 2014); Fini v. DISH Network, L.L.C., 955 F. Supp. 2d 1288 (M.D. Fla. 2013); Harris v. World Fin. Network Nat'l Bank, 867 F. Supp. 2d 888 (E.D. Mich. 2012); D.G. v. William W. Siegel & Associates, 791 F. Supp. 2d 622, 625 (N.D. Ill. 2011); Kane v. Nat'l Action Fin. Services, 2011 WL 6018403 (E.D. Mich. Nov. 7, 2011); Tang v. Medical Recovery Specialists, L.L.C., 2011 WL 6019221, at *3 (N.D. Ill. July 7, 2011) (actual recipient is "called party" and has standing to sue).

154 Osorio v. State Farm Bank, F.S.B., 746 F.3d 1242 (11th Cir. 2014); Soppet v. Enhanced Recovery Co., L.L.C., 679 F.3d 637, 640 (7th Cir. 2012); Swope v. Credit Mgmt., L.P., 2013 WL 607830 (E.D. Mo. Feb. 19, 2013).

155 Breslow v. Wells Fargo Bank, 755 F.3d 1265 (11th Cir. 2014); Osorio v. State Farm Bank, 746 F.3d 1242 (11th Cir. 2014); Soppet v. Enhanced Recovery Co., L.L.C., 679 F.3d 637 (7th Cir. 2012); King v. Time Warner Cable, ___ F. Supp. 3d ___, 2015 WL 4103689 (S.D.N.Y. July 7, 2015); Kane v. Nat'l Action Fin. Services, Inc., 2011 WL 6018403 (E.D. Mich. Nov. 7, 2011).

156 *In re* Rules & Regulations Implementing the Tel. Consumer Prot. Act of 1991 ¶ 91, CG Docket No. 02-278, WC Docket No. 07-135, 2015 WL 4387780, ___ F.C.C. ___ (July 10, 2015).

phone number has been reassigned.[157] The caller always has the burden of proving it had the requisite consent to call the person called, even after a number has been reassigned.[158]

6.3.4.4 Revocation of Consent

Consent may be revoked at any time, in any reasonable way. In 2015 the FCC issued a declaratory ruling that reiterated this specifically:

> Consumers have a right to revoke consent, using any reasonable method including orally or in writing. Consumers generally may revoke, for example, by way of a consumer-initiated call, directly in response to a call initiated or made by a caller, or at an in-store bill payment location, among other possibilities . . . . We conclude that callers may not abridge a consumer's right to revoke consent using any reasonable method.[159]

The caller cannot designate the exclusive means by which the consumer must revoke consent.[160] Moreover, the Commission emphasized that, "regardless of the means by which a caller obtains consent, under longstanding Commission precedent," if any question arises as to whether prior express consent was provided by a call recipient, the burden is on the caller to prove that it obtained the necessary prior express consent.[161]

The FCC's 2015 pronouncement followed on the heels of a similar conclusion by the Third Circuit.[162] The Third Circuit concluded the following:

1. A 2012 FCC ruling[163] that a consumer may "fully revoke" her prior express consent by transmitting an opt-out request to the sending party was entitled to deference.

2. Congress intended to use the common law concept of "consent," which is revocable.[164]

3. The TCPA is a remedial statute that was passed to protect consumers from unwanted automated telephone calls.[165]

4. There is no indication in the legislative history that Congress intended for the statute to limit a consumer's rights by imposing a temporal restriction on the right to revoke prior express consent.

5. A contract provision authorizing automated phone calls may not preclude revocation of consent because "the ability to use an autodialing system to contact a debtor is plainly not an essential term to a credit agreement."

6. Callers have a continuing responsibility to check the accuracy of their records to ensure that they are not inadvertently calling mobile numbers.[166]

The Eleventh Circuit[167] and subsequent lower court decisions have followed the Third Circuit.[168]

The FCC's 2015 declaratory ruling makes clear that any statement in which "the called party clearly express[es] his or her desire not to receive further calls" is sufficient to show revocation.[169] It also clarifies that revocation may be oral.[170] The Eleventh Circuit and several other courts took this position

---

157 *See id.* at ¶¶ 84, 86 (listing methods callers have to learn of reassigned numbers).

158 *In re* Rules & Regulations Implementing the Tel. Consumer Prot. Act of 1991 ¶ 85, CG Docket No. 02-278, WC Docket No. 07-135, 2015 WL 4387780, ___ F.C.C. ___ (July 10, 2015) ("The caller, and not the called party, bears the burden of demonstrating: (1) that he had a reasonable to basis to believe he had consent to make the call, and (2) that he did not have actual or constructive knowledge of reassignment prior to or at the time of this one-additional-call window we recognize as an opportunity for callers to discover reassignment.")

159 *In re* Rules & Regulations Implementing the Tel. Consumer Prot. Act of 1991 ¶ 64, CG Docket No. 02-278, WC Docket No. 07-135, 2015 WL 4387780, ___ F.C.C. ___ (July 10, 2015). *See* King v. Time Warner Cable, ___ F. Supp. 3d ___, 2015 WL 4103689, at *5 (S.D.N.Y. July 7, 2015) (applying FCC's 2015 declaratory ruling; consumer's revocation, communicated to caller, was effective).

160 *In re* Rules & Regulations Implementing the Tel. Consumer Prot. Act of 1991 ¶ 63, CG Docket No. 02-278, WC Docket No. 07-135, 2015 WL 4387780, ___ F.C.C. ___ (July 10, 2015).

161 *Id.* at ¶ 58.

162 Gager v. Dell Fin. Services, L.L.C., 727 F.3d 265 (3d Cir. 2013), *rev'g* Gager v. Dell Fin. Services, L.L.C., 2012 WL 1942079 (M.D. Pa. May 29, 2012).

163 *In re* Rules and Regulations Implementing the Telephone Consumer Protection Act of 1991, SoundBite Communications, Inc. ¶ 11 n.47, 27 F.C.C. Rcd. 15391 (Nov. 26, 2012). *See also id.* at ¶ 7 (stating that consumer may "request that no further text messages be sent"); *id.* at ¶ 13 (noting that consumer may opt out of receiving voice calls after prior express consent has been given); *id.* at ¶ 15 (suggesting that, after

consumer has received text messages, she may then send request for those messages to stop at any time).

164 Gager v. Dell Fin. Services, L.L.C., 727 F.3d 265, 270–272 (3d Cir. 2013). *See also* Adamcik v. Credit Control Services, Inc., 832 F. Supp. 2d 744 (W.D. Tex. 2011) (holding that consent is revocable and relying on common law meaning of "consent").

165 *See* S. Rep. 102-178, at 5 (1991), *reprinted in* 1991 U.S.C.C.A.N. 1968, 1972. *See also* Satterfield v. Simon & Schuster, Inc., 569 F.3d 946, 954 (June 19, 2009) (discussing TCPA's purpose of curbing calls that are a nuisance and an invasion of privacy); SoundBite, 27 F.C.C. Rcd. at 15391-92 ¶ 2 (discussing TCPA's purpose of protecting consumers against unwanted contact from automated dialing systems).

166 *See In re* Rules and Regulations Implementing the Telephone Consumer Protection Act of 1991, 19 F.C.C. Rcd. 19215, 19219-20 ¶ 11 (Sept. 21, 2004) (declining to extend safe harbor provisions to calls made erroneously or inadvertently to wireless numbers). *See also* Breslow v. Wells Fargo Bank, 857 F. Supp. 2d 1316, 1322 (S.D. Fla. 2012) ("[C]ompanies who make automated calls bear the responsibility of regularly checking the accuracy of their account records[.]"), *aff'd*, 755 F.3d 1265 (11th Cir. 2014).

167 Osorio v. State Farm Bank, 746 F.3d 1242 (11th Cir. 2014) .

168 Conklin v. Wells Fargo Bank, N.A., 2013 WL 6409731 (M.D. Fla. Dec. 9, 2013); Munro v. King Broad. Co., 2013 WL 6185233 (W.D. Wash. Nov. 26, 2013).

169 *In re* Rules & Regulations Implementing the Tel. Consumer Prot. Act of 1991 ¶ 67, CG Docket No. 02-278, WC Docket No. 07-135, 2015 WL 4387780, ___ F.C.C. ___ (July 10, 2015). *See* Morris v. Ocwen Loan Servicing, L.L.C., 2015 WL 5072011 (S.D. Fla. Aug. 24, 2015) (allowing consumer to proceed to trial on question whether revocation of consent set forth in a qualified written request sent to mortgage servicer, and repeated in a telephone call, was effective); Reardon v. Uber Technologies, Inc., ___ F. Supp. 3d ___, 2015 WL 4451209, at *10 (N.D. Cal. July 19, 2015) (applying FCC declaratory ruling; consent can be revoked in any reasonable manner)

170 *In re* Rules & Regulations Implementing the Tel. Consumer Prot. Act of 1991 ¶¶ 64, 70, CG Docket No. 02-278, WC Docket No. 07-135, 2015 WL 4387780, ___ F.C.C. ___ (July 10, 2015).

even before the FCC's ruling.[171] Earlier decisions that required the consumer to give written notice in accordance with the Fair Debt Collection Practices Act[172] to revoke consent to receive debt collection calls[173] should no longer be considered good law in light of these developments. Of course, written notice by means providing proof of receipt is preferable from the standpoint of proof.

When debt collection calls are involved, notice to the caller that the consumer has filed a bankruptcy petition is revocation of consent to make collection calls.[174] Revocation of consent is also accomplished when a law firm sends a creditor a letter stating that it represents an alleged debtor and that all calls regarding the debt should be directed to it.[175]

Recently, creditors have begun inserting provisions in form agreements purporting to authorize the use of automated equipment to contact consumers at any number furnished by the consumer or otherwise obtained by the creditor. Under *Gager*, this consent can be revoked.[176] By entering into a contractual relationship with a seller, a consumer does not waive the right to revoke consent to receive autodialed or prerecorded cell phone calls.[177]

Several decisions hold that consumers who revoke their consent to text messaging may be sent a final "confirmatory text message" confirming receipt of a recipient's unsubscribe request.[178] The FCC has also adopted this interpretation.[179]

6.3.4.5 No Established Business Relationship Exception

In contrast to the TCPA provisions dealing with junk faxes, there is no exception for autodialed or prerecorded calls to cell phone numbers of persons with whom the caller has an established business relationship.[180] The consent requirements described in the preceding subsections apply regardless of the existence of an established business relationship.[181]

6.3.5 Private Remedies; Who May Sue

The restrictions on autodialed or prerecorded calls to cell phones and other sensitive numbers are part of section 227(b) of the TCPA. Section 227(b) includes its own private right of action.[182] In contrast to the private cause of action for violating the do-not-call portion of the TCPA, even the first call that violates the restrictions on autodialed or prerecorded calls is actionable, and there is no defense for reasonable procedures.[183] Remedies for a prevailing plaintiff are the greater of actual damages or $500 per violation, and these damages can be trebled for knowing or willful violations.[184] Continuing to call a cell phone number after the consumer has told the caller that it is a wrong number establishes knowledge and willfulness.[185]

The person subscribing to the number called at the time a robocall is placed has standing to enforce the prohibition on robocalling, even if the call is a "wrong party" collection call.[186] The owner of a cell phone also has standing to sue for calls made while the phone was in the possession of an investigator hired by his attorney.[187] A subscriber may be the called party even if the subscriber's business shares the line.[188] Receipt of an unwanted call is actionable even if the plaintiff does not pay for the call.[189]

171 Osorio v. State Farm Bank, F.S.B., 746 F.3d 1242 (11th Cir. 2014); Adamcik v. Credit Control Services, Inc., 832 F. Supp. 2d 744 (W.D. Tex. 2011); Gutierrez v. Barclays Grp., 2011 WL 579238, at *4 (S.D. Cal. Feb. 9, 2011).

172 15 U.S.C. § 1692c(c).

173 Moore v. Firstsource Advantage, L.L.C., 2011 WL 4345703, at *30–31 (W.D.N.Y. Sept. 15, 2011); Moltz v. Firstsource Advantage, L.L.C., 2011 WL 3360010, at *5 (W.D.N.Y. Aug. 3, 2011); Cunningham v. Credit Mgmt., L.P., 2010 WL 3791104, at *5 (N.D. Tex. Aug. 30, 2010), *adopted by* 2010 WL 3791049 (N.D. Tex. Sept. 27, 2010); Starkey v. Firstsource Advantage, L.L.C., 2010 WL 2541756, at *6 (W.D.N.Y. Mar. 11, 2010), *adopted by* 2010 WL 2541731 (W.D.N.Y. June 21, 2010).

174 *In re* Hammond, 2014 WL 2761260 (Bankr. N.D. Tex. June 18, 2014).

175 Miceli v. Orange Lake Country Club, Inc., 2015 WL 5081621 (M.D. Fla. Aug. 5, 2015), *available at* www.nclc.org/unreported.

176 Gager v. Dell Fin. Services, L.L.C., 727 F.3d 265, 273–274 (3d Cir. 2013).

177 *Id.* at 274.

178 Ibey v. Taco Bell Corp., 2012 WL 2401972 (S.D. Cal. June 18, 2012) (when consumer sent a text message in response to defendant's invitation to complete a survey, then sent "STOP" message requesting that defendant cease sending him text messages, defendant's "single, confirmatory text message did not constitute unsolicited telemarketing" and therefore was not "an invasion of privacy contemplated by Congress in enacting the TCPA"). *Accord* Ryabyshchuk v. Citibank (South Dakota), 2012 WL 5379143 (S.D. Cal. Oct. 30, 2012).

179 *In re* Rules and Regulations Implementing the Telephone Consumer Protection Act of 1991, SoundBite Communications, Inc., Petition for Expedited Declaratory Ruling, CG Docket No. 02-278, FCC 12-143, 2012 FCC LEXIS 4874 (Nov. 29, 2012) (allowing organizations that send text messages to consumers from whom they have obtained prior express consent to continue practice of sending a final, one-time text to confirm receipt of a consumer's opt out request).

180 47 C.F.R. § 64.1200(a)(1).

181 *See* Gager v. Dell Fin. Services, L.L.C., 727 F.3d 265, 273 (3d Cir. 2013) (exemption in 47 C.F.R. § 64.1200(a)(2)(iii), (iv) to calls "made to any person with whom the caller has an established business relationship" and calls "made for a commercial purpose [that do] not include or introduce an unsolicited advertisement or constitute a telephone solicitation" apply only to autodialed calls made to land-lines); Zehala v. Am. Express, 2011 WL 4484297 (S.D. Ohio Sept. 26, 2011) (established business relationship exception inapplicable to calls to cell phones); Bentley v. Bank of Am., 773 F. Supp. 2d 1367 (S.D. Fla. Mar. 23, 2011) (declining to hold that established business relationship exception applies to autodialed or artificial voice calls to cell phones for debt collection purposes).

182 47 U.S.C. § 227(b)(3).

183 *See* §§ 6.9.1, 6.9.6, *supra.*

184 *See* §§ 6.9.2.1–6.9.2.3, *supra.*

185 Moore v. DISH Network L.L.C., 57 F. Supp. 3d 639, 657 (N.D. W. Va. 2014).

186 *See generally* § 6.3.4.3, *supra* (reassigned numbers).

187 Moore v. DISH Network L.L.C., 57 F. Supp. 3d 639, 648–650 (N.D. W. Va. 2014).

188 Thomas v. Dun & Bradstreet Credibility Corp., ___ F. Supp. 3d ___, 2015 WL 4698398, at *4 (C.D. Cal. Aug. 5, 2015).

189 De Los Santos v. Millward Brown, Inc., 2014 WL 2938605 (S.D. Fla. June 30, 2014). *See also* § 6.9.3.1, *infra* (Article III standing).

A person who carries and regularly uses a cell phone and who receives unwanted calls has standing to sue even if another person's name is on the bill.[190] Even if the right to sue is limited to subscribers, this term may include users whose names are not on the bill, as cellular customer agreements often refer to other "subscribers" on the contracting subscriber's plan.

Issues regarding TCPA litigation that are generally applicable to all its substantive prohibitions are discussed in § 6.9, *infra*.

6.3.6 Investigating and Documenting TCPA Cell Phone Cases

Prior express consent is often the definitive issue in a robocall case. The consumer may have provided a cell phone number at some point in the relationship with the caller or the caller's predecessor. Or there may have been an obscure provision in a document the consumer signed that the caller will argue amounts to prior express consent to receive autodialed and prerecorded calls. The consumer should be questioned in detail about how the caller might have gotten the consumer's cell phone number and should be asked to search for any documents that might constitute consent. Any basis on which the caller claims to have consent should be flushed out through discovery at the earliest possible point.

Whether or not the consumer remembers providing the cell phone number or consenting to receive robocalls, the consumer should immediately revoke any consent that may have been given and demand that the calls stop. The consumer should be advised to do so both orally and in writing by certified mail

with return receipt. The caller will not be able to claim consent for calls that continue after the consumer asks them to stop. In addition, it will be easier to establish willfulness or knowledge for the calls made after the consumer asked that the calls stop.[191]

Identifying the caller is another key issue. The caller's postal address is necessary in order to give written revocation of consent and will be necessary to investigate the caller's collectability and to serve process. It is common for consumers to have received only calls, not written correspondence. Callers may be reluctant to give out their addresses, particularly if they know they are violating the TCPA. The consumer should be instructed to ask callers for the full name and address of the entity on whose behalf they are calling. In the case of a collection call, one strategy is for the consumer to ask for a postal address in order to mail a paper check or money order in case he or she decides to make a payment. (The consumer should be prepared for the collector to press for telephone authorization for an electronic debit from the consumer's bank account). If these methods of identifying the caller do not work, people with expertise in the technical aspects of telecommunications may be able to provide ways to trace the call.

Consumers should be asked to keep a log of calls they receive, including the date and time of the call, the number from which the call was made as shown on the consumer's caller ID, the name of the caller and the company, any contact information the consumer was able to obtain, and the content of the call. They should also keep records of any charges they incur for the calls under their cell phone plans.

Consumers often undercount the number of calls they have received. Since the statute prohibits *making* autodialed or prerecorded calls to a cell phone without the prior express consent of the called party, regardless of whether the consumer answered the call,[192] and damages are available on a per-call basis, it is important to identify all calls that have been made. The calls that the consumer has actually answered are likely the tip of an iceberg. The consumer should obtain his or her phone carrier's records of all calls made. In addition, once suit is filed, formal discovery directed to the caller and the caller's carriers may produce records of even more calls. Discovery along these lines can require technical expertise.

If the caller is uncollectable or cannot be identified, the consumer should be encouraged to file a complaint with the FCC. The FCC offers an easy online complaint form.[193]

---

190 Gesten v. Stewart Law Grp., L.L.C., 67 F. Supp. 3d 1356 (S.D. Fla. 2014) (plaintiff need not be "called party" or charged for call to assert a TCPA claim); Olney v. Progressive Cas. Ins. Co., 993 F. Supp. 2d 1220 (S.D. Cal. 2014) ("Defendant's position that only the intended recipient has standing to bring a claim under the TCPA has been squarely rejected in no less than twenty cases"); Olney v. Job.com, Inc., 2013 WL 5476813 (E.D. Cal. Sept. 30, 2013) (evidence that plaintiff was not subscriber to his telephone line did not undermine statutory standing); Page v. Regions Bank, 917 F. Supp. 2d 1214 (N.D. Ala. 2012) (plaintiff was "subscriber" when he was "the regular user and carrier of the cellular telephone, as well as the person who need[ed] the telephone line to receive other calls," despite the phone not being registered to him); Breslow v. Wells Fargo Bank, N.A., 857 F. Supp. 2d 1316 (S.D. Fla. 2012), *aff'd*, 755 F.3d 1265 (11th Cir. 2014); Agne v. Papa John's Int'l, Inc., 286 F.R.D. 559, 565 (W.D. Wash. 2012) (authorized user of shared cell phone plan who is intended recipient of text message has standing even though her ex-husband is primary account holder); D.G. v. William W. Siegel & Associates, 791 F. Supp. 2d 622 (N.D. Ill. 2011) (plaintiff is a "called party" if caller intends to call plaintiff's number, plaintiff receives calls, and plaintiff is regular user and carrier of phone); Kane v. Nat'l Action Fin. Services, 2011 WL 6018403 (E.D. Mich. Nov. 7, 2011); Tang v. Med. Recovery Specialists, L.L.C., 2011 WL 6019221, at *3 (N.D. Ill. July 7, 2011) (finding "called party" was actual recipient). *Cf.* Soppet v. Enhanced Recovery Co., L.L.C., 679 F.3d 637, 640 (7th Cir. 2012) (defining "subscriber" in *dicta* as "the person who pays the bills or needs the line in order to receive other calls"). *But see* Jamison v. First Credit Services, Inc., 2013 WL 3872171 (N.D. Ill. July 29, 2013) (when plaintiff was using his mother's cell phone, he is not subscriber and cannot sue).

191 *See* § 6.9.2.3, *infra* (willfulness or knowledge as a requirement for treble damages).

192 *See* § 6.3.3, *supra*.

193 Fed. Communications Comm'n, Compaint Form, *available at* https://consumercomplaints.fcc.gov.

6.4   Prerecorded Calls to Residential Lines

6.4.1   General

The TCPA prohibits placing a call that uses an artificial or prerecorded voice to a residential telephone line.[194] When Congress adopted this provision, it found that:

> [b]anning such automated or prerecorded telephone calls to the home, except when the receiving party consents to receiving the call or when such calls are necessary in an emergency situation affecting the health and safety of the consumer, is the only effective means of protecting telephone consumers from this nuisance and privacy invasion.[195]

Because of a series of exceptions, this prohibition applies primarily to telemarketing calls.[196]

Unlike the provision dealing with cell phones,[197] this TCPA provision does not prohibit the use of autodialers to make live calls to a consumer's residence. As a result, it does not prevent telemarketing calls generally—just those using a prerecorded message. The FTC Telemarketing Sales Rule has a similar provision, which is not limited to calls to a residence but is limited to prerecorded calls by telemarketers.[198]

A live telemarketing call is prohibited if the residence's number is on the general do-not-call registry or the caller's company-specific do-not-call list.[199] But even if the phone number is not listed on those lists, the caller still cannot use a prerecorded message.[200]

6.4.2   Exceptions

The TCPA exempts calls made with the called party's prior express consent and calls for emergency purposes.[201] It also gives the FCC authority to exempt calls that are either not for a commercial purpose[202] or are for commercial purpose but will not adversely affect the privacy of the called parties and do not include unsolicited advertisements.[203] Taken together, the statute and the FCC rule create six exceptions to the prohibition of prerecorded calls to a residence:

- The caller has the prior express written consent of the called party;[204]
- The call is made for emergency purposes;[205]
- The call is not for a commercial purpose;[206]
- The call is a commercial call but does not include or introduce an advertisement or constitute telemarketing;[207]
- The call is made by or on behalf of a tax-exempt nonprofit;[208]
- The call delivers a "health care" message by a "covered entity" or its "business associate" as those terms are defined by the HIPAA Privacy Rule.[209]

The overall result of these exceptions is that the primary application of the prohibition is to telemarketing calls.

The FTC Telemarketing Sales Rule has similar exceptions.[210] However, it has no exception for calls made by a for-profit telemarketer on behalf of a nonprofit, so the FTC rule applies to prerecorded calls made on behalf of nonprofits when the FCC rule does not.[211] Prerecorded calls that one or more of the FCC or FTC exceptions allow still must disclose certain information.[212]

On November 2, 2015, the statute was amended by an appropriations bill to exempt calls "made solely pursuant to the collection of a debt owed to or guaranteed by the United States."[213] Since the FCC's rules already exempt commercial calls that do not include or introduce an advertisement or constitute telemarketing,[214] it does not appear that this amendment expands significantly upon the scope of the existing exceptions. An uncodified provision of the bill requires the FCC to adopt rules implementing this amendment within nine months after enactment.[215] Online updates to this treatise will address developments regarding this amendment.

At one time the FCC made an exception for calls made by a caller with an established business relationship with the called party.[216] That exception was eliminated in 2012, effective

---

194   47 U.S.C. § 227(b)(1)(B); 47 C.F.R. § 64.1200(a)(3).

195   Pub. L. 102–243, § 2, ¶ 12, 105 Stat. 2394 (1991). *See also* Leyse v. Bank of Am., ___ F.3d ___, 2015 WL 5946456, at *6 (3d Cir. Oct. 14, 2015) ("in passing the Act, Congress was animated by 'outrage[ ] over the proliferation' of prerecorded telemarketing calls to private residences, which consumers regarded as 'an intrusive invasion of privacy' and 'a nuisance.' ").

196   *See* § 6.4.2, *infra.*

197   *See* § 6.3, *supra.*

198   16 C.F.R. § 310.4(b)(1)(v).

199   *See* §§ 6.5.1, 6.5.2, *infra.*

200   State *ex rel.* Charvat v. Frye, 868 N.E.2d 270 (Ohio 2007).

201   47 U.S.C. § 227(b)(1)(B).

202   47 U.S.C. § 227(b)(2)(B)(i).

203   47 U.S.C. § 227(b)(2)(B)(ii).

204   47 C.F.R. § 64.1200(a)(3).

205   47 C.F.R. § 64.1200(a)(3)(i). *See also* 47 U.S.C. § 227(b)(1)(B).

206   47 C.F.R. § 64.1200(a)(3)(ii).

207   47 C.F.R. § 64.1200(a)(3)(iii).

208   47 C.F.R. § 64.1200(a)(3)(iv).

209   47 C.F.R. § 64.1200(a)(3)(v), *adopted by In re* Rules and Regulations Implementing the Telephone Consumer Protection Act of 1991 ¶¶ 57-65, 27 F.C.C. Rcd. 1830 (F.C.C.), 27 F.C.C.R. 1830, 55 Communications Reg. (P&F) 356, 2012 WL 507959 (Feb. 15, 2012).

210   16 C.F.R. § 310.4(b)(1)(v)(A) exempts calls with an express agreement in writing. Section 310.4(b)(1)(v)(D) exempts calls similar to the FCC's health care call exception. By limiting the FTC rule's scope to actions by telemarketers, it effectively excludes emergency calls and calls that are not for a commercial purpose or that do not introduce an advertisement or constitute telemarketing.

211   *See* § 5.2.3, *supra.*

212   *See* § 6.4.3, *infra.*

213   Pub. L. No. 114-74, § 301 (Nov. 2, 2015) (amending 47 U.S.C. § 227(b)(1)(B)).

214   47 C.F.R. § 64.1200(a)(3)(iii).

215   Pub. L. No. 114-74, § 301 (Nov. 2, 2015) ("Not later than 9 months after the date of enactment of this Act, the Federal Communications Commission, in consultation with the Department of Treasury, shall prescribe regulations to implement the amendments made by this section").

216   *See* 47 C.F.R. § 64.1200(f)(5) (defining "established business relationship"); Cubbage v. Talbots, Inc., 2010 WL 2710628 (W.D. Wash. July 7, 2010) (refusing to review validity of FCC rule allowing artificial voice calls if established business relationship exists; also holding that, if

---

October 16, 2013.[217] In addition, prior to that revision, the FCC's exception for consent was broader, applying to any prior express consent, even if it was not in writing. Now the consent must be in writing.[218] Prior express written consent is a defined term in the FCC regulations, meaning a signed agreement in writing clearly authorizing the seller to send solicitations using prerecorded voices to a designated phone number.[219] The writing must identify the number to which the signatory authorizes the calls to be made.[220] It must also disclose that agreeing to the recorded messages is not a precondition to purchasing the goods or services.[221]

The signature requirement can be met by an electronic or digital signature if federal and state law allow.[222] Obtaining consent during the call—for example, by asking the consumer to press numbers on the telephone keypad to hear a message—is insufficient.[223] In the similar context of autodialed or artificial voice calls to cell phones, courts have held that written consent can be revoked orally.[224]

The prohibition of prerecorded calls to a residence applies even to a call that contains free offers and information about goods and services that are commercially available.[225] The call is for a commercial purpose, and it constitutes telemarketing or an advertisement. The same is true of a call that purports to be a survey but that is preliminary to a sales call.[226] Even if such a call cannot be termed an advertisement because it does not mention the product being promoted, it constitutes

telemarketing if its intent is to promote the product.[227] Dual purpose "courtesy" calls to reward program members that encourage recipients to engage in future purchasing activity are also covered as solicitations, because neither the statute nor the regulations require an explicit mention of a good, product, or service when the implication is clear from the context.[228]

Debt collection calls to residential landlines are not subject to the FCC's restrictions on prerecorded calls because they do not transmit unsolicited advertisements or fall within the FCC's definition of telemarketing.[229] Telemarketing is defined in the FCC rule as the initiation of a telephone call or message for the purpose of encouraging the purchase or rental of, or investment in, property, goods, or services.[230] Nor do debt collection calls fall within the FTC rule, which applies only to telemarketing.[231] In addition, at the end of October 2015, as this chapter was being finalized, it appeared that the statute would be amended by an appropriations bill to require the FCC to adopt rules to create a specific exception for calls that were solely for the purpose of collecting debt owed to or guaranteed by the U.S. government.

6.4.3 Required Disclosures for All Prerecorded Calls

All artificial or prerecorded messages must at the beginning of the message state clearly the identity of the individual or other entity responsible for initiating the call.[232] In addition, during or after the message, the call must state the telephone number of the business, individual, or other entity that initiated the call.[233] The number cannot be a 900-number or any other number for which charges exceed local or long-distance transmission charges.[234]

---

caller has established business relationship exception with one member of a household, artificial voice calls are allowed even if another person answers). *See also* Schneider v. Susquehanna Radio Corp., 581 S.E.2d 603 (Ga. Ct. App. 2003) (no violation when consumer was enrolled in discount club operated by caller, even though call transmitted an unsolicited advertisement); Kaplan v. First City Mortg., 701 N.Y.S.2d 859 (N.Y. City Ct. 1999) (listing one's number in telephone directory does not constitute express consent).

217 Report and Order, *In re* Rules and Regulations Implementing the Telephone Consumer Protection Act of 1991, 27 F.C.C.R. 1830, 2012 WL 507959 (F.C.C. Feb. 15, 2012) (deleting former subsection (a)(2)(iv) of 47 C.F.R. § 64.1200).

218 47 C.F.R. § 64.1200(a)(3).

219 47 C.F.R. § 64.1200(f)(8).

220 47 C.F.R. § 64.1200(f)(8).

221 47 C.F.R. § 64.1200(f)(8)(i)(B).

222 47 C.F.R. § 64.1200(f)(8)(ii).

223 Margulis v. P & M Consulting, Inc., 121 S.W.3d 246 (Mo. Ct. App. 2003); Report and Order, *In re* Rules and Regulations Implementing the Telephone Consumer Protection Act of 1991, at 142, 18 F.C.C. Rcd. 14014, 2003 WL 21517853 (F.C.C. July 3, 2003). *See also* Reichenbach v. Chung Holdings, L.L.C., 823 N.E.2d 29 (Ohio Ct. App. 2004) (call is an advertisement even though it only asked recipient to press a keypad number for more information).

224 *See* § 6.3.4.4, *supra*.

225 Charvat v. Crawford, 799 N.E.2d 661 (Ohio Ct. App. 2003); Report and Order, *In re* Rules and Regulations Implementing the Telephone Consumer Protection Act of 1991, 18 F.C.C. Rcd. 14014 ¶¶139–141, 2003 WL 21517853 (F.C.C. July 3, 2003).

226 Golan v. Veritas Entm't, L.L.C., 788 F.3d 814 (8th Cir. 2015) (call was not an advertisement when it did not mention product being promoted, but it was telemarketing because its intent was to promote a movie); Margulis v. P & M Consulting, Inc., 121 S.W.3d 246 (Mo. Ct. App. 2003) (interpreting pre-2003 version of regulation, but citing FCC's 2003 amendments).

227 Golan v. Veritas Entm't, L.L.C., 788 F.3d 814 (8th Cir. 2015).

228 Chesbro v. Best Buy Stores, L.P., 705 F.3d 913 (9th Cir. 2012) (citing *In re Rules and Regulations Implementing the Telephone Consumer Protection Act of 1991, Report and Order*, 18 F.C.C. Rcd. 14014 ¶ 136, 2003 WL 21517853 (F.C.C. July 3, 2003)).

229 47 C.F.R. § 64.1200(a)(3)(iii), (f)(12). *See* Rantz-Kennedy v. Discover Fin. Services, 2013 WL 3167912 (D. Md. June 20, 2013), *aff'd*, 544 Fed. Appx. 183 (4th Cir. 2013); Zehala v. American Express, 2011 WL 4484297 (S.D. Ohio Sept. 26, 2011) (prohibition against artificial voice calls to residential lines is inapplicable to debt collection calls); Spencer v. Arizona Premium Fin. Co., 2011 WL 4473178 (W.D.N.Y. Sept. 26, 2011) (artificial voice collection call to non-debtor falls within exception for calls for commercial purposes that do not include unsolicited advertisements or amount to telephone solicitations); Santino v. NCO Financial Sys., Inc., 2011 WL 754874 (W.D.N.Y. Feb. 24, 2011) (TCPA does not prohibit artificial voice debt collection calls even to non-debtor); Bentley v. Bank of Am., 773 F. Supp. 2d 1367 (S.D. Fla. 2011) (established business relationship exception allows artificial voice debt collection calls to residential lines); Franasiak v. Palisades Collection, L.L.C., 822 F. Supp. 2d 320 (W.D.N.Y. 2011) (debt collection calls, even to non-debtors, fall within commercial purpose exception to artificial voice prohibition). *See also In re* Rules and Regulations Implementing the Telephone Consumer Protection Act of 1991, 23 F.C.C. Rcd. 559 (F.C.C. Jan. 4, 2008).

230 47 C.F.R. § 64.1200(f)(12).

231 16 C.F.R. § 310.4(b).

232 47 U.S.C. § 227(d)(3)(A); 47 C.F.R. § 64.1200(b)(1).

233 47 U.S.C. § 227(d)(3)(A); 47 C.F.R. § 64.1200(b)(2).

234 47 C.F.R. § 64.1200(b)(2).

These requirements apply to all artificial or prerecorded voice calls, whether to land lines or cell phones.[235] They apply even to calls that do not involve telemarketing or that fall within one of the other exceptions to the prohibition of such calls to residential lines.[236] They apply to lawful as well as unlawful messages.[237] The requirement that the caller's identity be disclosed applies to political campaign calls.[238] The entity that created the message is liable for the violation, even if another entity broadcast it.[239]

Application of these requirements to debt collectors raises special issues because the instigator of a prerecorded call does not know who is listening to the call and the Federal Fair Debt Collection Practices Act (FDCPA) prohibits communicating about the debt to third parties.[240] The FCC in 2005 advised collectors that they could identify themselves by an individual's name (thus not indicating that the call was about a debt) but that they still must provide a telephone number to allow the consumer to make a do-not-call request.[241] See NCLC's *Fair Debt Collection*[242] for more discussion of the interrelationship between FDCPA and TCPA requirements.

6.4.4 Requirement of Opt-Out Mechanism for Prerecorded Telemarketing Calls

A final disclosure requirement applies to prerecorded telemarketing calls to residential telephone subscribers (and, under the FCC rule, to any of the sensitive telephone numbers discussed in § 6.3, *supra*.[243] For these calls, there must be an automated, interactive-voice and/or key-press-activated opt-out mechanism for the called person to make a do-not-call request, with explanatory instructions.[244] This mechanism must be provided within two seconds after the caller provides certain identifying information required by the regulation.[245] If the prerecorded message is left on an answering machine, it must also provide a telephone number to which the consumer can make a do-not-call request.[246]

6.4.5 Private Remedies

The restriction on prerecorded messages sent to residential phones is found in section 227(b) of the TCPA. As a result, there is a private right of action for the first call and no defense for reasonable procedures.[247] Remedies for a prevailing plaintiff are the greater of actual damages or $500 per violation, and these damages can be trebled for knowing or willful violations.[248]

Less clear are TCPA private remedies for violation of the requirement that recorded calls include identifying disclosures. These requirements are found in section 227(d) of the TCPA, which does not provide for a private right of action.[249] But the FCC rule setting out identification requirements can also be viewed as promulgated pursuant to the authorization in section 227(b) to prescribe regulations to implement the exceptions to the prerecorded call prohibition,[250] and there is a private cause of action for violations of section 227(b). Alternatively, the identification requirement could be viewed as enacted pursuant to section 227(c) as a privacy protection regulation, since it relates to telephone solicitations and is essential if a company-specific do-not-call list is to function as intended. Section 227(c) violations are enforceable with a somewhat different private right of action than section 227(b) violations.[251]

The person to whose residence a call is placed has standing to sue for the violation even if some other household member answers the call.[252] A regular user of a residential line, even if not the subscriber, also falls within the zone of interests protected by the statute and is entitled to bring suit for violations.[253]

Issues regarding TCPA litigation that are generally applicable to all its substantive prohibitions are discussed in § 6.9, *infra*.

There is a direct private cause of action for violation of the FTC Telemarketing Sales Rule provisions on prerecorded calls and disclosures only if there is a minimum of $50,000 in actual

---

235 47 U.S.C. § 227(d)(3)(A) (requirements apply to "all artificial or prerecorded telephone messages").

236 *See* § 6.4.2, *supra*.

237 47 U.S.C. § 227(d)(3)(A) (requirements apply to "all artificial or prerecorded telephone messages"). *See State of Oklahoma ex rel. Edmondson v. Pope*, 505 F. Supp. 2d 1098 (W.D. Okla. 2007), *vacated on other grounds*, 516 F.3d 1214 (10th Cir. Feb. 26, 2008) (vacating decision because of failure to notify U.S. Attorney General of challenge to constitutionality of federal statute); *Boydston v. Asset Acceptance L.L.C.*, 496 F. Supp. 2d 1101, 1105 (N.D. Cal. 2007).

238 *Maryland v. Universal Elections*, 787 F. Supp. 2d 408 (D. Md. 2011).

239 *Maryland v. Universal Elections*, 787 F. Supp. 2d 408 (D. Md. 2011) (political consulting firm is liable when it provided artificial voice message and telephone numbers to another company that actually placed calls).

240 *See* 15 U.S.C. § 1692c(b).

241 70 Fed. Reg. 19,330 (Apr. 13, 2005).

242 National Consumer Law Center, Fair Debt Collection (8th ed. 2014), *updated at* www.nclc.org/library.

243 *See* 47 C.F.R. § 64.1200(b)(3).

244 16 C.F.R. § 310.4(b)(v)(B)(ii)(A); 47 C.F.R. § 64.1200(b)(3).

245 47 C.F.R. § 64.1200(b)(1), (3).

246 16 C.F.R. § 310.4(b)(v)(B)(ii)(B); 47 C.F.R. § 64.1200(b)(3).

247 *See* §§ 6.9.1, 6.9.6, *supra*.

248 *See* §§ 6.9.2.1–6.9.2.4, *infra*.

249 Burdge v. Association Health Care Mgmt., Inc., 2009 WL 414595 (S.D. Ohio Feb. 18, 2009) (slip copy); Boydston v. Asset Acceptance, L.L.C., 496 F. Supp. 2d 1101, 1105 (N.D. Cal. 2007); Worsham v. Ehrlich, 957 A.2d 161 (Md. Ct. Spec. App. 2008).

250 *See* Charvat v. Ryan, 858 N.E.2d 845 ¶ 26 (Ohio Ct. App. 2006); Report and Order, 7 F.C.C. Rcd. 8752, F.C.C. 92-443 ¶ 55 (F.C.C. 1992) ("TCPA provides consumers with a private right of action, if otherwise permitted by state law or court rules, for any violation of the autodialer or prerecorded voice message prohibitions and for any violation of the guidelines for telephone solicitations").

251 *See* §§ 6.9.1, 6.9.6, *supra*.

252 Margulis v. P & M Consulting, Inc., 121 S.W.3d 246 (Mo. Ct. App. 2003).

253 Leyse v. Bank of Am., ___ F.3d ___, 2015 WL 5946456 (3d Cir. Oct. 14, 2015) (subscriber's roommate, who was regular user of telephone, has standing to sue for prerecorded calls to that line even if caller intended to reach subscriber). *But cf.* Kopff v. World Research Grp., L.L.C., 568 F. Supp. 2d 39 (D.D.C. 2008) (administrative assistant who picks up fax addressed to business does not have claim; business has claim).

damages, but violations may be the basis for state UDAP claims or claims under a state telemarketing statute.[254] State attorneys general, the FTC, and other federal agencies can enforce the rule without regard to the $50,000 requirement.[255] Remedies for violations of the FTC Telemarketing Sales Rule are summarized at §§ 6.2.1, 6.2.2, *supra*, and examined in more detail at § 5.6, *supra*.

6.5 FTC and FCC Do-Not-Call Rules

6.5.1 Company-Specific Do-Not-Call Lists

The FTC Telemarketing Sales Rule prohibits a seller or telemarketer from calling a person who has previously asked to be placed on the seller's do-not-call list.[256] Each seller, including for-profit solicitors who solicit charitable donations, must maintain a company-specific do-not-call list[257] and must honor do-not-call requests made to its employees and agents.[258] The Fourth Circuit has held that the FTC's extension of this rule to for-profit solicitors for charities was constitutional and within the FTC's authority.[259]

Telemarketers are prohibited from denying or interfering in any way with a person's right to be placed on a do-not-call list.[260] Hanging up on a person who starts to ask not to be called is a violation.[261] It is also a FTC Telemarketing Sales Rule violation for any person to sell or purchase the list for any purpose other than rule compliance.[262]

The FCC also requires telemarketers to maintain company-specific do-not-call lists and to honor do-not-call requests until cancelled by the consumer or removed by the database administrator.[263] Companies must also have a do-not-call list policy and make it available to consumers upon request.[264] The FCC rules explicitly apply the company-specific do-not-call provision to cell phones.[265]

The FCC requirement of company-specific do-not-call lists was enacted pursuant to 47 U.S.C. § 227(c) as a protection of privacy rights. A private right of action is provided if a consumer receives a second call within twelve months that violates section 227(c), and a prevailing plaintiff is entitled to the greater of actual damages or $500 per violation.[266] These damages can be trebled for knowing or willful violations, but the caller is not liable if it has instituted reasonable procedures to prevent violations.[267] The private right of action under the FTC rule requires a minimum of $50,000 in actual damages, but there is no requirement that there be at least two calls violating a rule provision within a year.[268] Violations may also be the basis for state UDAP claims or claims under a state telemarketing statute.

6.5.2 Nationwide Do-Not-Call List

6.5.2.1 Authority

In 2003, the FTC expanded the Telemarketing Sales Rule to establish a national do-not-call registry,[269] but operation of the do-not-call list was made contingent on congressional funding.[270] Congress approved funding on March 11, 2003, at the same time directing the FCC to issue a final do-not-call rule that maximized consistency with the FTC's rule.[271] By July, 2003, the FCC had adopted a nationwide do-not-call rule.[272]

Litigation caused a slight delay in the launch of the do-not-call list. Shortly before it was to go into effect, a federal district court held that it exceeded the FTC's statutory authority.[273] Congress responded within days by passing a new law that made the FTC's authority clearer.[274] In 2004, the Tenth Circuit

254 15 U.S.C. § 6104(a). *See* § 5.6.1.1, *supra*.

255 15 U.S.C. §§ 6102(c), 6103(a), (f)(2), 6105.

256 16 C.F.R. § 310.4(b)(1)(iii)(A). *See* Fed. Trade Comm'n v. Health Formulas, L.L.C., 2015 WL 2130504 (D. Nev. May 6, 2015) (issuing preliminary injunction against defendants who were alleged to have repeatedly violated TSR's do-not-call provisions); Fed. Trade Comm'n v. Ivy Capital, Inc., 2013 WL 1224613 (D. Nev. Mar. 26, 2013) (finding defendants liable for calling consumers who had registered on do-not-call list and for continuing to call consumers who asked defendants to stop calling them), *aff'd in part, vacated in part on other grounds*, ___ Fed. Appx. ___, 2015 WL 5781664 (9th Cir. Oct. 5, 2015).

257 16 C.F.R. § 310.6(a). *See also* 68 Fed. Reg. 4580, 4636–37 (Jan. 29, 2003) (FTC's explanation of this provision).

258 United States v. DISH Network, L.L.C., 75 F. Supp. 3d 942, 1015–1018 (C.D. Ill. 2014) (company-specific do-not-call request is effective as to seller if it is communicated to seller's agent or employee), *vacated in part on other grounds*, 80 F. Supp. 3d 917 (C.D. Ill. 2015) (fact issue whether retailers were seller's agents).

259 Nat'l Fed'n of the Blind v. Fed. Trade Comm'n, 420 F.3d 331, 341–42 (4th Cir. 2005).

260 16 C.F.R. § 310.4(b)(1)(ii). *See also* 68 Fed. Reg. 4580, 4628 (Jan. 29, 2003) (directing another person to deny or interfere with a person's right to be placed on a do-not-call list is a violation).

261 68 Fed. Reg. 4580, 4628 (Jan. 29, 2003).

262 16 C.F.R. § 310.4(b)(2).

263 47 C.F.R. § 64.1200(c)(2), *as amended by* 73 Fed. Reg. 40,183 (July 14, 2008) (conforming to Do-Not-Call Improvement Act of 2007 by deleting requirement that registrations be renewed every five years).

264 47 C.F.R. § 64.1200(d)(1). *See* Reichenbach v. Chung Holdings, L.L.C., 823 N.E.2d 29 (Ohio Ct. App. 2004); Adamo v. AT&T, 2001 WL 1382757 (Ohio Ct. App. Nov. 8, 2001) (affirming award of treble damages for violation of requirement).

265 47 C.F.R. § 64.1200(e).

266 47 U.S.C. § 227(c)(5). *See* Wagner v. CLC Resorts & Developments, Inc., 32 F. Supp. 3d 1193 (M.D. Fla. 2014) (violation is making telemarketing call without having instituted required company-specific do-not-call list procedures). *See generally* §§ 6.9.1, 6.9.2.1–6.9.2.4, 6.9.6, *infra*.

267 *See* §§ 6.9.1, 6.9.2.1–6.9.2.4, 6.9.6, *infra*.

268 *See* §§ 5.6, 6.2.1, 6.2.2, *supra*.

269 16 C.F.R. § 310.4(b)(1)(iii)(B).

270 Telemarketing Sales Rule, 68 Fed. Reg. 4580, 4580 (Jan. 29, 2003) (statement of basis and purpose).

271 Do Not Call Implementation Act, Pub. L. No. 108-10, 117 Stat. 557 (Mar. 11, 2003).

272 47 C.F.R. § 64.1200(c)(2). *See* Report and Order, *In re* Rules and Regulations Implementing the Telephone Consumer Protection Act of 1991, 18 F.C.C. Rcd. 14014, 2003 WL 21517853 (F.C.C. July 3, 2003).

273 U.S. Sec. v. Fed. Trade Comm'n, 282 F. Supp. 2d 1285 (W.D. Okla. 2003), *rev'd*, 358 F.3d 1228 (10th Cir. 2004).

274 An Act to Ratify the Authority of the Fed. Trade Commission to Establish a Do-Not-Call Registry, Pub. L. No. 108-82, 117 Stat. 1006 (2003). *See* Mainstream Mktg., Inc. v. Fed. Trade Comm'n, 358 F.3d

upheld the constitutionality of both the FTC's and the FCC's do-not-call rules.[275] By September 1, 2006, consumers had registered 130 million telephone numbers with the national do-not-call list.[276]

6.5.2.2　Scope of the FTC and FCC Do-Not-Call-Rules

The FTC do-not-call rule applies only to telemarketing calls, not non-telemarketing calls such as debt collection calls.[277] Similarly, the FCC do-not-call rule applies only to telephone solicitations.[278]

The FCC do-not-call rule is somewhat broader in scope than the comparable FTC rule. The FCC's rule covers all entities engaged in telemarketing, even purely intrastate transactions.[279] By contrast, the FTC's rule extends only to telemarketing that involves more than one interstate call;[280] nor does it cover banks, credit unions, savings and loan associations, airlines, common carriers such as telephone companies, and insurance companies.[281]

The FTC rule prohibits any call to a "person" whose telephone number is on the do-not-call list, without limiting this prohibition to land lines or residential lines.[282] A court rejected a telemarketer's claim that the FTC had to prove that its calls were made to the person who originally registered the number on the do-not-call list; all that need be shown is that the telemarketer called a number that was on the list.[283] Similarly, the FCC rule includes cell phones, by virtue of a presumption that wireless phones registered on the list are residential telephones.[284] When it adopted this provision, the FCC indicated that a cell phone used to supplement a residential land line

qualifies as residential, even if the land line is the subscriber's primary phone.[285] The FCC noted that, if it took enforcement action, it might require a complaining wireless subscriber to provide further proof of the validity of its presumption.[286]

Calls can violate the FTC rule even if the call is not completed, as the rule prohibits initiating an improper telemarketing call.[287] The fact that the called party is a non-English speaker does not excuse an illegal call.[288]

6.5.2.3　Exemptions

Both the FTC and the FCC exempt calls by or on behalf of tax-exempt nonprofit organizations from the nationwide do-not-call list.[289] The FTC's rule exempts calls to businesses[290] (with a partial exception for "toner phoner" calls).[291] The FCC rule also creates an exception when the telemarketer has a personal relationship with the called party.[292]

Both rules exempt calls made to someone with whom the company has an "established business relationship."[293] Such a relationship lasts for eighteen months after the consumer's last purchase or transaction with the company or for three months after the consumer makes an inquiry or application regarding the company's products or services.[294] Even within the three- or eighteen-month window, the consumer can stop the calls by asking to be put on the company-specific do-not-call list and thus may continue to do business with a company while still preventing privacy-invading telemarketing calls.[295] The FTC

1228 (10th Cir. 2004) (rule was within FTC's authority both before and after the new law).

275　Mainstream Mktg., Inc. v. Fed. Trade Comm'n, 358 F.3d 1228 (10th Cir. 2004).

276　Proposed Rules, 71 Fed. Reg. 58,716, 58,725 (Oct. 4, 2006).

277　Bridge v. Ocwen Fed. Bank, 669 F. Supp. 2d 853, 859 (N.D. Ohio 2009). *Cf.* United States v. Corps. For Character, L.C., ___ F. Supp. 3d ___, 2015 WL 4577051 (D. Utah Mar. 31, 2015) (holding that calls with the purpose of selling movie tickets were telemarketing under TSR and not simply informational or advocacy calls, even though sales were not actually completed during call).

278　47 C.F.R. § 64.1200(c). *See also* 47 C.F.R. § 64.1200(f)(14) (definition of telephone solicitation).

279　Report and Order, *In re* Rules and Regulations Implementing the Telephone Consumer Protection Act of 1991 ¶ 212, 18 F.C.C. Rcd. 14014, 2003 WL 21517853 (F.C.C. July 3, 2003).

280　15 U.S.C. § 6106(4). *See* 68 Fed. Reg. 4580, 4587 (Jan. 29, 2003) (statement of basis and purpose for FTC rule).

281　68 Fed. Reg. 4580, 4586–4587 (Jan. 29, 2003).

282　16 C.F.R. § 310.4(b)(1)(iii). *See* United States v. DISH Network, L.L.C., 75 F. Supp. 3d 942, 1003 (C.D. Ill. 2014), *vacated in part*, 80 F. Supp. 3d 917 (C.D. Ill. 2015) (FTC's jurisdiction under do-not-call rule extends to wireless calls).

283　United States v. DISH Network, L.L.C., 75 F. Supp. 3d 942, 1007–1008 (C.D. Ill. 2014), *vacated in part on other grounds*, 80 F. Supp. 3d 917 (C.D. Ill. 2015).

284　47 C.F.R. § 64.1200(e). *See* United States v. DISH Network, L.L.C., 75 F. Supp. 3d 916, 926 (C.D. Ill. Dec. 11, 2014), *vacated in part on other grounds,* 80 F. Supp. 3d 917 (C.D. Ill. 2015).

285　*In re* Rules and Regulations Implementing the Telephone Consumer Protection Act of 1991 ¶¶ 35, CG Docket No. 02–278, F.C.C. 03–153, 2003 WL 21517853 (F.C.C. July 3, 2003) (FCC Report and Order).

286　*Id.* at ¶ 35.

287　United States v. DISH Network, L.L.C., 75 F. Supp. 3d 942, 1010 (C.D. Ill. 2014), *vacated in part on other grounds*, 80 F. Supp. 3d 917 (C.D. Ill. 2015).

288　*Id.*

289　16 C.F.R. § 310.6(a) (FTC rule); 47 C.F.R. § 64.1200(f)(14)(iii) (FCC rule) (excluding calls on behalf of nonprofits from definition of telephone solicitation; do-not-call rule's limits apply only to telephone solicitations). *See also* 68 Fed. Reg. 4580, 4629, 4634–37, 4654 (Jan. 29, 2003) (FTC rule).

290　16 C.F.R. § 310.6(b)(7). *See also* 68 Fed. Reg. 4580, 4632 (Jan. 29, 2003).

291　16 C.F.R. § 310.6(b)(7) (calls to induce retail sale of nondurable office or cleaning supplies to a business are covered by FTC rule except for nationwide do-not-call list). *See also* 68 Fed. Reg. 4580, 4632 (Jan. 29, 2003).

292　47 C.F.R. § 64.1200(c)(2)(iii) (creating the exception), (f)(16) (defining "personal relationship").

293　16 C.F.R. § 310.4(b)(1)(iii)(B)(ii) (FTC rule); 47 C.F.R. § 64.1200(f)(5) (FCC rule) (excluding calls to a person with whom the caller has an established business relationship from definition of "telephone solicitation," and thereby creating exception to do-not-call rule, which applies only to telephone solicitations). *See also* § 6.8.2.3, *infra* (established business relationship as exception to junk fax prohibition).

　　　The FCC's rule also makes an exception for calls to persons with whom the telemarketer has a "personal relationship," 47 C.F.R. § 64.1200(c)(2)(iii), while the FTC rule does not have this exception.

294　16 C.F.R. § 310.2(o) (FTC rule); 47 C.F.R. § 64.1200(f)(5) (FCC rule). *See* 68 Fed. Reg. 4580, 4591–94 (Jan. 29, 2003).

295　Report and Order, *In re* Rules and Regulations Implementing the Telephone Consumer Protection Act of 1991 ¶ 124, 18 F.C.C. Rcd.

rule also exempts calls in which the consumer has provided an express written agreement to receive calls from the caller.[296] The exemptions from the FTC rule are treated as affirmative defenses.[297]

6.5.2.4 Operation of the Do-Not-Call Rules

The FCC's do-not-call rule prohibits any telephone solicitation to a residential telephone subscriber whose number is registered on the national do-not-call list.[298] Similarly, the FTC's rule provides that it is an abusive telemarketing practice for a telemarketer to initiate, or for a seller to cause a telemarketer to initiate, an outbound telephone call to a person whose telephone number is registered on the list.[299]

Individuals can register their telephone numbers on the do-not-call list by calling 1-888-382-1222 (TTY 1-866-290-4236). The call must be made from the telephone number that the consumer wishes to register. In the alternative, a consumer can register one or more numbers through the FTC's website, www.ftc.gov. The do-not-call list includes cell phone numbers and pager numbers,[300] so consumers should register these as well as land line numbers.

The Do-Not-Call Improvement Act of 2007 provides that a registered telephone number shall not be removed from the registry except upon the consumer's request or the FTC's finding that the number has been disconnected and reassigned or is invalid.[301] The FTC and FCC rules provide that consumers who want to receive information from a specific company may give that company signed written permission to call, even though the consumer is on the national registry.[302]

Predictably, even the enactment of a do-not-call registry attracted scam artists. The FTC rule prohibits denying or interfering in any way with a person's right to be placed on the do-not-call registry.[303] It is also an FTC rule violation for any person to sell or purchase the list for any purpose other than rule compliance.[304] The FTC has obtained a consent order against an individual who induced consumers to pay him to pre-register them for the do-not-call list. Part of his goal was to get personal information from the consumers. He also sold a service that would allegedly block telemarketing calls and junk mail and faxes.[305]

6.5.2.5 Relationship to State Do Not Call Laws

The FTC's do-not-call registry requirements are intended to be at least as stringent as most state laws.[306] The TCPA provides that any state database must include the part of the national database that relates to that state.[307] However, the FTC declined to preempt state laws,[308] and states are able to continue to enforce their telemarketing laws, including their do-not-call lists, for intrastate telemarketing calls.[309]

The FTC has coordinated its do-not-call registry with the do-not-call lists of many states so that consumers can register for both the federal and state list at the same time.[310] Consumers in doubt about whether a single registration suffices should register for both the national do-not-call list and their respective state list.

6.5.3 Remedies for Rule Violations

The FCC do-not-call rule provision was enacted pursuant to 47 U.S.C. § 227(c) as a protection of privacy rights, and thus a private right of action is provided if a consumer receives more than one call within twelve months, providing a prevailing plaintiff with the greater of actual damages or $500 per violation.[311] These damages can be trebled for knowing or willful violations, but the caller is not liable if it has instituted reasonable procedures to prevent violations.[312]

The private right of action under the FTC rule requires a minimum of $50,000 in actual damages, but there is no requirement that there be at least two calls violating a rule provision within a year.[313] Violations may also be the basis for

---

14014, 2003 WL 21517853 (F.C.C. July 3, 2003).

   The FTC rule is the same. 68 Fed. Reg. 4580, 4634 (Jan. 29, 2003). *See also* Charvat v. Dispatch Consumer Services, 769 N.E.2d 829 (Ohio 2002) (an existing customer can terminate an "established business relationship" for purposes of the TCPA by asking to be placed on company do-not-call list).

296 *See* 16 C.F.R. § 310.4(b)(1)(iii)(B)(i). *See also* 47 C.F.R. § 64.1200(c)(2)(ii) (similar provision of FCC rule).

297 United States v. DISH Network, L.L.C., 75 F. Supp. 3d 942, 1008 (C.D. Ill. 2014), *vacated in part on other grounds*, 80 F. Supp. 3d 917 (C.D. Ill. 2015).

298 47 C.F.R. § 64.1200(c)(2). *See, e.g.*, Fed. Trade Comm'n v. Instant Response Sys., L.L.C., 2015 WL 1650914 (E.D.N.Y. Apr. 15, 2015) (granting summary judgment against defendant who purchased call lists but did not investigate whether they included registered numbers).

299 16 C.F.R. § 310.4(b)(1)(iii)(B).

300 68 Fed. Reg. 4580, 4632–33 (Jan. 29, 2003). *See* § 6.5.2.2, *supra*.

301 *See* Pub. L. No. 110-187 (Feb. 15, 2008), *codified at* 15 U.S.C. § 6101. *See also* 47 C.F.R. § 64.1200(c)(2), *as amended by* 73 Fed. Reg. 6041 (Feb. 1, 2008) (do-not-call registrations must be honored indefinitely).

302 16 C.F.R. § 310.4(b)(1)(iii)(B)(i), *adopted by* 68 Fed. Reg. 4580, 4634 (Jan. 29, 2003). *See also* 47 C.F.R. § 64.1200(c)(2)(ii) (allowing telemarketer to call person on do-not-call list who has given express written agreement to receive calls).

303 16 C.F.R. § 310.4(b)(1)(ii).

304 16 C.F.R. § 310.4(b)(2).

305 Fed. Trade Comm'n v. Kevin Chase, 5 Trade Reg. Rep. (CCH) ¶ 15407 (N.D. Cal. May 6, 2003) (complaint; order found at 5 Trade Reg. Rep. (CCH) ¶ 15,518 (N.D. Cal. Dec. 8, 2003)) (consent decree against individual who claimed that, for a fee, he could pre-register consumers for FTC's national do-not-call list). *See also* Fed. Trade Comm'n v. Telephone Prot. Agency, No. 5:04cv49, 5 Trade Reg. Rep. (CCH) ¶ 15,582 (W.D.N.C. Apr. 21, 2004) (complaint against defendants who billed consumers, without their consent, for listing them in do-not-call registry).

306 Q & A: The FTC's Changes to the Telemarketing Sales Rule, *available at* www.contactcenterworld.com.

307 47 U.S.C. § 227(f)(2).

308 68 Fed. Reg. 4580, 4638 (Jan. 29, 2003).

309 *Id.*

310 Fed. Reg. 4580, 4638, 4641 (Jan. 29, 2003).

311 *See* §§ 6.9.1, 6.9.2.1–6.9.2.4, 6.9.6, *infra*.

312 *See* §§ 6.9.1, 6.9.2.1–6.9.2.4, 6.9.6, *infra*.

313 *See* §§ 5.6, 6.2.1, 6.2.2, *supra*.

state UDAP claims or claims under a state telemarketing statute. The FTC[314] and the states also have enforcement authority.

Both the FCC and FTC rules provide a defense for a violation of the do-not-call provision when the caller (and, under the FTC rule, the seller) has instituted written procedures, training, and practices to avoid violations and (at least for the FTC Rule) when the call itself is the result of an error.[315]

The Securities and Exchange Commission has also approved proposals by the Financial Industry Regulatory Authority (FINRA), formerly the National Association of Securities Dealers (NASD),[316] and the New York Stock Exchange (NYSE)[317] to amend their rules to conform to the FCC's do-not-call rule. The entities governed by these rules are also subject to the FCC rule.[318] Thus, in addition to remedies under the TCPA, violations may result in administrative actions by either the FINRA or the NYSE.[319] Sanctions range from a censure or fine to a suspension, expulsion, or bar.

6.6 Other Restrictions on Unwanted Calls

6.6.1 Threats and Obscene Language; Harassment

The FTC Telemarketing Sales Rule prohibits threats, intimidation, and the use of profane or obscene language.[320] Harassment by repeated calls is also prohibited.[321]

These restrictions are found only in the FTC Telemarketing Sales Rule and not in the FCC's rule on telemarketing and junk faxes. The enabling statute for the Telemarketing Sales Rule makes a private cause of action available only if the plaintiff alleges at least $50,000 in actual damages.[322] However, violations of the rule may also be the basis for claims under a state UDAP or telemarketing statute. In addition, state attorneys general, the FTC, and other federal agencies can enforce the FTC rule.[323] Remedies for violations of the FTC Telemarketing Sales Rule are summarized at § 6.2.1, 6.2.2, *supra*, and examined in more detail at § 5.6, *supra*.

6.6.2 Misrepresentations and Disclosure of the Purpose of Telemarketing Calls

6.6.2.1 FTC Rule Requirements

The FTC Telemarketing Sales Rule requires that, in any outgoing call to induce the purchase of goods or services, the telemarketer must make prompt oral disclosure of the seller's identity, the call's purpose (to sell goods or services), and the nature of the goods or services.[324] Callers seeking charitable donations must make prompt oral disclosure of the identity of the charitable organization on behalf of which the call is made and that the purpose of the call is to solicit a charitable donation.[325]

Disclosures must be truthful, clear, and conspicuous.[326] In response to suggestions to clarify that prompt disclosure means "at the onset of a call," the FTC stated that no clarification was necessary because prompt means "at once or without delay, and before any substantive information about a prize, product or service is conveyed to the consumer."[327]

The Telemarketing Sales Rule also prohibits telemarketers from making any false or misleading statements to induce any person to pay for goods and services.[328] This provision is considered in more detail at § 5.3.2, *supra*.

While private rights of action under the FTC Rule require a minimum of $50,000 in actual damages, violations may be the basis for state UDAP claims or claims under a state telemarketing statute. State attorneys general, the FTC, and other

314 *See, e.g.*, Fed. Trade Comm'n v. E.M.A. Nationwide, Inc., 2013 WL 4545143 (N.D. Ohio Aug. 27, 2013) (granting summary judgment and permanent injunction against telemarketer; FTC produced records of over 1000 complaints of violations of do-not-call rule), *aff'd*, 767 F.3d 611 (6th Cir. 2014). *See generally* § 5.6.1, *supra*.

315 *See* 16 C.F.R. § 310.4(b)(3); 47 C.F.R. § 64.1200(c)(2)(i). *See also* 47 U.S.C. § 227(c)(5) (establishment and implementation of reasonable procedures as affirmative defense). *See generally* United States v. DISH Network, L.L.C., 75 F. Supp. 3d 942, 1008–1009 (C.D. Ill. 2014) (concluding that telemarketer failed to prove safe harbor defense), *vacated in part on other grounds*, 80 F. Supp. 3d 917 (C.D. Ill. 2015); United States v. Corps. For Character, L.C., ___ F. Supp. 3d ___, 2015 WL 4577051 (D. Utah Mar. 31, 2015) (looking to quantity of prohibited calls as possible evidence that proper procedures were not in place or that violations were not errors).

316 SR-NASD-2004-174 (Nov. 24, 2004). *See also* 69 Fed. Reg. 2801 (Jan. 20, 2004); SEC Rel. No. 34-49055 (Jan. 12, 2004).

317 70 Fed. Reg. 60,119 (Oct. 14, 2005); SEC Rel. No. 34-52579 (Oct. 7, 2005). *See also* 70 Fed. Reg. 49,961 (Aug. 25, 2005); SEC Rel. No. 34-52308 (Aug. 19, 2005).

318 *See* 70 Fed. Reg. 20,196, 20,198 n.6 (Apr. 18, 2005).

319 *See* New York Stock Exchange, NYSE Rule 476, *available at* http://rules.nyse.com ("Disciplinary Proceedings Involving Charges Against Members, Member Organizations, Principal Executives, Approved Persons, Employees, or Others"); Financial Industry Regulatory Authority, FINRA Manual, Rule 8310, *available at* http://finra.complinet.com ("Sanctions for Violations of the Rules"). *See also New York Stock Exchange*, NYSE Rule 3230, *available at* http://rules.nyse.com ("Telemarketing"); Financial Industry Regulatory Authority, FINRA Manual, Rule 3230, *available at* http://finra.complinet.com ("Telemarketing").

320 16 C.F.R. § 310.4(a)(1).

321 16 C.F.R. § 310.4(b)(1)(i).

322 *See* § 5.6.1.1, *supra*.

323 *See, e.g.*, Fed. Trade Comm'n v. Instant Response Sys., L.L.C., 2015 WL 1650914 (E.D.N.Y. Apr. 15, 2015) (granting summary judgment, permanent injunction, and monetary judgment against defendants who repeatedly called consumers, threatened them with lawsuits and ruined credit, and accused them of dishonesty when they refused to purchase services); Fed. Trade Comm'n v. City W. Advantage, Inc., 2008 WL 2844696 (D. Nev. July 22, 2008) (temporary restraining order against defendants who continued to contact consumers after consumers hung up or stated they were not interested in offer).

324 16 C.F.R. § 310.4(d).

325 15 U.S.C. § 6102(a)(3)(D); 16 C.F.R. § 310.4(e). *See* Nat'l Fed'n of the Blind v. Fed. Trade Comm'n, 420 F.3d 331, 343 (4th Cir. 2005) (rule is constitutional and within FTC's authority).

326 16 C.F.R. §§ 310.3(a)(1), 310.4(d), (e).

327 67 Fed. Reg. 4502, 4526–4527 (Jan. 30, 2002). *Accord* 68 Fed. Reg. 4580, 4648 (Jan. 29, 2003).

328 16 C.F.R. § 310.3(a)(4).

federal agencies can enforce the Telemarketing Sales Rule. Remedies for violations of the FTC rule are summarized at § 6.2.1, 6.2.2, *supra*, and examined in more detail at § 5.6, *supra*.

6.6.2.2 TCPA Disclosure Requirements

The FCC rule under the TCPA requires telemarketers to disclose the name of the individual caller, the name of the person or entity on whose behalf the call is being made, and a return telephone number, which may not be a 900-number.[329] However, it does not repeat the other disclosure requirements of the FTC rule or that rule's prohibition of misrepresentations.

It appears that the FCC's disclosure requirement is a privacy protection, promulgated pursuant to its section 227(c) authority, since it relates to telephone solicitations and is essential if a company-specific (or national) do-not-call list is to be enforceable.[330]

If it is a privacy protection, then a private cause of action is available under section 227(c)(5) if a person receives more than one call within any twelve-month period by or on behalf of the same entity in violation of the requirement.

The FCC's TCPA rule also requires disclosures at the beginning of all prerecorded telephone messages.[331] These requirements are discussed in §§ 6.3.1 and 6.4.3, *supra*.

6.6.3 Abandoned Calls

One problem with automatic dialing systems is that they lead to abandoned calls, because the called party may answer the call at a time when all of the solicitors are still on other calls. This may happen when a telemarketer uses automatic dialing equipment (predictive dialers) that calls too many numbers for the employees of the telemarketing company to handle. Consumers rightfully complain that they rush to answer the phone, only to find no one at the other end of the call.[332]

Both the FTC Telemarketing Sales Rule and the FCC rules implementing the TCPA contain provisions limiting abandoned calls. The FCC rule first requires that the caller not disconnect an unanswered telemarketing call prior to at least fifteen seconds or four rings.[333] The FTC Telemarketing Sales Rule has the same requirement, although it is presented less directly.[334] Both rules thus prevent callers from disconnecting before the consumer has time to reach the phone.

The FCC rule then provides that, if the call recipient does answer the call, a telemarketing call cannot be abandoned, which is defined as not connected to a live sales representative within two seconds of the called person's greeting.[335] "Telemarketing" calls are defined as calls for the purpose of encouraging the purchase or rental of, or investment in, property, goods, or services.[336] Calls made by or on behalf of tax-exempt nonprofits are explicitly excluded.[337]

In addition, the FCC rule allows telemarketers to abandon up to 3% of their calls in a single calling campaign, as measured over a thirty-day period.[338] The telemarketer must keep records establishing compliance.[339] For these calls not answered within two seconds by a live representative, there must be a prerecorded identification and opt-out option, including the ability to opt out during the call using an interactive voice and/or key-press-activated opt-out mechanism.[340]

The FTC Telemarketing Sales Rule also prohibits abandoning calls after the consumer picks up the call.[341] Its provisions are similar to the FCC rule, with a similar 3% allowance for abandoned calls, a similar record-keeping requirement, and a similar requirement that calls not answered within two seconds contain a recording identifying the caller and with a phone number to opt out.[342] Connecting the consumer to an artificial voice message within the two-second period is insufficient.[343]

Like the FCC rule, the FTC rule's abandoned call requirement only applies to telemarketers,[344] but the FTC Telemarketing Sales Rule, unlike the FCC rule, applies to those performing telemarketing for charities.[345] A federal court has held that the FTC restrictions are within the FTC's statutory authority.[346] They are not an unconstitutional restraint on speech, even as applied to charitable solicitations.[347] Many states also have statutes restricting autodialing, and the FCC has declined to preempt such laws.[348]

The FCC provision restricting abandoned calls should be viewed as enacted pursuant to 47 U.S.C. § 227(c) as a

329 47 C.F.R. § 64.1200(d)(4).
330 *See* §§ 6.5.1, 6.5.2, *infra*.
331 47 C.F.R. § 64.1200(b)(1).
332 73 Fed. Reg. 51,163, 51,196 (Aug. 29, 2008); 68 Fed. Reg. 4580, 4641, 4645 (Jan. 29, 2003). *See* Irvine v. Akron Beacon J., 770 N.E.2d 1105 (Ohio Ct. App. 2002).
333 47 C.F.R. § 64.1200(a)6).
334 16 C.F.R. § 310.4(b)(4)(ii) provides a partial defense from abandoned calls if the caller allows the phone to ring for fifteen seconds or four rings. *Cf.* United States v. DISH Network, L.L.C., 75 F. Supp. 3d 942, 1019 (C.D. Ill. 2014) (noting that safe harbor defense for do-not-call violations is not available for abandonment violations), *vacated in part on other grounds*, 80 F. Supp. 3d 917 (C.D. Ill. 2015).
335 47 C.F.R. § 64.1200(a)(7).
336 47 C.F.R. § 64.1200(f)(12).
337 47 C.F.R. § 64.1200(a)(7)(iv).
338 47 C.F.R. § 64.1200(a)(7).
339 47 C.F.R. § 64.1200(a)(7)(iii).
340 47 C.F.R. § 64.1200(a)7)(i).
341 16 C.F.R. § 310.4(b)(1)(iv).
342 16 C.F.R. § 310.4(b)(4). The FTC rule allows for technology that ensures there will be no more than 3% abandoned calls, while the FCC rule requires there be no more than 3% abandoned.
343 Fed. Trade Comm'n v. Asia Pac. Telecom, Inc., 802 F. Supp. 2d 925 (N.D. Ill. 2011).
344 *See* Michaelson v. CBE Grp., Inc., 2015 WL 2449038 (N.D. Ill. May 21, 2015) (TSR's abandoned call provision is inapplicable to debt collection calls).
345 *See* 16 C.F.R. § 310.2(dd).
346 U.S. Sec. v. Fed. Trade Comm'n, 282 F. Supp. 2d 1285 (W.D. Okla. 2003), *aff'd on other grounds*, 358 F.3d 1228 (10th Cir. 2004) (upholding do-not-call rule).
347 Nat'l Fed'n of the Blind v. Fed. Trade Comm'n, 420 F.3d 331, 341 (4th Cir. 2005).
348 *See* Report and Order, *In re* Rules and Regulations Implementing the Telephone Consumer Protection Act of 1991 ¶ 134, 18 F.C.C. Rcd. 14014, 2003 WL 21517853 (F.C.C. July 3, 2003).

protection of privacy rights. A private right of action is provided if a consumer receives more than one call within twelve months that violates section 227(c), and a prevailing plaintiff receives the greater of actual damages or $500 per violation.[349] These damages can be trebled for knowing or willful violations, but the caller is not liable if it has instituted reasonable procedures to prevent violations.[350] The private right of action under the FTC Telemarketing Sales Rule requires a minimum of $50,000 in actual damages, but violations may be the basis for state UDAP claims or claims under a state telemarketing statute, and there is no requirement that there be at least two calls within a year that violate the rule.[351]

6.6.4 Restrictions on Calling Times

The FCC and FTC Rules prohibit telephone solicitations before 8:00 a.m. or after 9:00 p.m., local time (determined by the called party's location).[352] Both rules allow calls at other times with the consumer's prior consent,[353] and the FCC rule allows calls at other times when there is an established business relationship.[354] Calls during the prohibited hours are violations even if the caller hangs up before the consumer answers.[355] The FCC restrictions apply to wireless telephones as well as land lines.[356]

The FTC rule provision applies to for-profit entities that solicit for charities,[357] and the Fourth Circuit has held that this restriction is constitutional.[358] The FCC provision does not apply to calls by or on behalf of tax-exempt nonprofits.[359]

The FCC provision restricting calling times should be viewed as enacted pursuant to 47 U.S.C. § 227(c) as a protection of privacy rights, and thus a private right of action is provided if a consumer receives more than one call within twelve months.[360] A prevailing plaintiff is entitled to the greater of

actual damages or $500 per violation.[361] These damages can be trebled for knowing or willful violations, but the caller is not liable if it has instituted reasonable procedures to prevent violations.[362] The private right of action under the FTC rule requires a minimum of $50,000 in actual damages, but there is no requirement that there be at least two calls violating a rule provision within a year.[363] Violations may also be the basis for state UDAP claims or claims under a state telemarketing statute.

6.6.5 Transmitting Caller ID Information and Prohibition of Caller ID Blocking

The FCC and FTC rules require any person or entity that engages in telemarketing to transmit caller ID information to the called party, and the rules prohibit caller ID blocking.[364] The Fourth Circuit has held that the FTC rule is constitutional and within the FTC's authority, even as applied to for-profit solicitors for charities.[365]

The telemarketer must transmit or cause to be transmitted either the telemarketer's name and telephone number or the name and telephone number (answered during regular business hours) of the business or organization on whose behalf the telemarketer is calling.[366] The FTC has indicated that technical failures outside the telemarketer's control will not be considered violations as long as the telemarketer has taken all available steps to comply with the rule.[367]

The FCC adopted these caller ID provisions along with revisions to its main TCPA rule in 2003.[368] In 2010, Congress passed the Truth in Caller ID Act as an amendment to the TCPA.[369] The FCC then amended its caller ID rule to include several additional definitions and to add a new provision, tracking the statute, prohibiting any person from engaging in caller ID spoofing.[370]

---

349 *See* §§ 6.9.1, 6.9.2.1–6.9.2.4, 6.9.6, *infra*.

350 *See* §§ 6.9.1, 6.9.2.1–6.9.2.4, 6.9.6, *infra*.

351 *See* §§ 5.6, 6.2.1, 6.2.2, *supra*.

352 16 C.F.R. § 310.4(c); 47 C.F.R. § 64.1200(c)(1). *See also* Irvine v. Akron Beacon J., 770 N.E.2d 1105 (Ohio Ct. App. 2002) (use of autodialer during prohibited hours a violation of TCPA).

353 16 C.F.R. § 310.4(c) (FTC rule); 47 C.F.R. § 64.1200(f)(14)(i) (excluding calls made with called party's prior express invitation or solicitation from definition of "telephone solicitation").

354 47 C.F.R. § 64.1200(c)(1), (c)(2)(iii) (applying calling time restriction to "telephone solicitations," defined by section 64.1200(f)(14)(ii) to exclude calls to a person with whom the caller has an established business relationship).

355 Irvine v. Akron Beacon J., 770 N.E.2d 1105 (Ohio Ct. App. 2002).

356 47 C.F.R. § 64.1200(e). *See also* Report and Order, *In re* Rules and Regulations Implementing the Telephone Consumer Protection Act of 1991 ¶ 167, 18 F.C.C. Rcd. 14014, 2003 WL 21517853 (F.C.C. July 3, 2003). *Cf.* 16 C.F.R. § 310.4(c) (phrasing FTC rule as applicable to outbound calls to a person's residence).

357 Nat'l Fed'n of the Blind v. Fed. Trade Comm'n, 420 F.3d 331, 341 (4th Cir. 2005).

358 *Id.* at 341.

359 *See* 47 C.F.R. § 64.1200(c)(1) (applying calling time restriction to "telephone solicitations," defined by section 64.1200(f)(14)(iii) to exclude calls by or on behalf of nonprofits).

360 47 U.S.C. § 227(c)(5). *See* § 6.9.2.2, *infra*.

361 *See* §§ 6.9.1, 6.9.2.1–6.9.2.4, 6.9.6, *infra*.

362 47 U.S.C. § 227(c)(5). *See* §§ 6.9.1, 6.9.2.1–6.9.2.4, 6.9.6, *infra*.

363 *See* §§ 5.6, 6.2.1, 6.2.2, *supra*.

364 16 C.F.R. § 310.4(a)(8); 47 C.F.R. § 64.1601(e). *See also* 73 Fed. Reg. 43196 (July 20, 2011) (Statement of Basis and Purpose for FTC's amended telemarketing rule); 68 Fed. Reg. 4580, 4623–4628 (Jan. 29, 2003) (amending FCC rule in light of Truth in Caller ID Act); Report and Order, *In re* Rules and Regulations Implementing the Telephone Consumer Protection Act of 1991 ¶ 184, 18 F.C.C. Rcd. 14014, 2003 WL 21517853 (F.C.C. July 3, 2003).
   "Caller identification service" is defined at 16 C.F.R. § 310.2(d).

365 Nat'l Fed'n of the Blind v. Fed. Trade Comm'n, 420 F.3d 331, 342 (4th Cir. 2005).

366 16 C.F.R. § 310.4(a)(8); 47 C.F.R. § 64.1601(e). *See* United States v. Corps. For Character, L.C., ___ F. Supp. 3d ___, 2015 WL 4577051 (D. Utah Mar. 31, 2015) (displaying name of product rather than name of seller was insufficient to comply with TSR's caller ID requirements).

367 68 Fed. Reg. 4580, 4626 (Jan. 29, 2003).

368 Report and Order, *In re* Rules and Regulations Implementing the Telephone Consumer Protection Act of 1991 ¶ 184, 18 F.C.C. Rcd. 14014, 2003 WL 21517853 (F.C.C. July 3, 2003).

369 Pub. L. No. 111-331 (2010). *See* 47 U.S.C. § 227(e).

370 47 C.F.R. § 64.1604, *added by* 76 Fed. Reg. 43196 (July 20, 2011). *Cf.* Teltech Sys., Inc. v. Bryant, 702 F.3d 232 (5th Cir. 2012) (state statute that prohibited all caller ID spoofing, even that done with intent

Unlike other sections of the TCPA, the section in which the Truth in Caller ID Act is codified does not explicitly provide for a special cause of action. However, a private cause of action may be available pursuant to section 207 of the Communications Act of 1934,[371] which provides a private cause of action for damages by any person who claims to be damaged by a common carrier that is subject to the provisions of the chapter of the U.S. Code that includes the TCPA.

In addition, the portion of the FCC rule that prohibits caller ID blocking was adopted years before the Truth in Caller ID Act was enacted. That prohibition should be viewed as enacted pursuant to 47 U.S.C. § 227(c) as part of the protections created by the nationwide do-not-call rule.[372] A private right of action should thus be available under section 227(c)(5) if a consumer receives more than one call within twelve months.[373] A prevailing plaintiff may recover the greater of actual damages or $500 per violation.[374] These damages can be trebled for knowing or willful violations, but the caller is not liable if it has instituted reasonable procedures to prevent violations.[375]

The private right of action under the FTC rule requires a minimum of $50,000 in actual damages, but there is no requirement that there be at least two calls violating a rule provision within a year.[376] Violations may also be the basis for state UDAP claims or claims under a state telemarketing statute.

6.6.6 State Statutes Limiting Unwanted Calls

Some state statutes take steps to protect the public from annoyance and inconvenience by restricting the time of calls or requiring the salesperson to hang up as soon as the consumer indicates a lack of interest.[377] Many prohibit telemarketers from calling people who have listed themselves on a statewide database or the nationwide do-not-call registry.[378]

A number of state telemarketing laws also prohibit telemarketers from blocking caller ID and restrict prerecorded calls, autodialers,[379] and junk faxes.[380]

State telemarketing statutes often provide for a private right of action and strong private remedies. State telemarketing statutes and private remedies under those statutes are summarized at Appendix D, *infra*, and these statutes are considered in more detail at § 5.9, *supra*.

6.7 Text Messages

6.7.1 Introduction

A relatively new form of unwanted telephone contact involves text messages sent to consumers' cell phones. A telemarketer or other entity sends over the Internet a large number of e-mails whose addresses identify unique cell phone numbers.[381] The cellular carriers convert these e-mails to text messages and forward them to the designated cell phones.[382] Such texts are generally unwanted—the texts may result in charges to the consumer, and consumers are used to text messages coming only from selected individuals.

While the CAN-SPAM Act[383] may regulate some aspects of this spam text messaging,[384] that statute does not provide a direct consumer remedy.[385] Because it prohibits the use of automatic dialers to "call" a cell phone,[386] the Telephone Consumer Protection Act (TCPA) generally prohibits spam text messaging and provides an explicit consumer private right of action with statutory and treble damages.[387] This section thus focuses on the applicability of this TCPA prohibition to unwanted text messages sent to the consumer's cell phone.

A more detailed discussion of the prohibition of autodialed calls to cell phones may be found in § 6.3, *supra*. Note that the fact that the CAN-SPAM Act may regulate certain aspects of Internet-originated text messages does *not* affect whether the TCPA also applies to such a practice.[388]

---

to deceive but not intent to defraud, is conflict-preempted by federal caller ID law, which requires intent to defraud; suit by vendors of caller ID spoofing services for mystery shopper use and personal use). *See generally* National Consumer Law Center, Fair Debt Collection § 8.3.3 (8th ed. 2014), *updated at* www.nclc.org/library (further discussion of Truth in Caller ID Act).

371 47 U.S.C. § 207.

372 68 Fed. Reg. 4580, 4623 (Jan. 29, 2003); Report and Order, *In re* Rules and Regulations Implementing the Telephone Consumer Protection Act of 1991 ¶¶ 173, 179, 182, 18 F.C.C. Rcd. 14014, 2003 WL 21517853 (F.C.C. July 3, 2003) (citing relationship to do-not-call rule enforcement as reason for prohibition).

373 47 U.S.C. § 227(c)(5). *See* § 6.9.2.2, *infra*.

374 *Id. See* §§ 6.9.1, 6.9.2.1–6.9.2.4, 6.9.6, *infra*.

375 *See* §§ 6.9.1, 6.9.2.1–6.9.2.4, 6.9.6, *infra*.

376 *See* §§ 5.6, 6.2.1, 6.2.2, *supra*.

377 *See* Appx. D, *infra*.

378 *See* Holcomb v. Steven D. Smith, Inc., 170 P.3d 815 (Colo. App. 2007) (state do-not-call law covers residential telephone numbers that are also used as business numbers); TSA Stores, Inc. v. Dep't of Agriculture & Consumer Services, 957 So. 2d 25 (Fla. Dist. Ct. App. 2007) (merely giving telephone number to sales clerk is not consent to receive telemarketing calls, but making purchase within past eighteen months creates existing business relationship allowing seller to call even if consumer is on do-not-call list). *See generally* Appx. D, *infra*.

379 *See, e.g.,* Indiana v. American Family Voices, Inc., 898 N.E.2d 293 (Ind. 2008) (reversing lower court dismissal of state's suit under the Indiana Autodialer Law).

380 *See* Appx. D, *infra*.

381 *See, e.g.,* Dominguez v. Yahoo, Inc., ___ Fed. Appx. ___, 2015 WL 6405811 (3d Cir. Nov. 21, 2014) (reversing dismissal of TCPA claim by consumer who received 27,809 unwanted text messages over seventeen months from a single sender despite multiple requests to stop and complaints to FTC and FCC).

382 *See* Joffe v. Acacia Mortg. Corp., 211 Ariz. 325 (Ct. App. 2006) (describing this technology).

383 *See* § 6.10, *infra*.

384 *See, e.g.,* Joffe v. Acacia Mortg. Corp., 211 Ariz. 325 (Ariz. Ct. App. 2006).

385 *See* § 6.10.2.2, *infra*.

386 *See* § 6.3, *supra*.

387 *See* §§ 6.7.2, 6.7.4, *infra*.

388 *See* Joffe v. Acacia Mortg. Corp., 211 Ariz. 325 (Ariz. Ct. App. 2006). *See also In re* Rules & Regulations Implementing the Telephone Consumer Protection Act of 1991 ¶¶ 120–121, CG Docket No. 02-278, WC Docket No. 07-135, 2015 WL 4387780, ___ F.C.C. ___ (July 10, 2015).

6.7.2 TCPA Prohibits Use of Automatic Dialing Systems to Send Text Messages Without Consent

With certain exceptions that will be listed *infra*, the TCPA prohibits any person from initiating a "call" using an automatic telephone dialing system to "any telephone number assigned to a paging service, cellular telephone service, specialized mobile radio service, or other radio common carrier service, or any service for which the called party is charged for the call."[389] As discussed below, this provision has been successfully used to challenge spam text messaging. The provision effectively makes illegal virtually any text message sent out in bulk without the recipient's prior express consent (which must be in writing in the case of telemarketing messages).[390]

The first question is whether an e-mail originating over the Internet and converted to a text message sent to a cell phone is a "call" as used for the purposes of the TCPA. The FCC has ruled that the TCPA prohibition "encompasses both voice calls and text calls to wireless numbers including, for example, short message service (SMS) calls."[391] Courts have reached the same conclusion.[392] There is no requirement that the call involve two-way communication[393] or that the consumer be charged for the text message.[394] Initiating an e-mail that will be converted to a text is sufficient for the TCPA provision to apply.

The next question is whether the text message initiates from "an automatic telephone dialing system." The FCC rule defines this term as "equipment which has the capacity to store or produce telephone numbers to be called using a random or sequential number generator and to dial such numbers."[395]

Courts generally find that this definition is met by sophisticated systems that generate large numbers of text messages.[396] Courts often focus on the word "capacity" and hold that it is not necessary for the plaintiff to prove that the device (for example, a computer) was used in a way that meets the definition, as long as the device has the capacity to be used in that way.[397] On the other hand, systems that send text messages triggered by the individualized action of a natural person may not be covered.[398]

Nor is it a defense to argue that the equipment merely sent an e-mail to a cellular carrier and not the consumer and that the carrier's equipment is what actually sent the message to the consumer's cell phone.[399] The equipment was instrumental in sending the message to the consumer.

Telemarketers and others sued for sending text messages to cell phones have raised various constitutional challenges to the TCPA and its application to text messaging. These challenges have not been successful.[400]

6.7.3 Extremely Limited Exceptions to the General Prohibition

The TCPA's prohibition on the use of autodialers to make voice calls and send text messages does not apply if the caller

389   *See* 47 U.S.C. 227(b)(1)(A). *See also* 47 C.F.R. § 64.1200(a)(1)(iii).
390   *See* § 6.7.3, *infra* (consent requirements).
391   Report and Order, *In re* Rules and Regulations Implementing the Telephone Consumer Protection Act of 1991 ¶ 165, 18 F.C.C. Rcd. 14014, 2003 WL 21517853 (F.C.C. July 3, 2003). *Accord In re* Rules & Regulations Implementing the Telephone Consumer Protection Act of 1991 ¶¶ 27, 107–108, 111–115, CG Docket No. 02-278, WC Docket No. 07-135, 2015 WL 4387780, ___ F.C.C. ___ (July 10, 2015).
392   Gomez v. Campbell-Ewald Co., 768 F.3d 871 (9th Cir. 2014), *cert. granted*, 135 S. Ct. 2311 (2015); Satterfield v. Simon & Schuster, Inc., 569 F.3d 946, 952 (9th Cir. 2009) ("a text message is a 'call' within the meaning of the TCPA."); Reardon v. Uber Technologies, Inc., ___ F. Supp. 3d ___, 2015 WL 4451209 (N.D. Cal. July 19, 2015); Scott v. Merchants Ass'n Collection Services, 2012 WL 4896175 (S.D. Fla. Oct. 15, 2012); Connelly v. Hilton Grand Vacations Co., 2012 WL 2129364 (S.D. Cal. June 11, 2012); Buslepp v. Improv Miami, Inc., 2012 WL 1560408 (S.D. Fla., May 4, 2012); Buslepp v. B&B Entm't, L.L.C., 2012 WL 1571410 (S.D. Fla. May 3, 2012); Pimental v. Google Inc., 2012 WL 691784 (N.D. Cal. Mar. 2, 2012); Lo v. Oxnard European Motors, L.L.C., 2011 WL 6300050 (S.D. Cal. Dec. 15, 2011); Kramer v. Autobytel, 759 F. Supp. 2d 1165 (N.D. Cal. 2010); Lozano v. Twentieth Century Fox Film Corp., 702 F. Supp. 2d 999 (N.D. Ill. 2010); Kazemi v. Payless Shoesource, Inc., 2010 WL 963225 (N.D. Cal. Mar. 12, 2010); Abbas v. Seeling Source, L.L.C., 2009 WL 4884471 (N.D. Ill. Dec. 14, 2009); Joffe v. Acacia Mortg. Corp., 211 Ariz. 325 (Ariz. Ct. App. 2006). *See also In re* Jiffy Lube Int'l, Inc., Text Spam Litig., 847 F. Supp. 2d 1253 (S.D. Cal. 2012); Daniel L. Hadjinian, *Reach Out and Text Someone: How Text Message Spam May Be a Call Under the TCPA*, 4 Shidler J. L. Com. & Tech. 3 (2007).
393   *See* Joffe v. Acacia Mortg. Corp., 121 P.3d 831 (Ariz. Ct. App. 2006).
394   *See* Agne v. Papa John's Int'l, Inc., 286 F.R.D. 559, 570 (W.D. Wash. 2012); Buslepp v. Improv Miami, Inc., 2012 WL 1560408 (S.D. Fla. May 4, 2012); Lozano v. Twentieth Century Fox Film Corp., 702 F. Supp. 2d 999 (N.D. Ill. 2010); Abbas v. Selling Source, L.L.C., 2009 WL 4884471 (N.D. Ill. Dec. 14, 2009).

395   47 C.F.R. § 64.1200(f)(2).
396   *See* Pimental v. Google Inc., 2012 WL 691784 (N.D. Cal. Mar. 2, 2012); *In re* Jiffy Lube Int'l, Inc., Text Spam Litig., 847 F. Supp. 2d 1253 (S.D. Cal. 2012); Lozano v. Twentieth Century Fox Film Corp., 702 F. Supp. 2d 999 (N.D. Ill. 2010); Abbas v. Selling Source, L.L.C., 2009 WL 4884471 (N.D. Ill. Dec. 14, 2009); Joffe v. Acacia Mortg. Corp., 121 P.3d 831 (Ariz. Ct. App. 2006).
397   Abbas v. Selling Source, L.L.C., 2009 WL 4884471 (N.D. Ill. Dec. 14, 2009). *See generally* § 6.3.2, *supra* (what is an autodialer).
398   Luna v. Shac, L.L.C., ___ F. Supp. 3d ___, 2015 WL 4941781 (N.D. Cal. Aug. 19, 2015) (Internet-based calling system was not autodialer when human intervention was involved in drafting message, determining its timing, and clicking "send"); Gragg v. Orange Cab Co., 995 F. Supp. 2d 1189 (W.D. Wash. 2014) (system that sent text message advising consumer that taxicab was en route when a taxicab driver accepted a service request is not an automated telephone dialing system because it requires human intervention on the part of the driver). *See also* Marks v. Crunch San Diego, L.L.C., 55 F. Supp. 3d 1288 (S.D. Cal. 2014) (characterizing FCC interpretation as unauthorized and overbroad; third-party web-based platform for sending text messages to numbers inputted by several methods and then selected by sender is not an autodialer).
399   *See* Satterfield v. Simon & Schuster, Inc., 569 F.3d 946, 952 (9th Cir. 2009); Pimental v. Google Inc., 2012 WL 691784 (N.D. Cal. Mar. 2, 2012); Joffe v. Acacia Mortg. Corp., 121 P.3d 831 (Ariz. Ct. App. 2006). *See also In re* Rules & Regulations Implementing the Telephone Consumer Protection Act of 1991 ¶¶ 30-31, CG Docket No. 02-278, WC Docket No. 07-135, 2015 WL 4387780, ___ F.C.C. ___ (July 10, 2015) (entity that offers a calling platform that others use to send text messages does not make or initiate the call as long as it does not knowingly allow illegal acts).
400   *See* § 6.3.1, *supra*.

or sender has the recipient's prior express consent.[401] If the text message constitutes telemarketing or introduces an advertisement, the recipient's consent must be written.[402] Senders of spam text messages are rarely able to establish that they had the recipient's consent.[403]

There are several other exceptions that rarely apply. There is an exception for emergency calls.[404] Certain health care messages are exempt from the requirement to obtain prior express written consent before using an autodialer to send a message to a cell phone that introduces an advertisement or constitutes telemarketing.[405] In 2015, the FCC announced a new exception for certain exigent health care text messages and certain messages from financial institutions relating to fraud and similar matters.[406] There is also an exception when the call is made to a phone number that was a land line and was converted to a cell phone number within the last fifteen days, provided that the number is not on the general do-not-call list or the caller's company-specific do-not-call list.[407] These exceptions are discussed in § 6.3, *supra*.

There is no exception for debt collection messages.[408] The prohibition applies whether or not the caller is seeking to solicit goods or services, although the consent requirements are stricter for messages that introduce an advertisement or constitute telemarketing.[409] There is no exception for a prior business relationship.[410] Thus anyone sending a debt collection text message with an automatic telephone dialing system without prior express consent[411] is violating the TCPA.

Sending a text message without using an automatic telephone dialing system does not violate this prohibition. However, other TCPA provisions, the Fair Debt Collection Practices Act, or the FTC Telemarketing Sales Rule may come into play.

6.7.4 Remedies

The restrictions on autodialing cell phones and other sensitive numbers is part of section 227(b) of the TCPA, so there is a private right of action for the first violation and no defense

for reasonable procedures.[412] Remedies for a prevailing plaintiff are the greater of actual damages or $500 per violation, and these damages can be trebled for knowing or willful violations.[413] Issues regarding TCPA litigation that are generally applicable to all its substantive prohibitions are discussed in § 6.9, *infra*.

6.8 Junk Faxes

6.8.1 TCPA Limits on Junk Faxes

The FTC Telemarketing Sales Rule does not regulate junk faxes. The TCPA and the FCC rule adopted under it prohibit the use of a telephone fax machine, a computer, or any other device to send an unsolicited advertisement to a telephone fax machine.[414] The impetus behind this prohibition is that junk faxes tie up recipients' fax lines and shift costs from advertisers to recipients.[415] It protects against faxes to business telephone subscribers as well as residential subscribers.[416]

The junk fax prohibition applies regardless of whether the message is sent to a fax server, which receives and stores the message for later printing, or to a conventional fax machine that automatically prints each message.[417] As long as the fax is sent over a telephone line, the TCPA applies to it, even if a fax

---

401 *See* § 6.3.4.2, *infra*.

402 47 C.F.R. § 64.1200(a)(2). *See* § 6.3.4.1, *infra*.

403 *See, e.g.*, Agne v. Papa John's Int'l, Inc., 286 F.R.D. 559, 570 (W.D. Wash. 2012) (sender has burden of providing individual consent).

404 47 C.F.R. § 64.1200(a)(1).

405 47 C.F.R. § 64.1200(a)(2). *See* Fed. Communications Comm'n, Public Notice, Consumer and Governmental Affairs Bureau Seeks Comment on Petition for Expedited Declaratory Ruling And Exemption from American Association of Health Care Administrative Management n.7 (Dec. 17, 2014), *available at* www.fcc.gov ("HIPAA-covered autodialed or prerecorded calls to a wireless number are exempt from the written consent requirement. *See* 47 C.F.R. § 64.1200(a)(2). These calls are still covered by the general consent requirement in 64.1200(a)(1).")

406 *See* § 6.3.3, *supra*.

407 47 C.F.R. § 64.1200(a)(1)(iv).

408 *See* § 6.3.3, *supra*.

409 *See* § 6.3.4.1, *supra*.

410 *See* § 6.3.4.5, *supra* (no exception for established business relationships).

411 *See* § 6.3.4, *supra* (consent requirements).

412 *See* §§ 6.9.1, 6.9.6, *infra*.

413 *See* §§ 6.9.2.1–6.9.2.4, *infra*.

414 47 U.S.C. § 227(b)(1)(C); 47 C.F.R. § 64.1200(a)(4); Lary v. Flasch Bus. Consulting, 878 So. 2d 1158 (Ala. Civ. App. 2003) (reversing dismissal of junk fax claim); Grady v. OTC Investor's Edge, 2003 WL 22828294 (Ohio Ct. Com. Pl. Oct. 15, 2003) (awarding $1500 treble damages plus $200 UDAP statutory damages for junk fax). *See* Minn. *ex rel.* Hatch v. Sunbelt Communications & Mktg., 282 F. Supp. 2d 976 (D. Minn. 2002) (granting preliminary injunction against unsolicited faxes); Nat'l Notary Ass'n v. U.S. Notary, 2002 WL 1265555 (Cal. Ct. App. June 7, 2002) (unpublished) (upholding nationwide injunction under California UDAP statute, limiting a California company from sending unsolicited faxes). *See also* Kaufman v. ACS Sys., Inc., 2 Cal. Rptr. 3d 296 (Cal. Ct. App. 2003) (summarizing legislative history and testimony in favor of junk fax prohibition); Chair King, Inc. v. GTE Mobilnet of Houston, Inc., 135 S.W.3d 365 (Tex. App. 2004) (quoting legislative history of junk fax prohibition), *rev'd on other grounds*, 184 S.W.3d 707 (Tex. 2006).

415 *See* Omerza v. Bryant & Stratton, 2007 WL 2822000 (Ohio Ct. App. Sept. 28, 2007) (unpublished) (summarizing legislative history). *See also* Stonecrafters, Inc. v. Wholesale Life Ins. Brokerage, 915 N.E.2d 51 (Ill. App. Ct. 2009) (class action complaint alleged that defendant had sent mass, unsolicited one-page facsimile advertisements to prospective clients without permission, actual damages resulted from wear and tear on fax equipment and unauthorized loss of plaintiffs' toner and paper).

416 Grady v. Lenders Interactive Services, 2004 WL 1799178 (Ohio Ct. App. Aug. 12, 2004) (unpublished).

417 47 U.S.C. § 227(a)(3) (defining telephone facsimile machine as one that has the *capacity* to transcribe text or images from an electronic signal onto paper); Holtzman v. Caplice, 2008 WL 2168762 (N.D. Ill. May 23, 2008); Report and Order, *In re* Rules and Regulations Implementing the Telephone Consumer Protection Act of 1991 ¶¶ 198–202, 18 F.C.C. Rcd. 14014, 2003 WL 21517853 (F.C.C. July 3, 2003); Covington & Burling v. Int'l Mktg. & Research, Inc., 2003 WL 21384825 (D.C. Super. Ct. Apr. 17, 2003), *as amended on reconsideration by* 2003 D.C. Super. LEXIS 28 (D.C. Super. Ct. May 17, 2003).

server on the receiving end converts it into an attachment to an e-mail that is forwarded to the recipient.[418] Since the statute prohibits the sending of the unsolicited fax, it should not be necessary to present evidence that the fax was received.[419]

The recipient is under no obligation to contact the sender and request that no further faxes be sent.[420] However, demonstrating that the recipient has asked the sender to stop can be important in obtaining an increased statutory damages award for willful or knowing violations.

6.8.2   Types of Junk Faxes Prohibited

6.8.2.1   Unsolicited Advertising

The junk fax rule generally prohibits "unsolicited advertisement[s]."[421] To meet the statutory definition of an "unsolicited advertisement," the fax must advertise the commercial availability or quality of property, goods, or services and be transmitted without prior express invitation or permission.[422] In determining whether an unsolicited fax is an advertisement, the court must consider circumstances such as the sender's identity and motives, not just the content of the fax itself.[423]

Fax messages that promote goods or services at no cost—such as free magazine subscriptions, catalogs, consultations, or seminars—are unsolicited advertisements because they often serve as part of an overall marketing campaign and because advertising the commercial availability or quality of an item does not require a sale.[424] The FCC has found that, when a promotion for "free" services serves as a pretext for later solicitations, the original promotional fax constitutes an advertisement.[425] It is not necessary for a fax to actually include a cost for what is being

---

418   *In re* Westfax, Inc. Petition for Consideration and Clarification, Rules and Regulations Implementing the Telephone Consumer Protection Act of 1991, No. 05-278, No. 05-338, 2015 WL 5120880 (Aug. 28, 2015) (also holding that ultimate recipient, not entity that provides fax server, is "recipient" for TCPA purposes).

419   Fun Services of Kan. City, Inc. v. Love, 2011 WL 1843253, at *2 (W.D. Mo. May 11, 2011) ("[a] violation occurs when the prohibited fax is sent"); Clearbrook v. Rooflifters, L.L.C., 2010 WL 2635781, at *3 (N.D. Ill. June 28, 2010) (TCPA requires only that an improper fax be sent; it does not require receipt); Hinman v. M & M Rental Ctr., Inc., 545 F. Supp. 2d 802, 805 (N.D. Ill. 2008) (listing elements of claim as merely sending an unsolicited fax advertisement via telephone fax machine, computer, or other device without listing receipt as an element); Eclipse Mfg. Co. v. M & M Rental Ctr., Inc., 521 F. Supp. 2d 739, 745 (N.D. Ill. 2007) (listing elements without mentioning any requirement of receipt); A Fast Sign Co. v. American Home Services, Inc., 734 S.E.2d 31 (Ga. 2012) (sender is liable for unsolicited advertisements it attempts to send to fax machines, whether or not the transmission is completed or received by the targeted recipient); Critchfield Physical Therapy v. Taranto Grp., Inc., 263 P.3d 767, 778–79 (Kan. 2011) ("The statute creates no requirement that a transmission be received," although it addresses exceptions for 'recipients' who had established business relationships or who gave permission for advertisers to send them fax promotions); Display South, Inc. v. Express Computer Supply, Inc., 961 So. 2d 451, 455 (La. Ct. App. 2007) (rejecting argument that an "unsolicited" fax must be received for a violation to occur). *Cf.* First Nat'l Collection Bureau, Inc. v. Walker, 348 S.W.3d 329, 338–42 (Tex. App. 2011) (if Texas law had required proof of receipt, it would have been a narrowing of the federal statute and thus preempted). *But see* Holtzman v. Turza, 728 F.3d 682 (7th Cir. 2013) (stating that defendant's contention that each recipient must prove receipt is "right on the law," but finding sender's log sufficient to prove receipt); Carnett's, Inc. v. Hammond, 610 S.E.2d 529 (Ga. 2005) ("The TCPA is violated only if a plaintiff receives an 'unsolicited' fax"). *But cf.* Targin Sign Systems, Inc. v. Preferred Chiropractic Ctr., Ltd., 679 F. Supp. 2d 894, 898–99 (N.D. Ill. 2010) (stating that, once class liability is established, class members will have to show receipt of the fax).

420   Hinman v. M & M Rental Ctr., Inc., 596 F. Supp. 2d 1152, 1161 (N.D. Ill. 2009); Stefano & Associates, Inc. v. Global Lending Grp., Inc., 2008 WL 186638 (Ohio Ct. App. Jan. 23, 2008); Manufacturers Auto Leasing, Inc. v. Autoflex Leasing, Inc., 139 S.W.3d 342 (Tex. App. 2004) (citing FCC rulings).

421   47 U.S.C. § 227(b)(1)(C). *See also* § 6.3.4.1, *supra* (interpretation of "advertisement" for purposes of restrictions on calls to cell phones).

422   47 U.S.C. § 227(a)(5); 42 C.F.R. § 64.1200(f)(15). *See* Sandusky Wellness Center, L.L.C. v. Medco Health Solutions, Inc., 788 F.3d 218 (6th Cir. 2015) (to be an advertisement, fax must promote goods or services to be bought or sold, with profit as aim; communication that covertly promotes a product may be an advertisement, but pharmacy benefit manager's faxes to health care provider, listing drugs in patients' health care plans' formularies, were not advertisements when benefit manager was not selling them and would not profit from their use); Green v. Time Ins. Co., 629 F. Supp. 2d 834 (N.D. Ill. 2009) (insurance company's fax to insurance agent, proposing that he become an agent and sell its insurance, meets definition of "unsolicited advertisement"); Hinman v. M & M Rental Ctr., Inc., 596 F. Supp. 2d 1152, 1162 (N.D. Ill. 2009) (fax was an advertisement even though it also contained an invitation to an open house); Sadowski v. Med1 Online, L.L.C., 2008 WL 489360 (N.D. Ill. Feb. 20, 2008) (refusing to dismiss claim that faxes that appeared geared toward acquiring new customers were advertisements). *But cf.* Phillips Randolph Enterprises, Inc. v. Adler-Weiner Research Chi., Inc., 526 F. Supp. 2d 851 (N.D. Ill. 2007) (unsolicited fax that sought participants for research study was not advertisement); Ameriguard, Inc. v. Univ. of Kansas Med. Ctr. Research Inst., Inc., 2006 WL 1766812 (W.D. Mo. 2006) (unsolicited fax that recruited participants in clinical trial was not an advertisement), *aff'd*, 222 Fed. Appx. 530 (8th Cir. Mar. 15, 2007).

423   Physicians Healthsource, Inc. v. Stryker Sales Corp., 65 F. Supp. 3d 482, 492–493 (W.D. Mich. 2015) (court can consider more than fax itself in determining whether invitation to "free" dinner and seminar is an advertisement; fact question whether only certain portions of seminar mentioned defendant's products); Rudgayzer & Gratt v. Enine, Inc., 779 N.Y.S.2d 882 (N.Y. App. Div. 2004). *See also* Accounting Outsourcing, L.L.C. v. Verizon Wireless Personal Communications, L.P., 329 F. Supp. 2d 789, 808 (M.D. La. 2004) (statute's definition of advertisement is not unconstitutionally vague).

424   71 Fed. Reg. 25,967, 25,973 (May 3, 2006). *See* Physicians Healthsource, Inc. v. Stryker Sales Corp., 65 F. Supp. 3d 482 (W.D. Mich. 2015) (fact question whether fax from orthopedic device manufacturer, inviting primary care physicians to free dinner and presentation about orthopedics advances, was advertisement); G.M. Sign, Inc. v. MFG.com, Inc., 2009 WL 1137751 (N.D. Ill. Apr. 24, 2009) (fax offering "free service to buyers" was unsolicited advertisement).

425   *In re* Presidential Who's Who dba Presidential Who's Who, Inc., Notice of Apparent Liability for Forfeiture ¶ 7, EB-08-TC-2507 (released Sep. 13, 2010) ("Instead we find that the faxes in question serve as a pretext to advertise a commercial product or service . . . . Although there is no cost for inclusion in the publication, the products associated with the publication, such as professional directories or plaques, are later commercially available."). *Accord* Drug Reform Coordination Network, Inc. v. Grey House Publ'g, Inc., ___ F. Supp. 3d ___, 2015 WL 2404695 (D.D.C. May 11, 2015) (denying motion to dismiss; fax offering free listing in directory was advertisement when seller followed up with e-mails advertising directory).

offered for the fax to constitute an advertisement, provided that the product or service is commercially available.[426]

Some courts hold that "informational messages" that are not primarily advertisements are not covered.[427] The Seventh Circuit rejects the existence of any such exception.[428] Thus, an attorney's fax that included his name, contact information, and specialties was an advertisement as a matter of law even though 75% of the content consisted of unsolicited generic informational material.[429]

A fax that pitches a product or service in the guise of conducting a survey or providing information about it is an advertisement.[430] Messages that only seek donations to political campaigns or charitable organizations,[431] or that encourage application for an award,[432] are not unsolicited advertisements, however. Faxes listing job openings may not be covered, as they do not offer goods or services for sale.[433] On the other hand, faxes advertising business opportunities that involve the provision of goods or services may be covered.[434]

6.8.2.2 Exemption When Fax Sent Pursuant to Express Invitation or Permission

The TCPA rule prohibits fax advertisements only if they are "unsolicited."[435] An advertisement is "unsolicited" if it "is transmitted to any person without that person's prior express invitation or permission."[436]

Publishing one's fax number in a publication such as a professional association's directory is not express permission in and of itself to fax an advertisement[437] (although it is one way in which a sender that has an established business relationship with the recipient may obtain the recipient's fax number, as discussed in § 6.8.2.3, *infra*). An invitation or permission cannot be in the form of a negative option[438] and cannot be inferred or implied.[439] The invitation or permission must be given before any faxes are sent.[440] However, express permission can be found when an individual provides a fax number, such as providing it as contact information on a seller's website form.[441]

Under the FCC regulations, fax advertisements that are sent to a recipient who has provided prior express invitation or permission must be accompanied by an opt-out notice, just as in the case of one sent pursuant to an established business relationship.[442] This requirement is discussed in § 6.8.2.4, *infra*.

The FCC has determined that "a sender should have the obligation to demonstrate that it complied with the rules, including that it had the recipient's prior express invitation or permission."[443] Courts have also followed this rule and placed the burden of proof on the sender of the communication.[444]

---

426 *In re* Presidential Who's Who dba Presidential Who's Who, Inc., Notice of Apparent Liability for Forfeiture, EB-08-TC-2507 at ¶ 7 (released Sep. 13, 2010).

427 Physicians Healthsource, Inc. v. Janssen Pharmaceuticals, Inc., 2013 WL 486207 (D.N.J., Feb. 6, 2013), *later op.*, 2014 WL 413534 (D.N.J. Feb. 4, 2014); Stern v. Bluestone, 911 N.E.2d 844 (N.Y. 2009) ("Attorney Malpractice Report" consisting of short essay about various topics related to attorney malpractice not an advertisement even though sender was an attorney who filed such cases).

428 Holtzman v. Turza, 728 F.3d 682 (7th Cir. 2013).

429 *Id.*

430 Peter Strojnik, P.C. v. Signalife, Inc., 2009 WL 605411 (D. Ariz. Mar. 9, 2009) (fax that touted company's stock was advertisement even though it did not include explicit sales offer); Rudgayzer & Gratt v. Enine, Inc., 779 N.Y.S.2d 882 (N.Y. App. Div. 2004). *See also* 71 Fed. Reg. 25,967, 25,973 (May 3, 2006). *But cf.* Omerza v. Bryant & Stratton, 2007 WL 2822000 (Ohio Ct. App. Sept. 28, 2007) (unpublished) (fax from one member of local chamber of commerce to other members, proposing various types of mutually beneficial partnerships, was not an advertisement).

431 71 Fed. Reg. 25,967, 25,972 (May 3, 2006).

432 N.B. Industries, Inc. v. Wells Fargo & Co., 465 Fed. Appx. 640, 642 (9th Cir. 2012) (holding faxes encouraging application for a business award not to be an unsolicited advertisement, because advertisements for a related business conference and logos, slogans, and websites of the senders were found to be a de minimis amount of advertising on the specific faxes).

433 Friedman v. Torchmark Corp., 2013 WL 1629084 (S.D. Cal. Apr. 16, 2013); Phillips Randolph Enterprises, L.L.C. v. Adler-Weiner Research Chi., Inc., 526 F. Supp. 2d 851 (N.D. Ill. 2007); Lutz Appellate Services v. Curry, 859 F. Supp. 180 (E.D. Pa. 1994) (job openings).

434 Brodsky v. Humana Dental Ins. Co., 2014 WL 2780089 (N.D. Ill. June 12, 2014).

435 47 U.S.C. § 227(a)(5). *See* § 6.8.2.1, *supra*.

436 47 U.S.C. § 227(a)(5); 47 C.F.R. § 64.1200(f)(15) (definition of "unsolicited advertisement"). *See* David L. Smith Associates v. Advanced

Placement Team, Inc., 2007 WL 969589 (Tex. App. Apr. 3, 2007) (unpublished) (question of fact whether help wanted advertisement that listed fax number was invitation to employment agency to fax information about candidates); § 6.8.2.4, *infra* (opt-out notice).

437 Travel Travel Kirkwood, Inc. v. Jen N.Y. Inc., 206 S.W.3d 387 (Mo. Ct. App. 2006); Report and Order, *In re* Rules and Regulations Implementing the Telephone Consumer Protection Act of 1991 ¶ 193, 18 F.C.C. Rcd. 14014, 2003 WL 21517853 (F.C.C. July 3, 2003). *But see* Travel 100 Grp., Inc. v. Mediterranean Shipping Co. (USA) Inc., 889 N.E.2d 781 (Ill. App. Ct. 2008) (agreement among members of trade association that new offers would be faxed).

438 71 Fed. Reg. 25,967, 25,972 (May 3, 2006) (sending a fax with an instruction to call a number if the recipient no longer wishes to receive such faxes would be an impermissible negative option); Report and Order, *In re* Rules and Regulations Implementing the Telephone Consumer Protection Act of 1991 ¶ 191, 18 F.C.C. Rcd. 14014, 2003 WL 21517853 (F.C.C. July 3, 2003).

439 Jemiola v. XYZ Corp., 802 N.E.2d 745 (Ohio Ct. Com. Pl. 2003).

440 71 Fed. Reg. 25,967, 25,972 (May 3, 2006).

441 *See* Practice Mgmt. Support Services, Inc. v. Appeal Solutions, Inc., 2010 WL 748170 (N.D. Ill. Mar. 1, 2010).

442 47 C.F.R. § 64.1200(a)(4)(iv). *See* § 6.8.2.4, *infra*.

443 *In re* Rules and Regulations Implementing the Telephone Consumer Protection Act of 1991, CG Docket No. 02-278; No. 05-338, FCC Release 06-42, 21 F.C.C. Rcd. 3787, at 3812, 2006 FCC LEXIS 1713, 38 Communications. Reg. (P & F) 167 (Apr. 6, 2006). *See also* Virtual Auto Loans, EB-09-TC-230, 2009 FCC LEXIS 4342 (Mar. 9, 2009); New York Sec. & Private Patrol, Inc., EB-09-TC-231, 2009 FCC LEXIS 4343 (Mar. 9, 2009).

444 Gutierrez v. Barclays Grp., 2011 WL 579238, at *2 (S.D. Cal. Feb. 9, 2011); Van Sweden Jewelers, Inc. v. 101 VT, Inc., 2012 WL 4127824 (W.D. Mich. June 21, 2012); Green v. Serv. Master on Location Services Corp., 2009 WL 1810769 (N.D. Ill. June 22, 2009); Hinman v. M & M Rental Ctr., Inc., 596 F. Supp. 2d 1152 (N.D. Ill. 2009) (finding that consent did not exist with respect to class because TCPA allocates burden of obtaining consent on senders of unsolicited faxes rather than requiring recipients to opt out); Sadowski v. Med1 Online, L.L.C., 2008 WL 2224892, at *3–4 (N.D. Ill. May 27, 2008) (consent is an affirmative defense); Covington & Burling v. Int'l Mktg. & Research, Inc., 2003 WL 21384825 (D.C. Super. Ct. Apr. 17, 2003), *as amended on reconsideration by* 2003 D.C. Super. LEXIS 28 (D.C. Super. Ct. May 17, 2003);

6.8.2.3 Exemption for Established Business Relationship

The TCPA contains an explicit exemption for fax advertisements when there is an established business relationship between the sender and recipient, but only if the sender obtains the recipient's fax number in a particular fashion and discloses an opt-out right.[445] The FCC defines an established business relationship as one created by a voluntary two-way communication on the basis of a purchase, transaction, inquiry, or application.[446] If there is an established business relationship, it extends only to the company with which the consumer has had the voluntary two-way communication, not affiliates of that company.[447] The sender has the burden of proving that the established business relationship exception applies.[448]

The TCPA authorizes the FCC to set time limits on an established business relationship for purposes of the junk fax restriction, and lists a number of issues that the FCC must address if it does so.[449] Nevertheless, the existing FCC rule does not set any expiration time for established business relationships in the context of junk faxes. It merely provides that the established business relationship is in effect unless "previously terminated by either party."[450] When it adopted this provision in 2006, the FCC promised to evaluate whether consumers were complaining about receiving faxes after they reasonably expected any established business relationship to have ended, and revisit the rule if necessary.[451] It has not, however, revised the rule in this respect. (The former established business relationship exception to the prohibition of telemarketing robocalls, which the FCC abolished in 2012, provided that the relationship expired after three months if it was based on an inquiry or application or eighteen months if it was based on a purchase or transaction.[452])

For a fax to be exempt from the TCPA's prohibition on the basis of an established business relationship, the sender must have obtained the recipient's fax number in one of two ways.[453] The sender must have obtained the fax number either by a voluntary communication from the recipient or by "a directory, advertisement, or site on the Internet to which the recipient voluntarily agreed to make available its facsimile number for public distribution."[454] Merely listing one's fax number in a directory or advertisement or on the Internet is insufficient if the sender does not have an established business relationship with the recipient.[455]

6.8.2.4 Notice Requirement If Fax Sent Pursuant to Explicit Permission or Established Business Relationship

Whenever a fax advertisement is sent pursuant to the established business relationship exemption, the first page of the

---

All Am. Printing, L.L.C. v. Fin. Solutions, 315 S.W.3d 719, 724–725 (Mo. 2010) (prior express permission is an affirmative defense rather than an element of a TCPA claim); Travel Travel Kirkwood, Inc. v. Jen N.Y. Inc., 206 S.W.3d 387 (Mo. Ct. App. 2006) (sender has burden and 'express' permission must be clear, definite, explicit, plain, direct, and unmistakable, not dubious or ambiguous); Jemiola v. XYZ Corp., 802 N.E.2d 745 (Ohio Ct. Com. Pl. 2003); Lampkin v. GGH, Inc., 146 P.3d 847 ¶ 27 (Okla. Ct. App. 2006) (recipient should not be charged with proving negative propositions that it did not give permission or did not have a business relationship with sender). *See generally* § 6.9.8, *infra*.

445 47 U.S.C. § 227(b)(1)(C), *as amended by* Pub. L. No. 109-21 (S 714), 119 Stat. 359 (July 9, 2005); 47 C.F.R. § 64.1200(a)(4). *See* Catalyst Strategic Design, Inc. v. Kaiser Found. Health Plan, Inc., 64 Cal. Rptr. 3d 55 (Cal. Ct. App. 2007) (unpublished) (reciting history of amendments); Report of the Comm. on Commerce, Science, and Transp. on the Junk Fax Prevention Act of 2005, S. Rep. No. 109-79 (June 7, 2005) (describing history of established business relationship exception to junk fax prohibition). *See generally* § 6.8.2.4, *infra* (opt-out notice requirement).

446 47 C.F.R. § 64.1200(f)(6). *See* Centerline Equip. Corp. v. Banner Pers. Serv., Inc., 2009 WL 1607587 (N.D. Ill. June 9, 2009) (fax sender's previous cold calls to recipient do not create established business relationship). *See also* 71 Fed. Reg. 25,967, 25,969 (May 3, 2006) ("[A]n inquiry about store location or the identity of the fax sender, for instance, would not alone form an EBR for purposes of sending facsimile advertisements. Merely visiting a Web site, without taking additional steps to request information or provide contact information, also does not create an EBR.").

447 71 Fed. Reg. 25,967, 25,969 (May 3, 2006).

448 71 Fed. Reg. 25,967 (May 3, 2006) ("[t]o ensure that the EBR exemption is not exploited, the Commission concludes that an entity that sends a facsimile advertisement on the basis of an EBR should be responsible for demonstrating the existence of the EBR").

449 47 U.S.C. § 227(b)(2)(G), *as amended by* Pub. L. No. 109-21 (S 714), 119 Stat. 359 (July 9, 2005).

450 47 C.F.R. § 64.1200(f)(6).

451 71 Fed. Reg. 25,967, 25,969 (May 3, 2006).

452 Former 47 C.F.R. § 64.1200(a)(4)(i), *as amended by* 68 Fed. Reg. 44,177 (July 25, 2003).

453 71 Fed. Reg. 25,967 (May 3, 2006) ("an EBR alone does not entitle a sender to fax an advertisement to an individual consumer or business"); Bromberg Law Office, P.C. v. Itkowitz & Harwood, 831 N.Y.S.2d 351 (N.Y. Civ. Ct. 2006) (sender must both have established business relationship with recipient and have obtained fax number in one of the specified ways).

These requirements do not apply, however, if the established business relationship existed prior to the date of enactment of the 2005 law. 47 U.S.C. § 227(b)(1)(C)(ii), *as amended by* Pub. L. No. 109-21, 119 Stat. 359 (July 9, 2005); 47 C.F.R. § 64.1200(a)(4)(ii)(C).

454 47 U.S.C. § 227(b)(1)(C)(ii)(II), *as amended by* Pub. L. No. 109-21, 119 Stat. 359 (July 9, 2005); 47 C.F.R. § 64.1200(a)(4)(ii)(B) (fax recipient voluntarily makes fax number available by listing it in recipient's own directory or advertisement; if it is listed in third-party compilation, faxer must take reasonable steps to verify that recipient voluntarily made it available). *See also* 71 Fed. Reg. 25,967, 25,968 (May 3, 2006).

455 47 U.S.C. § 227(b)(1)(C)(i), *as amended by* Pub. L. No. 109-21, 119 Stat. 359 (July 9, 2005). *See, e.g.*, City Select Auto Sales, Inc. v. David/ Randall Associates, Inc., 96 F. Supp. 3d 403 (D.N.J. 2015); Rossario's Fine Jewelry, Inc. v. Paddock Publications, Inc., 2007 WL 2409791 (N.D. Ill. Aug. 22, 2007) (granting summary judgment to faxer when facts showed that recipient voluntarily provided fax number). *See also* 71 Fed. Reg. 25,967, 25,968 (May 3, 2006) ("[S]enders of facsimile advertisements must have an EBR with the recipient in order to send the advertisement to the recipient's facsimile number. The fact that the facsimile number was made available in a directory, advertisement or Web site does not alone entitle a person to send a facsimile advertisement to that number."); Report and Order, *In re* Rules and Regulations Implementing the Telephone Consumer Protection Act of 1991 ¶ 193, 18 F.C.C. Rcd. 14014, 2003 WL 21517853 (F.C.C. July 3, 2003) (publishing one's fax number in, for example, a professional association's directory is not consent).

fax advertisement must contain a clear and conspicuous notice of the recipient's right to opt out of receiving additional faxes.[456] This same requirement applies to fax advertisements sent with the recipient's explicit permission.[457] The Sixth, Seventh, and Eighth Circuits have held that non-compliance results in negation of the consent and established business relationship defenses.[458] A compliant opt-out notice must contain all of the information specified in the statute and regulation.[459]

There must be at least one means of opting out that is cost-free.[460] The advertiser or faxer must have the ability to receive opt-out requests twenty-four hours a day, seven days a week.[461] It must comply with an opt-out request within the shortest reasonable time, not to exceed thirty days.[462] An advertiser or faxer must honor the opt-out request even if the consumer continues to do business with the advertiser.[463] The opt-out request expires if the consumer subsequently provides an express invitation or permission for the sender to resume sending faxes.[464] The advertiser is responsible for the failures of any third party who records or maintains opt-out requests for the advertiser.[465]

On October 30, 2014, the FCC released an order providing a six-month window during which senders of faxes could ask the FCC for a retroactive waiver of the requirement to include an opt-out notice in faxes sent with the recipient's prior consent.[466] Whether any retrospective waivers the FCC grants will insulate senders of faxes from liability remains to be seen. One of the first courts to address the question held that the ruling did not impact its decision that a defendant's advertisements were faxed without prior express permission because its ruling rested not merely on the FCC's ruling but on the statute itself.[467] The court also pointed out that the FCC's waiver did not invalidate the regulation, which remains in effect as promulgated. It also held that the FCC could, at most, decline to exercise its statutory enforcement power but could not use an administrative waiver to eliminate statutory liability. In any event, the FCC's order applies only to faxes sent with the recipient's prior consent,[468] not unsolicited faxes[469] or faxes sent pursuant to an established business relationship.[470] It also provides that granting a waiver should not be construed in any way to confirm or deny whether the petitioner had the prior express permission of the recipients to send the faxes.[471]

6.8.3 Other Junk Fax Restrictions and Requirements

"War dialing" (dialing numbers to determine whether they are fax or voice lines) is specifically prohibited.[472] The FCC's

---

456 47 U.S.C. § 227(b)(1)(C)(iii), (2)(D), *as amended by* Pub. L. No. 109-21, 119 Stat. 359 (July 9, 2005); 47 C.F.R. § 64.1200(a)(4)(iii). *See also* 71 Fed. Reg. 25,967, 25,969 (May 3, 2006) ("including an opt-out notice on a facsimile advertisement alone is not sufficient to permit the transmission of the fax; an EBR with the recipient must also exist"); Holtzman v. Turza, 728 F.3d 682 (7th Cir. 2013) (faxes without opt-out notices violated TCPA even if sent pursuant to established business relationship); Spine & Sports Chiropractic, Inc. v. Zirmed, Inc., 2014 WL 2946421 (W.D. Ky. June 30, 2014) (faxes without opt-out notices violated TCPA even if sent pursuant to established business relationship); Landsman & Funk, P.C. v. Lorman Bus. Ctr., Inc., 2009 WL 602019 (W.D. Wis. Mar. 9, 2009) (finding opt-out notice sufficient even though it stated that sender must comply with opt-out request within reasonable time, rather than within thirty days); Kovel v. Lerner, Cumbo & Associates, Inc., 927 N.Y.S.2d 286 (N.Y. App. Term 2011) (faxes without opt-out notices violated TCPA even if sent pursuant to established business relationship).

457 47 C.F.R. § 64.1200(a)(4)(iv). *See* Holtzman v. Turza, 728 F.3d 682 (7th Cir. 2013) (faxes without opt-out notices violated TCPA even if sent with permission); Nack v. Walburg, 715 F.3d 680 (8th Cir. 2013) (opt-out notice is required even for faxes sent with permission, and Hobbs Act precludes challenge to FCC regulation requiring this notice); MSG Jewelers, Inc. v. C & C Quality Printing, Inc., 2008 TCPA Rep. 1811 (Mo. Cir. Ct. July 17, 2008) (recipient of fax advertisement sent with express permission still had standing to sue for failure to include opt-out notice).

458 *In re* Sandusky Wellness Ctr., L.L.C., 788 F.3d 218 (6th Cir. 2014); Nack v. Walburg, 715 F.3d 680 (8th Cir. 2013); Holtzman v. Turza, 728 F.3d 682 (7th Cir. 2013). *Accord* Drug Reform Coordination Network, Inc. v. Grey House Publ'g, Inc., ___ F. Supp. 3d ___, 2015 WL 2404695 (D.D.C. May 11, 2015) (sender of a fax that does not include opt-out notice is not protected by established business relationship exception); Physicians Healthsource, Inc. v. Stryker Sales Corp., 65 F. Supp. 3d 482, 497 (W.D. Mich. 2015); City Select Auto Sales, Inc. v. David/Randall Associates, Inc., 96 F. Supp. 3d 403 (D.N.J. 2015); Spine & Sports Chiropractic, Inc. v. Zirmed, Inc., 2014 WL 2946421 (W.D. Ky. June 30, 2014); C-Mart, Inc. v. Metropolitan Life Ins. Co., 299 F.R.D. 679 (S.D. Fla. 2014); Bais Yaakov of Spring Valley v. Alloy, Inc., 936 F. Supp. 2d 272 (S.D.N.Y. 2013); A Aventura Chiropractic Ctr., Inc. v. Med Waste Mgmt., L.L.C., 2013 WL 3463489 (S.D. Fla. July 3, 2013).

459 Exclusively Cats Vet. Hosp. v. Fla. Infusion Services, Inc., 2013 WL 2318462 (E.D. Mich. May 28, 2013).

460 47 C.F.R. § 64.1200(a)(4)(iii)(D).

461 47 C.F.R. § 64.1200(a)(4)(iii)(E).

462 47 C.F.R. § 64.1200(a)(4)(vi). *See also* 47 C.F.R. § 64.1200(a)(4)(v) (requirements for opt-out request).

463 71 Fed. Reg. 25,967, 25,971 (May 3, 2006).

464 *Id.*

465 47 C.F.R. § 64.1200(a)(4)(vi).

466 *In re* Implementing the Rules & Regulations of the Tel. Consumer Protection Act of 1991, Application for Review filed by Anda, Inc., 29 F.C.C. Rcd. 13998, 29 F.C.C.R. 13998, 61 Communications Reg. (P&F) 671, 2014 WL 5493425 (Oct. 30, 2014).

467 Physicians Healthsource, Inc. v. Stryker Sales Corp., 65 F. Supp. 3d 482, 497–498 (W.D. Mich. 2015).

468 Fauley v. Haska Corp., ___ F. Supp. 3d ___, 2015 WL 4079189 (N.D. Ill. July 6, 2015).

469 *See* Simon v. Healthways Inc., 2015 WL 1568230 (C.D. Cal. Apr. 7, 2015); Physicians Healthsource, Inc. v. Doctor Diabetic Supply, L.L.C., 2014 WL 7366255 (S.D. Fla. Dec. 24, 2014) (certifying class; FCC's 2013 order irrelevant when defendant presented no evidence that any of its faxes were solicited); Around the World Travel, Inc. v. Unique Vacations, Inc., 2014 WL 6606953 (E.D. Mich. Nov. 19, 2014).

470 Simon v. Healthways, Inc., 2015 WL 1568230, at *4 (C.D. Cal. Apr. 7, 2015).

471 *In re* Implementing the Rules & Regulations of the Tel. Consumer Protection Act of 1991, Application for Review filed by Anda, Inc., 29 F.C.C. Rcd. 13998, 29 F.C.C.R. 13998, 61 Communications Reg. (P&F) 671, 2014 WL 5493425 (Oct. 30, 2014) ¶ 31.

472 47 C.F.R. § 64.1200(a)(8); Report and Order, *In re* Rules and Regulations Implementing the Telephone Consumer Protection Act of 1991 ¶ 135, 18 F.C.C. Rcd. 14014, 2003 WL 21517853 (F.C.C. July 3, 2003).
    The effective date was announced at 68 Fed. Reg. 44,144 (July 25, 2003).

war-dialing regulation has withstood an attack for allegedly exceeding the FCC's statutory authority under the TCPA.[473]

The TCPA also requires fax transmissions to include the date and time of the transmission and the identity and telephone number of the sender.[474] However, most courts have held that the TCPA does not create a private cause of action to enforce this requirement.[475]

6.8.4 Junk Fax Litigation and Remedies

The prohibition on junk faxes is found at 47 U.S.C. § 227(b), and consequently there is a private right of action for any violation, even the first junk fax that an individual receives.[476] The recipient of a junk fax need not be the owner of the fax machine in order to have standing to sue; Congress was concerned not just about the costs of paper and ink but also with the waste of time and disruption of the free flow of commerce that junk faxes cause.[477] However, the entity to which the phone line is issued or who pays for the toner and supplies consumed is a proper plaintiff. An employee who picks up the fax does not have an individual claim.[478]

There is no defense based on reasonable procedures.[479] Nor is there any requirement that the plaintiff have suffered actual damages.[480]

Remedies include actual damages or $500 per violation, whichever is greater, and the court may treble the award in the case of a willful or knowing violation.[481] Under the FCC rules, a fax broadcaster (faxer) is liable for violation of the junk fax rule, including failure to include the opt-out notice, if it demonstrates a high degree of involvement in, or actual notice of, the unlawful activity and fails to take steps to prevent such fax transmissions.[482]

Tips on investigating junk faxes and profiles of junk faxers may be found at www.junkfax.org. A review of FCC enforcement actions concerning junk faxes can also be helpful.[483] Sometimes useful information is also found on complaint board websites. Issues regarding TCPA litigation that are generally applicable to all its substantive prohibitions are discussed in § 6.9, *infra*.

6.8.5 State Junk Fax Claims

Many states have their own laws forbidding junk faxes. These statutes may make useful parallel claims, as they may have additional remedies and fewer jurisdictional issues.[484] For example, the TCPA does not provide for attorney fees for a prevailing plaintiff.

The TCPA explicitly allows states to prohibit junk faxes, automatic dialing systems, artificial or prerecorded voice messages, and telephone solicitations, and allows states to impose more restrictive intrastate requirements.[485] In 2005, the FCC opened a proceeding to decide whether to rule that the TCPA preempts certain state laws[486] but has taken no action on this proposal.

---

473 Baltimore-Washington Tel. Co. v. Hot Leads Co. L.L.C., 584 F. Supp. 2d 736 (D. Md. 2008).

474 47 U.S.C. § 227(d)(1)(B). *See also* 47 C.F.R. § 68.318(d).

475 Klein v. Vision Lab Telecommunications, Inc., 399 F. Supp. 2d 528 (S.D.N.Y. 2005) (no private cause of action to enforce statutory requirement or the regulation implementing it); Adler v. Vision Lab Telecommunications, Inc., 393 F. Supp. 2d 35 (D.D.C. 2005); Lary v. Flasch Bus. Consulting, 878 So. 2d 1158 (Ala. Civ. App. 2003); USA Tax Law Ctr., Inc. v. Office Warehouse Wholesale, L.L.C., 160 P.3d 428 (Colo. App. 2007); Ferron & Associates v. U.S. Four, Inc., 2005 WL 3550760 (Ohio Ct. App. Dec. 29, 2005) (unpublished). *See* Talty v. Strada Capital Corp., 2009 TCPA Rep. 1921 (Ohio Ct. Com. Pl. Sept. 30, 2009) (distinguishing cases finding no private right of action under 47 C.F.R. § 63.318(d) from actions brought under 47 U.S.C. § 227(b)(3) after the July 2005 TCPA amendment for failing to provide the notice required by 47 U.S.C. § 227(b)(2)(D), and finding a right of action for the latter). *But see* Schraut v. Rocky Mtn. Reclamation, No. 01-AC-002848 O CV, 2001 TCPA Rep. 1182 (Mo. Cir. Ct. Dec. 18, 2001) (violations of the header identification requirements in the statute are not actionable, but violations of similar requirements in the regulations are actionable under 47 U.S.C. § 227(b)(3)).

476 *See* Nack v. Walburg, 715 F.3d 680 (8th Cir. 2013) (Hobbs Act precludes challenge to FCC's determination to promulgate opt-out notice requirement under section 227(b), so there is a private cause of action). *See generally* §§ 6.9.1, 6.9.6, *infra*.

477 American Copper & Brass, Inc. v. Lake City Indus. Products, Inc., 757 F.3d 540, 544–545 (6th Cir. 2014); Holtzman v. Turza, 728 F.3d 682, 684 (7th Cir. 2013). *See generally* § 6.9.3.1, *infra* (standing).

478 Kopff v. World Research Grp., L.L.C., 568 F. Supp. 2d 39 (D.D.C. 2008) (administrative assistant who picks up fax addressed to business does not have claim).

479 *See generally* §§ 6.9.1, 6.9.6, *infra*.

480 Palm Beach Golf Center-Boca, Inc. v. John G. Sarris, D.D.S., P.A., 781 F.3d 1245, 1252–1253 (11th Cir. 2015). *See generally* § 6.9.3.1, *infra* (Art. III standing).

481 *See* §§ 6.9.2.1–6.9.2.4, *infra*.

482 47 C.F.R. § 64.1200(a)(4)(vii).

483 *See* Fed. Communications Comm'n, Headlines, available at www.fcc.gov.

484 *See, e.g.,* Md. Code Ann., Com. Law §§ 14-3201 to 14-3202 (West) (making violation of the TCPA a state law violation and providing for attorney fees); Oettinger v. Stevens Commercial Roofing, L.L.C., 2013 WL 3811765 (N.J. Super. Ct. App. Div. July 24, 2013) (recipient is entitled to statutory damages by showing receipt of junk fax and need not demonstrate additional injury).

485 47 U.S.C. § 227(f)(1). *See* Gottlieb v. Carnival Corp., 635 F. Supp. 2d 213, 224–26 (E.D.N.Y. 2009) (New York junk fax law covers both intrastate and interstate faxes and is not preempted); Weber v. U.S. Sterling Sec., Inc., 924 A.2d 816 (Conn. 2007) (state law that allows certain junk faxes does not override TCPA's prohibition); Utah Div. of Consumer Prot. v. Flagship Capital, 125 P.3d 894 (Utah 2005) (TCPA does not restrict stronger state restrictions on autodialers). *But see* Chamber of Commerce v. Lockyer, 2006 WL 462482 (E.D. Cal. Feb. 27, 2006) (construing 47 U.S.C. § 227(e)(1) to allow states to regulate only interstate faxes). *But cf.* Klein v. Vision Lab Telecommunications, Inc., 399 F. Supp. 2d 528 (S.D.N.Y. 2005) (construing state junk fax law to cover only intrastate faxes in light of view that TCPA preempts some state laws; called into doubt by Gottlieb v. Carnival Corp., 436 F.3d 335, 343 (2d Cir. 2006)). *See generally* § 6.2.4.2, *supra*.

486 70 Fed. Reg. 37,317 (June 29, 2005). *See also* 70 Fed. Reg. 9875 (Mar. 1, 2005) (request for comments on petition seeking ruling that TCPA preempts Florida restrictions on autodialed prerecorded voice calls); Charvat v. Telelytics, L.L.C., 2006 WL 2574019 (Ohio Ct. App. Aug. 31, 2006) (TCPA does not preempt even regulation of interstate calls unless they frustrate the federal objective of a uniform national standard). *Cf.* Worsham v. Ehrlich, 957 A.2d 161 (Md. Ct. Spec. App. 2008)

Courts are divided as to whether a TCPA violation is also a violation of the state UDAP statute, which may offer additional remedies such as attorney fees.[487] Courts are also divided regarding common law claims such as conversion, trespass, and invasion of privacy.[488]

6.9 TCPA Litigation and Remedies

6.9.1 Private Causes of Action Under the TCPA

The TCPA's substantive requirements are set out at 47 U.S.C. § 227(b)–(e). Subsections 227(b) and (c) each provide for an explicit (although somewhat different) private right of action.

Subsection 227(b) provides a private remedy for any violation of that section or of a regulation prescribed under that section.[489] Thus there is a private right of action for any violation of provisions dealing with restrictions on autodialed or prerecorded calls or texts to cell phones,[490] prerecorded telephone calls to land line telephones,[491] and junk faxes,[492] as well as the regulations under that section. A single violation is sufficient to create liability.[493]

Section 227(c), which requires the FCC to adopt rules concerning subscriber privacy rights, provides a private remedy when a person has received more than one telephone call within any twelve-month period by or on behalf of the same entity in violation of regulations prescribed under section 227(c).[494] It appears that the FCC's requirement that telemarketers identify the entity on whose behalf they are calling is a privacy protection, promulgated pursuant to this authority, since it relates to telephone solicitations and is essential if a company-specific (or national) do-not-call list is to be enforceable. Similarly, the FCC adopted the restrictions on calling times[495] and abandoned calls[496] pursuant to this authority concerning privacy. The same is true of the prohibition against blocking caller ID.[497] (The 2010 amendment of the TCPA by the Truth in Caller ID Act[498] imposes broader restrictions on caller ID falsification and does not include a special private cause of action, but the FCC's regulations were adopted many years before that amendment).[499] Thus, there may be a private right of action under section 227(c) for violation of the restrictions on calling times, the prohibition against blocking caller ID, the restrictions against abandoned calls, and the requirement that telemarketers identify the entity on whose behalf they are calling, all of which relate to privacy.

A consumer is not required to register with the nationwide do-not-call list as a precondition of maintaining a private cause of action for violations (other than the nationwide do-not-call provision) or to mitigate damages for repeated violations.[500] However, for violations that fall within section 227(c), there is an affirmative defense that the defendant established and implemented with due care reasonable procedures to prevent such violations.[501]

Subsections (d) and (e) contain no explicit private remedy. Several courts have held that there is no private cause of action to enforce the technical and procedural standards for telecommunications equipment set forth in section 227(d),[502] including the requirement that the sender's identity and telephone number be included in a fax.

Special issues regarding the private cause of action for violation of the restrictions on robocalls, prerecorded calls, and junk faxes are discussed in the sections addressing those substantive protections. As noted in § 6.2.3, *supra*, a private cause of action to enforce the FTC Rule is available only when the individual's damages exceed $50,000. Litigation under the FTC rule is not discussed here but only in § 6.2.3 and Chapter 5, *supra*.

(47 U.S.C. § 227(e)(1) preempts state regulation of certain requirements for prerecorded voice calls that are not solicitation calls).

487 *See* § 6.2.4.2, *supra*.

488 *See* Palm Beach Golf Center-Boca, Inc. v. John G. Sarris, D.D.S., P.A., 781 F.3d 1245, 1254–1255 (11th Cir. 2015) (Fla. law) (occupying telephone line and fax machine by sending junk fax may be conversion); Rossario's Fine Jewelry, Inc. v. Paddock Publications, Inc., 443 F. Supp. 2d 976 (N.D. Ill. 2006) (rejecting conversion claim as *de minimis* and as chattel property—ink, toner, paper—never came into defendant's possession); Adler v. Vision Lab Telecommunications, Inc., 393 F. Supp. 2d 35 (D.D.C. 2005) (dismissing negligence claim but refusing to dismiss invasion of privacy claim); U.S. Fax Law Ctr., Inc. v. iHire, Inc., 374 F. Supp. 2d 924 (D. Colo. 2005), *aff'd on other grounds*, 476 F.3d 1112 (10th Cir. 2007); Edwards v. Emperor's Garden Restaurant, 130 P.3d 1280 (Nev. 2006) (does not constitute conversion). *But see* Centerline Equip. Corp. v. Banner Personnel Serv., Inc., 545 F. Supp. 2d 768 (N.D. Ill. 2008) (denial of motion to dismiss) (Illinois allows class conversion claims even when each individual loss is *de minimis*).

489 47 U.S.C. § 227(b)(3).

490 *See* § 6.3, *infra*.

491 *See* § 6.4, *infra*.

492 *See* §§ 6.3.5 (special issues regarding private cause of action to enforce do-not-call provisions and prohibitions against robocalls to cell phones), 6.4.5 (special issues regarding private cause of action to enforce prohibitions against prerecorded calls to residential lines), 6.8.4 (special issues regarding private cause of action to enforce prohibitions against junk faxes), *supra*.

493 Lary v. Tom Taylor Agency, 878 So. 2d 1165 (Ala. Civ. App. 2003); Reichenbach v. Chung Holdings, L.L.C., 823 N.E.2d 29 (Ohio Ct. App. 2004) (prerecorded call); Reichenbach v. Fin. Freedom Centers, 2004 WL 2634624 (Ohio Ct. App. Nov. 19, 2004) (unpublished); Grady v. Lenders Interactive Services, 2004 WL 1799178 (Ohio Ct. App. Aug. 12, 2004) (unpublished).

494 47 U.S.C. § 227(c)(5). *See* Worsham v. Nationwide Ins. Co., 772 A.2d 868 (Md. Ct. Spec. App. 2001) (consumer has private cause of action if a repeat call is made after request to be placed on no-call list).

495 7 F.C.C. Rcd. 8752, at ¶ 26 (F.C.C. Oct. 16, 1992). *See* § 6.6.4, *infra*.

496 *Id.* ¶¶ 146–149. *See* § 6.6.3, *supra*.

497 *See* 68 Fed. Reg. 4580, 4623 (Jan. 29, 2003); Report and Order, *In re* Rules and Regulations Implementing the Telephone Consumer Protection Act of 1991 ¶ 183, 18 F.C.C. Rcd. 14014, 2003 WL 21517853 (F.C.C. July 3, 2003) (citing privacy concerns as reason for prohibition). *See generally* § 6.6.5, *infra*.

498 Pub. L. No. 111-331 (2010). *See* 47 U.S.C. § 227(e).

499 *See* § 6.6.5, *infra*.

500 State *ex rel.* Charvat v. Frye, 868 N.E.2d 270 (Ohio 2007).

501 47 U.S.C. § 227(c)(5).

502 Kopff v. Battaglia, 425 F. Supp. 2d 76, 91 (D.D.C. 2006); Lary v. Flasch Bus. Consulting, 878 So. 2d 1158 (Ala. Civ. App. 2003); Ferron & Associates v. U.S. Four, Inc., 2005 WL 3550760 (Ohio Ct. App. Dec. 29, 2005) (unpublished).

6.9.2 Private Remedies

6.9.2.1 Overview of TCPA Remedies

The plaintiff can recover actual monetary loss or $500 for each violation, whichever is greater.[503] The court may treble the damage award if it finds that the defendant's violation was willful or knowing.[504] However, the court is not obligated to treble the award.[505] A plaintiff can also seek an injunction against future violations,[506] and the consumer may not have to prove irreparable harm as is traditionally required for injunctive relief.[507]

The TCPA is a strict liability statute.[508] There is no bona fide error defense except to violations of the privacy protections, primarily the "do not call" prohibitions.[509]

The statutory damage award is intended both as compensation and as deterrence and is not so disproportionate to actual damages as to violate due process, including either individual or class actions.[510] Some courts have, however, suggested that after a class is certified it may be necessary to mitigate the award to comply with due process.[511] The treble damages provision is remedial rather than punitive.[512]

The consumer need not prove any monetary loss or actual damages in order to recover statutory damages.[513] Because such losses are likely to be minimal, statutory damages are necessary to motivate consumers to enforce the statute.[514]

Several courts have held that a TCPA statutory damages claim cannot be assigned.[515] There is, however, a contrary holding under the law of Illinois in a case in which the assignment was part of the sale of a business.[516]

6.9.2.2 Multiple Violations

In a junk fax case, each junk fax is a separate violation entitling the consumer to an award of damages.[517] A violation occurs when the prohibited fax is sent.[518] In one case, a

---

503   *See* First Nat'l Collection Bur., Inc. v. Walker, 348 S.W.3d 329, at *14 (Tex. App. 2011) (consumer is entitled to $500 statutory damages, not "up to" $500).

504   47 U.S.C. § 227(b)(3). *See* Irvine v. Akron Beacon J., 770 N.E.2d 1105 (Ohio Ct. App. 2002) (trial court has authority under TCPA to award treble damages in lieu of statutory damages but not in addition to them); Adamo v. AT&T, 2001 WL 1382757 (Ohio Ct. App. Nov. 8, 2001) (awarding treble damages for calls made after request to be placed on do-not-call list and for failure to provide written do-not-call policy on request); Grady v. OTC Investor's Edge, 2003 WL 22828294 (Ohio Ct. Com. Pl. Oct. 15, 2003) (awarding treble damages).

505   *See* Kopff v. Roth, 2007 WL 1748918 (D.D.C. June 15, 2007) (finding violations willful but exercising discretion not to treble award); Charvat v. Ryan, 879 N.E.2d 765, 771 (Ohio 2007) (if it is shown that violation is willful or knowing, then trial court "may, but need not," award treble damages)

506   47 U.S.C. § 227(b)(3), (5).

507   Meyer v. Portfolio Recovery Associates, L.L.C., 707 F.3d 1036 (9th Cir. 2012) (affirming preliminary injunction without need to reach issue).

508   Park Univ. Enterprises, Inc. v. American Cas. Co., 314 F. Supp. 2d 1094 (D. Kan. 2004), *aff'd*, 442 F.3d 1239 (10th Cir. 2006).

509   47 U.S.C. § 227(c)(5). *See* Morgan v. Branson Vacation Travel, L.L.C., 2013 WL 5532228 (W.D. Okla. Oct. 4, 2013); George v. Leading Edge Recovery Solutions, L.L.C., 2013 WL 3777034 (M.D. Fla. July 18, 2013). *But cf.* Chyba v. First Fin. Asset Mgmt., Inc., 2014 WL 1744136 (S.D. Cal. Apr. 30, 2014) (debt collector's good faith belief that debtor had consented to calls defeats liability).

510   Accounting Outsourcing, L.L.C. v. Verizon Wireless Personal Communications, L.P., 329 F. Supp. 2d 789, 808–809 (M.D. La. 2004) (statutory damages available under Telephone Consumer Protection Act do not raise *Gore* concerns because statute gives defendants fair notice of potential punishment; not overly severe and oppressive); Texas v. American Blast Fax, Inc., 121 F. Supp. 2d 1085 (W.D. Tex. 2000) (TCPA's $500 minimum damages provision is not overly severe in light of the public interest in deterring unsolicited fax advertising); ESI Ergonomic Solutions v. United Artists Theatre Cir., Inc., 50 P.3d 844 (Ariz. Ct. App. 2002) (TCPA penalties "not so disproportionate to actual damages as to violate due process"); Kaufman v. ACS Sys., Inc., 2 Cal. Rptr. 3d 296 (Cal. Ct. App. 2003) (damages provision legitimately addresses public harms); Harjoe v. Herz Fin., 108 S.W.3d 653 (Mo. 2003) (holding that Congress is entitled to determine a penalty sufficient to deter conduct); Chair King, Inc. v. GTE Mobilnet of Houston, Inc., 135 S.W.3d 365 (Tex. App. 2004), *rev'd on other grounds*, 184 S.W.3d 707 (Tex. 2006) (statutory penalty does not violate due process when it legitimately addresses and deters a public

harm). *See also* Critchfield Physical Therapy v. Taranto Grp., Inc., 263 P.3d 767, 781 (Kan. 2011) ("threat of catastrophic judgments should not protect parties that violate the law on a large scale and is not a relevant factor in determining where a plaintiff class should be certified"). *See generally* § 6.2.4.3, *supra*.

511   *Cf.* Kavu, Inc. v. Omnipak Corp., 246 F.R.D. 642 (W.D. Wash. 2007) (potential large damages for numerous violations of junk fax rule was not a sufficient reason to deny class certification; court will address constitutionality of large statutory damage award when determining appropriate amount of damages).

512   Motorists Mut. Ins. Co. v. Dandy-Jim, Inc., 912 N.E.2d 659 (Ohio Ct. App. 2009). *Cf.* Terra Nova Ins. Co. v. Fray-Witzer, 869 N.E.2d 565 (Mass. 2007) (for purposes of exclusions in sender's insurance policy, $500 statutory damage award serves as liquidated damages to compensate consumers for losses that are difficult to quantify and is not punitive, but if it is trebled it is punitive).

513   Holtzman v. Turza, 728 F.3d 682 (7th Cir. 2013) (plaintiff need not show printing of fax or other monetary loss; Lary v. American Med. Practice Services, 909 So. 2d 204 (Ala. Civ. App. 2005); Kaplan v. Democrat & Chron., 701 N.Y.S.2d 859 (N.Y. App. Div. 1999) (reversing dismissal of complaint of consumer who sued after receiving three telephone calls soliciting newspaper subscriptions in violation of TCPA but could not show any monetary loss; Kaplan v. First City Mortg., 701 N.Y.S.2d 859 (N.Y. City Ct. 1999). *See generally* § 6.9.3.1, *infra* (standing).

514   Kaplan v. Democrat & Chron., 698 N.Y.S.2d 799, 801 (N.Y. App. Div. 1999). *Cf.* J.A. Weitzman, Inc. v. Lerner, Cumbo & Associates, Inc., 847 N.Y.S.2d 679 (N.Y. App. Div. 2007) (denying actual damages because of plaintiff's inability to show damages from junk fax with reasonable certainty). *See generally* § 6.9.3.1, *infra* (Article III standing).

515   U.S. Fax. Law Ctr., Inc. v. iHire, 476 F.3d 1112 (10th Cir. 2007) (applying Colorado law; neither TCPA claim nor claim under Colorado junk fax law is assignable); Consumer Crusade, Inc. v. Everycontractor.com, 2008 WL 619296 (D. Colo. Mar. 4, 2008); Consumer Crusade, Inc. v. Crevecor Mortg., Inc., 2008 WL 619300 (D. Colo. Mar. 4, 2008); Martinez v. Green, 131 P.3d 492 (Ariz. Ct. App. 2006); Kruse v. McKenna, 178 P.3d 1198 (Colo. 2008) (TCPA claim is action for a penalty so is not assignable); McKenna v. Oliver, 159 P.3d 697 (Colo. App. 2006).

516   Eclipse Mfg. Co. v. M & M Rental Ctr., Inc., 521 F. Supp. 2d 739 (N.D. Ill. 2007).

517   47 U.S.C. § 227(b)(3) (authorizing damages "for each such violation"). *See* Meyer v. Howard S. Bixenholtz Constr., 952 A.2d 507 (N.J. Super. Ct. App. Div. 2008). *See also* Worsham v. Nationwide Ins. Co., 772 A.2d 868 (Md. Ct. Spec. App. 2001) ($500 is to be awarded per call, not per violation).

518   Fun Services of Kan. City, Inc. v. Love, 2011 WL 1843253, at *2 (W.D. Mo. May 11, 2011).

---

district court awarded a consumer $500 per fax for 7725 unsolicited fax advertisements, for a total award of $3,862,500.[519] In another, a court awarded over $4 million for 8430 faxes.[520] The same statutory damages provision applies to violations of the TCPA's robodialing and artificial voice prohibitions, so the same rule should apply to those violations.

The liability provisions for violations of the TCPA's do-not-call rules also authorize statutory damages "for each such violation."[521] Thus, in calculating the $500 per violation for purposes of section 227(c) (which allows a private right of action only after the second call), the consumer is entitled to damages for each call,[522] including the first one.[523]

If a defendant commits multiple violations of the TCPA in connection with a single call, fax, or text message, the Sixth Circuit has held that only one damage award is available per call.[524] Some other federal courts have agreed with this position.[525] However, in a later case the Sixth Circuit held that a consumer could recover two statutory damage awards where a single call violated both the prohibition against artificial voice telemarketing calls, made actionable by section 227(b)(3), and the do-not-call rule, made actionable by section 227(c)(5).[526] And the Eleventh Circuit, reading the plain language of the statute's authorization of damages "for each such violation," has held that a plaintiff can recover two awards when a single junk fax violated both the prohibition on the use of an automatic telephone dialing system to call an emergency line and the junk fax prohibition.[527] The Missouri Supreme Court has held that a two-page junk fax that contains a single advertisement is one, not two, violations.[528]

6.9.2.3 Willfulness or Knowledge As a Requirement for Treble Damages

Whether a defendant acts willfully or knowingly is relevant only to treble damages and is not a general prerequisite to a recovery of TCPA statutory damages.[529] In seeking a treble

damage award, the defendant's willfulness or knowledge need not be proven by clear and convincing evidence.[530] The plaintiff must prove that the violation was done willfully, or knowingly, but need not prove both.[531]

Some courts have held that, in order to show a willful or knowing violation of the TCPA, the plaintiff need only show that the defendant willfully or knowingly committed the act that violated the TCPA.[532] This is consistent with the FCC's interpretation, which is that "willful or knowing" requires merely that "the violator knew that he was doing the act in question . . . . A violator need not know that his action or inaction constitutes a violation."[533] However, other courts require "that the person have reason to know, or should have known, that his conduct would violate the statute."[534]

Discovery may reveal that the sender was advised of the law through other complaints, enforcement actions, or other suits. Note however that, if there is possible insurance coverage and a large claim, it may not be in the plaintiff's interest to prove willfulness, as many policies exclude coverage for willful conduct.

6.9.2.4 Remedies Under UDAP Statutes and Other State Laws

The TCPA does not provide for an attorney fee award, but the consumer may be able to assert a parallel claim under the state UDAP statute and win fees under that statute[535] or recover

---

519   *See* Hinman v. M & M Rental Ctr., Inc., 596 F. Supp. 2d 1152 (N.D. Ill. 2009). *See also* Lary v. Work-Loss Data Inst., 911 So. 2d 18 (Ala. Civ. App. 2005) (consumer is entitled to $500 for each of three faxes sent).

520   Holtzman v. Turza, 728 F.3d 682 (7th Cir. 2013).

521   47 U.S.C. § 227(c)(5). *See* Charvat v. NMP, L.L.C., 656 F.3d 440 (6th Cir. 2011).

522   Charvat v. NMP, L.L.C., 656 F.3d 440 (6th Cir. 2011).

523   Charvat v. GVN Mich., Inc., 561 F.3d 623, 630 (6th Cir. 2009).

524   Charvat v. GVN Mich., Inc., 561 F.3d 623, 632 (6th Cir. 2009).

525   Cellco P'ship v. Wilcrest Health Care Mgmt. Inc., 2012 WL 1638056 (D.N.J. May 8, 2012); Charvat v. DFS Services, L.L.C., 781 F. Supp. 2d 588 (S.D. Ohio 2011) (dismissing all but one TCPA claim for each call); Martin v. PPP, Inc., 719 F. Supp. 2d 967 (N.D. Ill. 2010).

526   Charvat v. NMP, L.L.C., 656 F.3d 440 (6th Cir. 2011).

527   Lary v. Trinity Physician Fin. & Ins. Services, 780 F.3d 1101 (11th Cir. 2015). *See also* Charvat v. Ryan, 858 N.E.2d 845 (Ohio Ct. App. 2006) (fax recipient may recover multiple awards of statutory damages, *aff'd in part, rev'd in part on other grounds*, 879 N.E.2d 765 (Ohio 2007). *Cf.* Charvat v. Echostar Satellite, L.L.C., 621 F. Supp. 2d 549 (S.D. Ohio 2008) (even though multiple recoveries for a single call are not allowed, plaintiff may plead multiple violations in the alternative for each call).

528   Harjoe v. Herz Fin., 108 S.W.3d 653 (Mo. 2003).

529   Lary v. American Med. Practice Services, 909 So. 2d 204 (Ala. Civ. App. 2005).

530   First Nat'l Collection Bureau, Inc. v. Walker, 348 S.W.3d 329, at *15 (Tex. App. 2011).

531   47 U.S.C. § 227(b)(3), (c)(5).

532   Stewart v. Regent Asset Mgmt. Solutions, Inc., 2011 WL 1766018, at *6–7 (N.D. Ga. May 4, 2011), *adopted by* 2011 U.S. Dist. LEXIS 58600 (N.D. Ga. May 31, 2011); Sengenberger v. Credit Control Services, Inc., 2010 WL 1791270, at *6 (N.D. Ill. May 5, 2010); Charvat v. Ryan, 879 N.E.2d 765, 770–771 (Ohio 2007). *Cf.* Lary v. Trinity Physician Fin. & Ins. Services, 780 F.3d 1101, 1106–1107 (11th Cir. 2015) (no liability when defendant did not know that telephone line was an emergency line or that fax was unsolicited).

533   *In re* Dynasty Mortg., L.L.C., 22 F.C.C. Rcd. 9453, 9470 n.86, 2007 WL 1427724 (F.C.C. May 14, 2007).

534   Harris v. World Fin. Network Nat'l Bank, 867 F.Supp.2d 888, 895 (E.D. Mich. 2012); Adamcik v. Credit Control Services, 832 F. Supp. 2d 744 (W.D. Tex. 2011); State of Tex. v. American Blastfax, Inc., 164 F. Supp. 2d 892, 899 (W.D. Tex. 2001); Covington & Burling v. Int'l Mktg. & Research, Inc., 2003 WL 21384825, at *8 (D.C. Super. Apr. 17, 2003); Brown v. Enterprise Recovery Sys., Inc., 2013 WL 4506582 (Tex. App. Aug. 22, 2013) (unpublished); Manufacturers Auto Leasing, Inc. v. Autoflex Leasing, Inc., 139 S.W.3d 342, 346 (Tex. App. 2004) (applying TCPA subsection regulating faxes and stating that "the TCPA is willfully or knowingly violated when the defendant knows of the TCPA's prohibitions, knows he does not have permission to send a fax ad to the plaintiff, and sends it anyway").

535   *See, e.g.,* Brodsky v. HumanaDental Ins. Co., 2011 WL 529302 (N.D. Ill. Feb. 8, 2011) (denying motion to dismiss claim that sending junk faxes is unfair practice under UDAP statute); Centerline Equip. Corp. v. Banner Personnel Serv., Inc., 545 F. Supp. 2d 768 (N.D. Ill. 2008) (denial of motion to dismiss). *See also* Charvat v. Telelytics, L.L.C., 2006 WL 2574019 (Ohio Ct. App. Aug. 31, 2006) (state UDAP claim that did not conflict with TCPA was not preempted and could proceed). *Cf.* Charvat v. Ryan, 879 N.E.2d 765, 771–72 (Ohio 2007) (to be eligible for UDAP fee award, plaintiff need only show that defendant who

fees from a fund created via a class action. Many courts hold that a TCPA violation is a state UDAP violation.[536] Some state UDAP or telemarketing statutes contain express prohibitions that parallel TCPA prohibitions such as junk faxing.[537]

One complication with UDAP claims is that in some states the consumer must show a loss of money or property in order to bring a claim.[538] This standard may be difficult to meet in the case of certain types of violations such as artificial voice telemarketing calls to a land line.[539] However, depletion of a limited number of cell phone minutes may be sufficient.[540]

Some UDAP statutes give companies standing to sue when the company's competitor engages in deceptive or illegal conduct, putting the competing company at a competitive advantage. Such a provision may give a company standing to sue its competitor for TCPA violations.[541]

6.9.3　Standing and Jurisdiction

6.9.3.1　Article III Standing

The Eighth Circuit has held that injury in fact sufficient to confer Article III standing can be established merely by invasion of a legal right created by the TCPA, such as the receipt of unsolicited prerecorded telephone calls.[542] Thus, the recipient of an unwanted call has Article III standing regardless of whether he or she pays for the call.[543] Occupying the recipient's fax machine by sending an unsolicited fax is sufficient to confer Article III standing, even if the recipient does not read or print the fax.[544] However, advocates should be aware that in 2015 the Supreme Court agreed to hear a case that may address the scope of Article III standing when the plaintiff suffers invasion of a statutory right but does not experience other losses.[545]

The question of which persons are authorized by the statute to bring suit is discussed elsewhere in this chapter, in the sections dealing with each statutory prohibition.[546]

6.9.3.2　Jurisdiction in Federal and State Court

In 2012 the U.S. Supreme Court held that there is federal question jurisdiction for private TCPA suits.[547] As a result, a plaintiff may file a TCPA suit in federal court for a single illegal solicitation by phone or fax, and a defendant may remove any TCPA case to federal court without regard to the amount in controversy.

The TCPA explicitly grants consumers the right to bring suit for violations in state court "if otherwise permitted by the laws or rules of court" of the state.[548] The legislative history suggests that Congress did not intend to override state court rules about venue, jurisdictional amounts, and similar matters.[549] Thus some courts hold that, while a state is not obligated to change its procedures to accommodate TCPA claims, it cannot refuse to entertain them.[550] Other courts have held that this language allows states to opt out of jurisdiction over these cases rather than requiring an affirmative act to opt in.[551] A third approach,

---

violated TCPA and UDAP statute by making prerecorded autodialed telemarketing call acted intentionally, not that it knew it was violating the law, but trial court has discretion whether to award fees).

536　*See, e.g.,* Brodsky v. HumanaDental Ins. Co., 2011 WL 529302 (N.D. Ill. Feb. 8, 2011) (upholding UDAP claim); Locklear Elec., Inc. v. Lay, 2009 WL 4678428 (S.D. Ill. Dec. 7, 2009); ABC Bus. Forms, Inc. v. Pridamor, Inc., 2009 WL 4679477 (N.D. Ill. Dec. 1, 2009) (plaintiff's TCPA claim not challenged, and UDAP claim survives, but conversion claim dismissed); ABC Bus. Forms, Inc. v. Pridamor, Inc., 2009 WL 4679477 (N.D. Ill. Dec. 1, 2009); Green v. Anthony Clark Int'l Ins. Brokers, Ltd., 2009 WL 2515594 (N.D. Ill. Aug. 17, 2009); R. Rudnick & Co. v. GF Prot., Inc., 2009 WL 112380 (N.D. Ill. Jan. 15, 2009); Centerline Equip. Corp. v. Banner Personnel Serv., Inc., 545 F. Supp. 2d 768 (N.D. Ill. 2008); Pollack v. Cunningham Fin. Grp., L.L.C., 2008 WL 4874195 (N.D. Ill. June 2, 2008); Sadowski v. Med1 Online, L.L.C., 2008 WL 2224892 (N.D. Ill. May 27, 2008); People v. Discovery Mktg., Inc., 99-3243 (C.D. Ill. Feb. 14, 2000). *But see* Paldo Sign & Display, Inc. v. Topsail Sportswear, Inc., 2010 WL 276701, at *3–5 (N.D. Ill. Jan. 15, 2010); G.M. Sign, Inc. v. Stergo, 681 F. Supp. 2d 929, 935–937 (N.D. Ill. 2009); Stonecrafters, Inc. v. Foxfire Printing & Packaging, Inc., 633 F. Supp. 2d 610, 616 (N.D. Ill. 2009); Rossario's Fine Jewelry, Inc. v. Paddock Publications, Inc., 443 F. Supp. 2d 976 (N.D. Ill. 2006) (TCPA claim could proceed, but state UDAP claim failed for lack of showing that fax advertisement was unfair); Western Ry. Devices Corp. v. Lusida Rubber Products, Inc., 2006 WL 1697119 (N.D. Ill. June 13, 2006) (junk faxes offend public policy but are not oppressive and do not cause substantial injury).

537　*See, e.g.,* Ind. Code 24-5-0.5-3(a)(19).

538　*See* National Consumer Law Center, Unfair and Deceptive Acts and Practices § 11.4.2 (8th ed. 2012), *updated at* www.nclc.org/library.

539　*See, e.g.,* Van Patten v. Vertical Fitness Grp., L.L.C., 22 F. Supp. 2d 1069 (S.D. Cal. 2014) (dismissing UDAP claim because of failure to allege that text message caused loss of money or property).

540　Thomas v. Dun & Bradstreet Credibility Corp., ___ F. Supp. 3d ___, 2015 WL 4698398, at *7 (C.D. Cal. Aug. 5, 2015).

541　*See* Nat'l Notary Ass'n v. U.S. Notary, 2002 WL 1265555 (Cal. Ct. App. June 7, 2002) (unpublished) (company that was harmed by its competitor's use of illegal junk faxes may bring UDAP suit even though it did not receive any faxes itself).

542　Golan v. Veritas Entm't, L.L.C., 788 F.3d 814 (8th Cir. 2015).

543　King v. Time Warner Cable, ___ F. Supp. 3d ___, 2015 WL 4103689, at *6 (S.D.N.Y. July 7, 2015) (no monetary loss need be shown); Gesten v. Stewart Law Grp., L.L.C., 67 F. Supp. 3d 1356 (S.D. Fla. 2014). *See also* §§ 6.9.2.1–6.9.2.3, *supra., infra.*

544　Palm Beach Golf Center-Boca, Inc. v. John G. Sarris, D.D.S., P.A., 781 F.3d 1245, 1250–1253 (11th Cir. 2015); Holtzman v. Turza, 728 F.3d 682, 684 (7th Cir. 2013).

545　Robins v. Spokeo, Inc., 742 F.3d 409 (9th Cir. 2015), *cert. granted* 135 S. Ct. 1892 (2015).

546　*See* §§ 6.3.5 (robocalls to cell phones), 6.4.5 (prerecorded calls to residential lines), 6.8.4 (junk faxes), *infra.*

547　Mims v. Arrow Fin. Services, L.L.C., 132 S. Ct. 740 (2012).

548　47 U.S.C. § 227(b)(3), (c)(5).

549　*See* Comments of Senator Hollings, 137 Cong. Rec. S16205–06 (Nov. 7, 1991) ("the bill does not, because of constitutional constraints, dictate to the States which court in each State shall be the proper venue for such an action, as this is a matter for State legislators to determine"). *See also* Accounting Outsourcing, L.L.C. v. Verizon Wireless Personal Communications, L.P., 329 F. Supp. 2d 789, 800–801 (M.D. La. 2004) (giving effect to legislative history; suit in state courts of general jurisdiction is allowed unless there is a procedural or jurisdictional bar); Schulman v. Chase Manhattan Bank, 710 N.Y.S.2d 368 (N.Y. App. Div. 2000) (relying on legislative history).

550　Italia Foods v. Sun Tours, 986 N.E.2d 55, 61–62 (Ill. 2011) (adopting this approach and terming it the "acknowledgment" approach).

551　Murphey v. Lanier, 204 F.3d 911 (9th Cir. 2000); Adler v. Vision Lab Telecommunications, Inc., 393 F. Supp. 2d 35 (D.D.C. 2005) (adopting the opt-in approach, is very much a minority view and interprets the TCPA as depriving states of jurisdiction unless a state takes affirmative steps to exercise jurisdiction over private TCPA claims through legislation or court rule.[552]

In any event, the state role in providing a forum for TCPA claims does not mean that it can lessen the federal statute's requirements or reduce the liability it provides. For example, a court held that, after opting in, Texas could not restrict TCPA claims to calls that the consumer actually received.[553]

A court can exercise personal jurisdiction over a defendant that purposely avails itself of the privilege of conducting activities in the forum state or purposefully directs its activities to residents of the forum state. Directing unwanted calls to cell phone numbers with area codes assigned to a state is sufficient to allow that state to exercise personal jurisdiction over the caller, even though some of the cell phone numbers may belong to persons in other states.[554]

6.9.4 Class Actions

Depending largely on the facts, courts have differed about whether class certification is appropriate for particular TCPA cases involving junk fax[555] and telephone/text

---

opt-out approach; District of Columbia did not opt out by declining to create a private right of action for unsolicited faxes when considering another bill); Biggerstaff v. Voice Power Telecommunications, Inc., 221 F. Supp. 2d 652 (D.S.C. 2002); Lary v. Flasch Bus. Consulting, 878 So. 2d 1158 (Ala. Civ. App. 2003); Lary v. Tom Taylor Agency, 878 So. 2d 1165 (Ala. Civ. App. 2003); Kaufman v. ACS Sys., Inc., 2 Cal. Rptr. 3d 296 (Cal. Ct. App. 2003) (California's enactment and later repeal of law to ban junk faxes until TCPA took effect does not show intent to close state courts to TCPA suits); McKenna v. Oliver, 159 P.3d 697 (Colo. App. 2006); Consumer Crusade, Inc. v. Keller-Lowry Ins., Inc., 2005 WL 2893842 (Colo. Dist. Ct. Denver Cnty. July 6, 2005) (Colorado's adoption of its own junk fax law did not amount to opting out); Portuguese Am. Leadership Council of the U.S., Inc. v. Investors' Alert, Inc., 956 A.2d 671 (D.C. 2008); Condon v. Office Depot, Inc., 855 So. 2d 644 (Fla. Dist. Ct. App. 2003); Carnett's, Inc. v. Hammond, 610 S.E.2d 529, 530 (Ga. 2005) (TCPA "provides private right of action in state court unless prohibited by state law"); R.A. Ponte Architects, Ltd. v. Investors' Alert, Inc., 857 A.2d 1 (Md. 2004); Worsham v. Nationwide Ins. Co., 772 A.2d 868 (Md. Ct. Spec. App. 2001) (allowing private cause of action in state court for violation of company-specific do-not-call rule); Mulhern v. MacLeod, 808 N.E.2d 778 (Mass. 2004) (state need not pass enabling legislation); Edwards v. Emperor's Garden Rest., 130 P.3d 1280, 1286 (Nev. 2006) ("private causes of action based on TCPA claims may be maintained in Nevada courts when consistent with Nevada's laws and court rules," but Nevada statute of limitations controls); Edwards v. Direct Access, L.L.C., 124 P.3d 1158 (Nev. 2005); Zelma v. Market U.S.A., 778 A.2d 591 (N.J. Super. Ct. Law. Div. 2001); Schulman v. Chase Manhattan Bank, 710 N.Y.S.2d 368 (N.Y. App. Div. 2000); Betor v. Quantalytics, Inc., 2003 WL 22407121 (Ohio Ct. Com. Pl. Oct. 3, 2003); Jemiola v. XYZ Corp., 802 N.E.2d 745 (Ohio Ct. Com. Pl. 2003); MLC Mortg. Corp. v. Sun Am. Mortg. Co., 212 P.3d 1199 (Okla. 2009); Aronson v. Fax.com Inc., 51 Pa. D & C.4th 421 (Pa. Ct. Com. Pl. Allegheny Cnty. 2001). *See* Reynolds v. Diamond Foods & Poultry, Inc., 79 S.W.3d 907 (Mo. 2002). *See also* Accounting Outsourcing, L.L.C. v. Verizon Wireless Personal Communications, L.P., 329 F. Supp. 2d 789, 800–801 (M.D. La. 2004) (suit in state courts of general jurisdiction is allowed unless there is a procedural or jurisdictional bar); Consumer Crusade, Inc. v. Affordable Health Care Solutions, Inc., 121 P.3d 350 (Colo. App. 2005) (states cannot refuse to entertain TCPA suits but need not adopt special procedural rules for them). *But see* Chair King v. GTE Mobilnet of Houston, Inc., 184 S.W.3d 707 (Tex. 2006) (recipients of junk faxes had no actionable claim in Texas prior to state's adoption of law explicitly permitting TCPA suits in state court).

552 *See* Chair King v. GTE Mobilenet of Houston, Inc., 184 S.W.3d 707 (Tex. 2006) (recipients of junk faxes had no actionable claim in Texas prior to state's adoption of law explicitly permitting TCPA suits in state court).

553 First Nat'l Collection Bur., Inc. v. Walker, 348 S.W.3d 329, at *8 (Tex. App. 2011) (after opting in, Texas cannot restrict TCPA claims to calls that consumer actually received).

554 Ott v. Mortg. Investors Corp., 65 F. Supp. 3d 1046 (D. Or. 2014).

555 *CLASS CERTIFICATION APPROPRIATE:* American Copper & Brass, Inc. v. Lake City Indus. Products, Inc., 757 F.3d 540 (6th Cir. 2014); Kaye v. Amicus Mediation & Arbitration Grp., Inc., 300 F.R.D. 67 (D. Conn. 2014); Jay Clogg Realty Grp., Inc. v. Burger King Corp., 298 F.R.D. 304 (D. Md. 2014); Spine and Sports Chiropractic, Inc. v. Zirmed, Inc., 2014 WL 2946421 (W.D. Ky. June 30, 2014); Chapman v. Wagener Equities, Inc., 2014 WL 540250 (N.D. Ill. Feb. 11, 2014), *leave to appeal denied*, 747 F.3d 489 (7th Cir. 2014); Michel v. WM Healthcare Solutions, Inc., 2014 WL 497031 (S.D. Ohio. Feb. 7, 2014); C-Mart, Inc. v. Metropolitan Life Ins. Co., 299 F.R.D. 679 (S.D. Fla. 2014); City Select Auto Sales, Inc. V. David Randall Associates, Inc., 2014 WL 413533 (D.N.J. Feb. 3, 2014); St. Louis Heart Ctr., Inc. v. Vein Centers for Excellence, Inc., 2013 WL 6498245 (E.D. Mo. Dec. 11, 2013); Lindsay Transmission, L.L.C. v. Office Depot, Inc., 2013 WL 275568 (E.D. Mo. Jan. 24, 2013); Agne v. Papa John's Int'l, Inc., 286 F.R.D. 559 (W.D. Wash. 2012) (certifying class of text message recipients); Targin Sign Sys. v. Preferred Chiropractic Ctr., Ltd., 679 F. Supp. 2d 894 (N.D. Ill. 2010); Garrett v. Ragle Dental Lab, Inc., 2010 WL 4074379 (N.D. Ill. Oct. 12, 2010); Clearbrook v. Rooflifters, L.L.C., 2010 WL 2635781 (N.D. Ill. June 28, 2010) (Cox, M.J.); Holtzman v. Turza, 2009 WL 3334909 (N.D. Ill. Oct. 14, 2009), *aff'd*, 728 F.3d 682 (7th Cir. 2013); G.M. Sign, Inc. v. Group C Communications, Inc., 2010 WL 744262 (N.D. Ill. Feb. 25, 2010); CE Design v. Beaty Const., Inc., 2009 WL 192481 (N.D. Ill. Jan. 26, 2009) (certifying class); CE Design Ltd. v. Cy's Crabhouse North, Inc., 259 F.R.D. 135 (N.D. Ill. 2009) (certifying class; accepting plaintiff's method of determining class membership); Hinman v. M & M Rental Ctr., Inc., 545 F. Supp. 2d 802 (N.D. Ill. 2008) (when defendant sent faxes *en masse* to numbers purchased from third-party vendor, possibility that some recipients might have separately consented does not preclude class certification); Sadowski v. Med1 Online, L.L.C., 2008 WL 2224892 (N.D. Ill. May 27, 2008); Kavu, Inc. v. Omnipak Corp., 246 F.R.D. 642 (W.D. Wash. 2007) (numerous violations of junk fax rule met commonality, typicality, and adequacy requirements for class certification); ESI Ergonomic Solutions, L.L.C. v. United Artists Theatre Circuit, Inc., 50 P.3d 844 (Ariz. Ct. App. 2002); Kaufman v. ACS Sys., Inc., 2 Cal. Rptr. 3d 296 (Cal. Ct. App. 2003) (TCPA does not foreclose class actions; must be decided on case-by-case basis); Hooters of Augusta, Inc. v. Nicholson, 537 S.E.2d 468 (Ga. Ct. App. 2000) (affirming class certification); CE Design Ltd. v. C & T Pizza, 32 N.E.3d 150 (Ill. App. Ct. 2015); JT's Frames, Inc. v. Sunhill NIC Co., 2012 WL 696814 (Ill. App. Ct. Mar. 26, 2012); Travel 100 Grp., Inc. v. Empire Cooler Serv., Inc., 2004 WL 3105679 (Ill. Cir. Ct. Cook Cnty. Oct. 19, 2004) (fact that TCPA allows faxes to people who have given express consent does not bar class certification; manner in which defendant selected recipients may raise inference that they had not consented); Core Funding Grp., L.L.C. v. Young, 792 N.E.2d 547 (Ind. Ct. App. 2003); Critchfield Physical Therapy v. Taranto Grp., Inc., 263 P.3d 767 (Kan. 2011); Display South, Inc. v. Graphics House Sports Promotions, Inc., 992 So. 2d 510 (La. Ct. App. 2008) (affirming certification of class; whether some class members gave consent to receive faxes will be addressed on individual basis after common issues are resolved); Display South, Inc. v. Express Computer Supply, Inc., 961 So. 2d 451 (La. Ct. App. 2007); Karen S. Little, L.L.C. v. Drury Inns,

message[556] claims.

Inc., 306 S.W.3d 577 (Mo. Ct. App. 2010); Dubsky v. Advanced Cellular Communications, Inc., 2004 WL 503757 (Ohio Ct. Com. Pl. Feb. 24, 2004) (unpublished) (granting class certification); Lampkin v. GGH, Inc., 146 P.3d 847 (Okla. Civ. App. 2006). *See also* Saf-T-Gard Int'l, Inc. v. Wagener Equities, Inc., 251 F.R.D. 312 (N.D. Ill. 2008) (junk fax class action can be certified despite possibility that some class members gave consent to receive faxes, but certification inappropriate here because class members cannot be identified); Accounting Outsourcing, L.L.C. v. Verizon Wireless Personal Communications, L.P., 329 F. Supp. 2d 789, 803 (M.D. La. 2004); Hypertouch, Inc. v. Superior Ct., 27 Cal. Rptr. 3d 839 (Cal. Ct. App. 2005) (ruling on manner of notifying TCPA class; propriety of class certification not an issue on appeal); Carnett's, Inc. v. Hammond, 610 S.E.2d 529 (Ga. 2005) (TCPA class actions can be certified, but trial court was within its discretion to find lack of commonality when plaintiff did not attempt to exclude consumers who had established business relationship with defendant); Anderson Office Supply, Inc. v. Advanced Med. Associates, P.A., 273 P.3d 786 (Kan. Ct. App. 2012) (recipient was not required to prove that purported class members all received advertisements and thus were injured prior to class certification); All American Painting, L.L.C. v. Chiropractic & Sports Injury Ctr. of Creve Coeur, P.C., 368 S.W.3d 244 (Mo. Ct. App. 2012).

CLASS CERTIFICATION NOT APPROPRIATE: Davies v. W. W. Granger, Inc., 2014 WL 2935905 (N.D. Ill. June 27, 2014) (class denied when there were serious issues concerning consent and established business relationship on part of named plaintiff); G.M. Sign, Inc. v. Franklin Bank, 2007 WL 4365359 (N.D. Ill. Dec. 13, 2007) (denying class certification because, *inter alia*, class definition included a component of a lack of defense, namely proof of express invitation or permission), *later decision at* 2008 WL 2410427 (N.D. Ill. June 11, 2008) (requiring class definition to condition class membership on absence of consent); Bridging Communities, Inc. v. Top Flite Fin., Inc., 2013 WL 2417939 (E.D. Mich. June 3, 2013); Kenro, Inc. v. Fax Daily, Inc., 962 F. Supp. 1162 (S.D. Ind. 1997) (determination of class membership would inappropriately require addressing merits of claim, particularly determining whether faxes were in fact unsolicited); Forman v. Data Transfer, Inc., 164 F.R.D. 400 (E.D. Pa. 1995) (same); Livingston v. U.S. Bank, 58 P.3d 1088 (Colo. App. 2002) (same). *See also* Paldo Sign & Display Co. v. Topsail Sportswear, Inc., 2010 WL 276701 (N.D. Ill. Jan. 15, 2010) (TCPA claim not at issue, but dismissing plaintiff's UDAP and conversion claims arising from unsolicited fax as *de minimis*; aggregating the harm of all potential class members would not raise injury to a substantial level when total actual damages would amount to $8); Paradise v. Al Copeland Investments, Inc., 22 So. 3d 1018 (La. Ct. App. 2009) (reversing grant of class certification because of inability to identify class members when lists of fax recipients would have to be reconstructed); Local Baking Products, Inc. v. Kosher Bagel Munch, Inc., 23 A.3d 469 (N.J. Super. Ct. App. Div. 2011) (class action not superior because an individual small claims case could be cost-effective). *Cf.* Gene & Gene, L.L.C. v. BioPay, L.L.C., 541 F.3d 318 (5th Cir. 2008) (TCPA violations are not per se unsuitable for class resolution, but class certification inappropriate when seller purchased some fax numbers from vendor but supplemented list with numbers of persons who had contacted it or with whom it had ongoing business relationships), *later op.*, 624 F.3d 698 (5th Cir. 2010); Sandusky Wellness Ctr. L.L.C. v. Medtox Scientific, Inc., 2014 WL 3846037 (D. Minn. Aug. 5, 2014); Lindsay Transmission, L.L.C. v. Office Depot, Inc., 2013 WL 275568 (E.D. Mo. Jan. 24, 2013); Conrad v. Gen. Motors Acceptance Corp., 283 F.R.D. 326 (N.D. Tex. 2012) (certification denied on predominance grounds and because only two class members were identified); Blitz v. Agean, Inc., 743 S.E.2d 247 (N.C. Ct. App. 2013); Kondos v. Lincoln Prop. Co., 110 S.W.3d 716 (Tex. App. 2003) (reversing class certification because of lack of rigorous analysis; plaintiffs may pursue certification again upon remand).

556 *CLASS CERTIFICATION APPROPRIATE:* Meyer v. Portfolio Recovery Associates, L.L.C., 707 F.3d 1036 (9th Cir. 2012); Abdeljalil v. Gen. Elec. Capital Corp., 306 F.R.D. 303 (S.D. Cal. 2015); Zyburo v. NCSPlus, Inc., 44 F. Supp. 3d 500 (S.D.N.Y. 2014); Birchmeier v.

A New York class action rule prohibits recovery of a minimum damage award in a class action, unless the statute creating the remedy specifically authorizes class actions.[557] Because of this rule, New York state courts have refused to certify TCPA class actions.[558] However, the U.S. Supreme Court has held that this rule cannot prevent certification of a statutory damages class action in federal court because certification in federal court is governed by Rule 23 of the Federal Rules of Civil Procedure.[559] Federal courts have applied this ruling to reject challenges to TCPA class actions based on other states' statutory or case law prohibiting class actions for statutory or minimum damages.[560]

Caribbean Cruise Line, Inc., 302 F.R.D. 240 (N.D. Ill. 2014); Stern v. DoCircle, Inc., 2014 WL 486262 (C.D. Cal. Jan. 29, 2014); Manno v. Healthcare Revenue Recovery Grp., L.L.C., 289 F.R.D. 674 (S.D. Fla. 2013); Lee v. Stonebridge Life Ins. Co., 289 F.R.D. 292 (N.D. Cal. 2013); Knutson v. Schwan's Home Serv., Inc., 2013 WL 4774763 (S.D. Cal. Sept. 5, 2013); Silbaugh v. Viking Magazine Services, 278 F.R.D. 389 (N.D. Ohio 2012) (text message class certified); Lo v. Oxnard European Motors, L.L.C., 2012 WL 1932283 (S.D. Cal. May 29, 2012); Mitchem v. Ill. Collection Serv., 271 F.R.D. 617 (N.D. Ill. 2011); Balbarin v. North Star Capital Acquisition, L.L.C., 2011 U.S. Dist. LEXIS 686 (N.D. Ill. Jan. 5, 2011), *later opinion*, 2011 WL 211013 (N.D. Ill. Jan. 21, 2011), *later opinion*, 2011 U.S. Dist. LEXIS 58761 (N.D. Ill. June 1, 2011).

CLASS CERTIFICATION INAPPROPRIATE: Boyer v. Diversified Consultants, Inc., 306 F.R.D. 536 (E.D. Mich. 2015) (class definition was impermissible fail-safe class); Zarichny v. Complete Payment Recovery Services, Inc., 80 F. Supp. 3d 610 (E.D. Pa. 2015) (class defined as persons who had not given prior express consent is impermissible fail-safe class); Warnick v. DISH Network, L.L.C., 301 F.R.D. 551 (D. Colo. 2014) (finding proposed class definition overbroad and not ascertainable); Smith v. Microsoft Corp., 297 F.R.D. 464 (S.D. Cal. 2014) (concluding that plaintiff has burden of showing lack of consent); Cullan & Cullan, L.L.C. v. M-Qube, Inc., 2014 WL 347034 (D. Neb. Jan. 30, 2014); Jamison v. First Credit Services, Inc., 2013 WL 3872171 (N.D. Ill. July 29, 2013); Gannon v. Network Tel. Services, Inc., 2013 WL 2450199 (C.D. Cal. June 5, 2013); O'Connor v. Diversified Consultants, Inc., WL 2319342 (E.D. Mo. May 28, 2013); Balthazor v. Central Credit Services, L.L.C., 2012 WL 6725872 (S.D. Fla. Dec. 27, 2012); Anderson v. Domino's Pizza, Inc., 2012 WL 2891804 (W.D. Wash. July 16, 2012); Vigus v. Southern Ill. Riverboat/Casino Cruises, Inc., 274 F.R.D. 229, 238 (S.D. Ill. 2011); Hicks v. Client Services, Inc., 2008 WL 5479111 (S.D. Fla. Dec. 11, 2008).

557 N.Y. C.P.L.R. 901(b) (McKinney).

558 J.A. Weitzman, Inc. v. Lerner, Cumbo & Associates, Inc., 847 N.Y.S.2d 679 (N.Y. App. Div. 2007); Rudgayzer & Gratt v. Cape Canaveral Tour & Travel, Inc., 799 N.Y.S.2d 795 (N.Y. App. Div. 2005); Rudgayzer & Gratt v. LRS Communications, Inc., 789 N.Y.S.2d 601 (N.Y. Sup. Ct. 2004); Giovanniello v. Hispanic Media Grp. USA, Inc., 780 N.Y.S.2d 720 (N.Y. Sup. Ct. 2004), *aff'd in relevant part, modified in part on other grounds*, 799 N.Y.S.2d 800 (N.Y. App. Div. 2005). *See also* Weber v. U.S. Sterling Sec., Inc., 924 A.2d 816 (Conn. 2007) (applying New York procedural rule).

559 Shady Grove Orthopedic Associates, P.A. v. Allstate Ins. Co., 559 U.S. 393 (2010).

560 Am. Copper & Brass, Inc. v. Lake City Indus. Products, Inc., 757 F.3d 540 (6th Cir. 2014) (Michigan court rule prohibiting class actions for statutory damages without regard to actual damages does not apply in federal court); Bank v. Independence Energy Grp., L.L.C., 736 F.3d 660 (2d Cir. 2013); Fitzgerald v. Gann Law Books, Inc., 956 F. Supp. 2d 581 (D.N.J. 2013); City Select Auto Sales, Inc. v. David Randall Associates, Inc., 296 F.R.D. 299 (D.N.J. 2013); A & L Indus., Inc. v. P. Cipollini,

In a fax case, one of the key questions is whether the lack of consent or the absence of an established business relationship can be proven without extensive individual adjudications. (The established business relationship defense applies only to fax cases.[561]) The fact that third parties were utilized to provide a list and conduct a "blast fax" advertisement campaign for the defendant gives rise to the conclusion that consent was lacking and that the faxes were not sent because of an existing business relationship.[562] A class may also be certified when the defendant omitted the opt-out notice that is a condition of both the consent and established business relationship defenses in a fax case.[563]

In a cell phone or text message case, the key issue is whether there is a class of persons who can be identified as having been subjected to a violation without the need for extensive individual inquiry regarding consent. For example, a situation comparable to a "blast fax" case based on a purchased list might be presented if a debt collector's records showed what numbers were obtained from skip-tracing or capturing incoming calls, so that the legality of the calls or text messages presents "uniform circumstances."[564] In any event, a caller's failure to maintain records showing which consumers had given consent cannot defeat class certification, as to do so would reward the caller for its poor record-keeping.[565]

A sample class action complaint for a violation of the TCPA is available online as companion material to this treatise.[566]

Discovery is proper prior to TCPA class certification, especially with a stipulated protective order.[567] However, a court may deny merits discovery if it is not relevant to certification.[568]

It is common for defendants to make a Rule 68 offer of the full amount of statutory damages to the named plaintiffs in a TCPA class action. If the class representatives reject the offer, the defendants argue that the action is moot. The Supreme Court has agreed to hear a case in which the Ninth Circuit rejected this position.[569]

6.9.5 Who Is Liable

6.9.5.1 "Any Person"

The TCPA's substantive restrictions apply to "any person,"[570] a term that includes individuals, partnerships, associations, joint-stock companies, trusts, and corporations.[571] However, the substantive provisions of the statute and rule use terms such as "initiate" or "make" a call or "send" a fax, so a second question is the level of involvement in these acts that is necessary for liability. The FCC's regulation addresses this question with respect to junk faxes, and it has issued declaratory rulings that address the issue with respect to several other types of TCPA violations. These issues are discussed in the subsections that follow.

Inc., 2013 WL 5503303, at *5 (D.N.J. Oct. 2, 2013); Weitzner v. Sanofi Pasteur, Inc., 2013 WL 5411729 (M.D. Pa. Sept. 26, 2013); Bais Yaakov of Spring Valley v. Peterson's Nelnet, L.L.C., 2012 WL 4903269, at *7 (D.N.J. Oct. 17, 2012), *appeal certified*, 2013 WL 663301 (D.N.J. Feb. 21, 2013); Landsman & Funk, P.C. v. Skinder-Strauss Associates, 2012 WL 6622120 (D.N.J. Dec. 19, 2012), *reconsideration denied*, 2013 WL 466448 (D.N.J. Feb. 8, 2013); Bank v. Spark Energy Holdings, L.L.C., 2012 WL 4097749, at *2 (S.D. Tex. Sept. 13, 2012) ("federal law permits plaintiffs to bring TCPA claims as class action"). *See also* Bailey v. Domino's Pizza, L.L.C., 867 F. Supp. 2d 835, 841 (E.D. La. 2012) (stating in context of statute of limitations question that § 227(b)(3), which refers to state laws and state court rules, "applies to TCPA claims brought in state court but by its plain language does not reach a TCPA claim brought in federal court").

561 *See* §§ 6.3.4.5, 6.8.2.3, *supra*.

562 Spine & Sports Chiropractic, Inc. v. Zirmed, Inc., 2014 WL 2946421 (W.D. Ky. June 30, 2014); Hawk Valley, Inc. v. Taylor, 301 F.R.D. 169 (E.D. Pa. 2014); St. Louis Heart Ctr., Inc. v. Vein Centers for Excellence, Inc., 2013 WL 6498245 (E.D. Mo. Dec. 11, 2013); Sandusky Wellness Center L.L.C. v. Medtox Scientific, Inc., 2013 WL 951143 (D. Minn. Mar. 12, 2013); Savanna Grp., Inc. v. Trynex, Inc., 90 Fed. R. Evid. Serv. 428, 2013 WL 66181 (N.D. Ill. Jan. 4, 2013); Siding & Insulation Co. v. Combined Ins. Grp. Ltd., Inc., 2012 WL 1425093, at *3 (N.D. Ohio Apr. 24, 2012) (certification cannot be defeated "by asserting the vague possibility that some of the individuals on the anonymous lists may have perchance consented to receiving the fax"); Targin Sign Sys. v. Preferred Chiropractic Ctr., Ltd., 679 F. Supp. 2d 894 (N.D. Ill. 2010); CE Design Ltd. v. Cy's Crabhouse North, Inc., 259 F.R.D. 135 (N.D. Ill. 2009); Exclusively Cats Veterinary Hosp. v. Anesthetic Vaporizer Services, 10-10620, 2010 WL 5439737 (E.D. Mich. Dec. 27, 2010); G.M. Sign, Inc. v. Group C Communications, Inc., 2010 WL 744262 (N.D. Ill. Feb. 25, 2010); G.M. Sign, Inc. v. Finish Thompson, Inc., 2009 WL 2581324 (N.D. Ill. Aug. 20, 2009); Hinman v. M & M Rental Ctr., 545 F. Supp. 2d 802 (N.D. Ill. 2008); Sadowski v. Med1 Online, L.L.C., 2008 WL 2224892 (N.D. Ill. May 27, 2008).

563 47 U.S.C. § 227(b)(2)(D), (E); 47 C.F.R. § 64.1200(a)(4)(iii); *In re* Sandusky Wellness Ctr., L.L.C., 570 Fed. Appx. 437 (6th Cir. 2014) (vacating denial of class certification and remanding for further consideration when trial court failed to recognize that commonality might be present if faxes lacked opt-out notices); Holtzman v. Turza, 728 F.3d 682 (7th Cir. 2013), *aff'g* Holtzman v. Turza, 2009 WL 3334909 (N.D. Ill. Oct. 14, 2009). *See generally* § 6.8.2.4, *supra*.

564 Connelly v. Hilton Grand Vacations Co., 294 F.R.D. 574 (S.D. Cal. 2013). *See also* Stonebridge Life Ins. Co., 289 F.R.D. 292, 295 (N.D. Cal. 2013) ("theoretical possibility that dialing lists selected through automatic processes might sometimes include individuals who, by happenstance, have previously consented" insufficient to defeat class certification on text messaging claim).

565 Zyburo v. NCSPlus, Inc., 44 F. Supp. 3d 500, 503 (S.D.N.Y. 2014).

566 National Consumer Law Center, Consumer Class Actions (8th ed. 2013) (see document entitled *Original Federal Jurisdiction, Post-CAFA Complaint—Telephone Consumer Protection Act*, available online as companion material to the *Consumer Class Actions* treatise).

567 Kane v. Nat'l Action Fin. Services, Inc., 2012 WL 1658643, at *6 (E.D. Mich. May 11, 2012).

568 Ketch, Inc. v. Heubel Material Handling, Inc., 2011 WL 4527881 (W.D. Okla. Sep. 28, 2011).

569 Gomez v. Campbell-Ewald Co., 768 F.3d 871 (9th Cir. 2014), *cert. granted*, 135 S. Ct. 2311 (2015). *See also* Stein v. Buccaneers Ltd. P'ship, 772 F.3d 698 (11th Cir. 2014) (unaccepted Rule 68 offer did not moot class action).

570 47 U.S.C. § 227(b)(1); 47 C.F.R. § 64.1200(a), (c), (d), (e) ("no person" shall violate restrictions).

571 City Select Auto Sales, Inc. v. David/Randall Associates, Inc., 96 F. Supp. 3d 403 (D.N.J. 2015) (company president may be liable if he personally participated in or authorized junk faxes); Maryland v. Universal Elections, 787 F. Supp. 2d 408 (D. Md. 2011) (individuals can be liable even when acting on behalf of a corporation); Accounting Outsourcing, L.L.C. v. Verizon Wireless Personal Communications, L.P., 329 F. Supp. 2d 789, 806 (M.D. La. 2004).

6.9.5.2 Fax Cases

6.9.5.2.1 *Liability of the person on whose behalf the advertisement is faxed*

In fax cases, an FCC regulation makes the party on whose behalf an advertisement is faxed responsible for any TCPA violations, without regard to technical agency law.[572] This is so, for example, even if the fax blaster is an independent contractor under agency law.[573] The FCC regulation to this effect has been sustained as a proper exercise of rulemaking authority.[574]

Even if the FCC had not provided by regulation that the party on whose behalf a fax is sent is the sender, sellers would still be liable on common law agency principles when their agents transmitted junk faxes. A 2013 FCC declaratory ruling, while dealing only with the TCPA's telemarketing restrictions, not its junk fax prohibition, recognizes that it is appropriate to apply common law agency principles to hold parties vicariously liable under federal statutes, including the TCPA.[575]

Several courts have erroneously held that the 2013 declaratory ruling displaces the regulation's strict liability standard for entities on whose behalf junk faxes are sent, and that liability can now be based only on common law agency principles.[576] These courts overlook the fact that the strict liability standard is part of a regulation that is specifically applicable to junk faxes. The declaratory ruling dealt only with the TCPA's telemarketing prohibitions. Moreover, in the ruling, the FCC made it clear that it could impose stricter vicarious liability standards on telemarketers through rulemaking[577]—a step it has already taken with respect to the TCPA's separate junk fax prohibition. Citing these reasons and an FCC amicus letter, both the Sixth and Eleventh Circuits have held that the FCC's 2013 declaratory ruling does not replace the regulation that casts liability on the party on whose behalf a junk fax is sent.[578]

6.9.5.2.2 *Fax blasters*

The FCC's regulation also provides that "[a] facsimile broadcaster will be liable for violations of paragraph (a)(3) of this section . . . if it demonstrates a high degree of involvement in, or actual notice of, the unlawful activity and fails to take steps to prevent such facsimile transmissions."[579] A "facsimile broadcaster" is defined as "a person or entity that transmits messages to telephone facsimile machines on behalf of another person or entity for a fee."[580] The FCC considers that a "fax broadcaster that serves as 'more than a mere conduit for third party faxes' is liable under the TCPA."[581] A fax broadcaster meets the FCC's standard if it supplies the fax numbers or determines the content of the advertisements.[582]

---

572   47 C.F.R. § 64.1200(f)(10) (defining "sender" for purposes of junk fax rule as person or entity on whose behalf a fax is sent or whose goods or services are advertised in it). *See* Imhoff Inv., L.L.C. v. Alfoccino, Inc., 792 F.3d 627 (6th Cir. 2015) (applying FCC's definition); Palm Beach Golf Center-Boca, Inc. v. John G. Sarris, D.D.S., P.A., 781 F.3d 1245, 1254–1255 (11th Cir. 2015); City Select Auto Sales, Inc. v. David/Randall Associates, Inc., 96 F. Supp. 3d 403 (D.N.J. 2015); Addison Automatics, Inc. v. RTC Grp., Inc., 2013 WL 3771423 (N.D. Ill. July 16, 2013); Glen Ellyn Pharmacy v. Promius Pharma, L.L.C., 2009 WL 2973046 (N.D. Ill. Sept. 11, 2009) (entity or entities on whose behalf facsimiles are transmitted are ultimately liable for compliance with rule banning unsolicited facsimile advertisements); Hooters of Augusta v. Nicholson, 537 S.E.2d 468, 472 (Ga. Ct. App. 2000) ("an advertiser may not avoid liability under the TCPA solely on the basis that the transmission was executed by an independent contractor"); Worsham v. Nationwide Ins. Co., 772 A.2d 868, 878 (Md. Ct. Spec. App. 2001) (independent contractor status of fax broadcaster does not shield from liability the person on whose behalf fax was sent); Chair King, Inc. v. GTE Mobilnet of Houston, Inc., 135 S.W.3d 365, 392–393 (Tex. App. 2004), *rev'd on other grounds*, 184 S.W.3d 707 (Tex. 2006); *In re* Rules and Regulations Implementing the Telephone Consumer Protection Act of 1991 ¶¶ 34–35, FCC Release No. 95-310, CC Docket No. 92-90, 10 F.C.C. Rcd. 12391, 1995 FCC LEXIS 5179, 78 Rad. Reg. 2d (P & F) 1258 (F.C.C. Aug. 7, 1995) (holding that "the entity or entities on whose behalf facsimiles are transmitted are ultimately liable for compliance with the rule banning unsolicited facsimile advertisements").

573   Hooters of Augusta, Inc. v. Nicholson, 537 S.E.2d 468 (Ga. Ct. App. 2000).

574   Palm Beach Golf Center-Boca, Inc. v. John G. Sarris, D.D.S., P.A., 781 F.3d 1245, 1257 (11th Cir. 2015); Asher & Simons, P.A. v. j2 Global Canada, Inc., 977 F. Supp. 2d 544 (D. Md. 2013). *See also* Accounting Outsourcing, L.L.C. v. Verizon Wireless Personal Communications, L.P., 329 F. Supp. 2d 789, 805–806 (M.D. La. 2004) (coverage of parties who hire others to do their fax advertising is not unconstitutionally vague).

575   *In re* The Joint Petition Filed by DISH Network, L.L.C., the United States of America, and the States of California, Illinois, North Carolina, and Ohio for Declaratory Ruling Concerning the Telephone Consumer Protection Act (TCPA) Rules, 2013 WL 1934349, F.C.C. 13-54 (F.C.C. May 9, 2013). *See also* American Soc'y of Mech. Engineers, Inc. v. Hydrolevel Corp., 456 U.S. 556, 565–574, 102 S. Ct. 1935, 72 L. Ed. 2d 330 (1982) (holding that "general principles of agency law," including "apparent authority theory," may establish a basis for liability in private antitrust actions under 15 U.S.C. § 15); American Tel. &

Tel. Co. v. Winback & Conserve Program, Inc., 42 F.3d 1421, 1427–1440 (3d Cir. 1994) (general agency principles, including apparent authority, apply to determine liability in private damages action for alleged false designation of origin under § 43(a) of the Lanham Act, 15 U.S.C. § 1125(a)); Accounting Outsourcing, L.L.C. v. Verizon Wireless Personal Communications, L.P., 329 F. Supp. 2d 789, 794–795, 805–806 (M.D. La. 2004) (liability in private TCPA action under § 227(b)(3) for violation of prohibitions against unsolicited fax advertisements may be predicated on agency doctrines of vicarious liability, because to construe statute otherwise would effectively allow "an end-run around the TCPA's prohibitions").

576   *See* Siding & Insulation Co. v. Alco Vending, Inc., 2015 WL 1858935 (N.D. Ohio Apr. 22, 2015); Savanna Grp., Inc. v. Trynex, Inc., 2013 WL 4734004, at *5 (N.D. Ill. Sept.3, 2013) ("Given the substantial similarity between the definitions of 'seller' and 'sender' and the broad language of the ruling concerning violations of § 227(b), the [*Dish Network*] ruling is controlling in this case").

577   *In re* The Joint Petition Filed by DISH Network, L.L.C., the United States of America, and the States of California, Illinois, North Carolina, and Ohio for Declaratory Ruling Concerning the Telephone Consumer Protection Act (TCPA) Rules ¶ 32, 2013 WL 1934349, F.C.C. 13-54 (F.C.C. May 9, 2013).

578   Imhoff Inv., L.L.C. v. Alfoccino, Inc., 792 F.3d 627 (6th Cir. 2015); Palm Beach Golf Center-Boca, Inc. v. John G. Sarris, D.D.S., P.A., 781 F.3d 1245, 1254–1255 (11th Cir. 2015).

579   47 C.F.R. § 64.1200(a)(4)(vii).

580   47 C.F.R. § 64.1200(f)(7).

581   *In re* Fax.com, Inc., 19 F.C.C. Rep. 748, 755 n.36 (2004).

582   71 Fed. Reg. 25,967, 25,971 (May 3, 2006); Report and Order, *In re* Rules and Regulations Implementing the Telephone Consumer

For example, in *State of Texas v. American Blastfax, Inc.*, the court refused to dismiss a TCPA claim against a fax broadcaster whose business was alleged to have centered around using a fax machine to send unsolicited advertisements—"the precise conduct outlawed by the TCPA."[583] With these allegations, the broadcaster "[wa]s more than a common carrier or service provider [because it] maintain[ed] and use[d] a database of recipient fax numbers, actively solicit[ed] third party advertisers and presumably review[ed] the content of the fax advertisements it sen[t] . . . . Blastfax is far more than a mere conduit for third party faxes."[584]

Other relevant facts include whether the broadcaster counseled customers how to bypass "spam filters," "do not call lists," and "do not fax lists"; advised the customers how to use their electronic fax service to reduce their advertising costs and shift the cost to recipients; assisted customers in generating a fax list of working fax numbers; allowed customers to use their services when defendants knew or should have known that the representations by their customers that there was a preexisting or established business relationship between the customers and recipients of the faxes, or that the recipients had opted in to receiving the faxes, were false; allowed faxes to be sent even though it knew that the faxes contained opt-out information that was illegible or too small to survive fax transmission; and advised customers how to use defendants' technology and skill to override and circumvent the wishes of recipients who did not want to receive unwanted commercial offers and solicitations.[585]

A fax broadcaster that is highly involved in the sender's messages must be identified on the fax along with the sender.[586] The advertiser and a fax broadcaster with a high degree of involvement may be jointly liable.[587]

6.9.5.3 Autodialed or Prerecorded Debt Collection and Other Calls to Cell Phones

Creditors are liable for improper autodialed or prerecorded calls to cell phones by their debt collection agents. In a 2008 ruling, the FCC determined that "a creditor on whose behalf an autodialed or prerecorded message call is made to a wireless number bears the responsibility for any violation of the Commission's rules. Calls placed by a third party collector on behalf of that creditor are treated as if the creditor itself placed the call."[588]

Even if the FCC had not issued this ruling, as a general rule creditors would be liable based on common law agency principles for the TCPA violations of the debt collectors they hire. A 2013 declaratory ruling by the FCC, while dealing only with telemarketers' TCPA violations, recognizes that it is appropriate to apply common law agency principles to hold parties vicariously liable under federal statutes, including the TCPA.[589] This ruling is discussed in more detail in § 6.9.5.4, *infra*.

The FCC's 2008 ruling addresses this question only as to calls by debt collectors and is silent about the principal's liability for non-debt collection calls that violate the TCPA. To the extent these calls are telemarketing calls, who is liable is discussed in § 6.9.5.4, *infra*.

6.9.5.4 Telemarketing Calls

Both the prohibition against prerecorded calls to residential lines and the company-specific and nationwide do-not-call rules are limited to telemarketing calls. In 2013, the FCC issued a declaratory ruling addressing the extent to which sellers are liable for their telemarketers' violation of these prohibitions.

The FCC started by examining the language of the statute and regulation, which prohibits "initiat[ing]" a call in violation of one of these provisions.[590] It interpreted "initiation" of a call to be confined to "tak[ing] the steps necessary to physically place a telephone call."[591] It held that a seller does not "initiate" a call when a third-party telemarketer places the call, unless the seller gives the telemarketer specific and comprehensive instructions as to the timing and manner of the call.[592] (It should be noted that other TCPA prohibitions use different language. For example, the prohibition against robocalls to cell phones provides that it is unlawful to "make" such a call without prior express consent.[593])

Protection Act of 1991 § 195, 18 F.C.C. Rcd. 14014, 2003 WL 21517853 (F.C.C. July 3, 2003). *See* Portuguese Am. Leadership Council of the U.S., Inc. v. Investors' Alert, Inc., 956 A.2d 671 (D.C. 2008) (reversing dismissal of claim against fax broadcaster).

583 State of Texas v. American Blastfax, Inc., 121 F. Supp. 2d 1085, 1089 (W.D. Tex. 2000).

584 *Id.* at 1089–1090.

585 Merchant & Gould, P.C. v. Premiere Global Services, 749 F. Supp. 2d 923, 937 (D. Minn. 2010).

586 47 C.F.R. § 68.318(d).

587 *Id.*

588 *In re* Rules and Regulations Implementing the Telephone Consumer Protection Act of 1991, Request of ACA Int'l for Clarification and Declaratory Ruling, No. 02-278, FCC Release 07-232, 23 F.C.C. Rcd. 559,

565, 2008 WL 65485, 43 Comm. Reg. (P & F) 877 (F.C.C. Jan. 4, 2008) ¶ 10. *See* Hartley-Culp v. Green Tree Servicing, L.L.C., 52 F. Supp. 3d 700 (M.D. Pa. 2014); Martin v. Cellco P'ship, 2012 WL 5048854 (N.D. Ill. Oct. 18, 2012) (rejecting Verizon's claim that "it cannot be held liable for automated dunning calls placed by Vantage and Chase to Plaintiff's cell phone," relying on the FCC ruling); *In re* The Joint Petition Filed by DISH Network, L.L.C., the United States of America, and the States of California, Illinois, North Carolina, and Ohio for Declaratory Ruling Concerning the Telephone Consumer Protection Act (TCPA) Rules ¶ 38, F.C.C. 13-54, No. 11-50 (F.C.C. May 9, 2013) (reiterating 2008 conclusion that creditors are liable for autodialed or prerecorded calls made on their behalf by collectors to wireless numbers).

589 *In re* The Joint Petition Filed by DISH Network, L.L.C., the United States of America, and the States of California, Illinois, North Carolina, and Ohio for Declaratory Ruling Concerning the Telephone Consumer Protection Act (TCPA) Rules, 2013 WL 1934349, F.C.C. 13-54 (F.C.C. May 9, 2013).

590 47 U.S.C. § 227(b)(1)(B); 47 C.F.R. § 64.1200(a)(3), (c).

591 *In re* The Joint Petition Filed by DISH Network, L.L.C., the United States of America, and the States of California, Illinois, North Carolina, and Ohio for Declaratory Ruling Concerning the Telephone Consumer Protection Act (TCPA) Rules ¶ 26, 2013 WL 1934349, F.C.C. 13-54 (F.C.C. May 9, 2013).

592 *Id.* at ¶¶ 26, 27. *Accord* Smith v. State Farm Mut. Auto. Ins. Co., 30 F. Supp. 3d 765, 771 (N.D. Ill. 2014) (no direct liability, and duty not to violate TCPA is not non-delegable).

593 47 U.S.C. § 227(b)(1)(A).

Nonetheless, the FCC went on to hold that a seller may be held vicariously liable under federal common law principles of agency for violations of either section 227(b) or section 227(c) that are committed by third-party telemarketers. The FCC noted:

> Our conclusion that a seller does not necessarily *initiate* a call that is placed by a third-party telemarketer on the seller's behalf does not end our inquiry. For even when a seller does not "initiate" a call under the TCPA, we conclude that it may be held vicariously liable for certain third-party telemarketing calls. In particular, we find that the seller may be held vicariously liable under federal common law principles of agency for TCPA violations committed by third-party telemarketers. In this regard, we explain below that a seller may be liable for violations by its representatives under a broad range of agency principles, including not only formal agency, but also principles of apparent authority and ratification.[594]

The FCC also considered the language of section 227(c)(5), which provides for liability for violation of the TCPA's do-not-call rules if a person has received more than one call within a twelve-month period "by or on behalf of the same entity." It did not rule out the possibility of interpreting this language to make sellers liable for their telemarketers' violation of the do-not-call rules beyond the common law principles of agency,[595] and some courts have adopted this view.[596] However, the FCC held that a rulemaking proceeding, rather than a declaratory judgment, would be required.

The 2013 declaratory ruling states that liability can be based not only on formal agency but also on principles of apparent authority and ratification.[597] By way of guidance, it provides several illustrative examples of evidence that may demonstrate that the telemarketer is the seller's authorized representative with apparent authority to make the seller vicariously liable for the telemarketer's section 227(b) violations:

> [A]pparent authority may be supported by evidence that the seller allows the outside sales entity access to information and systems that normally would be within the seller's exclusive control, including: access to detailed information regarding the nature and pricing of the seller's products and

services or to the seller's customer information. The ability by the outside sales entity to enter consumer information into the seller's sales or customer systems, as well as the authority to use the seller's trade name, trademark and service mark may also be relevant. It may also be persuasive that the seller approved, wrote or reviewed the outside entity's telemarketing scripts. Finally, a seller would be responsible under the TCPA for the unauthorized conduct of a third-party telemarketer that is otherwise authorized to market on the seller's behalf if the seller knew (or reasonably should have known) that the telemarketer was violating the TCPA on the seller's behalf and the seller failed to take effective steps within its power to force the telemarketer to cease that conduct. At a minimum, evidence of these kinds of relationships—which consumers may acquire through discovery, if they are not independently privy to such information—should be sufficient to place upon the seller the burden of demonstrating that a reasonable consumer would not sensibly assume that the telemarketer was acting as the seller's authorized agent.[598]

Even if the party directly committing the violation is an independent contractor, the principal may be liable if the independent contractor was also an agent acting within the scope of its agency.[599] A clause in the contract between the principal and the caller, stating that it does not create an agency relationship, is not dispositive.[600]

Many courts have agreed with the 2013 declaratory ruling that sellers can be vicariously liable under common law agency principles for their telemarketers' TCPA violations.[601] For

---

594   *In re* The Joint Petition Filed by DISH Network, L.L.C., the United States of America, and the States of California, Illinois, North Carolina, and Ohio for Declaratory Ruling Concerning the Telephone Consumer Protection Act (TCPA) Rules ¶ 28, 2013 WL 1934349, F.C.C. 13-54 (F.C.C. May 9, 2013).

595   *Id.* at ¶¶ 31–32, 40.

596   *See, e.g.,* Worsham v. Nationwide Ins. Co., 772 A.2d 868, 878–879 (Md. Ct. Spec. App. 2001). *But see* Lucas v. Telemarketer Calling from (407) 476-5670 & Other Tele. Numbers, 2014 WL 1119594, at *6–9 (S.D. Ohio Mar. 20, 2014) (Mag. recommendation) (finding that FCC's 2013 ruling is only basis for vicarious liability for calls by telemarketers).

597   *In re* The Joint Petition Filed by DISH Network, L.L.C., the United States of America, and the States of California, Illinois, North Carolina, and Ohio for Declaratory Ruling Concerning the Telephone Consumer Protection Act (TCPA) Rules ¶¶ 28, 34, 2013 WL 1934349, F.C.C. 13-54 (F.C.C. May 9, 2013).

598   *Id.* at ¶ 46 (footnotes omitted).

599   American Tel. & Tel. Co. v. Winback & Conserve Program, Inc., 42 F.3d 1421, 1437–1440 (3d Cir. 1994), cited with approval in note 84 of FCC's 2013 declaratory ruling) (listing many circumstances under which common law of agency makes principals liable for acts of independent contractors).

600   Toney v. Quality Resources, Inc., 75 F. Supp. 3d 727, 743–744 (N.D. Ill. 2014).

601   *See, e.g.,* Gomez v. Campbell-Ewald Co., 768 F.3d 871 (9th Cir. 2014) (affording *Chevron* deference to FCC's 2013 ruling), *cert. granted,* 135 S. Ct. 2311 (2015); Thomas v. Taco Bell Corp., 582 Fed. Appx. 678 (9th Cir. 2014) (applying FCC's reasoning in its 2013 declaratory ruling; vicarious liability can provide basis for liability for sending text message advertisements to cell phone without consent, but neither apparent authority nor ratification shown here); Toney v. Quality Resources, Inc., 75 F. Supp. 3d 727, 742–747 (N.D. Ill. 2014) (applying FCC's 2013 ruling; holding that allegations that seller, *inter alia*, authorized telemarketer to make calls, participated in developing script, and required that telemarketers follow it verbatim are sufficient, but rejecting arguments based on apparent authority and ratification); Smith v. State Farm Mut. Auto. Ins. Co., 30 F. Supp. 3d 765 (N.D. Ill. 2014) (agreeing with FCC's reasoning in 2013 ruling; holding that complaint stated a claim against insurer, who gave its agents authority to hire telemarketer, making telemarketer a subagent of the insurer); Lucas v. Telemarketer Calling from (407) 476-5670 & Other Tel. Numbers, 2014 WL 1119594, at *6–9 (S.D. Ohio Mar. 20, 2014) (mag. recommendation) (applying FCC's 2013 ruling; Mey v. Monitronics Int'l, Inc., 959 F. Supp. 2d 927 (N.D. W. Va. 2013) (holding that 2013 declaratory ruling was within FCC's authority; sufficient for plaintiff to allege that a telemarketer, acting on behalf of manufacturer and another seller, placed nineteen

example, a court refused to dismiss a claim that telemarketers were subagents of an insurance company when the company's insurance agents' contracts with a telemarketer controlled the timing, target location, and volume of its calls.[602] Another court held that allegations that the seller authorized a telemarketer to make calls, participated in developing the script, and required that telemarketers follow it verbatim were sufficient to withstand a motion to dismiss.[603]

6.9.5.5 Joint Venture, Aiding and Abetting, and Liability of Individuals, Parent Companies, Subsidiaries

The FCC did not address joint venture liability in its 2013 ruling. However, joint venture liability is entirely consistent with the common law agency principles it articulated in that ruling, so it is reasonable to conclude that a franchisor, parent company, or remote seller may be liable for TCPA violations if it is engaged in a joint venture with its franchisee, subsidiary, or dealer.[604] Many courts have also applied the general rule that corporate officers or other individuals can be liable if they personally participate in wrongful conduct.[605]

A parent company may be liable for the acts of its subsidiary if the parent company is so dominant that the subsidiary's corporate form is little more than a legal fiction.[606] Vicarious liability can extend to subcontractors who hire entities that violate the TCPA's telemarketing restrictions. For example, the Ninth Circuit held that a third-party marketing consultant hired by a merchant can be liable on agency principles if an entity to which it outsources the work violates the TCPA.[607] On the other hand, some courts have concluded that aiding and abetting liability is not available as a general rule under federal statutes, including the TCPA.[608]

6.9.6 Statute of Limitations

Most courts have held that the general four-year statute of limitations for federal claims applies to TCPA claims under sections 227(b) and (c).[609] Prior to the Supreme Court's decision in *Mims v. Arrow Financial Services, LLC*,[610] that the TCPA's permissive grant of jurisdiction to state courts does not deprive federal district courts of federal-question jurisdiction over private TCPA suits, a minority of courts applied state law limitations provisions.[611] These decisions are no longer good law after *Mims*.[612] Most recent decisions hold that the fact that TCPA cases can now always be brought in federal court

calls to a residential number on do-not-call list); Bridgeview Health Care Ctr. Ltd. v. Clark, 2013 WL 4495221, at *1 (N.D. Ill. Aug. 21, 2013). *See also In re* Jiffy Lube Int'l, Inc., Text Spam Litig., 847 F. Supp. 2d 1253 (S.D. Cal. 2012) (applying vicarious liability principles similar to those announced a year later in FCC's ruling; refusing to dismiss claim against entity that hired company to send text message advertisements to cell phones). *Cf.* Charvat v. Farmers Ins. Columbus, Inc., 897 N.E.2d 167 (Ohio Ct. App. 2008) (holding, prior to FCC's 2013 ruling, that telemarketer hired by insurance agent was not acting on behalf of insurance company whose insurance the agent sold, so insurer was not liable for telemarketer's violation of do-not-call rule.

602 Smith v. State Farm Mut. Auto. Ins. Co., 30 F. Supp. 3d 765, 775 (N.D. Ill. 2014).

603 Toney v. Quality Resources, Inc., 75 F. Supp. 3d 727, 742–744 (N.D. Ill. 2014) (applying FCC's 2013 ruling).

604 Mey v. Honeywell Int'l, Inc., 2013 WL 1337295, at *5 (S.D. W. Va. Mar. 29, 2013) (holding that plaintiff stated a claim against Honeywell for its dealers' TCPA telemarketing violations on ground that a partnership or joint venture was alleged, and "congressional tort actions implicitly include the doctrine of vicarious liability, whereby employers are liable for the acts of their agents and employees"); Agne v. Papa John's Int'l, Inc., 286 F.R.D. 559, 565 (W.D. Wash. 2012) (allowing consumer to proceed against franchisor that encouraged its franchisees to contract with robodialer to send text messages to cell phones).

605 Jackson Five Star Catering, Inc. v. Beason, 2013 WL 5966340 (E.D. Mich. Nov. 8, 2013); Brennan v. Nat'l Action Fin. Services, Inc., 2012 WL 3888218 (E.D. Mich. Sept. 7, 2012); Baltimore-Washington Tel. Co. v. Hot Leads Co., L.L.C., 584 F. Supp. 2d 736 (D. Md. 2008) (dismissing civil conspiracy claim, but noting that individual officers could still be liable jointly and severally for violating TCPA's prohibition of "war dialing"); Texas v. American Blast Fax, Inc., 164 F. Supp. 2d 892 (W.D. Tex. 2001); Weber v. U.S. Sterling Sec., Inc., 924 A.2d 816 (Conn. 2007) (while principals of limited liability company cannot be held liable for junk faxes solely because of their position with company, they can be held liable for their own wrongful acts); Covington & Burling v. Int'l Mktg. & Research, Inc., 2003 WL 21384825 (D.C. Super. Ct. Apr. 17, 2003), *as amended on reconsideration by* 2003 D.C. Super. LEXIS 28 (D.C. Super. Ct. May 17, 2003).

606 *See* Zarichny v. Complete Payment Recovery Services, Inc., 80 F. Supp. 3d 610 (E.D. Pa. 2015) (articulating this test, but finding allegations insufficient; company not liable for autodialed prerecorded debt collection calls made by its debt collection subsidiary on behalf of a third-party creditor).

607 Gomez v. Campbell-Ewald Co., 768 F.3d 871 (9th Cir. 2014), *cert. granted*, 135 S. Ct. 2311 (2015).

608 Clark v. Avatar Technologies, 2014 WL 309079 (S.D. Tex. Jan. 28, 2014); Baltimore-Washington Tel. Co. v. Hot Leads Co., 584 F. Supp. 2d 736, 738 (D. Md. 2008).

609 28 U.S.C. § 1658(a). *See* Bank v. Independence Energy Grp., L.L.C., 736 F.3d 660 (2d Cir. 2013); Benedia v. Super Fair Cellular, Inc., 2007 WL 2903175 (N.D. Ill. Sept. 26, 2007); Sznyter v. Malone, 66 Cal. Rptr. 3d 633 (Cal. Ct. App. 2007) (rejecting argument that TCPA incorporates state statute of limitations); Zelma v. Konikow, 879 A.2d 1185 (N.J. Super. Ct. App. Div. 2005) (absent state adoption of specific, shorter statute of limitations for TCPA claims, federal four-year limitation period applies); Stern v. Bluestone, 850 N.Y.S.2d 90 (N.Y. App. Div. 2008), *rev'd on other grounds*, 911 N.E.2d 844 (N.Y. 2009); Jemiola v. XYZ Corp., 802 N.E.2d 745 (Ohio Ct. Com. Pl. 2003); Grady v. OTC Investor's Edge, 2003 WL 22828294 (Ohio Ct. Com. Pl. Oct. 15, 2003). *See also* Bailey v. Domino's Pizza, L.L.C., 867 F. Supp. 2d 835 (E.D. La. 2012); Wellington Homes, Inc. v. West Dundee China Palace Rest., Inc., 984 N.E.2d 554 (Ill. App. Ct. Feb. 4, 2013); Anderson Office Supply, Inc. v. Advanced Med. Associates, P.A., 273 P.3d 786 (Kan. Ct. App. 2012); Worsham v. Fairfield Resorts, Inc., 981 A.2d 24 (Md. Ct. Spec. App. 2009) (holding that four-year statute of limitations under 28 U.S.C. § 1658 applies to private suit in Maryland state court).

610 Mims v. Arrow Fin. Services, L.L.C., ___ U.S. ___, 132 S. Ct. 740, 751–753 (2012).

611 *See, e.g.*, Edwards v. Emperor's Garden Rest., 130 P.3d 1280 (Nev. 2006) (since TCPA claim can be pursued in state court only when consistent with state laws and rules, shorter state statute of limitations applies); Weitzner v. Vaccess Am. Inc., 5 Pa. D. & C. 5th 95, 123–127 (Pa. Ct. Com. Pl. 2008); David L. Smith & Associates, L.L.P. v. Advanced Placement Team, Inc., 169 S.W.3d 816 (Tex. App. 2005).

612 Giovanniello v. ALM Media, L.L.C., 726 F.3d 106 (2d Cir. 2013).

requires application of the federal statute of limitations.[613] The Seventh Circuit held that the four-year limitations period was tolled during pendency of a prior state court putative class action.[614]

6.9.7 Pleadings and Discovery in TCPA Litigation

A TCPA complaint need not be pleaded with particularity.[615] It need not identify the number that was called.[616] However, the complaint must plead the necessary facts to support the legal claims made,[617] including some specificity regarding the defendant's use of an "automatic telephone dialing system," if applicable.[618] For example, the complaint should allege that the defendant uses automatic telephone dialing equipment and that the call bore telltale signs of an automated call, such as an obviously artificial voice, a message asking the consumer to press one of several keys, or a gap between picking up the call and a human being coming on the line.[619]

One way to investigate whether a defendant uses an automated telephone dialing equipment is to check the defendant's website, as defendants will often boast of their use of the latest technology. Another step is to determine whether the defendant has made a filing with the Texas Public Utility Commission, which requires a license to use automated telephone dialing equipment to contact persons in that state.[620]

The TCPA statute of limitations is four years, so discovery may seek records going back at least four years.[621] Discovery from telecommunication companies and other non-parties may be necessary due to the technical nature of automatic dialing systems, fax broadcasting, and sending text messages, and should be initiated as soon as possible.[622] Experts may be required to prove that an "automatic telephone dialing system" was used.[623] The differing scopes of discovery for the two claims was one reason a court denied consolidation of a TCPA case with an FDCPA case.[624]

Discovery of other suits alleging TCPA violations has been compelled from a defendant.[625] On the other hand, a court

---

613 Giovanniello v. ALM Media, L.L.C., 726 F.3d 106 (2d Cir. 2013); Compressor Eng'g Corp. v. Chicken Shack, Inc., 2013 WL 4413752 (E.D. Mich. Aug. 15, 2013); Warnick v. DISH Network, L.L.C., 2013 WL 1151884 (D. Colo. Mar. 19, 2013); Bridging Communities, Inc. v. Top Flite Fin., Inc., 2013 WL 185397 (E.D. Mich. Jan. 17, 2013); Bailey v. Domino's Pizza, L.L.C., 867 F. Supp. 2d 835 (E.D. La. 2012); Bais Yaakov of Spring Valley v. Peterson's Nelnet, L.L.C., 2012 WL 4903269 (D.N.J. Oct. 17, 2012).

614 Sawyer v. Atlas Heating & Sheet Metal Works, Inc., 642 F.3d 560 (7th Cir. 2011).

615 Jackson v. Caribbean Cruise Line, Inc., 88 F. Supp. 3d 129, 138 (E.D.N.Y. 2015) (complaint need not be pleaded with particularity, but this one has insufficient non-conclusory allegations that sender of text messages was cruise line's agent); McCabe v. Caribbean Cruise Line, 2014 WL 3014874, at *4 (E.D.N.Y. July 3, 2014). *See also* Dr. Stuart T. Zaller, L.L.C. v. Pharmawest Pharmacy, Ltd., 2011 WL 5508912 (D. Md. Nov. 8, 2011) (allegations against 'Defendants' or 'all Defendants,' without specifying which defendant did or knew what, put named defendant clearly on notice).

616 Margulis v. Generation Life Ins. Co., 91 F. Supp. 3d 1165 (E.D. Mo. 2015) (complaint need not identify complete telephone number that was called or number from which call was made); Buslepp v. B&B Entm't, L.L.C., 2012 WL 1571410 (S.D. Fla. May 3, 2012) (complaint need not state number called or identify class members); Sterling v. Mercantile Adjustment Bureau, L.L.C., 2011 WL 4915813 (W.D.N.Y. Oct. 17, 2011) (denying motion for more definite statement; complaint need not identify number called).

617 Augustin v. Santander Consumer USA, Inc., 43 F. Supp. 3d 1251 (M.D. Fla. 2012) (complaint insufficient when it alleges no dates, details, or identifying phone numbers); Myers v. Stoneleigh Recovery Associates, 2012 WL 1356752 (E.D. Cal. Apr. 18, 2012) (dismissing *pro se* complaint, with leave to amend, for failing to allege any facts to support TCPA claim).

618 Jackson v. Caribbean Cruise Line, Inc., 88 F. Supp. 3d 129, 139–140 (E.D.N.Y. 2015) (finding allegations upon information and belief sufficient); Ibey v. Taco Bell Corp., 2012 WL 2401972 (S.D. Cal. June 18, 2012) (granting motion to dismiss, with leave to amend, because complaint's allegations that defendant used an "automatic telephone dialing system" were conclusory).

619 *See* Soular v. Northern Tier Energy, L.P., 2015 WL 5024786 (D. Minn. Aug. 25, 2015) (allegations regarding generic and promotional content of text messages—that they were sent en masse from defendant's text message service and sent with an autodialer—are sufficient); Thomas

v. Dun & Bradstreet Credibility Corp., ___ F. Supp. 3d ___, 2015 WL 4698398, at *6 (C.D. Cal. Aug. 5, 2015) (allegation of pause after plaintiff answered phone, and defendant's likely need for an autodialer, are sufficient); Gragg v. Orange Cab Co., 942 F. Supp. 2d 1111 (W.D. Wash. 2013) (allegation that defendants' equipment sent tens of thousands of substantially similar text messages, and that there was temporal disconnection between using defendants' service and receiving text message, are sufficient to raise inference that autodialer was used); Vaccaro v. CVS Pharmacy, Inc., 2013 WL 3776927 (S.D. Cal. July 16, 2013); Connelly v. Hilton Grand Vacations Co., 2012 WL 2129364 (S.D. Cal. June 11, 2012) (allegation that, after recipient answered call, there was a delay before a live person spoke to recipient is sufficient until discovery can be conducted), *later opinion at* 995 F. Supp. 2d 1189 (W.D. Wash. 2014) (finding on facts that defendant's system did not meet definition of autodialer). *See also* Kramer v. Autobytel, Inc., 759 F. Supp. 2d 1165 (N.D. Cal. 2010) (for purposes of motion to dismiss, autodialed nature of text message can be inferred from allegation that message was impersonal in nature and was sent from a code registered to defendant).

620 *See* Pub. Util. Comm'n of Tex., ADA—Automatic Dial Announcing Device Permits, *available at* www.puc.texas.gov.

621 Jenkins v. G.C. Services, Ltd. P'ship, 2012 WL 1067947 (W.D.N.C. Mar. 29, 2012) (defendant ordered to identify date and time of all calls to plaintiff's number for four years and whether made by a person or an automatic telephone dialing system).

622 Kaffko v. Quepasa Corp., 2011 WL 4442654 (D. Nev. Sep. 22, 2011) (denying non-party's motion to quash production of records related to text messages).

623 Mudgett v. Navy Fed. Credit Union, 998 F. Supp. 2d 722 (E.D. Wis. 2012) (neither defendant's "Phone Skills Manual" or plaintiff's submissions contained sufficient evidence to conclude that placed calls were connected to computer capable of autodialing).

624 Martin v. Midland Funding, L.L.C., 2011 WL 3876965 (N.D. Ill. Aug. 31, 2011).

625 Castro v. Green Tree Servicing, L.L.C., 2012 WL 2428190 (S.D.N.Y. June 22, 2012) (compelling list of past suits alleging FDCPA or TCPA violations); Chang v. Cavalry Portfolio Services, L.L.C., 2011 WL 6101952 (E.D.N.Y. Dec. 1, 2011) (same; also compelling documents related to defendant's automatic telephone dialing system). *But cf.* Charvat v. Travel Services, ___ F. Supp. 3d ___, 2015 WL 3917046 (N.D. Ill. June 24, 2015) (defendant is not entitled to discover plaintiff's tax returns to show how much income he derives from TCPA litigation).

denied an attempt to discover the amounts a plaintiff received from other TCPA suits as not being relevant.[626]

Courts have dismissed defendants' counterclaims against TCPA plaintiffs to collect on the underlying debt as noncompulsory.[627] Furthermore, courts have declined to exercise supplemental jurisdiction over these counterclaims because doing so would contradict federal policy concerns against automated telemarketing.[628]

A variety of pleadings and discovery materials in TCPA cases can be found on the companion website.

6.9.8 Burden of Proof Regarding Exceptions

The general rule under the TCPA is that a person making a call has the burden of demonstrating that it falls within an exception to one of the TCPA's prohibitions.[629] Accordingly,

the existence of prior express consent to make an autodialed or an artificial or prerecorded call to a cell phone is an affirmative defense for which the caller bears the burden of proof.[630] This is consistent with the general rule that the party claiming the benefit of an exception in a federal statute has the burden of coming forward with at least some evidence of the applicability of the exception.[631]

This burden of proof was reiterated several times in a 2015 FCC declaratory ruling.[632] The Commission emphasized that, "regardless of the means by which a caller obtains consent, under longstanding Commission precedent, if any question arises as to whether prior express consent was provided by a call recipient, the burden is on the caller to prove that it obtained the necessary prior express consent."[633] Indeed, the Commission advises that callers seeking to meet their burden of proof maintain adequate business records:

> The well-established evidentiary value of business records means that callers have reasonable ways to carry their burden of proving consent. We expect that responsible callers, cognizant of their duty to ensure that they have prior express consent under the TCPA and their burden to prove that they have such consent, will maintain proper business records tracking consent. Thus, we see no reason to shift the TCPA compliance burden onto consumers and affirm that they do not bear the burden of proving that a caller did not have prior express consent for a particular call."[634]

6.9.9 Recovering from Defendant's Insurance Policy

There is an extensive body of law addressing whether TCPA claims and related state claims are covered under insurance policies. Potentially applicable coverages include (a) the "right of privacy" portion of "advertising injury" coverage typically provided by general liability policies, (b) property damage, (c) errors and omissions and professional liability policies, typically issued to debt collectors and collection attorneys, and (d) modified directors and officers

---

626 Desai v. ADT, 2012 WL 1755739 (N.D. Ill. May 11, 2012).

627 Watkins v. Synchrony Bank, 2015 WL 5178134 (M.D. Pa. Sept. 4, 2015); Ayres v. Nat'l Mgmt. Corp., 1991 WL 66845 (E.D. Pa. Apr. 25, 1991). *See also* Sparrow v. Mazda Am. Credit, 385 F. Supp. 2d 1063 (E.D. Cal. 2005) (FDCPA suit); Hart v. Clayton-Parker & Associates, Inc., 869 F. Supp. 774 (D. Ariz. 1994) (dismissing counterclaim in FDCPA suit for lack of jurisdiction). *But see* Miller v. 3G Collect, LLC, 302 F.R.D. 333 (E.D. Pa. 2014) (counterclaim was compulsory); Horton v. Calvary Portfolio Services, L.L.C., 301 F.R.D. 547 (S.D. Cal. 2014) (counterclaim for breach of contract was compulsory).

628 Watkins v. Synchrony Bank, 2015 WL 5178134 (M.D. Pa. Sept. 4, 2015) (exercising supplemental jurisdiction over counterclaim "would likely frustrate the federal policy of deterring automated telephone calls embodied within the TCPA"); Sparrow v. Mazda Am. Credit, 385 F. Supp. 2d 1063 (E.D. Cal. 2005) (declining to exercise supplemental jurisdiction in FDCPA suit because "[s]trong policy reasons exist to prevent the chilling effect of trying FDCPA claims in the same case as state law claims for collection of the underlying debt"); Ayres v. Nat'l Mgmt. Corp., 1991 WL 66845 (E.D. Pa. Apr. 25, 1991) (allowing counterclaims on underlying debts "discourag[es] plaintiffs from bringing meritorious claims in federal court"). *But see* Hunt v. 21st Mortg. Corp., 2012 WL 3903783 (N.D. Ala. Sept. 7, 2012); Wilson v. Discover Bank, 2012 WL 1899539 (W.D. Wash. May 24, 2012) (exercising supplemental jurisdiction).

629 *See In re* Rules and Regulations Implementing the Tel. Consumer Prot. Act of 1991, 27 F.C.C. Rcd. 1830, n.68 (F.C.C. 2012) (in a dispute, telemarketer has burden to prove that consumer gave written consent for the call); Van Sweden Jewelers, Inc. v. 2012 WL 4074620 (W.D. Mich. June 21, 2012); Gutierrez v. Barclays Grp., 2011 WL 579238, at *2 (S.D. Cal. Feb. 9, 2011); Virtual Auto Loans, 2009 FCC LEXIS 4342 (Mar. 9, 2009); Hinman v. M & M Rental Ctr., Inc., 596 F. Supp. 2d 1152 (N.D. Ill. 2009); Green v. Serv. Master on Location Services Corp., 2009 WL 1810769 (N.D. Ill. June 22, 2009); Sadowski v. Med 1 Online, L.L.C., 2008 WL 2224892, at *3–4 (N.D. Ill. May 27, 2008) (observing that issue of consent is an affirmative defense); Lampkin v. GGH, Inc., 146 P.3d 847, ¶ 27 (Okla. Ct. App. 2006) (recipient should not be charged with proving the negative propositions that it did not give permission or did not have a business relationship with sender); *In re* Rules and Regulations Implementing the Telephone Consumer Protection Act of 1991, Request of ACA Int'l for Clarification and Declaratory Ruling ¶ 10, 23 F.C.C. Rcd. 559, 565, 2008 WL 65485 (F.C.C. Jan. 4, 2008) ("we conclude that the creditor should be responsible for demonstrating that the consumer provided prior express consent."); *In re* Rules and Regulations Implementing the Tel. Consumer Prot. Act of 1991, 21 F.C.C. Rcd. 3787, 3812 (F.C.C. 2006) (determining that "a sender should have the obligation to demonstrate that it complied with the rules, including that it had the recipient's prior express invitation or

permission"); New York Sec. & Private Patrol, Inc., 2009 FCC LEXIS 4343 (Mar. 9, 2009). *See also* § 6.8.2.2, *supra* (burden of proof in junk fax cases).

630 Grant v. Capital Mgmt. Services, L.P., 449 Fed. Appx. 598, 600 n. 1 (9th Cir. 2011); King v. Time Warner Cable, ___ F. Supp. 3d ___, 2015 WL 4103689, at *5 (S.D.N.Y. July 7, 2015); Echevvaria v. Diversified Consultants, Inc., 2014 WL 929275, at *7 (S.D.N.Y. Feb. 28, 2014).

631 Meacham v. Knolls Atomic Power Lab., 554 U.S. 84, 128 S. Ct. 2395, 2400, 171 L. Ed. 2d 283 (2008) ("[T]he burden of proving justification or exemption under a special exception to the prohibitions of a statute generally rests on one who claims its benefits."); FTC v. Morton Salt Co., 334 U.S. 37, 44–45, 68 S. Ct. 822, 92 L. Ed. 1196 (1948); E.E.O.C. v. Chi. Club, 86 F.3d 1423, 1429–1430 (7th Cir. 1996); Irwin v. Mascott, 96 F. Supp. 2d 968 (N.D. Cal. 1999).

632 *In re* Rules & Regulations Implementing the TCPA of 1991 ¶¶ 47, 58, 70, 85, 27 F.C.C. Rcd. 15391, 2015 WL 4387780 (July 10, 2015).

633 *Id.* at ¶ 58.

634 *In re* Rules & Regulations Implementing the TCPA of 1991 ¶ 70, 27 F.C.C. Rcd. 15391, 2015 WL 4387780 (July 10, 2015).

liability policies, which often provide for coverage for the company itself.[635] Since the mid-2000s, many but not all policies have included specific exclusions for conduct that can give rise to TCPA claims.[636]

In pursuing TCPA cases, care should be taken to preserve and avoid negating necessary insurance coverage. For example, the plaintiff should give notice to any insurance companies and brokers. Asking for $1500 treble damages for each offending communication may not be advisable if the defendant is not able to pay damages from its own assets but has insurance coverage with exclusions for willful violations of statutes.

6.9.10 Government Enforcement

The TCPA authorizes state attorneys general to seek damages or injunctive relief in federal court.[637] Consumers may also file complaints with the FCC.[638] Complaints are important because the FCC often bases policy decisions on the complaints it receives. The FCC can issue citations and fine violators of TCPA rules, and FCC citations and resulting enforcement actions can provide useful statements of agency expectations and interpretations of both the TCPA and FCC rules. However, to seek individual damages under the TCPA, consumers should file a civil suit.

6.10 Unsolicited Bulk Commercial E-Mail (Spam)

6.10.1 Background

Unsolicited bulk commercial e-mail, commonly known as "spam,"[639] is a problem for consumers for a number of reasons. Its low cost and anonymity attract fraudulent sellers. Pyramid schemes, miracle cures, pornography, and a host of bogus products are marketed by spam.[640] Spam can contain viruses. Any response to spam, even to request that no further solicitations be sent, gives information to the entity that sent the spam and can undermine the consumer's privacy.

635 Western Heritage Ins. Co. v. Asphalt Wizards, 795 F.3d 832 (8th Cir. 2015) ($1000-per-claim deductible excludes all class members' claims for $500 TCPA statutory damages); Nationwide Mutual Ins. Co. v. David Randall Associates, Inc., 551 Fed. Appx. 6388 (3d Cir. 2014); Park Univ. Enterprises, Inc. v. American Cas. Co. of Reading, Pa., 442 F.3d 1239, i249 (10th Cir. 2006); Resource Bankshares Corp. v. St. Paul Mercury Ins. Co., 407 F.3d 631 (4th Cir. 2005); Universal Underwriters Insurance Co. v. Lou Fusz Automotive Network, 401 F.3d 876, 881, 883 (8th Cir. 2005); Hooters of Augusta, Inc. v. American Global Ins. Co., 157 Fed. Appx. 201, 208 (11th Cir. 2005), aff'g 272 F. Supp. 2d 1365 (S.D. Ga. 2003); American States Ins. Co. v. Capital Associates of Jackson Cnty., Inc., 392 F.3d 939, 942 (7th Cir. 2004); Western Rim Inv. Advisors, Inc. v. Gulf Ins. Co., 96 Fed. Appx. 960 (5th Cir. 2004), aff'g 269 F. Supp. 2d 836 (N.D. Tex. 2003); American Cas. Co. of Reading, Pa. v. Superior Pharmacy, L.L.C., 86 F. Supp. 3d 1307 (M.D. Fla. 2015); Maxum Indem. Co. v. Eclipse Mfg. Co., 2013 WL 5993389 (N.D. Ill. Nov. 12, 2013); Cincinnati Ins. Co. v. Gage Ctr. Dental Grp., P.A., 2013 WL 5913751 (D. Kan., Nov. 1, 2013); Cincinnati Ins. Co. v. All Plumbing, Inc., 64 F. Supp. 3d 69 (D.D.C. 2014); Encore Receivable Mgmt., Inc. v. Ace Property & Cas. Ins. Co., 2013 WL 3354571 (S.D. Ohio July 3, 2013); RPM Pizza, L.L.C. v. Argonaut Great Cent. Ins. Co., 2013 WL 1296678 (M.D. La. Mar. 28, 2013); BCS Ins. Co. v. Big Thyme Enterprises, Inc., 2013 WL 594858 (D.S.C. Feb. 14, 2013); Melrose Hotel Co. v. St. Paul Fire & Marine Ins. Co., 432 F. Supp. 2d 488 (E.D. Pa. 2006), aff'd, 503 F.3d 339, 340 (3d Cir. 2007); New Century Mortg. Corp. v. Great N. Ins. Co., 2006 WL 2088198 (N.D. Ill. July 25, 2006); American Home Assurance Co. v. McLeod USA, Inc., 2006 WL 1895704 (N.D. Ill. July 5, 2006); Erie Ins. Exch. v. Watts, 2006 WL 1547109 (S.D. Ind. May 30, 2006); Nutmeg Ins. Co. v. Employers Ins. Co. of Wausau, 2006 WL 453235 (N.D. Tex. Feb. 24, 2006); St. Paul Fire & Marine Ins. Co. v. Brunswick Corp., 405 F. Supp. 2d 890, 895 (N.D. Ill. 2005); Registry Dallas Associates, L.P. v. Wausau Bus. Ins. Co., 2004 WL 614836 (N.D. Tex. Feb. 26, 2004); Prime TV, L.L.C. v. Travelers Ins. Co., 223 F. Supp. 2d 744 (M.D.N.C. 2002); Standard Mut. Ins. Co. v. Lay, 989 N.E.2d 591 (Ill. May 23, 2013); Valley Forge Ins. Co. v. Swiderski Electronics, Inc., 860 N.E.2d 307 (Ill. 2006); G.M. Sign, Inc. v. Pennswood Partners, Inc., 9 N.E.3d 49 (Ill. App. Ct. Mar. 24, 2014); State Farm Fire & Cas. Co. v. Kapraun, 2014 WL 3047309 (Mich. Ct. App. July 3, 2014); Telecommunications Network Design Inc. v. Brethren Mut. Ins. Co., 5 A.3d 331 (Pa. Super. Ct. 2010); TIG Ins. Co. v. Dallas Basketball, Ltd., 129 S.W.3d 232 (Tex. App. 2004).

636 Emcasco Ins. Co. v. CE Design, Ltd., 784 F.3d 1371 (10th Cir. 2015) (conversion and UDAP claims as well as TCPA claims fall within exclusion for "distribution of material in violation of statutes"); Interline Brands, Inc. v. Chartis Specialty Ins. Co., 749 F.3d 962 (11th Cir. 2014); James River Ins. Co. v. Med Waste Mgmt., L.L.C., 46 F. Supp. 3d 1350 (S.D. Fla. 2014) (giving effect to exclusion of acts that violate TCPA and applying it to conversion claim as well); MDC Acquisition Co. v. Traveler's Prop. Cas. Co., 545 Fed. Appx. 398 (6th Cir. 2013).

637 47 U.S.C. § 227(g)(1). See Virginia ex rel. Jagdmann v. Real Time Int'l, Inc., 2005 WL 1162937 (E.D. Va. Apr. 26, 2005); Texas v. American Blast Fax, Inc., 164 F. Supp. 2d 892 (W.D. Tex. 2001).

638 Complaints can be filed through the FCC's website at www.fcc.gov.

639 "SPAM" is a trademark of the Hormel Food Co., but that company states on its website that it does not object to the use of the term to mean unsolicited bulk commercial e-mail as long as the term is printed in lower case letters. For discussions of issues regarding spam, see John Soma, Spam Still Pays: The Failure of the CAN-SPAM Act of 2003 and Proposed Legal Solutions, 45 Harv. J. on Legis. 165 (Winter 2008); Jasmine E. McNealey, Angling for Phishers: Legislative Responses to Deceptive E-Mail, 13 Comm. L. & Pol'y 275 (Spring 2008); David E. Sorkin, Technical and Legal Approaches to Unsolicited Electronic Mail, 35 U.S.F.L. Rev. 325 (Winter 2001), available at repository.jmls.edu; David E. Sorkin, Unsolicited Commercial E-Mail and the Telephone Consumer Protection Act of 1991, 45 Buffalo L. Rev. 1001 (1997), available at repository.jmls. edu; Sabra-Anne Kalin, Note, 16 Berkeley Tech. L.J. 435 (2001); Max. P. Ochoa, Case Note: Legislative Note: Recent State Laws Regulating Unsolicited Electronic Mail, 16 Computer & High Tech L.J. 459 (May 2000); Gary S. Moorefield, Note, SPAM: It's Not Just for Breakfast Anymore: Federal Legislation and the Fight to Free the Internet from Unsolicited Commercial E-Mail, 5 B.R. J. Sci. & Tech. L. 10 (Spring 1999).

640 See, e.g., Fed. Trade Comm'n v. Trustsoft, Inc., 2005 WL 1523915 (S.D. Tex. June 14, 2005) (false representations that spyware had been detected on consumers' computers and that spammer's product would remove it); Fed. Trade Comm'n v. Global Net Solutions, Inc., 2005 WL 221836 (D. Nev. Jan. 3, 2005) (pornography); Fed. Trade Comm'n v. Bryant, 2004 WL 2504357 (M.D. Fla. Oct. 4, 2004) (business opportunities marketed in violation of telemarketing law); Fed. Trade Comm'n v. Phoenix Avatar, Inc., 2004 WL 1746698 (N.D. Ill. July 30, 2004) (weight loss patch). See also Fed. Trade Comm'n v. Sili Nutraceuticals, L.L.C., 2007 WL 2415849 (N.D. Ill. Aug. 13, 2007) (rapid weight loss product); United States v. Cyberheat, Inc., 2007 WL 686678 (D. Ariz. Mar. 2, 2007) (discussing pornographic spam).

There is debate within the Internet community about whether spam ought to be regulated, and some favor technological solutions. These solutions are imperfect, however. Filtering programs can overscreen or underscreen, and spam senders can devise ways to evade filtering systems. Technological solutions also carry costs that are passed on to consumers in the form of increased prices: the costs Internet Service Providers (ISPs) incur to add increased capacity, add customer service staff to deal with consumer complaints about spam, and purchase or develop spam filtering programs.[641]

Spam also increases direct costs for individual consumers. The time spent receiving spam ties up the consumer's wireless system or Internet access line. If the consumer pays for Internet access by the hour instead of a flat monthly fee, receiving spam increases the charges. Receipt of spam also occupies the resources of the consumer's computer system.

Perhaps the worst problem caused by spam is that it undermines legitimate use of e-mail. When Congress passed the federal E-Sign statute in 2000,[642] it imagined that e-mail would be an efficient, cost-effective way for companies to communicate with consumers. Spam undermines this goal. A consumer who is flooded by an ocean of spam is likely to overlook important legitimate e-mail messages. Spam can fill up the consumer's e-mail storage capacity and prevent the consumer from receiving legitimate messages. Worse yet, the consumer or the consumer's ISP may use a spam filtering program that overscreens, blocking legitimate messages along with the spam. There is particular danger if E-Sign or other statutes are interpreted to allow notices to be considered sent without proof that the consumer actually received and opened the message.

The main federal response to the spam problem is the Controlling the Assault of Non-Solicited Pornography and Marketing Act of 2003 (CAN-SPAM).[643] The Act has been criticized by some for preempting more aggressive state laws that combat spam,[644] although it does not preempt state laws which prohibit falsity or deception in commercial e-mail messages.

CAN-SPAM requires that subject headings not be misleading to a reasonable recipient.[645] In addition, commercial e-mail must provide the valid postal address and actual e-mail address of the sender, and senders must honor recipients' requests not to receive further communications.[646] Unfortunately, these requirements are widely ignored and are ill-considered in any event since a consumer must open, read, and respond to spam in order to opt out.

Despite the passage of CAN-SPAM, there has been no decrease in spam.[647] Spammers continue to hide their identities and locations, and spam is increasingly originated overseas, thereby creating further enforcement problems.[648] The FCC has rejected the idea of a do-not-spam list out of fear that the list itself would become a source of e-mail addresses that spammers could exploit.[649]

Enforcement of CAN-SPAM is made even more difficult by the fact that the statute does not permit an individual consumer right of action.[650] Instead, the statute must be enforced by various state and federal agencies or by ISPs.[651] The provisions of CAN-SPAM and other legal theories for suing spam senders are discussed below.

---

641 America Online v. Smith, 2006 WL 181674 (E.D. Va. Jan. 24, 2006) (findings as to cost of spam). *See also* Adam Hamel, Note, *Will the CAN-SPAM Act of 2003 Finally Put a Lid on Unsolicited E-Mail?*, 39 New. Eng. L. Rev. 961 (2005) (discussing costs). *But cf.* Jaynes v. Commonwealth, 666 S.E.2d 303 (Va. 2008) (holding that statute prohibiting false routing information in dissemination of e-mails was unconstitutionally overbroad because it prohibits anonymous transmission of *all* unsolicited bulk e-mails and noting that there was nothing in the record showing that unsolicited *non-commercial* bulk e-mails increased costs to Internet service providers).

642 15 U.S.C. §§ 7001–7031. *See* National Consumer Law Center, Consumer Banking and Payments Law (5th ed. 2013), *updated at* www.nclc.org/library.

643 15 U.S.C. §§ 7701–7713.

644 15 U.S.C. § 7707(b). *See* Elizabeth A. Alongi, Note, *Has the U.S. Canned Spam?*, 46 Ariz. L. Rev. 263, 287–89 (2004); Andre R. Jaglom, *Internet, Distribution, E-Commerce and Other Computer Related Issues*, SJ075 ALI-ABA 505, 517–20 (2004). *See also* Lily Zhang, Note, *The CAN-SPAM Act, An Insufficient Response to the Growing Spam Problem*, 20 Berkeley Tech. L.J. 301 (2005); Stephanie A. Joyce & Glenn B. Manishin, *Overview of Current Spam Law and Policy*, 784

PLI/Pat 9, 15–16 (2004) (stating that far-reaching federal preemption is an achievement of CAN-SPAM).

645 15 U.S.C. § 7704(a)(1), (2); Fed. Trade Comm'n v. Optin Global, Inc., 2005 WL 1027108 (N.D. Cal. Apr. 13, 2005) (granting TRO forbidding subject lines that falsely suggest recipient has already submitted a mortgage application or otherwise has a relationship with sender or another).

646 15 U.S.C. § 7704(a)(3)–(5).

647 John Soma, *Spam Still Pays: The Failure of the Can-Spam Act of 2003 and Proposed Legal Solutions*, 45 Harv. J. on Legis. 165 (Winter 2008); Elizabeth A. Alongi, Note, *Has the U.S. Canned Spam?*, 46 Ariz. L. Rev. 263, 288 (2004). *See also* Matthew Hettrich, Comment, *Data Privacy Regulation in the Age of Smartphones*, 31 Touro L. Rev. 981, 990–991 (2015) ("While CAN-SPAM has many positive aspects, overall, the statute has not accomplished its purpose of deterring spammers"); Symantec Intelligence Report (Jan., 2012), *available at* www.symantec.com; FTC Spam Summit: The Next Generation of Threats and Solutions 5 (Nov. 2007), *available at* www.ftc.gov.

648 Unspam Techs., Inc. v. Chernuk, 716 F.3d 322 (4th Cir. 2013) (concluding that there was no personal jurisdiction over overseas banks that processed payments made to spammers); Fed. Trade Comm'n v. Phoenix Avatar, L.L.C., 2004 WL 1746698 (N.D. Ill. July 30, 2004) (detailed description of tricks used by spammers, here sellers of fake diet patches, to cover their tracks). *See also* America Online, Inc. v. Smith, 2006 WL 181674 (E.D. Va. Jan. 24, 2006) (describing methods of evasion; concluding that spammer obtained ISP's services "without authority" and "by false pretenses" within meaning of statute).

649 Fed. Trade Comm'n v. Phoenix Avatar, L.L.C., 2004 WL 1746698 (N.D. Ill. July 30, 2004). *See also* Mary Kissel, *FTC Says "Do Not E-mail List" Isn't Feasible*, Wall St. J., June 16, 2004, at D12.

650 Madorsky v. Does, 2006 WL 1587349 (N.D. Ohio June 8, 2006) (dismissing *pro se* complaint by individual because CAN-SPAM Act does not create private cause of action).

651 15 U.S.C. § 7706. *See* Adam Zitter, Note, *Good Laws for Junk Fax? Government Regulation of Unsolicited Solicitations*, 72 Fordham L. Rev. 2767, 2789 (2004).

6.10.2 *Federal CAN-SPAM Act*

6.10.2.1 Substantive Prohibitions

The Controlling the Assault of Non-Solicited Pornography and Marketing Act of 2003 (CAN-SPAM)[652] contains six important requirements concerning the content of unsolicited commercial e-mail:

- False or misleading "header information" (the source, destination, and routing information of an e-mail) is prohibited.[653]
- Deceptive subject headings are prohibited.[654]
- Each message must contain a working electronic return address conspicuously displayed so that recipients can opt out of receiving further spam.[655] This link must operate for thirty days from the transmission of the message.

- It is unlawful for a sender to continue sending commercial e-mail to the recipient more than ten days after receiving an opt-out request.[656]
- Each message must provide the "valid physical postal address of the sender" and include a clear statement that it is an advertisement or solicitation and that the recipient has a right to not receive further spam from the sender.[657]
- Pornographic e-mails must be identified as such in their subject headings if they are being sent without the prior consent of the recipient.[658] Failure to provide this notice could result in up to five years' imprisonment.[659]

As used in the statute, "electronic mail message" includes messages transmitted within the MySpace or Facebook websites.[660]

CAN-SPAM also seeks to outlaw the techniques used by spammers to saturate e-mail accounts, making it unlawful for spammers to harvest e-mail addresses with an automatic address finding program and to generate e-mail addresses alphabetically in what is known as a dictionary attack.[661] CAN-SPAM also prohibits the creation of multiple e-mail accounts through automated means in order to transmit spam that is unlawful under the Act.[662]

The FTC has issued a CAN-SPAM rule that clarifies the statutory prohibitions.[663] The rule defines with more precision a number of terms found in the Act, clarifies when the primary purpose of an e-mail is commercial and thus covered by the Act, sets out requirements as to subject headers for sexually oriented material, and prohibits charging a fee to recipients who wish to opt out.

6.10.2.2 CAN-SPAM Remedies

Only federal and state officials and Internet service providers (ISPs) can enforce CAN-SPAM. There is no private consumer right of action.[664] Any consumer private action must be

---

652 15 U.S.C. §§ 7701–7713.

653 15 U.S.C. § 7704(a)(1), 7702. *See* Facebook, Inc. v. Power Ventures, Inc., 844 F. Supp. 2d 1025 (N.D. Cal. 2012) (defendant "initiated" spam e-mails when it created a promotion, imported Facebook users' friends to the guest list, and authored e-mail text even though plaintiff's servers then automatically generated e-mails; using plaintiff's name in header was misleading); Fed. Trade Comm'n v. Westby, 2004 WL 1175047 (N.D. Ill. Mar. 4, 2004) (defining and enjoining "spoofing": disguising origin of e-mail by using "from" or "reply to" address of non-consenting third party). *See also* Omega World Travel, Inc. v. Mummagraphics, Inc., 469 F.3d 348 (4th Cir. 2006) (certain inaccuracies in header did not make header materially false or misleading because headers were otherwise "replete with accurate identifiers of the sender"); Aitken v. Commc'n Workers of Am., 496 F. Supp. 2d 653 (E.D. Va. 2007) (holding misleading headers to be material); MySpace, Inc. v. Wallace, 498 F. Supp. 2d 1293 (C.D. Cal. 2007) ("hijacking" member accounts to send out mass commercial messages amounts to illegal conduct; "Congress intended to prohibit not only sending messages with *inaccurate* header information, but also sending messages with *accurate* header information, access to which was obtained through false or fraudulent pretenses." (italics in original)). *But cf.* Facebook, Inc. v. ConnectU, L.L.C., 489 F. Supp. 2d 1087 (N.D. Cal. 2007) (no violation of Act absent allegations that headers were misleading or false as source of origination even though Facebook competitor sent solicitations in fraudulent and deceptive manner); Internet Access Serv. Providers, L.L.C. v. Real Networks, Inc., 2005 WL 1244961 (D. Idaho May 25, 2005) (allegation of false or misleading information in the body of an e-mail fails to state claim under section 7704(a)(1), which forbids false or misleading header information). *See generally* Katherine Wong, *The Future of Spam Litigation After Omega World Travel v. Mummagraphics*, 20 Harv. J.L. & Tech. 459 (2007).

654 15 U.S.C. § 7704(a)(2). *See* Fed. Trade Comm'n v. Optin Global, Inc., 2005 WL 1027108 (N.D. Cal. Apr. 13, 2005) (granting TRO forbidding subject lines that falsely suggest recipient has already submitted a mortgage application or otherwise has a relationship with sender or another).

655 15 U.S.C. § 7704(a)(3).
An ISP can bring an action under section 7704(a)(3), but it must demonstrate a "pattern or practice" of prohibited conduct. 15 U.S.C. § 7706(g)(1). *See also* Aitken v. Communication Workers of Am., 496 F. Supp. 2d 653 (E.D. Va. 2007) (claim survives motion to dismiss; opt-out information not conspicuously displayed, nor was manner to opt out specified). *Compare* MySpace, Inc. v. Wallace, 498 F. Supp. 2d 1293 (C.D. Cal. 2007) (pattern and practice demonstrated), *with* Omega World Travel, Inc. v. Mummagraphics, Inc., 469 F.3d 348 (4th Cir. 2006) (dismissing claim; one violation does not amount to pattern or practice).

656 15 U.S.C. § 7704(a)(4).

657 15 U.S.C. § 7704(a)(5).

658 15 U.S.C. § 7704(d)(1); 16 C.F.R. § 316.4, *adopted by* 69 Fed. Reg. 21,024 (Apr. 19, 2004).

659 15 U.S.C. § 7704(d)(5). *See* United States v. Kilbride, 2007 WL 2774487 (D. Ariz. Sept. 21, 2007) (defendants sentenced to five years each).

660 Facebook, Inc. v. MaxBounty, Inc., 274 F.R.D. 279 (N.D. Cal. 2011); MySpace v. Wallace, 498 F. Supp. 2d 1293, 1300 (C.D. Cal. 2007).

661 15 U.S.C. § 7704(b). *See* S. Rep. 108-102, 2004 U.S.C.C.A.N. 2348, 2363 (July 16, 2003). *See also* Asis Internet Services v. Rausch, 2010 WL 1838752 (N.D. Cal. May 3, 2010) (finding dictionary attack to be aggravated violation of statute warranting treble damages). *Cf.* United States v. Simpson, 796 F.3d 548, 555 (5th Cir. 2015) (noting, in context of enhancement of a criminal sentence for aiding and abetting transmission of spam, that CAN–SPAM Act makes it unlawful to send e-mail to addresses obtained by a dictionary attack).

662 15 U.S.C. § 7704(b). *See* S. Rep. 108-102, 2004 U.S.C.C.A.N. 2348, 2363 (July 16, 2003). *See also* Asis Internet Services v. Rausch, 2010 WL 1838752 (N.D. Cal. May 3, 2010) (finding dictionary attack to be aggravated violation of statute warranting treble damages).

663 16 C.F.R. Part 316, *adopted by* 73 Fed. Reg. 29,654 (May 21, 2008). *See also* Notice of Proposed Rulemaking, 70 Fed. Reg. 25,426 (May 12, 2005). *See also* 70 Fed. Reg. 3110 (Jan. 19, 2005) (adopting § 316.3).

664 *See* Elizabeth A. Alongi, Note, *Has the U.S. Canned Spam?*, 46 Ariz. L. Rev. 263, 288 (2004) (criticizing CAN-SPAM Act for pre-empting

based on one of the other theories examined at §§ 6.10.3 and 6.10.4, *infra*.

Federal and state officials and ISPs need not limit their enforcement to those sending out the spam. Persons knowingly promoting their business through prohibited spam are subject to the remedies available under the CAN-SPAM Act.[665] This obviates the need to seek out the often hard to find spammer and allows those enforcing the Act to "follow the money" to the company that is knowingly benefiting from spam.[666]

State attorneys general can bring enforcement actions if they believe that a violation has caused harm to citizens of the state.[667] ISPs are authorized to enforce the CAN-SPAM Act by demonstrating that they have been "adversely affected" by a violation.[668] However, the Ninth Circuit has held that a small-scale operator of a website that provides only e-mail accounts cannot bring suit under this provision because it would be an overly broad interpretation of "Internet access service" that ignores congressional intent of only allowing "bona fide" ISPs to bring suit.[669]

State attorneys general and ISPs must show a pattern or practice for violations relating to provisions allowing opt-out of future spam.[670] ISPs must also show a pattern or practice for violation of the provision concerning deceptive subject headings.[671] A pattern or practice need not be shown for other violations.

State attorneys general can seek actual damages on behalf of their residents, and ISPs can also seek actual damages. In the alternative, the state may seek statutory damages of $250 per e-mail, and an ISP may seek statutory damages of $25 to $100 per e-mail, depending on the type of violation.[672] Damages are limited to $2 million in actions by state attorneys general and to $1 million in actions by ISPs but may be increased if a knowing or willful violation of the CAN-SPAM Act is demonstrated.[673] In addition, the prevailing party in a CAN-SPAM action may be awarded attorney fees at the court's discretion.[674]

---

state laws that did include a private right of action). *But cf.* Gordon v. Ascentive, L.L.C., 2007 WL 1795334 (E.D. Wash. June 19, 2007) (denying motion to dismiss suit under CAN-SPAM Act by consumer who was sole proprietor of website that enabled users to access content and e-mail).

665 15 U.S.C. § 7705. *See* S. Rep. 108-102, 2004 U.S.C.C.A.N. 2348, 2363. *See also* United States v. Cyberheat, 2007 WL 686678 (D. Ariz. Mar. 2, 2007) (knowledge and control over affiliates are questions of fact; contract provisions between defendant and affiliates disallowing spam are not dispositive); United States v. Impulse Media Grp., Inc., 2007 WL 1725560 (W.D. Wash. June 8, 2007) (discussing knowledge and intent requirements); Asis Internet Services v. Optin Global, Inc., 2006 WL 1820902 (N.D. Cal. June 30, 2006) (to show that company initiated or procured offending spam, must show that company paid for messages and knew or consciously avoided knowing that sender would violate law); Beyond Systems, Inc. v. Kennedy W. Univ., 2006 WL 1554847 (D. Md. May 31, 2006) (in determining whether business promoted by spam has sufficient contacts with forum state to confer jurisdiction, key issue is nature of relationship with sender of spam); Hypertouch, Inc. v. Kennedy-W. Univ., 2006 WL 648688 (N.D. Cal. Mar. 8, 2006) (liability requires showing that company whose services were promoted knew or consciously avoided knowing that sender would violate law; decision also addresses qualifications for ISP status).

666 *See* S. Rep. 108-102, 2004 U.S.C.C.A.N. 2348, 2363 (July 16, 2003); Fed. Trade Comm'n v. Phoenix Avatar, Inc., 2004 WL 1746698 (N.D. Ill. July 30, 2004) (describing complex and lengthy investigation leading to seller whose weight-loss patch was marketed by misleading spam; source of e-mail effectively disguised, but agency traced funds from its test purchases).

667 15 U.S.C. § 7706(f). *See, e.g.,* Washington v. Avtech Direct, 2006 WL 1419354 (W.D. Wash. May 19, 2006) (granting permanent injunction, civil penalty, and attorney fees in suit by state for violations of CAN-SPAM Act, Washington anti-spam statute, and UDAP statute).

668 15 U.S.C. § 7706(g). *See, e.g.,* Zoobuh, Inc. v. Better Broad., L.L.C., 2013 WL 2407669 (D. Utah May 31, 2013) (ISP was adversely harmed when considering proportion of number of messages to number of employees, and number of users); Anytime Fitness, L.L.C. v. Roberts, 2013 WL 1760950 (D. Minn. Apr. 24, 2013) (host of franchisees' e-mail addresses was adversely affected by "disruption in business relationships with [plaintiff's] franchisees" and increased bandwidth); Facebook, Inc. v. Power Ventures, Inc., 844 F. Supp. 2d 1025 (N.D. Cal. 2012) (ISP was adversely affected when it took steps to block this defendant's specific e-mail); Microsoft Corp. v. Neoburst.net, L.L.C., 2004 WL 2043093 (N.D. Cal. Sept. 3, 2004) (granting injunction forbidding spammer from violating ISP's terms of use). *See also* Aitken v. Communication Workers of Am., 496 F. Supp. 2d 653 (E.D. Va. 2007); MySpace, Inc. v. The Globe.com, Inc., 2007 WL 1686966 (C.D. Cal. Feb. 27, 2007) (plaintiff is an ISP; granting summary judgment on most grounds); MySpace, Inc. v. Wallace, 498 F. Supp. 2d 1293 (C.D.

Cal. 2007) (granting preliminary injunction); Asis Internet Services v. Optin Global, Inc., 2006 WL 1820902 (N.D. Cal. June 30, 2006) (suit by ISP against spammers and company whose services they promoted); America Online, Inc. v. Smith, 2006 WL 181674 (E.D. Va. Jan. 24, 2006); America Online, Inc. v. Ambro Enterprises, 2005 WL 2218433 (E.D. Va. Sept. 8, 2005).

669 Gordon v. Virtumundo, Inc., 575 F.3d 1040 (9th Cir. 2009) (small-scale operator of website who provides e-mail accounts is not ISP entitled to bring suit under CAN-SPAM Act). *See also* Ferguson v. Active Response Grp., 348 Fed. Appx. 255 (9th Cir. 2009) (unpublished), *aff'g* Ferguson v. Quinstreet, Inc., 2008 WL 3166307 (W.D. Wash. Aug. 5, 2008) (individual who controls twenty-nine registered domain names, has built and maintains webpages for himself and third parties, and provides an e-mail forwarding service for a few people lacks standing); Haselton v. Quicken Loans, Inc., 2010 WL 1180353 (W.D. Wash. Mar. 23, 2010) (only bona fide ISPs have standing under CAN-SPAM Act). *But see* Hypertouch, Inc. v. Kennedy-W. Univ., 2006 WL 648688 (N.D. Cal. Mar. 8, 2006) (holding plaintiff e-mail service provider was ISP that could sue under CAN-SPAM Act because it operated servers that support over 120 e-mail accounts which could be impacted by spam). *But cf.* Asis Internet Services v. Rausch, 2010 WL 1838752 (N.D. Cal. May 3, 2010) (corporation that is licensed to do business in state, provides dial-up, broadband, Internet, and e-mail service to 1000 customers, provides services with its own equipment, has contracts with outside vendors, has four employees, and has suffered financial loss due to spam is ISP and has standing).

670 State attorneys general and ISPs must show a pattern or practice to enforce violations of 15 U.S.C. § 7704(a)(3), (4), (5). *See* 15 U.S.C. § 7706(f)(1), (g)(1).

671 ISPs must show a pattern or practice to enforce violations of 15 U.S.C. § 7704(a)(2). *See* 15 U.S.C. § 7706(g)(1).

672 15 U.S.C. § 7706(f)(3), (g)(3).

673 15 U.S.C. § 7706(f)(3)(B)–(C), (g)(3)(B)–(C).

674 15 U.S.C. § 7706(f)(4), (g)(4). *See also* Asis Internet Services v. Optin Global, Inc., 2010 WL 2035327 (N.D. Cal. May 19, 2010) (awarding $806,979 in attorney fees to deter casting such a "wide net" against plaintiff who unreasonably continued litigation after discovery turned up no evidence that defendant sent or procured e-mails). *Compare* Gordon v. Virtumundo, Inc., 2007 WL 2253296 (W.D. Wash. Aug. 1,

A number of federal and state agencies can also enforce the CAN-SPAM Act. The main federal agency is the FTC, which can enforce the statute as if a violation were a violation of an FTC trade regulation rule.[675] The FTC does not have jurisdiction in certain areas wherein regulation is authorized for other federal, or even state, agencies. Instead, in these areas the CAN-SPAM Act is enforced by various banking agencies as to actions by banks; by the SEC for violations by dealers, brokers, registered investment advisors, or investment companies; by state insurance regulators to the extent that the state seeks to regulate the practice; by the Department of Transportation for air carriers; by the FCC for persons subject to FCC jurisdiction; and by the Secretary of Agriculture and the Farm Credit Administration for certain entities under their jurisdiction.[676]

For example, violation by a securities broker would give the SEC the ability to bring an enforcement action.[677] In enforcement actions by the FTC or other commissions, the enforcement powers are described by the statute which governs that commission.[678]

6.10.3 Other Federal Restrictions on Spam

6.10.3.1 The Telephone Consumer Protection Act

The Telephone Consumer Protection Act (TCPA) prohibits sending of unsolicited advertisements to a "telephone facsimile machine."[679] "Telephone facsimile machine" is defined as "equipment which has the capacity . . . (B) to transcribe text or images (or both) from an electronic signal received over a regular telephone line onto paper."[680] On its face, this definition appears to include e-mail messages that are transmitted over a telephone line to a computer that has the capacity to print the message. It might also include messages sent to a computer that was not attached to a printer if it was able to save the message to disk for later printing.[681] At least one court, however, has held that the TCPA does not apply to unsolicited bulk e-mail.[682]

If the TCPA were interpreted to apply to spam, it would provide an attractive private cause of action for consumers. It provides for a private cause of action for $500 per violation, which is to be trebled if the violation was willful or knowing.[683]

6.10.3.2 FTC Rules

The FTC's Mail or Telephone Order Merchandise Rule[684] provides a remedy for online fraud when the problem is failure to deliver or a delay in delivering merchandise. The rule broadly provides that it covers sales made by "any direct or indirect use of the telephone to order merchandise, regardless of whether the telephone is activated by, or the language used is that of human beings, machines, or both."[685] This language clearly includes sales conducted online when the connection is through a telephone line.[686]

In general, FTC rules that apply to written or printed advertisements also apply to online advertisements.[687] For example, the FTC's trade regulation rules on franchising and business opportunities[688] require certain disclosures in connection with the advertisement and sale of franchises and business opportunities and apply to transactions over the Internet. Failure to comply with these rules is a per se violation of most state UDAP statutes. If an e-mail message invites consumers to call the sender to purchase goods or services, the FTC's Telemarketing Sales Rule applies to the telephone call and the sale in a number of different types of transactions, including investment opportunities, debt relief services, certain business opportunities, credit card protection plans, credit repair, recovering funds lost to a telemarketing scam, and advance fee loans.[689]

6.10.3.3 Federal Criminal Statutes

Some ISPs and commercial websites have successfully sued spam senders under two provisions of the federal criminal

---

intended to cover e-mail). *See also* Prukala v. Elle, 11 F. Supp. 3d 443, 448–449 (M.D. Pa. 2014) (holding that prohibitions of TCPA do not apply to e-mail messages, and the fact that plaintiff received e-mails on same device that she used as a telephone (that is, a smart phone) did not bring such communications under the TCPA's reach).

683   *See* §§ 6.9.2.1–6.9.2.4, *supra.*

684   16 C.F.R. § 435. *See* § 2.6 *supra.*

685   16 C.F.R. § 435.2(b).

686   *See* Fed. Trade Comm'n v. Auctionsaver, 5 Trade Reg. Rep. (CCH) ¶ 15252 (S.D. Cal. Apr. 22, 2002) (consent decree against Internet-based computer seller that violated mail order rule); Fed. Trade Comm'n v. Bargains & Deals Magazine, L.L.C. (W.D. Wash. Oct. 11, 2001), *available at* www.ftc.gov (complaint for permanent injunction and other equitable relief); Fed. Trade Comm'n v. Computers by Us, Inc., 5 Trade Reg. Rep. (CCH) ¶ 15148 (D. Md. Aug. 30, 2001) (proposed consent decree against web-based auction that made slow delivery and did not honor cancellation requests; also bars misrepresentation that auction owns the items it is auctioning); Fed. Trade Comm'n v. Brandzel, 5 Trade Reg. Rep. (CCH) ¶ 23,999 (N.D. Ill. 1996) (filing of complaint).

687   Fed. Trade Comm'n, .com Disclosures (2013), *available at* www .ftc.gov. *See generally* National Consumer Law Center, Unfair and Deceptive Acts and Practices § 4.2.14.3.9 (8th ed. 2012), *updated at* www.nclc.org/library.

688   16 C.F.R. pts. 436, 437. *See* § 2.8. *supra.*

689   *See* § 5.2.2, *supra.*

2007) (finding plaintiffs' suit "ill-motivated, unreasonable, and frivolous" and awarding $111,440 in fees and costs), *aff'd*, 575 F.3d 1040 (9th Cir. 2009), *with* Phillips v. Worldwide Internet Solutions, Inc., 2007 WL 184719 (Jan. 22, 2007) (denying defendants' motion for attorney fees when suit was deemed neither frivolous nor unreasonable).

675   15 U.S.C. § 7706(a). FTC enforcement authority for such a violation is examined at § 2.2.5, *supra.*

676   15 U.S.C. § 7706(b).

677   15 U.S.C. § 7706(b)(3).

678   15 U.S.C. § 7706(c).

679   47 U.S.C. § 227(b)(1)(C).

680   47 U.S.C. § 227(a)(3).

681   *See* Covington & Burling v. Int'l Mktg. & Research, Inc., 2003 WL 21384825 (D.C. Super. Ct. Apr. 17, 2003), *as amended on reconsideration by* 2003 D.C. Super. LEXIS 28 (D.C. Super. Ct. May 17, 2003); David E. Sorkin, *Unsolicited Commercial E-Mail and the Telephone Consumer Protection Act of 1991*, 45 Buffalo L. Rev. 1001 (1997), *available at* repository.jmls.edu (detailed analysis of statutory construction issues).

682   Aronson v. Bright-Teeth Now, L.L.C., 824 A.2d 320 (Pa. Super. Ct. 2003) (unsolicited bulk e-mail does not place the same burdens on recipient as faxes; legislative history does not indicate that statute was

code: 18 U.S.C. § 2701, which prohibits unlawful access to stored communications, and 18 U.S.C. § 1030, which includes a prohibition against hacking into a computer.[690] These cases involved spammers who harvested consumers' e-mail addresses from websites, contrary to the website's posted policy, or sent spam with a forged return address so that replies and bounced-back messages went to the ISP. These statutes may apply in a consumer context.[691]

6.10.3.4 Trademark Infringements

ISPs have won trademark claims when spammers used the ISP's name in a counterfeit return address.[692]

6.10.4 State Anti-Spam Laws

6.10.4.1 General

About two-thirds of the states have anti-spam laws,[693] and these are attractive to private litigants because they typically provide a private right of action.[694] The substantive provisions of these laws vary.[695] Some prohibit deception in headers—the routing information that accompanies an e-mail message—or subject lines. A few require the message to include a specific marker, such as "ADV," in the subject line so that recipients can identify and screen out unsolicited commercial messages if they choose.

6.10.4.2 Preemption

The application of state anti-spam laws has been sharply limited by enactment of the federal Controlling the Assault of Non-Solicited Pornography and Marketing Act of 2003 (CAN-SPAM), that preempts much of the state law governing spam.[696] CAN-SPAM preempts state law "that expressly regulates the use of electronic mail to send commercial messages" but does not supersede state laws that prohibit "falsity or deception in any portion of a commercial electronic mail message."[697] Thus, a UDAP statute's prohibition of deception can

---

690 *See* Craigslist, Inc. v. Naturemarket, Inc., 694 F. Supp. 2d 1039 (N.D. Cal. 2010) (granting permanent injunction, damages, and attorney fees); America Online, Inc. v. LCGM, 46 F. Supp. 2d 444 (E.D. Va. 1998); Hotmail Corp. v. Van$ Money Pie Inc., 1998 WL 388389 (N.D. Cal. Apr. 16, 1998) (granting preliminary injunction). *But cf.* Czech v. Wall Street on Demand, Inc., 674 F. Supp. 2d 1102 (D. Minn. 2009) (dismissing 18 U.S.C. § 1030 claim by cell phone owner, based on receipt of unwanted text messages, for failure to allege, *inter alia*, damage or loss caused by alleged violations).

691 *See, e.g.,* Mortenson v. Bresnan Commc'n, L.L.C., 2010 WL 5140454 (D. Mont. Dec. 13, 2010) (denying motion to dismiss consumer claim under 18 U.S.C. § 1030).

692 Yahoo! Inc. v. XYZ Cos., 872 F. Supp. 2d 300 (S.D.N.Y. 2011); Craigslist, Inc. v. Naturemarket, Inc., 694 F. Supp. 2d 1039 (N.D. Cal. 2010) (granting permanent injunction, damages, and attorney fees); Classified Ventures v. Softcell Mktg., Inc., 109 F. Supp. 2d 898 (N.D. Ill. 2000) (stipulated judgment); America Online, Inc. v. LCGM, 46 F. Supp. 2d 444 (E.D. Va. 1998); America Online, Inc. v. IMS, 24 F. Supp. 2d 548 (E.D. Va. 1998); Hotmail Corp. v. Van$ Money Pie Inc., 1998 WL 388389 (N.D. Cal. Apr. 16, 1998) (granting preliminary injunction).

693 *See* Spam Laws, www.spamlaws.com.

694 *See* § 6.10.4.4, *infra*.

695 *See* Kleffman v. Vonage Holdings Corp., 232 P.3d 625 (Cal. 2010) (an e-mail with an accurate and traceable domain name does not misrepresent header information; rejecting claim that sending unsolicited commercial e-mail advertisements from multiple domain names for purpose of bypassing spam filters constituted falsified, misrepresented, or forged header information under state law), *aff'd without op.*, 387 Fed. Appx. 696 (9th Cir. 2010).

696 15 U.S.C. § 7707(b). *See also* Gage E. Services, L.L.C. v. AngelVision Technologies, Inc., 2013 WL 286247 (D.S.D. Jan. 24, 2013) (concluding that CAN-SPAM Act completely preempts state claims, so ISP's state law action can be removed to federal court). *But cf.* White Buffalo Ventures v. Univ. of Tex., 420 F.3d 366 (5th Cir. 2005) (CAN-SPAM Act does not prevent state university's use of spam filter; although CAN-SPAM Act preempts state regulation of non-deceptive spam, university was acting as an ISP, and CAN-SPAM Act explicitly permits ISPs to filter e-mail messages); 150 Cong. Rec. E72-02, E73 (2004) (remarks of Representative Dingell). *See generally* Andre R. Jalgom, Am. Law Inst. *Internet, Distribution, E-Commerce and Other Computer Related Issues*, SJ075 ALI-ABA 505, 517–18 (2004).

697 15 U.S.C. § 7707(b); 150 Cong. Rec. E72-02, E73 (2004) (remarks of Representative Dingell). *See* Asis Internet Services v. Member Source Media, L.L.C., 2010 WL 1610066 (N.D. Cal. Apr. 20, 2010) (reliance and damages not required to avoid preemption of claim under state anti-spam law); Asis Internet Services v. Consumerbargaingiveaways, L.L.C., 622 F. Supp. 2d 935 (N.D. Cal. 2009) (state laws prohibiting fraud and those prohibiting deception that does not meet common law fraud standards fall into exception from preemption); Hypertouch, Inc. v. Azoogle.com, Inc., 2009 WL 734674 (N.D. Cal. Mar. 19, 2009) (CAN-SPAM Act does not preempt trespass to chattels claim or claim that e-mails contained fraudulent and false statements), *aff'd on other grounds*, 386 Fed. Appx. 701 (9th Cir. 2010); Ferguson v. Quinstreet, Inc., 2008 WL 3166307 (W.D. Wash. Aug. 5, 2008) (state law's prohibition of unintentional errors in e-mail goes beyond "falsity or deception" so is preempted), *aff'd*, 348 Fed. Appx. 255 (9th Cir. 2009); Beyond Systems, Inc. v. Keynetics, Inc., 422 F. Supp. 2d 523 (D. Md. 2006) (requirement of truthful header and other information explicitly not preempted by CAN-SPAM Act); Gordon v. Impulse Mktg. Grp., Inc., 375 F. Supp. 2d 1040 (E.D. Wash. 2005) (Washington statute that forbids misleading subject lines "falls squarely within" this exception to preemption); Andre R. Jalgom, Am. Law Inst. *Internet, Distribution, E-Commerce and Other Computer Related Issues*, SJ075 ALI-ABA 505, 517–18 (2004) (explaining that laws such as Virginia's, which criminalize the falsifying of header information in violation of an ISP's policy, are undisturbed by CAN-SPAM Act). *See also* Beyond Systems, Inc. v. Kraft Foods, Inc., 777 F.3d 712, 716 (4th Cir. 2015) (finding that state law claims were not preempted, since they were "in the vein of a tort," but affirming summary judgment for defendants when plaintiff invited injury for which relief was later sought), *aff'g* 972 F. Supp. 2d 748 (D. Md. 2013); Hoang v. Reunion.com, Inc., 2010 WL 1340535 (N.D. Cal. Mar. 31, 2010) (allegation of detrimental reliance on alleged false statements in e-mails is not required to avoid preemption); Hypertouch, Inc. v. ValueClick, Inc., 123 Cal. Rptr. 3d 8 (Cal. Ct. App. 2011) (exception to preemption applies to any state law prohibiting material falsity or material deception in e-mail even if it does not require every element of common law fraud). *But see* Omega World Travel, Inc. v. Mummagraphics, Inc., 469 F.3d 348 (4th Cir. 2006) (state law preempted to the extent that it encompasses errors not sounding in tort). *But cf.* Wagner v. Spire Vision, L.L.C., 2015 WL 876514, at *3 (N.D. Cal. Feb. 27, 2015) (plaintiff required to demonstrate that header information in e-mails not only violated state statute but contained material misrepresentations; any other claims are preempted if they apply to immaterial misrepresentations); Martin v. CCH, Inc., 784 F. Supp. 2d 1000 (N.D. Ill. 2011) (less than comprehensive information outside the body of an e-mail is a technical

be applied to spam and is not preempted.[698] However, a state cannot regulate the manner of sending commercial e-mail (as opposed to the deceptive content) simply by calling the regulation an anti-fraud law.[699]

There has been considerable debate over what constitutes "deception" in headers or elsewhere in the e-mail for purposes of state anti-spam laws. For example, one issue is whether fanciful names are truly deceptive if no reasonable person would believe that such a name truly identified the "sender" (for example, "Mickey Mouse," "Santa Claus").[700]

Any state law requiring certain information to be incorporated into spam is now preempted.[701] State laws requiring

spammers to refrain from e-mailing users who have opted not to receive spam (opt-out laws) and/or to refrain from spamming until an e-mail user has opted to receive spam (opt-in laws) are superseded by CAN-SPAM.[702] Also, CAN-SPAM preempts requirements that spammers place abbreviations such as "ADV" in subject headings to identify an e-mail as spam.[703] However, a state law is preempted only if it "expressly regulates" spam, so a state law that prohibits merchants from requesting personal identification information from their customers can be applied to prohibit collection of e-mail addresses that the merchant then uses to send spam.[704]

6.10.4.3 Constitutional Challenges to State Anti-Spam Statutes

State anti-spam statutes have been upheld against challenges that they impermissibly regulate interstate commerce. In *State v. Heckel*, the Washington Supreme Court upheld the constitutionality of an anti-spam statute that prohibited deception in headers and subject lines.[705] A number of other courts have held that a requirement for truthful information does not heavily burden—and may indeed facilitate—interstate commerce.[706]

The risk of conflicting state laws is minimal, because no state is likely to welcome deceptive spam.[707] A California appellate decision upheld a similar prohibition against deception in spam.[708] The court was particularly persuaded by the fact that the California statute applied only to spam that was delivered to California residents via an ISP's service or equipment located in the state. Anti-spam statutes have also been challenged on First Amendment grounds but upheld as permissible regulation of commercial speech to prevent deception.[709]

---

allegation with no basis in traditional tort theories and is therefore outside the exception to CAN-SPAM Act's preemption clause); Gordon v. Virtumundo, Inc., 2007 WL 1459395 (W.D. Wash. May 15, 2007) (claims preempted because no falsity or deception alleged), aff'd, 575 F.3d 1040 (9th Cir. 2009).

698 Hoang v. Reunion.com, Inc., 2010 WL 1340535 (N.D. Cal. Mar. 31, 2010) (allegation of detrimental reliance on alleged false statements in e-mails is not required to avoid preemption); Ferron v. SubscriberBase Holdings, Inc., 2009 WL 650731 (S.D. Ohio Mar. 11, 2009); Asis Internet Services v. Vistaprint USA, Inc., 617 F. Supp. 2d 989 (N.D. Cal. 2009) (federal law does not preempt state statute that prohibits deceptive e-mails even if statute sets a standard less than common law fraud); Balsam v. Trancos, 138 Cal. Rptr. 3d 108 (Cal. Ct. App. 2012) (falsified "from" line is materially deceptive, so claim is not preempted).

699 150 Cong. Rec. E72-02, E73 (2004) (remarks of Representative Dingell).

700 *See* Balsam v. Trancos, Inc. 203 Cal. App. 4th 1083 (2012) (header information is deceptive when it uses a sender domain name that neither identifies actual sender on its face nor is readily traceable to sender using a publicly available online database; admitted motivation for use of multiple, random domain names was to prevent recipients of e-mails from being able to identify defendant as their true source). *See also* Facebook, Inc. v. Power Ventures, Inc., 844 F. Supp. 2d 1025 (N.D. Cal. 2012) (e-mail that omits any means to contact the sender is misleading); Hypertouch, Inc. v. Valueclick, Inc., 192 Cal. App. 4th 805 (2011) (actual fraud not required to escape preemption of state statute by CAN-SPAM). *But see* Wagner v. Spire Vision L.L.C., 2015 WL 876514, at *5 (N.D. Cal. Feb. 27, 2015) (e-mails contained identifying information in their bodies, and that information suggests defendants were not trying to conceal senders' identities); DeWitt v. DeVry Univ., Inc., 2015 WL 4120482, at *5 (Cal. Ct. App. July 8, 2015) (unpublished) (plaintiff conceded that headers identified defendants and admitted he did not need to open e-mails in order to determine advertising entity; because headers identified actual sender, they did not violate state law); DeWitt v. Foot Locker Retail, Inc., 2015 WL 3417439 (Cal. Ct. App. May 28, 2015) (unpublished); Rosolowsky v. Guthy-Renker L.L.C., 230 Cal. App. 4th 1403 (Cal. Ct. App. 2014) (regardless of allegedly untraceable domain names involved, sender's identity was readily ascertainable from body of e-mails, and therefore no cause of action for misrepresented header information was stated; also, because e-mails provided a hyperlink to sender's website and provided an "unsubscribe" notice as well as a physical address, plaintiffs could not plausibly allege that sender attempted to conceal its identity); Rosolowski v. Bosley Med. Grp., 2014 WL 6645881 (Cal. Ct. App. Nov. 20, 2014) (unpublished) (as long as sender's identity is readily ascertainable from body of e-mail, a header line in a commercial e-mail advertisement does not misrepresent sender's identity merely because it does not identify official name of sending entity or because it does not identify an entity whose domain name is traceable from an online database).

701 15 U.S.C. § 7707(b). *See* Ferron v. SubscriberBase Holdings, Inc., 2009 WL 650731 (S.D. Ohio Mar. 11, 2009); Ferron v. Echostar Satellite,

L.L.C., 2008 WL 4377309 (S.D. Ohio Sept. 24, 2008), *aff'd without op.*, 410 Fed. Appx. 903 (6th Cir. 2010).

702 *See* 150 Cong. Rec. E72-02, E73 (2004) (remarks of Representative Dingell); Andre R. Jaglom, *Internet, Distribution, E-Commerce and Other Computer Related Issues*, SJ075 ALI-ABA 505, 517–18 (2004). *See also* John T. A. Rosenthal, *Consent or No Consent, That is the Question: How the Pre-Emption Provision in CAN-SPAM Act Precludes State Law Statutes That Require Specific Consent for Commercial E-mails*, 18 No. 4 J. Internet L. 1 (October 2014).

703 150 Cong. Rec. E72-02, E73 (2004). *See also* Martin v. CCH, Inc., 784 F. Supp. 2d 1000 (N.D. Ill. 2011) (CAN-SPAM Act clearly preempts state laws that require labels such as "ADV").

704 Capp v. Nordstrom, Inc., 2013 WL 5739102 (E.D. Cal. Oct. 22, 2013).

705 State v. Heckel, 24 P.3d 404 (Wash. 2001).

706 Beyond Systems, Inc. v. Keynetics, Inc., 422 F. Supp. 2d 523 (D. Md. 2006) (requirement to obey preexisting law not burdensome); MaryCLE, L.L.C. v. First Choice Internet, Inc., 890 A.2d 818 (Md. 2006) (burden was not to weed out Maryland addresses but simply to provide truthful headers, and so forth; commerce clause not violated).

707 MaryCLE, L.L.C. v. First Choice Internet, Inc., 890 A.2d 818 (Md. 2006).

708 Ferguson v. Friendfinders, Inc., 115 Cal. Rptr. 2d 258 (Cal. Ct. App. 2002).

709 White Buffalo Ventures v. Univ. of Tex., 420 F.3d 366 (5th Cir. 2005) (university that provided e-mail service was both arm of the state and ISP; no First Amendment violation when "user-efficiency" that is the burden on recipients of uncontrolled spam was legitimate state interest, and spam filter was reasonably tailored to prevent this; note however

---

6.10.4.4 Remedies Under State Anti-Spam Laws

Most state anti-spam laws give recipients of spam a private cause of action, often including statutory damages, such as $10 per message or a flat award of $500.[710] Many of these state statutes also allow a prevailing plaintiff to recover costs and attorney fees. While the damage amounts are small, they could be very significant in a class action. Even in an individual action, many people will have received so many e-mail messages that the cumulative statutory damages could be significant. The private right of action provided by many state anti-spam laws should survive the CAN-SPAM Act to the extent that the state statute's substantive provision is not preempted. Whether an owner of a spamming business may be liable even if others actually send the messages will likely depend on the specific language of the applicable state anti-spam statute.[711]

Some state anti-spam laws provide for a reduction in statutory damages when the defendant established and implemented practices and procedures reasonably designed to prevent the unsolicited commercial e-mail advertisements that violate the law.[712] However, such practices and procedures must have been in place at the time the e-mails were sent.[713]

Instead of creating its own private cause of action, some anti-spam laws are amendments to the state UDAP statute, so a violation is redressed under that statute.[714] A few other anti-spam state statutes provide only criminal penalties, but a UDAP cause of action may still be available for violations, as in many states a violation of a consumer protection law is a per se UDAP violation.[715]

One significant potential problem is the question of whether a recipient of spam must show an actual injury in order to recover statutory damages. Some anti-spam statutes, such as those in Colorado and Nevada, do not have an explicit requirement of actual damage,[716] but others provide a private cause of action only for actual damages or only for a person who has been injured. Some UDAP statutes also require a showing of actual damage, and some specify an "ascertainable loss of money or property."[717]

A person who falls for a fraudulent spam advertisement and pays out money has clearly satisfied any injury requirement. A harder question is whether the simple receipt of spam is sufficient to support a claim. An FTC decision has held that receipt of deceptive spam contrary to the privacy policy of the website from which addresses were harvested amounts to substantial consumer injury as required by the FTC's definition of unfairness.[718]

Consumers might also be able to draw some support from decisions holding that spammers committed trespass to chattels when their e-mails occupied an ISP's capacity due to the receipt of unwanted e-mail.[719] These decisions recognize that there is some injury just from the temporary reduction in a computer's capacity due to the receipt of unwanted e-mail.

A consumer who pays for Internet access by the hour rather than on a flat monthly rate will probably be able to show some monetary loss due to receipt of spam. Businesses might also be able to show damage in the form of wages paid to employees whose time was wasted receiving and deleting unwanted e-mail messages.

The consumer who receives an unsolicited e-mail is not the only one injured by spam. If the spammer forges the return address or "header," an innocent third party may be inundated by bounce-back messages and protest e-mails. The FTC's

---

that "server-efficiency" not shown—that is, a less restrictive method might have sufficed to protect servers). *See also* Joffe v. Acacia Mortg. Co., 121 P.3d 831 (Ariz. Ct. App. 2005) (ban on unsolicited computer-generated Internet-to-cell phone messages was permissible restriction on time, place, and manner when protection of privacy was significant interest). *But cf.* Jaynes v. Commonwealth, 666 S.E.2d 303 (Va. 2008) (holding that statute prohibiting false routing information in dissemination of e-mails was unconstitutionally overbroad because it prohibits anonymous transmission of *all* unsolicited bulk e-mails).

710 Asis Internet Services v. Subscriberbase, 2010 WL 3504792 (N.D. Cal. Sept. 8, 2010) (statute provides for liquidated damages of $1000 for each e-mail in violation of statute); Hypertouch, Inc. v. ValueClick, Inc., 123 Cal. Rptr. 3d 8 (Cal. Ct. App. 2011) (statute of limitations for actual damages is three years; one year for liquidated damages).

711 Kramer v. Perez, 595 F.3d 825 (8th Cir. 2010) (no liability for violating statute without evidence that defendant shareholder used an "interactive computer service" to initiate the sending of spam). *Cf.* Hypertouch, Inc. v. ValueClick, Inc., 123 Cal. Rptr. 3d 8 (Cal. Ct. App. 2011) (issue is not whether defendants sent or had knowledge of e-mails, but whether they advertised in e-mails).

712 *See, e.g.,* Cal. Bus. & Prof. Code §§ 17529.5(b)(2) and 17529.8(b) (West); S.D. Codified Laws § 37-24-48.

713 Wagner v. Spire Vision L.L.C., 2015 WL 876514, at *8 (N.D. Cal. Feb. 27, 2015) (finding that it was "irrelevant whether defendants currently have sufficient compliance procedures in place" and that key issue is "whether defendants had established and implemented sufficient compliance procedures when defendants sent the emails at issue").

714 *See* Gordon v. Impulse Mktg. Grp., Inc., 375 F. Supp. 2d 1040 (E.D. Wash. 2005) (Washington UDAP statute forbids conspiracy with another person to initiate transmission of an e-mail that contains false or misleading information in subject line); Ferguson v. Friendfinders, Inc., 115 Cal. Rptr. 2d 258 (Cal. Ct. App. 2002) (reversing dismissal of consumer's claims against spammer under state UDAP statutes).

715 *See* National Consumer Law Center, Unfair and Deceptive Acts and Practices § 11.4.2 (8th ed. 2012), *updated at* www.nclc.org/library.

716 Wagner v. Spire Vision, 2014 WL 889483 (N.D. Cal. Mar. 3, 2014) (holding that state law determining "deception and falsity" is not preempted by federal statue, therefore no harm or reliance needed to be proved).

717 *See* National Consumer Law Center, Unfair and Deceptive Acts and Practices § 12.5.2 (8th ed. 2012), *updated at* www.nclc.org/library. *See also* Gordon v. BAC Home Loans Servicing, L.P., 2011 WL 1565363 (E.D. Wash. Apr. 25, 2011) (mere receipt of unsolicited commercial e-mail is not UDAP violation without allegation of actual damage), *aff'd,* 465 Fed. Appx. 731 (9th Cir. 2012); Madorsky v. Does, 2006 WL 1587349 (N.D. Ohio June 8, 2006) (dismissing claim because no showing of damages, as required by Ohio Computer Crimes Act). *But cf.* Asis Internet Services v. Member Source Media, L.L.C., 2010 WL 1610066 (N.D. Cal. Apr. 20, 2010) (reliance and damages not required to avoid preemption of claim under state anti-spam law); Asis Internet Services v. Subscriberbase Inc., 2010 WL 1267763 (N.D. Cal. Apr.1, 2010) (same).

718 Fed. Trade Comm'n v. Reverseauction.com, Inc., 5 Trade Reg. Rptr. (CCH) ¶ 24,688 (D.D.C. Jan. 6, 2000) (decision to accept consent decree). *See also* Register.com, Inc. v. Verio, Inc., 126 F. Supp. 2d 238 (S.D.N.Y. 2000), *aff'd,* 356 F.3d 393 (2d Cir. 2004).

719 *See* § 6.10.5.2, *infra.*

proceedings against spammers in these circumstances are authority that these acts are unfair and deceptive.[720]

California's and Maryland's anti-spam statutes allow ISPs to sue, but a federal court concluded that the ISP must be "bona fide" and that an ISP that was created solely to attract and trap spam, and whose income derived primarily from anti-spam suits, was not bona fide.[721] The court held that the claim was also barred because the ISP's activity amounted to consent to the harm for which it brought suit and deprived it of standing. On appeal, the court found that the ISP did have Article III standing but agreed with the lower court that the ISP, by consenting to the harm from spam e-mails, was precluded from recovering under the California and Maryland anti-spam statutes.[722]

6.10.5 Other State Law Claims

6.10.5.1 UDAP Claims

There should be no room for dispute that general UDAP prohibitions apply to online fraud. However, some states are amending their UDAP statutes to make it clear that advertising, offers, and publications that are transmitted electronically or over the Internet fall within the statute.[723] The CAN-SPAM Act does not preempt state laws of general application that could be used to attack spammers, such as UDAP claims.[724]

6.10.5.2 Common Law Tort Claims

ISPs have successfully asserted against spammers the ancient common law claim of trespass to chattels—the use of a chattel without or exceeding the consent of the owner and impairing the use, value, or condition of the chattel.[725] These

cases have held that a spammer who temporarily intrudes on a computer electronically to harvest e-mail addresses, or temporarily takes up a part of the computer's capacity with spam messages, sufficiently impairs the chattel to support the cause of action. It is conceivable that a consumer could also assert a trespass to chattels claim based on the temporary reduction in the computer's capacity due to receipt of spam.[726]

If a company causes a third party to send offending spam, a complaint for civil conspiracy may also be available.[727] The CAN-SPAM Act does not preempt state laws of general application that could be used to attack spammers, such as computer fraud laws or common law theories arising under trespass, contract, or tort.[728]

6.10.5.3 State Telemarketing and Door-to-Door Statutes

Whether state telephone sales laws apply to online sales will depend on their language. Georgia's telemarketing law explicitly applies to theft offenses committed while

---

720   Jessica Farrah Drees, Nos. 022-3234 to 022-3237, 022-3077, 022-3302, 5 Trade Reg. Rep. (CCH) ¶ 15323 (Nov. 13, 2002).

721   Beyond Systems, Inc. v. Kraft Foods, Inc., 972 F. Supp. 2d 748 (D. Md. 2013), *aff'd*, 777 F.3d 712 (4th Cir. 2015).

722   Beyond Systems, Inc. v. Kraft Foods, Inc., 777 F.3d 712, 716 (4th Cir. 2015) ("It claimed a harm—receiving spam e-mail—and Maryland and California law create an interest in being free from such harm.").

723   *See, e.g.*, Cal. Bus. & Prof. Code § 17538 (West). *See also* Specht v. Netscape Communications Corp., 306 F.3d 17, 34 n.17 (2d Cir. 2002) (discussing California statute and other standards for online disclosures).

724   15 U.S.C. § 7707(b)(2). *See* 150 Cong. Rec. E72-02, E73 (2004) (remarks of Representative Dingell); S. Rep. 108-102, 2004 U.S.C.C.A.N. 2348, 2365 (July 16, 2003). *See also* White Buffalo Ventures v. Univ. of Tex., 420 F.3d 366 (5th Cir. 2005) (CAN-SPAM Act does not preempt state statutes not specific to electronic transactions, here state university's anti-solicitation policy).

725   Register.com, Inc. v. Verio, Inc., 126 F. Supp. 2d 238 (S.D.N.Y. 2000) (intruding electronically into business' database to harvest e-mail addresses, without authorization, causes harm by reducing the system's capacity), *aff'd*, 356 F.3d 393 (2d Cir. 2004); America Online, Inc. v. Nat'l Health Care Discount, Inc., 121 F. Supp. 2d 1255 (N.D. Iowa 2000); America Online, Inc. v. LCGM, Inc., 46 F. Supp. 2d 444 (E.D. Va. 1998); Hotmail Corp. v. Van$ Money Pie, Inc., 1998 WL 388389 (N.D. Cal. Apr. 16, 1998); America Online, Inc. v. IMS, 24 F. Supp. 2d 548 (E.D. Va. 1998) (granting summary judgment against

spammer on trespass to chattels and other claims); CompuServe, Inc. v. CyberPromotions, Inc., 962 F. Supp. 1015, 1022 (S.D. Ohio 1997) (issuing preliminary injunction against spammer on theory of trespass to chattels); Sch. of Visual Arts v. Kuprewicz, 771 N.Y.S.2d 804 (N.Y. Sup. Ct. 2003) (facts alleged constituting elements of trespass to chattels claim). *See also* Microsoft Corp. v. Does 1–18, 2014 WL 1338677, at *9–10 (E.D. Va. Apr. 2, 2014) ("The unauthorized intrusion into an individual's computer system through hacking, malware, or even unwanted communications supports actions under these claims"; plaintiff alleged facts sufficient to show that defendant committed common law trespass to chattels by using "botnet" to access computers and servers without authorization). *But see* Intel Corp. v. Hamidi 71 P.3d 296, 303–04 (Cal. 2003) (rejecting plaintiff's claim that defendant's spamming of its computer system constituted trespass to chattels). *But cf.* Omega World Travel, Inc. v. Mummagraphics, Inc., 469 F.3d 348 (4th Cir. 2006) (trespass to chattels claim based upon computer intrusion requires more than allegation of nominal damages; evidence failed to show that receipt of eleven e-mail messages placed "meaningful burden" on computer system or other resources).

726   *See, e.g.*, Sotelo v. DirectRevenue, L.L.C., 384 F. Supp. 2d 1219 (N.D. Ill. 2005) (trespass to chattel may be claimed by individual consumer if unauthorized electronic contact with computer system causes harm). *See also* Mortensen v. Bresnan Commc'n, L.L.C., 2010 WL 5140454 (D. Mont. Dec. 13, 2010) (must establish that defendant intentionally and without authorization interfered with plaintiff's possessory interest in computer system, causing damage to plaintiff). *Cf.* Burgess v. Eforce Media, Inc., 2007 WL 3355369 (W.D.N.C. Nov. 9, 2007) (in trespass to chattels claim based on unsolicited pop-up advertisements, actual damages not required when claim is based on unlawful interference).

727   Asis Internet Services v. Optin Global, Inc., 2006 WL 1820902 (N.D. Cal. June 30, 2006) (if plaintiff ISP could state claim for CAN-SPAM or California false advertising statute violations, claim for civil conspiracy would also be good).

728   15 U.S.C. § 7707(b)(2). *See* 150 Cong. Rec. E72-02, E73 (2004) (remarks of Representative Dingell); S. Rep. 108-102, 2004 U.S.C.C.A.N. 2348, 2365 (July 16, 2003). *See also* White Buffalo Ventures v. Univ. of Tex., 420 F.3d 366 (5th Cir. 2005) (CAN-SPAM Act does not preempt state statutes not specific to electronic transactions, here state university's anti-solicitation policy).

"engaged in any activity involving or using a computer or computer network."[729] Virginia's home solicitation sales law covers sales conducted by telephone "or other electronic means."[730]

6.10.6 Available Defendants in a Private Cause of Action

The first practical problem in suing a spammer is finding the perpetrator. Spammers take great pains to conceal their actual identities and locations.[731] Some people in the Internet community may have the ability to track down spammers.[732] Established companies may also sometimes violate state anti-spam laws.

Vicarious liability may be established via agency, conspiracy or *respondeat superior.* "[I]ronically enough, [the Defendant's] very attempt to control its affiliates by banning the use of bulk mail, among other restrictions it imposes, implies control which in turn is suggestive of a principal's control of an agent."[733]

The anti-spam statutes in some states expressly provide for liability via conspiracy. Anti-spam statutes in other states (for example, Tennessee and Rhode Island) explicitly cover certain aiders and abettors.[734] In other states, the UDAP statute or standard tort law may extend liability to other entities that are involved in sending spam.[735] Thus, the knowledge and intent of the various participants in the promotional scheme that involves the use of spam, any agreement among them, steps taken to carry out the illegal acts, and resulting damage become key facts. Prior complaints that may have been ignored by those who participated in any such conspiracy will obviously be of interest.

A state court action will be successful, however, only if personal jurisdiction can be obtained over the selected defendant. Personal jurisdiction will be available when the potential defendant "purposefully availed" itself of the privilege of doing business in the forum state and when the cause of action arose from that forum-related activity. Because e-mail addresses do not disclose the geographical address of the recipient, spammers argue that this requirement is not fulfilled. A number of courts have concluded, however, that one who sends out massive quantities of e-mail at random must know that it can reach—and cause harm in—any one of the states.[736]

Fraudulent promoters who use the Internet may argue that only their home state, and not the consumer's home

---

729 Ga. Code Ann. § 10-1-393.5(b).

730 Va. Code Ann. § 59.1-21.2.

731 Fed. Trade Comm'n v. Phoenix Avatar, Inc., 2004 WL 1746698 (N.D. Ill. July 30, 2004) (expert testimony about use of false routing information and "open proxies" to disguise source of e-mails; FTC traced funds from its test purchase to seller of weight loss patches); Fed. Trade Comm'n v. Westby, 2004 WL 1175047 (N.D. Ill. Mar. 4, 2004) (defining and enjoining "spoofing": disguising origin of e-mail by using "from" or "reply to" address of non-consenting third party); Optinrealbig.com v. Ironport Sys., Inc., 323 F. Supp. 2d 1037 (N.D. Cal. 2004) (detailed discussion of methods by which spammers cover their tracks).

732 *See generally* Fed. Trade Comm'n, A CAN-SPAM Informant Reward System: A Report to Congress (Sept. 2004), *available at* www.ftc.gov.

733 Beyond Systems, Inc. v. Keynetics, Inc. 422 F. Supp. 2d 523 (2006).

734 *See* America Online, Inc. v. Nat'l Health Care Discount, Inc., 121 F. Supp. 2d 1255 (N.D. Iowa 2000) (declining to grant summary judgment on issue of whether merchant was liable for acts of spammer it hired). *But see* Seidl v. Greentree Mortg. Co., 30 F. Supp. 2d 1292 (D. Colo. 1998) (spammer was seller's independent contractor, so seller was not liable for harm caused by spammer's forged use of plaintiff's return address).

735 *See* National Consumer Law Center, Unfair and Deceptive Acts and Practices Ch. 11 (8th ed. 2012), *updated at* www.nclc.org/library.

736 Ferron v. 411 Web Directory, 2009 WL 2047780 (S.D. Ohio July 6, 2009) (sending 168 e-mails to plaintiff located in Ohio); Ferron v. E360insight, L.L.C., 2008 WL 4411516 (S.D. Ohio Sept. 29, 2008); Asis Internet Services v. Imarketing Consultants, Inc., 2008 WL 2095498 (N.D. Cal. May 16, 2008) (purposeful availment shown by sending mass unsolicited commercial e-mails for commercial gain); Gordon v. Virtumundo, Inc., 2006 WL 1495770 (W.D. Wash. May 24, 2006) (purposeful availment shown by sending of "mass unsolicited e-mails"; fact that sender earned revenue in forum state also significant); Microsoft Corp. v. JDO Media, Inc., 2005 WL 1838609 (W.D. Wash. Aug. 1, 2005) (principal of corporation knew or should have known that some of mass e-mails would reach Washington); America Online, Inc. v. Ambro Enterprises, 2005 WL 2218433 (E.D. Va. 2005) (jurisdiction proper under several prongs of state long-arm statute; defendants could reasonably expect to be brought to court in state where most harm occurred, here the site of ISP's servers). *See also* Melaleuca, Inc. v. Hansen, 2008 WL 2788470 (D. Idaho July 18, 2008); Aitken v. Communication Workers of Am., 496 F. Supp. 2d 653 (E.D. Va. 2007) (purposeful availment test satisfied when non-resident defendants intentionally sent e-mails to residents in forum state; rejecting argument that defendants believed e-mails would be received only by resident recipients, as argument "ignores the essential nature of spamming and other intentional torts committed via computers and the harm these torts cause"); Omni Innovations, L.L.C. v. Impulse Mktg. Grp., Inc., 2007 WL 2110337 (W.D. Wash. July 18, 2007); Verizon Online Services, Inc. v. Ralsky, 203 F. Supp. 2d 601 (E.D. Va. 2002) (in trespass-to-chattel case, transmission of unsolicited bulk e-mail through plaintiff ISP by out-of-state defendant is sufficient minimum contacts to satisfy due process personal jurisdiction requirements); Internet Doorway, Inc. v. Parks, 138 F. Supp. 2d 773 (S.D. Miss. 2001) (in suit by ISP for trespass to chattel, personal jurisdiction proper over defendant who sent e-mail to state resident; active nature of e-mail satisfies minimum contact with state; tort occurred when state resident opened e-mail); MaryCLE, L.L.C. v. First Choice Internet, Inc., 890 A.2d 818 (Md. 2006) (purposeful availment shown by sending of mass unsolicited e-mails); Jaynes v. Commonwealth, 634 S.E.2d 357 (Va. Ct. App. 2006) (upholding jurisdiction over out-of-state spammer), *rev'd on other grounds*, 666 S.E.2d 303 (Va. 2008). *Cf.* Beyond Systems, Inc. v. Keynetics, Inc., 422 F. Supp. 2d 523 (D. Md. 2006) (allowing further discovery on complicated question of jurisdiction). *But cf.* Phillips v. Worldwide Internet Solutions, 2006 WL 1709189 (N.D. Cal. June 20, 2006) (ISP failed to allege that California court had jurisdiction over Canadian website hosting service, websites or individual; appears to have sued wrong ones of several closely related entities); Beyond Systems, Inc. v. Kennedy W. Univ., 2006 WL 1554847 (D. Md. May 31, 2006) (remotely-sent spam does not meet requirements of Maryland's long-arm statute); Silverstein v. Experienced Internet.com, 2005 WL 1629935 (N.D. Cal. July 11, 2005) (allegations that Florida company's e-mails were received in California, based on information and belief, not sufficient to show minimum contacts), *aff'd*, 266 Fed. Appx. 678 (9th Cir. 2008); Fenn v. Mleads Enterprises, Inc., 137 P.3d 706 (Utah 2006) (sending one e-mail to one state resident not sufficient for personal jurisdiction).

---

state, has jurisdiction over them. Courts have rejected this argument, analogizing a posting on the Internet to the placement of an advertisement in a national publication, both of which are purposeful attempts to reach consumers in distant states.[737]

---

737 National Consumer Law Center, *Consumer Credit Regulation* § 7.9.2 (2d ed. 2015), *updated at* www.nclc.org/library.

6.10.7 Consumer's Consent As a Defense

Defendants may argue that they used an "opt-in list" of e-mail addresses of persons who gave prior consent and that this is a defense to liability. Any specific evidence of such consent should be explored during discovery. An alleged "opt-in" list may have been assembled by a third party having no actual evidence of such claimed consent. Furthermore, any actual "opt-in" may have taken place on a webpage entirely unrelated to the e-mails at issue.

Chapter 7 The Federal Racketeer Influenced and Corrupt Organizations Act (RICO)

7.1 Overview

7.1.1 The Structure of RICO

The Federal Racketeer Influenced and Corrupt Organization Act provisions of the Organized Crime Control Act of 1970 (RICO)[1] is a complex federal statute that imposes criminal and civil penalties and permits treble damages when a defendant uses one of two methods to engage with an identified enterprise in any one of four prohibited ways. The two methods are (1) a pattern of racketeering activity and (2) the collection of an unlawful debt.[2] The four prohibited practices are spelled out in RICO § 1962:

(a) It shall be unlawful for any person who has received any income derived, directly or indirectly, from a pattern of racketeering activity or through collection of an unlawful debt . . . to use or invest, directly or indirectly, any part of such income, or the proceeds of such income, in acquisition of any interest in, or the establishment or operation of, any enterprise which is engaged in, or the activities of which affect, interstate or foreign commerce. . . .

(b) It shall be unlawful for any person through a pattern of racketeering activity or through collection of an unlawful debt to acquire or maintain, directly or indirectly, any interest in or control of any enterprise which is engaged in, or the activities of which affect, interstate or foreign commerce.

(c) It shall be unlawful for any person employed by or associated with any enterprise engaged in, or the activities of which affect, interstate or foreign commerce, to conduct or participate, directly or indirectly, in the conduct of such enterprise's affairs through a pattern of racketeering activity or collection of unlawful debt.

(d) It shall be unlawful for any person to conspire to violate any of the provisions of subsections (a), (b), or (c) of this section.[3]

Each of these four prohibited practices are triggered by the defendant's use of *either* a pattern of racketeering activity or the "collection of an unlawful debt," the two methods that RICO targets.

"Racketeering activity" is defined in the statute to include nine generic state crimes and a longer list of specified federal offenses such as bribery, extortion, narcotics, and obstruction of justice.[4] The crimes are called predicate offenses, and only the enumerated crimes establish racketeering activity. Mail fraud[5] and wire fraud are the most significant predicate offenses, especially for consumer plaintiffs.[6]

A "pattern of racketeering activity" requires at least two acts of "racketeering activity" within ten years of each other.[7] Pattern, in RICO, is a complex and intensely fact-specific element that has been the subject of abundant litigation. This topic is covered at § 7.3.3, *infra*.

An "unlawful debt" is defined as either illegal gambling debts or usury, under either state or federal law, at a rate at least twice the enforceable rate.[8] To establish a RICO violation based on the collection of an unlawful debt, a plaintiff need not show a pattern of racketeering activity, just one instance of collection of a debt.[9]

Violators of RICO are subject to criminal penalties,[10] to forfeiture of their interest in the enterprise,[11] and to other sanctions.[12] RICO also provides private litigants with federal court jurisdiction for actions seeking treble damages plus attorney fees:

Any person injured in his business or property by reason of a violation of section 1962 of this chapter may sue therefor in any appropriate United States district court and shall recover threefold the damages he sustains and the cost of the suit, including reasonable attorney fees.[13]

7.1.2 Advantages and Disadvantages of RICO Claims

The advantages of a RICO claim are straightforward: federal court jurisdiction, treble damages, attorney fees, an extremely broad scope, and the ability to raise claims against third parties not directly dealing with the consumer. Because of the increased monetary exposure resulting from the threat of treble damages and attorney fees, a RICO claim may cause a defendant to settle more quickly or for more money than it might do in the ordinary civil lawsuit. RICO also provides a cause of action for violations of statutes, such as mail fraud and wire fraud, that omit or provide only a limited private cause of

---

1   18 U.S.C. §§ 1961–1968, *reprinted at* Appx. E.1, *infra*.
2   18 U.S.C. § 1962(a)–(d).
3   18 U.S.C. § 1962.
4   18 U.S.C. § 1961(1).

5   18 U.S.C. § 1341. *See* §§ 7.3.2.1–7.3.2.4, *infra*.
6   18 U.S.C. § 1343. *See* § 7.3.2.5, *infra*.
7   18 U.S.C. § 1961(5).
8   18 U.S.C. § 1961(6).
9   18 U.S.C. §§ 1961(6), 1962(a)–(c) (pattern of racketeering *or* collection of unlawful debt). *See* § 7.3.4, *infra*.
10 18 U.S.C. § 1963.
11 *Id. See* U.S. Dep't of Justice, Criminal Div., Criminal Forfeitures Under the RICO and Continuing Enterprise Statutes (1980).
12 *E.g.*, 18 U.S.C. § 1964(a) (court-ordered restrictions on future business activities, dissolution or reorganization of any enterprise).
13 18 U.S.C. § 1962(c).

action.[14] Although federal RICO was partially devised to fight organized crime, its broad provisions for criminal and civil liability were deliberately drawn to encompass types of business-related misconduct that are not peculiar to "gangsters."[15]

On the other hand, the RICO statute is complex and important ambiguities remain to be resolved by the courts.[16] Including a RICO claim in a simple lawsuit may needlessly complicate the case and lead to numerous procedural motions. The law is in flux, the volume of civil RICO litigation is high, and practitioners must keep abreast of recent developments.[17] In addition, some defendants will see the added exposure of a RICO claim as justifying a more vigorous defense. While RICO does not require that the defendants have been convicted of a crime, courts are likely to react less hostilely to RICO claims if clear criminal activity underlies the claim.

Civil plaintiffs struggle to succeed at RICO claims: One court examined all the RICO cases filed in the southern district of New York between 2004 and 2007 and determined that every case resolved on the merits had been resolved against the plaintiffs.[18] Of course, one explanation for this statistic is that cases resolved on the merits were mostly dismissed at the motion-to-dismiss stage, lost for failure to properly plead a RICO claim. Cases that made it past this stage were then settled, but these settlements (many favorable to the plaintiffs) were not counted in the statistic.

7.1.3   Relation to and Displacement by Other Statutes

Federal statutes may bar RICO claims based on conduct such statutes already cover. RICO itself excludes securities fraud claims from its scope.[19] However, when the purchase

of securities is merely "incidental" to the fraudulent conduct underlying the claim, the Private Litigation Securities Reform Act will not bar the RICO claim.[20] Whistle-blower claims arising in the nuclear industry are preempted by the Energy Reorganization Act.[21] Some RICO claims relating to workers' benefits have been preempted by the National Labor Relations Act,[22] while others have survived preemption.[23] The Fair Labor Standards Act and the Food, Drug, and Cosmetics Act may also preempt RICO claims covered by those respective

---

14 The federal mail fraud statute does not allow for a private cause of action for damages, 18 U.S.C. § 1341, but a defrauded victim may be able to recover for a violation of the statute through RICO's remedies. *See, e.g.,* Wisdom v. First Midwest Bank of Poplar Bluff, 167 F.3d 402, 408 (8th Cir. 1999); Moss v. Morgan Stanley, Inc., 553 F. Supp. 1347, 1361 (S.D.N.Y.), *aff'd,* 719 F.2d 5 (2d Cir. 1983).

15 For the legislative history of RICO, see 115 Cong. Rec. 6994, 6995, 9567 (1969); 1970 U.S.C.C.A.N. 4007, 4032–4036; Blakey, *The RICO Civil Fraud Action in Context: Reflections on Bennett v. Berg,* 58 Notre Dame L. Rev. 237 (1982) (Prof. G. Robert Blakey, the author of this article, was principal draftsman of RICO); and sources cited in Strafer, Massumi & Skolnick, *Civil RICO in the Public Interest: "Everybody's Darling,"* 19 Am. Crim. L. Rev. 655, 680 n.193 (1982).

16 *See, e.g.,* § 7.9.5, *infra* (injunctive relief for private plaintiffs).

17 Two reporting services, RICO Law Reporter and RICO Business Disputes Guide (CCH), are devoted exclusively to RICO. RICO cases are regularly featured in bar journals and the legal press.

18 Gross v. Waywell, 628 F. Supp. 2d 475, 479–480 (S.D.N.Y. 2009) ("experience bears out that overwhelmingly the RICO plaintiffs' gilded vision of threefold damages and attorney's fees dispels into a mirage").

19 18 U.S.C. § 1964(a), *as amended by* the Private Litig. Sec. Reform Act of 1995, Pub. L. No. 104-67, 109 Stat. 758 (1995). *See, e.g.,* Licht v. Watson, 567 Fed. Appx. 689, 2014 WL 2121219, at *4 (11th Cir. May 22, 2014); MLSMK Inv. Co. v. JP Morgan Chase & Co., 651 F.3d 268, 277 (2d Cir. 2011) (PSLRA bars RICO claim even when plaintiff cannot pursue a securities fraud claim); Affco Inv. 2001, L.L.C. v. Proskauer Rose, L.L.P., 625 F.3d 185, 191 (5th Cir. 2010) (affirming

dismissal of claim); Swartz v. KPMG L.L.P., 476 F.3d 756, 761 (9th Cir. 2007) (affirming dismissal of claim as barred by the Private Securities Litigation Reform Act); *In re* LIBOR-Based Fin. Instruments Antitrust Litig., 935 F. Supp. 2d 666, 728-29 2013 WL 1285338, at *54 (S.D.N.Y. Mar. 29, 2013) (PSLRA bars plaintiffs' RICO claim when some of the predicate acts could have given rise to a securities fraud action); Dorn v. Berson, 2012 WL 1004907, at *4 (E.D.N.Y. Mar. 1, 2012) (magistrate's report and recommendation) (reasoning that the PSLRA barred plaintiff's RICO claim), *adopted by* 2012 WL 1004905 (E.D.N.Y. Mar. 23, 2012); Picard v. Kohn, 907 F. Supp. 2d 392, 398–400 (S.D.N.Y. 2012) (stating that the PSLRA bars RICO claims even when no valid fraud claim provides an alternative); Boudinot v. Shrader, 2012 WL 489215, at *5 (S.D.N.Y. Feb. 15, 2012) (reasoning that the PSLRA barred RICO claims based on defendant's fraudulent acts that forced or induced plaintiffs to sell their shares); Alack v. Jaybar, L.L.C., 2011 WL 3626687, at *3 (E.D. La. Aug. 17, 2011) (dismissing claims based on predicate acts of bank fraud when the alleged fraud was "undertaken in connection with the purchase of a security"); Holland v. TD Ameritrade, 2011 WL 23086, at *4 (E.D. Cal. Jan. 4, 2011) (magistrate's findings and recommendation, *report and recommendation adopted,* 2011 WL 346204 (E.D. Cal. Feb. 1, 2011); Trachsel v. Buchholz, 2009 WL 86698, at *4–5 (N.D. Cal. Jan. 9, 2009). *See also* Gilmore v. Gilmore, 503 Fed. Appx. 97, 99–100 (2d Cir. 2012) (trial court did not err in refusing to allow plaintiffs to split the alleged predicate acts between two separate enterprises to avoid PSLRA); Bixler v. Foster, 596 F.3d 751, 759–760 (10th Cir. 2010) (construing exception broadly and upholding dismissal of RICO claim); Powers v. Wells Fargo Bank N.A., 439 F.3d 1043, 1044–1045 (9th Cir. 2006) (affirming dismissal of claim based on securities fraud).

20 Ouwinga v. Benistar 419 Plan Services, Inc., 694 F.3d 783, 790–791 (6th Cir. 2012) (reversing dismissal of RICO claims that were based on misrepresentation of tax consequences of welfare benefit plan; it was merely incidental that the policies were securities).

21 Norman v. Niagara Mohawk Power Corp., 873 F.2d 634, 637 (2d Cir. 1989); Masters v. Daniel Int'l Corp., 1991 U.S. Dist. LEXIS 7595 (D. Kan. May 3, 1991).

22 Tamburello v. Comm-Tract Corp., 67 F.3d 973 (1st Cir. 1995); Brennan v. Chestnut, 973 F.2d 644 (8th Cir. 1992); Mann v. Air Line Pilots Ass'n, 848 F. Supp. 990 (S.D. Fla. 1994); Graveley Roofing Corp. v. United Union of Roofers, Waterproofers & Allied Workers Local Union No. 30, 1994 U.S. Dist. LEXIS 7489 (E.D. Pa. June 2, 1994); Domestic Linen Supply & Laundry Co. v. Int'l Bhd. of Teamsters, 1992 U.S. Dist. LEXIS 22201 (E.D. Mich. Oct. 30, 1992); Butchers' Union, Local 498 v. SDC Inv., Inc., 631 F. Supp. 1001 (E.D. Cal. 1986). *See also* Danielson v. Burnside-Ott Aviation Training Ctr., Inc., 941 F.2d 1220 (D.C. Cir. 1991) (Service Contract Act preempts RICO); Goulart v. United Airlines, Inc., 1996 U.S. Dist. LEXIS 2894 (N.D. Ill. Mar. 8, 1996) (Railway Labor Act). *But see* Hood v. Smith's Transfer Corp., 762 F. Supp. 1274 (W.D. Ky. 1991) (suit by employee participants in ESOP plan against their company not preempted by National Labor Relations Act).

23 Trollinger v. Tyson Foods, Inc., 370 F.3d 602, 610 (6th Cir. 2004) (holding that suit by workers who were union members that alleged that their employer had violated RICO in scheming to depress their wage scale was not preempted by the NLRA).

statutory schemes.[24] Similarly, the federal Defense Base Act and Longshore Act preempt a contractor's RICO claims, as those acts contain exclusive remedies.[25] Conduct that could give rise to another statutory claim may nonetheless form the basis of a RICO claim, so long as the two statutes do not conflict.[26]

RICO claims based on fraud in the insurance industry will generally survive, notwithstanding the reverse preemption provision of the McCarran-Ferguson Act,[27] which ousts federal regulation of certain insurance matters that a state regulates. In *Humana Inc. v. Forsyth*, the Supreme Court ruled that the reverse preemption provision does not apply to federal RICO claims unless the RICO statute invalidates, impairs, or supersedes a state insurance statute.[28] Accordingly, even if a state insurance law provides a remedial scheme for insurance fraud, the additional availability of RICO remedies for the same misconduct does not "impair" the insurance regulatory scheme.[29]

7.1.4 RICO's Interstate or Foreign Commerce Requirement

RICO claims must allege an enterprise that "is engaged in, or [that] the activities of which affect, interstate or foreign commerce."[30] The requisite connection with commerce need only be "minimal"[31] or "insubstantial."[32] Use of the mail to execute a fraudulent scheme satisfies the requirement; in other words, predicate offenses of mail fraud sufficiently meet the interstate commerce requirement in and of themselves.[33] However, allegations of intrastate mail may not be sufficient.[34] The enterprise's effects can themselves also provide the nexus to commerce.[35] Sufficient effects will exist when the enterprise utilizes the interstate mail or wires[36] or when supplies are shipped through interstate commerce.[37] Even when most of the activities of an enterprise's member take place outside of the United States, the element will be met if they had "substantial direct effects" on the United States.[38] However, RICO does not

---

24 Gordon v. Kaleida Health, 847 F. Supp. 2d 479, 490 (W.D.N.Y. Jan. 17, 2012) (reasoning that "allowing plaintiffs to recover under civil RICO for alleged substantive violations of the FLSA would thwart Congress's careful, comprehensive scheme to remedy wage and hour violations falling within the FLSA's scope"); *In re* Epogen & Aranesp Off-Label Mktg. & Sales Practices Litig., 590 F. Supp. 2d 1282, 1290–1291 (C.D. Cal. 2008) (though Food, Drug, and Cosmetic Act preempted plaintiffs' claims, stating that RICO claims for true mail or wire fraud could escape preemption).

25 Brink v. Cont'l Ins. Co., 787 F.3d 1120, 1127 (D.C. Cir. 2015).

26 *See, e.g.*, Ray v. Spirit Airlines, Inc., 767 F.3d 1220, 1224–1229 (11th Cir. 2014) (concluding that Airline Deregulation Act did not preempt RICO; reasoning that "[w]e apply a strong presumption against finding repeals by implication precisely because so many involve so much speculation about congressional intent"); Johnson v. KB Home, 720 F. Supp. 2d 1109 (D. Ariz. 2010) (RESPA did not displace plaintiff's RICO claim based on allegedly inflated appraisals, even if allegations could have supported a RESPA violation); Schwartz v. Lawyers Title Ins. Co., 680 F. Supp. 2d 690, 702 (E.D. Pa. 2010) (state title insurance claims act did not provide exclusive remedy against title insurance company, so did not preclude RICO claim).

27 15 U.S.C. § 1012(b).

28 525 U.S. 299, 119 S. Ct. 710, 142 L. Ed. 2d 753 (1999).
      The Court stated that, "[w]hen federal law does not directly conflict with state regulation, and when application of the federal law would not frustrate any declared state policy or interfere with a State's administrative regime, the McCarran-Ferguson Act does not preclude its application." 525 U.S. at 310.

29 *See, e.g.*, State Farm Mut. Auto. Ins. Co. v. Pointe Physical Therapy, L.L.C., 68 F. Supp. 3d 744, 751 (E.D. Mich. 2014) (holding that state insurance fraud claim did not override federal RICO claim because to apply RICO would not "invalidate, impair or supersede [the state's] insurance laws"); Jackson v. U.S. Bank, N.A., 44 F. Supp. 3d 1210, 1217–1218 (S.D. Fla. 2014) (ruling that state's regulation of insurance did not preempt RICO claim arising from force-placed insurance on borrowers because the acts alleged—sending misleading notices to borrowers and paying kickbacks—did not involve "business of insurance"). *But see* Riverview Health Inst., L.L.C. v. Medical Mut. of Ohio, 601 F.3d 505, 519 (6th Cir. 2010) (concluding RICO conflicts with state's insurance regulatory scheme, so McCarran-Ferguson Act requires dismissal of RICO claims).

30 18 U.S.C. § 1962(a), (b), (c).

31 United States v. Chance, 306 F.3d 356, 373 (6th Cir. 2002) (need only show a *de minimis* connection with interstate commerce); United States v. Juvenile Male, 118 F.3d 1344 (9th Cir. 1997); United States v. Miller, 116 F.3d 641 (2d Cir. 1997); R.A.G.S. Couture, Inc. v. Hyatt, 774 F.2d 1350, 1353 (5th Cir. 1985); United States v. Robinson, 763 F.2d 778, 781 (6th Cir. 1985); United States v. Rone, 598 F.2d 564, 573 (9th Cir. 1979); Spencer v. Hartford Fin. Services Grp., Inc., 256 F.R.D. 284, 287 (D. Conn. 2009).

32 United States v. Qaoud, 777 F.2d 1105, 1116 (6th Cir. 1985); Adorno-Bezares v. City of New Brunswick Dep't of Planning, Cmty., & Econ. Dev., 2012 WL 4505339, at *4 (D.N.J. Sept. 27, 2012) (denying motion to dismiss when it was "conceivable" that interstate commerce requirement was met); Owl Constr. Co. v. Ronald Adams Contractors, Inc., 642 F. Supp. 475 (E.D. La. 1986).

33 *See* United States v. Maloney, 71 F.3d 645, 663–664 (7th Cir. 1995); Illinois Dep't of Revenue v. Phillips, 771 F.2d 312, 313 (7th Cir. 1985).

34 Calica v. Independent Mortg. Bankers, Ltd., 1989 WL 117057, at *2 (E.D.N.Y. Sept. 28, 1989). *See also* Utz v. Correa, 631 F. Supp. 592, 596 (S.D.N.Y. 1986) (intrastate telephone calls did not violate wire fraud statute).

35 United States v. Conn, 769 F.2d 420, 423–424 (7th Cir. 1985); United States v. Murphy, 768 F.2d 1518, 1531 (7th Cir. 1985); Wiwa v. Royal Dutch Petroleum Co., 2002 WL 319887, at *22 (S.D.N.Y. Feb. 28, 2002) (claim that unlawful exploitation of Nigerian oil fields resulted in an unfair advantage in the United States oil market established commercial nexus); Karel v. Kroner, 635 F. Supp. 725, 728 (N.D. Ill. 1986). *See also* Breslin Realty Dev. Corp. v. Schackner, 457 F. Supp. 2d 132, 137 (E.D.N.Y. 2006) (denying defendants' motion for summary judgment, noting that the enterprise's effects on interstate commerce can satisfy the element).

36 *See* United States v. Bagnariol, 665 F.2d 877, 892, 893 (9th Cir. 1981); Moore v. It's All Good Auto Sales, Inc., 907 F. Supp. 2d 915, 924 (W.D. Tenn. 2012) (use of interstate electronic communication to advertise satisfies interstate commerce requirement when such advertising is vital to fraudulent scheme); Marini v. Adamo, 812 F. Supp. 2d 243, 267 (E.D.N.Y. 2011) (intrastate faxes do not satisfy the interstate commerce requirement). *See also* Environmental Services, Inc. v. Recycle Green Services, Inc., 7 F. Supp. 3d 260, 273 (E.D.N.Y. 2014) (refusing to dismiss complaint that failed to specifically allege that wire transmissions were sent through interstate commerce, permitting additional discovery). *But see* Utz v. Correa, 631 F. Supp. 592, 596 (S.D.N.Y. 1986) (intrastate phone calls do not satisfy interstate commerce requirement of wire fraud statute).

37 *See* Meineke Discount Muffler Shops, Inc. v. Noto, 548 F. Supp. 352, 354 (E.D.N.Y. 1982) (memorandum).

38 United States v. Philip Morris USA, Inc., 566 F.3d 1095 (D.C. Cir. 2009), *order clarified*, 778 F. Supp. 2d 8 (D.D.C. 2011).

extend to extraterritorial activities, even if some fraudulently obtained funds eventually reach the United States.[39]

7.1.5 Liberal Construction

Many federal courts initially reacted with hostility to civil RICO actions in scenarios remote from organized crime conducted by professional criminals. Courts interpreted RICO—especially civil RICO—restrictively, dismissing many actions at the pleading stage. However, by its own terms, RICO "shall be liberally construed to effectuate its remedial purposes,"[40] and the Supreme Court has rebuffed several lower court efforts to limit its scope, supporting an expansive construction of the statute.[41] It has done this despite acknowledging the fact that civil RICO has been used far more often against "legitimate" businesses than against "the archetypal, intimidating gangster."[42] Among the limitations that have been rejected by the Supreme Court or the great weight of authority are the following:

- *Organized Crime Nexus*: The defendant need not be a member of or involved with "organized crime."[43]
- *Racketeering Enterprise Injury*: The injury to the plaintiff need not derive from the racketeering enterprise instead of resulting simply from the predicate offenses themselves.[44]

- *Criminal Conviction*: The defendant need not have been criminally convicted of the acts alleged as predicate offenses.[45]
- *Association for Wholly Criminal Purposes*: RICO applies not only to racketeering in relation to otherwise lawful enterprises but to associations whose purposes are wholly criminal.[46]
- *Commercial or Competitive Injury*: A RICO action does not require a distinctively commercial or competitive injury.[47]
- *"Garden-Variety" Fraud*: Perhaps most important in consumer cases, RICO does not exclude "garden variety" business or consumer fraud that otherwise satisfies the requirements of a RICO cause of action.[48]

Defendants may attempt to interject new substantive RICO limitations that may be only relabeled versions or minor variants of discredited restrictions. For example, the Supreme Court in *American Bank & Trust Co. v. Haroco* rejected a proposed limitation revolving around whether the defendant enterprise was "conducted" through a pattern of racketeering activity.[49] This, held the Court, was essentially a restatement of the "racketeering injury" restriction it had just rejected in *Sedima*: "The submission that the injury must flow not from the predicate offenses themselves but from the fact that they were performed as part of the conduct of an enterprise suffers from the same defects as the amorphous and unfounded restrictions on the RICO private action we rejected in [*Sedima*]."[50] Any proposed limitation, old or new, without explicit support in the language of the statute should be vigorously contested on the basis of the liberal construction that Congress mandated[51] and that the Supreme Court has consistently avowed. The expansive use of civil RICO against "legitimate" businesses has aroused criticism and occasioned various proposals to restrict

---

39   *See* United States v. Chao Fan Xu, 706 F.3d 965, 978 (9th Cir. 2013), *as amended on denial of reh'g* (Mar. 14, 2013).

40   Organized Crime Control Act of 1970, Pub. L. No. 91-452, tit. IX, § 304(a), 84 Stat. 92, 947 (1970) (uncodified provision). *See* Sedima, S.P.R.L. v. Imrex Co., 473 U.S. 479, 497–498 (1985) (quoting this provision to support its holding that a RICO plaintiff need only show injury from the predicate offenses themselves and not a "racketeering injury"). *See also* Biasch v. Gallina, 346 F.3d 366, 372 (2d Cir. 2003) (quoting provision in holding that civil RICO plaintiff had standing).

41   *See* Sedima, S.P.R.L. v. Imrex Co., 473 U.S. 479, 497–499, 105 S. Ct. 3275, 87 L. Ed. 2d 346 (1985); United States v. Turkette, 452 U.S. 576, 586, 587 (1981).

42   Sedima, S.P.R.L. v. Imrex Co., 473 U.S. 479, 499, 105 S. Ct. 3275, 87 L. Ed. 2d 346 (1985).

43   The U.S. Supreme Court, in reiterating this position, has stated that Congress' failure to limit the application of RICO to organized crime resulted from its acknowledgment that organized crime is heavily involved in legitimate enterprises, making it impossible to adequately define organized crime. H.J. Inc. v. Northwestern Bell Tel. Co., 492 U.S. 229, 109 S. Ct. 2893, 106 L. Ed. 2d 195 (1989). *See also* United States v. Hunt, 749 F.2d 1078, 1088 (4th Cir. 1984); Owl Constr. Co. v. Ronald Adams Contractors, Inc., 727 F.2d 540, 542 (5th Cir. 1984); Schacht v. Brown, 711 F.2d 1343, 1353 (7th Cir. 1983); Bennett v. Berg, 685 F.2d 1053, 1063 (8th Cir. 1982), *aff'd en banc*, 710 F.2d 1361 (8th Cir. 1983); United States v. Campanale, 518 F.2d 352, 363, 364 (9th Cir. 1975); Prudential Ins. Co. v. U.S. Gypsum Co., 711 F. Supp. 1244 (D.N.J. 1989) (suit for property damage caused by asbestos in buildings). *But cf.* US Airline Pilots Ass'n v. Awappa, L.L.C., 615 F.3d 312, 317 (4th Cir. 2010) ("[t]hese penalties are primarily designed to provide society with a powerful response to the dangers of organized crime").

44   Sedima, S.P.R.L. v. Imrex Co., 473 U.S. 479, 495, 105 S. Ct. 3275, 87 L. Ed. 2d 346 (1985).

     According to this theory, now rejected, an injury "caused by the defendant's predicate offenses, rather than by its use of a pattern of racketeering injury in connection with a RICO enterprise," was not

considered to be caused by a violation of section 1962. Bankers Trust Co. v. Rhoades, 741 F.2d 511, 517 (2d Cir. 1984), *vacated and remanded*, 473 U.S. 922 (1985).

45   Sedima, S.P.R.L. v. Imrex Co., 473 U.S. 479, 493, 105 S. Ct. 3275, 87 L. Ed. 2d 346 (1985).

     A criminal conviction, though not a requirement, is not an impediment either. Conduct resulting in convictions for predicate offenses may be used in subsequent RICO proceedings. United States v. Persico, 774 F.2d 30 (2d Cir. 1985) (criminal case). *See* § 7.8.4, *infra* (offensive collateral estoppel).

46   United States v. Turkette, 452 U.S. 576, 584, 585 (1981).

47   Callan v. State Chem. Mfg. Co., 584 F. Supp. 619, 622, 623 (E.D. Pa. 1984) (memorandum); Crocker Nat'l Bank v. Rockwell Int'l Corp., 555 F. Supp. 47, 49 (N.D. Cal. 1982).

     As a commentator has pointed out, "[t]here appears to be some overlap between the concepts of a 'racketeering enterprise injury' and a 'commercial injury.' " Litig. Research Grp., Civil RICO: A Review of the Case Law 20 (1985). *See also* Strafer, Massumi & Skolnick, *Civil RICO in the Public Interest: "Everybody's Darling,"* 79 Am. Crim. L. Rev. 655, 689–691 (1982).

48   Tabas v. Tabas, 47 F.3d 1280 (3d Cir. 1995); Schacht v. Brown, 711 F.2d 1343, 1353–1356 (7th Cir. 1983).

49   473 U.S. 606, 607 (1985) (per curiam).

50   *Id.* at 609.

51   *See also* Note, *Civil RICO: The Temptation and the Impropriety of Judicial Restriction*, 95 Harv. L. Rev. 1101 (1982).

its scope;[52] nonetheless, civil RICO survives as a potent tool with which to combat corporate abuses of consumers.

7.2 The RICO Defendant

RICO refers to the RICO defendant as the "person" and defines "person" as "including any individual or entity capable of holding a legal or beneficial interest in property."[53] Only certain narrow exceptions to this broad definition of person exist.

Municipalities and municipal corporations such as school boards are immune from suit,[54] either on the theory that they cannot form the necessary criminal intent[55] or because treble damages would punish the very taxpayers that RICO was designed to protect.[56] General immunity principles prevent RICO suits against the Internal Revenue Service,[57] tribal councils,[58] legislators,[59] judges,[60] and the FDIC.[61] As with other federal statutes, the Eleventh Amendment may bar claims against state agencies or state officials.[62] The *Noerr-Pennington* doctrine—which, stated generally, provides that attempts to influence government decisions are not actionable under the Sherman Act—has been extended by one court to bar a RICO suit based on prepetition demand letters sent to consumers.[63]

7.3 Pattern of Racketeering Activity or Collection of an Unlawful Debt

7.3.1 Introduction

RICO targets two types of methods of engaging with an enterprise: "a pattern of racketeering activity" and "collection of an unlawful debt." RICO prohibits these methods only when they have one of four enumerated relationships to an enterprise, as described in § 7.5, *infra*.

7.3.2 Racketeering Activity

7.3.2.1 General

The first method of engaging with an enterprise that RICO targets is the use of a pattern of racketeering activity.[64] RICO defines racketeering activity as an indictable act under one of nine generic categories of state crimes or under one of about fifty enumerated federal crimes.[65] These are called "predicate offenses." A violation of a statute, such as a UDAP statute, cannot be a predicate offense if it is not enumerated in RICO.[66] Most consumer RICO litigation focuses on two of the

---

52 *See, e.g.*, The Private Securities Litigation Reform Act of 1995, 104 Pub. L. No. 104-67, 109 Stat. 758 (1995) (amending 18 U.S.C. § 1964(a) to exclude "any conduct that would have been actionable as fraud in the purchase or sale of securities" as the basis of a civil RICO action); Howard v. Am. Online Inc., 208 F.3d 741, 749 (9th Cir. 2000) (PSLRA bars claim when it was "actionable" as securities fraud even if plaintiffs themselves would not have standing to bring such a claim); Bald Eagle Area Sch. Dist. v. Keystone Fin., Inc., 189 F.3d 321, 329 (3d Cir. 1999) (affirming dismissal on basis of PSLRA). *See also* Grell, *Exorcising RICO from Product Litigation*, 24 Wm. Mitchell L. Rev. 1089 (1998); Bradley, *Long Arm of the Rackets Law Draws Fire From White-Collar Targets*, Christian Science Monitor, Feb. 7, 1986, at 21, col. 1; Zimroth, *Legislative Proposals to Amend the Civil RICO Statute*, Practicing Law Institute, 1985 Civil RICO at 427–444.

53 18 U.S.C. § 1961(3).

Each of the four subsections defining the conduct prohibited by RICO begins with the phrase "[i]t shall be unlawful for *any person* to." 18 U.S.C. § 1962(a)–(d) (emphasis added). *See also* St. Paul Mercury Ins. Co. v. Williamson, 224 F.3d 425, 440 (5th Cir. 2000) (a RICO person is the defendant, while a RICO enterprise can be either a legal entity or an association in fact).

54 *See, e.g.*, Rogers v. City of N.Y., 359 Fed. Appx. 201, 204 (2d Cir. 2009) (affirming dismissal of claim against a city); Ochoa v. Housing Auth. of City of L.A., 47 Fed. Appx. 484, 486 (9th Cir. 2002) (neither a municipal corporation nor its employees in their official capacities are subject to RICO liability); Lattanzio v. Ackerman, 2010 WL 1610459, at *3 (E.D. Ky. Apr. 20, 2010); Pilitz v. Incorporated Vill. of Rockville Ctr., 2008 WL 4326996, at *5 (E.D.N.Y. Sept. 22, 2008); Wood v. Incorporated Vill. of Patchogue, 311 F. Supp. 2d 344, 354 (E.D.N.Y. 2004); Dickerson v. City of Denton, 298 F. Supp. 2d 537, 549 (E.D. Tex. 2004); Frooks v. Town of Cortlandt, 997 F. Supp. 438, 457 (S.D.N.Y. 1998), *aff'd without op.*, 182 F.3d 899 (2d Cir. 1999); Dammon v. W.L. Folse, 846 F. Supp. 36, 37–38 (E.D. La. 1994); Nu-Life Constr. Corp. v. Board of Educ. of the City of N.Y., 779 F. Supp. 248, 252 (E.D.N.Y. 1991).

55 *See, e.g.*, Lancaster Cmty. Hosp. v. Antelope Valley Hosp. Dist., 940 F.2d 397, 404 (9th Cir. 1991); BEG Investments, L.L.C. v. Alberti, 85 F. Supp. 3d 13, 28–30 (D.D.C. 2015); Nationwide Pub. Ins. Adjusters Inc. v. Edcouch-Elsa I.S.D., 913 F. Supp. 2d 305 (S.D. Tex. 2012) (dismissing claims against a school district); Pilitz v. Incorporated Vill. of Rockville Ctr., 2008 WL 4326996, at *5 (E.D.N.Y. Sept. 22, 2008); Interstate Flagging, Inc. v. Town of Darien, 283 F. Supp. 2d 641, 645–646 (D. Conn. 2003); Nu-Life Constr. Corp. v. Board of Educ. of the City of N.Y., 779 F. Supp. 248, 251 (E.D.N.Y. 1991).

56 Gil Ramirez Grp., L.L.C. v. Houston Indep. Sch. Dist., 786 F.3d 400, 412 (5th Cir. 2015); Genty v. Resolution Trust Corp., 937 F.2d 899, 914 (3d Cir. 1991) (township).

57 Chow v. Giordano, 24 F.3d 245 (9th Cir. 1994) (unpublished, text at 1994 U.S. App. LEXIS 11048) (relying on agency's sovereign immunity).

58 Smith v. Babbitt, 875 F. Supp. 1353 (D. Minn. 1995) (relying on tribe's sovereign immunity).

59 Chappell v. Robbins, 73 F.3d 918 (9th Cir. 1995).

60 Rolfes v. MBNA Am. Bank N.A., 416 F. Supp. 2d 745, 749 (D.S.D. 2005), *aff'd*, 219 Fed. Appx. 613 (8th Cir. 2007).

61 McNeily v. United States, 6 F.3d 343 (5th Cir. 1993) (relying on misrepresentation exception of the Federal Tort Claims Act, 28 U.S.C. § 2680(h)).

62 Bair v. Krug, 853 F.2d 672, 675 (9th Cir. 1988) (action against state officials acting in their official capacities barred); Rogers v. Mitchell, 2003 WL 21976743, at *1–2 (N.D. Tex. Aug. 19, 2003) (action against state lottery commission barred). *See also* Doe v. Board of Trustees of Univ. of Ill., 429 F. Supp. 2d 930, 941 (N.D. Ill. 2006) (suit barred by state sovereign immunity statute).

63 Sosa v. DIRECTV, Inc., 437 F.3d 923, 936–937 (9th Cir. 2006).

64 18 U.S.C. § 1962(a)–(d).

65 18 U.S.C. § 1961(1).

66 Zito v. Leasecomm Corp., 2003 WL 105652, at *9 (S.D.N.Y. Sept. 30, 2003) (UDAP violation not a predicate offense; neither is obstruction of state justice because RICO only enumerates the federal obstruction of justice crime relating to federal court proceedings). *Cf.* St. Clair v. Citizens Fin. Grp., 340 Fed. Appx. 62, 67 (3d Cir. July 23, 2009) (dismissing bank customer's RICO claim arising from collection of overdraft charges; since defendants were not state actors, they could not violate Hobbs Act, so their conduct could not be a predicate act).

enumerated federal crimes: mail fraud and wire fraud, detailed immediately below. In addition, it is not sufficient to plead racketeering activity—there must be a pattern of such activity, as discussed at § 7.3.3, *infra*.

7.3.2.2 Elements of Mail Fraud

The elements of mail fraud are a scheme to defraud and a mailing made for the purpose of executing the scheme.[67] The mail and wire fraud statutes address a broader scope of fraud than common law fraud does.[68] It is not necessary that anyone actually be defrauded.[69] Nor is it necessary that the mailings themselves include any misrepresentations or contribute directly to the deception of the plaintiffs, so long as they are part of a scheme to defraud.[70] Misrepresentations arising in the course of legal proceedings are not exempt: one district court rejected the argument of the defendants, who had been accused of running a default judgment mill, that "mail and wire fraud committed in the course of litigation activities cannot, as a matter of law, constitute predicate acts for RICO

offenses."[71] As always under the RICO, the plaintiff must have suffered injury to business or property "by reason of" the RICO violation.[72]

In 2008, in *Bridge v. Phoenix Bond & Indemnity Co.*, the Supreme Court resolved a circuit split to hold that a RICO plaintiff asserting mail or wire fraud need not claim first party reliance.[73] In this case, the plaintiffs were participants in a county's auction of tax liens that the county had acquired on the property of delinquent taxpayers.[74] The Court ruled that they could base a RICO claim on misrepresentations made to the county, rather than to the participants themselves. Appellate courts have followed *Bridge* to conclude that RICO plaintiffs need not allege reliance in order to properly plead a predicate act of mail fraud.[75]

Since *Bridge*, plaintiffs should be able to withstand a motion to dismiss that challenges a complaint for failing to allege reliance.[76] However, at least one court has concluded that a plaintiff must still show reliance in order to successfully allege a RICO claim based on mail or wire fraud,[77] although the court may have characterized a proximate cause issue as a reliance issue.[78]

A scheme to defraud encompasses anything "designed to defraud as to representations as to the past or present, or suggestions and promises as to the future."[79] It includes the

---

67 Schmuck v. United States, 489 U.S. 705, 109 S. Ct. 1443, 103 L. Ed. 2d 734 (1989) (mailing incidental to fraudulent scheme sufficient); Pereira v. United States, 347 U.S. 1, 8, 74 S. Ct. 358, 98 L. Ed. 2d 435 (1954); United States v. Dick, 744 F.2d 546, 550 (7th Cir. 1984); Anderson v. Smithfield Foods, Inc., 207 F. Supp. 2d 1358, 1362 (M.D. Fla. 2002); Jordan (Berm.) Inv. Co. v. Hunter Green Investments Ltd., 154 F. Supp. 2d 682, 691 (S.D.N.Y. 2001); Emcore Corp. v. PricewaterhouseCoopers L.L.P., 102 F. Supp. 2d 237, 245 (D.N.J. 2000); Polycast Tech. Corp. v. Uniroyal, Inc., 728 F. Supp. 926 (S.D.N.Y. 1989); Austin v. Merrill Lynch, Pierce, Fenner & Smith, 570 F. Supp. 667, 669 (W.D. Mich. 1983). *See also* Heinrich v. Waiting Angels Adoption Services, Inc., 668 F.3d 393, 408–409 (6th Cir. 2012) (identifying the necessary elements as "a scheme to defraud, the use of the mail or wires in furtherance of the scheme and a sufficient factual basis from which to infer *scienter*" and reversing the lower court's granting of a motion to dismiss); Manax v. McNamara, 660 F. Supp. 657 (W.D. Tex. 1987) (no scheme to defraud), *aff'd*, 842 F.2d 808 (5th Cir. 1988).

68 Regency Communications v. Cleartel Communications Inc., 160 F. Supp. 2d 36, 44 (D.D.C. 2001) (breach of contract accompanied by use of mail to deceive plaintiffs could fulfill mail fraud statute's requirements) (citing McEvoy Travel Bureau, Inc. v. Heritage Travel, Inc., 904 F.2d 786 (1st Cir. 1990)).

   Furthermore, the party deprived of money or property need not be the same person who was deceived. *In re* Lupron Mktg. & Sales Practices Litig., 295 F. Supp. 2d 148, 168 (D. Mass. 2001) (citing United States v. Evans, 844 F.2d 36, 39 (2d Cir. 1988)).

69 United States v. Reid, 533 F.2d 1255, 1264 n.34 (D.C. Cir. 1976); United States v. Andreadis, 366 F.2d 423, 431 (2d Cir. 1966); Unocal Corp. v. Superior Court, 244 Cal. Rptr. 540 (Cal. Ct. App. 1988) (unpublished).

70 Schmuck v. United States, 489 U.S. 705, 714 (1989); Jones v. Ram Med., Inc., 807 F. Supp. 2d 501, 513 (D.S.C. 2011) (denying motion to dismiss); Charleswell v. Chase Manhattan Bank, N.A., 308 F. Supp. 2d 545, 577 (D. V.I. 2004); Shapo v. O'Shaugnessy, 246 F. Supp. 2d 935 (N.D. Ill. 2002); Silvershein v. Fruman, 1997 WL 531310 (S.D.N.Y. 1997) (mailings may constitute mail fraud even if they occur after the fraud is completed). *See also In re* American Investors Life Ins. Co. Annuity Mktg. & Sales Practices Litig., 2006 WL 1531152, at *11 (E.D. Pa. June 2, 2006) (stating that complaint was adequate if it alleged that mailings were " 'incident to an essential part' " of scheme, but dismissing complaint on other grounds); Eva v. Midwest Nat'l Mortg. Banc, Inc., 143 F. Supp. 2d 862, 877 (N.D. Ohio 2001) (incidental use of the mail sufficient).

71 Mayfield v. Asta Funding, Inc., 2015 WL 1501100, at *8 (S.D.N.Y. Mar. 31, 2015)

72 18 U.S.C. § 1962(c); § 7.6, *infra*.

73 553 U.S. 639, 170 L. Ed. 2d 1012, 128 S. Ct. 2131, 2145 (2008) (abrogating VanDenBroeck v. CommonPoint Mortg. Co., 210 F.3d 696 (6th Cir. 2000) and Sikes v. Teleline, Inc., 281 F.3d 1350 (11th Cir. 2002)).

74 Bridge v. Phoenix Bond & Indemnity Co., 553 U.S. 639, 170 L. Ed. 2d 1012, 128 S. Ct. 2131, 2138, 2145 (2008).

75 *See, e.g.*, Biggs v. Eaglewood Mortg., L.L.C. 353 Fed. Appx. 864, 867 (4th Cir. 2010) (upholding summary judgment for defendant on other grounds); Schoedinger v. United Healthcare of Midwest, Inc., 557 F.3d 872, 877 (8th Cir. 2009) (upholding dismissal of RICO claim on other grounds). *See also* § 7.6.3, *infra*.

   Some plaintiffs were even able to convince courts to reverse and remand summary judgments for reconsideration based on the intervening change in the law by *Bridge. See, e.g.*, Chaz Concrete Co., L.L.C. v. Codell, 545 F.3d 407, 409 (6th Cir. 2008).

76 *See, e.g.*, Montoya v. PNC Bank, N.A., 2015 WL 1311482, at *12–13 (S.D. Fla. Mar. 23, 2015) (citing Wallace v. Midwest Fin. & Mortg. Services, 714 F.3d 414, 419–420 (6th Cir. 2013)).

77 Biggs v. Eaglewood Mortg., L.L.C. 582 F. Supp. 2d 707, 714–716 (D. Md. 2008) (in a case in which plaintiffs, older borrowers, claimed that defendant had made false statements to them in order to induce them to execute a loan far less favorable to them than their existing mortgage, evidence that they had a history of repeatedly refinancing their mortgage on a variety of terms refuted their argument that the misrepresentations were material), *aff'd without op.*, 353 Fed. Appx. 864 (4th Cir. 2009).

78 *See* § 7.6.3, *infra*.

79 Durland v. United States, 161 U.S. 306, 313 (1896). *See also* United States v. Philip Morris USA Inc., 566 F.3d 1095, 1116–1117 (D.C. Cir. 2009) (upholding the trial court's conclusion that defendants had engaged in a scheme to defraud smokers and potential smokers, noting that the court had described the multiple components of the scheme and enumerated the 108 racketeering acts supporting the scheme), *order clarified*, 778 F. Supp. 2d 8 (D.D.C. 2011); Williams v. Aztar Ind. Gaming Corp., 351 F.3d 294, 299 (7th Cir. 2003) (plaintiff must allege

assertion of "half-truths" or the concealment of material facts.[80] A statement is material if it "would be important to a reasonable person" engaged in that type of transaction.[81] Statements that are "mere puffery," however, are not actionable as material misstatements.[82] If relying on a fraudulent failure to disclose

information, the plaintiff should be sure to specifically plead that the defendant had a duty to disclose.[83]

The mail and wire fraud statutes include schemes to defraud a person of intangible rights, as opposed to just money and property.[84] Nonetheless, a RICO plaintiff must still meet RICO's requirement of "injury to business or property."[85]

Mail fraud requires a specific intent to defraud,[86] or the making of representations in reckless disregard for their truth or falsity.[87] The intent requirement is satisfied by the existence of a scheme reasonably calculated to deceive persons of ordinary prudence and comprehension.[88]

---

a misrepresentation in order to allege mail fraud); Wilson v. Parisi, 549 F. Supp. 2d 637, 659 (M.D. Pa. 2008) (home buyers who alleged a fraudulent lending scheme could meet scheme to defraud element by showing that they paid more than fair market value for their property as a result of a fraudulent appraisal); In re American Investors Life Ins. Co. Annuity Mktg. & Sales Practices Litig., 2007 WL 2541216, at *21 (E.D. Pa. Aug. 29, 2007) (in case alleging that defendants engaged in a fraudulent scheme to sell elders unnecessary and unsuitable estate planning instruments, concluding that plaintiffs sufficiently alleged a scheme to defraud). But see Westways World Travel, Inc. v. AMR Corp., 265 Fed. Appx. 472 (9th Cir. 2008) (defendant's communication of its interpretation of a contract and its demand for payment pursuant to that interpretation could not fulfill scheme element); D'Orange v. Feely, 894 F. Supp. 159 (S.D.N.Y. 1995) (mailings sent by attorney regarding pending litigation cannot be mail fraud predicates even if contain fraudulent material), aff'd on other grounds, 101 F.3d 1393 (2d Cir. 1996) (table).

80 Nat'l Sec. Sys., Inc. v. Iola, 700 F.3d 65, 107 (3d Cir. 2012) (trial court abused its discretion by failing to instruct jury on a concealed commissions theory, which could have constituted a scheme to defraud); Emery v. American Gen. Fin., Inc., 71 F.3d 1343, 1348 (7th Cir. 1995) (omission or concealment of loan information can constitute mail fraud); United States v. Beecroft, 608 F.2d 753, 757 (9th Cir. 1979); Parish v. Beneficial Illinois, Inc., 1996 U.S. Dist. LEXIS 4453 (N.D. Ill. Apr. 10, 1996) (loan refinancing forms which were misleading as to costs were basis for mail fraud); In re Lupron Mktg. & Sales Practices Litig., 295 F. Supp. 2d 148 (D. Mass. 2001). See Williams v. Duke Energy Int'l, Inc., 681 F.3d 788, 802–803 (6th Cir. 2012) (concluding that the failure to disclose side rebates with some customers could be sufficiently fraudulent, reversing lower court's dismissal of RICO claims); In re Nat'l W. Life Ins. Deferred Annuities Litig., 2012 WL 440820, at *4–5 (S.D. Cal. Feb. 10, 2012) (concluding that a rational jury could conclude that defendant's sales materials misrepresented features of its annuities such that it had a duty to disclose its commissions, denying defendant's motion for summary judgment). See also Zimmerman v. Poly Prep Country Day Sch., 888 F. Supp. 2d 317, 328–329 (E.D.N.Y. 2012) (holding that plaintiffs adequately alleged that the purpose of a scheme to conceal a coach's sexual abuse of students was "for obtaining money and property" by alleging that defendants sought to "derive substantial revenue" from alumni contributions and otherwise). But see Decatur Ventures, L.L.C. v. Daniel, 485 F.3d 387 (7th Cir. 2007) (since under Indiana law, an appraiser's report is considered merely a statement of opinion, rather than fact, it could not be the basis of mail fraud unless plaintiff could show that the speaker disbelieved his or her own words); Nolan v. Galaxy Scientific Corp., 269 F. Supp. 2d 635, 640 (E.D. Pa. 2003) (no RICO liability based on omission in mailed literature when "the causal link between the alleged mail fraud and the purported fraudulent activity [was] too attenuated"); Pappas v. NCNB, 653 F. Supp. 699 (M.D.N.C. 1987) (no mail fraud when no fiduciary duty existed to disclose prime lending rate).

81 United States v. Philip Morris USA Inc., 566 F.3d 1095, 1122 (D.C. Cir. 2009) (false statements regarding the addiction of cigarettes found material), order clarified, 778 F. Supp. 2d 8 (D.D.C. 2011). See also Schoedinger v. United Healthcare of Midwest, Inc., 557 F.3d 872 (8th Cir. 2009) (RICO claim failed because no demonstration that the asserted misrepresentations were false).

82 See, e.g., In re Countrywide Fin. Corp. Mortg. Mktg. & Sales Practices Litig., 601 F. Supp. 2d 1201, 1217–1218 (S.D. Cal. 2009) (statements that loans were "the best available" or "ideal" for a particular borrower were "too prevalent" to rise to actionable misrepresentation).

83 See Eller v. EquiTrust Life Ins. Co., 778 F.3d 1089, 1091–1095 (9th Cir. 2015) (concluding that an annuity purchaser failed to establish that seller had a duty to disclose its internal pricing methods, notwithstanding assertions about bonuses that were to have accrued to purchaser); American United Life Ins. Co. v. Martinez, 480 F.3d 1043, 1065 (11th Cir. 2007) (upholding dismissal of complaint that failed to allege that the defendant owed a duty to disclose the material information); In re Countrywide Fin. Corp. Mortg. Mktg. & Sales Practices Litig., 601 F. Supp. 2d 1201, 1218 (S.D. Cal. 2009) (refusing to dismiss RICO claim based on defendants' failure to disclose specific terms to plaintiffs, but concluding that defendants had no independent duty to disclose their overarching fraudulent scheme).

84 Pub. L. No. 100-690, § 7603(a), 102 Stat. 4508 (1988), codified at 18 U.S.C. § 1346. See also BCS Services, Inc. v. BG Investments, Inc., 728 F.3d 633 (7th Cir. 2013) (intangible rights such as tax liens qualify as property for purposes of a RICO claim comprising predicate acts of mail fraud). The section reads "[f]or the purposes of this chapter, the term 'scheme or artifice to defraud' includes a scheme or artifice to deprive another of the intangible right of honest services."

Congress amended the statute after the Supreme Court ruled in McNally v. United States, 483 U.S. 350, 107 S. Ct. 2875, 97 L. Ed. 292 (1987) that the mail and wire fraud statutes were limited to the protection of money and property, not intangible rights.

85 See § 7.6, infra.

86 United States v. Philip Morris USA Inc., 566 F.3d 1095, 1118–1122 (D.C. Cir. 2009) (upholding the trial court's conclusion that evidence that defendants' "chief executive officers and other highly placed officials . . . made or approved statements they knew to be false or misleading, evince[ed] their specific intent to defraud consumers"), order clarified, 778 F. Supp. 2d 8 (D.D.C. 2011); Blu-J, Inc. v. Kemper C.P.A. Grp., 916 F.2d 637 (11th Cir. 1990); Abell v. Potomac Ins. Co., 858 F.2d 1104 (5th Cir. 1988) (fraudulent intent required; materiality and reliance not required); Haroco v. American Nat'l Bank & Trust Co., 747 F.2d 384, 403 (7th Cir. 1984), aff'd per curiam, 473 U.S. 606 (1985); United States v. Rasheed, 663 F.2d 843, 847 (9th Cir. 1981); Buyers & Renters United to Save Harlem v. Pinnacle Grp. N.Y. L.L.C., 575 F. Supp. 2d 499, 508 (S.D.N.Y. 2008) (refusing to dismiss RICO claim); Mount Prospect State Bank v. Grossman, 1989 U.S. Dist. LEXIS 2086 (N.D. Ill. Feb. 24, 1989) (default on loans not sufficient to make RICO claim because no showing of intent to defraud at time loans made). See also Selman v. American Sports Underwriters, Inc., No. 84-0099C (W.D. Va. Mar. 23, 1987) (plaintiff's mail and wire fraud allegations insufficient to show specific intent to defraud).

87 United States v. Munoz, 233 F.3d 1117, 1136 (9th Cir. 2000); United States v. Cogle, 63 F.3d 1239 (3d Cir. 1995); United States v. Dick, 744 F.2d 546, 551 (7th Cir. 1984); United States v. Hopkins, 744 F.2d 716, 717–718 (10th Cir. 1984); United States v. Farris, 614 F.2d 634, 638 (9th Cir. 1979); Flag Co. v. Maynard, 2006 WL 1030173, at *9 (D. Or. Apr. 17, 2006).

88 Berent v. Kemper Corp., 973 F.2d 1291 (6th Cir. 1992); Sun Sav. & Loan Ass'n v. Dierdorff, 825 F.2d 187 (9th Cir. 1987); United States v. Green, 745 F.2d 1205 (9th Cir. 1984). See also Hale v. State Farm Mut. Auto. Ins. Co., 2013 WL 1287054, at *18–19 (S.D. Ill. Mar. 28, 2013)

In contrast, claims based on negligent or unintentional conduct will not meet the intent requirement. Accordingly, a defendant's good faith belief in even an impractical or "somewhat visionary" scheme is a defense.[89] However, honest belief does not justify baseless, false, or reckless representations or promises even if made by someone who was subjectively sincere.[90] Thus mail fraud includes more conduct than covered by common law fraud but probably somewhat less conduct than covered by the UDAP "deceptive" standard.

7.3.2.3 Mail Fraud's Mailing Requirement

The defendant itself need not have mailed the material so long as the defendant caused it to be mailed.[91] Nor need the mailing itself contain the fraudulent representation; it is enough if the mailing somehow aids others in executing the fraudulent scheme.[92] So, for example, once victims have been defrauded, a mailing meant to prevent or delay them from detecting the fraud could suffice.[93]

Under the mail fraud statute, each mailing in furtherance of a scheme to defraud is a separate offense, separately punishable.[94] It does not follow, though, for purposes of RICO, that two or more acts indictable as mail fraud will always establish a "pattern" of racketeering activity.[95] But, so far as the mail fraud statute itself is concerned, multiple mailings in furtherance of a single scheme to defraud provide multiple RICO predicate offenses: the mail fraud statute punishes not the "scheme to defraud" but *mailings* which further it.[96] For mail fraud, unlike wire fraud, the communication need not have been interstate.[97]

7.3.2.4 Aiding and Abetting Mail Fraud

Can aiding and abetting mail fraud itself be a predicate act under RICO? Note that this question differs from that of whether RICO imposes liability for aiding and abetting a RICO violation; most circuit courts have ruled that it does not, at least for claims arising under section 1962(c).[98] RICO defines, as a predicate offense, "any act which is indictable under . . . § 1341 (relating to mail fraud), [or] § 1343 (relating to wire fraud) . . . ."[99] One who aids and abets a federal crime is treated as a principal.[100] Accordingly, aiding and abetting mail fraud or one of the other federal offenses listed should constitute a predicate offense under RICO.[101] However, in a RICO § 1962(c) claim one will still have to prove that the defendant, in addition to aiding and abetting the underlying crime, "conduct[ed] or participate[d] . . . in the conduct of [the] enterprise's affairs" through the pattern of racketeering activity or collection of an unlawful debt.

(concluding that mailed submissions to state supreme court intended to conceal defendant's financial support of a justice's election campaign sufficed); Barsky v. Metro Kitchen & Bath, Inc., 587 F. Supp. 2d 976, 991 (N.D. Ill. 2008) (concluding that plaintiffs failed to prove intent when evidence from both sides indicated that defendant acted in good faith); Royal Indem. Co. v. Pepper Hamilton L.L.P., 479 F. Supp. 2d 419, 428–429 (D. Del. 2007) (denying defendants' motion to dismiss); United States v. Philip Morris USA, Inc., 566 F.3d 1095 (D.C. Cir. 2009), *order clarified*, 778 F. Supp. 2d 8 (D.D.C. 2011) (holding that plaintiff had sufficiently established mail fraud, stating that "[t]he individual components must be viewed not independently but in context of the entire scheme to defraud . . . [i]t is sufficient to prove by the totality of the circumstances that the defendant devised a scheme intended to defraud which included one or more of the individual component schemes alleged").

89 South Atlanta Ltd. P'ship v. Riese, 284 F.3d 518, 531 (4th Cir. 2002); United States v. Smith, 13 F.3d 1421, 1426 (10th Cir. 1994); United States v. Hopkins, 744 F.2d 716, 717, 718 (10th Cir. 1984).

90 United States v. Smith, 13 F.3d 1421, 1426 (10th Cir. 1994); United States v. Stoll, 743 F.2d 439, 445, 446 (6th Cir. 1984); Sparrow v. United States, 402 F.2d 826, 828, 829 (10th Cir. 1968).

91 United States v. Maze, 414 U.S. 395, 399, 400, 94 S. Ct. 645, 38 L. Ed. 2d 603 (1974); Pereira v. United States, 347 U.S. 1, 8, 74 S. Ct. 358, 98 L. Ed. 2d 435 (1954); City of N.Y. v. Smokes-Spirits.com, Inc., 541 F.3d 425, 446 (2d Cir. 2008), *related case*, 911 N.E.2d 834 (N.Y. 2009) (answering unrelated questions that Second Circuit has certified to state supreme court), *rev'd on other grounds*, 130 S. Ct. 983 (2010); Dale v. Ala Acquisitions, Inc., 203 F. Supp. 2d 694, 702 (S.D. Miss. 2002) (defendant need not have made the communication personally, enough whether the use of the mail was reasonably foreseeable).
The mailing must have been made by the defendant or its agent. Armbruster v. K-H Corp., 206 F. Supp. 2d 870, 897 (E.D. Mich. 2002).

92 Schmuck v. United States, 489 U.S. 705, 109 S. Ct. 1443, 103 L. Ed. 2d 734 (1989) (mailing incidental to fraudulent scheme sufficient); Hofstetter v. Fletcher, 905 F.2d 897 (6th Cir. 1988) (mailings after initial sales based on fraud may be considered to show scheme existed); United States v. Reid, 533 F.2d 1255, 1265 (D.C. Cir. 1976). *See also* American Eagle Credit Corp. v. Gaskins, 920 F.2d 352, 354 (6th Cir. 1990) (mailings need not be essential element of scheme); United States v. Philip Morris USA, Inc., 449 F. Supp. 2d 1 (D.D.C. 2006) (a mailing incidental to the scheme can suffice), *aff'd in part, rev'd in part on other grounds*, 566 F.3d 1095 (D.C. Cir. 2009). *But see* Nakahata v. New York-Presbyterian Healthcare Sys., Inc., 723 F.3d 192, 204–205 (2d Cir. 2013) (alleged mailing did not further any fraudulent scheme); Hinterberger v. Catholic Health Sys., Inc., 536 Fed. Appx. 14, 16 (2d Cir. 2013) (same).

93 United States v. Brutzman, 731 F.2d 1449, 1454 (9th Cir. 1984); United States v. Jones, 712 F.2d 1316, 1320, 1321 (9th Cir. 1983).

94 United States v. Stoll, 743 F.2d 439, 444, 445 (6th Cir. 1984); United States v. Ledesma, 632 F.2d 670, 679 (7th Cir. 1980).

95 *See* § 7.3.3, *infra. See also* Anton Motors, Inc. v. Powers, 644 F. Supp. 299, 303 (D. Md. 1986); Millers Cove Energy Co. v. Domestic Energy Services Co., 646 F. Supp. 520, 521–522 (E.D. Mich. 1986).

96 United States v. Weatherspoon, 581 F.2d 595, 601, 602 (7th Cir. 1978).

97 United States v. Cady, 567 F.2d 771, 776 n.7 (8th Cir. 1977); Barsky v. Metro Kitchen & Bath, Inc., 587 F. Supp. 2d 976, 990 (N.D. Ill. 2008) (concluding that plaintiffs were able to support mail fraud allegations based on a mailing from a defendant's attorney to plaintiffs); Hinsdale Women's Clinic v. Women's Health Care of Hinsdale, 690 F. Supp. 658, 663 (N.D. Ill. 1988).

98 *See also* § 7.3.2.2, *supra*.

99 18 U.S.C. § 1961(B).

100 18 U.S.C. § 2. *See also* Petro-Tech, Inc. v. Western Co., 824 F.2d 1349, 1357 (3d Cir. 1987) (one who has aided and abetted the commission of two predicate offenses is guilty of those offenses).

101 *See, e.g.*, Aetna Cas. Sur. Co. v. P&B Autobody, 1994 U.S. App. LEXIS 36770, at *94 (1st Cir. Dec. 29, 1994) (aiding or abetting mail fraud is also a "predicate act," because aiding and abetting mail fraud is a violation of the mail fraud statute itself). *See also* Dayton Monetary Associates v. Donaldson, Lufkin, & Jenrette Sec. Corp., 1995 U.S. Dist. LEXIS 1198, at *12 (S.D.N.Y. Feb. 2, 1995) (holding that Supreme Court's decision in *Central Bank v. Interstate Bank* did not affect whether aiding and abetting mail fraud was a predicate offense, but whether aiding and abetting a RICO violation was a RICO violation).

7.3.2.5 Wire Fraud

For RICO purposes, wire fraud[102] and mail fraud are treated in virtually identical fashion.[103] The only difference is that wire fraud requires an interstate communication,[104] typically by the Internet, e-mail, or telephone. The requirement is met if a telephone call, though originating and arriving in the same state, is routed out of the state along the way.[105] The element of specific intent is the same,[106] and it is enough if the defendant foreseeably caused the telephone call, whether or not he or she placed it.[107] As with mail fraud, each use of the wires is a separate offense, even if they all facilitate the same scheme,[108] and schemes to defraud a person of intangible rights are actionable.[109]

7.3.3 "Pattern" of Racketeering Activity

7.3.3.1 Introduction

Racketeering activity is not actionable unless there is a "pattern" of racketeering activity.[110] A pattern of racketeering activity "requires at least two acts of racketeering activity."[111] However, these acts can both serve the same criminal scheme.[112] Courts have great difficulty defining "pattern" of racketeering activity, and this remains one of the haziest aspects of RICO law. The United States Supreme Court has addressed the issue twice, but uncertainty still remains.

7.3.3.2 Supreme Court Guidance

The first Supreme Court case to address the "pattern" requirement, *Sedima, S.P.R.L. v. Imrex Co.*,[113] did not define the term but indicated that the commission of two predicate offenses, while necessary, may not suffice to establish a pattern:

> As many commentators have pointed out, the definition of a "pattern of racketeering activity" differs from the other provisions in § 1961 in that it states that a pattern "requires at least two acts of racketeering activity," . . . not that it "means" two such acts. The implication is that while two acts are necessary, they may not be sufficient. Indeed, in common parlance two of anything do not generally form a "pattern."[114]

The Court quoted from RICO's Senate Report: "[t]he target of [RICO] is thus not sporadic activity. The infiltration of legitimate business normally requires more than one "racketeering activity" and the threat of continuing activity to be effective. It is this factor of continuity plus relationship which combines to produce a pattern."[115] The Court also pointed out a non-RICO provision of the Organized Crime Control Act which defined pattern as follows: "criminal conduct forms a pattern if it embraces criminal acts that have the same or similar purposes, results, participants, victims, or methods of commission, or otherwise are interrelated by distinguishing characteristics and are not isolated events."[116] The Supreme Court, by deploring "the failure of Congress and the courts to develop a meaningful concept of 'pattern,' "[117] in effect invited the lower courts to redress their neglect of the problem.

The second Supreme Court case to consider the pattern requirement, *H.J. Inc. v. Northwestern Bell Telephone Co.*,[118] specifically states that a pattern of racketeering need not involve organized crime, cannot be shown merely by proving two predicate offenses, and does not require predicate offenses that are part of separate illegal schemes.[119] The Court noted that the dictionary definition of pattern is "an arrangement or

---

102 18 U.S.C. § 1343. The statute states:

> Whoever, having devised or intending to devise any scheme or artifice to defraud, or for obtaining money or property by means of false or fraudulent pretenses, representations, or promises, transmits or causes to be transmitted by means of wire, radio, or television communication in interstate or foreign commerce, any writings, signs, signals, pictures, or sounds for the purpose of executing such scheme or artifice, shall be fined not more than $1000 or imprisoned not more than five years, or both. If the violation affects a financial institution, such person shall be fined not more than $1,000,000 or imprisoned not more than twenty years, or both.

103 *See* Carpenter v. United States, 484 U.S. 19, 108 S. Ct. 316, 98 L. Ed. 2d 275 (1987); United States v. Giovengo, 637 F.2d 941, 944 (3d Cir. 1980); D'Iorio v. Adonizio, 554 F. Supp. 222, 264 n.3 (M.D. Pa. 1982) (memorandum).

104 Smith v. Ayres, 845 F.2d 1360 (5th Cir. 1988); First Pac. Bancorp, Inc. v. Bro, 847 F.2d 542 (9th Cir. 1988); Hall v. Tressic, 381 F. Supp. 2d 101, 108 (N.D.N.Y. 2005) (dismissing claim); Harris Trust & Sav. Bank v. Ellis, 609 F. Supp. 1118, 1122 (N.D. Ill. 1985) (memorandum), *aff'd on other grounds*, 810 F.2d 700 (7th Cir. 1987); Efron v. Embassy Suites (P.R.), Inc., 47 F. Supp. 2d 200, 205 (D. P.R. 1999) (allegations of facsimile transmissions without allegations of use of telephone lines were insufficient to allege predicate offense of wire fraud), *aff'd*, 223 F.3d 12 (1st Cir. 2000); Utz v. Correa, 631 F. Supp. 592 (S.D.N.Y. 1986); Gitterman v. Vitoulis, 579 F. Supp. 423 (S.D.N.Y. 1983).

105 *See, e.g.,* United States v. Davila, 592 F.2d 1261, 1263, 1264 (5th Cir.), *reh'g denied en banc*, 597 F.2d 283 (5th Cir. 1978). *But see* Barsky v. Metro Kitchen & Bath, Inc., 587 F. Supp. 2d 976, 989 (N.D. Ill. 2008) (allegations that a defendant made calls from one Chicago suburb to plaintiffs in another did not support wire fraud).

106 United States v. Cusino, 694 F.2d 185, 187 (9th Cir. 1982).

107 *Id.* at 188; Renwick v. Bonnema, 2009 WL 592341, at *2 (E.D. Tex. Mar. 6, 2009) (denying defendants' motion to dismiss claim that alleged that they had perpetrated a scheme to sell life insurance policies through a plan that was not valid under ERISA).

108 United States v. Benmuhar, 658 F.2d 14, 16 (1st Cir. 1981).

109 Pub. L. No. 100-690, § 7603(a), 102 Stat. 4508 (1988) (codified at 18 U.S.C. § 1346). The section reads "[f]or the purposes of this chapter, the term 'scheme or artifice to defraud' includes a scheme or artifice to deprive another of the intangible right of honest services."

110 18 U.S.C. § 1962(a), (b), (c).

111 18 U.S.C. § 1961(5).

112 Blake v. Dierdorff, 856 F.2d 1365, 1368 (9th Cir. 1988); Madden v. Gluck, 815 F.2d 1163, 1164 (8th Cir. 1987).

113 473 U.S. 479 (1985).

114 473 U.S. 479, 496 n.14 (1985).

115 *Id.* (quoting S. Rep. No. 617, 91st Cong., 1st Sess. 158 (1969)).

116 *Id.* (quoting 18 U.S.C. § 3575(e)).

117 *Id.* at 500.

118 492 U.S. 229, 109 S. Ct. 2893, 106 L. Ed. 2d 195 (1989).
    After remand, the district court again dismissed this case because of the court's unwillingness to second guess the state public utility commission's authority. H.J. Inc. v. Northwestern Bell Tel. Co., 734 F. Supp. 879 (D. Minn. 1990), *aff'd*, 954 F.2d 485 (8th Cir. 1992).

119 492 U.S. 229, 236–237, 109 S. Ct. 2893, 106 L. Ed. 2d 195 (1989).

order of things or activity."[120] Therefore, the Court reasoned, it does not matter how many predicate offenses there are, unless they are related to one another in some order or arrangement.[121]

In *H.J., Inc.*, the Supreme Court held that the concept of "pattern" has two separate properties that a plaintiff must establish: relationship and continuity.[122] Reiterating its reasoning in *Sedima*, the Court concluded that the relationship criterion is met if the acts have " 'the same or similar purposes, results, participants, victims, or methods of commission, or are otherwise interrelated.' "[123] As for continuity, while the Court declined to express a specific test, it did rough out the requirement by providing that a plaintiff could meet the requirement by showing either closed-ended or open-ended continuity.[124] Closed-ended continuity could be shown "by proving a series of related predicates extending over a substantial period of time."[125] Alternatively, a plaintiff could show "open-ended" continuity by proving a threat of continued racketeering activity.[126] These different means of establishing the continuity criterion have received significant attention from the courts.

7.3.3.3 Closed-Ended Continuity

The scheme's duration is the primary factor in closed-ended continuity. Courts rarely find that a scheme, measured from first predicate offense to last,[127] that lasted less than two years qualifies for closed-ended continuity.[128] However, though

---

120   *Id.* at 238.

121   *Id.*

122   *Id.* at 239.

123   *Id.* at 240 (quoting 18 U.S.C. § 3575(e)).

124   *Id.* at 241.

125   *Id.* at 242 (emphasis added).

> Predicate acts committed over just a few weeks or months would not satisfy closed-ended continuity, in such a case the plaintiff would have to show "open-ended" continuity to meet the continuity property of the pattern element. *Id.*

126   *Id.* at 242.

> While declining to define open-ended continuity, the Court offered a couple of examples: open-ended continuity could be met if the racketeering acts themselves included a specific threat of repetition, extending indefinitely into the future, as with a "protection" racket, or if the predicate offenses or offenses were part of an ongoing entity's regular way of doing business. *Id.* at 242, 243.
>
> Given the facts alleged by the plaintiffs, that the defendants had paid five bribes to a utility commission over the course of six years, the Court reversed the lower court's dismissal of the claim and remanded. The court held that the bribes could be found to be related for a common purpose, meeting the relationship property, and the plaintiffs could meet the continuity property either under a closed-ended analysis, given the frequency of the acts, or under an open-ended analysis, either by showing that the bribes were a regular way of conducting the defendant's ongoing business, or that bribery was a regular way of conducting or participating in the conduct of the alleged RICO enterprise, the utility company. *Id.* at 250.

127   *See* Cofacredit, S.A. v. Windsor Plumbing Supply Co., 187 F.3d 229, 243 (2d Cir. 1999) (acts that do not constitute RICO predicate offenses are not included in the calculation, refusing to consider later acts that did not involve interstate commerce).

128   *See, e.g.,* W & D Imports, Inc. v. Lia, 563 Fed. Appx. 19, 2014 WL 1465383, at *4 (2d Cir. Apr. 16, 2014) (one-and-a-half years' duration was insufficient); Heinrich v. Waiting Angels Adoption Services, Inc.,

668 F.3d 393, 410–411 (6th Cir. 2012) (two months insufficient); Spool v. World Child Int'l Adoption Agency, 520 F.3d 178, 184 (2d Cir. 2008) (sixteen months insufficient); Jackson v. BellSouth Telecomms., 372 F.3d 1250 (11th Cir. 2004) (nine months insufficient, given that allegations related to a single scheme); Turner v. Cook, 362 F.3d 1219, 1230 (9th Cir. 2004) (in suit by judgment debtor against judgment creditors, no closed-ended continuity when bulk of alleged predicate offenses took place in two-month period with remaining acts occurring in the preceding year); Soto-Negron v. Taber Partners I, 339 F.3d 35, 38–39 (1st Cir. 2003) (wrongful cashing of six checks within days of one another did not satisfy continuity requirement); Pizzo v. Bekin Van Lines Co., 258 F.3d 629, 633 (7th Cir. 2001) (consumer who received substandard furniture could not demonstrate pattern of fraud by store with evidence of only one other dissatisfied customer); GE Inv. Private Placement Partners II v. Parker, 247 F.3d 543, 550 (4th Cir. 2001) (two years insufficient, in light of other circumstances); GICC Capital Corp. v. Technology Fin. Grp., Inc., 67 F.3d 463, 467 (2d Cir. 1992); Metromedia Co. v. Fugazy, 983 F.2d 350, 369 (2d Cir. 1992) (over two years); Jacobson v. Cooper, 882 F.2d 717, 720 (2d Cir. 1989) ("matter of years"). *See also* Coquina Investments v. TD Bank, N.A., 760 F.3d 1300, 1320–1322 (11th Cir. 2014) (affirming denial of plaintiff's motion to amend its closed-ended continuity theory that was based on predicate acts spanning only five months, reasoning that plaintiff had been on notice that "the relevant period for determining continuity is not the time during which the underlying scheme operated, but rather the time during which 'the specific incidents . . . actually charged' occurred") (citation omitted)); De Falco v. Bernas, 2001 U.S. App. LEXIS 5256, at *92 (2d Cir. Mar. 13, 2001) (year and a half insufficient for closed-ended continuity); Wisdom v. First Midwest Bank, 167 F.3d 402, 407 (8th Cir. 1999) (six months insufficient); GICC Capital Corp. v. Technology Fin. Grp., Inc., 67 F.3d 463, 468 (2d Cir. 1992) (less than one year insufficient); Hughes v. Consol-Pa. Coal Co., 945 F.2d 594, 611 (3d Cir. 1991) (twelve months insufficient); J.D. Marshall Int'l, Inc. v. Redstart, Inc., 935 F.2d 815, 821 (7th Cir. 1991) (thirteen months insufficient); Monasco v. Wasserman, 886 F.2d 681, 684 (4th Cir. 1989) (one year insufficient); Sky Med Supply Inc. v. SCS Support Claims Services, Inc., 17 F. Supp. 3d 207, 227 (E.D.N.Y. 2014) (closed-ended continuity did not exist for plaintiffs who failed to allege acts of fraud extending over a year or more); De Sole v. Knoedler Gallery, L.L.C., 974 F. Supp. 2d 274, 309 (S.D.N.Y. 2013) (nine months insufficient); Walther v. Patel, 2011 WL 382752, at *6 (E.D. Pa. Feb. 4, 2011) (scheme that lasted merely weeks insufficient); Miller v. Countrywide Home Loans, 747 F. Supp. 2d 947, 964 (S.D. Ohio 2010) (five months insufficient); Monroe v. Hyundai of Manhattan & Westchester, 2008 WL 4891223, at *1–9 (S.D.N.Y. Nov. 12, 2008) (single act of fraud that took place over four days could not satisfy either the closed- or open-ended continuity property of pattern) (adopting magistrate's report and recommendation), *aff'd with op.*, 372 Fed. Appx 147 (2d Cir. 2010); Metcalf v. Death Row Records, Inc., 2003 WL 22097336, at *3 (N.D. Cal. Sept. 3, 2003) (one to two months insufficient); Maryland-Nat'l Capital Park & Planning Comm'n v. Boyle, 203 F. Supp. 2d 468, 478 (D. Md. 2002) (eighteen months insufficient), *aff'd*, 2003 WL 1879017 (4th Cir. Apr. 16, 2003); Special Purpose Accounts Receivable Coop. Corp. v. Prime One Capital Co. L.L.C., 202 F. Supp. 2d 1339, 1350 (S.D. Fla. 2002) (five-and-a-half months insufficient); Vicon Fiber Optics Corp. v. Scrivo, 201 F. Supp. 2d 216, 220 (S.D.N.Y. 2002) (four months insufficient); Shapo v. O'Shaugnessy, 246 F. Supp. 2d 935 (N.D. Ill. 2002) (seven years sufficed); G-I Holdings, Inc. v. Baron & Budd, 238 F. Supp. 2d 521 (S.D.N.Y. 2002) (seven months insufficient); Arboireau v. Adidas Salomon AG, 2002 WL 31466557 (D. Or. Mar. 19, 2002), *aff'd in part, vacated in part on other grounds*, 347 F.3d 1158 (4th Cir. 2003); First Capital Asset Mgmt. v. Brickelbush, Inc., 150 F. Supp. 2d 624, 635 (S.D.N.Y. 2001) (less than a year insufficient); Dempsey v. Sanders, 132 F. Supp. 2d 222, 228 (S.D.N.Y. 2001); Oak Beverages, Inc. v. TOMRA of Mass., L.L.C., 96 F. Supp. 2d 336 (S.D.N.Y. 2000) (fourteen months insufficient); Staiger v. Bentley Mortg. Corp., 1999 Conn. Super.

closed-ended continuity is primarily a temporal concept, time span alone does not necessarily determine its existence; the number and variety of predicate offenses, the number of both participants and victims, and the presence of separate schemes are also relevant in determining whether closed-ended continuity exists.[129] A scheme aimed at only a handful of victims

may be less likely to meet the closed-ended continuity requirement of pattern.[130] In any event, these factors can be particularly influential when the time span falls on the short side of two years.[131] Correspondingly, when a plaintiff can establish

---

LEXIS 2407, at *14–*15 (Sept. 7, 1999) (one year insufficient when single scheme). *But see* Ferrer v. International Longshoremen's Ass'n, 2009 WL 1361953, at *7 (D. P.R. May 11, 2009) (plaintiff sufficiently alleged closed-ended continuity, notwithstanding that events underlying the claim spanned only eleven months, reasoning that further discovery could reveal a longer span of time); Wilson v. De Angelis, 156 F. Supp. 2d 1335, 1339 (S.D. Fla. 2001) (refusing to dismiss RICO claim based on ten acts over ten months); Williams v. Waldron, 14 F. Supp. 2d 1334, 1340 (N.D. Ga. 1998) (one year sufficient), *aff'd without op.*, 248 F.3d 1180 (11th Cir. 2001).

129 Cofacredit, S.A. v. Windsor Plumbing Supply Co., 187 F.3d 229, 242 (2d Cir. 1999) (citing GICC Capital Corp. v. Technology Fin. Grp., Inc., 67 F.3d 463, 468 (2d Cir. 1992)); Vicom, Inc. v. Harbridge Merchant Services, 20 F.3d 771, 780 (7th Cir. 1994); Brandon Apparel Grp. v. Quitman Mfg. Co., 52 F. Supp. 2d 913, 918 (N.D. Ill. 1999) (court should consider (1) the number and variety of predicate offenses; (2) the length of time over which the predicate offenses were committed; (3) the number of victims; (4) the presence of separate schemes; and (5) the occurrence of distinct injuries) (citing Morgan v. Bank of Waukegan, 804 F.2d 970, 975 (7th Cir. 1986)). *See also* Whitney, Bradley & Brown, Inc. v. Kammermann, 436 Fed. Appx. 257, 259 (4th Cir. 2011) (in calculating number of victims, only the corporate victim and not its shareholders counted; concluding that plaintiff failed to establish closed-ended continuity); DeGuelle v. Camilli, 664 F.3d 192, 203–204 (7th Cir. 2011) (concluding that plaintiff sufficiently alleged closed-ended continuity by identifying fraudulent acts occurring over five years and involving several actors and commission methods); Hall v. Witteman, 584 F.3d 859, 867–868 (10th Cir. 2009) (no pattern existed when plaintiff alleged only "a closed-ended series of predicate acts constituting a single scheme to accomplish a discrete goal"); Efron v. Embassy Suites (P.R.), Inc., 223 F.3d 12, 19 (1st Cir. 2000) (when alleged scheme involved only one venture against three plaintiffs, it was merely a "single effort" and did not have closed-ended continuity); Vicom v. Harbridge Merch. Services, Inc., 20 F.3d 771, 780 (7th Cir. 1994); Day v. DB Capital Grp., L.L.C., 2011 WL 887554, at *12 (D. Md. Mar. 11, 2011) (denying motion to dismiss when foreclosure rescue scheme operated for more than two years and involved additional victims); Spencer v. Hartford Fin. Services Grp., Inc., 256 F.R.D. 284, 296 (D. Conn. 2009) (in certifying class, concluding that allegations that defendant fraudulently administered 8000 structured settlements over several years sufficiently alleged continuity); Beta Health Alliance MD PA v. Kelley Witherspoon L.L.P., 2009 WL 2195882, at *4 (N.D. Tex. July 22, 2009) (plaintiff sufficiently alleged a pattern by alleging a scheme that took place over a span of five years and involved thirty-four instances of fraud); Kurins v. Silverman, 2009 WL 321011, at *5 (S.D.N.Y. Feb. 10, 2009) (as amended Feb. 13, 2009) (closed-ended continuity properly alleged when plaintiff claimed multiple acts of fraud involving multiple participants and taking place over a period of nearly five years); Gavin v. AT&T Corp., 543 F. Supp. 2d 885, 906 (N.D. Ill. 2008) (no closed ended continuity when alleged predicate offenses comprised multiple mailings over the period of a few months that all related to the same alleged fraud scheme); Ellipso, Inc. v. Mann, 541 F. Supp. 2d 365, 376–377 (D.D.C. 2008) (no pattern when conduct consisted of a single scheme to deceive as to a single loan); AB Mauri Food, Inc. v. Harold, 2008 WL 878451, at *3 (E.D. Mo. Mar. 27, 2008) (no pattern when conduct involved only a single scheme and a single victim); Javitch v. Capwill, 284 F. Supp. 2d 848, 855–856 (N.D. Ohio 2003); Meyer Material Co. v. Mooshol, 188 F. Supp. 2d 936, 941 (N.D. Ill. 2002) (citing factors to find pattern); Teti v. Towamencin Township,

2001 U.S. Dist. LEXIS 15600, at *24–25 (E.D. Pa. Aug. 17, 2001), *aff'd without op.*, 2002 WL 31758388 (3d Cir. Nov. 6, 2002); Regency Communications v. Cleartel Communications, Inc., 160 F. Supp. 2d 36, 46 (D.D.C. 2001); Jordan (Berm.) Inv. Co. v. Hunter Green Investments Ltd., 154 F. Supp. 2d 682, 694 (S.D.N.Y. 2001).

130 *See, e.g.*, Home Orthopedics Corp. v. Rodriguez, 781 F.3d 521, 529–530 (1st Cir. 2015) (affirming dismissal of RICO claim that court characterized as involving a "single financial endeavor"; stating that "[w]e have 'consistently declined to find continuity where the RICO claim concerns a single, narrow scheme targeting few victims' ") (citation omitted)); Crest Const. II, Inc. v. Doe, 660 F.3d 346, 357 (8th Cir. 2011) (seven months insufficient); Pringle v. Garcia, 2014 WL 1651976, at * 5 (N.D. Ind. Apr. 23, 2014)(wire transfers made up only one scheme that involved only one type of racketeering activity and one victim); Bailey v. Atlantic Auto. Corp., 992 F. Supp. 2d 560, 584–585 (D. Md. 2014) (only one specific instance of fraud directed solely at plaintiff, rejecting "conclusory" assertion that defendant must have engaged in similar fraud with other customers); Manley v. Doby, 2012 WL 5866210, at *3 (E.D.N.Y. Nov. 19, 2012) (no pattern when all of defendants' alleged criminal activity took place over the course of a single eviction proceeding against a single victim); Busby v. Capital One, N.A., 772 F. Supp. 2d 268, 282 (D.D.C. 2011) (pattern not established when victim of wrongful foreclosure failed to identify similar actions against other homeowners); Holding v. Cook, 521 F. Supp. 2d 832, 840 (C.D. Ill. 2007) (no pattern when single scheme to defraud a single victim into believing the rollover of an IRA account would be tax free); Williams v. Equity Holding Corp., 498 F. Supp. 2d 831, 844 (E.D. Va. 2007) (no closed-ended continuity when scheme took place over a period of one year and consisted of only four predicate acts directed towards the single purpose of defrauding one couple); Caravella v. Hearthwood Homes Inc., 2007 WL 2886507, at *9 (N.D.N.Y. Sept. 27, 2007) (no closed-ended continuity when conduct extended over only fourteen months and involved a single scheme of selling homes in a single development); Polzin v. Barna & Co., 2007 WL 2710705, at *8 (E.D. Tenn. Sept. 14, 2007) (no closed-ended continuity when plaintiff alleged a single fraudulent scheme involving the sale of one log home package and when conduct occurred over a period of only thirteen months); Lefkowitz v. Bank of N.Y., 2003 WL 22480049, at *8 (S.D.N.Y. Oct. 31, 2003); *In re* AmerLink, Ltd., 2011 WL 802794, at *4 (Bankr. E.D.N.C. Mar. 2, 2011). *See also* Rowe v. U.S. Bancorp, 569 Fed. Appx. 701, 704–705 (11th Cir. 2014) (concluding that, under Georgia's RICO statute, "[a] pattern of racketeering activity cannot be based on a single transaction" and, accordingly, affirming dismissal of claim based on allegedly forged assignment of plaintiffs' mortgage that preceded a foreclosure); Kearney v. Foley & Lardner, 2012 WL 6004225, at *5 (S.D. Cal. Nov. 29, 2012) (no pattern when "the allegations at best amount to a single, finite scheme (not a continuous one) intended to deprive Plaintiff (and not other victims) of the fair market value of her property"). *But see* Dickey v. Kennedy, 583 F. Supp. 2d 183, 188 (D. Mass. 2008) (pattern adequately alleged, even though only three victims were targeted by the scheme, when each victim was "targeted separately through repetitions of similar criminal conduct over a three-year period"); Warnock v. State Farm Mut. Auto. Ins. Co., 2008 WL 4594129, at *8 (S.D. Miss. Oct. 14, 2008) (pattern adequately alleged based on multiple transmissions of fraudulent litigation documents over the course of several years).

131 *See, e.g.*, Roger Whitmore's Auto. Services, Inc. v. Lake Cnty., Ill., 2002 WL 959587, at *5 (N.D. Ill. May 9, 2002) (short duration of scheme outweighed by the number of victims, number of injuries, variety of predicate acts and existence of two separate schemes); Kayne v. MTC Elecs. Techs. Co. 74 F. Supp. 2d 276, 286 (E.D.N.Y. 1998)

a fairly substantial time span, the importance of those factors recedes.[132]

7.3.3.4   Open-Ended Continuity

In contrast to closed-ended continuity, which primarily depends on time, open-ended continuity depends primarily on a threat that the defendant will continue its criminal activity.[133] To ascertain such a threat, courts will examine the nature of the predicate offenses alleged or the nature of the enterprise on whose behalf the predicate offenses were performed.[134] To show open-ended continuity when the enterprise is primarily a legitimate business, a plaintiff should show that the predicate offenses were the regular way of running the business, or that the acts were of a sort that imply a threat of continued criminal activity.[135] So, for example, the Second Circuit has held that

plaintiffs sufficiently pleaded pattern when they alleged that the defendants, owners of apartments being offered as condominiums, mailed 8000 copies of a single marketing letter that allegedly misrepresented the condition of the apartments.[136] Although the mailing was a single act, because the defendants owned several other apartments in the same complex that remained to be sold, they could be expected to offer them with similar fraudulent letters, and accordingly open-ended continuity existed.[137]

(rejecting "bright line test" in favor of evaluation of factors, ruling that plaintiffs adequately alleged open-ended continuity of scheme that spanned fifteen months).

132   *See, e.g.*, Fresh Meadow Food Services, L.L.C. v. RB 175 Corp., 282 Fed. Appx. 94, 99 (2d Cir.2008) (three-and-a-half years); Marini v. Adamo, 812 F. Supp. 2d 243, 263–264 (E.D.N.Y. 2011) (six years).

133   H.J. Inc. v. Northwestern Bell Tel. Co., 492 U.S. 229, 242–243, 109 S. Ct. 2893, 106 L. Ed. 2d 195 (1989). *See also* Merritt v. Lake Jovita Homeowner's Ass'n, Inc., 358 Fed. Appx. 47, 49–50 (11th Cir. 2009) (plaintiffs could not establish a pattern simply from acts of mail and wire fraud when the predicate acts did not indicate a threat of continuing racketeering activity); Craig Outdoor Adver., Inc. v. Viacom Outdoor, Inc., 528 F.3d 1001, 1028–1029 (8th Cir. 2008) (no open ended continuity when there was no evidence that alleged fraudulent activity would continue in the future); Turner v. Cook, 362 F.3d 1219, 1229 (9th Cir. 2004) (plaintiff must allege misconduct that threatens to repeat in the future); United States v. Connolly, 341 F.3d 16, 30 (1st Cir. 2003) (finding threat of future criminal conduct fulfilled when racketeering acts were part of an ongoing criminal enterprise); Jordan (Berm.) Inv. Co. v. Hunter Green Investments Ltd., 154 F. Supp. 2d 682, 694 (S.D.N.Y. 2001).

134   GICC Capital Corp. v. Technology Fin. Grp., Inc., 67 F.3d 463, 468 (2d Cir. 1992).

135   *See* H.J., Inc. v. Northwestern Bell Tel. Co., 492 U.S. 229, 242–243, 109 S. Ct. 2893, 106 L. Ed. 2d 195 (1989) (such a threat exists when there is "a specific threat of repetition," "the predicates are a regular way of conducting [an] ongoing legitimate business," or "the predicates can be attributed to a defendant operating as part of a long-term association that exists for criminal purposes"); Kalitta Air, L.L.C. v. GSBD & Associates, 591 Fed. Appx. 338, 343–347 (6th Cir. 2014) (finding that plaintiff had sufficiently alleged open-ended continuity, and ruling that trial court had erred in concluding that alleged scheme had a " 'built-in ending point' "); W & D Imports, Inc. v. Lia, 563 Fed. Appx. 19, 2014 WL 1465383, at *4 (2d Cir. Apr. 16, 2014) (insufficient evidence of threat of continued criminal activity); TAGC Mgmt., L.L.C. v. Lehman, Lee & Xu, Ltd., 536 Fed. Appx. 45, 47 (2d Cir. 2013) (failure to allege a plausible threat of continuing criminal conduct); Jackson v. BellSouth Telecomms., 372 F.3d 1250 (11th Cir. 2004) (no open-ended continuity in case brought by plaintiffs against their former attorneys, arising from defendants' allegedly unethical settlement of plaintiffs' employment discrimination suit, when plaintiffs did not show that the predicate acts were part of defendants' usual way of doing business or that acts might be repeated in the future); GE Inv. Private Placement Partners II v. Parker, 247 F.3d 543, 549 (4th Cir. 2001); Llewellyn-Jones v. Metro Prop. Grp., L.L.C., 22 F. Supp. 3d 760, 793–794 (E.D. Mich. 2014) (allegations of continuing criminal conduct were not too "vague and conclusory"); Seikaly & Stewart, P.C. v. Fairley, 18 F. Supp. 3d

989, 995–996 (D. Ariz. 2014) (sufficient allegation of continuing threat of illicit activities to survive motion for judgment on the pleadings); Environmental Services, Inc. v. Recycle Green Services, Inc., 7 F. Supp. 3d 260, 273 (E.D.N.Y. 2014) (sufficient allegation alleged that defendants continued to "pose a criminal threat" in part by alleging that one defendant continued in the illegal activity even after plaintiff filed its complaint); Savage v. MTF Relocation, Inc., 2012 WL 822954, at *5 (N.D. Cal. Mar. 9, 2012) (magistrate's report and recommendation) (in case arising from moving company's fraud, recommending that plaintiff's motion for default judgment be granted when plaintiff alleged that defendant used websites to solicit business, along with emails and phone calls to complete transactions, indicating that "the alleged predicate acts are the means by which defendant regularly conducts its business"); Burford v. Cargill, Inc., 2011 WL 4382124, at *8 (W.D. La. Sept. 20, 2011) (denying motion to dismiss when plaintiff identified acts indicating that offenses were part of "an ongoing entity's regular way of doing business"); Pacheco v. Golden Living Ctr.-Summit, 2011 WL 744656, at *5 (M.D. Pa. Feb. 23, 2011) (continuity sufficiently alleged; allegations that nursing home resident's assets were fraudulently transferred to defendant, along with allegations that defendant did the same to other residents, indicated that such fraud was defendant's regular way of conducting business); Bloodstock Research Info. Services, Inc. v. Edbain.com, L.L.C., 622 F. Supp. 2d 504, 515 (E.D. Ky. 2009) (continuity sufficiently alleged by showing that nature of defendant's business suggested a threat of repetition); McNulty v. Reddy Ice Holdings, Inc., 2009 WL 1508381, at *15 (E.D. Mich. May 29, 2009) (concluding that a defendant's retaliatory act against plaintiff can indicate a threat of continued criminal activity, supporting open-ended continuity), *rev'd on reconsideration on other grounds*, 2009 WL 2168231 (E.D. Mich. July 17, 2009); Heaven & Earth, Inc. v. Wyman Props. Ltd. P'ship, 2003 WL 22680935, at *9 (D. Minn. Oct. 21, 2003) (finding continuity when plaintiff alleged that defendants' fraudulent billing practices were part of their regular business practice); First Guar. Mortg. Corp. v. Procopio, 217 F. Supp. 2d 633, 637 (D. Md. 2002); First Capital Asset Mgmt. v. Brickelbush, Inc., 150 F. Supp. 2d 624, 633–634 (S.D.N.Y. 2001). *See also* Cofacredit, S.A. v. Windsor Plumbing Supply Co., 187 F.3d 229, 243 (2d Cir. 1999); GICC Capital Corp. v. Technology Fin. Grp., Inc., 67 F.3d 463, 466 (2d Cir. 1992) (holding that plaintiffs' evidence of a "discrete and relatively short-lived scheme to defraud a handful of victims" did not sufficiently demonstrate that such fraud was an ordinary part of the operations of the enterprise, a plumbing supply company. Accordingly, no open-ended continuity); AT&T Corp. v. Schroeder, 2006 WL 1806187, at *3 (W.D. Wash. June 28, 2006) (granting summary judgment to plaintiff after holding that it had shown open-ended continuity); Lefkowitz v. Bank of New York, 2003 WL 22480049, at *9 (S.D.N.Y. Oct. 31, 2003) (plaintiff, the beneficiary of her parents' estates, failed to show that defendants, the estates' executor and its counsel, regularly used fraud to administer estates).

136   Beauford v. Helmsley, 865 F.2d 1386, 1392 (2d Cir.) (en banc), *vacated and remanded*, 492 U.S. 914, *adhered to on remand*, 843 F.2d 1433 (2d Cir. 1989).

137   Beauford v. Helmsley, 865 F.2d 1386, 1391, 1392 (2d Cir.). *See also* De Falco v. Bernas, 244 F.3d 286 (2d Cir. 2001) (open-ended continuity sufficiently pleaded when escalating nature of defendants' extortion

Showing that the defendants have committed similar predicate offenses with regard to other consumers can also establish open-ended continuity.[138] The court should measure the threat at the time the racketeering activity occurred; subsequent events that may ultimately negate the threat, for instance a subsequent closing of the business, are immaterial.[139]

Lower court decisions reveal a good deal of doctrinal confusion with respect to the meaning of an open-ended continuity pattern, some of which may be particularly important in some consumer cases that are framed around a single fraudulent scheme. For instance, a typical consumer case might involve identical fraudulent representations that are made to a large number of potential purchasers.[140] These facts may generate multiple mail and wire fraud violations to serve as predicate offenses, but a restrictively-minded court might hold that there is only one

scheme and one criminal episode and therefore no threat of continued criminal activity and no pattern.[141]

However, such identical fraudulent representations may actually establish open-ended continuity under the criteria established in *H.J., Inc.*, because they reveal the defendant's regular manner of doing business and thus establish the future threat that is key to proving open-ended continuity. For instance, in one case a lender was accused of using a fraudulent loan agreement and extortionate means of collection; the court concluded that allegations of identical fraudulent documents and letters could establish the continuity aspect of pattern by showing that they were part of the defendant's regular way of conducting business.[142] Other courts have also held that

---

demands implied a threat that the demands would continue); G-I Holdings, Inc. v. Baron & Budd, 238 F. Supp. 2d 521 (S.D.N.Y. 2002) (finding threat of continuing illegal activity in scheme to fix affidavits).

138 *See, e.g.*, Corley v. Rosewood Care Ctr., Inc., 142 F.3d 1041, 1046 (7th Cir. 1998) (reversing summary judgment for defendant, which operated a number of nursing homes, and remanding to allow further discovery to substantiate the pattern element because plaintiff alleged that there were other victims, in other nursing homes, of defendant's bait-and-switch scheme who taken together would establish continuity), *on remand*, Corley v. Rosewood Care Ctr., Inc., 152 F. Supp. 2d 1099, 1110 (C.D. Ill. 2001) (again entering summary judgment, on ground that plaintiff had still failed to show that misrepresentations regarding the nursing homes were a regular activity of defendants in their transactions with other customers); Jones v. Ram Med., Inc., 807 F. Supp. 2d 501, 514–515 (D.S.C. 2011) (in scheme to distribute and sell counterfeit surgical mesh, concluding that plaintiffs sufficiently pleaded open-ended continuity with allegations that fraudulent activities presented an ongoing threat because defendants used existing networks that remained in operation); Ifill v. West, 1999 U.S. Dist. LEXIS 21320, at *20–*21 (E.D.N.Y. Aug. 24, 1999) (open-ended continuity sufficiently pleaded when plaintiffs alleged an ongoing agreement between defendants to continue the scheme and alleged that defendant had used the same modus operandi to defraud other consumers). *See also* G-I Holdings, Inc. v. Baron & Budd, 238 F. Supp. 2d 521 (S.D.N.Y. 2002) (threat of criminal activity by law firm who allegedly falsified affidavits continued while asbestos litigation existed, therefore pattern element satisfied). *But see* Crest Const. II, Inc. v. Doe, 660 F.3d 346, 357–358 (8th Cir. 2011) (concluding that plaintiff's allegations that defendants' activities threatened multiple victims were too conclusory to raise open-ended continuity).

139 Heinrich v. Waiting Angels Adoption Services, Inc., 668 F.3d 393, 410–411 (6th Cir. 2012) (reversing lower court's dismissal of plaintiffs' claim); City of New York v. LaserShip, Inc., 33 F. Supp. 3d 303, 312 (S.D.N.Y. 2014) (open-ended continuity adequately alleged by demonstrating threat of future criminal activity); Allstate Ins. Co. v. Lyons, 843 F. Supp. 2d 358 (E.D.N.Y. 2012) (concluding that plaintiff sufficiently pleaded open-ended continuity by alleging that defendant's inflated billings constituted a regular way of conducting its business).

140 *E.g.*, Hofstetter v. Fletcher, 905 F.2d 897, 904 (6th Cir. 1988) (injuring numerous investors over the course of several years sufficient); Terre Du Lac Ass'n, Inc. v. Terre Du Lac, Inc., 772 F.2d 467, 472–473 (8th Cir. 1985) (suit against subdivision promoters by land purchasers alleging unfulfilled promises to pave roads). *See also* Lawaetz v. Bank of Nova Scotia, 653 F. Supp. 1278, 1287 (D. V.I. 1987) (bank's fraudulent promise to extend credit through phone calls and letters to six plaintiffs constitutes pattern).

141 *See* GE Inv. Private Placement Partners II v. Parker, 247 F.3d 543, 549 (4th Cir. 2001) (no pattern when scheme had single goal of defrauding investors in the sale of a single enterprise); Saglioccolo v. Eagle Ins. Co., 112 F.3d 226 (6th Cir. 1997) (insurer's refusal to provide documentation needed to sell cab medallions due to unpaid premiums on cab's insurance not pattern when it took place over one month); Leonard v. J.C. Pro Wear, Inc., 64 F.3d 657 (4th Cir. 1995) (unpublished disposition text available on Westlaw) (single purpose, single set of victims, seven months insufficient; Fourth Circuit refused, however, to hold that a seven month scheme is per se insufficient); Tudor Associates Ltd., II v. AJ & AJ Servicing, Inc., 36 F.3d 1094 (4th Cir. 1994) (no pattern when scheme lasted more than ten years and involved many predicates, but single injury and single victim); Vemco, Inc. v. Camardella, 23 F.3d 129 (6th Cir. 1994) (seventeen month scheme, one goal and one victim, is not a pattern); Primary Care Investors v. PHP Healthcare Corp., 986 F.2d 1208 (8th Cir. 1993) (no continuity when less than one year); Wade v. Hopper, 993 F.2d 1246 (7th Cir. 1993); 420 E. Ohio Ltd. P'ship v. Cocose, 980 F.2d 1122 (7th Cir. 1992) (despite high number of mail and wire fraud predicate acts, six months is not a substantial period of time under *H.J., Inc.*); Fleet Credit Corp. v. Sion, 893 F.2d 441 (1st Cir. 1990) (ninety-five predicate acts of mail fraud over four and a half years is not a pattern). *See also* Schroeder v. Acceleration Life Ins. Co., 972 F.2d 41 (3d Cir. 1992) (reversing summary judgment for defendant on grounds that an alleged "benefits reduction scheme" based on a large number of credit disability insurance policies issued over a long period of time met definition of "pattern"); Walther v. Patel, 2011 WL 382752, at *8 (E.D. Pa. Feb. 4, 2011) ("conclusory allegation" of "institutional pattern" of deception is insufficient); Schneider Rucinski Enterprises v. Stratasoft, Inc., 2009 WL 559827, at *10 (S.D. Cal. Mar. 3, 2009) (no pattern when allegations established only a single fraud perpetrated on a single victim); Gilman v. Trott, 2008 WL 4057542, at *1–4 (W.D. Mich. Aug. 28, 2008) (no pattern when plaintiffs alleged only a single mailing of a demand for payment) (adopting magistrate's report and recommendation); Johnson v. Andrews, RICO Business Disputes Guide (CCH) ¶ 8643, 1994 U.S. Dist. LEXIS 11880 (D. Mass. Aug. 17, 1994) (with mail and wire fraud, sheer numbers do not make a pattern); Becher v. Feller, 884 N.Y.S.2d 83 (N.Y. App. Div. July 21, 2009) (no pattern when scheme was limited to one real estate transaction and spanned only one year). *But see* Libertad v. Welch, 53 F.3d 428 (1st Cir. 1995) (abortion protestors' three-month campaign could be long enough when it was its regular way of doing business).

142 Brown v. C.I.L., Inc., 1996 U.S. Dist. LEXIS 4917 (N.D. Ill. Jan. 26, 1996). *See also* Arenson v. Whitehall Convalescent & Nursing Home, 880 F. Supp. 1202 (N.D. Ill. 1995) (allegations that nursing home sent seventy-five bills fraudulently overcharging for drugs over five-year period established closed-end continuity and additionally established open-ended continuity by showing such fraud was part of defendant's regular way of conducting business; Robinson v. Empire of Am. Realty Credit Corp., 1991 U.S. Dist. LEXIS 2084 (N.D. Ill. Feb. 20, 1991) (allegations that mortgagor sent thousands of statements over a

multiple acts arising from one criminal episode can form a pattern.[143]

Consumer cases that involve a scheme that by its nature projects into the future, a "recidivist" scheme, may well meet the requirements of an "open-ended" type pattern. For example, some homeowners pleaded that they had been victimized by a scheme through which a finance company illegally diverted loan proceeds; the court concluded that the scheme, which took place over just nine months, satisfied the pattern requirement by virtue of being "open-ended."[144] In contrast, a

case alleging a single transaction with a single victim, such as in the sale of a piece of real estate, may have more difficulty meeting the open-ended continuity requirement, even when the plaintiff alleges several predicate offenses.[145]

When a scheme is "inherently terminable," such as when it plots the looting of funds that have already been exhausted, there is no threat of continued activity and accordingly no

---

period of several years demanding excess escrow deposits met continuity requirement). *But see* Polzin v. Barna & Co., 2007 WL 2710705, at *9 (E.D. Tenn. Sept. 14, 2007) (no open-ended continuity when plaintiff alleged only that the seller of a log home did business with other consumers using the same contract).

143 Young v. Hamilton, 92 Fed. Appx. 389, 392 (9th Cir. 2003) (predicate acts that related to a single fraudulent investment scheme could establish pattern); Corley v. Rosewood Care Ctr., Inc., 142 F.3d 1041 (7th Cir. 1998) (plaintiff's allegations that nursing home's alleged bait-and-switch scheme involved not just plaintiff but many other residents over a period of twelve to fourteen months were sufficient evidence of pattern to withstand summary judgment); Busby v. Crown Supply, Inc., 896 F.2d 833 (4th Cir. 1990) (scheme to defraud salesmen of their commissions, which extended over ten years, sufficient). *See also* United States v. Connolly, 341 F.3d 16, 30 (1st Cir. 2003) (stating that a "single criminal episode" is "narrow in scope and purpose"); Walk v. Baltimore & Ohio R.R., 847 F.2d 1100 (4th Cir. 1988) (not necessary to show more than one fraudulent scheme to establish a pattern), *vacated*, 492 U.S. 914 (1989), *on remand*, 890 F.2d 698 (4th Cir. 1989); Sky Med. Supply Inc. v. SCS Support Claims Services, Inc., 17 F. Supp. 3d 207, 227–228 (E.D.N.Y. 2014) (open-ended continuity established by allegation that mail fraud was involved in primary operations of the defendants' business); Heaven & Earth, Inc. v. Wyman Props. Ltd. P'ship, 2003 WL 22680935, at *6–7 (D. Minn. Oct. 21, 2003) (plaintiffs could establish pattern based on acts committed as part of single scheme to overcharge tenant for utility charges); Matthews v. New Century Mortg. Corp., 185 F. Supp. 2d 874, 892 (S.D. Ohio 2002) (finding that plaintiffs had adequately alleged pattern in state RICO claim brought against defendants who had allegedly been part of a fraudulent home improvement loan scheme targeted toward older women). *But see* GE Inv. Private Placement Partners II v. Parker, 247 F.3d 543, 550 (4th Cir. 2001) (lender fraud that stopped with plaintiff's investment did not demonstrate that defendants regularly did business that way); Eastern Publ'g & Adver., Inc. v. Chesapeake Publ'g & Advert., Inc., 895 F.2d 971 (4th Cir. 1990) (single closed-ended scheme, which posed no threat of continuity and lasted only three months, insufficient).

144 Thomas v. Ross & Hardies, 9 F. Supp. 2d 547, 553 (D. Md. 1998) (plaintiffs alleged that the principals had targeted minority homeowners and had convinced them to mortgage their homes for the maximum amount possible in return for paying off prior mortgages and extending a line of credit, then failed to pay off the prior loans). *See also* Reyes v. Zion First Nat'l Bank, 2012 WL 947139, at *6 (E.D. Pa. Mar. 21, 2012) (plaintiff could satisfy open-ended continuity with allegations that the defendant bank, as a regular part of its business, processed unauthorized debits from multiple victims' accounts on behalf of fraudulent telemarketers during a fourteen-month period); Johnson v. KB Home, 720 F. Supp. 2d 1109 (D. Ariz. 2010) (plaintiffs who alleged the defendants developed a scheme to defraud based on appraisal inflation and who identified three mailings in support of the allegations sufficiently alleged a threat of continuing activity for purposes of an open-ended pattern); Proctor v. Metropolitan Money Store Corp., 645 F. Supp. 2d 464, 480–481 (D. Md. 2009) (plaintiffs who alleged that the defendants engaged in an equity-stripping foreclosure rescue scheme successfully alleged pattern); Flag Co. v. Maynard, 2006 WL 1030173, at *4–6 (D.

Or. Apr. 17, 2006) (holding that plaintiff sufficiently demonstrated that it was just one of several victims of defendants' fraud, supporting open-ended continuity). *But see* Corley v. Rosewood Care Ctr., Inc., 152 F. Supp. 2d 1099, 1110 (C.D. Ill. 2001) (not inferring that, if nursing home company misrepresented prices in one home, it must have made the same misrepresentations with respect to other homes).

145 *See, e.g.*, Crawford v. Franklin Credit Mgmt. Corp., 758 F.3d 473, 488–489 (2d Cir. 2014) (affirming dismissal of complaint that alleged a single scheme involving a single victim of an alleged foreclosure rescuer); Margaritis v. BAC Home Loans Servicing, L.P., 579 Fed. Appx. 574, 2014 WL 2750004, at *1 (9th Cir. June 18, 2014) (affirming dismissal); Soto-Negron v. Taber Partners I, 339 F.3d 35, 38–39 (1st Cir. 2003) (wrongful cashing of six checks within days of one another did not satisfy continuity requirement); Nugent v. Saint Agnes Med. Ctr., 53 Fed. Appx. 828, 829 (9th Cir. 2002) (no threat of continuity when scheme involves single fraud with single victim); Castrillo v. American Home Mortg. Serv., Inc., 670 F. Supp. 2d 516, 531 (E.D. La. 2009) (mortgagee's allegations that defendants sought to wrongfully foreclose on his home were insufficient to establish continuity); Martinez v. Martinez, 207 F. Supp. 2d 1303, 1306 (D.N.M. 2002) (no pattern when scheme involved only ex-wife and ran only over the course of divorce litigation), *aff'd in part, vacated in part on other grounds*, 2003 WL 1904807 (10th Cir. 2003); Singh v. Parnes, 199 F. Supp. 2d 152, 161–162 (S.D.N.Y. 2002) (no pattern when all activities related to purchase and sale of one property); Mathon v. Marine Midland Bank, 875 F. Supp. 986 (E.D.N.Y. 1985) (no continuity). *See also* Liggon-Redding v. Willingboro Township, 351 Fed. Appx. 674, 678 (3d Cir. 2009) (plaintiff, who alleged that defendants had acted fraudulently in attempting to collect real estate taxes, failed to fulfill the continuity requirement); GE Inv. Private Placement Partners II v. Parker, 247 F.3d 543, 550 (4th Cir. 2001) (fraud in association with sale of single enterprise did not satisfy continuity); GICC Capital Corp. v. Technology Fin. Grp., 67 F.3d 463, 468 (2d Cir. 1995) (when just one victim, continuity not established); Welch v. Centex Home Equity Co., 323 F. Supp. 2d 1087 (D. Kan. 2004) (no continuity when fraud arose from a single scheme, the forgery of plaintiff's signature on loan documents for the purchase of a home); Dempsey v. Sanders, 132 F. Supp. 2d 222, 227 (S.D.N.Y. 2001) (thirteen predicate acts comprising a single scheme to defraud a single victim were not sufficiently continuous); Hobson v. Lincoln Ins. Agency, Inc., 2000 U.S. Dist. LEXIS 13314 (N.D. Ill. Sept. 7, 2000) (plaintiff's allegations of ten payments made over a ten month period as part of a single, allegedly fraudulent, insurance transaction do not constitute a "pattern"); China Trust Bank v. Standard Chartered Bank, PLC, 981 F. Supp. 282, 287–288 (S.D.N.Y. 1997) (predicate acts by single defendant against single victim met neither open-ended nor closed-ended continuity tests); Travis v. Boulevard Bank, 1994 U.S. Dist. LEXIS 14615 (N.D. Ill. Oct. 14, 1994) (when alleged acts of mail fraud all related to the single alleged wrongful act of defendant's procurement of force placed insurance on plaintiff's RISC, no continuity). *Cf.* Rowe v. U.S. Bancorp, 2014 WL 2700203, at *3 (11th Cir. June 16, 2014) (per curiam) (a "single transaction could not constitute a pattern of racketeering activity" under Georgia's RICO statute). *But see* Cypress/Spanish Ft. I, L.P. v. Professional Serv. Indus., Inc., 814 F. Supp. 2d 698, 714 (N.D. Tex. 2011) (stating that "[i]n order to establish a pattern of racketeering activity, a plaintiff need not demonstrate multiple schemes," and denying defendant's motion to dismiss).

open-ended continuity.[146] However, when the scheme involves representations made to many consumers, courts should allow plaintiffs the opportunity to discover other targets of the scheme and the representations made to them in order to establish a threat of continued crimes, that is, open-ended continuity.[147]

7.3.3.5 Relationship Aspect of Pattern

In *H.J. Inc. v. Northwestern Bell Telephone Co.*, both continuity and a relationship were required to create a pattern of racketeering activity.[148] Predicate offenses of racketeering satisfy the relationship test if they "have the same or similar purposes, results, participants, victims, or methods of commission, or otherwise are interrelated by distinguishing characteristics and are not isolated events."[149] This criterion "exists to ensure that RICO is not used to penalize a series of disconnected criminal acts."[150] Attorneys must be careful to demonstrate a relationship between acts (beyond that they were performed by the same defendant).[151]

---

146 US Airline Pilots Ass'n v. Awappa, L.L.C., 615 F.3d 312, 318 (4th Cir. 2010) (union failed to establish open-ended continuity when allegation that defendant sought to destroy the union entailed a "built-in ending point"); Bixler v. Foster, 596 F.3d 751, 761 (10th Cir. 2010) (complaint alleging a single scheme to arrange the transfer of one corporation's assets to another is insufficient to establish the threat of future criminal conduct necessary for open-ended continuity); Spool v. World Child Int'l Adoption Agency, 520 F.3d 178, 186 (2d Cir. 2008) (ruling no open-ended continuity existed when scheme was "inherently terminable"); Turner v. Cook, 362 F.3d 1219, 1229 (9th Cir. 2004) (no open-ended continuity in suit against judgment creditors "since the alleged activities were finite in nature [and] would cease once appellees collected the outstanding tort judgment"); Kenda Corp. v. Pot O'Gold Money Leagues, Inc., 329 F.3d 216, 233 (1st Cir. 2003) (no open-ended continuity when all acts directed toward one transaction); GICC Capital Corp. v. Technology Fin. Grp., Inc., 67 F.3d 463, 467 (2d Cir. 1992); GE Inv. Private Placement Partners II v. Parker, 247 F.3d 543, 549 (4th Cir. 2001) (when fraud was limited to sale of a single enterprise, no threat of continued criminal activity); Caravella v. Hearthwood Homes Inc., 2007 WL 2886507, at *11 (N.D.N.Y. Sept. 27, 2007) (no open-ended continuity when conduct concerned the selling of homes in a single development and therefore was "inherently terminable); Gavin v. AT&T Corp., 543 F. Supp. 2d 885, 906–908 (N.D. Ill. 2008) (no open ended continuity when scheme, which involved a corporate merger, had a natural ending point at the termination of the post-merger cleanup); First Capital Asset Mgmt. v. Brickelbush, Inc., 150 F. Supp. 2d 624, 634 (S.D.N.Y. 2001) (bankruptcy fraud scheme inherently terminable by the conclusion of the case). *See also* Home Orthopedics Corp. v. Rodriguez, 781 F.3d 521, 531 (1st Cir. 2015) (no open-ended continuity when scheme involved a single contract, and defendant's lawsuit based on that contract, was, even if frivolous, " 'not indefinite' "); Howard v. America Online, Inc., 208 F.3d 741, 750 (9th Cir. 2000) (no open-ended continuity when basis of plaintiff's complaint was an advertising program to promote a one-time change in pricing policy, no threat that would be repeated in the future); Kurins v. Silverman, 2009 WL 321011, at *4 (S.D.N.Y. Feb. 10, 2009) (as amended Feb. 13, 2009) (no open-ended continuity when plaintiff failed to allege a threat of ongoing criminal activity); Metcalf v. Death Row Records, Inc., 2003 WL 22097336, at *4 (N.D. Cal. Sept. 3, 2003) (no open-ended continuity when only one scheme with one victim). *But see* CVLR Performance Horses v. Wynne, 524 Fed. Appx. 924 (4th Cir. 2013) (fact that these victims had already been bilked and would likely not do business again with defendant does not establish lack of continuity).

147 *See* Corley v. Rosewood Care Ctr., 142 F.3d 1041, 1049 (7th Cir. 1998) (reversing summary judgment in favor of defendant, a nursing home owner, when plaintiff alleged that there were other victims of defendant's bait-and-switch scheme). *But see* Pizzo v. Bekin Van Lines Co., 258 F.3d 629 (7th Cir. 2001) (refusing plaintiff the opportunity to discover additional fraud victims).

148 *See* § 7.3.3.4, *supra*.

149 H.J. Inc. v. Northwestern Bell Tel. Co., 492 U.S. 229, 240, 109 S. Ct. 2893, 106 L. Ed. 2d 195 (1989) (internal quotation omitted); Kehr Packages, Inc. v. Fidelcor, Inc., 926 F.2d 1406, 1414 (3d Cir. 1991) ("[t]he relatedness test will nearly always be satisfied in cases alleging at least two acts of mail fraud stemming from the same fraudulent transaction"); Pacheco v. Golden Living Ctr.-Summit, 2011 WL 744656, at *5 (M.D. Pa. Feb. 23, 2011) (acts to forge documents to transfer nursing home resident's pension and benefits to defendant were sufficiently related because they had a similar purpose); Fischbein v. Sayer, 2009 WL 2170349, at *6 (S.D.N.Y. July 16, 2009) (plaintiff adequately alleged the relatedness requirement of pattern). *See also* DeGuelle v. Camilli, 664 F.3d 192, 202–204 (7th Cir. 2011) (plaintiff sufficiently alleged that defendants' acts of retaliation for his whistleblowing were sufficiently related to the fraudulent acts revealed); Brown v. Cassens Transp. Co., 546 F.3d 347, 355 (6th Cir. 2008) (relatedness exists when a plaintiff shows that predicate acts have the same purpose and the same result); Heller Fin., Inc. v. Grammco Computer Sales, Inc., 71 F.3d 518, 524 (5th Cir. 1996) (relationship requirement not met when "[t]he purposes of the alleged predicate acts were distinct and dissimilar"); United States v. Eufrasio, 935 F.2d 553, 565 (3d Cir. 1991) (finding requirement met, affirming defendants' convictions); Jones v. Ram Med., Inc., 807 F. Supp. 2d 501, 514 (D.S.C. 2011) (concluding that plaintiffs sufficiently pleaded relatedness by alleging common features of a scheme to distribute and sell counterfeit surgical mesh, including the method, fraudulent purpose, results, participants, and method of commission); Jones v. Deutsche Bank AG, 2005 WL 1683614, at *4 (N.D. Cal. July 19, 2005) (holding that plaintiff sufficiently alleged pattern); Anderson v. Smithfield Foods, Inc., 207 F. Supp. 2d 1358, 1363 (M.D. Fla. 2002); Maryland-Nat'l Capital Park & Planning Comm'n v. Boyle, 203 F. Supp. 2d 468, 475 (D. Md. 2002), *aff'd*, 2003 WL 1879017 (4th Cir. Apr. 16, 2003); Meyer Material Co. v. Mooshol, 188 F. Supp. 2d 936, 941 (N.D. Ill. 2002) (relationship element satisfied when acts related to common purpose of embezzlement); Wilson v. De Angelis, 156 F. Supp. 2d 1335, 1340 (S.D. Fla. 2001) (fraud in connection with ten purchases of gold bullion coins over ten-month period was sufficiently related for purposes of fulfilling pattern element); Dempsey v. Sanders, 132 F. Supp. 2d 222, 227 (S.D.N.Y. 2001); Ifill v. West, 1999 U.S. Dist. LEXIS 21320, at *19 (E.D.N.Y. Aug. 24, 1999) (when refinancing and foreclosure scheme designed to acquire inflated, federally-insured mortgages had common participants and common goals, relationship established).

150 United States v. Eufrasio, 935 F.2d 553, 565 (3d Cir. 1991) (finding requirement met, affirming defendants' convictions).

151 For example, in Brown v. Coleman Investments, Inc., 993 F. Supp. 416, 430 (M.D. La. 1998), the court took a miserly view of the pattern requirement, finding that there is no pattern of racketeering activity if the alleged acts are part of the usual endeavors of the enterprise; thus, a RICO claim could not be based on a loan funded by an enterprise to a dealer even though the loan necessarily included funding upcharges for license fees and taxes wrongfully charged by the dealer. *See also* Proctor v. Metro. Money Store Corp., 645 F. Supp. 2d 464, 480–481 (D. Md. 2009) (relationship properly met when plaintiffs alleged that foreclosure rescue scam's predicate acts had similar purpose of stripping homeowners' equity and the same methods of commission); Maryland-Nat'l Capital Park & Planning Comm'n v. Boyle, 203 F. Supp. 2d 468, 476 (D. Md. 2002) (suggesting caution about finding RICO claims in episodes of "garden variety fraud") (citations omitted), *aff'd*, 2003 WL

7.3.3.6 Factors Facilitating Proof of a Pattern

Although the "pattern" and "enterprise" elements of a RICO claim are distinct and each must be independently proven, the same evidence may prove both.[152] In addition, most courts hold that a plaintiff need not be injured by a practice to plead it as part of the pattern of racketeering activity,[153] so long as the plaintiff otherwise meets the requirement of injury to business or property.[154]

7.3.4 *Collection of an Unlawful Debt*

Attorneys can easily overlook the "collection of an unlawful debt" method of violation as an alternative to the other covered RICO method, pattern of racketeering activity.[155] An unlawful debt is defined to include a usurious debt that is unenforceable in whole or in part as to interest or principal and that bears an interest rate of at least twice the enforceable rate.[156]

Virtually all usury laws specify that usurious loans are unenforceable, at least as to the portion of interest exceeding the enforceable rate. Consequently, the key to proving a RICO violation based on collection of an unlawful debt is showing that a creditor collected a debt when the interest rate exceeded twice the enforceable rate.[157] Violating a lending law is not enough—the law must set a maximum amount of interest that can be charged and the creditor must have charged more than twice that set amount. Collection of an unlawful debt thus cannot be based merely on violations of laws dealing with the method of collecting interest or the kind of property that can be received for a loan.[158] Counsel should be careful to identify and plead the specific interest rates.[159]

Showing that a lender charged more than twice the permissible amount of a specific component of the overall interest rate may not suffice to meet the element. A RICO claim has been disallowed based on a mortgage lender's practice of charging more than twice the legally allowable points on a mortgage loan, because the total amount charged was not more than twice the legally permissible interest rate of 24%.[160] The court held that charging more than twice the allowable points was not twice the allowable "rate." In another case, the court dismissed federal and state RICO claims by mortgagors against their lenders because, although the first month's interest rate exceeded the permitted percentage, the interest calculated over the life of the loan did not.[161] An action can proceed if the total of all interest-related charges (as opposed to a single component) is twice the allowable rate.[162] In addition to alleging an excessive rate, the action must also allege that the usurious debt is unenforceable.[163]

Collection of an unlawful debt may apply in the following situations:

- If a rent-to-own transaction is treated under state law as a disguised credit transaction, the imputed interest rate (calculated by assigning a fair market value for the appliance and dividing lease payments between principal and interest) will probably exceed twice the allowed rate.[164]

1879017 (4th Cir. Apr. 16, 2003); Majchrowski v. Norwest Mortg., 6 F. Supp. 2d 946, 946 (N.D. Ill. 1998) (describing plaintiff's claim that mortgagee imposed fraudulent fees against mortgagors as illustrating that "the line between civil RICO, a formidable weapon authorizing treble damages and attorney fees, and conventional breach of contract actions, has faded considerably").

152 United States v. Turkette, 452 U.S. 576, 582–583 (1981); United States v. Qaoud, 777 F.2d 1105, 1115 (6th Cir. 1985); United States v. Mazzei, 700 F.2d 85, 89 (2d Cir. 1983); United States v. Bagnariol, 665 F.2d 877, 890, 891 (9th Cir. 1981); United States v. Perholtz, 657 F. Supp. 603 (D.D.C. 1988). *See also* § 7.4, *infra.*

153 Marshall v. Ilsley Trust Co. v. Pate, 819 F.2d 806, 809 (7th Cir. 1987); Town of Kearney v. Hudson Meadows Urban Renewal Corp., 829 F.2d 1263, 1268 (3d Cir. 1987).

154 *See* § 7.6, *infra.*

155 *See* Ukwuoma v. Marine, No. CV-85-6557 DWW (KX), 6 RICO L. Rep. 94,220 (C.D. Cal. verdict June 9, 1987) ($1.1 million for collection of unlawful debt and pattern of lender fraud involving 36% loan to restaurant owners).

156 *See* Merly v. D'Arcangelo, 1992 WL 11182, at *1 (Conn. Super. Ct. Jan. 16, 1992) (finding pleading sufficient when it alleged that lender was associated with Gambino crime family, that each defendant was engaged in interstate commerce, and that notes called for usurious interest (104%); note that a plaintiff should also plead that the usury laws affect the enforceability of the loans). *Cf.* Goldenstein v. Repossessors, Inc., 2014 WL 3535112, at *8 (E.D. Pa. July 17, 2014) (repossession of collateral is not collection of an unlawful debt).

157 Bellizan v. Easy Money of La., Inc., 2002 WL 1611648, at *6 (E.D. La. July 19, 2002) (rejecting argument that, when loan was illegally split into two transactions to avoid interest rate limitations, allowable interest on second loan was zero for purposes of RICO's interest rate element). *See* Hernandez v. Vanderbilt Mortg. & Fin., Inc., 2010 WL 3359559, at *11 (S.D. Tex. Aug. 25, 2010) (debt not unlawful when stated interest rate was lower than state maximum); Dimas v. Vanderbilt Mortg. & Fin., Inc., 2010 WL 3342216, at *11 (S.D. Tex. Aug. 25, 2010) (same as *Hernandez*); Soto v. Vanderbilt Mortg. & Fin., Inc., 2010 WL 3363657, at *11 (S.D. Tex. Aug. 23, 2010) (same as *Hernandez*).

158 Sundance Land Corp. v. Community First Fed. Sav. & Loan Ass'n, 840 F.2d 653, 666, 667 (9th Cir. 1988). *See also* Montclair v. L.O.I., Inc., 246 Fed. Appx. 535, 537 (9th Cir. Sept. 4, 2007) (affirming dismissal of RICO claim based on collection agency's pursuit of bad check charges; ruling that collection agency was not subject to statutory restrictions on bad check penalties that applied to payday lenders, notwithstanding that the agency took the assignment of the debt from a payday lender); Klein v. U.S. Bank, N.A., 2010 WL 703255, at *2 (M.D. Pa. Feb. 25, 2010) (dismissing RICO claim based on alleged illegal foreclosure on plaintiff's home).

159 *See* Day v. DB Capital Grp., L.L.C., 2011 WL 887554, at *14 (D. Md. Mar. 11, 2011) (dismissing claim when plaintiff failed to identify specific interest rate or other facts that would indicate usury).

160 Reidy v. Meritor Sav., 888 F.2d 898 (table), 1989 WL 132673, at *1 (D.C. Cir. 1989).

161 Johnson v. Fleet Fin., Inc., 785 F. Supp. 1003, 1010 (S.D. Ga. 1992).

162 *See* Nolen v. Nucentrix Broadband Networks, Inc., 293 F.3d 926, 929 (5th Cir. 2002) (late fee not interest under Texas law).

163 Cannarozzi v. Fiumara, 371 F.3d 1, 6 (1st Cir. 2004) (because the allegedly unlawful loans could be enforced through an exception to the usury laws, they could not support plaintiff's RICO claims).

164 *See* Starks v. Rent-A-Center, 1990 U.S. Dist. LEXIS 20099 (D. Minn. May 15, 1990), *aff'd on other grounds*, 58 F.3d 358 (8th Cir. 1995); Miller v. Colortyme, Inc., 518 N.W.2d 544, 548 (Minn. 1994) (Minnesota's usury statute applies to rent-to-own contracts); Fogie v. Rent-A-Center, Inc., 518 N.W.2d 544, 548 (Minn. 1994) (rent-to-own contracts are consumer credit sales under Minnesota law).

- Interest hidden or mislabeled in a sham "post-dated check-cashing" loan scheme may increase the relevant effective interest rate.[165]
- If a house sale and lease-back arrangement can be treated instead as a direct loan with an imputed interest rate, the effective rate may significantly exceed the allowable rate.[166]
- A number of installment sales acts only allow creditors to exceed the general usury rate (for example, 8%) with a higher rate (for example, 18%) only when the installment sales act is complied with. Failure to comply should make the general rate, and not the higher installment sales rate, the "enforceable" rate for purposes of RICO.
- Federal law allows manufactured-home lenders to charge rates far in excess of the rate allowed by state usury law, but only if the creditor complies with certain OTS regulations; noncompliance returns the transaction to the state usury rate.[167]
- If hidden interest, such as fictitious fees, broker's commissions, inflation of the cash sales price for credit customers, or points are treated as interest under state law, the actual rate may exceed twice the allowable rate.[168]
- When an auto pawnbroker or other pawnbroker incorrectly believes that state usury rates do not apply, the customer may be charged effective interest rates as high as 200 or 300%, likely far in excess of twice the permissible rate.[169]

- When a creditor thinks it is not, but actually is, covered by a state credit limit, the creditor may exceed twice the enforceable rate.[170]

The RICO statute prohibits four different types of relationships with an enterprise through either of the two violation methods: a pattern of racketeering activity or the collection of an unlawful debt.[171] The grammar of the RICO statute makes clear that the pattern requirement applies only to racketeering activity and not to collection of an unlawful debt. As a result, one instance of collection of an unlawful debt should be enough to trigger liability, if the plaintiff establishes one of the four prohibited relationships between the defendant's debt collection and the enterprise.[172]

Accordingly, the plaintiff should not have to show that the defendant was in the business of collecting unlawful debts; an occasional instance of loansharking should suffice.[173] While a state appellate court has held otherwise,[174] the state's supreme court made a special effort to point out the error of that holding.[175]

7.4 The "Enterprise"

7.4.1 General

To prove a RICO violation, a plaintiff must establish more than a pattern of racketeering activity or collection of an unlawful debt. The plaintiff must connect the illegal conduct

---

165 *See* Cashback Catalog Sales, Inc. v. Price, 102 F. Supp. 2d 1375, 1380 (S.D. Ga. 2000) (denying summary judgment to defendant who took post-dated checks in return for a reduced amount of cash plus an allegedly valueless certificate to a mail-order catalog company for the difference); Arrington v. Colleen, Inc., 2000 WL 34001056, at *6 (D. Md. Aug. 7, 2000) (denying lender's motion for summary judgment); Burden v. York, Clearinghouse No. 52,502, No. 98-268 (E.D. Ky. Sept. 29, 1999); Hamilton v. HLT Check Exch., 987 F. Supp. 953, 957–958 (E.D. Ky. 1997) (denying the motion of defendant, a check cashing business, to dismiss RICO claim alleging the collection of an unlawful debt). *See also* Henry v. Cash Today, Inc., 199 F.R.D. 566, 572–573 (S.D. Tex. 2000) (class certification granted in cash back ad sale case); National Consumer Law Center, Foreclosures and Mortgage Servicing Ch. 18 (4th ed. 2012), *updated at* www.nclc.org/library.

166 *In re* Eyler, 2008 WL 4833096, at *4–5 (Bankr. D. Md. Oct. 28, 2008) (amended proposed findings of fact and conclusions of law) (awarding damages in foreclosure rescue scheme). *See* Proctor v. Metropolitan Money Store Corp., 645 F. Supp. 2d 464, 481–482 (D. Md. 2009) (construing a foreclosure rescue arrangement as creating an equitable mortgage under Maryland law and characterizing rent as interest. Accordingly, sellers stated a class action RICO claim for collection of an unlawful debt by alleging that the loans made entailed interest in excess of twice Maryland's usury limit).

167 *See* National Consumer Law Center, Consumer Credit Regulation § 3.7 (2d ed. 2015), *updated at* www.nclc.org/library.

168 National Consumer Law Center, Consumer Credit Regulation Ch. 5 (2d ed. 2015), *updated at* www.nclc.org/library. *See also* Faircloth v. Certified Fin. Inc., 2001 U.S. Dist. LEXIS 6793 (E.D. La. May 15, 2001) (approving settlement agreement in class action that alleged defendants flipped loans to impose excessive interest). *But see* Rivera v. AT&T Corp., 141 F. Supp. 2d 719, 723–725 (S.D. Tex. 2001) (since late fee was not interest under state law, no usury that would establish collection of an unlawful debt), *aff'd without op.*, 2002 WL 663707 (5th Cir. Mar. 25, 2002).

169 *See* Burnett v. Ala Moana Pawn Shop, Clearinghouse No. 46,771 (D. Haw. 1991) (RICO not pleaded), *aff'd*, 3 F.3d 1261 (9th Cir. 1993).

170 *See* National Consumer Law Center, Consumer Credit Regulation § 3.9 (2d ed. 2015), *updated at* www.nclc.org/library. *But see* State v. Roderick, 704 So. 2d 49, 54 (Miss. 1997) (holding Mississippi RICO statute void for vagueness as applied to a criminal prosecution of check cashing business for violation of usury law).

171 18 U.S.C. § 1962(a)–(d).

172 *See* United States v. Oreto, 37 F.3d 739 (1st Cir. 1994) (unlawful debt section does not require pattern—this does not render the statute unconstitutional); Ballen v. Prudential Bache Sec., 23 F.3d 335 (10th Cir. 1994); United States v. Weiner, 3 F.3d 17 (1st Cir. 1993); Davis v. Mutual Life Ins. Co. of N.Y., 6 F.3d 367 (6th Cir. 1993); United States v. Giovanelli, 945 F.2d 479 (2d Cir. 1991) (only single collection of unlawful debt need be proved); Eyler v. 3 Vista Court L.L.C., 2008 WL 4844962, at *3 (D. Md. Aug. 26, 2008) (a plaintiff need not demonstrate a pattern of collection of an unlawful debt).

173 *See, e.g.,* Cashback Catalog Sales, Inc. v. Price, 102 F. Supp. 2d 1375 (S.D. Ga. 2000) (denying summary judgment on RICO claim); Arrington v. Colleen, Inc., 2000 WL 34001056, at *7 (D. Md. Aug. 7, 2000) (denying lender's motion for summary judgment); Burden v. York, Clearinghouse No. 52,502, No. 98-268 (E.D. Ky. Sept. 29, 1999); Hamilton v. HLT Check Exch., 987 F. Supp. 953 (E.D. Ky. 1997) (denying the motion of defendant, a check-cashing business, to dismiss RICO claim alleging the collection of an unlawful debt). *See also* Henry v. Cash Today, Inc., 199 F.R.D. 566 (S.D. Tex. 2000) (class certification granted in cash back ad sale case). *But see* Cannarozzi v. Fiumara, 371 F.3d 1, 4 n.4 (1st Cir. 2004); Wright v. Sheppard, 919 F.2d 665 (11th Cir. 1990); Durante Bros. & Sons, Inc. v. Flushing Nat'l Bank, 755 F.2d 239 (2d Cir. 1985); Weisel v. Pischel, 197 F.R.D. 231 (E.D.N.Y. 2000); Robidoux v. Conti, 741 F. Supp. 1019 (D.R.I. 1990).

174 Bandas v. Citizens State Bank of Silver Lake, 412 N.W.2d 818, 821 (Minn. Ct. App. 1987), *remanded on other grounds sub nom.* VanderWeyst v. First State Bank, 425 N.W.2d 803 (Minn. 1988).

175 425 N.W.2d 803 (Minn. 1988).

to an "enterprise." In *Scheidler*, the Supreme Court characterized the "enterprise" as the vehicle through which the unlawful pattern of racketeering is committed.[176] The exact nature of that connection is discussed at § 7.5, *infra*, including such connections as investing the income from the illegal conduct in the enterprise, using the illegal activity to control the enterprise, or participating in the enterprise's affairs through the illegal activity. This section examines the requirements for the consumer as to pleading an enterprise.

Enterprise includes "any individual, partnership, corporation, or other legal entity, and any . . . group of individuals associated in fact although not a legal entity."[177] This is a broad definition, and courts construe the term broadly.[178]

Because of the difficulty of proving injury under the other subsections of section 1962,[179] most RICO litigation is brought under RICO § 1962(c). However, that subsection requires that the enterprise be distinct from the defendant.[180] This may mean that the corporate defendant conducting the fraud cannot also be the enterprise. In addition, courts have held that the same entity cannot be both a RICO claimant and the RICO enterprise.[181] In practice, this frequently means that the plaintiff, in designating an enterprise, must rely on the last item in the definition of enterprise: "any union or group of individuals associated in fact although not a legal entity." The corporate wrongdoer is the defendant and an association in fact of related entities is the enterprise.

An association in fact is "a group of persons associated together for a common purpose of engaging in a course of conduct."[182] To show an association in fact, a plaintiff must allege both component entities (the associates) and a relationship among those entities (the association).

7.4.2 Entities Making Up an "Association in Fact"

A group of corporations can be an association in fact,[183] as can a group of individuals associated with several corporations.[184] An institution and its customer may form an association in fact: one court concluded that a lender had worked closely enough with a development company it financed to create an association in fact enterprise.[185]

An association in fact enterprise may include non-culpable associates that do not have a criminal purpose in common with the other entities included in the enterprise.[186] A complaint that names a discreet and specific number of constituents to the enterprise, as opposed to an amorphous group as a whole (such as all members of the secondary market), is more likely to succeed.[187]

7.4.3 Level of Association Necessary for an Association in Fact

7.4.3.1 Introduction

Once a plaintiff has identified the associates, the plaintiff must show an association among them to establish an association in fact enterprise. In *United States v. Turkette*,[188] the Supreme Court concluded that such an enterprise is "proved by evidence of an ongoing organization, formal or informal,

---

176 Nat'l Org. for Women v. Scheidler, 510 U.S. 249, 259, 114 S. Ct. 748, 804, 127 L. Ed. 2d 99, 109 (1994).

177 18 U.S.C. § 1961(4).

178 United States v. Connolly, 341 F.3d 16, 28 (1st Cir. 2003) (upholding conviction of FBI agent); Pruitt v. County of Sacramento, 2010 WL 3717302, at *3 (E.D. Cal. Sept. 15, 2010) (governmental drug task force can be RICO enterprise). *See also* SKS Constructors, Inc. v. Drinkwine, 458 F. Supp. 2d 68, 79 (E.D.N.Y. 2006) (ruling that allegations of an enterprise sufficed to withstand a motion to dismiss); World Wrestling Entm't, Inc. v. Jakks Pac., Inc., 425 F. Supp. 2d 484, 493–495 (S.D.N.Y. 2006) (stating that the pattern of racketeering activity alleged can itself suffice to establish an enterprise), *aff'd*, 328 Fed. Appx. 695 (2d Cir. 2009).

179 *See* § 7.6, *infra*.

180 *See* § 7.4.4, *infra*.

181 Jaguar Cars v. Royal Oaks Motor Car Co., 46 F.3d 258, 267 (3d Cir. 1995); Simon Prop. Grp., Inc. v. Palombaro, 2009 WL 1549293, at *5 (W.D. Pa. June 2, 2009).

182 United States v. Turkette, 452 U.S. 576, 583 (1981).

183 *See, e.g.*, United States v. Philip Morris USA Inc., 566 F.3d 1095, 1112 (D.C. Cir. 2009) (association in fact enterprise may comprise corporations), *order clarified*, 778 F. Supp. 2d 8 (D.D.C. 2011); Shearin v. E.F. Hutton Grp., Inc., 885 F.2d 1162, 1165 (3d Cir. 1989). *See also* Smith v. Bank of Am. Home Loans, 968 F. Supp. 2d 1159, 1169 (M.D. Fla. 2013) (mortgagee bank, and Mortgage Electronic Registration System of which the bank was a member, could together constitute a RICO enterprise). *But see* Roberts v. Heim, 670 F. Supp. 1466 (N.D. Cal. 1987) (association in fact can only comprise of natural persons).

184 United States v. London, 66 F.3d 1227, 1244 (1st Cir. 1995) (business owner can be enterprise with corporation); Ocean Energy II, Inc. v. Alexander & Alexander, Inc., 868 F.2d 740 (5th Cir. 1989) (individuals and corporations who attempted to sell worthless and illegal insurance policies on at least one occasion may be deemed association in fact); United States v. Perholtz, 842 F.2d 343, 353 (D.C. Cir. 1988) (association in fact enterprise can be a mixed group of individuals, corporations, and partnerships); United States v. Thevis, 665 F.2d 616, 625, 626 (5th Cir. 1982). *See also* United States v. Benny, 786 F.2d 1410 (9th Cir. 1986) (sole proprietor can associate with enterprise consisting of sole proprietorship and other individuals working for the proprietorship); American Manufacturers' Mut. Ins. Co. v. Townson, 912 F. Supp. 291 (E.D. Tenn. 1995) (marriage can be an enterprise/association in fact for insurance fraud purposes); Allstate Ins. Co. v. A.M. Pugh Associates, Inc., 604 F. Supp. 85, 100 (M.D. Pa. 1984) (memorandum). *But see* Foval v. First Nat'l Bank of Commerce in New Orleans, 841 F.2d 126 (5th Cir. 1988) (no association in fact if no continuing relationship).

185 Rodriguez v. Banco Cent., 777 F. Supp. 1043 (D. P.R. 1991), *aff'd on other grounds*, 990 F.2d 7 (1st Cir. 1993).

186 United States v. Cianci, 210 F. Supp. 2d 71, 73–75 (D.R.I. 2002) (a legitimate organization, such as a city agency, may be a non-culpable member of a RICO enterprise operated by a defendant for criminal purposes).

187 *See, e.g.*, VanDenBroeck v. CommonPoint Mortg. Co., 210 F.3d 696, 700 (6th Cir. 2000); Dirt Hogs, Inc. v. Natural Gas Pipeline Co., 2000 U.S. App. LEXIS 6463, at *9 (10th Cir. Apr. 10, 2000) (criticizing allegations of a string of participants, known and unknown, as a "moving target" approach); Richmond v. Nationwide Cassel L.P. 52 F.3d 640, 645 (7th Cir. 1995) ("a nebulous, open-ended description of the enterprise does not sufficiently identify this essential element").

188 452 U.S. 576, 583, 101 S. Ct. 2524, 2528 (1981) (entity is proved by existence of an ongoing organization, formal or informal, and by evidence that the various associates function as a continuing unit).

and by evidence that the various associates function as a continuing unit."[189] In 2009, the Supreme Court in *Boyle v. United States* loosened the definition of an association in fact enterprise.[190] In *Boyle*, the Court emphasized the "breadth of the 'enterprise' concept in RICO."[191] The Court agreed that an association in fact enterprise must have a structure and then looked to common dictionary definitions of "structure": "In the sense relevant here, the term 'structure' means '[t]he way in which parts are arranged or put together to form a whole' and '[t]he interrelation or arrangement of parts in a complex entity.' "[192] To satisfy this definition of structure, an association in fact enterprise must have three structural features: (1) a purpose; (2) relationships among those associated with the enterprise; and (3) longevity sufficient to permit these associates to pursue the enterprise's purpose.[193] However, the Court reasoned from *Turkette* that the enterprise could be "loosely and informally organized" while still having the requisite structure.[194]

The Court identified features that the structure of an enterprise did *not* need to have: (1) it does not need a leader; (2) it does not need to have a hierarchy; and (3) it does not need to have a long-term master plan or agreement.[195] Furthermore, a court's instructions to the jury need not include the word "structure."[196] Rather, the Court approved of the *Boyle* trial court's instructions that, "in order to establish the existence of such an enterprise, the Government had to prove that: '(1) There [was] an ongoing organization with some sort of framework, formal or informal, for carrying out its objectives; and (2) the various members and associates of the association function[ed] as a continuing unit to achieve a common purpose.' "[197]

The petitioner, who was the criminal defendant below, objected to the trial court's instruction that the jury could " 'find an enterprise where an association of individuals, without structural hierarchy, form[ed] solely for the purpose of carrying out a pattern of racketeering acts' and that '[c]ommon sense suggests that the existence of an association

in fact is oftentimes more readily proven by what it does, rather than by abstract analysis of its structure.' "[198] The Supreme Court, however, approved the lower court's language, noting the broad discretion that trial court judges have in framing instructions.[199] In fact, the Court cautioned that a trial judge should not instruct a jury that it must find an "ascertainable" structure in order to conclude that an association in fact enterprise existed.[200]

7.4.3.2 The Enterprise's "Ongoing Organization"

Under *Boyle*, to show that an association in fact enterprise has some sort of ongoing organization, a plaintiff must show that the enterprise has the following three structural features: (1) a purpose; (2) relationships among those associated with the enterprise; and (3) longevity sufficient to permit these associates to pursue the enterprise's purpose.[201] However, the association in fact need not have a structural hierarchy, a chain of command, or any kind of dues, rules, or rituals.[202] Rather, "decisions may be made on an *ad hoc* basis and by any number of methods—by majority vote, consensus, a show of strength, etc."[203] Members of the group need not have fixed roles; different members may perform different roles at different times.[204] *Boyle* appears to override the decisions of other courts that required the plaintiff to show that the enterprise had a hierarchical or consensual decision-making structure with evidence of a chain of command or similar evidence.[205] Subsequent to

---

189 *Id.* at 580, 583.

190 Boyle v. United States, 129 S. Ct. 2237 (2009).

191 *Id.* at 2246.

192 *Id.* at 2244 (citing American Heritage Dictionary 1718 (4th ed. 2000)).

193 *Id.*

194 *Id.* at 2241, 2244, 2246 (affirming the petitioner's conviction).

195 *Id.* at 2241, 2246 (affirming the petitioner's conviction notwithstanding that the association in fact enterprise in which he was a member had none of these features). *See also* United States v. Henley, 766 F.3d 893, 906–907 (8th Cir. 2014) (stating that, in a criminal RICO case, prosecution must show "(1) a common or shared purpose that animates the individuals associated with it, (2) a formal or informal organization of the participants in which they function as a unit, including some continuity of both structure and personnel, and (3) an ascertainable structure distinct from that inherent in the conduct of a pattern of racketeering activity"); Sykes v. Mel Harris & Associates, L.L.C., 757 F. Supp. 2d 413, 426 (S.D.N.Y. 2010) (allegation that entity was "formed for the common purpose of securing default judgments through fraudulent means" sufficient to allege enterprise), *class action certification aff'd*, 780 F.3d 70 (2d Cir. 2015).

196 Boyle v. United States, 129 S. Ct. 2237, 2244 (2009).

197 *Id.* at 2242.

198 *Id.*

199 *Id.* at 2244.

200 *Id.* at 2244–2245.

      The Court reasoned that, "[w]henever a jury is told that it must find the existence of an element beyond a reasonable doubt, that element must be 'ascertainable' or else the jury could not find that it was proved. Therefore, telling the members of the jury that they had to ascertain the existence of an 'ascertainable structure' would have been redundant and potentially misleading." *Id.*

201 Boyle v. United States, 129 S. Ct. 2237, 2244 (2009).

202 *Id.* at 2245.

203 *Id.*

204 *Id.*

205 *See, e.g.*, Wagh v. Metris Direct, Inc., 363 F.3d 821 (9th Cir. 2003); VanDenBroeck v. CommonPoint Mortg. Co., 210 F.3d 696, 700 (6th Cir. 2000); Simon v. Value Behavioral Health, Inc., 208 F.3d 1073, 1083 (9th Cir. 2000) (allegations that merely show collaboration or collective activity will not support enterprise element); Chang v. Chen, 80 F.3d 1293, 1295 (9th Cir. 1996) (dismissing complaint that did not allege a "system of authority" among the members of the association in fact); Crowe v. Henry, 43 F.3d 198, 205 (5th Cir. 1995) (association in fact enterprise must have an existence separate and apart from the pattern of racketeering, must be an ongoing organization, and have members that function as a continuing unit as shown by a hierarchical or consensual decision making structure); Landry v. Air Line Pilots Ass'n Int'l AFL-CIO, 901 F.2d 404 (5th Cir. 1990); Wooley v. Jackson Hewitt, Inc., 540 F. Supp. 2d 964, 975 (N.D. Ill. 2008) (in suit against tax preparation company, dismissing claim when plaintiff failed to allege a "command structure" separate and distinct from defendants themselves); Cedar Swamp Holdings, Inc. v. Zaman, 487 F. Supp. 2d 444 (S.D.N.Y. 2007) (alleged "hub and spoke" structure did not suffice to satisfy structure element of enterprise); German Free State of Bavaria v. Toyobo Co., Ltd., 480 F. Supp. 2d 958, 967–968 (W.D. Mich. 2007)

Boyle, lower court decisions have applied a relaxed construction of the structural requirement.[206]

Even prior to *Boyle*, several courts of appeal rejected the idea that a plaintiff must show a decision-making framework and have allowed less formal associations to suffice as enterprises.[207] Under these decisions, to establish an enterprise, the plaintiff need only show "evidence of an ongoing organization, formal or informal," and "evidence that the various associates function as a continuing unit."[208] Furthermore, the purpose of the enterprise need not align perfectly with the purposes of the members of the enterprise.[209]

It appears that *Boyle* did not impact decisions that concluded that a plaintiff can use evidence of acts other than predicate offenses to demonstrate the decision-making framework of the association in fact.[210] Furthermore, the plaintiff need not prove that the members' whole purpose in organizing together was to engage in *prohibited* conduct, so long as the members intended to engage together in *some* form of conduct.[211]

(plaintiff failed to establish a structure for the enterprise alleged); Progressive N. Ins. Co. v. Alivio Chiropractic Clinic, Inc., 2005 WL 3526581, at *3 (D. Minn. Dec. 22, 2005) (plaintiff successfully alleged an enterprise comprising defendants along with others that engaged in a scheme to defraud plaintiff, an insurance company); State Farm Mut. Auto Ins. Co. v. Giventer, 212 F. Supp. 2d 639, 650 (N.D. Tex. 2002); *In re* Mastercard Int'l Inc., 132 F. Supp. 2d 468, 484–485 (E.D. La. 2001) (enterprise must have an existence separate from the pattern itself; test is whether enterprise would continue if pattern of racketeering ceased), *aff'd*, 313 F.3d 257 (5th Cir. 2003).

206   *See, e.g.*, Slorp v. Lerner, Sampson & Rothfuss, 587 Fed. Appx. 249, 265–266 (6th Cir. 2014) (plaintiff, who alleged fraudulent scheme to wrongfully foreclose on his home, adequately alleged an enterprise among a bank, its law firm, and Mortgage Electronic Registration Systems, Inc.; reversing dismissal of his RICO claim); United States v. Hutchinson, 573 F.3d 1011 (10th Cir. 2009) (affirming criminal conviction when trial court's jury instructions were nearly identical to those in *Boyle*); Javier v. Beck, 2014 WL 3058456, at *7 (S.D.N.Y. July 3, 2014) ("[t]he Complaint is spare regarding the interrelationship of the various corporate defendants and their roles in the enterprise . . . the unity of ownership and purpose across a four-year period is sufficient to allege the existence of a RICO enterprise"); Llewellyn-Jones v. Metro Prop. Grp., LLC, 22 F. Supp. 3d 760, 791–792 (E.D. Mich. 2014) (enterprise sufficiently pleaded by alleging that defendants had a common purpose to defraud investors, along with a relationship to supply forged documents, false information, and eviction records); Hale v. State Farm Mut. Auto. Ins. Co., 2013 WL 1287054, at *16 (S.D. Ill. Mar. 28, 2013) (refusing to dismiss RICO claim that alleged that defendant and others created an enterprise that had the goal of electing a specific justice to the Illinois Supreme Court in order to obtain the reversal of a $1.06 billion judgment); Fremont Reorganizing Corp. v. Duke, 811 F. Supp. 2d 1323, 1337–1338 (E.D. Mich. 2011) (denying motion to dismiss, reasoning that plaintiff alleged that the enterprise functioned as a continuing unit); Beta Health Alliance MD PA v. Kelley Witherspoon L.L.P., 2009 WL 2195882 (N.D. Tex. July 22, 2009) (plaintiffs properly alleged an association in fact enterprise by claiming "that there is an ongoing organization with a continuity of structure and a shared purpose"); McNulty v. Reddy Ice Holdings, Inc., 2009 WL 2168231, at *4 (E.D. Mich. July 17, 2009) (plaintiff adequately pleaded facts sufficient to allege an association in fact enterprise under *Boyle*'s construction); *In re* Nat'l W. Life Ins. Deferred Annuities Litig., 635 F. Supp. 2d 1170 (S.D. Cal. 2009) (plaintiff had supplied facts adequate to show that alleged enterprise's participants had a common purpose, rejecting argument that participants "must share all of their purposes in common"). *See also* Mayfield v. Asta Funding, Inc., 2015 WL 1501100, at *10 (S.D.N.Y. Mar. 31, 2015) (plaintiffs, who each had stale default judgments filed against them, sufficiently pleaded an enterprise comprising a debt-buying company, its subsidiary, a law firm, attorneys, and other individuals whom plaintiffs alleged had each played a role in a scheme to fraudulently collect default judgments); Liberty Mut. Fire Ins. Co. v. Acute Care Chiropractic Clinic P.A., 88 F. Supp. 3d 985, 1002–1003 (D. Minn. 2015) (plaintiffs sufficiently alleged " 'existence of an enterprise that extend[s] beyond the minimal association surrounding the pattern of racketeering activity' ") (citation omitted)); De Sole v. Knoedler Gallery, L.L.C., 974 F. Supp. 2d 274, 301 (S.D.N.Y. 2013) (plaintiffs sufficiently alleged an enterprise comprising several different individuals who joined together to sell forged artworks); Coleman v. Commonwealth Land Title Ins. Co., 684 F. Supp. 2d 595, 612–613 (E.D. Pa. 2010) (contractual arrangement between defendant title company and its title agents helped establish an association in fact enterprise that had as its common purpose the deliberate overstating to insureds of the amount due on title insurance). *But see* Brink v. Cont'l Ins. Co., 787 F.3d 1120, 1127 (D.C. Cir. 2015) (ruling that plaintiffs'

claims were preempted, but also concluding that they failed to establish required elements of a RICO enterprise); Crichton v. Golden Rule Ins. Co., 576 F.3d 392, 400 (7th Cir. 2009) (concluding that plaintiff had failed to adequately establish that intended enterprise had an organizational hierarchy or structure); *In re* Trilegiant Corp., Inc., 11 F. Supp. 3d 82, 98–99 (D. Conn2014) (concluding that, even after *Boyle*, allegations of a "hub-and-spoke" organization fail to allege an enterprise without some allegations of coordinated behavior among the "spokes"); Rocha v. FedEx Corp., 15 F. Supp. 3d 796, 806–807 (N.D. Ill. Jan. 17, 2014) (plaintiffs failed to allege a RICO enterprise among various related corporate entities of a home package delivery "corporate family" because they failed to allege either a RICO purpose or adequate structure of the enterprise).

207   *See, e.g.*, Odom v. Microsoft Corp., 486 F.3d 541 (9th Cir. 2007); United States v. Patrick, 248 F.3d 11, 19 (1st Cir. 2001); United States v. Perholtz, 842 F.2d 343, 354 (D.C. Cir. 1988) (concluding that enterprise is "established by common purpose among the participants, organization, and continuity"); United States v. Bagaric, 706 F.2d 42, 56 (2d Cir. 1983), *abrogated on other grounds by* Nat'l Org. for Women, Inc. v. Scheidler, 510 U.S. 249, 114 S. Ct. 798, 127 L. Ed. 2d 99 (1994); United States v. Cagnina, 697 F.2d 915, 921 (11th Cir. 1983) (the enterprise need not have a distinct, formalized structure).

208   Odom v. Microsoft Corp., 486 F.3d 541 (9th Cir. 2007) (concluding that plaintiffs had sufficiently demonstrated an enterprise comprising Best Buy and Microsoft to fraudulently charge Best Buy customers for MSN Internet accounts). *See also* Newcal Industries, Inc. v. Ikon Office Solution, 513 F.3d 1038, 1056 (9th Cir. 2008) (plaintiff need not allege or prove a separate organizational structure).

209   Williams v. Mohawk Indus., Inc., 465 F.3d 1277, 1285–1286 (11th Cir. 2006) (stating that "there has never been any requirement that the 'common purpose' of the enterprise be the sole purpose of each and every member of the enterprise," rejecting the Seventh Circuit's contrary holding in Baker v. IBP, Inc., 357 F.3d 685 (7th Cir. 2004)). *See* Allen *ex rel.* Allen v. Devine, 726 F. Supp. 2d 240, 247 (E.D.N.Y. 2010) (common purpose sufficiently alleged even though individual defendants victimized a corporate member of the enterprise).

210   United States v. Connolly, 341 F.3d 16, 26 (1st Cir. 2003) (testimony of several payments made to FBI agent that were not part of alleged predicate acts supported jury's finding that agent had participated in an ongoing association in fact). *See also* Royal Indem. Co. v. Pepper Hamilton L.L.P., 479 F. Supp. 2d 419, 426 (D. Del. 2007) (plaintiff successfully alleged a RICO enterprise by alleging that one member conducted the business of borrowing money, making loans, and obtaining insurance while others provided the necessary legal and financial advice, guidance, and information).

211   Richmond v. Nationwide Cassel L.P. 52 F.3d 640, 644 (7th Cir. 1995). *See also* Williams v. Mohawk Indus., Inc., 465 F.3d 1277, 1285–1286

7.4.3.3 A Continuing Unit

Boyle v. United States also gives some guidance on the "continuing unit" aspect of an enterprise.[212] The Court provided that, "[w]hile the group must function as a continuing unit and remain in existence long enough to pursue a course of conduct, nothing in RICO exempts an enterprise whose associates engage in spurts of activity punctuated by periods of quiescence."[213] Thus, a plaintiff need not show that the group engaged in an uninterrupted chain of illicit conduct. Associates belonging to an association in fact enterprise may function as a "continuing unit" by "persist[ing] as an identifiable entity through time . . . ."[214] Such continuity can be shown from a pre-existing corporate relationship, such as among a corporation and its parent or subsidiaries.[215] Legitimate associations in fact may serve as enterprises.

7.4.3.4 Relation of Enterprise to the Racketeering Activity

In *Boyle v. United States*,[216] the petitioner argued that the structure of an association in fact enterprise must extend "beyond that inherent in the pattern of racketeering activity in which it engages." The Supreme Court agreed only to the extent that a plaintiff must establish the element of enterprise separate from the element of a pattern of racketeering activity, asserting that "proof of one does not necessarily establish the other."[217] However, the Court rejected the argument that "the existence of an enterprise may never be inferred from the evidence showing that persons associated with the enterprise engaged in a pattern of racketeering activity."[218] Rather, the Court confirmed that "the evidence used to prove the pattern of racketeering activity and the evidence establishing an enterprise 'may in particular cases coalesce.' "[219] Accordingly, although the *association* must exist separate from the pattern of racketeering activity in order to keep the two elements of "enterprise" and "pattern" from collapsing into one, the enterprise need not have *purposes* or *goals* (as opposed to structures) separate from the pattern of racketeering activity.[220] *Boyle* should allow cases to withstand motions to dismiss so long as the plaintiff carefully pleads sufficient facts to satisfy both the pattern and the enterprise elements.[221]

Different circuits approach the enterprise requirement differently, though practitioners should note that pre-*Boyle* pronouncements may be infirm. In analyzing whether the enterprise is separate and apart from the racketeering, the Eighth Circuit asks whether "the enterprise would still exist were the predicate acts removed from the equation."[222] A more conservative

(11th Cir. 2006) (so long as the members of an enterprise share a common purpose, that purpose need not be the sole purpose of each member of the enterprise, disagreeing with Baker v. IBP, Inc., 357 F.3d 685 (7th Cir. 2004)); *In re* Pharmaceutical Indus. Average Wholesale Price Litig., 263 F. Supp. 2d 172, 184 (D. Mass. 2003) (mere awareness by participants in fraudulent scheme that there were others in parallel schemes did not sufficiently establish an association in fact). *Cf.* Craig Outdoor Adver., Inc. v. Viacom Outdoor, Inc., 528 F.3d 1001 (8th Cir. 2008) (declining to decide whether common purpose of the enterprise must be fraudulent; affirming summary judgment for defendants on RICO claim on grounds that plaintiffs failed to demonstrate that members shared a common purpose); Allstate Ins. Co. v. Michael Kent Plambeck, D.C., 2014 WL 1303000, at *3 (N.D. Tex. Mar. 31, 2014) (jury could have reasonably found an enterprise when plaintiffs supplied evidence of a shared common purpose of a "desire to make money" along with evidence of an "existence separate and apart from the alleged racketeering activity" and evidence that the enterprise "functioned as a continuing unit"), *aff'd*, 2015 WL 5472433 (5th Cir. Sept. 17, 2015).

212 Boyle v. United States, 129 S. Ct. 2237, 2245 (2009).

213 *Id. See also* Winger v. Best Buy Co., 2011 WL 995937, at *6 (D. Ariz. Mar. 21, 2011) (twenty-seven months sufficient).

214 Burdett v. Miller, 957 F.2d 1375, 1379 (7th Cir. 1992). *See also* Landry v. Air Line Pilots Ass'n Int'l AFL-CIO, 901 F.2d 404, 433 (5th Cir. 1990) (no continuing unit when the alleged enterprise "briefly flourished and faded"); Cannon v. Wells Fargo Bank N.S., 2014 WL 324556, at *3 (N.D. Cal. Jan. 29, 2014) (insurance company, along with a loan servicer and its associate, functioned as a "continuing unit" to force-place flood and hazard insurance at artificially inflated prices on home mortgagors); Manhattan Telecomms. Corp. v. DialAmerica Mktg., 156 F. Supp. 2d 376, 382 (S.D.N.Y. 2001).

215 *See, e.g., In re* American Investors Life Ins. Co. Annuity Mktg. & Sales Practices Litig., 2007 WL 2541216, at *17 (E.D. Pa. Aug. 29, 2007) (in case alleging that defendants engaged in a fraudulent scheme to sell elders unnecessary and unsuitable estate planning instruments, concluding that plaintiffs sufficiently met second characteristic when they alleged that sales agents and attorneys played specific roles over time); Majchrowski v. Norwest Mortg., Inc. 6 F. Supp. 2d 946, 954 (N.D. Ill. 1998) (plaintiff met characteristic in case alleging that mortgage service company, its parent, and its parent's parent formed an enterprise that the mortgage company used to charge improper fees to borrowers).

216 Boyle v. United States, 129 S. Ct. 2237, 2245 (2009).

217 *Id.* at 2244.

218 *Id.*

219 *Id.*

220 United States v. Phillips, 239 F.3d 829, 844 (7th Cir. 2001). *See also* Crowe v. Clark, 552 Fed. Appx. 796, 800 (10th Cir. 2014) (while failed to properly allege an enterprise, "an enterprise need not exist separate and apart from a pattern of racketeering activity").

221 *See, e.g.,* Burford v. Cargill, Inc., 2011 WL 4382124, at *8 (W.D. La. Sept. 20, 2011) (denying motion to dismiss, citing *Boyle*); Fremont Reorganizing Corp. v. Duke, 811 F. Supp. 2d 1323, 1337–1338 (E.D. Mich. 2011) (denying motion to dismiss when plaintiff alleged that one member, not directly involved in the fraud, had separate standard business operations of managing and renting property).

222 Handeen v. Lemaire, 112 F.3d 1339, 1351–1352 (8th Cir. 1997) (enterprise must have a common or shared purpose, continuity of personnel, and an ascertainable structure distinct from the pattern of racketeering activity). *See also* Crest Const. II, Inc. v. Doe, 660 F.3d 346, 355 (8th Cir. 2011) (granting defendants' motion to dismiss, describing plaintiff's allegations of association as "conclusory"); Kearney v. Dimanna, 195 Fed. Appx. 717, 720–721 (10th Cir. 2006) (no association-in-fact enterprise when the only allegations of association were those forming the wrongful behavior toward plaintiff); Williams Elec. Games, Inc. v. Garrity, 366 F.3d 569, 579 (7th Cir. 2004) (rejecting enterprise comprising briber and the corporation he bribed); Asa-Brandt, Inc. v. ADM Investor Services, Inc., 344 F.3d 738, 752–53 (8th Cir. 2003) (citing *Handeen* in affirming summary judgment for defendants); Harwood v. Int'l Estate Planners, 33 Fed. Appx. 903, 905 (9th Cir. 2002); Crowe v. Henry, 43 F.3d 198, 205 (5th Cir. 1995) (finding enterprise existed beyond the alleged predicate acts); Landry v. Airline Pilots Assoc., 901 F.2d 404 (5th Cir. 1990) (when only purpose is to commit predicate acts, no separate enterprise); Liberty Mut. Fire Ins. Co. v. Acute Care Chiropractic Clinic P.A., 88 F. Supp. 3d 985, 1003–1004 (D. Minn. 2015) (plaintiffs sufficiently alleged an enterprise distinct from racketeering activity; reasoning that enterprise need not have a purpose distinct from the overall fraud and that plaintiffs alleged the enterprise

approach harkens back to the image of a Mafia crime family, looking for evidence that a group engaged in a diverse number of predicate offenses or had an organizational system of authority beyond what was purely necessary to commit the predicate offenses.[223] The Seventh Circuit has noted that criminal gangs "have a less formal, a less reticulated and differentiated structure" than do formal enterprises,[224] concluding that while "[t]here must be some structure . . . there need not be much." In any event, the enterprise need not have had an economic goal that was separate from the commission of the racketeering acts.[225] One court has characterized the correct question as being "not for what purpose the enterprise was formed, but rather . . . whether the structure of the enterprise is definite enough to *enable* it to function as a racketeering organization for other purposes."[226]

Thus, the evidence of illegal activity may serve dual, albeit separate, functions: pattern and enterprise.[227] Enterprise

is proved by evidence that the participants functioned as a continuing unit, while pattern is proved by evidence of the requisite number of acts of racketeering committed by the participants in the enterprise.[228] Accordingly, a plaintiff should not have to offer different evidence to meet the pattern element. Nonetheless, because a plaintiff must show that the organization's structure existed separate from the pattern, plaintiffs should carefully distinguish the function of evidence offered to show the purpose of the enterprise's existence from the function of that same evidence offered to show the racketeering activity itself.[229]

7.4.4 Enterprise Must Be Distinct from Defendant for Section 1962(c) Claims

7.4.4.1 General

RICO § 1962(c) prohibits one "employed by or associated with" an enterprise from "[conducting or participating] . . . in the conduct of such enterprise's affairs" in a defined manner. The other three subsections of 1962 do not have comparable language, and this has led the Supreme Court to construe subsection (c) as imposing a "distinctness" requirement[230] that

---

existed separately from the fraud); Capogreco v. Pro Ins. Agency, Inc., 2007 WL 4510266, at *7 (N.D. Ohio Dec. 18, 2007) (concluding that plaintiffs, investors who alleged that defendant had fraudulently marketed and sold payphone investments, had sufficiently alleged an entity separate and distinct from the alleged racketeering activity); *In re* American Investors Life Ins. Co. Annuity Mktg. & Sales Practices Litig., 2007 WL 2541216, at *18 (E.D. Pa. Aug. 29, 2007) (in case alleging that defendants engaged in a fraudulent scheme to sell elders unnecessary and unsuitable estate planning instruments, concluding that plaintiffs sufficiently met third characteristic when they alleged that the members engaged in activities other than those giving rise to the suit); *In re* Nat'l W. Life Ins. Deferred Annuities Litig., 467 F. Supp. 2d 1071, 1080–1082 (S.D. Cal. 2006) (plaintiff had sufficiently alleged an enterprise when it had alleged "the existence of a common communication network through which enterprise participants share information on a regular basis for the purposes of fraudulently selling deferred annuities to senior citizens").

223 Gunderson v. ADM Investor Services, Inc., 2001 U.S. Dist. LEXIS 3383, at *58, *59 (N.D. Iowa Feb. 13, 2001). *See also* Ochoa v. Housing Auth. of City of Los Angeles, 47 Fed. Appx. 484, 486 (9th Cir. 2002) (dismissing claim when plaintiffs did not allege an organization with a structure outside of that inherent in the alleged predicate acts); State Farm Mut. Auto Ins. Co. v. Giventer, 212 F. Supp. 2d 639, 650 (N.D. Tex. 2002) (no enterprise when nothing held constituent members together beyond the predicate acts themselves).

224 Burdett v. Miller, 957 F.2d 1375, 1379 (7th Cir. 1992) (rejecting argument of defendants, investment advisors to plaintiff, that though they may have conspired to defraud plaintiff they did not form an enterprise). *See also* Carnegie v. Household Int'l, Inc., 220 F.R.D. 542, 546 (N.D. Ill. 2004) (in case by taxpayer against tax service based on alleged fraud in refund anticipation loans, suggesting that plaintiff has a lighter burden in establishing an enterprise at the pleading stage of the litigation), *aff'd on other issues*, 376 F.3d 656 (7th Cir. 2004) (affirming certification of class).

225 *In re* Sumitomo Copper Litig., 104 F. Supp. 2d 314 (S.D.N.Y. 2000); Moss v. Morgan Stanley, 719 F.2d 5, 22 (2d Cir. 1983).

226 Montoya v. PNC Bank, N.A., 2015 WL 1311482, at *18 (S.D. Fla. Mar. 23, 2015) (denying defendants' motion to dismiss claim alleging that defendants conducted an enterprise to force-place insurance coverage on borrowers at inflated costs and with kickbacks to lender) (emphasis in original)).

227 *In re* Sumitomo Copper Litig., 104 F. Supp. 2d 314, 318 (S.D.N.Y. 2000) (the same evidence may be offered to prove both the enterprise and the pattern of racketeering, so long as plaintiff shows an ascertainable structure that is more than the sum of the predicate acts); Schmidt

v. Fleet Bank, 16 F. Supp. 2d 340, 349 n.5 (S.D.N.Y. 1998). *See also* Ouwinga v. Benistar 419 Plan Services, Inc., 694 F.3d 783, 794–795 (6th Cir. 2012); United States v. Phillips, 239 F.3d 829, 844 (7th Cir. 2001); United States v. Rogers, 89 F.3d 1326, 1337 (7th Cir. 1997) ("it would be nonsensical to require proof that an enterprise had purposes or goals separate and apart from the pattern of racketeering activity"; finding evidence sufficient); Moss v. Morgan Stanley, 719 F.2d 5, 22 (2d Cir. 1983) (evidence offered to prove racketeering acts and that offered to prove the existence of an enterprise will not always be distinct); World Wrestling Entm't, Inc. v. Jakks Pac., Inc., 425 F. Supp. 2d 484, 493–495 (S.D.N.Y. 2006) (pattern of racketeering activity alleged can itself suffice to establish an enterprise), *aff'd*, 328 Fed. Appx. 695 (2d Cir. 2009); United States v. Ganim, 225 F. Supp. 2d 145, 161 (D. Conn. 2002) (rejecting argument that proof of enterprise must be distinct from proof of pattern).

228 United States v. Turkette, 452 U.S. 576, 583 (1981).

229 *Cf.* Wagh v. Metris Direct, Inc., 363 F.3d 821, 831 (9th Cir. 2003) (dismissing complaint when plaintiff did not allege that defendants "established a system of making decisions in furtherance of their alleged criminal activities, independent from their respective regular business practices," practices such as routine credit card transactions); Crissen v. Gupta, 994 F. Supp. 2d 937, 947–948 (S.D. Ind. 2014) (plaintiff argued merely that a defendant's activities constituted its "own business affairs and . . . not . . . acts to further the goals of a separate enterprise"); Hemmerdinger Corp. v. Ruocco, 976 F. Supp. 2d 401, 413–414 (E.D.N.Y. 2013) (adequately alleged *Boyle*'s three structural requirements); Johnson v. JP Morgan Chase Bank, 2008 WL 1925026, at *4 (E.D. Cal. Apr. 29, 2008) (dismissing claim of consumer against bank, alleging a conspiracy to unlawfully collect a debt, on grounds that the complaint failed to allege an organization with an existence separate from the racketeering activity).

230 Cedric Kushner Promotions Ltd. v. King, 533 U.S. 158, 161, 121 S. Ct. 2087, 2090, 150 L. Ed. 2d 198 (2001); Switzer v. Coan, 261 F.3d 985, 992 (10th Cir. 2000) (affirming dismissal of claim); Bessette v. Arco Fin. Services, Inc., 230 F.3d 439, 449 (1st Cir. 2000); Begala v. PNC Bank, Ohio, N.A., 214 F.3d 776, 781 (6th Cir. 2000); Jaguar Cars, Inc. v. Royal Oaks Motor Car Co., 46 F.3d 258, 268 (3d Cir. 1995); Crowe v. Henry, 43 F.3d 198, 205, 206 (5th Cir. 1995); Puckett v. Tennessee Eastman Co., 889 F.2d 1481, 1489 (6th Cir. 1989).

subsections (a) and (b) and (d) do not necessarily have.[231] The theory is that the language of RICO § 1962(c) clearly envisions a defendant separate and apart from the subject enterprise. Thus, ordinarily in a RICO § 1962(c) case one cannot simply allege that a defendant conducted the defendant's own affairs through a pattern of racketeering activity or collection of an unlawful debt, but rather must allege that the defendant conducted someone *else's* affairs that way.[232]

The distinctness requirement between enterprise and person in a RICO § 1962(c) case does not lack case law, but it does lack consistent interpretation. For instance, each of the following enterprise constructions raises the question of whether the enterprise is sufficiently distinct from the defendant person or persons:

- An enterprise that includes the defendant person as one member,
- An enterprise that consists of nothing but defendant persons,
- An enterprise that consists of a defendant along with that defendant's employees or agents, and
- An enterprise that consists of a defendant's subsidiary or parent.

The issue arises often because the most attractive defendant may well be a corporation that has been active in the commission of the unlawful activity. Furthermore, the corporation has likely acted within a sphere in which the only obvious characters to fill out an association in fact are in fact related in some way to that corporation, and the plaintiff must distinguish the enterprise from the corporate defendant.

Legal formalities can establish distinctness. The Supreme Court held in *Cedric Kushner Promotions Ltd. v. King*[233] that the distinctness requirement is satisfied when the defendant person and the corporation are distinctly different legal entities, even though they may be connected. The decision respects legal formalities, holding that for purposes of RICO § 1962(c), an employee person is distinct from a corporation enterprise notwithstanding that the employee is the president and sole shareholder of the corporation.[234] However, the Supreme Court expressly chose not to decide the merits of those cases in which the defendant person was also a member of an association in fact enterprise along with other parties related to that person;[235] decisions addressing these sorts of enterprises are discussed below. The decision may signal, however, that a

legal distinction will satisfy the requirement of a distinction between the person and the enterprise, notwithstanding some substantive identification between those serving the roles.[236]

7.4.4.2 The Defendant-Employees Enterprise

Some courts appear to hold that the legal distinction between a corporation and its employees is sufficient to meet the distinctness requirement, so long as the corporation's actions can be shown to be separate from those of its agents.[237]

---

231 *See* § 7.4.5, *infra. But see* Kredietbank, N.V. v. Joyce Morris, Inc., 1986 WL 5926, at *5 (D.N.J. Jan. 9, 1986), *aff'd*, 808 F.2d 1516 (3d Cir. 1986) ("person" and "enterprise" must be distinct under each subsection of section 1962).

232 *See* Reves v. Ernst & Young, 507 U.S. 170, 113 S. Ct. 1163, 122 L. Ed. 2d 525 (1993); Cruz v. FXDirectDealer, L.L.C., 720 F.3d 115, 119–120 (2d Cir. 2013) (dismissing claim, stating that "a corporate person cannot violate the statute by corrupting itself"). *See also* Miller v. Countrywide Home Loans, 747 F. Supp. 2d 947, 964 (S.D. Ohio 2010) (dismissing claim when defendant lender was also the enterprise).

233 Cedric Kushner Promotions Ltd. v. King, 533 U.S. 158, 121 S. Ct. 2087, 150 L. Ed. 2d 198 (2001).

234 533 U.S. at 163, 164–165.

235 *Id.* (calling it "less natural to speak of a corporation as 'employed by' or 'associated with' [such an] oddly constructed entity").

236 *See, e.g.*, Ad-X Int'l, Inc. v. Kolbjornsen, 97 Fed. Appx. 263, 266–267 (10th Cir. 2004) (debtor is distinct from debtor's bankruptcy estate for purposes of RICO, citing Cedric Kushner); Allstate Ins. Co. v. Lyons, 843 F. Supp. 2d 358 (E.D.N.Y. 2012) (denying motion to dismiss when plaintiff alleged that employees were RICO defendants and the enterprise the employers, reasoning that natural persons are distinct from the corporations that employ them); Winger v. Best Buy Co., 2011 WL 995937, at *6 (D. Ariz. Mar. 21, 2011) (plaintiff adequately established an enterprise distinct from the defendants, who, along with others, were members of the enterprise); Vanderbilt Mortg. & Fin., Inc. v. Flores, 735 F. Supp. 2d 679, 703 (S.D. Tex. 2010) (plaintiff sufficiently established a distinct enterprise); Medina v. Vanderbilt Mortg. & Fin., Inc., 2010 WL 3359541, at *7 (S.D. Tex. Aug. 25, 2010) (concluding that plaintiff sufficiently distinguished defendants from the enterprise); Soto v. Vanderbilt Mortg. & Fin., Inc., 2010 WL 3363657, at *18 (S.D. Tex. Aug. 23, 2010) (complaint sufficient when it clearly identified each defendant's role and the structure of the enterprise); HT of Highlands Ranch, Inc. v. Hollywood Tanning Sys., Inc., 590 F. Supp. 2d 677, 689 (D.N.J. 2008) (noting that named defendants were legal entities distinct from associates that constituted association in fact enterprise); Allstate Ins. Co. v. Rozenberg, 590 F. Supp. 2d 384, 391–392 (E.D.N.Y. 2008) (plaintiffs sufficiently alleged an enterprise consisting of corporations that were legally distinct from the defendant persons, who were officers and employees of those corporations); Jones v. Deutsche Bank AG, 2005 WL 1683614, at *3–4 (N.D. Cal. July 19, 2005) (denying defendant's motion to dismiss when defendants alleged to be part of the enterprise each had its own legal existence, separate from the racketeering activity); United States v. Philip Morris USA, 327 F. Supp. 2d 13, 18 (D.D.C. 2004) (defendants that were each individual legal entities were distinct from an enterprise consisting of two or more defendants); Chen v. Mayflower Transit, Inc., 315 F. Supp. 2d 886, 903 (N.D. Ill. 2004) (defendant could be sufficiently distinct from enterprise comprising defendant and affiliates); Crawford & Sons Lt. Profit Sharing Plan v. Besser, 216 F.R.D. 228, 237 (E.D.N.Y. 2003) (shareholder and officer of corporation were sufficiently distinct from corporation itself); G-I Holdings, Inc. v. Baron & Budd, 238 F. Supp. 2d 521, 547 (S.D.N.Y. 2002) (name partners of law firm were separate and distinct entities from firm, citing *Cedric Kushner*); Wilson v. De Angelis, 156 F. Supp. 2d 1335, 1338 (S.D. Fla. 2001) (relying on *Cedric Kushner* to hold that the legal distinction between a corporation and its officer suffices to establish RICO distinctness); Eva v. Midwest Nat'l Mortg. Banc, Inc., 143 F. Supp. 2d 862, 871 (N.D. Ohio 2001) (allowing enterprise of association in fact comprising all the named defendants). *See also* Spencer v. Hartford Fin. Services Grp., Inc., 256 F.R.D. 284, 288 (D. Conn. 2009) (plaintiffs sufficiently showed class predominance on the issue of enterprise when alleged enterprise comprised independent brokers that were distinct legal entities and not employees of any defendant).

237 *See, e.g.*, Jaguar Cars, Inc. v. Royal Oaks Motor Car Co., 46 F.3d 258, 268 (3d Cir. 1995) ("[a] corporation is an entity legally distinct from its officers or employees, which satisfies the 'enterprise' definition of [RICO]"); Adam Grp., Inc. of Middle Tenn. v. Tunnell, 2014 WL 2781128, at *6 (M.D. Tenn. June 19, 2014) (defendants, employees of the enterprise alleged, were sufficiently distinct from the enterprise because

---

Showing that the two had different goals for their actions may be one way to demonstrate this separation. However, in general an enterprise that consists of an association in fact of the defendant corporation along with its employees may not be sufficiently distinct from the defendant itself, at least when the employees were acting within the scope of their employment.[238] Courts reason that a corporation must always act through its employees and agents, and accordingly any corporate act will be accomplished through an association of the employees or subsidiaries and their corporation.[239] Nonetheless, a RICO plaintiff may be able to satisfy the distinctness requirement by showing that the corporation's agents included in the enterprise took separate roles in the racketeering activities, such as by showing the agents conducted racketeering acts in their private capacity and to their own benefit, as opposed to within the scope of their employment.[240]

7.4.4.3 The Defendant-Employer Enterprise

When employees are the named defendants and the employing corporation is the alleged enterprise, some courts find no distinctness problem,[241] while others require the plaintiff to show that the employees were somehow acting outside the scope of their authority while engaging in the predicate offenses in order to establish that they were distinct from the enterprise they were conducting.[242]

7.4.4.4 The Defendant-Parent Corporation Enterprise

Many courts refuse to find a parent corporation to be a distinct enterprise from subsidiary defendants, at least when the plaintiff fails to allege that the enterprise included some person or entity operating outside of the defendant's normal scope of business.[243] However, other courts have ruled that a subsidiary

---

they were "legally distinct entities"); Heslep v. Americans for African Adoption, Inc., 890 F. Supp. 2d 671, 677 (N.D. W. Va. 2012) (consumers, allegedly defrauded in a foreign adoption scheme, successfully alleged an enterprise comprising the corporate adoption agency, some employees, and individual members of the corporation's board of directors); Emcore Corp. v. PricewaterhouseCoopers L.L.P., 102 F. Supp. 2d 237, 257 (D.N.J. 2000) (defendant partners were distinct from association in fact enterprise comprising partners and the partnership, however, partners were not distinct from enterprise consisting of nothing but the partnership). *See also* Vanderbilt Mortg. & Fin., Inc. v. Flores, 746 F. Supp. 2d 819, 844 (S.D. Tex. 2010) (denying summary judgment; distinctness can exist when an association in fact enterprise comprised various corporations, including the RICO person, and their employees).

238 Anatian v. Coutts Bank (Switz.) Ltd., 193 F.3d 85, 89–90 (2d Cir. 1999); Bachman v. Bear, Stearns & Co., 178 F.3d 930, 932 (7th Cir. 1999); Riverwoods Chappaqua Corp. v. Marine Midland Bank, 30 F.3d 339, 344 (2d Cir. 1994) ("plain language" of subsection 1962(c) requires that defendant be distinct from the enterprise); Brittingham v. Mobil Corp., 943 F.2d 297, 300, 301 (3d Cir. 1991) (distinctness not met when enterprise alleged to consist of defendant corporation and its subsidiary together with advertising agencies); Zimmerman v. Poly Prep Country Day Sch., 888 F. Supp. 2d 317, 327 (E.D.N.Y. 2012) (distinctness not met when plaintiffs alleged an association in fact of a school and its employees, but sufficient for an association in fact comprising a school and its board members); Sykes v. Mel Harris & Associates, L.L.C., 757 F. Supp. 2d 413, 425 (S.D.N.Y. 2010) (corporate defendant and its employees cannot form a sufficiently distinct enterprise, but enterprise can be made up of three corporations and their employees), *class action certification aff'd*, Sykes v. Mel S. Harris & Associates, L.L.C., 780 F.3d 70 (2d Cir. 2015); Mear v. Sun Life Assurance Co. of Canada (U.S.)/Keyport Life Ins. Co., 2008 WL 245217, at *9 (D. Mass. Jan. 24, 2008) (in suit alleging that defendants fraudulently marketed and sold equity-indexed annuities to older consumers, concluding that plaintiff failed to allege that the a corporation was distinct from an enterprise comprising the corporation and its sales agents); *In re* Parmalat Secs. Litig., 479 F. Supp. 2d 332, 346–347 (S.D.N.Y. 2007); Eva v. Midwest Nat'l Mortg. Banc, Inc., 143 F. Supp. 2d 862, 874 (N.D. Ohio 2001) (individual defendants who are employees or agents of enterprise are too identified with it to be considered distinct); Larobina v. First Union Nat'l Bank, 2006 WL 437396, at *6–7 (Conn. Super. Ct. Feb. 1, 2006) (distinctness not met when plaintiff alleged an enterprise consisting of defendant and its employees and agents).

239 Brittingham v. Mobil Corp., 943 F.2d 297, 300 (3d Cir. 1991), *criticized by* Emcore Corp. v. PricewaterhouseCoopers, L.L.P., 102 F. Supp. 2d 237, 261 (D.N.J. 2000) ("the conception that a corporation must always act through its agents has become outdated").

240 Emcore Corp. v. PricewaterhouseCoopers L.L.P., 102 F. Supp. 2d 237, 258 (D.N.J. 2000).

241 *See, e.g.*, City of N.Y. v. Smokes-Spirits.com, Inc., 541 F.3d 425, 447–448 (2d Cir. 2008), *related case*, 911 N.E.2d 834 (N.Y. 2009) (answering unrelated questions that Second Circuit has certified to state supreme court), *rev'd on other grounds*, 130 S. Ct. 983 (2010); Abraham v. Singh, 480 F.3d 351, 357 (5th Cir. 2007) (distinctness requirement satisfied when RICO person was an employee of the alleged enterprise, defendant's employer); United States v. Najjar, 300 F.3d 466, 485 (4th Cir. 2002) (so long as employee is a distinct legal entity, employee is sufficiently distinct from corporation); Oklahoma *ex rel.* AG v. Stifel, Nicolaus & Co., 1998 U.S. App. LEXIS 18291 (10th Cir. Aug. 7, 1998); Khurana v. Innovative Health Care Sys., Inc., 130 F.3d 143, 155 (5th Cir. 1997), *vacated as moot sub nom.* Teel v. Khurana, 525 U.S. 979 (1998); Marini v. Adamo, 812 F. Supp. 2d 243, 269–270 (E.D.N.Y. 2011) (denying defendant's motion for summary judgment when plaintiff alleged an enterprise, of which he was also a co-owner, comprising the RICO defendant and his employer); Caravella v. Hearthwood Homes Inc., 2007 WL 2886507, at *5 (N.D.N.Y. Sept. 27, 2007) (in suit alleging that defendants made misrepresentations in the sale of homes, concluding that realtors were sufficiently distinct from their agency, the alleged enterprise); Eva v. Midwest Nat'l Mortg. Banc, Inc., 143 F. Supp. 2d 862 (N.D. Ohio 2001) (distinctness requirement satisfied when alleged enterprise consisted of more than the defendant corporation associated with individual defendant employees, mere affiliation with third-party corporation completing the enterprise did not destroy distinctness). *See also* Burford v. Cargill, Inc., 2011 WL 4382124, at *6 (W.D. La. Sept. 20, 2011) (refusing to dismiss a complaint alleging that defendant, an employee, and other legally distinct entities yielded an enterprise).

242 *See, e.g.*, George Lussier Enterprises, Inc. v. Subaru of New England, Inc., 2002 WL 1349523, at *2 (D.N.H. June 3, 2002) (executive vice president and general manager could be RICO person conducting employer-enterprise); Allen v. New World Coffee, Inc., 2001 U.S. Dist. LEXIS 3269, at *27 (S.D.N.Y. Mar. 27, 2001) (complaint that alleged that employee defendants associated together in the course of their employment and on behalf of the corporation was insufficient to establish the corporation as a distinct enterprise); Emcore Corp. v. PricewaterhouseCoopers L.L.P., 102 F. Supp. 2d 237, 261 (D.N.J. 2000) (defendant partners were not distinct from enterprise consisting of nothing but partnership). *See also* Kovian v. Fulton Cnty. Nat'l Bank & Trust Co., 100 F. Supp. 2d 129 (N.D.N.Y. 2000) (dismissing claim against defendant bank and two of its employees when enterprise alleged to be association in fact among the three on grounds that, if employees acted outside of the scope of their employment, than claim against defendant bank failed).

243 *See, e.g.*, Fogie v. THORN Ams., Inc., 190 F.3d 889, 897, 898 (8th Cir. 1999) (subsidiary not liable for conducting an enterprise comprising

can be sufficiently distinct from a parent to satisfy the requirement, when the parent is alleged to be the enterprise.[244]

The subsidiary-as-defendant scenario has been distinguished from that of parent-as-defendant on the grounds that while ordinarily a subsidiary is the agent of its parent, the reverse is not true.[245] In this framework, courts appear to look

for an irregular relationship, something beyond the ordinary corporate activities of a corporation acting through its employees or a parent controlling the affairs of its subsidiary. Thus, in the Seventh Circuit one may be able to fulfill the distinctness requirement by showing that the parent corporation "somehow made it easier to commit or conceal the fraud of which the plaintiff complains."[246] The author of the two key Seventh Circuit decisions, Chief Judge Posner, describes the appropriate analysis as the "family resemblance" test to "determine how close to the prototype the case before the court is."[247] As examples of such a prototype he cited:

> [O]ne in which a person bent on criminal activity seizes control of a previously legitimate firm and uses the firm's resources, contacts, facilities, and appearance of legitimacy to perpetrate more, and less easily discovered, criminal acts than he could do in his own person, that is, without channeling his criminal activities through the enterprise that he has taken over.[248]

The expressed fear of some courts, that allowing a claim against a subsidiary conducting the affairs of its parent corporation will allow unintended RICO liability,[249] is constrained by the separate requirement in RICO § 1962(c) that the defendant must have conducted or participated in the conduct of the enterprise and not just its own affairs.[250] To read distinctness expansively does not correspondingly expand RICO liability for corporations, as a plaintiff must still show that the subsidiary corporation itself engaged in racketeering activity.

7.4.4.5 The Defendant-Subsidiary Enterprise

When the parent corporation serves the role of defendant and one or more of its subsidiaries as the enterprise, courts are also reluctant to find a distinct enterprise without some evidence that the subsidiary acted outside an ordinary parent/subsidiary relationship,[251] unless additional parties had roles

---

solely the parent of the subsidiary and related businesses; however, court suggests that, if sufficient evidence of distinction beyond the mere fact of legal entities were offered, liability might arise); Brannon v. Boatmen's First Nat'l Bank, 153 F.3d 1144, 1149 (10th Cir. 1998) (bank's holding company was not a distinct enterprise plaintiff showed nothing more than ordinary parent-subsidiary relationship); Discon, Inc. v. NYNEX Corp., 93 F.3d 1055, 1064 (2d Cir. 1996), *rev'd on other grounds*, 525 U.S. 128 (1998) (distinctness requirement not satisfied when NYNEX Group was alleged to be the RICO enterprise and its subsidiaries were named defendants when they "were acting within the scope of a single corporate structure, guided by a single corporate consciousness"); NCNB Nat'l Bank v. Tiller, 814 F.2d 931, 936 (4th Cir. 1987) (defendant bank was not distinct from its holding company, the alleged enterprise); *overruled on other grounds*, Busby v. Crown Supply, Inc., 896 F.2d 833 (4th Cir. 1990); Atkinson v. Anadarko Bank & Trust Co., 808 F.2d 438, 441 (5th Cir. 1987) (no evidence that defendant bank was distinct from the alleged enterprise, its holding company); Panix Promotions v. Lewis, 2002 U.S. Dist. LEXIS 784, at *19 (S.D.N.Y. Jan. 15, 2002) (a division or subsidiary of an alleged enterprise may not serve as the RICO "person"); Dow Chem. Co. v. Exxon Corp., 30 F. Supp. 2d 673, 700, 701 (D. Del. 1998); Metcalf v. Painewebber Inc., 886 F. Supp. 503, 513 (W.D. Pa. 1995) (defendant corporation was not distinct from enterprise alleged to comprise corporation with its subsidiaries and agents when all the members of the alleged enterprise were acting in furtherance of defendant's business), *aff'd without op.*, 79 F.3d 1138 (3d Cir. 1996) (table); Nebraska Sec. Bank v. Dain Bodsworth, Inc., 838 F. Supp. 1362, 1369 (D. Neb. 1993) (neither a parent nor its wholly owned subsidiary can constitute a section 1962(c) enterprise if the other is named as the defendant person). *See also* Bailey v. Atlantic Auto. Corp., 992 F. Supp. 2d 560, 582–583 (D. Md. 2014) (distinct enterprise inadequate when identifying parent and its subsidiaries as RICO defendants, and an association in fact comprising those entities along with other defendants); Wooley v. Jackson Hewitt, Inc., 540 F. Supp. 2d 964, 974 (N.D. Ill. 2008) (in suit against tax preparation company, concluding that a franchisor and its franchisees could not be an enterprise); Bodam v. GTE Corp., 197 F. Supp. 2d 1225 (C.D. Cal. 2002) (units within enterprise were not sufficiently distinct to be RICO person); Pavlov v. Bank of N.Y. Co., 135 F. Supp. 2d 426, *vacated and remanded on other grounds*, 2002 WL 63576 (2d Cir. Jan. 14, 2002) (enterprise sufficiently alleged; continuity need not extend beyond acts forming pattern) (division of defendant corporation is not a distinct enterprise).

244 *See, e.g.*, Begala v. PNC Bank, Ohio, N.A., 214 F.3d 776, 781 (6th Cir. 2000) (a corporation may not be liable under subsection 1962(c) for participating in the affairs of an enterprise that consists only of its own subdivisions, agents or members); Dirt Hogs, Inc. v. Natural Gas Pipeline Co., 2000 U.S. App. LEXIS 6463, at *9, *10 (10th Cir. Apr. 10, 2000); Haroco v. American Nat'l Bank, 747 F.2d 384, 402 (7th Cir. 1984) (section 1962(c) "requires only some separate and distinct existence for the person and the enterprise, and a subsidiary is certainly a legal entity distinct from its parent"), *aff'd on other grounds*, 473 U.S. 606 (1985); Majchrowski v. Norwest Mort., 6 F. Supp. 2d 946, 956 (N.D. Ill. 1998) (*Haroco* dictates that a subsidiary is presumptively distinct from its parent in a case when a subsidiary is cast as the defendant and its parent as the enterprise, therefore manufacturer's dealer alleged to have fraudulently sold an extended service contract to plaintiff was distinct from enterprise comprising manufacturer and its dealers).

245 Majchrowski v. Norwest Mort., 6 F. Supp. 2d 946, 956 (N.D. Ill. 1998).

246 Emery v. American Gen. Fin., Inc., 134 F.3d 1321, 1324 (7th Cir. 1998); Fitzgerald v. Chrysler Corp., 116 F.3d 225, 227 (7th Cir. 1997).

247 Fitzgerald v. Chrysler Corp., 116 F.3d 225, 227 (7th Cir. 1997).

248 *Id.*

249 Brannon v. Boatmen's First Nat'l Bank, 153 F.3d 1144, 1147 (10th Cir. 1998); Bodtker v. Forest City Trading Grp., 1999 U.S. Dist. LEXIS 15345, at *20 (D. Or. Sept. 9, 1999).

250 *See* § 7.5.3, *infra*. Indeed, some courts confuse the distinctness requirement with this separate element of RICO.

251 *See, e.g.*, N. Cypress Med. Ctr. Operating Co. v. Cigna Healthcare, 781 F.3d 182, 202–203 (5th Cir. 2015) (affirming dismissal); Shields v. UnumProvident Corp., 415 Fed. Appx. 686, 691 (6th Cir. 2011) (affirming dismissal); Chagby v. Target Corp., 358 Fed. Appx. 805, 808 (9th Cir. Nov. 19, 2009) (affirming dismissal of claim when alleged enterprise consisted of defendant and its wholly-owned subsidiaries); Shorter v. Metropolitan Life Ins. Co., 216 Fed. Appx. 689, 692–693 (9th Cir. 2007) (distinctness not met when the enterprise alleged was a division of the RICO defendant); Bucklew v. Hawkins, Ash, Baptie & Co., 329 F.3d 923, 934 (7th Cir. 2003) (affirming dismissal of complaint against parent and subsidiary); Brannon v. Boatmen's First Nat'l Bank, 153 F.3d 1144, 1148 (10th Cir. 1998); Emery v. American Gen. Fin., Inc., 134 F.3d 1321, 1324 (7th Cir. 1998) (no distinctness when defendant corporation was merely exercising power that is inherent in

in the enterprise. However, when the plaintiff can show that the defendant parent facilitated illicit activity through the enterprise in a manner distinct from the usual activities of the constituent subsidiary members of the enterprise, the plaintiff may successfully establish that the defendant parent was sufficiently distinct from the enterprise.[252] Correspondingly, a principal and its agent who do not have a corporate relationship may be separate persons in a RICO enterprise when the agent is not acting in the scope of the agency relationship.[253]

7.4.5 Subsections 1962(a), (b), and (d) Generally Do Not Require a Distinct Enterprise

The issue of distinct entities generally arises only in claims brought under RICO § 1962(c). Since RICO § 1962(a) and 1962(b) do not refer to the liable "person" as being "employed by or associated with" an enterprise, no need for the distinction arises from their language.[254] Under subsection (a), most courts have accepted the argument that the liable "person" and the affected "enterprise" may be the same.[255] Subsection 1962(a) may be useful in consumer situations in which a business invests the proceeds of mail fraud in its own operations,[256] for instance, or when a bank converts the contents of a customer's IRA for its own use, such as to pay off a defaulted loan of which it was guarantor.[257]

Under subsection (b), the "distinct" requirement has been the subject of conflicting judicial opinions.[258] With respect to

its ownership of wholly-owned subsidiaries); Khurana v. Innovative Health Care Sys., Inc., 130 F.3d 143, 155 (5th Cir. 1997); Fitzgerald v. Chrysler Corp., 116 F.3d 225, 227 (7th Cir. 1997); Compagnie de Reassurance d'Ile de France v. New England Reinsurance Corp., 57 F.3d 56, 92 (1st Cir. 1995) (distinctness not met when alleged enterprise, a subsidiary, took no actions independent of its defendant parent); Lorenz v. CSX Corp., 1 F.3d 1406, 1412 (3d Cir. 1993) (subsidiary not a distinct enterprise when it "merely acts on behalf of, or to the benefit of, its parent"); Bendzak v. Midland Nat'l Life Ins. Co., 440 F. Supp. 2d 970, 988–989 (S.D. Iowa 2006) (plaintiff, who had purchased an annuity that she alleged was fraudulently represented to her, sufficiently alleged an enterprise consisting of an insurance company and its agents); Waddell & Reed Fin., Inc. v. Torchmark Corp., 223 F.R.D. 566 (D. Kan. 2004) (subsidiary not distinct without allegation that parent corporation was able to more easily commit or conceal the fraud by using the subsidiary); Blue Cross & Blue Shield of N.J., Inc. v. Philip Morris, Inc., 113 F. Supp. 2d 345, 368 (E.D.N.Y. 2000) (distinctness not met when enterprise consisted solely of defendant corporation's subsidiaries and when they and the corporation "operated within a generally unified corporate structure and were guided by a single corporate consciousness"). *But see* Fleischhauer v. Feltner, 879 F.2d 1290, 1297 (6th Cir. 1989) (that one of the individual defendants alleged to be part of the enterprise owned 100% of the corporate defendants alleged to be part of the same enterprise did not vitiate distinctness, corporations were separate legal entities); U1IT4less, Inc. v. FedEx Corp., 896 F. Supp. 2d 275, 287–288 (S.D.N.Y. 2012) (concluding that, given that the parent corporation and its subsidiary are separate legal entities, each was distinct from the other for purposes of RICO); Johnson v. KB Home, 720 F. Supp. 2d 1109 (D. Ariz. 2010) (defendant parent corporation was sufficiently distinct from appraisal companies, its subsidiaries); Marlow v. Allianz Life Ins. Co., 2009 WL 1328636, at *6 (D. Colo. May 12, 2009) (parent corporation not distinct from an enterprise consisting of the parent's subsidiaries and agents); Florida v. Tenet Healthcare Corp., 420 F. Supp. 2d 1288, 1305–1306 (S.D. Fla. 2005) (denying defendant's motion to dismiss when complaint alleged an enterprise consisting of defendant and wholly-owned subsidiaries of the defendant, among others).

252 *In re* Countrywide Fin. Corp. Mortg. Mktg. & Sales Practices Litig., 601 F. Supp. 2d 1201, 1214 (S.D. Cal. 2009) (plaintiff mortgagors adequately alleged enterprise consisting of defendant mortgagee and others who had participated in loan-making process, though dismissing RICO class action on other grounds). *See also* Negrete v. Allianz Life Ins. Co. of N. Am., 926 F. Supp. 2d 1143, 1151-53 (C.D. Cal. 2013) (denying motion to dismiss; annuity purchasers sufficiently alleged that an enterprise comprising defendant annuity seller, along with nineteen field marketing organizations in most of which it had an ownership interest, was sufficiently distinct from defendant).

253 Mitchell Tracey v. First Am. Title Ins. Co., 935 F. Supp. 2d 826, 843 (D. Md. Mar. 28, 2013) (title insurance companies could be distinct from an association in fact formed with their insurance agents); Wiwa v. Royal Dutch Petroleum Co., 2002 WL 319887, at *23 (S.D.N.Y. Feb. 28, 2002) (denying motion to dismiss). *See also* Coleman v. Commonwealth Land Title Ins. Co., 684 F. Supp. 2d 595, 610 (E.D. Pa. 2010) (distinction requirement satisfied when defendant was a title insurance company and the enterprise was an association in fact of that company and its

title agents); Levine v. First Am. Title Ins. Co., 682 F. Supp. 2d 442, 457 (E.D. Pa. 2010) (same as *Coleman*); Schwartz v. Lawyers Title Ins. Co., 680 F. Supp. 2d 690, 705 (E.D. Pa. 2010) (same as *Coleman*, noting that the title agents were not employees); Chen v. Mayflower Transit, Inc., 315 F. Supp. 2d 886, 903 (N.D. Ill. 2004) (corporation and its affiliates).

254 *See* Bowman v. Western Auto Supply Co., 773 F. Supp. 174 (W.D. Mo. 1991) (section 1962(a) and (b) do not require enterprise distinct from person), *rev'd on other grounds*, 985 F.2d 383 (8th Cir. 1993); Gervase v. Superior Ct., 37 Cal. Rptr. 875, 889 (Cal. Ct. App. 1995) (no other subsection requires distinction).

255 Busby v. Crown Supply, Inc., 896 F.2d 833 (4th Cir. 1990) (overruling United States v. Computer Sciences Corp., 689 F.2d 1181 (4th Cir. 1982)); Petro-Tech, Inc. v. Western Co., 824 F.2d 1349 (3d Cir. 1987); Schreiber Distrib. Co. v. Serv-Well Furniture, 806 F.2d 1393 (9th Cir. 1986); Smith v. MCI Telecomms. Corp., 678 F. Supp. 823 (D. Kan. 1987); Welek v. Solomon, 650 F. Supp. 972 (E.D. Mo. 1987); *In re* Dow Co. "Sarabond" Products Liab. Litig., 660 F. Supp. 270 (D. Colo. 1987), *aff'd in part, rev'd in part on other grounds*, 875 F.2d 278 (10th Cir. 1989); Prodex, Inc. v. Legg Mason Wood Walker, Inc., 1987 U.S. Dist. LEXIS 866 (E.D. Pa. Feb. 5, 1987); Conan Properties, Inc. v. Mattel, 619 F. Supp. 1167, 1171 (S.D.N.Y. 1985); Gervase v. Superior Ct., 37 Cal. Rptr. 875, 889 (Cal. Ct. App. 1995). *But see* McEvoy Travel Bureau, Inc. v. Heritage Travel, Inc., 721 F. Supp. 15 (D. Mass. 1989), *aff'd on other grounds*, 904 F.2d 786 (1st Cir. 1990); Garbade v. Great Divide Mining & Milling Corp., 645 F. Supp. 808 (D. Colo. 1986), *aff'd*, 831 F.2d 212 (10th Cir. 1987).

256 Haroco, Inc. v. American Nat'l Bank & Trust Co., 747 F.2d 384, 401 (7th Cir. 1984), *aff'd per curiam*, 473 U.S. 606 (1985) ("under subsection (a), therefore, the liable person may be a corporation using the proceeds of a pattern of racketeering activity in its operations"). *See also* Gutierrez v. Givens, 1 F. Supp. 2d 1077 (S.D. Cal. 1998) (reasonable to infer from allegations that bank received beneficial income from alleged racketeering activities which was likely invested in the bank's operations in violation of section 1962(a)).

257 Masi v. Ford City Bank & Trust Co., 779 F.2d 397, 401, 402 (7th Cir. 1985).

258 Landry v. Air Line Pilots Ass'n Int'l AFL-CIO, 901 F.2d 404 (5th Cir. 1990) (two may be the same); Hillard v. Shell W. E & P, Inc., 836 F. Supp. 1365, 1374 (W.D. Mich. 1993), *rev'd on other grounds*, 149 F.3d 1183 (6th Cir. 1998); Robinson v. City Colleges of Chicago, 656 F. Supp. 555, 560 (N.D. Ill. 1987); Prodex, Inc. v. Legg Mason Wood Walker, Inc., 1987 U.S. Dist. LEXIS 866 (E.D. Pa. Feb. 5, 1987); Medallion TV Enterprises Inc. v. SelecTV of Cal., 627 F. Supp. 1290, 1294–1295 (C.D. Cal. 1985) (distinction required), *aff'd*, 833 F.2d 1360 (9th Cir. 1987). *But see* Vietnam Veterans of Am. v. Guerdon Indus.,

subsection (d), at least one court has ruled that the defendant and the enterprise need not be distinct when the substantive provision subject to the conspiracy, RICO § 1962(b), did not require such distinction.[259]

7.4.6 Strategies to Find the Corporation Liable

7.4.6.1 Introduction

The major implication of having to plead an enterprise distinct from the defendant is that the corporation involved in a scheme will often present itself as the obvious enterprise, and corporate employees or officers as the apparent defendants. But the corporation may be the party with the deep pocket and the individuals largely judgment proof. One approach is to make the corporation the defendant and argue that the enterprise is an association in fact among the corporation and its officers.[260] This approach, though, may raise concerns about whether the defendant and the enterprise are sufficiently distinct.[261] This subsection reviews other approaches to reach the corporation's deep pockets, even though the employees are named as the parties engaging in the predicate offenses.

7.4.6.2 Respondeat Superior

The corporation may be vicariously liable under principles of *respondeat superior*,[262] but several decisions have held that

---

644 F. Supp. 951, 957 (D. Del. 1986) (distinct entities not required); Commonwealth of Pa. v. Perry Constr. Co., 617 F. Supp. 940, 943 (W.D. Pa. 1985).

259 Gordon v. Tyndall, 1987 U.S. Dist. LEXIS 13664, at *3 (N.D. Cal. Feb. 5, 1987).

260 Jaguar Cars Inc. v. Royal Oaks Motor Car Co., 46 F.3d 258, 261 (3d Cir. 1995) (officers and directors of a corporation can be named as RICO persons when the corporation is named as the enterprise). *See also* Miranda v. Ponce Fed. Bank, 948 F.2d 41, 45 (1st Cir. 1991) (officers of corporate enterprise can be personally liable for RICO violations on behalf of corporation); United States v. Perholtz, 842 F.2d 343, 354 (D.C. Cir. 1988); Petro-Tech v. Western Co. of N.A., 824 F.2d 1349 (3d Cir. 1987); Cullen v. Margiotta, 811 F.2d 698 (2d Cir. 1987); United States v. Benny, 786 F.2d 1410 (9th Cir. 1986); United States v. Local 560, IBT, 780 F.2d 267 (3d Cir. 1985); Gassner v. Stotler & Co., 671 F. Supp. 1187 (N.D. Ill. 1987); Portnoy v. E.F. Hutton & Co., 1987 U.S. Dist. LEXIS 17337 (D.N.J. Jan. 15, 1987); Huntsman-Christensen Corp. v. Mountain Fuel Supply Co., 1986 U.S. Dist. LEXIS 17337 (D. Utah Nov. 24, 1986); Brainerd & Bridges v. Weingeroff Enterprises, Inc., 1986 U.S. Dist. LEXIS 22478 (N.D. Ill. July 21, 1986); Chicago HMO v. Trans Pac. Life Ins. Co., 622 F. Supp. 489, 494, 495 (N.D. Ill. 1985) (memorandum). *But see* Rhodes v. Consumers' Buyline, 868 F. Supp. 368 (D. Mass. 1993) (directors and officers acting on behalf of corporate enterprise are not distinct from it).

261 *See* § 7.4.4, *supra*.

262 Oki Semiconductor Co. v. Wells Fargo Bank, N.A., 298 F.3d 768, 775–776 (9th Cir. 2002) (*respondeat superior* liability may be imposed if employer benefited from acts); Crowe v. Henry, 43 F.3d 198, 206 (5th Cir. 1995) (law firm could be vicariously liable under section 1962(a) and (b) when it was alleged to have derived some benefit from its agent's wrongdoing in the form of unauthorized legal fees); Cox v. Administrator, United States Steel & Carnegie, 17 F.3d 1386, 1407 (corporation could be liable when union negotiators fraudulently

respondeat superior should not be available to circumvent the RICO § 1962(c) requirement that the "person" and the "enterprise" be distinct.[263] When the employer is not the alleged

---

received pension benefits from corporation in exchange for concessions which ultimately damaged the union), *op. amended*, 30 F.3d 1347 (11th Cir. 1994); Davis v. Mutual Life Ins. Co. of New York, 6 F.3d 367 (6th Cir. 1993) (vicarious liability under RICO against insurer for fraudulent actions of one of its agents; no prohibition against such liability when corporation benefited from agent's acts); Quick v. Peoples Bank of Cullman Cnty., 993 F.2d 793, 798 (11th Cir. 1993) (*respondeat superior* liability when bank benefited from loan officer's wrongdoing and some evidence of acquiescence); Brady v. Dairy Fresh Products Co., 974 F.2d 1149, 1153–1154 (9th Cir. 1992) (*respondeat superior* allowed when corporation is not the enterprise and the employer receives some benefit from the employee's actions); Petro-Tech, Inc. v. Western Co., 824 F.2d 1349, 1361 (3d Cir. 1987) (*respondeat superior* liability may be imposed for violations of subsection 1962(a)); United States v. Philip Morris USA, Inc., 566 F.3d 1095 (D.C. Cir. 2009), *order clarified*, 778 F. Supp. 2d 8 (D.D.C. 2011); Moy v. Adelphi Inst., 866 F. Supp. 696 (E.D.N.Y. 1994) (vocational school could be vicariously liable for statements made by its recruiters); Western Auto Supply Co. v. Northwestern Mut. Life Ins. Co., 1994 U.S. Dist. LEXIS 13574 (W.D. Mo. Apr. 25, 1994) (insurer could be liable for acts of its agents when it was named as part of association in fact, had not been named as the enterprise, and was alleged to have benefited from the agent's actions); Mylan Labs., Inc. v. Akzo, N.V., 770 F. Supp. 1053 (D. Md. 1991); Connors v. Lexington Ins. Co., 666 F. Supp. 434 (E.D.N.Y. 1987); Temple Univ. v. Salla Bros., 656 F. Supp. 97 (E.D. Pa. 1986); Bernstein v. IDT Corp., 582 F. Supp. 1079, 1082–1084 (D. Del. 1984). *See also In re* American Investors Life Ins. Co. Annuity Mktg. & Sales Practices Litig., 2006 WL 1531152, at *12 (E.D. Pa. June 2, 2006) (stating that certain defendants could be liable under the doctrine of *respondeat superior*, but dismissing complaint on other grounds); Clark v. Security Life Ins. Co., 509 S.E.2d 602 (Ga. 1998) (vicarious liability in civil suit under RICO law should be decided under criminal law principles rather than tort law; superior is liable for agent's act if superior authorized, requested, commanded, performed, or recklessly tolerated it); Brian & Lee, *Vicarious Liability of Corporations and Corporate Enterprises Under RICO*, 7 RICO Law Rep. 560 (1988); Dwyer & Kelly, *Vicarious Civil Liability Under the Racketeer-Influenced and Corrupt Organizations Act*, 21 Cal. W. L. Rev. 324 (1985). *But see* Laro, Inc. v. Chase Manhattan Bank, 866 F. Supp. 132 (S.D.N.Y. 1994) (no corporate liability for independent fraudulent acts of its employees unless corporation actually benefited), *aff'd without op.*, 60 F.3d 810 (1995); Jeffreys v. Exten, 784 F. Supp. 146 (D. Del. 1992) (defendant which has itself been victimized not liable for third-party RICO violation); Albert Einstein Med. Ctr. v. Physicians Clinical Services, Ltd., 1991 U.S. Dist. LEXIS 13302 (E.D. Pa. Sept. 18, 1991) (same as *Jeffreys*).

263 Miller v. Yokohama Tire Corp., 358 F.3d 616, 620 (9th Cir. 2004) (no vicarious liability when the employer is not distinct from the RICO enterprise); Gasoline Sales, Inc. v. Aero Oil Co. 39 F.3d 70, 73 (3d Cir. 1994) (subsidiary corporation could not be held vicariously liable for actions of subsidiary's vice president); Brady v. Dairy Fresh Products Co., 974 F.2d 1149 (9th Cir. 1992) (vicarious liability not allowed when it would violate the distinctness requirement or if the company was not benefited); Miranda v. Ponce Fed. Bank, 948 F.2d 41 (1st Cir. 1991) (attempt to invoke *respondeat superior* "lame"—section 1962(c) does not recognize corporate liability on that basis); D&S Auto Parts, Inc. v. Schwartz, 838 F.2d 964, 967 (7th Cir. 1988) (imposing vicarious liability would defeat the purposes of RICO); Liquid Air Corp. v. Rogers, 834 F.2d 1297 (7th Cir. 1987); Luthi v. Tonka Corp., 815 F.2d 1229 (8th Cir. 1987) (no vicarious liability); Schofield v. First Commodity Corp., 793 F.2d 28 (1st Cir. 1986) (*respondeat superior* at odds with congressional intent behind section 1962(c)); Sea-Land Serv. v. Atlantic

enterprise, however, other courts have pointed out that *respondeat superior* liability can both motivate employers to monitor their employees and keep them from engaging in racketeering activity and force employers who have benefited from their employee's illegal activity to compensate the victims.[264]

Courts that have ruled against *respondeat superior* liability in RICO § 1962(c) cases have often cited to the congressional intent behind that subsection, which was to protect corporations from criminal infiltration; to hold them liable would be to use RICO to hold liable the very entities it was designed to protect.[265] However, other courts have reasoned that this intent is not subverted when the defendant corporation is not the same as the RICO § 1962(c) enterprise, and accordingly *respondeat superior* may be appropriate in those cases.[266] The non-identity concerns are not raised in a RICO § 1962(d) case, and accordingly *respondeat superior* liability may be less controversial there.[267]

To avoid undermining congressional intent, some courts have sought to distinguish those cases in which the defendant corporation was a "central figure" or "aggressor" in the scheme and for which *respondeat superior* liability may be appropriate,[268] from those cases in which the corporation was merely passive, even though perhaps benefiting from the scheme. To show that the defendant was a central figure or aggressor, the plaintiff may have to show that one of the officers or directors either knew of, or was recklessly indifferent to, the illegal activities.[269] It may be sufficient in other courts to show that the defendant corporation's agents actively promoted the scheme.[270] The question is fact-specific and therefore not appropriate for a section 12(b)(6) motion.[271]

In pleading *respondeat superior*, it is wise to plead both that the employee took the alleged action on behalf of the employer and that the employer benefited from the action.[272]

Pac. Int'l, 61 F. Supp. 2d 1102 (D. Haw. 1999) (vicarious liability not appropriate when it would impose liability on the enterprise); Williams Elecs. Games, Inc. v. Barry, 42 F. Supp. 2d 785, 791 (N.D. Ill. 1999), *aff'd*, 366 F.3d 569 (7th Cir. 2004); Soanes v. Empire Blue Cross/Blue Shield, 26 RICO L. Rep. 241, No. 91 Civ. 8698 (S.D.N.Y. July 3, 1997) (union and its welfare fund not vicariously liable for local's president's participation in fraudulent insurance brokerage transaction); Pollack v. Laidlaw Holdings, Inc., 1993 U.S. Dist. LEXIS 459 (S.D.N.Y. Jan. 19, 1993), *rev'd on other grounds*, 27 F.3d 808 (2d Cir. 1994), *on remand* 1995 U.S. Dist. LEXIS 15935 (S.D.N.Y. Oct. 30, 1995); Ram Inv. Associates v. Citizens Fid. Bank & Trust Co., 1992 WL 240581 (S.D.N.Y. 1992) (if no apparent authority, no *respondeat superior*); Metro Furniture Rental, Inc. v. Alessi, 770 F. Supp. 198 (S.D.N.Y. 1991) (bank could not be liable for actions of low-level employee when no corporate policy shown); First Nat'l Bank v. Lustig, 727 F. Supp. 276 (E.D. La. 1989); Grimsley v. First Alabama Bank, 1988 WL 156777, 1988 U.S. Dist. LEXIS 16042 (S.D. Ala. 1988); American Bonded Warehouse Corp. v. Compagnie Nationale Air France, 653 F. Supp. 861 (N.D. Ill. 1987); Banque Worms v. Luis A. Duque Pena E Hijos Ltd., 652 F. Supp. 770 (S.D.N.Y. 1987); Gilbert v. Prudential Bache Sec., 643 F. Supp. 107 (E.D. Pa. 1986); Lynn Elecs. v. Automation Mach. & Dev. Corp., 1986 U.S. Dist. LEXIS 19433 (E.D. Pa. Oct. 6, 1986). *See also* D&S Auto Parts, Inc. v. Schwartz, 838 F.2d 964 (7th Cir. 1988) (principal liable under section 1962(a) only if principal also is perpetrator); *In re* Citisource, Inc., Sec. Litig., 694 F. Supp. 1069 (S.D.N.Y. 1988) (municipal corporation cannot be held vicariously liable under RICO); Gruber v. Prudential-Bache Sec., 679 F. Supp. 165 (D. Conn. 1987) (non-enterprise vicariously liable under section 1962(c) only when it is central figure in the alleged scheme); Kovian v. Fulton Cnty. Nat'l Bank, 647 F. Supp. 830 (N.D.N.Y. 1986) (limited vicarious liability in unlawful debt collection action); Sea State Bank v. Visiting Nurses Ass'n of Telfair Cnty., Inc., 568 S.E.2d 491, 492 (Ga. Ct. App. 2002) (no *respondeat superior* liability unless evidence that employer profited from acts).

264 *See, e.g.*, Thomas v. Ross & Hardies, 9 F. Supp. 2d 547, 557 (D. Md. 1998) (holding law firm partnership could be held liable under RICO under traditional partnership agency principles for racketeering acts of partner); Baker *ex rel.* Hall Brake Supply, Inc. v. Stewart Title & Trust, Inc., 197 Ariz. 535, 5 P.3d 249, 259 (2000).

265 Landry v. Air Line Pilots Ass'n Int'l AFL-CIO, 901 F.2d 404 (5th Cir. 1990); Yellow Bus Lines, Inc. v. Drivers, Chauffeurs & Helpers Local Union 639, 883 F.2d 132, 140 (D.C. Cir. 1989), *rev'd in part on other grounds*, 913 F.2d 948 (D.C. Cir. 1990) (en banc); D&S Auto Parts, Inc. v. Schwartz, 838 F.2d 964, 967 (7th Cir. 1988); Liquid Air Corp. v. Rogers, 834 F.2d 1297, 1306 (7th Cir. 1987); Luthi v. Tonks Corp., 815 F.2d 1229, 1230 (8th Cir. 1987); Schofield v. First Commodity Corp. of Boston, 793 F.2d 28, 32–34 (1st Cir. 1986); Kovian v. Fulton Cnty. Nat'l Bank & Trust Co., 100 F. Supp. 2d 129, 133 (N.D.N.Y. 2000); Qatar Nat'l Navigation & Transp. Co. v. Citibank, N.A., 1992 U.S. Dist. LEXIS 14784 (S.D.N.Y. Sept. 29, 1992), *aff'd*, 182 F.3d 901 (2d Cir. 1999); Kahn v. Chase Manhattan Bank, N.A., 760 F. Supp. 369, 373 (S.D.N.Y. 1991) ("the independent acts of an employee not acting in his employer's interest are not a sufficient basis to hold the employer liable

under RICO"); Banque Worms v. Luis A. Duque Pena E Hijos, Ltda., 652 F. Supp. 770, 772 (S.D.N.Y. 1986); Rush v. Oppenheimer & Co., 628 F. Supp. 1188, 1194, 1195 (S.D.N.Y. 1985).

266 *See, e.g.*, Davis v. Mutual Life Ins. Co., 6 F.3d 367, 379, 380 (6th Cir. 1994) (when defendant is not the enterprise, and "knowingly sponsored and benefited from the activity," vicarious liability may be appropriate); Brady v. Dairy Fresh Products Co., 974 F.2d 1149, 1154 (9th Cir. 1992); Petro-Tech, Inc. v. Western Co. of N. Am., 824 F.2d 1349, 1361, 1362 (3d Cir. 1987); United States v. Philip Morris USA, Inc., 566 F.3d 1095 (D.C. Cir. 2009), *order clarified*, 778 F. Supp. 2d 8 (D.D.C. 2011); Connors v. Lexington Ins. Co., 666 F. Supp. 434, 453 (E.D.N.Y. 1987) (ordinary rules of agency apply to RICO cases); Bernstein v. IDT Corp., 582 F. Supp. 1079, 1083 (D. Del. 1984).

267 *Cf.* Baker *ex rel.* Hall Brake Supply, Inc. v. Stewart Title & Trust, Inc., 5 P.3d 249, 259 (Ariz. 2000) (describing goals of *respondeat superior* liability and concluding that the particular circumstances of the case did not justify such liability for the employer).

268 *See* USA Certified Merchants, L.L.C. v. Koebel, 273 F. Supp. 2d 501, 504 (S.D.N.Y. 2003); Dubai Islamic Bank v. Citibank, N.A., 256 F. Supp. 2d 158, 165 (S.D.N.Y. 2003); Kovian v. Fulton Cnty. Nat'l Bank & Trust Co., 100 F. Supp. 2d 129, 133 (N.D.N.Y. 2000) (not enough to show that employer benefited from the scheme); Nystrom v. Associated Plastic Fabricators, Inc., 1999 U.S. Dist. LEXIS 9480 (N.D. Ill. June 1999) (not enough to show that employer benefited from the scheme); Schmidt v. Fleet Bank, 16 F. Supp. 2d 340, 352 (S.D.N.Y. 1998) (must show employer was more than mere beneficiary); Gruber v. Prudential-Bache Sec. Inc., 679 F. Supp. 165, 181 (D. Conn. 1987).

269 Kovian v. Fulton Cnty. Nat'l Bank & Trust Co., 100 F. Supp. 2d 129, 133 (N.D.N.Y. 2000).

270 Gunderson v. ADM Investor Services, Inc., 2001 U.S. Dist. LEXIS 3383, at *72–*73 (N.D. Iowa Feb. 13, 2001). *But see* Kovian v. Fulton Cnty. Nat'l Bank & Trust Co., 100 F. Supp. 2d 129, 133 (N.D.N.Y. 2000) (respondeat superior liability inappropriate when high-ranking officers were acting outside the scope of their employment).

271 Bank Brussels Lambert v. Credit Lyonnais (Suisse) S.A., 2000 U.S. Dist. LEXIS 16399, at *33 (S.D.N.Y. Nov. 13, 2000).

272 Pollack v. Laidlaw Holdings, Inc., 1995 U.S. Dist. LEXIS 15935 (S.D.N.Y. Oct. 30, 1995) (corporation could be liable when these two elements proved). *See also* Heritage Christian Sch., Inc. v. ING N. Am.

If there is evidence of ratification by the principal, that should be pleaded as well.

7.4.6.3 Indemnification and Insurance

The corporation may be required to indemnify individual employees who incur RICO liability. Indemnification is not always favored.[273] Consequently, care should be taken to name as the defendant an officer, director, or agent of an enterprise for whose actions the enterprise is responsible or whom it will indemnify. Similarly, the individual defendant may have liability insurance. Liability insurance normally does not cover intentional wrongdoing, so it is important to plead a RICO claim in a manner designed to maximize the chance of recovery by incorporating such considerations.

7.4.6.4 Aiding and Abetting

A party can be liable under RICO for aiding and abetting the RICO violation even if that party did not have the requisite participation in the enterprise. However, a Supreme Court decision construing the Securities Exchange Act may hinder aider and abettor liability under RICO. In *Central Bank v. First Interstate Bank*,[274] the Court held that civil liability under the Securities Exchange Act of 1934 did not include those who merely aid and abet a section 10(b) violation because the act does not provide for aider and abettor liability. Some RICO courts have ruled that *Central Bank* does not affect RICO aider and abettor liability because RICO liability depends on whether the defendant is criminally liable for the predicate offense, and one who

aids and abets a federal crime is principally liable.[275] However, recent opinions have agreed almost universally that *Central Bank* destroyed any aider and abettor cause of action under RICO, at least with respect to actions brought under RICO § 1962(c).[276] Furthermore, any action asserting aiding and abetting of securities fraud may be barred by the Private Securities Litigation Reform Act.[277]

Nonetheless, an aiding and abetting claim may still be viable under RICO § 1962(a) because, unlike the other subsections, RICO § 1962(a) incorporates by reference the general criminal aiding and abetting statute, 18 U.S.C. § 2.[278] To state a claim of aider and abettor liability under RICO, the plaintiff must allege the following: (1) the existence of an independent wrong committed by the primary offender; (2) the rendering of substantial assistance to the primary wrongdoer by the

---

Ins. Corp., 851 F. Supp. 2d 1154, 1159–1162 (E.D. Wis. 2012) (ruling that corporations did not have respondeat superior liability for agents' RICO violations when agents were acting to further their own goals rather than those of their principals); *In re* Hydrox Chem. Co., 194 B.R. 617, 627–628 (Bankr. N.D. Ill. 1996) (while no vicarious liability for actions of corporate officers, corporation that benefited could be directly liable).

273 Several courts have agreed that contribution and indemnification are not available under RICO. *See, e.g.*, The Cnty. of Hudson v. Janiszewski, 2007 WL 2688882, at *6 (D.N.J. Sept. 13, 2007) (holding no indemnification under RICO, reasoning that the treble damages provision indicated that Congress intended to punish violators and not to relieve their liability), *aff'd*, 351 Fed. Appx. 662 (3d Cir. 2009); THC Holdings Corp. v. Tishman, 1998 WL 305639, at *2 n.1 (S.D.N.Y. June 9, 1998) (dismissing contribution and indemnification claims); Academic Indus., Inc. v. Untermeyer Mace Partners, Ltd., 1992 WL 73473, at *6 (S.D.N.Y. Apr. 1, 1992); Andrews v. Fitzgerald, 1992 U.S. Dist. LEXIS 9315 (M.D.N.C. Feb. 7, 1992); Friedman v. Hartmann, 787 F. Supp. 411, 415 (S.D.N.Y. 1992); Feldman v. Sergeant, 1990 WL 74477, at *2 (D.N.J. June 4, 1990) (dismissing third-party complaint to extent it sought indemnification or contribution under RICO). *See also* Sequa v. Gelmin, 851 F. Supp. 106, 108 (S.D.N.Y. 1994) (corporation did not have to indemnify person it sued, despite indemnification agreement); Sikes v. AT&T Co., 841 F. Supp. 1572 (S.D. Ga. 1993) (contribution, but not indemnification, rights will be honored); Sequa Corp. v. Gelmin, 828 F. Supp. 203, 205–206 (S.D.N.Y. 1993) (indemnification for costs of defense only). *But see* Vanguard Sav. & Loan Ass'n v. Banks, 1995 U.S. Dist. LEXIS 961 (E.D. Pa. Jan. 26, 1995) (contribution is not available to a RICO defendant).

274 511 U.S. 164, 114 S. Ct. 1439, 128 L. Ed. 2d 119 (1994).

275 Crowe v. Henry, 43 F.3d 198 (5th Cir. 1995); First Am. Corp. v. Al-Nahyan, 17 F. Supp. 2d 10 (D.D.C. 1998) (finding RICO sufficiently different from the Securities Exchange Act that *Central Bank* did not control); *In re* American Honda Motor Co. Dealership Relations Litig., 958 F. Supp. 1045 (D. Md. 1997); Am. Auto. Accessories, Inc. v. Fishman, 1996 U.S. Dist. LEXIS 12207 (N.D. Ill. Aug. 22, 1996); Dayton Monetary Associates v. Donaldson, Lufkin & Jenrette Sec. Corp., RICO Business Disputes Guide (CCH) ¶ 8748, 1995 U.S. Dist. LEXIS 1198 (S.D.N.Y. Feb. 1, 1995); Standard Chlorine of Delaware, Inc. v. Sinibaldi, RICO Business Disputes Guide (CCH) ¶ 8780, 1994 U.S. Dist. LEXIS 20541 (D. Del. Dec. 8, 1994); Succession of Lula Belle Wardlaw v. Whitney Nat'l Bank, RICO Business Disputes Guide (CCH) ¶ 8711, 1994 U.S. Dist. LEXIS 15215 (E.D. La. Oct. 17, 1994).

276 Pennsylvania Ass'n of Edwards Heirs v. Rightenour, 235 F.3d 839, 844 (3d Cir. 2001) (no aiding and abetting liability under RICO after *Central Bank*); Rolo v. City Investing Co. Liquidating Trust, 155 F.3d 644 (3d Cir. 1998) (relying on *Central Bank*, no aiding and abetting liability); *In re* Countrywide Fin. Corp. Mortg. Mktg. & Sales Practices Litig., 601 F. Supp. 2d 1201, 1219 (S.D. Cal. 2009); Wiwa v. Royal Dutch Petroleum Co., 2002 WL 319887, at *25 n.33 (S.D.N.Y. Feb. 28, 2002) (no aider-and-abettor liability); *In re* Mastercard Int'l Inc., 132 F. Supp. 2d 468 (E.D. La. 2001); Goldfine v. Sichenzia, 118 F. Supp. 2d 392, 406 (S.D.N.Y. 2000) (no aiding and abetting liability under section 1962(c)); Jubelirer v. Mastercard Int'l, 68 F. Supp. 2d 1049 (W.D. Wis. 1999) (no aiding and abetting liability under RICO after *Central Bank*); Niles v. Palmer, 1999 U.S. Dist. LEXIS 17759, at *28 (S.D.N.Y. Oct. 26, 1999); Touhy v. Northern Trust Bank, 1999 U.S. Dist. LEXIS 7967, at *7 (N.D. Ill. May 17, 1999) (no aiding and abetting liability for section 1962(c)); Soranno v. New York Life Ins. Co., 1999 U.S. Dist. LEXIS 1963 (N.D. Ill. Feb. 22, 1999) (no aiding and abetting liability under section 1962(d)); Hayden v. Paul, Weiss, Rifkind, Wharton & Garrison, 955 F. Supp. 248 (S.D.N.Y. 1997); Kaiser v. Stewart, 1997 U.S. Dist. LEXIS 12788 (E.D. Pa. Aug. 19, 1997); *In re* Lake States Commodities, Inc., 936 F. Supp. 1461 (N.D. Ill. 1996) (no aiding and abetting liability under section 1962(c)); Rosenheck v. Rieber, 932 F. Supp. 626 (S.D.N.Y. 1996); Dep't of Economic Dev. v. Arthur Andersen & Co., 924 F. Supp. 449 (S.D.N.Y. 1996) (no aiding and abetting liability under civil RICO); Bowdoin Constr. Corp. v. Rhode Island Hosp. Trust Nat'l Bank, N.A., 869 F. Supp. 1004 (D. Mass. 1994) (aiding and abetting securities fraud cannot be a predicate act for RICO; under *Reves*, to be liable under section 1962(c), a defendant must participate in the operation or management of the enterprise itself), *aff'd on other grounds*, 94 F.3d 721 (1st Cir. 1996).

277 *See* § 7.1.3, *supra*.

278 18 U.S.C. § 1962(a). However, the reference is made specifically with respect to collection of an unlawful debt, so arguably only those actions based upon such collection, rather than on a pattern of racketeering activity, will be eligible for an aiding and abetting claim.

aider and abettor; and (3) the requisite scienter of the aider and abettor.[279]

7.5 Enterprise's Relationship to the Predicate Offenses

7.5.1 Introduction

RICO prohibits a defendant from engaging in a pattern of racketeering activity or collection of an unlawful debt with an identified enterprise in any of four prohibited ways. These four prohibited practices are discussed below. Section 7.4, *supra*, discussed the nature of an "enterprise."

7.5.2 Proceeds of Illegal Conduct Invested in the Enterprise: Section 1962(a)

RICO § 1962(a) addresses the investment of ill-gotten gains in an enterprise, prohibiting any person who receives income from a pattern of racketeering activity from using that income to acquire any interest in, or to establish or operate any enterprise engaged in, interstate or foreign commerce.[280] "This provision was primarily directed at halting the investment of racketeering proceeds into legitimate businesses, including the practice of money laundering."[281] Under this section, a plaintiff must allege the following: (1) that the defendant received money from a pattern of racketeering activity; (2) that the defendant invested that money in an enterprise; and (3) that the enterprise affected interstate commerce.[282]

7.5.3 Acquiring an Interest in the Enterprise Through Illegal Conduct: Section 1962(b)

RICO § 1962(b) prohibits a person from acquiring or maintaining, directly or indirectly, through a pattern of racketeering activity or collection of an unlawful debt, any interest in or control of an enterprise engaged in interstate or foreign commerce.[283] The purpose of RICO § 1962(b) is "to prohibit the takeover of a legitimate business through racketeering, typically extortion or loansharking."[284] To establish a claim the plaintiffs must allege the following: (1) the defendants acquired or maintained an interest in or control of the enterprise through a pattern of racketeering activity or the collection of an unlawful debt, and (2) the plaintiffs suffered injury as a result.[285] One court has held that acquiring control through legal means, such as a legitimate stock purchase, will nullify the first element.[286]

The "interest" that section 1962(b) refers to means a proprietary interest,[287] and the element can be satisfied with the purchase of stock[288] or any other property right in the enterprise.[289] However, a plaintiff who seeks to show that a defendant acquired control through racketeering activity must show more than mere influence. "[T]he 'control' contemplated is in the nature of the control one gains through the acquisition of sufficient stock to affect the composition of a board of directors."[290] Or, even more restrictively, "control connotes domination. It signifies the kind of power that an owner of 51% or more of an entity would normally enjoy."[291]

---

279 Touhy v. Northern Trust Bank, 1999 U.S. Dist. LEXIS 7967 (N.D. Ill. May 14, 1999) (deliberate indifference to scheme insufficient for aider and abettor liability) (citing R.E. Davis Chem. Corp. v. Nalco Chem. Co., 757 F. Supp. 1499 (N.D. Ill. 1990)).

280 18 U.S.C. § 1962(a). *See also* Ducote Jax Holdings L.L.C. v. Bradley, 335 Fed. Appx. 392, 399 (5th Cir. 2009) (defendant's act of sending money received from plaintiff to another defendant in the enterprise sufficed to allege investment requirement of section 1962); Kauthar SDN BHD v. Sternberg, 149 F.3d 659, 672 (7th Cir. 1998) (affirming dismissal of RICO claims); Kashelkar v. Rubin & Rothman, 97 F. Supp. 2d 383, 394 (S.D.N.Y. 2000) (section 1962(a) complaint dismissed for failing to allege that defendant received income from racketeering activity, acquired an interest in an enterprise, or established an enterprise), *aff'd*, 242 F.3d 365 (2d Cir. 2001); Proctor v. Metropolitan Money Store Corp., 645 F. Supp. 2d 464, 482–483 (D. Md. 2009) (denying motion to dismiss claim alleging that as part of a foreclosure rescue scam, certain individuals reinvested excessive fees that they collected into new transactions; Tran v. Tran, 2000 U.S. Dist. LEXIS 10946, at *43 (S.D.N.Y. Aug. 4, 2000) (plaintiff proved violation of subsection 1962(a) by showing that the defendant, who owned hotels, underpaid their employees, the savings from which could be considered income which defendants than used or invested in the enterprise comprising the hotels), *aff'd in part, reversed in part on other grounds*, 281 F.3d 23 (2d Cir. 2002) (holding that RICO claim was time barred); Morin v. Trupin, 835 F. Supp. 126, 131, 132 (S.D.N.Y. 1985).

281 Brittingham v. Mobil Corp., 943 F.2d 297, 303 (3d Cir. 1991).

282 Nolen v. Nucentrix Broadband Networks, Inc., 293 F.3d 926, 929, 930 (5th Cir. 2002) (injury from allegedly illegal late fees did not arise from use or investment of racketeering income); Shearin v. E.F. Hutton Grp., Inc., 885 F.2d 1162, 1165 (3d Cir. 1989) (citing B.F. Hirsch, Inc. v. Enright Ref. Co., 617 F. Supp. 49, 51, 52 (D.N.J. 1985)); Allen v. New

World Coffee, Inc., 2002 WL 432685 (S.D.N.Y. Mar. 19, 2002) (investment of racketeering income is essence of section 1962(a) violation).

283 18 U.S.C. § 1962(b). *See also* Kauthar SDN BHD v. Sternberg, 149 F.3d 659, 672 (7th Cir. 1998) (affirming dismissal of RICO claims); Kashelkar v. Rubin & Rothman, 97 F. Supp. 2d 383, 394 (S.D.N.Y. 2000) (section 1962(b) complaint dismissed for failing to allege that defendant acquired or maintained an interest in an enterprise), *aff'd*, 242 F.3d 365 (2d Cir. 2001); Morin v. Trupin, 835 F. Supp. 126, 133 (S.D.N.Y. 1985).

284 David B. Smith & Terrance G. Reed, Civil RICO, P 5.01, p.5-2 (1997).

285 Jordan (Berm.) Inv. Co. v. Hunter Green Investments Ltd., 154 F. Supp. 2d 682 (S.D.N.Y. 2001); Morin v. Trupin, 832 F. Supp. 93, 99 (S.D.N.Y. 1993).

286 Acro-Tech, Inc. v. Robert Jackson Family Trust, 84 Fed. Appx. 747, 750 (9th Cir. 2003).

287 Guerrier v. Advest, Inc., 1993 U.S. Dist. LEXIS 3975, at *30, *31 (D.N.J. Mar. 25, 1993).

288 Moffatt Enterprises, Inc. v. Borden, Inc., 763 F. Supp. 143, 147 (W.D. Pa. 1990).

289 *See* Welch Foods, Inc. v. Gilchrist, 1996 U.S. Dist. LEXIS 15819, at *7 (W.D.N.Y. Oct. 18, 1996).

290 Moffatt Enterprises, Inc. v. Borden, Inc., 763 F. Supp. 143, 147 (W.D. Pa. 1990). *But see* Kukuk v. Fredal, 2001 U.S. Dist. LEXIS 16419, at *27–28 (E.D. Mich. Aug. 1, 2001) (refusing to dismiss section 1962(b) claim against defendant who did not own stock in allegedly sham fund and was employed by fund but who had simply earned commissions on sales of interests in the fund).

291 Kaiser v. Stewart, 1997 U.S. Dist. LEXIS 12788, at *9 (E.D. Pa. Aug. 19, 1997). *See also* Browne v. Abdelhak, 2000 U.S. Dist. LEXIS 12064, at *30–*31 (E.D. Pa. Aug. 23, 2000) (plaintiff failed to sufficiently allege control when only alleged that defendants were officers of the

Once the plaintiff has shown the acquisition of an interest in or control of the enterprise, the plaintiff must further demonstrate a relationship between the pattern of racketeering activity and the acquisition or maintenance of the interest.[292]

7.5.4 Participation in the Enterprise Through Illegal Conduct: Section 1962(c)

RICO § 1962(c) declares it unlawful for "any person *employed by* or *associated with* any enterprise . . . *to conduct or participate*, directly or indirectly, in the conduct of such enterprise's affairs through a pattern of racketeering activity or collection of unlawful debt."[293] A plaintiff must identify the appropriate defendant as someone employed by or associated with the enterprise and then identify the enterprise itself and establish their respective roles in the RICO scheme while ensuring that they are sufficiently distinct from each other.[294] The plaintiff must then demonstrate that the relationship between the defendant person and the enterprise meets the requirements of RICO § 1962(c). That is, the plaintiff must show that the defendant conducted or participated in the conduct of the enterprise's affairs.

The Supreme Court, in *Reves v. Ernst & Young*, gave some guidance about the requisite participation in an enterprise's affairs.[295] In that case, the defendants were auditors who had issued a series of false financial statements but who did not otherwise participate in the enterprise's affairs. "Conduct," stated the majority, "requires an element of direction."[296] To participate, the defendant must have had "*some* part in directing the enterprise's affairs."[297] The requirement is not control but direction.[298] Although the Court held that the behavior of the third-party professionals in this case did not rise to this level, the Court stressed that RICO § 1962(c) does not limit liability to upper-level professionals:

> An enterprise is "operated" not just by upper management but also by lower rung participants in the enterprise who are under the direction of upper management. An enterprise also might be "operated" or "managed" by others "associated with" the enterprise who exert control over it as, for example, by bribery.[299]

While acknowledging that the interpretation limits the liability of "outsiders" who have no official position within the enterprise, the Court noted that its test allowed outsiders to be liable if they conducted or participated in the enterprise's affairs, consistent with the limiting language of that subsection. The Court also pointed out that that limiting language is specific to RICO § 1962(c) and accordingly had no effect on RICO §§ 1962(a) and (b), which were still appropriate for the infiltration of legitimate organizations by "outsiders."[300]

Since *Reves*, plaintiffs have not had great success with claims against outside professionals.[301] Some courts require that the plaintiff show more than a legitimate business relationship between the defendant and the enterprise. That is, when the defendant is outside the enterprise's chain of command, an ordinary contractual relationship will not be considered conduct or participation.[302]

---

300 *Id.* at 185.

301 *See, e.g.,* James Cape & Sons Co. v. PCC Constr. Co., 453 F.3d 396, 403 (7th Cir. 2006) (ruling that plaintiff, a disappointed construction bidder, did not adequately allege that defendant, which plaintiff alleged had conspired to rig the bidding system, had sufficient control over the core functions of the enterprise, the contract-awarding agency, to satisfy the *Reves* test); Azrielli v. Cohen Law Offices, 21 F.3d 512 (2d Cir. 1994) (attorneys); United States v. Quintanilla, 25 F.3d 694 (8th Cir. 1993) (attorneys); Baumer v. Pachl, 8 F.3d 1341 (9th Cir. 1993) (attorney); McNew v. People's Bank of Ewing, 999 F.2d 540 (6th Cir. 1993) (bank); Nolte v. Pearson, 994 F.2d 1311 (8th Cir. 1993) (preparer of opinion letters); Jordan (Berm.) Inv. Co. v. Hunter Green Investments Ltd., 154 F. Supp. 2d 682, 693 (S.D.N.Y. 2001) (law firm and lawyer); Feirstein v. Nanbar Realty Corp., 963 F. Supp. 254 (S.D.N.Y. 1997); Hayden v. Paul, Weiss, Rifkind, Wharton & Garrison, 955 F. Supp. 248 (S.D.N.Y. 1997) (auditor); Vickers Stock Research Corp. v. Quotron Sys., Inc., 26 RICO L. Rep. 246, No. 96 Civ. 2269 (HB) (S.D.N.Y. July 22, 1997); Resolution Trust Corp. v. S&K Chevrolet Co., 918 F. Supp. 1235 (C.D. Ill.) (outside insurance broker who just provided services for a car dealership did not operate or manage it; encouraging fraudulent scheme is not enough), *vacated in part on other issues*, 923 F. Supp. 135 (C.D. Ill. 1996); Reynolds v. Condon, 908 F. Supp. 1494 (N.D. Iowa 1995) (lawyer who merely did work for client did not participate in the conduct of its affairs); In re Phar-Mor, Inc. Sec. Litig., 893 F. Supp. 484 (W.D. Pa. 1995) (auditors who ignored fraudulent financials of client did not manage or operate it for RICO purposes); Succession of Lula Belle Wardlaw v. Whitney Nat'l Bank, RICO Business Disputes Guide (CCH) ¶ 8711, 1994 U.S. Dist. LEXIS 15215 (E.D. La. Oct. 17, 1994) (lender did not meet RICO's participation requirement when all it did was honor withdrawal requests even if it knew they were fraudulent; it had no duty to watch for breach of fiduciary duty). *See also* Sykes v. Mel Harris & Associates, L.L.C., 757 F. Supp. 2d 413, 427 (S.D.N.Y. 2010) (dismissing RICO claims against individual process servers because they were not alleged to have directed the enterprise's affairs), *class action certification aff'd*, Sykes v. Mel S. Harris & Associates, L.L.C., 780 F.3d 70 (2d Cir. 2015). *But see* Resolution Trust Corp. v. Stone, 998 F.2d 1534 (10th Cir. 1993) (insurance group liable because participation sufficient).

In one post-*Reves* case, the court considered the possible liability of a lender that did not exercise direct control over the enterprise and ruled that it is not enough that the enterprise might not have been able to function without the financing—provision of services essential to the operation of the RICO enterprise is not the same as participating in the conduct of its affairs. De Wit v. Firstar Corp., 879 F. Supp. 947 (N.D. Iowa 1995).

The quality of job done by the professional is irrelevant. Baumer v. Pachl, 8 F.3d 1341 (9th Cir. 1993); University of Maryland at Baltimore v. Peat, Marwick, Main & Co., 996 F.2d 1534 (3d Cir. 1993).

302 *See, e.g.,* Crichton v. Golden Rule Ins. Co., 576 F.3d 392, 400 (7th Cir. 2009) (conduct element failed when plaintiff alleged only "ordinary

---

corporation who had received large bonuses, salary increases, and payments from the enterprise's stock option plan).

292 Browning Ave. Realty Corp. v. Rosenshein, 774 F. Supp. 129, 140 (S.D.N.Y. 1991); Litton Indus., Inc. v. Lehman Bros. Kuhn Loeb Inc., 709 F. Supp. 438, 452 (S.D.N.Y. 1989).

293 Emphasis added.

294 *See* § 7.4.4, *supra*.

295 Reves v. Ernst & Young, 507 U.S. 170, 113 S. Ct. 1163, 122 L. Ed. 2d 525 (1993).

296 *Id.* at 178.

297 *Id.* at 179 (emphasis in original).

298 *Id.*

299 *Id.* at 184 (footnotes deleted).

So, for example, when a bank's involvement with the enterprise was limited to processing deposits and withdrawals, it did not sufficiently participate for RICO § 1962(c) liability, even though it knew the deposits and withdrawals were fraudulent.[303] Similarly, a lender that had financed a real estate developer that was accused of defrauding lot buyers evaded liability under the *Reves* test.[304] The Eighth Circuit has warned that courts "must carefully distinguish between the bank conducting its own affairs as creditor, and the bank taking additional steps as an outsider to direct the operation or management of its customer, the RICO enterprise."[305] Thus, a bank that urges a debtor to take actions that will benefit the bank, perhaps to the detriment of others, may well fail the *Reves* test.[306]

Even when the outside professional had influence over the enterprise,[307] and even when the goods or services provided benefited the enterprise, the element will not be satisfied without additional evidence of actual direction.[308] Allegations

of assistance that do not show direction will not suffice.[309] However, when the defendants do more than just provide services and participate in the functions of the allegedly illegal activity, then they come within RICO § 1962(c).[310] Accordingly,

---

operation of a garden-variety marketing arrangement" between defendant health insurer and other members of the enterprise); Brannon v. Boatmen's First Nat'l Bank, 153 F.3d 1144, 1148 (10th Cir. 1998); *In re* Mastercard Int'l Inc., 132 F. Supp. 2d 468,489 (E.D. La. 2001).

303 Goren v. New Vision Int'l Inc., 156 F.3d 721, 728 (7th Cir. 1998) ("simply performing services for an enterprise, even with knowledge of the enterprise's illicit nature, is not enough to subject an individual to RICO liability under § 1962(c)"); Jubelirer v. MasterCard Int'l, 68 F. Supp. 2d 1049, 1053 (W.D. Wis. 1999) (merely having a business relationship with and performing services for an enterprise does not give rise to RICO liability); Succession of Wardlaw v. Whitney Nat'l Bank, 1994 U.S. Dist. LEXIS 15215, at *5 (E.D. La. 1994).

304 Dongelewicz v. PNC Bank Nat'l Ass'n, 2004 WL 1661863, at *5 (3d Cir. July 23, 2004) (affirming summary judgment in favor of lender).

305 Dahlgren v. First Nat'l Bank of Holdrege, 533 F.3d 681, 690 (8th Cir. 2008).

306 *Id.* (plaintiffs accused bank of misleading them into continuing to do business with a company by concealing company's increasing financial weakness; plaintiffs had sufficiently alleged one act that indicated *Reves*-type control, the altering of notes to create the appearance of a security interest in assets the bank otherwise had no security interest in; however, accepting the bank's characterization of the event as an "isolated incident" that had occurred long before the predicate acts alleged by plaintiffs in support of their RICO claim; thus concluding that the one act could not alone demonstrate sufficient control over the enterprise's actions).

307 *In re* Taxable Mun. Bond Sec. Litig., 1993 U.S. Dist. LEXIS 17978, at *14 (E.D. La. 1993) (attorney not liable even though had influence in the enterprise).

308 Slaney v. International Amateur Athletic Fed'n, 244 F.3d 580, 598 (7th Cir. 2001) (U.S. Olympic Committee did not engage in conduct of alleged enterprise merely by providing drug testing services); The Univ. of Maryland v. Peat, Marwik, Main & Co., 996 F.2d 1534, 1539 (3d Cir. 1993) (auditor). *See also* City of N.Y. v. Smokes-Spirits.com, Inc., 541 F.3d 425, 449 (2d Cir. 2008) (allegations that defendant provided services that may have been helpful to an enterprise does not suffice to show that defendant "exert[ed] any control over the enterprise"), *related case at* 911 N.E.2d 834 (N.Y. 2009) (answering unrelated questions that Second Circuit has certified to state supreme court), *rev'd on other grounds*, 130 S. Ct. 983 (2010); Paycom Billing Services, Inc. v. Payment Res. Int'l, 212 F. Supp. 2d 732, 740 (W.D. Mich. 2002) (mere participation of non-employee is not enough, must show some exertion of control); Roger Whitmores Auto. Services, Inc. v. Lake Cnty., Ill., 2002 WL 959587, at *6 (N.D. Ill. May 9, 2002); Brown v. Coleman Investments, Inc., 993 F. Supp. 416 (M.D. La. 1998) (automobile

credit corporation who merely made and approved loans had no part in directing affairs of enterprise that included dealer alleged to have charged inflated fees and taxes).

309 Walter v. Drayson, 538 F.3d 1244, 1249 (9th Cir. 2008) (plaintiff's allegations failed to show that an attorney for a trustor, a member of an associated-in-fact enterprise, satisfied the *Reves* test when allegations did not show that attorney knowingly implemented decisions of upper management of enterprise nor showed that she was indispensable to achievement of enterprise's goal); Mayo, Lynch & Associates, Inc. v. Pollack, 799 A.2d 12, 21, 22 (N.J. Super. Ct. App. Div. 2002) (attorney who issued opinion letters only gave routine legal services that did not constitute direction of the enterprise's affairs and therefore did not violate RICO regardless of whether letters were fraudulent). *See also* Crete v. Resort Condos. Int'l, L.L.C., 2011 WL 666039, at *11 (D.N.J. Feb. 14, 2011) (general allegation of support and direction insufficient); Johnson v. Equity Title & Escrow Co. of Memphis, L.L.C., 476 F. Supp. 2d 873, 877–879 (W.D. Tenn. 2007) (holding that plaintiff, a victim of a predatory loan scheme, successfully alleged that a title company that participated in the scheme had participated sufficiently to meet the "conduct" requirement, distinguishing the acts of the actors from those of outsiders); Carr v. Home Tech Co., 476 F. Supp. 2d 859, 863–865 (W.D. Tenn. 2007) (same as *Johnson*); Javitch v. Capwill, 284 F. Supp. 2d 848, 854 (N.D. Ohio 2003) (allegations that defendant acted pursuant to instructions of others while ignoring illicit nature of scheme did not meet *Reves'* operation or management test); Schmidt v. Fleet Bank, 16 F. Supp. 2d 340, 347 (S.D.N.Y. 1998) (allegations that bank allowed defrauder access to escrow accounts, approving overdrafts, and helping him to conceal scheme did not sufficiently allege conduct or participation).

310 *See, e.g.*, Ouwinga v. Benistar 419 Plan Services, Inc., 694 F.3d 783, 792 (6th Cir. 2012); City of New York v. LaserShip, Inc., 33 F. Supp. 3d 303, 310 (S.D.N.Y. 2014) (sufficient demonstration that defendant had "some part in directing the affairs" of the enterprise); International Floor Crafts, Inc. v. Adams, 578 F. Supp. 2d 231, 235 (D. Mass. 2008) (denying lender's motion for summary judgment when facts indicated that lender did not receive periodic interest payments but rather received a portion of profits, yielding a question of fact as to whether she was an active participant); Royal Indem. Co. v. Pepper Hamilton, L.L.P., 479 F. Supp. 2d 419, 427 (D. Del. 2007) (denying defendant's motion to dismiss); State Farm Mut. Auto. Ins. Co. v. Weiss, 410 F. Supp. 2d 1146, 1158 (M.D. Fla. 2006) (denying motion for summary judgment of one defendant, a physician who allegedly participated in a scheme to defraud plaintiffs, insurers, by ordering unnecessary medical tests); Roger Whitmores Auto. Services, Inc. v. Lake Cnty., Ill., 2002 WL 959587, at *5 (N.D. Ill. May 9, 2002) (defendants' accompaniment of allegedly corrupt sheriff on visits to extort campaign contributions could satisfy conduct element when defendants knew the purpose of the visits); *In re* Lupron Mktg. & Sales Practices Litig., 295 F. Supp. 2d 148, 172 n.25 (D. Mass. 2001) (rejecting defendant's argument that *Reves* required defendant to have had "control" of the enterprise); Ifill v. West, 1999 U.S. Dist. LEXIS 21320, at *27–*28 (E.D.N.Y. Aug. 24, 1999) (denying motion to dismiss RICO claim against lender when plaintiff alleged that lender recruited prospective targets for the fraudulent scheme by distributing brochures and giving seminars and applied to HUD before making loans for protection from possible losses from the contemplated mortgages); Sikes v. AT&T, 179 F.R.D. 342, 353 (S.D. Ga. 1998) (denying summary judgment to AT&T for its part in operating a 900-number game when defendant had not just rendered telephone services but had allegedly approved and edited the scripts and advertising used in the game, reviewed and altered the prize structure and game rules, and exercised control over the length

attorneys can be liable under RICO if they participated in the fraud, as opposed to merely providing the traditional functions of giving legal advice.[311] An insurance company that provides force-placed insurance to borrowers at a lender's behest may have sufficient control over an alleged enterprise as well.[312] The question of just how much participation the outside professional had is not usually appropriate to resolve at the pleadings stage.[313]

When the defendant is within the enterprise, however, "[s]pecial care is required in translating *Reves*' concern with 'horizontal' connections—focusing on the liability of an outside adviser—to the 'vertical' question of how far RICO liability may extend within the enterprise but down the organizational ladder."[314] *Reves* was concerned with those cases in which the defendant had a horizontal relationship with the enterprise. It has less of a limiting effect on those cases in which the defendant is within the structure of the enterprise, that is, when the defendant has a vertical relationship with the enterprise.

Courts have repeated the Supreme Court's instruction that lower rung participants may be liable, for example by "knowingly implementing decisions, as well as by making them."[315] Evidence that a defendant had decision-making power can show that a defendant participated in the operation of an enterprise, but *Reves* does not require such evidence.[316] Moreover, the commission of crimes by lower level employees may be found to indicate participation in the operation or management of the enterprise but does not prove it.[317] The plaintiff

---

and price of calls to the game); Heller v. First Town Mortg. Corp., 1998 U.S. Dist. LEXIS 14427, at *24–*25 (S.D.N.Y. Sept. 14, 1998) (declining to dismiss RICO claim against mortgage escrow account servicer, finding that the functions that defendant performed for the enterprise, which comprised investors or lenders who pool their mortgages, rose to level of participation in the operation and management of the enterprise's affairs); Bowdoin Constr. Corp. v. Rhode Island Hosp. Trust Nat'l Bank, N.A., 869 F. Supp. 1004 (D. Mass. 1994) (developer and lead lender for a resort exercised actual control over the resort), *aff'd on other grounds*, 94 F.3d 721 (1st Cir. 1996). *See also* Philadelphia Reserve Supply Co. v. Nowalk & Associates, Inc., 864 F. Supp. 1456 (E.D. Pa. 1994) (under N.J. RICO statute, accountants who assisted in formulation and implementation of fraudulent scheme operated or managed the RICO enterprise; went well beyond the normal provision of accounting services).

311 Ouwinga v. Benistar 419 Plan Services, Inc., 694 F.3d 783, 792 (6th Cir. 2012) (reversing dismissal of section 1962(c) claim against lawyers who falsely promoted benefit plan by knowingly providing misleading opinion letters that contributions were tax-deductible); Thomas v. Ross & Hardies, 9 F. Supp. 2d 547, 555 (D. Md. 1998) (*Reves* did not limit liability of attorney who allegedly persuaded homeowners to obtain mortgages and then diverted proceeds to enterprise instead of paying prior mortgagors, as agreed); Arons v. Lalime, 3 F. Supp. 2d 314, 322 (W.D.N.Y. 1998) (document that showed that defendant attorney helped establish and create procedures for fraudulent "roll program" which would pay attorney percentage of financial benefits raised factual question as to whether attorney exercised sufficient control over the enterprise to incur RICO liability); Mruz v. Caring, Inc., 991 F. Supp. 701, 719–720 (D.N.J. 1998) (plaintiffs, whistleblower employees, overcame *Reves* by alleging that attorneys seized power and control of enterprise for purposes of dissuading plaintiffs from revealing fraud and to defame and intimidate them; alleged behavior was more than the mere provision of legal services); Mathon v. Marine Midland Bank, N.A., 875 F. Supp. 986, 995 (E.D.N.Y. 1995) (concluding that plaintiffs sufficiently pleaded that attorneys had sufficient managerial control to meet the conduct requirement, though dismissing RICO claim on other grounds); Tribune Co. v. Purcigliotti, 869 F. Supp. 1076, 1098 (S.D.N.Y. 1994) (attorneys who assisted in filing and prosecution false workers' compensation claims participated in the operation or management of an enterprise comprising their law firm, several unions, and a doctor when they were alleged to have conceived of and executed the scheme), *aff'd*, 66 F.3d 12 (2d Cir. 1995). *See also* Roger Whitmores Auto. Services, Inc. v. Lake Cnty., Ill., 2002 WL 959587, at *6 (N.D. Ill. May 9, 2002) (dismissing attorneys from suit); Mayo, Lynch & Associates, Inc. v. Pollack, 799 A.2d 12, 18 (N.J. Super. Ct. App. Div. 2002) (jury could conclude that attorney's failure to comply with bid law indicated an intent to participate in illegal scheme in violation of state RICO statute).

312 Montoya v. PNC Bank, N.A., 2015 WL 1311482, at *10 (S.D. Fla. Mar. 23, 2015) (denying motion to dismiss when plaintiffs alleged that an insurer "managed the day-to-day operations of Defendants' RICO scheme by, for example, tracking [the lender's] portfolio for lapses [and] mailing notices that borrowers that included misleading 'half-truths' ").

313 *See, e.g.,* MCM Partners, Inc. v. Andrews-Bartlett & Assoc., Inc., 62 F.3d 967, 979 (7th Cir. 1995) (lower level employees can be deemed

to participate in RICO enterprise even if participation was coerced); United States v. Starrett, 55 F.3d 1525, 1546 (11th Cir. 1995) (lower level employees can be liable if they knowingly implement management decisions); Ifill v. West, 1999 U.S. Dist. LEXIS 21320, at *25 (E.D.N.Y. Aug. 24, 1999); Friedman v. Hartmann, 1994 U.S. Dist. LEXIS 9727, at *2 (S.D.N.Y. July 15, 1994); LaVornia v. Rivers, 669 So. 2d 288 (Fla. Dist. Ct. App. 1996) (employee does not have to be in control of decisions to be deemed to have participated). *See also* Renwick v. Bonnema, 2009 WL 393967, at *2 (E.D. Tex. Feb. 13, 2009) (denying defendant's motion to dismiss on the grounds that plaintiffs had sufficiently alleged that defendant had directed the enterprise's affairs).

314 United States v. Oreto, 37 F.3d 739, 750 (1st Cir. 1994).

315 United States v. Diaz, 176 F.3d 52, 93 (2d Cir. 1999) (affirming convictions of gang members when "the record makes clear that [the defendants] were both on the ladder, rather than under it"); MCM Partners, Inc. v. Andrews-Bartlett & Associates, Inc., 62 F.3d 967, 978 (5th Cir. 1995) (citing United States v. Oreto, 37 F.3d 739, 750 (1st Cir. 1994)).

316 DeFalco v. Bernas, 244 F.3d 286, 312 (2d Cir. 2001) (affirming verdict in case arising from alleged corruption in town affairs against defendants who did not have any official role in managing the town when there was sufficient evidence that defendants participated in that management); United States v. Posada-Rios, 158 F.3d 832, 856 (5th Cir. 1998); Dale v. Frankel, 131 F. Supp. 2d 852 (S.D. Miss. 2001). *See also* Williams v. Mohawk Indus., Inc., 465 F.3d 1277, 1286 (11th Cir. 2006) (holding that plaintiffs had sufficiently pleaded control to withstand a motion to dismiss); Baisch v. Gallina, 346 F.3d 366, 376 (2d Cir. 2003) (vacating summary judgment for a defendant, a shareholder and officer of participant in an allegedly fraudulent financing scheme, because plaintiff "demonstrated his discretionary authority and direction of the enterprise"); United States v. Shifman, 124 F.3d 31, 36 (1st Cir. 1997) (a defendant who is plainly integral to carrying out the enterprise's activities may be liable; denying summary judgment to defendant, an indebted borrower, who allegedly made referrals to his loansharker in exchange for relief on his debts); Barsky v. Metro Kitchen & Bath, Inc., 587 F. Supp. 2d 976, 988–989 (N.D. Ill. 2008) (individual who functionally controlled one of the associate corporations in alleged association in fact enterprise could not avoid RICO liability by identifying himself as a mere employee).

317 United States v. Allen, 155 F.3d 35, 42 (2d Cir. 1998) (denying summary judgment when evidence could show that defendant's acts of bribery could be found to be participation).

---

must demonstrate that the defendant's conduct related to the enterprise and was not just the defendant's own wrongdoing.[318] Ordinary employment duties, such as clerical work, will likely not satisfy the conduct requirement.[319]

When the enterprise is alleged to be an association in fact of which the defendants are alleged to be members, the structure is vertical, not horizontal, and the level of the defendant's participation should be judged accordingly.[320] By knowingly implementing management's decisions, and thereby enabling the enterprise to achieve its goals, the defendants meet the participation test of *Reves*.[321] Similarly, in a case against a subsidiary, a plaintiff may be able to adequately establish the conduct requirement by showing that the subsidiary used its responsibilities to commit fraud and then upstreamed that income to the corporate group enterprise in a manner that influenced the operation of the enterprise beyond a mere financial benefit.[322]

Members of an enterprise not related to each other by direct corporate ownership may still satisfy the conduct requirement by making non-trivial contributions such as controlling sales or advertising documents that other members of the enterprise use to execute the fraud.[323] However, when the enterprise comprises defendants not related by corporate ownership, the plaintiff must demonstrate that a given defendant conducted the enterprise's affairs, as opposed to the defendant's own affairs.[324]

7.5.5 Conspiracy: Section 1962(d)

RICO § 1962(d) declares it unlawful for any person to conspire to violate any of the provisions of subsections (a), (b), or (c) of RICO § 1962. *Salinas v. United States*[325] resolved a split in the circuits as to the requirements of RICO § 1962(d) by choosing the broader of two possible readings. Relying on traditional conspiracy law, which provides that, so long as they share a common purpose, conspirators are liable for the acts of their co-conspirators, the Court ruled that RICO does not require that the defendant must commit or agree to commit two or more predicate offenses in order to violate RICO § 1962(d).[326] Rather, the conspirator need only "intend to further an endeavor which, if completed, would satisfy all of the elements of a substantive criminal offense, . . . it suffices that he adopt the goal of furthering or facilitating the criminal endeavor."[327] While the commission of two predicate offenses may prove this intent, it is not the only means of proving it.[328] Based on this holding, the Court affirmed the conviction of a sheriff's deputy who knew about and agreed to facilitate a bribery scheme but who had not accepted or agreed to accept two bribes.

Lower court decisions since *Salinas* have generally held that the plaintiff or prosecutor need only show that the defendant agreed that predicate offenses would be committed on behalf of the conspiracy.[329] The Eleventh Circuit has taken

---

318 *See, e.g.*, Williams v. Ford Motor Co., 11 F. Supp. 2d 983, 986 (N.D. Ill. 1998) (dismissing complaint against Ford Motor Company based on dealer's fraudulent charges under extended service plan, dealer's fraud was its own act, not that of the enterprise consisting of Ford and dealership). *See also* Davis-Lynch, Inc. v. Moreno, 667 F.3d 539, 551 (5th Cir. 2012), *as revised*, (Jan. 12, 2012) (husband and son-in-law of embezzling employee did not conduct the enterprise by merely receiving funds or materials generated by the fraudulent scheme); Richardson v. Cella, 2013 WL 4525642, at *5 (E.D. La. Aug. 26, 2013) (allegations that a defendant's use of employees and other resources of companies under his control sufficed).

319 *See, e.g.*, Barsky v. Metro Kitchen & Bath, Inc., 587 F. Supp. 2d 976, 988 (N.D. Ill. 2008).

320 *See* MCM Partners v. Andrews-Bartlett & Associates, 62 F.3d 967, 979 (7th Cir. 1995) (reversing dismissal of claims against defendant).

321 *Id. See also* Leonard v. City of Los Angeles, 208 Fed. Appx. 517, 519 (9th Cir. 2006) (ruling that plaintiff met the conduct requirement by alleging that some of the defendants had bribed members of the enterprise); Williams v. Mohawk Indus., Inc., 465 F.3d 1277, 1285 (11th Cir. 2006) (ruling that plaintiff had sufficiently alleged the conduct element for purposes of a motion to dismiss); United States v. Oreto, 37 F.3d 739, 750, 751 (1st Cir. 1994) (section 1962(c) applies to foot soldiers as well as to generals); United States v. Philip Morris USA, 566 F.3d 1095 (D.C. Cir. 2009), *order clarified*, 778 F. Supp. 2d 8 (D.D.C. 2011); Phoenix Bond & Indem. Co. v. Bridge, 911 F. Supp. 2d 661 (N.D. Ill. 2012) (plaintiffs met the conduct element by alleging that defendants made "a conscious decision to adopt a particular structure" with the enterprise to participate in rigged tax sales); Tuscano v. Tuscano, 403 F. Supp. 2d 214, 227 (E.D.N.Y. 2005) (denying the motion of defendants, employees, to dismiss).

322 *See* Miller v. Chevy Chase Bank, 1998 U.S. Dist. LEXIS 3651, at *3 (N.D. Ill. Mar. 24, 1998); Majchrowski v. Norwest Mortg., 6 F. Supp. 2d 946, at 44, 45 (N.D. Ill. 1998).

323 *See, e.g.*, Negrete v. Allianz Life Ins. Co. of N. Am., 2011 WL 4852314, at *6–7 (C.D. Cal. Oct. 13, 2011) (denying defendant's motion for summary judgment, reasoning that defendant's participation exceeded mere control of document content but extended to training and control over other members of the enterprise).

324 United Food & Commercial Workers Unions & Emp'rs Midwest Health Benefits Fund v. Walgreen Co., 719 F.3d 849, 854–856 (7th Cir. 2013) (rejecting argument that simply because each member of the association in fact needed the other to have accomplished the scheme, each was thereby acting on behalf of the enterprise).

325 522 U.S. 52, 118 S. Ct. 469, 139 L. Ed. 2d 352 (1997).

326 522 U.S. at 65 ("[t]he interplay between subsections (c) and (d) does not permit us to excuse from the reach of the conspiracy provision an actor who does not himself commit or agree to commit the two or more predicate acts requisite to the underlying offense").

327 *Id.*

328 *Id.*

329 United States v. Harris, 695 F.3d 1125, 1131 (10th Cir. 2012) (existence of an enterprise is not an element of a section 1962(d) claim); Heinrich v. Waiting Angels Adoption Services, Inc., 668 F.3d 393, 411 (6th Cir. 2012) (" '[a]n agreement can be shown if the defendant objectively manifested an agreement to participate directly or indirectly in the affairs of an enterprise through the commission of two or more predicate crimes' ") (citation omitted); United States v. Philip Morris USA, Inc., 566 F.3d 1095 (D.C. Cir. 2009), *order clarified*, 778 F. Supp. 2d 8 (D.D.C. 2011); United States v. Corrado, 286 F.3d 934, 937 (6th Cir. 2002) (section 1962(d) does not require an overt or specific act to further the RICO enterprise; Smith v. Berg, 247 F.3d 532, 538 (3d Cir. 2001) (defendant may be liable under section 1962(d) if he knowingly agrees to facilitate a scheme that includes the operation or management of an enterprise; rejecting construction that would require defendants to have conspired to do something for which the defendant would, if successful, be liable under section 1962(c)); Goren v. New Vision Int'l, Inc., 156 F.3d 721 (7th Cir. 1998) (defendant must agree that someone would commit two predicate acts on behalf of the enterprise); United States v. To, 144 F.3d 737 (11th Cir. 1998); New York Dist. Council of

the expansive view that such an agreement can be shown by proving an agreement on an overall objective, which in turn can be proven by circumstantial evidence that each defendant must reasonably have known that others were also conspiring to participate in the same enterprise through a pattern of racketeering activity.[330] However, a few courts have ruled that

a RICO civil conspiracy claim can stand only if the plaintiff proves that the defendant agreed to commit predicate offenses.[331] Given that these cases did not analyze the impact of *Salinas*, their holdings are frail.

The issue that arises most often under RICO § 1962(d) is whether a corporation has conspired with its own parent, subsidiaries, officers, or directors. While some courts have ruled that a corporation cannot, in effect, conspire with itself for RICO purposes,[332] other courts accept intra-corporate conspiracies.[333]

Carpenters Pension Fund v. Forde, 939 F. Supp. 2d 268, 283 (S.D.N.Y. 2013) (refusing to dismiss conspiracy claim, concluding that section 1962(d) does not require a plaintiff to allege an enterprise or continuity of pattern as to each individual conspiracy defendant); Brock v. Thomas, 782 F. Supp. 2d 133 (E.D. Pa. 2011) (plaintiff need not show that defendant herself committed the substantive violation in order to establish a conspiracy claim); Strayer v. Bare, 2008 WL 1924092, at *7 (M.D. Pa. Apr. 28, 2008) (a defendant can be part of a conspiracy even when that defendant does not participate in all the elements of the conspiracy); Roger Whitmore's Auto. Services, Inc. v. Lake Cnty., Ill., 2002 WL 959587, at *10 (N.D. Ill. May 9, 2002) (conspiracy claim could survive if one of the defendants agreed that someone else should commit two predicate acts constituting a pattern); Wiwa v. Royal Dutch Petroleum Co., 2002 WL 319887, at *26 (S.D.N.Y. Feb. 28, 2002) (co-conspirators need not know of all violations by the other conspirators in furtherance of the conspiracy, finding plaintiff alleged RICO conspiracy claim); Eva v. Midwest Nat'l Mortg. Banc, Inc., 143 F. Supp. 2d 862, 880 (N.D. Ohio 2001) (refusing to dismiss conspiracy claim, since it could be logically inferred from plaintiff's allegations that defendant voluntarily involved itself in the scheme); BCCI Holdings v. Khalil, 56 F. Supp. 2d 14 (D.D.C. 1999) (co-conspirator need only agree to a scheme that will violate section 1962(c) and need not commit or agree to commit the predicate acts himself), *aff'd in part, rev'd in part on other grounds*, 214 F.3d 168 (D.C. Cir. 2000); American Auto. Accessories, Inc. v. Fishman, 991 F. Supp. 995 (N.D. Ill. 1998). *See also* Sky Med. Supply Inc. v. SCS Support Claims Services, Inc., 17 F. Supp. 3d 207, 227, 228, 229–231 (E.D.N.Y 2014) (detailed allegations of specific role of each defendant in scheme stated a plausible claim); Wilson v. Parisi, 549 F. Supp. 2d 637, 660 (M.D. Pa. 2008) (in claim arising from allegedly fraudulent lending scheme, upholding claim against appraiser based on the inflated appraisal of plaintiff's home); Johnson v. Equity Title & Escrow Co. of Memphis, L.L.C., 476 F. Supp. 2d 873, 880 (W.D. Tenn. 2007) (same as *Carr*); Carr v. Home Tech Co., 476 F. Supp. 2d 859, 866 (W.D. Tenn. 2007) (denying defendants' motion to dismiss when plaintiffs alleged that they "formed an enterprise and agreed that one or more of them would take criminal actions to further their alleged predatory lending scheme"); In re American Investors Life Ins. Co. Annuity Mktg. & Sales Practices Litig., 2007 WL 2541216, at *27 (E.D. Pa. Aug. 29, 2007) (in case alleging that defendants engaged in a fraudulent scheme to sell elders unnecessary and unsuitable estate planning instruments, denying motion to dismiss RICO conspiracy claim against certain defendants); In re Nat'l W. Life Ins. Deferred Annuities Litig., 467 F. Supp. 2d 1071, 1086 (S.D. Cal. 2006) (denying defendant's motion to dismiss); SKS Constructors, Inc. v. Drinkwine, 458 F. Supp. 2d 68, 80–81 (E.D.N.Y. 2006) (denying defendant's motion to dismiss); Baker v. Family Credit Counseling Corp., 440 F. Supp. 2d 392, 411 (E.D. Pa. 2006) (denying motion of credit counseling services to dismiss claim of consumers who had entered into debt management plans that they alleged worsened their financial condition); The Flag Co. v. Maynard, 2006 WL 1030173, at *11–12 (D. Or. Apr. 17, 2006) (holding that plaintiff sufficiently alleged that defendants agreed to participate in an enterprise and to the commission of two predicate acts); Florida v. Tenet Healthcare Corp., 420 F. Supp. 2d 1288, 1307 (S.D. Fla. 2005).

330 United States v. To, 144 F.3d 737 (11th Cir. 1998). *See also* Angermeir v. Cohen, 14 F. Supp. 3d 134, 154–156 (S.D.N.Y. 2014) (though allegations were somewhat "conclusory," defendants' agreement " 'can be inferred from circumstantial evidence of the defendant[s'] status in the enterprise or knowledge of wrongdoing' ").

Alternatively, a violation of section 1962(d) can be shown by proving the defendant agreed to commit two predicate acts. Angermeir v. Cohen, 2014 WL 1613016, at *14–15 (S.D.N.Y. Mar. 27, 2014). *But see* Zito v. Leasecomm Corp., 2003 WL 22251352, at *20 (S.D.N.Y. Sept. 30, 2003) (allegation that defendant should have known of fraudulent scheme insufficient to support conspiracy claim because a RICO plaintiff must show that a defendant joined the conspiracy with the intent to commit the offenses that are the object of the scheme) (citing United States v. Ceballos, 340 F.3d 115, 123–124 (2d Cir. 2003)).

331 Jordan (Berm.) Inv. Co. v. Hunter Green Investments Ltd., 154 F. Supp. 2d 682, 695 (S.D.N.Y. 2001) (holding, contrary to *Salinas*, that defendants must have agreed to commit two predicate acts in order to sustain section 1962(d) liability); First Capital Asset Mgmt. v. Brickelbush, Inc., 150 F. Supp. 2d 624, 636 (S.D.N.Y. 2001) (no conspiracy without claim that defendants agreed to commit predicate acts sufficient for a pattern). *See also* Abraham v. Singh, 480 F.3d 351, 357 (5th Cir. 2007) (holding that plaintiff sufficiently alleged a violation of section 1962(d) by alleging that each defendant had agreed to commit at least two predicate acts of racketeering).

332 Fogie v. THORN Americas, Inc., 190 F.3d 889 (8th Cir. 1999) (as a matter of law, a parent corporation and its wholly-owned subsidiaries are incapable of forming a conspiracy with one another); WW, L.L.C. v. Coffee Beanery, Ltd., 2012 WL 3728184, at *16 (D. Md. Aug. 27, 2012) (concluding that neither exception to the intracorporate conspiracy doctrine existed and dismissing RICO claim); Broussard v. Meineke Discount Muffler Shops, Inc., 903 F. Supp. 16 (W.D.N.C. 1996); Brown v. Siegel, 1995 U.S. Dist. LEXIS 1945 (E.D. Pa. Feb. 14, 1995); Northeast Jet Ctr., LTD. v. Lehigh-Northampton Airport Auth., 767 F. Supp. 672 (E.D. Pa. 1991); U.S. Concord, Inc. v. Harris Graphics Corp., 757 F. Supp. 1053 (N.D. Cal. 1991); Rosemount Cogeneration Joint Venture v. Northern States Power Co., 1991 U.S. Dist. LEXIS 1504 (D. Minn. Jan. 18, 1991); Gaudette v. Panos, 650 F. Supp. 912 (D. Mass. 1987), *rev'd on other grounds*, 852 F.2d 30 (1st Cir. 1988); Satellite Fin. Planning Corp. v. First Nat'l Bank, 633 F. Supp. 386 (E.D. Pa. 1986); Yancoski v. E.F. Hutton, 581 F. Supp. 88 (E.D. Pa. 1983). *See also* Bellizan v. Easy Money of La., Inc., 2001 U.S. Dist. LEXIS 1731 (E.D. La. Feb. 12, 2001) (refusing to dismiss conspiracy claim when plaintiff avoided self-conspiracy problem by excluding primary defendant, a payday loan company, from the conspiracy claims).

333 Webster v. Omnitriton Int'l, Inc., 79 F.3d 776 (9th Cir. 1996) (extends section 1962(d) liability to a wholly intra-corporate conspiracy); Shearin v. E.F. Hutton Grp., Inc., 885 F.2d 1162 (3d Cir. 1989); Fleischhauer v. Feltner, 879 F.2d 1290 (6th Cir. 1989); Haroco, Inc. v. American Nat'l Bank & Trust Co. of Chicago, 747 F.2d 384, 403 n.22 (7th Cir. 1984), *aff'd on other grounds*, 473 U.S. 606 (1985); United States v. Hartley, 678 F.2d 961, 970–972 (11th Cir. 1982) (dicta); Mitchell Tracey v. First Am. Title Ins. Co., 935 F. Supp. 2d 826, 846 (D. Md. 2013) (applying "independent personal stake" exception to the intracorporate conspiracy doctrine; refusing to dismiss section 1962(d) claim when plaintiffs alleged that defendant had a personal interest that was "independent and 'wholly separable' " from corporation's interests); Dist. 65 Retirement Trust v. Prudential Sec. Inc., 925 F. Supp. 1551 (N.D. Ga. 1996); Pappas v. NCNB, 653 F. Supp. 699 (M.D.N.C. 1987); Ashland Oil, Inc. v. Arnett, 656 F. Supp. 950 (N.D. Ind. 1987), *aff'd in part, rev'd in part*

A plaintiff pleading a violation of RICO § 1962(d) must meet the restrictive injury pleading rules for that section in addition to pleading the substantive violation.[334]

7.6　Required Injury

7.6.1　General

"Any person injured in his business or property by reason of a violation of section 1962" may sue for treble RICO damages.[335] The Supreme Court has explicitly rejected any constrictive constructions of this injury requirement that would require private RICO plaintiffs to prove "racketeering" or "competitive" or "commercial" injury.[336] Furthermore, RICO is not limited to domestic injuries.[337]

The injury must be "by reason of a violation of section 1962," not by reason of the predicate offense. As described at § 7.6.2, *infra*, this significantly complicates proof of injury under most RICO section 1962 subsections, but not under RICO section 1962(c). As a result, most RICO consumer litigation is under section 1962(c).

The injury requirement raises issues as to proximate cause, the type of injury required, and the injury's directness, concreteness, and ripeness. While a plaintiff must have suffered an injury, that plaintiff need not have been injured by each predicate offense alleged, but only by one of the defendant's predicate offenses.[338]

The Sixth Circuit has ruled that while a direct injury is necessary, RICO's standing requirement is not a jurisdictional issue.[339] At the pleading stage, it should be sufficient to allege that the plaintiff has suffered an injury caused by the violations; the plaintiff need not plead factual detail such as the components of the damages.[340]

7.6.2　Injury from Predicate Offense's Relationship to the Enterprise

7.6.2.1　Injury Under Section 1962(a)

RICO § 1962(a) prohibits a person who has derived income from a pattern of racketeering activity or collection of an unlawful debt to invest that income in an enterprise. In most circuits, the plaintiff must prove injury not by the predicate offenses, but by the defendant's investment of illegally gotten profits into the enterprise.[341] In these circuits, the plaintiff has to show that the use or investment of the income was a "substantial factor" in causing the plaintiff's injury; simply showing that the racketeering activity continued through the

---

339　Stooksbury v. Ross, 528 Fed. Appx. 547, 2013 WL 2665596, at *7 (6th Cir. June 13, 2013) (affirming jury verdict for damages that came after the court entered a default judgment on liability as a discovery sanction).

340　Zito v. Leasecomm Corp., 2003 WL 22251352, at *18–19 (S.D.N.Y. Sept. 30, 2003).

341　*See, e.g.*, N. Cypress Med. Ctr. Operating Co. v. Cigna Healthcare, 781 F.3d 182, 202 (5th Cir. 2015) (affirming dismissal of claim); Ideal Steel Supply Corp. v. Anza, 652 F.3d 310, 324 (2d Cir. 2011) (concluding that plaintiff was able to establish injury by claiming that its competitor did not charge sales tax on cash transactions and used money saved to open a competitive store near plaintiff); Kolar v. Preferred Real Estate Inv., Inc., 361 Fed. Appx. 354, 360 (3d Cir. 2010) (affirming dismissal of claim); Rao v. BP Products N. Am., Inc., 589 F.3d 389, 398–399 (7th Cir. 2009) (affirming dismissal of claim); Sybersound Records, Inc. v. UAV Corp., 517 F.3d 1137, 1149 (9th Cir. 2008) ("[r]einvestment of proceeds from alleged racketeering activity back into the enterprise to continue its racketeering activity is insufficient to show proximate causation"); Abraham v. Singh, 480 F.3d 351, 356–357 (5th Cir. 2007); St. Paul Mercury Ins. Co. v. Williamson, 224 F.3d 425, 443 (5th Cir. 2000); Fogie v. THORN Ams., Inc., 190 F.3d 889, 894 (8th Cir. 1999); Parker & Parsley Petroleum Co. v. Dresser Indus., 972 F.2d 580, 584 (5th Cir. 1992); Vemco, Inc. v. Camardella, 23 F.3d 129, 132 (6th Cir. 1994); Nugget Hydroelec. L.P. v. Pacific Gas & Elec. Co., 981 F.2d 429, 437, 438 (9th Cir. 1992); Glessner v. Kenny, 952 F.2d 702, 708–710 (3d Cir. 1991); Danielsen v. Burnside-Ott Aviation Training Ctr., Inc., 941 F.2d 1220, 1229, 1230 (D.C. Cir. 1991); Ouaknine v. McFarlane, 897 F.2d 75, 82 (2d Cir. 1990); Grider v. Texas Oil & Gas Corp., 868 F.2d 1147, 1150 (10th Cir. 1989); Proctor v. Metropolitan Money Store Corp., 645 F. Supp. 2d 464, 482–483 (D. Md. 2009) (denying motion to dismiss when plaintiffs alleged that as part of foreclosure rescue scam, certain individuals reinvested excessive fees that they collected into new transactions); Marlow v. Allianz Life Ins. Co., 2009 WL 1328636, at *3 (D. Colo. May 12, 2009). *See also* Carnegie v. Household Int'l, Inc., 220 F.R.D. 542, 546 (N.D. Ill. 2004) (noting that while the Seventh Circuit has not ruled on the issue, following the majority to hold that a plaintiff "must allege an investment injury which can be distinguished from the injuries resulting from the predicate acts of fraud"), *aff'd on other grounds*, 376 F.3d 656 (7th Cir. 2004) (affirming certification of class); Allen v. New World Coffee, Inc., 2002 WL 432685, at *3–4 (S.D.N.Y. Mar. 19, 2002) (claim that alleged injury arose from reinvestment of racketeering income into the enterprise did not state section 1962(a) claim). *But see* Busby v. Crown Supply, Inc., 896 F.2d 833, 836–840 (4th Cir. 1990) (rejecting "investment injury" rule).

---

on other grounds, 875 F.2d 1271 (7th Cir. 1989); Pandick v. Rooney, 632 F. Supp. 1430, 1435 (N.D. Ill. 1986); Callan v. State Chem. Mfg. Co., 584 F. Supp. 619, 623 (E.D. Pa. 1984). *See also* Hernandez v. Vanderbilt Mortg. & Fin., Inc., 2010 WL 3359559, at *19 (S.D. Tex. Aug. 25, 2010) (refusing to dismiss claim when no defendant had a parent/subsidiary relationship with another defendant); Dimas v. Vanderbilt Mortg. & Fin., Inc., 2010 WL 3342216, at *19 (S.D. Tex. Aug. 25, 2010); Soto v. Vanderbilt Mortg. & Fin., Inc., 2010 WL 3363657, at *19 (S.D. Tex. Aug. 23, 2010). *Cf.* Hoxworth v. Blinder, Robinson & Co., 903 F.2d 186 (3d Cir. 1990) (leaving issue unresolved). *See generally* D. Abrams, The Law of Civil RICO § 4.8 (1995).

334　*See* § 7.6.2.4, *infra*.

335　18 U.S.C. § 1964(c); Sedima, S.P.R.L. v. Imrex Co., 473 U.S. 479, 496, 105 S. Ct. 3275, 87 L. Ed. 2d 346 (1985) (a "plaintiff only has standing if, and can only recover to the extent that, he has been injured in his business or property by the conduct constituting the violation"). *See also* Ironworkers Local Union 68 v. AstraZeneca Pharm., L.P., 634 F.3d 1352, 1360 (11th Cir. 2011) ("injury is an essential element that must be alleged"); Price v. Pinnacle Brands, Inc., 138 F.3d 602, 606–607 (5th Cir. 1998) (injury to plaintiff's business or property is a prerequisite under section 1964); Nodine v. Textron, Inc., 819 F.2d 347, 348–349 (1st Cir. 1987) (a plaintiff who cannot show injury to business or property lacks standing).

336　Sedima, S.P.R.L. v. Imrex Co., 473 U.S. 479, 495, 105 S. Ct. 3275, 87 L. Ed. 2d 346 (1985).

337　European Cmty. v. RJR Nabisco, Inc., 764 F.3d 149, 150 (2d Cir. 2014).

338　Terminate Control Corp. v. Horowitz, 28 F.3d 1335 (2d Cir. 1994); Town of Kearny v. Hudson Meadows Urban Renewal Corp., 829 F.2d 1263 (3d Cir. 1987); Marshall & Ilsley Trust Co. v. Pate, 819 F.2d 806 (7th Cir. 1987); Hunt v. Gouverneur Townhouse Partners, 1991 U.S. Dist. LEXIS 16749 (S.D.N.Y. Nov. 18, 1991).

reinvestment of racketeering proceeds will be considered too remote an injury to establish standing.[342]

This interpretation of the injury element will hamper use of the subsection in typical consumer cases. For example, a district court held that a plaintiff who alleged that a bank violated RICO § 1962(a) by collecting improper late charges through mail fraud, then reinvesting those charges to finance the bank's operations, failed to allege that he was injured by reason of the investment.[343] In another case, the injury requirement failed when profits from fraudulent advertising were reinvested in the company, resulting in the company continuing to sell the deceptively advertised product.[344]

7.6.2.2 Injury Under Section 1962(b)

RICO § 1962(b) prohibits a person through a pattern of racketeering activity or collection of an unlawful debt from acquiring or maintaining an interest in or control of an enterprise. Similar to the discussion regarding RICO § 1962(a), courts hold that, when alleging a violation of subsection 1962(b), the plaintiff must plead that the injury suffered was caused by the defendant's acquisition or maintenance of an interest in or control of an enterprise, as distinct from an injury resulting from the predicate offenses.[345]

---

342 Guy's Mech. Sys., Inc. v. FIA Card Services, N.A., 339 Fed. Appx. 193 (3d Cir. 2009) ("the mere use of racketeering proceeds to support a business that continues to engage in the racketeering activities that produced those profits does not qualify as an investment injury for purposes of a section 1962(a) claim"); Wagh v. Metris Direct, Inc., 363 F.3d 821, 829 (9th Cir. 2003) (rejecting argument that a plaintiff need only allege an injury caused by the use or investment of funds received from anyone through racketeering activity); R.R. Brittingham v. Mobil Corp. 943 F.2d 297, 304 (3d Cir. 1991) ("If this remote connection were to suffice, the use-or-investment injury requirement would be almost completely eviscerated where the alleged pattern of racketeering is committed on behalf of a corporation."); Hernandez v. Vanderbilt Mortg. & Fin., Inc., 2010 WL 3359559, at *16 (S.D. Tex. Aug. 25, 2010) (dismissing claim when plaintiffs failed to allege that they were injured by defendants' investment in an enterprise); Wood v. General Motors Corp., 2010 WL 3613812, at *8 (E.D.N.Y. Aug. 23, 2010) (magistrate's report and recommendation), *report and recommendation adopted*, 2010 WL 3613809 (E.D.N.Y. Sept. 15, 2010); Soto v. Vanderbilt Mortg. & Fin., Inc., 2010 WL 3363657, at *16 (S.D. Tex. Aug. 23, 2010); Carnegie v. Household Int'l, Inc., 220 F.R.D. 542, 546 (N.D. Ill. 2004) (dismissing section 1962(a) claim arising from alleged kickbacks for refund anticipation loans on grounds that plaintiff alleged only that the enterprise, rather than defendants' ownership of the enterprise, caused her injuries), *aff'd on other issues*, 376 F.3d 656 (7th Cir. 2004) (affirming certification of class); Charleswell v. Chase Manhattan Bank, N.A., 308 F. Supp. 2d 545, 575 (D. V.I. 2004) (dismissing section 1962(a) claim arising from mortgagee's procurement of forced placed hazard insurance that did not insure plaintiffs' equity in their homes on grounds that plaintiffs failed to distinguish the harm resulting from defendants' reinvestment of proceeds from the harm that was caused by their allegedly fraudulent activities); Calabrese v. CSC Holdings, Inc., 283 F. Supp. 2d 797, 812 (E.D.N.Y. 2003) (dismissing section 1962(a) claim against cable company on plaintiffs' failure to specifically allege how racketeering income was invested and how that investment directly caused their injuries); Dangerfield v. Merrill Lynch, Pierce, Fenner & Smith, Inc., 2003 WL 22227956, at *10 (S.D.N.Y. Sept. 26, 2003); Berk v. Tradewell, Inc., 2003 WL 21664679, at *1–4 (S.D.N.Y. July 16, 2003) (section 1962(a) requires a plaintiff to allege an injury caused by defendant's investment of racketeering income, dismissing claim against offices of employee that allegedly underpaid commissions and issued false W-2 statements); Roger Whitmore's Auto. Services, Inc. v. Lake Cnty., Ill., 2002 WL 959587, at *7 (N.D. Ill. May 9, 2002) (mere reinvestment insufficient); Bodtker v. Forest City Trading Grp., 1999 U.S. Dist. LEXIS 15345, at *11–*12 (D. Or. Sept. 9, 1999) (dismissing section 1962(a) claim when plaintiff alleged that defendant reinvested racketeering proceeds back into parent corporation, which allowed the racketeering activities to continue through "normal business operations"); Birnbaum v. Law Offices of G. David Westfall, P.C., 120 S.W.3d 470, 475 (Tex. App. 2003) (affirming summary judgment in favor of law firm on counterclaim brought by former client).

343 Turner v. Union Planters Bank, 974 F. Supp. 890, 893, 894 (S.D. Miss. 1997).

344 Brittingham v. Mobil Corp., 943 F.2d 297 (3d Cir. 1991). *See also* Bellizan v. Easy Money of La., Inc., 2001 U.S. Dist. LEXIS 1731, at *10 (E.D. La. Feb. 12, 2001) (since the injury suffered by plaintiff borrowers arose from payday lender's collection of allegedly usurious loans and not from the reinvestment of the profits from those loans in the business, their section 1962(a) claim failed).

345 *See, e.g.*, N. Cypress Med. Ctr. Operating Co. v. Cigna Healthcare, 781 F.3d 182, 203 (5th Cir. 2015) (affirming dismissal of claim); Abraham v. Singh, 480 F.3d 351, 357 (5th Cir. 2007); Leonard v. City of Los Angeles, 208 Fed. Appx. 517, 519 (9th Cir. 2006) (reversing trial court's dismissal of section 1962(b) claim of plaintiffs, a restaurant and related parties, who alleged that they were injured by the bribery of city police officers by a seafood supplier); Discon, Inc. v. Nynex Corp., 93 F.3d 1055, 1062, 1063 (2d Cir. 1996); Compagnie de Reassurance d'Ile de France v. New England Reinsurance Corp., 57 F.3d 56, 92 (1st Cir. 1995); Lightning Lube, Inc. v. Witco Corp., 4 F.3d 1153, 1191 (3d Cir. 1993); Danielson v. Burnside-Ott-Aviation Training Ctr., Inc., 941 F.2d 1220, 1229, 1230 (D.C. Cir. 1991); Old Time Enterprises, Inc. v. Int'l Coffee Corp., 862 F.2d 1213, 1219 (5th Cir. 1989); Hernandez v. Vanderbilt Mortg. & Fin., Inc., 2010 WL 3359559, at *17 (S.D. Tex. Aug. 25, 2010); Wood v. General Motors Corp., 2010 WL 3613812, at *8 (E.D.N.Y. Aug. 23, 2010) (magistrate's report and recommendation), *report and recommendation adopted*, 2010 WL 3613809 (E.D.N.Y. Sept. 15, 2010); Soto v. Vanderbilt Mortg. & Fin., Inc., 2010 WL 3363657, at *17 (S.D. Tex. Aug. 23, 2010); Carmona v. Spanish Broad. Sys., Inc., 2009 WL 890054, at *8 (S.D.N.Y. Mar. 30, 2009) (dismissing claim); Lester v. Percudani, 556 F. Supp. 2d 473 (M.D. Pa. 2008) (upholding claim against bank that allegedly participated in a fraudulent home lending conspiracy); *In re* Nat'l W. Life Ins. Deferred Annuities Litig., 467 F. Supp. 2d 1071, 1084 (S.D. Cal. 2006) (plaintiffs, who alleged that the defendants, insurance companies and agents, defrauded them by selling them unsuitable investments, sufficiently pleaded a violation of section 1962(b)); Carnegie v. Household Int'l, Inc., 220 F.R.D. 542, 546 (N.D. Ill. 2004) (dismissing section 1962(b) claim arising from alleged kickbacks for refund anticipation loans on grounds that plaintiff failed to allege a separate injury arising from defendants' ownership of the enterprise), *aff'd on other issues*, 376 F.3d 656 (7th Cir. 2004) (affirming certification of class); Crawford & Sons, Ltd. Profit Sharing Plan v. Besser, 216 F.R.D. 228, 238 (E.D.N.Y. 2003); Berk v. Tradewell, Inc., 2003 WL 21664679, at *1–4 (S.D.N.Y. July 16, 2003) (holding that plaintiff failed to allege acquisition or maintenance injuries under section 1962(b)); Allen v. New World Coffee, Inc., 2002 WL 432685, at *3–*4 (S.D.N.Y. Mar. 19, 2002) (plaintiff who failed to allege injury from defendant's acquisition or maintenance of an interest in the enterprise, but who only alleged injury from predicate acts, could not sustain section 1862(b) claim); Roger Whitmore's Auto. Services, Inc. v. Lake Cnty., Ill., 2002 WL 959587, at *8 (N.D. Ill. May 9, 2002) (dismissing plaintiffs' claim that failed to allege racketeering activity was a "but-for" cause of injury); Bellizan v. Easy Money of La., Inc., 2001 U.S. Dist. LEXIS 1731 (E.D. La. Feb. 12, 2001) (dismissing claim

7.6.2.3   Injury Under Section 1962(c)

Under RICO § 1962(c), when a consumer is injured by the predicate offenses themselves, the consumer can seek treble damages because the consumer was injured by *reason of* the violation, in contrast to RICO § 1962(a) and (b), which require an injury from the specific, prohibited relationship between the defendant and the enterprise.[346] RICO § 1962(c) prohibits a person employed or associated with an enterprise to conduct or participate in the conduct of that enterprise through a pattern of racketeering activity or collection of an unlawful debt. The Supreme Court has construed this language to mean that, "under § 1962(c), the compensable injury necessarily is the harm caused by predicate offenses sufficiently related to constitute a pattern, for the essence of the violation is the commission of those acts in connection with the conduct of an enterprise."[347] It is for this reason that section 1962(c) is the most common violation pleaded in a RICO case.

7.6.2.4   Injury Under Section 1962(d)

As for subsection 1962(d), the conspiracy subsection, a plaintiff must show that the injury was caused by an overt act that is an act of racketeering, or otherwise wrongful under RICO, and not just injury from an act that furthered the conspiracy.[348] The Supreme Court in *Beck v. Prupis* affirmed the dismissal of the case of a former employee who alleged that his firing was part of the defendant's conspiracy to violate RICO.[349] The firing itself was not an overt act of racketeering or otherwise prohibited by the statute and therefore the claim failed to meet RICO's injury requirement.[350] However, the Court expressly declined to decide whether "whether a plaintiff suing under § 1964(c) for a RICO conspiracy must allege an actionable violation under § 1962(a)–(c), or whether it is sufficient for the plaintiff to allege an agreement to complete a substantive violation and the commission of at least one act of racketeering that caused him injury."[351] Based on dicta, it does not appear that a plaintiff must necessarily have a claim under section 1962(c) in order to allege a violation of section 1962(d), which would functionally render section 1962(d) superfluous: "a plaintiff could, through a § 1964(c) suit for a violation of § 1962(d), sue co-conspirators who might not themselves have violated one of the substantive provisions of § 1962." The Third

Circuit subsequently upheld such an interpretation, ruling that a defendant alleged to have conspired to violate section 1962(c) did not have to commit or agree to commit predicate acts to be liable for conspiracy under section 1962(d), so long as he knowingly agreed to facilitate a scheme that included operation or management of a RICO enterprise.[352]

7.6.3   *Proximate and "But For" Causation*

The plaintiff must show that the defendant's RICO violation proximately caused the plaintiff's injury; it is insufficient to show merely that the injury would not have occurred "but for" the violation. In *Holmes v. Securities Investor Protection Corp.*,[353] the Supreme Court rejected a RICO construction that would have allowed a plaintiff to recover simply by showing that the plaintiff was injured, that the defendant had violated RICO § 1962, and that "but for" that violation, the plaintiff would not have suffered the injury.[354] Rather, a RICO plaintiff may not recover unless the plaintiff can demonstrate that the injuries were directly and proximately caused by a defendant's racketeering activity.[355]

---

352 Smith v. Berg, 247 F.3d 532, 538 (3d Cir. 2001).

353 Holmes v. Securities Investor Prot. Corp.,503 U.S. 258, 112 S. Ct. 1311, 117 L. Ed. 2d 532 (1992).

354 *Id.* at 503 U.S. 258, 265, 266.

355 *See* Phoenix Bond & Indem. Co. v. Bridge, 553 U.S. 639, 128 S. Ct. 2131, 170 L. Ed. 2d 1012 (2008); Empress Casino Joliet Corp. v. Johnston, 763 F.3d 723, 729–735 (7th Cir. 2014) (finding plaintiffs—casinos alleging that defendants, members of horseracing industry, had bribed state's governor to obtain favorable tax legislation—sufficiently established proximate cause with respect to one bill, but concluding plaintiffs failed to show it for a different bill; reversing summary judgment for defendants); Rock v. BAE Sys., Inc., 556 Fed. Appx. 869, 871–872 (11th Cir. 2014) (affirming dismissal of RICO claim); Jackson v. Nat'l Ass'n for Advancement of Colored People, 546 Fed. Appx. 438, 442–444 (5th Cir. 2013) (former employee failed to show that mail and wire fraud her employer allegedly committed did not proximately cause employer's inability to reinstate her); Wallace v. Midwest Fin. & Mortg. Services, Inc., 714 F.3d 414 (6th Cir. 2013) (causation may be shown if inflated appraisal furthered the fraudulent scheme that caused homeowner's financial injuries, even if he did not rely on the appraisal); *In re* Neurontin Mktg. & Sales Practices Litig., 712 F.3d 51, 57–58 (1st Cir. 2013) (reversing summary judgment for defendant, concluding that plaintiff provided sufficient evidence of both "but for" and proximate causation); BCS Services, Inc. v. Heartwood 88, L.L.C., 637 F.3d 750, 758–759 (7th Cir. 2011) (statistical evidence could suffice to defeat summary judgment on issue of causation); Southeast Laborers Health & Welfare Fund v. Bayer Corp., 444 Fed. Appx. 401, 409–410 (11th Cir. 2011) (affirming lower court's grant of defendant's motion to dismiss when plaintiff insufficiently demonstrated that defendant's alleged fraud regarding safety and efficacy of a prescription drug led directly to plaintiff's decision to pay for the drug); Stancuna v. New Haven Legal Assist. Inc., 383 Fed. Appx. 23, 24 (2d Cir. 2010) (affirming dismissal of claim); Bixler v. Foster, 596 F.3d 751, 756 (10th Cir. 2010) (affirming dismissal of claim); RWB Services, L.L.C. v. Hartford Computer Grp., Inc., 539 F.3d 681, 687 (7th Cir. 2008) (plaintiff lender who sought recovery for injuries allegedly caused by a scheme to repackage and resell used cameras as new, had adequately alleged both aspects of proximate cause); V-Tech Services, Inc. v. Street, 215 Fed. Appx. 93, 95–96 (3d Cir. 2007) (disappointed bidder could not meet RICO injury requirement when bidder might not have won the disputed contract even without the alleged fraudulent conduct); Williams v.

---

against payday lender because plaintiffs were injured only by the predicate acts, not by defendant's acquiring or maintaining an interest or control in the enterprise); *In re* Motel 6 Sec. Litig., 161 F. Supp. 2d 227 (S.D.N.Y. 2001); Redtail Leasing v. Bellezza, 1997 U.S. Dist. LEXIS 14821, at *3 (S.D.N.Y. Sept. 30, 1997); Domberger v. Metropolitan Life Ins. Co., 961 F. Supp. 506, 525 (S.D.N.Y. 1997).

346 18 U.S.C. § 1964(c).

347 Sedima, S.P.R.L. v. Imrex, Co., 473 U.S. 479, 497, 105 S. Ct. 3275, 87 L. Ed. 2d 346 (1985) (under section 1962(c)). Presumably the same reasoning applies if the method of violation is a collection of an unlawful debt, as opposed to a pattern of racketeering activity.

348 Beck v. Prupis, 529 U.S. 494, 120 S. Ct. 1608, 146 L. Ed. 2d 561 (2000).

349 529 U.S. 494, 505 (2002).

350 529 U.S. 494, 507 (2002).

351 *Id.* at 506 n.10.

Mohawk Indus., Inc., 465 F.3d 1277, 1287–1291 (11th Cir. 2006) (plaintiffs, members of a class of legal workers, sufficiently alleged that defendant's practices of hiring illegal immigrants proximately caused injury to plaintiffs by depressing wages); James Cape & Sons Co. v. PCC Constr. Co., 453 F.3d 396, 404 (7th Cir. 2006) (affirming judgment on the pleadings for the defendant in case in which plaintiff alleged the defendant had participated in rigging bids on the grounds that plaintiff could not show what portion of profits it alleged it had lost were caused by defendant's conduct); Evans v. City of Chicago, 434 F.3d 916, 931–933 (7th Cir. 2006) (plaintiff, who had allegedly been wrongfully imprisoned, could not base standing on the income lost from being incarcerated when he could not show that he had been gainfully employed before his arrest); George Lussier Enterprises, Inc. v. Subaru of New England, Inc., 393 F.3d 36 (1st Cir. 2004) (injuries of car dealers from alleged scheme by distributor to pack options onto vehicles were not caused by any misrepresentations and therefore did not support RICO claim); Green Leaf Nursery v. E.I. DuPont De Nemours and Co., 341 F.3d 1292 (11th Cir. 2003) (owners of nursery who alleged that defendant falsified evidence and tampered with witnesses could not establish proximate cause); Oki Semiconductor Co. v. Wells Fargo Bank, N.A., 298 F.3d 768, 774 (9th Cir. 2002) (plaintiff failed to show that defendant's money laundering of proceeds from armed robbery proximately caused loss); Ove v. Gwinn, 264 F.3d 817, 825 (9th Cir. 2001) (plaintiffs, whose blood was taken by defendant's employees upon arrest for driving under the influence, could not show causation as they did not allege that the fact that employees were unlicensed caused their blood alcohol levels to register above the legal limit); Byrne v. Nezhat, 261 F.3d 1075, 1111 (11th Cir. 2001) (injury to plaintiff arising from surgery by defendant did not result from misrepresentations allegedly made in medical journals or on bills, therefore no RICO injury); Proctor & Gamble Co. v. Amway Corp., 242 F.3d 539, 565 (5th Cir. 2001) (company could not demonstrate that competitor's alleged illegal pyramid structure proximately caused its injury); Maio v. Aetna Inc., 221 F.3d 472, 483 (3d Cir. 2000) (RICO plaintiff must show business or property suffered injury and that injury was proximately caused by defendant's violation of section 1962); Summit Props. v. Hoechst Celanese Corp., 214 F.3d 556, 561 (5th Cir. 2000) (rejecting "fraud on the market" theory of causation for RICO injury); Steamfitters Local Union No. 420 Welfare Fund v. Phillip Morris, Inc., 171 F.3d 912, 933 (3d Cir. 1999) (union health and welfare funds did not have standing to sue tobacco companies to recover monies paid for funds' participants' smoking-related illnesses; causation "much too speculative and attenuated to support a RICO claim"); Bonilla v. Volvo Car Corp., 150 F.3d 62 (1st Cir. 1998) (defendant's excise fraud, which presumably lowered the cost of cars purchased by plaintiffs, could not support a RICO claim because plaintiffs were not injured by reason of the fraud); Price v. Pinnacle Brands, Inc., 138 F.3d 602 (5th Cir. 1998) (no RICO injury when plaintiffs, purchasers of trading cards packages manufactured by defendant, alleged that defendant's practice of randomly inserting limited edition cards in packages was illegal gambling; plaintiffs had mere expectancy interests, not tangible property interests, declining to follow Schwartz v. Upper Deck Co., 967 F. Supp. 405 (S.D. Cal. 1997)); First Nationwide Bank v. Gelt Funding Corp., 27 F.3d 763 (2d Cir. 1994); Wilson v. EverBank, N.A., 77 F. Supp. 3d 1202, 1226–1228 (S.D. Fla. 2015) (dismissing claims of borrowers who alleged a scheme to force-place hazard insurance, reasoning that they failed to show that their injuries in paying for unauthorized charges were proximately caused by defendants' scheme); City of New York v. LaserShip, Inc., 33 F. Supp. 3d 303, 312–313 (S.D.N.Y. 2014) (S.D.N.Y. 2014) (plaintiff adequately alleged that defendant's selling, shipping, and transporting of unstamped cigarettes caused plaintiff a RICO injury of lost tax revenue); Negrete v. Allianz Life Ins. Co. of N. Am., 2011 WL 4852314, at *12 (C.D. Cal. Oct. 13, 2011) (concluding that plaintiffs, annuities purchasers, could establish proximate causation through evidence that they relied on defendant's sales materials; denying defendant's motion for summary judgment); Gagliardi v. Equifax Info.

The Supreme Court in 2006 resoundingly reaffirmed and provided guidance for the *Holmes* proximate cause rule in *Anza v. Ideal Steel Supply Corp.*, in which business owners sued a competitor that had failed to charge its customers sales

Services, L.L.C., 2011 WL 337331, at *6 (W.D. Pa. Feb. 3, 2011) (granting summary judgment to defendant when plaintiff failed to establish a link between his injuries and defendant's actions); Sykes v. Mel Harris & Associates, L.L.C., 757 F. Supp. 2d 413, 427–428 (S.D.N.Y. 2010) (defendants' pursuit of default judgments and attempts to enforce them proximately caused plaintiff's injuries), *class action certification aff'd*, Sykes v. Mel S. Harris & Associates, L.L.C., 780 F.3d 70 (2d Cir. 2015); Levine v. Torino Jewelers, Ltd., 2006 WL 709098, at *3–4 (S.D.N.Y. Mar. 22, 2006) (holding that plaintiff sufficiently alleged that defendants' acts would have been "a substantial factor in the sequence of responsible causation," and plaintiff's injury would have been "reasonably foreseeable or anticipated as a natural consequence") (citation omitted); Anglo-Iberia Underwriting Mgmt. Co. v. Lodderhose, 282 F. Supp. 2d 126, 133 (S.D.N.Y. 2003) (defamation damages too speculative to be recoverable, and therefore able to be trebled, under RICO); G-I Holdings, Inc. v. Baron & Budd, 238 F. Supp. 2d 521 (S.D.N.Y. 2002) (plaintiffs who alleged that they paid higher settlements to defendants' clients due to defendants' fraud alleged RICO injury); First Capital Asset Mgmt., Inc. v. Brickelbush, Inc., 218 F. Supp. 2d 369, 381 (S.D.N.Y. 2002) (plaintiffs failed to show that their inability to collect debts was proximately caused by defendants' predicate acts of bankruptcy crimes); Anderson v. Smithfield Foods, Inc., 207 F. Supp. 2d 1358, 1364 (M.D. Fla. 2002) (plaintiffs failed to allege causation when they did not allege that defendants targeted plaintiffs with scheme to defraud); Emcore Corp. v. PricewaterhouseCoopers, L.L.P., 102 F. Supp. 2d 237, 243 (D.N.J. 2000); Medgar Evers Houses Tenants Ass'n v. Medgar Evers Houses Associates, L.P., 25 F. Supp. 2d 116 (E.D.N.Y. 1998) (plaintiffs who alleged that housing management company made fraudulent statements to HUD had not suffered an injury proximately caused by the fraud; plaintiffs must show that their injuries are the "preconceived purpose," "specifically intended consequence," "necessary result" or "foreseeable consequences" of the racketeering); Line v. Astro Mfg. Co., 993 F. Supp. 1033 (E.D. Ky. 1998) (plaintiff who had paid no more than fair market value for manufactured home did not suffer an injury from the manufacturer's alleged concealment of the fire hazards of such homes); Skeete v. IVF Am., Inc., 972 F. Supp. 206 (S.D.N.Y. 1997) (no standing when injury did not arise from claimed predicate acts); Moore v. Painewebber, Inc., 1997 U.S. Dist. LEXIS 13884 (S.D.N.Y. Sept. 9, 1997) (investor who sued brokerage firm alleging misrepresentation could not proceed without alleging either "transaction causation" (would not have purchased but for the misrepresentations) or "loss causation" (misrepresentations were the reason the transaction turned out to be a losing one)); Red Ball Interior Demolition Corp. v. Palmadessa, 874 F. Supp. 576 (S.D.N.Y. 1995) (plaintiff must show direct relationship between plaintiff's injury and defendant's conduct). *See also* CGC Holding Co., L.L.C. v. Broad & Cassel, 773 F.3d 1076, 1099 (10th Cir. 2014) (rejecting defendant's challenge to standing, concluding that plaintiffs sufficiently pleaded proximate cause for purpose of class certification).

When mail fraud is involved, plaintiffs must show not only that they relied on fraudulent representations but that their reliance was the cause of their injury. Red Ball Interior Demolition Corp. v. Palmadessa, 874 F. Supp. 576 (S.D.N.Y. 1995). *See also* Lerner v. Fleet Bank, N.A., 459 F.3d 273, 283–286 (2d Cir. 2006) (discussing the differences between common law proximate cause and the more stringent RICO standard); Johnson v. Hoffa, 196 Fed. Appx. 88, 90–91 (3d Cir. 2006) (plaintiff, a former union employee who alleged that he was fired after he investigated corruption within the union, could not establish standing because the termination was not "independently wrongful" under any substantive RICO provision).

tax and had submitted fraudulent tax returns to the state.[356] The Court rejected the plaintiffs' argument that the practice allowed the defendant to charge lower prices and that those lower prices cost the plaintiffs sales.[357] The injury alleged, the Court reasoned, was too attenuated from the violating act, the tax fraud, to satisfy proximate cause.[358] The fact that a competitor commits tax fraud does not mean that it will charge lower prices, nor are a business's lost sales necessarily the product of a competitor's lower prices.[359]

The Supreme Court revisited the question of causation again in 2010, concluding in *Hemi Group, L.L.C. v. City of New York* that a city's RICO claim against an online cigarette seller failed for lack of proximate cause.[360] The city alleged mail fraud based on the defendant's failure to comply with a statute requiring it to report its customers to state authorities so that taxes could be collected from the cigarette buyers. Without the customer information, the city could not pursue non-taxpaying buyers for payment of the tax, which, according to the city, cost it lost revenue. In a plurality opinion, the Court confirmed that to successfully state a RICO claim, the plaintiff must demonstrate not just "but for" cause but also "proximate cause" between the alleged predicate acts and the ultimate injury.[361] In doing so, the Court restated guidance from *Holmes* that " '[t]he general tendency of the law, in regard to damages, at least, is not to go beyond the first step.' "[362] The Court characterized the city's theory of damages as requiring the Court to go "well beyond the first step," in part because it required reference to third parties, as the direct cause of the city's damages was the failure of the cigarette buyers, the defendant's customers, to pay the taxes that the state required them to pay.[363] Stretching proximate cause to cover the subsequent failure of the seller to file the statutorily-mandated report on customer information stretched the link between initial cause and ultimate injury too far.

Thus, a RICO plaintiff must establish causation by showing that the violation was both the factual (the "but for") cause of the plaintiff's injury and additionally that the violation proximately caused that injury: the violation was a substantial factor in the sequence of responsible causation and the injury was reasonably foreseeable or a natural consequence of the violation.[364] A liberal view of proximate cause requires only

---

356 Anza v. Ideal Steel Supply Corp., 547 U.S. 451, 164 L. Ed. 2d 720, 126 S. Ct. 1991, 1993 (2006).

357 *Id.* at 126 S. Ct. 1991, 1997 (2006).

358 *Id.*

359 *Id.* The Ninth Circuit construed *Anza* in holding that a governmental entity could not establish that the defendants' hiring of illegal aliens proximately caused its increased costs of law enforcement and public health care. Canyon Cnty. v. Syngenta Seeds, Inc., 519 F.3d 969, 981–982 (9th Cir. 2008). *See also* Treadway v. Lisotta, 2008 WL 3850462, at *4 (E.D. La. Aug. 15, 2008) (concluding, in case brought by insureds against a state-run entity providing insurance to high-risk applicants, that alleged financial mismanagement by entity was too attenuated from asserted injuries of excess assessments to satisfy RICO's proximate cause requirements).

   However, a city may base standing on a loss of tax revenue allegedly caused by a merchant's fraudulent evasion of use taxes. City of N.Y. v. Smokes-Spirits.com, Inc., 541 F.3d 425, 441 (2d Cir. 2008), *related case*, 911 N.E.2d 834 (N.Y. 2009) (answering unrelated questions that Second Circuit has certified to state supreme court), *rev'd on other grounds*, 130 S. Ct. 983 (2010).

360 Hemi Grp., L.L.C. v. City of New York, 130 S. Ct. 983, 988 (2010).

361 *Id.* (four Justices joined this aspect of the opinion; Justice Ginsburg concurred in the judgment).

362 *Id.* (citation omitted).

363 *Id.* at 990.

364 Williams v. Duke Energy Int'l, Inc., 681 F.3d 788, 803 (6th Cir. 2012) (reversing dismissal of claim brought by utility customers against utility and related entities arising from alleged unlawful rebates to large customers; concluding that plaintiffs adequately alleged proximate cause; rejecting argument that, since plaintiffs would have had to bring a case before a utility commission to recover the loss proximate cause was destroyed); Baisch v. Gallina, 346 F.3d 366, 369–371 (2d Cir. 2003); First Nationwide Bank v. Gelt Funding Corp., 27 F.3d 763, 769 (2d Cir. 1994); Lerner v. Fleet Bank, N.A., 318 F.3d 113, 116–130 (2d Cir. 2003); Brittingham v. Mobil Corp., 943 F.2d 297, 304 (3d Cir. 1991); New Mexico Oncology & Hematology Consultants, Ltd. v. Presbyterian Healthcare Services, 54 F. Supp. 3d 1189, 1241–1244 (D.N.M. 2014) (dismissing claim based on misrepresentations made by defendants, competitors of plaintiff, to pharmaceutical companies, reasoning that misrepresentations did not proximately cause any injury to plaintiff because it was merely an indirect victim); Lawson v. Full Tilt Poker Ltd., 930 F. Supp. 2d 476, 488-89 (S.D.N.Y. 2013) (intervening cause between racketeering activities and alleged injury disrupted proximate causation); Johnson v. KB Home, 720 F. Supp. 2d 1109 (D. Ariz. 2010) (purchasers of homes established proximate cause by alleging that their mortgage lenders would not have approved their loans but for defendants' fraudulently inflated appraisals); Spencer v. Hartford Fin. Services Grp., Inc., 256 F.R.D. 284, 298 (D. Conn. 2009). *See also* Newcal Indus., Inc. v. Ikon Office Solution, 513 F.3d 1038, 1055 (9th Cir. 2008) (proximate cause depends on three factors: "(1) whether there are more direct victims of the alleged wrongful conduct who can be counted on to vindicate the law as private attorneys general; (2) whether it will be difficult to ascertain the amount of plaintiff's damages attributable to defendant's wrongful conduct; and (3) whether the courts will have to adopt complicated rules apportioning damages to obviate the risk of multiple recoveries"); Sybersound Records, Inc. v. UAV Corp., 517 F.3d 1137, 1148–1149 (9th Cir. 2008) (decreased sales could not fulfill injury element when decrease could result from causes other than defendant's mail or wire fraud); Brandenburg v. Seidel, 859 F.2d 1179, 1189 (4th Cir. 1988) (proximate cause inquiry considers factors such as the foreseeability of the particular injury, the intervention of other independent causes, and the factual directness of the causal connection); Negrete v. Allianz Life Ins. Co. of N. Am., 287 F.R.D. 590, 606–607 (C.D. Cal. 2012) (class members who did not rely on alleged misrepresentations could nonetheless satisfy proximate cause by showing that reliance by *some* members of the class allowed defendant to raise the price of its products, thereby overcharging all class members); Burford v. Cargill, Inc., 2011 WL 4382124, at *10 (W.D. La. Sept. 20, 2011) (denying motion to dismiss when plaintiffs, cow feed purchasers, alleged that a cow feed manufacturer had reengineered the feed formula to the detriment of the cows' health and milk production); Circiello v. Alfano, 612 F. Supp. 2d 111, 116 (D. Mass. 2009) (plaintiff, who had alleged that her father had died because of a doctor's malpractice, could not establish proximate cause for any RICO injury from the acts of the defendants, a system of health care institutions and a board certification agency); Ficken v. AMR Corp., 578 F. Supp. 2d 134, 141 (D.D.C. 2008) (dismissing RICO claim on grounds that plaintiff merely alleged that airline falsely told him that frequent flyer mileage was not recoverable and did not allege that he lost that mileage as a result of a deliberate misrepresentation); Lester v. Percudani, 556 F. Supp. 2d 473 (M.D. Pa. 2008) (plaintiffs who alleged that defendants' scheme to finance home purchases for plaintiffs who

---

that it "be a substantial cause of a succession of events that in a logical sequence ultimately causes a plaintiff injury."[365]

would otherwise be unable to afford homes could establish causation even though not all of plaintiffs participated in the financing program because plaintiffs alleged that defendants' actions artificially increased home prices in the area when each of the plaintiffs had purchased property); Hearns v. Parisi, 548 F. Supp. 2d 132, 138 (M.D. Pa. 2008) (plaintiff who asserted that he was the victim of a predatory lending scheme was unable to show that the appraisal overvalued his house); Wallace v. BCS Ins. Co., 2008 WL 149150 (E.D. Cal. Jan. 14, 2008) (denying summary judgment on proximate cause issue in case alleging that the defendants, sellers of trip cancellation and interruption insurance, falsely represented to plaintiffs, purchaser of the insurance, that the coverage required a physician to cancel or interrupt the trip, rejecting defendants' argument that an independent ground for denial negated proximate cause); Florida v. Tenet Healthcare Corp., 420 F. Supp. 2d 1288, 1305–1306 (S.D. Fla. 2005) (allegations that hospital group's Medicare fraud lowered pool payments to plaintiffs, other hospitals, sufficiently satisfied the proximate cause requirement to withstand defendant's motion to dismiss); Hy Cite Corp. v. badbusinessbureau .com, L.L.C., 418 F. Supp. 2d 1142, 1151 (D. Ariz. 2005) (allegations that defendant's website, which disparaged plaintiff, caused plaintiff to lose customers sufficiently satisfied proximate cause requirement); Dale v. Ala Acquisitions, Inc., 203 F. Supp. 2d 694, 702 (S.D. Miss. 2002) (plaintiffs sufficiently pleaded standing).

365 *In re* Lupron Mktg. & Sales Practices Litig., 295 F. Supp. 2d 148, 175 (D. Mass. 2003). *See also* Slorp v. Lerner, Sampson & Rothfuss, 587 Fed. Appx. 249, 264 (6th Cir. 2014) (reversing dismissal of RICO claim, concluding that mortgagor sufficiently established that an allegedly fraudulent assignment of his mortgage to defendant bank caused his injuries incurred from fighting foreclosure; rejecting defendants' argument that it was mortgagor's default, and not the assignment, that caused his injuries); Wallace v. Midwest Fin. & Mortg. Services, Inc., 714 F.3d 414 (6th Cir. 2013) (causation may be shown if inflated appraisal furthered the fraudulent scheme that caused homeowner's financial injuries, even if he did not rely on the appraisal); *In re* Neurontin Mktg. & Sales Practices Litig., 712 F.3d 21, 38 (1st Cir. 2013) (rejecting defendant's argument that "there [were] too many steps in the causal chain between its misrepresentation and [plaintiff's] alleged injury" to establish proximate cause); Walters v. McMahen, 684 F.3d 435, 443–444 (4th Cir. 2012) (plaintiffs could not show that the predicate acts alleged, the fraudulent use of false identification documents by an employer that allegedly employed illegal immigrants, proximately caused their alleged injury of depressed wages); Southeast Laborers Health & Welfare Fund v. Bayer Corp., 444 Fed. Appx. 401, 409–410 (11th Cir. 2011) (affirming lower court's grant of defendant's motion to dismiss when plaintiff insufficiently alleged facts demonstrating that defendant's alleged fraud regarding safety and efficacy of a prescription drug led directly to plaintiff's decision to pay for the drug); RWB Services, L.L.C. v. Hartford Computer Grp., Inc., 539 F.3d 681, 688 (7th Cir. 2008) (rejecting lower court's reasoning that since other potential plaintiffs could show a more direct injury, this plaintiff did not sufficiently allege proximate cause, stating that "[t]he existence of multiple victims with different injuries does not foreclose a finding of proximate cause; in fact, one of the hallmarks of a RICO violation is 'the occurrence of distinct injuries' affecting several victims"); Trollinger v. Tyson Foods, Inc., 370 F.3d 602, 619 (6th Cir. 2004) (overturning dismissal of complaint by plaintiffs, unionized employees who alleged that their wages were depressed by employer's transportation and employment of illegal immigrants); Phoenix Bond & Indem. Co. v. Bridge, 911 F. Supp. 2d 661 (N.D. Ill. 2012) (concluding that a plaintiff need not establish 100% certainty that the damages were caused by a RICO violation; preponderance suffices); Heaven & Earth, Inc. v. Wyman Props. Ltd. P'ship, 2003 WL 22680935, at *1–2 (D. Minn. Oct. 21, 2003) (denying motion to dismiss).

However, a plaintiff in a section 1962(c) case based on a pattern of mail or wire fraud need not allege that the injury was caused by the plaintiff's reliance on any false representations. In 2008 the Supreme Court ruled in *Bridge v. Phoenix Bond & Indemnity Company* that such a RICO plaintiff could satisfy the proximate cause requirement by pleading that the injury suffered was proximately caused by misrepresentations made to a third party that relied on them, rather than to the plaintiff, who could not have relied on them.[366] Accordingly, the plaintiffs, who were participants in a county's auction of tax liens that the county had acquired on the property of delinquent taxpayers, could base a RICO claim on misrepresentations made to the county, rather than to the participants themselves.[367] Nonetheless, some sort of reliance by *someone* may be necessary to adequately establish proximate causation when the predicate act is mail or wire fraud.[368]

7.6.4 Type of Injury Required for a RICO Claim

The term "business or property" in RICO § 1964(c) limits compensable injuries to those that are proprietary in nature.[369] Personal injury and mental suffering do not confer RICO standing.[370] Courts have even held that pecuniary losses

In proposing a more restrictive construction of standing, Justice Scalia has argued that a plaintiff has RICO standing only by meeting the traditional elements of statutory standing under the predicate acts giving rise to the claim. Holmes v. Security Investor Prot. Corp., 503 U.S. 258, 287–289 (1992) (Scalia, J., concurring).

One such element is the "zone-of-interests" test, which asks, apart from the directness of the injury, whether plaintiff is in the class of persons that Congress intended the statute to benefit. *Id.* at 287 (Scalia, J., concurring).

366 553 U.S. 639, 170 L. Ed. 2d 1012, 128 S. Ct. 2131, 2145 (2008) (abrogating VanDenBroeck v. CommonPoint Mortg. Co., 210 F.3d 696 (6th Cir. 2000) and Sikes v. Teleline, Inc., 281 F.3d 1350 (11th Cir. 2002)). *See also* Slorp v. Lerner, Sampson & Rothfuss, 587 Fed. Appx. 249, 262–266 (6th Cir. 2014) (plaintiff, a mortgagor who had to fight an allegedly illegitimate foreclosure by one defendant, a bank, sufficiently established proximate cause by alleging that a defendant law firm misrepresented to him that his mortgage had been assigned to defendant bank through filing a state-court complaint against him and serving a fraudulent assignment in connection with it); Winger v. Best Buy Co., 2011 WL 995937, at *3 (D. Ariz. Mar. 21, 2011) (applying *Bridge*).

367 128 S. Ct. 2131, 2138, 2145. *See also* Johnson v. KB Home, 720 F. Supp. 2d 1109 (D. Ariz. 2010) (plaintiffs who alleged mail fraud arising from allegedly fraudulent appraisals of the properties that they purchased did not need to prove reliance).

368 *See* Herbert v. HSBC Mortg. Services, 2014 WL 3756360, at *8 (E.D.N.Y. June 30, 2014) (recommending dismissal), *report and recommendation adopted in relevant part*, 2014 WL 3756367 (E.D.N.Y. July 30, 2014); Lynch v. Capital One Bank (USA), 2013 WL 2915734, at *3–4 (E.D. Pa. June 14, 2013) (granting motion to dismiss).

369 *See* Living Designs, Inc. v. E.I. Dupont de Nemours & Co., 431 F.3d 353, 361–362 (9th Cir. 2005) (looking to state law to determine whether a particular harm is a loss of property, and holding that plaintiffs' claim that defendant's fraudulent inducement led to them settling their claims for less damages than they would have otherwise received satisfied RICO's standing requirement).

370 *See, e.g.,* Dysart v. BankTrust, 516 Fed. Appx. 861, 864 (11th Cir. Apr. 16, 2013) (personal injuries such as mental anguish, stress, physical

caused by personal injuries, such as medical expenses and lost wages, are not actionable injuries.[371] Nonetheless, the defendant need not have had an economic motive in order to cause

an actionable injury.[372] The Second Circuit has ruled that, for a municipality, financial losses from unpaid taxes are compensable injuries.[373] However, the Fifth Circuit has concluded that a county land recorder's loss of recording fees are not.[374]

Out-of-pocket expenses, such as attorney fees and travel expenses, may satisfy the injury requirement, even if they were only indirectly caused by the defendant's illegal conduct.[375] A plaintiff who pays interest at a higher rate than

---

discomfort, and emotional distress were not actionable); Santana v. Cook Cnty. Bd. of Review, 679 F.3d 614 (7th Cir. 2012) (ruling that any injury to plaintiff's reputation was personal and therefore did not meet the "business or property" requirement); Tal v. Hogan, 453 F.3d 1244 (10th Cir. 2006); Chadda v. Burcke, 180 Fed. Appx. 370 (3d Cir. 2006); Evans v. City of Chicago, 434 F.3d 916, 925–926 (7th Cir. 2006) (plaintiff's allegations that defendant's malicious prosecution and false imprisonment of him caused him to lose potential employment income failed to meet RICO's injury requirement; pecuniary losses that flow from personal injuries are insufficient); Moore v. Potter, 141 Fed. Appx. 803, 805 (11th Cir. 2005); Fleischhauer v. Feltner, 879 F.2d 1290, 200 (6th Cir. 1989); Grogan v. Platt, 835 F.2d 844, 847 (1st Cir. 1988) (income lost by FBI agents who were shot by defendants was not injury to "business or property" because they derived from personal injuries); Bougopoulos v. Altria Grp., Inc., 954 F. Supp. 2d 54, 66, at *10 (D.N.H. June 18, 2013) (dismissing claim alleging physical and mental injuries from plaintiff's chronic obstructive pulmonary disease along with loss of income from plaintiff's inability to work); Echeverria v. BAC Home Loans Servicing, L.P., 900 F. Supp. 2d 1299, 1303–1304 (M.D. Fla. 2012) (personal injuries caused by defendants' threatening mail and telephone communications were insufficient), aff'd, 523 Fed. Appx. 675 (11th Cir. July 18, 2013); Jones v. Ram Med., Inc., 807 F. Supp. 2d 501, 511–512 (D.S.C. 2011) (in case arising from the defendant's sale of allegedly inferior surgical mesh, concluding that though RICO does not provide a remedy for personal injuries, plaintiff had pleaded economic damages related to costs of purchasing, implanting, and removing the mesh sufficient to survive a motion to dismiss); Robinson v. Castle, 2011 WL 3813292, at *6 (S.D. Tex. Aug. 29, 2011) (dismissing claim alleging physical injuries and past and future medical expenses); Dermesropian v. Dental Experts, L.L.C., 718 F. Supp. 2d 143, 153 (D. Mass. 2010); Warnock v. State Farm Mut. Auto. Ins. Co., 2008 WL 4594129, at *4 (S.D. Miss. Oct. 14, 2008); Giannone ex rel. Giannone v. Ayer Inst., 290 F. Supp. 2d 553, 565 (E.D. Pa. 2003) (neither frostbite nor emotional distress suffered by student in a wilderness camp fulfilled RICO's requirement of injury to "business or property"); Burnett v. Al Baraka Inv. and Dev. Corp., 274 F. Supp. 2d 86, 101 (D.D.C. 2003) (losses suffered on Sept. 11, 2001, from terrorist attacks did not grant standing to victims' family members and representatives in suit against entities that allegedly supported the terrorists); LaBarbera v. Angel, 2000 U.S. Dist. LEXIS 1195, at *8–*9 (E.D. Tex. Jan. 20, 2000); Bryan v. American Med. Sys., Inc., 2008 WL 1795237, at *9 (Cal. Ct. App. Apr. 22, 2008). But cf. Diaz v. Gates, 420 F.3d 897, 898–903 (9th Cir. 2005) (en banc) (reversing dismissal of RICO claim of plaintiff, who claimed that police falsely imprisoned him; plaintiff could base standing on the property injury of interference with current or prospective contractual relations).

371 See, e.g., Walker v. Gates, 2002 WL 1065618, at *8 (C.D. Cal. May 28, 2002) (plaintiff's lost wages and other pecuniary losses resulting from allegedly illegal incarceration do not meet injury requirement because they derived from a personal, not proprietary, injury); Ehrich v. B.A.T. Indus., P.L.C., 964 F. Supp. 164 (D.N.J. 1997) (expenses resulting from addiction to defendants' tobacco products, such as lost wages, medical expenses, and costs incurred in attempting to quit smoking, are not actionable); Borskey v. Medtronics, Inc., RICO Bus. Disputes Guide (CCH) ¶ 8811, 1995 WL 120098 (E.D. La. Mar. 15, 1995) (expenses for surgery to remove defective medical device are not compensable under RICO because they are too closely tied to personal injury); In re Orthopedic Bone Screw Products Liab. Litig., 1995 WL 273600 (E.D. Pa. Mar. 2, 1995) (medical expenses to remove defective bone screw are too closely tied to personal injury to be recoverable under RICO).

372 The Supreme Court has made clear that an economic motive on the defendant's part is not required for the plaintiff to have a compensable RICO injury. The Court reversed the dismissal of a section 1962(c) claim against several anti-abortion groups that allegedly conspired to close clinics through a pattern of extortion. Nat'l Org. for Women, Inc. v. Scheidler, 510 U.S. 249, 114 S. Ct. 798, 127 L. Ed. 2d 99 (1994). But see Buyers & Renters United to Save Harlem v. Pinnacle Grp. N.Y. L.L.C., 575 F. Supp. 2d 499 (S.D.N.Y. 2008) (tenant organization failed to establish RICO injury based upon frustration of organization's efforts to advocate and organize tenants).

373 City of New York v. Smokes-Spirits.com, Inc., 541 F.3d 425, 445 (2d Cir. 2008), related case, 911 N.E.2d 834 (N.Y. 2009), rev'd on other grounds, 130 S. Ct. 983 (2010).

374 Welborn v. Bank of New York Mellon Corp., 557 Fed. Appx. 383, 387 (5th Cir. 2014) (loss rose not from a "commercial activity" but rather a "governmental function").

375 See, e.g., Clements v. LSI Title Agency, Inc., 779 F.3d 1269, 1272–1273 (11th Cir. 2015) (plaintiff's allegation that she would have received a refund of closing costs satisfied injury requirement, notwithstanding that she had received a credit for an equal amount); Slorp v. Lerner, Sampson & Rothfuss, 587 Fed. Appx. 249, 263 (6th Cir. 2014) (attorney fees incurred by plaintiff to contest an allegedly illegitimate foreclosure action was a sufficient injury to provide standing; reversing dismissal of RICO claim); Angermeir v. Cohen, 14 F. Supp. 3d 134, 153–154 (S.D.N.Y. 2014) (legal fees to respond to the defendants' allegedly fraudulent law suits conferred standing); Stitt v. Citibank, 942 F. Supp. 2d 944, 948 954at *1, *8 (N.D. Cal. 2013) (concluding that plaintiffs adequately alleged standing based on overcharges paid to defendants who "allegedly adopted a uniform practice designed to maximize fees assessed on delinquent borrowers' accounts," though dismissing the case on other grounds); Hale v. State Farm Mut. Auto. Ins. Co., 2013 WL 1287054, at *14 (S.D. Ill. Mar. 28, 2013) (plaintiffs sufficiently alleged an interest to business or property arising from defendants' alleged manipulation of a state supreme court in order to escape liability for a $1.05 billion judgment, effectively depriving plaintiffs, policy holders, of rightful damages); Warnock v. State Farm Mut. Auto. Ins. Co., 2008 WL 4594129, at *4 (S.D. Miss. Oct. 14, 2008) (attorney fees expended in allegedly fraudulent subrogation action brought by the defendant conferred standing); Geraci v. Women's Alliance, Inc., 436 F. Supp. 2d 1022, 1039 (D.N.D. 2006) (dismissing complaint on other grounds); The Flag Co. v. Maynard, 2006 WL 1030173, at *12–13 (D. Or. Apr. 17, 2006) (settlement sums paid by plaintiff after relying on defendant's misrepresentations as to the legality of a blast fax service satisfied RICO's standing requirement). See, e.g., Williams v. Mohawk Indus., Inc., 465 F.3d 1277, 1286–1287 (11th Cir. 2006) (plaintiffs, members of a class of legal workers, sufficiently alleged that the defendant's practices of hiring illegal immigrants proximately caused a compensable injury to plaintiffs by depressing wages); Zareas v. Bared-San Martin, 209 Fed. Appx. 1 (1st Cir. 2006); Leonard v. City of Los Angeles, 208 Fed. Appx. 517, 519 (9th Cir. 2006) (plaintiffs, a restaurant and associated parties, could satisfy element by showing that defendants' fraud caused them to switch to another seafood provider that charged higher prices and reduced plaintiffs' sales); Michalowski v. Rutherford, 82 F. Supp. 3d 775, 785–786 (N.D. Ill. 2015) (former state employee who alleged that he had been forced to bear costs of a campaign signature drive and do unpaid political work

that for which he was approved can establish injury, as can a plaintiff who establishes that the defendant filed a false lien against the plaintiff's property.[376] However, temporary charges that are later withdrawn or reimbursed may be insufficient to establish standing.[377] Furthermore, a claim for statutory entitlements, such as workers' compensation benefits, does not constitute a property interest injury that confers RICO standing.[378] Similarly, the deprivation of honest services, without more, may not confer RICO standing.[379]

A cause of action can be a form of "property," the loss of which will confer RICO standing.[380] Similarly, the loss of a right to compete is an injury to "business."[381] A group of documented workers successfully alleged that they suffered a direct injury from the actions of a defendant, an employer that they alleged hired undocumented workers at lower rates, which allegedly depressed wages available to the plaintiffs.[382]

7.6.5 Indirect Injury to Third Parties

The plaintiff in a RICO action must have suffered direct injury; indirectly injured third parties do not have RICO standing. Creditors do not have standing to sue for injury to the direct victim[383] and union members do not have standing to sue for injuries to the union.[384] An employee who is fired for his refusal to participate in a fraudulent scheme may or may not be able to bring a RICO claim.[385] Depositors in a

---

376 sufficiently met RICO's injury requirement); Breslin Realty Dev. Corp. v. Schackner, 457 F. Supp. 2d 132, 137 (E.D.N.Y. 2006) (plaintiff, an employer, could show injury from the alleged payroll fraud of former employees). *But see* Evans v. City of Chicago, 434 F.3d 916, 931–933 (7th Cir. 2006) (attorney fees that flowed from defendant's infliction of personal injury do not confer standing; also, insufficient showing that these fees were proximately caused by racketeering activity); Zimmerman v. Poly Prep Country Day Sch., 888 F. Supp. 2d 317, 330 (E.D.N.Y. 2012) (personal injuries are not injuries to business or property, and lost wages and out-of-pocket expenses " 'closely associated with the personal injuries' " do not establish RICO standing).

376 Hernandez v. Vanderbilt Mortg. & Fin., Inc., 2010 WL 3359559, at *14 (S.D. Tex. Aug. 25, 2010); Dimas v. Vanderbilt Mortg. & Fin., Inc., 2010 WL 3342216, at *14 (S.D. Tex. Aug. 25, 2010). *But see* Hopson v. Chase Home Fin., L.L.C., 14 F. Supp. 3d 774, 791–792 (S.D. Miss. 2014) (no RICO injury for false promises not to foreclose and by loan's securitization).

377 Indigo LR L.L.C. v. Advanced Ins. Brokerage of Am., Inc., 717 F.3d 630, 633–634 (8th Cir. 2013) (receiver's reimbursement of employer's payment of employee's health care costs after insurer was placed in receivership redressed employer's injury); Kim v. BMW of Manhattan, Inc., 827 N.Y.S.2d 129, 130 (N.Y. App. Div. 2006) (no compensable injury through either the withholding of their car or a temporary charge to their credit card). *See also* Vanderbilt Mortg. & Fin., Inc. v. Flores, 747 F. Supp. 2d 794, 821–822 (S.D. Tex. 2010) (temporary imposition of fraudulent liens on plaintiffs' real properties did not cause financial loss).

378 Jackson v. Sedgwick Claims Mgmt. Services, Inc., 731 F.3d 556, 562–570 (6th Cir. 2013), *overruling* Brown v. Cassens Transp. Co., 675 F.3d 946, 958 (6th Cir. 2012), *cert. denied*, 134 S. Ct. 2133 (U.S. 2014); Brown v. Ajax Paving Indus., Inc., 752 F.3d 656, 657 (6th Cir. 2014).

379 *See* Portfolio Investments, L.L.C. v. First Sav. Bank Nw., 583 Fed. Appx. 814, 816 (9th Cir. 2014); Ove v. Gwinn, 264 F.3d 817, 825 (9th Cir. 2001).

380 *See, e.g.*, Deck v. Engineered Laminates, 349 F.3d 1253, 1259 (10th Cir. 2003) (plaintiff alleged standing by claiming that settlement agreement reached in prior litigation with defendant, in which plaintiff relinquished certain claims, arose from mail fraud). *But see* Magnum v. Archdiocese of Phila., 253 Fed. Appx. 224 (3d Cir. 2007) (the lost opportunity to bring state law personal injury claims does not fulfill injury to "business or property" element of a RICO claim); Circiello v. Alfano, 612 F. Supp. 2d 111, 114– 115 (D. Mass. 2009) (daughter's alleged injury—of loss of opportunity to file a claim for wrongful death over death of her father—not sufficiently concrete).

381 Deck v. Engineered Laminates, 349 F.3d 1253, 1259 (10th Cir. 2003) (plaintiff fulfilled RICO's standing requirement by alleging that plaintiff relinquished right to compete in fraudulently induced settlement agreement). *See* Ideal Steel Supply Corp. v. Anza, 652 F.3d 310, 324 (2d Cir. 2011) (concluding that plaintiff was able to establish injury by claiming that its competitor did not charge sales tax on cash transactions and used money saved to open a competitive store near plaintiff).

382 *See, e.g.*, Williams v. Mohawk Indus., Inc., 465 F.3d 1277, 1291–1292 (11th Cir. 2006); Trollinger v. Tyson Foods, Inc., 370 F.3d 602, 605, 615–620 (6th Cir. 2004); Mendoza v. Zirkle Fruit Co., 301 F.3d 1163, 1168–1172 (9th Cir. 2002). *But see* Varela v. Gonzales, 773 F.3d 704, 709 (5th Cir. 2014) (without determining whether standing may ever exist in such circumstances, concluding that plaintiffs' allegations were insufficient); Simpson v. Sanderson Farms, Inc., 744 F.3d 702, 708–713 (11th Cir. 2014) (dismissing claims).

383 Nat'l Enterprises, Inc. v. Mellon Fin. Services Corp., 847 F.2d 251 (5th Cir. 1988). *But see* Bauder v. Ralston Purina Co., 1989 U.S. Dist. LEXIS 14091 (E.D. Pa. Nov. 21, 1989) (puppy food buyers who relied on ads had RICO claim against dog food manufacturer which misrepresented beneficial effects of dog food).

384 Adams-Lundy v. Ass'n of Prof'l Flight Attendants, 844 F.2d 245 (5th Cir. 1988). *See also* Gherini v. Lagomarsino, 258 Fed. Appx. 81 (9th Cir. 2007) (plaintiff did not have standing because he never had a property interest in the subject alleged to have been damaged); Commer v. American Fed'n of State, Cnty. and Mun. Employees, 2003 WL 21697873, at *3–4 (S.D.N.Y. July 22, 2003) (acts that caused removal of plaintiff from presidency of union damaged union, not plaintiff). *But see* Trollinger v. Tyson Foods, Inc., 370 F.3d 602, 617 (6th Cir. 2004) (plaintiffs, unionized employees who sued employer claiming that employer schemed to depress wages by transporting and hiring illegal immigrants, had standing, rejecting defendant's argument that only union could bring the suit).

385 Courts split on this issue. *Compare* Schiffels v. Kemper Fin. Services, Inc., 978 F.2d 344 (7th Cir. 1992) (whistleblower's termination and removal from executive bonus pool is injury to property), *appeal after remand*, 1993 U.S. Dist. LEXIS 6283 (N.D. Ill. May 10, 1993), *and* Miranda v. Ponce Fed. Bank, 948 F.2d 41 (1st Cir. 1991) (standing), *and* McNulty v. Reddy Ice Holdings, Inc., 2009 WL 1508381, at *16 (E.D. Mich. May 29, 2009), *rev'd on reconsideration on other grounds*, 2009 WL 2168231 (E.D. Mich. July 17, 2009), *and* Mruz v. Caring, Inc., 991 F. Supp. 701 (D.N.J. 1998) (fired whistleblower employees had suffered RICO injury), *with* Bowman v. Western Auto Supply Co., 985 F.2d 383 (8th Cir. 1993) (no standing, noting that firing an employee is not a predicate act and that it is irrelevant that the employer engaged in predicate acts which did not injure the employee), *and* Reddy v. Litton Indus., Inc., 912 F.2d 291 (9th Cir. 1990) (no standing), *and* Shearin v. E.F. Hutton Grp., Inc., 885 F.2d 1162 (3d Cir. 1989) (standing), *and* Hecht v. Commerce, 897 F.2d 21 (2d Cir. 1990) (no standing), *and* O'Malley v. O'Neill, 887 F.2d 1557 (11th Cir. 1989) (no standing), *and* Cullom v. Hibernia Nat'l Bank, 859 F.2d 1211, 1214, 1215 (5th Cir. 1988) (no standing), *and* Hjermstad v. Central Livestock Ass'n, Inc., 2003 WL 21658260, at *3–4 (D. Minn. July 14, 2003) (employee fired after he refused to participate in an allegedly illegal scheme of his employer's did not have standing), *and* Dunn v. Board of Incorporators of African Methodist Episcopal Church, 2002 WL 1000920, at *2–3 (N.D. Tex. May 14, 2002) (no standing), *and* Dugan v. Bell Tel. of Pa., 876 F. Supp.

failed financial institution lack standing to sue because of the derivative nature of their injuries.[386] Hospitals and insurers may not recover their expenses incurred for the medical care of smokers who were allegedly injured by RICO violations.[387] Similarly, those who have suffered increased health care costs from the effects of others' smoking have been unable to assert standing.[388] Following this reasoning, the Ninth Circuit held that a governmental entity cannot recover for increased expenditures for law enforcement and health care services sustained in its sovereign or quasi-sovereign capacity, because it does not have a property interest in those expenditures.[389] The county had argued that it had suffered these increased expenditures because of the defendants' employment of illegal aliens. Likewise, overpayments by health and welfare benefit administrators for prescription drugs have been considered to be too attenuated from allegedly fraudulent advertising to establish standing.[390] Though shareholders may not have standing to sue for their own injuries from racketeering activity conducted through the corporation,[391] they have standing to sue derivatively on behalf of the corporation.[392]

Circuits vary slightly in the factors they evaluate to determine whether an injury is sufficiently direct, a concept similar to but distinct from the "proximate cause" requirement. The Ninth Circuit considers three factors in evaluating whether an injury is too remote to state a RICO claim: (1) whether more direct victims of the alleged wrongful conduct exist; (2) whether the amount of damages attributable to the conduct will be too difficult to ascertain; and (3) whether courts will have to use complicated apportioning rules to avoid awarding multiple recoveries.[393] The Fifth Circuit has adopted a slightly different three-part test, drawn from shareholder derivative suits, in which the plaintiffs are shareholders or analogous to shareholders: (1) whether the racketeering activity was directed against the corporation; (2) whether the alleged injury to the shareholders merely derived from the injury to the corporation; and (3) whether state law provides that the sole cause of action accrues in the corporation.[394]

7.6.6　Is the Injury Concrete and Ripe?

The injury must be sufficiently concrete, or ripe, to confer RICO standing. For example, the loss of *potential* business does not satisfy RICO's injury requirement.[395] Likewise, the possibility of a future injury is not a present injury compensable under RICO.[396] Lost opportunity does not qualify as a RICO injury.[397] Injury to mere expectancy interests will not confer RICO standing, such as when one purchases a pack of trading cards in the hope that it holds a special promotional card, at least when the plaintiff cannot show that the value of the pack was less than what was paid.[398] In a case in which homeowners

713 (W.D. Pa. 1994) (former employee had no standing to sue when his alleged injury stemmed from his firing and not from the predicate act he alleged), *and* Hoydal v. Prime Opportunities, Inc., 856 F. Supp. 327 (E.D. Mich. 1994) (employee who resigned rather than engaging in what she saw as fraudulent acts has no standing), *and* Nicholson v. Windham, 571 S.E.2d 466, 469 (Ga. Ct. App. 2002) (plaintiff's injury from being fired did not meet state RICO's injury requirement). *See also* Bess v. Cate, 422 Fed. Appx. 569, 571 (9th Cir. Mar. 16, 2011) (injury arising from a personnel decision to transfer plaintiff was not caused by a racketeering injury).

386　*In re* Sunrise Sec. Litig., 916 F.2d 874 (3d Cir. 1990). *See also* Niemi v. Lasshofer, 728 F.3d 1252, 1260–1261 (10th Cir. 2013) (injuries of investors in and guarantors for the corporate target of the alleged scheme lacked standing as their injuries were derivative of the corporation's); Schrager v. Aldana, 542 Fed. Appx. 101, 104 (3d Cir. 2013) (beneficiary of an estate that was the target of the alleged scheme lacked standing).

387　*See, e.g.*, Association of Wash. Pub. Hosp. Districts v. Philip Morris, Inc., 241 F.3d 696 (9th Cir. 2001); Blue Cross & Blue Shield of N.J., Inc. v. Philip Morris, Inc., 113 F. Supp. 2d 345, 369 (E.D.N.Y. 2000).

388　*See, e.g.*, Perry v. American Tobacco Co., 324 F.3d 845, 850 (6th Cir. 2003); Service Employees Int'l Union Health & Welfare Fund v. Philip Morris Inc., 249 F.3d 1068 (D.C. Cir. 2001); Lyons v. Philip Morris Inc., 225 F.3d 909 (8th Cir. 2000); Texas Carpenters Health Benefit Fund v. Philip Morris Inc., 199 F.3d 788 (5th Cir. 2000); Int'l Bhd. of Teamsters, Local 734 Health & Welfare Trust Fund v. Philip Morris Inc., 196 F.3d 818 (7th Cir. 1999); Laborers Local 17 Health & Benefit Fund v. Philip Morris Inc., 191 F.3d 229 (2d Cir. 1999); Or. Laborers-Employers Health & Welfare Trust Fund v. Philip Morris Inc., 185 F.3d 957 (9th Cir. 1999); Steamfitters Local Union No. 420 Welfare Fund v. Philip Morris Inc., 171 F.3d 912 (3d Cir. 1999).

389　Canyon Cnty. v. Syngenta Seeds, Inc., 519 F.3d 969, 979 (9th Cir. 2008).

390　*In re* Yasmin & Yaz (Drospirenone) Mktg., Sales Practices & Products Liab. Litig., 2010 WL 3119499, at *7 (S.D. Ill. Aug. 5, 2010) (emphasizing the "multiple steps" separating wrongful conduct from the injuries).

391　*See, e.g.*, Manson v. Stacescu, 11 F.3d 1127, 1131 (2d Cir. 1993) ("[a] shareholder generally does not have standing to bring an individual action under RICO to redress injuries to the corporation in which he owns stock"); Barry v. Curtin, 993 F. Supp. 2d 347, 352–353 (E.D.N.Y. 2014) (dismissing shareholder's claim).

392　Bivens Gardens Office Bldg., Inc. v. Barnett Banks of Fla., Inc., 140 F.3d 898 (11th Cir. 1998) ("[a]llowing shareholders to state a RICO

claim on behalf of the corporation functions as an important safety valve, because otherwise executives looting a corporation would be insulated from RICO liability as a result of no one having standing to sue them"). *See also* Finch v. Finch, 2009 WL 310776, at *4 (S.D. Ill. Feb. 9, 2009) (trust beneficiary had standing to sue, distinguishing a shareholder's suit against a corporation); Fischbein v. Sayer, 2009 WL 2170349, at *7 (S.D.N.Y. July 16, 2009) (diminution in or denial of limited partnership interests could satisfy RICO's standing requirement).

393　Mendoza v. Zirkle Fruit Co., 301 F.3d 1163, 1169 (9th Cir. 2002) (finding that plaintiffs who alleged an illegal scheme to hire illegal immigrants in order to depress the labor market stated a claim).

394　Joffroin v. Tufaro, 606 F.3d 235, 238 (5th Cir. 2010) (homeowners did not have standing to bring a RICO claim based on fraudulent overcharges to the homeowners' association). *See also* Bridgewater v. Double Diamond-Delaware, Inc., 2011 WL 1671021, at *6 (N.D. Tex. Apr. 29, 2011) (plaintiffs adequately pleaded standing when state law accrued claim in the individual homeowners, not the homeowners' association).

395　Imagineering, Inc. v. Kiewit Pac. Co., 976 F.2d 1303, 1312 (9th Cir. 1992).

396　Calobrace v. American Nat'l Can Co., 1995 U.S. Dist. LEXIS 915 (N.D. Ill. Jan. 25, 1995).

397　*In re* Taxable Mun. Bond Sec. Litig., 51 F.3d 518 (5th Cir. 1995). *See also* Warnock v. State Farm Mut. Auto. Ins. Co., 2008 WL 4594129, at *4 (S.D. Miss. Oct. 14, 2008) (asserted damage to credit score arising from defendant's allegedly meritless subrogation action against plaintiff too speculative to confer standing).

398　Price v. Pinnacle Brands, 138 F.3d 602, 604, 605 (5th Cir. 1998). *See also* Chaset v. Fleer/Skybox Int'l, L.P., 300 F.3d 1083, 1087 (9th Cir. 2002) (no injury from trading card purchase); Strates Shows, Inc. v.

brought suit against their mortgage holders, alleging that those holders were not entitled to enforce the mortgages, the court held that the asserted prospective injuries—that they may have to pay more money than owed on the mortgage or pay additional attorney fees—were not sufficiently concrete.[399] The increased risk of loss suffered by a lender who made loans secured by artificially inflated collateral was not sufficiently ripe to confer standing.[400] Similarly, buyers of light cigarettes, which they alleged the defendants marketed with misrepresentations, could not establish injury based on a price impact theory, the amount by which the defendants would have had to reduce their prices to account for the reduced demand that would have existed had the defendants not made the misrepresentations.[401] Such an injury is too vague and speculative to fulfill the injury element.[402] However, a plaintiff may be able to survive summary judgment by demonstrating the fact of loss even if the plaintiff cannot demonstrate a legal entitlement.[403]

The Second Circuit has refused to recognize as compensable the injury of receiving a product less valuable than that paid for.[404] Car buyers who had purchased vehicles equipped with defective Firestone tires were also held not to have suffered a RICO injury from the mere fact that the value of their vehicles had diminished.[405] Similarly, in *Maio v. Aetna Inc.*,[406] the Third Circuit ruled that insurance purchasers, who alleged that the health insurance plan the defendant provided was inferior to that which had been advertised, could not demonstrate that they had received something worth less than they paid unless they could show some sort of adverse medical consequences, such as denial of benefits or medical malpractice.[407] Meanwhile, the Eighth Circuit has followed the Second Circuit, ruling that home buyers who alleged that they were overcharged appraisal fees and received an appraisal of their home that was less than the market value of a valid, independent appraisal did not adequately allege a concrete financial loss as a result of the appraisals.[408]

However, one court recently distinguished *Maio*, in which a plaintiff alleged not that she was given an inferior insurance policy but that she would not have purchased the policy in the first place but for the defendant's fraudulent misrepresentations.[409] The court concluded that the plaintiff had sufficiently alleged that the defendants had caused her injury of lost monies spent on premiums.[410] Similarly, another court ruled that annuities purchasers could establish sufficiently concrete financial losses by alleging that the annuities they had purchased from the defendant had measurably lower yields, higher surrender charges, lost principal, and premium overcharges.[411] Purchasers of a product that they were told was new but was in fact used could establish a sufficiently concrete injury.[412] Similarly, pleading that a consumer overpaid for a product that was marketed as having features it did not have can sufficiently allege standing.[413]

In one unique case, the Third Circuit expanded usual notions of who qualifies as a victim for RICO purposes. An American businessman had bribed Nigerian officials to get a contract with Nigeria. The Third Circuit held that the victims of the scheme included American and foreign citizens who suffered no economic injury, on the theory that bribery

Amusements of Am., Inc., 379 F. Supp. 2d 817, 828 (E.D.N.C. 2005); Moccio v. Cablevision Sys. Corp. 208 F. Supp. 2d 361, 373 (E.D.N.Y. 2002) (plaintiffs who complained that cable company failed to broadcast every Yankee game broadcast failed to state an injury because they did not allege a right to all such games); Dumas v. Major League Baseball Props., Inc., 104 F. Supp. 2d 1220 (S.D. Cal. 2000).

399 Izenberg v. ETS Services, L.L.C., 589 F. Supp. 2d 1193, 1204 (C.D. Cal. 2008). *See also* Chagby v. Target Corp., 358 Fed. Appx. 805, 808 (9th Cir. Nov. 19, 2010) (in suit arising from allegedly fraudulent advertising in sale of beverages, $0.96 price paid by plaintiff for a beverage did not establish a cognizable RICO injury when price was correct amount under state law such that plaintiff was not overcharged); Johnson v. KB Home, 720 F. Supp. 2d 1109, 1117 (D. Ariz. 2010) (purchasers of homes who alleged that defendants had inflated the appraisals for their homes could not establish standing when, notwithstanding inflated appraisals, they had paid less than properties were worth); Ivar v. Elk River Partners, L.L.C., 705 F. Supp. 2d 1220, 1234–1235 (D. Colo. 2010) (buyers of properties could not establish a RICO injury when they paid less than properties were worth, notwithstanding that properties were worth less than represented).

400 First Nationwide Bank v. Gelt Funding Corp., 27 F.3d 763, 769 (2d Cir. 1994).

401 McLaughlin v. American Tobacco Co., 522 F.3d 215, 222, 230 (2d Cir. 2008).

402 *Id.*

403 Gil Ramirez Grp., L.L.C. v. Houston Indep. Sch. Dist., 786 F.3d 400, 411 (5th Cir. May 18, 2015) (finding that plaintiff, a contractor with a school district alleging that corruption had hurt its success in receiving work, successfully created a fact issue as to standing; stating that "[a] plaintiff need not show that the other party *would have been obliged* to confer a benefit, only that the other party *would have conferred* the benefit") (emphasis in original)).

404 McLaughlin v. American Tobacco Co., 522 F.3d 215, 222, 228 (2d Cir. 2008) (injury arising from loss of value model, the difference between the price cigarette buyers paid for light cigarettes as represented by defendants and the price they would have paid but for the misrepresentations, did not give rise to RICO standing). *But see* Bailey v. Atl. Auto. Corp., 992 F. Supp. 2d 560, 579 (D. Md. 2014) (car purchaser established RICO injury from her reliance upon the false representation that the car was not a former short-term rental vehicle).

405 *In re* Bridgestone/Firestone, Inc. v. Wilderness Tires Products Liab. Litig., 155 F. Supp. 2d 1069, 1090–1091 (S.D. Ind. 2001) (also holding that even plaintiffs who had expended money in replacing allegedly defective tires because of fear they might fail did not establish a RICO injury).

406 Maio v. Aetna Inc., 221 F.3d 472 (3d Cir. 2000).

407 *Id.* at 483. *But see In re* Managed Care Litig., 185 F. Supp. 2d 1310 (S.D. Fla. 2002) (plaintiffs who alleged that they were injured by paying more for insurance coverage than they would have absent defendants' alleged omissions and misrepresentations established RICO standing).

408 Gomez v. Wells Fargo Bank, N.A., 676 F.3d 655, 661–662 (8th Cir. 2012).

409 McClain v. Coverdell & Co., 272 F. Supp. 2d 631, 637–638 (E.D. Mich. 2003).

410 *Id.*

411 Negrete v. Allianz Life Ins. Co. of N. Am., 2011 WL 4852314, at *10 (C.D. Cal. Oct. 13, 2011).

412 Jordan v. Scott Fetzer Co., 2009 WL 1885063, at *5 (M.D. Ga. June 30, 2009) ("[a]llegations that purchasers of a good received something materially different than what was represented to them in their purchase satisfies the requirement of injury to property under § 1964(c)").

413 Winger v. Best Buy Co., 2011 WL 995937, at *3 (D. Ariz. Mar. 21, 2011).

of foreign officials injures the people whose officials accepted bribes and diminishes the stature and influence of the United States abroad.[414]

7.7 Pleading

7.7.1 Local Requirements for Case Statements

Prior to filing any RICO claim, be sure to check to see if the relevant court has issued a standing order or a local court rule that requires a plaintiff to file a RICO case statement. The popularity and complexity of RICO claims have led many courts to institute special procedures specific to cases including RICO counts. Failing to file the required statement can lead to dismissal of the RICO claim.[415] Some of the case statements are extremely detailed and may impose a set outline that demands the attorney to pinpoint each element of the RICO claim.[416]

The RICO "case statement" requirement has withstood a plaintiff's challenge that it imposed an impermissibly heightened pleading standard or court-issued discovery.[417] The court concluded that it was neither but was simply a case management tool.[418] At least one plaintiff has argued that the Supreme Court's decision in *Swierkiewicz v. Sorema N.A.*,[419] which held that courts may not require a plaintiff to plead a prima facie case in an employment discrimination suit, prohibits the heightened pleading requirements of RICO standing orders.[420] The court avoided the issue by finding that the plaintiff's complaint failed to meet even the basic requirements of Rule 8(a).

Even should such a case statement not be required by the relevant jurisdiction, running through such a statement before filing a RICO claim can help to ensure that every element of the RICO claim has been properly pleaded, to expose potential points of litigation, such as identity between enterprise and defendant,[421] to try out different organizations as enterprise and defendants, and to organize a presentation of evidence.

7.7.2 Pleading Fraud—Particularity Requirement in Rule 9(b)

Pleading a RICO claim properly requires reasonably detailed allegations of fraud and a multi-faceted claim for relief. Many local courts have their own special requirements for pleading RICO cases, and these should be followed carefully.[422]

Most consumer RICO cases assert the predicate offenses of mail fraud or wire fraud and, for purposes of RICO, the Federal Rules of Civil Procedure apply, requiring that fraud be pleaded with particularity.[423] The rule's purposes include providing

---

414 Environmental Tectonics v. W.S. Kirkpatrick, Inc., 847 F.2d 1052 (3d Cir. 1988) (number of victims considered in deciding whether acts constituted a pattern), *aff'd on other grounds*, 493 U.S. 400 (1990).

415 *See, e.g.*, Ruiz v. Alegria, 905 F.2d 545 (1st Cir. 1990) (dismissal with prejudice); Snyder v. U.S. Equities Corp., 2014 WL 317189, at *6 (W.D.N.Y. Jan. 28, 2014) (dismissing claim); Oginsky v. Paragon Props. of Costa Rica L.L.C., 784 F. Supp. 2d 1353 (S.D. Fla. 2011) (dismissing claim for failure to comply with local case statement rule); Kapner v. Riverside Wine & Liquor, Inc., 2011 WL 5154608, at *8 (W.D.N.Y. Oct. 28, 2011) (dismissing claims); Barrus v. Dick's Sporting Goods, Inc., 732 F. Supp. 2d 243, 259 (W.D.N.Y. 2010) (dismissing claim for failing to file case statement required by local rule); McDonald v. Heaton, 2006 WL 1704604, at *5 (W.D. Okla. June 16, 2006) (directing plaintiff to file a RICO case statement); Pierce v. Ritter, 133 F. Supp. 2d 1344, 1346 (S.D. Fla. 2001) (dismissing both federal and state RICO claims for failing to comply with local rule). *But see* Commercial Cleaning Services, L.L.C. v. Colin Serv. Sys., 271 F.3d 374, 386 (2d Cir. 2001) (complaint's failure to allege an essential element of the RICO predicate offense was not fatal, allowing plaintiff to cure by re-pleading).

416 *See, e.g.*, Gen. Order #14, U.S. District Court for the Northern District of New York; RICO Standing Order, U.S. District Court for the Eastern District of Louisiana; RICO Case Statement, U.S. District Court for the Southern District of California; Barsekian v. First Am. Loanstar Tr. Services, 2009 WL 56893, at *2 (C.D. Cal. Jan. 6, 2009) (requiring plaintiff to supply RICO case statement and designating the form to be supplied); Greer v. Stulp, 2002 U.S. Dist. LEXIS 1482 (N.D. Ill. Feb. 1, 2002) (listing elements of required case statement). *See also* Cruz v. Cinram Int'l, Inc., 574 F. Supp. 2d 1227, 1235 (N.D. Ala. 2008) (while plaintiff need not file a separate RICO case statement, plaintiff must file a more definite statement in that form).

417 Northland Ins. Co. v. Shell Oil Co., 930 F. Supp. 1069, 1076 (D.N.J. 1996).

418 *Id.* at 1075. *See also* Figueroa Ruiz v. Alegria, 896 F.2d 645, 646 (1st Cir. 1990) (affirming dismissal for failure to comply with order); Elliott v. Foufas, 867 F.2d 877 (5th Cir. 1989) (rejecting argument that standing order conflicted with Federal Rule of Civil Procedure 8(a)); Old Time Enterprises v. Int'l Coffee Corp., 862 F.2d 1213, 1217 (5th Cir. 1989) (affirming dismissal). *But see* Commercial Cleaning Services, L.L.C. v. Colin Serv. Sys., Inc., 271 F.3d 374, 385–386 (2d Cir. 2001)

(finding that the standing order called for more than the "essential elements of a RICO claim").

419 534 U.S. 506, 511 (2002).

420 Wagh v. Metris Direct, Inc., 363 F.3d 821, 826–827 (9th Cir. 2003).

421 *See* § 7.4.4, *supra*.

422 *See* § 7.7.1, *supra*.

423 Nitro Distrib., Inc. v. Alitcor, Inc., 565 F.3d 417, 428–429 (8th Cir. 2009); Lum v. Bank of Am., 361 F.3d 217, 223–224 (3d Cir. 2004) (complaint must put defendants " 'on notice of the precise misconduct with which they are charged,' " holding that "conclusory" allegations that do not state the date, time, or place of the alleged misrepresentations do not satisfy the rule) (quoting Seville Indus. Mach. Corp. v. Southmost Mach. Corp., 742 F.2d 786, 791 (3d Cir. 1984)); Edwards v. Marin Park, Inc., 356 F.3d 1058, 1066 (9th Cir. 2004); Murr Plumbing Inc. v. Scherer Bros. Fin. Services Co., 48 F.3d 1066 (8th Cir. 1995) (while mail and wire fraud statutes do not require proof of a misrepresentation of fact, still must be specificity regarding the elements of the statutory fraud); Mills v. Polar Molecular Corp., 12 F.3d 1170 (2d Cir. 1993); Farlow v. Peat, Marwick, Mitchell & Co., 956 F.2d 982 (10th Cir. 1992); Cayman Exploration Corp. v. United Gas Pipe Line Corp., 873 F.2d 1357 (10th Cir. 1989); Durham v. Business Mgmt. Associates, 847 F.2d 1505, 1512 (11th Cir. 1988) (allegations necessary to fulfill Rule 9(b) need not necessarily be in complaint, finding rule satisfied by allegations in filed affidavit along with complaint); Flowers v. Continental Grain Co., 775 F.2d 1051, 1054 (8th Cir. 1985) (mail fraud); Allen v. New World Coffee, Inc., 2001 U.S. Dist. LEXIS 3269, at *13 (S.D.N.Y. Mar. 27, 2001); Brown v. Coleman Investments, Inc., 993 F. Supp. 416 (M.D. La. 1998) (in case against assignee of retail installment sales contract, plaintiff's complaint failed to adequately plead fraud when it alleged only that defendant knew assignor had inflated fees but did not allege defendant had specific intent); Prudential Ins. Co. v. U.S. Gypsum Co., 711 F. Supp. 1244 (D.N.J. 1989) (fraud sufficiently pleaded when plaintiff alleged that defendants conspired in printing materials of various sorts which hid the dangers of asbestos); Wabash Valley Power Ass'n v. Public Serv. Co., 678 F. Supp. 757 (S.D. Ind. 1988); McLendon v. Continental Grp., Inc., 602 F. Supp. 1492, 1507 (D.N.J. 1985); Doxieu

---

defendants with fair notice of the claims against them, protecting defendants from harm to their reputations by unfounded fraud allegations, and reducing the number of strike suits.[424] Many cases with potentially valid RICO claims are dismissed each year because the complaints do not explain clearly and in sufficient detail the fraudulent behavior allegedly constituting the RICO predicate offenses.[425] Some courts now require

that all predicate offenses—not just those based on fraud—be pleaded with equal particularity.[426] However, the plaintiff need not plead damages with the particularity of Rule 9(b).[427] Furthermore, a plaintiff need only plead the intent element of fraud in general terms.[428]

---

v. Ford Motor Credit Co., 603 F. Supp. 624, 627, 628 (S.D. Ga. 1984) (memorandum); Saine v. A.I.A., Inc., 582 F. Supp. 1299, 1303 (D. Colo. 1984); Taylor v. Bear Stearns & Co., 572 F. Supp. 667, 682 (N.D. Ga. 1983). *See also* Chang v. California Canadian Bank, 823 F.2d 554 (9th Cir. 1987) (holding that Rule 9(b) is not satisfied by conclusory allegation of "intimate knowledge").

If it is impossible to meet specificity requirements because the necessary information is in the defendant's control, one might request limited discovery for the purpose of refining the RICO claim. Blue Line Coal Co. v. Equibank, 683 F. Supp. 493 (E.D. Pa. 1988).

424 New England Data Services, Inc. v. Becher, 829 F.2d 286, 288, 290 (1st Cir. 1987) (deciding however that, when mail and wire fraud are pleaded as predicate acts in RICO cases, court should follow a more lenient process of dismissal, in light of the probability that information needed to satisfy Rule 9(b) will be in exclusive control of a defendant, *id.* at 290); DiVittorio v. Equidyne Extractive Indus., Inc., 822 F.2d 1242, 1247 (2d Cir. 1987); G-I Holdings, Inc. v. Baron & Budd, 238 F. Supp. 2d 521 (S.D.N.Y. 2002). *See also In re* Nat'l W. Life Ins. Deferred Annuities Litig., 467 F. Supp. 2d 1071, 1082–1083 (S.D. Cal. 2006) (denying motion to dismiss when the complaint provided "a strong basis" that plaintiffs "were contacted through use of the mails and interstate wires in connection with the alleged fraud"); *In re* Lupron Mktg. & Sales Practices Litig., 295 F. Supp. 2d 148, 171 (D. Mass. 2001) (suggesting that, given the improbability that defendants communicated without using the mail or interstate wires, plaintiffs should be able to cure their pleading deficiencies in an amended complaint).

425 *See* Mierzwa v. Safe & Secure Self Storage, L.L.C., 493 Fed. Appx. 273, 274–276 (3d Cir. 2012) (affirming dismissal of claim alleging insurance fraud when complaint "did not provide when, where, or between whom any alleged illicit agreement was made"); United Food & Commercial Workers Cent. Pa. & Reg'l Health & Welfare Fund v. Amgen, Inc., 400 Fed. Appx. 255, 257 (9th Cir. 2010) (dismissing claim when plaintiffs failed to identify statements that were literally false and misleading at the time they were made); Todaro v. Richman, 170 Fed. Appx. 236, 238 (3d Cir. 2006) (affirming dismissal of claim); Smith v. Figa & Burns, 69 Fed. Appx. 922, 926 (10th Cir. 2003) (affirming dismissal of RICO counterclaim when pleading contained no details about the timing and nature of the predicate acts alleged); *In re* Nordeen, 495 B.R. 468, 474 (B.A.P. 9th Cir. 2013) (dismissing claim when defaulting borrowers failed to specifically allege fraudulent acts or concrete financial loss from defendants' actions); Waldrup v. Countrywide Fin. Corp., 2014 WL 3715131, at *4–5 (C.D. Cal. July 23, 2014) (borrower's allegations against a mortgage company arising from its alleged representation that she would be required to obtain an appraisal of her home from a specific appraiser failed Rule 9(b) when they did not specify when and how defendant made representations and how plaintiff received appraisals); Herbert v. HSBC Mortg. Services, 2014 WL 3756360, at *4–6 (E.D.N.Y. June 30, 2014) (conclusory statements and those phrased in general terms did not meet Rule 9(b)), *report and recommendation adopted in relevant part*, 2014 WL 3756367 (E.D.N.Y. July 30, 2014); Mitchell v. Lenoir, 2013 WL 6231158 (W.D. Tenn. Dec. 2, 2013) (failure to "identify any false statement . . . much less the time and date of any false representation"); Buena Vista, L.L.C. v. New Res. Bank, 2011 WL 250361, at *3 (N.D. Cal. Jan. 26, 2011) (dismissing claim when plaintiff failed to identify the particular deceptive statements that were mailed or how the fraud was furthered by any particular mailings); Wood v. General Motors Corp., 2010 WL

3613812, at *6 (E.D.N.Y. Aug. 23, 2010) (magistrate's report and recommendation) (allegations that warranty coverage was denied did not evidence knowledge of fraud), *report and recommendation adopted*, 2010 WL 3613809 (E.D.N.Y. Sept. 15, 2010); *In re* Countrywide Fin. Corp. Mortg. Mktg. & Sales Practices Litig., 601 F. Supp. 2d 1201, 1216–1217 (S.D. Cal. 2009) (in case brought by mortgagors alleging that defendants engaged in a scheme to steer borrowers into subprime loans, concluding that allegations by one group of plaintiffs that failed to allege a specific time frame did not satisfy Rule 9(b)); *In re* Parmalat, 383 F. Supp. 2d 587, 604 (S.D.N.Y. 2005) (dismissing claim); International Telecom, Inc. v. Generadora Electrica del Oriente S.A., 2002 WL 465291, at *7 (S.D.N.Y. Mar. 27, 2002) (noting trend to apply the rule "strictly" to dismiss civil RICO claims). *See also* Brink v. Cont'l Ins. Co., 787 F.3d 1120, 1127 (D.C. Cir. 2015) (finding plaintiffs' RICO claims were preempted, but also stating that they failed to comply with Rule 9(b), characterizing allegations as "threadbare"). *But cf.* Pacheco v. Golden Living Ctr.-Summit, 2011 WL 744656, at *5 (M.D. Pa. Feb. 23, 2011) (allegations that defendant's employee used forgery to access nursing home resident's pension and benefits to transfer them to the defendant adequately notified defendant of the circumstances of alleged fraud).

426 *See* Shapo v. O'Shaugnessy, 246 F. Supp. 2d 935 (N.D. Ill. 2002); Jordan (Berm.) Inv. Co. v. Hunter Green Investments Ltd., 154 F. Supp. 2d 682, 692 (S.D.N.Y. 2001); Brooks v. Bank of Boulder, 891 F. Supp. 1469 (D. Colo. 1995) ("a charge of racketeering should not be easier to make than an allegation of fraud"); Biddle Sawyer Corp. v. Charket Chem. Corp., 1991 U.S. Dist. LEXIS 4599 (S.D.N.Y. Apr. 2, 1991); Market Services, Inc. v. Ying, No. 90-CIV-3152 (S.D.N.Y. Feb. 1, 1991). *Accord* Holbrook v. Master Prot. Corp., 883 P.2d 295 (Utah Ct. App. 1994) (unlawful activity under Utah's RICO statute must be pleaded with particularity). *But see* Liquidation Comm'n of Banco Intercontinental, S.A. v. Renta, 530 F.3d 1339, 1355–1356 (11th Cir. 2008) ("We now hold that RICO predicate acts not sounding in fraud need not necessarily be pleaded with the particularity required by Fed. R. Civ. P. 9(b). When fraud is pleaded as an alternative claim, the non-fraud claims in the complaint need not be pleaded with particularity unless the same misrepresentation forms the basis of both the fraud and non-fraud claim."); Abels v. Farmers Commodities Corp., 259 F.3d 910, 919 (8th Cir. 2001) (plaintiff need not meet Rule 9(b) when pleading non-fraud predicate offenses); Proctor v. Metropolitan Money Store Corp., 645 F. Supp. 2d 464, 476 (D. Md. 2009) (Rule 9(b) applies only to pleading of predicate acts of mail and wire fraud); Cruz v. Cinram Int'l, Inc., 574 F. Supp. 2d 1227 (N.D. Ala. 2008) (RICO predicate acts not sounding in fraud need not comply with Rule 9(b) but, when fraud is pleaded, non-fraud claims that are based on the same misrepresentation as the fraud claims must also be pleaded with particularity); Panix Promotions v. Lewis, 2002 U.S. Dist. LEXIS 784, at *26 (S.D.N.Y. Jan. 15, 2002) (allegations of a RICO conspiracy need not meet heightened pleading allegations in Rule 9(b)); CNBC v. Alvarado, RICO Business Disputes Guide (CCH) ¶ 8629, 1994 U.S. Dist. LEXIS 11505 (S.D.N.Y. Aug. 17, 1994) (specificity not required when pleading commercial bribery as predicate act); Towers Fin. Corp. v. Solomon, 126 F.R.D. 531 (N.D. Ill. 1989) (only fraud allegations, not whole RICO claim, need meet Rule 9(b) specificity requirements); Gentry v. Yonce, 522 S.E.2d 137 (S.C. 1999) (pleading need not comply with state Rule 9's particularity requirements unless fraud is alleged as a predicate act).

427 Robbins v. Wilkie, 300 F.3d 1208, 1211 (10th Cir. 2002).

428 Odom v. Microsoft Corp., 486 F.3d 541, 554 (9th Cir. 2007) (en banc) ("[t]he only aspects of wire fraud that require particularized allegations are the factual circumstances of the fraud itself"); Andrews Farms

The degree of pleading that will sufficiently satisfy the particularity requirement in Rule 9(b) varies with the type of fraud. However, generally courts require a RICO plaintiff to plead the time, place, and particular context of the false representations as well as the identity of the party making the representations and the consequences of making them.[429] The consumer lawyer should be as factually specific as possible about the fraud.

In alleging mail fraud, the plaintiff should identify the sender and recipient, the date and location of mailing and receipt, the contents of the mailings and their relationship to the fraud, and the consequences of the mailings.[430] Mere recitation of the

---

v. Calcot, Ltd., 527 F. Supp. 2d 1239, 1255 (E.D. Cal. 2007); Jordan (Berm.) Inv. Co. v. Hunter Green Investments Ltd., 154 F. Supp. 2d 682 (S.D.N.Y. 2001) (plaintiff pleads fraudulent intent adequately either by pleading that defendants consciously engaged in fraudulent behavior or that they had both the motive and the "clear opportunity" to commit fraud). *See* Allstate Ins. Co. v. Lyons, 843 F. Supp. 2d 358 (E.D.N.Y. 2012) (reasoning that a plaintiff may sufficiently allege scienter by either alleging facts showing that the defendant had both opportunity and motive to commit fraud, or by alleging facts constituting "circumstantial evidence of conscious misbehavior or recklessness," and concluding that plaintiff had met this standard). *See also* Winger v. Best Buy Co., 2011 WL 995937, at *4 (D. Ariz. Mar. 21, 2011). *But see* Heinrich v. Waiting Angels Adoption Services, Inc., 668 F.3d 393, 405–406 (6th Cir. 2012) (reasoning that Rule 9(b) requires plaintiffs to identify the basis for inferring intent with specific facts).

429   *E.g.*, Lundy v. Catholic Health Sys. of Long Island, Inc., 711 F.3d 106, 119–120 (2d Cir. 2013) (affirming dismissal of RICO claims); Knoll v. Schectman, 275 Fed. Appx. 50 (2d Cir. 2008) (complaint's allegations of "fraudulent accounting" or "fraudulent Escrow accounting statement" or "complaint . . . containing numerous false statements and instances of perjury" or "fraudulent statement of purchase of mortgage" did not suffice); Lum v. Bank of Am., 361 F.3d 217, 223–224 (3d Cir. 2004); Edwards v. Marin Park, Inc., 356 F.3d 1058, 1066 (9th Cir. 2004) (affirming dismissal of RICO claim when complaint failed to allege contents of fraudulent documents); Walls v. Int'l Longshoremen's & Warehousemen's Union, 2001 U.S. App. LEXIS 9746, at *4–5 (9th Cir. May 11, 2001) (dismissing RICO complaint that contained only "general and conclusory allegations" regarding the predicate acts of fraud); Corley v. Rosewood Care Ctr., 142 F.3d 1041, 1050 (7th Cir. 1998); Emery v. American Gen. Fin., Inc., 134 F.3d 1321 (7th Cir. 1998); Murr Plumbing Inc. v. Scherer Bros. Fin. Services Co., 48 F.3d 1066 (8th Cir. 1995); Bankers Trust Co. v. Rhoades, 859 F.2d 1096 (2d Cir. 1988); Schreiber Distrib. Co. v. Serv Well Furniture Co., 806 F.2d 1393 (9th Cir. 1986); Haroco v. American Nat'l Bank & Trust Co., 747 F.2d 384, 405 (7th Cir. 1984), *aff'd*, 473 U.S. 606 (1985); Moss v. Morgan Stanley, Inc., 719 F.2d 5, 19 (2d Cir. 1983); Bennett v. Berg, 685 F.2d 1053, 1062 (8th Cir. 1982), *aff'd en banc*, 710 F.2d 1361 (8th Cir. 1983); Seikaly & Stewart, P.C. v. Fairley, 18 F.Supp.3d 989, 995–996 (D. Ariz. 2014) (plaintiff met Rule 9(b) by specifically pleading "the content of the fraud, the approximate time frame that the fraud was committed, the manner of transmission of the fraud, and from where and from whom the fraud originated"); Allstate Ins. Co. v. Tacoma Therapy, Inc., 2013 WL 4763607 (W.D. Wash. Sept. 4, 2013) (Rule 9(b) met, which "does not require the pleading of detailed evidentiary matter"); Allstate Ins. Co. v. Lyons, 843 F. Supp. 2d 358 (E.D.N.Y. 2012) (concluding that plaintiff sufficiently identified the respect in which the statements were fraudulent, when and where statements were made, and who made them); CVLR Performance Horses, Inc. v. Wynne, 852 F. Supp. 2d 705, 723 (W.D. Va. 2012) (concluding that plaintiff had complied with Rule 9(b), though dismissing complaint on other grounds), *rev'd on other grounds*, 524 Fed. Appx. 924 (4th Cir. 2013) (holding that district court erred in dismissing on grounds of failure to plead continuity); Allstate Ins. Co. v. Bogoraz, 818 F. Supp. 2d 544, 551 (E.D.N.Y. 2011) (concluding that plaintiff had complied with Rule 9(b)); Reed v. Countrywide Home Loans, Inc., 2008 WL 2447136, at *1 (E.D. Mich.) (dismissing complaint); Hall v. Tressic, 381 F. Supp. 2d 101, 109 (N.D.N.Y. 2005); Welch v. Centex Home Equity Co., 323 F. Supp. 2d 1087 (D. Kan. 2004) (dismissing complaint of borrower arising from forgery of plaintiff's name on loan documents because plaintiff had alleged fraud

"conclusorily"); DeNune v. Consolidated Capital of N. Am., Inc., 288 F. Supp. 2d 844, 857 (N.D. Ohio 2003) (holding plaintiff pleaded RICO allegations with sufficient particularity); Tierney and Partners, Inc. v. Rockman, 274 F. Supp. 2d 693, 699 (E.D. Pa. 2003) (RICO plaintiff alleging mail or wire fraud must plead the means of transmission of the material in complaint, along with the material's date, sender, recipient, and an explanation of its relationship to the pattern); Crawford & Sons, Ltd. Profit Sharing Plan v. Besser, 216 F.R.D. 228, 234 (E.D.N.Y. 2003) (stating that allegations of intent need not meet such a high standard; holding that plaintiff met rule's requirements); Paycom Billing Services, Inc. v. Payment Res. Int'l, 212 F. Supp. 2d 732, 735 (W.D. Mich. 2002); Sony Music Entertainment Inc. v. Robison, 2002 WL 272406, at *5 (S.D.N.Y. Feb. 26, 2002), *reconsideration granted*, 2002 WL 550967 (S.D.N.Y. Apr. 11, 2002); Eva v. Midwest Nat'l Mortg. Banc, Inc., 143 F. Supp. 2d 862, 877 (N.D. Ohio 2001). *See also* Burke v. Ability Ins. Co., 926 F. Supp. 2d 1056, 1067 (D.S.D. 2013) (dismissing claim when plaintiff failed to identify which participants formed the RICO enterprise); Shepard v. Lustig, 912 F. Supp. 2d 698 (N.D. Ill. 2012) (plaintiff satisfied Rule 9(b), but dismissing RICO claim on other grounds); Heslep v. Americans for African Adoption, Inc., 890 F. Supp. 2d 671, 6883 (N.D. W. Va. 2012) (allegations sufficed); Sykes v. Mel Harris & Associates, L.L.C., 757 F. Supp. 2d 413, 425 (S.D.N.Y. 2010) (plaintiff complied with Rule 9(b) by pleading facts giving "rise to a 'strong inference of fraudulent intent' because defendants had a motive and opportunity to do so"), *class action certification aff'd*, Sykes v. Mel S. Harris & Associates, L.L.C., 780 F.3d 70 (2d Cir. 2015). *But see* Rolo v. City Investing Co. Liquidating Trust 155 F.3d 644, 658 (3d Cir. 1998) (plaintiffs "need not, however, plead the 'date, place or time' of the fraud, so long as they use an 'alternative means of injecting precision and some measure of substantiation into their allegations of fraud' "); Perlberger v. Caplan & Luber, L.L.P., 152 F. Supp. 2d 650, 653 (E.D. Pa. 2001) (in a case involving *pro se* plaintiff's claim against attorneys who had represented her, requirements in Rule 9(b) "must be read in conjunction with the liberal pleading rules that the Rules embrace"; denying motion to dismiss); Metro Furniture Rental, Inc. v. Alessi, 770 F. Supp. 198 (S.D.N.Y. 1991); Azurite Corp. Ltd. v. Amster Co., 730 F. Supp. 571 (S.D.N.Y. 1990); Frank E. Basil, Inc. v. Leidesdorf, 713 F. Supp. 1194 (N.D. Ill. 1989); UNR Indus., Inc. v. Continental Ins. Co., 623 F. Supp. 1319, 1329 (N.D. Ill. 1985) (memorandum); Mitchell Energy Corp. v. Martin, 616 F. Supp. 924 (S.D. Tex. 1985); Harris Trust & Sav. Bank v. Ellis, 609 F. Supp. 1118, 1123 (N.D. Ill. 1985) (memorandum), *aff'd on other grounds*, 810 F.2d 700 (7th Cir. 1987); Rudolph v. Merrill Lynch, Pierce, Fenner & Smith, Inc., 100 F.R.D. 807, 809 (N.D. Ill. 1984).

430   Ambrosia Coal & Constr. Co. v. Pages Morales, 482 F.3d 1309, 1316–1317 (11th Cir. 2007); Silverstein v. Percudani, 207 Fed. Appx. 238, 239–240 (3d Cir. 2006) (affirming dismissal when plaintiff failed to describe the content of the alleged misrepresentation and failed to specify which defendants he met with, when he met with them, and what misrepresentations they made); Liberty Mut. Fire Ins. Co. v. Acute Care Chiropractic Clinic P.A., 88 F. Supp. 3d 985, 1001–1002 (D. Minn. 2015) (allegations of "the who, what, where, when, and how of the alleged fraud" satisfied Rule 9(b) even though plaintiff did not plead representative examples of fraudulent claims; relying on "indicia of reliability" that included "the identities of the entities and individuals involved; statements from confidential informants; deposition testimony from prior litigation; and the methods used to commit the alleged fraud," along with the fraudulent content); WW, L.L.C. v. Coffee Beanery, Ltd., 2012 WL 3728184, at *11, *14 (D.

Md. Aug. 27, 2012) (finding complaint sufficient); Walther v. Patel, 2011 WL 382752, at *6 (E.D. Pa. Feb. 4, 2011) ("failure to identify the speaker of the deceptive statements is alone sufficient to dismiss the RICO claim"); Myers v. Lee, 2010 WL 2757115, at *3–4 (E.D. Va. July 12, 2010) (plaintiff adequately pleaded misrepresentations, even though he generally attributed some statements and did not allege the specific dates); Proctor v. Metropolitan Money Store Corp., 645 F. Supp. 2d 464, 474 (D. Md. 2009) (plaintiffs met Rule 9(b) by pleading both dates and substantive details of the documents, correspondence, and other acts allegedly taken in pursuit of foreclosure rescue scam); *In re* Nat'l Century Fin. Enterprises, Inc., Inv. Litig., 617 F. Supp. 2d 700, 715–716 (S.D. Ohio 2009) (allegations sufficed as to both affirmative misrepresentations and failure to disclose); Ferrer v. International Longshoremen's Ass'n, 2009 WL 1361953, at *5–6 (D. P.R. May 11, 2009) (complaint satisfied Rule 9(b)); HT of Highlands Ranch, Inc. v. Hollywood Tanning Sys., Inc., 590 F. Supp. 2d 677 (D.N.J. 2008) (allegations satisfied Rule 9(b)); Izenberg v. ETS Services, L.L.C., 589 F. Supp. 2d 1193, 1204 (C.D. Cal. 2008) (complaint failed Rule 9(b) when it included no allegations as to time, place, or specific content of alleged misrepresentations and did not identify the manner in which scheme involved U.S. mail); Meeks-Owens v. Indymac Bank, F.S.B., 557 F. Supp. 2d 566 (M.D. Pa. 2008) (in case alleging a predatory lending scheme, concluding that plaintiffs' allegations regarding their section 1962(d) claim were sufficiently particularized when they addressed " 'the period of the conspiracy, the object of the conspiracy, and certain actions of the alleged conspirators taken to achieve that purpose' ") (citations omitted); Kattula v. Jade, 2008 WL 1837226, at *7 (M.D. Pa. Apr. 11, 2008) (ruling that plaintiffs had satisfied Rule 9(b) with detailed allegations as to the fraudulent scheme); Williams v. Equity Holding Corp., 498 F. Supp. 2d 831, 842 (E.D. Va. 2007) (in claim alleging scheme to defraud consumers of their home, complaint sufficed when plaintiffs outlined the alleged scheme and plead a time frame for the scheme, along with the specific persons, entities, and times connected with the fraud and the general contents of the communications); Best Deals on TV, Inc. v. Naveed, 2007 WL 2825652, at *10 (N.D. Cal. Sept. 26, 2007) (allegations sufficed when the complaint set forth specific dates, amounts, and particular transactions between various individuals and financial institutions); First Guar. Mortg. Corp. v. Procopio, 217 F. Supp. 2d 633, 637 (D. Md. 2002); Int'l Telecom, Inc. v. Generadora Electrica del Oriente S.A., 2002 WL 465291, at *7 (S.D.N.Y. Mar. 27, 2002) (plaintiff failed to show the whom, what, where, when and why surrounding the allegedly fraudulent communications); Kukuk v. Fredal, 2001 U.S. Dist. LEXIS 16419, at *16 (E.D. Mich. Aug. 1, 2001) (plaintiffs, who set forth the months and years of alleged misrepresentations, sufficiently described the time-period requirement of Rule 9(b)); Kerby v. Mortg. Funding Corp., 992 F. Supp. 787 (D. Md. 1998) (in claim by borrowers alleging initial mortgage funder had received a kickback from the subsequent purchaser of the mortgage, plaintiffs sufficiently pleaded fraud by producing internal document listing payments passed from purchaser to funder to mortgage broker and by showing that funder failed to timely provide the Good Faith Estimate required by RESPA and received compensation for holding a risk-free note two weeks; not fatal that funder was not differentiated in the generalized descriptions of the acts of mail and wire fraud); Grafman v. Century Broad. Corp., 727 F. Supp. 432 (N.D. Ill. 1989); Tkaczuk v. Weil, 1988 U.S. Dist. LEXIS 14080, 1988 U.S. Dist. LEXIS 14080, Fed. Sec. L. Rep. (CCH) ¶ 94,347 (N.D. Ill. Dec. 9, 1988). *See also* Moon v. Harrison Piping Supply, 465 F.3d 719, 723–24 (6th Cir. 2006) (plaintiff adequately alleged the predicate acts behind a scheme to defraud him of workers' compensation benefits, but ruling that plaintiff failed to establish a RICO claim on other grounds); Tilbury v. Aames Home Loan, 199 Fed. Appx. 122, 126 (3d Cir. 2006) (affirming dismissal of RICO complaint when plaintiffs provided only "conclusory allegations" of the underlying predicate acts); *In re* Countrywide Fin. Corp. Mortg. Mktg. & Sales Practices Litig., 601 F. Supp. 2d 1201, 1216–17 (S.D. Cal. 2009) (allegations that failed to

time and place letters were sent is not enough.[431] Nonetheless, a plaintiff may be able to avoid identifying specific instances of mailings if the plaintiff does identify the specific details of the nature of the materials that allegedly furthered the scheme.[432] Furthermore, when the plaintiff identifies a mailing

<hr/>

allege a specific time frame did not satisfy Rule 9(b), but other allegations did satisfy Rule 9(b) when they identified a "specific and limited time frame"); Natomas Gardens Inv. Grp. L.L.C. v. Sinadinos, 2009 WL 1363382 at *24 (E.D. Cal. May 12, 2009) (allegations satisfied Rule 9(b)); Destfino v. Kennedy, 2009 WL 63566, at *5–6 (E.D. Cal. Jan. 8, 2009) (in case asserting that defendants made misrepresentations in the financing of homes and cars, condemning " 'shotgun' " pleading that alleged that each defendant "engaged in each and every fraudulent conduct and . . . uttered each and every fraudulent statement"; concluding that complaint failed both Rule 9(b) and Rule 8(a)), *aff'd without op.*, 630 F.3d 952 (9th Cir. 2011); Renwick v. Bonnema, 2009 WL 592341, at *2 (E.D. Tex. Mar. 6, 2009) (complaint sufficiently complied with Rule 9(b) when allegations were "supported by the 'particulars of time, place and contents' "); Strayer v. Bare, 2008 WL 1924092, at *5–6 (M.D. Pa. Apr. 28, 2008) (concluding that complaint alleging bank's participation in scheme to defraud sufficed to meet Rule 9(b) when plaintiffs alleged that the bank "was aware" that the account in dispute was being misused); SKS Constructors, Inc. v. Drinkwine, 458 F. Supp. 2d 68, 78–79 (E.D.N.Y. 2006) (plaintiff adequately alleged mail and wire fraud in connection with a scheme to defraud by alleging dates and amounts of checks evidencing the scheme); Baker v. Family Credit Counseling Corp., 440 F. Supp. 2d 392, 409 (E.D. Pa. 2006) (plaintiffs, credit counseling applicants, adequately met particularity requirements of Rule 9(b) when they alleged dates, senders, and contents of a facsimile and other communications); *In re* Reciprocal of Am. (ROA) Sales Practices Litig., 2006 WL 1627802, at *13 (W.D. Tenn. June 12, 2006) (dismissing complaint because plaintiff failed to sufficiently plead detrimental reliance element of mail fraud); Martinez v. Martinez, 207 F. Supp. 2d 1303, 1307 (D.N.M. 2002), *aff'd in part, vacated in part on other grounds*, 62 Fed. Appx. 309 (10th Cir. 2003); Karreman v. Evergreen Int'l Spot Trading, Inc., 2002 WL 31119429, at *6 (S.D.N.Y. Sept. 24, 2002).

431 DeLorean v. Cork Gully, 118 B.R. 932 (E.D. Mich. 1990). *See* American Dental Ass'n v. Cigna Corp., 605 F.3d 1283, 1292 (11th Cir. 2010) (dismissing complaint that provided a list of mailings and wires, without ever identifying any actual fraud); Burnett v. Amrein, 243 Fed. Appx. 393, 395 (10th Cir. 2007) (general allegations that certain unknown mailings were false but that did not identify the specific falsity did not suffice); Rogers v. Nacchio, 241 Fed. Appx. 602, 608 (11th Cir. 2007) (affirming dismissal when plaintiffs failed to allege specific facts identifying which defendants made which statements, which conduct constituted the predicate acts, the reliance on any of the specific statements, or the manner in which plaintiffs were misled by any statement); Propst v. Ass'n of Flight Attendants, 546 F. Supp. 2d 14, 25 (E.D.N.Y. 2008) (plaintiffs must provide " 'more than labels and conclusions, and a formulaic recitation of the elements of a cause of action will not do' ") (citation omitted), *aff'd*, 330 Fed. Appx. 304 (2d Cir. 2009); Polzin v. Barna & Co., 2007 WL 2710705, at *5 (E.D. Tenn. Sept. 14, 2007) (identifying the specific dates of the communications not sufficient; a plaintiff must also allege which defendant sent which mailing or made which telephone call); Schweitzer v. Testaverde, 1990 U.S. Dist. LEXIS 1672 (S.D.N.Y. Feb. 15, 1990) (must set forth contents of the items mailed and specify how each item was false and misleading). *See also* Maersk, Inc. v. Neewra, Inc., 554 F. Supp. 2d 424, 463 (S.D.N.Y. 2008) (when plaintiffs do not allege that a defendant himself made the fraudulent mailings and calls, plaintiff must allege with particularity that defendant "caused" the mailings and calls; upholding complaint).

432 *See* Cypress/Spanish Ft. I, L.P. v. Professional Serv. Indus., Inc., 814 F. Supp. 2d 698, 711–713 (N.D. Tex. 2011) (concluding that plaintiff

as merely furthering a fraudulent scheme, rather than as false or misleading itself, Rule 9(b) may not require the time and place details, so long as the plaintiff has identified the specific circumstances constituting the scheme elsewhere in the complaint.[433] Some courts also read Rule 9(b) as requiring the plaintiff to plead the purpose of the mailing within the defendant's scheme.[434]

In the case of wire fraud, the plaintiff must provide similarly detailed information and also must allege an interstate telephone call or other interstate wire communication in the furtherance of the fraudulent scheme.[435] When the plaintiff relies on a violation based on the collection of an unlawful debt (as opposed to a pattern of racketeering activity), the plaintiff must, in addition to specifying the details of the transaction, specify the prescribed interest rate which the defendant has exceeded.[436]

A plaintiff may not plead fraud simply on information and belief without some elaboration of the facts supporting that belief, subject to two primary exceptions.[437] First, many courts will make an exception to the rule of pleading fraud with particularity when the information needed to do so is within the exclusive control of the defendant and will permit the plaintiff to conduct discovery in order to plead more specifically.[438]

Second, the pleading based on information and belief may be sufficient if the "information and belief" pertains to information from a pending criminal complaint.[439] A RICO claim that alleges mail fraud against third parties in addition to the plaintiff may also be subject to more lenient particularity requirements.[440] However, mere allegations that a defendant also defrauded unidentified others will not suffice.[441]

The safest approach is to draft the civil RICO complaint so as to resemble, as closely as possible, a criminal indictment.[442]

---

did not need to identify any specific mailing sent for purposes of furthering a fraudulent scheme or to allege that mailing or wiring of any document was made for the purpose of executing scheme).

433 Crabhouse of Douglaston Inc. v. Newsday Inc., 801 F. Supp. 2d 64, 87–89 (E.D.N.Y. 2011) (denying defendant's motion to dismiss); Burford v. Cargill, Inc., 2011 WL 4382124, at *13 (W.D. La. Sept. 20, 2011) (denying defendant's motion to dismiss).

434 Allen v. New World Coffee, Inc., 2001 U.S. Dist. LEXIS 3269, at *12 (S.D.N.Y. Mar. 27, 2001) (citing *McLaughlin v. Anderson*, 962 F.2d 187, 191 (2d Cir. 1992)).

435 DeLorean v. Cork Gully, 118 B.R. 932 (E.D. Mich. 1990); Harris Trust & Sav. Bank v. Ellis, 609 F. Supp. 1118, 1122 (M.D. Ill. 1985) (memorandum), *aff'd on other grounds*, 810 F.2d 700 (7th Cir. 1987). *See* Heinrich v. Waiting Angels Adoption Services, Inc., 668 F.3d 393, 405–406 (6th Cir. 2012) (identifying failure of allegations to include the date plaintiffs received allegedly fraudulent email and the manner in which the misrepresentations proximately caused any injury the plaintiffs suffered).

436 Blount Fin. Services, Inc. v. Walter E. Heller & Co., 632 F. Supp. 240 (E.D. Tenn. 1986), *aff'd*, 819 F.2d 151 (6th Cir. 1987).

437 *See* Saporito v. Combustion Eng'g, Inc., 843 F.2d 666 (3d Cir. 1988), *remanded on other grounds*, 489 U.S. 1049 (1989), *remanded in part to district court*, 879 F.2d 859 (3d Cir. 1989).

438 Williams v. Duke Energy Int'l, Inc., 681 F.3d 788, 802–803 (6th Cir. 2012) (reversing dismissal of claim brought by utility customers against utility and related entities arising from alleged unlawful rebates to large customers); Corley v. Rosewood Care Ctr., 142 F.3d 1041, 1050 (7th Cir. 1998); Saporito v. Combustion Eng'g, Inc., 843 F.2d 666 (3d Cir. 1988), *remanded on other grounds*, 489 U.S. 1049 (1989), *remanded in part to district court*, 879 F.2d 859 (3d Cir. 1989); New England Data Serv., Inc. v. Becher, 829 F.2d 286 (1st Cir. 1987); Turi v. Main St. Adoption Services, L.L.P., 2012 WL 4510858, at *11 (E.D. Pa. Oct. 1, 2012) (plaintiffs satisfied Rule 9(b) given that some necessary information about what defendants knew and when they knew it was within their exclusive control); Berk v. Tradewell, Inc., 2003 WL 21664679, at *13 (S.D.N.Y. July 16, 2003) (Rule 9(b) should be read permissively when the relevant information is in defendant's exclusive possession or when the complaint is filed against a corporate

insider); Shapo v. O'Shaugnessy, 246 F. Supp. 2d 935, 956 (N.D. Ill. 2002) (appropriate to loosen particularity requirement when information on extent of defendants' use of wires and mails exclusively in their control); Taylor v. Bob O'Connor Ford, Inc., 1999 U.S. Dist. LEXIS 4028, at *11 (N.D. Ill. Mar. 26, 1999); Spira v. Nick, 876 F. Supp. 553 (S.D.N.Y. 1995); CNBC v. Alvarado, RICO Business Disputes Guide (CCH) ¶ 8629, 1994 U.S. Dist. LEXIS 11505 (S.D.N.Y. Aug. 17, 1994); Official Publications, Inc. v. Kable News Co., 775 F. Supp. 631 (S.D.N.Y. 1991); Economou v. Physicians Weight Loss Centers, 756 F. Supp. 1024 (N.D. Ohio 1991); Vista Co. v. Columbia Pictures Indus., Inc. 725 F. Supp. 1286 (S.D.N.Y. 1989); Philan Ins. Ltd. v. Frank B. Hall Co., 712 F. Supp. 339 (S.D.N.Y. 1989); Blue Line Coal Co. v. Equibank, 683 F. Supp. 493 (E.D. Pa. 1988). *See* Grant v. Turner, 505 Fed. Appx. 107 (3d Cir. 2012) (trial court should not dismiss claim without allowing discovery when plaintiffs allege that defendants deliberately concealed the identities of some of those making false statements). *But see* Nitro Distrib., Inc. v. Alitcor, Inc., 565 F.3d 417, 429 (8th Cir. 2009) (denying motion for extension of time); Stanley v. Int'l Broth. of Elec. Workers, AFL-CIO CLC, 207 Fed. Appx. 185, 188–189 (3d Cir. 2006) (rejecting plaintiffs' argument that a "log" in the defendants' possession could provide the necessary details, describing it as "too speculative"); Stark v. Monson, 2008 WL 189959, at *9 (D. Minn. Jan. 22, 2008) (although a plaintiff need not plead the exact dates and contents of communications when the specifics are in defendants' exclusive control, nonetheless the plaintiff must identify the speaker and the recipient of fraud, especially when multiple defendants have been sued); Polzin v. Barna and Co., 2007 WL 2710705, at *5 (E.D. Tenn. Sept. 14, 2007) (a plaintiff must allege that defendants are in control of the records containing the information); Denison v. Kelly, 759 F. Supp. 199 (M.D. Pa. 1991) (plaintiff not allowed to do discovery as to elements of complaint; reasonable investigations to be completed *before* complaint is filed). *But cf.* Cordero-Hernandez v. Hernandez-Ballesteros, 449 F.3d 240, 247 (1st Cir. 2006) (affirming dismissal of complaint when district court found that additional discovery was unlikely to yield the information that plaintiff needed to state a RICO claim).

439 Epstein v. Haas Sec. Corp., 731 F. Supp. 1166, 1183 (S.D.N.Y. 1990).

440 Corley v. Rosewood Care Ctr., Inc., 142 F.3d 1041, 1050 (7th Cir. 1998) (in case alleging that nursing home company ran bait-and-switch scheme, particularity requirements in Rule 9(b) "must be relaxed where the plaintiff lacks access to all facts necessary to detail his claim, and that is most likely to be the case where, as here, the plaintiff alleges a fraud against one or more third parties [other residents]").

441 Goren v. New Vision Int'l, Inc., 156 F.3d 721 (7th Cir. 1998) (affirming dismissal of RICO claim that alleged defendants had sold bogus health products not just to plaintiff but to other, unidentified, customers); Emery v. American Gen. Fin., Inc., 134 F.3d 1321 (7th Cir. 1998) (affirming dismissal of RICO claim based on defendant's alleged loan-flipping scheme when plaintiff had failed to produce fraud-containing solicitation letters mailed to other borrowers).

442 Blakey, *How to Tell If You Have a RICO Case*, 5 Law. Alert, Oct. 28, 1985, at 28; Harris, *A Framework for Pleading Civil RICO*, in Practicing Law Institute, Civil RICO 1985, at 165. Five examples of RICO civil complaints and criminal indictments are reproduced in Harris, *A Framework for Pleading Civil RICO*, in Practicing Law Institute, 1985 Civil RICO, at 189–318.

Claims should be framed as specifically as possible, including particular factual allegations that establish two or more predicate offenses. While most courts have rejected this as a legal requirement,[443] a few older federal district court decisions held that RICO claims based on predicate offenses of fraud must be pleaded with as much detail as a bill of particulars in a federal criminal indictment, sufficient to furnish probable cause to conclude that the predicate offenses were committed.[444] In any event, the closer to a criminal indictment, the less potential there is for the defendant to even raise the issue. Similarly, drafting a complaint in close compliance with any required RICO case statement (or, if the jurisdiction does not require such a statement, in line with one of the more detailed case statements required by other jurisdictions)[445] should forestall allegations that the complaint fails to meet Rule 9(b).

7.7.3 Avoiding Rule 11 Claims

Careful drafting, an understanding of the RICO statute and its elements, and knowledge of local requirements will all help protect against a Rule 11 claim.[446] So long as a claim has not been established as clearly non-viable, courts in RICO cases have been reluctant to impose Rule 11 sanctions against lawyers using RICO in novel ways.[447]

Counsel can easily avoid some of the highest exposure missteps. Be careful to plead only those predicate offenses that are recognized by the statute, as including other acts may lead to sanctions.[448] Also, when pleading fraud, an attorney's failure to plead with particularity in accordance with Rule 9(b) can lead to sanctions.[449] Finally, be sure to allege each element of a RICO claim; omitting an element may lead to sanctions.[450]

Even if there is a good faith basis for a RICO complaint, attorneys should reevaluate the RICO claim as the case progresses.[451] Courts in two circuits have affirmed Rule 11

---

443 Haroco v. American Nat'l Bank & Trust Co., 747 F.2d 384, 403, 404 (7th Cir. 1984), *aff'd per curiam*, 473 U.S. 606 (1985); Cincinnati Gas & Elec. Co. v. General Elec. Co., 656 F. Supp. 49 (S.D. Ohio 1986); Kamin v. Colorado Nat'l Bank of Denver, 648 F. Supp. 52 (D. Colo. 1986); *In re* Nat'l Mortg. Equity Corp., 636 F. Supp. 1138 (C.D. Cal. 1986); Chicago HMO v. Trans Pac. Life Ins. Co., 622 F. Supp. 489, 494, 495 (N.D. Ill. 1985); Electronic Relays (India) Pvt. Ltd. v. Pascente, 610 F. Supp. 648, 649 (N.D. Ill. 1985) (memorandum).

444 Rhoades v. Powell, 644 F. Supp. 645 (E.D. Cal. 1986), *aff'd without op.*, 961 F.2d 217 (9th Cir. 1992); Gregoris Motors v. Nissan Motor Corp., 630 F. Supp. 902 (E.D.N.Y. 1986); Allington v. Carpenter, 619 F. Supp. 474 (C.D. Cal. 1985); Bennett v. E.F. Hutton Co., 597 F. Supp. 1547, 1560 (N.D. Ohio 1984); Taylor v. Bear Stearns & Co., 572 F. Supp. 667 (N.D. Ga. 1983); Bache Halsey Stuart Shields, Inc. v. Tracy Collins Bank & Trust Co., 558 F. Supp. 1042, 1045, 1046 (D. Utah 1983).

445 *See* § 7.7.1, *supra.*

446 Fed. R. Civ. P. 11.

447 *E.g.*, Official Publications, Inc. v. Kable News Co., 884 F.2d 664 (2d Cir. 1989) (reversing award of sanctions); Smith Int'l, Inc. v. Texas Commerce Bank, 844 F.2d 1193 (5th Cir. 1988); Beeman v. Fiester, 852 F.2d 206 (7th Cir. 1988); Blackburn v. Calhoun, 2008 WL 850191, at *29 (N.D. Ala. Mar. 4, 2008) (denying motion for sanctions), *aff'd*, 296 Fed. Appx. 788 (11th Cir. 2008); Clifford v. Hughson, 992 F. Supp. 661 (S.D.N.Y. 1998) (no Rule 11 sanctions when plaintiffs amended complaint each time with leave of court, in a good faith effort to supply missing RICO elements); Rochester Midland Corp. v. Mesko, 696 F. Supp. 262 (E.D. Mich. 1988); Arnold v. Moran, 687 F. Supp. 232 (E.D. Va. 1988); Design Time, Inc. v. Synthetic Diamond Tech., Inc., 674 F. Supp. 1564 (N.D. Ind. 1987). *See also* Blakey, *How to Tell If You Have a RICO Case*, 5 Law. Alert 27 (Oct. 28, 1985). *But see* Kearney v. Dimanna, 195 Fed. Appx. 717, 721–723 (10th Cir. 2006) (ruling that an attorney may be sanctioned for mixing frivolous claims with meritorious ones); Avirgan v. Hull, 932 F.2d 1572 (11th Cir. 1991) (affirming award of one million dollars in sanctions and fees when no proof established of RICO claim after two years of discovery and no basis for original claim); Hartz v. Friedman, 919 F.2d 469 (7th Cir. 1990) (sanctions for filing frivolous appeal); O'Malley v. New York City

Transit Auth., 896 F.2d 704 (2d Cir. 1990) (sanctions are mandatory if court finds suit baseless); Lodal, Inc. v. Great Am. Ins. Cos., 2001 U.S. Dist. LEXIS 22123, at *28 (W.D. Mich. Sept. 19, 2001) (awarding sanctions against attorney for RICO claims that "lacked any factual or legal basis and were asserted for an improper basis" in case arising from dispute between manufacturer and two insurers over coverage of policies); Brandt v. Schal Associates, Inc., 131 F.R.D. 512 (N.D. Ill. 1990) ($350,000 sanctions awarded against plaintiff's lawyer for turning simple contract case into RICO claim); Wardwell v. Metmor Fin., Inc., 1988 WL 156801 (D. Mass. 1988) (sanctions imposed when no reasonable investigation into the law prior to bringing baseless RICO claim); *In re* Young, 639 S.E.2d 674, 677–678 (S.C. 2007) (imposing a public reprimand against attorney for his conduct in bringing a "retaliatory" RICO claim, based on state ethical rules); Davies v. Thiessen, 1999 Wash. App. LEXIS 1242 (Wash. Ct. App. July 6, 1999) (upholding sanctions against attorney who filed UDAP and RICO claims arising from sale of an allegedly defective house; finding suit baseless and filed for an improper purpose).

One development RICO's drafters probably did not expect is that several marital disputes have resulted in RICO litigation. *See* Grimmett v. Brown, 75 F.3d 506 (9th Cir. 1996) (spouse claimed to have been defrauded out of assets); Reynolds v. Condon, 908 F. Supp. 1494 (N.D. Iowa 1995) (man sued former wife and others alleging they defrauded him out of marital home and other assets).

448 Binghamton Masonic Temple, Inc. v. Bares, 1999 U.S. App. LEXIS 18139, at *4 (2d Cir. July 30, 1999) (affirming sanctions against attorney who pleaded non-recognized acts in addition to the recognized predicate acts of mail fraud, wire fraud, bank fraud and securities fraud); Browning v. Weichert, 1999 U.S. App. LEXIS 2307, at *3 (9th Cir. Feb. 12, 1999) (affirming sanctions when plaintiff pleaded slander as a predicate act); Williams v. Select Media Services, L.L.C., 2008 WL 544914, at *4–5 (M.D. Ala. Feb. 27, 2008) (granting motion for sanctions when the attorney had asserted a RICO claim based in part on a violation of 18 U.S.C. § 1466 (sale or transfer of obscene material), which is not a predicate act, and when an investigation prior to filing would have revealed that the claim was frivolous).

449 *See, e.g.*, Binghamton Masonic Temple, Inc. v. Bares, 1999 U.S. App. LEXIS 18139, at *4 (2d Cir. July 30, 1999) (affirming sanctions against attorney when, among other defects, he failed to plead scienter with particularity). *See also* Gerstenfeld v. Nitsberg, 190 F.R.D. 127 (S.D.N.Y. 1999) (denying sanctions in dismissal of RICO claim for failure to comply with Rule 9(b), but warning that sanctions could be imposed if the attorney reasserted the claim without pleading facts supporting both particularity and substantive RICO elements); § 7.7.2, *supra.*

450 *See, e.g.*, Dangerfield v. Merrill Lynch, Pierce, Fenner & Smith, Inc., 2003 WL 22227956, at *13 (S.D.N.Y. Sept. 26, 2003) (imposing sanctions in light of court's conclusion that "no attorney conducting a reasonable inquiry into the legal viability of [the plaintiff's] RICO claim could have thought that it had any chance to succeed").

451 *See* Smith v. Our Lady of the Lake Hosp., Inc., 960 F.2d 439 (5th Cir. 1992) (while attorney's Rule 11 duty is particularly strong in RICO cases, sanctions for withdrawn RICO claim were inappropriate because law was not clear when complaint was filed in good faith); Divot Golf

sanctions for failure to dismiss a RICO claim when it was clear after discovery that the claim was not valid,[452] and one circuit imposed sanctions against attorneys for filing a class action securities fraud suit based on a *Wall Street Journal* article and an earlier-filed complaint, without conducting their own investigation.[453]

A federal district judge's sanctions will be reviewed only for abuse of discretion on appeal.[454] On appeal, Federal Rule of Appellate Procedure 38 allows an appellate court to impose sanctions for frivolously filed appeals as well.[455]

7.8 Litigation

7.8.1 Service of Process, Venue, and Jurisdiction

Most courts have construed RICO as having a nationwide service of process provision,[456] so that suit can be brought in a convenient forum without concern for whether the defendant has minimum contacts with the state.[457] However, circuit courts of appeals cases are split as to whether the nationwide service of process provision itself provides a sufficient basis for personal jurisdiction,[458] or whether a plaintiff must first establish personal jurisdiction over one of the defendants before relying on RICO's nationwide service of process provision to obtain personal jurisdiction over other defendants.[459] Furthermore, one court has construed RICO's jurisdictional provision as extending to only those defendants " 'residing in any other district' " and accordingly not to foreign defendants.[460]

Circuits also split on whether, in assessing personal jurisdiction, a defendant need only have minimum contacts with

---

Corp. v. Citizens Bank of Mass., 2003 WL 61287, at *2–3 (D. Mass. Jan. 8, 2003) (imposing sanctions, noting that plaintiffs repeated factual misstatements and failed to properly allege pattern even after put on notice of complaint's deficiencies by defendants); Anderson v. Smithfield Foods, Inc., 209 F. Supp. 2d 1278, 1281 (S.D. Fla. 2002) (imposing sanctions for failing to make a "reasonable inquiry" before filing second amended complaint after previous two complaints had been dismissed); Miller v. Norfolk S. Ry. Co., 208 F. Supp. 2d 851, 852 (N.D. Ohio 2002) (ordering reprimand against attorney who filed motion to reconsider that contained no new facts or legal theories); Martinez v. Martinez, 207 F. Supp. 2d 1303, 1309 (D.N.M. 2002) (imposing sanctions when attorney failed to follow court's explicit warnings upon dismissing initial complaint but rather filed amended complaint that still failed to properly allege RICO claim), *aff'd in part, vacated in part on other grounds*, 62 Fed. Appx. 309 (10th Cir. 2003). *See also* Byrne v. Nezhat, 261 F.3d 1075, 1116 (11th Cir. 2001) ("any doubt" as to meritlessness of state RICO claim dissolved when state court dismissed similar action brought on behalf of a different client against same defendants; affirming sanctions against attorney who nonetheless continued to pursue claim).

452 Fahrenz v. Meadow Farm P'ship, 850 F.2d 207 (4th Cir. 1988) (affirming sanctions against attorney for unreasonable opposition to summary judgment motion after three key deponents repudiated critical facts); Flip Side Productions, Inc. v. Jam Productions, Ltd., 843 F.2d 1024, 1037 (7th Cir. 1988) (affirming sanctions for failure to dismiss after discovery showed no claim); Fred A. Smith Lumber Co. v. Edidin, 845 F.2d 750 (7th Cir. 1988) (law clearly against plaintiff). *See also In re Taxable Mun. Bond Sec. Litig.*, 1994 U.S. Dist. LEXIS 1072 (E.D. La. Feb. 3, 1994) (imposing sanctions when plaintiff refused to dismiss claims which were clearly invalidated by new case).

453 Garr v. U.S. Healthcare, Inc., 22 F.3d 1274, 1279, 1280 (3d Cir. 1994).
    Now that securities fraud no longer serves as a predicate act such a case would have further reason to draw sanctions. *See* The Private Sec. Litig. Reform Act of 1995, 104 Pub. L. No. 104-67, 109 Stat. 758 (1995) (amending 18 U.S.C. § 1964(a) to exclude "any conduct that would have been actionable as fraud in the purchase or sale of securities" as the basis of a civil RICO action).

454 *See, e.g.*, Olson Farms, Inc. v. Barbosa, 134 F.3d 933, 936 (9th Cir. 1998). *See also* Byrne v. Nezhat, 261 F.3d 1075, 1116–1117 (11th Cir. 2001) (affirming sanctions against attorney but vacating sanctions against client in medical malpractice case framed as a RICO claim, finding record "replete with instances of bad faith and dilatory tactics"); Birnbaum v. Law Offices of G. David Westfall, P.C., 120 S.W.3d 470, 476 (Tex. App. 2003) (affirming sanctions against plaintiff when plaintiff failed to properly specify his objections to the order in the lower court).

455 *See, e.g.*, Horoshko v. Citibank, N.A., 373 F.3d 248 (2d Cir. 2004) (per curiam) (awarding fees for "gross[]" abuse of the appellate process); Williams v. Aztar Ind. Gaming Corp., 351 F.3d 294, 300 (7th Cir. 2003) (finding that RICO claim was filed solely to invoke federal court jurisdiction and directing plaintiff to show cause as to why he should not be sanctioned). *See also* St. Germain v. Howard, 556 F.3d 261, 264 (5th Cir. 2009) (declining to assess sanctions).

456 Although courts agree that the nationwide service of process provision is found within 18 U.S.C. § 1965, some base the finding on section 1965(b), which allows nationwide service when required for "ends of justice," while others base it on section 1965(d). *See also* Gatz v. Ponsoldt, 271 F. Supp. 2d 1143, 1153 (D. Neb. 2003) (personal jurisdiction appropriate). *Compare* PT United Can Co. v. Crown Cork & Seal Co., 138 F.3d 65, 71 (2d Cir. 1998) (section 1965(b), but nationwide service only authorized when ends of justice require it), *and* Stauffacher v. Bennett, 969 F.2d 455, 460 (7th Cir. 1992) (section 1965(b)), *and* Butcher's Union Local No. 498 v. SDC Inv., Inc., 788 F.2d 535, 538 (9th Cir. 1986) (section 1965(b), however court must have personal jurisdiction over at least one of the participants in the alleged multidistrict conspiracy, and plaintiff must show that there is no other district in which a court will have personal jurisdiction over all of the alleged co-conspirators), *and* Suarez Corp. Indus. v. McGraw, 71 F. Supp. 2d 769, 777 (N.D. Ohio 1999) (section 1965(b)), *with* ESAB Grp., Inc. v. Centricut, Inc., 126 F.3d 617, 626 (4th Cir. 1997) (section 1965(d)), *and* Republic of Panama v. BCCI Holdings (Luxembourg) S.A., 119 F.3d 935, 942 (11th Cir. 1997) (section 1965(d)).

457 ESAB Grp., Inc. v. Centricut, Inc., 126 F.3d 617 (4th Cir. 1997); Lisak v. Mercantile Bancorp, Inc., 834 F.2d 668, 671 (7th Cir. 1987); Tsai v. Karlik, 2014 WL 3687201, at *1 (E.D. Mo. July 24, 2014); Sadighi v. Daghighfekr, 36 F. Supp. 2d 267, 274 (D.S.C. 1999); Monarch Normandy Square Partners v. Normandy Square Associates Ltd. P'ship, 817 F. Supp. 896 (D. Kan. 1993). *But cf.* Courboin v. Scott, 596 Fed. Appx. 729, 733–734 (11th Cir. 2014) (because plaintiff failed to state "a colorable federal RICO claim . . . he may not rely on RICO's nationwide service-of-process provision"; affirming dismissal); Flores v. Koster, 2013 WL 4874115, at *5 (N.D. Tex. June 28, 2013) (dismissing claim on ground that plaintiffs failed to properly serve defendant).

458 ESAB Grp., Inc. v. Centricut, Inc., 126 F.3d 617, 626–627 (4th Cir. 1997); Republic of Panama v. BCCI Holdings (Luxembourg) S.A., 119 F.3d 935, 942 (11th Cir. 1997).

459 FC Inv. Grp. LC v. IFX Markets, Ltd., 529 F.3d 1087, 1100 (D.C. Cir. 2008); PT United Can Co. Ltd. v. Crown Cork & Seal Co., 138 F.3d 65, 70 (2d Cir. 1998); Butcher's Union Local No. 498 v. SDC Inv. Inc., 788 F.2d 535, 538 (9th Cir. 1986).

460 Elsevier, Inc. v. Grossman, 77 F. Supp. 3d 331, 342, 343 (S.D.N.Y. Jan. 5, 2015) (quoting 18 U.S.C. § 1965(b) and concluding that therefore plaintiffs who sue foreign defendants must rely on state's long-arm statute).

the United States,[461] or whether the Fifth Amendment requires a court to consider issues of fairness and reasonableness after the defendant has shown that litigating in the plaintiff's chosen forum will implicate the liberty interests of the defendant.[462] RICO does not authorize international service.[463]

As for venue, RICO § 1965(a) provides that venue is proper in any district in which the defendant resides, is found, has an agent, or transacts his affairs. This section has been ruled to supplement, without nullifying, general venue provisions, so the court will weigh all relevant factors.[464] One court concluded that a defendant cannot succeed on a venue defense on the basis that he merely conducted the affairs of his employer in the forum.[465]

Though the RICO statute, which expressly confers jurisdiction upon the federal district courts,[466] says nothing about whether state courts have concurrent jurisdiction over civil RICO claims, the Supreme Court in *Tafflin v. Levitt* held that they do.[467] While *Tafflin* did not speak to the issue of removability, the RICO statute contains no express prohibition on removal, so defendants may remove RICO claims to federal court pursuant to 28 U.S.C. § 1441.[468]

7.8.2 RICO Statute of Limitations

The Supreme Court has ruled that the statute of limitations in RICO cases is four years.[469] When the statute of limitations begins to run remains a question answered differently in different jurisdictions.

The first issue to determine is whether the claim is yet in existence. In this connection, the Second Circuit holds that, when a separate bankruptcy proceeding is pending in which the plaintiff stands to recover all or some of his or her damages, a RICO claim has yet to accrue.[470]

The next issue is to determine when the claim, if in existence, has accrued. While the Supreme Court has yet to sanction a specific accrual method, it has expressly disapproved of two of them. In *Klehr v. A.O. Smith Corp.*,[471] the Court outlawed the Third Circuit's "last predicate act" approach, which provided that so long as any predicate act causing injury occurred within the limitations period, the RICO claim will have accrued within the statute of limitations.[472] The next year, in *Rotella v. Wood*,[473] the Court eliminated an even

---

461 *See, e.g.*, Cory v. Aztec Steel Bldg., Inc., 468 F.3d 1226, 1229 (10th Cir. 2006); Busch v. Buchman, Buchman & O'Brien, Law Firm, 11 F.3d 1255, 1258 (4th Cir. 1994); United States v. Tillem, 906 F.2d 814 (2d Cir. 1990); Go-Video, Inc. v. Akai Elec. Co., 885 F.2d 1406, 1416 (9th Cir. 1989); Lisak v. Mercantile Bancorp, Inc., 834 F.2d 668, 671 (7th Cir. 1987) (RICO); David v. Signal Int'l, L.L.C., 588 F. Supp. 2d 718, 727 (E.D. La. 2008); BankAtlantic v. Coast to Coast Contractors, Inc., 947 F. Supp. 480 (S.D. Fla. 1996); Headwear, U.S.A., Inc. v. Stange, 166 F.R.D. 36 (D. Kan. 1996). *See also* FC Inv. Grp. LC v. IFX Markets, Ltd., 529 F.3d 1087, 1099–1100 (D.C. Cir. 2008) (affirming dismissal of RICO action against foreign currency broker, on the grounds that the court could not obtain personal jurisdiction over the defendant, and rejecting argument that the nationwide service of process provision conferred jurisdiction without minimum contacts).

However, notwithstanding the nationwide service provisions, a court will most likely not exercise jurisdiction over a potential RICO claim involving an Indian intra-tribal dispute.

462 *See, e.g.*, Republic of Panama v. BCCI Holdings (Luxembourg) S.A., 119 F.3d 935, 945, 946 (11th Cir. 1997).

463 Archangel Diamond Corp. Liquidating Trust v. OAO Lukoil, 75 F. Supp. 3d 1343, 1360–1361 (D. Colo. 2014); Forbes v. Eagleson, 1996 U.S. Dist. LEXIS 10583 (E.D. Pa. July 23, 1996).

464 *See* Bigham v. Envirocare of Utah, Inc., 123 F. Supp. 2d 1046 (S.D. Tex. 2000) (though venue proper in forum sought by plaintiff, court transferred venue to another district after balancing the statutory factors and finding that action overwhelmingly involved conduct in and persons situated in transferee district); Kunkler v. Palko Mgmt. Corp., 992 F. Supp. 780, 781, 782 (E.D. Pa. 1998) (transferring venue); Cobra Partners L.P. v. Liegl, 990 F. Supp. 332, 335 (S.D.N.Y. 1998); BankAtlantic v. Coast to Coast Constr., 947 F. Supp. 480, 485 (S.D. Fla. 1996) (denying motion to dismiss); Quirk v. Gilsenan, RICO Business Disputes Guide (CCH) ¶ 8666, 1994 U.S. Dist. LEXIS 14041, at *6–*7 (S.D.N.Y. Sept. 29, 1994) (transferring venue).

465 Phoenix Home Mut. Ins. Co. v. Brown, 857 F. Supp. 7 (W.D.N.Y. 1994).

466 18 U.S.C. § 1964(a), (c).

467 493 U.S. 455, 110 S. Ct. 792, 107 L. Ed. 2d 887 (1990).

468 Emrich v. Touche Ross & Co., 846 F.2d 1190, 1195, 1196 (9th Cir. 1988) (RICO claims are removable pursuant to 28 U.S.C. § 1441(a), federal court may exercise jurisdiction over pendent state claims); Kabealo v. Davis, 829 F. Supp. 923, 927 (S.D. Ohio 1993), *aff'd without op.*, 72 F.3d 129 (6th Cir. 1995); Lichtenberger v. Prudential-Bache Sec., Inc.,

737 F. Supp. 43 (S.D. Tex. 1990). *See also* Bass v. First Pac. Networks, Inc., 219 F.3d 1052 (9th Cir. 2000) (RICO claim that had been filed in state court removed to federal court, district court retained jurisdiction over pendent state claim after dismissing federal RICO claim). *But see* Murphy v. Bank of Am. Nat'l Trust & Sav. Ass'n, 1999 U.S. App. LEXIS 3575, at *7 (9th Cir. Mar. 4, 1999) (holding it was without jurisdiction to review district court's remand order that RICO claim did not meet the statutory requirement in section 1331(c) of being a "separate and independent" cause of action because it was too inextricably intertwined with the state causes of action).

It is also worth noting that a federal court to which a RICO claim has been removed may abstain from hearing it if there is a pending state action. Farkas v. D'Oca, 857 F. Supp. 300 (S.D.N.Y. 1994) (abstention proper when state case involving difficult marital issues was pending); Lawrence v. Cohn, 778 F. Supp. 678 (S.D.N.Y. 1991). *But see* New Beckley Mining Corp. v. Int'l Union, United Mine Workers of Am., 946 F.2d 1072 (4th Cir. 1991) (abuse of discretion for federal court judge to abstain in favor of state court action).

One federal court declined to abstain from hearing a RICO claim filed in federal court that duplicated a state court action, stating that federal courts should decide RICO claims. Macy's E., Inc. v. Emergency Envtl. Services, Inc., 925 F. Supp. 191 (S.D.N.Y. 1996).

One federal court remanded to state court a case that was removed on the basis of the RICO count in the counterclaim, deciding that the complaint was essentially state-based and that it is the complaint, not the counterclaim, that determines whether a case is removable. Barnhart-Graham Auto Inc. v. Green Mountain Bank, 786 F. Supp. 394 (D. Vt. 1992).

469 Agency Holding Corp. v. Malley-Duff & Associates, 483 U.S. 143, 107 S. Ct. 2759, 2764, 97 L. Ed. 2d 121 (1987).

470 *See* Bankers Trust v. Rhodes, 859 F.2d 1096, 1106 (2d Cir. 1988). *See also* First Nationwide Bank v. Gelt Funding Corp., 27 F.3d 763 (2d Cir. 1994); Lincoln House v. Dupree, 903 F.3d 845 (1st Cir. 1990); Barnett v. Stern, 909 F.2d 973, 977 n.4 (7th Cir. 1990). *But cf.* Grimmett v. Brown, 75 F.3d 506 (9th Cir. 1996).

471 Klehr v. A.O. Smith Corp., 521 U.S. 179, 117 S. Ct. 1984, 138 L. Ed. 2d 373 (1997).

472 Keystone Ins. Co. v. Houghton, 863 F.2d 1125 (3d Cir. 1988); Norris v. Wirtz, 703 F. Supp. 1322 (N.D. Ill. 1989); Armbrister v. Roland Int'l Corp., 667 F. Supp. 802 (M.D. Fla. 1987); Wabash Pub. Co. v. Dermer, 650 F. Supp. 212 (N.D. Ill. 1986).

473 Rotella v. Wood, 528 U.S. 549, 120 S. Ct. 1075, 145 L. Ed. 2d 1047 (1998).

---

more popular rule, the "injury and pattern" discovery rule, which had been used by the Sixth,[474] Eighth,[475] Tenth,[476] and Eleventh[477] Circuits, and which provided that a RICO claim accrues when the claimant discovers, or should have discovered, both an injury and a pattern of racketeering activity. The Court reasoned that, "By tying the start of the limitations period to a plaintiff's reasonable discovery of a pattern rather than to the point of injury or its reasonable discovery, the rule would extend the potential limitations period for most civil RICO cases well beyond the time when a plaintiff's cause of action is complete," which would undercut the principal policies behind a statute of repose.[478]

While expressly refusing to endorse a final rule,[479] the Court left open the possibility that two remaining rules may be valid. One, the "injury discovery" rule, provides that the cause of action accrues as soon as the plaintiff knew, or should have known, that the plaintiff had been injured, regardless of the plaintiff's knowledge of the pattern. This rule has been used by the First,[480] Second,[481] Third,[482] Fourth,[483] Fifth,[484] Sixth[485]

Seventh,[486] and Ninth[487] Circuits. The other, the more draconian "injury" rule, would deem the action accrued as soon as the injury occurred, with discovery of that injury irrelevant.[488]

The injury discovery rule provides that a civil RICO claim accrues when the plaintiff discovers, or should have discovered, the injury. When a pattern of RICO activity causes a continuing series of separate injuries, the "separate accrual" rule allows a civil RICO claim to accrue for each injury when the plaintiff discovers, or should have discovered, that injury.[489] Under the "separate accrual" rule, which has been adopted by the Second,[490] Third,[491] Seventh,[492] Eighth,[493] Ninth,[494] Tenth,[495] and Eleventh[496] Circuits, discovery of each separate RICO violation triggers a new limitations period. The Fifth Circuit recently adopted the separate accrual rule after analyzing *Rotella* and finding that it did not bar adoption of the rule.[497]

The Supreme Court conceded that the "injury discovery" rule leaves open the possibility that the four-year period could expire before a second predicate offense—necessary for a RICO violation—occurred but declined to rule on that contingency because it was not a part of the case before it.[498] The Sixth Circuit has since rejected the argument that the "injury discovery" period could begin to run before the RICO cause of action accrued.[499]

With respect to RICO conspiracy actions, most courts follow the "conspiracy" rule, under which the limitation period

---

474   Caproni v. Prudential Sec., Inc., 15 F.3d 614, 619, 620 (6th Cir. 1994).

475   Granite Falls Bank v. Henrikson, 924 F.2d 150 (8th Cir. 1991).

476   Bath v. Bushkin, Gaims, Gaines, & Jonas, 913 F.2d 817 (10th Cir. 1990).

477   Bivens Gardens Office Bldg., Inc. v. Barnett Bank of Florida, Inc., 906 F.2d 1546 (11th Cir. 1990).

478   Rotella v. Wood, 528 U.S. 558 (1998).

479   *Id.* at 554 n.2.

480   Lares Grp., II v. Tobin, 221 F.3d 41, 44 (1st Cir. 2000); Rodriguez v. Banco Cent., 917 F.2d 664 (1st Cir. 1990).

481   Cohen v. S.A.C. Trading Corp., 711 F.3d 353, 362–363 (2d Cir. 2013) (reversing dismissal of claims; plaintiff did not have sufficient inquiry notice to trigger the running of the limitations period); Koch v. Christie's Int'l, P.L.C., 699 F.3d 141, 153 (2d Cir. 2012) (limitations period begins "once there are sufficient 'storm warnings' to trigger the duty to inquire"); Frankel v. Cole, 313 Fed. Appx. 418 (2d Cir. 2009) (remanding to determine when injuries occurred and when plaintiffs should have discovered them); Riverwoods Chappaqua Corp. v. Marine Midland Bank, 30 F.3d 339 (2d Cir. 1994) (concluding that federal, not state tolling rules apply to civil RICO and overruling *Cullen* in this regard; holding that federal tolling rule does not apply on the facts); Bankers Trust Co. v. Rhoades, 859 F.2d 1096 (2d Cir. 1988); Ward v. Chanana, 2008 WL 5383582, at *3 (N.D. Cal. Dec. 23, 2008) (applying the injury discovery rule); Lapides v. Tarlow, 2002 WL 31682382, at *2 (S.D.N.Y. Nov. 27, 2002); Strother v. Harte, 171 F. Supp. 2d 203, 209 (S.D.N.Y. 2001). *See also* Denny v. Ford Motor Co., 959 F. Supp. 2d 262, 273-74 (N.D.N.Y. 2013) (applying discovery rule; dismissing claim); Allstate Ins. Co. v. Valley Physical Medicine & Rehabilitation, P.C., 475 F. Supp. 2d 213, 228–231 (E.D.N.Y. 2007) (applying injury discovery rule to bar recovery for some of plaintiff's claims), *vacated in part on other grounds on reconsideration*, 555 F. Supp. 2d 335 (E.D.N.Y. 2008).

482   Cetel v. Kirwan Fin. Grp., Inc., 460 F.3d 494, 507 (3d Cir. 2006) (citing rule and applying two-step process to determine when plaintiffs should have become aware of their claim); Mathews v. Kidder, Peabody & Co., 260 F.3d 239, 247 (3d Cir. 2001) (RICO injury from overpriced securities occurs at time of purchase); Forbes v. Eagleson, 228 F.3d 471, 482 (3d Cir. 2000); Annulli v. Panikkar, 200 F.3d 189, 195 (3d Cir. 1995).

483   Detrick v. Panalpina, Inc., 108 F.3d 529 (4th Cir. 1997) (Fourth Circuit declines to reconsider its accrual rule); Pocahontas Supreme Coal Co. v. Bethlehem Steel Corp., 828 F.2d 211 (4th Cir. 1987).

484   Rotella v. Wood, 147 F.3d 438 (5th Cir.), *aff'd*, 528 U.S. 549 (1998).

485   Sims v. Ohio Cas. Ins. Co., 151 Fed. Appx. 433, 435 (6th Cir. 2005).

486   Graves v. Combined Ins. Co., 95 F.3d 1154 (7th Cir. 1996) (accrual when plaintiff discovers or should have discovered, his injury); McCool v. Strata Oil Co., 972 F.2d 1452 (7th Cir. 1992). *See also* Heaven & Earth, Inc. v. Wyman Props. Ltd. P'ship, 2003 WL 22680935, at *6–7 (D. Minn. Oct. 21, 2003) (each of landlord's allegedly fraudulent billing statements that overcharged for utilities was a separate act of fraud for purposes of the statute of limitations); Quanstrom v. Kirkwood, 2002 WL 1770526, at *5 (N.D. Ill. July 31, 2002) (dismissing suit).

487   Grimmett v. Brown, 75 F.3d 506 (9th Cir. 1996) (Ninth Circuit declines to change from discovery of injury rule to knowledge of extent to damage rule; must be clear and definite damages before statute will begin to run).

488   Rotella v. Wood, 528 U.S. 549, 554 n.2 (1998).

489   Bankers Trust Co. v. Rhoades, 859 F.2d 1096, 1102 (2d Cir. 1988).

490   Bingham v. Zolt, 66 F.3d 553 (2d Cir. 1995); Bankers Trust Co. v. Rhoades, 859 F.2d 1096 (2d Cir. 1988).

491   Annulli v. Panikkar, 200 F.3d 189, 197, 198 (3d Cir. 1999); Keystone Ins. Co. v. Houghton, 863 F.2d 1125 (3d Cir. 1988).

492   McCool v. Strata Oil Co., 972 F.2d 1452 (7th Cir. 1992). This approach was specifically rejected by the Fourth Circuit in Cherrey v. Diaz, 991 F.2d 787 (4th Cir. 1993).

493   Granite Falls Bank v. Henrickson, 924 F.2d 150, 154 (8th Cir. 1991), *abrogated on other grounds by* Rotella v. Wood, 528 U.S. 549 (2000).

494   Grimmett v. Brown, 75 F.3d 506, 514 (9th Cir. 1996) (subsequent injury must be "new and independent" to extend limitations period).

495   Bath v. Bushkin, Gaims, Gaines & Jonas, 913 F.2d 817, 820 (10th Cir. 1990), *abrogated on other grounds by* Rotella v. Wood, 528 U.S. 549 (2000).

496   Lehman v. Lucom, 727 F.3d 1326, 1331 (11th Cir. 2013); Pilkington v. United Airlines, 112 F.3d 1532, 1535 (11th Cir. 1997) (however, injury must be "new and independent" to extend limitations period).

497   Love v. Nat'l Med. Enterprises, 230 F.3d 765, 774 (5th Cir. 2000).

498   Rotella v. Wood, 528 U.S. 549, 559 (1998).

499   Bygrave v. Van Reken, 238 F.3d 419 (6th Cir. 2000), *reported in full at* 2000 U.S. App. LEXIS 29377 (Nov. 14, 2000) (dismissing plaintiff's case on other grounds).

runs from the date of the last predicate offense.[500] The First Circuit's conspiracy rule provides that the statute of limitations does not begin to run until the objectives of the conspiracy are either accomplished or abandoned.[501]

An additional statute of limitations issue involves the situation in which the statute of limitations for the predicate offenses underlying the RICO claim *has* expired, although the RICO statute of limitations itself has not yet run. Two courts have held that so long as the RICO statute of limitations has not run, the predicate offenses remain available to be proved.[502]

The doctrine of equitable tolling is also relevant to limitations issues. To raise equitable tolling as a statute of limitations defense, the plaintiff must be prepared to plead and prove the following elements: (1) the use of fraudulent means by the party raising the statute of limitations; (2) successful concealment from the injured party; and (3) evidence that the party claiming fraudulent concealment did not know or by the exercise of due diligence could not have known that he might have a cause of action.[503] At least one court has stated that the doctrine of equitable tolling may well delay the running of the RICO statute of limitations while the victim diligently investigates the possible existence and extent of a pattern of racketeering.[504] In *Rotella*, the Supreme Court responded to concerns that the "injury discovery" rule might bring Rule 9(b)

fraud pleading problems by stating that their decision did not disturb general equitable principles of tolling.[505]

Equitable tolling can be based on a defendant's fraudulent concealment.[506] Fraudulent concealment refers to a defendant's active steps to prevent the plaintiff from suing in time, such as by hiding evidence or promising not to plead the statute of limitations.[507] However, the Supreme Court ruled in *Klehr* that to assert fraudulent concealment, the plaintiff must have been reasonably diligent in seeking to discover the injury.[508] The plaintiff must also show that he or she was actively misled by the defendant.[509]

7.8.3 RICO Standard of Proof

Since civil RICO claims are essentially fraud claims, at least one commentator has suggested they should be proven by clear and convincing evidence, the traditional standard of proof in fraud cases.[510] However, federal courts have ruled with near universal agreement that civil RICO claims, even those based on mail and wire fraud, need only be established by a preponderance of the evidence.[511] These courts have found support in

---

500 Charter Oak Fire Ins. Co. v. Domberg, 1987 WL 15413, 1987 U.S. Dist. LEXIS 7153 (N.D. Ill. Aug. 3, 1987); Citicorp Sav. of Ill. v. Streit, 1987 WL 9318, 1987 U.S. Dist. LEXIS 2860 (N.D. Ill. Apr. 6, 1987); Carlstead v. Holiday Inns, Inc., 1987 WL 9024, 1987 U.S. Dist. LEXIS 2546 (N.D. Ill. Mar. 26, 1987).

The Sixth Circuit rejected the last predicate act rule in Agristor Fin. Corp. v. Van Sickle, 967 F.2d 233 (6th Cir. 1992), and the Seventh Circuit rejected it in McCool v. Strata Oil Co., 972 F.2d 1452 (7th Cir. 1992).

501 United States v. Lopez, 851 F.2d 520 (1st Cir. 1988).

502 Hoxworth v. Blinder, Robinson & Co., 980 F.2d 912 (3d Cir. 1992); Leroy v. Paytel III Mgmt. Associates, 1992 U.S. Dist. LEXIS 17864 (S.D.N.Y. 1992). *See also* Toto v. McMahan, Brafman, Morgan & Co., 1995 U.S. Dist. LEXIS 1399 (S.D.N.Y. Feb. 7, 1995) (even though underlying Sec. fraud predicates untimely, RICO claims viable); Kress v. Hall-Houston Oil Co., 1993 U.S. Dist. LEXIS 6350 (D.N.J. May 12, 1993) (same as *Toto*).

503 Klehr v. A.O. Smith Corp., 521 U.S. 179, 117 S. Ct. 1984, 138 L. Ed. 2d 373 (1997) (requiring exercise of due diligence). *See also* Ballen v. Prudential Bache Sec., 23 F.3d 335 (10th Cir. 1994).

504 McCool v. Strata Oil Co., 972 F.2d 1452 (7th Cir. 1992). *See also* Hale v. State Farm Mut. Auto. Ins. Co., 2013 WL 1287054, at *11 (S.D. Ill. Mar. 28, 2013) (applying equitable tolling to deny defendant's motion to dismiss); New York Dist. Council of Carpenters Pension Fund v. Forde, 939 F. Supp. 2d 268, 279 (S.D.N.Y. 2013) (applying doctrine; denying defendants' motion to dismiss); Shapo v. O'Shaugnessy, 246 F. Supp. 2d 935 (N.D. Ill. 2002) (recognizing tolling doctrine); G-I Holdings, Inc. v. Baron & Bodd, 238 F. Supp. 2d 521 (S.D.N.Y. 2002) (standard tolling exceptions apply to civil RICO claims). *But see* Graves v. Combined Ins. Co., 95 F.3d 1154 (7th Cir. 1996) (no equitable tolling of claims of life insurance purchasers when original contract and mailed policies put them on notice of possible fraud); Bontknowski v. First Nat'l Bank, 998 F.2d 459 (7th Cir. 1993) (no equitable tolling when with due diligence the plaintiff could have discovered the facts); Calabrese v. State Farm Mut. Automobile Ins. Co., 996 F.2d 1219 (7th Cir. 1993) (to show equitable tolling, plaintiff must allege affirmative acts of concealment; inadequate responses to discovery in earlier litigation do not constitute such acts).

505 528 U.S. 549, 560 (1998).

506 *See, e.g.*, Love v. Nat'l Med. Enterprises, 230 F.3d 765, 780 (5th Cir. 2000) (finding material fact as to issue of fraudulent concealment).

507 Reeves v. Frierdich, 2000 U.S. App. LEXIS 416, at *16 (7th Cir. Jan. 4, 2000) (citing Hentosh v. Herman M. Finch Univ., 167 F.3d 1170, 1174 (7th Cir. 1999)).

508 Klehr v. A.O. Smith Corp., 521 U.S. 179, 194–195, 117 S. Ct. 1984, 138 L. Ed. 2d 373 (1997). *See also* Rolo v. City Investing Co. Liquidating Trust, 155 F.3d 644, 656 n.12 (3d Cir. 1998) (plaintiff did not meet burden of showing diligence); Whitehall Tenants Corp. v. Whitehall Realty Co., 1997 U.S. App. LEXIS 30264, at *5–*6 (2d Cir. Oct. 31, 1997) (plaintiff did not meet burden of showing diligence); Allstate Ins. Co. v. Valley Physical Medicine & Rehabilitation, P.C., 475 F. Supp. 2d 213, 222–233 (E.D.N.Y. 2007) (ruling that the statute of limitations on plaintiff's RICO claims were not tolled because plaintiff did not exercise due diligence in discovering the claim), *vacated in part on other grounds on reconsideration*, 555 F. Supp. 2d 335 (E.D.N.Y. 2008).

509 Forbes v. Eagleson, 228 F.3d 471, 486 (3d Cir. 2000) (refusing to toll period).

510 Strafer, Massumi & Skolnick, *Civil RICO in the Public Interest: "Everybody's Darling,"* 19 Am. Crim. L. Rev. 655, 715–717 (1985). *See also* Hofstetter v. Fletcher, 905 F.2d 897 (6th Cir. 1988) (explicitly refusing to adopt clear and convincing standard, rejecting argument that standard should be higher because finding of RICO liability implied criminal wrongdoing).

511 NMB Air Operations Corp. v. McEvoy, 1999 U.S. App. LEXIS 22991 (9th Cir. 1999) (preponderance of evidence is the proper standard of proof for RICO claims based on predicate acts of mail and wire fraud, rejecting claim that trial court should have held plaintiff to a clear and convincing standard); Fleischhauer v. Feltner, 879 F.2d 1290 (6th Cir. 1989); Liquid Air Corp. v. Rogers, 834 F.2d 1297 (7th Cir. 1987); Wilcox v. First Interstate Bank of Or., 815 F.2d 522, 532 (9th Cir. 1987); Cullen v. Margiotta, 811 F.2d 698 (2d Cir. 1987); Armco Indus. Credit Corp. v. SLT Warehouse Co., 782 F.2d 475, 481 (5th Cir. 1986); United States v. Local 560 of Int'l Brotherhood of Teamsters, 780 F.2d 267, 279 n.12 (3d Cir. 1985); United States v. Capetto, 502 F.2d 1351, 1358 (7th Cir. 1974); City of N.Y. v. Liberman, 1988 U.S. Dist. LEXIS 580 (S.D.N.Y. Jan. 25, 1988); Eaby v. Richmond, 561 F. Supp. 131, 133, 134 (E.D. Pa. 1983); Heinhold Commodities, Inc. v. McCarty, 513 F. Supp. 311, 313 (N.D. Ill. 1979); Farmers Bank of Del. v. Bell Mortg. Corp., 452 F. Supp. 1278, 1280 (D. Del. 1978).

Sedima, in which the Supreme Court, while refusing to decide the issue, strongly suggested that the ordinary civil standard of preponderance of the evidence should apply to civil RICO:

> In a number of settings, conduct that can be punished as criminal only upon proof beyond a reasonable doubt will support civil sanctions under a preponderance standard. [Citations omitted.] There is no indication that Congress sought to depart from this general principle here.[512]

7.8.4 Offensive Collateral Estoppel

RICO § 1964(d) specifically allows a successful government prosecutor to prevent the defendant from denying a final criminal judgment in a subsequent civil RICO action based on the same issues. So, it appears possible that in government actions, a civil RICO action would follow automatically from a successful criminal prosecution.[513]

However, the RICO statute does not specifically allow private parties to use offensive collateral estoppel in civil suits following criminal convictions.[514] Nonetheless, a few courts, including the Ninth Circuit, have decided that a private RICO claimant can use offensive collateral estoppel based on a prior RICO criminal conviction.[515] In contrast, some other courts, including the Seventh Circuit, have denied plaintiffs the use of offensive collateral estoppel.[516]

Assuming offensive collateral estoppel is available to private RICO plaintiffs, its normal principles should apply. Thus the private plaintiff must first allege that issues in the subsequent civil case were actually litigated and necessary to the outcome of the first criminal case;[517] and second must show that, under the doctrine of *Parklane Hosiery*, use of offensive collateral estoppel would not involve any of the following four situations unfair to the defendant:

- It would have been practical to join the civil plaintiff in the prior action;
- The judgment in the first case was inconsistent with any prior decisions;
- The defendant in the first case lacked the incentive to litigate vigorously;
- The first case did not provide procedural opportunities that are available to the defendant in the second case and that could readily cause a different result.[518]

7.8.5 Defensive Collateral Estoppel

Conversely, plaintiffs may also find that res judicata (claim preclusion)[519] and collateral estoppel (issue preclusion)[520] may be used defensively against them. Res judicata can preclude litigation of all claims that could have been raised in the earlier proceeding, even if they were not.[521] The doctrine of res judicata requires that the parties in the present suit be the

---

512 Sedima, S.P.R.L. v. Imrex Co., 473 U.S. 479, 491, 105 S. Ct. 3275, 87 L. Ed. 2d 346 (1985).

513 *See* United States v. Ianniello, 808 F.2d 184 (2d Cir. 1986) (criminal RICO acquittal does not estop government civil RICO action); Buchanan Cnty., Va. v. Blankenship, 496 F. Supp. 2d 715, 719 (W.D. Va. 2007) (permitting plaintiff to use collateral estoppel to preclude relitigation of facts established in the previous criminal case); County of Cook v. Lynch, 560 F. Supp. 136 (N.D. Ill. 1982) (county successfully used offensive collateral estoppel after criminal conviction in United States v. Marubeni Am. Corp., 611 F.2d 763 (9th Cir. 1980)), *aff'd*, United States v. Lynch, 692 F.2d 759 (7th Cir. 1982); Maryland v. Buzz Berg Wrecking Co., 496 F. Supp. 245 (D. Md. 1980) (civil suit following criminal conviction in United States v. Grande, 620 F.2d 1026 (4th Cir. 1980)). *But see In re* Lewisville Properties, Inc., 849 F.2d 946 (5th Cir. 1988) (no collateral estoppel when civil pleading identified different enterprises and patterns of racketeering).

514 *Cf.* 18 U.S.C. § 1964(d) (only specifies the United States may estop denials in civil actions following criminal convictions).

515 Fireman's Fund Ins. Co. v. Stites, 258 F.3d 1016, 1020–1021 (9th Cir. 2001) (reasoning that RICO statute, enacted in 1970, omitted such estoppel because federal common law only adopted it in 1979, with the Supreme Court's decision in *Parklane Hosiery v. Shore*); Buchanan Cnty., Virginia v. Blankenship, 496 F. Supp. 2d 715, 718–720 (W.D. Va. 2007) (permitting offensive collateral estoppel); Anderson v. Janovich, 543 F. Supp. 1124, 1128, 1129 (W.D. Wash. 1982) (permitting collateral estoppel, reasoning that it is an existing civil remedy and an uncodified RICO section, section 904(b), provides that RICO does not supplant existing federal or state civil remedies). *See also* Parklane Hosiery Co. v. Shore, 439 U.S. 322, 326–328, 99 S. Ct. 645, 58 L. Ed. 2d 552 (1979) (use of offensive collateral estoppel is within the broad discretion of the trial court, and even strangers to the original suit may rely on it); County of Oakland v. City of Detroit, 776 F. Supp. 1211 (E.D. Mich. 1991) (convicted sewage haulers collaterally estopped from re-litigating issues necessarily decided in prior judgments); Ross v. Jackie Fine Arts, Inc., 1991 U.S. Dist. LEXIS 13535, at *3 (D.S.C. Sept. 4, 1991) (relying on offensive collateral estoppel to grant plaintiff summary judgment on RICO claims though without analyzing its applicability).

516 Henry v. Farmer City State Bank, 808 F.2d 1228 (7th Cir. 1987). *See also* Federal Deposit Ins. Corp. v. Bayles & Co. of Am., 1992 U.S. Dist. LEXIS 10138 (M.D. Fla. June 30, 1992; City of N.Y. v. Liberman, 1988 U.S. Dist. LEXIS 580 (S.D.N.Y. Jan. 25, 1988); State Farm Fire & Cas. Co. v. Estate of Caton, 540 F. Supp. 673, 683 (N.D. Ind. 1982) (concluding that offensive collateral estoppel may not be used against a defendant when prior criminal conviction against him was abated due to his death, but leaving open possibility that "upon appropriate motion collateral estoppel may be available against [other] defendants").

517 *See, e.g.*, Schaafsma v. Marriner, 641 F. Supp. 576 (D. Vt. 1986) (no bar to RICO suit when predicate acts not at issue in earlier proceeding and controlling law changed).

518 Parklane Hosiery Co. v. Shore, 439 U.S. 322, 330, 99 S. Ct. 645, 58 L. Ed. 2d 552 (1979). *See also* Narumanchi v. Adanti, 101 F.3d 108 (2d Cir. 1996) (table; text at 1996 U.S. App. LEXIS 39274) (res judicata barred RICO claims that could have been asserted in prior action); County of Cook v. Lynch, 648 F. Supp. 738 (N.D. Ill. 1986) (collateral estoppel precludes defendant who vigorously contested her guilt of mail fraud and bribery from re-litigating issues in civil suit).

519 To establish a defense of res judicata, defendants must show: (1) identity of claims; (2) identity of parties; and (3) a prior final judgment on the merits. Perry v. Globe Auto Recycling, Inc., 227 F.3d 950, 952 (7th Cir. 2000).

520 Defendants, to establish the defense of collateral estoppel, must show that: (1) the issue sought to be precluded was the same as that involved in the prior action; (2) the issue was actually litigated; (3) the determination of the issue was essential to the final judgment; and (4) the party against whom estoppel is invoked fully represented in the prior action. Haroco of Am., Ltd. v. Freeman, Atkins & Coleman, Ltd., 58 F.3d 303, 307 (7th Cir. 1995).

521 Greenberg v. Bd. of Governors of the Fed. Reserve Sys., 968 F.2d 164, 168 (2d Cir. 1992).

same as those in the prior suit.[522] However, identity of parties is not necessarily an element of collateral estoppel,[523] so that doctrine may be used to bar a RICO claim even when the defendant in the present suit was not a party to the prior suit.[524] However, the doctrine will not bar a suit that presents different causes of action.[525]

7.8.6 In Pari Delicto *Defense*

RICO is silent as to common-law defenses such as *in pari delicto* (the plaintiff is equally at fault), but some circuit courts

---

of appeals have concluded that *in pari delicto* is a valid defense to a civil RICO claim.[526]

7.9 Private Remedies

7.9.1 *Actual Damages*

Although the Supreme Court has not established a measure of damages available in RICO claims,[527] it has stated that "the compensable injury necessarily is the harm caused by predicate offenses sufficiently related to constitute a pattern."[528] Accordingly, a court should consider any reasonable basis for assessing the injury. A plaintiff injured by a RICO violation is entitled to a complete recovery.[529] It is wise to delineate the source of various categories of damages and to be prepared to show the court that the various components are not duplicative.[530]

An important exclusion from RICO's general availability to remedy injury is personal injury.[531] Personal injury—whether manifested by physical injury or emotional distress—is neither directly nor indirectly compensable.[532] Nor are pecuniary

---

522 Saboff v. St. John's River Water Mgmt. Dist., 200 F.3d 1356, 1360 (11th Cir. 2000). *See also* Pierce v. Ritter, 133 F. Supp. 2d 1344 (S.D. Fla. 2001) (refusing to apply doctrine of res judicata when defendants in present suit were the attorneys for the defendants in the prior suit, not those defendants themselves).

523 Blonder-Tongue Lab. v. University of Ill. Found., 402 U.S. 313, 91 S. Ct. 1434, 28 L. Ed. 2d 788 (1970).

524 *See, e.g.*, Rodriguez v. Doe, 549 Fed. Appx. 141, 144 (4th Cir. Dec. 11, 2013) (new claims barred by *res judicata* because based on the same conspiracy); Saud v. Bank of N.Y., 929 F.2d 916 (2d Cir. 1991) (holding that plaintiffs who failed to raise fraud and forgery as defenses in an earlier state foreclosure action had their federal RICO claim that was based on the same allegations barred by res judicata); Central Transp., Inc. v. Four Phase Sys., Inc., 936 F.2d 256 (6th Cir. 1991) (holding that a breach-of-contract arbitration panel's decision precluded plaintiff from litigating a related RICO claim); Feminist Women's Health Ctr. v. Codispoti, 63 F.3d 863 (9th Cir. 1995). *See also* Xiangyuan Zhu v. St. Francis Health Ctr., 215 Fed. Appx. 717, 718–720 (10th Cir. 2007) (res judicata barred consumer's RICO claim when allegations arose out of a relationship that was the "focal point" of a previous state complaint); Cahill v. Jewell, 1999 U.S. App. LEXIS 9268 (6th Cir. May 12, 1999) (plaintiff's RICO action against insurance seller barred by res judicata effect of prior state court class action when plaintiffs were members of the class); Pierce v. Ritter, 133 F. Supp. 2d 1344, 1347 (S.D. Fla. 2001) (holding that collateral estoppel doctrine barred plaintiff's RICO action); Miller Hydro Grp. v. Popovitch, 851 F. Supp. 7 (D. Me. 1994) (dismissing plaintiff's RICO claims on grounds of defensive collateral estoppel); Wyckoff v. Zaiderman, 1987 WL 14295 (D.D.C. June 3, 1987); State Farm Fire & Cas. Co. v. Estate of Caton, 540 F. Supp. 673, 682, 683 (N.D. Ind. 1982); Strates Shows, Inc. v. Amusements of Am., Inc., 646 S.E.2d 418, 424–425 (N.C. Ct. App. 2007) (dismissing plaintiff's state UDAP claim when an earlier federal RICO claim had had been dismissed on the grounds that plaintiff had failed to show that its injury was proximately caused by the illegal conduct, reasoning that he element of causation was the same as that in a federal RICO claim). *But see* Green Tree Fin. Corp. v. Honeywood Dev. Corp., 2001 U.S. Dist. LEXIS 654, at *18–20 (when prior arbitration demand did not specifically assert a RICO conspiracy violation nor use the word "conspiracy," collateral estoppel would not bar plaintiff's RICO conspiracy claim).

525 Empress Casino Joliet Corp. v. Johnston, 763 F.3d 723, 728 (7th Cir. 2014) (concluding that *res judicata* did not bar RICO claim brought by casinos against horsetracks, alleging that defendants had bribed state's governor to ensure that a favorable tax bill was enacted; applying state's transactional test). *See also* Klein v. Gutman, 994 N.Y.S.2d 654, 655–658 (N.Y. App. Div. 2014) (ruling that an action alleging RICO violations arising from allegations of fraud did not have *res judicata* effect on suit based on breach of fiduciary duty and similar claims when prior action was in favor of entity defendants rather than defendant personally; reasoning that two actions did not "rest 'on the same claims based upon the same harm' ") (citation omitted).

526 *E.g.*, Republic of Iraq v. ABB AG, 768 F.3d 145, 163 (2d Cir. 2014); Official Comm. of Unsecured Creditors of PSA, Inc. v. Edwards, 437 F.3d 1145, 1152-56 (11th Cir. 2006); Rogers v. McDorman, 521 F.3d 381, 387–391 (5th Cir. 2008).

527 Fleischhauer v. Feltner, 879 F.2d 1290 (6th Cir. 1989).

528 Sedima, S.P.R.L. v. Imrex Co., 473 U.S. 479, 497, 105 S. Ct. 3275, 87 L. Ed. 2d 346 (1985) (rejecting requirement of a racketeering injury); Liquid Air Corp. v. Rogers, 834 F.2d 1297, 1310 (7th Cir. 1987); City of Chi. Heights v. Lobue, 914 F. Supp. 279, 283 (N.D. Ill. 1996) (plaintiff failed to show causation); County of Oakland by Kuhn v. Vista Disposal, 900 F. Supp. 879, 890 (E.D. Mich. 1995) (plaintiff showed injury caused by RICO conspiracy). *See also* D'Orange v. Feely, 894 F. Supp. 159, 163 (S.D.N.Y. 1995) (damages sustained by RICO victim were, at a minimum, equal to the damages resulting from the sum of the predicate acts of mail fraud).

529 Liquid Air Corp. v. Rogers, 834 F.2d 1297, 1310 (7th Cir. 1987) (citing Carter v. Berger, 777 F.2d 1173, 1176 (7th Cir. 1985)).

530 *See* Alcorn Cnty. v. U.S. Interstate Supplies, Inc., 731 F.2d 1160, 1171 (5th Cir. 1984) (court should not allow duplicative damages under RICO and state common law); Interpool Ltd. v. Patterson, 1994 U.S. Dist. LEXIS 16897 (S.D.N.Y. Nov. 28, 1994); Burdett v. Miller, 1990 U.S. Dist. LEXIS 16098, at *34 (N.D. Ill. Nov. 28, 1990) (declining to award damages for breach of fiduciary duty as those would be duplicative of RICO damages), *vacated on other grounds*, 957 F.2d 1375 (7th Cir. 1992). *See also* Cormier v. Discover Bank, 207 Fed. Appx. 866, 867–868 (9th Cir. 2006) (affirming summary judgment when plaintiffs did not identify the specific injury caused by the defendants' racketeering activity).

531 Grogan v. Platt, 835 F.2d 844 (11th Cir. 1988); Bankers Trust Co. v. Rhoades, 741 F.2d 511, 515 (2d Cir. 1984), *vacated and remanded on other grounds*, 473 U.S. 922 (1985); East v. A.H. Robins Co., 616 F. Supp. 333, 335 (E.D. Wis. 1985).

532 Maio v. Aetna Inc., 221 F.3d 472, 482 (3d Cir. 2000); Hamm v. Rhone-Poulenc Rorer Pharms., 187 F.3d 941, 948 (8th Cir. 1999); Price v. Pinnacle Brands, 138 F.3d 602, 607 n.20 (5th Cir. 1998) (no recovery for gambling addiction injury); Pilkington v. United Airlines, 112 F.3d 1532, 1526 (11th Cir. 1997); Genty v. Resolution Trust Corp., 937 F.2d 899 (3d Cir. 1991); Berg v. First State Ins. Co., 915 F.2d 460 (9th Cir. 1990); Fleischhauer v. Feltner, 879 F.2d 1290 (6th Cir. 1989); Grogan v. Platt, 835 F.2d 844 (11th Cir. 1988); LaBarbera v. Angel, 2000 U.S. Dist. LEXIS 1195, at *8–*9 (E.D. Tex. Jan. 20, 2000). *See also* § 7.6, *supra*.

---

losses connected with physical injury or emotional distress.[533] The Ninth Circuit requires the plaintiff to prove "concrete financial loss."[534]

7.9.2   *Treble and Punitive Damages*

A successful RICO claimant will be awarded treble damages. The jury will not normally be told about either the triple damages provision or the attorney fee provision.[535] The courts are divided as to availability of punitive damages.[536] A treble damage provision should not replace a punitive damages remedy because treble damages are remedial rather than punitive.[537] However, the Fifth Circuit has ruled that only one-third of RICO's trebled damages are deemed compensatory for purposes of the single-recovery rule, and the other two-thirds are penal.[538]

7.9.3   *Attorney Fees and Costs*

The RICO statute provides that an injured person "shall" recover costs, including a reasonable attorney fee.[539] The attorney fees awarded need not be in proportion to the amount of damages.[540] Singling out RICO defendants for the imposition of attorney fee liability does not deny them equal protection of the laws.[541] A prevailing defendant, however, is not entitled to fees.[542]

It is important to itemize the time spent and the work performed during the course of investigation and litigation, and, to the extent possible, to separate work done on the RICO claim from work done on other aspects of the case. Under *Hensley v. Eckerhart*, a plaintiff who is entitled to fees arising from a successful RICO claim may also obtain fees for other claims arising from the same common nucleus of facts.[543] Nonetheless, since the party seeking to recover attorney fees bears the burden of "[d]ocumenting the appropriate hours expended and hourly rates," it is best to present the court with a detailed affidavit rather than to leave the matter to conjecture. It is the plaintiff's job to establish what fees are being sought and to justify them, and courts occasionally refuse to award fees if they are not presented with proper evidence of the appropriate dollar amount.[544] In settling a case, explicit provision for attorney fees should be made, to avoid any question as to whether the right to attorney fees have been waived.[545]

---

533   Grogan v. Platt, 835 F.2d 844 (11th Cir. 1988). *See also* Rodriguez v. Quinones, 813 F. Supp. 924 (D. P.R. 1993) (reputation injury not RICO injury).

534   Imagineering, Inc. v. Kiewit Pac. Co., 976 F.2d 1303, 1310 (9th Cir. 1992) (affirming dismissal); Oscar v. University Students Co-Op Ass'n, 965 F.2d 783, 785–787 (9th Cir. 1992) (en banc) ("injury" must consist of concrete financial loss and not injury to a valuable, but intangible, property interest).

535   HBE Leasing Corp. v. Frank, 22 F.3d 41, 45 (2d Cir. 1994); St. James v. Future Fin., 776 A.2d 849, 870 (N.J. Super. Ct. App. Div. 2001).

536   *See also* BCS Services, Inc. v. BG Investments, Inc., No. 12-3235, 728 F.3d 633 (7th Cir. 2013) (rejecting defendant's argument that punitive damages awarded on claim for tortious interference with business relations double-counted with treble damages awarded on RICO claim, reasoning that RICO's treble damages were not punishment but a mechanism to compensate for "undercompensation"). *Compare* Com-Tech Associates v. Computer Associates Int'l, Inc., 753 F. Supp. 1078 (E.D.N.Y. 1991) (declining to strike a claim for punitive damages "at the pleading stage"), *aff'd on other grounds*, 938 F.2d 1574 (2d Cir. 1991), *and* Ross v. Jackie Fine Arts, Inc., 1991 U.S. Dist. LEXIS 13535 (D.S.C. Sept. 4, 1991) (awarding actual, trebled, and punitive damages); Al-Kazemi v. General Acceptance & Inv. Corp., 633 F. Supp. 540 (D.D.C. 1986) (same), *with* Toucheque v. Price Bros. Co., 5 F. Supp. 2d 341, 350 (D. Md. 1998) (RICO does not authorize punitive damages), *and* Galerie Furstenberg v. Coffaro, 697 F. Supp. 1282, 1289 (S.D.N.Y. 1998) (dismissing punitive damages claim), *and* Bingham v. Zolt, 823 F. Supp. 1126, 1135 (S.D.N.Y. 1993) (RICO does not authorize punitive damages), *aff'd*, 66 F.3d 553 (2d Cir. 1995), *and* Standard Chlorine of Del., Inc. v. Sinibaldi, 821 F. Supp. 232, 252–253 (D. Del. 1992) (RICO does not authorize punitive damages), *and* Mylan Labs., Inc. v. Akzo, N.V., 770 F. Supp. 1053 (D. Md. 1991) (striking RICO punitive damages claim), *and In re* VMS Sec. Litig., 752 F. Supp. 1373 (N.D. Ill. 1990) (treble damages are outer limit), *and* Southwest Marine, Inc. v. Triple A Mach. Shop, Inc., 720 F. Supp. 805 (N.D. Cal. 1989) (treble damages are outer limit).

537   *See* Neibel v. Trans World Assurance Co., 108 F.3d 1123 (9th Cir. 1997); Rhue v. Dawson, 841 P.2d 215 (Ariz. Ct. App. 1992) (allowing punitive damages in addition to treble damages under Arizona RICO statute; jury not to be told of trebling when it determines amount of punitive damages).

    Many courts recognize that RICO is a remedial statute, not punitive. *See, e.g.*, Agency Holding Corp. v. Malley-Duff & Associates, 483 U.S. 143, 107 S. Ct. 2759, 2764, 97 L. Ed. 2d 121 (1987) (RICO was designed to remedy injury); County of Oakland v. City of Detroit, 784 F. Supp. 1275, 1285 (E.D. Mich. 1992).

538   Abell v. Potomac Ins. Co., 858 F.2d 1104, *vacated on other grounds sub. nom.* Fryar v. Abell, 492 U.S. 914 (1989).

539   18 U.S.C. § 1964(c).

540   Rosario v. Livaditis, 963 F.2d 1013 (7th Cir. 1992); FMC Corp. v. Varonos, 892 F.2d 1308 (7th Cir. 1990); Northeast Women's Ctr. v. McMonagle, 889 F.2d 466 (3d Cir. 1989); Nu-Life Constr. Corp. v. Board of Educ., 795 F. Supp. 602 (E.D.N.Y. 1992).

    One court has held that adding a multiplier to the attorney fee is inappropriate. Burdett v. Miller, 957 F.2d 1375 (7th Cir. 1992).

541   Dee v. Sweet, 489 S.E.2d 823 (Ga. 1997) (upholding state RICO statute).

542   Jackson v. County of Rockland, 450 Fed. Appx. 15, 19–20 (2d Cir. 2011) (reasoning that defendant was not injured in his business or property by reason of a RICO violation).

543   461 U.S. 424, 435 (1983). *See also* Uniroyal Goodrich Tire Co. v. Mutual Trading Corp., 63 F.3d 516, 525 (7th Cir. 1995) (citing *Hensley* in reversing the trial court's refusal to award fees in case that alleged a RICO violation along with state unfair trade practices and other state claims); Tran v. Tran, 2002 WL 31108362, at *3 (S.D.N.Y Sept. 23) (refusing to reduce award of fees notwithstanding that plaintiff failed to prevail on her RICO count given that she prevailed on her Fair Labor Standards Act count, the facts of which were "inextricably intertwined" with those of the RICO count), *aff'd*, 67 Fed. Appx. 40 (2d Cir. June 3, 2003).

544   *See* International Floor Crafts, Inc. v. Adams, 847 F. Supp. 2d 254 (D. Mass. 2012) (noting that appellate fees are included in allowable fees but reducing fee award by one-half from that requested while awarding costs in full). *See also* Serin v. Northern Leasing Sys., Inc., 501 Fed. Appx. 39, 41 (2d Cir. 2012) (rejecting argument that trial court should have further reduced fees of attorneys who did not keep contemporaneous time records, when it had already reduced their fees by 35% in part because of that failure).

545   *See* Buckhannon Bd. & Care Home v. West Va. Dep't of Health & Human Res., 532 U. S. 598, 121 S. Ct. 1835, 149 L. Ed. 2d 855 (2001) (plaintiff who obtains enforceable judgment on merits or court-ordered consent decree is prevailing party and may seek fee award, but "private settlement" is insufficient); Nusom v. COMH Woodburn, Inc., 122 F.3d

Over and above attorney fees, a prevailing plaintiff is entitled to costs, which can be substantial. One court included among recoverable costs: photocopying, paralegal assistance, travel, telephone, videotaped depositions, postage, investigative fees, process server fees, witness fees, delivery, and any other costs for which an attorney generally bills the client separately. The court drew the line at parking and office supplies, however, finding that they are items of overhead.[546]

7.9.4 Prejudgment Interest

The United States Supreme Court let stand a Fourth Circuit denial of prejudgment interest in a RICO case on the basis that the district courts have discretion to award prejudgment interest to RICO plaintiffs.[547] One district court imposed prejudgment interest because the defendants had unreasonably delayed and obstructed the course of litigation.[548] Another district court ruled that prejudgment interest should only be awarded under special circumstances.[549]

7.9.5 Injunctive and Other Equitable Relief

The district courts have jurisdiction to prevent and restrain RICO violations by means including, but not limited to, the compelled divestiture of interests in an enterprise, reasonable restrictions on a person's future activities or investments, and even the dissolution or reorganization of an enterprise.[550] The United States Attorney General is expressly authorized to seek such relief,[551] but whether private civil litigants may obtain it is a question that has divided the courts. The Supreme Court in 2003 declined to resolve the circuits' split on the issue.[552] Some have indicated that such relief is available,[553] often in dictum;

others have said that it was not, again usually in dictum.[554] The Ninth Circuit has expressly considered the issue and held that it was not available.[555] The Sixth Circuit has ruled that

---

other grounds, 537 U.S. 393 (2003); Huyer v. Wells Fargo & Co., 295 F.R.D. 332, 344 (S.D. Iowa 2013) (following Seventh Circuit's reasoning); Suburban Buick, Inc. v. Gargo, 2009 WL 1543709 (N.D. Ill. May 29, 2009) (injunctive relief possible, but prematurely sought); United States v. Philip Morris USA, 316 F. Supp. 2d 6, 12 (D.D.C. 2004) (denying defendants' motion for partial summary judgment); *In re* Managed Care Litig., 298 F. Supp. 2d 1259, 1283 (S.D. Fla. 2003) (RICO authorizes injunctive relief); Motorola Credit Corp. v. Uzan, 202 F. Supp. 2d 239, 243 (S.D.N.Y. 2002) (injunctive relief available), *remanded on other grounds*, 322 F.3d 130 (2d Cir. 2003); Bernard v. Taub, 1990 WL 34680 (E.D.N.Y. 1990); Federal Deposit Ins. Corp. v. Antonio, 649 F. Supp. 1352 (D. Colo. 1986) (discussed, but did not decide availability), *aff'd*, 843 F.2d 1311 (10th Cir. 1988); Abel v. Bonfanti, 625 F. Supp. 263 (S.D.N.Y. 1986) (assuming availability based on traditional equitable factors); Miller v. Affiliated Fin. Corp., 600 F. Supp. 987, 994 (N.D. Ill. 1984) (denying injunction and declaratory relief); DeMent v. Abbott Capitol Corp., 589 F. Supp. 1378, 1382–1384 (N.D. Ill. 1984) (memorandum) (denying equitable relief except forms amounting to monetary payment); Kaufman v. Chase Manhattan Bank, 581 F. Supp. 350, 359 (S.D.N.Y. 1984); Kaushal v. State Bank of India, 556 F. Supp. 576, 581–584 (N.D. Ill. 1983) (denying orders for divestiture and against sale of business); Nakash v. Superior Court, 241 Cal. Rptr 578 (Cal. Ct. App. 1987) (state not bound by Ninth Circuit).

For arguments in favor of the availability of injunctive relief to private civil plaintiffs, see Blakey, *The RICO Civil Fraud Action in Context: Reflections on Bennett v. Berg*, 58 Notre Dame L. Rev. 237, 330–341 (1982); Note, *The Availability of Equitable Relief in Causes of Action in RICO*, 59 Notre Dame L. Rev. 945 (1984).

554   Matek v. Murat, 862 F.2d 720 (9th Cir. 1988); Religious Tech. Ctr. v. Wollersheim, 796 F.2d 1076 (9th Cir. 1986); USACO Coal Co. v. Carbomin Energy, 689 F.2d 94, 97, 98 (6th Cir. 1982); Minter v. Wells Fargo Bank, N.A., 593 F. Supp. 2d 788, 795–796 (D. Md. 2009) (citing *Religious Tech. Ctr. v. Wollerstein*); Amari Co. v. Burgess, 2008 WL 268698, at *3 (N.D. Ill. Jan. 28, 2008) (denying motion for a preliminary injunction on grounds that only the attorney general may seek preliminary relief); Sterling Suffolk Racecourse Ltd. P'ship v. Burrillville Racing Assoc., Inc., 802 F. Supp. 662 (D.R.I. 1992); P.R.F., Inc. v. Philips Credit Corp., 1992 U.S. Dist. LEXIS 19696 (D. P.R. Dec. 21, 1992); Curley v. Cumberland Farms Dairy, Inc., 728 F. Supp. 1123 (D.N.J. 1989); Town of W. Hartford v. Operation Rescue, 726 F. Supp. 371 (D. Conn. 1989), *vacated, remanded on other grounds*, 915 F.2d 92 (2d Cir. 1990); Raymark Indus., Inc. v. Stemple, 714 F. Supp. 460 (D. Kan. 1988); First Nat'l Bank & Trust Co. v. Hollingsworth, 701 F. Supp. 701 (W.D. Ark. 1988); Anderson-Myers Co. v. Roach, 660 F. Supp. 106 (D. Kan. 1987); Leff v. Olympic Fed. S&L, No. 86 C 3026 (N.D. Ill. June 18, 1987); Philatelic Found. v. Alan Kaplan, 647 F. Supp. 1344 (S.D.N.Y. 1986); Vietnam Veterans of Am., Inc. v. Guerdon Indus., 644 F. Supp. 951 (D. Del. 1986); Chambers Dev. Co. v. Browning-Ferris Indus., 590 F. Supp. 1528, 1540, 1541 (W.D. Pa. 1984); Vietnamese Fishermen's Ass'n v. Knights of the Ku Klux Klan, 518 F. Supp. 993, 1014 (S.D. Tex. 1981); United States v. Barber, 476 F. Supp. 182, 189 (S.D. W. Va. 1979); United States v. Mandel, 415 F. Supp. 997, 1021 (D. Md. 1976), *aff'd on other grounds by equally divided court*, 602 F.2d 653 (4th Cir. 1979). *See also* Burnham Broad. Co. v. Williams, 629 So. 2d 1335 (La. Ct. App. 1993) (Louisiana appellate court affirmed preliminary injunction in private RICO action without comment).

555   Or. Laborers-Employers Health & Welfare Trust Fund v. Philip Morris, Inc., 185 F.3d 957, 967 (9th Cir. 1999); Ganey v. Raffone, 91 F.3d 143 (6th Cir. 1988) (noting in dictum that it is questionable whether injunctions are available to RICO private plaintiffs); Religious Tech. Ctr. v. Wollersheim, 796 F.2d 1076 (9th Cir. 1986). *See also In re* Fredeman Litig., 843 F.2d 821 (5th Cir. 1988) (court could not use general

---

830 (9th Cir. 1997) (construing acceptance of Rule 68 offer for money judgment "together with costs" not to waive TILA and state RICO attorney fees).

546   Hertz Corp. v. Caulfied, 796 F. Supp. 225 (E.D. La. 1992).

547   *See* Bseirani v. Abou-Khadra, 4 F.3d 1071 (4th Cir. 1993). *See also* Securitron Magnalock Corp. v. Schnabolk, 1994 U.S. Dist. LEXIS 14894 (S.D.N.Y. Oct. 18, 1994) (prejudgment interest not available under RICO except in the most unusual case), *aff'd on other grounds*, 65 F.3d 256 (2d Cir. 1995).

548   Miltland Raleigh-Durham v. Myers, 807 F. Supp. 1025 (S.D.N.Y. 1993). *See also* D'Orange v. Feely, 894 F. Supp. 159 (S.D.N.Y. 1995) (prejudgment interest awarded), *aff'd*, 101 F.3d 1393 (2d Cir. 1996) (table).

549   Farberware, Inc. v. Groben, 1995 U.S. Dist. LEXIS 15409 (S.D.N.Y. Sept. 15, 1995) (magistrate's recommendation), *adopted by* 1995 U.S. Dist. LEXIS 14492 (Oct. 4, 1995).

550   18 U.S.C. § 1964(a).

551   18 U.S.C. § 1964(b). *See also* United States v. Philip Morris USA, Inc., 449 F. Supp. 2d 1 (D.D.C. 2006) (awarding injunctive relief), *aff'd in part, vacated in part on other grounds*, 566 F.3d 1095 (D.C. Cir. 2009) (largely upholding lower court's injunction), *order clarified*, 778 F. Supp. 2d 8 (D.D.C. 2011).

552   Scheidler v. Nat'l Org. for Women, Inc., 537 U.S. 393 (2003).

553   *See* Aetna v. Liebowitz, 730 F.2d 905, 906 (2d Cir. 1984) (suggesting private injunctive relief might be available); Trane Co. v. O'Connor Sec., 718 F.2d 26, 28, 29 (2d Cir. 1983); Dan River, Inc. v. Icahn, 701 F.2d 278, 290 (4th Cir. 1983); NOW, Inc. v. Scheidler, 267 F.3d 687 (7th Cir. 2001) (affirming injunction against abortion protestors), *rev'd on*

injective relief is available in private RICO actions, without commenting on its reasons for departing from the more usual rule.[556] Some inclination to avoid the issue is discernible.[557] Without ruling on the issue of equitable relief as such, the Fifth Circuit has held that disgorgement is not a remedy available under civil RICO when it is sought only to compensate losses, not to prevent future misconduct.[558]

7.10 RICO Consumer Cases in the Courts

7.10.1 Examples of Successful Consumer RICO Cases

7.10.1.1 Mortgage Lending

A number of RICO claims have successfully challenged mortgage lending practices:

- A complaint by borrowers victimized by a mortgage lender survived a motion to dismiss. The plaintiffs alleged that the lender, among other abuses, padded loans with fraudulent charges. The borrowers sued the subsequent holders of the notes who had purchased them on the secondary mortgage market (the lender itself was in bankruptcy). The defendant had sought to dismiss the claims based on mail fraud to the extent the suit alleged that the note purchasers knew of the mortgage lender's fraudulent conduct. The lenders subsequently settled the case by agreeing to reform the borrower's notes, for a savings to the class conservatively estimated at $2.5 million, plus attorney fees.[559]

- In a case alleging that defendants engaged in a predatory lending scheme, a Pennsylvania district court concluded that the plaintiffs, home purchasers, had raised genuine issues of material fact with respect to whether developers knowingly participated in a scheme to defraud and whether

the appraiser colluded with the developers in inflating the representation of the homes' fair market value.[560]

- In a case alleging a predatory lending scheme that targeted first time home buyers and minorities and arranged for inflated appraisals of home values, a Pennsylvania district court refused to dismiss the plaintiff's complaint.[561]

- In a case that alleged that a real estate developer, appraiser, and mortgage lender had schemed to artificially inflate real estate values denying the defendants' motion for summary judgment, ruling that the plaintiffs sufficiently established injury.[562]

- A Tennessee district court ruled that plaintiffs, victims of a predatory lending scheme, successfully alleged a RICO enterprise consisting of a title company, a mortgage lender, and other participants in the scheme.[563]

- A court refused to dismiss a claim by mortgage loan customers against a bank that they alleged charged inflated legal fees. The court found that the plaintiffs had sufficiently alleged an enterprise, an association in fact comprising the bank and a law firm, and that the bank conducted a pattern of racketeering activity consisting in part of a scheme to defraud by means of affirmative representations that the legal fees were genuine and not excessive.[564]

- A court of appeals panel affirmed a district court's ruling that a title insurance agency and lending companies, who allegedly conspired with another defendant to defraud the plaintiffs into purchasing homes they could not afford by misrepresenting that the homes would be entitled to tax abatements and mortgage credit certificates, could be liable under RICO's conspiracy provision by knowingly agreeing to facilitate a scheme which included operation or management of a RICO enterprise, even if they did not commit or agree to commit predicate offenses.[565]

- An Arizona district court refused to dismiss the RICO claims of custom home purchasers who alleged that the defendants schemed to create fraudulent appraisals that inflated the values of the homes so that they could sell them for more than they were worth.[566] The court concluded that the plaintiffs adequately established standing, an enterprise, and a pattern of racketeering activity.

- A claim against home equity strippers has survived a motion to dismiss because the homeowners have properly alleged

---

556   NCR Corp. v. Feltz, 1993 WL 11876 (6th Cir. Jan. 21, 1993).

557   *E.g.*, Northeast Women's Ctr., Inc. v. McMonagle, 813 F.2d 53 (3d Cir. 1987) (vacating denial of preliminary injunction due to failure to make factual findings of irreparable harm without mentioning whether private injunctive relief is available); Revlon, Inc. v. Pantry Pride, Inc., 621 F. Supp. 804, 816 (D. Del. 1985) (denying a preliminary injunction on the ground of lack of probability of success on the merits without deciding whether such relief is available); McLendon v. Continental Grp., Inc., 602 F. Supp. 1492, 1518, 1519 (D.N.J. 1985) (reviewing the arguments and reserving decision as "the law is in great flux"). *See also In re* Fredeman Litig., 843 F.2d 821 (5th Cir. 1988) (declining to decide whether all forms of injunctive relief are foreclosed to private RICO plaintiffs).

558   Richard v. Hoechst Celanese Chem. Grp., Inc., 355 F.3d 345, 354–355 (5th Cir. 2003) (reasoning that equitable relief under RICO would only be available to address future violations); United States v. Carson, 52 F.3d 1173, 1182 (2d Cir. 1995) (disgorgement limited to those funds "being used to fund or promote the illegal conduct, or [that] constitute capital available for that purpose"). *See also* United States v. Philip Morris USA, Inc., 396 F.3d 1190 (D.C. Cir. 2005) (disgorgement not available as remedy).

559   Anderson v. Federal Nat'l Mortg. Ass'n, Clearinghouse No. 42,568 (E.D. Va. Nov. 25, 1987) (order denying motion to dismiss).

---

        equitable powers to enjoin sale of assets in RICO case). *But cf.* Nakash v. Superior Court, 241 Cal. Rptr 578 (Cal. Ct. App. 1987) (state court is not bound by Ninth Circuit precedent).

---

560   Wilson v. Parisi, 549 F. Supp. 2d 637 (M.D. Pa. 2008).

561   Meeks-Owens v. Indymac Bank, F.S.B., 557 F. Supp. 2d 566 (M.D. Pa. 2008).

562   Lester v. Percudani, 556 F. Supp. 2d 473 (M.D. Pa. 2008). *See also* Wallace v. Midwest Fin. & Mortg. Services, Inc., 714 F.3d 414 (6th Cir. 2013) (reversing summary judgment against homeowner on RICO claim based on procurement of falsified appraisal that enabled fraudulent mortgage lending scheme to succeed).

563   Carr v. Home Tech Co., 476 F. Supp. 2d 859, 863–865 (W.D. Tenn. 2007) (referring to prior order of the court).

564   Weil v. Long Island Sav. Bank, F.S.B., 77 F. Supp. 2d 313 (E.D.N.Y. 1999).

565   Smith v. Berg, 247 F.3d 532 (3d Cir. 2001).

566   Johnson v. KB Home, 720 F. Supp. 2d 1109 (D. Ariz. 2010).

predicate acts of mail fraud and an association in fact enterprise.[567]

- A court refused to dismiss a claim brought by homeowners against their mortgagee and related entities alleging that the mortgagee had charged unauthorized and illicit fees related to the plaintiffs' bankruptcy.[568]
- A court refused to dismiss claims brought by former residential property owners against a Christian corporation, a mortgage company and others alleging a scheme to defraud the plaintiffs of their property and profit from inflated mortgages. The court found that the plaintiffs had sufficiently alleged an enterprise, a pattern of racketeering activity and proximate cause of their injuries, which included the loss of their home equity and the amount of their monthly rent payments that exceeded their prior mortgage obligations.[569]
- A Third Circuit panel upheld a lower court's decision that refused to dismiss a class action RICO conspiracy claim by plaintiff home buyers against several realty-related corporations. The plaintiffs alleged that the corporations had conspired with another defendant, a developer, to induce the plaintiffs to purchase homes they could not afford, by using fraudulent financial incentives. On appeal, the court held that the plaintiffs need not show that the defendant corporations committed a substantive violation of RICO, but only that the defendant knowingly agreed to assist a scheme that included the operation or management of a RICO enterprise.[570]
- A court refused to dismiss RICO claims brought by a class of loan applicants against a lender and affiliated mortgage brokers, alleging that the lender bribed the brokers to induce their business. The court said the alleged association in fact was sufficiently distinct from the defendants itself when the brokers were an integral part of the scheme and indeed benefited from it.[571]
- A court refused to dismiss a complaint brought by homeowners who had allegedly been victimized by a scheme by which a financial services company convinced them to mortgage their homes for the maximum amount possible in return for paying off prior loans and extending a line of credit. The homeowners sued the company, its principals, and its attorney. The court ruled that the plaintiffs had sufficiently alleged a pattern of racketeering activity.[572]
- A court reversed the dismissal of a RICO claim brought by a mortgagor who claimed that a law firm had fraudulently executed an assignment of the mortgage to another bank, which had then relied on the assignment to bring an illegitimate foreclosure action against the plaintiff.[573]

- A Maryland district court denied a motion to dismiss a claim alleging that the defendants engaged in a foreclosure rescue scam.[574] The plaintiffs alleged that the defendants created a sale-and-leaseback operation intended to siphon off the homeowners' equity. The court concluded that the plaintiffs pleaded mail and wire fraud with sufficient particularity and that the sale/leaseback transaction could be characterized as an equitable mortgage that was an unlawful debt under state law. The complaint alleged that the title company, due to its association with other RICO defendants, received a large volume of referrals and then charged excessive fees which benefited the settlement agents; that settlement agents reinvested fees into the title company and channeled fees to two other entities; and that fees were then reinvested in the mortgage foreclosure rescue scam, which resulted in additional referrals to title company and settlement agents.
- A North Carolina district court refused to dismiss a claim alleging that the defendants operated a fraudulent mortgage modification business, making false promises to lower the mortgage payments of the plaintiffs, who were struggling homeowners.[575]

7.10.1.2 Predatory Non-Mortgage Lending and Rent to Own

A number of RICO claims have successfully challenged non-mortgage lending practices and rent-to-own transactions:

- A complaint by a taxpayer against a tax return preparation service and lender based on alleged fraud in refund anticipation loans survived a motion to dismiss.[576]
- The Seventh Circuit reversed the dismissal of RICO claims by a loan applicant against a lender in which she alleged that the lender fraudulently induced her to refinance her existing personal loan at exorbitant rates. She did not allege that Truth in Lending requirements or other statutory requirements were violated, but the lender did not make clear that it would be less expensive to take out a new loan than to refinance the old one. The Seventh Circuit noted that a careful reading of the Truth in Lending statement would have shown that the refinancing was not a good deal but noted that not everyone is capable of being a careful reader. It summarized the allegation as being that the complainant belonged to a class of borrowers who are not competent interpreters of Truth in Lending forms and that the lender took advantage of that fact.[577]
- A RICO class action against a lender that charged interest rates between 179% and 557% and used threats in the collection process withstood a motion to dismiss.[578]

567 Bryant v. Bigelow, 311 F. Supp. 2d 666, 671 (S.D. Ohio 2004).

568 Majchrowski v. Norwest Mortg., 6 F. Supp. 2d 946 (N.D. Ill. 1998).

569 Ifill v. West, 1999 U.S. Dist. LEXIS 21320 (E.D.N.Y. Aug. 24, 1999).

570 Smith v. Berg, 247 F.3d 532, 538 (3d Cir. 2001). The trial court later declined to certify the class of homebuyers, but on other grounds. Smith v. Berg, 2001 U.S. Dist. LEXIS 15814 (E.D. Pa. Oct. 1, 2001).

571 Epps v. The Money Store, No. 96 C 2703, 26 RICO L. Rep. 631 (N.D. Ill. Sept. 30, 1997).

572 Thomas v. Ross & Hardies, 9 F. Supp. 2d 547 (D. Md. 1998).

573 Slorp v. Lerner, Sampson & Rothfuss, 587 Fed. Appx. 249 (6th Cir. 2014).

574 Proctor v. Metropolitan Money Store Corp., 645 F. Supp. 2d 464 (D. Md. 2009).

575 Manuel v. Gembala, 2012 WL 3957918, at *8–10 (E.D.N.C. Aug. 17, 2012), *adopted by* 2012 WL 3958174 (E.D.N.C. Sept. 10, 2012).

576 Carnegie v. Household Intl, Inc., 220 F.R.D. 542 (N.D. Ill. 2004), *aff'd on other issues*, 376 F.3d 656 (7th Cir. 2004) (affirming certification of class).

577 Emery v. American Gen. Fin., Inc., 71 F.3d 1343 (7th Cir. 1995).

578 Brown v. C.I.L., Inc., 1996 WL 164294 (N.D. Ill. Mar. 29, 1996).

- When the implicit interest in rent-to-own (RTO) contracts was usurious under state law and was more than twice the applicable rate, the RICO predicate element of "unlawful debt" was established.[579]
- A district court's dismissal on the ground that there was no RICO injury, separate from the injury caused by the predicate offenses,[580] was reversed by the Seventh Circuit[581] in a case in which corporations sued a bank alleging that it had fraudulently charged an excessive interest rate on loans by lying about the prime rate to which the interest rates were pegged; the deceptive statements, sent by mail, were the predicate offenses of mail fraud. The decision was, in turn, affirmed by the Supreme Court.[582]
- The Second Circuit affirmed the certification of a class action against defendants that the plaintiffs alleged bought debt portfolios and then filed debt collection actions with mass-produced fraudulent affidavits in order to obtain default judgments and then enforce them.[583]

7.10.1.3   Auto Financing, Leasing, and Repossessions

A number of RICO claims have successfully challenged auto financing, leasing, and repossession practices:

- The Fourth Circuit twice reversed the district court's dismissal of RICO claims by a class of used car buyers against a car wholesaler and a related finance company. The consumer alleged that the defendants had engaged in a fraudulent "churning" scheme to sell cars at inflated rates, repossess them, conduct sham repossession sales, and bill consumers for alleged deficiencies.[584]
- A RICO class was certified against an auto dealership and finance company in a case in which the plaintiffs alleged that the defendants had violated both RICO provisions and the TILA in connection with discounts associated with certain retail installment sales contracts and sales of extended warranties.[585]
- A court refused to dismiss a class action brought against a finance company for failing to include a provision in car loan documents that would allow the debtor to raise seller-related

defenses to any attempt to collect the loan. The court ruled that the plaintiff had alleged a sufficient pattern.[586]

7.10.1.4   Land Sales, Retirement Communities, and Nursing Homes

A number of RICO claims have successfully challenged land sale, retirement community, and nursing home practices:

- Past and present residents sued the corporation which owned and operated their retirement community for fraudulently inducing them to purchase lifetime occupancy agreements by misrepresenting the financial soundness of the corporation and falsely promising affordable "life care." In a wide-ranging opinion, the Eighth Circuit rejected the district court's imposition of commercial or competitive racketeering injury requirements. The court also allowed the corporations' mortgage lender and former accountant to be sued as persons "associated with" the enterprise, rejecting any "RICO relationship" requirement linking these defendants to the enterprise; and held that an enterprise had been alleged which was sufficiently distinct from the "pattern of racketeering activity." However, the court called for greater particularity in the pleading of the predicate offenses of mail fraud and for pleading of a culpable "person" apart from the corporate "enterprise."[587] On remand, the owner of the retirement community turned out to be judgment-proof, but its mortgagee, a defendant "associated with" the enterprise and alleged to have known of and concealed its mismanagement, settled the case for $62.8 million.[588]
- The Eighth Circuit held that plaintiffs had sufficiently alleged injury in a case in which an association of purchasers of land in a subdivision sued the developer, relying upon mail fraud predicate offenses, alleging that the developer had not lived up to its promises. The alleged failure to pave roads as promised, and the sale of additional lots by a mail fraud scheme, leading to heavier road use and greater need for maintenance (which was the landowners' responsibility) were held to be sufficient direct or indirect injury under the statute.[589]

A motion to dismiss was denied in a RICO case based on nursing home president's use of dummy drug invoices to overbill patients.[590]

---

579   *See* Fogie v. Rent-A-Center, Inc., 1995 WL 649575 (D. Minn. 1995), *aff'd sub nom.* Fogie v. Thorn Americas, Inc., 95 F.3d 645 (8th Cir. 1996) (RICO issue was not addressed on appeal). *See also* Starks v. Rent-A-Center, 1990 U.S. Dist. LEXIS 20099 (D. Minn. May 15, 1990), *aff'd on other grounds*, 58 F.3d 358 (8th Cir. 1995).

580   Haroco, Inc. v. American Nat'l Bank & Trust Co., 577 F. Supp. 111, 114 (N.D. Ill. 1983).

581   Haroco, Inc. v. American Nat'l Bank & Trust Co., 747 F.2d 384, 387–398 (7th Cir. 1984).

582   American Nat'l Bank & Trust Co. v. Haroco, Inc., 473 U.S. 606, 105 S. Ct. 3291, 87 L. Ed. 2d 437 (1985) (per curiam).

583   Sykes v. Mel S. Harris & Associates, L.L.C., 780 F.3d 70 (2d Cir. 2015).

584   Chisolm v. TranSouth Fin. Corp., 95 F.3d 331 (4th Cir. 1996), *appeal after remand*, 164 F.3d 623 (4th Cir. 1998) (table, full text at 1998 U.S. App. LEXIS 24632), *on remand*, 184 F.R.D. 556 (E.D. Va. 1999) (certifying class), *later op. at* 194 F.R.D. 538 (E.D. Va. 2000) (defining subclasses and ruling on trial plans).

585   Johnson v. Rohr-Ville Motors, Inc., 189 F.R.D. 363 (N.D. Ill. 1999).

586   Brown v. LaSalle Northwest Nat'l Bank, 820 F. Supp. 1078 (N.D. Ill. 1993).

587   Bennett v. Berg, 685 F.2d 1053 (8th Cir. 1982), *aff'd en banc*, 710 F.2d 1361 (8th Cir. 1983). *See* Blakey, *The RICO Civil Fraud Action in Context: Reflections on Bennett v. Berg*, 58 Notre Dame L. Rev. 237 (1982).

588   *"Indirect" RICO Defendant Settles for $62.8 Million*, 5 Law. Alert, Feb. 24, 1986, at 5.

589   Terre Du Lac Ass'n, Inc. v. Terre Du Lac, Inc., 772 F.2d 467 (8th Cir. 1985).

590   Arenson v. Whitehall Convalescent & Nursing Home, 880 F. Supp. 1202 (N.D. Ill. 1995). *See also* Nat'l Senior Citizens Law Ctr., *Applying Racketeering Laws to Nursing Homes*, 19 Clearinghouse Rev. 1306 (1986).

7.10.1.5   Trade Schools

Successful RICO claims against trade school abuses include:

- A RICO class was certified against a vocational school and its parent company when the class alleged that the defendants had fraudulently represented to students the education they would receive.[591]
- A court tentatively certified a class of students on a RICO claim they brought against the former president of a trade school. The students alleged that the defendant had fraudulently caused them to get student loans while misrepresenting their qualifications to the government.[592]

7.10.1.6   Insurance, Annuities

A number of RICO claims have successfully challenged practices relating to insurance and to annuities:

- In a case asserting fraud in the denial of claims for trip interruption and cancellation insurance, alleging that the denials falsely represented that a doctor's statement was necessary to receive coverage, a California district court ruled that the plaintiffs were able to establish proximate cause.[593]
- In a case arising from the sale to elders of estate planning instruments and annuities alleged to be unnecessary and unsuitable, and that contained undisclosed deferral periods and surrender charges, a Pennsylvania district court ruled that the plaintiffs had pleaded an appropriate injury and thus had standing.[594]
- The Second Circuit overturned the dismissal of a claim by life insurance policy buyers who alleged that the defendant had marketed the policy as a kind of IRA. If the plaintiff were able to prove that the defendant had "misdescribed the economic value of the bargain," that foregone returns of an IRA or other similar savings plan would have been greater than the investment plaintiffs selected, and that the difference was a foreseeable consequence of the misrepresentation, the court ruled that the allegations would show loss causation and confer standing under RICO.[595]
- A California district court ruled that a plaintiff, who had been induced to buy an annuity, successfully alleged a RICO enterprise consisting of insurance companies that allegedly schemed to convince annuity purchasers to buy annuities inappropriate for them.[596]
- A court certified a class of persons in a suit against an insurance company that alleged that the company charged the insureds a copayment for the generic drug Tamoxifen as if it were a prescription drug; the court refused to dismiss the

case, ruling that the plaintiff had adequately alleged a pattern to defraud.[597]
- A court ruled that several policyholders had alleged sufficient injury in a suit against an insurance agent that alleged that he fraudulently induced them to buy life insurance policies by misrepresenting the benefits. The issue was whether the plaintiffs, who were proceeding under subsection 1962(a), had to prove they were injured because of the defendant's investment of the racketeering proceeds.[598]
- In a case alleging that an insurance company misrepresented the pricing features of annuities, a California district court denied summary judgment to the defendant, concluding that the plaintiff had sufficiently raised fact issues as to the existence of an enterprise among the defendant and its sales agents, the control the defendant exercised over the enterprise, and a concrete injury suffered by the plaintiffs.[599]
- A Nevada district court denied a motion to dismiss a RICO claim against a life insurance company, a benefits company, and the benefits company's president that alleged that they had schemed to prey upon older consumers, some of whom were mentally incapacitated, acquiring the consumers' personal financial information through deceptive marketing schemes and then using that information to target the consumers for annuities and life insurance policies.[600]

7.10.1.7   Miscellaneous

A number of RICO claims have successfully challenged other consumer law abuses:

- The Sixth Circuit reversed the dismissal of a claim brought by electric utility customers against a state-regulated public utility, its subsidiaries, and one of its large customers that alleged that the utility had paid unlawful rebates to certain large customers.[601] The court rejected the defendants' arguments that the utility bills issued by the utility were not fraudulent and that the plaintiffs could not adequately establish damages.

---

591   Cullen v. Whitman Med. Corp., 188 F.R.D. 226 (E.D. Pa. 1999).

592   Rodriguez v. McKinney, 156 F.R.D. 112 (E.D. Pa. June 6, 1994).

593   Wallace v. BCS Ins. Co., 2008 WL 149150 (E.D. Cal. Jan. 14, 2008).

594   *In re* American Investors Life Ins. Co. Annuity Mktg. & Sales Practices Litig., 2007 WL 2541216 (E.D. Pa. Aug. 29, 2007).

595   Moore v. PaineWebber, Inc., 189 F.3d 165 (2d Cir. 1999).

596   *In re* Nat'l W. Life Ins. Deferred Annuities Litig., 467 F. Supp. 2d 1071, 1085–1086 (S.D. Cal. 2006).

597   Morse v. Bankers Life & Cas. Co., 2000 U.S. Dist. LEXIS 2211 (N.D. Ill. Feb. 24, 2000) (finding that two acts could form a pattern).

598   Pinski v. Adelman, 1995 U.S. Dist. LEXIS 16550 (N.D. Ill. Nov. 2, 1995).

        This issue of whether a section 1962(a) injury may arise from the predicate acts or must arise from the investment of the proceeds of the predicate acts has arisen in many cases. *See* Compagnie de Reassurance D'Ille de France v. New England Reinsurance Corp., 57 F.3d 56 (1st Cir. 1995) (Supreme Court let stand First Circuit ruling which required injury from the investment of the proceeds, not just from the predicate acts). *See also* R.C.M. Executive Gallery Corp. v. ROLS Capital Corp., 901 F. Supp. 630 (S.D.N.Y. 1995) (section 1962(a) action by restaurant investors dismissed when they did not allege injury from investment of the proceeds of usurious loan).

599   Negrete v. Allianz Life Ins. Co. of N. Am., 2011 WL 4852314 (C.D. Cal. Oct. 13, 2011).

600   Sommers v. Cuddy, 2012 WL 359339 (D. Nev. Feb. 2, 2012).

601   Williams v. Duke Energy Int'l, Inc., 681 F.3d 788 (6th Cir. 2012).

- A class action was certified in a case in which prescription drug purchasers alleged that the defendant, a publisher of prescription drug prices, conspired to artificially inflate the published prices of prescription drugs.[602]
- A court refused to dismiss a claim that a retailer, working with a manufacturer, procured speakers in which one of the three drivers was phony and then sold them to consumers as three-way speakers.[603]
- A district court refused to dismiss a RICO claim brought against the operator of adult dating websites that alleged that the defendant used false testimonials and similar devices to induce individuals to buy or upgrade their memberships.[604]
- A Pennsylvania district court denied the motions to dismiss of a bank, third-party payment processors, and a telemarketer that the plaintiff alleged had constructed a scheme to fraudulently withdraw funds from the plaintiff's account.[605] The court noted that the plaintiff had identified specific red flags that should have alerted the payment processors to the fraudulent nature of the telemarketing practices.[606]
- In a case alleging that the defendants conspired to repackage and sell used vacuum cleaners as new, a Georgia district court concluded that the plaintiffs had successfully alleged an enterprise with a common purpose of minimizing the market for used vacuum cleaners furthered, among other acts, by providing distributors with registration cards directed to new purchasers that the distributors could provide to secondhand purchasers.[607]
- A court of appeals vacated the dismissal of a RICO claim that alleged that the defendants created fraudulent travel clubs and swindled the plaintiffs by "promis[ing] Plaintiffs a variety of free trips and travel services in return for their purchase of 'Travel Club' memberships."[608]
- A court refused to dismiss a case brought by a class of AT&T calling card holders against AT&T, claiming AT&T said the cards were "free" without disclosing that there was a substantial fee for using them. The lawsuit alleged fraud, RICO violation, deceptive acts, and false advertising. The RICO predicate offenses alleged were mail and wire fraud.[609]
- False advertising has become a far more common subject of RICO claims in recent years.[610]

7.10.2 Examples of Unsuccessful Consumer RICO Cases

Consumer cases in which the plaintiffs were for one reason or another unsuccessful include the following:

- Three circuits have ruled that telephone ratepayers do not have the right to have courts award damages that effectively reset filed rates.[611]
- A court dismissed a class action that credit card holders filed against three financial institutions which gave credit cards to bad credit risks upon payment of a deposit. The deposits were misused and the marketer went bankrupt. The court held that the 16% to 18% interest rate charged was not twice the allowable credit card rate of 24%, so the RICO claim for unlawful debt collection was dismissed.[612]

An Illinois district court dismissed a case alleging that a tax preparation firm and its franchises violated RICO by engaging in a pattern of racketeering activity involving the wire transmission of thousands of fraudulently prepared tax returns and the processing of credit card charges for its tax return guarantee program.[613]

In a suit brought by home purchasers against home builders and real estate agents alleging that they fraudulently induced the plaintiffs to buy homes without an adequate water supply, a New York district court ruled that the plaintiffs could not establish a pattern of racketeering activity given that the scheme lasted only fourteen months and defrauded only ten sets of individuals.[614]

- A court dismissed a suit filed by a charge card holder that claimed mail and wire fraud as to a scheme to waive fees for some cardholders. The court dismissed the case, stating that even if the claims were true, there was no mail fraud. RICO, the court said, was not meant to protect consumers against the irritation of learning that others have gotten a better deal.[615]
- A court held that a bank's practice of buying insurance which protected its loan at the expense of automobile purchasers who did not produce evidence of insurance did not violate RICO when the three plaintiffs (who owned one car) did not produce evidence of a pattern or of continuity.[616] The plaintiffs argued that there were numerous events of mail fraud because the bank sent several letters, but the court said that the Seventh Circuit does not look favorably on relying on many instances of mail fraud to establish a pattern of racketeering activity.

---

602 New England Carpenters Health Benefits Fund v. First Databank, Inc., 244 F.R.D. 79 (D. Mass. 2007).

603 Winger v. Best Buy Co., 2011 WL 995937 (D. Ariz. Mar. 21, 2011).

604 Badella v. Deniro Mktg. L.L.C., 2011 WL 227668 (N.D. Cal. Jan. 24, 2011).

605 Reyes v. Zion First Nat'l Bank, 2012 WL 947139 (E.D. Pa. Mar. 21, 2012).

606 *Id.* at *6. *See also* Reyes v. Netdeposit, L.L.C., 2015 WL 5131287 (3d Cir. Sept. 2, 2015) (vacating and remanding denial of class certification in the case).

607 Jordan v. Scott Fetzer Co., 2007 WL 4287719 (M.D. Ga. Dec. 4, 2007).

608 Grant v. Turner, 505 Fed. Appx. 107, 110 (3d Cir. 2012).

609 Gelb v. American Tel. & Tel., 813 F. Supp. 1022 (S.D.N.Y. 1993).

610 A.B. Weissman, *Watch Out Joe Isuzu, the Civil RICO Police Are on Your Trail: Misleading Advert. as a Potential Civil RICO Growth Indus.*, 13 RICO L. Rep. 5 (May 1991).

611 Wegoland, Ltd. v. NYNEX Corp., 27 F.3d 17 (2d Cir. 1994); Taffet v. Southern Co., 967 F.2d 1483 (11th Cir. 1992); H.J. Inc. v. Northwestern Bell Tel. Co., 954 F.2d 485 (8th Cir. 1992).

612 Iacobucci v. Universal Bank of Md., 1991 WL 102460 (S.D.N.Y. June 5, 1991), *aff'd*, 962 F.2d 1 (2d Cir. 1992).

613 Wooley v. Jackson Hewitt, Inc., 540 F. Supp. 2d 964 (N.D. Ill. 2008).

614 Caravella v. Hearthwood Homes Inc., 2007 WL 2886507 (N.D.N.Y. Sept. 27, 2007).

615 Litwin v. American Express Co., 838 F. Supp. 855 (S.D.N.Y. 1993).

616 Travis v. Boulevard Bank, N.A., No. 93 C 6847 (N.D. Ill. Oct. 7, 1994).

- In a suit brought by survivors of deceased people against a number of funeral homes based on the funeral homes' knowing dealings with a cemetery with a reputation for mistreating corpses, the court found no RICO violation. It said that while the funeral homes may have been negligent, there was no pattern to defraud, the plaintiffs having shown no motive and no benefit to the funeral homes.[617]
- The Sixth Circuit granted summary judgment to a bank on RICO claims brought by a class of automobile purchasers who alleged that the bank had fraudulently purchased unauthorized insurance coverage on their loans. The court found the language of the loan documents not sufficiently misleading to constitute fraud. It also found that allegations of kickbacks the bank received from the insurance company were not sufficiently particularized.[618]
- The Seventh Circuit declined to find mail fraud when consumers complained that their insurance certificates said they would receive unearned premiums back on prepayment, but the insurer did not pay the premiums back until asked to do so. The court found that the insurance certificates did not say anything incorrect and that the complaint did not state a cause of action for mail fraud.[619]
- When a car buyer claimed that the assignee of her finance contract bought more insurance than necessary and demanded that she pay for it, a court found that there was no mail fraud because there was no allegation of a misrepresentation. The assignee said it was going to buy the insurance and did so. The car buyer did not allege any intent to defraud. The allegations were not sufficient for mail fraud.[620]
- A court dismissed the case of frustrated former property owners who had sued their mortgage holder, alleging that it had a practice of fraudulently imposing early payoff charges. The enterprises alleged, consisting of the defendants' corporate parents, were insufficiently distinct from the defendant itself when there was an integrated operational relationship between the three entities.[621]
- A consumer class action for warranty fraud brought by two purchasers of automobile service contracts against Chrysler, alleging fraudulent inducement by misrepresentation of coverage, was dismissed because Chrysler was insufficiently distinct from a claimed enterprise consisting of its affiliates and agents.[622]
- A RICO claim filed by allegedly defrauded franchisees was deemed barred by a waiver of liability signed by franchisees.[623]

- The First Circuit overturned a $43 million RICO verdict against Volvo Car Corporation, ruling that there was insufficient evidence that Volvo knew of fraud by a Volvo dealer and distributor and that the Monroney Act violations by Volvo could not support the verdict because they are not predicate offenses.[624]
- A used car buyer brought section 1962(a) claim against the financier of his vehicle, alleging that the defendant had fraudulently charged excessive late fees which were later used to replenish, in part, the general operating funds of the enterprise so the scheme could continue. Requisite investment injury was lacking. If there was any claim it was based on predicate offenses, not investment injury.[625]
- A court dismissed a claim against the successor to a company that had allegedly lent money to the plaintiffs at usurious rates, ruling that the plaintiffs cannot claim themselves as part of an associated-in-fact enterprise when the group existed to defraud them.[626]
- A court found that a claimed association in fact was indistinct from the alleged pattern when the only activities alleged were the scheme itself. Homebuyers brought a RICO claim against parties who participated in selling them unstable homes built over a landfill. The court ruled that the enterprise was the same as the pattern of activity and must be proved separately.[627]
- A court dismissed a claim that due to the defendant's allegedly fraudulent forced placement of collateral protection insurance (CPI), the plaintiffs had lost money spent on overpriced insurance that insured only the defendant's interest. The court held that the injury alleged did not arise from the reinvestment of racketeering proceeds and that the claim was insufficient to allege that the defendant invested the money obtained in the alleged enterprise.[628]
- The Eleventh Circuit affirmed the dismissal of a RICO claim brought by a bankrupt homeowner against the foreclosing mortgagee, concluding that RICO did not provide a remedy for a scheme with but one goal, that of divesting a mortgagor of her home.[629]

In a case alleging that an insurance company deceptively marketed and sold equity-indexed annuities to elders, a Massachusetts district court ruled that the plaintiff could not base her claim on an enterprise comprising the insurance company and its sales agents because the two were not sufficiently distinct.[630]

---

617 *In re* Cedar Hill Cemetery Litig., 853 F. Supp. 706 (S.D.N.Y. 1994).

618 Kenty v. Bank One, Columbus, N.A., 92 F.3d 384 (6th Cir. 1996).

619 Richards v. Combined Ins. Co. of Am., 55 F.3d 247 (7th Cir. 1995). *See also* Hoban v. USLIFE Credit Life Ins. Co., 163 F.R.D. 509 (N.D. Ill. 1995), a similar case.

620 Dixon v. TCF Bank Ill., F.S.B., 1995 U.S. Dist. LEXIS 15706 (N.D. Ill. 1995).

621 Deane v. Weyerhaeuser Mortg. Co., 967 F. Supp. 30 (D. Mass. 1997).

622 Fitzgerald v. Chrysler Corp., 116 F.3d 225 (7th Cir. 1997).

623 Williams v. Stone, 109 F.3d 890 (3d Cir. 1997).

624 Bonilla v. Volvo Car Corp., 150 F.3d 62 (1st Cir. 1998).

625 Turner v. Union Planters Bank, 974 F. Supp. 890 (S.D. Miss. 1997) (class action alleging RICO violations and violations of Mississippi Motor Vehicle Sales Finance Act).

626 R.C.M. Executive Gallery Corp. v. Rols Capital Co., 1997 U.S. Dist. LEXIS 565 (S.D.N.Y. Jan. 23, 1997).

627 McDonough v. Nat'l Home Ins. Co., 108 F.3d 174 (8th Cir. 1997).

628 Weathersby v. Associated Fin. Services Co., 1999 U.S. Dist. LEXIS 6392 (E.D. La. Apr. 28, 1999).

629 Dysart v. BankTrust, 516 Fed. Appx. 861(11th Cir. Apr. 16, 2013).

630 Mear v. Sun Life Assurance Co. of Canada (U.S.)/Keyport Life Ins. Co., 2008 WL 245217 (D. Mass. Jan. 24, 2008).

Chapter 8   State RICO and Civil Theft Statutes

8.1   Introduction

The preceding chapter analyzed federal Racketeer Influenced and Corrupt Organizations Act (RICO) statutes. This chapter analyzes their state counterparts: state RICO statutes and state civil theft laws.

Approximately half the states have enacted state racketeering laws that are similar to the federal RICO statute discussed in the preceding chapter.[1] All but a few of these statutes[2] create a private cause of action. State RICO statutes often have important advantages over federal RICO and state UDAP statutes.[3] State civil theft laws, discussed in § 8.8, *infra*, are somewhat harder to adapt to consumer cases but can present similar advantages if they apply.

8.2   Advantages of State RICO Statutes

8.2.1   *Strategic Advantages of State RICO Statutes As Compared to Federal RICO*

State RICO laws offer a number of strategic advantages over a federal RICO claim. A consumer who prefers to stay in state court may not wish to file a federal RICO claim, because it creates federal question jurisdiction. As a result, a defendant can remove the case to federal court. A state RICO claim does not usually create federal question jurisdiction,[4] so the claim can be removed to federal court only if there is another basis, such as diversity of citizenship, for federal jurisdiction.

Another advantage is that the additional predicate offenses that state RICO statutes list may allow a RICO recovery when a predicate offense recognized by federal RICO cannot be proven. For example, some statute RICO statutes list fraud, usury, telemarketing fraud, or violations of the state credit services law as predicate offenses.[5]

Furthermore, many state RICO statutes have simplified versions of federal RICO's complex requirements about how the defendant's acts have affected an enterprise.[6] For example, many state RICO statutes allow a civil suit if the defendant used the proceeds of racketeering activity to acquire an interest in either an enterprise or real property, in contrast to the requirement of the corresponding RICO provision, section 1962(b), that the defendant acquire an interest in the enterprise itself.[7] Several state RICO statutes allow suit whenever the plaintiff has suffered damage due to a pattern of racketeering activity on the part of the defendant.[8] In contrast, a federal RICO plaintiff must show an injury by reason of the substantive violation of the RICO statute, that is, from the defendant's forbidden interaction with the enterprise.[9] Courts have often interpreted such departures from federal RICO as intentional and significant and have given them their plain meaning.[10] As another example, Georgia's RICO statute also goes beyond its federal counterpart in prohibiting not only conspiracies but also attempted conspiracies.[11]

Another difference between state and federal RICO statutes is that state RICO statutes do not require a nexus between racketeering activity and interstate commerce.[12] Another possible advantage is that most state RICO statutes set forth a specific, concrete pattern requirement that may be easier to deal with than federal RICO standard.[13]

Many state RICO statutes explicitly state that a civil RICO defendant who has been criminally convicted is precluded from denying commission of the criminal acts. Some specifically allow recovery for personal injury as well as financial losses.

Another possible advantage of a state RICO claim is that it may trigger less of a "full battle" response on the defendant's part. In addition, many state RICO statutes explicitly afford a right to trial by jury. The objection that federal RICO was not intended to federalize state tort law cannot be used to confine the impact of state RICO.[14]

---

1   State RICO statutes are summarized at Appendix F, *infra*. Some states also have forfeiture laws that are similar in some ways to RICO statutes but apply only to drug offenses. *See, e.g.*, 725 Ill. Comp. Stat. §§ 175/1 to 175/9.

2   Statutes that do not provide a private cause of action include: Cal. Penal Code §§ 186 to 186.8 (West); Conn. Gen. Stat. §§ 53-393 to 53-403; Mich. Comp. Laws §§ 750.159f–750.159x; Minn. Stat. §§ 609.901 to 609.912; N.Y. Penal Law art. 460 (McKinney); Okla. Stat. tit. 22, §§ 1401 to 1419; 18 Pa. Cons. Stat. § 911. *See* Ferris, Baker Watts, Inc. v. Deutsche Bank Sec. Ltd., 2004 WL 2501563 (D. Minn. Nov. 5, 2004) (using choice of law analysis to apply New Jersey RICO law, which provides a private cause of action, rather than Minn. RICO law, which does not, when alleged unlawful acts occurred in or emanated from New Jersey, even though plaintiffs did not suffer injury there); Federal Ins. Co. v. Ayers, 741 F. Supp. 1179 (E.D. Pa. 1990) (no private cause of action under Pennsylvania RICO); Town of W. Hartford v. Dadi, 2002 Conn. Super. LEXIS 325 (Feb. 1, 2002).

3   *See* § 8.2, *infra*.

4   *See* § 8.6.1, *infra*.

5   *See* § 8.4.1, *infra* (discussion of predicate offenses).

6   *See* § 8.4.3, *infra*.

7   *See, e.g.*, Fla. Stat. §§ 895.03, 895.05(6); Miss. Code Ann. §§ 97-43-5, 97-43-9(6). *See also* Ga. Code Ann. § 16-14-6 (allowing private RICO suit when the defendant has acquired an interest in an enterprise, real property, or personal property).

8   *See, e.g.*, Ariz. Rev. Stat. Ann. § 13-2314.04.

9   18 U.S.C. § 1964(c). *See* § 7.6.2, *supra*.

10   Reaugh v. Inner Harbour Hosp., Ltd., 447 S.E.2d 617 (Ga. Ct. App. 1994); Siragusa v. Brown, 971 P.2d 801 (Nev. 1998).

11   Faillace v. Columbus Bank & Trust Co., 605 S.E.2d 450 (Ga. Ct. App. 2004).

12   Baines v. Superior Court, 688 P.2d 1037, 1041 (Ariz. Ct. App. 1984).

13   *See* § 7.3.3, *supra* (federal RICO pattern requirement).

14   State *ex rel.* Corbin v. Pickrell, 667 P.2d 1304 (Ariz. 1983).

8.2.2 Strategic Advantages of State RICO Laws As Compared to UDAP Statutes

State RICO laws offer an approach to fill in some of the gaps in state UDAP statutes:

Private right of action. Although there is a private right of action under every state's UDAP statute, there are gaps and exclusions in many states. Iowa, for example, precludes private UDAP claims against banks, insurance companies, and a number of other potential defendants. Many state UDAP statutes do not afford a private cause of action for non-consumer transactions. The state RICO statute may provide a cause of action in these situations.

Scope restrictions. A number of state UDAP statutes exclude banks, insurance companies, utilities, landlords, or others. While state RICO statutes have their own coverage complexities, they do not exclude whole categories of potential defendants. Any defendant who commits the required number of predicate offenses, has whatever involvement with an enterprise that the statute requires, and causes damage to the victim is covered by the state RICO statute. State RICO laws also cover both business and consumer transactions. In Florida, Louisiana, Ohio, Rhode Island, and Utah, where the state UDAP statutes have significant coverage gaps, a private cause of action under the state RICO statute can be a particularly attractive alternative.

On the other hand, some states make it harder to use RICO, rather than unfair and deceptive acts and practices (UDAP), statutes in some instances. For example, Wisconsin prohibits RICO actions against the estate of a deceased defendant.[15] The Georgia Supreme Court has refused to apply to state RICO claims the rule that an employer is liable for its employees' tortious acts committed within the scope of their employment but instead requires application of the criteria for criminal liability.[16]

Exhaustion of administrative remedies. Plaintiffs may not be subject to an exhaustion of administrative remedies requirement in a RICO action that they might face with another type of claim. For example, in a Georgia case, the court ruled that the plaintiffs did not have to exhaust insurance department administrative remedies when making a RICO claim based on violation of insurance laws and other fraudulent acts.[17]

Substantive prohibitions. While the substantive prohibitions of most UDAP statutes are broad, cases sometimes arise that do not fit cleanly into any UDAP substantive prohibition. This is particularly true in states where the UDAP statute does not prohibit unfair conduct or has a limited "catch-all" for acts that are not specifically listed. The state RICO law is worth investigating in these cases. While all state RICO laws require proof of acts that would constitute a criminal offense, many include such offenses as fraud, usury, violation of certain consumer protection laws, and federal mail and wire fraud.

Treble damages provisions. The UDAP statutes in Arizona, Florida, Idaho, Indiana, Michigan, Oregon, and Rhode Island do not authorize treble damages. Yet each of those states has a RICO statute that authorizes a private cause of action for treble damages.

In Arizona, for example, a private cause of action under the state UDAP statute is available only because the courts have implied one, and the courts have not implied a treble damages remedy. The state RICO statute, on the other hand, allows suit for treble damages, costs, and attorney fees. Predicate offenses include usury, fraud, and extortionate extensions of credit.

Attorney fee provisions. A number of state UDAP statutes do not provide for an award of attorney fees or make the award discretionary. Most state RICO statutes, by contrast, mandate an award of attorney fees if the plaintiff is successful. However, some state RICO statutes also allow an attorney fee award to a prevailing defendant.[18]

Statutes of limitations. Many state RICO statutes have more generous statutes of limitations than the state UDAP statute. For example, the statute of limitations is just one year for Louisiana and Oregon UDAP claims but five years for a state RICO suit. Even when the UDAP and state RICO statutes of limitations are similar, the state RICO statute may have better rules about tolling. For example, most state RICO statutes of limitations are tolled during the pendency of a related criminal or civil action.

Notice letters and public interest preconditions. Some UDAP statutes require the plaintiff to send the defendant a notice a certain number of days before filing suit.[19] In a handful of states, the UDAP statute has been restrictively interpreted to allow a private cause of action only if the matter affects the public interest.[20] RICO claims offer the possibility of avoiding both of these limitations.

8.3 Validity and Interpretation of State RICO Statutes

State RICO statutes have been upheld against a variety of constitutional challenges.[21] Courts are unlikely to hold that

---

15 *See* Schimpf v. Gerald, Inc., 2 F. Supp. 2d 1150 (E.D. Wis. 1998) (concluding that state RICO action is punitive in nature and so cannot survive defendant's death).

16 Clark v. Security Life Ins. Co., 509 S.E.2d 602 (Ga. 1998).

17 Provident Indemnity Life Ins. Co. v. James, 506 S.E.2d 892 (Ga. Ct. App. 1998).

18 *See* § 8.6.3, *infra.*

19 National Consumer Law Center, Unfair and Deceptive Acts and Practices § 11.4.4 (8th ed. 2012), *updated at* www.nclc.org/library.

20 National Consumer Law Center, Unfair and Deceptive Acts and Practices § 11.4.3 (8th ed. 2012), *updated at* www.nclc.org/library.

21 Fort Wayne Books, Inc. v. Indiana, 489 U.S. 46, 109 S. Ct. 916, 103 L. Ed. 2d 34 (1989) (state RICO statute is not unconstitutionally vague and does not violate First Amendment, but pre-trial seizure of adult bookstore's entire stock was unconstitutional prior restraint); Lemaster v. Ohio, 119 F. Supp. 2d 754 (S.D. Ohio 2000) (not unconstitutionally vague); Bowden v. State, 402 So. 2d 1173 (Fla. 1981) (criminal case; state RICO statute not unconstitutionally vague or overbroad); Freeman v. State, 554 So. 2d 621 (Fla. Dist. Ct. App. 1989) (not unconstitutionally vague); Dee v. Sweet, 489 S.E.2d 823 (Ga. 1997) (finding fee award provision constitutional); State v. Bates, 933 P.2d 48 (Haw. 1997) (term "associated with any enterprise" is not unconstitutionally

other state or federal statutes displace the state or federal RICO statute in the absence of very clear statutory language.[22]

Because of the similarities between federal and state RICO statutes, courts will often look to federal court decisions in interpreting state RICO provisions that track federal RICO closely.[23] Courts construing state RICO statutes have rejected some of the same limitations on RICO liability that the United States Supreme Court and the federal courts have rejected with regard to the federal RICO statute. For example, there is no requirement that the defendant be a member of or involved with organized crime[24] or that "racketeering injury" be shown.[25] Nonetheless, state courts have not hesitated to reject federal RICO cases when interpreting state RICO provisions that appear to have a different legislative intent.[26]

---

vague, and RICO statutes do not implicate freedom of association); State v. Hansen, 877 P.2d 898 (Idaho 1994) (criminal prosecution; state RICO statute not unconstitutionally vague); Flinn v. State, 563 N.E.2d 536 (Ind. 1990) (not unconstitutionally vague or overbroad); State v. Passante, 542 A.2d 952 (N.J. 1987) (state RICO act constitutional); State v. Ball, 661 A.2d 251, 265 (N.J. 1995) (pattern requirement not unconstitutionally vague); State v. Romig, 700 P.2d 293 (Or. Ct. App. 1985) (state RICO Act constitutional); State v. Thompson, 751 P.2d 805 (Utah Ct. App. 1988) (same); Wisconsin v. O'Connell, 508 N.W.2d 23 (Wis. Ct. App. 1993). *But cf.* State v. Feld, 745 P.2d 147 (Ariz. Ct. App. 1987) (certain remedies given to state under state RICO constitutional, certain are not); State v. Roderick, 704 So. 2d 49 (Miss. 1997) (state RICO statute's predicate offense of usury is unconstitutionally vague as applied to check-cashing fees); State v. Thomas, 14 P.3d 854 (Wash. Ct. App. 2000) (finding repeal of state RICO statute's sunset provision void because of violation of state constitution's procedural requirements, so entire statute except for certain severable insurance fraud provisions is no longer in effect; legislature responded by enacting Laws 2001, ch. 222, effective May 9, 2001, which reenacted the RICO statute without substantive change).

22 S.C. Johnson & Son, Inc. v. Transport Corp., 697 F.3d 544 (7th Cir. 2012) (Federal Aviation Administration Authorization Act does not preempt state RICO claim alleging that motor carriers bribed manufacturer's employee to obtain favored treatment, even though their actions affected rates they were able to charge); AGS Capital Corp. v. Product Action Int'l, L.L.C., 884 N.E.2d 294 (Ind. Ct. App. 2008) (state trade secrets law's displacement of all laws pertaining to misappropriation of trade secrets except contract law and criminal law does not displace civil RICO statute because it is derivative of criminal law). *But cf.* Kilminster v. Day Mgmt. Corp., 919 P.2d 474 (Or. 1996) (workers compensation statute displaces state RICO statute if injury occurred during course and scope of plaintiff's employment).

23 Jackson v. BellSouth Telecommunications, 372 F.3d 1250, 1263–1264 (11th Cir. 2004) (Florida RICO); Acro-Tech, Inc. v. Robert Jackson Family Trust, 2003 WL 22783349 (9th Cir. Nov. 24, 2003) (Or. law); Meadaa v. K.A.P. Enterprises, 2014 WL 6801636 (W.D. La. Dec. 1, 2014) (federal RICO decisions are persuasive); Robins v. Global Fitness Holdings, L.L.C., 838 F. Supp. 2d 631, 651 (N.D. Ohio 2012) (stating that elements of federal and state RICO statutes are the same and analyzing them together); Merrill Lynch Bus. Fin. Services, Inc. v. Kupperman, 441 Fed. Appx. 938 (D.N.J. 2010) (finding federal and New Jersey RICO claims to be the same in all material respects; granting summary judgment for cross-claimant on both), *aff'd*, 2011 WL 3328492 (3d Cir. Aug. 3, 2011); Direct Dev., Inc. v. At World Props., L.L.C., 2010 WL 2079958 (E.D. Wis. May 24, 2010) (adopting elements from federal RICO); State, Office of Att'y Gen. v. Tenet Healthcare Corp., 420 F. Supp. 2d 1288 (S.D. Fla. 2005); DeNune v. Consol. Capital, 288 F. Supp. 2d 844 (N.D. Ohio 2003); Allocco v. City of Coral Gables, 221 F. Supp. 2d 1317 (S.D. Fla. 2002) (following federal RICO decisions that require reliance when mail and wire fraud are predicate acts); Nat'l Union Fire Ins. Co. v. Kozeny, 115 F. Supp. 2d 1210 (D. Colo. 2000), *aff'd*, 2001 WL 1149327 (10th Cir. Sept. 28, 2001); Planned Parenthood v. American Coal., 945 F. Supp. 1355 (D. Or. 1996); Lifeflite Med. Air Transp., Inc. v. Native Am. Air Services, Inc., 7 P.3d 158 (Ariz. Ct. App. 2000); Gross v. State, 765 So. 2d 39 (Fla. 2000); Simpson Consulting, Inc. v. Barclays Bank, 490 S.E.2d 184 (Ga. Ct. App. 1997) (Georgia will follow federal RICO interpretations except when Georgia's public policy differs); State v. Bates, 933 P.2d 48 (Haw. 1997); State v. Ontai, 929 P.2d 69 (Haw. 1996) (following

federal interpretations about how much structure an enterprise must have); Jackson v. State, 33 N.E.3d 1173 (Ind. Ct. App. 2015) (adopting pattern requirements from federal RICO statute even though Indiana RICO statute's language is different); Allum v. Valley Bank, 849 P.2d 297 (Nev. 1993) (Nevada will impose proximate causation requirement because United States Supreme Court did so); State v. Ball, 661 A.2d 251, 258 (N.J. 1995) (federal decisions are of use in construing state RICO statute despite the differences between the statutes); State v. Bisaccia, 724 A.2d 836 (N.J. Super. Ct. App. Div. 1999) (following federal court rules that conspiracy can be a predicate offense; noting that New Jersey RICO statute covers broader spectrum of behavior than federal RICO); State v. Beverly, 37 N.E.3d 116 (Ohio 2015) (using U.S. Supreme Court interpretations of "enterprise" as guidance); State v. Schlosser, 681 N.E.2d 911 (Ohio 1997); State v Walker, 333 P.3d 316 (Or. 2014) (finding interpretations of federal RICO's enterprise requirement persuasive); Loewen v. Galligan, 882 P.2d 104 (Or. Ct. App. 1994) (federal decisions persuasive); Sanchez v. Guerrero, 885 S.W.2d 487 (Tex. App. 1994); Hill v. Estate of Allred, 216 P.3d 929 (Utah 2009); Trujillo v. Northwest Trustee Services, Inc., 355 P.3d 1100 (Wash. 2015) (following U.S. Supreme Court's definition of "enterprise"); State v. Evers, 472 N.W.2d 828 (Wis. Ct. App. 1991).

24 Doxieu v. Ford Motor Credit Co., 603 F. Supp. 624 (S.D. Ga. 1984); Banderas v. Banco Cent. del Ecuador, 461 So. 2d 265 (Fla. Dist. Ct. App. 1985); Patterson v. Proctor, 514 S.E.2d 37 (Ga. Ct. App. 1999) (Georgia RICO statute does not require conspiracy or connection to organized crime); Dee v. Sweet, 460 S.E.2d 110 (Ga. Ct. App. 1995) (need not demonstrate a nexus with organized crime in order to prevail on a Georgia RICO claim); Larson v. Smith, 391 S.E.2d 686 (Ga. Ct. App. 1990). *But see* Georgia Gulf Corp. v. Ward, 701 F. Supp. 1556 (N.D. Ga. 1987) (plaintiff must allege organized crime nexus under Georgia RICO statute).

25 State *ex rel.* Corbin v. Pickrell, 667 P.2d 1304 (Ariz. 1983).

26 Federal Deposit Ins. Corp. v. First Interstate Bank of Denver, 937 F. Supp. 1461 (D. Colo. 1996) (declining to follow federal RICO precedent in interpreting Colorado RICO statute); Phila. Reserve Supply Co. v. Nowalk & Associates, Inc., 864 F. Supp. 1456 (E.D. Pa. 1994) (finding New Jersey RICO statute to have less strict definition of "pattern" than federal RICO); People v. Chaussee, 880 P.2d 749, 757 (Colo. 1994) (declining to follow federal RICO interpretations in light of differences in statutory language); People v. James, 40 P.3d 36 (Colo. App. 2001) (declining to follow federal precedent because of differences between federal and Colorado RICO); Faillace v. Columbus Bank & Trust Co., 605 S.E.2d 450, 454 (Ga. Ct. App. 2004); Southern-Intermodal Logistics, Inc. v. D.J. Powers Co., 555 S.E.2d 478 (Ga. Ct. App. 2000) (U.S. Supreme Court ruling on RICO statute of limitations has no bearing on interpretation of Georgia RICO); Siragusa v. Brown, 971 P.2d 801 (Nev. 1998) (even though Nevada RICO is patterned after federal RICO, it differs in that it does not require a pattern, so there is no pattern or continuity requirement); Franklin Med. Associates v. Newark Pub. Sch., 828 A.2d 966 (N.J. Super. Ct. App. Div. 2003) (construing New Jersey RICO definition of enterprise more broadly than federal); State v. Wilson, 682 N.E.2d 5 (Ohio Ct. App. 1996) (declining to follow federal precedent about whether the enterprise must be separate and apart from the corrupt activity); Bowcutt v. Delta N. Star Corp., 976 P.2d 643 (Wash. Ct. App. 1999) (declining to follow federal precedent when state statutory language differed from federal).

State RICO statutes should be entitled to a liberal construction, at least in civil suits.[27] For example, Georgia's Supreme Court holds that its RICO statute is to be liberally construed.[28] A Wisconsin decision holds that the civil remedy provisions of that state's RICO statute are remedial and entitled to a liberal construction, even though other portions of the statute are penal.[29]

8.4 Elements of a State RICO Claim
8.4.1 Predicate Offenses

The typical state RICO statute lists a variety of state offenses that constitute predicate offenses, and some also add certain federal crimes as predicate offenses. Many state RICO statutes include the same offenses as federal RICO, providing a parallel cause of action to a federal RICO claim. Some state RICO statutes also allow a claim to be based upon collection of an unlawful debt.[30]

Generally, state RICO statutes recognize only the more serious crimes as predicate offenses.[31] The statute may require the predicate offenses to have been committed in the state.[32] If the predicate offenses impose strict liability, without the need to prove criminal intent, it may be possible to establish state RICO liability without any showing of intent.[33]

State RICO statutes are particularly useful for consumer claims because they often include fraud and usury as predicate offenses.[34] Some list violations of specific consumer protection laws, such as laws prohibiting equity skimming or telemarketing fraud.[35] Ohio's RICO statute includes operation of an unregistered credit service organization as a predicate offense,[36] and Wisconsin includes identity theft.[37] Even if specific consumer fraud offenses are not among the listed predicate offenses, theft offenses are often included and will be applicable to many types of consumer fraud.[38] Ohio's RICO statute, however, requires that at least one predicate offense not be a form of securities fraud, mail fraud, or wire fraud.[39]

Generally, there is no requirement that the defendant be criminally convicted of the acts alleged as predicate offenses,[40] but a defendant who has been convicted may be stopped

---

27 *See, e.g.,* Nat'l Credit Union Bd. v. Regine, 749 F. Supp. 401 (D.R.I. 1990) (applying statutory provision that Rhode Island's RICO statute is to be construed liberally).

28 Williams Gen. Corp. v. Stone, 632 S.E.2d 376 (Ga. 2006).

29 S.C. Johnson & Son, Inc. v. Morris, 779 N.W.2d 19 (Wis. Ct. App. 2009). *Accord* MBS Certified Pub. Accountants, L.L.C. v. Wisconsin Bell Inc., 828 N.W.2d 575, 586 (Wis. Ct. App. 2013).

30 *See, e.g.,* Passa v. City of Columbus, 748 F. Supp. 2d 804 (S.D. Ohio 2010) (Ohio RICO claim can be based on collection of unlawful debt, but not shown here since payday loan rates were legal).

31 Byrne v. Nezhat, 261 F.3d 1075 (11th Cir. 2001) (misdemeanors are not predicate offenses under Georgia RICO); Dowling v. Select Portfolio Servicing, Inc., 2006 WL 571895 (S.D. Ohio Mar. 7, 2006) (must include at least one felony; perjury allegation sufficient).

32 Arthur v. JP Morgan Chase Bank, 569 Fed. Appx. 669 (11th Cir. 2014) (Florida RICO statute does not apply extraterritorially, but out-of-state plaintiffs might be able to state a claim if defendants' criminal acts occurred at least partially in Florida; not shown here); Trans USA Products, Inc. v. Howard Berger Co., 2008 WL 3154753, at *5 (D.N.J. Aug. 4, 2008); Riha v. State Farm Mut. Auto. Ins. Co., 2007 WL 42976 (S.D. Ind. Jan. 3, 2007). *See also* Brown v. Kerkhoff, 504 F. Supp. 2d 464, 538–539 (S.D. Iowa 2007) (predicate act under Iowa RICO must be punishable as an indictable offense under the laws of the state where it occurred and under the laws of Iowa). *See generally* § 8.6.1, *infra* (RICO suits by out-of-state residents).

33 State v. Schlosser, 681 N.E.2d 911 (Ohio 1997) (Ohio's RICO statute allows a strict liability statute).

34 *See, e.g.,* Royale Luau Resort, L.L.C. v. Kennedy Funding, Inc., 2008 WL 482327 (D.N.J. Feb. 19, 2008) (predicate offenses include fraudulent practices such as issuing loan commitment containing false statements); Kennedy Funding, Inc. v. Ruggers Acquisition & Dev., Inc., 2007 WL 2212859 (D.N.J. July 31, 2007) (allegation that lender issued false loan commitment letter is sufficient allegation of predicate act).

35 *But cf.* State v. Roderick, 704 So. 2d 49 (Miss. 1997) (when usury is not listed in RICO statute as a predicate offense, and is a civil rather than a criminal offense under Mississippi law, check casher's charging of interest in excess of allowable amount will not constitute a RICO violation).

35 Fla. Stat. § 895.02(1)(a)(34) (listing telemarketing fraud as a predicate offense); Wash. Rev. Code § 9A.82.010(4)(cc) (includes equity skimming as a predicate offense). *See also* Iowa Code § 706A.1 (any indictable offense committed for financial gain on a continuing basis); Or. Rev. Stat § 166.715(6)(a)(SS) (offenses involving real estate and escrow); Canterbury v. Columbia Gas, 2001 WL 1681132 (S.D. Ohio Sept. 25, 2001) (telecommunication fraud is predicate offense but plaintiff must plead detrimental reliance). *But see* State v. Gusow, 724 So. 2d 135 (Fla. Dist. Ct. App. 1998) (loan broker fraud and violations of advance fee prohibitions not predicate offenses since they did not involve interest or usurious practices); Clark v. Security Life Ins. Co., 509 S.E.2d 602 (Ga. 1998) (failure to file insurance policy with state insurance department is not a predicate offense); State v. Roderick, 704 So. 2d 49 (Miss. 1997) (state RICO statute's predicate offense of usury is unconstitutionally vague as applied to check-cashing fees).

36 State v. Schlosser, 681 N.E.2d 911 (Ohio 1997).

37 Wis. Stat. §§ 946.82, 943.201.

38 *Cf.* Blanton v. Bank of Am., 567 S.E.2d 313 (Ga. Ct. App. 2002) (theft by conversion is predicate offense, but not shown by bank's disregard of oral escrow agreement).

39 Ohio Rev. Code Ann. § 2923.34 (West). *See In re* Nat'l Century Fin. Enterprises, Inc., Inv. Litig., 604 F. Supp. 2d 1128 (S.D. Ohio 2009) (finding predicate offenses sufficiently alleged); Rahimi v. St. Elizabeth Med. Ctr., 1997 WL 33426269 (S.D. Ohio July 16, 1997). *See also* Synergy Fin., L.L.C. v. Zarro, 329 F. Supp. 2d 701, 714 (W.D.N.C. 2004) (noting similar requirement under North Carolina RICO statute).

40 Black v. State, 819 So. 2d 208, 212 n.2 (Fla. Dist. Ct. App. 2002) (criminal case); Harvey v. State, 617 So. 2d 1144 (Fla. Dist. Ct. App. 1993); 4447 Corp. v. Goldsmith, 504 N.E.2d 559 (Ind. 1987), *aff'd in relevant part, rev'd in part on other grounds,* 489 U.S. 46, 109 S. Ct. 916, 103 L. Ed. 2d 34 (1989) (liability despite lack of conviction is constitutional); Commonwealth of Pa. v. Stocker, 622 A.2d 333 (Pa. Super. Ct. 1993); Baxter v. Jones, 614 N.E.2d 1094 (Ohio Ct. App. 1992); Computer Concepts v. Brandt, 801 P.2d 800 (Or. 1990) (interpreting version of Oregon statute before 1995 amendment); Cruze v. Hudler, 267 P.3d 176 (Or. Ct. App. 2011) (conviction unnecessary when predicate act is forgery, even though forgery arose in securities context and statute requires conviction if predicate act is one of certain securities crimes); Hill v. Estate of Allred, 216 P.3d 929 (Utah 2009) (Utah RICO statute allows person injured by pattern of unlawful activity to bring civil suit even if no criminal action is pursued). *Cf.* Rolin Mfg. Inc. v. Mosbrucker, 544 N.W.2d 132 (N.D. 1996) (under North Dakota's RICO statute, either a prior conviction or probable cause must be alleged with reference to predicate acts). *But see* Or. Rev. Stat. § 166.725(6), (7) (allowing RICO suit based on certain predicate offenses only after conviction); Rubicon Global Ventures, Inc. v. Chongqing Zongshen Grp. Import/Exp. Corp.,

from denying the facts necessary for the conviction.[41] In the absence of a conviction, the plaintiff must prove all elements of the predicate offenses, including any required mental state.[42] Some state RICO statutes require that economic gain motivate the commission of the predicate crimes.[43] A defendant who has not personally committed the requisite number of predicate offenses may still be liable under a state RICO statute that makes actionable a conspiracy to violate its prohibitions.[44]

8.4.2 Pattern Requirements

Some state RICO statutes are explicit about matters as to which federal RICO is silent or vague, such as the meaning of a "pattern of racketeering activity."[45] Hawaii's RICO statute only requires one predicate offense.[46] Others require at least three predicate offenses.[47] A pattern under the Florida[48] and Idaho[49] RICO statutes is at least two predicate offenses. They

cannot be simultaneous but must be separate incidents.[50] Proof of two predicate offenses is also sufficient under the Oregon[51] and Georgia[52] RICO statutes. In Georgia, each defendant need not commit the requisite number of predicate offenses, as long as the pattern requirement is satisfied collectively.[53]

Several states have no pattern requirement.[54] The Nevada RICO statute does not require a "pattern of racketeering" and instead defines racketeering as "two predicate offenses of the type described" in the state statute.[55] However, a federal court holds that the plaintiff must show a relationship and continuity of the criminal acts.[56]

Some courts interpret "pattern" for purposes of a state RICO statute more liberally than courts interpret the term under federal RICO.[57] For example, the Colorado RICO statute does not require that proof of a pattern include proof that predicate offenses are related to another or proof of continuity.[58] Continuity is similarly not required in Georgia and Oregon,[59] nor, according to some courts, in Ohio.[60] In Florida, Idaho, and Louisiana, however, there must be proof of a relationship between the predicate offenses and that the acts pose a threat of continuing activity.[61] An Indiana court adopted the

---

2010 WL 4812860 (D. Or. Nov. 19, 2010) (for some predicate acts, Oregon RICO statute requires a conviction). *But cf.* Black v. Arizala, 95 P.3d 1109 (Or. 2004) (Oregon amendment requiring conviction does not apply retroactively).

41 Cox v. Mayan Lagoon Estates Ltd., 734 S.E.2d 883 (Ga. App. Ct. 2012) (criminal conviction has estoppel effect pursuant to state RICO statute even if it is on appeal, but criminal restitution proceedings do not establish injury element of a civil RICO claim).

42 Occidental Fire & Cas. Co. v. Great Plains Capital Corp., 1999 WL 96433 (9th Cir. Feb. 22, 1999) (Ariz. law) (company owner's civil liability as principal for acts of agent does not create state RICO liability when owner not shown to have criminal intent); *In re* Caribbean K Line, Ltd., 288 B.R. 908 (S.D. Fla. 2002) (felonious intent is element of Florida Civil Theft claim); Arwood v. Dunn (*In re* Caribbean K Line, Ltd.), 288 B.R. 908 (S.D. Fla. 2002) (finding allegation of felonious intent sufficient at pleading stage); Mayo, Lynch & Associates v. Pollack, 799 A.2d 12 (N.J. Super. Ct. App. Div. 2002) (trier of fact may infer defendant attorney's knowledge of bid-rigging scheme from his egregiously wrong legal advice approving the rigged bid).

43 *See* Occidental Fire & Cas. Co. v. Great Plains Capital Corp., 1999 WL 96433 (9th Cir. Feb. 22, 1999) (Arizona requires that offense be committed for financial gain); Kaplan v. Prolife Action League, 493 S.E.2d 416 (N.C. 1997) (North Carolina RICO statute requires causal nexus between racketeering activity and pecuniary gain); Winchester v. Stein, 959 P.2d 1077 (Wash. 1998).

44 Bradley v. Miller, 2015 WL 1469153, at *17 (S.D. Ohio Mar. 30, 2015); De la Osa v. State, 158 So. 3d 712 (Fla. Dist. Ct. App. 2015) (affirming conviction of conspiracy to violate Florida RICO statute when defendant agreed that others would commit criminal acts to further conspiracy).

45 *See, e.g.,* Idaho Code Ann. § 18-7803(d); Ind. Code § 35-45-6-1; N.M. Stat. Ann. § 30-42-3(D); Wis. Stat. § 946.82. *See also* Patterson v. Proctor, 514 S.E.2d 37 (Ga. Ct. App. 1999) (thefts may be considered separate transactions, even though related, to meet Georgia's requirement of at least two offenses); Trujillo v. Northwest Trustee Services, Inc., 355 P.3d 1100 (Wash. 2015) (applying Washington RICO statute's very detailed definition of "pattern").

46 Hawaii v. Ontai, 929 P.2d 69 (Haw. 1996).

47 *See, e.g.,* Minn. Stat. § 609.902(6); Wash. Rev. Code § 9A.82.010(12); Wis. Stat. § 946.82(3). *See also* State v. Huynh, 519 N.W.2d 191 (Minn. 1994).

48 Watts v. Dep't of Prof'l Regulation, 571 So. 2d 483 (Fla. Dist. Ct. App. 1990) (table).

49 Spence v. Howell, 890 P.2d 714 (Idaho 1995).

50 Lockheed Martin Corp. v. Boeing Co., 314 F. Supp. 2d 1198, 1222 (M.D. Fla. 2004).

51 Computer Concepts v. Brandt, 801 P.2d 800 (Or. 1990).

52 Larson v. Smith, 391 S.E.2d 686 (Ga. Ct. App. 1990).

53 Faillace v. Columbus Bank & Trust Co., 605 S.E.2d 450 (Ga. Ct. App. 2004).

54 *See, e.g.,* R.I. Gen. Laws § 7-15-2. *See also* State *ex rel.* Corbin v. Pickrell, 667 P.2d 1304 (Ariz. 1983); Siragusa v. Brown, 971 P.2d 801 (Nev. 1998) (Nevada requires two predicate acts but does not require pattern); Commonwealth v. Peetros, 535 A.2d 1026 (Pa. 1987); State v. Brown, 486 A.2d 595 (R.I. 1985) (elements are the commission of one predicate offense and investment of proceeds in establishment, conduct, or operation of an enterprise).

55 *See* Siragusa v. Brown, 971 P.2d 801 (Nev. 1998).

56 Rapaport v. Soffer, 2012 WL 2522069 (D. Nev. June 29, 2012).

57 *See, e.g.,* State v. Pierce, 962 P.2d 35 (Or. Ct. App. 1998) (separate acts taking place within a very short period of time, even a few minutes, can establish a pattern, and thus eight identical letters sent by attorney constituted pattern of mail fraud, not single episode). *But see* Lifeflite Med. Air Transp., Inc. v. Native Am. Air Services, Inc., 7 P.3d 158 (Ariz. Ct. App. 2000) (interpreting Arizona's RICO statute, which had been amended to parallel federal RICO more closely, to require that related predicate acts extend over a substantial period of time); Gross v. State, 765 So. 2d 39 (Fla. 2000) (Florida requires continuity, similarity, and interrelatedness). *But cf.* Bradley v. Tibbles, 2009 WL 3242101 (N.D. Ind. Sept. 30, 2009) (following federal RICO decisions defining pattern); Perimeter Realty v. GAPI, Inc., 533 S.E.2d 136 (Ga. Ct. App. 2000) (two real estate closings, part of a single transaction, constitute just one predicate act).

58 People v. Chaussee, 880 P.2d 749 (Colo. 1994).

59 Marshall v. City of Atlanta, 195 B.R. 156 (N.D. Ga. 1996); Newman v. Comprehensive Care Corp., 794 F. Supp. 1513 (D. Or. 1992); Dover v. State, 385 S.E.2d 417 (Ga. Ct. App. 1989). *See also* Altamont Summit Apts. v. Wolff Props. L.L.C., 2002 U.S. Dist. LEXIS 2761 (D. Or. Feb. 13, 2002).

60 *See* State v. Hicks, 2003 WL 23095414 (Ohio Ct. App. Dec. 31, 2003). *But see* Morrow v. Reminger & Reminger, L.P.A., 915 N.E.2d 696 (Ohio Ct. App. 2009).

61 Meadaa v. K.A.P. Enterprises, 2014 WL 6801636 (W.D. La. Dec. 1, 2014); Gross v. State, 765 So. 2d 39 (Fla. 2000) (Florida requires continuity, similarity, and interrelatedness); Mannos v. Moss, 155 P.3d 1166,

federal RICO statute's continuity requirement even though the Indiana RICO statute was silent.[62] New Jersey cases require some showing of continuity but less than would be required under federal RICO.[63]

The Utah Supreme Court interprets the pattern requirement of its RICO statute, like that of the federal statute, to require a showing of both continuity and relationship, but all the predicate acts may be part of a single scheme.[64] The Arizona statute requires the plaintiff to show that the acts of racketeering were continuous or threatened to be continuous, and courts follow federal RICO cases in interpreting this requirement.[65]

In New Jersey, some courts hold that a pattern may consist of a short-term pattern of activity, provided that the related incidents are not disconnected or isolated.[66] In Georgia, the pattern of racketeering activity can consist of two acts that harm the same individual and that are linked to each other.[67] But in Ohio, conduct that involves a single victim and a single transaction and takes place over a short period of time does not constitute a pattern.[68] Likewise, in Idaho a single scheme cannot constitute a pattern unless there is a threat of continuing racketeering activity.[69]

In Oregon, one court held that separate acts taking place within a very short period of time, even a few minutes, can establish a pattern, so eight identical letters sent by an attorney constituted a pattern of mail fraud.[70] A federal court held that a series of predicate offenses that were part of a single fraudulent scheme to sell a single property to a single buyer did not constitute a pattern under Oregon's RICO statute.[71]

8.4.3 *Enterprise Requirements*

Some courts, in interpreting state RICO statutes, simply follow U.S. Supreme Court definitions of "enterprise."[72] However, many state RICO statutes have simplified requirements about the relationship between the defendant's racketeering acts and an enterprise. Some allow suit by anyone who suffers damage as a result of the racketeering acts, without any requirement that those acts have an effect on an enterprise.[73] Georgia's counterpart to section 1962(b) of the federal RICO statute is broader than the federal statute in that it outlaws the use of a pattern of racketeering activity to acquire or maintain an interest in any property, not just in an enterprise.[74] Under Rhode Island's statute, however, the plaintiff must have suffered harm from the defendant's acquisition or maintenance of an interest in or control of an enterprise or from the defendant's conduct or participation in the conduct of the affairs of an enterprise.[75] Connecticut's statute (which does not provide for a private cause of action) also requires that the racketeering activity have a nexus to an enterprise.[76] Utah requires there to be an enterprise, but there need not be more than one enterprise.[77]

1175 (Idaho 2007) (must show "connected pattern" of racketeering activity; single scheme may be sufficient if acts amount to a threat of continuing racketeering activity).

62   Jackson v. State, 33 N.E.3d 1173, 1179 (Ind. Ct. App. 2015).

63   State v. Ball, 661 A.2d 251, 264 (N.J. 1995) (while continuity is not an element, pattern of racketeering activity should be, or threaten to be, ongoing, and underlying incidents should not be isolated events). *See also* Emcore Corp. v. PricewaterhouseCoopers, L.L.P., 102 F. Supp. 2d 237 (D.N.J. 2000) (New Jersey RICO definition of pattern is more flexible and generous to plaintiffs than federal definition and requires only relatedness among incidents; continuity may be considered as a circumstance favoring finding of relatedness); Metz v. United Counties Bancorp, 61 F. Supp. 2d 364, 373 (D.N.J. 1999) (acts must be related and pose a threat of continued criminal activity, but New Jersey stresses continuity less than relatedness).

64   Hill v. Estate of Allred, 216 P.3d 929 (Utah 2009). *See also* Miller v. Basic Research, Inc., 2008 WL 4755787 (D. Utah Oct. 27, 2008) (multiple predicate acts committed over several months as part of advertising campaign meet pattern requirement).

65   Warfield v. Gardner, 346 F. Supp. 2d 1033 (D. Ariz. 2004).

66   Ford Motor Co. v. Edgewood Props., Inc., 2009 WL 150951, at *13 (D.N.J. Jan. 20, 2009), *on reconsideration in part*, 2009 WL 2488174 (D.N.J. Aug. 11, 2009) (allowing RICO claim to go forward). *But cf.* Stoecker v. Echevarria, 975 A.2d 975 (N.J. Super. Ct. App. Div. 2009) (no pattern when RICO claim relates to single transaction).

67   Brown v. Freedman, 474 S.E.2d 73 (Ga. Ct. App. 1996). *See also* O'Neal v. Garrison, 263 F.3d 1317 (11th Cir. 2001) (pattern established by two related acts toward plaintiff plus a similar act toward another person), *amended on other grounds and reh'g denied*, 270 F.3d 1323 (11th Cir. 2001). *Accord* Colonial Penn Ins. Co. v. Value Rent-A-Car, Inc., 814 F. Supp. 1084 (S.D. Fla. 1992) (Florida RICO statute requires continuity).

68   Hanlin v. Ohio Builders & Remodelers, Inc., 196 F. Supp. 2d 572 (S.D. Ohio 2001). *See also* Morrow v. Reminger & Reminger L.P.A., 915 N.E.2d 696 (Ohio Ct. App. 2009) (single scheme that involves several predicate acts is insufficient).

69   Mannos v. Moss, 155 P.3d 1166, 1175 (Idaho 2007); Spence v. Howell, 890 P.2d 714, 726 (Idaho 1995).

70   State v. Pierce, 962 P.2d 35 (Or. Ct. App. 1998).

71   Altamont Summit Apts. L.L.C. v. Wolff Props., L.L.C., 2002 WL 31972359 (D. Or. Aug. 21, 2002).

72   *See, e.g.,* Trujillo v. Northwest Trustee Services, Inc., 355 P.3d 1100 (Wash. 2015).

73   *See, e.g.,* Ariz. Rev. Stat. Ann. § 13-2314.04; Or. Educ. Ass'n v. Parks, 291 P.3d 789 (Or. Ct. App. Nov. 21, 2012); Kotera v. Daioh Int'l, U.S.A., 40 P.3d 506, 524 (Or. Ct. App. 2002) (plaintiff must show that defendant participated in pattern of racketeering activity as part of an enterprise, but need only show that the predicate acts themselves caused damage). *But see* Riha v. State Farm Mut. Auto. Ins. Co., 2007 WL 42976 (S.D. Ind. Jan. 3, 2007) (no state RICO claim if only injuries plaintiff suffers are those caused by the predicate acts themselves); Abbott v. Good Shepherd Med. Ctr., 2004 WL 2847903 (D. Or. Dec. 9, 2004) (plaintiff must allege injury arising from defendant's acquisition or control of interest in enterprise); Schlenker Enterprises, L.P. v. Reese, 2010 WL 4323662 (Ohio Ct. App. Nov. 1, 2010) (must show that defendant not only received proceeds of corrupt activity but also used them to acquire interest in real estate or an enterprise); State v. Bradshaw, 99 P.3d 359, 369–370 (Utah Ct. App. 2004) (must show that defendant used or invested proceeds in acquisition, establishment, or operation of an enterprise), *rev'd on other grounds*, 152 P.3d 288 (Utah 2006) (addressing non-RICO counts).

74   Reaugh v. Inner Harbour Hosp., Ltd., 447 S.E.2d 617, 622 (Ga. Ct. App. 1994). *See also* Nat'l Union Fire Ins. Co. v. Kozeny, 2001 U.S. App. LEXIS 21211 (10th Cir. Sept. 28, 2001) (applying Colorado's version, which prohibits use of proceeds to acquire interest in enterprise or real property).

75   Carlsten v. Widecom Grp., Inc., 2003 WL 21688263 (R.I. Super. Ct. July 1, 2003).

76   State v. Rodriguez-Roman, 3 A.3d 783, 792 (Conn. 2010).

77   Alta Indus. Ltd. v. Hurst, 846 P.2d 1282 (Utah 1993). *But see* Dawson v. Goldman Sachs & Co., 2014 WL 5465127 (D. Colo. Oct. 27, 2014)

When an enterprise is required, many courts have rejected the position that it must have a "distinct" or "ascertainable" structure.[78] In New Jersey, the enterprise element is satisfied if there is a group of people, no matter how loosely defined, whose existence or association provides or implements the common purpose of committing one or more predicate offenses.[79] An ascertainable structure need not be shown but only the interactions that are necessary when a group divides among its members functions that are necessary to achieve a common purpose.[80] In Utah there must be an ongoing organization; a sporadic, temporary alliance is insufficient.[81] In Ohio, the enterprise may be merely an association-in-fact: "a continuing unit that functions with a common purpose."[82] Florida requires an ongoing organization, formal or informal, with a common purpose of engaging in a course of conduct, which functions as a continuing unit.[83]

In defining the term "enterprise" under its RICO statute, the Minnesota Supreme Court has required a showing of "an organizational set-up, whether formal or informal, that not only exists to commit the predicate offenses but also does more, such as coordinating those acts into an overall pattern of criminal activity."[84] Idaho requires evidence of an association or agreement or a common purpose to engage in the predicate offenses.[85] The enterprise must be an ongoing organization whose members function as a continuing unit, and it must have some structure separate from the pattern of racketeering activity.[86]

In Oregon, an enterprise must be "some kind of entity that can either employ or be associated with a version" and "something that an individual can conduct or participate in through a pattern of racketeering activity."[87] It must have "some kind of recognizable or ascertainable existence," but the enterprise need not "exist separately from its associates, as opposed to existing as a result of the association itself."[88] It need not have any organizational formality.[89]

The U.S. Supreme Court has stated that a federal RICO enterprise may be inferred from the evidence establishing the pattern of criminal activity.[90] New Jersey[91] and Ohio[92] likewise hold that the existence of an enterprise and the existence of a pattern may be established by the same proof, even though they are separate elements. Similarly, in Connecticut[93] and Florida,[94] the evidence of the existence of the enterprise may be the same as the evidence that establishes the pattern. But Oklahoma requires the enterprise to have some structure apart from the crimes it is alleged to have committed, and separate proof is required.[95]

Some courts hold that an enterprise cannot be composed simply of a corporation and its officers or employees.[96] The

---

(equating Colorado RICO and federal RICO enterprise requirements; allegation that subsidiary conducted affairs of a parent corporation is insufficient).

78 Acro-Tech, Inc. v. Robert Jackson Family Trust, 2003 WL 22783349 (9th Cir. Nov. 24, 2003)(Oregon law); Warfield v. Gardner, 346 F. Supp. 2d 1033 (D. Ariz. 2004); Martin v. State, 376 S.E.2d 888 (Ga. Ct. App. 1988); State v. Ball, 661 A.2d 251 (N.J. 1995) (enterprise must have an "organization," but this organization need not feature an ascertainable structure or a structure with a particular configuration); State v. Hughes, 767 P.2d 382 (N.M. Ct. App. 1988); State v. Cheek, 786 P.2d 1305 (Or. Ct. App. 1990). *See also* Wesleyan Pension Fund, Inc. v. First Albany Corp., 964 F. Supp. 1255 (S.D. Ind. 1997) (association in fact consisting of a corporation, its officers, and either two sister corporations or a parent and subsidiary and their officers and employees are sufficiently distinct from named defendants); State v. Rodriguez-Roman, 3 A.3d 783, 793 (Conn. 2010) (no proof of ascertainable structure separate from pattern of unlawful activity is required; enterprise may be an informal, unchartered partnership); Gross v. State, 765 So. 2d 39 (Fla. 2000); Helmadollar v. State, 811 So. 2d 819 (Fla. Dist. Ct. App. 2002) (short-term informal organization is enterprise). *Cf. In re Schering-Plough Corp. Intron/Temodar Consumer Class Action*, 2009 WL 2043604, at *29 n.20 (D.N.J. July 10, 2009) (noting split among New Jersey courts as to whether a corporation can conduct an enterprise consisting of an association-in-fact between it and a subsidiary, but finding it unnecessary to decide the issue). *But see* State v. Ontai, 929 P.2d 69 (Haw. 1996) (requiring proof of ongoing organization with a structure distinct from that inherent in the conduct of the racketeering activity); Knutson v. County of Barnes, 642 N.W.2d 910 (N.D. 2002) (enterprise must be distinct); Carlsten v. Widecom Grp., Inc., 2003 WL 21688263 (R.I. Super. Ct. July 1, 2003). *See generally* § 7.4.4, *supra* (related issues under the federal RICO statute).

79 Franklin Med. Associates v. Newark Pub. Sch., 828 A.2d 966 (N.J. Super. Ct. App. Div. 2003). *See also* Ford Motor Co. v. Edgewood Props., Inc., 2009 WL 150951 (D.N.J. Jan. 20, 2009) (noting that New Jersey definition of "enterprise" is broader than that of federal RICO statute; plaintiff may name enterprise as a defendant), *on reconsideration in part*, 2009 WL 2488174 (D.N.J. Aug. 11, 2009) (allowing RICO claim to go forward).

80 State v. Ball, 661 A.2d 251, 261 (N.J. 1995).

81 State v. Bradshaw, 99 P.3d 359 (Utah Ct. App. 2004), *rev'd on other grounds*, 152 P.3d 288 (Utah 2006) (addressing non-RICO counts).

82 State v. Beverly, 37 N.E.3d 116 (Ohio 2015).

83 Gross v. State, 765 So. 2d 39 (Fla. 2000).

84 State v. Huynh, 519 N.W.2d 191, 196 (Minn. 1994).

85 Mannos v. Moss, 155 P.3d 1166, 1175 (Idaho 2007).

86 State v. Hansen, 877 P.2d 898 (Idaho 1994).

87 State v Walker, 333 P.3d 316, 323 (Or. 2014).

88 *Id.*

89 *Id.*

90 Boyle v. United States, 129 S. Ct. 2237, 2244 (2009).

91 State v. Ball, 661 A.2d 251, 261 (N.J. 1995).

92 State v. Beverly, 37 N.E.3d 116 (Ohio 2015).

93 State v. Rodriguez-Roman, 3 A.3d 783, 793 (Conn. 2010).

94 Gross v. State, 765 So. 2d 39 (Fla. 2000).

95 Miskovsky v. State, 31 P.3d 1054 (Okla. Crim. App. 2001) (note that Oklahoma RICO statute does not explicitly afford a private cause of action).

96 Colonial Penn Ins. Co. v. Value Rent-A-Car, Inc., 814 F. Supp. 1084 (S.D. Fla. 1992) (a corporation and its officers cannot conspire with each other for purposes of RICO); State v. Gertsch, 2000 Ida. App. LEXIS 92 (Idaho Ct. App. Dec. 5, 2000) (sole proprietorship made up of single person is not an enterprise with which that person may be associated); Turchyn v. Nakonachny, 811 N.E.2d 119, 123 (Ohio Ct. App. 2004). *See also* Cooke v. AT&T Corp., 2007 WL 912222 (S.D. Ohio Mar. 23, 2007) (requirements of statute not satisfied if a defendant corporation, through its agents, commits the predicate acts in the conduct of its own business). *Cf.* Royale Luau Resort, L.L.C. v. Kennedy Funding, Inc., 2008 WL 482327 (D.N.J. Feb. 19, 2008) (if corporation is the enterprise, it cannot be liable under New Jersey RICO statute, but individuals who control it can be); Abbott v. Good Shepherd Med. Ctr., 2004 WL 2847903 (D. Or. Dec. 9, 2004) (corporation cannot be both the person and the enterprise). *But see* Miskovsky v. State, 31 P.3d 1054 (Okla. Crim. App. 2001) (enterprise need not be incorporated but can be a sole proprietorship that defendant owns and works for).

Wisconsin RICO statute has been interpreted to require that the "person" or defendant be separate from the enterprise.[97] A federal decision interprets the New Jersey RICO statute in the same way,[98] but other courts disagree.[99] In Colorado, the enterprise must include at least one person or entity besides the defendant,[100] but it can be a corporation over which the defendant has some control.[101] In Florida, although the defendant may be part of the enterprise, the defendant may not be the sole entity comprising the enterprise.[102] Colorado follows federal cases that hold that, when a separate entity is formed by the act of incorporation, the corporation constitutes an enterprise within the meaning of the state RICO law, separate from the person engaged in the pattern of racketeering activity.[103] But the jury need not be instructed that the enterprise must be an ongoing organization, operate as a continuing unit, and be separate and apart from the pattern of activity in which it engages.[104] An Ohio decision holds that a city can be an enterprise, defined by the statute to include government agencies, and the state's sovereign immunity law does not protect it from state RICO liability.[105]

8.5   Statute of Limitations

Most state RICO statutes set forth a statute of limitations period as well as a requirement for the timing between predicate offenses. Statutes of limitations vary from one year to ten years and are typically about five years.[106] Most are tolled while related cases are pending. Some state RICO statutes also extend the time allowed between predicate offenses when the offender has been incarcerated. North Dakota's RICO statute

has a discovery rule,[107] and Florida[108] and Georgia[109] also recognize the rule. The Ohio Supreme Court holds that the statute of limitations does not run from the date of discovery of the pattern of unlawful activity but leaves open the question of whether it might run from discovery of some other element.[110] An intermediate appellate court in Ohio, following federal decisions, adopts an injury discovery rule.[111]

Colorado's RICO statute does not specify a limitations period, but a court has used the two-year Colorado general limitations period and ruled that the two years do not begin to run until the plaintiff knew or should have known of all elements of the RICO claim, including the existence of a pattern.[112] A New Jersey appellate court has suggested that either a four-year or a five-year statute of limitations applies to New Jersey civil RICO claims.[113]

In addition to applying the discovery rule, Georgia applies the "separate accrual" rule to its RICO statute.[114] Under this rule, when a new and independent injury is incurred from the same violation, the statute of limitations for damages from that injury runs from the date the plaintiff should have discovered it.

8.6   Litigating State RICO Cases

8.6.1   Jurisdictional and Procedural Issues

State RICO actions will generally be tried in state court, but in the alternative a state RICO claim can usually supplement a related federal RICO claim in federal court.[115] The Eleventh

---

97   Johnson v. Bankers Life & Cas. Co., 973 F. Supp. 2d 950 (W.D. Wis. 2013).

98   Prudential Ins. Co. v. Bank of Am., 14 F. Supp. 3d 591 (D.N.J. 2014), *reconsideration granted in part*, 2014 WL 2999065 (D.N.J. July 2, 2014).

99   Prudential Ins. Co. v. Credit Suisse Secs., L.L.C., 2013 WL 5467093, at *21 (Sept. 30, 2013) (New Jersey RICO statute does not require that the person and the enterprise be distinct; a purely intra-corporate enterprise is sufficient). *See also* Prudential Ins. Co. v. Goldman, Sachs & Co., 2013 WL 1431680 (Apr. 9, 2013) (corporate affiliates, such as a parent corporation and its subsidiaries, can associate with each other to form an enterprise).

100 People v. James, 40 P.3d 36 (Colo. App. 2001).

101 Nat'l Union Fire Ins. Co. v. Kozeny, 2001 U.S. App. LEXIS 21211 (10th Cir. Sept. 28, 2001) (Colorado law).

102 Palmas y Bambu v. E.I. DuPont De Nemours & Co., 881 So. 2d 565 (Fla. Dist. Ct. App. 2004). *See also* Lockheed Martin Corp. v. Boeing Co., 314 F. Supp. 2d 1198, 1222 (M.D. Fla. 2004); Florida Evergreen Foliage v. E.I. DuPont de Nemours & Co., 336 F. Supp. 2d 1239, 1260–1261 (S.D. Fla. 2004), *aff'd on other grounds*, 470 F.3d 1036, 1041–1042 (11th Cir. 2006).

103 People v. Pollard, 3 P.3d 473 (Colo. App. 2000).

104 People v. James, 40 P.3d 36 (Colo. App. 2001).

105 Thornton v. Cleveland, 890 N.E.2d 353 (Ohio Ct. App. 2008). *See also* Bratton v. Couch, 2003 WL 21652166 (Ohio Ct. App. July 8, 2003) (Ohio RICO statute includes governmental agencies in definition of enterprise).

106 *See* Burr v. Kulas, 564 N.W.2d 631 (N.D. 1997) (applying state RICO statute's seven-year limitations period instead of other limitations period urged by defendant).

107 *See* N.D. Cent. Code § 12.1-06.1-05(7). *See also* Burr v. Kulas, 564 N.W.2d 631 (N.D. 1997).

108 Huff Groves Trust v. Caulkins Indiantown Citrus Co., 829 So. 2d 923 (Fla. Dist. Ct. App. 2002).

109 Southern-Intermodal Logistics, Inc. v. D.J. Powers Co., 555 S.E.2d 478 (Ga. Ct. App. 2000). *See also* Cochran Mill Associates v. Stephens, 648 S.E.2d 764 (Ga. Ct. App. 2007) (only when partners in real estate partnership began questioning managing partner regarding checks written to himself did state RICO statute of limitations begin to run).

110 Doe v. Archdiocese of Cincinnati, 849 N.E.2d 268 (Ohio 2006) (rejecting argument that statute of limitations runs only upon discovery of pattern; here, when plaintiff knew of the sexual abuse crimes, the identity of the perpetrator, and the perpetrator's affiliation with the defendant archdiocese at age fifteen, it began to run when he reached age of majority).

111 Tri-State Computer Exch., Inc. v. Burt, 2003 WL 21414688 (Ohio Ct. App. June 20, 2003).

112 Federal Deposit Ins. Corp. v. Refco Grp., Ltd., 989 F. Supp. 1052 (D. Colo. 1997).

113 Fraser v. Bovino, 721 A.2d 20 (N.J. Super. Ct. App. Div. 1998).

114 Southern Intermodal Logistics, Inc. v. D.J. Powers Co., 555 S.E.2d 478 (Ga. Ct. App. 2001) (adopting separate accrual rule). *But cf.* Cochran Mill Associates v. Stephens, 648 S.E.2d 764 (Ga. Ct. App. 2007) (under state RICO claim involving real estate partnership's managing partner's use of checks written to himself to convert partnership funds, no new cause of action for each act of conversion as the act was not new and independent).

115 *See, e.g.,* Doxieu v. Ford Motor Credit Co., 603 F. Supp. 624 (S.D. Ga. 1984) (Georgia and federal RICO claims by automobile buyer against assignee under retail installment contract); Bache Halsey Stuart Shields Inc. v. Tracy Collins Bank & Trust Co., 558 F. Supp. 1042 (D. Utah 1983) (Utah and federal RICO claims).

Circuit has held that federal courts have original jurisdiction over a state RICO claim that alleges only federal crimes as predicate offenses and raises very substantial federal questions, and such a case is removable to federal court.[116]

Most states require state RICO claims to be pleaded with particularity.[117] Nevada requires that claims under its RICO statute be as specific as would be required in a criminal indictment or information.[118]

An out-of-state resident has the right to file a state RICO case.[119] The fact that some acts occurred outside the state does not make the RICO statute inapplicable as long as acts in furtherance of the conspiracy occurred in the state.[120]

A Georgia appellate court has ruled that a plaintiff who alleges Insurance Code violations in a RICO suit need not exhaust administrative remedies.[121] The Ohio Supreme Court holds that a plaintiff whose injuries occurred before the state RICO statute's effective date cannot assert a claim under the statute.[122]

Some state RICO statutes specify a standard of proof.[123] The Georgia Supreme Court has interpreted its statute, which is silent on the standard of proof, to require proof only by a preponderance of the evidence.[124]

8.6.2 Who May Be a Defendant in a State RICO Suit?

Georgia,[125] Indiana,[126] and New Jersey[127] RICO defendants need not have played a part in directing the enterprise's affairs; providing advice or otherwise participating is sufficient. Idaho, on the other hand, has determined that a defendant must have some level of managerial control over the enterprise in order to implicate the state statute.[128]

A corporation is included in the definition of "person" and can be held liable in a civil case under Georgia's RICO statute.[129] A state may have sovereign immunity from a state RICO claim,[130] but one decision holds that a city does not.[131]

Wisconsin prohibits RICO actions against the estate of a deceased defendant.[132] The Georgia Supreme Court has refused to apply to state RICO claims the rule that an employer is liable for its employees' tortious acts committed within the scope of their employment.[133] Instead, the criteria for criminal liability must be applied.

8.6.3 Private Remedies Under State RICO Statutes

Most state RICO statutes, like federal RICO, provide for actual damages,[134] treble damages,[135] costs, and attorney fees,[136]

---

116 Ayres v. General Motors Corp., 234 F.3d 514 (11th Cir. 2000). *But see* Local 1 FLM-FJC UFCWIV v. Caputo, 1988 WL 13774 (S.D.N.Y. Feb. 18, 1988). *But cf. In re* United Container L.L.C., 284 B.R. 162, 173 (Bankr. S.D. Fla. 2002) (removal not allowed when complaint alleged both federal and state predicate acts).

117 WMCV Phase 3, L.L.C. v. Shushok & McCoy, Inc., 750 F. Supp. 2d 1180 (D. Nev. 2010); Girgis v. Countrywide Home Loans, Inc., 733 F. Supp. 2d 835 (N.D. Ohio 2010) (Florida and Ohio RICO claims must be pleaded with particularity); Canterbury v. Columbia Gas, 2001 WL 1681132 (S.D. Ohio Sept. 25, 2001); Cobb County v. Jones Grp., P.L.C., 460 S.E.2d 516 (Ga. Ct. App. 1995) (dismissing claim because complaint did not contain specific allegations of fraud); Knutson v. County of Barnes, 642 N.W.2d 910 (N.D. 2002); Rolin Mfg., Inc. v. Mosbrucker, 544 N.W.2d 132 (N.D. 1996); Patton v. Wilson, 2003 WL 21473566 (Ohio Ct. App. June 26, 2003); Kondrat v. Morris, 692 N.E.2d 246 (Ohio Ct. App. 1997) (conclusory allegations of corrupt activity do not satisfy requirement that claim alleging state civil RICO violation be pleaded with particularity); Carlton v. Brown, 323 P.3d 571, 583 (Utah 2014). *See also* Girgis v. Countrywide Home Loans, Inc., 733 F. Supp. 2d 835, 853 (N.D. Ohio 2010) (dismissing state RICO claim because of insufficient specificity of allegations); Altamont Summit Apts. v. Wolff Props. L.L.C., 2002 U.S. Dist. LEXIS 2761 (D. Or. Feb. 13, 2002) (specifying elements that must be pleaded).

118 Cummings v. Charter Hosp. of Las Vegas, Inc., 896 P.2d 1137 (Nev. 1995); Hale v. Burkhardt, 764 P.2d 866 (Nev. 1988).

119 State *ex rel*. Corbin v. Pickrell, 667 P.2d 1304, 1312 (Ariz. 1983).

120 Black v. State, 819 So. 2d 208 (Fla. Dist. Ct. App. 2002) (criminal case). *See also* § 8.4.1, *supra* (whether predicate acts must be committed in the state).

121 Provident Indemnity Life Ins. Co. v. James, 506 S.E.2d 892 (Ga. Ct. App. 1998).

122 Doe v. Archdiocese of Cincinnati, 849 N.E.2d 268 (Ohio 2006).

123 *See, e.g.*, Arwood v. Dunn (*In re* Caribbean K Line, Ltd.), 288 B.R. 908 (S.D. Fla. 2002) (applying Florida's statutory requirement of clear and convincing evidence); Alta Indus. Ltd. v. Hurst, 846 P.2d 1282, 1288 (Utah 1993) (noting Utah's statutory requirement of clear and convincing evidence).

124 Williams Gen. Corp. v. Stone, 614 S.E.2d 758 (Ga. 2005).

125 Faillace v. Columbus Bank & Trust Co., 605 S.E.2d 450 (Ga. Ct. App. 2004).

126 Keesling v. Beegle, 880 N.E.2d 1202 (Ind. 2008).

127 State v. Ball, 661 A.2d 251, 267–268 (N.J. 1995); Mayo, Lynch & Associates v. Pollack, 799 A.2d 12 (N.J. Super. Ct. App. Div. 2002).

128 *See* State of Idaho v. Nunez, 981 P.2d 738 (Idaho 1999) (concluding officer who stole money and drugs from police station was not involved in a criminal enterprise because he was not conducting his employer's affairs when he committed his crimes).

129 Williams Gen. Corp. v. Stone, 614 S.E.2d 758 (Ga. 2005).

130 Long v. Kroger, 2013 WL 4244474 (D. Or. Feb. 1, 2013) (state's waiver of sovereign immunity for tort claims does not apply to state RICO claim); Anderson v. Dep't of Revenue, 828 P.2d 1001 (Or. 1992).

131 Thornton v. Cleveland, 890 N.E.2d 353 (Ohio Ct. App. 2008).

132 *See* Schimpf v. Gerald, Inc., 2 F. Supp. 2d 1150 (E.D. Wis. 1998) (concluding that state RICO action is punitive in nature and so cannot survive defendant's death).

133 Clark v. Security Life Ins. Co., 509 N.E.2d 602 (Ga. 1998).

134 *See, e.g.*, CSAHA/UHHS-Canton, Inc. v. Aultman Health Found., 2012 WL 750972, at *9–10 (Ohio Ct. App. Mar. 5, 2012) (unpublished) (damages indirectly caused by corrupt activity are compensable).

135 *See, e.g.*, Vairo v. Clayden, 734 P.2d 110 (Ariz. Ct. App. 1987) (treble damages mandatory; treble *before* deducting amount received in settlement; treble prejudgment interest); Nelson v. Taff, 499 N.W.2d 685 (Wis. Ct. App. 1993).

136 *See* Dial Mfg. Int'l, Inc. v. McGraw-Edison Co. Int'l, 657 F. Supp. 248 (D. Ariz. 1987) (discussing apportionment of state RICO attorney fees relating to non-RICO counts), *aff'd without op.*, 833 F.2d 1015 (9th Cir. 1987); Sullivan v. Metro Productions, Inc., 724 P.2d 1242 (Ariz. Ct. App. 1986) (treble damages and attorney fees are mandatory); Tallitsch v. Child Support Services, Inc., 926 P.2d 143 (Colo. App. 1996) (discussing calculation of attorney fees under Colorado RICO statute); Dee v. Sweet, 489 S.E.2d 823 (Ga. 1997) (upholding award of fees and finding fee award provision constitutional); Dee v. Sweet, 460 S.E.2d 110 (Ga. Ct. App. 1995) (damages award of one dollar sufficient to justify awarding of attorney fees; discussing apportionment of state RICO

but several provide for double damages[137] or just compensatory damages.[138] Additional punitive damages are often authorized.[139] Some state RICO statutes provide for an award of attorney fees to whichever party prevails, creating a risk of a fee award to a prevailing defendant.[140]

A New Jersey court has ruled that the plaintiff cannot get both punitive damages on a non-RICO claim and treble damages on a state RICO claim.[141] At least one court in a state RICO case has followed the federal rule that the jury should not be told that its compensatory damages award will be trebled.[142]

The purpose of the treble damages provision under the Georgia RICO statute is not to impose sanctions, as is the case with punitive damages, but rather to compensate victims and provide incentives for private attorneys general to enforce the law.[143] In some states, the multiple damages remedy is mandatory once a violation is found.[144] A Wisconsin decision holds

that, when a case involved both RICO claims and related non-RICO claims, the entire damage award could be trebled even though the jury did not identify any particular part of the award that related to the RICO claim.[145]

State RICO statutes typically require the plaintiff to have suffered an injury as a condition of a private cause of action.[146] Some state statutes, unlike federal RICO, allow recovery for injury to the person as well as to property or business.[147] The plaintiff may have to show that the injury flowed directly from the racketeering activity.[148] In some states, the statute sets a cap on damage awards.

Florida courts disagree about whether the economic loss doctrine limits state RICO claims.[149] A federal court has held that the economic loss rule does not apply to the Nevada RICO statute, even if the predicate offenses also amount to a breach of contract.[150] The court will, however, reject a state RICO claim that is merely an artfully pleaded contract claim.[151] A Wisconsin court rejected the application

---

attorney fees relating to non-RICO counts); Franklin Med. Associates v. Newark Pub. Sch., 828 A.2d 966 (N.J. Super. Ct. App. Div. 2003) (error for trial court to disallow attorney fee petition because it was filed after judgment); Kmotorka v. Wylie, 2013 WL 425866 (Ohio Ct. App. Feb. 1, 2013) (RICO plaintiff who wins equitable relief by a preponderance of the evidence can recover attorney fees, but otherwise must prevail by clear and convincing evidence in order to recover fees).

137 *See, e.g.,* Utah Code Ann. § 76-10-1605(1) (West); Wis. Stat. § 946.87(4).

138 *See, e.g.,* Wash. Rev. Code § 9A.82.100(1)(a).

139 *See, e.g.,* Del. Code Ann. tit. 11, § 1505(c); Ga. Code Ann. § 16-14-6(c); Ind. Code § 34-24-2-6(b); Miss. Code Ann. § 97-43-9(6); Or. Rev. Stat. § 166.725(7)(a); Wis. Stat. § 946.87(4). *See also* Rhue v. Dawson, 841 P.2d 215 (Ariz. Ct. App. 1992).

140 *See, e.g.,* Ohio Rev. Code Ann. § 2923.34(G) (West) (allowing court to award fees to prevailing defendant as interests of justice may require unless it finds that special circumstances would make an award unjust). *See also* Accident Care Specialists of Portland, Inc. v. Allstate Fire & Cas. Ins. Co., 2014 WL 2747632 (D. Or. June 16, 2014) (awarding fees to prevailing defendant after considering factors set forth in state RICO statute); Albright v. Attorneys' Title Ins. Fund, 2009 WL 1065401 (D. Utah Apr. 20, 2009) (awarding fees to prevailing defendant; fees are mandatory to prevailing party under Utah RICO statute); RLS Bus. Ventures v. Second Chance Wholesale, Inc., 784 So. 2d 1194 (Fla. Dist. Ct. App. 2001) (denying prevailing defendant's claim for fees because plaintiffs were advancing in good faith a novel but credible interpretation); Peirce v. Szymanski, 2013 WL 1933148 (Ohio Ct. App. May 10, 2013) (affirming trial court's discretion to deny fees to prevailing defendant); Holbrook v. Master Prot. Corp., 883 P.2d 295 (Utah Ct. App. 1994) (no error in awarding attorney fees to defendant on state RICO claim).

141 St. James v. Future Fin., 776 A.2d 849 (N.J. Super. Ct. App. Div. 2001).

142 *Id. See also* National Consumer Law Center, Unfair and Deceptive Acts and Practices § 12.4.2.8 (8th ed. 2012), *updated at* www.nclc.org/library.

143 Williams Gen. Corp. v. Stone, 614 S.E.2d 758 (Ga. 2005). *But see* Alta Indus. Ltd. v. Hurst, 846 P.2d 1282, 1292 (Utah 1993) (double damages under state RICO statute are punitive, so punitive damages cannot be awarded on a related count).

144 *See, e.g.,* Allstate Ins. Co. v. Nassiri, 2013 WL 3716444 (D. Nev. July 15, 2013) (interpreting Nevada treble damages provision as mandatory); Daggett v. Jackie Fine Arts, Inc., 733 P.2d 1142 (Ariz. Ct. App. 1986) (treble damages mandatory); Sullivan v. Metro Productions, Inc., 724 P.2d 1242 (Ariz. Ct. App. 1986) (treble damages and attorney fees are mandatory).

145 S.C. Johnson & Son, Inc. v. Morris, 779 N.W.2d 19 (Wis. Ct. App. 2009).

146 *See, e.g.,* Ford Motor Co. v. Edgewood Props., Inc., 2009 WL 150951, at *10 (D.N.J. Jan. 20, 2009), *on reconsideration in part*, 2009 WL 2488174 (D.N.J. Aug. 11, 2009) (allowing RICO claim to go forward); Weaver v. Aetna Life Ins. Co., 2008 WL 4833035 (D. Nev. Nov. 4, 2008) (dismissing suit because of insufficient showing of injury; taking an extremely cramped reading of this requirement), *aff'd without op.*, 370 Fed. Appx. 822 (9th Cir. 2010).

147 *See, e.g.,* Ariz. Rev. Stat. Ann. § 13-2314.04(A); Idaho Code Ann. § 18-7805; N.M. Stat. Ann. § 30-42-6(A); Utah Code Ann. § 76-10-1605(1) (West). *See also* Southern-Intermodal Logistics, Inc. v. D.J. Powers Co., 555 S.E.2d 478 (Ga. Ct. App. 2000) (Georgia RICO statute allows suit by any person who has been injured, with no requirement that injury be to person or property).

148 Rubicon Global Ventures, Inc. v. Chongqing Zongshen Grp. Import/Exp. Corp., 2010 WL 4812860 (D. Or. Nov. 19, 2010) (predicate act must be proximate cause of plaintiff's injuries; dismissing claim when causation was too remote); Nicor Int'l Corp. v. El Paso Corp., 292 F. Supp. 2d 1357, 1378 (S.D. Fla. 2003) (dismissing claim because of failure to show causation); Nicholson v. Windham, 571 S.E.2d 466 (Ga. Ct. App. 2002) (causation too remote when injury was termination of employment because employee refused to participate in criminal activity); Franklin Med. Associates v. Newark Pub. Sch., 828 A.2d 966 (N.J. Super. Ct. App. Div. 2003) (must show that predicate acts were proximate cause of the harm); City of Cleveland v. JP Morgan Chase Bank, 2013 WL 1183332 (Ohio Ct. App. Mar. 21, 2013) (unpublished) (affirming dismissal of state RICO claim; damage to city from lender's pattern of foreclosing on city residents' homes by submitting fraudulent paperwork is too remote and derivative). *But cf.* American Fed'n of Teachers v. Oregon Taxpayers United PAC, 189 P.3d 9 (Or. 2008) (causation sufficient when defendant forged signatures on ballot initiative that would have restricted plaintiff teacher's union's ability to collect dues, forcing plaintiff to spend money to oppose the measure; defendant's false reports to state that it met requirements for non-profit status caused similar injury and also satisfied injury requirement).

149 *See* Wilson v. De Angelis, 156 F. Supp. 2d 1335 (S.D. Fla. 2001) (economic loss doctrine is no bar). *Contra* Sarkis v. Pafford Oil Co., 697 So. 2d 524 (Fla. Dist. Ct. App. 1997); Delgado v. J.W. Courtesy Pontiac GMC-Truck, Inc., 693 So. 2d 602 (Fla. Dist. Ct. App. 1997).

150 G.K. Las Vegas Ltd. P'ship v. Simon Prop. Grp., Inc., 460 F. Supp. 2d 1222, 1236 (D. Nev. 2006).

151 *Id.*

of the voluntary payment defense to a RICO claim, holding that allowing the defense would frustrate the purpose of the RICO statute.[152]

Many state RICO statutes expressly authorize injunctive relief for private plaintiffs.[153] A Washington court ordered an injunction to be issued without bond under the state RICO law to prevent a predatory lender from foreclosing on a home, even though the state Deeds of Trust Act authorized an injunction against foreclosure only upon posting a substantial bond.[154] State RICO statutes may also provide that property acquired through an offense under the statute is held under an involuntary trusteeship.[155]

8.7 Application of State RICO Statutes to Consumer Fraud

Like federal RICO statutes, state RICO statutes constitute a proper weapon for use against "garden variety" fraud.[156]

Indeed, many state RICO statutes explicitly list fraud, usury, and violations of certain consumer protection statutes as predicate offenses.[157] These statutes demonstrate the legislative intent to treat consumer fraud as organized crime and to afford victimized consumers the powerful remedies of the RICO laws.

Examples of the application of state civil RICO laws to consumer issues include:

- A utility company's payment of illegal rebates to certain large customers to induce them to withdraw objections to a proposed rate structure, and its subsequent attempt to cover up these payments.[158]
- A telecommunications company's fraudulent billing for telephone-based gambling charges.[159]
- A subprime mortgage lender's alleged conspiracy with various mortgage brokers to defraud single, elderly women out of great sums of money or the equity in their homes.[160]
- A foreclosure trustee's demands and lien filings for allegedly unpaid homeowner assessments that far exceeded the amount at which the delinquent assessments were growing.[161]
- A Ponzi scheme that targeted elderly, unsophisticated, and inexperienced investors.[162]

However, the Washington Supreme Court rejected a claim that a trustee that was conducting a non-judicial foreclosure violated the state RICO statute by misrepresenting the identity of the holder of the obligation.[163]

---

152 MBS Certified Pub. Accountants, L.L.C. v. Wisconsin Bell Inc., 828 N.W.2d 575 (Wis. Ct. App. 2013).

153 *See, e.g.*, Ind. Code § 34-24-2-6(a); Or. Rev. Stat. § 166.725(6). *See* Federal Deposit Ins. Corp. v. Antonio, 843 F.2d 1311 (10th Cir. 1988) (injunction preventing dissipation of assets not traceable to alleged racketeering permitted under Colorado RICO statute); Nat'l Union Fire Ins. Co. v. Kozeny, 115 F. Supp. 2d 1210 (D. Colo. 2000) (granting injunctive relief to prevent dissipation of assets), *aff'd*, 2001 U.S. App. LEXIS 21211 (10th Cir. Sept. 28, 2001); Marsellis-Warner Corp. v. Rabens, 51 F. Supp. 2d 508 (D.N.J. 1999) (New Jersey statute does not expressly preclude equitable actions by private plaintiffs and its plain language appears to allow courts to grant equitable relief); Bowcutt v. Delta N. Star Corp., 976 P.2d 643 (Wash. Ct. App. 1999) (interpreting Washington statute as allowing private plaintiffs to obtain injunctive relief). *But see* Curley v. Cumberland Farms Dairy, Inc., 728 F. Supp. 1123 (D.N.J. 1989) (no injunctions for private litigants under New Jersey RICO statute).

154 Bowcutt v. Delta N. Star Corp., 976 P.2d 643 (Wash. Ct. App. 1999).

155 *See, e.g.*, Ariz. Rev. Stat. Ann. § 13-2314.04. *But cf.* Allied Mortg. Grp., Inc. v. Peter Strojnik, P.C., 2009 WL 2581400 (Ariz. Ct. App. Aug. 20, 2009) (notice placed in land records asserting claim under state RICO statute was groundless and land owner was entitled to attorney fees to quiet title).

156 *See, e.g.*, Kemp v. AT&T, 393 F.3d 1354 (11th Cir. 2004) (upholding judgment under federal and state RICO statutes for telecommunications company's fraudulent billing for telephone-based gambling charges, but reducing punitive damages from $1 million to $250,000); Matthews v. New Century Mortg. Corp., 185 F. Supp. 2d 874 (S.D. Ohio 2002) (predatory lending and home improvement fraud); Eva v. Midwest Nat'l Mortg. Banc, Inc., 143 F. Supp. 2d 862 (N.D. Ohio 2001) (denying motion to dismiss state RICO claim against predatory lender based on wire fraud); Stroik v. State, 671 A.2d 1335 (Del. 1996) (upholding state RICO criminal conviction against perpetrators of vehicle sublease scam); Bandaras v. Banco Central del Ecuador, 461 So. 2d 265, 269–270 (Fla. Dist. Ct. App. 1985); Faillace v. Columbus Bank & Trust Co., 605 S.E.2d 450 (Ga. Ct. App. 2004) (upholding state RICO judgment against telemarketer in favor of bank that was duped into approving fraudulent charges to customers' credit cards); Reaugh v. Inner Harbour Hosp., Ltd., 447 S.E.2d 617 (Ga. Ct. App. 1994) (suit against juvenile treatment center for abuse and failure to provide treatment); Larson v. Smith, 391 S.E.2d 686 (Ga. Ct. App. 1990); Sanchez v. Guerrero, 885 S.W.2d 487 (Tex. App. 1994); State v. Thompson, 751 P.2d 805 (Utah Ct. App. 1988); Dorr v. Sacred Heart Hosp., 597 N.W.2d 462 (Wis. App. Ct. 1999) (hospital's filing of false

lien on consumer's tort recovery could be criminal slander of title, which would support RICO suit). *But see* Daniels v. True, 547 N.E.2d 425 (Ohio Mun. Ct. 1988) (state RICO statute not intended to reach contractor's use of false name and failure to perform work); Griswold v. U.S. Sprint Communications Co., 506 N.W.2d 426 (Wis. Ct. App. 1993) (no fraud claims allowed for simple refusal to do business in manner claimant wanted).

157 *See* § 8.4.1, *supra.*

158 Williams v. Duke Energy Int'l, 681 F.3d 788, 803–804 (6th Cir. 2012) (Ohio law) (reversing dismissal of state RICO claim; predicate acts are money laundering, telecommunications fraud, and obstruction of justice).

159 Kemp v. AT&T, 393 F.3d 1354 (11th Cir. 2004) (upholding judgment under federal and state RICO statutes, but reducing punitive damages from $1 million to $250,000). *See also* MBS Certified Pub. Accountants, L.L.C. v. Wisconsin Bell Inc., 828 N.W.2d 575 (Wis. Ct. App. 2013) (reversing dismissal of state RICO complaint against telecommunications provider for cramming).

160 Matthews v. New Century Mortg. Corp., 185 F. Supp. 2d 874 (S.D. Ohio 2002) (allowing claim to proceed).

161 Ellis v. Alessi Trustee Corp., 2015 WL 3708733 (D. Nev. June 15, 2015) (denying defendants' renewed motion for judgment as a matter of law after jury verdict in favor of homeowner).

162 Bradley v. Miller, 2015 WL 1469153 (S.D. Ohio Mar. 30, 2015) (granting summary judgment in favor of consumers against some defendants).

163 Trujillo v. Northwest Trustee Services, Inc., 355 P.3d 1100 (Wash. 2015) (holding that complaint failed to plead enterprise requirements). *See also* Rowe v. U.S. Bancorp, 569 Fed. Appx. 701 (11th Cir. 2014) (affirming dismissal of Georgia RICO claim; fact that signatory of mortgage assignment did not actually sign it is not forgery so is not a predicate offense).

8.8 State Civil Theft and Crime Victims Statutes

8.8.1 Civil Theft Statutes

A number of states have civil theft laws that offer a private cause of action for conduct that violates state criminal laws. Because there is no requirement that there be an enumerated nexus to an enterprise, and there is no pattern requirement, these statutes are often more appropriate than state or federal RICO statutes for consumer claims. For transactions within their scope, these statutes may provide significant advantages over the state UDAP statute.

A *Colorado* statute allows the owner of property that was taken by theft, robbery, or burglary to recover $200 or treble damages, whichever is greater, plus costs and attorney fees.[164] Unlike the state UDAP statute, there is no requirement of a showing that the act or practice has a significant impact on the public as consumers.[165] However, the economic loss doctrine could bar a civil theft claim if proof of theft is contingent upon proof of breach of contract.[166]

A *Connecticut* statute provides treble damages for theft.[167] An advantage of a claim under this statute is that, unlike the Connecticut UDAP statute, it offers treble damages. However, because the civil theft statute requires a showing of larceny, intent must be shown.[168]

Florida's civil theft statute[169] gives a cause of action for treble damages, minimum statutory damages of $200, and attorney fees to any person injured by a violation of any of a variety of theft statutes or a state law regarding financial abuse of elders. One of the theft offenses is dealing in property on which identifying features such as serial numbers have been removed or altered without the manufacturer's consent,[170] a crime that may be applicable to sales of rebuilt wrecks or reassembled motor vehicles. A pre-suit demand letter is required. For the transactions it covers, the Florida civil theft statute has certain advantages over a claim under the Florida UDAP statute, which does not provide for multiple damages, allows fees to be awarded against the consumer if the defendant prevails,[171] and has broadly-phrased exclusions for banks, utilities, and

insurers. The economic loss doctrine does not bar a civil theft claim even if the parties' duties are governed by a contract.[172] A consumer won a judgment under this statute against a car dealer who took his deposit then drove the car 200 miles, blew out the engine, and refused to return the deposit.[173]

Georgia allows compensatory damages, plus exemplary damages of up to triple the amount of the loss if the total claim, including exemplary damages, is less than $5000 for willful damage to or theft of personal property (including unlawful conversion).[174] Pre-suit notice is required and attorney fees are available.[175] Georgia's UDAP statute has been interpreted extremely narrowly,[176] so this statute offers a number of advantages if a transaction falls within its scope.

In *Indiana*, a person who has suffered a pecuniary loss as a result of a theft or fraud crime, or certain other types of crimes, may sue for treble damages, costs, attorney fees, certain travel expenses and court costs, and collection costs.[177] There is no requirement that the defendant has been convicted of the underlying offense, and proof of the offense need only be by a preponderance of the evidence.[178] Courts have applied this statute to consumer fraud,[179] and to claims that creditors wrongfully repossessed property from consumers.[180] This

---

164 Colo. Rev. Stat. § 18-4-405. *See* Lykins v. Teta (*In re* Teta), 2011 WL 2435948 (Bankr. D. Colo. June 16, 2011) (awarding treble damages; dealer committed theft offense by accepting car on consignment and then selling it but failing to pay off lien or deliver title to new buyer). *But cf.* Mats v. Mazin, 2012 WL 3242951 (D. Colo. Aug. 6, 2012) (interpreting statute not to apply to aiding and abetting).

165 *See* National Consumer Law Center, Unfair and Deceptive Acts and Practices § 11.4.3.2 (8th ed. 2012), *updated at* www.nclc.org/library.

166 Makoto USA, Inc. v. Russell, 250 P.3d 625, 628 (Colo. App. 2009); Van Rees v. Unleaded Software, Inc., 2013 WL 6354532 (Colo. App. Dec. 5, 2013), *cert. granted*, 2014 WL 5473799 (Colo. Oct. 14, 2014).

167 Conn. Gen. Stat. § 52-564.

168 Suarez-Negrete v. Trotta, 705 A.2d 215 (Conn. App. 1998).

169 Fla. Stat. § 772.11.

170 Fla. Stat. § 812.016.

171 Florida's civil theft statute allows defendants to recover attorney fees, but only upon a finding that the claim was without substantial factual or legal support. Fla. Stat. § 772.11(1).

172 Fahey v. Am. Home Mortg. Servicing, Inc., 2012 WL 6114849 (S.D. Fla. Dec. 10, 2012).

173 Belle Glade Chevrolet-Cadillac Buick Pontiac Oldsmobile, Inc., v. Figgie, 54 So. 3d 991 (Fla. Dist. Ct. App. 2011).

174 Ga. Code Ann. § 51-10-6.

175 *Id.* Attorney fees are available to the prevailing defendant upon a showing that the claim was brought without reasonable factual or legal support.

176 *See* National Consumer Law Center, Unfair and Deceptive Acts and Practices §§ 4.2.15.3, 11.4.3.3 (8th ed. 2012), *updated at* www.nclc.org/library.

177 Ind. Code § 34-24-3-1.

178 Klinker v. First Merchants Bank, 964 N.E.2d 190 (Ind. 2012).

179 *See, e.g.*, Auto Liquidation Ctr., Inc. v. Bates, 969 N.E.2d 139 (Ind. Ct. App. 2012) (table, text at 2012 WL 2130886) (affirming award of treble damages under civil theft statute against car dealer who refused buyer's payments yet refused to release car or return down payment); Palmer Dodge, Inc. v. Long, 791 N.E.2d 788 (Ind. Ct. App. 2003) (criminal conversion, the knowing exercise of control over property of another to a greater extent than that consented to by the other, will support award of attorney fees; dealer refused to return trade-in after financing fell through, although contract explicitly required return). *But cf.* Riha v. State Farm Mut. Auto. Ins. Co., 2007 WL 42976 (S.D. Ind. Jan. 3, 2007) (rejecting claim under civil theft law against insurer that concealed vehicle's salvage history; this did not amount to theft, and any deceptive acts occurred out of state; Kesling v. Hubler Nissan, Inc., 997 N.E.2d 327 (Ind. 2013) (civil theft claim can be based on violation of criminal deception law, but there must be a misrepresentation of fact, not merely puffing). *See generally* National Consumer Law Center, Repossessions § 13.4.4 (8th ed. 2013), *updated at* www.nclc.org/library.

180 Ind. Code § 34-24-3-1 (criminal conversion). *See* Greco v. KMA Auto Exch., 765 N.E.2d 140 (Ind. Ct. App. 2002) (dealer committed criminal conversion and is liable under civil theft statute for repossessing car when it had no right to do so). *See also* Auto Liquidation Ctr., Inc. v. Bates, 969 N.E.2d 139 (Ind. Ct. App. 2012) (table) (repossession without reasonable basis amounted to criminal conversion, which is actionable under civil theft statute; affirming liability of repossessing dealer); Smith v. Brown, 778 N.E.2d 490 (Ind. Ct. App. 2002) (when contract allowing creditor to record deed was void as against public policy and

---

statute offers some advantages over Indiana's UDAP statute, which requires a pre-suit notice, requires a showing of knowledge or intent, allows attorney fees to be awarded against the consumer if the defendant prevails, excludes real estate transactions, and does not provide for multiple damages.

Michigan allows a private cause of action for treble damages and attorney fees for certain theft offenses.[181] This statute has been applied to claims that creditors wrongfully repossessed consumer goods.[182] An advantage of this statute over the state UDAP statute is that the scope of the UDAP statute has been construed extremely narrowly.[183] However, one court has held that, when the predicate act is conversion, the economic loss doctrine will bar the claim unless the defendant's conduct is alleged to have breached a duty that is separate and distinct from any breach of contract.[184]

Minnesota provides civil liability for double damages for theft of personal property, and a criminal complaint is not a prerequisite.[185] Fraudulently inducing buyers to pay the purchase price for real property states a claim.[186] This statute has advantages over the state UDAP statute in that it offers double damages and does not include the restrictive public benefit requirement that courts have read into Minnesota's UDAP statutes.[187]

North Carolina provides a civil action for damages, punitive damages up to $1000 in most cases, and attorney fees for certain theft offenses without the need for a criminal prosecution.[188]

Ohio offers a private cause of action for damages, attorney fees, costs, and, in certain cases, punitive damages to anyone injured in person or property by a criminal act.[189] Treble and minimum damages are available if the crime is one of certain theft offenses.[190] The statute also provides for treble damages and statutory damages in some circumstances[191] if the defendant does not respond properly to a thirty-day demand letter.[192] A cause of action can be maintained even if the defendant has not been convicted of the crime.[193] This statute has been applied to an auto dealer's failure to follow through on a promise to assume the payments on the car the consumers were trading in,[194] and to a mortgage lender's failure to apply loan modification payments to the mortgage debt as promised.[195] The broad scope of Ohio's civil theft statute is an advantage over its UDAP statute, which excludes insurers, utility companies, and many creditors and financial institutions.

Utah allows treble damages, costs, and attorney fees for certain theft offenses.[196] The multiple damages provision is an advantage of this statute over the state UDAP statute. In addition, the state UDAP statute excludes a number of types of transactions and actors.

Texas offers a civil remedy of actual damages, statutory damages up to $1000, and attorney fees for certain theft offenses.[197] Claims under this statute will avoid the pre-suit notice requirement of the Texas UDAP statute and its limited scope, which excludes many loan transactions. The Texas UDAP statute also lacks a statutory damages provision. However, one court has held that attorney fees are available to a prevailing defendant without the need to show that the claim was groundless, frivolous, or brought in bad faith.[198]

Wisconsin's civil theft statute grants a private cause of action for treble damages and all reasonably-incurred costs of investigation and litigation against a defendant who obtains title to property through intentional, knowing misrepresentations.[199] A criminal conviction is not required to bring a complaint.[200]

8.8.2 Other Statutes That Provide a Private Cause of Action for Crime Victims

In addition, some states have general crime victims' civil liability statutes that provide a private right of action. For example, an Arkansas statute provides for actual damages and attorney fees for any conduct that would constitute a felony,

was also procured by fraud, recording the deed was conversion; triple damages pursuant to civil theft statute were proper). *But cf.* DBS Constr. Inc. v. New Equip. Leasing, Inc., 2011 WL 1157531 (N.D. Ind. Mar. 28, 2011) (must show knowledge of a high degree of probability that exercise of control over property is unauthorized; not shown when creditor who seized equipment loaned by plaintiff to debtor reasonably believed that equipment belonged to debtor).

181 Mich. Comp. Laws § 600.2919a.
182 Williams v. Delamar Car Co., 2011 WL 1811061 (W.D. Mich. May 12, 2011) (awarding treble damages, costs, and attorney fees for repossession while consumer was current on payments and engaged in dispute over extended warranty); Shoup v. Iliana Recovery Sys., Inc., 2002 U.S. Dist. LEXIS 674 (W.D. Mich. Jan. 8, 2002) (ruling on damages after default judgment). *But cf.* El Camino Res., Ltd. v. Huntington Nat'l Bank, 712 F.3d 917 (6th Cir. 2013) (showing of actual knowledge that property was converted is required; dismissing claim that bank should have known of customer's egregiously fraudulent conduct).
183 *See* National Consumer Law Center, Unfair and Deceptive Acts and Practices § 2.3.3.3.2 (8th ed. 2012), *updated at* www.nclc.org/library.
184 Llewellyn-Jones v. Metro Prop. Grp., L.L.C., 22 F. Supp. 3d 760 (E.D. Mich. 2014).
185 Minn. Stat. Ann. § 604.14.
186 Damon v. Groteboer, 937 F. Supp. 2d 1048 (D. Minn. 2013).
187 *See* National Consumer Law Center, Unfair and Deceptive Acts and Practices § 11.4.3.4 (8th ed. 2012), *updated at* www.nclc.org/library.
188 N.C. Gen. Stat. § 1-538.2.
189 Ohio Rev. Code Ann. § 2307.60 (West).
190 Ohio Rev. Code Ann. § 2307.61 (West). *See* Corbett v. Beneficial Ohio, Inc., 847 F. Supp. 2d 1019 (S.D. Ohio 2012) (section 2913.61 applies if theft involves personal property, but not if it involves real property).

191 Ohio Rev. Code § 2307.61 (West).
192 *See* Buckeye Check Cashing, Inc. v. Proctor, 1999 Ohio App. LEXIS 2678 (June 15, 1999) (interpreting ambiguous statutory language).
193 CitiMortgage, Inc. v. Rudzik, 2014 WL 1384596 (Ohio Ct. App. Mar. 31, 2014) (unpublished).
194 Gonzalez v. Spofford, 2005 WL 1541016 (Ohio Ct. App. June 30, 2005).
195 CitiMortgage, Inc. v. Rudzik, 2014 WL 1384596 (Ohio Ct. App. Mar. 31, 2014) (unpublished) (reversing dismissal of complaint).
196 Utah Code Ann. § 76-6-412 (West).
197 Tex. Civ. Prac. & Rem. Code §§ 134.001 to 134.005 (West).
198 Arrow Marble, L.L.C. v. Estate of Killion, 441 S.W.3d 702 (Tex. App. 2014).
199 Wis. Stat. § 895.446 (providing a civil cause of action for theft and certain other crimes). *Cf.* Malzewski v. Rapkin, 723 N.W.2d 156 (Wis. Ct. App. 2006) (civil theft claim requires proof of elements of tort of fraud; rejecting plaintiff's claim because of failure to establish reliance).
200 Wis. Stat. § 895.446(2).

and the proof is only by a preponderance of the evidence.[201] Alabama provides a civil action for any injury to person or property that amounts to a felony, whether or not the offender is criminally prosecuted.[202] Rhode Island provides a private cause of action for damages to any person who suffers injury to the person, reputation, or estate by reason of the commission of any crime or offense, and the law specifies that it is not a defense that no criminal complaint has been filed.[203]

Even if they do not have more generally applicable laws allowing civil actions for injuries caused by theft or other crimes, a number of states provide a civil remedy for certain consumer crimes such as identity theft,[204] theft from a vulnerable adult,[205] or theft in the mortgage lending process.[206] Many states also have laws allowing a private cause of action for dishonored-check offenses. These statutes often provide for a civil penalty or multiple damages and are widely used by collection agencies that specialize in dishonored checks. They are discussed in NCLC's treatise, *Collection Actions*.[207]

---

201 Ark. Code Ann. § 16-118-107.

202 Ala. Code § 6-5-370.

203 R.I. Gen. Laws § 9-1-2.

204 Conn. Gen. Stat. § 52-571h; Colo. Rev. Stat. §§ 13-21-109.5 (fraudulent use of social security number), 13-21-125 (unlawful use of personal identifying information); 720 Ill. Comp. Stat. § 5/16-33 (applicable only if defendant has been convicted); Okla. Stat. tit. 21, § 1533.1; 42 Pa. Cons. Stat. Ann. § 8315 (West) (actual damages or $500 plus costs and attorney fees); Tenn. Code Ann. § 47-18-2104 (treble damages for willful or knowing violation); Utah Code Ann. § 78B-6-1701 (West) ($1000 or three times actual damages, whichever is greater, plus costs and attorney fees, and punitive damages in the court's discretion; no requirement of criminal conviction; proof by preponderance of the evidence); Wyo. Stat. Ann. § 1-1-128 (injunction, damages, costs, and attorney fees; no requirement of criminal conviction).

205 Miss. Code Ann. § 11-7-165 (treble damages for embezzlement from vulnerable adult; includes conversion, embezzlement, extortion, theft, or fraud). *See also* Tenn. Code Ann. § 71-6-120 (private right of action for various theft offenses against older or disabled person; punitive damages in accordance with applicable common law standards; attorney fees if theft resulted from intentional, fraudulent, or malicious conduct).

206 Colo. Rev. Stat. § 13-21-125.

207 National Consumer Law Center, Collection Actions § 8.3.1 (3d ed. 2014), *updated at* www.nclc.org/library.

Chapter 9   The Federal False Claims Act

9.1   Background

9.1.1   Introduction

The Federal False Claims Act (FCA) and similar state false claims acts impose liability on government contractors who make false or fraudulent claims for payment of services and products.[1] Although false claims act cases have traditionally been used to file claims against government defense and health care contractors and suppliers, they are expanding into other areas—such as insurance, housing, government entitlement programs, government loan programs, and environmental and labor laws—that offer potential use by consumer lawyers.[2]

Unlike almost all other federal fraud statutes or common law causes of action, federal and state false claims acts,[3] with their unique *qui tam*[4] provisions, allow consumers to file and prosecute a lawsuit in the name of a state or of the United States.[5] Because false claims act cases are brought on behalf of the government, the individual plaintiff—or relator—need not suffer any individual or direct harm to bring the action.[6] By authorizing suits in these situations, the FCA and similar state false claims acts offer a tremendous opportunity for individuals and organizations to remedy and prevent fraud and other improper marketplace conduct.

The FCA and similar state false claims acts empower individuals and organizations with knowledge of private fraud against the government to file lawsuits to recover damages and penalties for the government. Its express intent is to encourage *qui tam* suits by giving consumers the tools and incentive to represent the government in actions against individuals and organizations who falsely bill for services not rendered or goods not delivered.

As powerful a tool as the FCA represents, the inexperienced practitioner should also recognize its challenges. The Supreme Court has noted that "[t]he False Claims Act's *qui tam* provisions present many interpretative challenges," such that it may not always be possible, even for the Supreme Court itself, "to make them operate together smoothly like a fine tuned machine."[7]

9.1.2   History of the Federal False Claims Act

9.1.2.1   Early History

Qui tam actions originated in England[8] around the end of the thirteenth century, when private individuals who had suffered injury began bringing actions in the royal courts on both their own and the Crown's behalf.[9] In the fourteenth century, Parliament began enacting statutes that specifically provided for *qui tam* suits. These suits were of two types—suits that allowed a party to sue for injury to themselves as well as the Crown and "those that allowed informers to obtain a portion of the penalty as a bounty for their information, even if they had not suffered an injury themselves."[10] These statutes were known as "informer" statutes, and it is the latter type of suit—when no individual injury is required to bring the suit—that provided the genesis for *qui tam* statutes enacted in the United States.

Because these early statutes were "highly subject to abuse,"[11] many early statutes were repealed over the ensuing centuries, although laws allowing *qui tam* suits by informers continued to exist in England until 1951. However, *qui tam* statutes crossed the Atlantic to the colonies, some of which enacted their own *qui tam* statutes. The use of "informer" acts carried over after the American Revolution and the first United States Congress passed a considerable number of *qui tam* statutes.[12]

9.1.2.2   Civil War Origins of the Federal False Claims Act

The False Claims Act[13] was originally known as the "Informer's Act" or the "Lincoln Law." It was enacted during the height of the Civil War at the urging of President Abraham

---

1   *See generally* Claire M. Sylvia, The False Claims Act: Fraud Against the Government (2d ed. 2010). For an overview of the statute, see Grande, *An Overview of the Federal False Claims Act*, Ann. 2002 ATLA-CLE 1177 (July 2002).

2   *See generally* Grande, The False Claims Act: A Consumer's Tool to Combat Fraud Against the Government, 12 Loy. Consumer L. Rev. 129 (2000).

3   31 U.S.C. § 3729 (1983).
    The Act, originally known as the "Informer's Act" or the "Lincoln Law," was enacted during the Civil War to deal with widespread fraud by private military supply contractors. United States *ex rel.* Newsham v. Lockheed Missiles and Space Co., 722 F. Supp. 607, 609 (N.D. Cal. 1989).

4   *Qui tam* is the abbreviation of the Latin phrase "*qui tam pro domino rege quam pro si ipso in hac parte sequitur*," which means, "[w]ho sues on behalf of the King as well as for himself." Black's Law Dictionary 1282 (8th ed. 2004).

5   There are several jurisdictions that have county or city false claims acts, for example, New York City Administrative Code, Title 7, Chapter 8. There are also state laws that include actions on behalf of counties, for example, Hawai'i Revised Statutes Chapter 46-171 *et seq.*

6   The FCA also allows for supplemental jurisdiction over related state law claims, including wrongful termination claims and claims that may be brought under the various state false claims acts. 31 U.S.C. § 3732(b).

---

7   Kellogg Brown & Root Services, Inc. v. United States *ex rel.* Carter, 135 S. Ct. 1970, 1979, 191 L. Ed. 2d 899 (2015).

8   *See generally* Note, The History and Development of Qui Tam, 1972 Wash. U.L.Q. 81.

9   Vermont Agency of Natural Res. v. United States *ex rel.* Stevens, 529 U.S. 765 (2002).

10   *Id.*

11   *Id.*

12   *Id.*

13   31 U.S.C. § 3729 (1983).

Lincoln when dramatically increased government spending on military procurement led to widespread fraud by private contractors.[14] The most glaring examples of fraud included sawdust sold as munitions and transported to Union soldiers; supplies such as horses and mules sold to units of the Union cavalry and then resold to other units; and unseaworthy ships freshly painted and delivered to the Navy as newly built.[15]

By 1863, the fraud and profiteering in military supplies for the Union Army severely imperiled the Union war effort. In Lincoln's words, "worse than traitors in arms are the men who pretend loyalty to the flag, feast and fatten on the misfortunes of the Nation while patriotic blood is crimsoning the plains of the South and their countrymen are moldering in the dust."[16] Unfortunately, in the 1860s, there were no federal law agencies (such as a centralized Department of Justice or Federal Bureau of Investigation) to spearhead the enforcement effort. This situation left the United States—and the Union Army—with neither the tools nor the institutions to combat the fraud that the President viewed as threatening the very existence of the United States.[17] In response to President Lincoln's concerns, Congress enacted the False Claims Act of 1863, which the President immediately signed into law.[18] It allowed private parties—called *qui tam* plaintiffs or relators[19]—to bring private actions on behalf of the government and share in a portion of the recovered monies.

9.1.2.3   1943 Federal False Claims Act Revisions

After the Civil War, the False Claims Act fell into disuse, but the military build-up prior to World War II and expansion of the federal government's economic role provided new opportunities for private contractors to profit through fraud.[20]

However, because of what was perceived to be an abuse of the system by *qui tam* plaintiffs who had no direct knowledge of the fraud, yet were able to recover monies under the Act after a public disclosure of a government criminal investigation, amendments were made in 1943 that restricted the statute. The 1943 amendments prohibited a *qui tam* recovery when there was any prior government knowledge of the false billing. The 1943 amendments also gave the government discretion to award nothing to the *qui tam* plaintiff and reduced to 25% the maximum amount the *qui tam* plaintiff could obtain.[21] The effects of these changes reduced the incentives for private individuals to file *qui tam* actions and virtually eliminated the availability of the False Claims Act as a means of combating government fraud.

9.1.2.4   Defense Industry Fraud Prompts 1986 FCA Liberalization

After passage of the 1943 amendments, another period of relative disuse followed. However, the number of filings of False Claims Act complaints increased dramatically after 1986, when Congress liberalized some of its provisions making it easier to bring lawsuits under the Act and increasing the incentives for *qui tam* plaintiffs to pursue False Claims Act lawsuits.

During the early 1980s increasing congressional concern over rampant fraud, particularly in the defense industry, prompted Congress to liberalize the FCA's application.[22] Just as the Civil War and pre-World War II military build-ups presented defense contractors with increased opportunities to profit from false billings, the dramatic increase in military spending after 1980 again created the climate for government contractors to steal from the government.[23]

During this time period, Congress was increasingly confronted with reports of fraud and fraudulent billings that permeated virtually every government program.[24] For example, in 1985 the Department of Defense Inspector General reported that nine of the top ten defense contractors were under investigation for multiple fraud offenses, including four of the largest which were later convicted of criminal offenses against the government.[25] Estimates of public money lost to fraud ranged from hundreds of millions of dollars to $50 billion per year.[26] In considering amendments to the False Claims Act, Congress recognized that "the most serious problem plaguing effective

---

14   United States v. Bornstein, 423 U.S. 303, 309, 96 S. Ct. 523, 46 L. Ed. 2d 514 (1976) (FCA was enacted in 1863 with the principal goal of "stopping the massive frauds perpetrated by large [private] contractors during the Civil War"). *See also* U.S. *ex rel.* Newsham v. Lockheed Missiles & Space Co., 722 F. Supp. 607, 609 (N.D. Cal. 1989).

15   *See generally* 132 Cong. Rec. 22339-40 (1986) (remarks of Representatives Berman and Bedell).

16   *See* 89 Cong. Rec. 10847 (1943).

17   Helmer, Lugbill, & Neff, False Claims Act: Whistleblower Litigation § 3-3, at 27 (1994).

18   12 Stat. 696 (1863).

19   Neither the Federal False Claims Act nor the Hawaii False Claims Act use the term "relator" and instead refer to "*qui tam* plaintiff." 31 U.S.C. § 3730(d); Haw. Rev. Stat. § 661-27 (2002 Supp.).

    However, the federal courts have used the historical term "relator." Vermont Agency of Natural Res. v. United States *ex rel.* Stevens, 529 U.S. 765 (2000) ("a private person (the 'relator') may bring a *qui tam* civil action . . .") Black's Law Dictionary defines "relator" as:

    > [a]n informer. The person upon whose complaint, or at whose instance certain writs are issued such as information or writ of quo warranto, and who is quasi the plaintiff in the proceeding. For example if John Smith is the relator and Jones is the defendant, the citation would read, State ex rel. John Smith v. Jones.

    Black's Law Dictionary (6th ed. 1990).

20   John T. Boese, Civil False Claims and Qui Tam Actions 1-12 (1999 Supp.).

21   *See generally* 31 U.S.C. §§ 232, 233, 235 (1976).

22   Helmer, Lugbill, & Neff, False Claims Act: Whistleblower Litigation § 3-6(b), at 38 (1994).

23   *Id.* at 33 (1994).

24   S. Rep. No. 99-345, at 2 (1986), *reprinted in* 1986 U.S.C.C.A.N. 5266, 5267.

25   *Id.* (citing *Testimony of Department of Defense Inspector General Joseph Sherick, Hearings on Federal Securities Laws and Defense Contracting before the Subcomm. on Oversight and Investigations of the Comm. on Energy and Commerce, House of Representatives*, 99th Congress (1985)).

26   S. Rep. No. 99-345, at 3 (1986), *reprinted in* 1986 U.S.C.C.A.N. 5266, 5268.

enforcement [of federal anti-fraud laws] is a lack of resources on the part of Federal enforcement agencies."[27] Congressional leaders thus acknowledged that in many instances the government's enforcement team was overmatched by the legal teams retained by major contractors. Faced with this untenable situation, Congress took action by strengthening private enforcement tools to supplement inadequate government resources and specifically sought to increase the number of *qui tam* filings to achieve this goal: "The Committee believes that the amendments in S. 1562 which allow and encourage assistance from the private citizenry can make a significant impact on bolstering the Government's fraud enforcement effort."[28]

9.1.2.5 2009 and 2010 Amendments

In 2009, Congress passed the Fraud Enforcement and Recovery Act of 2009 (FERA),[29] which was designed to address a broad range of issues relating to fraud and fraud enforcement, particularly as it related to the economic stimulus package. FERA amended the False Claims Act (FCA) to reverse a number of restrictive court interpretations and to clarify congressional intent in enacting the 1986 amendments. These amendments clarified that a false claim need not be presented directly to the government, ensuring that the submission of false claims by subcontractors came within the reach of the statute. The amendments also clarified that the government need not prove that a false statement was made for the purpose of getting a false claim paid.

In 2010, the Patient Protection and Affordable Health Care Act amended the FCA to limit the categories that may constitute a public disclosure, to authorize the United States to block dismissal of a case based on a public disclosure and to clarify the term "original source."[30] In 2010, Congress amended the FCA to provide a three-year statute of limitation for actions when an individual alleges that a company took retaliatory action against the individual for whistleblowing.[31]

9.2 Advantages and Disadvantages of the Federal False Claims Act

9.2.1 *Advantages*

False claims acts provide a unique weapon in the consumer attorney's arsenal—not one used every day, but one whose impact can be dramatic for the wrongdoer and extremely important for the public interest. Consider a whistleblower or other individual who comes to an attorney's office with inside information about systematic wrongdoing that involves government funding, but a major class action is impractical because:

- The costs of the action are prohibitive;
- The whistleblower may not stick the case out because individual damages are small;
- An arbitration clause prevents a court action;
- The lack of federal jurisdiction forces an action into state court, which will not be an effective venue in a particular state; or
- The UDAP or fraud statute of limitations has run for all or some affected consumers.

The solution may be to use the federal False Claims Act or a parallel state statute. The whistleblower brings what is called a *qui tam*[32] action for treble the damages suffered by the government and gets to keep up to 30% of the recovery plus attorney fees. This recovery may be enough of an incentive to keep the whistleblower committed to the case.

Similarly, arbitration clauses should not apply because the individual is bringing the case for the government, and no arbitration agreement exists between the government and the wrongdoer.[33] Class action requirements do not apply either, since the plaintiff is the United States and not a class of individuals. In the most successful false claims cases, private counsel and the government combine their resources in a public-private partnership if the government intervenes in the case. While the government taking over the case decreases the whistleblower's percentage recovery somewhat, the chances to prevail in an intervened action are much greater than a non-intervened action.

Claims under the federal False Claims Act are brought in federal court, and supplemental jurisdiction applies to related state law claims, including wrongful termination claims and claims that may be brought under the various state false claims acts.[34] The statute of limitations under the federal Act is six years but can be extended up to ten years when the fraud has not been discovered until later.[35]

9.2.2 *Disadvantages*

There are a number of disadvantages of false claims act cases. The cases are brought on behalf of the government, which means that ultimate control over the case rests with government counsel. Even if the government declines to intervene in the case, government and court approval is required for dismissal or settlement.

Private counsel does not have the ability to conduct pre-filing discovery, and the government is under no obligation to inform private counsel of the status of its investigation. The government also often takes months or even years to make its intervention decision and the cases often take years to resolve.

---

27 S. Rep. No. 99-345, at 7 (1986), *reprinted in* 1986 U.S.C.C.A.N. 5266, 5267.

28 *Id.*

29 Pub. L. No. 111-21, 123 Stat. 1617 (2009).

30 Pub. L. No. 111-148, § 10104(j)(2), 124 Stat. 119 (2010).

31 Dodd-Frank Wall Street Reform and Consumer Protection Act, Pub. L. No 111-203, § 1079(A), 124 Stat. 1376, 2079 (2010).

32 *Qui tam* is the abbreviation of the Latin phrase "*qui tam pro domino rege quam pro si ipso in hac parte sequitur*," which means: "Who sues on behalf of the King as well as for himself." Black's Law Dictionary 1282 (8th ed. 2004).

33 Courts have held that retaliation claims under § 3730(h) may be subject to arbitration. *See generally* Sylvia, The False Claims Act: Fraud Against the Government § 5:32 (2d ed. 2010).

34 31 U.S.C. § 3732(b).

35 31 U.S.C. § 3731(b).

9.3   Elements of an FCA Case

9.3.1   *False Claims Covered by the Statute*

Almost any action that involves fraud in trying to obtain payment of government funds or avoid lawful payment of government funds may impose liability under the Act.[36] The FCA is "intended to reach all types of fraud, without qualification, that might result in financial loss to the Government."[37]

The most common actions are "mischarge" cases in which the government has been overcharged for a service not rendered, or charged more than it should have been. Other types of false claims include the submission of false claims for payment or in contract negotiations, the submission of false statements to create eligibility for federal programs, and the supplying of substandard services or products.[38]

Importantly, the FCA also imposes liability when the contractor has certified explicitly or implicitly that it will comply with federal statutes and laws but fails to do so.[39] The Act excludes claims that a person or company failed to pay federal taxes.[40]

9.3.2   *Standards for Liability*

In order to prevail on an FCA claim, the false claim must be proven by a preponderance of the evidence.[41] The standard for liability under the FCA makes it clear that it is not a fraud statute to which common law fraud principles apply, although the requirements of Federal Rule of Civil Procedure 9(b) to plead with particularity are imposed.[42] Instead, it is a false claim or false statement statute, which imposes liability based upon a *scienter* standard.[43]

Before 1986, some courts had incorrectly interpreted the Act to require intentional acts to find a contractor liable for submission of false claims.[44] In 1986 Congress clarified the standard and imposed liability when the defendant knows the information is false or acts in deliberate ignorance or reckless disregard of its truth or falsity.[45] The intent of these amendments was to impose liability for conduct that was more than merely negligent but less than intentional.[46] Congress wanted to impose liability when "an individual 'buried his head in the sand' and failed to make simple inquiries which would alert him that false claims are being submitted."[47]

9.3.3   *Who May File a False Claims Act Case*

9.3.3.1   Introduction

Most often relators are employees or former employees who have direct knowledge of fraudulent activity and have complained directly or indirectly to their company. Relators may also be outside consultants or even competitors who have discovered fraudulent activity by another company.

9.3.3.2   Persons Excluded from Bringing a False Claims Act Case

The FCA contains few restrictions barring an individual from serving as a relator in a *qui tam* action. A present or former member of the armed forces is, for example, barred from serving as a relator in a suit against another "member of the armed forces."[48] Such an individual may, however, bring suit against government contractors working for the armed forces.[49] Relators also may not bring *qui tam* actions *pro se*. This is, at least in part, to protect the government's underlying claim when a relator acting *pro se* might be "unable effectively to litigate [the claim]."[50]

---

36 *See* John T. Boese, Civil False Claims and *Qui Tam* Actions § 1-4 (2d ed. 2000).

37 United States v. Neifert-White Co., 390 U.S. 228, 232 (1968).

38 31 U.S.C. § 3730(a)(1)–(7).
    Subsection 3730(a)(1)(A) imposes liability when the defendant (1) knowingly (2) presents or causes to be presented for payment or approval or a claim (3) that is false or fraudulent. Subsection 3730(a)(1)(B) imposes liability when the defendant (1) made or used a record or statement (2) the record or statement was false (3) the defendant knew it was false and (4) the record or statement was material to the false or fraudulent claim.

39 *See* United States *ex rel.* Hendow v. Univ. of Phoenix, 461 F.3d 1166 (9th Cir. 2006) (explaining false certification imposes liability when there is a false statement of compliance with government regulation); United States *ex rel.* Main v. Oakland City Univ., 426 F.3d 914 (7th Cir. 2005) (university's false statement on application for eligibility for student loans subjects it to False Claims Act suit, even though students had to make separate applications for loans); McNutt *ex rel.* United States v. Haleyville Medical Supplies, Inc., 423 F.3d 1256 (11th Cir. 2005) (approving False Claims Act suit against medical provider that was ineligible for Medicare reimbursement because of its violation of Anti-Kickback statute); Sylvia, The False Claims Act: Fraud Against the Government § 4:33 (2d ed. 2010).

40 31 U.S.C. § 3729(e).
    There is a separate federal statute that allows whistleblowers to bring actions involving tax fraud. *See* § 9.11, *infra*.

41 31 U.S.C. § 3731(c).

42 *See* Claire M. Sylvia, The False Claims Act: Fraud Against the Government § 5:31 (2d ed. 2010). *See also* United States *ex rel.* Fowler v. Caremark RX, L.L.C., 496 F.3d 730 (7th Cir. 2007); Mitchell v. Beverly Enterprises Inc., 248 Fed. Appx. 73 (11th Cir. 2007); United

States *ex rel.* Atkins v. McInteer, 470 F.3d 1350 (11th Cir. 2006); Bly-Magee v. Lungren, 214 Fed. Appx. 642 (9th Cir. 2006).

43 *See* John T. Boese, Civil False Claims and *Qui Tam* Actions §§ 1-3, 2-5 (2d ed. 2000). *See also* United States *ex rel.* Hefner v. Hackensack Univ. Med. Ctr., 495 F.3d 103 (3d Cir. 2007).

44 *Compare* United States v. Hughes, 585 F.2d 284, 286–288 (7th Cir. 1978) (no specific intent to defraud required to satisfy knowing violation), *with* United States v. Mead, 426 F.2d 118, 122–123 (9th Cir. 1970) (specific intent to defraud required to show knowing violation), *and* United States v. Ekelman & Associates, Inc., 532 F.2d 545, 548 (6th Cir. 1976) (actual knowledge of falsity of claims required).

45 31 U.S.C. § 3729(b).

46 S. Rep. No. 99-345, at 21 (1986), *reprinted in* 1986 U.S.C.C.A.N. 5266, 5286.

47 S. Rep. No. 99-345, at 20, 21 (1986), *reprinted in* 1986 U.S.C.C.A.N. 5266, 5285, 5286.

48 31 U.S.C. §3730(e)(1); United States *ex rel.* Karr v. Castle, 746 F. Supp. 1231, 1248 (D. Del. 1990), *aff'd sub nom.* U.S. v. Carper, 22 F.3d 303 (3d Cir. 1994).

49 United States *ex rel.* LeBlanc v. Raytheon Co., 913 F.2d 17, 20 (1st Cir. 1990).

50 Riley v. St. Luke's Episcopal Hosp., 252 F.3d 749, 763 (5th Cir. 2001).

When an individual has signed a release of claims against the defendant, the court will consider the extent of the release, as well as the public policy interests weighing against a release of the claims, in determining whether the individual may serve as a relator.[51]

9.3.3.3 Relator Must Introduce Non-Public Information or Qualify As an Original Source

The FCA contains provisions barring certain claims that are based on "substantially the same allegations or transactions" as have already been "publicly disclosed." The provisions barring such claims have been significantly amended as recently as 2010.

At this time, the FCA provides that "public disclosure" may occur in a number of venues: in hearings at which the government is a party; in government reports, audits, or investigations; and from the news media.[52] When such public disclosure has already occurred, the court "shall" dismiss an action or claim with two exceptions.[53]

First, and only as of 2010, the government now has the authority to oppose the dismissal of an action or claim based upon previous public disclosure.[54] When the government provides notice of such opposition, the court may not dismiss the case.[55]

Second, despite a public disclosure, an individual may still qualify to be a relator when he or she is an "original source" for the action or claims.[56] Though this "original source" exception is long-standing, the statutory requirements for qualifying as an "original source" have also changed with the 2010 amendments of the Act.[57] When a relator has already voluntarily provided the government with information concerning the false claims, that individual may qualify as an original source despite public disclosure. Similarly, when a relator has knowledge "that is independent of and materially adds to" the publicly disclosed allegations, that relator may qualify as an original source if he or she voluntarily provides the information to the government prior to filing.[58]

9.3.3.4 Relator May Not File Action Based on Same Facts As Pending Case

In addition, the FCA bars an individual from bringing a false claims action "based on the facts underlying" an already pending false claims action.[59] This is often referred to as the "first-to-file" rule. Courts have asserted that this provision is intended to prevent the filing of "parasitic" or "opportunistic" actions based on the same facts as pending actions.[60] The Supreme Court has further clarified that this prohibition only bars the filing of an additional action when the original action is actively pending.[61] When an original action has been dismissed, that action no longer bars the filing of an additional action based on the same facts.

In order to determine whether a subsequent action is "based on the facts underlying the pending action," courts have most often applied an "essential claim" or "material facts" test. There is general agreement that such a test involves a simple comparison of complaints, but no uniform set of criteria apply in such a test.[62] The FCA suggests, and courts agree, that when complaints contain multiple FCA claims each claim will be analyzed separately.[63]

9.4 The FCA's Litigation Procedures

The statute of limitations is six years from the date of the violation, but a tolling provision can extend the period to as long as ten years.[64] To commence an FCA case, the relator files a complaint under seal and serves a copy upon the United States Attorney.[65] Unlike any other civil action, the relator and relator's attorney are acting on behalf of two interests—that of the person filing the complaint and that of the United States.[66]

Courts interpret Federal Rule of Civil Procedure 9(b) to require that the facts in a *qui tam* case be pleaded with particularity, but they differ in their application of this requirement. Some courts require that the relator allege all elements with particularity—that is, specifying the who, what, when, and where of the fraudulent activity, including details as to the specific false claims actually presented to the government

---

51 United States v. Purdue Pharma, L.P., 600 F.3d 319, 329 (4th Cir. 2010); United States *ex rel.* Ritchie v. Lockheed Martin Corp., 558 F.3d 1161, 1168–1169 (10th Cir. 2009); United States ex. rel. Nowak v. Medtronic, Inc., 806 F. Supp. 2d 310, 336 (D. Mass. 2011).

52 31 U.S.C. § 3730(e)(4).

53 31 U.S.C. § 3730(e)(4)(A).

54 31 U.S.C. § 3730(e)(4)(A).

55 United States *ex rel.* Szymoniak v. Am. Home Mortg. Servicing, Inc., 2014 WL 1910845, at *1 (D.S.C. May 12, 2014).

56 31 U.S.C. § 3730(e)(4)(B); United States *ex rel.* Spay v. CVS Caremark Corp., 913 F. Supp. 2d 125 (E.D. Pa. 2012).

57 Many cases discussing the nature of an "original source" were decided prior to this amendment. *See, e.g.,* Rockwell Int'l Corp. v. United States, 549 U.S. 457, 167 L. Ed. 2d 190, 127 S. Ct. 1397 (2007). *See also* United States *ex rel.* Boothe v. Sun Healthcare Grp., Inc., 496 F.3d 1169 (10th Cir. 2007); United States *ex rel.* Fowler v. Caremark RX, L.L.C., 496 F.3d 730 (7th Cir. 2007); United States *ex rel.* Atkinson v. PA Shipbuilding Co., 473 F.3d 506 (3d Cir. 2007); United States *ex rel.* Bly-Magee v. Premo, 470 F.3d 914 (9th Cir. 2006).

58 31 U.S.C. § 3730(e)(4)(B).

59 31 U.S.C. § 3730(b)(5) (providing in full that, "[w]hen a person brings an action under this subsection, no person other than the Government may intervene or bring a related action based on the facts underlying the pending action.").

60 United States *ex rel.* Boise v. Cephalon, Inc., 2014 WL 5038393 (E.D. Pa. Oct. 9, 2014).

61 Kellogg Brown & Root Services, Inc. v. United States *ex rel.* Carter, 135 S. Ct. 1970, 1978–1979 (2015).

62 *See, e.g.,* United States *ex rel.* Kurnik v. PharMerica Corp., 2015 WL 1524402 (D.S.C. Apr. 2, 2015); United States *ex rel.* Moore v. Pennrose Properties, L.L.C., 2015 WL 1358034, at *4 (W.D. Ohio Mar. 24, 2015).

63 31 U.S.C. § 3730(b)(1). *See, e.g.,* United States *ex rel.* Tillson v. Lockheed Martin Energy Systems, Inc., 2004 WL 2403114, at *6 (W.D. Ky. Sept. 30, 2014).

64 31 U.S.C. § 3731(b).

65 31 U.S.C. § 3730(b)(1).

66 31 U.S.C. § 3730(b).

for payment.[67] Other courts assert that relators are unlikely to have specific billing information for every individual false claim and require that the relator only plead "particular details of a scheme . . . paired with reliable indicia that lead to a strong inference that claims were actually submitted."[68]

The complaint, which must be accompanied by a written disclosure of evidence and information possessed by the relator, is then evaluated by government attorneys who decide whether or not to intervene in the case.[69] Although the statute requires the government to make its decision to intervene within sixty days,[70] the government often seeks multiple extensions[71] and may possibly take two or three years or more to decide whether to intervene in the action.

If the government chooses to intervene, the U.S. Attorney's Office will either attempt to settle the action or ask that the complaint be unsealed. When the complaint is unsealed, it is served upon the defendant and the government will have primary responsibility for prosecuting the action.[72] The relator, however, still has a statutory right to participate in the lawsuit, unless the government seeks to limit the relator's involvement by court order.[73] Congress wanted the relator to stay in the case to make sure that the government did not neglect evidence, cause undue delay, or drop the case without legitimate reason.[74]

If the government declines to intervene, the relator may continue the action on his or her own, while continuing to inform the government of the course of the litigation.[75] The government also retains its right to intervene at a later stage in the case. Regardless of whether the government decides to intervene, court approval must be sought for any settlement.[76] While the relator's percentage of the proceeds is greater if the government does not intervene, the vast majority of *qui tam* recoveries have occurred in cases in which the government has intervened.[77]

Venue is proper in the judicial district where any defendant can be found, resides, transacts business, or in which any act alleged as a violation is alleged to have occurred.[78] The Act provides for international service of process[79] and national service of trial and hearing subpoenas.[80]

9.5   FCA Claims Are Not Subject to Arbitration Requirements

The United States Supreme Court has made clear that, as a general rule, the Federal Arbitration Act (FAA) requires that, if the parties agree, any potential claims under either federal or state law may be subject to a forced arbitration agreement.[81] This is true even if the plaintiff's private claims serve a public purpose.[82]

Claims brought under the FCA or state false claims acts, however, present an important exception to this general rule. Claims brought on behalf of the government—whether federal or state government—should not be subject to arbitration agreements between the relator and the defendant.

Courts arriving at this conclusion ground their analysis in at least two different theories. First, claims brought by an employee or consumer under a false claims act are not within the scope of the arbitration agreement because, even at their broadest, such clauses can only cover the relationship between the consumer or employee and the defendant. But false claims act claims have nothing to do with this relationship. As one court has explained:

> Because plaintiff's qui tam action is completely outside the scope of the Agreement, it is not covered by the arbitration clause. The Agreement relates solely to the terms of plaintiff's employment by PCCA. However, plaintiff's qui tam claims in no way impinge on her employee status. Even if plaintiff had never been employed by defendants, assuming other conditions were met, she would still be able to bring a suit against them for presenting false claims to the government.[83]

Second, many courts conclude correctly that *qui tam* claims are not subject to arbitration agreements between the relator and the defendant because the relator does not have the authority to select a forum for these claims: in the *qui tam* context,

---

67   *See, e.g.*, United States *ex rel.* Nathan v. Takeda Pharmaceuticals N. Am., Inc., 707 F.3d 451, 457–458 (4th Cir. 2013).

68   *See, e.g.*, United States *ex rel.* Grubbs v. Kanneganti, 565 F.3d 180, 190 (5th Cir. 2009).

69   31 U.S.C. § 3730(b)(2).

70   *Id.*

71   *See* 31 U.S.C. § 3730(b)(3), (4).

72   31 U.S.C. § 3730(c).

73   31 U.S.C. § 3730(c)(1), (2)(C).

74   S. Rep. No. 99-345, at 26 (1986), *reprinted in* 1986 U.S.C.C.A.N. 5266, 5291.

75   31 U.S.C. § 3730(c)(3).

76   *Id.*

77   *See* TAF Educ. Fund, Taxpayers Against Fraud: Qui Tam Statistics, *available at* www.taf.org.

78   31 U.S.C. § 3732(a).

79   *Id.*

80   *Id.*

81   *See* National Consumer Law Center, Consumer Arbitration Agreements Ch. 4 (7th ed. 2015), *updated at* www.nclc.org/library.

82   *See, e.g.*, Kilgore v. Key Bank Ass'n, 718 F.3d 1052 (9th Cir. 2013) (en banc).

83   Mikes v. Strauss, 889 F. Supp. 746, 754 (S.D.N.Y. 1995). *Cf.* Nguyen v. City of Cleveland, 138 F. Supp. 2d 938, 939 (N.D. Ohio 2001) (addressing FCA retaliation claims and concluding that "the case of a *qui tam* relator is fundamentally different from the case of others seeking to avoid arbitration, because the relator has acted for the public rather than for himself. Therefore, the Court's holding is not an expression of common law judicial hostility towards arbitration that the Arbitration Act was meant to overcome, but rather a recognition of a conflict between the policies of the False Claims Act and the Arbitration Act that does not exist in other contexts." (internal citations omitted)).

    Although there are relatively few cases besides *Mikes* that address the arbitrability of FCA claims in themselves (as distinct from FCA retaliation claims), even those courts concluding that FCA retaliation claims *are* subject to arbitration clauses—and the defendants moving to compel arbitration of such claims—seem to assume that FCA *qui tam* claims, meaning claims brought on behalf of the federal government pursuant to the procedures spelled out in the False Claims Act, are not arbitrable. *See, e.g.*, United States *ex rel.* McBride v. Halliburton Co., 2007 WL 1954441, at *4 (D.D.C. July 5, 2007).

the relator brings claims on behalf of the government, and he or she cannot waive the *government*'s right to a public forum for these claims.[84]

Both of these rationales find support in the Supreme Court's decision in *E.E.O.C. v. Waffle House*, in which the Court held that Waffle House could not compel arbitration of the EEOC's enforcement action to seek victim-specific relief for a particular employee, even though that employee had agreed to arbitrate her employment disputes.[85] Because the EEOC's claims belonged to the EEOC, they were not subject to an arbitration agreement to which the EEOC was not a party.

This analysis is supported by the proposition that the government is not subject to private arbitration agreements, and it is not based on an argument that federal statutory schemes somehow trump or alter the purported "federal policy in favor of arbitration" embodied in the FAA. For this reason, *qui tam* claims brought on behalf of a state are no more likely to be subject to arbitration clauses than *qui tam* claims brought on behalf of the federal government, and state rules invalidating arbitration clauses that purport to require arbitration of *qui tam* claims brought on behalf of the state are not preempted by the FAA.[86]

9.6 Remedies

The FCA provides for the recovery of civil penalties and damages. Civil penalties are adjusted per the Federal Civil Penalties Inflation Adjustment Act of 1990. At this time, such penalties are not less than $5500 and not more than $11,000 per false claim. The magnitude of the civil penalty within that range is within the discretion of the court.[87] It may be based upon the "totality of the circumstances" and include factors such as the seriousness of the misconduct, the scienter of the defendants, and the amount of damages suffered.[88]

Because each false claim qualifies for a separate monetary penalty, parties often debate how to calculate the number of violations committed. In such cases, the relator or government may allege, for example, that penalties are appropriate for each invoice submitted, while a defendant may argue that a single overarching contract constitutes the basis for the claim. Courts make determinations concerning such matters on a case-by-case basis and have focused on what qualifies as the defendant's "causative act" triggering the false claims liability—and how many separate causative acts occurred.[89]

The FCA also provides additional liability for "3 times the amount of damages which the Government sustains because of the act of that person."[90] When the violator cooperates with the government, liability may be reduced to "not less than 2 times the amount of damages[.]"[91] Just as with the civil penalties, parties often debate the proper method for determining damages. Courts have made clear that, given the variety of false claims, there cannot be a single method for calculating damages in a *qui tam* action.[92] Damages, however, must be actual in nature and may be offset by "compensatory payments" that have been made from "any source."[93]

Courts have split on whether only these net damages, or instead gross damages, are subject to trebling. The majority of courts, however, have held that only the government's net (or actual) damages are subject to trebling.[94]

9.7 Incentives Available to the Relator

The relator is entitled to a percentage of the proceeds of the case. As a general matter, if the government intervenes in the case, the minimum award to the relator is 15% (but not more than 25%). In cases in which the action is substantially based on publicly disclosed information, the relator may not receive an award exceeding 10% of the recovery.[95] If the government declines to intervene, the minimum award is 25% (but not more than 30%).[96]

84 Mikes v. Strauss, 889 F. Supp. 746, 755 (S.D.N.Y. 1995) ("[A]s a relator plaintiff stands as a private representative of the government, participating in any recovery to which the government may be entitled. Since the government was not a party to the Agreement, even granting defendants' contention that the arbitration clause encompasses more than employment issues, we are not convinced that plaintiff, suing on the government's behalf, is necessarily bound by its terms."). *See also* Iskanian v. CLS Transp. Los Angeles, L.L.C., 327 P.3d 129, 152–153 (Cal. 2004), *cert. denied*, 135 S. Ct. 1155, 190 L. Ed. 2d 911 (2015) ("In sum, the FAA aims to promote arbitration of claims belonging to the private parties to an arbitration agreement. It does not aim to promote arbitration of claims belonging to a government agency, and that is no less true when such a claim is brought by a statutorily designated proxy for the agency as when the claim is brought by the agency itself.").

85 E.E.O.C. v. Waffle House, Inc., 534 U.S. 279, 296 (2002) ("[When the] EEOC chooses from among the many charges filed each year to bring an enforcement action in a particular case, the agency may be seeking to vindicate a public interest, not simply provide make-whole relief for the employee, even when it pursues entirely victim-specific relief. To hold otherwise would undermine the detailed enforcement scheme created by Congress simply to give greater effect to an agreement between private parties that does not even contemplate the EEOC's statutory function.").

86 Sakkab v. Luxottica Retail N. Am., Inc., 2015 WL 5667912, at *4 (9th Cir. Sept. 28, 2015).

87 *See* United States *ex rel.* Longhi v. Lithium Power Technologies, Inc., 530 F. Supp. 2d 888, 901 (S.D. Texas 2008) (assessing maximum penalties when "fraud was systematic and knowing"), *aff'd*, 575 F.3d 458 (5th Cir. 2009).

88 *See* United States *ex rel.* Purcell v. MWI Corp., 15 F. Supp. 3d 18, 31 (D.C. Cir. 2014).

89 *See* United States v. Bornstein, 423 U.S. 303, 313 (1976) ("[a] correct application of the statutory language requires . . . that the focus in each case be upon the specific conduct of the person from whom the Government seeks to collect the statutory forfeitures"); United States *ex rel.* Longhi v. Lithium Power Technologies, Inc., 530 F. Supp. 2d 888, 901 (S.D. Texas 2008) (finding "four causative acts" and assessing four civil penalty awards), *aff'd*, 575 F.3d 458 (5th Cir. 2009).

90 31 U.S.C. § 3729(a).

91 31 U.S.C. § 3729(a)(2).

92 *See* United States *ex rel.* Humane Soc. of U.S. v. Hallmark Meat Packing Co., 2013 WL 5753784, at *7 (C.D. Cal. Apr. 30, 2013).

93 *See* United States *ex rel.* Purcell v. MWI Corp., 15 F. Supp. 3d 18, 31 (D.C. Cir. 2014).

94 *See* United States v. Anchor Mortg. Corp., 711 F.3d 745, 750–751 (7th Cir. 2013) (collecting cases). *But see also* United States v. Eghbal, 548 F.3d 1281, 1285 (9th Cir. 2008).

95 31 U.S.C. § 3730(d)(1).

96 31 U.S.C. § 3730(d)(2).

In considering the appropriate percentage which a relator should receive, courts have looked to the Senate's discussion of factors to consider in determining an award.[97] Such factors include the significance of the information provided, the relator's contribution to the outcome, and the government's previous knowledge of the fraud.

Courts have also considered the Department of Justice's internal guidelines, which consist of over two dozen non-exhaustive factors, in determining such awards. These factors include the relator's opposition to or involvement in the fraud, the hardships borne by the relator in bringing the action, and the efforts of the relator's counsel. As courts have noted, however, the guidelines are "merely internal standards and not federal regulations."[98] Furthermore, the guidelines do not attempt to establish any single test or coherent theory for determining an award.[99] As such, these factors may provide "common sense" guidance but certainly do not limit the courts' discretion.[100]

A relator may also receive an award against the violator for reasonable expenses incurred in the action as well as "reasonable attorneys' fees and costs."[101]

9.8　Examples of False Claims Act Cases

The fact patterns giving rise to False Claims Act liability are extremely varied. Traditional areas include fraud in marketing and selling drugs, Medicare and Medicaid fraud by health care providers, health care contractors and private insurance companies administering government health insurance programs. Such areas offer tremendous opportunity for a consumer attorney seeking to establish a false claims act practice. However, less traditional areas also exist and may provide a focus for use of the Act:

Banks: A FCA settlement was reached with Gold Bank–Oklahoma for charging excessive interest rates. The bank charged excessive interest rates and fees to individuals on agricultural loans guaranteed by the Farm Service Agency.[102]

Environmental Statutes: The False Claims Act imposes liability when a contractor knowingly fails to satisfy the environmental requirements of a government contract but seeks payment even though it has not complied with the contractual requirements.[103]

Education: A False Claims Act case was settled by the City of San Francisco against Strategic Resource Solutions, a city contractor that was supposed to install energy efficient equipment in San Francisco Schools.[104] The government has also settled cases with school counseling programs whose payments were made in part with Medicaid funds.[105] A university's false statement on its application for eligibility for student loans subjected it to suit under the False Claims Act, even though individual students had to make separate applications for loans.[106] An FCA action was also properly brought when a school certified to the government (to qualify for federal loans and grants) that it did not pay incentive compensations to its "enrollment counselors."[107] This incentive compensation could lead to enrollment of students who were not qualified and could not benefit from the course, harming both the students and the government.

FDCPA: A law firm that acted as a collection agency for the federal government has been sued under the False Claims Act for failing to credit consumers' accounts on the day that payment was received. The firm was collecting student loans on behalf of the Illinois Student Assistance Commission. The failure to credit the accounts resulted in excessive interest payments by the students and an inflated fee earned by the law firm because its fees were based upon a percentage of the amount collected.[108]

There is also an argument that a private collector hired by the government violates the FCA when it violates the federal Fair Debt Collection Practices Act (FDCPA). A condition the government imposes on the private collection agencies it hires is compliance with the FDCPA. Non-compliance with the FDCPA should thus lead to the collectors making false claims for reimbursement from the government for their collection efforts. Disallowance of student loan collection fees results in a sharply reduced student obligations.

Financial Services Industry: The FCA can be used when misconduct in the financial services industry involves federal funds. Cases have been brought involving investment banking firms diverting proceeds from municipal bond transactions that should have gone to the federal government and against accounting firms for preparing false hospital cost reports.[109]

Insurance: When the government agrees to provide insurance and applications for either coverage or benefits are

---

97　*See* United States *ex rel.* Alderson v. Quorum Health Grp., 171 F. Supp. 2d 1323, 1331–1332 (M.D. Fla. 2001).

98　*See* United States *ex rel.* Johnson-Pochardt v. Rapid City Reg'l Hosp., 252 F. Supp. 2d 892, 899–900 (D.S.D. 2003); United States *ex rel.* Alderson v. Quorum Health Grp., 171 F. Supp. 2d 1323, 1333 (M.D. Fla. 2001).

99　*See* United States *ex rel.* Johnson-Pochardt v. Rapid City Reg'l Hosp., 252 F. Supp. 2d 892, 899–900 (D.S.D. 2003); United States *ex rel.* Alderson v. Quorum Health Grp., F. Supp. 2d 1323, 1331–1332 (M.D. Fla. 2001).

100　*See* United States *ex rel.* Alderson v. Quorum Health Grp., 171 F. Supp. 2d 1323, 1333 (M.D. Fla. 2001).

101　31 U.S.C. § 3730(d)(1), (2).

102　*See* Gold Banc Reaches Agreement in Principle to Settle Qui Tam Lawsuit, Bus. Wire, Aug. 9, 2004. *See generally* D. Jean Veta & Jennifer Xi, *Government Loan Programs Spawn New Liability: False Claims Act Prosecutions*, www.bloomberglaw.com (2012), *available at* http://about.bloomberglaw.com.

103　*See, e.g.,* United States *ex rel.* Made in the USA Found. v. Billington, 985 F. Supp. 604 (D. Md. 1997). *See generally* Claire Sylvia, The False Claims Act: Fraud Against the Government § 2:16 (2d ed. 2013).

104　Bay City News, June 30, 2004.

105　N.J. Express Times, May 7, 2004.

106　United States *ex rel.* Main v. Oakland City Univ., 426 F.3d 914 (7th Cir. 2005).

107　United States *ex rel.* Hendow v. University of Phoenix, 461 F.3d 1166 (9th Cir. 2006). *See also* Ab-Tech Constr., Inc. v. United States, 31 Fed. Cl. 429, 432–433 (1994).

108　8 Consumer Fin. Servs. Law Report, No. 1 (June 2, 2004).

109　Sylvia, The False Claims Act: Fraud Against the Government § 2:17 (2d ed. 2010).

fraudulent, a False Claims Act claim may be brought. For example, the Third Circuit has held that a lender's claim for mortgage insurance benefits is a false claim, when the lender fraudulently induced the government to issue the insurance policy.[110] Another example is a settlement against Bankers Insurance Company, when Bankers, authorized to collect flood insurance premiums for deposit into the U.S. Treasury's national flood insurance fund and to use federal money to pay flood insurance claims, submitted monthly statements that failed to report $1.1 million in interest due the government.[111]

Loan Applications: A false application for a government loan is a false claim.[112] For example, if there are false representations made to obtain a government loan, the False Claims Act may impose liability.[113]

New Vehicles Not as Represented: The federal government is a major purchaser of new automobiles. When a vehicle does not include equipment as specified, the manufacturer's collection of payment for the vehicle is a false claim. The resulting settlement or a follow-up case is likely to obtain similar relief for consumer purchasers of similar vehicles.

Nursing Home and Other Medicare-Related Charges: A classic use of the False Claims Act involves Medicare and Medicaid fraud, so it is well-suited to investigations of, and challenges to, charges made at nursing homes and related institutions.[114] These can include false billing, overbilling, "upcoding," billing for unnecessary services, and various schemes involving improper referrals.

Overbilling of GSA: The False Claims Act has been used to reach numerous settlements with defendants improperly overbilling the General Services Administration (GSA), which supports and manages basic services for other federal agencies. Cases have included overcharges for software licensing[115] and overbilling for long-distance communications charges.[116]

Pharmaceutical and Medical Device Charges: Relators have brought numerous actions against companies engaged in "off-label" marketing of drugs, price fraud (when companies are statutorily required to offer certain prices to the government), and the marketing of defective medical devices at standard prices.

Purchases under Government Benefit Programs: When a government program limits charges that providers can assess (such as not marking up goods or services higher than their normal retail price), overcharges can be recovered under the False Claims Act, and these amounts should be refunded to those who were forced to purchase overly expensive goods with their benefits. Similarly, when the government buys manufactured homes for disaster victims, defects in those homes should be actionable under the false claims statute.

Underpayment of Government Royalties: Relators have brought numerous actions in cases in which the defendants underpaid royalties to the government based on profits earned from land leased from federal land.[117]

9.9 The FCA's Whistleblower Protection

9.9.1 General

The FCA prohibits discriminatory or retaliatory acts against an employee who takes actions in furtherance of an FCA case.[118] The federal FCA and most state false claims acts provide protection to *qui tam* relators who are discharged, demoted, suspended, threatened, harassed, or in any other manner discriminated against in the terms and conditions of their employment as a result of their furtherance of an action under the false claims act.[119]

Remedies include reinstatement with comparable seniority as the *qui tam* relator would have had but for the discrimination, two times the amount of any back pay, interest on any back pay, and compensation for any special damages sustained as a result of the discrimination, including litigation costs and reasonable attorney fees. Causes of action may also be available under state whistleblower statutes and state common law retaliation claims.

FCA whistleblower retaliation claims as well as similar state law claims are brought by the individual for the individual. Relator's counsel should ensure that the relator understands that a matter may involve two separate claims—a claim brought on behalf of the government because of a false claim to the government (over which the relator may have limited authority) and the individual's own retaliation claims, which are solely the relator's.

Because FCA complaints must be filed under seal, often discovery and other information relating to the whistleblower's claim must await the outcome of the government's investigation of the FCA claim. This is not necessarily a bad strategy, since a strong FCA case may bolster a less strong retaliation claim.

However, there are a number of pitfalls inherent in this dual representation. For example, an employee who is covered by a collective bargaining agreement may be required to submit a

---

110   United States v. Venziale, 268 F.2d 504 (3d Cir. 1959).

111   The Daily Record (Baltimore, MD) July 2, 2004.

112   United States v. Neifer-White Co., 390 U.S. 228 (1968). *See also* United States *ex rel.* Hunt v. Citigroup Inc. et al., No. 11-05473 (S.D.N.Y.) (Citigroup $158 million settlement of false HUD loan certification).

113   United States *ex rel.* Main v. Oakland City Univ., 426 F.3d 914 (7th Cir. 2005); United States v. Entin, 750 F. Supp. 512 (S.D. Fla. 1990).

114   *See* United States *ex rel.* Frazier v. IASIS Healthcare Corp., 812 F. Supp. 2d 1008, 1014 (D. Ariz. 1998).

115   Press Release, U.S. Dep't of Justice, Government Files Complaint Against CA Inc. for False Claims on GSA Contract (May 29, 2014), *available at* www.justice.org. *See also* United States *ex rel.* Smith v. VMWARE, INC. et al., No. 10-cv-00769 (E.D. Va. 2010).

116   L.A. Times, May 5, 2004. *See also* United States *ex rel.* Shea v. Verizon Communications, Inc., 844 F. Supp. 2d 78, 80 (D.D.C. 2012).

117   *See* Press Release, U.S. Dep't of Justice, Chevron to Pay U.S. More Than $45 Million to Resolve Allegations of False Claims for Royalties Underpayment (Dec. 23, 2009), *available at* www.justice.org.

118   31 U.S.C. § 3730(h). *See generally* McKnight, Lugbill & Grande, Cause of Action by Employee for Retaliation and Reprisal Pursuant to the False Claims Act 31 U.S.C. § 3730(h), 22 Causes of Action 2d 217 (2008).

119   31 U.S.C. § 3730(h).

pre-filing administrative claim before having a statutory cause of action. However, submission of the administrative pre-filing requirement would be a violation of the sealed *qui tam* complaint. As such, it is simply not clear how a *qui tam* relator can or should properly proceed to bring an action in certain circumstances.

9.9.2 Arbitration Requirements and Whistleblower Retaliation Claims

While the false claims act claim itself is not subject to an arbitration requirement,[120] the majority of courts now conclude that the federal False Claims Act's protections against retaliation for whistleblowers are subject to arbitration agreements.[121] Whereas *qui tam* claims belong to the government, retaliation claims—though perhaps part of a statutory scheme that supports false claims acts—run to the benefit of the whistleblower.

This analysis is further bolstered by the Dodd-Frank Act's prohibition on the arbitration of certain retaliation claims brought by whistleblowers under federal securities laws.[122] Some courts have concluded that the decision by Congress not to similarly carve out False Claims Act retaliation supports the proposition that those retaliation claims are subject to the FAA's general mandates.[123] Of course, although retaliation claims are subject to an arbitration requirement, there are still a number of challenges to an arbitration requirement, depending on the requirement itself and the facts of the case, as discussed in another NCLC treatise.[124]

9.10 State False Claims Acts

9.10.1 Relation of State and Federal False Claims Acts

Over half of all states, as well as the District of Columbia, have enacted false claims acts. The reach of these statutes, however, varies widely and may also differ greatly from the federal False Claims Act. Thus claims based upon differing state false claims acts, even when brought upon the same theory of fraud, may achieve diametrically different outcomes.[125]

One clear difference between the federal and state statutes is that the federal statute deals with false claims submitted to the federal government while the state acts apply to false claims submitted to the state government. Additionally, it is the federal government that decides whether to intervene in an FCA claim, as it is the state government's decision whether to intervene in the case under a state false claims act. And of course the federal claim is brought in federal court, and the state claim is brought in state court.

The FCA does, however, allows for supplemental jurisdiction over related state law claims, including claims that may be brought under the various state false claims acts, as well as wrongful termination claims.[126] As such, when both a state and the federal government have received false claims, the relator may file a consolidated case involving both claims in federal court.[127]

The statutes, along with their most important provisions, are summarized in Appendix G, *infra*. Because the state statutes continue to evolve—especially in response to federal acts in 2009 and 2010—practitioners are advised to consult each state's laws directly. As recently as May 2015, Vermont signed into effect its own false claims act.[128] In contrast, only two months later in July 2015, Wisconsin repealed its act in its entirety.[129]

9.10.2 Who May File a State False Claims Act Case

The majority of state false claims acts allow—as does the federal False Claims Act—private individuals to bring an action as a relator. Certain states, however, have enacted false claims acts that entirely lack such *qui tam* provisions.[130] That is, though the state itself may bring suits based upon false claims, the private individual is not empowered to bring suit on behalf of the state. In such states, the false claim act may provide for whistleblower rewards, but in most cases it does not.[131]

Furthermore, several states limit those cases in which state employees may act as relators. In some states, this limitation applies only to current employees who have disregarded internal reporting procedures, while in other states

---

120   *See* § 9.5, *supra*.

121   *See, e.g.,* Stirrup v. Educ. Mgmt., L.L.C., 2014 WL 4655438, at *11 (D. Ariz. Sept. 17, 2014); James v. Conceptus, Inc., 851 F. Supp. 2d 1020, 1038 (S.D. Tex. 2012). *But see* Nguyen v. City of Cleveland, 121 F. Supp. 2d 643, 647 (N.D. Ohio 2000) ("Thus while this Court does not find that the plain text of the whistleblower statute or the legislative history clearly demonstrate Congress's intention to except whistleblower retaliation claims from the Arbitration Act, it does find that a conflict exists between arbitration and the underlying purposes of the FCA.").

122   Pub. L. No. 111–203, 124 Stat. 1376, 1746, 1848, *codified as amended at* 7 U.S.C. § 26(n) and 18 U.S.C. § 1514A(e)) (amending Sarbanes-Oxley Act and Commodities Exchange Act).

123   James v. Conceptus, Inc., 851 F. Supp. 2d 1020, 1038 (S.D. Tex. 2012).

124   *See* National Consumer Law Center, Consumer Arbitration Agreements (7th ed. 2015), *updated at* www.nclc.org/library.

125   *See, e.g.,* United States *ex rel.* Notorfransesco v. Surgical Monitoring Assoc., 2014 U.S. Dist. LEXIS 122402, at *2 (E.D. Pa. Sept. 2, 2014).

126   31 U.S.C. § 3732(b).

127   *See, e.g.,* United States *ex rel.* Anthony v. Burke Eng'g Co., 356 F. Supp. 2d 1119, 1120 (C.D. Cal. 2005).

128   False Claims Act, H.B. 120, 2014 Gen. Assemb., Reg. Sess. (Vt. 2015).

129   Wis. Stat. §§ 20.931 *et seq., repealed* July 12, 2015.

130   States with false claims acts lacking *qui tam* provisions or whistleblower rewards include Kansas (Kan. Stat. Ann. §§ 75-7501 *et seq.*), Mississippi (Miss. Code Ann. §§ 43-13-213 *et seq.*), Nebraska (Neb. Rev. Stat. §§ 68-936 *et seq.*), Oregon (Or. Rev. Stat. §§ 180.750 *et seq.*), and Utah (Utah Code Ann. §§ 26-20-1 *et seq.*).
      Under Arkansas law (Ark. Code Ann. §§ 20-77-901 *et seq.*) and Missouri law (Mo. Rev. Stat. §§ 191.900 *et seq.*), a whistleblower may not file suit but may receive a reward for providing information.

131   Under Arkansas law (Ark. Code Ann. §§ 20-77-901 *et seq.*) and Missouri law (Mo. Rev. Stat. §§ 191.900 *et seq.*), a whistleblower may not file suit but may receive a reward for providing information.

it is a blanket exclusion extended to current and former employees.[132]

Because of these and other limitations placed upon those individuals who may act as a relator, a practitioner should consult both Appendix G, *infra*, concerning individual state laws and the laws themselves before assuming a client may bring a suit as a relator.

9.10.3 Claims Covered and Exemptions Provided

State false claims acts with *qui tam* provisions often closely mimic the federal statute, allowing actions that target any type of fraud upon the state.[133] In certain cases, state acts expand upon the federal act and allow relators to bring additional claims—for example, based upon tax violations.[134] This is, however, the exception. More often, state acts introduce greater limitations upon potential claims than does the federal act.

Most dramatically, in a substantial minority of states, in response to specific incentives provided by the federal government, state legislatures have enacted false claims acts that provide only for the prosecution of Medicaid fraud or fraud upon other state health care funds.[135]

State false claims acts also differ from the federal False Claims Act insofar as some allow actions brought on behalf of any of the state "governmental entities" or "political subdivisions."[136] Other states have no such provision.[137] In a relatively few cases, a political subdivision—such as a county or city—may itself have enacted a false claims act.[138]

9.10.4 State Procedural Requirements

The majority of state acts closely mimic the procedural requirements of the federal False Claims Act. Relators, for example, must file suit under seal. The suit remains under seal for a period of time—ranging most often from sixty to 120 days[139]—by which time the government must determine whether it will intervene in the matter. As in the federal False Claims Act, in most states, even should the state decline to intervene, the relator may continue to pursue the action. However, in a small minority of states, should the state choose to not intervene, the action is ended.[140]

Similarly, under most state laws, should the relator not file suit within a set period of time, the defendant may plead the statute of limitations as a defense. Most often, states have followed the federal example and included a limitation of six years after the date the violation has occurred when parties had knowledge of the violation or a limitation of three years from the discovery of the right of action (so long as the tolled period does not exceed ten years from the date the violation was committed). Certain states, however, have adopted other limitation periods—both shorter and longer than in the federal act—while others do not specify any time limitation.[141]

9.10.5 Other Considerations

Other considerations for practitioners—such as the elements of proof required to establish a claim, anti-retaliation provisions, as well as provisions governing relator awards and attorney fees—are summarized in Appendix G, *infra*. Appendix G is not intended to summarize all pertinent provisions but instead provides the practitioner with a quick reference guide to some of the most important provisions in the various state false claims acts. Especially given the relative rapidity with which the state acts continue to evolve, any practitioner intending to bring a state claim must consult the laws of that state directly.

---

132 *See, e.g.,* D.C. Code § 2-381.03(c)(4); Fla. Stat. §§68.087(4), (5); Ga. Code Ann. §23-3-122(i); Mass. Gen. Laws, ch. 12, §5G(4).

133 States with false claims acts that enable *qui tam* actions on the basis of fraud generally include California (Cal. Gov't Code §§12650 *et seq.* (West)); Delaware (Del. Code Ann. tit. 6, §§1201 *et seq.*); District of Columbia (D.C. Code §§2-381.01 *et seq.*); Florida (Fla. Stat. §§ 68.081 *et seq.*); Hawaii (Haw. Rev. Stat. §§ 661-21 *et seq.*); Illinois (740 Ill. Comp. Stat. Ann. §§ 175/1 *et seq.*); Indiana (Ind. Code §§ 5-11-5.5 *et seq.*); Iowa (Iowa Code §§ 685.1 *et seq.*); Massachusetts (Mass. Gen. Laws ch. 12, §§ 5 *et seq.*); Minnesota (Minn. Stat. §§ 15C.01 *et seq.*); Montana (Mont. Code Ann §§ 17-8-401 *et seq.*); Nevada (Nev. Rev. Stat. §§ 357.010 *et seq.*); New Jersey (N.J. Stat. Ann. §§ 2A:32C-1 *et seq.* (West)); New Mexico (N.M. Stat. Ann. §§ 44-9-1 *et seq.*); New York (N.Y. State Fin. Law §§ 188 *et seq.* (McKinney)); North Carolina (N.C. Gen. Stat. §§ 1-605 *et seq.*); Rhode Island (R.I. Gen. Laws §§ 9-1.1-1 *et seq.*); Tennessee (Tenn. Code Ann. §§ 4-18-101 *et seq.*); and Virginia (Va. Code Ann. §§ 8.01-216.1 *et seq.*).

134 *See, e.g.,* N.Y. State Fin. Law § 189(4)(a) (McKinney).

135 The Deficit Reduction Act of 2005 incentivized the implementation of many such acts by allowing states to recover additional percentages of the damages recovered in Medicaid false claims act cases. States that limit *qui tam* actions to healthcare-related false claims include Colorado (Colo. Rev. Stat. §§ 25.4-4-303.4 *et seq.*); Connecticut (Conn. Gen. Stat. §§ 17b-301a-17b-301p); Georgia (Ga. Code. Ann. § 49-4-168 *et seq.*); Louisiana (La. Rev. Stat. Ann. §§ 6:438.1 *et seq.*); Maryland (Md. Code Ann. Health-Gen. §§ 2-601 *et seq.* (West)); Michigan (Mich. Comp. Laws Serv. §§ 400.601 *et seq.*); New Hampshire (N.H. Rev. Stat. Ann. §§ 167:61-b *et seq.*); Oklahoma (Okla. Stat. tit. 63, §§ 5053 *et seq.*); Texas (Tex. Hum. Res. Code Ann. §§ 36.001 *et seq.* (West)); and Washington (Wash. Rev. Code § 74.66.005 *et seq.*).

New Mexico (N.M. Stat. Ann. §§ 27-14-1 *et seq.*) and Tennessee (Tenn. Code Ann. §§ 71-5-181 *et seq.*) also have false claims acts specific to Medicaid, but those states also have separate general false claims acts.

136 *See, e.g.,* Mass. Gen. Laws ch. 12, §§ 5 *et seq.* (providing for actions on behalf of "political subdivisions"); Mont. Code Ann. §§ 17-8-401 *et seq.* (providing for actions on behalf of any governmental entity).

137 *See, e.g.,* Ind. Code §§ 5-11-5.5 *et seq.*

138 Such municipalities include Alleghany County, Pennsylvania, Broward County, Florida, and Miami-Dade County, Florida, as well as the cities of Chicago, New York, and Philadelphia.

139 *But see* Tex. Hum. Res. Code Ann. §§ 36.102 (West) (mandating false claims act complaint be kept under seal for 180-day period).

140 *See, e.g.,* Md. Code Ann., Gen. Provisions, §§ 2-601 to 2-604 (West).

141 *See, e.g.,* N.M. Stat. Ann. §§ 44-9-12 (noting that a "civil action pursuant to the Fraud Against Taxpayers Act may be brought at any time."); Wash. Rev. Code § 74.66.100(2) (noting a civil action may be brought "at any time, without limitation" after the violation is committed).

9.11 Other Statutes That Give Rewards to Whistleblowers

In the last several years, Congress has enacted several federal statutes that broaden the areas within which whistleblowers may receive incentives for reporting fraud. The Internal Revenue Code was amended in 2006 to allow whistleblowers to file complaints involving major tax fraud and tax underpayment.[142] There are a number of restrictions, the most notable of which is that the statute applies only if there is an underpayment in excess of $2 million. Like the FCA, any person may be a whistleblower. Whistleblowers need not file a lawsuit to recover a reward and may fill in IRS Form 211, *Application for Reward for Original Information*.[143]

Like the FCA, this statute offers an award of at least 15% or up to 30% of the monetary damages awarded on success of the suit. Unlike the FCA, if the contributions of the relator are not considered significant enough, a diminished award of less than 10% may be awarded. Unsurprisingly, any award that is submitted under this statute may be revoked if the Whistleblower Office of the IRS determines that the relator planned or initiated the actions that lead to a violation of the statute. While the FCA's whistleblower award has fewer restrictions attached, it is arguably much easier to be a relator under this statute, able to simply fill out a form instead of bringing suit.

Another relatively new statute is the Sarbanes-Oxley Act of 2002. The Act protects employees who provide information regarding conduct that violates the rules of the SEC. This protection includes discharge, demotion, and harassment and also rewards whistleblowers with compensation for any time or costs incurred during the action. This award is more compensatory than incentivizing though, which may have contributed to the construction of the later created 15 U.S.C. § 78u-6.

Like the amendment to the Internal Revenue Code, this statute has some severe limitations on its applicability. The Sarbanes-Oxley Act whistleblower protection provision applies only to publicly traded companies. Additionally, the monetary award is only awarded if the disputed amount exceeds $2 million. This makes the award not nearly as strong of an incentive under this statute as the award offered under the FCA.

Shortly after the Sarbanes-Oxley Act was instituted, a statute was enacted that authorized awards to whistleblowers who submitted information to the Securities and Exchange Commission that resulted in monetary sanctions.[144] The SEC must pay awards to whistleblowers who voluntarily provide original information to the SEC that leads to the successful enforcement of actions relating to a violation of the federal securities laws resulting in monetary sanctions exceeding $1,000,000.[145]

The awards range from at least 10% to a maximum of 30% of the monetary sanctions collected in the case. Awards are paid from the SEC Investor Protection Fund. This fund is supplied by the monetary sanctions won from cases brought forth by whistleblowers. The new statute also prohibits retaliation by employers against individuals who provide the SEC with information about possible securities law violations.[146] It does not permit a private individual to file a *qui tam* lawsuit, however.

A similar statute was enacted to create a procedure for whistleblowers to report to the Commodities Futures Trading Commission any illegal trading in commodities, such as oil, minerals, and agricultural products.[147] Like the previous statute, awards are paid from a fund specifically set aside to award whistleblowers who voluntarily provide information regarding violations of the CEA. By setting aside a fund and making awards available for whistleblowers, the CFTC encourages whistleblowers to come forth.

9.12 False Claims Act Checklist

Because of the procedural and substantive differences in the FCA, it is extremely important that any attorney considering filing an FCA case associate or at the least consult with an experienced practitioner in this area. However, the following checklist should provide some guidance in assessing whether a potential False Claims Act cause of action is possible:

(1) Is there government funding involved?
(2) Does the false or fraudulent action involve a claim for payment or involve a certification of compliance with governmental statutes?
(3) Is the conduct of the contract knowing or in reckless disregard (as opposed to merely negligent)?
(4) Has the government suffered actual or potential loss as a result of the false or fraudulent action?
(5) Is the problem systemic or systematic in nature?

If the answers to these five questions are "yes," then the procedural aspects of the statute must be analyzed:

(1) Has there been a public disclosure of the basis of the fraudulent activity?
(2) If there has been a public disclosure, is the relator the original source of the publicly disclosed information?
(3) What documentation does the relator have to support the claim?
(4) Are there sufficient facts to plead the fraud with particularity as required under Federal Rule of Civil Procedure 9(b)?
(5) What is the proper venue for the case?
(6) Is it a case in which the government is likely to intervene?
(7) Are there other individual claims that the relator has (wrongful termination, retaliation)?

---

142 *See* 26 U.S.C. § 7623.
143 *Available at* www.irs.gov.
144 15 U.S.C. § 78u-6. Regulations implementing the whistleblower protection provisions are at 17 C.F.R. pts. 240, 241.
145 15 U.S.C. § 78u-6.

146 15 U.S.C. § 78u-6(h).
147 7 U.S.C. § 26.

Chapter 10   Regulation of Debt Relief Services

10.1   Introduction

This chapter deals with entities that solicit consumers burdened with *unsecured* debt and promise them a path to relief. The range of scams involving debt relief seems to have no limit other than the scammers' creativity. There have been scams claiming to help consumers get relief from home mortgage, credit card, auto loan, payday loan, student loan, and many other kinds of debts. Some of those topics are more thoroughly discussed in other NCLC publications:

- Mortgage-related scams are discussed in *Foreclosure and Mortgage Servicing*.[1]
- The type of credit counseling required for those seeking to file a bankruptcy proceeding or to emerge from bankruptcy is discussed in *Consumer Bankruptcy Law and Practice*.
- Student loans and scams targeting borrowers are discussed in *Student Loan Law*.[2] But the laws addressed in this chapter are also likely to cover student-loans-related scams because they are unsecured debt.
- Debt relief scams involving automobile subleases in which a broker offers to get the consumer out from under an unaffordable car loan or lease by leasing the vehicle to another consumer, are examined in *Automobile Fraud*.[3]
- Credit repair services are extensively regulated by the federal Credit Repair Organizations Act (CROA), by state credit repair statutes, and by the FTC Telemarketing Sales Rule. Chapter 5, *supra*, examines the credit repair provisions of the Telemarketing Sales Rule. Section 10.4.2, *infra*, analyzes the CROA's application to debt relief services. But NCLC's most detailed description of credit repair law is found in *Fair Credit Reporting*.[4]

This chapter focuses on services offering relief from unsecured debt. In particular, this chapter discusses credit counselors offering debt management plans, debt settlement companies, debt negotiation companies, and debt elimination companies. These scams also frequently involve criminal misconduct, which is not discussed in this chapter.[5]

10.2   Debt Management, Settlement, Negotiation, and Elimination Services Distinguished

10.2.1   Credit Counselors and Debt Management Plans

10.2.1.1   General

Credit counselors may offer advice and help develop a budget for the consumer but, in most cases, credit counselors feature helping consumers set up a debt management plan (DMP). Through a DMP, a consumer sends a lump sum to the credit counseling agency, usually on a monthly basis. The agency then distributes that payment to the consumer's various unsecured creditors, again usually on a monthly basis.

Creditor attitudes toward DMPs have varied over time and by creditor. DMPs rarely involve principal reductions, but creditors may be more amenable to alter interest rates and other charges in a DMP. In 2009, the nation's top ten credit card issuers agreed to provide additional relief to struggling consumers,[6] but it is unclear how significant these changes are since they retain the basic DMP model of paying the entire debt over time.

The credit counseling industry first began with a number of largely legitimate nonprofit providers that performed useful functions, including consumer financial education, counseling, and setting up DMPs. Most of these counseling agencies were members of the National Foundation for Credit Counseling (NFCC). The individual agencies and even the NFCC itself often relied on creditor funding, through a system known as "fair share" in which creditors returned a portion of DMP payments to the individual agencies that set up the plans.

Creditors have begun to move away from this model, in part because of a 2006 revision to the Internal Revenue Code that caps the aggregate revenues a nonprofit credit counseling agency may receive from creditor payments attributable to DMPs.[7] But the IRS ruling was only one factor, because now these agencies receive less than 10% of their revenue from fair share payments,[8] far less than the required IRS cap of 50%.[9]

In addition, IRS regulations limit the percentage of total revenue that is both from consumers' creditors and attributable to debt management plan services. For credit counseling organizations already in existence, the percentage starts at

---

1   National Consumer Law Center, Foreclosures and Mortgage Servicing Ch. 18 (5th ed. 2014), *updated at* www.nclc.org/library.

2   National Consumer Law Center, Student Loan Law (5th ed. 2015), *updated at* www.nclc.org/library (in particular see § 1.12.4, which discusses debt relief scams focused on student loan borrowers).

3   National Consumer Law Center, Automobile Fraud § 4.8 (5th ed. 2015), *updated at* www.nclc.org/library.

4   National Consumer Law Center, Fair Credit Reporting Ch. 15 (8th ed. 2013), *updated at* www.nclc.org/library.

5   *See, e.g.*, United States v. Ventura-Oliver, 2014 WL 2712294 (D. Haw. June 13, 2014), *appeal dismissed* (May 8, 2015) (preliminary forfeiture order after conviction based on debt elimination scheme); Christine Dempsey, Guilty Verdict in Federal Fraud Trial, The Hartford Courant, June 25, 2013, *available at* www.courant.com (conviction for mail

fraud and fictitious obligations for scam involving sale of fake bonds sold to pay off consumer debts).

6   Press Release, Nat'l Found. for Credit Counseling, Top Credit Card Issuers Support the NFCC's "Call to Action" for Consumer Repayment Relief (Apr. 15, 2009).

7   26 U.S.C. § 501(q).

8   75 Fed. Reg. 48,458, 48,460 (Aug. 10, 2010).

9   *See* 26 U.S.C. § 501(q).

80% and gradually decreases after three years to 50%. The 50% limit applies to new credit counseling organizations.

Credit counseling agencies, however, continue to receive significant creditor contributions. Some creditors have simply changed to a grant format, awarding funding to agencies based on various criteria that are not tied to individual DMP accounts. Of course, the major new source of revenue for credit counseling agencies is payments from the consumers themselves. This change occurred about the same time as a dramatic growth in the credit counseling industry.[10]

During the 1990s, the credit counseling industry grew rapidly, from about 200 agencies to more than a 1000 by 2002; as of 2011, the NFCC reported that more than three million people received counseling and educational services just from NFCC member agencies.[11]

Initially, most credit counseling agencies were affiliated with NFCC, but the NFCC began to lose market share over time to more aggressive agencies. As the industry grew, predatory practices also become more prevalent.[12] Newcomers to the industry, including both agencies that were literally new to the field and older agencies that adopted the business strategies of the newer players, generally offer services by phone or Internet only and are more likely to steer consumers into DMPs, to sell their services aggressively, and to charge high fees.

A credit counseling agency's nonprofit status is also no guarantee against such predatory practices. The founder of one credit counseling nonprofit also owned part of numerous for-profit businesses involved in payday lending.[13] In recent years, many consumers have been victimized by organizations that purport to be nonprofit credit counseling agencies but in fact funnel consumer payments to affiliated for-profit corporations.[14] One common scheme is to have a nonprofit organization act as a front for a group of related for-profit organizations. The nonprofit solicits and enrolls consumers in DMPs but contract out the operation of the plans and many other functions to the related for-profits, funneling most of its revenue to them.[15]

Membership in the NFCC also is not a guarantee of quality services. Even credit counseling organizations that operate on the more traditional nonprofit model may give consumers one-sided information or steer them into inappropriate debt management plans.

10.2.1.2 The Requirement of Credit Counseling Before Filing Bankruptcy

One area of credit counseling that has exploded, in terms of the number of consumers served, is the credit counseling required by the United States Bankruptcy Code for consumers entering and leaving a bankruptcy proceeding. Consumers must obtain counseling from an approved credit counseling agency no more than six months before filing bankruptcy[16] and then undergo a second counseling session, termed a "personal financial management" course, prior to obtaining a discharge in a bankruptcy case.[17] Most of this counseling is by phone or over the Internet.

There is much less room for abuse in credit counseling required through the bankruptcy process—the main concern is whether the requirements prevent consumers from exercising needed bankruptcy rights. As such, this chapter will not focus on this form of credit counseling. For more on bankruptcy-related credit counseling, see NCLC's *Consumer Bankruptcy Law and Practice*.[18]

The reasons why there is much less room for abuse are clear—there is little room for out-of-pocket injury to consumers from either type of bankruptcy-related credit counseling. In order to conduct either type of counseling, an agency must be approved by the Executive Office of the U.S. Trustee (EOUST), and the list of approved agencies is available on the EOUST website.[19]

The Bankruptcy Code states that counseling agencies can only charge a reasonable fee and provide services without regard to the consumer's ability to pay the fee.[20] Studies to

---

10 *See, e.g.*, King v. Capital One Bank (USA), N.A., 2012 WL 5570624 (W.D. Va. Nov. 15, 2012) (allegations that creditors contributions to nonprofit credit counseling agency compromised agency's independence).

11 Nat'l Found. for Credit Counseling, On-Line Press Kit Fact Sheet (2011), *available at* www.nfcc.org.

12 The U.S. Senate Permanent Committee on Investigations held a series of hearings in 2005 on abuses in the industry. *See* U.S. Senate Permanent Subcomm. on Investigations, Comm. on Homeland Sec. Governmental Affairs, Profiteering in a Non-Profit Industry: Abusive Practices in Credit Counseling, S. Rep. No. 109-55 (Apr. 13, 2005), *available at* http://frwebgate.access.gpo.gov. *See generally* National Consumer Law Center & Consumer Fed'n of Am., Credit Counseling in Crisis (Apr. 2003), *available at* www.nclc.org.

13 Jason Zweig and Rachel Louise Ensign, Credit Counselor Has Ties to High-Interest Lenders, Wall St. J., Jan. 12, 2015, *available at* www.wsj .com. Note that, interestingly, the name of the credit counseling agency discussed in this article is Consolidated Credit Counseling Services, which has an acronym (CCCS) that is easily confused with the more widely known non-profit Consumer Credit Counseling Services.

14 *See* National Consumer Law Center & Consumer Fed'n of Am., Credit Counseling in Crisis (Apr. 2003), *available at* www.nclc.org.

15 *See, e.g.*, Zimmerman v. Cambridge Credit Counseling Corp., 529 F. Supp. 2d 254 (D. Mass. 2008) (describing scheme and rejecting

argument that company was exempt from CROA because of IRS tax exemption), *aff'd sub nom.* Zimmerman v. Puccio, 613 F.3d 60 (1st Cir. 2010); Federal Trade Comm'n v. Integrated Credit Solutions, Inc., No. 8:06-CV-00806-SCB-TGW (M.D. Fla. May 3, 2006), *available at* www.ftc.gov (complaint and stipulated judgments filed) (describing purported nonprofit organization's participation as part of for-profit enterprise with related for-profit companies); Federal Trade Comm'n v. Debt Mgmt. Found. Services, No. 8:04-CIV-1674-T-17-MSS (M.D. Fla. July 29, 2004) (complaint filed), *available at* www.ftc.gov (describing use of nonprofit as front to funnel revenue to related for-profit companies).

16 11 U.S.C. §§ 109(h) (counseling requirement), 521(b) (counseling certification filing requirement). *See* National Consumer Law Center, Consumer Bankruptcy Law and Practice §§ 3.2.1.4, 7.3.5 (10th ed. 2012), *updated at* www.nclc.org/library.

17 11 U.S.C. §§ 111(d) (course requirement), 727(a)(11), 1328(g) (condition to discharge). *See* National Consumer Law Center, Consumer Bankruptcy Law and Practice § 8.3.3 (10th ed. 2012), *updated at* www .nclc.org/library.

18 National Consumer Law Center, Consumer Bankruptcy Law and Practice (10th ed. 2012), *updated at* www.nclc.org/library.

19 *See* www.justice.gov.

20 11 U.S.C. § 111(c)(2)(B).

date have found that most agencies typically charge $50 or less for each of the two required bankruptcy courses.[21] The U.S. trustee recommends that the fee should be in the range of $0 to $50.[22] Fees must be waived for those who cannot afford the fees.[23]

In addition, there is no room for abuse concerning the debt management plan (DMP). Counseling that fulfills the two bankruptcy requirements does not involve a DMP, since payment of creditors is instead handled through the bankruptcy process.

10.2.2 Debt Settlement Services

In contrast to credit counseling agencies that provide debt management plans, debt settlement firms do not send regular monthly payments to creditors. Instead, they claim that they will negotiate a lump-sum payoff of the consumer's debts after the consumer accumulates enough money in a special savings account (though few consumers are able to).[24] In the meantime, the firm tells the consumer to cease payments to the creditor and instead send a monthly payment to the debt settler or a third party connected to it.[25] The justification for stopping payments to creditors is that doing so will make the creditor more willing to negotiate a settlement.[26]

The debt settlement companies will often use third parties to hold the consumer's money in an attempt to avoid various forms of state or federal regulation.[27] The third party holds the clients' payments in separate accounts. But the debt settlement companies can withdraw funds from the accounts to pay their fees. One third party was reported to have contracted with over 500 different debt settlement firms and managed for them over 600,000 accounts.[28] (However, in the worst case scenario, these unlicensed, unregulated, unbonded organizations may simply disappear with the consumer's funds.[29]) Unless subject to state or federal restrictions on advance fees,[30] the debt settlement firm and the third party pay themselves a fee out of the monthly payments—making it even harder for the consumer to save enough to negotiate a settlement.

Some debt settlement providers have attempted to evade state regulations and create the appearance of respectability by affiliating themselves with an attorney.[31] There are numerous variations, but generally the attorney or law firm involved does little or no work on each client's case. Instead the attorney is merely—as one court explained—"fronting" his law license for a third-party debt settlement firm.[32] This has also been more charitably described as "the attorney model."[33] This is discussed further in § 10.7.3, *infra*.

The main problems with debt settlement, as set out in various reports,[34] are the following:

---

21 *See, e.g.,* Gov't Accounting Office, Bankruptcy Reform: Dollar Costs Associated with the Bankruptcy Abuse Prevention and Consumer Protection Act of 2005, at 31 (June 2008) (finding typical cost of $100 to fulfill both counseling requirements in a bankruptcy case).

22 *See* www.usdoj.gov.

23 28 C.F.R. §§ 58.15(e) (credit counseling), 58.25 (j) (personal financial management instruction course).

24 *See* § 10.5.3.2, *infra*(discussing account requirements for debt relief services). *See also* 75 Fed. Reg. 48,457, 48,461–48,462 (Aug. 10, 2010) (describing a typical debt settlement scenario).

25 *See Debt Settlement: Fraudulent, Abusive, and Deceptive Practices Pose Risk to Consumers, Gov't Accountability Office Before Comm. on Commerce, Science, and Transportation, U.S. Senate*, GAO Report No. GAO-10-593T (Apr. 22, 2010) (statement of Gregory D. Kutz). *See also* Estrella v. Freedom Fin. Network, L.L.C., 2010 WL 2231790 (N.D. Cal. June 2, 2010) (certifying class action alleging UDAP violation for tortious interference with contractual relationship when defendant instructed clients to stop paying creditors).

26 *See* F.T.C. v. E.M.A. Nationwide, Inc., 767 F.3d 611, 621–622 (6th Cir. 2014) (quoting telemarketing script that included a response to the question "Why should I stop paying my creditors?"; response stated, among other things: "When creditors do not receive payments, this impacts their bottom line and in so doing you effectively take back control and force the creditors to negotiate with you!") (citations omitted).

27 *See* §§ 10.5.2, 10.7.1–10.7.3, *infra*.

28 Carlsen v. Global Client Solutions, L.L.C., 256 P.3d 321 (Wash. 2011).

29 *See* Press Release, Attorney General McCollum Warns About Credit Repair Scams, Sues Debt Negotiation Companies (Feb. 21, 2008) (reporting on suit against debt settlement outfit that simply pocketed consumers' payments).

30 *See* §§ 10.5.3.1 (federal restrictions), 10.7 (state regulation), *infra*.

31 *See, e.g., In re* Allegro Law, L.L.C., 2010 WL 2712256, at *1 (Bankr. M.D. Ala. July 6, 2010) (describing deceptive debt settlement service in which lawyer recruited clients but work was done by non-attorneys at separate company; finding attorney was deceiving clients and company was practicing law without license); Brown v. Consumer Law Associates, L.L.C., 283 F.R.D. 602 (E.D. Wash. 2012) (describing debt settlement company using guise of legal services to evade state law; licensed attorneys whose primary business was debt adjustment not eligible for state attorney exemption); Federal Trade Comm'n v. Nat'l Consumer Council, No. SACV04-0474 CJC(JWJX), at 2 (C.D. Cal. June 10, 2004) (supplement to report of temporary receiver's activities, first report to court) (defendant would assign certain debt settlement contracts with consumers to a law firm because of certain state qualification restrictions); Fed. Trade Comm'n, Bureau of Consumer Prot., Debt Relief Services and the Telemarketing Sales Rule: What People Are Asking (Oct. 2010), *available at* www.ftc.gov.

32 *In re* Allegro Law, L.L.C., 2010 WL 2712256, at *1 (Bankr. M.D. Ala. July 6, 2010). *See* 75 Fed. Reg. 48,457, 48,468 (Aug. 10, 2010) (discussing whether FTC should exempt attorneys from debt relief provisions of Telemarketing Sales Rule); Disciplinary Counsel v. Lorenzon, 978 N.E.2d 183 (Ohio 2012) (attorney disciplined for allowing debt relief firm to use his electronic signature and registration number without adequate supervision).

33 *See, e.g.,* Consumer Fin. Prot. Bureau v. Morgan Drexen, Inc., 60 F. Supp. 3d 1082, 1085 (C.D. Cal. 2014) (complaint describing defendant's use of "attorney model"); Elizabeth Ody, *Debt Firms Play 'Whack-a-Mole' Using Lawyers to Skirt Fee Ban*, www.bloomberg.com (Sept. 30, 2011) (referring to use of attorney model to benefit from loopholes in state laws). *See also* Huffman v. Legal Helpers Debt Resolution, L.L.C. (*In re* Huffman), 505 B.R. 726, 734–738 (S.D. Miss. 2014) (describing extensively attorney involvement in national debt settlement operation).

34 *See* Final Rule Amendments, Federal Trade Commission Telemarketing Sales Rule, 75 Fed. Reg. 48,457, 48,463 (Aug. 10, 2010); New York City Bar, Profiteering from Financial Distress: An Examination of the Debt Settlement Industry (May 2012), *available at* www2.nycbar .org; *Debt Settlement: Fraudulent, Abusive, and Deceptive Practices Pose Risk to Consumers, Gov't Accountability Office Before Comm. on Commerce, Science, and Transportation, U.S. Senate*, GAO Rpt. No. GAO-10-593T (Apr. 22, 2010) (statement of Gregory D. Kutz); National Consumer Law Center, An Investigation of Debt Settlement

- The consumers targeted by debt settlement companies are generally the least likely to benefit.[35] Companies target consumers who are unemployed, whose income is exempt from debt collection, or who may be better served by bankruptcy.

- Very few consumers ever complete a debt settlement program,[36] forfeiting all the fees they have paid the company and that the company takes out of the consumer's payments to date. In the meantime, consumers in debt settlement programs continue to face collection efforts. Their debts also continue to grow as creditor fees accumulate and interest accrues.[37]

- Despite advertisements and promises, consumers often suffer damaged credit-worthiness and increased debt as creditors pile on fees and penalty interest.

- Initial debt settlement fees may be very high, and then fees are taken out of each amount sent to the debt settlement company, so consumers do not end up saving much in the "reserve accounts."

- It is unclear what, if any, professional services are offered by most debt settlement companies to assist debtors.

- The marketing of debt settlement and negotiation plans often includes false, misleading, or unsubstantiated representations about how much customers are likely to save, that creditor and debt collector harassment will end, and that the provider has special relationships with creditors or special techniques for reducing debts.

- Many debt settlement providers tell customers to stop paying or communicating with their creditors, missing the chance to avail themselves of offers of help from the creditor.[38]

Debt settlement firms often promote their service as a way to avoid bankruptcy,[39] but their customers often end up in bankruptcy nevertheless.[40] Generally it is questionable whether debt settlement services provide anything of value.[41]

For example, the FTC alleged in one case that a debt settlement company promised to reduce consumers' unsecured debt to fifty-five cents on the dollar, enable them to pay off all their debts in three years, and improve their financial situation. The company also said it would start forwarding the consumer's payments to creditors within several weeks after enrollment. In fact, the company required consumers to pay 45% of the total program fee up front—which often took many months—before the company paid any of the consumer's creditors. Customers saw their debt increase due to late fees and finance charges. Many were sued and then subjected to wage garnishment or other collection remedies, all of which damaged their credit reports.[42]

10.2.3 Debt Negotiation Services

Debt negotiation companies for a fee promise to negotiate interest rate reductions or other concessions from creditors in order to lower customers' monthly payments. Unlike debt management plans or debt settlement, debt negotiators generally do not claim to implement full balance payment plans or obtain lump sum settlements.[43] Companies targeting student loan

---

Companies: An Unsettling Business for Consumers (Mar. 2005), *available at* www.nclc.org.

35 National Consumer Law Center, An Investigation of Debt Settlement Companies: An Unsettling Business for Consumers (Mar. 2005), *available at* www.nclc.org. *See* Kendall v. Able Debt Settlement, Inc. (*In re Kendall*), 440 B.R. 526 (B.A.P. 8th Cir. 2010) (debt settlement firm accepted client despite knowing client had negative net income).

36 According to the Colorado Attorney General, "only 7.81% of Colorado consumers who had entered a debt settlement program since the beginning of 2006 had completed their programs by the end of 2008" and 53% had dropped-out. 75 Fed. Reg. 48,457, 48,469–48,470 (Aug. 10, 2010). *See also id.* 48,471–48,476 (Aug. 10, 2010) (discussing available data regarding effectiveness of debt settlement); *id.* at 48,471 n.194 ("the record indicates that many consumers either receive no settlements or save less than the fees and other costs that they pay"); Cuomo v. Nationwide Asset Services, Inc., 888 N.Y.S.2d 850 (N.Y. Super. Ct. 2009) (defendant admitted that only about 5% of customers completed program).

37 National Consumer Law Center, An Investigation of Debt Settlement Companies: An Unsettling Business for Consumers (Mar. 2005). *See* Ctr. for Responsible Lending, The State of Lending: Debt Settlement (June 30, 2014), *available at* www.responsiblelending.org (estimating that consumers must settle at least two-thirds of enrolled debt to benefit from program after accounting for accretion and debt settlement fees). *See also In re* Sinnot, 845 A.2d 373 (Vt. 2004) (describing the lack of actual work performed by a law firm offering debt settlement services).

38 *See, e.g.,* Duran v. J. Hass Grp. L.L.C., 2012 WL 3233818 (E.D.N.Y. June 8, 2012) (alleging consumer was told to stop paying creditors; consumer was later sued by creditor).

39 *See, e.g.,* Consumer Fin. Prot. Bureau v. Morgan Drexen, Inc., 60 F. Supp. 1082, 1085 (C.D. Cal. 2014) (complaint alleging services were advertised as way to avoid bankruptcy).

40 *See, e.g.,* Kendall v. Able Debt Settlement, Inc. (*In re Kendall*), 440 B.R. 526 (B.A.P. 8th Cir. 2010); Huffman v. Legal Helpers Debt Resolution, L.L.C. (*In re* Huffman), 505 B.R. 726, 747–748 (S.D. Miss. 2014) (consumer filed chapter 7, "the very contingency she had hoped to avoid by enrolling in the debt settlement program"); Baer v. Persels & Assoc. (*In re* Chance), 2013 WL 501392 (D. Kan. Jan. 16, 2013) (debtor filed bankruptcy after paying $2097 over nine months for debt management), *adopted by* 2013 WL 501413 (D. Kan. Feb. 6, 2013); Morris v. Persels & Assoc. (*In re* Good), 2012 WL 3066885 (Bankr. D. Kan. July 27, 2012) (debtors filed bankruptcy after paying thousands of dollars for debt settlement); Moore v. Allied Consumer Services, 2012 WL 1345196 (Bankr. D. Kan. Apr. 16, 2012) (debtor paid debt settlement firm $6722 over eleven months, was sued by several creditors, and ultimately filed bankruptcy); *In re* Beebe, 435 B.R. 95 (Bankr. N.D.N.Y. 2010) (bankruptcy filed after nearly a year of unsuccessful payments to debt settlement company). *See also* Elizabeth O'Brien, *10 Things Bankruptcy Court Won't Tell You*, SmartMoney Magazine, Sept. 30, 2009, *available at* www.tnj.com (reporting that debt settlement companies "bill their services as an alternative to bankruptcy, but in many cases they can hurt more than they help" because their "business model works squarely against the debtors' interests").

41 *See, e.g., In re* Sinnot, 845 A.2d 373 (Vt. 2004) (describing the lack of actual work performed by a law firm offering debt settlement services).

42 Federal Trade Comm'n v. Edge Solutions, Inc., No. CV-07-4087 (E.D.N.Y. Oct. 1, 2007), *available at* www.ftc.gov (complaint filed) (similar allegations). *See also* Stipulated Final Judgment and Order, Consumer Fin. Prot. Bureau v. Am. Debt Settlement Solutions, Inc., No. 9:13-cv-80548-DMM (S.D. Fl. entered June 7, 2013) (detailing typical practices of debt settlement firm, violations of TSR, and UDAPs).

43 75 Fed. Reg. 48,457, 48,464 (Aug. 10, 2010).

borrowers could be considered a version of debt negotiators.[44] These companies charge fees for assistance in navigating free government programs to assist student loan borrowers or pass off government programs as their own, often providing misinformation and bad advice in the process. Even if these services do not meet a state definition of debt negotiation, they are likely to meet the FTC's definition of a debt relief service.[45]

10.2.4 Debt Elimination

Purveyors of debt elimination schemes offer specious plans to eliminate debt without paying anything to the creditor. The variations of these schemes seems limited only by the creativity of the scammers and the desperation of distressed consumers.[46] Some schemes purport to obtain the lender's consent to a power of attorney authorizing the debt elimination company to satisfy the debt. Consumers, believing that the debt is now eliminated, stop making their payments and then not only lose the fee that they paid to the fraud artist, but also face seizure of any collateral for the loan—such as a home or car. Sometimes the company goes even further and obtains a new loan against the property, keeping the bulk of the proceeds. The consumer then ends up in a worse position than before, with two lenders claiming security interests in the property.[47]

Others set up an arbitration that is programmed to produce a ruling that the debt is invalid.[48] A number of courts have refused to give effect to arbitration awards enforced as part of debt elimination schemes.[49] Another debt elimination scheme

sells consumers a set of documents and pleadings setting forth incomprehensible legal theories about why the debt is not owed, such as a claim that the lender wrongfully "monetized" debt.[50] Another scheme involves sending multiple frivolous dispute letters under the Fair Credit Billing Act.[51] These schemes induce consumers to file *pro se* suits to litigate these issues. The suits are invariably dismissed and some consumers have faced motions for sanctions.[52] Yet another version sells the consumer an instrument, such as a "bond for discharge of debt" or "redemption

---

44 *See* National Consumer Law Center, Searching for Relief: Desperate Borrowers and the Growing Student Loan "Debt Relief" Industry (June 2013), *available at* www.nclc.org.

45 *See* § 10.5, *infra* (describing the FTC Telemarketing Sales Rule and debt relief services).

46 *See, e.g.,* Baer v. Daley, 2012 WL 5200029 (D. Kan. Oct. 22, 2012) (scammer claimed to assume consumers' debts then force accord and satisfaction on creditor through restrictive endorsement on check offering partial payment).

47 *See* United States v. Johnson, 610 F.3d 1138 (9th Cir. 2010) (upholding conviction of principals of scheme); Frances Kenny Family Trust v. World Sav. Bank, 2005 WL 106792 (N.D. Cal. Jan. 19, 2005) (awarding sanctions and referring attorney involved in scheme to state bar association).

48 *See* Buczek v. Trans Union, L.L.C., 2006 WL 3666635 (S.D. Fla. Nov. 9, 2006) (granting judgment against consumer on claims based on debt elimination scheme); Chase Manhattan Bank v. Nat'l Arbitration Council, Inc., 2005 WL 1270504 (M.D. Fla. May 27, 2005) (describing scheme and granting creditor's motion for preliminary injunction against it). *See also* BMI Fed. Credit Union v. Burkitt, 2010 WL 2637930 (Ohio Ct. App. June 30, 2010) (describing variant in which a panel of notaries purports to issue a judgment).

49 *See, e.g.,* Chase Bank USA v. Naes, Inc., 2010 WL 94020 (D. Nev. Jan. 8, 2010); Citibank (South Dakota) N.A. v. Dahlquist, 152 P.3d 693 (Mont. 2007) (arbitration award in consumer's favor was void ab initio because arbitrator was not one of the ones listed in arbitration agreement); Citibank v. Wood, 894 N.E.2d 57 (Ohio Ct. App. 2008) (arbitration award in consumer's favor was a legal nullity, not subject to statutory time limits on moving to vacate an award); Citibank S.D., N.A. v. Schmidt, 744 N.W.2d 829 (S.D. 2008). *See also* United States v. Wickline, 2008 WL 2498107 (S.D. Ohio June 16, 2008) (refusing to allow defendants, indicted for mail fraud, wire fraud, and money

laundering in connection with sale of arbitration-based debt elimination scheme, to introduce evidence that scheme validly took advantage of banking law loophole, as no such loophole exists).

50 *See, e.g.,* Gallant v. Deutsche Bank Nat'l Trust Co., 766 F. Supp. 2d 714 (W.D. Va. 2011); Brown v. Moynihan, 2010 WL 4642492 (D. Ariz. Nov. 9, 2010); Bank of Am. v. Derisme, 2010 WL 3211066 (D. Conn. Aug. 13, 2010); McLaughlin v. CitiMortgage, Inc., 726 F. Supp. 2d 101 (D. Conn. June 11, 2010) (carefully describing nature and origins of debt elimination theories), *leave to amend denied*, 2010 WL 3037810 (D. Conn. Aug. 4, 2010); Thomas v. Countrywide Home Loans, 2010 WL 1328644 (N.D. Ga. Mar. 29, 2010); Andrews v. Select Portfolio Servicing, Inc., 2010 WL 1176667 (D. Md. Mar. 24, 2010); Buckley v. Bayrock Mortg. Corp., 2010 WL 476673 (N.D. Ga. Feb. 5, 2010); Barber v. Countrywide Home Loans, Inc., 2010 WL 398915 (W.D.N.C. Jan. 25, 2010); Johnson v. Deutsche Bank Nat'l Trust Co., 2009 WL 2575703 (S.D. Fla. July 1, 2009); Gentsch v. Ownit Mortg. Solutions Inc., 2009 WL 1390843 (E.D. Cal. May 14, 2009) (dismissing "vapor money" claims as "absurd"), *later op. at* 2009 WL 1468988 (E.D. Cal. May 26, 2009) (dismissing case); Urzua v. Indymac Bank, 2008 WL 1846768 (N.D. Cal. Apr. 14, 2008) (urging lender to report purveyor of unintelligible admiralty law debt elimination claim to federal banking authorities); Indymac Bank v. Dye, 2008 WL 4394667 (Del. Super. Ct. Apr. 18, 2008) (denying debtor's motions and counterclaims based on incomprehensible legal theories sold by now-suspended accountant as part of debt elimination scheme); Citibank S.D., N.A. v. Schmidt, 744 N.W.2d 829, 833 (S.D. 2007) (characterizing as "bizarre" debtor's claim that he did not have to repay credit card debt because bank "monetized" his signature); Brook v. Woodall, 257 P.3d 456 (Utah Ct. App. 2011).

51 *See, e.g.,* Langenfeld v. Chase Bank USA, 537 F. Supp. 2d 1181 (N.D. Okla. 2008); Kryszak v. Chase Bank USA, 2008 WL 822015 (W.D.N.Y. Mar. 26, 2008); Eicken v. USAA Fed. Sav. Bank, 498 F. Supp. 2d 954 (S.D. Tex. 2007) (rejecting FCBA claims because of insufficient evidence that consumer who submitted them as part of a debt elimination program had an actual belief that there were billing errors); Washington Mut. Bank v. Forgue, 2007 WL 4232708 (W.D.N.Y. Nov. 27, 2007) (awarding sanctions). *See* Press Release, Fla. Office of the Att'y Gen., Attorney General McCollum Warns About Credit Repair Scams, Sues Debt Negotiation Companies (Feb. 21, 2008), *available at* www.creditfactors.com (reporting on suit against debt elimination scheme involving FCBA dispute letters).

52 *See, e.g.,* Esquibel v. Chase Manhattan Bank, 276 Fed. Appx. 393 (5th Cir. 2008); Thomas v. Countrywide Home Loans, 2010 WL 1328644 (N.D. Ga. Mar. 29, 2010); Buckley v. Bayrock Mortg. Corp., 2010 WL 476673 (N.D. Ga. Feb. 5, 2010) (denying lender's motion for sanctions in "vapor money" case, subject to renewal if consumer files future frivolous pleadings); Daniel v. Chase Bank USA, 650 F. Supp. 2d 1275 (N.D. Ga. 2009); Millan v. Chase Bank USA, 533 F. Supp. 2d 1061 (C.D. Cal. 2008); Carmack v. Chase Manhattan Bank, 521 F. Supp. 2d 1017 (N.D. Cal. 2007); Adams v. Bank of Am., 2007 WL 2746871 (M.D.N.C. Sept. 19, 2007) (granting motion to dismiss; complaint "consists of thirty-three pages of indecipherable allegations"); League v. Citibank, 663 S.E.2d 266 (Ga. Ct. App. 2008).

certificate," that the consumer is to present to the creditor and that supposedly forces the creditor to abandon the debt.[53]

Another team of scammers set up a Ponzi Scheme in which some initial customers had their debts satisfied with "processing fees" paid by others. By the time the scheme collapsed, the scammers had promised to eliminate debts worth $950,000,000 but controlled assets of only $17,000,000.[54] Although the scammers were convicted, a court-appointed receiver obtained judgments for unjust enrichment against some consumers who benefited from the scam.[55]

Federal banking agencies have warned banks against these schemes, characterizing them as bogus and asserting that creating or presenting such instruments may be a federal crime.[56] One major lender has claimed that debt elimination schemes caused credit card debtors to withhold over $75 million in payments.[57]

10.3 Nonprofit Versus For-Profit Services

10.3.1 Background

An important distinction in the regulation of debt relief services is whether the entity is nonprofit, for-profit, or a for-profit entity masquerading as a nonprofit. Some state laws limit certain debt relief services only to nonprofits.[58] The FTC Telemarketing Sales Rule, a major source of federal regulation of debt relief agencies,[59] does not apply to legitimate nonprofits. Another major source of federal regulation, the Credit Repair Organizations Act[60] (CROA) does not apply to nonprofit agencies that have gained 501(c)(3) status and are legitimate nonprofits. State UDAP and other state law theories may also not apply to nonprofits.[61]

In addition, many agencies stress their nonprofit nature when they market their services.[62] Consumers are less likely to be on their guard if they believe they are dealing with a nonprofit organization.

The likelihood of a debt relief entity claiming nonprofit status varies depending on the type of service offered. Credit counselors offering debt management plans often claim nonprofit status. Such status is far rarer for debt settlement, debt negotiation, or debt elimination companies,[63] and, when it is alleged, it may be bogus.

Whether a debt relief agency is truly a nonprofit involves a two-part test. The first is whether it has filed the proper papers and received the proper approval (if any) to claim nonprofit status. The second is whether the actual operation of the agency belies its nonprofit status.

Whether an agency is a true nonprofit will of course depend on the facts, and it may also depend on the statute at issue that distinguishes for-profit from nonprofit entities. Nevertheless, precedent under the federal CROA, the FTC Telemarketing Sales Rule, and state debt relief laws may all be relevant to interpreting true nonprofit status under the other laws as well.

10.3.2 IRS Standards for Nonprofit Status

To be exempt from the federal CROA, an agency must be more than a nonprofit. It must apply for and be approved by the IRS to be tax exempt under section 501(c)(3) of the Internal Revenue Code.[64] In addition, it must operate in fact as a nonprofit.[65] Current IRS standards offer useful guidelines as to whether a debt relief agency is a true nonprofit.

Do not view an agency's section 501(c)(3) status as determinative. The IRS granted this status in the 1990s and early 2000s to many "for-profits in disguise" during a time of great growth in the credit counseling industry—1215 agencies applied for section 501(c)(3) status from 1994 through early 2004.[66] It was not until many of these agencies had been granted section

---

53   *See* Christine Dempsey, Guilty Verdict in Federal Fraud Trial, The Hartford Courant, June 25, 2013, *available at* www.courant.com (describing scam involving sale of fake bonds sold to consumers for purpose of paying off debts).

54   Ashmore v. Cook, 2013 WL 6283508 (D.S.C. Dec. 4, 2013).

55   *See, e.g.,* Ashmore v. Taylor, 2014 WL 6473714 (D.S.C. Nov. 18, 2014); Ashmore v. Cook, 2013 WL 6283508 (D.S.C. Dec. 4, 2013).

56   *See* Office of the Comptroller of the Currency, Illegal Financial Activity: Fictitious Debt Elimination Schemes, OCC Alert 2003-12 (Oct. 1, 2003), *available at* www.occ.treas.gov. *See also* Office of the Comptroller of the Currency, Fraudulent Debt Elimination Schemes, OCC Alert 2007-55 (Sept. 5, 2007), *available at* www.occ.treas.gov; Bd. of Governors of the Federal Reserve Sys., On Debt Elimination Scams, Supervisory Letter SR 04-3 (Jan. 28, 2004), *available at* www.federalreserve.gov.

57   Chase Bank v. Hess, 2011 WL 45132 (D. Del. Jan. 6, 2011). *See also* Chase Bank USA, N.A. v. Consumer Law Ctr. of DelRay Beach, L.L.C., 2015 WL 4556650 (D. Del. July 29, 2015) (summary judgment to Chase in debt elimination scheme); Chase Bank USA, N.A. v. Allegro Law, L.L.C., 2013 WL 3149461 (E.D.N.Y. June 19, 2013) (default judgment to Chase in debt elimination scheme).

58   *See* § 10.7.1, *infra.*

59   *See* § 10.5, *infra.*

60   *See* § 10.4, *infra.*

61   *See* National Consumer Law Center, Unfair and Deceptive Acts and Practices § 2.3.5.1 (8th ed. 2012), *updated at* www.nclc.org/library.

62   *See, e.g.,* Federal Trade Comm'n v. Integrated Credit Solutions, Inc., No. 8:06-CV-00806-SCB-TGW (M.D. Fla. May 3, 2006), *available at* www.ftc.gov (complaint and stipulated judgments filed) (describing how purported nonprofit stressed its nonprofit nature when selling its services to consumers).

63   *See* Cuomo v. Nationwide Asset Services, Inc., 888 N.Y.S.2d 850 (N.Y. Super. Ct. 2009) (extensively describing a debt settlement operation). There are at least some nonprofit agencies that will negotiate settlements for consumers, but these agencies generally do not hold or escrow consumers' monthly payments. Instead, these agencies attempt to negotiate lump sum pay-offs of a consumer's debts based on funds the consumer already has or can easily obtain.

64   *See* National Consumer Law Center, Fair Credit Reporting § 15.2.2.3.2 (8th ed. 2013), *updated at* www.nclc.org/library.

65   *Id.*

66   U.S. Senate Permanent Subcomm. on Investigations, Comm. on Homeland Sec. Governmental Affairs, Profiteering in a Non-Profit Industry: Abusive Practices in Credit Counseling, S. Rep. No. 109-55 (Apr. 13, 2005), *available at* www.gpo.gov.

501(c)(3) status did the IRS finally begin taking a closer look at the agencies' actual operations.[67]

In 2010, the IRS Credit Counseling Compliance Project stated that it has revoked, terminated, or proposed revocation of over half of the credit counseling organizations examined.[68] While this has certainly weeded out a number of bogus nonprofits, it is very likely that many consumer credit counseling agencies with section 510(c)(3) status are not in fact true nonprofits.

The IRS itself has stated that organizations offering only debt management plans without significant education and counseling should not qualify for section 501(c)(3) status.[69] The IRS provided additional guidance on these standards in a 2004 memorandum.[70] According to the IRS chief counsel, section 501(c)(3) status is not proper for agencies if "they are not providing any meaningful education or relief of the poor."[71] The counsel states further that in some cases there may be a basis for arguing for revocation based on inurement.[72]

An additional chief counsel memorandum, published on May 9, 2006, provides the legal framework to determine whether a credit counseling agency that offers counseling and debt management plans to the general public will qualify as under section 501(c)(3).[73] This memorandum does not discuss inurement or private benefit because those issues were addressed in the 2004 memorandum. According to the IRS, the critical inquiry is whether a credit counseling organization conducts its counseling program to improve an individual debtor's understanding of the individual's financial problems and improve his or her ability to address those problems. The IRS memorandum states further that "[t]he process the organization uses to interview clients and develop recommendations, train its counselors and market its services can distinguish between an organization whose object is to improve a person's knowledge and skills to manage his personal debt, and an organization that is offering counseling primarily as a mechanism to enroll individuals in a specific option (e.g., debt management plans) without considering the individual's best interest."[74]

In addition, 2006 legislation further clarified the requirements for a consumer credit counseling being granted section 510(c)(3) status.[75] Credit counseling agencies provide services tailored to the specific needs and circumstances of consumers; provide services for the purpose of improving a consumer's credit record, credit history, or credit rating only to the extent that such services are incidental to providing credit counseling services and without charging separately for such services; and establish and implement a fee policy so that fees charged are reasonable and fee waivers are given to consumers who are unable to pay.

Except as allowed by state law, fees based in whole or in part on a percentage of the consumer's debt, the consumer's payments to be made pursuant to a debt management plan, or on the projected or actual savings to the consumer resulting from enrolling in a debt management plan are prohibited. Loans to debtors are also prohibited.

10.3.3 FTC Standards for Nonprofit Status

To be exempt from the FTC Telemarketing Sales Rule, a debt relief agency must be organized to carry on business neither for profit nor for the profit of its members.[76] This standard under the FTC Act does not rely on the IRS's section 501(3)(c) standard, nor is it dependent on a state law determination as to nonprofit status.

The FTC Act applies to nonprofits to the extent to which they engage in business activities.[77] If a nonprofit is really engaged in a profit-making enterprise, it is covered by the FTC Act.[78]

---

67 *See, e.g.,* Solution Plus, Inc. v. Commissioner of Internal Revenue, 2008 WL 312764 (T.C. Feb. 5, 2008) (upholding denial of tax exempt status when organization provided only minimal educational activities and its primary activity was sale of debt management plans); Priv. Ltr. Rul. 2004-52-036, 2004 WL 2968115 (Dec. 24, 2004); Priv. Ltr. Rul. 2004-50-039, 2004 WL 2832021 (Dec. 10, 2004); Priv. Ltr. Rul. 2004-47-046, 2004 WL 2636501 (Nov. 19, 2004).

68 *See* www.irs.gov.

69 Fed. Trade Comm'n, IRS and State Regulators Urge Care When Seeking Help from Credit Counseling Organizations (Oct. 14, 2003), *available at* www.ftc.gov. *See also* Solution Plus, Inc. v. Commissioner of Internal Revenue, 2008 WL 312764 (T.C. Feb. 5, 2008) (upholding denial of tax exempt status when organization provided only minimal educational activities and its primary activity was sale of debt management plans).

70 Internal Revenue Serv., Chief Counsel Advice Memo., CCA 200431023, IRC Section 501—Exemption from Tax on Corporations, Certain Trusts, etc., 2004 WL 1701316 (July 13, 2004). *See generally* David Lander & Deanne Loonin, *Restoring "Nonprofitness" and "Quality" to the Credit Counseling Industry*, Norton Bankr. L. Adviser (Apr. 2005).

71 Internal Revenue Serv., Chief Counsel Advice Memo., CCA 200431023, IRC Section 501—Exemption from Tax on Corporations, Certain Trusts, etc., 2004 WL 1701316 (July 13, 2004). *See generally* David Lander & Deanne Loonin, *Restoring "Nonprofitness" and "Quality" to the Credit Counseling Industry*, Norton Bankr. L. Adviser (Apr. 2005).

72 Internal Revenue Serv., Chief Counsel Advice Memo., CCA 200431023, IRC Section 501—Exemption from Tax on Corporations, Certain Trusts, etc., 2004 WL 1701316 (July 13, 2004). *See generally* David Lander & Deanne Loonin, *Restoring "Nonprofitness" and "Quality" to the Credit Counseling Industry*, Norton Bankr. L. Adviser (Apr. 2005).

73 Internal Revenue Serv., Office of Chief Counsel Memo. (May 9, 2006), *available at* www.irs.gov.

74 *Id.* at 2.

75 Pub. L. No. 109-280 (Aug. 17, 2006), *codified at* 26 U.S.C. § 501(q).

76 15 U.S.C. § 44.

77 *See* American Med. Ass'n v. Federal Trade Comm'n, 638 F.2d 443 (2d Cir. 1980), *aff'd per curiam*, 455 U.S. 676 (1982); Federal Trade Comm'n v. Nat'l Comm'n on Egg Nutrition, 517 F.2d 485 (7th Cir. 1975). *See also* Community Blood Bank, Inc. v. Federal Trade Comm'n, 405 F.2d 1011 (8th Cir. 1969); Miller v. Risk Mgmt. Found., 632 N.E.2d 841 (Mass. App. Ct. 1994).

78 Community Blood Bank, Inc. v. Federal Trade Comm'n, 405 F.2d 1011 (8th Cir. 1969); Federal Trade Comm'n v. AmeriDebt, Inc., 343 F. Supp. 2d 451 (D. Md. 2004); *In re* Ohio Christian Coll., 80 F.T.C. 815 (Fed. Trade Comm'n 1972) (issue is whether business carried on "for their own profit or that of their members"; FTC had jurisdiction when diploma mill was incorporated as nonprofit but controlled by one individual, who treated its assets as his own). *See also* California Dental Ass'n v. Federal Trade Comm'n, 526 U.S. 756, 119 S. Ct. 1604, 143 L. Ed. 2d 935 (U.S. 1999) (nonprofit association that provides

The FTC has made it clear that it does not consider *faux* nonprofit debt relief organizations exempt from its jurisdiction.[79] A federal court has found that the FTC Act applies to a counselor that was incorporated as a nonprofit but failed to provide promised educational services and participated in common enterprise with closely related for-profit corporations.[80] The Federal Trade Commission has pursued a number of other allegedly nonprofit credit counseling agencies, claiming their nonprofit status is not legitimate.[81]

10.4 Federal and State Credit Repair Laws

10.4.1 Introduction

The federal Credit Repair Organizations Act (CROA)[82] and analogous state statutes, if applicable, provide strong consumer protections and potent private remedies concerning any form of debt relief services. If applicable, these statutes may be a consumer's first approach to challenging abuses by any form of debt relief services.

Nevertheless, for these statutes to be applicable to debt relief services, there must be a representation that the service can assist the consumer in improving the consumer's credit record. Additional limits relate to nonprofits. Thus it is possible for a debt relief service to limits its advertising and other representations to avoid coverage by these statutes,[83] but doing so deprives the debt relief service of the opportunity to appeal to a major consumer concern (repairing a consumer's credit record).

CROA and analogous state statutes are examined in detail in another NCLC treatise, *Fair Credit Reporting*.[84] This section summarizes the key points of the statutes and discusses their applicability to debt relief services.

10.4.2 Scope and Applicability to Debt Relief Services

Most of CROA's restrictions apply only to "credit repair organizations," but this term is broadly defined. It encompasses any person who performs or offers to perform any service, for a fee or other valuable consideration, for the express or implied purpose of (1) improving any consumer's credit record, credit history, or credit rating or (2) providing advice and assistance to any consumer with regard to any such activity or service.[85]

CROA exempts from the definition of credit repair organization entities that have received section 501(c)(3) nonprofit status from the IRS and that operate as a nonprofit in actual practice.[86] The IRS determination of section 501(c)(3) status is not determinative,[87] so false nonprofits are still covered by CROA. State credit repair statutes may have different scope provisions regarding nonprofit status and whether activities other than credit repair are covered.[88]

Credit counseling services are more likely to be organized as section 501(c)(3) nonprofits than other forms of debt relief services, so the nonprofit exemption is particularly relevant to them. But the CROA will still apply to such credit counseling services if it can be shown that they are for-profit businesses in disguise, either because they focus entirely on selling debt management plans or because of close connections to for-profit affiliates.[89]

Thus the CROA's provision regarding credit repair organizations should apply to any type of debt relief service that expressly or impliedly offers to improve a consumer's credit record, as long as the entity does not meet the nonprofit test.

---

substantial economic benefit to its for-profit members comes under FTC jurisdiction).

79 *Prepared Statement of the Fed. Trade Comm'n on Bus. Practices of Debt Relief Cos Before the Sen. Comm. on Commerce, Science, and Transp.* 4, 12 (Aug. 12, 2010), *available at* www.ftc.gov.

80 Federal Trade Comm'n v. AmeriDebt, Inc., 343 F. Supp. 2d 451 (D. Md. 2004); Federal Trade Comm'n v. AmeriDebt Inc., DebtWorks, Inc., Andris Pukke, & Pamela Pukke (D. Md. Nov. 19, 2003), *available at* www.ftc.gov (complaint filed), *preliminary injunction granted*, 373 F. Supp. 2d 558 (D. Md. 2005), *motions to dismiss granted in part, denied in part*, 343 F. Supp. 2d 451 (D. Md. 2004) (AmeriDebt's bankruptcy does not preclude FTC action; FTC Act applies if organization that purported to be a nonprofit was in fact operating for profit), *consent orders entered*, www.ftc.gov (ordering company to cease doing business; banning its principal from credit counseling and debt management businesses and requiring him to turn over nearly all of his assets to the court-appointed receiver, up to $35 million).

81 *See, e.g.,* Federal Trade Comm'n v. Integrated Credit Solutions, Inc., No. 8:06-CV-00806-SCB-TGW (M.D. Fla. May 3, 2006), *available at* www.ftc.gov (complaint and stipulated judgments filed) (allegations of purported nonprofit organization's participation as part of for-profit enterprise with related for-profit companies, and deceptive marketing); Federal Trade Comm'n v. Ballenger Grp., L.L.C., & Ballenger Holdings, L.L.C. (D. Md. Nov. 19, 2003) (complaint filed), *available at* www.ftc.gov (complaint and stipulated final judgment). *See generally Prepared Statement of the Fed. Trade Comm'n on Bus. Practices of Debt Relief Cos Before the Sen. Comm. on Commerce, Science, and Transp.* (Aug. 12, 2010), *available at* www.ftc.gov (listing FTC enforcement actions).

82 15 U.S.C. §§ 1679–1679j. *See* National Consumer Law Center, Fair Credit Reporting Ch. 15 (8th ed. 2013), *updated at* www.nclc.org/library.

83 *See* Pavlov v. Debt Resolvers USA, Inc., 907 N.Y.S.2d 798 (N.Y. Civ. Ct. 2010).

84 National Consumer Law Center, Fair Credit Reporting Ch. 15 (8th ed. 2013), *updated at* www.nclc.org/library.

85 15 U.S.C. § 1679a(3)(A); National Consumer Law Center, Fair Credit Reporting § 15.2.2.2 (8th ed. 2013), *updated at* www.nclc.org/library.

86 15 U.S.C. § 1679a(3)(B)(i).

87 Zimmerman v. Cambridge Credit Counseling Corp., 409 F.3d 473 (1st Cir. 2005) (IRS determination of tax-exempt status not dispositive). *Accord* Baker v. Family Credit Counseling Corp., 440 F. Supp. 2d 392 (E.D. Pa. 2006) (section 501(c)(3) classification by the IRS is not dispositive in deciding whether an organization is exempt from CROA). *But see* Limpert v. Cambridge Credit Counseling, 328 F. Supp. 2d 360 (E.D.N.Y. 2004) (CROA may apply to credit counseling agencies that make representations regarding credit reports, but claims against section 501(c)(3) agencies dismissed).

88 *See* National Consumer Law Center, Fair Credit Reporting Ch. 15 (8th ed. 2013), *updated at* www.nclc.org/library.

89 *See* Zimmerman v. Cambridge Credit Counseling Corp., 529 F. Supp. 2d 254 (D. Mass. 2008) (rejecting argument that spurious nonprofit credit counseling organization that funneled revenues to related for-profits fell within CROA's exemption), *aff'd sub nom.* Zimmerman v. Puccio, 613 F.3d 60 (1st Cir. 2010).

Many credit counseling agencies should fit this definition.[90] So should debt settlement, debt negotiation, and debt elimination services. Applicability does not depend on the nature of the debt relief service but on the entity's representations concerning credit repair and its nonprofit status.

For example, debt settlement companies are generally for-profit, so there should be no question that the CROA applies as long as the threshold definitional requirements of a credit repair organization are met. If a debt settlement provider advertises that its service will repair bad credit or improve credit scores, the provider will meet the CROA's definition of credit repair organization.[91] One federal court held that, while the debt settlement activity itself did not meet CROA's definition of credit repair, the provider's "Post Closing Credit Restoration Program" did.[92]

In addition, although most CROA provisions apply only to entities meeting the definition of a credit repair organization, other provisions apply to "any person."[93] These prohibitions have two applications to debt relief services. They can establish a cause of action against individuals or entities that participate in debt relief services with the debt relief company. For example, one federal court has applied these prohibitions to for-profit corporations and individuals that are involved with a purported nonprofit credit counseling organization in its deceptive marketing of debt management plans.[94]

In addition, when a debt relief service may not qualify as a credit repair organization, there may be cases in which the debt relief service violates a CROA prohibition applicable to any person. While the prohibitions relate in various ways to credit repair, there may be situations in which a debt settlement service that is not a credit repair organization will still violate the CROA, as described at § 10.4.3, *infra*.

The CROA also excludes from the definition of "credit repair organization" depository institutions such as banks, savings associations, and credit unions.[95] This exemption does not apply to a non-bank company that, in cooperation with a debt settlement provider, sets up and administers bank accounts into which consumers deposit payments that will be used to settle their debts.[96]

10.4.3 CROA Requirements

CROA prevents any credit repair organization from charging or receiving any money for the performance of any service before such service is fully performed.[97] For example, when a debt settlement company states it will settle a consumer's debt with a creditor for less than the outstanding obligation, then, if the CROA applies, it should not charge any fees or take money out of the consumer's escrow payments until the debt is settled. A debt elimination company should not charge a fee until the debt is eliminated.

The CROA also has extensive required disclosures for credit service organizations that is unlikely to be provided by any debt relief service.[98] No services may be provided until three days after the contract containing these disclosures has been signed.[99] The CROA also sets out detailed requirements as to the contract itself, including a three-day cooling-off period.[100] Any waiver of the CROA provisions is void.[101]

Other provisions apply to "any person."[102] Even if a debt relief service does not qualify as a credit repair organization (for example, it has section 501(c)(3) status), no person (including the debt relief service entity) may make an untrue or misleading statement or advise a consumer to make an untrue or misleading statement to the consumer's creditor with respect to the consumer's credit worthiness, credit standing, or credit capacity.[103]

In addition, if a debt relief service qualifies as a credit repair organization, then no person (such as affiliated companies or individuals employed by the debt relief service) can make any untrue or misleading representations about the debt relief service provided.[104] Nor can any person engage even indirectly in any act that constitutes or results in deception in connection with the services of a credit repair organization.[105]

---

90 *See* Zimmerman v. Cambridge Credit Counseling Corp., 529 F. Supp. 2d 254 (D. Mass. 2008) (spurious nonprofit credit counseling organization meets definition of credit repair organization), *aff'd sub nom.* Zimmerman v. Puccio, 613 F.3d 60 (1st Cir. 2010); Baker v. Family Credit Counseling Corp., 440 F. Supp. 2d 392 (E.D. Pa. 2006); Polacsek v. Debticated Consumer Counseling, Inc., 413 F. Supp. 2d 539 (D. Md. 2005); Limpert v. Cambridge Credit Counseling Corp., 328 F. Supp. 2d 360 (E.D.N.Y. 2004). *But cf.* Plattner v. Edge Solutions, Inc., 422 F. Supp. 2d 969 (N.D. Ill. 2006) (CROA does not apply to debt settlement organization when organization stated that its program would probably worsen participants' credit ratings but that it would help them restore their credit ratings after they completed the program).

91 Reynolds v. Credit Solutions, Inc., 541 F. Supp. 2d 1248 (N.D. Ala. 2008), *vacated*, Picard v. Credit Solutions, Inc., 564 F.3d 1249 (11th Cir. 2009) (question of whether company was credit reporting organization should have been decided by arbitrator).

92 Cortese v. Edge Solutions, Inc., 2007 WL 2782750 (E.D.N.Y. 2007). *But see* Plattner v. Edge Solutions, Inc., 422 F. Supp. 2d 969 (N.D. Ill. 2006) (CROA does not apply to debt settlement organization when organization stated that its program would probably worsen participants' credit ratings but that it would help them restore their credit ratings after they completed the program). *See generally* National Consumer Law Center, Fair Credit Reporting § 15.2.2.2 (8th ed. 2013), *updated at* www.nclc.org/library.

93 *See* 15 U.S.C. § 1679b(a).

94 Zimmerman v. Cambridge Credit Counseling Corp., 529 F. Supp. 2d 254 (D. Mass. 2008), *aff'd sub nom.* Zimmerman v. Puccio, 613 F.3d 60 (1st Cir. 2010).

95 15 U.S.C. § 1679(a)(3)(B)(iii).

96 Willis v. Debt Care, USA, Inc., 2011 WL 7121288 (D. Or. Oct. 24, 2011).

97 15 U.S.C. § 1679b(b).

98 15 U.S.C. § 1679c.

99 15 U.S.C. § 1679d(a).

100 15 U.S.C. §§ 1679d(b), 1679e.

101 15 U.S.C. § 1679f(a).

102 15 U.S.C. § 1679b(a).

103 15 U.S.C. § 1679b(a)(1).

104 15 U.S.C. § 1679b(a)(3).

105 15 U.S.C. § 1679b(a)(4).

10.4.4　CROA Remedies

Contracts not in compliance with the CROA's extensive disclosure and terms requirements are void and unenforceable.[106] Any person who fails to comply with the CROA is liable to the consumer for either actual damages or the amount paid by the consumer to the credit repair organization, whichever is greater, plus punitive damages and attorney fees.[107] The statute explicitly provides for consumer class actions.[108]

The CROA statute of limitations is five years and can be extended when the violation is material to establishing the liability of the credit repair organization.[109] Both the FTC and state attorneys general can enforce the statute as well.[110] The CROA provides for federal court jurisdiction; if the consumer prefers to stay in state court, the best approach is to bring a claim under an analogous state credit repair statute.

10.5　The FTC Telemarketing Sales Rule

10.5.1　Introduction

The FTC's Telemarketing Sales Rule ("the TSR") imposes specific restrictions and requirements on debt relief service that will often be applicable to credit counseling, debt settlement, debt negotiation, and debt elimination companies.[111] The FTC Telemarketing Sales Rule is examined in detail in Chapter 5, *supra*. This section is limited to the TSR's application to debt relief services.

The TSR prohibits debt relief services covered by the TSR from collecting fees until the debt has been settled, altered, or reduced; requires certain disclosures in marketing these services; and prohibits certain specific misrepresentations. The federal law under which the TSR was adopted provides a private cause of action, but only when the consumer's actual damages exceed $50,000.[112] However, in most states the TSR will be enforceable as a UDAP violation.[113]

10.5.2　Debt Relief Services Covered

Certain FTC Telemarketing Sales Rule provisions apply to any "debt relief service," defined as any program or service that is represented or implied to renegotiate, settle, or alter the terms of a debt between a person and one or more unsecured creditors or debt collectors.[114] Similar services addressing

mortgage debt are the subject of a separate rule,[115] examined in another NCLC treatise.[116] Although the debt relief services provisions of the Telemarketing Sales Rule are limited to unsecured debt, the rest of the TSR may apply to other debt-related scams that otherwise meet the requirements of the TSR, and many do.[117]

The TSR's definition of debt relief services applies to credit counseling and debt management, debt elimination, debt settlement, debt negotiation, and the seemingly infinite number of variations that have developed.[118] The TSR is thus applicable as long as the rule's general coverage applies to the transaction.

The TSR applies to telemarketers and sellers. A telemarketer is any person who, in connection with telemarketing, initiates or *receives* telephone calls to or from a customer.[119] Telemarketing "means a plan, program, or campaign conducted to induce the purchase of goods or services by use of one or more telephones, and which involves more than one interstate telephone call."[120]

The TSR thus requires use of the telephone, so it does not apply to purely Internet-based sales, even when a consumer is directly solicited by an email,[121] since a telephone call is not involved. The TSR does, however, apply to debt relief services when the seller sends the consumer an email or advertises on the Internet and the consumer responds by telephone.[122] Therefore, how the consumer found and contacted the provider should be among the first questions advocates ask clients dealing with debt relief providers.

Seller is defined as "any person who, in connection with a telemarketing transaction, provides, offers to provide, or arranges for others to provide goods or services to the customer in exchange for consideration."[123] Thus, the TSR reaches

---

106　15 U.S.C. § 1679f(c).

107　15 U.S.C. § 1679g(a).

108　15 U.S.C. § 1679g(a)(2)(B).

109　15 U.S.C. § 1679i.

110　15 U.S.C. § 1679h.

111　16 C.F.R. § 310. *See* 75 Fed. Reg. 48,458 (Aug. 10, 2010) (supplemental information concerning the Rule's debt relief services provisions).

112　*See* § 5.6.1.1, *supra*.

113　*See* § 5.6.1.2, *supra*.

114　16 C.F.R. § 310.2(m). The FTC has produced a guide to the Telemarketing Sales Rule's coverage of debt relief services that elaborates on the scope of the rule and other provisions. It is available at www.ftc.gov.

115　Mortgage Assistance Relief Services Rule, 16 C.F.R. pt. 1015 [pt. 322].

116　National Consumer Law Center, Foreclosures and Mortgage Servicing Ch. 18 (5th ed. 2014), *updated at* www.nclc.org/library.

117　*See, e.g.*, Press Release, Fed. Trade Comm'n, Auto Loan Relief Scammer Banned from Telemarketing, Debt Relief Services Under FTC Settlement (July 10, 2015), *available at* www.ftc.gov.

118　*See, e.g.*, Press Release, Fed. Trade Comm'n, FTC Sues to Stop Deceptive Debt Relief Operation (Feb. 24, 2015) (announcing first use of debt relief services rule against organization promising relief from payday loans), *available at* www.ftc.gov.

119　16 C.F.R. § 310.2(cc).

120　16 C.F.R. § 310.2(dd).

121　See the statement of basis and purpose for the FTC's Telemarketing Rule at the proposal stage, 60 Fed. Reg. 30,411 (June 8, 1995). *See also* 800-JR Cigar, Inc. v. GoTo.com, Inc., 437 F. Supp. 2d 273 (D.N.J. 2006).

122　See the discussion later in this subsection of consumer initiated calls.

123　16 C.F.R. § 310.2(aa). *See* Federal Trade Comm'n v. Stefanchik, 559 F.3d 924 (9th Cir. 2009) (explaining that, under 16 C.F.R. § 310.2(z), the TSR applies to "any seller," defined as "any person who, in connection with a telemarketing transaction, provides, offers to provide, or arranges for others to provide goods or services to the customer in exchange for consideration"); United States v. DISH Network, 667 F. Supp. 2d 952 (C.D. Ill. 2009) (rule may create strict liability unless seller demonstrates that safe harbor provision applies through, for example, having written procedures and routine business practices to comply with the rule), *later op. at* 754 F. Supp. 2d 1004 (C.D. Ill. 2011)

entities who hire telemarketers to sell their goods or services, not just to the telemarketers themselves.[124]

The TSR also prohibits anyone from providing substantial assistance or support while knowing (or consciously avoiding knowing) that the seller or telemarketer has violated certain provisions of the Telemarketing Sales Rule.[125] Application of the TSR to those providing substantial assistance extends the scope of the TSR to the myriad lead generators, back-office services, and affiliated companies often used by more sophisticated operations to evade liability or to protect assets.[126] This also includes payment processors, without whom debt relief services could not operate. For example, the FTC has taken action against a payment processor for assisting and facilitating a violation of the TSR because the processor continued handling charges for the telemarketer despite high chargeback rates and knowing other details of the telemarketer's business practices.[127] This raises the question of whether the debt relief service provider's bank could also be exposed to similar liability—particularly because banks are obliged to exercise due diligence when working with third-party payment processors.[128] This obligation includes understanding who the payment processor does business with.[129] In 2013, the CFPB used this aspect of the rule to shut down a company that maintained accounts and processed payments for debt relief service providers despite knowing that the providers were charging illegal advance fees.[130]

Unlike many transactions covered by the TSR, it applies to debt relief services not only when the debt relief service initiates the call but also when the customer initiates a call in response to the seller's advertisement in any medium or to direct mail solicitation (via mail, email, or fax).[131] Thus the TSR generally applies to any debt relief service when consumers obligate themselves via a telephone communication.

A important exception to the TSR's coverage is that it does not apply when a sale may be initiated over the phone but is not completed, or payment not authorized, until after a face-to-face meeting.[132] This exemption is intended to apply only to substantive meetings, so debt relief providers should not be able to exploit the exemption by organizing a token document signing with a notary or the office receptionist. If the face-to-face meeting is at the customer's home or away from the seller's place of business, the seller must comply with the FTC's Door-to-Door Sales Rule.[133] But neither rule applies when the debt relief service succeeds in having the consumer come to the seller's office and complete the transaction there.

Attorneys are not specifically exempt from the Telemarketing Sales Rule,[134] but the FTC assumes most will be exempt in practice because the TSR only applies to interstate telemarketing and because of the "face-to-face meeting" exemption.[135] The FTC has produced a guide for businesses, including attorneys, that lists questions and answers regarding the exemptions.[136] Section 10.7.3, *infra*, discusses whether attorneys are exempt from state laws.

The TSR also does not apply when the customer initiates a call that is not in response to any form of solicitation by the seller or telemarketer.[137] However, this exemption does not apply to "upselling,"[138] which is when the consumer initiates the call and the seller seeks to solicit the purchase of

---

(claim stated; giving weight to seller's failure to effectively monitor dealers' telemarketing). *See also* Federal Trade Comm'n v. Global Mktg. Grp., Inc., 594 F. Supp. 2d 1281 (M.D. Fla. 2008) (granting FTC motion for summary judgment against defendant for violating the Telemarketing Sales Rule when defendant was intimately involved in day-to-day operations of twenty-four corporations that assisted telemarketers that induced consumers to pay fees for credit cards and credit card loss protection services which consumers never received).

124 *See, e.g.*, Fed. Trade Comm'n v. Stefanchik, 559 F.3d 924, 930 (9th Cir. 2009) (individual and his company liable under telemarketing rule when they arranged for telemarketer to promote sales, retained authority to review and approve all marketing materials, and decided what products would be sold); United States v. DISH Network, L.L.C., 2011 WL 98951 (C.D. Ill. Jan. 10, 2011) (key issue is whether seller of satellite television services caused telemarketing violations by its network of dealers), *later op. at* 754 F. Supp. 2d 1004 (C.D. Ill. 2011) (claim stated; giving weight to seller's failure to effectively monitor telemarketing by dealers).

125 16 C.F.R. § 310.3(b) ("It is a deceptive telemarketing act or practice and a violation of this Rule for a person to provide substantial assistance or support to any seller or telemarketer when that person knows or consciously avoids knowing that the seller or telemarketer is engaged in any act or practice that violates §§ 310.3(a), (c) or (d), or § 310.4 of this Rule.").

126 *See, e.g.*, Zimmerman v. Puccio, 613 F.3d 60 (1st Cir. 2010) (describing elaborate business arrangement involving sham nonprofit credit counseling firm and numerous, related, for-profit entities).

127 *See, e.g.*, FTC v. Innovative Wealth Builders, Inc., No. 8:13-cv-123-T-33EAJ, First Amended Complaint (June 4, 2013) and Stipulated Order for Permanent Injunction (Sept. 9, 2013), *available at* www.ftc.gov (detailing numerous misrepresentations and unsubstantiated claims regarding debt settlement services).

128 Federal Financial Institutions Examination Council, Bank Secrecy Act/Anti-Money Laundering Examination Manual, Third-Party Payment Processors—Overview (2010), *available at* www.ffiec.gov.

129 *Id.*

130 Stipulated Final Judgment and Consent Order, CFPB v. Meracord, L.L.C., No. 3:13-cv-05871 (W.D. Wash. Oct. 4, 2013).

131 16 C.F.R. § 310.6(b)(5), (6).

132 16 C.F.R. § 310.6(b)(3). *See* Fed. Trade Comm'n, Bureau of Consumer Prot., Complying with the Telemarketing Sales Rule (Feb. 2011), *available at* www.ftc.gov (in section titled "Calls That Are Part of a Transaction Involving a Face-to-Face Sales Presentation," discussing extent of this exemption).

133 FTC Rule Concerning Cooling-Off Period for Sales Made at Homes or at Certain Other Locations, 16 C.F.R. pt. 429; § 2.5, *supra*.

134 *Cf.* Consumer Fin. Prot. Bureau v. Morgan Drexen, Inc., 60 F. Supp. 1082, 1094 (C.D. Cal. 2014) (exemption to CFPB's authority over practice of law does not apply to the extent that attorney is otherwise subject to any of enumerated consumer laws transferred to CFPB) (applying 12 U.S.C. § 5517(e)(3)).

135 Fed. Trade Comm'n, Bureau of Consumer Prot., Debt Relief Services & the Telemarketing Sales Rule: A Guide for Business (July 2010), *available at* www.ftc.gov (see section titled "Who's Covered by the New Rule?").

136 Fed. Trade Comm'n, Bureau of Consumer Prot., Debt Relief Services & the Telemarketing Sales Rule: What People Are Asking (Oct. 2010), *available at* www.ftc.gov.

137 16 C.F.R. § 310.6(b)(4).

138 *Id.*

additional goods or services other than those the customer is calling about.[139]

The TSR exempts sales in which the customer responds to a mailed catalog and initiates the call.[140] For this exception to apply, the catalog must describe the goods offered for sale, include multiple pages, and have been issued at least annually.[141] In addition, the exception applies only if the entity sending the catalog never solicits customers by telephone and only takes catalog orders without soliciting further orders.[142]

The TSR only applies to transactions within the FTC's general jurisdiction and so does not apply to banks and certain other depositories that may assist in a debt relief scheme.[143] The FTC Act only applies to acts by a company organized to carry on business for profit or for the profit of their members.[144] As such, the TSR does not apply to true nonprofit enterprises but does apply to sham nonprofits.[145] In addition, for-profit entities that telemarket on behalf of debt relief services are within the scope of the TSR.[146]

Given the remedial purpose of the Telemarketing Sales Rule, courts should interpret it broadly. Debt relief services should not be permitted to evade the TSR through deceptive sales tactics or complicated contractual arrangements.[147]

10.5.3   Rule Requirements for Debt Relief Services

10.5.3.1   Prohibition Against Collection of Fees Before Results Are Achieved

Some of the most important protections in the FTC Telemarketing Sales Rule for debt relief customers are the limits on when and how providers may be paid.[148] Under the TSR, sellers and telemarketers may not be paid until they achieve results.

This one provision largely prohibits any debt elimination or debt settlement service within the scope of the Telemarketing Sales Rule. Since debt elimination schemes do not actually result in debt elimination, receipt of any payment from the consumer is a violation. Similarly, debt settlement companies will not be able to seek fees until they in fact achieve results from consumers, which is entirely opposite to their business model.

Specifically, the FTC Rule states that the provider may not request or receive payment for any debt relief service until:

- The seller or telemarketer has renegotiated, settled, reduced, or otherwise altered the terms of at least one debt pursuant to a settlement agreement, debt management plan, or other valid contractual agreement executed by the customer;[149] and
- The customer has made at least one payment pursuant to the settlement agreement, debt management plan, or other agreement.[150]

If and when the debt relief provider achieves results, the Telemarketing Sales Rule limits the ways in which the fee can be calculated. These restrictions are designed to support the prohibition against up-front fees by preventing providers from front-loading their fees if a consumer has enrolled multiple debts in a debt relief program.[151]

The fee for settling each individual debt may only be calculated in one of two ways: in proportion to the total amount of debt enrolled in the service[152] or as a percentage of the amount saved by settling the specific debt.[153] Whichever method the provider chooses, it must be used consistently for all debts enrolled by the customer who owns the debts. The provider cannot use the proportional method for some debts and the percentage method for others.[154] The amount of debt used to calculate the fee must be the amount owed to the creditor at the time the customer enrolled in the debt relief service.[155]

If the debt relief service provider opts for the proportional method of calculating fees, the fee for each debt settled must be in the same proportion to the total fee (for all of the debts enrolled) as the individual debt bears to the entire amount of debt enrolled.[156] If the provider uses the percentage method, the percentage charged must be the same for each individual debt enrolled by the customer.[157]

For example, compare two debt settlement contracts, each for settling two debts—one debt being for $2000 and the other for $8000. Contract A sets the total fee at $1000 for settling both the debts. Contract B says the fee will be 35% of the amount saved by settling the debts. If the service provider

---

139   *Id.* § 310.2(ee).

140   16 C.F.R. § 310.2(dd). *Cf.* Distributel, Inc. v. State, 933 P.2d 1137 (Alaska 1997) (similar language in Alaska telemarketing law does not exclude sales made when the seller called the consumer after having sent a catalog).

141   16 C.F.R. § 310.2(dd).

142   *Id.*

143   68 Fed. Reg. 4580, 4581 n.19 (Jan. 29, 2003); Fed. Trade Comm'n, Complying with the Telemarketing Sales Rule 7 (Apr. 1996). *But cf.* Navarro v. Sears Life Ins. Co., 2008 WL 3863451 (E.D. Cal. Aug. 18, 2008) (applying rule to telemarketing sale of insurance; McCarran-Ferguson Act does not prevent application of rule).

144   15 U.S.C. § 44.

145   68 Fed. Reg. 4580, 4581 n.19 (Jan. 29, 2003).

146   Section 5.2.3.4, *supra.*

147   Consumer Fin. Prot. Bureau v. Morgan Drexen, Inc., 60 F. Supp. 3d 1082, 1094 (C.D. Cal. 2014).

148   16 C.F.R. § 310.4(a)(5).

149   16 C.F.R. § 310.4(a)(5)(i)(A).

150   16 C.F.R. § 310.4(a)(5)(i)(B).

151   *Prepared Statement of the Fed. Trade Comm'n on Bus. Practices of Debt Relief Cos. Before the Sen. Comm. on Commerce, Science, and Transp.* (Aug. 12, 2010), *available at* www.ftc.gov.

152   16 C.F.R. § 310.4(a)(5)(i)(C)(*1*).

153   16 C.F.R. § 310.4(a)(5)(i)(C)(*2*).

154   *See* 16 C.F.R. § 310.4(a)(5)(i)(C)(*2*) ("The percentage charged cannot change from one individual debt to another"). If, for example, the provider used a contract that allowed charging the greater of the amount allowed by clause (C)(*1*) or (C)(*2*), applying that provision would result in charging different percentage rates for different individual debts, which would violate the rule.

155   16 C.F.R. § 310.4(a)(5)(i)(C)(*1*), (*2*).

156   16 C.F.R. § 310.4(a)(5)(i)(C)(*1*); 75 Fed. Reg. 48,457, 48,469 (Aug. 10, 2010) ("the fee must be proportional, i.e., the same fraction of the total fee as the size of the debt resolved is of the total debt enrolled").

157   16 C.F.R. § 310.4(a)(5)(i)(C)(*2*).

settles the $2000 debt for $1500, the maximum fee allowed for settling that debt would be $200[158] under the proportional method used in Contract A and $175[159] under Contract B.

10.5.3.2 Escrowing Fees

Even though debt relief service providers may not seek payment until they deliver results, they are allowed to require customers to regularly pay into an account the money necessary to cover the provider's fee and to fund anticipated settlement agreements with creditors.[160] These payments may be required before the provider performs any work on the contract, but the Telemarketing Sales Rule imposes a number of restrictions on the provider's ability to impose such a requirement:[161]

- The funds must be held in an account at an insured financial institution;
- The customer owns the funds held in the account and must be paid accrued interest on the account, if any;
- The entity administering the account must not be owned or controlled by, or in any way affiliated with, the debt relief service;
- The entity administering the account must not give or accept any kickbacks for referrals involving the debt relief service;
- The customer must be allowed to withdraw from the debt relief service at any time without penalty; and
- When the customer withdraws, he or she must, within seven business days of the customer's request, receive all the money in the account, other than funds legally earned by the debt relief service.

10.5.3.3 Disclosures

When a telemarketing call involves a debt relief service, the seller or telemarketer must make a number of disclosures to the customer in addition to those required for other calls covered by the Telemarketing Sales Rule.[162] The disclosures must be made truthfully, in a clear and conspicuous manner, and before the customer enrolls in the service or consents to pay for any goods or other services offered.[163] Failure to meet this requirement is a deceptive act or practice and a violation of the Telemarketing Sales Rule.[164]

For calls involving debt relief services, the seller or telemarketer must disclose how long it will take to achieve the represented results.[165] When the service may include making

a settlement offer to any of the customer's creditors or debt collectors,[166] the seller or telemarketer must also disclose:

- When the provider will make a bona fide settlement offer to each creditor or debt collector;[167] and
- The amount of money or the percentage of each debt the customer must accumulate before the provider will make a settlement offer.[168]

If any aspect of the debt relief service relies upon or results in the consumer failing to pay creditors or debt collectors, sellers and telemarketers must disclose that using the service:

- Will adversely affect the customer's creditworthiness;
- May result in the customer being sued or subject to debt collection activities; and
- May cause the customer's debt to grow from the accrual of fees and interest.[169]

The Telemarketing Sales Rule allows debt relief providers to request or require customers to pay into an account funds that will be used for the provider's fees and for payments to creditors.[170] If the provider does so, the seller or telemarketer must disclose that:

- The customer owns the funds;
- The customer may withdraw from the service at any time without penalty; and
- If the customer withdraws, he or she is entitled to a full refund of all money in the account, other than fees earned by the service provider in accordance with the payment provisions of the Telemarketing Sales Rule.[171]

10.5.3.4 Deceptive Telemarketing Acts and Practices

It is a deceptive telemarketing act or practice and a violation of the Telemarketing Sales Rule for telemarketers and sellers to misrepresent "any material aspect of any debt relief service."[172] The rule gives several examples of aspects of the debt relief service that cannot be misrepresented, including the information covered by the required disclosures,[173] any effect the service will have on collection efforts by creditors or debt collectors, the provider's success rate, and whether the service is offered by a nonprofit entity.[174]

10.5.3.5 Unsubstantiated Claims

Another highly important FTC Rule requirement is that debt relief providers must have a reasonable basis to substantiate

---

158 The total amount of debt enrolled is $10,000 ($2000 + $8000). The $2000 debt is 20% of the total amount of debt enrolled ($2000 ÷ $10,000 = 0.2). Twenty percent of the $1000 total fee is $200.

159 The amount saved was $500 ($2000 − $1500 = $500). Thirty-five percent of $500 is $175 ($500 × 0.35 = $175).

160 16 C.F.R. § 310.4(a)(5)(ii).

161 16 C.F.R. § 310.4(a)(5)(ii)(A)–(E).

162 These other disclosures are set out at § 5.3.2, *supra*.

163 16 C.F.R. § 310.3(a)(1).

164 16 C.F.R. § 310.3(a)(1).

165 16 C.F.R. § 310.3(a)(1)(viii)(A).

166 16 C.F.R. § 310.3(a)(1)(viii)(A).

167 16 C.F.R. § 310.3(a)(1)(viii)(A).

168 16 C.F.R. § 310.3(a)(1)(viii)(B).

169 16 C.F.R. § 310.3(a)(1)(viii)(C).

170 16 C.F.R. § 310.4(a)(5)(ii).

171 16 C.F.R. § 310.3(a)(1)(viii)(D). *See* § 10.5.3.1, *supra*.

172 16 C.F.R. § 310.3(a)(2)(x).

173 *See* § 10.5.3.3, *supra*.

174 16 C.F.R. § 310.3(a)(2)(x).

any claims regarding specific savings or other results.[175] The FTC's Statement of Basis and Purpose provides extensive guidance about the evidence providers must possess before they make such claims. First, debt service providers must account for the additional debt and costs consumers incur as a result of interest, late fees, and other charges imposed by creditors during the course of the program.

Second, in calculating any savings, providers must account for the fees paid to the provider by the consumer. Third, they must include in their calculation of savings those consumers who dropped out or were otherwise unable to complete the program. Finally, they must account for individual accounts that were not settled successfully.

Thus, providers may not exclude debts they have failed to settle from their calculations of the average savings consumers achieve.[176] These requirements are particularly significant because they will prevent providers from making claims about their success rates that are based on anecdotal evidence or manipulated statistics. Any claim regarding a provider's results should be considered deceptive if it cannot produce this data.

10.5.4 Recordkeeping Requirements

The Telemarketing Sales Rule requires those subject to the rule to maintain a list of records that should be discoverable in litigation. Even when an aggrieved consumer has no right of action under the Rule, records maintained pursuant to the Rule may prove invaluable to establishing other causes of action.[177]

Telemarketers and sellers are required to maintain materials—including advertising and promotional materials, telemarketing scripts, and names and addresses of customers—for twenty-four months. If the company goes out of business, its principal is required to maintain the records. If the company is sold or changes ownership, the new owner is required to maintain the records.[178]

10.5.5 Private Remedies and Government Enforcement

FTC Telemarketing Sales Rule violations can be remedied as set out in the Telemarketing and Consumer Fraud and Abuse Prevention Act.[179] Private remedies, government enforcement under this statute, and remedies under UDAP and other statutes for Rule violations are examined in more detail at § 5.6, *supra*.

In brief, the statute provides that any person adversely affected by any pattern or practice of Telemarketing Sales Rule violations may bring an action in federal court if the amount in controversy exceeds $50,000 in actual damages for each person adversely affected by such telemarketing.[180] The reference to actual damages excludes punitive damages[181] and possibly attorney fees from the computation of those damages but should include consequential damages, including damage to a consumer's credit worthiness (for example, having to pay a higher interest rate to obtain a mortgage), physical ailments as a result of the violation, and perhaps pain and suffering.[182] The $50,000 threshold can thus be met when the debt relief services in fact worsens the consumer's credit rating for years into the future or causes serious emotional distress, particularly with physical symptoms.

The court may award to the prevailing party costs of suit and reasonable fees for attorneys and expert witnesses.[183] While this presents some risk to a plaintiff having to pay the telemarketer's attorney fees and costs, the Supreme Court in a Civil Rights Act case has said that, when the court may issues fees to the prevailing party, a successful civil rights plaintiff should recover "in all but special circumstances" and that prevailing defendants should recover only when the claim is frivolous, unreasonable, or without foundation.[184]

Consumers can also bring suit in state court under their state UDAP statute for Telemarketing Sales Rule violations, since a violation of an FTC rule will be treated as a per se UDAP violation in most states,[185] and the practice violating the rule may be unfair and deceptive in its own right.

State attorneys general and other state consumer protection authorities are authorized under the Telemarketing and Consumer Fraud and Abuse Prevention Act to file suit in federal court when there is a pattern or practice of FTC Telemarketing Sales Rule violations.[186] The statute authorizes them to seek an injunction to stop the telemarketing practice and to recover damages, restitution, or other compensation on

---

175 75 Fed. Reg. 48,458, 48,500–48,501 (Aug. 10, 2010). *See, e.g.*, FTC v. Innovative Wealth Builders, Inc., No. 8:13-cv-123-T-33EAJ, First Amended Complaint (June 4, 2013) and Stipulated Order for Permanent Injunction (Sept. 9, 2013), *available at* www.ftc.gov (detailing numerous misrepresentations and unsubstantiated claims regarding debt settlement services).

176 75 Fed. Reg. 48,458, 48,500–48,501 (Aug. 10, 2010). *See also Prepared Statement of the Fed. Trade Comm'n on Bus. Practices of Debt Relief Cos. Before the Sen. Comm. on Commerce, Science, and Transp.* (Aug. 12, 2010), *available at* www.ftc.gov (summarizing substantiation requirements).

177 *See, e.g.*, Zimmerman v. Puccio, 613 F.3d 60 (1st Cir. 2010) (telemarketing scripts used to prove violation of Credit Repair Organizations Act).

178 16 C.F.R. § 310.5.

179 15 U.S.C. §§ 6101–6108.

180 15 U.S.C. § 6104(a).

The legislative history indicates that federal courts will have exclusive jurisdiction and also that the $50,000 threshold applies to any action under the Act irrespective of the court before which the case is brought. *See* H. Rep. No. 103-20, 4 U.S.C.C.A.N. 1635 (103d Cong. 2d Sess. 1994).

181 *See* H. Rep. No. 103-20, 4 U.S.C.C.A.N. 1635 (103d Cong. 2d Sess. 1994).

182 *See* Federal Aviation Admin. v. Cooper, 132 S. Ct. 1441 (2012) (discussing the meaning of actual damages as provided in federal statutes).

183 15 U.S.C. § 6104(d).

184 Christianburg Garment Co. v. Equal Employment Opportunity Comm'n, 434 U.S. 412 (1978).

185 *See* National Consumer Law Center, Unfair and Deceptive Acts and Practices §§ 3.2.6, 3.4.5 (8th ed. 2012), *updated at* www.nclc.org/library.

186 15 U.S.C. § 6103(a), (f)(2).

behalf of the state's citizens.[187] The FTC and CFPB both have authority to enforce the Rule,[188] with the same enforcement authorities that those agencies have to enforce other rules.[189]

10.6 Fair Debt Collection Practices Act

There is an argument that debt relief organizations receiving payments from consumers and distributing them to creditors meets the definition of "debt collector" under the Fair Debt Collection Practices Act (FDCPA), as they are collecting debts that are "owed or due another."[190] If so, they will be covered by the FDCPA and probably a number of state debt collection laws as well.[191]

The FDCPA prohibits unfair and deceptive practices and enumerates many different requirements, including required notices and consumer rights.[192] Private remedies include actual damages, statutory damages up to $1000, and attorney fees.[193]

Factual investigation is likely to show that the credit counseling organization acts only as an intermediary between the consumer and the creditor without assuming any part of the consumer's legal liability for the debt. Thus one federal court has refused to read into the FDCPA a categorical exclusion for credit counseling services retained by the debtor and instead required additional fact-finding to determine if the debt relief service fell within the FDCPA's scope.[194]

On the other hand another court has held that a credit counseling organization was not a debt collector because the consumer, rather than the creditor, retained it.[195] However, the court appears to have based this conclusion on the view that the credit counseling organization "assume[d] the consumer's debts," which is not the case.[196]

The FDCPA does exempt "any nonprofit organization which, at the request of consumers, performs bona fide consumer credit counseling and assists consumers in the liquidation of their debts by receiving payments from such consumers and distributing such amounts to creditors."[197] While this exemption applies to legitimate nonprofit credit counseling, the very existence of the exemption for nonprofits implies that for-profit credit counselors and other debt relief services are covered by the FDCPA.[198] Thus, when a consumer alleged that a credit counseling organization was not in fact operating as a nonprofit, a federal court held that it was a fact question whether the organization fell within this exception.[199]

10.7 State Regulation of Debt Relief Services

10.7.1 Statutes Requiring Registration and Licensing

Most states have enacted legislation requiring at least certain debt relief agencies to be registered or licensed. This section will generally use the term "licensed" to also include "registered" and similar concepts. These statutes can be significant because often debt settlement or other debt relief agencies argue that they are not covered by the licensing requirement. If courts hold otherwise, then consumers have strong remedies against these entities selling services while unlicensed.

The statute itself may or may not provide a private remedy for unlicensed agencies engaging in debt relief, but the practice is clearly a state UDAP violation.[200] In addition, in many states the contract with the consumer is void and the consumer must be returned all monies paid.[201]

A number of issues arise as to whether a debt relief service must be, or even can be, licensed. A few state debt relief statutes only allow nonprofits to be licensed, so for-profit credit counseling or other types of for-profit debt relief services covered by the statute are prohibited.[202] In other states, the licensing requirement only applies to for-profit entities, so truly nonprofit agencies need not be registered or licensed. Statutes may also apply the licensing requirement to only those organizations that charge fees or receive consideration for services.

The state law summaries in Appendix I, *infra*, indicate which states require certain debt relief service providers to obtain a license or registration. The appendix specifies whether the registration or licensing law explicitly exempts nonprofit agencies or other providers that do not charge for services. (For example, the Uniform Law Commission's (ULC) Debt Management Services Act does not apply to providers that receive no compensation from either their customers or from their creditors, thus applying to nonprofits that accept payments).

---

187 15 U.S.C. § 6103(a). *See, e.g.,* Tennessee v. Lexington Law Firms, 1997 U.S. Dist. LEXIS 7403, 1997-1 Trade Cas. (CCH) ¶ 71,8201 (M.D. Tenn. May 14, 1997) (seeking a permanent injunction and other equitable relief); New York v. Fin. Services Network, 930 F. Supp. 865 (W.D.N.Y. 1996) (granting preliminary injunction in suit brought by New York and North Carolina). *See also* Iowa Code § 714.16 (authorizing Iowa Attorney General to bring suit under the federal statute on behalf of Iowa residents).

188 15 U.S.C. §§ 6102(c), 6105. *See* Federal Trade Comm'n v. Micom Corp., 1997 U.S. Dist. LEXIS 3404, 1997-1 Trade Cas. (CCH) ¶ 71,753 (S.D.N.Y. Mar. 12, 1997).

189 *See* §§ 2.2.5, 3.9, *supra.*

190 15 U.S.C. § 1692a(6).

191 15 U.S.C. §§ 1692–1692p.

192 *See* National Consumer Law Center, Fair Debt Collection (8th ed. 2014), *updated at* www.nclc.org/library.

193 National Consumer Law Center, Fair Debt Collection Ch. 6 (8th ed. 2014), *updated at* www.nclc.org/library.

194 Yang v. DTS Fin. Grp., 570 F. Supp. 2d 1257, 1260 (S.D. Cal. 2008) (denying defendants' motion to dismiss).

195 Limpert v. Cambridge Credit Counseling, 328 F. Supp. 2d 360 (E.D.N.Y. 2004).

196 *Id.* at 363.

197 15 U.S.C. § 1692a(6)(E).

198 Yang v. DTS Fin. Grp., 570 F. Supp. 2d 1257, 1260 (S.D. Cal. 2008).

199 *Id.*

200 *See* § 10.7.6, *infra.*

201 *See* § 10.7.6, *infra.*

202 *See, e.g.,* N.J. Stat. Ann. §§ 2C:21-19, 17:16G-2 (West); N.Y. Banking Law, § 579 (McKinney) (budget planning services).

Among the states that require licensing or registration, the trend is to require both nonprofit and for-profit agencies to obtain a license. This trend can be explained, at least in part, by the 2005 and 2008 versions of the ULC Debt Management Act that gives states the option of restricting debt management to nonprofit organizations or allowing for-profits to operate as well. The 2011 version does not even provide an option to restrict the statute only to nonprofits. Many states that previously restricted debt management to nonprofits are opening up the business in their states to for-profits.[203]

A number of states, instead of licensing or registering debt management agencies, prohibit debt management and debt settlement outright but provide that certain entities are exempt from this prohibition, typically including nonprofits and sometimes attorneys.[204] These statutes effectively limit debt management to nonprofit and certain other providers such as licensed attorneys. Finally, a few states do not license or register debt adjustment agencies and do not prohibit them outright but do regulate them extensively.[205]

10.7.2 Types of Debt Relief Services That Must Be Licensed or Registered

A key question is whether a state statute requiring licensing or registration of debt relief services applies just to consumer credit counseling or whether it also applies to debt settlement, debt negotiation, and debt elimination services. Most of the cases consider the application to debt settlement.

In 2005, the Uniform Law Commission enacted a model debt management law (ULC Debt Management Act), amended it in 2008, and again in 2011.[206] The basic coverage of the law remains unchanged in all three versions, applying to "debt management services," broadly defined as intermediary services between an individual and one or more creditors of the individual for the purpose of obtaining concessions. This model has been adopted in seven states,[207] and a number of other states have enacted statutes with similar coverage.[208] The 2008 and 2011 versions of the Act are summarized in Appendix I, *infra*.

This should encompass credit counseling agencies that provide DMPs, debt settlement companies that purport to reduce debts through settlement, and debt negotiation services that negotiate with creditors for consumers. It will also cover certain debt elimination services as well, such as when a service sets up an arbitration forum to hear the consumer's dispute with the creditor or perhaps even when the agency provides documents to submit to the creditor. In all these cases, the debt relief service agency provides "intermediary" services between the consumer and the creditor.

At other times, debt management statutes covering credit counseling with DMPs also explicitly apply to debt settlement services.[209] Another way in which states deal with debt

---

203 Examples include Maine and Texas, which eliminated the nonprofit requirement for debt management in 2007. New Hampshire and Rhode Island made similar changes in 2004, as did Virginia in 2005 and Mississippi in 2006. Pennsylvania followed the trend in 2008, passing a law that allows for-profits to provide debt management and debt settlement services as long as they are licensed. The previous Pennsylvania law prohibiting "debt pooling" did not apply to nonprofit organizations. This old law is still in effect, but agencies that comply with the new licensing procedures are not subject to liability under the debt pooling law unless the license is denied, suspended, or revoked or its renewal is refused. 63 Pa. Stat. Ann. §§ 2401 to 2449 (West).

204 Ark. Code Ann. §§ 5-63-301 to 5-63-305 (debt management or debt settlement); Haw. Rev. Stat. §§ 446-1 to 446-4 (debt management and debt settlement); Mass. Gen. Laws Ann. ch. 221, § 46C (defining debt management and debt settlement as the practice of law), ch. 180, § 4A (allowing nonprofit charitable credit counseling corporations to provide debt management plans); N.M. Stat. Ann. §§ 56-2-1 to 56-2-4 (debt management and debt settlement); N.C. Gen. Stat. §§ 14-432 to 14-426 (debt adjustment and debt settlement); Okla. Stat. tit. 24, §§ 15 to 18 (debt management); W. Va. Code § 61-10-23 (debt management); Wyo. Stat. Ann. §§ 33-14-101 to 33-14-103 (debt management or debt settlement).

205 *See* Fla. Stat. §§ 817.801 to 817.806 (credit counseling and debt management; caps fees); Ga. Code Ann. §§ 18-5-1 to 18-5-4 (debt management and debt settlement; limits fees); Ohio Rev. Code Ann. §§ 4710.02 to 4710.99 (West) (debt management and debt settlement; auditing, insurance, handling of funds, caps fees); Wash Rev. Code §§ 18.28.010 to 18.28.910 (debt management and debt settlement; detailed regulation).

206 Unif. Law Comm'n, Uniform Debt-Management Act, *available at* www.uniformlaws.org.

207 Colo. Rev. Stat. §§ 12-14.5-201 to 12-14.5-242; Del. Code Ann. tit. 6, §§ 2401A to 2439A; Nev. Rev. Stat. §§ 676A.010 to 676A.780; N.D. Cent. Code §§ 13-11-101 to 13-11-29; R.I. Gen. Laws §§ 19-14.8-1 to 19-14.8-43; Tenn. Code Ann. §§ 47-18-5501 to 47-18-5541; Utah Code §§ 13-42-101 to 13-42-141. *See also* V.I. Code Ann. tit. 12A §§ 401 to 441.

208 *See* Ky. Rev. Stat. Ann. §§ 380.010(3) (West); Me. Rev. Stat. tit. 32, § 6172(2)(D); Miss. Code Ann. §§ 81-22-3(b)(iv); N.J. Stat. Ann. §§ 17:16G-1(c) (West); Ore. Rev. Stat. §§ 697.602(2)(d); Tex. Fin. Code Ann. §§ 394.202(3-a), (6) (West); Vt. Stat. Ann. tit. 8, §§ 2751(2).

209 *See, e.g.*, Colo. Rev. Stat. § 12-14.5-201; Del. Code Ann. tit. 6, § 2401A; Ind. Code § 24-5-15-2; Iowa Code § 533A.1 (defining "debt management" to include debt settlement); Idaho Code Ann. §§ 26-2222(9), 26-2223(7) (defining debt counselor and credit counselor to include providers of both pro-rating and debt settlement); Kan. Stat. Ann. § 50-1117(d)(3) (defining "debt management service" to include negotiating or offering to negotiate to defer or reduce a consumer's credit obligations); Ky. Rev. Stat. Ann. § 380.010 (West); Me. Rev. Stat. tit. 32, § 6172 (defining "debt management service" to include acting as an intermediary for the purpose of settling the consumer's obligation); Minn. Stat. § 332A.02; Miss. Code Ann. § 81-22-3 ("debt management service" includes adjusting, compromising, negotiating, settling, discharging or otherwise deferring, reducing or altering the terms of payment of the consumer's obligation); Nev. Rev. Stat. § 676A.140; N.H. Rev. Stat. Ann. § 399-D:2 ("debt adjustment" means negotiating on behalf of a consumer); N.Y. Gen. Bus. Law § 455 (McKinney) ("budget planning" includes distributing, or supervising, coordinating or controlling the distribution of debtor's money); Or. Rev. Stat. § 697.602 ("debt management service" includes acting as an intermediary on a consumer's behalf to obtain a concession from a creditor); 63 Pa. Stat. Ann. §§ 2401 to 2448 (West) (debt settlement provisions are in flux after a state appellate court found some provisions to be unconstitutional); R.I. Gen. Laws §§ 19-14.8-2; S.C. Code §§ 37-7-101 (defining credit counseling services to include debt management, debt settlement, and credit repair); Tenn. Code Ann. §§ 47-18-5501 to 47-18-5541; Tex. Fin. Code Ann. § 394.202 (West); Utah Code Ann. § 13-42-101 (West); Vt. Stat. Ann. tit. 8, § 2751 ("debt adjustment" includes

---

settlement is to exclude it from the debt management statute[210] but enact a separate licensing statute specifically for debt settlement.[211] Consumers Union and the National Consumer Law Center jointly issued a model debt settlement law in 2012.[212]

In some situations, the language is more ambiguous as to whether debt settlement is covered by a debt management licensing statute. Debt adjustment statutes are enacted to protect consumers and, as a remedial statute, should be construed liberally in favor of the consumer.[213]

Often courts will be asked to determine if a debt settlement company is covered by a "debt adjuster" law that applies to agencies that collect payments from consumer for distribution to creditors, sometimes called prorating debt, that will typically apply to entities that escrow, handle, manage, or otherwise control client funds.[214] The debt settlement companies argue that they do not escrow, handle, manage, or otherwise

control their clients' funds[215] but instead ask the consumer to forward the money to a third party that places the funds in a separate account, authorizing the debt settlement agency to receive fees directly out of that account.[216] For example, one recent case cited to the fact that the third party contracted with over 500 different debt settlement firms and managed for them over 600,000 accounts.[217] The debt settlement companies claim solely to negotiate for the consumer, while the third party holds the money in escrow.

However, courts frequently reject this argument that the debt settlement company does not manage or control the funds,[218] so the debt settlement company must be licensed under the debt adjustment or similar law.[219] Courts hold that the debt settlement company need not be in physical possession of the funds to be covered by the statute.[220] The companies maintain sufficient control over customer funds, through authorizations and other arrangements, to be covered by the statute and would not provide services until those funds are deposited in the third-party account.[221] The debt settlement

---

services as an intermediary between a debtor and one or more of the debtor's creditors for the purpose of obtaining concessions); Va. Code §§ 6.2-2000 (defining credit counselor as one who engages in debt management, financial planning or debt settlement); V.I. Code Ann. tit. 12A, § 401; Wash. Rev. Code § 18.28.010.

In 2007, Missouri enacted a law that eliminated the prohibition on debt adjustment services for consideration as long as the debt adjuster is working under a debt management plan. Debt adjusting services include settling of debts. Mo. Rev. Stat. §§ 425.010, 425.020.

The California statute exempts nonprofit debt settlement agencies from the licensing requirements as long as the agencies charge fees below the required fee limits. Cal. Fin. Code § 12104 (West).

The majority of debt settlement agencies are for-profit and should not be exempted from licensing even if they did charge fees under the limits.

210 Conn. Gen. Stat.§§ 36a-656 (defining debt adjustment as receiving funds for distribution to creditors), 36a-671(c) (exempting licensed debt adjusters from licensing pursuant to debt settlement statute); 205 Ill. Comp. Stat. § 665/2 (defining debt management to exclude debt settlement covered by Debt Settlement Consumer Protection Act); Ind. Code § 28-1-29-1(2) (defining debt management company to exclude provider of debt settlement services); Md. Code Ann., Fin. Inst. §§ 12-901 (specifying the services to be provided by debt management services provider), 12-1001(d)(1) (specifying that debt settlement does not include debt management) (West); Minn. Stat. §§ 332A(9), (13) (defining debt management and debt settlement provider), 332B.02(13) (debt settlement does not include debt management).

211 *See, e.g.*, Conn. Gen. Stat. §§ 36a-671 to 36a-671(e); 225 Ill. Comp. Stat. §§ 429/1 to 429/155; Ind. Code §§ 24-5-15-2.5 (part of credit repair statute); Md. Code Ann., Fin. Inst. §§ 12-1001 to 12-1017 (West); Minn. Stat. §§ 332B.02 to 332B.14; Mont. Code Ann. §§ 30-14-2101 to 30-14-2104 (does not apply to for-profit or nonprofit providers that are subject to separate debt management act); 63 Pa. Stat. Ann. §§ 2401–2449 (West). *But see* U.S. Organizations for Bankruptcy Alternatives v. Dep't of Banking, 991 A.2d 370 (Pa. Commw. Ct. 2010) (Pennsylvania requirement that the state regulator issue separate regulations governing the conduct of debt settlement services struck down as violating the state constitution).

212 National Consumer Law Center & Consumers Union, Model Debt Settlement Law for States (Jan. 2012), *available at* www.nclc.org.

213 Smith v. Legal Helpers Debt Resolution, L.L.C., 2011 WL 5166494 (W.D. Wash. Oct. 31, 2011).

214 *See, e.g.*, Ariz. Rev. Stat. Ann. § 6-701(4); Cal. Fin. Code § 12002.1 (West); La. Rev. Stat. Ann. § 37:2582; Mich. Comp. Laws § 451.412(d); Neb. Rev. Stat. § 69-1201(1); N.H. Rev. Stat. Ann. § 399:D-2(IV); N.Y. Gen. Bus. Law. § 455 (McKinney); Wis. Stat. § 218.02(1)(a). *See also* Morgan Drexen, Inc. v. Wis. Dep't of Fin. Institutions, 862 N.W.2d 329 (Wis. Ct. App. 2015) (affirming decision finding company was debt

adjustment service company under state prorater law and ordering disgorgement of unlawfully collected fees).

215 *See, e.g.*, Kendall v. Able Debt Settlement, Inc. (*In re* Kendall), 440 B.R. 526 (B.A.P. 8th Cir. 2010) (debt settlement company not subject to state "debt adjuster" law because it does not collect payments from consumer for distribution to creditors).

216 *See* Ass'n of Settlement Cos., Position Paper (Mar. 9, 2006), *available at* www.ftc.gov. *See also* Association of Settlement Cos. v. Dep't of Banking, 977 A.2d 1257 (Pa. Commw. Ct. 2009) (debt settlement trade organization claimed that most debt settlement companies do not hold, handle, or control their clients' funds).

217 Carlsen v. Global Client Solutions, L.L.C., 256 P.3d 321 (Wash. 2011).

218 *See* 225 Ill. Comp. Stat. §§ 429/1 to 429/155; Nationwide Asset Services, Inc. v. DuFauchard, 79 Cal. Rptr. 3d 844 (Cal. Ct. App. 2008); *In re* SDS W. Corp., No. 07CC148 (Ill. Dep't of Fin. & Prof'l Reg., Div. of Fin. Institutions Jan. 11, 2008), *available at* www.nclc.org/unreported (Illinois has since adopted a new debt settlement law); Pavlov v. Debt Resolvers USA, Inc., 907 N.Y.S.2d 798 (N.Y. Civ. Ct. 2010); Carlsen v. Global Client Solutions, L.L.C., 256 P.3d 321 (Wash. 2011) (interpreting Wash. Rev. Code §§ 18.28.010(1)–(2), 18.28.080); JK Harris Fin. Recovery Sys., 718 N.W.2d 739 (Wis. Ct. App. 2006) (citing Wis. Stat. § 218.02). *See also* Smith v. Legal Helpers Debt Resolution, L.L.C., 2011 WL 5166494 (W.D. Wash. Oct. 31, 2011); Estrella v. Freedom Fin. Network, L.L.C., 778 F. Supp. 2d 1041 (N.D. Cal. 2011) (discussing evidence at length; fact question whether debt settlement company was in constructive receipt of consumers' funds).

219 *See* Nationwide Asset Services, Inc. v. DuFauchard, 79 Cal. Rptr. 3d 844 (Cal. Ct. App. 2008); JK Harris Fin. Recovery Sys., 718 N.W.2d 739 (Wis. Ct. App. 2006) (citing Wis. Stat. § 218.02). *See also* Press Release, State of Cal., Dep't of Corps., Order Prohibits Debt Reduction Companies from Operating Without a License (Aug. 28, 2006), *available at* www.businesswire.com.

220 *See* Nationwide Asset Services, Inc. v. DuFauchard, 79 Cal. Rptr. 3d 844 (Cal. Ct. App. 2008); Pavlov v. Debt Resolvers USA, Inc., 907 N.Y.S.2d 798 (N.Y. Civ. Ct. 2010); Carlsen v. Global Client Solutions, L.L.C., 256 P.3d 321 (Wash. 2011) (interpreting Wash. Rev. Code §§ 18.28.010(1)–(2), 18.28.080); JK Harris Fin. Recovery Sys., 718 N.W.2d 739 (Wis. Ct. App. 2006) (citing Wis. Stat. § 218.02). *See also* Estrella v. Freedom Fin. Network, L.L.C., 778 F. Supp. 2d 1041 (N.D. Cal. 2011) (discussing evidence at length; fact question whether debt settlement company was in constructive receipt of consumers' funds).

221 *See* 225 Ill. Comp. Stat. §§ 429/1 to 429/155; Nationwide Asset Services, Inc. v. DuFauchard, 79 Cal. Rptr. 3d 844 (Cal. Ct. App. 2008); *In re*

company can also be seen as being covered by a statute applying to entities that "coordinate" the funds going to a creditor.[222]

State debt management statutes have also been found to apply to the third party holding the funds in a debt settlement scheme, whether or not the debt settlement company itself is covered.[223] The third party's cooperation with the debt settlement provider and its involvement in receiving and distributing the funds have been found to be sufficient to meet the statutory definition of "debt management service."[224]

10.7.3 Whether Attorneys Are Exempt

Many state debt management statutes include a blanket exemption or a narrower exemption for attorneys who provide debt relief services that are incidental to the practice of law. These exemptions are summarized in Appendix I, *infra*. In addition, in most states the attorney must be licensed in the state to claim the exemption.[225] An out-of-state law firm cannot exempt itself from a state statute by hiring an in-state attorney as an independent contractor,[226] but the contractor may be exempt.

Such an exemption certainly protects an attorney who occasionally helps a client settle a debt to avoid litigation or bankruptcy. But the exemption is more often disputed when invoked by organizations that regularly settle large numbers of debts for many clients—frequently employing non-attorneys to do all the work and only nominally involving licensed attorneys.

The tactic of involving an attorney so a non-attorney can claim an exemption has become known as the "attorney model." This practice has been the subject of extensive litigation.[227] The role of non-attorney service providers is always central to disputes over whether someone may claim

the exemption. Are the non-attorneys working for the attorney under proper supervision, as they would in a stereotypical law firm? Or is the attorney superfluous and little more than a name on the contract?

The Colorado Supreme Court addressed the role of non-attorneys in a case involving one of the country's largest debt relief services providers, Morgan Drexen.[228] The company portrayed itself as employing non-attorneys who would provide debt relief services under the supervision of independent attorneys. The attorneys would purportedly hire Morgan Drexen as a form of back-office support. The arrangement used contracts portraying Morgan Drexen as subordinate to the attorneys who hired it. However, after looking at the substance of the relationship, the court found that "Morgan Drexen [was] not acting for the lawyer in rendition of the lawyer's professional services; rather, the lawyer [was] acting for Morgan Drexen[]"[229] by lending the auspices of his or her law license. Therefore, because the attorney did not supervise the non-attorneys providing the debt relief service, the transaction was not eligible for the attorney exemption.

The Connecticut Supreme Court has described similar factors that regulators should use in determining whether a debt negotiation service provider qualifies for an attorney exemption. Focusing on the attorney's conduct, the provider does not qualify for an exemption if a Connecticut-licensed attorney does not:

- Exercise meaningful oversight over the non-attorney staff;
- Provide any genuine legal advice or services; or
- Maintain a bona fide attorney-client relationship with the client.[230]

Even though non-attorney involvement is often the focus of exemption disputes, the Connecticut factors indicate that the attorney's own conduct is always relevant. For example, if an attorney's sole practice is comprised of debt relief services, the exemption may not apply.[231]

As explained in the official comments to the Uniform Debt Management Services Act, the legal services exemption only applies if the services are rendered in an attorney-client

---

SDS W. Corp., No. 07CC148 (Ill. Dep't of Fin. & Prof'l Reg., Div. of Fin. Institutions Jan. 11, 2008), *available at* www.nclc.org/unreported (Illinois has since adopted a new debt settlement law; Carlsen v. Global Client Solutions, L.L.C., 256 P.3d 321 (Wash. 2011) (interpreting Wash. Rev. Code §§ 18.28.010(1)–(2), 18.28.080). *See also* Estrella v. Freedom Fin. Network, L.L.C., 778 F. Supp. 2d 1041 (N.D. Cal. 2011) (discussing evidence at length; fact question whether debt settlement company was in constructive receipt of consumers' funds).

222 Pavlov v. Debt Resolvers USA, Inc., 907 N.Y.S.2d 798 (N.Y. Civ. Ct. 2010).

223 Willis v. Debt Care, USA, Inc., 2011 WL 7121288 (D. Or. Oct. 24, 2011); Carlsen v. Global Client Solutions, L.L.C., 256 P.3d 321 (Wash. 2011) (interpreting Wash. Rev. Code §§ 18.28.010(1)–(2), 18.28.080).

224 Willis v. Debt Care, USA, Inc., 2011 WL 7121288 (D. Or. Oct. 24, 2011); Carlsen v. Global Client Solutions, L.L.C., 256 P.3d 321 (Wash. 2011) (interpreting Wash. Rev. Code §§ 18.28.010(1)–(2), 18.28.080).

225 Smith v. Legal Helpers Debt Resolution, L.L.C., 2011 WL 5166494 (W.D. Wash. Oct. 31, 2011); Kinderknecht v. Persels & Associates, L.L.C., 470 B.R. 149 (Bankr. D. Kan. 2012).

226 Kinderknecht v. Persels & Associates, L.L.C. (*In re* Kinderknecht), 470 B.R. 149 (Bankr. D. Kan. 2012).

227 *See, e.g.*, Coffman v. Williamson, 348 P.3d 929 (Colo. 2015) (service provider not eligible for legal services exemption despite involvement of in-state attorneys; legal services exemption did not violate state constitution).

228 Coffman v. Williamson, 348 P.3d 929 (Colo. 2015).

229 Coffman v. Williamson, 348 P.3d 929, 939 (Colo. 2015).

230 Persels & Associates, L.L.C. v. Banking Comm'r, ___ A.3d ___, 318 Conn. 652 (Conn. 2015). Note that the court used the ambiguous conjunction "and/or" when itemizing these requirements. Given the nature of the requirements, it is likely that all are necessary to qualify for the exemption.

231 Brown v. Consumer Law Associates, L.L.C., 283 F.R.D. 602 (E.D. Wash. 2012) (describing debt settlement company using guise of legal services to evade state law; licensed attorneys whose primary business was debt adjustment not eligible for state attorney exemption); Smith v. Legal Helpers Debt Resolution, L.L.C., 2011 WL 5166494 (W.D. Wash. Oct. 31, 2011). *See also* Parks v. Persels & Associates, L.L.C., 509 B.R. 345, 351 (D. Kan. 2014) ("apparent abandonment of the ordinary requirements of legal representation [by in-state attorney/independent contractor hired by out-of-state debt settlement firm] was so comprehensive that a rational fact finder could conclude that he was not actually engaged in the practice of law at all").

relationship.[232] The logic of this should apply to all states with attorney exclusions, even when the requirement is not expressly stated. The exclusion is based on the work the attorney performs and not the coincidental fact that the attorney has a license to practice law.[233]

Whenever an attorney is involved, the local rules of professional conduct are also relevant.[234] The American Bar Association has issued an ethics opinion saying lawyers who outsource work to non-attorneys are responsible for supervising them and remain ultimately responsible for rendering competent legal services to the client.[235] Attorneys involved in large debt-relief organizations may have difficulty proving that their practice meets professional standards—particularly the duty to adequately supervise staff.[236] Attorneys who own large operations dependent on non-attorneys may be liable for aiding and abetting the unauthorized practice of law.[237] This exposes the attorney to discipline from the state bar and to claims for malpractice.[238]

If the provider advertised that it offered the services of an attorney, consumers may also have claims for fraud, misrepresentation, or unfair and deceptive acts and practices.[239] When an attorney is just a front for a debt relief service agency, both the attorney and the agency performing the real services can be liable for violating the state's debt relief services statute.[240]

The exclusion for legal services should be considered an affirmative defense, rather than a jurisdictional matter.[241] So a provider waives it by failing to properly assert the exclusion in response to a complaint.

10.7.4 Substantive Provisions

Debt management statutes and other laws regulating debt relief services also may limit the fees agencies can charge, require written contracts, require that agencies maintain consumer payments in separate trust accounts and post bonds, and restrict other practices.[242] If the state debt management law applies to debt settlement, the typical for-profit debt settlement agency will most likely be violating the law in numerous ways.

Most clearly, the average debt settlement agency charges fees substantially higher than the fee limits in many state debt management laws. Some states use percentage limits for monthly fees, based on the level of the consumer's indebtedness (compared to income) or the total amount of the monthly DMP payment. The percentages allowed are as high as 12% or 15% in some states. In other states, a maximum dollar

---

232 Colorado v. Johnson Law Grp., P.L.L.C., 350 P.3d 961, 966 (Colo. App. 2014) (quoting Uniform Debt Management Services Act § 2, 7A U.L.A. 107 cmt. 10 (Supp. 2005)).

233 *See* Smith v. Legal Helpers Debt Resolution, L.L.C., 2011 WL 5166494 (W.D. Wash. Oct. 31, 2011); Persels & Associates, L.L.C. v. Banking Comm'r, ___ A.3d ___, 318 Conn. 652 (Conn. 2015) ("[t]o the extent attorneys engaged in these enterprises are not acting as attorneys, their conduct would fall outside the scope of the Rules of Professional Conduct and should therefore be included in the statutory scheme") (quoting Association of the Bar of the City of New York, *Profiteering from Financial Distress: An Examination of the Debt Settlement Industry* 3 (May 2012)). *See also* Parks v. Persels & Associates, L.L.C., 509 B.R. 345, 351 (D. Kan. 2014) ("apparent abandonment of the ordinary requirements of legal representation [by in-state attorney/independent contractor hired by out-of-state debt settlement firm] was so comprehensive that a rational fact finder could conclude that he was not actually engaged in the practice of law at all.").

234 Gorden v. Lloyd Ward & Assoc., P.C., 323 P.3d 1074, 1079 (Wash. Ct. App. 2014) (finding rules of professional conduct required voiding arbitration clause in retainer for debt settlement). *Accord* Meyer v. Island Grp. Partners, L.L.C., No. 2013-CV-192 (Ohio Ct. Com. Pl. Dec. 2, 2013) (applying Ohio ethics rules; voiding arbitration agreement in engagement agreement), *available at* www.nclc.org/unreported.

235 *See* ABA Formal Op. 08-451 (August 5, 2008). *See also* Model Rule of Professional Conduct 5.3 (Responsibilities Regarding Nonlawyer Assistance).

236 *See, e.g., In re* Huang, 5 Cal. State Bar Rptr. 296, 2014 WL 232686, at *1 (Cal. Bar Ct. Jan. 16, 2014), *publ'n ordered sub nom. In re* Huang, 2014 WL 866184 (Cal. Bar Ct. Mar. 4, 2014) ("[t]his case illustrates ethical problems that arise when an attorney fails to supervise nonlawyers in a high-volume law practice"; regarding mortgage loan modification services).

237 *See In re* Huang, 5 Cal. State Bar Rptr. 296, 2014 WL 232686 (Cal. Bar Ct. Jan. 16, 2014), *publ'n ordered sub nom. In re* Huang, 2014 WL 866184 (Cal. Bar Ct. Mar. 4, 2014) (attorney aided and abetted unauthorized practice of law by allowing non-attorneys to perform all work in large-scale mortgage loan modification firm).

238 *See, e.g.,* Report and Recommendation, *In re* Macey, Comm'n No. 2012PR00057 (Ill. Disciplinary Comm'n Hearing Bd. Dec. 2014); Suspension Order, M.R. 27212 (Ill. June 4, 2015) (failure to supervise non-attorney employee of debt settlement company and assisting non-attorneys in unauthorized practice of law).

239 *See, e.g.,* Bumpus v. Ward, 2012 WL 4789768, at *7 (Ohio Ct. App. Oct. 9, 2012) (consumer stated claim for fraud and fraudulent inducement by alleging that she was led to believe an attorney would perform services actually provided by non-attorneys; consumer also stated claims for violation of Credit Repair Organizations Act, state UDAP law, and had grounds to pierce corporate veil).

240 Smith v. Legal Helpers Debt Resolution, L.L.C., 2011 WL 5166494 (W.D. Wash. Oct. 31, 2011). *Cf.* Persels & Associates, L.L.C. v. Banking Comm'r, ___ A.3d ___, 318 Conn. 652 (2015) ("If the [banking] commissioner were to determine . . . that . . . the plaintiff or another debt negotiation company was merely using Connecticut attorneys as a front or facade to circumvent the debt negotiation statutes, then there would be no separation of powers problem and the commissioner would not be barred from exercising his full statutory authority.").

241 Colorado v. Johnson Law Grp., P.L.L.C., 350 P.3d 961 (Colo. App. 2014) (interpreting 2008 version of Act).

242 Ark. Code Ann. §§ 5-63-301 to 5-63-305; Del. Code Ann. tit. 11, § 910 (criminal law provision, but with an exception for providers licensed under debt management services law that became effective on Jan. 1, 2007); Fla. Stat. §§ 817.801 to 817.806 (credit counseling), §§ 559.10 to 559.13 (budget planners); Ga. Code Ann. §§ 18-5-1 to 18-5-4; 14 Guam Code Ann. §§ 7101 to 7113 (although no licensing or registration requirement, agencies must file a notice of intent and must be bonded); Haw. Rev. Stat. §§ 446-1 to 446-4; Mass. Gen. Laws ch. 180, § 4A; Mo. Rev. Stat. §§ 425.010 to 425.040 (reporting requirements and other substantive limitations); N.M. Stat. Ann. §§ 56-2-1 to 56-2-4; N.C. Gen. Stat. §§ 14-423 to 14-426; Ohio Rev. Code Ann. §§ 4710.01 to 4710.99 (West) (no registration or licensing requirement, but extensive reporting requirements and other substantive regulations); Okla. Stat. tit. 24, §§ 15 to 18; 18 Pa. Cons. Stat. § 7312; S.D. Codified Laws §§ 37-34-1 to 37-34-3; Wash. Rev. Code §§ 18.28.010 to 18.28.900; W. Va. Code § 61-10-23; Wyo. Stat. Ann. §§ 33-14-101 to 33-14-103.

cap is used.[243] At least a few states simply limit fees to bona fide and reasonable costs.[244] However, it is more common for states to use the more general standard when regulating fees for counseling and education and to set specific limits when regulating fees for debt management plans. An Illinois administrative decision imposed a $120,000 fine on a debt settlement company that was operating in the state without a license and charging fees in excess of those allowed by the state debt management service law.[245]

10.7.5 Constitutional and Jurisdictional Challenges to State Debt Relief Statutes

Debt relief service providers have attacked state regulations on constitutional grounds in a number of cases.

So far, all of the cases asserting violations of the federal constitution have failed:

- Kansas' debt relief laws have been attached and upheld a number of times. The U.S. Supreme Court ruled that the Kansas debt adjustment statute did not violate due process and its exclusion of attorneys did not violation the Equal Protection Clause.[246] Another court has upheld the application of Kansas' statute to attorneys against constitutional arguments that the statute is vague and violates the separation of powers.[247] And a third case upheld the law against a challenge under the Commerce Clause.[248]

- The Colorado Supreme Court held that Colorado's implementation of the Uniform Debt Management Services Act violated neither the federal Commerce Clause nor the Privileges and Immunities Clause.[249]

- A federal court has also upheld the Washington debt management statute against constitutional challenges that the statute impairs contracts and violates due process, equal protection, and privileges and immunities law.[250]

Cases finding no violation of the Commerce Clause are particularly important because some of the larger debt relief service providers operate across state lines. A number of state debt management laws explicitly cover organizations that do business in the state or serve consumers in the state regardless of where the organization is located.[251]

Cases alleging violations of state constitutions have had mixed results:

- The Connecticut Supreme Court held that the attorney exception to the state's debt relief services law violated the separation of powers requirements of the state constitution to the extent that it gave the banking commissioner authority to regulate the practice of law.[252]

- The Colorado Supreme Court held that the legal services exemption in Colorado's Debt Management Services Act did not violate the state constitution's separation of powers clause.[253]

- Pennsylvania's act delegating regulation of debt settlement services to the state Banking Department was struck down because it provided no standards for setting fees and because the department did not have authority to issue the regulations called for by the department.[254] (The act was replaced effective November 2014).[255]

---

243 For example, New Jersey sets a fee limit of no more than 1% of a consumer's monthly gross income but, in any case, no more than $15. N.J. Stat. Ann. § 17:16G-6 (West). *See also* Mo. Rev. Stat. § 425.010 (requires "reasonable fees"—cap of $50 for initial setup and monthly, the greater of $35 or 8% of the amount distributed monthly to creditors); Ohio Rev. Code Ann. § 4710.02 (West) (maximum initial fee of $75 and monthly, the greater of $30 or 8.5% of the amount distributed monthly to creditors); R.I. Gen. Laws § 19-14.8-23 (cap of $50 for monthly service fee); Utah Code Ann. § 13-42-123(4) (West) (cap of $50 for monthly service fee).

244 *See, e.g.,* 14 Guam Code Ann. § 7109; Tex. Fin. Code § 394.210 (West) (fees must be fair and reasonable).

245 *In re* SDS W. Corp., No. 07CC148 (Ill. Dep't of Fin. & Prof'l Reg., Div. of Fin. Institutions Jan. 11, 2008), *available at* www.nclc.org/unreported.

Illinois has since adopted a new debt settlement law. *See* 225 Ill. Comp. Stat. §§ 429/1 to 429/155.

246 Ferguson v. Skrupa, 372 US 726 (1963). *See also* Smith v. Legal Helpers Debt Resolution, L.L.C., 2011 WL 5166494 (W.D. Wash. Oct. 31, 2011).

247 Kinderknecht v. Persels & Ass'ns, L.L.C., 470 B.R. 149 (Bankr. D. Kan. 2012).

248 Cambridge Credit Counseling Corp. v. Foulston, 303 F. Supp. 2d 1188 (D. Kan. 2003), *judgment vacated, appeal dismissed,* 2004 WL 3266802 (10th Cir. Oct. 19, 2004) (dismissing appeal because of mootness), *on remand to* 2005 WL 846225 (D. Kan. Feb. 2, 2005) (dismissing case as moot).

249 Coffman v. Williamson, 348 P.3d 929, 942 (Colo. 2015).

250 Smith v. Legal Helpers Debt Resolution, L.L.C., 2011 WL 5166494 (W.D. Wash. Oct. 31, 2011).

251 *See, e.g.,* Ariz. Rev. Stat. Ann. § 6-701 (definition of debt management explicitly covers persons or companies that receive money in this state or from residents of the state); Kan. Stat. Ann. § 50-1118 (no person shall engage in debt management business with a resident of this state without first obtaining registration); Ky. Rev. Stat. Ann. § 380.040(1) (West) (debt adjusting law applies whether or not provider is located in the state); Me. Rev. Stat. tit. 32, § 6172; Md. Code Ann., Fin. Inst. § 12-906 (West) (a person who provides debt management services is subject to licensure whether or not the person maintains an office in the state); Mich. Comp. Laws § 451.414(l) (business of debt management is defined to mean providing or offering to provide debt management to one or more residents of this state); Mont. Code Ann. § 30-14-2002 (Debt Management Services Act applies to any person who provides or offers to provide debt management plans to residents of the state); N.H. Rev. Stat. Ann. § 399-D:1 (debt adjustment services are conducted in the state whenever services are performed in this state or on behalf of a person located in this state); N.Y. Gen. Bus. Law § 455 (McKinney) (an entity shall be considered as engaged in budget planning in the state if it solicits business within the state and, in connection with such solicitation, enters into a contract for budget planning with an individual then resident in the state); Tex. Fin. Code Ann. § 394.202 (West) (defining debt management services provider as a person who provides or offers to provide to a consumer in this state a debt management service); Vt. Stat. Ann. tit. 8, § 2751.

252 Persels & Associates, L.L.C. v. Banking Comm'r, ___ A.3d ___, 318 Conn. 652 (Conn. 2015).

253 Coffman v. Williamson, 348 P.3d 929 (Colo. 2015).

254 U.S. Organizations for Bankr. Alternatives, Inc. v. Dep't of Banking, 991 A.2d 370, 375 (Pa. Commw. Ct. 2010).

255 *See* Appx. I, *infra* (describing Pennsylvania's regulation of debt relief services).

10.7.6 Private Remedies

Older state debt relief laws sometimes are contained in the state criminal codes or otherwise do not provide for private enforcement. Nevertheless, there is a growing trend that state debt relief legislation provide an explicit private right of action.[256] The statutes of the seven states enacting the ULC Debt Management Act provide for the greater of compensatory damages (including non-economic injury) or $5000, treble the amount of impermissible fees collected, punitive damages, costs, and attorney fees.[257]

At other times, the statute will explicitly provide that a violation of the debt management law is a violation of the state UDAP law.[258] Even in other states, violations of these laws should be UDAP violations regardless of whether this explicit language is included.[259]

If an agency is required to be licensed but is not, a number of the debt relief services statutes provide that the contract is void or voidable, requiring money paid to be returned.[260] Thus the statutes for the seven states enacting the ULC Debt Management Act provide that, when the entity is unlicensed or takes impermissible fees, the contract is voidable, allowing the consumer to recover all amounts paid except those amounts forwarded to the consumer's creditors.[261] In addition, other law in many states provides that contracts entered into by the unlicensed entity is either void or voidable.[262]

In any action against an insolvent but licensed or registered debt relief service, one source of funds to pay for a judgment may be a bond. State licensing laws typically require the agency to purchase a bond to cover consumer claims. Another way to reach deep pockets is to sue third parties involved with the scheme, such as the party holding consumer accounts in a debt settlement scheme[263] or any other party aiding and abetting the scheme.[264]

10.8 Other Claims

10.8.1 UDAP Claims

Abuses by credit counseling, debt settlement, debt negotiation, and debt relief services are actionable under state unfair and deceptive acts and practices (UDAP) statutes.[265] Every

---

256 *See, e.g.,* Cal. Fin. Code § 12316 (West) (if prorater contracts for, receives, or makes excessive charge, contract is void and all payments must be returned to debtor); Conn. Gen. Stat. § 36a-661a (if debt management provider imposes unauthorized fee, contract is voidable, and debtor may recover any fees paid), 36a-671b (debt settlement contract that does not comply with statute is voidable); Ind. Code § 24-5-15-9 (debt settlement; greater of twice actual damages or $1000; attorney fees); Kan. Stat. Ann. § 50-1133 (private right of action for not less than the amount paid to provider; costs and attorney fees; punitive damages may be awarded); Ky. Rev. Stat. Ann. § 380.110 (West) (for ascertainable loss of money or property, right of action for actual damages; equitable relief and prevailing party attorney fees at court's discretion; punitive damages if appropriate); Me. Rev. Stat. tit. 32, § 6181 (actual damages, costs and attorney fees; if violation involved transfer of real property, consequential damages available); Md. Code Ann., Fin. Inst. §§ 12-918, 12-930 (West) (debt management: if provider imposes unauthorized fee, contract is void and funds must be returned; for any violation of statute, private right of action for actual damages, costs, and attorney fees); Mich. Comp. Laws § 451.428(5) (provider who charges excessive fee must return to debtor all payments, less the amount distributed to creditors, plus a penalty equal to the excessive fee); Minn. Stat. §§ 332A.17, 332A.18(2), 332B.12, 332B.13(2) (right to rescind contract and return of all sums not paid to creditors; private right of action for actual, incidental, and consequential damages, statutory damages up to $1000 (debt management) or $5000 (debt settlement), costs and attorney fees; class actions explicitly permitted); Miss. Code Ann. § 81-22-23(2)(d) (actual damages, costs, and attorney fees); Mont. Code Ann. § 30-14-2015 (greater of actual damages or $500; costs and attorney fees; violation is also a UDAP violation); N.J. Stat. Ann. § 17:16G-8 (West) (debtor injured by violation has private right of action for damages); Or. Rev. Stat. § 697.718 (for ascertainable loss of money or property; damages and prevailing party attorney fees); S.C. Code Ann. § 37-7-117 (actual and punitive damages, costs, and attorney fees); Tex. Fin. Code Ann. § 394.215 (West) (actual and punitive damages, costs, and attorney fees); Vt. Stat. Ann. tit. 8, § 2764(c); Va. Code Ann. § 6.2-2023 (any person who suffers loss by reason of violation has private right of action to enforce statute and may recover attorney fees, expert witness fees, and costs). *See also* Craft v. North Seattle Cmty. College Found., 2008 WL 961325 (M.D. Ga. Apr. 8, 2008) (refusing to dismiss claim under private cause of action provision of state debt adjusting law against provider that charged fees in excess of those permitted by the statute).

257 Colo. Rev. Stat. § 12-14.5-235; Del. Code Ann. tit. 6 § 2435A; Nev. Rev. Stat. § 676A.760; N.D. Cent. Code § 13-11-29 (greater of actual restitution or $2000); R.I. Gen. Laws § 19-14.8-35; Tenn. Code Ann. § 47-18-5535; Utah Code Ann. § 13-42-135 (West). *See also* V.I. Code tit. 12A, § 435.

258 225 Ill. Comp. Stat. § 429/155; Ind. Code § 24-5-15-11 (debt settlement); Kan. Stat. Ann. § 50-1132; Ky. Rev. Stat. Ann. § 380.990(3) (West);

Md. Code Ann., Fin. Inst. § 12-1016 (West); Minn. Stat. §§ 332A.18(1), 332B.13(1); Mont. Code Ann. § 30-14-2015(2), 30-14-2104(3); 63 Pa. Stat. Ann. § 2416(c) (West); S.C. Code Ann. § 37-7-118; Va. Code Ann. § 6.2-2025; Wash Rev. Code § 18.28.080(1). *See also* Kinderknecht v. Persels & Associations, L.L.C., 470 B.R. 149 (Bankr. D. Kan. 2012) (engaging in debt relief without a license violates statute and thus UDAP violation).

259 *See, e.g.,* Estrella v. Freedom Fin. Network, L.L.C., 778 F. Supp. 2d 1041 (N.D. Cal. 2011) (violation of state debt prorater law would be violation of UDAP statute); Kinderknecht v. Persels & Associations, L.L.C., 470 B.R. 149 (Bankr. D. Kan. 2012); *In re* Fricker, 115 B.R. 809 (Bankr. E.D. Pa. 1990); Pavlov v. Debt Resolvers USA, Inc., 907 N.Y.S.2d 798 (N.Y. City Civ. Ct. 2010). *See also* National Consumer Law Center, Unfair and Deceptive Acts and Practices § 3.2.7 (8th ed. 2012), *updated at* www.nclc.org/library.

260 *See* 205 Ill. Comp. Stat. § 665/16b (debt management), 225 Ill. Comp. Stat. § 429/80b (debt settlement); La. Rev. Stat. Ann. § 37:2596; Md. Code Ann., Fin. Inst. § 12-916(c) (West) (debt management); Tex. Fin. Code § 394.215(a), (b) (West).

261 Colo. Rev. Stat. § 12-14.5-225; Del. Code Ann., tit. 6 § 2425A; Nev. Rev. Stat. § 676A.610; N.D. Cent. Code § 13-11-28; R.I. Gen. Laws § 19-14.8-25; Tenn. Code Ann. § 47-18-5525; Utah Code Ann. § 13-42-125 (West). *See also* V.I. Code tit. 12A, § 425.

262 *See* Pavlov v. Debt Resolvers USA, Inc., 907 N.Y.S.2d 798 (N.Y. Civ. Ct. 2010). *See also* National Consumer Law Center, Consumer Credit Regulation § 7.8.5 (2d ed. 2015), *updated at* www.nclc.org/library.

263 Carlsen v. Global Client Solutions, L.L.C., 256 P.3d 321 (Wash. 2011) (interpreting Wash. Rev. Code §§ 18.28.010(1)–(2), 18.28.080).

264 Carlsen v. Global Client Solutions, L.L.C., 256 P.3d 321 (Wash. 2011) (interpreting Wash. Rev. Code §§ 18.28.010(1)–(2), 18.28.080).

265 *See, e.g.,* Willis v. Debt Care, USA, Inc., 2011 WL 7121288 (D. Or. Oct. 24, 2011) (refusing to dismiss UDAP claim against company that, in cooperation with a debt settlement provider, set up and administered

state has a UDAP statute, and every state affords consumers a private cause of action for violations.[266]

Thus a consumer who has paid for an unsuccessful debt elimination service should have a UDAP claim for the provider's misrepresentation of the features, legality, and likelihood of success of the technique.[267] There has also been extensive federal enforcement of unfair and deceptive debt settlement practices.[268]

A state court has also found that a debt consolidation service violated the state UDAP statute by promising to stop all bill collectors' calls, when actually some creditors would not agree to the plan but would continue to look to the debtor for money. Furthermore, the debt consolidation service promised to stop interest from accruing, but the service charged such large fees that the debtor's payments were often increased.[269] The court also held that it was a UDAP violation

not to disclose an initial sixty-day delay in forwarding payments to creditors; the fact that certain creditors would not agree to debt pooling arrangements; the penalties for missed payments and termination; the total number of payments; and the total of fees.[270]

The FTC has also brought a large number of cases against various types of debt relief services for engaging in unfair and deceptive acts and practices.[271] Because of the similarities in the substantive standards in the FTC Act and state UDAP statutes, the suits filed by the FTC against deceptive credit counseling agencies are persuasive precedent that the same acts violate state UDAP statutes.[272] Any practice found to be unfair and deceptive under the FTC Act should also be found to be deceptive under a state UDAP statute. Indeed, many state UDAP statutes explicitly provide that FTC actions are to be given great weight in interpreting state UDAP statutes.[273] Of course, this includes the debt relief services provisions in the FTC's Telemarketing Sales Rule.[274]

There will be few issues of scope in bringing a UDAP claim, since debt relief services certainly involves the sale of services to consumers. One possible issue of coverage is whether a UDAP statute applies to true nonprofits, but, depending on the wording of a particular UDAP statute, it may even apply to true nonprofits.[275] Another coverage issue is whether the UDAP statute applies to transactions regulated by a state agency; in general, however, such an exemption only applies to practices permitted by such an agency.[276] When an attorney fronts for a debt relief service or is the one engaging in the service, issues arise as to whether attorneys are within the scope of a UDAP statute.[277]

---

bank accounts into which consumers deposit payments that will be used to settle their debts); Estrella v. Freedom Fin. Network, L.L.C., 2010 WL 2231790 (N.D. Cal. June 2, 2010) (UDAP claim based on defendants instructing clients to cease paying creditors; class certified); Citibank (South Dakota) N.A. v. Nat'l Arbitration Council, Inc., 2006 WL 2691528 (M.D. Fla. Sept. 19, 2006) (debt elimination scam); Cuomo v. Nationwide Asset Services, Inc., 888 N.Y.S.2d 850 (N.Y. Super. Ct. 2009) (attorney general raising UDAP claims based on deceptive advertising); Pavlov v. Debt Resolvers USA, Inc., 907 N.Y.S.2d 798 (N.Y. Civ. Ct. 2010) (finding debt settlement firm to be unlicensed "budget planner" and consequently in violation of UDAP statute); Fithian v. Accredited Fin., Inc., No. 10 OT 06-0352 (Knox Co., Ohio Ct. Com. Pl. Jan. 18, 2011) (default judgment listing defendants' unfair, deceptive, and unconscionable acts and practices), *available at* www.nclc.org/unreported; David Jason West & Pydia, Inc. v. State, 212 S.W.3d 513 (Tex. App. 2006) (affirming grant of temporary injunction under state UDAP statute against debt elimination company); Carlsen v. Global Client Solutions, L.L.C., 256 P.3d 321 (Wash. 2011) (recognizing UDAP claim for aiding and abetting violation of debt adjustment statute). *See also* Baker v. Family Credit Counseling Corp., 440 F. Supp. 2d 392 (E.D. Pa. July 28, 2006); Harmon v. Meek, 2008 WL 918513 (Tenn. Ct. App. Apr. 4, 2008).

266 *See* National Consumer Law Center, Unfair and Deceptive Acts and Practices Appx. A (8th ed. 2012), *updated at* www.nclc.org/library.

267 *See* David Jason West & Pydia, Inc. v. State, 212 S.W.3d 513 (Tex. App. 2006) (affirming grant of temporary injunction under state UDAP statute against debt elimination company). *See also* United States v. Hirmer, 767 F. Supp. 2d 1305, 1315–1316 (N.D. Fla. 2011) (pointing out that consumers who paid for fraudulent tax debt elimination scheme are probably victims who are entitled to restitution in criminal case); Citibank (South Dakota) N.A. v. Nat'l Arbitration Council, Inc., 2006 WL 2691528 (M.D. Fla. Sept. 19, 2006) (describing NAC arbitration awards and procedures as "nothing more than a sham" and enjoining future arbitrations; granting summary judgment on claims of tortious interference with contractual relationship and violation of state UDAP law).

268 Federal Trade Comm'n v. Innovative Sys. TeCh., Inc., No. CVO 4-0728 (C.D. Cal. Feb. 4, 2004) (permanent injunction), *available at* www .ftc.gov. *See also* Federal Trade Comm'n v. Edge Solutions, Inc., CV-07-4087 (E.D.N.Y. Oct. 1, 2007), *available at* www.ftc.gov (complaint filed). *See generally Prepared Statement of the Fed. Trade Comm'n on Bus. Practices of Debt Relief Cos. Before the Sen. Comm. on Commerce, Science, and Transp.* (Aug. 12, 2010), *available at* www .ftc.gov (citing FTC and state enforcement actions).

269 Commonwealth v. Legal Credit Counselors, Inc., Clearinghouse No. 41,271 (Mass Super. Ct. 1983).

270 *Id.*

271 *See, e.g.*, Federal Trade Comm'n v. American Tax Relief L.L.C., 751 F. Supp. 2d 972 (N.D. Ill. 2010) (granting preliminary injunction for deceptive representations regarding ability to settle tax debts); Federal Trade Comm'n v. Edge Solutions, Inc., No. CV-07-4087 (E.D.N.Y. Oct. 1, 2007), *available at* www.ftc.gov (complaint filed) (debt settlement); Stipulated Final Judgment and Order, Federal Trade Comm'n & State of Wash. v. Debt Solutions, Inc., No. CV06-0298JLR (W.D. Wash. filed May 22, 2007), *available at* www.ftc.gov (permanently enjoining defendant business owners and telemarketers from engaging in debt elimination business; entering $23,255,420 judgment but suspending it due to an inability to pay); Stipulated Final Judgment and Order for Permanent Injunction, Federal Trade Comm'n v. Innovative Sys. TeCh., Inc., No. CVO 4-0728 (C.D. Cal. Feb. 4, 2004) (debt settlement service), *available at* www.ftc.gov. *See generally Prepared Statement of the Fed. Trade Comm'n on Bus. Practices of Debt Relief Cos. Before the Sen. Comm. on Commerce, Science, and Transp.* (Aug. 12, 2010), *available at* www.ftc.gov (citing FTC and state enforcement actions).

272 *See* National Consumer Law Center, Unfair and Deceptive Acts and Practices § 3.4.5 (8th ed. 2012), *updated at* www.nclc.org/library.

273 *Id.*

274 *See* § 10.5, *supra.*

275 *See* National Consumer Law Center, Unfair and Deceptive Acts and Practices § 2.3.5.1 (8th ed. 2012), *updated at* www.nclc.org/library.

276 National Consumer Law Center, Unfair and Deceptive Acts and Practices § 2.3.3 (8th ed. 2012), *updated at* www.nclc.org/library.

277 *See* Kinderknecht v. Persels & Associations, L.L.C., 470 B.R. 149 (Bankr. D. Kan. 2012) (UDAP statute does apply to attorneys).

10.8.2 Unauthorized Practice of Law; Attorney Malpractice

Debt elimination schemes may run afoul of state statutes and regulations governing the unauthorized practice of law[278] when the scheme provides the debtor with pleadings, discovery requests, briefs, and other legal services. The same may be the case with a non-attorney involved in a debt settlement service that offers legal advice.[279] If an attorney participates in a debt relief service scam, the attorney may be liable for malpractice,[280] deception, and violations of state ethics rules.[281]

10.8.3 RICO Claims

Federal and state RICO claims should be considered for fraudulent debt services transactions.[282] Mail or wire fraud will often provide the predicate acts. For example, the principals behind a debt elimination scheme were convicted of over thirty counts of mail fraud.[283]

RICO claims provide for treble damages and attorney fees. They are well suited to bring claims against third-party "deep pockets" involved with the debt relief service, such as attorneys involved in the scheme or the principals of the company. Federal and state RICO claims are examined in detail earlier in this treatise.[284]

10.8.4 Common Law Claims

Clearly, common law claims such as breach of contract, negligent misrepresentation, breach of fiduciary duty,[285] and fraud may apply to debt relief services. Fraud claims may be particularly appropriate for debt elimination schemes.[286] Because debt relief operations sometimes involve the assistance of third parties (such as banks, payment processors, or attorneys) that may not be subject to state debt relief laws, advocates should investigate liability for aiding and abetting a violation of state law.[287] Causes of action based on joint venture, civil conspiracy, and allegations sufficient to pierce the corporate veil may help reach assets needed to pay a judgment in the consumer's favor.[288] Creditors have also obtained injunctions and money judgments against debt elimination scams on various theories, including interference with contractual relations.[289]

10.8.5 Bankruptcy

While some consumers are attracted to debt relief services because they hope to avoid bankruptcy, for-profit debt relief programs often force consumers deeper into debt, leaving bankruptcy as the only source of relief. Filing bankruptcy may be particularly attractive as an option to recover funds lost to a debt relief program. A consumer or bankruptcy trustee may be able to recover funds paid to a debt relief service provider by showing that the payment was a fraudulent transfer under the Bankruptcy Code.[290] Fraudulent transfers are discussed

---

278 *See* National Consumer Law Center, *Unfair and Deceptive Acts and Practices* § 10.4 (8th ed. 2012), *updated at* www.nclc.org/library. *See generally* Lea Krivinskas, *Don't File: Rehabilitating Unauthorized Practice of Law-Based Policies in the Credit Counseling Industry*, 79 Am. Bankr. L. J. 51 (Winter 2005).

279 *See* Griggs v. Credit Solutions of Am., Inc. 2010 WL 2976209 (N.D. Tex. July 28, 2010); *In re* Nelms, 2010 WL 2712258 (Bankr. M.D. Ala. July 6, 2010).

280 *See, e.g.,* Bryson v. Berges, 2015 WL 5000850, at *5 (S.D. Fla. Aug. 24, 2015) (denying attorney's motion for summary judgment in malpractice claim involving debt relief and credit repair scam). Note that less than a month later a jury awarded this consumer compensatory and punitive damages totaling nearly $22,000 against the law firm and other defendants. Final Judgment, Bryson v. Berges, No. 14-cv-62323-JIC (Sept. 18, 2015).

281 Kinderknecht v. Persels & Associates, L.L.C., 470 B.R. 149 (Bankr. D. Kan. 2012); *In re* Allegro Law, L.L.C., 2010 WL 2712256, at *1 (Bankr. M.D. Ala. July 6, 2010); North Carolina State Bar v. Erickson, 702 S.E.2d 555 (N.C. Ct. App. 2010) (upholding decision to suspend attorney for five years for assistance in bond scheme). *See also* Gorden v. Lloyd Ward & Assoc., P.C., 323 P.3d 1074, 1079 (Wash. Ct. App. 2014) (finding rules of professional conduct required voiding arbitration clause in retainer for debt settlement); Meyer v. Island Grp. Partners, L.L.C., No. 2013-CV-192 (Ohio Ct. Com. Pl. Dec. 2, 2013) (applying Ohio ethics rules; voiding arbitration agreement in engagement agreement), *available at* www.nclc.org/unreported.

282 *See, e.g.,* Baker v. Family Credit Counseling Corp., 440 F. Supp. 2d 392 (E.D. Pa. 2006) (plaintiffs successfully alleged RICO claim). *See also* Guidotti v. Legal Helpers Debt Resolution, L.L.C., 866 F. Supp. 2d 315 (D.N.J. 2011) (consumer stated New Jersey RICO claim), *vacated and remanded on other grounds*, 716 F.3d 764 (3rd Cir. 2013).

283 United States v. Johnson, 610 F.3d 1138 (9th Cir. 2010).

284 *See* Chs. 7, 8, *supra*.

285 Smith v. Legal Helpers Debt Resolution, L.L.C., 2011 WL 5166494 (W.D. Wash. Oct. 31, 2011); Kinderknecht v. Persels & Associations, L.L.C., 470 B.R. 149 (Bankr. D. Kan. 2012).

286 *See* Isenberg v. Chase Bank USA, 661 F. Supp. 2d 627 (N.D. Tex. 2009) (awarding damages to credit card lender against operator of debt elimination scheme; noting that "[defendant's] actions worked to defraud both credit-card holders and credit institutions. The result was [defendant's] receipt of hundreds of thousands of dollars, while both credit-card holders and credit institutions suffered equivalent losses.").

287 *See* Newton v. American Debt Services, Inc., 2013 WL 5592620, at *11 (N.D. Cal. Oct. 10, 2013) (discussing liability of bank that was exempt from state prorater law).

288 *See, e.g.,* Zimmerman v. Puccio, 613 F.3d 60 (1st Cir. 2010) (owners of credit counseling agency held personally liable for violations); Newton v. American Debt Services, Inc., 2013 WL 5592620 (N.D. Cal. Oct. 10, 2013) (discussing civil conspiracy).Smith v. Legal Helpers Debt Resolution, L.L.C., 2011 WL 5166494 (W.D. Wash. Oct. 31, 2011).

289 *See, e.g.,* Chase Bank USA, N.A. v. Hess, 2013 WL 867542 (D. Del. Mar. 7, 2013) (tortious interference with contractual relations), *adopted by* 2013 WL 5314706 (D. Del. Sept. 20, 2013); Capitol One Bank v. Carefree Debt, Inc., 2010 WL 2228418 (D.S.C. June 1, 2010); Citibank (South Dakota) N.A. v. Nat'l Arbitration Council, Inc., 2006 WL 2691528 (M.D. Fla. Sept. 19, 2006) (enjoining sham arbitrations; granting summary judgment on claims of tortious interference with contractual relationship and violation of state UDAP law); Bank of Am. v. Malfatti (*In re* Malfatti), 430 B.R. 555 (Bankr. N.D. Cal. 2010), *rev'd on other grounds*, 2012 WL 3590751 (9th Cir. B.A.P. Aug. 21, 2012) (holding that state tort court judgments did not have issue preclusion effect in bankruptcy discharge proceedings).

290 *See, e.g.,* Huffman v. Legal Helpers Debt Resolution, L.L.C. (*In re* Huffman), 505 B.R. 726, 753–757 (S.D. Miss. 2014).

in another NCLC treatise, *Consumer Bankruptcy Law and Practice*.[291]

If the debt relief service meets the Bankruptcy Code's definition of a "debt relief agency"[292] (which is very different from the FTC's definition of a "debt relief service"), a number of restrictions and requirements are placed upon the service. Violations may lead to claims for damages, attorney fees, and—for intentional abuse or a pattern or practice of abuse—civil penalties.[293] A debt relief service can easily meet the Bankruptcy Code's definition by including information or references to bankruptcy in its contract or other documents.[294]

---

291 National Consumer Law Center, Consumer Bankruptcy Law and Practice (10th ed. 2012), *updated at* www.nclc.org/library.

292 *See* 11 U.S.C. §§ 526–527; National Consumer Law Center, Consumer Bankruptcy Law and Practice § 16.8 (10th ed. 2012), *updated at* www.nclc.org/library.

293 11 U.S.C. §§ 526–527. *See* Huffman v. Legal Helpers Debt Resolution, L.L.C. (*In re* Huffman), 505 B.R. 726, 765–766 (S.D. Miss. 2014) (civil penalty of $28,000 against debt relief service for violating Bankruptcy Code rules regarding debt relief agencies).

294 *See, e.g.,* Huffman v. Legal Helpers Debt Resolution, L.L.C. (*In re* Huffman), 505 B.R. 726, 760–763 (S.D. Miss. 2014) (finding debt relief service to qualify as "debt relief agency" under Bankruptcy Code).

Chapter 11   Other Statutes Protecting Consumers

11.1   Antitrust Statutes

11.1.1   Federal Antitrust Laws

Federal antitrust law is comprised of a series of federal statutes prohibiting various types of anti-competitive commercial activity. The most important of these are the Sherman Act, the Clayton Act, and the Robinson-Patman Act. The Sherman Act prohibits contracts or combinations that unreasonably restrain trade—including price fixing, market allocation, and illegal tie-ins—as well as the abuse of monopoly power.[1] The Clayton Act prohibits seller requirements that purchasers not contract with certain other competitors when the effect is to reduce competition and also prohibits certain other forms of anti-competitive conduct.[2] The Robinson-Patman Act prohibits price discrimination that has the effect of reducing competition.[3] Private suits are allowed to recover trebled damages, injunctive relief, and attorney fees (to a prevailing plaintiff only).[4]

At first blush, these statutes may appear appealing potential tools available to consumers who have purchased products at prices increased by anti-competitive behavior. However, in *Illinois Brick Co. v. Illinois*,[5] the U.S. Supreme Court ruled that only "direct" purchasers of products priced anti-competitively can recover antitrust damages. Because consumers generally purchase from retailers, and not directly from the manufacturers, this doctrine has severely limited the usefulness of the federal antitrust laws from a consumer practice standpoint.[6] It is possible that the advent of sales over the Internet directly to consumers by manufacturers will result in increasing use of the federal antitrust laws by consumers. However, few such suits have been noted in the case law to date.

In addition, several kinds of transactions are excluded from the scope of the federal antitrust laws or are affected by special considerations. For example, the McCarran-Ferguson Act provides that the Sherman and Clayton Acts "shall be applicable to the business of insurance [only] to the extent that such business is not regulated by State law."[7] The Capper-Volstead Act provides express authority for certain joint marketing agreements between competing producers of agricultural products, thus exempting such arrangements from antitrust challenge.[8] Special considerations apply when addressing intellectual property issues, labor issues, or transactions involving regulated industries.

11.1.2   State Antitrust Laws

Following the Supreme Court's *Illinois Brick* decision, discussed in § 11.1.1, *supra*, many states enacted so-called "Illinois Brick Repealer Statutes," expressly authorizing recovery of damages under state antitrust law to "indirect purchasers" of a price-fixed product.[9] In *California v. ARC America Corporation*,[10] the U.S. Supreme Court upheld such state laws as proper exercises of state authority, rejecting the argument that the Court's *Illinois Brick* decision interpreting federal antitrust law preempted contrary conclusions under state antitrust laws. Thus, in any state with either a statutory or judicially-crafted "Illinois Brick Repealer" rule, antitrust damages under state law may be sought by "indirect" as well as direct purchasers.

State antitrust laws vary widely. The provisions in most states include prohibitions similar to those set forth in the federal Sherman Act, though often with different wording and often excluding any express prohibition on unilateral monopoly.[11] Additionally, however, the laws in many states address in disparate fashion various competitive pricing and other

---

1   15 U.S.C. §§ 1–7.

2   15 U.S.C. §§ 12–27.

3   15 U.S.C. §§ 13, 13a, 13b, 21a.

4   15 U.S.C. §§ 15, 26. *See* 15 U.S.C. § 12(a) (listing of the antitrust statutes to which these remedies apply).

5   431 U.S. 720 (1977).

6   The *Illinois Brick* doctrine applies only to recovery of damages, not injunctive relief or attorney fees. However, given the difficulty in proving an antitrust violation, and the considerable expense required to present expert opinion on the economic issues, it would rarely be practical for a consumer attorney to assert a federal antitrust claim without the possibility of a significant damages recovery.

7   15 U.S.C. § 1012(b).

8   7 U.S.C. § 291. *See* Bell v. Fur Breeders Agric. Co-op., 348 F.3d 1224, 1231 (10th Cir. 2003).

9   Ala. Code § 6-5-60; Cal. Bus. & Prof. Code § 16750 (West); D.C. Code Ann. § 28-4509; Haw. Rev. Stat. § 480-13; Kan. Stat. Ann., § 50-161; Me. Rev. Stat. Ann. tit. 10, § 1104; Mich. Comp. Laws § 445.778; Minn. Stat. § 325D.57; Miss. Code Ann. § 75-21-9; Neb. Rev. Stat. § 59-821; Nev. Rev. Stat. § 598A.210; N.M. Stat. Ann. § 57-1-3; N.Y. Gen. Bus. § 340 (McKinney); N.D. Cent. Code § 51-08.1-08; Or. Rev. Stat. § 646.780; Utah Code Ann. § 76-10-919 (West); Vt. Stat. Ann. tit. 9, § 2465; Wis. Stat. § 133.18.

In addition, the courts of several states have interpreted their state statutes to permit indirect purchaser standing: Bunker's Glass Co. v. Pilkington, P.L.C., 75 P.3d 99 (Ariz. 2003); Comes v. Microsoft Corp. 646 N.W.2d 440 (Iowa 2002); Hyde v. Abbott Labs., Inc. 473 S.E.2d 680 (N.C. 1996); Freeman Industries, L.L.C. v. Eastman Chem. Co., 172 S.W.3d 512, 516 (Tenn. 2005).

In West Virginia, the attorney general issued a legislative ruling permitting indirect purchaser standing that was ratified by the West Virginia legislature. *See In re* New Motor Vehicles Canadian Exp. Antitrust Litig., 350 F. Supp. 2d 160, 173–174 (D. Me. 2004).

10   490 U.S. 93 (1989).

11   *See, e.g.*, Cal. Bus. & Prof. Code §§ 16700 to 16770 (West) ("Cartwright Act"); Conn. Gen. Stat. §§ 35-24 to 35-49; Fla. Stat. §§ 542.15 to 542.36; Md. Code Ann., Com. Law §§ 11-201 to 11-213 (West); N.Y. Gen. Bus. Laws §§ 340 to 347 (McKinney) ("Donnelly Act").

arrangements.[12] The full panoply of state law is beyond the scope of this treatise.[13]

Consumer litigation asserting violations of state antitrust law remains relatively uncommon, with one important exception: class actions alleging price-fixing on behalf of consumers as "indirect" purchasers.[14] Hundreds of such class actions have been brought on behalf of indirect consumer purchasers over the last twenty years. The cases often have excellent facts, as shown by the fact that parallel criminal prosecutions of defendants' executives have often resulted in large fines and guilty pleas.[15] Many of these cases have settled and others have been litigated to a successful conclusion. However, the cases are inherently complex and present complicated questions surrounding class certification, particularly due to issues involving the assessment or apportionment of recoverable damages sought by both direct and indirect purchasers of the same product.[16] Because the conspiracies are often global in scope, a sufficient nexus to commerce within the United States also may become a cornerstone of the defense.[17]

Another set of anti-competitive practices that might be challenged by consumers is that surrounding "tying" requirements—that is, when "a supplier agrees to sell a buyer a product (the tying product), but only on the condition that the buyer also purchases a different (or tied) product."[18] However, because a tying arrangement must "injure competition" to violate the antitrust laws, the usual plaintiffs asserting claims of illegal tying are other businesses who want to compete with the defendant in sales of the "tied" product.

In the consumer context, allegations of illegal tying have usually been couched as UDAP violations rather than as direct antitrust claims.[19]

In a series of cases flowing from the Department of Justice's successful monopolization case against Microsoft Corporation alleging the tying of Internet Explorer to sales of Windows software, several substantial recoveries were obtained through settlement on behalf of consumers in private state court litigation.[20] However, many similar suits were dismissed when the applicable state laws did not permit recovery by indirect purchasers.[21]

11.2 Statutes Regulating Unsolicited Goods

Selling unsolicited goods occurs when a seller delivers goods that the consumer has never ordered and then charges the consumer for the price of those goods. The "seller" may threaten to turn over accounts to a debt collection agency or report the delinquency to a credit reporting agency. Consumers who refuse to accept unsolicited goods may also be threatened with liability for storage charges. Consumers, unsure of their legal rights, may find it inconvenient and costly to mail the goods back and may pay the seller for them in the face of debt collection efforts.

Federal law prohibits use of the mail to send unordered merchandise, with the exception of free gifts, and requires that a notice accompany the gift disclosing that the consumer may treat unsolicited merchandise as a gift.[22] Infractions are per se violations of the Federal Trade Commission Act,[23] and the FTC has filed many enforcement actions for violating these requirements.[24] In a "toner phoner" scheme, a telemarketer uses the ruse of promising free gifts in order to get the names of a company's employees, then places the employees' names on invoices for unordered office supplies as a means of leading the company to believe that the merchandise had been properly ordered.[25] Other schemes involve representing that the telemarketer is the customer's

---

12 *See, e.g.*, Cal. Bus. & Prof. Code § 17040 (West) (geographic price discrimination); Ind. Code §§ 24-1-5 (forbidding anti-competitive practices in motion picture distribution).

13 *See* Am. Bar Ass'n Section on Antitrust Law, State Antitrust Practice and Statutes (4th ed. 2009) (a comprehensive review of all state antitrust laws).

14 Sullivan v. DB Investments, Inc., 667 F.3d 273 (3d Cir. 2011); *In re* TFT-LCD (Flat Panel) Antitrust Litig., 2012 WL 253298 (N.D. Cal. Jan. 26, 2012).

15 *See, e.g., In re* Vitamins Antitrust Class Actions 215 F.3d 26, 28 (D.C. Cir. 2000); *In re* TFT-LCD (Flat Panel) Antitrust Litig., 2011 WL 3566419 (N.D. Cal. Aug. 12, 2011).

16 *In re* Flash Memory Antitrust Litig., 2010 WL 2332081 (N.D. Cal. June 9, 2010), *reconsideration denied*, 2011 WL 1301527 (N.D. Cal. Mar. 31, 2011); *In re* Graphics Processing Units Antitrust Litig., 253 F.R.D. 478, 507 (N.D. Cal. 2008) (denying class certification of an indirect purchaser class because there was no "reliable method for proving common impact on all purchasers of defendants' products throughout the chain of distribution"); Clayworth v. Pfizer, Inc., 49 Cal. 4th 758 (Cal. 2010)

17 Animal Science Products, Inc. v. China Minmetals Corp., 654 F.3d 462 (3d Cir. 2011); *In re* TFT-LCD (Flat Panel) Antitrust Litig., 2012 WL 3763616 (N.D. Cal. 2012).

18 Brantley v. NBC Universal, Inc., 675 F.3d 1192, 1199 (9th Cir. 2012) (quoting North Pac. Ry. Co. v. United States, 356 U.S. 1, 5 (1958)); Belton v. Comcast Cable Holdings, L.L.C., 151 Cal. App. 4th 1224, 1234 (Cal. 2007).

19 *See* National Consumer Law Center, Unfair and Deceptive Acts and Practices § 5.8 (8th ed. 2012), *updated at* www.nclc.org/library.

20 *In re* Microsoft I-V Cases, 135 Cal. App. 4th 706 (2006); *In re* South Dakota Microsoft Antitrust Litig., 707 N.W.2d 85, 92 (S.D. 2005).

21 Pomerantz v. Microsoft Corp., 50 P.3d 929, 934–935 (Colo. App. 2002); Berghausen v. Microsoft Corp., 765 N.E.2d 592, 596 (Ind. Ct. App. 2002); Minuteman, L.L.C. & Assoc. v. Microsoft Corp., 795 A.2d 833, 840–841 (N.H. 2002); Major v. Microsoft Corp., 60 P.3d 511, 515 (Okla. Civ. App. 2002); Siena v. Microsoft Corp., 796 A.2d 461, 465 (R.I. 2002).

22 39 U.S.C. § 3009.

23 39 U.S.C. § 3009(a).

24 Innumerable FTC actions against the senders of unordered merchandise may be found on the FTC's website, www.ftc.gov. *See, e.g., In re* Sunshine Art Studios, Inc. et al., 81 F.T.C. 836 (1972), *aff'd*, 481 F.2d 1171 (1st Cir. 1973).

25 Innumerable FTC actions against operators of "toner phoner" and related schemes are available on the FTC's website, www.ftc.gov. *See, e.g.*, Federal Trade Comm'n v. Ambus Registry, Inc., 5 Trade Reg. Rep. (CCH) ¶ 15,591, No. CV03-1294RBL (W.D. Wash. Apr. 26, 2004) (stipulated final judgment against telemarketer that misrepresented to small businesses that they had already agreed to make purchases).

usual supplier,[26] substituting more expensive items in place of those ordered,[27] and billing for advertising that was never requested.[28] It is similarly deceptive to deliver products in quantities greater than ordered and then to bill the consumer for them.[29]

Some decisions have found an implied private remedy for violation of the federal law.[30] One court has interpreted the prohibition as inapplicable to independent jobbers or wholesalers who receive merchandise from a distributor for resale.[31]

Some state UDAP regulations include prohibitions similar to the federal "unordered merchandise" statute.[32] States may also have enacted legislation in this area. For example, a Vermont statute allows consumers to deem unsolicited goods or services as gifts, although there is a mechanism for the sender to promptly notify the consumer that the goods were sent in error and giving the sender certain rights.[33] In addition, any violation of the FTC rule or the federal statute is likely to be considered a UDAP violation, either because it is a per se UDAP violation to violate an FTC rule or because the conduct is deceptive in and of itself.[34]

Most unordered merchandise scams also involve deceptive billing practices, which are discussed in another NCLC treatise.[35] For example, it is a UDAP violation to send the consumer a document that looks like an invoice as part of an offer for services in an attempt to lead the consumer to believe that the services have already been ordered.[36]

11.3 Plain English Statutes

A number of states have enacted plain language laws[37] that apply broadly to many types of transactions.[38] Other states have plain language requirements that apply to certain types of transactions, such as rent-to-own (RTO), insurance, consumer credit, and hearing aids transactions.[39]

---

26 *See, e.g.*, Federal Trade Comm'n v. United Wholesalers, Inc., 5 Trade Reg. Rep. (CCH) ¶ 23,965 (S.D. Fla. 1996) (proposed consent order requiring transfer of $1.3 million assets and payment of $202,000). *See also* Federal Trade Comm'n v. Datacom Mktg. Inc., 2006 WL 1472644 (N.D. Ill. May 24, 2006) (granting preliminary injunction against similar scheme).

27 Federal Trade Comm'n v. Freedom Med., Inc., 5 Trade Reg. Rep. (CCH) ¶ 23,964 (S.D. Ohio 1996) (consent decree); Federal Trade Comm'n v. Motion Med., Inc., 5 Trade Reg. Rep. (CCH) ¶ 24,036 (S.D. Ohio 1996) (consent order).

28 Innumerable FTC actions against schemes involving billing for advertising that was never ordered may be found on the FTC's website, www.ftc.gov. *See, e.g.*, Federal Trade Comm'n v. Datacom Mktg., Inc., 2006 WL 1472644 (N.D. Ill. May 24, 2006) (telemarketer called small businesses to "confirm" directory listing, then sent and billed for $400 directory).

29 *In re* Commercial Lighting Products, 95 F.T.C. 750 (1980) (consent order); *In re* Star Office Supply Co. et al., 77 F.T.C. 383 (1970).

30 Kipperman v. Academy Life Ins. Co., 554 F.2d 377 (9th Cir. 1977); Crosley v. Lens Express, Inc., 2001 WL 650728 (W.D. Tex. Feb. 12, 2001). *But see* Wisniewski v. Rodale, Inc., 510 F.3d 294 (3d Cir. 2007).

31 Blakemore v. Superior Court, 27 Cal. Rptr. 3d 877 (Cal. Ct. App. 2005).

32 *See* Idaho Admin. Code r. 04.02.01.220 (unordered goods or services); Mo. Code Regs. Ann. tit. 15, § 60-8.060. *See also* Huch v. Charter Communications, Inc., 290 S.W.3d 721 (Mo. 2009) (violation of regulation prohibiting unsolicited goods is UDAP violation).

33 Vt. Stat. Ann. tit. 9, § 4401.

34 *See* Blakemore v. Superior Court, 27 Cal. Rptr. 3d 877 n.17 (Cal. Ct. App. 2005). *See also* § 2.2.4.2, *supra*.

35 National Consumer Law Center, Unfair and Deceptive Acts and Practices § 5.7.7 (8th ed. 2012), *updated at* www.nclc.org/library.

36 Telcom Directories, Inc. v. Commonwealth *ex rel.* Cowan, 833 S.W.2d 848 (Ky. Ct. App. 1992).

37 Conn. Gen. Stat. §§ 42-151 to 42-158 (consumer loans or credit, purchase, or lease of consumer goods up to $25,000, residential leases); Haw. Rev. Stat. §§ 487A-1 to 487A-4 (consumer loans or credit, purchase, or lease of consumer goods up to $25,000, residential leases); Me. Rev. Stat. tit. 10, §§ 1121 to 1126 (consumer loans and leases up to $100,000); Minn. Stat. §§ 325G.29 to 325G.37 (consumer sales, leases, loans, credit, residential leases, up to $50,000, but not purchases of realty); Mont. Code Ann. §§ 30-14-1101 to 30-14-1113 (consumer sales, leases, loans, under $50,000, but not insurance, transfers of real estate); N.Y. Gen. Obl. Law § 5-702 (McKinney) (consumer sales, lease, loan or credit, and residential leases); N.J. Stat. Ann. §§ 56:12-1 to 56:12-13 (West); Or. Rev. Stat. §§ 180.540 to 180.555 (consumer sales, credit, loans, up to $50,000, insurance; real estate specifically included); 73 Pa. Stat. Ann. §§ 2201 to 2212 (West) (consumer sales, credit, loans, up to $50,000, but not insurance, real estate, or regulated financial institutions); W. Va. Code § 46A-6-109 (consumer sales or leases, residential leases).

38 *But see* Schwab v. Sears, Roebuck & Co. (*In re* Dirienzo), 254 B.R. 334 (Bankr. M.D. Pa. 2000) (retailer's captive national bank falls within exemption in Plain Language Law for financial institutions; monthly bill statements are also not covered).

39 *See, e.g.*, Alaska Stat. § 45.50.471(b)(13) (consumer installment sales); Ark. Code Ann. § 4-88-107(a)(8) (UDAP); Cal. Civ. Code § 1793.1 (West) (express warranties); Colo. Rev. Stat. § 6-1-105(1)(m) (UDAP); Conn. Gen. Stat. §§ 38a-295 to 38a-300 (insurance policies); Conn. Gen. Stat. § 42-241 (rent-to-own); Del. Code Ann. tit. 6, § 2732 (consumer contracts); D.C. Code Ann. § 28-3904(r)(5) (UDAP); Fla. Stat. §§ 627.4145 (insurance policies), 636.016 (prepaid limited health centers); Ga. Code Ann. § 33-3-25 (insurance policies); Haw. Rev. Stat. §§ 431:10-101 to 431:10-108 (insurance policies); 815 Ill. Comp. Stat. § 655/2 (rent-to-own); Ind. Code §§ 24-4.5-6-111(3)(e) (consumer credit code), 24-7-3-4 (RTO), 27-1-26-3 (insurance policies); Iowa Code §§ 537.3606(1) (RTO), 537.5108(4)(e) (factor listed for consideration in regard to unconscionability in actions by state administrator/consumer credit code); Kan. Stat. Ann. §§ 16a-6-111(3)(e) (factor listed for consideration in regard to unconscionability in actions by state administrator/consumer credit code), 50-627(b)(1) (UDAP; factor for court to consider in determining unconscionability); Ky. Rev. Stat. Ann. § 367.978(3), (6) (West) (RTO); Mass. Gen. Laws ch. 175, § 2B (insurance policies); Mich. Comp. Laws §§ 445.903(1)(x) (UDAP), 500.2236(3) (insurance); Minn. Stat. § 72C.01-.13 (insurance policies); Miss. Code Ann. § 83-65-111 (motor vehicle service); Mo. Rev. Stat. § 346.020 (hearing aids); Mont. Code Ann. §§ 33-15-321 to 33-15-329 (insurance policies); Neb. Rev. Stat. § 69-2105(3), (6) (RTO); Nev. Rev. Stat. §§ 687B.122 to 687B.128 (insurance policies); N.Y. Gen. Bus. Law §§ 399-pp(6)(b) (McKinney) (telemarketing), 771 (home improvement contracts); N.C. Gen. Stat. §§ 58-38-1 to 58-38-40 (insurance policies); N.D. Cent. Code §§ 26.1-36-13 to 26.1-36-16, 26.1-37-09 (insurance); Ohio Rev. Code Ann. §§ 1345.03 (UDAP), 3902.01 to 3902.08 (insurance) (West); Okla. Stat. tit. 14A, § 6-111(3)(e) (factor listed for consideration in regard to unconscionability in actions by state administrator/consumer credit code); Okla. Stat. tit. 36, §§ 3641 to 3651 (insurance policies); Or. Rev. Stat. §§ 743.100 to 743.109 (insurance policies); S.C. Code Ann. §§ 37-5-108(4)(a) (inability to understand language of agreement is factor in determining if creditor remedy is unconscionable), 38-61-20 to 38-61-50 (insurance); S.D. Codified Laws §§ 58-11A-1 to 58-11A-9 (insurance policies); Tenn. Code Ann. §§ 56-7-1601 to 56-7-1609 (insurance policies); Tex. Bus. & Com. Code Ann. § 92.051 (West) (rent-to-own); Tex. Fin. Code § 341.502 (West) (certain loans and retail installment sales); Tex. Ins. Code Ann. §§ 1301.157 and 1501.260

Plain English statutes typically require that contracts be written in a clear and coherent manner using words with common and everyday meanings and be appropriately divided into subsections with captions. Some statutes also require type of a readable size and ink that contrasts with the paper.[40]

Some statutes specify that the consumer can recover actual damages or small statutory damages (for example, $50 in an individual action and $10,000 in a class action) for violations.[41] Other statutes limit enforcement to a state agency or provide no explicit remedy. Some statutes specifically state that a violation does not make the contract void or provide a defense for a breach of contract action.[42]

Some statutes, such as Minnesota's, allow a seller, creditor, or lessor to submit proposed contracts to the attorney general for review to determine whether the contract complies with the plain language requirements.[43] Plain language determinations by the attorney general are not appealable.[44]

A violation of a plain language statute may be a per se UDAP violation.[45] Uniform Commercial Code (UCC) unconscionability concepts may also be helpful here.[46] The landmark case of *Commonwealth v. Monumental Properties, Inc.*, holds that the use of residential lease forms with "archaic and technical language beyond the easy comprehension of the consumer of average intelligence" may state a UDAP cause of action.[47]

11.4 Statutes Protecting Non-English Speakers

11.4.1 Introduction

New immigrants are often new to the English language as well. Many scam artists prey on this vulnerability, coercing non-English-speaking consumers to sign contracts or other documents that they do not understand. There are a number of ways to challenge contract transactions based on language barriers, and these include state statutes requiring the use of a non-English language, state UDAP laws, contract claims and defenses, and affirmative fraud claims.

11.4.2 Federal Requirements Regarding Use of Non-English Language

The FTC requires in both its rule concerning door-to-door sales[48] and its business opportunities rule[49] that the mandated disclosures be in the language in which the transaction is conducted. The FTC's Used Car Rule has a similar requirement.[50] There is no private right of action under the FTC Used Car Rule, but a violation of the rule may be actionable under a state UDAP statute.[51] Since the Used Car Rule was in part promulgated under the federal Magnuson-Moss Act, a good argument can also be made that it is a violation of the Magnuson-Moss Act to violate the Used Car Rule.[52]

In addition, the FTC has issued a policy statement that, when any rule, guide, statement, or cease-and-desist order requires "clear and conspicuous" disclosure of certain information in an advertisement or sales material in a publication that is not in English, then the disclosure shall appear in the predominant language of the publication. In the case of any other advertisement or sales material, the disclosure is required to appear in the language of the target audience, which is ordinarily the language principally used in the advertisement or sales material.[53]

The Truth in Lending Act allows but does not compel translation of its required disclosures.[54]

(health insurance), 2301.053 (automobile insurance), 2703.101 (residential title insurance) (West); Va. Code Ann. § 38.2-3735 (credit insurance policies); W. Va. Code §§ 33-29-1 to 33-29-9 (life, accident, and health insurance); Wis. Stat. § 426.108 (UDAP). *See also* N.Y. Gen. Oblig. Law § 5-1706 (McKinney) (structured settlement protection act; requires that documents assigning or transferring rights to payment conform to plain language requirements of N.Y. Gen. Oblig. Law § 5-702).

40 *See* Conn. Gen. Stat. § 42-152(b); Mont. Code Ann. § 30-14-1103; 73 Pa. Stat. Ann. § 2205 (West); W. Va. Code § 46A-6-109.

41 Haw. Rev. Stat. § 487A-1(b).

42 DelPonte v. Coral World Virgin Islands, Inc., 233 Fed. Appx. 178 (3d Cir. 2007) (violation of plain language act does not render contract void or voidable, unless enforcement would be unconscionable; not shown here; narrowly construing "consumer contract" not to include contract for underwater tourist expedition).

43 Minn. Stat. § 325G.35, subdiv. 1.

44 Minn. Stat. § 325G.35, subdiv. 2.

45 *See* National Consumer Law Center, Unfair and Deceptive Acts and Practices § 3.2.7 (8th ed. 2012), *updated at* www.nclc.org/library. *See also* 73 Pa. Stat. Ann. § 2207(b) (West).

46 *See* National Consumer Law Center, Consumer Warranty Law § 11.2 (5th ed. 2015), *updated at* www.nclc.org/library.

47 329 A.2d 812 (Pa. 1974). *See also* Kan. Stat. Ann. § 50-627(b)(1); Oldendorf v. General Motors Corp., 751 N.E.2d 214 (Ill. App. Ct. 2001) (deliberate obfuscation of warranty's coverage through use of vague, misleading, and contradictory language may be UDAP violation). *But see* Gonsalves v. First Ins. Co., 516 P.2d 720 (Haw. 1975).

48 16 C.F.R. § 429.1(a).

49 16 C.F.R. § 437.5.

50 16 C.F.R. § 455.5. *See* § 2.4, *supra* (general discussion of used car rule).

51 Martinez v. Rick Case Cars, Inc., 278 F. Supp. 2d 1371 (S.D. Fla. 2003) (refusing to dismiss claim that violation of FTC rule requiring Buyer's Guide and window sticker to be in Spanish was violation of Florida's UDAP statute).

52 *See* Currier v. Spencer, 772 S.W.2d 309 (Ark. 1989) (upholding trial court's award of Magnuson-Moss attorney fees for violation of FTC Used Car Rule); § 2.4.4, *supra*. *See generally* National Consumer Law Center, Consumer Warranty Law §§ 15.6.3.3, 15.6.9.1, 15.6.9.2 (5th ed. 2015), *updated at* www.nclc.org/library.

53 16 C.F.R. § 14.9(a).

54 12 C.F.R. § 1026.27 [§ 226.27]; Official Interpretations of Reg. Z, 12 C.F.R. pt. 1026 [pt. 226], Supp. I, pt. 3 § 1026.27 [§ 226.27]. *See* Nevarez v. O'Connor Chevrolet, Inc., 303 F. Supp. 2d 927 (N.D. Ill. 2004) (car dealer not required to provide consumer with a Spanish copy of the retail installment contract under TILA, even if Illinois law has such a requirement); Equicredit Corp. v. Turcios, 752 N.Y.S.2d 684 (N.Y. App. Div. 2002) (while TILA disclosures "may" be made in a language other than English, it does not require them, even when borrowers read, write, and speak only Spanish); County Trust Co. v. Mora, 383 N.Y.S.2d 468, 470 (N.Y. Rockland Cnty. Ct. 1975) (TILA does not require disclosures in Spanish even when consumers cannot understand English). *Cf.* Zamarippa v. Cy's Car Sales, Inc., 674 F.2d 877, 879 (11th Cir. 1982) (defective disclosure statement in English that Spanish-only speaking consumer could not understand was no defense to liability).

Disparate treatment based on ethnicity or practices having a disparate impact on minorities or other protected group may violate provisions of the federal civil rights acts, 42 U.S.C. §§ 1981 and 1982, and/or the Fair Housing Act and Equal Credit Opportunity Act.[55] These statutes provide strong private remedies.[56]

11.4.3 State Statutes Requiring Use of a Non-English Language

Several states have addressed the problem of immigrant fraud by passing statutes and regulations that specifically require translations of contracts for certain transactions or under certain circumstances.[57] The provisions vary by state. In some states, the statute applies only to specific types of transactions like rent-to-own or door-to-door sales. California's statute exempts loans secured by real property except for a few types of loans, such as reverse mortgages, but it applies to real estate brokers and mortgage brokers.[58] Translations may be required in any language in which the negotiations occurred or only in a specific language such as Spanish.

Illinois law formerly required sellers to provide a translated written contract if a retail transaction was negotiated in a language other than English, but, based on a 2001 amendment, the seller need only have the buyer sign a form in the language of negotiation stating that the seller explained the contract in that language.[59]

When a statute does not provide an explicit private right of action, a violation of a state law requiring translation of documents into languages other than English may be a per se UDAP violation.[60] In any event, the practice of providing contracts or disclosures knowing the consumer cannot understand them may be a state UDAP violation in its own right.

Several states have passed "English-only" laws,[61] which might trump state laws requiring certain documents to be translated[62] or even prevent courts from ordering documents to be translated as a matter of case law.[63] The constitutionality of the more expansive of these "English-only" laws is questionable on freedom of speech and equal protection grounds.[64]

---

55 *See* National Consumer Law Center, Credit Discrimination (6th ed. 2013), *updated at* www.nclc.org/library.

56 *Id.*

57 Ariz. Rev. Stat. Ann. §§ 44-1797.05 (applies to discount buying services), 44-5004 (door-to-door sales); Cal. Civ. Code §§ 1632 (Spanish, Chinese, Tagalog, Vietnamese, and Korean; exception if consumers supply their own interpreters), 1689.21 (solicited seminar sales contracts) (West); Del. Code Ann. tit. 6, § 4404 (door-to-door sales); Fla. Stat. §§ 636.015 (prepaid limited health services organizations), 641.305 (health maintenance organization), 641.421 (prepaid health clinics); 815 Ill. Comp. Stat. §§ 505/2B (home solicitation sales), 655/2 (rent-to-own); Kan. Stat. Ann. § 50-640 (door-to-door sales); 940 Mass. Code Regs. §§ 3.09 (prohibiting door-to-door sellers from inducing purchaser to sign documents if seller has reason to know that buyer cannot read or write under understand the terms), 8.05(3) (mortgage disclosures); Neb. Rev. Stat. § 69-1604 (door-to-door sales); N.J. Stat. Ann. §§ 17:16C-61.6, 17:16C-100 (West) (retail installment sales); Nev. Rev. Stat. §§ 482.3277 (dealer who advertises or negotiates in Spanish must provide approved Spanish forms upon request), 97.299 (state must prescribe motor vehicle applications and contracts and translate them into Spanish); N.M. Stat. Ann. § 57-26-4 (rent-to-own advertisements in languages other than English require companies to have purchase agreements in the same languages as the advertisements and make agreements available to consumers); N.Y. Pers. Prop. Law art. 10-A, § 428 (McKinney) (door-to-door); N.Y. Gen. Bus. Law § 369-ee (McKinney) (cancellation notices for prize awards); N.Y. Gen. Bus. Law § 394-c(7)(b) (McKinney) (dating services); N.Y. Real Prop. Law § 265-a(3) (McKinney); N.C. Gen. Stat. §§ 14-401.13 (cancellation notice), 25A-40 (door-to-door sales), 66-240 (membership camping); Or. Rev. Stat. § 646A.124 (lease-purchase agreements; exception if consumers supply their own interpreters); 73 Pa. Stat. Ann. § 201-7 (West) (door-to-door); P.R. Laws Ann. tit. 20, § 3055; P.R. Laws. Ann. tit. 17, § 510 (certain property sales); P.R. Laws. Ann. tit. 10, § 741 (retail installment contracts); Tex. Bus. & Com. Code Ann. §§ 92.051 (rent-to-own), 601.052(b) (home solicitation sales) (West); Tex. Fin. Code § 348.006(d) (West) (documentary fees in motor vehicle sales); Vt. Stat. Ann. tit. 9, § 2454 (door-to-door); Wis. Stat. § 423.203 (notice of cancellation); Wis. Admin. Code ATCP §§ 127.06(3), 127.34(2), 127.64(3) (door-to-door); Wyo. Stat. Ann. § 40-19-106 (rent-to-own). *See* Cal. Civ. Code § 1632.5 (West) (supervised financial institution can comply with language-of-negotiation requirement by delivering a summary of the loan terms in the borrower's language); Tex. Fin. Code § 341.502 (West) (certain loans and retail installment sales); ING Bank v. Ahn, 717 F. Supp. 2d 931 (N.D. Cal. 2010) (lender must provide translation of loan documents if negotiation was conducted in Korean, even if one of the borrowers is also fluent in English); Reyes v. Premier Home Funding, Inc., 640 F. Supp. 2d 1147 (N.D. Cal. 2009) (California translation law applies to certain real estate loans arranged by mortgage brokers and is not preempted by Home Owners Loan Act);

Gutierrez v. PCH Roulette, Inc., 2003 WL 22422431 (Cal. Ct. App. Oct. 24, 2003) (unpublished) (auto dealer who negotiated primarily in Spanish required to translate contract into Spanish). *Cf.* Nevarez v. O'Connor Chevrolet, Inc., 426 F. Supp. 2d 806, 816–8S7 (N.D. Ill. 2006) (car dealer's violation of language-of-negotiation law by failing to translate contract into Spanish is not equivalent to concealment of the information in that contract). *See generally* Jo Carrillo, *In Translation for the Latino Market Today: Acknowledging the Rights of Consumers in a Multilingual Housing Market*, 11 Harv. Latino L. Rev. 1 (2008) (analyzing Cal. Civ. Code § 1632).

58 *See* Arias v. Capital One, N.A., 2011 WL 835610 (N.D. Cal. Mar. 4, 2011) (applies to mortgage brokers); Gonzalez v. Alliance Bancorp, 2010 WL 1575963 (N.D. Cal. Apr. 19, 2010) (statute inapplicable to mortgage loan in absence of evidence that defendant was real estate broker); Castaneda v. Saxon Mortg. Services, Inc., 687 F. Supp. 2d 1191 (E.D. Cal. 2009) (claim based on mortgage loan not viable absent allegations that defendants were real estate brokers); Ortiz v. Accredited Home Lenders, Inc., 639 F. Supp. 2d 1159 (S.D. Cal. 2009) (dismissing claim when mortgagors did not allege that assignee acted as real estate broker or had principal-agent relationship with broker who negotiated loan); Delino v. Platinum Cmty. Bank, 628 F. Supp. 2d 1226 (S.D. Cal. 2009) (only applies to real estate brokers, not lenders or subsequent servicers).

59 815 Ill. Comp. Stat. § 505/2N, *as amended eff.* Aug. 23, 2001.

60 *See* National Consumer Law Center, Unfair and Deceptive Acts and Practices § 3.2.7 (8th ed. 2012), *updated at* www.nclc.org/library.

61 *See, e.g.*, Ariz. Const. art. 28, § 3; S.C. Code Ann. § 1-1-697.

62 *See* Steven W. Bender, *Consumer Protection for Latinos: Overcoming Language Fraud and English-Only in the Marketplace*, 45 Am. U. L. Rev. 1027, 1046 (1996).

63 *See id.* at 1053 n.143.

64 *See* Yniguez v. Arizonans for Official Language, 69 F.3d 920 (9th Cir. 1995) (declaring law unconstitutional), *vacated and remanded*, 520 U.S. 43 (1997), *on remand*, 118 F.3d 667 (9th Cir. 1997) (remanding to district court with instructions to dismiss case on procedural grounds); Alaskans for a Common Language, Inc. v. Kritz, 170 P.3d 183 (Alaska 2007) (striking down English-only provision as violative of state right to

The much more prevalent state laws that declare English to be the "official language" of the state are unlikely to have any substantive impact on consumer protections.[65] A California court rejected a car dealer's argument that the translation requirement conflicts with the California Constitution, which makes English the official language of the state.[66]

Many statutes and rules require "clear and conspicuous" disclosures to consumers without mentioning non-English languages. Nevertheless, implicit in these requirements may be the requirement that disclosures be in the same language as a transaction is conducted.

According to an FTC interpretation, when disclosures in an advertisement or other sales material are required to be clear and conspicuous, they must be in the language of the target audience—normally the language in which the advertisement or sales material is written—or the language of the periodical in which the advertisement appears.[67] State statutes that require clear and conspicuous disclosure may implicitly require the same standard.

11.4.4   *UDAP and Unconscionability Claims*

Uniform Commercial Code and other unconscionability concepts also provide a basis to claim that disclosures should be made in the same language as the transaction. It would be unconscionable for a seller to use the buyer's inability to understand contract provisions to include oppressive terms in the agreement.[68]

There is also precedent that it is unfair or deceptive not to translate important information into the same language as principally used in the transaction.[69] UDAP claims are preferable to contract law claims because the general presumption in contract law is that consumers have a duty to read documents or contracts that they sign or to find someone who can help them.[70]

Failure to translate a contract or disclosures is deceptive because the consumer is obviously confused and deceived if required disclosures are made in a manner the consumer cannot understand. In addition, non-English disclosure falls nicely into the FTC's unfairness approach.[71] A non-English-speaking consumer cannot reasonably avoid the fact that he or she cannot understand English disclosures. The confusion can lead to substantial injury. In a situation in which a seller has a large number of non-English-speaking customers, it would not be costly to add disclosures in a second language.[72]

Several UDAP statutes explicitly require that retailers not take advantage of a consumer's inability to understand the language of an agreement.[73] The FTC has accepted numerous consent agreements requiring that consumers be provided with contracts, other pertinent documents, and written disclosures in the same language as used in the sales presentation.[74] These documents must be provided in a timely manner.[75]

11.5   Restore Online Shoppers' Confidence Act

The Restore Online Shoppers' Confidence Act, enacted in 2010, provides several protections to consumers in online transactions. It requires disclosure of all material terms of the transaction before charging or attempting to charge a

---

free speech); Ruiz v. Hull, 957 P.2d 984 (Ariz. 1998) (holding English-only law violates both free speech and equal protection); *In re* Initiative Petition No. 366, 46 P.3d 123 (Okla. 2002) (English-only provisions on ballot initiative would infringe on state constitutional rights to freedom of speech and right to petition government for redress of grievances).

65   *See* Steven W. Bender, *Consumer Protection for Latinos: Overcoming Language Fraud and English-Only in the Marketplace,* 45 Am. U. L. Rev. 1027, 1049 n.124 (1996).

66   Gutierrez v. PCH Roulette, Inc., 2003 WL 22422431 (Cal. Ct. App. Oct. 24, 2003) (unpublished).

67   16 C.F.R. § 14.9(a).

68   Prevot v. Phillips Petroleum, Inc., 133 F. Supp. 2d 937 (S.D. Tex. 2001) (arbitration agreements signed by Spanish-speaking employees who did not understand English were unconscionable and unenforceable). *See generally* National Consumer Law Center, Unfair and Deceptive Acts and Practices § 4.4 (8th ed. 2012), *updated at* www.nclc.org/library (see especially § 4.4.4); Steven W. Bender, *Consumer Protection for Latinos: Overcoming Language Fraud and English-Only in the Marketplace,* 45 Am. U. L. Rev. 1027, 1040 (1996).

69   *In re* Kelcor Corp. et al., 93 F.T.C. 9 (1979) (consent order). *See also* Cantu v. Butron, 921 S.W.2d 344 (Tex. App. 1996) (upholding fraud verdict against attorney who took advantage of clients' inability to speak English).

70   *See also* Cathy Lesser Mansfield & Alan M. White, *Literacy and Contract,* 13.2 Stan. Law. & Pol. Rev. 233 (2002). *See generally* Steven

W. Bender, *Consumer Protection for Latinos: Overcoming Language and English-Only in the Marketplace,* 45 Am. U. L. Rev. 1027 (1996).

71   *See* National Consumer Law Center, Unfair and Deceptive Acts and Practices § 4.3.2 (8th ed. 2012), *updated at* www.nclc.org/library.

72   *See generally* Steven W. Bender, *Consumer Protection for Latinos: Overcoming Language Fraud and English-Only in the Marketplace,* 45 Am. U. L. Rev. 1027 (1996).

73   *UDAP statutes that explicitly forbid taking advantage of consumer's inability to understand:* Ark. Rev. Stat. Ann. § 4-88-107(a)(8); Mich. Comp. Laws § 445.903; Ohio Rev. Code Ann. § 1345.031(B)(13) (West) (residential mortgages).

    UDAP statutes that make it a factor to be considered in determining whether an act or practice is unconscionable: D.C. Code § 28-3904(r)(5); Ind. Code § 24-4.5-6-111(3)(e); Iowa Code § 537.5108(4)(e); Kan. Stat. Ann. § 50-627(b)(1); Ohio Rev. Code Ann. § 1345.03(B)(1) (West); Okla. Stat. tit. 15, § 761.1((B); S.C. Code Ann. § 37-5-108(4)(a)(iv); Wis. Stat. § 425.107(3)(d).

74   *See, e.g.,* Consent Decree, United States v. United Recovery Sys., Inc., No. H-02-1410 (sl) (S.D. Tex. 2002), *available at* www.ftc.gov; *In re* Cavanaugh Communities Corp. et al., 93 F.T.C. 559 (1979) (consent order); *In re* Hiken Furniture Co., 91 F.T.C. 1115 (1978) (consent order); *In re* Insilco Corp. et al., 91 F.T.C. 706 (1978) (consent order); *In re* Hallcraft Jewelers, Inc. et al., 89 F.T.C. 415 (1977) (consent order); *In re* Lafayette United Corp. et al., 88 F.T.C. 683 (1976); *In re* Carl Stepp, 88 F.T.C. 409 (1976) (consent order); *In re* J. Kurtz & Sons, Inc. et al., 87 F.T.C. 1300 (1976); *In re* Mutual Home Equip. Co. et al., 87 F.T.C. 606 (1976) (consent order); *In re* Weilt Co., 87 F.T.C. 406 (1976) (consent order); *In re* Almacenes Hernandez Corp. et al., 87 F.T.C. 400 (1976) (consent order); *In re* Buch's Jewelry Co. et al., 87 F.T.C. 394 (1976) (consent order); *In re* Daby's Furniture Corp. et al., 87 F.T.C. 389 (1976); *In re* J&J Furniture Corp. et al., 87 F.T.C. 383 (1976) (consent order); *In re* Library Mktg. Serv. Inc. et al., 85 F.T.C. 957 (1975) (consent order); *In re* Atlantic Indus. et al., 85 F.T.C. 903 (1975) (consent order).

75   *In re* Grand Spaulding Dodge, Inc., 90 F.T.C. 406 (1977) (consent order).

consumer for goods or services sold over the Internet through a negative option feature.[76] The seller must obtain the consumer's express informed consent before making the charge and must provide a simple mechanism for the consumer to stop recurring charges.[77] These protections are intended, among other things, to prohibit negative option sales.[78]

The Act also imposes specific restrictions on "post-transaction third party sellers." These are defined as entities that sell goods or services on the Internet after the consumer has made an Internet purchase from another merchant but that are not affiliated with the initial merchant.[79] These solicitations often appear as pop-up boxes during or immediately after the consumer's completion of the original transaction and imply that the offer is from the original merchant rather than an unrelated third party.[80] The statute requires disclosure of all material terms of the transaction, including a description of the goods or services being offered and their cost, and the fact that the post-transaction third-party seller is not affiliated with the initial merchant.[81] The statute also prohibits the initial merchant from sharing the consumer's billing information with the third-party seller and prohibits the third-party seller from billing the consumer unless the consumer has affirmatively provided his or her contact information and the full account number for the account that is to be charged.[82] The consumer must also perform some additional affirmative action, such as clicking on a confirmation button.[83]

The Act is enforceable by the FTC and state attorneys general.[84] It is not directly enforceable by consumers, but violations will be actionable as UDAP violations in many states.[85] In addition, compliance with the requirements imposed by the Act might be a condition of contract formation, rendering consumers' obligations void or voidable if the online seller did not comply with them.[86] The Act does not preempt other claims, including claims under state UDAP statutes.[87]

11.6 The Federal Computer Fraud and Abuse Act

11.6.1 Introduction

The federal Computer Fraud and Abuse Act (CFAA) provides for criminal and private remedies for accessing a computer without authorization and certain related practices.[88] Some of the prohibitions relate to unauthorized access to government information, including national security information. In addition, the statute enumerates a number of criminal penalties for conduct violating various act prohibitions. This section, however, focuses only on statutory prohibitions relevant to consumers and on private remedies available to consumers for violation of those prohibitions.

11.6.2 CFAA Prohibitions Relevant to Consumers

The CFAA prohibits the intentional access to a computer without authorization or in excess of authorized access when the person obtains:

- Information contained in a financial record of a card issuer or a financial institution;
- Information on a consumer contained in a file of a consumer reporting agency;
- Information from any federal department or agency; or
- Information from any "protected computer," whose definition includes a computer used in or affecting interstate commerce.[89]

For example, when a company has the ability to access consumer reports only when it has a permissible purpose to do so, the CFAA prohibits the company from accessing the reporting agency's computer to obtain consumer information when the company does not have such a permissible purpose. The

---

76 15 U.S.C. § 8403(1). *See* Appx. K, *infra* (full text of the Act).

77 15 U.S.C. § 8403(2), (3). *See* F.T.C. v. Health Formulas, L.L.C., 2015 WL 2130504 (D. Nev. May 6, 2015); Washington v. Internet Order, L.L.C., 2015 WL 918694 (W.D. Wash. Mar. 2, 2015).

78 15 U.S.C. § 8401(8) (Congressional findings).

79 15 U.S.C. § 8403(d). *See also* Letter from James A. Kohm, Assoc. Director, FTC Div. of Enforcement Bureau of Consumer Protection (Nov. 17, 2011) ("ROSCA does not define 'initiate a transaction' and no courts have addressed the issue"), *available at* www.ftc.gov.

80 *See* 15 U.S.C. § 8401 (congressional findings).

81 15 U.S.C. § 8402(a)(1).

82 15 U.S.C. § 8402(a)(2), (b). *See* Park v. Webloyalty.com, Inc., 2014 WL 4829465, at *7 (S.D. Cal. Sept. 29, 2014) (". . . ROSCA prohibits the 'data pass' method of sharing credit card information with third-party sellers, and the practice of authorizing financial transactions by email address alone".

83 15 U.S.C. § 8402(a)(2)(B).

84 15 U.S.C. §§ 8404, 8405. *See* F.T.C. v. Health Formulas, L.L.C., 2015 WL 2130504 (D. Nev. May 6, 2015) (granting preliminary injunction; FTC alleged *that defendants violated ROSCA by charging consumers without their permission through a* negative option). *See also* Washington v. Internet Order, L.L.C., 2015 WL 918694 (W.D. Wash. Mar. 2, 2015) (denying defendant's motion for stay).

85 *See, e.g.,* Marsh v. Zaazoom Solutions, L.L.C., 2012 WL 6522749, at *21 (N.D. Cal. Dec. 13, 2012). *See also* National Consumer Law Center, Unfair and Deceptive Acts and Practices § 3.2.7 (8th ed. 2012), *updated at* www.nclc.org/library.

86 *But cf.* Trilegiant Corp. v. Orbitz, L.L.C., 993 N.Y.S.2d 462, 468 (N.Y. Sup. Ct. 2014) (ROSCA does not render violating contracts unenforceable as between marketers using data pass as a tool), *aff'd,* 5 N.Y.S.3d 366 (N.Y. App. Div. 2015).

87 Marsh v. Zaazoom Solutions, L.L.C., 2012 WL 952226 (N.D. Cal. Mar. 20, 2012).

88 18 U.S.C. § 1030. *See* Sewell v. Bernardin, 795 F.3d 337 (2d Cir. 2015).

89 18 U.S.C. §§ 1030(a)(2), 1030(e)(2)(B). *See In re* Sony PS3 Other OS Litig., 551 Fed. Appx. 916, 922 (9th Cir. 2014) (users who voluntarily install software that allegedly caused harm cannot plead unauthorized access under CFAA); Bittman v. Fox, 2015 WL 3484335 (N.D. Ill. June 1, 2015) (purpose of CFAA is to punish trespassers and hackers); Tan v. Doe, 2014 WL 1779048 (S.D.N.Y. May 5, 2014) (to meet "protected computer" element, allegations must support plausible inference of substantial use of computer for ends related to interstate commerce); Mahoney v. DeNuzzio, 2014 WL 347624, at *5 (D. Mass. Jan. 29, 2014) (denying motion to dismiss CFAA claim when complaint alleged that Yahoo! and Facebook computers are "protected computers" used in interstate commerce, and defendant obtained access without authorization and obtained information from those computers).

---

company will be accessing the reporting agency's computer in excess of its authorized access, which access is limited only to when it has a permissible purpose to obtain the information.

The CFAA also prohibits:

- Knowingly causing the transmission of a program, information, code, or command that intentionally causes damage without authorization to a protected computer (for example, sending a virus to a protected computer);[90] or

- Knowingly, and with intent to defraud, trafficking in any password or similar information through which a computer may be accessed without authorization, when such trafficking affects interstate commerce.[91]

The CFAA applies to any person—there are no exclusions. The section on prohibitions applies to "whoever."[92] No exemptions or exclusions are found in the statute.

11.6.3 Consumer Remedies

Any person who suffers damage or loss by reason of a CFAA violation may maintain a civil action against the violator to obtain compensatory damages and injunctive or other equitable relief.[93] The action is only available if the conduct involves at least one of five factors:

1. That total economic damage to all affected persons aggregates to at least $5000;

2. The conduct affects the potential modification or impairment of a medical examination, diagnosis, treatment, or care of an individual;

3. The conduct causes physical injury;

4. The conduct threatens public health or safety; *or*

5. The conduct damages a federal computer used in the administration of justice, national defense, or national security.[94]

There is a two-year statute of limitations starting from when the injured party discovers the damage.[95] No action may be brought for negligent design or manufacture of computer hardware, software, or firmware.[96]

---

90 18 U.S.C. § 1030(a)(5)(A).

91 18 U.S.C. § 1030(a)(6).

92 18 U.S.C. § 1030(a).

93 18 U.S.C. § 1030(g).

94 18 U.S.C. §§ 1030(g), 1030(a)(4)(A)(i). *See* Halperin v. Int'l Web Services, L.L.C., 70 F. Supp. 3d 893 (N.D. Ill. 2014) (dismissing CFAA claim for failure to plausibly plead damages exceeding $5000 when considered in aggregate over one-year period; plaintiffs must meet damages themselves and cannot rely on absent members of putative class; noting that damages of absent class members may be aggregated only if arising from a single act); Walsh v. Microsoft Corp., 63 F. Supp. 3d 1312, 1320 (W.D. Wash. 2014) (dismissing CFAA claim for failure to plausibly plead damages exceeding $5000 when considered in aggregate over one-year period; plaintiffs must meet damages themselves and cannot rely on absent members of putative class); *In re* Google Android Consumer Privacy Litig., 2014 WL 988889 (N.D. Cal. Mar. 10, 2014) (same).

95 18 U.S.C. § 1030(g). *See* Sewell v. Bernardin, 795 F.3d 337 (2d Cir. 2015) (statute of limitations runs from the date that plaintiff discovered that someone had impaired integrity of each of her relevant Internet accounts).

96 18 U.S.C. § 1030(g).

Appendix A   FTC Trade Regulation Rules

A.1   Introduction

Appendix A.2, *infra*, reprints portions of the Federal Trade Commission (FTC) Act relating to FTC authority to enact trade regulation rules (TRRs), the scope of those TRRs, and FTC remedies to enforce the TRRs. This appendix then reprints nine of the more important FTC TRRs at appendices A.3–A.11, *infra*. Eight of these nine TRRs are analyzed at Chapter 2, *supra*. The TRR concerning preservation of consumer claims and defenses (FTC Holder Rule) is detailed at Chapter 4, *supra*. An important FTC advisory opinion on the FTC Holder Rule is reprinted at Appendix A.5.2, *infra*. A listing of seven TRRs *not* reprinted here is found at § 2.1.2, *supra*, and their full text is found at 16 C.F.R. ch. I, subch. D.

The FTC has also enacted a number of other types of rules under other statutory authority, and those are not reprinted in this appendix. One such rule, the FTC Telemarketing Sales Rule, is reprinted in Appendix C.1.2, *infra*, and detailed in Chapters 5 and 6, *supra*. Other FTC rules not reproduced here are listed at § 2.1.2, *supra*, where references can be found to other NCLC treatises that reprint a number of those rules; all of these rules are also available at title 16 of the Code of Federal Regulations. FTC industry guides are not reprinted in this appendix but are listed at § 2.10, *supra*, and can also found at title 16 of the Code of Federal Regulations.

The online version of this treatise, under Primary Sources, reprints materials interpreting the TRRs (including FTC statements of basis and purpose), TRR enforcement statements, staff interpretations, and FTC advisory opinions. This material is searchable and can be downloaded, printed, or even emailed.

A.2   Selected FTC Statutory Provisions

A.2.1   FTC Standard Rulemaking Authority

15 U.S.C.

* * *

§ 44.   Definitions
§ 45.   Unfair methods of competition unlawful; prevention by Commission

* * *

§ 57a.   Unfair or deceptive acts or practices rulemaking proceedings

* * *

§ 57b.   Civil actions for violations of rules and cease and desist orders respecting unfair or deceptive acts or practices

* * *

15 U.S.C. § 44.   Definitions

The words defined in this section shall have the following meaning when found in this subchapter, to wit:

"Commerce" means commerce among the several States or with foreign nations, or in any Territory of the United States or in the District of Columbia, or between any such Territory and another, or between any such Territory and any State or foreign nation, or between the District of Columbia and any State or Territory or foreign nation.

"Corporation" shall be deemed to include any company, trust, so-called Massachusetts trust, or association, incorporated or unincorporated, which is organized to carry on business for its own profit or that of its members, and has shares of capital or capital stock or certificates of interest, and any company, trust, so-called Massachusetts trust, or association, incorporated or unincorporated, without shares of capital or capital stock or certificates of interest, except partnerships, which is organized to carry on business for its own profit or that of its members.

* * *

[C. 311, § 4, 38 Stat. 719 (Sept. 26, 1914); C. 49, § 2, 52 Stat. 111 (Mar. 21, 1938); Pub. L. No. 102-242, tit. II, § 212(g)(1), 105 Stat. 2302 (Dec. 19, 1991); Pub. L. No. 107-273, Div. C, tit. IV, § 14102(c)(2)(B), 116 Stat. 1921 (Nov. 2, 2002); Pub. L. No. 109-455, § 2, 120 Stat. 3372 (Dec. 22, 2006)]

15 U.S.C. § 45.   Unfair methods of competition unlawful; prevention by Commission

(a) Declaration of unlawfulness; power to prohibit unfair practices; inapplicability to foreign trade

(1) Unfair methods of competition in or affecting commerce, and unfair or deceptive acts or practices in or affecting commerce, are hereby declared unlawful.

(2) The Commission is hereby empowered and directed to prevent persons, partnerships, or corporations, except banks, savings and loan institutions described in section 57a(f)(3) of this title, Federal credit unions described in section 57a(f)(4) of this title, common carriers subject to the Acts to regulate commerce, air carriers and foreign air carriers subject to part A of subtitle VII of Title 49, and persons, partnerships, or corporations insofar as they are subject to the Packers and Stockyards Act, 1921, as amended [7 U.S.C.A. § 181 *et seq.*], except as provided in section 406(b) of said Act [7 U.S.C.A. § 227(b)], from using unfair methods of competition in or affecting commerce and unfair or deceptive acts or practices in or affecting commerce.

* * *

[c. 311, § 5, 38 Stat. 719 (Sept. 26, 1914); c. 49, § 3, 52 Stat. 111 (Mar. 21, 1938); c. 601, tit. XI, § 1107(f), 52 Stat. 1028 (June 23, 1938); c. 646, § 32(a), 62 Stat. 991 (June 25, 1948); c. 139, § 127, 63 Stat. 107 (May 24, 1949); c. 61, § 4(c), 64 Stat. 21 (Mar. 16, 1950); c. 745, § 2, 66 Stat. 632 (July 14, 1952); Pub. L. No. 85-726, tit. XIV, §§ 1401(b), 1411, 72 Stat. 806, 809 (Aug. 23, 1958); Pub. L. No. 85-791, § 3, 72 Stat. 942 (Aug. 28, 1958); Pub. L. No. 85-909, § 3, 72 Stat. 1750 (Sept. 2, 1958); Pub. L. No. 86-507, § 1(13), 74 Stat. 200 (June 11, 1960); Pub. L. No. 93-153, tit. IV, § 408(c), (d), 87 Stat. 591, 592 (Nov. 16, 1973); Pub. L. No. 93-637, tit. II, §§ 201(a), 204(b), 205(a), 88 Stat. 2193, 2200 (Jan. 4, 1975); Pub. L. No. 94-145, § 3, 89 Stat. 801 (Dec. 12, 1975); Pub. L. No. 96-37, § 1(a), 93 Stat. 95 (July 23, 1979); Pub. L. No. 96-252, § 2, 94 Stat. 374 (May 28, 1980); Pub. L. No. 97-290, tit. IV, § 403, 96 Stat. 1246 (Oct. 8, 1982); Pub. L. No. 98-620, tit. IV, § 402(12), 98 Stat. 3358 (Nov. 8, 1984); Pub. L. No. 100-86, tit. VII, § 715(a)(1), 101 Stat. 655 (Aug. 10, 1987); Pub. L. No. 103-312, §§ 4, 6, 9, 108 Stat. 1691, 1692, 1695 (Aug. 26, 1994); Pub. L. No. 109-455, § 3, 120 Stat. 3372 (Dec. 22, 2006)]

* * *

15 U.S.C. § 57a. Unfair or deceptive acts or practices rulemaking proceedings

(a) Authority of Commission to prescribe rules and general statements of policy

(1) Except as provided in subsection (h) of this section, the Commission may prescribe—

(A) interpretive rules and general statements of policy with respect to unfair or deceptive acts or practices in or affecting commerce (within the meaning of section 45(a)(1) of this title), and

(B) rules which define with specificity acts or practices which are unfair or deceptive acts or practices in or affecting commerce (within the meaning of section 45(a)(1) of this title), except that the Commission shall not develop or promulgate any trade rule or regulation with regard to the regulation of the development and utilization of the standards and certification activities pursuant to this section. Rules under this subparagraph may include requirements prescribed for the purpose of preventing such acts or practices.

(2) The Commission shall have no authority under this subchapter, other than its authority under this section, to prescribe any rule with respect to unfair or deceptive acts or practices in or affecting commerce (within the meaning of section 45(a)(1) of this title). The preceding sentence shall not affect any authority of the Commission to prescribe rules (including interpretive rules), and general statements of policy, with respect to unfair methods of competition in or affecting commerce.

(b) Procedures applicable

(1) When prescribing a rule under subsection (a)(1)(B) of this section, the Commission shall proceed in accordance with section 553 of Title 5 (without regard to any reference in such section to sections 556 and 557 of such title), and shall also (A) publish a notice of proposed rulemaking stating with particularity the text of the rule, including any alternatives, which the Commission proposes to promulgate, and the reason for the proposed rule; (B) allow interested persons to submit written data, views, and arguments, and make all such submissions publicly available; (C) provide an opportunity for an informal hearing in accordance with subsection (c) of this section; and (D) promulgate, if appropriate, a final rule based on the matter in the rulemaking record (as defined in subsection (e)(1)(B) of this section), together with a statement of basis and purpose.

(2)

(A) Prior to the publication of any notice of proposed rulemaking pursuant to paragraph (1)(A), the Commission shall publish an advance notice of proposed rulemaking in the Federal Register. Such advance notice shall—

(i) contain a brief description of the area of inquiry under consideration, the objectives which the Commission seeks to achieve, and possible regulatory alternatives under consideration by the Commission; and

(ii) invite the response of interested parties with respect to such proposed rulemaking, including any suggestions or alternative methods for achieving such objectives.

(B) The Commission shall submit such advance notice of proposed rulemaking to the Committee on Commerce, Science, and Transportation of the Senate and to the Committee on Energy and Commerce of the House of Representatives. The Commission may use such additional mechanisms as the Commission considers useful to obtain suggestions regarding the content of the area of inquiry before the publication of a general notice of proposed rulemaking under paragraph (1)(A).

(C) The Commission shall, 30 days before the publication of a notice of proposed rulemaking pursuant to paragraph (1)(A), submit such notice to the Committee on Commerce, Science, and Transportation of the Senate and to the Committee on Energy and Commerce of the House of Representatives.

(3) The Commission shall issue a notice of proposed rulemaking pursuant to paragraph (1)(A) only where it has reason to believe that the unfair or deceptive acts or practices which are the subject of the proposed rulemaking are prevalent. The Commission shall make a determination that unfair or deceptive acts or practices are prevalent under this paragraph only if—

(A) it has issued cease and desist orders regarding such acts or practices, or

(B) any other information available to the Commission indicates a widespread pattern of unfair or deceptive acts or practices.

(c) Informal hearing procedure

The Commission shall conduct any informal hearings required by subsection (b)(1)(C) of this section in accordance with the following procedure:

(1)

(A) The Commission shall provide for the conduct of proceedings under this subsection by hearing officers who shall perform their functions in accordance with the requirements of this subsection.

(B) The officer who presides over the rulemaking proceedings shall be responsible to a chief presiding officer who shall not be responsible to any other officer or employee of the Commission. The officer who presides over the rulemaking proceeding shall make a recommended decision based upon the findings and conclusions of such officer as to all relevant and material evidence, except that such recommended decision may be made by another officer if the officer who presided over the proceeding is no longer available to the Commission.

(C) Except as required for the disposition of ex parte matters as authorized by law, no presiding officer shall consult any person or party with respect to any fact in issue unless such officer gives notice and opportunity for all parties to participate.

(2) Subject to paragraph (3) of this subsection, an interested person is entitled—

(A) to present his position orally or by documentary submission (or both), and

(B) if the Commission determines that there are disputed issues of material fact it is necessary to resolve, to present such rebuttal submissions and to conduct (or have conducted under paragraph (3)(B)) such cross-examination of persons as the Commission determines (i) to be appropriate, and (ii) to be required for a full and true disclosure with respect to such issues.

(3) The Commission may prescribe such rules and make such rulings concerning proceedings in such hearings as may tend to avoid unnecessary costs or delay. Such rules or rulings may include (A) imposition of reasonable time limits on each interested person's oral presentations, and (B) requirements that any cross-examination to which a person may be entitled under paragraph (2) be conducted by the Commission on behalf of that person in such manner as the Commission determines (i) to be appropriate, and (ii) to be required for a full and true disclosure with respect to disputed issues of material fact.

(4)

(A) Except as provided in subparagraph (B), if a group of persons each of whom under paragraphs (2) and (3) would be entitled to conduct (or have conducted) cross-examination and who are determined by the Commission to have the same or similar interests in the proceeding cannot agree upon a single representative of such interests for purposes of cross-examination, the Commission may make rules and rulings (i) limiting the representation of such interest, for such purposes, and (ii) governing the manner in which such cross-examination shall be limited.

(B) When any person who is a member of a group with respect to which the Commission has made a determination under subparagraph (A) is unable to agree upon group representation with the other members of the group, then such person shall not be denied under the authority of subparagraph (A) the opportunity to conduct (or have conducted) cross-examination as to issues affecting his particular interests if (i) he satisfies the Commission that he has made a reasonable and good faith effort to reach agreement upon group representation with the other members of the group and (ii) the Commission determines that there are substantial and relevant issues which are not adequately presented by the group representative.

(5) A verbatim transcript shall be taken of any oral presentation, and cross-examination, in an informal hearing to which this subsection applies. Such transcript shall be available to the public.

* * *

[c. 311, § 18 (Sept. 26, 1914), *as added by* Pub. L. No. 93-637, tit. II, § 202(a), 88 Stat. 2193 (Jan. 4, 1975), *and amended by* Pub. L. No. 96-37, § 1(c), 93 Stat. 95 (July 23, 1979); Pub. L. No. 96-221, tit. VI, § 610(b), 94 Stat. 174 (Mar. 31, 1980); Pub. L. No. 96-252, §§ 7 to 11(a), 12, 94 Stat. 376 to 379 (May 28, 1980); Pub. L. No. 100-86, tit. VII, § 715(c), 101 Stat. 655 (Aug. 10, 1987); Pub. L. No. 101-73, tit. VII, § 744(t), 103 Stat. 441 (Aug. 9, 1989); Pub. L. No. 102-242, tit. II, § 212(g)(2), 105 Stat. 2302 (Dec. 19, 1991); Pub. L. No. 102-550, tit. XVI, § 1604(a)(9), 106 Stat. 4082 (Oct. 28, 1992); Pub. L. No. 103-312, §§ 3, 5, 108 Stat. 1691, 1692 (Aug. 26, 1994); Pub. L. No. 103-437, § 5(a), 108 Stat. 4582 (Nov. 2, 1994); Pub. L. No. 109-351, tit. VII, § 725(g), 120 Stat. 2002 (Oct. 13, 2006); Pub. L. No. 109-356, § 123(g), 120 Stat. 2029 (Oct. 16, 2006); Pub. L. No. 111-203, tit. X, § 1092, 124 Stat. 2094 (July 21, 2010)]

* * *

15 U.S.C. § 57b. Civil actions for violations of rules and cease and desist orders respecting unfair or deceptive acts or practices

(a) Suits by Commission against persons, partnerships, or corporations; jurisdiction; relief for dishonest or fraudulent acts

(1) If any person, partnership, or corporation violates any rule under this subchapter respecting unfair or deceptive acts or practices (other than an interpretive rule, or a rule violation of which the Commission has provided is not an unfair or deceptive act or practice in violation of section 45(a) of this title), then the Commission may commence a civil action against such person, partnership, or corporation for relief under subsection (b) of this section in a United States district court or in any court of competent jurisdiction of a State.

* * *

(b) Nature of relief available
The court in an action under subsection (a) of this section shall have jurisdiction to grant such relief as the court finds necessary to redress injury to consumers or other persons, partnerships, and corporations resulting from the rule violation or the unfair or deceptive act or practice, as the case may be. Such relief may include, but shall not be limited to, rescission or reformation of contracts, the refund of money or return of property, the payment of damages, and public notification respecting the rule violation or the unfair or deceptive act or practice, as the case may be; except that nothing in this subsection is intended to authorize the imposition of any exemplary or punitive damages.

* * *

(d) Time for bringing of actions
No action may be brought by the Commission under this section more than 3 years after the rule violation to which an action under subsection (a)(1) of this section relates, or the unfair or deceptive act or practice to which an action under subsection (a)(2) of this section relates; except that if a

cease and desist order with respect to any person's, partnership's, or corporation's rule violation or unfair or deceptive act or practice has become final and such order was issued in a proceeding under section 45(b) of this title which was commenced not later than 3 years after the rule violation or act or practice occurred, a civil action may be commenced under this section against such person, partnership, or corporation at any time before the expiration of one year after such order becomes final.

* * *

[C. 311, § 19 (Sept. 26, 1914), *as added by* Pub. L. No. 93-637, tit. II, § 206(a), 88 Stat. 2201 (Jan. 4, 1975)]

* * *

A.2.2 *FTC Streamlined Rulemaking Authority Regarding Automobile Dealers*

Introduction

In 2010, the Dodd-Frank Wall Street Reform and Consumer Protection Act provided to the Consumer Financial Protection Bureau extensive authority to regulate consumer financial products, but excluded many automobile dealers from that authority. Instead, the Act gave the FTC streamlined rulemaking authority concerning automobile dealers. The statutory extracts *infra* detail those auto dealers excluded and provides for the streamlined rulemaking authority.

12 U.S.C. § 5519. Exclusion for auto dealers

(a) Sale, servicing, and leasing of motor vehicles excluded
Except as permitted in subsection (b), the Bureau may not exercise any rulemaking, supervisory, enforcement or any other authority, including any authority to order assessments, over a motor vehicle dealer that is predominantly engaged in the sale and servicing of motor vehicles, the leasing and servicing of motor vehicles, or both.

* * *

(d) Federal Trade Commission authority
Notwithstanding section 57a of Title 15, the Federal Trade Commission is authorized to prescribe rules under sections 45 and 57a(a)(1)(B) of Title 15.1 in accordance with section 553 of Title 5, with respect to a person described in subsection (a).

[Pub. L. No. 111-203, tit. X, § 1029, 124 Stat. 2004 (July 21, 2010)]

A.3   Negative Option Rule—16 C.F.R. § 425

16 C.F.R. § 425.1   The rule.

(a) In connection with the sale, offering for sale, or distribution of goods and merchandise in or affecting commerce, as "commerce" is defined in the Federal Trade Commission Act, it is an unfair or deceptive act or practice, for a seller in connection with the use of any negative option plan to fail to comply with the following requirements:

(1) Promotional material shall clearly and conspicuously disclose the material terms of the plan, including:

(i) That aspect of the plan under which the subscriber must notify the seller, in the manner provided for by the seller, if he does not wish to purchase the selection;

(ii) Any obligation assumed by the subscriber to purchase a minimum quantity of merchandise;

(iii) The right of a contract-complete subscriber to cancel his membership at any time;

(iv) Whether billing charges will include an amount for postage and handling;

(v) A disclosure indicating that the subscriber will be provided with at least ten (10) days in which to mail any form, contained in or accompanying an announcement identifying the selection, to the seller;

(vi) A disclosure that the seller will credit the return of any selections sent to a subscriber, and guarantee to the Postal Service or the subscriber postage to return such selections to the seller when the announcement and form are not received by the subscriber in time to afford him at least ten (10) days in which to mail his form to the seller;

(vii) The frequency with which the announcements and forms will be sent to the subscriber and the maximum number of announcements and forms which will be sent to him during a 12–month period.

(2) Prior to sending any selection, the seller shall mail to its subscribers, within the time specified by paragraph (a)(3) of this section:

(i) An announcement identifying the selection;

(ii) A form, contained in or accompanying the announcement, clearly and conspicuously disclosing that the subscriber will receive the selection identified in the announcement unless he instructs the seller that he does not want the selection, designating a procedure by which the form may be used for the purpose of enabling the subscriber so to instruct the seller, and specifying either the return date or the mailing date.

(3) The seller shall mail the announcement and form either at least twenty (20) days prior to the return date or at least fifteen (15) days prior to the mailing date, or provide a mailing date at least ten (10) days after receipt by the subscriber, provided, however, that whichever system the seller chooses for mailing the announcement and form, such system must provide the subscriber with at least ten (10) days in which to mail his form.

(b) In connection with the sale or distribution of goods and merchandise in or affecting commerce, as "commerce" is defined in the Federal Trade Commission Act, it shall constitute an unfair or deceptive act or practice for a seller in connection with the use of any negative option plan to:

(1) Refuse to credit, for the full invoiced amount thereof, the return of any selection sent to a subscriber, and to guarantee to the Postal Service or the subscriber postage adequate to return such selection to the seller, when:

(i) The selection is sent to a subscriber whose form indicating that he does not want to receive the selection was received by the seller by the return date or was mailed by the subscriber by the mailing date;

(ii) Such form is received by the seller after the return date, but has been mailed by the subscriber and postmarked at least 3 days prior to the return date;

(iii) Prior to the date of shipment of such selection, the seller has received from a contract-complete subscriber, a written notice of cancellation of membership adequately identifying the subscriber; however, this provision is applicable only to the first selection sent to a canceling contract-complete subscriber after the seller has received written notice of cancellation. After the first selection shipment, all selection shipments thereafter are deemed to be unordered merchandise pursuant to Section 3009 of the Postal Reorganization Act of 1970, as adopted by the Federal Trade Commission in its public notice, dated September 11, 1970;

(iv) The announcement and form are not received by the subscriber in time to afford him at least ten (10) days in which to mail his form.

(2) Fail to notify a subscriber known by the seller to be within any of the circumstances set forth in paragraphs (b)(1)(i) through (iv) of this section, that if the subscriber elects, the subscriber may return the selection with return postage guaranteed and receive a credit to his account.

(3) Refuse to ship within 4 weeks after receipt of an order merchandise due subscribers as introductory and bonus merchandise, unless the seller is unable to deliver the merchandise originally offered due to unanticipated circumstances beyond the seller's control and promptly makes a reasonably equivalent alternative offer. However, where the subscriber refuses to accept alternatively offered introductory merchandise, but instead insists upon termination of his membership due to the seller's failure to provide the subscriber with his originally requested introductory merchandise, or any portion thereof, the seller must comply with the subscriber's request for cancellation of membership, provided the subscriber returns to the seller any introductory merchandise which already may have been sent him.

(4) Fail to terminate promptly the membership of a properly identified contract-complete subscriber upon his written request.

(5) Ship, without the express consent of the subscriber, substituted merchandise for that ordered by the subscriber.

(c) For the purposes of this part:

(1) *Negative option plan* refers to a contractual plan or arrangement under which a seller periodically sends to subscribers an announcement which identifies merchandise (other than annual supplements to previously acquired merchandise) it proposes to send to subscribers to such plan, and the subscribers thereafter receive and are billed for the merchandise identified in each such announcement, unless by a date or within a time specified by the seller with respect to each such announcement the subscribers, in conformity with the provisions of such plan, instruct the seller not to send the identified merchandise.

(2) *Subscriber* means any person who has agreed to receive the benefits of, and assume the obligations entailed in, membership in any negative option plan and whose membership in such negative option plan has been approved and accepted by the seller.

(3) *Contract-complete subscriber* refers to a subscriber who has purchased the minimum quantity of merchandise required by the terms of membership in a negative option plan.

(4) *Promotional material* refers to an advertisement containing or accompanying any device or material which a prospective subscriber sends to the seller to request acceptance or enrollment in a negative option plan.

(5) *Selection* refers to the merchandise identified by a seller under any negative option plan as the merchandise which the subscriber will receive and be billed for, unless by the date, or within the period specified by the seller, the subscriber instructs the seller not to send such merchandise.

(6) *Announcement* refers to any material sent by a seller using a negative option plan in which the selection is identified and offered to subscribers.

(7) *Form* refers to any form which the subscriber returns to the seller to instruct the seller not to send the selection.

(8) *Return date* refers to a date specified by a seller using a negative option plan as the date by which a form must be received by the seller to prevent shipment of the selection.

(9) *Mailing date* refers to the time specified by a seller using a negative option plan as the time by or within which a form must be mailed by a subscriber to prevent shipment of the selection.

[38 Fed. Reg. 4896 (Feb. 22, 1973); 38 Fed. Reg. 6991 (Mar. 15, 1973); 63 Fed. Reg. 44,562 (Aug. 20, 1998)]

* * *

A.4 FTC Rule Concerning Cooling-Off Period For Sales Made at Homes or at Certain Other Locations

16 C.F.R.

SOURCE: 53 Fed. Reg. 45,459 (Nov. 10, 1988); 60 Fed. Reg. 54,186 (Oct. 20, 1995), unless otherwise noted.

AUTHORITY: Sections 1–23, F.T.C. Act, 15 U.S.C. §§ 41–58.

16 C.F.R. § 429.0   Definitions.

For the purposes of this part the following definitions shall apply:

(a) Door-to-Door Sale—A sale, lease, or rental of consumer goods or services in which the seller or his representative personally solicits the sale, including those in response to or following an invitation by the buyer, and the buyer's agreement or offer to purchase is made at a place other than the place of business of the seller (e.g., sales at the buyer's residence or at facilities rented on a temporary or short-term basis, such as hotel or motel rooms, convention centers, fairgrounds and restaurants, or sales at the buyer's workplace or in dormitory lounges), and which has a purchase price of $25 or more if the sale is made at the buyer's residence or a purchase price of $130 or more if the sale is made at locations other than the buyer's residence, whether under single or multiple contracts. The term *door-to-door sale* does not include a transaction:

(1) Made pursuant to prior negotiations in the course of a visit by the buyer to a retail business establishment having a fixed permanent location where the goods are exhibited or the services are offered for sale on a continuing basis; or

(2) In which the consumer is accorded the right of rescission by the provisions of the Consumer Credit Protection Act (15 U.S.C. 1635) or regulations issued pursuant thereto; or

(3) In which the buyer has initiated the contact and the goods or services are needed to meet a bona fide immediate personal emergency of the buyer, and the buyer furnishes the seller with a separate dated and signed personal statement in the buyer's handwriting describing the situation requiring immediate remedy and expressly acknowledging and waiving the right to cancel the sale within 3 business days; or

(4) Conducted and consummated entirely by mail or telephone; and without any other contact between the buyer and the seller or its representative prior to delivery of the goods or performance of the services; or

(5) In which the buyer has initiated the contact and specifically requested the seller to visit the buyer's home for the purpose of repairing or performing maintenance upon the buyer's personal property. If, in the course of such a visit, the seller sells the buyer the right to receive additional services or goods other than replacement parts necessarily used in performing the maintenance or in making the repairs, the sale of those additional goods or services would not fall within this exclusion; or

(6) Pertaining to the sale or rental of real property, to the sale of insurance, or to the sale of securities or commodities by a broker-dealer registered with the Securities and Exchange Commission.

(b) Consumer Goods or Services—Goods or services purchased, leased, or rented primarily for personal, family, or household purposes, including courses of instruction or training regardless of the purpose for which they are taken.

(c) Seller—Any person, partnership, corporation, or association engaged in the door-to-door sale of consumer goods or services.

(d) Place of Business—The main or permanent branch office or local address of a seller.

(e) Purchase Price—The total price paid or to be paid for the consumer goods or services, including all interest and service charges.

(f) Business Day—Any calendar day except Sunday or any federal holiday (*e.g.,* New Year's Day, President's Day, Martin Luther King's Birthday, Memorial Day, Independence Day, Labor Day, Columbus Day, Veterans' Day, Thanksgiving Day, and Christmas Day.)

[60 Fed. Reg. 54,186 (Oct. 20, 1995); 80 Fed. Reg. 1332 (Jan. 9, 2015)]

16 C.F.R. § 429.1   The Rule.

In connection with any door-to-door sale, it constitutes an unfair and deceptive act or practice for any seller to:

(a) Fail to furnish the buyer with a fully completed receipt or copy of any contract pertaining to such sale at the time of its execution, which is in the same language, e.g., Spanish, as that principally used in the oral sales presentation and which shows the date of the transaction and contains the name and address of the seller, and in immediate proximity to the space reserved in the contract for the signature of the buyer or on the front page of the receipt if a contract is not used and in bold face type of a minimum size of 10 points, a statement in substantially the following form:

"You, the buyer, may cancel this transaction at any time prior to midnight of the third business day after the date of this transaction. See the attached notice of cancellation form for an explanation of this right."

The seller may select the method of providing the buyer with the duplicate notice of cancellation form set forth in paragraph (b) of this section, *provided however*, that in the event of cancellation the buyer must be able to retain a complete copy of the contract or receipt. Furthermore, if both forms are not attached to the contract or receipt, the seller is required to alter the last sentence in the statement above to conform to the actual location of the forms.

(b) Fail to furnish each buyer, at the time the buyer signs the door-to-door sales contract or otherwise agrees to buy consumer goods or services from the seller, a completed form in duplicate, captioned either "NOTICE OF RIGHT TO CANCEL" or "NOTICE OF CANCELLATION," which shall (where applicable) contain in ten point bold face type the following information and statements in the same language, *e.g.*, Spanish, as that used in the contract.

Notice of Cancellation

[enter date of transaction]

_____

(Date)

You may CANCEL this transaction, without any Penalty or Obligation, within THREE BUSINESS DAYS from the above date.

If you cancel, any property traded in, any payments made by you under the contract or sale, and any negotiable instrument executed by you will be returned within TEN BUSINESS DAYS following receipt by the seller of your cancellation notice, and any security interest arising out of the transaction will be canceled.

If you cancel, you must make available to the seller at your residence, in substantially as good condition as when received, any goods delivered to you under this contract or sale, or you may, if you wish, comply with the instructions of the seller regarding the return shipment of the goods at the seller's expense and risk.

If you do make the goods available to the seller and the seller does not pick them up within 20 days of the date of your Notice of Cancellation, you may retain or dispose of the goods without any further obligation. If you fail to make the goods available to the seller, or if you agree to return the goods to the seller and fail to do so, then you remain liable for performance of all obligations under the contract.

To cancel this transaction, mail or deliver a signed and dated copy of this Cancellation Notice or any other written notice, or send a telegram, to [*Name of seller*], at [*address of seller's place of business*] NOT LATER THAN MIDNIGHT OF [*date*].

I HEREBY CANCEL THIS TRANSACTION.

(Date)_____

(Buyer's signature)_____

(c) Fail, before furnishing copies of the "Notice of Cancellation" to the buyer, to complete both copies by entering the name of the seller, the address of the seller's place of business, the date of the transaction, and the date, not earlier than the third business day following the date of the transaction, by which the buyer may give notice of cancellation.

(d) Include in any door-to-door contract or receipt any confession of judgment or any waiver of any of the rights to which the buyer is entitled under this section including specifically the buyer's right to cancel the sale in accordance with the provisions of this section.

(e) Fail to inform each buyer orally, at the time the buyer signs the contract or purchases the goods or services, of the buyer's right to cancel.

(f) Misrepresent in any manner the buyer's right to cancel.

(g) Fail or refuse to honor any valid notice of cancellation by a buyer and within 10 business days after the receipt of such notice, to: (i) Refund all payments made under the contract or sale; (ii) return any goods or property traded in, in substantially as good condition as when received by the seller; (iii) cancel and return any negotiable instrument executed by the buyer in connection with the contract or sale and take any action necessary or appropriate to terminate promptly any security interest created in the transaction.

(h) Negotiate, transfer, sell, or assign any note or other evidence of indebtedness to a finance company or other third party prior to midnight of the fifth business day following the day the contract was signed or the goods or services were purchased.

(i) Fail, within 10 business days of receipt of the buyer's notice of cancellation, to notify the buyer whether the seller intends to repossess or to abandon any shipped or delivered goods.

[37 Fed. Reg. 22,934 (Oct. 26, 1972), *as amended at* 38 Fed. Reg. 30,105 (Nov. 1, 1973); 38 Fed. Reg. 31,828 (Nov. 19, 1973); 53 Fed. Reg. 45,459 (Nov. 10, 1988); 60 Fed. Reg. 54,186 (Oct. 20, 1995)]

16 C.F.R. § 429.2   Effect on State laws and municipal ordinances.

(a) The Commission is cognizant of the significant burden imposed upon door-to-door sellers by the various and often inconsistent State laws that provide the buyer the right to cancel a door-to-door sales transaction. However, it does not believe that this constitutes sufficient justification for preempting all of the provisions of such laws and the ordinances of the political subdivisions of the various States. The rulemaking record in this proceeding supports the view that the joint and coordinated efforts of both the Commission and State and local officials are required to insure that consumers who have purchased from a door-to-door seller something they do not want, do not need, or cannot afford, be accorded a unilateral right to rescind, without penalty, their agreement to purchase those goods or services.

(b) This part will not be construed to annul, or exempt any seller from complying with, the laws of any State or the ordinances of a political subdivision thereof that regulate door-to-door sales, except to the extent that such laws or ordinances, if they permit door-to-door selling, are directly inconsistent with the provisions of this part. Such laws or ordinances which do not accord the buyer, with respect to the particular transaction, a right to cancel a door-to-door sale that is substantially the same or greater than that provided in this part, which permit the imposition of any fee or penalty on the buyer for the exercise of such right, or which do not provide for giving the buyer a notice of the right to cancel the transaction in substantially the same form and manner provided for in this part, are among those which will be considered directly inconsistent.

[60 Fed. Reg. 54,187 (Oct. 20, 1995)]

16 C.F.R. § 429.3   Exemptions.

(a) The requirements of this part do not apply for sellers of automobiles, vans, trucks or other motor vehicles sold at auctions, tent sales or other temporary places of business, provided that the seller is a seller of vehicles with a permanent place of business.

(b) The requirements of this part do not apply for sellers of arts or crafts sold at fairs or similar places.

[60 Fed. Reg. 54,187 (Oct. 20, 1995)]

A.5   FTC Rule Concerning Preservation of Consumers' Claims and Defenses

A.5.1   The Rule

16 C.F.R. § 433.1   Definitions.

(a) Person. An individual, corporation, or any other business organization.

(b) Consumer. A natural person who seeks or acquires goods or services for personal, family, or household use.

(c) Creditor. A person who, in the ordinary course of business, lends purchase money or finances the sale of goods or services to consumers on a deferred payment basis; *provided,* such person is not acting, for the purposes of a particular transaction, in the capacity of a credit card issuer.

(d) Purchase money loan. A cash advance which is received by a consumer in return for a "Finance Charge" within the meaning of the Truth in Lending Act and Regulation Z, which is applied, in whole or substantial part, to a purchase of goods or services from a seller who (1) refers consumers to the creditor or (2) is affiliated with the creditor by common control, contract, or business arrangement.

(e) Financing a sale. Extending credit to a consumer in connection with a "Credit Sale" within the meaning of the Truth in Lending Act and Regulation Z.

(f) Contract. Any oral or written agreement, formal or informal, between a creditor and a seller, which contemplates or provides for cooperative or concerted activity in connection with the sale of goods or services to consumers or the financing thereof.

(g) Business arrangement. Any understanding, procedure, course of dealing, or arrangement, formal or informal, between a creditor and a seller, in connection with the sale of goods or services to consumers or the financing thereof.

(h) Credit card issuer. A person who extends to cardholders the right to use a credit card in connection with purchases of goods or services.

(i) Consumer credit contract. Any instrument which evidences or embodies a debt arising from a "Purchase Money Loan" transaction or a "financed sale" as defined in paragraphs (d) and (e) of this section.

(j) Seller. A person who, in the ordinary course of business, sells or leases goods or services to consumers.

[40 Fed. Reg. 53,506 (Nov. 18, 1975)]

16 C.F.R. § 433.2   Preservation of consumers' claims and defenses, unfair or deceptive acts or practices.

In connection with any sale or lease of goods or services to consumers, in or affecting commerce as "commerce" is defined in the Federal Trade

Commission Act, it is an unfair or deceptive act or practice within the meaning of Section 5 of that Act for a seller, directly or indirectly, to:

(a) Take or receive a consumer credit contract which fails to contain the following provision in at least ten point, bold face, type:

> NOTICE
>
> ANY HOLDER OF THIS CONSUMER CREDIT CONTRACT IS SUBJECT TO ALL CLAIMS AND DEFENSES WHICH THE DEBTOR COULD ASSERT AGAINST THE SELLER OF GOODS OR SERVICES OBTAINED PURSUANT HERETO OR WITH THE PROCEEDS HEREOF. RECOVERY HEREUNDER BY THE DEBTOR SHALL NOT EXCEED AMOUNTS PAID BY THE DEBTOR HEREUNDER.

or,

(b) Accept, as full or partial payment for such sale or lease, the proceeds of any purchase money loan (as purchase money loan is defined herein), unless any consumer credit contract made in connection with such purchase money loan contains the following provision in at least ten point, bold face, type:

> NOTICE
>
> ANY HOLDER OF THIS CONSUMER CREDIT CONTRACT IS SUBJECT TO ALL CLAIMS AND DEFENSES WHICH THE DEBTOR COULD ASSERT AGAINST THE SELLER OF GOODS OR SERVICES OBTAINED WITH THE PROCEEDS HEREOF. RECOVERY HEREUNDER BY THE DEBTOR SHALL NOT EXCEED AMOUNTS PAID BY THE DEBTOR HEREUNDER.

[49 Fed. Reg. 53,506 (Nov. 18, 1975); 40 Fed. Reg. 58,131 (Dec. 15, 1975)]

16 C.F.R. § 433.3 Exemption of sellers taking or receiving open end consumer credit contracts before November 1, 1977, from requirements of § 433.2(a).

(a) Any seller who has taken or received an open end consumer credit contract before November 1, 1977, shall be exempt from the requirements of 16 C.F.R. Part 433 with respect to such contract provided the contract does not cut off consumers' claims and defenses.

(b) Definitions. The following definitions apply to this exemption:

    (1) All pertinent definitions contained in 16 C.F.R. 433.1.

    (2) *Open end consumer credit contract*: a consumer credit contract pursuant to which "open end credit" is extended.

    (3) *Open end credit*: consumer credit extended on an account pursuant to a plan under which a creditor may permit an applicant to make purchases or make loans, from time to time, directly from the creditor or indirectly by use of a credit card, check, or other device, as the plan may provide. The term does not include negotiated advances under an open-end real estate mortgage or a letter of credit.

    (4) *Contract which does not cut off consumers' claims and defenses*: a consumer credit contract which does not constitute or contain a negotiable instrument, or contain any waiver, limitation, term, or condition which has the effect of limiting a consumer's right to assert against any holder of the contract all legally sufficient claims and defenses which the consumer could assert against the seller of goods or services purchased pursuant to the contract.

[42 Fed. Reg. 19,490 (Apr. 14, 1977), *as amended at* 42 Fed. Reg. 46,510 (Sept. 16, 1977)]

A.5.2 FTC Advisory Opinion

UNITED STATES OF AMERICA
FEDERAL TRADE COMMISSION
WASHINGTON, D.C. 20580

Office of the Secretary

May 3, 2012

Jonathan Sheldon
Carolyn Carter
National Consumer Law Center
7 Winthrop Square
Boston, Massachusetts 02110

Dear Mr. Sheldon and Ms. Carter:

This letter is in response to the National Consumer Law Center's request for a Commission advisory opinion regarding the Federal Trade Commission's Trade Regulation Rule Concerning Preservation of Consumers' Claims and Defenses, 16 C.F.R. § 433, commonly known as the Holder Rule.[1] Specifically, you ask the Commission to affirm that the Holder Rule does not limit a consumer's right to an affirmative recovery to circumstances where the consumer can legally rescind the transaction or where the goods or services sold to the consumer are worthless. Your letter states that even though the plain language of the Rule is clear—which FTC staff confirmed in a 1999 opinion letter[2]—some courts continue to bar consumers from affirmative recoveries unless rescission is warranted.[3]

The Holder Rule protects consumers who enter into credit contracts with a seller of goods or services by preserving their right to assert claims and defenses against any holder of the contract, even if the original seller subsequently assigns the contract to a third-party creditor. In particular, the Holder Rule requires sellers that arrange for or offer credit to finance consumers' purchases to include in their credit contracts the following Notice:

> ANY HOLDER OF THIS CONSUMER CREDIT CONTRACT IS SUBJECT TO ALL CLAIMS AND DEFENSES WHICH THE DEBTOR COULD ASSERT AGAINST THE SELLER OF GOODS OR SERVICES OBTAINED [PURSUANT HERETO OR] WITH THE PROCEEDS HEREOF. RECOVERY HEREUNDER BY THE DEBTOR SHALL NOT EXCEED AMOUNTS PAID BY THE DEBTOR HEREUNDER.

16 C.F.R. § 433.2.

---

1 Your letter requesting an advisory opinion 1 is co-signed by representatives from Public Citizen, U.S. PIRG, the Center for Responsible Lending, and the National Association of Consumer Advocates.

2 *See* Attachment, FTC Staff Letter (Sept. 25, 1999). [*Editor's note:* The staff letter is not reprinted here but is available online as companion material to this treatise.]

3 Your letter lists six cases that have been decided since the issuance of the 1999 FTC staff opinion letter that have held that a consumer may only obtain an affirmative recovery against a creditor under the Holder Rule when the seller's breach is so substantial that rescission and restitution are justified or where the goods or services sold to the consumer are worthless: *Rollins v. Drive-1 of Norfolk, Inc.*, No. 2:06cv375, 2007 WL 602089 (E.D. Va. Feb. 21, 2007); *Phillips v. Lithia Motors, Inc.*, No. 03-3109-HO, 2006 WL 1113608 (D. Or. Apr. 27, 2006); *Costa v. Mauro Chevrolet, Inc.*, 390 F. Supp. 2d 720 (N.D. Ill. 2005); *Comer v. Person Auto Sales, Inc.*, 368 F. Supp. 2d 478 (M.D.N.C. 2005); *Herrara v. North & Kimball Group, Inc.*, No. 01C7349, 2002 U.S. Dist. LEXIS 2640 (N.D. Ill. Feb. 15, 2002); *Bellik v. Bank of America*, 869 N.E.2d 1179 (Ill. App. Ct. 2007). You cite *Comer* as pointedly rejecting the FTC staff opinion letter. *Comer* notes that the staff letter is "not binding on the Commission." 368 F. Supp. 2d at 490.

A creditor or assignee of the contract is thus subject to all claims or defenses that the consumer could assert against the seller. The Holder Rule does not create any new claims or defenses for the consumer; it simply protects the consumer's existing claims and defenses. The *only* limitation included in the Rule is that a consumer's recovery "shall not exceed amounts paid" by the consumer under the contract.

Thus, the plain language of the Rule permits a consumer to assert a seller's misconduct (1) to defend against a creditor's lawsuit for amounts owed under the contract and/or (2) to maintain a claim against the creditor for a refund of money the consumer has already paid under the contract (*i.e.,* an affirmative recovery). Despite the Rule's plain language, however, some courts have imposed additional limitations on a consumer's right to affirmative recovery. Beginning with *Ford Motor Credit Co. v. Morgan*, 536 N.E.2d 587 (Mass. 1989),[4] these courts have allowed affirmative recovery only if the consumer is entitled to rescission or similar relief under state law.[5] Courts following the *Morgan* approach have not imposed any similar limitation on a consumer's right to raise the seller's misconduct as a defense in a lawsuit.

The Commission affirms that the Rule is unambiguous, and its plain language should be applied.[6] No additional limitations on a consumer's right to an affirmative recovery should be read into the Rule, especially since a consumer would not have notice of those limitations because they are not included in the credit contract. Had the Commission meant to limit recovery to claims subject to rescission or similar remedy, it would have said so in the text of the Rule and drafted the contractual provision accordingly. It remains the Commission's intent that the plain language of the Rule be applied, which many courts have done.[7]

The purpose of the Holder Rule, as stated in the Rule's Statement of Basis and Purpose ("SBP"), supports this plain reading. The Commission adopted the Rule to provide recourse to consumers who otherwise would be legally obligated to make full payment to a creditor despite breach of warranty, misrepresentation, or even fraud on the part of the seller.[8] The

Commission found that "the creditor is *always* in a better position than the buyer to return seller misconduct costs to sellers, the guilty party,"[9] and therefore concluded that "[s]ellers and creditors will be responsible for seller misconduct."[10] Moreover, the Commission considered, but firmly rejected, a suggestion by industry representatives that the Rule be amended so that a consumer "may assert his rights only as a matter of defense or setoff against a claim by the assignee or holder," finding instead that "[t]he practical and policy considerations which militate against such a limitation on affirmative actions by consumers are far more persuasive."[11] For example, the Commission noted that some consumers may feel compelled to continue payments because of the threat of negative credit reporting and that "a stronger potential consumer remedy will encourage greater policing of merchants by finance institutions."[12]

Thus, to give full effect to the Commission's original intent to shift seller misconduct costs away from consumers, consumers must have the right to recover funds already paid under the contract if such recovery is necessary to fully compensate the consumer for the misconduct—even if rescission of the transaction is not warranted. Otherwise, whether a consumer is able to be fully compensated would depend on how much the consumer paid under the contract at the time of the dispute. For example, consider a consumer who finances the purchase of an automobile, later discovered to be defective, for $10,000 and is entitled to compensation of $3,000 based on the seller's misrepresentations regarding the condition of the automobile. If the consumer has paid $4,000 under the financing contract and still owes $6,000, the consumer could withhold $3,000 of the balance due and be fully compensated—a defensive posture sanctioned by *Morgan*. If, however, the consumer has paid $8,000 and owes $2,000, the *Morgan* approach would permit the consumer to withhold the remaining $2,000 payment, but not affirmatively recover the additional $1,000 that would be necessary to make the consumer whole.[13] There is no basis under the plain language and the intent of the Rule for such an anomalous result.

Courts that have followed the *Morgan* approach have misinterpreted two isolated comments in the SBP that accompanies the Rule. In part, the SBP states that affirmative recovery by the consumer "will only be available where a seller's breach is so substantial that a court is persuaded that rescission and restitution are justified"[14] and that consumers "will not be in a position to obtain an affirmative recovery from a creditor, unless they have actually commenced payments and received little or nothing of value from the seller."[15] However, when read in context of the entire SBP, including the SBP language highlighted above, the two SBP comments cited by *Morgan* and its progeny do not undermine the plain language of the Rule. As explained by one court that rejected the *Morgan* approach, "[w]here one or more parts of the [SBP] fully comport with the text of the rule while another, read in a particular way, is at odds with the plain

---

4   In *Morgan*, the court faced extensive consumer misconduct in connection with the financing of a car purchase. After experiencing problems with the car, the consumer concealed the automobile, removed the battery, removed or deflated the tires, and surrendered the automobile only after being found in contempt by the trial judge. He also delayed the sale of the automobile, during which time it was extensively vandalized, resulting in a total loss that was not recoverable due to the consumer's failure to obtain insurance. The creditor sued the consumer for the balance due under the contract, and the consumer filed a counterclaim based on the dealer's misrepresentations. Notably, in contravention of the one express limitation in the Holder Rule, the consumer sought recovery of an amount in excess of what the consumer had paid under the contract. The court ultimately held that the consumer was not entitled to any affirmative recovery, but he did not have to pay the remaining balance due. 536 N.E.2d at 588.

5   *See, e.g.,* n.3, *supra.*

6   *See Qwest Corp. v. Colorado Public Utilities Comm'n*, 656 F.3d 1093, 1099 (10th Cir. 2011) ("We begin with the plain language of the regulation. . . . If the regulation's language is clear, our analysis ends and we must apply its plain meaning.") (internal citations and quotations omitted); *Lozada v. Dale Baker Oldsmobile, Inc.,* 91 F. Supp. 2d 1087, 1095 (W.D. Mich. 2000) ("No basis exists for referring to the commentary to understand the meaning of language that is unambiguous on its face.").

7   *See, e.g., Lozada,* 91 F. Supp. 2d at 1094-95; *Simpson v. Anthony Auto Sales, Inc.,* 32 F. Supp. 2d 405, 409 n.10 (W.D. La. 1998); *Riggs v. Anthony Auto Sales,* 32 F. Supp. 2d 411, 416 n.13 (W.D. La. 1998); *Beemus v. Interstate Nat'l Dealer Servs., Inc.,* 823 A.2d 979, 984-85 (Pa. Super. Ct. 2003); *Jaramillo v. Gonzalez,* 50 P.3d 554, 561 (N.M. Ct. App. 2002); *Scott v. Mayflower Home Improvement Corp.,* 831 A.2d 564, 573-74 (N.J. Super. Ct. Law Div. 2001).

8   *See* 40 Fed. Reg. 53,506, 53,507 (Nov. 18, 1975) ("The rule is directed at what the Commission believes to be an anomaly. . . . The creditor may

assert his right to be paid by the consumer despite misrepresentation, breach of warranty or contract, or even fraud on the part of the seller, and despite the fact that the consumer's debt was generated by the sale.")

9   *Id.* at 53,523 (emphasis added); *see also id.* at 53,509 ("Between an innocent consumer, whose dealings with an unreliable seller are, at most, episodic, and a finance institution qualifying as 'a holder in due course,' the financer is in a better position both to protect itself and to assume the risk of a seller's reliability."); *id.* at 53,523 ("We believe that a rule which compels creditors to either absorb seller misconduct costs or return them to sellers, by denying sellers access to cut-off devices, will discourage many of the predatory practices and schemes. . . . The market will be policed in this fashion and all parties will benefit accordingly.").

10   *Id.* at 53,524.

11   *Id.* at 53,526.

12   *Id.* at 53,527.

13   This example is drawn from Michael Greenfield & Nina Ross, *Limits on a Consumer's Ability to Assert Claims and Defenses Under the FTC's Holder in Due Course Rule*, 46 Bus. Law. 1135, 1140 (1991).

14   40 Fed. Reg. at 53,524.

15   *Id.* at 53,527.

language of the regulation, there exists no basis for giving controlling weight to an interpretation which narrows the language of the rule itself."[16] These statements should be read as practical observations or predictions, instead of as contradicting the Rule. In most instances where there is significant consumer injury associated with seller misconduct but rescission is not warranted, the consumer is likely to find out about the injury shortly after the transaction is consummated, and thus is likely to stop payments before the claim amount is larger than the balance due. In other words, affirmative recoveries will be rare in cases where rescission is not justified because such recoveries occur only if the consumer's claim is larger than what the consumer still owes on the loan.[17] When read in this context, the two SBP comments do not conflict with the rest of the SBP and the plain language of the Rule.

Thus, the Commission affirms the plain language of the Holder Rule and the intent of the Rule as discussed in the entire SBP. Specifically, the Rule places no limits on a consumer's right to an affirmative recovery other than limiting recovery to a refund of monies paid under the contract. Further, the Rule does not limit affirmative recovery only to those circumstances where rescission is warranted or where the goods or services sold to the consumer are worthless.

By direction of the Commission.

Donald S. Clark
Secretary

A.6 Mail or Telephone Order Merchandise

16 C.F.R.
§ 435.1 Definitions.
§ 435.2 Mail, Internet, or telephone order sales.
§ 435.3 Limited applicability.

SOURCE: 79 Fed. Reg. 55615 (Sept. 17, 2014), unless otherwise noted.

AUTHORITY: 15 U.S.C. § 57a.

16 C.F.R. § 435.1   Definitions.

For purposes of this part:

(a) *Mail, Internet, or telephone order sales* shall mean sales in which the buyer has ordered merchandise from the seller by mail, via the Internet, or by telephone, regardless of the method of payment or the method used to solicit the order.

(b) *Prompt refund* shall mean:
(1) Where a refund is made pursuant to paragraph (d)(1), (d)(2)(ii), (d)(2)(iii), or (d)(3) of this section, a refund sent by any means at least as fast and reliable as first class mail within seven (7) working days of the date on which the buyer's right to refund vests under the provisions of this part. Provided, however, that where the seller cannot provide a refund by the same method payment was tendered, *prompt refund* shall mean a refund sent in the form of cash, check, or money order, by any means at least as fast and reliable as first class mail, within seven (7) working days of the date on which the seller discovers it cannot provide a refund by the same method as payment was tendered;
(2) Where a refund is made pursuant to paragraph (d)(2)(i) of this section, a refund sent by any means at least as fast and reliable as first class mail within one (1) billing cycle from the date on which the buyer's right to refund vests under the provisions of this part.

(c) *Receipt of a properly completed order* shall mean, where the buyer tenders full or partial payment in the proper amount in the form of cash, check, or money order; authorization from the buyer to charge an existing charge account; or other payment methods, the time at which the seller receives both said payment and an order from the buyer containing all of the information needed by the seller to process and ship the order. Provided, however, that where the seller receives notice that a payment by means other than cash or credit as tendered by the buyer has been dishonored or that the buyer does not qualify for a credit sale, *receipt of a properly completed order* shall mean the time at which:
(1) The seller receives notice that a payment by means other than cash or credit in the proper amount tendered by the buyer has been honored;
(2) The buyer tenders cash in the proper amount; or
(3) The seller receives notice that the buyer qualifies for a credit sale.

(d) *Refund* shall mean:
(1) Where the buyer tendered full payment for the unshipped merchandise in the form of cash, check, or money order, a return of the amount tendered in the form of cash, check, or money order sent to the buyer;
(2) Where there is a credit sale:
(i) And the seller is a creditor, a copy of a credit memorandum or the like or an account statement sent to the buyer reflecting the removal or absence of any remaining charge incurred as a result of the sale from the buyer's account;
(ii) And a third party is the creditor, an appropriate credit memorandum or the like sent to the third party creditor which will remove the charge from the buyer's account and a copy of the credit memorandum or the like sent to the buyer that includes the date that the seller sent the credit memorandum or the like to the third party creditor and the amount of the charge to be removed, or a statement from the seller acknowledging the cancellation of the order and representing that it has not taken any action regarding the order which will result in a charge to the buyer's account with the third party;
(iii) And the buyer tendered partial payment for the unshipped merchandise in the form of cash, check, or money order, a return of the amount tendered in the form of cash, check, or money order sent to the buyer;
(3) Where the buyer tendered payment for the unshipped merchandise by any means other than those enumerated in paragraph (d)(1) or (2) of this section:
(i) Instructions sent to the entity that transferred payment to the seller instructing that entity to return to the buyer the amount tendered in the form tendered and a statement sent to the buyer setting forth the instructions sent to the entity, including the date of the instructions and the amount to be returned to the buyer; or
(ii) A return of the amount tendered in the form of cash, check, or money order sent to the buyer; or
(iii) A statement from the seller sent to the buyer acknowledging the cancellation of the order and representing that the seller has not taken any action regarding the order which will access any of the buyer's funds.

(e) *Shipment* shall mean the act by which the merchandise is physically placed in the possession of the carrier.

(f) *Telephone* refers to any direct or indirect use of the telephone to order merchandise, regardless of whether the telephone is activated by, or the language used is that of human beings, machines, or both.

(g) The *time of solicitation* of an order shall mean that time when the seller has:
(1) Mailed or otherwise disseminated the solicitation to a prospective purchaser;
(2) Made arrangements for an advertisement containing the solicitation to appear in a newspaper, magazine or the like or on radio or

16 *Lozada*, 91 F. Supp. 2d at 1096.
17 *See id.* at 1095 (noting that the SBP "is susceptible of being understood as a statement of agency prediction that affirmative recoveries will occur only when courts are persuaded that the equities so require and when damages exceed the amount due on the account"); *accord Jaramillo*, 50 P.3d at 561.

television which cannot be changed or cancelled without incurring substantial expense; or

(3) Made arrangements for the printing of a catalog, brochure or the like which cannot be changed without incurring substantial expense, in which the solicitation in question forms an insubstantial part.

16 C.F.R. § 435.2   Mail, Internet, or telephone order sales

In connection with mail, Internet, or telephone order sales in or affecting commerce, as "commerce" is defined in the Federal Trade Commission Act, it constitutes an unfair method of competition, and an unfair or deceptive act or practice for a seller:

(a)(1) To solicit any order for the sale of merchandise to be ordered by the buyer through the mail, via the Internet, or by telephone unless, at the time of the solicitation, the seller has a reasonable basis to expect that it will be able to ship any ordered merchandise to the buyer:

 (i) Within that time clearly and conspicuously stated in any such solicitation; or

 (ii) If no time is clearly and conspicuously stated, within thirty (30) days after receipt of a properly completed order from the buyer. Provided, however, where, at the time the merchandise is ordered the buyer applies to the seller for credit to pay for the merchandise in whole or in part, the seller shall have fifty (50) days, rather than thirty (30) days, to perform the actions required in this paragraph (a)(1)(ii).

(2) To provide any buyer with any revised shipping date, as provided in paragraph (b) of this section, unless, at the time any such revised shipping date is provided, the seller has a reasonable basis for making such representation regarding a definite revised shipping date.

(3) To inform any buyer that it is unable to make any representation regarding the length of any delay unless:

 (i) The seller has a reasonable basis for so informing the buyer; and

 (ii) The seller informs the buyer of the reason or reasons for the delay.

(4) In any action brought by the Federal Trade Commission, alleging a violation of this part, the failure of a respondent-seller to have records or other documentary proof establishing its use of systems and procedures which assure the shipment of merchandise in the ordinary course of business within any applicable time set forth in this part will create a rebuttable presumption that the seller lacked a reasonable basis for any expectation of shipment within said applicable time.

(b)(1) Where a seller is unable to ship merchandise within the applicable time set forth in paragraph (a)(1) of this section, to fail to offer to the buyer, clearly and conspicuously and without prior demand, an option either to consent to a delay in shipping or to cancel the buyer's order and receive a prompt refund. Said offer shall be made within a reasonable time after the seller first becomes aware of its inability to ship within the applicable time set forth in paragraph (a)(1) of this section, but in no event later than said applicable time.

 (i) Any offer to the buyer of such an option shall fully inform the buyer regarding the buyer's right to cancel the order and to obtain a prompt refund and shall provide a definite revised shipping date, but where the seller lacks a reasonable basis for providing a definite revised shipping date the notice shall inform the buyer that the seller is unable to make any representation regarding the length of the delay.

 (ii) Where the seller has provided a definite revised shipping date which is thirty (30) days or less later than the applicable time set forth in paragraph (a)(1) of this section, the offer of said option shall expressly inform the buyer that, unless the seller receives, prior to shipment and prior to the expiration of the definite revised shipping date, a response from the buyer rejecting the delay and cancelling the order, the buyer will be deemed to have consented to a delayed shipment on or before the definite revised shipping date.

 (iii) Where the seller has provided a definite revised shipping date which is more than thirty (30) days later than the applicable time set forth in paragraph (a)(1) of this section or where the seller is unable to provide a definite revised shipping date and therefore informs the buyer that it is unable to make any representation regarding the length of the delay, the offer of said option shall also expressly inform the buyer that the buyer's order will automatically be deemed to have been cancelled unless:

  (A) The seller has shipped the merchandise within thirty (30) days of the applicable time set forth in paragraph (a)(1) of this section, and has received no cancellation prior to shipment; or

  (B) The seller has received from the buyer within thirty (30) days of said applicable time, a response specifically consenting to said shipping delay. Where the seller informs the buyer that it is unable to make any representation regarding the length of the delay, the buyer shall be expressly informed that, should the buyer consent to an indefinite delay, the buyer will have a continuing right to cancel the buyer's order at any time after the applicable time set forth in paragraph (a)(1) of this section by so notifying the seller prior to actual shipment.

 (iv) Nothing in this paragraph shall prohibit a seller who furnishes a definite revised shipping date pursuant to paragraph (b)(1)(i) of this section, from requesting, simultaneously with or at any time subsequent to the offer of an option pursuant to paragraph (b)(1) of this section, the buyer's express consent to a further unanticipated delay beyond the definite revised shipping date in the form of a response from the buyer specifically consenting to said further delay. Provided, however, that where the seller solicits consent to an unanticipated indefinite delay the solicitation shall expressly inform the buyer that, should the buyer so consent to an indefinite delay, the buyer shall have a continuing right to cancel the buyer's order at any time after the definite revised shipping date by so notifying the seller prior to actual shipment.

(2) Where a seller is unable to ship merchandise on or before the definite revised shipping date provided under paragraph (b)(1)(i) of this section and consented to by the buyer pursuant to paragraph (b)(1)(ii) or (iii) of this section, to fail to offer to the buyer, clearly and conspicuously and without prior demand, a renewed option either to consent to a further delay or to cancel the order and to receive a prompt refund. Said offer shall be made within a reasonable time after the seller first becomes aware of its inability to ship before the said definite revised date, but in no event later than the expiration of the definite revised shipping date. Provided, however, that where the seller previously has obtained the buyer's express consent to an unanticipated delay until a specific date beyond the definite revised shipping date, pursuant to paragraph (b)(1)(iv) of this section or to a further delay until a specific date beyond the definite revised shipping date pursuant to paragraph (b)(2) of this section, that date to which the buyer has expressly consented shall supersede the definite revised shipping date for purposes of paragraph (b)(2) of this section.

 (i) Any offer to the buyer of said renewed option shall provide the buyer with a new definite revised shipping date, but where the seller lacks a reasonable basis for providing a new definite revised shipping date, the notice shall inform the buyer that the seller is unable to make any representation regarding the length of the further delay.

 (ii) The offer of a renewed option shall expressly inform the buyer that, unless the seller receives, prior to the expiration of the old definite revised shipping date or any date superseding the old definite revised shipping date, notification from the buyer specifically consenting to the further delay, the buyer will be deemed to have rejected any further delay, and to have cancelled the order if the seller is in fact unable to ship prior to the expiration of the old definite revised shipping date or any date superseding the old definite revised shipping date. Provided, however, that where the seller offers the buyer the option to consent to an indefinite delay the offer shall expressly inform the buyer that, should the buyer so consent to an indefinite delay, the buyer shall have a continuing right to cancel the buyer's order at any time after the old definite revised shipping date or any date superseding the old definite revised shipping date.

(iii) Paragraph (b)(2) of this section shall not apply to any situation where a seller, pursuant to the provisions of paragraph (b)(1)(iv) of this section, has previously obtained consent from the buyer to an indefinite extension beyond the first revised shipping date.

(3) Wherever a buyer has the right to exercise any option under this part or to cancel an order by so notifying the seller prior to shipment, to fail to furnish the buyer with adequate means, at the seller's expense, to exercise such option or to notify the seller regarding cancellation.

(4) Nothing in paragraph (b) of this section shall prevent a seller, where it is unable to make shipment within the time set forth in paragraph (a)(1) of this section or within a delay period consented to by the buyer, from deciding to consider the order cancelled and providing the buyer with notice of said decision within a reasonable time after it becomes aware of said inability to ship, together with a prompt refund.

(c) To fail to deem an order cancelled and to make a prompt refund to the buyer whenever:

(1) The seller receives, prior to the time of shipment, notification from the buyer cancelling the order pursuant to any option, renewed option or continuing option under this part;

(2) The seller has, pursuant to paragraph (b)(1)(iii) of this section, provided the buyer with a definite revised shipping date which is more than thirty (30) days later than the applicable time set forth in paragraph (a)(1) of this section or has notified the buyer that it is unable to make any representation regarding the length of the delay and the seller:

(i) Has not shipped the merchandise within thirty (30) days of the applicable time set forth in paragraph (a)(1) of this section, and

(ii) Has not received the buyer's express consent to said shipping delay within said thirty (30) days;

(3) The seller is unable to ship within the applicable time set forth in paragraph (b)(2) of this section, and has not received, within the said applicable time, the buyer's consent to any further delay;

(4) The seller has notified the buyer of its inability to make shipment and has indicated its decision not to ship the merchandise;

(5) The seller fails to offer the option prescribed in paragraph (b)(1) of this section and has not shipped the merchandise within the applicable time set forth in paragraph (a)(1) of this section.

(d) In any action brought by the Federal Trade Commission, alleging a violation of this part, the failure of a respondent-seller to have records or other documentary proof establishing its use of systems and procedures which assure compliance, in the ordinary course of business, with any requirement of paragraph (b) or (c) of this section will create a rebuttable presumption that the seller failed to comply with said requirement.

16 C.F.R. § 435.3   Limited applicability.

(a) This part shall not apply to:

(1) Subscriptions, such as magazine sales, ordered for serial delivery, after the initial shipment is made in compliance with this part;

(2) Orders of seeds and growing plants;

(3) Orders made on a collect-on-delivery (C.O.D.) basis;

(4) Transactions governed by the Federal Trade Commission's Trade Regulation Rule entitled "Use of Prenotification Negative Option Plans," 16 CFR Part 425.

(b) By taking action in this area:

(1) The Federal Trade Commission does not intend to preempt action in the same area, which is not inconsistent with this part, by any State, municipal, or other local government. This part does not annul or diminish any rights or remedies provided to consumers by any State law, municipal ordinance, or other local regulation, insofar as those rights or remedies are equal to or greater than those provided by this part. In addition, this part does not supersede those provisions of any State law, municipal ordinance, or other local regulation which impose obligations or liabilities upon sellers, when sellers subject to this part are not in compliance therewith.

(2) This part does supersede those provisions of any State law, municipal ordinance, or other local regulation which are inconsistent with this part to the extent that those provisions do not provide a buyer with rights which are equal to or greater than those rights granted a buyer by this part. This part also supersedes those provisions of any State law, municipal ordinance, or other local regulation requiring that a buyer be notified of a right which is the same as a right provided by this part but requiring that a buyer be given notice of this right in a language, form, or manner which is different in any way from that required by this part. In those instances where any State law, municipal ordinance, or other local regulation contains provisions, some but not all of which are partially or completely superseded by this part, the provisions or portions of those provisions which have not been superseded retain their full force and effect.

(c) If any provision of this part, or its application to any person, partnership, corporation, act or practice is held invalid, the remainder of this part or the application of the provision to any other person, partnership, corporation, act or practice shall not be affected thereby.

A.7   FTC Franchise Rule—16 C.F.R. § 436

16 C.F.R.
§ 436.1   Definitions.
§ 436.2   Obligation to furnish documents.
§ 436.3   Cover page.
§ 436.4   Table of contents.
§ 436.5   Disclosure items.
§ 436.6   Instructions for preparing disclosure documents.
§ 436.7   Instructions for updating disclosures.
§ 436.8   Exemptions.
§ 436.9   Additional prohibitions.
§ 436.10   Other laws and rules.
§ 436.11   Severability.
Appendix A to Part 436—Sample Item 10 Table
Appendix B to Part 436—Sample Item 20(1) Table
Appendix C to Part 436—Sample Item 20(2) Table
Appendix D to Part 436—Sample Item 20(3) Table
Appendix E to Part 436—Sample Item 20(4) Table
Appendix F to Part 436—Sample Item 20(5) Table

SOURCE: 72 Fed. Reg. 15,544 (Mar. 2007), unless otherwise noted.

AUTHORITY: 15 U.S.C. 41–58.

16 C.F.R. § 436.1   Definitions.

Unless stated otherwise, the following definitions apply throughout part 436:

(a) *Action* includes complaints, cross claims, counterclaims, and third-party complaints in a judicial action or proceeding, and their equivalents in an administrative action or arbitration.

(b) *Affiliate* means an entity controlled by, controlling, or under common control with, another entity.

(c) *Confidentiality clause* means any contract, order, or settlement provision that directly or indirectly restricts a current or former franchisee from discussing his or her personal experience as a franchisee in the franchisor's system with any prospective franchisee. It does not include clauses that protect franchisor's trademarks or other proprietary information.

(d) *Disclose, state, describe,* and *list* each mean to present all material facts accurately, clearly, concisely, and legibly in plain English.

(e) *Financial performance representation* means any representation, including any oral, written, or visual representation, to a prospective franchisee, including a representation in the general media, that states, expressly or by implication, a specific level or range of actual or potential sales, income, gross profits, or net profits. The term includes a chart, table, or mathematical calculation that shows possible results based on a combination of variables.

(f) *Fiscal year* refers to the franchisor's fiscal year.

(g) *Fractional franchise* means a franchise relationship that satisfies the following criteria when the relationship is created:

    (1) The franchisee, any of the franchisee's current directors or officers, or any current directors or officers of a parent or affiliate, has more than two years of experience in the same type of business; and

    (2) The parties have a reasonable basis to anticipate that the sales arising from the relationship will not exceed 20% of the franchisee's total dollar volume in sales during the first year of operation.

(h) *Franchise* means any continuing commercial relationship or arrangement, whatever it may be called, in which the terms of the offer or contract specify, or the franchise seller promises or represents, orally or in writing, that:

    (1) The franchisee will obtain the right to operate a business that is identified or associated with the franchisor's trademark, or to offer, sell, or distribute goods, services, or commodities that are identified or associated with the franchisor's trademark;

    (2) The franchisor will exert or has authority to exert a significant degree of control over the franchisee's method of operation, or provide significant assistance in the franchisee's method of operation; and

    (3) As a condition of obtaining or commencing operation of the franchise, the franchisee makes a required payment or commits to make a required payment to the franchisor or its affiliate.

(*i*) *Franchisee* means any person who is granted a franchise.

(j) *Franchise seller* means a person that offers for sale, sells, or arranges for the sale of a franchise. It includes the franchisor and the franchisor's employees, representatives, agents, subfranchisors, and third-party brokers who are involved in franchise sales activities. It does not include existing franchisees who sell only their own outlet and who are otherwise not engaged in franchise sales on behalf of the franchisor.

(k) *Franchisor* means any person who grants a franchise and participates in the franchise relationship. Unless otherwise stated, it includes subfranchisors. For purposes of this definition, a "subfranchisor" means a person who functions as a franchisor by engaging in both pre-sale activities and post-sale performance.

(*l*) *Leased department* means an arrangement whereby a retailer licenses or otherwise permits a seller to conduct business from the retailer's location where the seller purchases no goods, services, or commodities directly or indirectly from the retailer, a person the retailer requires the seller to do business with, or a retailer-affiliate if the retailer advises the seller to do business with the affiliate.

(m) *Parent* means an entity that controls another entity directly, or indirectly through one or more subsidiaries.

(n) *Person* means any individual, group, association, limited or general partnership, corporation, or any other entity.

(o) *Plain English* means the organization of information and language usage understandable by a person unfamiliar with the franchise business. It incorporates short sentences; definite, concrete, everyday language; active voice; and tabular presentation of information, where possible. It avoids legal jargon, highly technical business terms, and multiple negatives.

(p) *Predecessor* means a person from whom the franchisor acquired, directly or indirectly, the major portion of the franchisor's assets.

(q) *Principal business address* means the street address of a person's home office in the United States. A principal business address cannot be a post office box or private mail drop.

(r) *Prospective franchisee* means any person (including any agent, representative, or employee) who approaches or is approached by a franchise seller to discuss the possible establishment of a franchise relationship.

(s) *Required payment* means all consideration that the franchisee must pay to the franchisor or an affiliate, either by contract or by practical necessity, as a condition of obtaining or commencing operation of the franchise. A required payment does not include payments for the purchase of reasonable amounts of inventory at bona fide wholesale prices for resale or lease.

(t) *Sale of a franchise* includes an agreement whereby a person obtains a franchise from a franchise seller for value by purchase, license, or otherwise. It does not include extending or renewing an existing franchise agreement where there has been no interruption in the franchisee's operation of the business, unless the new agreement contains terms and conditions that differ materially from the original agreement. It also does not include the transfer of a franchise by an existing franchisee where the franchisor has had no significant involvement with the prospective transferee. A franchisor's approval or disapproval of a transfer alone is not deemed to be significant involvement.

(u) *Signature* means a person's affirmative step to authenticate his or her identity. It includes a person's handwritten signature, as well as a person's use of security codes, passwords, electronic signatures, and similar devices to authenticate his or her identity.

(v) *Trademark* includes trademarks, service marks, names, logos, and other commercial symbols.

(w) *Written* or *in writing* means any document or information in printed form or in any form capable of being preserved in tangible form and read. It includes: type-set, word processed, or handwritten document; information on computer disk or CD–ROM; information sent via email; or information posted on the Internet. It does not include mere oral statements.

16 C.F.R. § 436.2   Obligation to furnish documents.

In connection with the offer or sale of a franchise to be located in the United States of America or its territories, unless the transaction is exempted under Subpart E of this part, it is an unfair or deceptive act or practice in violation of Section 5 of the Federal Trade Commission Act:

(a) For any franchisor to fail to furnish a prospective franchisee with a copy of the franchisor's current disclosure document, as described in Subparts C and D of this part, at least 14 calendar-days before the prospective franchisee signs a binding agreement with, or makes any payment to, the franchisor or an affiliate in connection with the proposed franchise sale.

(b) For any franchisor to alter unilaterally and materially the terms and conditions of the basic franchise agreement or any related agreements attached to the disclosure document without furnishing the prospective franchisee with a copy of each revised agreement at least seven calendar-days before the prospective franchisee signs the revised agreement. Changes to an agreement that arise out of negotiations initiated by the prospective franchisee do not trigger this seven calendar-day period.

(c) For purposes of paragraphs (a) and (b) of this section, the franchisor has furnished the documents by the required date if:

    (1) A copy of the document was hand-delivered, faxed, emailed, or otherwise delivered to the prospective franchisee by the required date;

    (2) Directions for accessing the document on the Internet were provided to the prospective franchisee by the required date; or

    (3) A paper or tangible electronic copy (for example, computer disk or CD–ROM) was sent to the address specified by the prospective franchisee by first-class United States mail at least three calendar days before the required date.

16 C.F.R. § 436.3   Cover page.

Begin the disclosure document with a cover page, in the order and form as follows:

(a) The title "FRANCHISE DISCLOSURE DOCUMENT" in capital letters and bold type.

(b) The franchisor's name, type of business organization, principal business address, telephone number, and, if applicable, email address and primary home page address.

(c) A sample of the primary business trademark that the franchisee will use in its business.

(d) A brief description of the franchised business.

(e) The following statements:

(1) The total investment necessary to begin operation of a [franchise system name] franchise is [the total amount of Item 7 (§ 436.5(g))]. This includes [the total amount in Item 5 (§ 436.5(e))] that must be paid to the franchisor or affiliate.

(2) This disclosure document summarizes certain provisions of your franchise agreement and other information in plain English. Read this disclosure document and all accompanying agreements carefully. You must receive this disclosure document at least 14 calendar-days before you sign a binding agreement with, or make any payment to, the franchisor or an affiliate in connection with the proposed franchise sale. [The following sentence in bold type] Note, however, that no governmental agency has verified the information contained in this document.

(3) The terms of your contract will govern your franchise relationship. Don't rely on the disclosure document alone to understand your contract. Read all of your contract carefully. Show your contract and this disclosure document to an advisor, like a lawyer or an accountant.

(4) Buying a franchise is a complex investment. The information in this disclosure document can help you make up your mind. More information on franchising, such as "A Consumer's Guide to Buying a Franchise," which can help you understand how to use this disclosure document, is available from the Federal Trade Commission. You can contact the FTC at 1–877–FTC–HELP or by writing to the FTC at 600 Pennsylvania Avenue, NW., Washington, D.C. 20580. You can also visit the FTC's home page at www.ftc.gov for additional information. Call your state agency or visit your public library for other sources of information on franchising.

(5) There may also be laws on franchising in your state. Ask your state agencies about them.

(6) [The issuance date].

(f) A franchisor may include the following statement between the statements set out at paragraphs (e)(2) and (3) of this section: "You may wish to receive your disclosure document in another format that is more convenient for you. To discuss the availability of disclosures in different formats, contact [name or office] at [address] and [telephone number]."

(g) Franchisors may include additional disclosures on the cover page, on a separate cover page, or addendum to comply with state pre-sale disclosure laws.

16 C.F.R. § 436.4   Table of contents.

Include the following table of contents. State the page where each disclosure Item begins. List all exhibits by letter, as shown in the following example.

Table of Contents

1. The Franchisor and any Parents, Predecessors, and Affiliates
2. Business Experience
3. Litigation
4. Bankruptcy
5. Initial Fees
6. Other Fees
7. Estimated Initial Investment
8. Restrictions on Sources of Products and Services
9. Franchisee's Obligations
10. Financing
11. Franchisor's Assistance, Advertising, Computer Systems, and Training
12. Territory
13. Trademarks
14. Patents, Copyrights, and Proprietary Information
15. Obligation to Participate in the Actual Operation of the Franchise Business
16. Restrictions on What the Franchisee May Sell
17. Renewal, Termination, Transfer, and Dispute Resolution
18. Public Figures
19. Financial Performance Representations
20. Outlets and Franchisee Information
21. Financial Statements
22. Contracts
23. Receipts

Exhibits

A. Franchise Agreement

16 C.F.R. § 436.5   Disclosure items.

(a) Item 1: The Franchisor, and any Parents, Predecessors, and Affiliates.
Disclose:

(1) The name and principal business address of the franchisor; any parents; and any affiliates that offer franchises in any line of business or provide products or services to the franchisees of the franchisor.

(2) The name and principal business address of any predecessors during the 10–year period immediately before the close of the franchisor's most recent fiscal year.

(3) The name that the franchisor uses and any names it intends to use to conduct business.

(4) The identity and principal business address of the franchisor's agent for service of process.

(5) The type of business organization used by the franchisor (for example, corporation, partnership) and the state in which it was organized.

(6) The following information about the franchisor's business and the franchises offered:

(i) Whether the franchisor operates businesses of the type being franchised.

(ii) The franchisor's other business activities.

(iii) The business the franchisee will conduct.

(iv) The general market for the product or service the franchisee will offer. In describing the general market, consider factors such as whether the market is developed or developing, whether the goods will be sold primarily to a certain group, and whether sales are seasonal.

(v) In general terms, any laws or regulations specific to the industry in which the franchise business operates.

(vi) A general description of the competition.

(7) The prior business experience of the franchisor; any predecessors listed in § 436.5(a)(2) of this part; and any affiliates that offer franchises in any line of business or provide products or services to the franchisees of the franchisor, including:

(i) The length of time each has conducted the type of business the franchisee will operate.

(ii) The length of time each has offered franchises providing the type of business the franchisee will operate.

(iii) Whether each has offered franchises in other lines of business. If so, include:

(A) A description of each other line of business.

(B) The number of franchises sold in each other line of business.

(C) The length of time each has offered franchises in each other line of business.

(b) Item 2: Business Experience. Disclose by name and position the franchisor's directors, trustees, general partners, principal officers, and any other individuals who will have management responsibility relating to the sale or operation of franchises offered by this document. For each person listed in this section, state his or her principal positions and employers during the past five years, including each position's starting date, ending date, and location.

(c) Item 3: Litigation.

(1) Disclose whether the franchisor; a predecessor; a parent or affiliate who induces franchise sales by promising to back the franchisor financially or otherwise guarantees the franchisor's performance; an affiliate who offers franchises under the franchisor's principal trademark; and any person identified in § 436.5(b) of this part:

(i) Has pending against that person:

(A) An administrative, criminal, or material civil action alleging a violation of a franchise, antitrust, or securities law, or alleging fraud, unfair or deceptive practices, or comparable allegations.

(B) Civil actions, other than ordinary routine litigation incidental to the business, which are material in the context of the number of franchisees and the size, nature, or financial condition of the franchise system or its business operations.

(ii) Was a party to any material civil action involving the franchise relationship in the last fiscal year. For purposes of this section, "franchise relationship" means contractual obligations between the franchisor and franchisee directly relating to the operation of the franchised business (such as royalty payment and training obligations). It does not include actions involving suppliers or other third parties, or indemnification for tort liability.

(iii) Has in the 10–year period immediately before the disclosure document's issuance date:

(A) Been convicted of or pleaded nolo contendere to a felony charge.

(B) Been held liable in a civil action involving an alleged violation of a franchise, antitrust, or securities law, or involving allegations of fraud, unfair or deceptive practices, or comparable allegations. "Held liable" means that, as a result of claims or counterclaims, the person must pay money or other consideration, must reduce an indebtedness by the amount of an award, cannot enforce its rights, or must take action adverse to its interests.

(2) Disclose whether the franchisor; a predecessor; a parent or affiliate who guarantees the franchisor's performance; an affiliate who has offered or sold franchises in any line of business within the last 10 years; or any other person identified in § 436.5(b) of this part is subject to a currently effective injunctive or restrictive order or decree resulting from a pending or concluded action brought by a public agency and relating to the franchise or to a Federal, State, or Canadian franchise, securities, antitrust, trade regulation, or trade practice law.

(3) For each action identified in paragraphs (c)(1) and (2) of this section, state the title, case number or citation, the initial filing date, the names of the parties, the forum, and the relationship of the opposing party to the franchisor (for example, competitor, supplier, lessor, franchisee, former franchisee, or class of franchisees). Except as provided in paragraph (c)(4) of this section, summarize the legal and factual nature of each claim in the action, the relief sought or obtained, and any conclusions of law or fact.[18] In addition, state:

(i) For pending actions, the status of the action.

(ii) For prior actions, the date when the judgment was entered and any damages or settlement terms.[19]

(iii) For injunctive or restrictive orders, the nature, terms, and conditions of the order or decree.

(iv) For convictions or pleas, the crime or violation, the date of conviction, and the sentence or penalty imposed.

(4) For any other franchisor-initiated suit identified in paragraph (c)(1)(ii) of this section, the franchisor may comply with the requirements of paragraphs (c)(3)(i) through (iv) of this section by listing individual suits under one common heading that will serve as the case summary (for example, "royalty collection suits").

(d) Item 4: Bankruptcy.

(1) Disclose whether the franchisor; any parent; predecessor; affiliate; officer, or general partner of the franchisor, or any other individual who will have management responsibility relating to the sale or operation of franchises offered by this document, has, during the 10–year period immediately before the date of this disclosure document:

(i) Filed as debtor (or had filed against it) a petition under the United States Bankruptcy Code ("Bankruptcy Code").

(ii) Obtained a discharge of its debts under the Bankruptcy Code.

(iii) Been a principal officer of a company or a general partner in a partnership that either filed as a debtor (or had filed against it) a petition under the Bankruptcy Code, or that obtained a discharge of its debts under the Bankruptcy Code while, or within one year after, the officer or general partner held the position in the company.

(2) For each bankruptcy, state:

(i) The current name, address, and principal place of business of the debtor.

(ii) Whether the debtor is the franchisor. If not, state the relationship of the debtor to the franchisor (for example, affiliate, officer).

(iii) The date of the original filing and the material facts, including the bankruptcy court, and the case name and number. If applicable, state the debtor's discharge date, including discharges under Chapter 7 and confirmation of any plans of reorganization under Chapters 11 and 13 of the Bankruptcy Code.

(3) Disclose cases, actions, and other proceedings under the laws of foreign nations relating to bankruptcy.

(e) Item 5: Initial Fees. Disclose the initial fees and any conditions under which these fees are refundable. If the initial fees are not uniform, disclose the range or formula used to calculate the initial fees paid in the fiscal year before the issuance date and the factors that determined the amount. For this section, "initial fees" means all fees and payments, or commitments to pay, for services or goods received from the franchisor or any affiliate before the franchisee's business opens, whether payable in lump sum or installments. Disclose installment payment terms in this section or in § 436.5(j) of this part.

(f) Item 6: Other Fees. Disclose, in the following tabular form, all other fees that the franchisee must pay to the franchisor or its affiliates, or that the franchisor or its affiliates impose or collect in whole or in part for a third party. State the title "OTHER FEES" in capital letters using bold type. Include any formula used to compute the fees.[20]

---

18 Franchisors may include a summary opinion of counsel concerning any action if counsel consent to use the summary opinion and the full opinion is attached to the disclosure document.

19 If a settlement agreement must be disclosed in this Item, all material settlement terms must be disclosed, whether or not the agreement is confidential. However, franchisors need not disclose the terms of confidential settlements entered into before commencing franchise sales. Further, any franchisor who has historically used only the Franchise Rule format, or who is new to franchising, need not disclose confidential settlements entered prior to the effective date of this Rule.

20 If fees may increase, disclose the formula that determines the increase or the maximum amount of the increase. For example, a percentage of gross sales is acceptable if the franchisor defines the term "gross sales."

Item 6 Table
OTHER FEES

Column 1	Column 2	Column 3	Column 4
Type of fee	Amount	Due Date	Remarks

(1) In column 1, list the type of fee (for example, royalties, and fees for lease negotiations, construction, remodeling, additional training or assistance, advertising, advertising cooperatives, purchasing cooperatives, audits, accounting, inventory, transfers, and renewals).

(2) In column 2, state the amount of the fee.

(3) In column 3, state the due date for each fee.

(4) In column 4, include remarks, definitions, or caveats that elaborate on the information in the table. If remarks are long, franchisors may use footnotes instead of the remarks column. If applicable, include the following information in the remarks column or in a footnote:

　(i) Whether the fees are payable only to the franchisor.

　(ii) Whether the fees are imposed and collected by the franchisor.

　(iii) Whether the fees are non-refundable or describe the circumstances when the fees are refundable.

　(iv) Whether the fees are uniformly imposed.

　(v) The voting power of franchisor-owned outlets on any fees imposed by cooperatives. If franchisor-owned outlets have controlling voting power, disclose the maximum and minimum fees that may be imposed.

(g) Item 7: Estimated Initial Investment. Disclose, in the following tabular form, the franchisee's estimated initial investment. State the title "YOUR ESTIMATED INITIAL INVESTMENT" in capital letters using bold type. Franchisors may include additional expenditure tables to show expenditure variations caused by differences such as in site location and premises size.

Item 7 Table:
YOUR ESTIMATED INITIAL INVESTMENT

Column 1	Column 2	Column 3	Column 4	Column 5
Type of expenditure	Amount	Method of payment	When due	To whom payment is to be made
Total.				

(1) In column 1:

　(i) List each type of expense, beginning with pre-opening expenses. Include the following expenses, if applicable. Use footnotes to include remarks, definitions, or caveats that elaborate on the information in the Table.

　　(A) The initial franchise fee.

　　(B) Training expenses.

　　(C) Real property, whether purchased or leased.

　　(D) Equipment, fixtures, other fixed assets, construction, remodeling, leasehold improvements, and decorating costs, whether purchased or leased.

　　(E) Inventory to begin operating.

　　(F) Security deposits, utility deposits, business licenses, and other prepaid expenses.

　(ii) List separately and by name any other specific required payments (for example, additional training, travel, or advertising expenses) that the franchisee must make to begin operations.

　(iii) Include a category titled "Additional funds— [initial period]" for any other required expenses the franchisee will incur before operations begin and during the initial period of operations. State the initial period. A reasonable initial period is at least three months or a reasonable period for the industry. Describe in general

terms the factors, basis, and experience that the franchisor considered or relied upon in formulating the amount required for additional funds.

(2) In column 2, state the amount of the payment. If the amount is unknown, use a low-high range based on the franchisor's current experience. If real property costs cannot be estimated in a low-high range, describe the approximate size of the property and building and the probable location of the building (for example, strip shopping center, mall, downtown, rural, or highway).

(3) In column 3, state the method of payment.

(4) In column 4, state the due date.

(5) In column 5, state to whom payment will be made.

(6) Total the initial investment, incorporating ranges of fees, if used.

(7) In a footnote, state:

　(i) Whether each payment is non-refundable, or describe the circumstances when each payment is refundable.

　(ii) If the franchisor or an affiliate finances part of the initial investment, the amount that it will finance, the required down payment, the annual interest rate, rate factors, and the estimated loan repayments. Franchisors may refer to § 436.5(j) of this part for additional details.

(h) Item 8: Restrictions on Sources of Products and Services. Disclose the franchisee's obligations to purchase or lease goods, services, supplies, fixtures, equipment, inventory, computer hardware and software, real estate, or comparable items related to establishing or operating the franchised business either from the franchisor, its designee, or suppliers approved by the franchisor, or under the franchisor's specifications. Include obligations to purchase imposed by the franchisor's written agreement or by the franchisor's practice.[21] For each applicable obligation, state:

(1) The good or service required to be purchased or leased.

(2) Whether the franchisor or its affiliates are approved suppliers or the only approved suppliers of that good or service.

(3) Any supplier in which an officer of the franchisor owns an interest.

(4) How the franchisor grants and revokes approval of alternative suppliers, including:

　(i) Whether the franchisor's criteria for approving suppliers are available to franchisees.

　(ii) Whether the franchisor permits franchisees to contract with alternative suppliers who meet the franchisor's criteria.

　(iii) Any fees and procedures to secure approval to purchase from alternative suppliers.

　(iv) The time period in which the franchisee will be notified of approval or disapproval.

　(v) How approvals are revoked.

(5) Whether the franchisor issues specifications and standards to franchisees, subfranchisees, or approved suppliers. If so, describe how the franchisor issues and modifies specifications.

(6) Whether the franchisor or its affiliates will or may derive revenue or other material consideration from required purchases or leases by franchisees. If so, describe the precise basis by which the franchisor or its affiliates will or may derive that consideration by stating:

　(i) The franchisor's total revenue.[22]

　(ii) The franchisor's revenues from all required purchases and leases of products and services.

21　Franchisors may include the reason for the requirement. Franchisors need not disclose in this Item the purchase or lease of goods or services provided as part of the franchise without a separate charge (such as initial training, if the cost is included in the franchise fee). Describe such fees in Item 5 of this section. Do not disclose fees already described in § 436.5(f) of this part.

22　Take figures from the franchisor's most recent annual audited financial statement required in § 436.5(u) of this part. If audited statements are not yet required, or if the entity deriving the income is an affiliate, disclose the sources of information used in computing revenues.

(iii) The percentage of the franchisor's total revenues that are from required purchases or leases.

(iv) If the franchisor's affiliates also sell or lease products or services to franchisees, the affiliates' revenues from those sales or leases.

(7) The estimated proportion of these required purchases and leases by the franchisee to all purchases and leases by the franchisee of goods and services in establishing and operating the franchised businesses.

(8) If a designated supplier will make payments to the franchisor from franchisee purchases, disclose the basis for the payment (for example, specify a percentage or a flat amount). For purposes of this disclosure, a "payment" includes the sale of similar goods or services to the franchisor at a lower price than to franchisees.

(9) The existence of purchasing or distribution cooperatives.

(10) Whether the franchisor negotiates purchase arrangements with suppliers, including price terms, for the benefit of franchisees.

(11) Whether the franchisor provides material benefits (for example, renewal or granting additional franchises) to a franchisee based on a franchisee's purchase of particular products or services or use of particular suppliers.

(*i*) Item 9: Franchisee's Obligations. Disclose, in the following tabular form, a list of the franchisee's principal obligations. State the title "FRANCHISEE'S OBLIGATIONS" in capital letters using bold type. Cross-reference each listed obligation with any applicable section of the franchise or other agreement and with the relevant disclosure document provision. If a particular obligation is not applicable, state "Not Applicable." Include additional obligations, as warranted.

Item 9 Table:
FRANCHISEE'S OBLIGATIONS

	Obligation	Section in agreement	Disclosure document item
a.	Site selection and acquisition/lease		
b.	Pre-opening purchase/leases		
c.	Site development and other pre-opening requirements		
d.	Initial and ongoing training		
e.	Opening		
f.	Fees		
g.	Compliance with standards and policies/operating manual		
h.	Trademarks and proprietary information		
i.	Restrictions on products/services offered		
j.	Warranty and customer service requirements		
k.	Territorial development and sales quotas		
l.	Ongoing product/service purchases		
m.	Maintenance, appearance, and remodeling requirements		
n.	Insurance		
o.	Advertising		
p.	Indemnification		
q.	Owner's participation/management/staffing		
r.	Records and reports		
s.	Inspections and audits		
t.	Transfer		
u.	Renewal		
v.	Post-termination obligations		
w.	Non-competition covenants		
x.	Dispute resolution		
y.	Other (describe)		

(j) Item 10: Financing.

(1) Disclose the terms of each financing arrangement, including leases and installment contracts, that the franchisor, its agent, or affiliates offer directly or indirectly to the franchisee.[23] The franchisor may summarize the terms of each financing arrangement in tabular form, using footnotes to provide additional information. For a sample Item 10 table, see Appendix A of this part. For each financing arrangement, state:

(i) What the financing covers (for example, the initial franchise fee, site acquisition, construction or remodeling, initial or replacement equipment or fixtures, opening or ongoing inventory or supplies, or other continuing expenses).[24]

(ii) The identity of each lender providing financing and their relationship to the franchisor (for example, affiliate).

(iii) The amount of financing offered or, if the amount depends on an actual cost that may vary, the percentage of the cost that will be financed.

(iv) The rate of interest, plus finance charges, expressed on an annual basis. If the rate of interest, plus finance charges, expressed on an annual basis, may differ depending on when the financing is issued, state what that rate was on a specified recent date.

(v) The number of payments or the period of repayment.

(vi) The nature of any security interest required by the lender.

(vii) Whether a person other than the franchisee must personally guarantee the debt.

(viii) Whether the debt can be prepaid and the nature of any prepayment penalty.

(ix) The franchisee's potential liabilities upon default, including any:

(A) Accelerated obligation to pay the entire amount due;

(B) Obligations to pay court costs and attorney's fees incurred in collecting the debt;

(C) Termination of the franchise; and

(D) Liabilities from cross defaults such as those resulting directly from non-payment, or indirectly from the loss of business property.

(x) Other material financing terms.

(2) Disclose whether the loan agreement requires franchisees to waive defenses or other legal rights (for example, confession of judgment), or bars franchisees from asserting a defense against the lender, the lender's assignee or the franchisor. If so, describe the relevant provisions.

(3) Disclose whether the franchisor's practice or intent is to sell, assign, or discount to a third party all or part of the financing arrangement. If so, state:

(i) The assignment terms, including whether the franchisor will remain primarily obligated to provide the financed goods or services; and

(ii) That the franchisee may lose all its defenses against the lender as a result of the sale or assignment.

(4) Disclose whether the franchisor or an affiliate receives any consideration for placing financing with the lender. If such payments exist:

(i) Disclose the amount or the method of determining the payment; and

(ii) Identify the source of the payment and the relationship of the source to the franchisor or its affiliates.

---

23 Indirect offers of financing include a written arrangement between a franchisor or its affiliate and a lender, for the lender to offer financing to a franchisee; an arrangement in which a franchisor or its affiliate receives a benefit from a lender in exchange for financing a franchise purchase; and a franchisor's guarantee of a note, lease, or other obligation of the franchisee.

24 Include sample copies of the financing documents as an exhibit to § 436.5(v) of this part. Cite the section and name of the document containing the financing terms and conditions.

(k) Item 11: Franchisor's Assistance, Advertising, Computer Systems, and Training. Disclose the franchisor's principal assistance and related obligations of both the franchisor and franchisee as follows. For each obligation, cite the section number of the franchise agreement imposing the obligation. Begin by stating the following sentence in bold type: "Except as listed below, [the franchisor] is not required to provide you with any assistance."

(1) Disclose the franchisor's pre-opening obligations to the franchisee, including any assistance in:

(i) Locating a site and negotiating the purchase or lease of the site. If such assistance is provided, state:

(A) Whether the franchisor generally owns the premises and leases it to the franchisee.

(B) Whether the franchisor selects the site or approves an area in which the franchisee selects a site. If so, state further whether and how the franchisor must approve a franchisee-selected site.

(C) The factors that the franchisor considers in selecting or approving sites (for example, general location and neighborhood, traffic patterns, parking, size, physical characteristics of existing buildings, and lease terms).

(D) The time limit for the franchisor to locate or approve or disapprove the site and the consequences if the franchisor and franchisee cannot agree on a site.

(ii) Conforming the premises to local ordinances and building codes and obtaining any required permits.

(iii) Constructing, remodeling, or decorating the premises.

(iv) Hiring and training employees.

(v) Providing for necessary equipment, signs, fixtures, opening inventory, and supplies. If any such assistance is provided, state:

(A) Whether the franchisor provides these items directly or only provides the names of approved suppliers.

(B) Whether the franchisor provides written specifications for these items.

(C) Whether the franchisor delivers or installs these items.

(2) Disclose the typical length of time between the earlier of the signing of the franchise agreement or the first payment of consideration for the franchise and the opening of the franchisee's business. Describe the factors that may affect the time period, such as ability to obtain a lease, financing or building permits, zoning and local ordinances, weather conditions, shortages, or delayed installation of equipment, fixtures, and signs.

(3) Disclose the franchisor's obligations to the franchisee during the operation of the franchise, including any assistance in:

(i) Developing products or services the franchisee will offer to its customers.

(ii) Hiring and training employees.

(iii) Improving and developing the franchised business.

(iv) Establishing prices.

(v) Establishing and using administrative, bookkeeping, accounting, and inventory control procedures.

(vi) Resolving operating problems encountered by the franchisee.

(4) Describe the advertising program for the franchise system, including the following:

(i) The franchisor's obligation to conduct advertising, including:

(A) The media the franchisor may use.

(B) Whether media coverage is local, regional, or national.

(C) The source of the advertising (for example, an in-house advertising department or a national or regional advertising agency).

(D) Whether the franchisor must spend any amount on advertising in the area or territory where the franchisee is located.

(ii) The circumstances when the franchisor will permit franchisees to use their own advertising material.

(iii) Whether there is an advertising council composed of franchisees that advises the franchisor on advertising policies. If so, disclose:

(A) How members of the council are selected.

(B) Whether the council serves in an advisory capacity only or has operational or decision-making power.

(C) Whether the franchisor has the power to form, change, or dissolve the advertising council.

(iv) Whether the franchisee must participate in a local or regional advertising cooperative. If so, state:

(A) How the area or membership of the cooperative is defined.

(B) How much the franchisee must contribute to the fund and whether other franchisees must contribute a different amount or at a different rate.

(C) Whether the franchisor-owned outlets must contribute to the fund and, if so, whether those contributions are on the same basis as those for franchisees.

(D) Who is responsible for administering the cooperative (for example, franchisor, franchisees, or advertising agency).

(E) Whether cooperatives must operate from written governing documents and whether the documents are available for the franchisee to review.

(F) Whether cooperatives must prepare annual or periodic financial statements and whether the statements are available for review by the franchisee.

(G) Whether the franchisor has the power to require cooperatives to be formed, changed, dissolved, or merged.

(v) Whether the franchisee must participate in any other advertising fund. If so, state:

(A) Who contributes to the fund.

(B) How much the franchisee must contribute to the fund and whether other franchisees must contribute a different amount or at a different rate.

(C) Whether the franchisor-owned outlets must contribute to the fund and, if so, whether it is on the same basis as franchisees.

(D) Who administers the fund.

(E) Whether the fund is audited and when it is audited.

(F) Whether financial statements of the fund are available for review by the franchisee.

(G) How the funds were used in the most recently concluded fiscal year, including the percentages spent on production, media placement, administrative expenses, and a description of any other use.

(vi) If not all advertising funds are spent in the fiscal year in which they accrue, how the franchisor uses the remaining amount, including whether franchisees receive a periodic accounting of how advertising fees are spent.

(vii) The percentage of advertising funds, if any, that the franchisor uses principally to solicit new franchise sales.

(5) Disclose whether the franchisor requires the franchisee to buy or use electronic cash registers or computer systems. If so, describe the systems generally in non-technical language, including the types of data to be generated or stored in these systems, and state the following:

(i) The cost of purchasing or leasing the systems.

(ii) Any obligation of the franchisor, any affiliate, or third party to provide ongoing maintenance, repairs, upgrades, or updates.

(iii) Any obligations of the franchisee to upgrade or update any system during the term of the franchise, and, if so, any contractual limitations on the frequency and cost of the obligation.

(iv) The annual cost of any optional or required maintenance, updating, upgrading, or support contracts.

(v) Whether the franchisor will have independent access to the information that will be generated or stored in any electronic cash register or computer system. If so, describe the information that the franchisor may access and whether there are any contractual limitations on the franchisor's right to access the information.

(6) Disclose the table of contents of the franchisor's operating manual provided to franchisees as of the franchisor's last fiscal year-end or a more recent date. State the number of pages devoted to each subject and the total number of pages in the manual as of this date. This disclosure may be omitted if the franchisor offers the prospective franchisee the opportunity to view the manual before buying the franchise.

(7) Disclose the franchisor's training program as of the franchisor's last fiscal year-end or a more recent date.

(i) Describe the training program in the following tabular form. Title the table "TRAINING PROGRAM" in capital letters and bold type.

Item 11 Table
TRAINING PROGRAM

Column 1	Column 2	Column 3	Column 4
Subject	Hours of Classroom Training	Hours of On-The-Job Training	Location

(A) In column 1, state the subjects taught.

(B) In column 2, state the hours of classroom training for each subject.

(C) In column 3, state the hours of on-the-job training for each subject.

(D) In column 4, state the location of the training for each subject.

(ii) State further:

(A) How often training classes are held and the nature of the location or facility where training is held (for example, company, home, office, franchisor-owned store).

(B) The nature of instructional materials and the instructor's experience, including the instructor's length of experience in the field and with the franchisor. State only experience relevant to the subject taught and the franchisor's operations.

(C) Any charges franchisees must pay for training and who must pay travel and living expenses of the training program enrollees.

(D) Who may and who must attend training. State whether the franchisee or other persons must complete the program to the franchisor's satisfaction. If successful completion is required, state how long after signing the agreement or before opening the business the training must be completed. If training is not mandatory, state the percentage of new franchisees that enrolled in the training program during the preceding 12 months.

(E) Whether additional training programs or refresher courses are required.

(*l*) Item 12: Territory.
Disclose:

(1) Whether the franchise is for a specific location or a location to be approved by the franchisor.

(2) Any minimum territory granted to the franchisee (for example, a specific radius, a distance sufficient to encompass a specified population, or another specific designation).

(3) The conditions under which the franchisor will approve the relocation of the franchised business or the franchisee's establishment of additional franchised outlets.

(4) Franchisee options, rights of first refusal, or similar rights to acquire additional franchises.

(5) Whether the franchisor grants an exclusive territory.

(i) If the franchisor does not grant an exclusive territory, state: "You will not receive an exclusive territory. You may face competition from other franchisees, from outlets that we own, or from other channels of distribution or competitive brands that we control."

(ii) If the franchisor grants an exclusive territory, disclose:

(A) Whether continuation of territorial exclusivity depends on achieving a certain sales volume, market penetration, or other contingency, and the circumstances when the franchisee's territory may be altered. Describe any sales or other conditions. State the franchisor's rights if the franchisee fails to meet the requirements.

(B) Any other circumstances that permit the franchisor to modify the franchisee's territorial rights (for example, a population increase in the territory giving the franchisor the right to grant an additional franchise in the area) and the effect of such modifications on the franchisee's rights.

(6) For all territories (exclusive and non-exclusive):

(i) Any restrictions on the franchisor from soliciting or accepting orders from consumers inside the franchisee's territory, including:

(A) Whether the franchisor or an affiliate has used or reserves the right to use other channels of distribution, such as the Internet, catalog sales, telemarketing, or other direct marketing sales, to make sales within the franchisee's territory using the franchisor's principal trademarks.

(B) Whether the franchisor or an affiliate has used or reserves the right to use other channels of distribution, such as the Internet, catalog sales, telemarketing, or other direct marketing, to make sales within the franchisee's territory of products or services under trademarks different from the ones the franchisee will use under the franchise agreement.

(C) Any compensation that the franchisor must pay for soliciting or accepting orders from inside the franchisee's territory.

(ii) Any restrictions on the franchisee from soliciting or accepting orders from consumers outside of his or her territory, including whether the franchisee has the right to use other channels of distribution, such as the Internet, catalog sales, telemarketing, or other direct marketing, to make sales outside of his or her territory.

(iii) If the franchisor or an affiliate operates, franchises, or has plans to operate or franchise a business under a different trademark and that business sells or will sell goods or services similar to those the franchisee will offer, describe:

(A) The similar goods and services.

(B) The different trademark.

(C) Whether outlets will be franchisor owned or operated.

(D) Whether the franchisor or its franchisees who use the different trademark will solicit or accept orders within the franchisee's territory.

(E) The timetable for the plan.

(F) How the franchisor will resolve conflicts between the franchisor and franchisees and between the franchisees of each system regarding territory, customers, and franchisor support.

(G) The principal business address of the franchisor's similar operating business. If it is the same as the franchisor's principal business address stated in § 436.5(a) of this part, disclose whether the franchisor maintains (or plans to maintain) physically separate offices and training facilities for the similar competing business.

(m) Item 13: Trademarks.

(1) Disclose each principal trademark to be licensed to the franchisee. For this Item, "principal trademark" means the primary trademarks, service marks, names, logos, and commercial symbols the franchisee will use to identify the franchised business. It may not include every trademark the franchisor owns.

(2) Disclose whether each principal trademark is registered with the United States Patent and Trademark Office. If so, state:

(i) The date and identification number of each trademark registration.

(ii) Whether the franchisor has filed all required affidavits.

(iii) Whether any registration has been renewed.

(iv) Whether the principal trademarks are registered on the Principal or Supplemental Register of the United States Patent and Trademark Office.

(3) If the principal trademark is not registered with the United States Patent and Trademark Office, state whether the franchisor has filed any trademark application, including any "intent to use" application or an application based on actual use. If so, state the date and identification number of the application.

(4) If the trademark is not registered on the Principal Register of the United States Patent and Trademark Office, state: "We do not have a federal registration for our principal trademark. Therefore, our trademark does not have many legal benefits and rights as a federally registered trademark. If our right to use the trademark is challenged, you may have to change to an alternative trademark, which may increase your expenses."

(5) Disclose any currently effective material determinations of the United States Patent and Trademark Office, the Trademark Trial and Appeal Board, or any state trademark administrator or court; and any pending infringement, opposition, or cancellation proceeding. Include infringement, opposition, or cancellation proceedings in which the franchisor unsuccessfully sought to prevent registration of a trademark in order to protect a trademark licensed by the franchisor. Describe how the determination affects the ownership, use, or licensing of the trademark.

(6) Disclose any pending material federal or state court litigation regarding the franchisor's use or ownership rights in a trademark. For each pending action, disclose:[25]

(i) The forum and case number.

(ii) The nature of claims made opposing the franchisor's use of the trademark or by the franchisor opposing another person's use of the trademark.

(iii) Any effective court or administrative agency ruling in the matter.

(7) Disclose any currently effective agreements that significantly limit the franchisor's rights to use or license the use of trademarks listed in this section in a manner material to the franchise. For each agreement, disclose:

(i) The manner and extent of the limitation or grant.

(ii) The extent to which the agreement may affect the franchisee.

(iii) The agreement's duration.

(iv) The parties to the agreement.

(v) The circumstances when the agreement may be canceled or modified.

(vi) All other material terms.

(8) Disclose:

(i) Whether the franchisor must protect the franchisee's right to use the principal trademarks listed in this section, and must protect the franchisee against claims of infringement or unfair competition arising out of the franchisee's use of the trademarks.

(ii) The franchisee's obligation to notify the franchisor of the use of, or claims of rights to, a trademark identical to or confusingly similar to a trademark licensed to the franchisee.

(iii) Whether the franchise agreement requires the franchisor to take affirmative action when notified of these uses or claims.

(iv) Whether the franchisor or franchisee has the right to control any administrative proceedings or litigation involving a trademark licensed by the franchisor to the franchisee.

---

25 The franchisor may include an attorney's opinion relative to the merits of litigation or of an action if the attorney issuing the opinion consents to its use. The text of the disclosure may include a summary of the opinion if the full opinion is attached and the attorney issuing the opinion consents to the use of the summary.

(v) Whether the franchise agreement requires the franchisor to participate in the franchisee's defense and/or indemnify the franchisee for expenses or damages if the franchisee is a party to an administrative or judicial proceeding involving a trademark licensed by the franchisor to the franchisee, or if the proceeding is resolved unfavorably to the franchisee.

(vi) The franchisee's rights under the franchise agreement if the franchisor requires the franchisee to modify or discontinue using a trademark.

(9) Disclose whether the franchisor knows of either superior prior rights or infringing uses that could materially affect the franchisee's use of the principal trademarks in the state where the franchised business will be located. For each use of a principal trademark that the franchisor believes is an infringement that could materially affect the franchisee's use of a trademark, disclose:

(i) The nature of the infringement.

(ii) The locations where the infringement is occurring.

(iii) The length of time of the infringement (to the extent known).

(iv) Any action taken or anticipated by the franchisor.

(n) Item 14: Patents, Copyrights, and Proprietary Information.

(1) Disclose whether the franchisor owns rights in, or licenses to, patents or copyrights that are material to the franchise. Also, disclose whether the franchisor has any pending patent applications that are material to the franchise. If so, state:

(i) The nature of the patent, patent application, or copyright and its relationship to the franchise.

(ii) For each patent:

(A) The duration of the patent.

(B) The type of patent (for example, mechanical, process, or design).

(C) The patent number, issuance date, and title.

(iii) For each patent application:

(A) The type of patent application (for example, mechanical, process, or design).

(B) The serial number, filing date, and title.

(iv) For each copyright:

(A) The duration of the copyright.

(B) The registration number and date.

(C) Whether the franchisor can and intends to renew the copyright.

(2) Describe any current material determination of the United States Patent and Trademark Office, the United States Copyright Office, or a court regarding the patent or copyright. Include the forum and matter number. Describe how the determination affects the franchised business.

(3) State the forum, case number, claims asserted, issues involved, and effective determinations for any material proceeding pending in the United States Patent and Trademark Office or any court.[26]

(4) If an agreement limits the use of the patent, patent application, or copyright, state the parties to and duration of the agreement, the extent to which the agreement may affect the franchisee, and other material terms of the agreement.

(5) Disclose the franchisor's obligation to protect the patent, patent application, or copyright; and to defend the franchisee against claims arising from the franchisee's use of patented or copyrighted items, including:

(i) Whether the franchisor's obligation is contingent upon the franchisee notifying the franchisor of any infringement claims or whether the franchisee's notification is discretionary.

(ii) Whether the franchise agreement requires the franchisor to take affirmative action when notified of infringement.

(iii) Who has the right to control any litigation.

(iv) Whether the franchisor must participate in the defense of a franchisee or indemnify the franchisee for expenses or damages in a proceeding involving a patent, patent application, or copyright licensed to the franchisee.

(v) Whether the franchisor's obligation is contingent upon the franchisee modifying or discontinuing the use of the subject matter covered by the patent or copyright.

(vi) The franchisee's rights under the franchise agreement if the franchisor requires the franchisee to modify or discontinue using the subject matter covered by the patent or copyright.

(6) If the franchisor knows of any patent or copyright infringement that could materially affect the franchisee, disclose:

(i) The nature of the infringement.

(ii) The locations where the infringement is occurring.

(iii) The length of time of the infringement (to the extent known).

(iv) Any action taken or anticipated by the franchisor.

(7) If the franchisor claims proprietary rights in other confidential information or trade secrets, describe in general terms the proprietary information communicated to the franchisee and the terms for use by the franchisee. The franchisor need only describe the general nature of the proprietary information, such as whether a formula or recipe is considered to be a trade secret.

(o) Item 15: Obligation to Participate in the Actual Operation of the Franchise Business.

(1) Disclose the franchisee's obligation to participate personally in the direct operation of the franchisee's business and whether the franchisor recommends participation. Include obligations arising from any written agreement or from the franchisor's practice.

(2) If personal "on-premises" supervision is not required, disclose the following:

(i) If the franchisee is an individual, whether the franchisor recommends on-premises supervision by the franchisee.

(ii) Limits on whom the franchisee can hire as an on-premises supervisor.

(iii) Whether an on-premises supervisor must successfully complete the franchisor's training program.

(iv) If the franchisee is a business entity, the amount of equity interest, if any, that the on-premises supervisor must have in the franchisee's business.

(3) Disclose any restrictions that the franchisee must place on its manager (for example, maintain trade secrets, covenants not to compete).

(p) Item 16: Restrictions on What the Franchisee May Sell. Disclose any franchisor-imposed restrictions or conditions on the goods or services that the franchisee may sell or that limit access to customers, including:

(1) Any obligation on the franchisee to sell only goods or services approved by the franchisor.

(2) Any obligation on the franchisee to sell all goods or services authorized by the franchisor.

(3) Whether the franchisor has the right to change the types of authorized goods or services and whether there are limits on the franchisor's right to make changes.

(q) Item 17: Renewal, Termination, Transfer, and Dispute Resolution. Disclose, in the following tabular form, a table that cross-references each enumerated franchise relationship item with the applicable provision in the franchise or related agreement. Title the table "THE FRANCHISE RELATIONSHIP" in capital letters and bold type.

(1) Describe briefly each contractual provision. If a particular item is not applicable, state "Not Applicable."

(2) If the agreement is silent about one of the listed provisions, but the franchisor unilaterally offers to provide certain benefits or protections to franchisees as a matter of policy, use a footnote to describe the policy and state whether the policy is subject to change.

(3) In the summary column for Item 17(c), state what the term "renewal" means for your franchise system, including, if applicable, a statement that franchisees may be asked to sign a contract with materially different terms and conditions than their original contract.

---

26 If counsel consents, the franchisor may include a counsel's opinion or a summary of the opinion if the full opinion is attached.

Item 17 Table:
THE FRANCHISE RELATIONSHIP

	Provision	Section in franchise or other agreement	Summary
a.	Length of the franchise term		
b.	Renewal or extension of the term		
c.	Requirements for franchisee to renew or extend		
d.	Termination by franchisee		
e.	Termination by franchisor without cause		
f.	Termination by franchisor with cause		
g.	"Cause" defined—curable defaults		
h.	"Cause" defined—non-curable defaults		
i.	Franchisee's obligations on termination/non-renewal		
j.	Assignment of contract by franchisor		
k.	"Transfer" by franchisee—defined		
l.	Franchisor approval of transfer by franchisee		
m.	Conditions for franchisor approval of transfer		
n.	Franchisor's right of first refusal to acquire franchisee's business		
o.	Franchisor's option to purchase franchisee's business		
p.	Death or disability of franchisee		
q.	Non-competition covenants during the term of the franchise		
r.	Non-competition covenants after the franchise is terminated or expires		
s.	Modification of the agreement		
t.	Integration/merger clause		
u.	Dispute resolution by arbitration or mediation		
v.	Choice of forum		
w.	Choice of law		

(r) Item 18: Public Figures.

Disclose:

(1) Any compensation or other benefit given or promised to a public figure arising from either the use of the public figure in the franchise name or symbol, or the public figure's endorsement or recommendation of the franchise to prospective franchisees.

(2) The extent to which the public figure is involved in the management or control of the franchisor. Describe the public figure's position and duties in the franchisor's business structure.

(3) The public figure's total investment in the franchisor, including the amount the public figure contributed in services performed or to be performed. State the type of investment (for example, common stock, promissory note).

(4) For purposes of this section, a public figure means a person whose name or physical appearance is generally known to the public in the geographic area where the franchise will be located.

(s) Item 19: Financial Performance Representations.

(1) Begin by stating the following:

The FTC's Franchise Rule permits a franchisor to provide information about the actual or potential financial performance of its franchised and/or franchisor-owned outlets, if there is a reasonable basis for the information, and if the information is included in the disclosure document. Financial performance information that differs from that included in Item 19 may be given only if: (1) a franchisor provides the actual records of an existing outlet you are considering buying; or (2) a franchisor supplements the information provided in this Item 19, for example, by providing information about possible performance at a particular location or under particular circumstances.

(2) If a franchisor does not provide any financial performance representation in Item 19, also state:

We do not make any representations about a franchisee's future financial performance or the past financial performance of company-owned or franchised outlets. We also do not authorize our employees or representatives to make any such representations either orally or in writing. If you are purchasing an existing outlet, however, we may provide you with the actual records of that outlet. If you receive any other financial performance information or projections of your future income, you should report it to the franchisor's management by contacting [name, address, and telephone number], the Federal Trade Commission, and the appropriate state regulatory agencies.

(3) If the franchisor makes any financial performance representation to prospective franchisees, the franchisor must have a reasonable basis and written substantiation for the representation at the time the representation is made and must state the representation in the Item 19 disclosure. The franchisor must also disclose the following:

(i) Whether the representation is an historic financial performance representation about the franchise system's existing outlets, or a subset of those outlets, or is a forecast of the prospective franchisee's future financial performance.

(ii) If the representation relates to past performance of the franchise system's existing outlets, the material bases for the representation, including:

(A) Whether the representation relates to the performance of all of the franchise system's existing outlets or only to a subset of outlets that share a particular set of characteristics (for example, geographic location, type of location (such as free standing vs. shopping center), degree of competition, length of time the outlets have operated, services or goods sold, services supplied by the franchisor, and whether the outlets are franchised or franchisor-owned or operated).

(B) The dates when the reported level of financial performance was achieved.

(C) The total number of outlets that existed in the relevant period and, if different, the number of outlets that had the described characteristics.

(D) The number of outlets with the described characteristics whose actual financial performance data were used in arriving at the representation.

(E) Of those outlets whose data were used in arriving at the representation, the number and percent that actually attained or surpassed the stated results.

(F) Characteristics of the included outlets, such as those characteristics noted in paragraph (3)(ii)(A) of this section, that may differ materially from those of the outlet that may be offered to a prospective franchisee.

(iii) If the representation is a forecast of future financial performance, state the material bases and assumptions on which the projection is based. The material assumptions underlying a forecast include significant factors upon which a franchisee's future results are expected to depend. These factors include, for example, economic or market conditions that are basic to a franchisee's operation, and encompass matters affecting, among other things, a franchisee's sales, the cost of goods or services sold, and operating expenses.

(iv) A clear and conspicuous admonition that a new franchisee's individual financial results may differ from the result stated in the financial performance representation.

(v) A statement that written substantiation for the financial performance representation will be made available to the prospective franchisee upon reasonable request.

(4) If a franchisor wishes to disclose only the actual operating results for a specific outlet being offered for sale, it need not comply with this section, provided the information is given only to potential purchasers of that outlet.

(5) If a franchisor furnishes financial performance information according to this section, the franchisor may deliver to a prospective franchisee a supplemental financial performance representation about a particular location or variation, apart from the disclosure document. The supplemental representation must:

(i) Be in writing.

(ii) Explain the departure from the financial performance representation in the disclosure document.

(iii) Be prepared in accordance with the requirements of paragraph (s)(3)(i)-(iv) of this section.

(iv) Be furnished to the prospective franchisee.

(t) Item 20: Outlets and Franchisee Information.

(1) Disclose, in the following tabular form, the total number of franchised and company-owned outlets for each of the franchisor's last three fiscal years. For purposes of this section, "outlet" includes outlets of a type substantially similar to that offered to the prospective franchisee. A sample Item 20(1) Table is attached as Appendix B to this part.

(i) In column 1, include three outlet categories titled "franchised," "company-owned, and "total outlets."

(ii) In column 2, state the last three fiscal years.

(iii) In column 3, state the total number of each type of outlet operating at the beginning of each fiscal year.

(iv) In column 4, state the total number of each type of outlet operating at the end of each fiscal year.

Item 20 Table No. 1
Systemwide Outlet Summary
For years [ ] to [ ]

Column 1	Column 2	Column 3	Column 4	Column 5
Outlet Type	**Year**	**Outlets at the Start of the Year**	**Outlets at the End of the Year**	**Net Change**
Franchised	2004			
	2005			
	2006			
Company-	2004			
Owned	2005			
	2006			
Total Outlets	2004			
	2005			
	2006			

(v) In column 5, state the net change, and indicate whether the change is positive or negative, for each type of outlet during each fiscal year.

(2) Disclose, in the following tabular form, the number of franchised and company-owned outlets and changes in the number and ownership of outlets located in each state during each of the last three fiscal years. Except as noted, each change in ownership shall be reported only once in the following tables. If multiple events occurred in the process of transferring ownership of an outlet, report the event that occurred last in time. If a single outlet changed ownership two or more times during the same fiscal year, use footnotes to describe the types of changes involved and the order in which the changes occurred.

(i) Disclose, in the following tabular form, the total number of franchised outlets transferred in each state during each of the franchisor's last three fiscal years. For purposes of this section, "transfer" means the acquisition of a controlling interest in a franchised outlet, during its term, by a person other than the franchisor or an affiliate. A sample Item 20(2) Table is attached as Appendix C to this part.

Item 20 Table No. 2
Transfers of Outlets from Franchisees to New Owners
(other than the Franchisor)
For years [ ] to [ ]

Column 1	Column 2	Column 3
State	Year	Number of Transfers
	2004	
	2005	
	2006	
	2004	
	2005	
	2006	
Total	2004	
	2005	
	2006	

(A) In column 1, list each state with one or more franchised outlets.

(B) In column 2, state the last three fiscal years.

(C) In column 3, state the total number of completed transfers in each state during each fiscal year.

(ii) Disclose, in the following tabular form, the status of franchisee-owned outlets located in each state for each of the franchisor's last three fiscal years. A sample Item 20(3) Table is attached as Appendix D to this part.

(A) In column 1, list each state with one or more franchised outlets.

(B) In column 2, state the last three fiscal years.

(C) In column 3, state the total number of franchised outlets in each state at the start of each fiscal year.

(D) In column 4, state the total number of franchised outlets opened in each state during each fiscal year. Include both new outlets and existing company-owned outlets that a franchisee purchased from the franchisor. (Also report the number of existing company-owned outlets that are sold to a franchisee in Column 7 of Table 4).

(E) In column 5, state the total number of franchised outlets that were terminated in each state during each fiscal year. For purposes of this section, "termination" means the franchisor's termination of a franchise agreement prior to the end of its term and without providing any consideration to the franchisee (whether by payment or forgiveness or assumption of debt).

(F) In column 6, state the total number of non-renewals in each state during each fiscal year. For purposes of this section, "non-renewal" occurs when the franchise agreement for a franchised outlet is not renewed at the end of its term.

(G) In column 7, state the total number of franchised outlets reacquired by the franchisor in each state during each fiscal year. For purposes of this section, a "reacquisition" means the franchisor's acquisition for consideration (whether by payment or forgiveness or assumption of debt) of a franchised outlet during its term. (Also report franchised outlets reacquired by the franchisor in column 5 of Table 4).

(H) In column 8, state the total number of outlets in each state not operating as one of the franchisor's outlets at the end of each fiscal year for reasons other than termination, non-renewal, or reacquisition by the franchisor.

(I) In column 9, state the total number of franchised outlets in each state at the end of the fiscal year.

(iii) Disclose, in the following tabular form, the status of company-owned outlets located in each state for each of the franchisor's last three fiscal years. A sample Item 20(4) Table is attached as Appendix E to this part.

Item 20 Table No. 3
Status of Franchised Outlets
For years [ ] to [ ]

Column 1 State	Column 2 Year	Column 3 Outlets at Start of Year	Column 4 Outlets Opened	Column 5 Terminations	Column 6 Non-Renewals	Column 7 Reacquired by Franchisor	Column 8 Ceased Operations— Other Reasons	Column 9 Outlets at End of the Year
	2004							
	2005							
	2006							
	2004							
	2005							
	2006							
Totals	2004							
	2005							
	2006							

Item 20 Table No. 4
Status of Company-Owned Outlets
For years [ ] to [ ]

Column 1 State	Column 2 Year	Column 3 Outlets at Start of Year	Column 4 Outlets Opened	Column 5 Outlets Re-acquired From Franchisee	Column 6 Outlets Closed	Column 7 Outlets Sold to Franchisee	Column 8 Outlets at End of the Year
	2004						
	2005						
	2006						
	2004						
	2005						
	2006						
Totals	2004						
	2005						
	2006						

(A) In column 1, list each state with one or more company-owned outlets.

(B) In column 2, state the last three fiscal years.

(C) In column 3, state the total number of company-owned outlets in each state at the start of the fiscal year.

(D) In column 4, state the total number of company-owned outlets opened in each state during each fiscal year.

(E) In column 5, state the total number of franchised outlets reacquired from franchisees in each state during each fiscal year.

(F) In column 6, state the total number of company-owned outlets closed in each state during each fiscal year. Include both actual closures and instances when an outlet ceases to operate under the franchisor's trademark.

(G) In column 7, state the total number of company-owned outlets sold to franchisees in each state during each fiscal year.

(H) In column 8, state the total number of company-owned outlets operating in each state at the end of each fiscal year.

(3) Disclose, in the following tabular form, projected new franchised and company-owned outlets. A sample Item 20(5) Table is attached as Appendix F to this part.

    (i) In column 1, list each state where one or more franchised or company-owned outlets are located or are projected to be located.

    (ii) In column 2, state the total number of franchise agreements that had been signed for new outlets to be located in each state as of the end of the previous fiscal year where the outlet had not yet opened.

    (iii) In column 3, state the total number of new franchised outlets in each state projected to be opened during the next fiscal year.

    (iv) In column 4, state the total number of new company-owned outlets in each state that are projected to be opened during the next fiscal year.

(4) Disclose the names of all current franchisees and the address and telephone number of each of their outlets. Alternatively, disclose this information for all franchised outlets in the state, but if these franchised outlets total fewer than 100, disclose this information for franchised outlets from contiguous states and then the next closest states until at least 100 franchised outlets are listed.

(5) Disclose the name, city and state, and current business telephone number, or if unknown, the last known home telephone number of every franchisee who had an outlet terminated, canceled, not renewed, or otherwise voluntarily or involuntarily ceased to do business under the franchise agreement during the most recently completed fiscal year or who has not communicated with the franchisor within 10 weeks of the disclosure document issuance date.[27] State in immediate conjunction with this information: "If you buy this franchise, your contact information may be disclosed to other buyers when you leave the franchise system."

(6) If a franchisor is selling a previously-owned franchised outlet now under its control, disclose the following additional information for that outlet for the last five fiscal years. This information may be attached as an addendum to a disclosure document, or, if disclosure has already been made, then in a supplement to the previously furnished disclosure document.

Item 20 Table No. 5
Projected Openings As Of [Last Day of Last Fiscal Year]

Column 1 State	Column 2 Franchise Agreements Signed But Outlet Not Opened	Column 3 Projected New Franchised Outlet in The Next Fiscal Year	Column 4 Projected New Company-Owned Outlet in the Next Fiscal Year
Total			

27 Franchisors may substitute alternative contact information at the request of the former franchisee, such as a home address, post office address, or a personal or business email address.

(i) The name, city and state, current business telephone number, or if unknown, last known home telephone number of each previous owner of the outlet;

(ii) The time period when each previous owner controlled the outlet;

(iii) The reason for each previous change in ownership (for example, termination, non-renewal, voluntary transfer, ceased operations); and

(iv) The time period(s) when the franchisor retained control of the outlet (for example, after termination, non-renewal, or reacquisition).

(7) Disclose whether franchisees signed confidentiality clauses during the last three fiscal years. If so, state the following: "In some instances, current and former franchisees sign provisions restricting their ability to speak openly about their experience with [name of franchise system]. You may wish to speak with current and former franchisees, but be aware that not all such franchisees will be able to communicate with you." Franchisors may also disclose the number and percentage of current and former franchisees who during each of the last three fiscal years signed agreements that include confidentiality clauses and may disclose the circumstances under which such clauses were signed.

(8) Disclose, to the extent known, the name, address, telephone number, email address, and Web address (to the extent known) of each trademark-specific franchisee organization associated with the franchise system being offered, if such organization:

(i) Has been created, sponsored, or endorsed by the franchisor. If so, state the relationship between the organization and the franchisor (for example, the organization was created by the franchisor, sponsored by the franchisor, or endorsed by the franchisor).

(ii) Is incorporated or otherwise organized under state law and asks the franchisor to be included in the franchisor's disclosure document during the next fiscal year. Such organizations must renew their request on an annual basis by submitting a request no later than 60 days after the close of the franchisor's fiscal year. The franchisor has no obligation to verify the organization's continued existence at the end of each fiscal year. Franchisors may also include the following statement: "The following independent franchisee organizations have asked to be included in this disclosure document."

(u) Item 21: Financial Statements.

(1) Include the following financial statements prepared according to United States generally accepted accounting principles, as revised by any future United States government mandated accounting principles, or as permitted by the Securities and Exchange Commission. Except as provided in paragraph (u)(2) of this section, these financial statements must be audited by an independent certified public accountant using generally accepted United States auditing standards. Present the required financial statements in a tabular form that compares at least two fiscal years.

(i) The franchisor's balance sheet for the previous two fiscal year-ends before the disclosure document issuance date.

(ii) Statements of operations, stockholders equity, and cash flows for each of the franchisor's previous three fiscal years.

(iii) Instead of the financial disclosures required by paragraphs (u)(1)(i) and (ii) of this section, the franchisor may include financial statements of any of its affiliates if the affiliate's financial statements satisfy paragraphs (u)(1)(i) and (ii) of this section and the affiliate absolutely and unconditionally guarantees to assume the duties and obligations of the franchisor under the franchise agreement. The affiliate's guarantee must cover all of the franchisor's obligations to the franchisee, but need not extend to third parties. If this alternative is used, attach a copy of the guarantee to the disclosure document.

(iv) When a franchisor owns a direct or beneficial controlling financial interest in a subsidiary, its financial statements should reflect the financial condition of the franchisor and its subsidiary.

(v) Include separate financial statements for the franchisor and any subfranchisor, as well as for any parent that commits to perform post-sale obligations for the franchisor or guarantees the franchisor's obligations. Attach a copy of any guarantee to the disclosure document.

(2) A start-up franchise system that does not yet have audited financial statements may phase-in the use of audited financial statements by providing, at a minimum, the following statements at the indicated times:

(i) The franchisor' first partial or full fiscal year selling franchises.	An unaudited opening balance sheet.
(ii) The franchisor' second fiscal year selling franchises.	Audited balance sheet opinion as of the end of the first partial or full fiscal year selling franchises.
(iii) The franchisor' third and subsequent fiscal years selling franchises.	All required financial statements for the previous fiscal year, plus any previously disclosed audited statements that still must be disclosed according to paragraphs (u)(1)(i) and (ii) of this section.

(iv) Start-up franchisors may phase-in the disclosure of audited financial statements, provided the franchisor:

(A) Prepares audited financial statements as soon as practicable.

(B) Prepares unaudited statements in a format that conforms as closely as possible to audited statements.

(C) Includes one or more years of unaudited financial statements or clearly and conspicuously discloses in this section that the franchisor has not been in business for three years or more, and cannot include all financial statements required in paragraphs (u)(1)(i) and (ii) of this section.

(v) Item 22: Contracts. Attach a copy of all proposed agreements regarding the franchise offering, including the franchise agreement and any lease, options, and purchase agreements.

(w) Item 23: Receipts. Include two copies of the following detachable acknowledgment of receipt in the following form as the last pages of the disclosure document:

(1) State the following:

Receipt

This disclosure document summarizes certain provisions of the franchise agreement and other information in plain language. Read this disclosure document and all agreements carefully.

If [name of franchisor] offers you a franchise, it must provide this disclosure document to you 14 calendar-days before you sign a binding agreement with, or make a payment to, the franchisor or an affiliate in connection with the proposed franchise sale.

If [name of franchisor] does not deliver this disclosure document on time or if it contains a false or misleading statement, or a material omission, a violation of federal law and state law may have occurred and should be reported to the Federal Trade Commission, Washington, D.C. 20580 and [state agency].

(2) Disclose the name, principal business address, and telephone number of each franchise seller offering the franchise.

(3) State the issuance date.

(4) If not disclosed in paragraph (a) of this section, state the name and address of the franchisor's registered agent authorized to receive service of process.

(5) State the following:

I received a disclosure document dated _____ that included the following Exhibits:

(6) List the title(s) of all attached Exhibits.

(7) Provide space for the prospective franchisee's signature and date.

(8) Franchisors may include any specific instructions for returning the receipt (for example, street address, email address, facsimile telephone number).

16 C.F.R. § 436.6   Instructions for preparing disclosure documents.

(a) It is an unfair or deceptive act or practice in violation of Section 5 of the FTC Act for any franchisor to fail to include the information and follow the instructions for preparing disclosure documents set forth in Subpart C (basic disclosure requirements) and Subpart D (updating requirements) of part 436. The Commission will enforce this provision according to the standards of liability under Sections 5, 13(b), and 19 of the FTC Act.

(b) Disclose all required information clearly, legibly, and concisely in a single document using plain English. The disclosures must be in a form that permits each prospective franchisee to store, download, print, or otherwise maintain the document for future reference.

(c) Respond fully to each disclosure Item. If a disclosure Item is not applicable, respond negatively, including a reference to the type of information required to be disclosed by the Item. Precede each disclosure Item with the appropriate heading.

(d) Do not include any materials or information other than those required or permitted by part 436 or by state law not preempted by part 436. For the sole purpose of enhancing the prospective franchisee's ability to maneuver through an electronic version of a disclosure document, the franchisor may include scroll bars, internal links, and search features. All other features (e.g., multimedia tools such as audio, video, animation, pop-up screens, or links to external information) are prohibited.

(e) Franchisors may prepare multi-state disclosure documents by including non-preempted, state-specific information in the text of the disclosure document or in Exhibits attached to the disclosure document.

(f) Subfranchisors shall disclose the required information about the franchisor, and, to the extent applicable, the same information concerning the subfranchisor.

(g) Before furnishing a disclosure document, the franchisor shall advise the prospective franchisee of the formats in which the disclosure document is made available, any prerequisites for obtaining the disclosure document in a particular format, and any conditions necessary for reviewing the disclosure document in a particular format.

(h) Franchisors shall retain, and make available to the Commission upon request, a sample copy of each materially different version of their disclosure documents for three years after the close of the fiscal year when it was last used.

(*i*) For each completed franchise sale, franchisors shall retain a copy of the signed receipt for at least three years.

16 C.F.R. § 436.7   Instructions for updating disclosures.

(a) All information in the disclosure document shall be current as of the close of the franchisor's most recent fiscal year. After the close of the fiscal year, the franchisor shall, within 120 days, prepare a revised disclosure document, after which a franchise seller may distribute only the revised document and no other disclosure document.

(b) The franchisor shall, within a reasonable time after the close of each quarter of the fiscal year, prepare revisions to be attached to the disclosure document to reflect any material change to the disclosures included, or required to be included, in the disclosure document. Each prospective franchisee shall receive the disclosure document and the quarterly revisions for the most recent period available at the time of disclosure.

(c) If applicable, the annual update shall include the franchisor's first quarterly update, either by incorporating the quarterly update information into the disclosure document itself, or through an addendum.

(d) When furnishing a disclosure document, the franchise seller shall notify the prospective franchisee of any material changes that the seller knows or should have known occurred in the information contained in any financial performance representation made in Item 19 (section 436.5(s)).

(e) Information that must be audited pursuant to § 436.5(u) of this part need not be audited for quarterly revisions; provided, however, that the franchisor states in immediate conjunction with the information that such information was not audited.

16 C.F.R. § 436.8   Exemptions.

(a) The provisions of part 436 shall not apply if the franchisor can establish any of the following:

(1) The total of the required payments, or commitments to make a required payment, to the franchisor or an affiliate that are made any time from before to within six months after commencing operation of the franchisee's business is less than $540.

(2) The franchise relationship is a fractional franchise.

(3) The franchise relationship is a leased department.

(4) The franchise relationship is covered by the Petroleum Marketing Practices Act, 15 U.S.C. 2801.

(5)(i) The franchisee's initial investment, excluding any financing received from the franchisor or an affiliate and excluding the cost of unimproved land, totals at least $1,084,900 and the prospective franchisee signs an acknowledgment verifying the grounds for the exemption. The acknowledgment shall state: "The franchise sale is for more than $1,084,900—excluding the cost of unimproved land and any financing received from the franchisor or an affiliate— and thus is exempted from the Federal Trade Commission's Franchise Rule disclosure requirements, pursuant to 16 CFR 436.8(a)(5)(i)";[28] or

(ii) The franchisee (or its parent or any affiliates) is an entity that has been in business for at least five years and has a net worth of at least $5,424,500.

(6) One or more purchasers of at least a 50% ownership interest in the franchise: within 60 days of the sale, has been, for at least two years, an officer, director, general partner, individual with management responsibility for the offer and sale of the franchisor's franchises or the administrator of the franchised network; or within 60 days of the sale, has been, for at least two years, an owner of at least a 25% interest in the franchisor.

(7) There is no written document that describes any material term or aspect of the relationship or arrangement.

(b) For purposes of the exemptions set forth in this section, the Commission shall adjust the size of the monetary thresholds every fourth year based upon the Consumer Price Index. For purposes of this section, "Consumer Price Index" means the Consumer Price Index for all urban consumers published by the Department of Labor.

[77 Fed. Reg. 36,150 (June 18, 2012)]

16 C.F.R. § 436.9   Additional prohibitions.

It is an unfair or deceptive act or practice in violation of Section 5 of the Federal Trade Commission Act for any franchise seller covered by part 436 to:

(a) Make any claim or representation, orally, visually, or in writing, that contradicts the information required to be disclosed by this part.

(b) Misrepresent that any person:

---

28 The large franchise exemption applies only if at least one individual prospective franchisee in an investor-group qualifies for the exemption by investing at the threshold level stated in this section.

(1) Purchased a franchise from the franchisor or operated a franchise of the type offered by the franchisor.

(2) Can provide an independent and reliable report about the franchise or the experiences of any current or former franchisees.

(c) Disseminate any financial performance representations to prospective franchisees unless the franchisor has a reasonable basis and written substantiation for the representation at the time the representation is made, and the representation is included in Item 19 (§ 436.5(s)) of the franchisor's disclosure document. In conjunction with any such financial performance representation, the franchise seller shall also:

(1) Disclose the information required by §§ 436.5(s)(3)(ii)(B) and (E) of this part if the representation relates to the past performance of the franchisor's outlets.

(2) Include a clear and conspicuous admonition that a new franchisee's individual financial results may differ from the result stated in the financial performance representation.

(d) Fail to make available to prospective franchisees, and to the Commission upon reasonable request, written substantiation for any financial performance representations made in Item 19 (§ 436.5(s)).

(e) Fail to furnish a copy of the franchisor's disclosure document to a prospective franchisee earlier in the sales process than required under § 436.2 of this part, upon reasonable request.

(f) Fail to furnish a copy of the franchisor's most recent disclosure document and any quarterly updates to a prospective franchisee, upon reasonable request, before the prospective franchisee signs a franchise agreement.

(g) Present for signing a franchise agreement in which the terms and conditions differ materially from those presented as an attachment to the disclosure document, unless the franchise seller informed the prospective franchisee of the differences at least seven days before execution of the franchise agreement.

(h) Disclaim or require a prospective franchisee to waive reliance on any representation made in the disclosure document or in its exhibits or amendments. Provided, however, that this provision is not intended to prevent a prospective franchisee from voluntarily waiving specific contract terms and conditions set forth in his or her disclosure document during the course of franchise sale negotiations.

(*i*) Fail to return any funds or deposits in accordance with any conditions disclosed in the franchisor's disclosure document, franchise agreement, or any related document.

16 C.F.R. § 436.10　Other laws and rules.

(a) The Commission does not approve or express any opinion on the legality of any matter a franchisor may be required to disclose by part 436. Further, franchisors may have additional obligations to impart material information to prospective franchisees outside of the disclosure document under Section 5 of the Federal Trade Commission Act. The Commission intends to enforce all applicable statutes and rules.

(b) The FTC does not intend to preempt the franchise practices laws of any state or local government, except to the extent of any inconsistency with part 436. A law is not inconsistent with part 436 if it affords prospective franchisees equal or greater protection, such as registration of disclosure documents or more extensive disclosures.

16 C.F.R. § 436.11　Severability.

If any provision of this part is stayed or held invalid, the remainder will stay in force.

Appendix A to Part 436—Sample Item 10 Table

SUMMARY OF FINANCING OFFERED

Item Financed	Source of Financing	Down Payment	Amount Financed	Term (Yrs)	Interest Rate	Monthly Payment	Prepay Penalty	Security Required	Liability Upon Default	Loss of Legal Right on Default
Initial Fee										
Land/Constr										
Leased Space										
Equip. Lease										
Equip. Purchase										
Opening Inventory										
Other Financing										

Appendix B to Part 436—Sample Item 20(1) Table

Systemwide Outlet Summary
For years 2004 to 2006

Column 1 Outlet Type	Column 2 Year	Column 3 Outlets at the Start of the Year	Column 4 Outlets at the End of the Year	Column 5 Net Change
Franchised	2004	859	1,062	+203
	2005	1,062	1,296	+234
	2006	1,296	2,720	+1,424
Company Owned	2004	125	145	+20
	2005	145	76	-69
	2006	76	141	+65
Total Outlets	2004	984	1,207	+223
	2005	1,207	1,372	+165
	2006	1,372	2,861	+1,489

Appendix C to Part 436—Sample Item 20(2) Table

Transfers of Franchised Outlets from Franchisees to New Owners (other than the Franchisor)
For years 2004 to 2006

Column 1 State	Column 2 Year	Column 3 Number of Transfers
NC	2004	1
	2005	0
	2006	2
SC	2004	0
	2005	0
	2006	2
Total	2004	1
	2005	0
	2006	4

Appendix D to Part 436—Sample Item 20(3) Table

Status of Franchise Outlets
For years 2004 to 2006

Column 1 State	Column 2 Year	Column 3 Outlets at Start of Year	Column 4 Outlets Opened	Column 5 Terminations	Column 6 Non-Renewals	Column 7 Reacquired by Franchisor	Column 8 Ceased Operations- Other Reasons	Column 9 Outlets at End of the Year
AL	2004	10	2	1	0	0	1	10
	2005	11	5	0	1	0	0	15
	2006	15	4	1	0	1	2	15
AZ	2004	20	5	0	0	0	0	25
	2005	25	4	1	0	0	2	26
	2006	26	4	0	0	0	0	30
Totals	2004	30	7	1	0	0	1	35
	2005	36	9	1	1	0	2	41
	2006	41	8	1	0	1	2	45

Appendix E to Part 436—Sample Item 20(4) Table

Status of Company-Owned Outlets
For years 2004 to 2006

Column 1 State	Column 2 Year	Column 3 Outlets at Start of Year	Column 4 Outlets Opened	Column 5 Outlets Reacquired From Franchisees	Column 6 Outlets Closed	Column 7 Outlets Sold to Franchisees	Column 8 Outlets at End of the Year
NY	2004	1	0	1	0	0	2
	2005	2	2	0	1	0	3
	2006	3	0	0	3	0	0
OR	2004	4	0	1	0	0	5
	2005	5	0	0	2	0	3
	2006	3	0	0	0	1	2
Totals	2004	5	0	2	0	0	7
	2005	7	2	0	3	0	6
	2006	6	0	0	3	1	2

Appendix F to Part 436—Sample Item 20(5) Table

Projected New Franchised Outlets
As of December 31, 2006

Column 1 State	Column 2 Franchise Agreements Signed But Outlet Not Opened	Column 3 Projected New Franchised Outlets in the Next Fiscal Year	Column 4 Projected New Company-Owned Outlets in the Current Fiscal Year
CO	2	3	1
NM	0	4	2
Total	2	7	3

A.8　FTC Business Opportunity Rule—16 C.F.R. § 437

16 C.F.R.

AUTHORITY: 15 U.S.C. 41–58.

SOURCE: 76 Fed. Reg. 76,860 (Dec. 8, 2011), unless otherwise noted.

16 C.F.R. § 437.1　Definitions.

The following definitions shall apply throughout this part:

(a) *Action* means a criminal information, indictment, or proceeding; a civil complaint, cross claim, counterclaim, or third party complaint in a judicial action or proceeding; arbitration; or any governmental administrative proceeding, including, but not limited to, an action to obtain or issue a cease and desist order, an assurance of voluntary compliance, and an assurance of discontinuance.

(b) *Affiliate* means an entity controlled by, controlling, or under common control with a business opportunity seller.

(c) *Business opportunity* means a commercial arrangement in which:

(1) A seller solicits a prospective purchaser to enter into a new business; and

(2) The prospective purchaser makes a required payment; and

(3) The seller, expressly or by implication, orally or in writing, represents that the seller or one or more designated persons will:

(i) Provide locations for the use or operation of equipment, displays, vending machines, or similar devices, owned, leased, controlled, or paid for by the purchaser; or

(ii) Provide outlets, accounts, or customers, including, but not limited to, Internet outlets, accounts, or customers, for the purchaser's goods or services; or

(iii) Buy back any or all of the goods or services that the purchaser makes, produces, fabricates, grows, breeds, modifies, or provides, including but not limited to providing payment for such services as, for example, stuffing envelopes from the purchaser's home.

(d) *Designated person* means any person, other than the seller, whose goods or services the seller suggests, recommends, or requires that the purchaser use in establishing or operating a new business.

(e) *Disclose* or *state* means to give information in writing that is clear and conspicuous, accurate, concise, and legible.

(f) *Earnings claim* means any oral, written, or visual representation to a prospective purchaser that conveys, expressly or by implication, a specific level or range of actual or potential sales, or gross or net income or profits. Earnings claims include, but are not limited to:

(1) Any chart, table, or mathematical calculation that demonstrates possible results based upon a combination of variables; and

(2) Any statements from which a prospective purchaser can reasonably infer that he or she will earn a minimum level of income (e.g., "earn enough to buy a Porsche," "earn a six-figure income," or "earn your investment back within one year").

(g) *Exclusive territory* means a specified geographic or other actual or implied marketing area in which the seller promises not to locate additional purchasers or offer the same or similar goods or services as the purchaser through alternative channels of distribution.

(h) *General media* means any instrumentality through which a person may communicate with the public, including, but not limited to, television, radio, print, Internet, billboard, Web site, commercial bulk email, and mobile communications.

(i) *Material* means likely to affect a person's choice of, or conduct regarding, goods or services.

(j) *New business* means a business in which the prospective purchaser is not currently engaged, or a new line or type of business.

(k) *Person* means an individual, group, association, limited or general partnership, corporation, or any other business entity.

(l) *Prior business* means:

(1) A business from which the seller acquired, directly or indirectly, the major portion of the business' assets; or

(2) Any business previously owned or operated by the seller, in whole or in part.

(m) *Providing locations, outlets, accounts, or customers* means furnishing the prospective purchaser with existing or potential locations, outlets, accounts, or customers; requiring, recommending, or suggesting one or more locators or lead generating companies; providing a list of locator or lead generating companies; collecting a fee on behalf of one or more locators or lead generating companies; offering to furnish a list of locations; or otherwise assisting the prospective purchaser in obtaining his or her own locations, outlets, accounts, or customers, *provided, however,* that advertising and general advice about business development and training shall not be considered as "providing locations, outlets, accounts, or customers."

(n) *Purchaser* means a person who buys a business opportunity.

(o) *Quarterly* means as of January 1, April 1, July 1, and October 1.

(p) *Required payment* means all consideration that the purchaser must pay to the seller or an affiliate, either by contract or by practical necessity, as a condition of obtaining or commencing operation of the business opportunity. Such payment may be made directly or indirectly through a third party. A required payment does not include payments for the purchase of reasonable amounts of inventory at bona fide wholesale prices for resale or lease.

(q) *Seller* means a person who offers for sale or sells a business opportunity.

(r) *Signature* or *signed* means a person's affirmative steps to authenticate his or her identity. It includes a person's handwritten signature, as well as an electronic or digital form of signature to the extent that such signature is recognized as a valid signature under applicable federal law or state contract law.

(s) *Written* or *in writing* means any document or information in printed form or in any form capable of being downloaded, printed, or otherwise preserved in tangible form and read. It includes: type-set, word processed, or handwritten documents; information on computer disk or CD–ROM; information sent via email; or information posted on the Internet. It does not include mere oral statements.

16 C.F.R. § 437.2　The obligation to furnish written documents.

In connection with the offer for sale, sale, or promotion of a business opportunity, it is a violation of this Rule and an unfair or deceptive act or practice in violation of Section 5 of the Federal Trade Commission Act ("FTC Act") for any seller to fail to furnish a prospective purchaser with the material information required by §§437.3(a) and 437.4(a) of this part in writing at least seven calendar days before the earlier of the time that the prospective purchaser:

(a) Signs any contract in connection with the business opportunity sale; or

(b) Makes a payment or provides other consideration to the seller, directly or indirectly through a third party.

16 C.F.R. § 437.3 The disclosure document.

In connection with the offer for sale, sale, or promotion of a business opportunity, it is a violation of this Rule and an unfair or deceptive act or practice in violation of Section 5 of the FTC Act, for any seller to:

(a) Fail to disclose to a prospective purchaser the following material information in a single written document in the form and using the language set forth in appendix A to this part; or if the offer for sale, sale, or promotion of a business opportunity is conducted in Spanish, in the form and using the language set forth in appendix B to this part; or if the offer for sale, sale, or promotion of a business opportunity is conducted in a language other than English or Spanish, using the form and an accurate translation of the language set forth in appendix A to this part:

(1) *Identifying information.* State the name, business address, and telephone number of the seller, the name of the salesperson offering the opportunity, and the date when the disclosure document is furnished to the prospective purchaser.

(2) *Earnings claims.* If the seller makes an earnings claim, check the "yes" box and attach the earnings statement required by §437.4. If not, check the "no" box.

(3) *Legal actions.*

(i) If any of the following persons has been the subject of any civil or criminal action for misrepresentation, fraud, securities law violations, or unfair or deceptive practices, including violations of any FTC Rule, within the 10 years immediately preceding the date that the business opportunity is offered, check the "yes" box:

(A) The seller;

(B) Any affiliate or prior business of the seller; or

(C) Any of the seller's officers, directors, sales managers, or any individual who occupies a position or performs a function similar to an officer, director, or sales manager of the seller.

(ii) If the "yes" box is checked, disclose all such actions in an attachment to the disclosure document. State the full caption of each action (names of the principal parties, case number, full name of court, and filing date). For each action, the seller may also provide a brief accurate statement not to exceed 100 words that describes the action.

(iii) If there are no actions to disclose, check the "no" box.

(4) *Cancellation or refund policy.* If the seller offers a refund or the right to cancel the purchase, check the "yes" box. If so, state all material terms and conditions of the refund or cancellation policy in an attachment to the disclosure document. If no refund or cancellation is offered, check the "no" box.

(5) *References.*

(i) State the name, state, and telephone number of all purchasers who purchased the business opportunity within the last three years. If more than 10 purchasers purchased the business opportunity within the last three years, the seller may limit the disclosure by stating the name, state, and telephone number of at least the 10 purchasers within the past three years who are located nearest to the prospective purchaser's location. Alternatively, a seller may furnish a prospective buyer with a list disclosing all purchasers nationwide within the last three years. If choosing this option, insert the words "See Attached List" without removing the list headings or the numbers 1 through 10, and attach a list of the references to the disclosure document.

(ii) Clearly and conspicuously, and in immediate conjunction with the list of references, state the following: "If you buy a business opportunity from the seller, your contact information can be disclosed in the future to other buyers."

(6) *Receipt.* Attach a duplicate copy of the disclosure document to be signed and dated by the purchaser. The seller may inform the prospective

purchaser how to return the signed receipt (for example, by sending to a street address, email address, or facsimile telephone number).

(b) Fail to update the disclosures required by paragraph (a) of this section at least quarterly to reflect any changes in the required information, including, but not limited to, any changes in the seller's refund or cancellation policy, or the list of references; *provided, however,* that until a seller has 10 purchasers, the list of references must be updated monthly.

16 C.F.R. § 437.4 Earnings claims.

In connection with the offer for sale, sale, or promotion of a business opportunity, it is a violation of this Rule and an unfair or deceptive act or practice in violation of Section 5 of the FTC Act, for the seller to:

(a) Make any earnings claim to a prospective purchaser, unless the seller:

(1) Has a reasonable basis for its claim at the time the claim is made;

(2) Has in its possession written materials that substantiate its claim at the time the claim is made;

(3) Makes the written substantiation available upon request to the prospective purchaser and to the Commission; and

(4) Furnishes to the prospective purchaser an earnings claim statement. The earnings claim statement shall be a single written document and shall state the following information:

(i) The title "EARNINGS CLAIM STATEMENT REQUIRED BY LAW" in capital, bold type letters;

(ii) The name of the person making the earnings claim and the date of the earnings claim;

(iii) The earnings claim;

(iv) The beginning and ending dates when the represented earnings were achieved;

(v) The number and percentage of all persons who purchased the business opportunity prior to the ending date in paragraph (a)(4)(iv) of this section who achieved at least the stated level of earnings;

(vi) Any characteristics of the purchasers who achieved at least the represented level of earnings, such as their location, that may differ materially from the characteristics of the prospective purchasers being offered the business opportunity; and

(vii) A statement that written substantiation for the earnings claim will be made available to the prospective purchaser upon request.

(b) Make any earnings claim in the general media, unless the seller:

(1) Has a reasonable basis for its claim at the time the claim is made;

(2) Has in its possession written material that substantiates its claim at the time the claim is made; and

(3) States in immediate conjunction with the claim:

(i) The beginning and ending dates when the represented earnings were achieved; and

(ii) The number and percentage of all persons who purchased the business opportunity prior to the ending date in paragraph (b)(3)(i) of this section who achieved at least the stated level of earnings.

(c) Disseminate industry financial, earnings, or performance information unless the seller has written substantiation demonstrating that the information reflects, or does not exceed, the typical or ordinary financial, earnings, or performance experience of purchasers of the business opportunity being offered for sale.

(d) Fail to notify any prospective purchaser in writing of any material changes affecting the relevance or reliability of the information contained in an earnings claim statement before the prospective purchaser signs any contract or makes a payment or provides other consideration to the seller, directly or indirectly, through a third party.

16 C.F.R. § 437.5 Sales conducted in Spanish or other languages besides English.

(a) If the seller conducts the offer for sale, sale, or promotion of a business opportunity in Spanish, the seller must provide the disclosure document required by §437.3(a) in the form and language set forth in appendix B to this part, and the disclosures required by §§437.3(a) and 437.4 must be made in Spanish.

(b) If the seller conducts the offer for sale, sale, or promotion of a business opportunity in a language other than English or Spanish, the seller must provide the disclosure document required by §437.3(a) using the form and an accurate translation of the language set forth in appendix A to this part, and the disclosures required by §§437.3(a) and 437.4 must be made in that language.

16 C.F.R. § 437.6   Other prohibited practices.

In connection with the offer for sale, sale, or promotion of a business opportunity, it is a violation of this part and an unfair or deceptive act or practice in violation of Section 5 of the FTC Act for any seller, directly or indirectly through a third party, to:

(a) Disclaim, or require a prospective purchaser to waive reliance on, any statement made in any document or attachment that is required or permitted to be disclosed under this Rule;

(b) Make any claim or representation, orally, visually, or in writing, that is inconsistent with or contradicts the information required to be disclosed by §§437.3 (basic disclosure document) and 437.4 (earnings claims document) of this Rule;

(c) Include in any disclosure document or earnings claim statement any materials or information other than what is explicitly required or permitted by this Rule. For the sole purpose of enhancing the prospective purchaser's ability to maneuver through an electronic version of a disclosure document or earnings statement, the seller may include scroll bars and internal links. All other features (e.g., multimedia tools such as audio, video, animation, or pop-up screens) are prohibited;

(d) Misrepresent the amount of sales, or gross or net income or profits a prospective purchaser may earn or that prior purchasers have earned;

(e) Misrepresent that any governmental entity, law, or regulation prohibits a seller from:

(1) Furnishing earnings information to a prospective purchaser; or

(2) Disclosing to prospective purchasers the identity of other purchasers of the business opportunity;

(f) Fail to make available to prospective purchasers, and to the Commission upon request, written substantiation for the seller's earnings claims;

(g) Misrepresent how or when commissions, bonuses, incentives, premiums, or other payments from the seller to the purchaser will be calculated or distributed;

(h) Misrepresent the cost, or the performance, efficacy, nature, or central characteristics of the business opportunity or the goods or services offered to a prospective purchaser;

(*i*) Misrepresent any material aspect of any assistance offered to a prospective purchaser;

(j) Misrepresent the likelihood that a seller, locator, or lead generator will find locations, outlets, accounts, or customers for the purchaser;

(k) Misrepresent any term or condition of the seller's refund or cancellation policies;

(*l*) Fail to provide a refund or cancellation when the purchaser has satisfied the terms and conditions disclosed pursuant to §437.3(a)(4);

(m) Misrepresent a business opportunity as an employment opportunity;

(n) Misrepresent the terms of any territorial exclusivity or territorial protection offered to a prospective purchaser;

(o) Assign to any purchaser a purported exclusive territory that, in fact, encompasses the same or overlapping areas already assigned to another purchaser;

(p) Misrepresent that any person, trademark or service mark holder, or governmental entity, directly or indirectly benefits from, sponsors, participates in, endorses, approves, authorizes, or is otherwise associated with the sale of the business opportunity or the goods or services sold through the business opportunity;

(q) Misrepresent that any person:

(1) Has purchased a business opportunity from the seller or has operated a business opportunity of the type offered by the seller; or

(2) Can provide an independent or reliable report about the business opportunity or the experiences of any current or former purchaser.

(r) Fail to disclose, with respect to any person identified as a purchaser or operator of a business opportunity offered by the seller:

(1) Any consideration promised or paid to such person. Consideration includes, but is not limited to, any payment, forgiveness of debt, or provision of equipment, services, or discounts to the person or to a third party on the person's behalf; or

(2) Any personal relationship or any past or present business relationship other than as the purchaser or operator of the business opportunity being offered by the seller.

16 C.F.R. § 437.7   Record retention.

To prevent the unfair and deceptive acts or practices specified in this Rule, business opportunity sellers and their principals must prepare, retain, and make available for inspection by Commission officials copies of the following documents for a period of three years:

(a) Each materially different version of all documents required by this Rule;

(b) Each purchaser's disclosure receipt;

(c) Each executed written contract with a purchaser; and

(d) All substantiation upon which the seller relies for each earnings claim from the time each such claim is made.

16 C.F.R. § 437.8   Franchise exemption.

The provisions of this Rule shall not apply to any business opportunity that constitutes a "franchise," as defined in the Franchise Rule, 16 CFR part 436; *provided, however,* that the provisions of this Rule shall apply to any such franchise if it is exempted from the provisions of part 436 because, either:

(a) Under §436.8(a)(1), the total of the required payments or commitments to make a required payment, to the franchisor or an affiliate that are made any time from before to within six months after commencing operation of the franchisee's business is less than $500, or

(b) Under §436.8(a)(7), there is no written document describing any material term or aspect of the relationship or arrangement.

16 C.F.R. § 437.9   Outstanding orders; preemption.

(a) A business opportunity required by prior FTC or court order to follow the Franchise Rule, 16 CFR part 436, may petition the Commission to amend the order or to stipulate to an amendment of the court order so that the business opportunity may follow the provisions of this part.

(b) The FTC does not intend to preempt the business opportunity sales practices laws of any state or local government, except to the extent of any conflict with this part. A law is not in conflict with this Rule if it affords prospective purchasers equal or greater protection, such as registration of disclosure documents or more extensive disclosures. All such disclosures, however, must be made in a separate state disclosure document.

16 C.F.R. § 437.10   Severability.

The provisions of this part are separate and severable from one another. If any provision is stayed or determined to be invalid, the remaining provisions shall continue in effect.

Appendix A to Part 437—Disclosure of Important Information About Business Opportunity

Required by the Federal Trade Commission, Rule 16 C.F.R. Part 437

Name of Seller: Address:

Phone: Salesperson: Date:

[Name of Seller] has completed this form, which provides important information about the business opportunity it is offering you. The Federal Trade Commission, an agency of the federal government, requires that [Name of Seller] complete this form and give it to you. However, the Federal Trade Commission has <u>not</u> seen this completed form or checked that the information is true. **Make sure that this information is the same as what the salesperson told you about this opportunity.**

LEGAL ACTIONS: Has [Name of Seller] or any of its key personnel been the subject of a civil or criminal action involving misrepresentation, fraud, securities law violation, or unfair or deceptive practices, including violations of any FTC Rule, within the past 10 years?

  ☐ **YES** → *If the answer is yes, [Name of Seller] must attach a list of all such legal actions to this form.*
  ☐ **NO**

CANCELLATION OR REFUND POLICY: Does [Name of Seller] offer a cancellation or refund policy?

  ☐ **YES** → *If the answer is yes, [Name of Seller] must attach a statement describing this policy to this form.*
  ☐ **NO**

EARNINGS: Has [Name of Seller] or its salesperson discussed how much money purchasers of this business opportunity can earn or have earned? In other words, have they stated or implied that purchasers can earn a specific level of sales, income, or profit?

  ☐ **YES** → *If the answer is yes, [Name of Seller] must attach an Earnings Claims Statement to this form. Read this statement carefully. You may wish to show this information to an advisor or accountant.*
  ☐ **NO**

REFERENCES: In the section below, [Name of Seller] must provide you with contact information for at least 10 people who have purchased a business opportunity from them. If fewer than 10 are listed, this is the total list of all purchasers. **You may wish to contact the people below to compare their experiences with what [Name of Seller] told you about the business opportunity.**

Note: If you purchase a business opportunity from [Name of Seller], your contact information can be disclosed in the future to other potential buyers.

Name	State	Telephone Number	Name	State	Telephone Number
1.			6.		
2.			7.		
3.			8.		
4.			9.		
5.			10		

Signature: _____   Date: _____

By signing above, you are acknowledging that you have received this form. This is <u>not</u> a purchase contract. To give you enough time to research this opportunity, the Federal Trade Commission requires that after you receive this form, [Name of Seller] must wait <u>at least seven calendar days</u> before asking you to sign a purchase contract or make any payments.

For more information about business opportunities in general: Visit the FTC's website at <u>www.ftc.gov/bizopps</u> or call 1-877-FTC-HELP (877-382-4357). You can also contact your state's Attorney General.

Appendix B to Part 437—Disclosure of Important Information About Business Opportunity

(Spanish-Language Version)

Formulario requerido por la Comisión Federal de Comercio (FTC)
Regla 16 de la Parte 437 del Código de Regulaciones Federales

Nombre del Vendedor: Domicilio:
Teléfono: Representante de Ventas: Fecha:

[Nombre del Vendedor] completó el presente formulario y en el mismo le suministra información importante sobre la oportunidad de negocio que le está ofreciendo. La Comisión Federal de Comercio (*Federal Trade Commission*, FTC), una agencia del gobierno federal, le requiere a la compañía [Nombre del Vendedor] que complete el presente formulario y que se lo entregue a usted. Pero la FTC no ha visto este formulario completado por la compañía ni ha verificado que la información indicada sea veraz. **Asegúrese de que la información contenida en el presente formulario coincida con lo que le dijo el representante de ventas respecto de esta oportunidad.**

ACCIONES LEGALES: ¿La compañía [Nombre del Vendedor] o alguno de los principales miembros de su personal ha sido sujeto de una acción civil o penal, que involucre falsedad, fraude, infracción de las leyes de títulos y valores, o prácticas desleales o engañosas, incluyendo infracciones de las Reglas o Normas de la FTC, dentro de los 10 últimos años?

❑ **SI** → *Si la respuesta es afirmativa, [Nombre del Vendedor] debe adjuntar al formulario una lista completa de dichas acciones legales.*

❑ **NO**

POLÍTICA DE CANCELACIÓN O REINTEGRO: ¿Ofrece [Nombre del Vendedor] una política de cancelación o reintegro?

❑ **SÍ** → *Si la respuesta es afirmativa, [Nombre del Vendedor] debe adjuntar al formulario una declaración con la descripción de dicha política.*

❑ **NO**

INGRESOS: ¿La compañía [Nombre del Vendedor] o alguno de sus representantes de ventas ha manifestado la cantidad de dinero que pueden ganar o que han ganado los compradores de esta oportunidad de negocio? ¿Dicho en otras palabras, han expresado de manera explícita o implícita que los compradores pueden alcanzar un nivel específico de ventas, o ganar un nivel específico de ingresos?

❑ **SÍ** → *Si la respuesta es afirmativa, [Nombre del Vendedor] debe adjuntar a este formulario una Declaración de los Ingresos Proclamados. Lea esta declaración atentamente. Puede que desee analizar esta información con un asesor o contador.*

❑ **NO**

REFERENCIAS: En esta sección del formulario, [Nombre del Vendedor] debe listar la información de contacto de por lo menos 10 personas que le hayan comprado una oportunidad de negocio. Si le suministran los datos de menos de 10 personas, es porque ésa es la lista completa de todos los compradores. **Puede que desee comunicarse con las personas listadas a continuación para comparar sus respectivas experiencias con lo que le dijo [Nombre del Vendedor] sobre la oportunidad de negocio que le está ofreciendo.**

Nota: Si usted compra una oportunidad de negocio de [Nombre del Vendedor], podrá divulgarse su información de contacto a otros posibles compradores.

Nombre	Estado	Número de Teléfono		Nombre	Estado	Número de Teléfono
1.			6.			
2.			7.			
3.			8.			
4.			9.			
5.			10.			

Firma: _____   Fecha: _____

Por medio de su firma, usted acusa recibo del presente formulario. Esto no es un contrato de compra. La Comisión Federal de Comercio (FTC) establece que con el fin de concederle el tiempo necesario para que usted investigue esta oportunidad, [Nombre del Vendedor] debe esperar un mínimo de siete días naturales o corridos a partir de la fecha en que le entregue este formulario antes de pedirle que firme un contrato de compra o que efectúe un pago.

Para más información sobre oportunidades de negocio en general: Visite el sitio Web de la FTC www.ftc.gov/bizopps o llame al 1-877-FTC-HELP (877-382-4357). Usted también puede establecer contacto con el Fiscal General de su estado de residencia.

A.9   FTC Credit Practices Rule

16 C.F.R.
§ 444.1   Definitions.
§ 444.2   Unfair credit practices.
§ 444.3   Unfair or deceptive cosigner practices.
§ 444.4   Late charges.
§ 444.5   State exemptions.

SOURCE: 49 Fed. Reg. 7789 (Mar. 1, 1984), unless otherwise noted.

AUTHORITY: Sec. 18(a), 88 Stat. 2193, *as amended by* 93 Stat. 95 (15 U.S.C. § 57a); 80 Stat. 383, *as amended by* 81 Stat. 54 (5 U.S.C. § 552).

16 C.F.R. § 444.1   Definitions.

(a) Lender. A person who engages in the business of lending money to consumers within the jurisdiction of the Federal Trade Commission.

(b) Retail installment seller. A person who sells goods or services to consumers on a deferred payment basis or pursuant to a lease-purchase arrangement within the jurisdiction of the Federal Trade Commission.

(c) Person. An individual corporation, or other business organization.

(d) Consumer. A natural person who seeks or acquires goods, services, or money for personal, family, or household use.

(e) Obligation. An agreement between a consumer and a lender or retail installment seller.

(f) Creditor. A lender or a retail installment seller.

(g) Debt. Money that is due or alleged to be due from one to another.

(h) Earnings. Compensation paid or payable to an individual or for his or her account for personal services rendered or to be rendered by him or her, whether denominated as wages, salary, commission, bonus, or otherwise, including periodic payments pursuant to a pension, retirement, or disability program.

(*i*) Household goods. Clothing, furniture, appliances, one radio and one television, linens, china, crockery, kitchenware, and personal effects (including wedding rings) of the consumer and his or her dependents, provided that the following are not included within the scope of the term *household goods*:

(1) Works of art;
(2) Electronic entertainment equipment (except one television and one radio);
(3) Items acquired as antiques; and
(4) Jewelry (except wedding rings).

(j) Antique. Any item over one hundred years of age, including such items that have been repaired or renovated without changing their original form or character.

(k) Cosigner. A natural person who renders himself or herself liable for the obligation of another person without compensation. The term shall include any person whose signature is requested as a condition to granting credit to another person, or as a condition for forbearance on collection of another person's obligation that is in default. The term shall not include a spouse whose signature is required on a credit obligation to perfect a security interest pursuant to state law. A person who does not receive goods, services, or money in return for a credit obligation does not receive compensation within the meaning of this definition. A person is a cosigner within the meaning of this definition whether or not he or she is designated as such on a credit obligation.

16 C.F.R. § 444.2   Unfair credit practices.

(a) In connection with the extension of credit to consumers in or affecting commerce, as commerce is defined in the Federal Trade Commission Act, it is an unfair act or practice within the meaning of Section 5 of that Act for a lender or retail installment seller directly or indirectly to take or receive from a consumer an obligation that:

(1) Constitutes or contains a cognovit or confession of judgment (for purposes other than executory process in the State of Louisiana), warrant of attorney, or other waiver of the right to notice and the opportunity to be heard in the event of suit or process thereon.

(2) Constitutes or contains an executory waiver or a limitation of exemption from attachment, execution, or other process on real or personal property held, owned by, or due to the consumer, unless the waiver applies solely to property subject to a security interest executed in connection with the obligation.

(3) Constitutes or contains an assignment of wages or other earnings unless:

(i) The assignment by its terms is revocable at the will of the debtor, or

(ii) The assignment is a payroll deduction plan or preauthorized payment plan, commencing at the time of the transaction, in which the consumer authorizes a series of wage deductions as a method of making each payment, or

(iii) The assignment applies only to wages or other earnings already earned at the time of the assignment.

(4) Constitutes or contains a nonpossessory security interest in household goods other than a purchase money security interest.

(b) [Reserved]

16 C.F.R. § 444.3   Unfair or deceptive cosigner practices.

(a) In connection with the extension of credit to consumers in or affecting commerce, as commerce is defined in the Federal Trade Commission Act, it is:

(1) A deceptive act or practice within the meaning of section 5 of that Act for a lender or retail installment seller, directly or indirectly, to misrepresent the nature or extent of cosigner liability to any person.

(2) An unfair act or practice within the meaning of section 5 of that Act for a lender or retail installment seller, directly or indirectly, to obligate a cosigner unless the cosigner is informed prior to becoming obligated, which in the case of open end credit shall mean prior to the time that the agreement creating the cosigner's liability for future charges is executed, of the nature of his or her liability as cosigner.

(b) Any lender or retail installment seller who complies with the preventive requirements in paragraph (c) of this section does not violate paragraph (a) of this section.

(c) To prevent these unfair or deceptive acts or practices, a disclosure, consisting of a separate document that shall contain the following statement and no other, shall be given to the cosigner prior to becoming obligated, which in the case of open end credit shall mean prior to the time that the agreement creating the cosigner's liability for future charges is executed:

NOTICE TO COSIGNER

You are being asked to guarantee this debt. Think carefully before you do. If the borrower doesn't pay the debt, you will have to. Be sure you can afford to pay if you have to, and that you want to accept this responsibility.

You may have to pay up to the full amount of the debt if the borrower does not pay. You may also have to pay late fees or collection costs, which increase this amount.

The creditor can collect this debt from you without first trying to collect from the borrower. The creditor can use the same collection methods against you that can be used against the borrower, such as suing you, garnishing your wages, etc. If this debt is ever in default, that fact may become a part of *your* credit record. This notice is not the contract that makes you liable for the debt.

16 C.F.R. § 444.4   Late charges.

(a) In connection with collecting a debt arising out of an extension of credit to a consumer in or affecting commerce, as commerce is defined in the Federal Trade Commission Act, it is an unfair act or practice within the meaning of section 5 of that Act for a creditor, directly or indirectly, to levy or collect any delinquency charge on a payment, which payment is otherwise a full payment for the applicable period and is paid on its due date or within an applicable grace period, when the only delinquency is attributable to late fee(s) or delinquency charge(s) assessed on earlier installment(s).

(b) For purposes of this section, *collecting a debt* means any activity other than the use of judicial process that is intended to bring about or does bring about repayment of all or part of a consumer debt.

16 C.F.R. § 444.5   State exemptions.

(a) If, upon application to the Federal Trade Commission by an appropriate State agency, the Federal Trade Commission determines that:

    (1) There is a State requirement or prohibition in effect that applies to any transaction to which a provision of this rule applies; and

    (2) The State requirement or prohibition affords a level of protection to consumers that is substantially equivalent to, or greater than, the protection afforded by this rule;

Then that provision of the rule will not be in effect in that State to the extent specified by the Federal Trade Commission in its determination, for as long as the State administers and enforces the State requirement or prohibition effectively.

(b) [Reserved]

A.10   FTC Funeral Industry Practices Rule

16 C.F.R.
§ 453.1   Definitions.
§ 453.2   Price disclosures.
§ 453.3   Misrepresentations.
§ 453.4   Required purchase of funeral goods or funeral services.
§ 453.5   Services provided without prior approval.
§ 453.6   Retention of documents.
§ 453.7   Comprehension of disclosures.
§ 453.8   Declaration of intent.
§ 453.9   State exemptions.

SOURCE: 59 Fed. Reg. 1611 (Jan. 11, 1994), unless otherwise noted.

AUTHORITY: 15 U.S.C. § 57a(a); 15 U.S.C. § 46(g); 5 U.S.C. § 552.

16 C.F.R. § 453.1   Definitions.

(a) Alternative container. An "alternative container" is an unfinished wood box or other non-metal receptacle or enclosure, without ornamentation or a fixed interior lining, which is designed for the encasement of human remains and which is made of fiberboard, pressed-wood, composition materials (with or without an outside covering) or like materials.

(b) Cash advance item. A "cash advance item" is any item of service or merchandise described to a purchaser as a "cash advance," "accommodation," "cash disbursement," or similar term. A cash advance item is also any item obtained from a third party and paid for by the funeral provider on the purchaser's behalf. Cash advance items may include, but are not limited to, the following items: cemetery or crematory services; pallbearers; public transportation; clergy honoraria; flowers; musicians or singers; nurses; obituary notices; gratuities and death certificates.

(c) Casket. A "casket" is a rigid container which is designed for the encasement of human remains and which is usually constructed of wood, metal, fiberglass, plastic or like material, and ornamented and lined with fabric.

(d) Commission. "Commission" refers to the Federal Trade Commission.

(e) Cremation. "Cremation" is a heating process which incinerates human remains.

(f) Crematory. A "crematory" is any person, partnership or corporation that performs cremation and sells funeral goods.

(g) Direct cremation. A "direct cremation" is a disposition of human remains by cremation, without formal viewing, visitation, or ceremony with the body present.

(h) Funeral goods. "Funeral goods" are the goods which are sold or offered for sale directly to the public for use in connection with funeral services.

(*i*) Funeral provider. A "funeral provider" is any person, partnership or corporation that sells or offers to sell funeral goods and funeral services to the public.

(j) Funeral services. "Funeral services" are any services which may be used to:

    (1) care for and prepare deceased human bodies for burial, cremation or other final disposition; and

    (2) arrange, supervise or conduct the funeral ceremony or the final disposition of deceased human bodies.

(k) Immediate burial. An "immediate burial" is a disposition of human remains by burial, without formal viewing, visitation, or ceremony with the body present, except for a grave-side service.

(*l*) Memorial service. A "memorial service" is a ceremony commemorating the deceased without the body present.

(m) Funeral ceremony. A "funeral ceremony" is a service commemorating the deceased with the body present.

(n) Outer burial container. An "outer burial container" is any container which is designed for placement in the grave around the casket including, but not limited to, containers commonly known as burial vaults, grave boxes, and grave liners.

(o) Person. A "person" is any individual, partnership, corporation, association, government or governmental subdivision or agency, or other entity.

(p) Services of funeral director and staff. The "services of funeral director and staff" are the services, not included in prices of other categories in § 453.2(b)(4) that are furnished by a funeral provider in arranging any funeral, such as conducting the arrangements conference, planning the funeral, obtaining necessary permits, and placing obituary notices.

16 C.F.R. § 453.2   Price disclosures.

(a) Unfair or deceptive acts or practices. In selling or offering to sell funeral goods or funeral services to the public, it is an unfair or deceptive act or practice for a funeral provider to fail to furnish accurate price information disclosing the cost to the purchaser for each of the specific funeral goods and funeral services used in connection with the disposition of deceased human bodies, including at least the price of embalming, transportation of remains, use of facilities, caskets, outer burial containers, immediate burials, or direct cremations, to persons inquiring about the purchase of funerals. Any funeral provider who complies with the preventive requirements in paragraph (b) of this section is not engaged in the unfair or deceptive acts or practices defined here.

(b) Preventive requirements. To prevent these unfair or deceptive acts or practices, as well as the unfair or deceptive acts or practices defined in § 453.4(b)(1), funeral providers must:

    (1) *Telephone price disclosures*. Tell persons who ask by telephone about the funeral provider's offerings or prices any accurate information from the price lists in paragraphs (b)(2) through (4) of this section and any other readily available information which reasonably answers the question.

(2) *Casket price list.*

(i) Give a printed or typewritten price list to people who inquire in person about the offerings or prices of caskets or alternative containers. The funeral provider must offer the list upon beginning discussion of, but in any event before showing caskets. The list must contain at least the retail prices of all caskets and alternative containers offered which do not require special ordering, enough information to identify each, and the effective date for the price list. In lieu of a written list, other formats, such as notebooks, brochures, or charts may be used if they contain the same information as would the printed or typewritten list, and display it in a clear and conspicuous manner. *Provided, however*, that funeral providers do not have to make a casket price list available if the funeral providers place on the general price list, specified in paragraph (b)(4) of this section, the information required by this section.

(ii) Place on the list, however produced, the name of the funeral provider's place of business and a caption describing the list as a "casket price list."

(3) *Outer burial container price list.*

(i) Give a printed or typewritten price list to persons who inquire in person about outer burial container offerings or prices. The funeral provider must offer the list upon beginning discussion of, but in any event before showing the containers. The list must contain at least the retail prices of all outer burial containers offered which do not require special ordering, enough information to identify each container, and the effective date for the prices listed. In lieu of a written list, the funeral provider may use other formats, such as notebooks, brochures, or charts, if they contain the same information as the printed or typewritten list, and display it in a clear and conspicuous manner. *Provided, however*, that funeral providers do not have to make an outer burial container price list available if the funeral providers place on the general price list, specified in paragraph (b)(4) of this section, the information required by this section.

(ii) Place on the list, however produced, the name of the funeral provider's place of business and a caption describing the list as an "outer burial container price list."

(4) *General price list.*

(i)(A) Give a printed or typewritten price list for retention to persons who inquire in person about the funeral goods, funeral services or prices of funeral goods or funeral services offered by the funeral provider. The funeral provider must give the list upon beginning discussion of any of the following:

(1) the prices of funeral goods or funeral services;

(2) the overall type of funeral service or disposition; or

(3) specific funeral goods or funeral services offered by the provider.

(B) The requirement in paragraph (b)(4)(i)(A) of this section applies whether the discussion takes place in the funeral home or elsewhere. *Provided, however*, that when the deceased is removed for transportation to the funeral home, an in-person request at that time for authorization to embalm, required by § 453.5(a)(2), does not, by itself, trigger the requirement to offer the general price list if the provider in seeking prior embalming approval discloses that embalming is not required by law except in certain special cases, if any. Any other discussion during that time about prices or the selection of funeral goods triggers the requirement under paragraph (b)(4)(i)(A) of this section to give consumers a general price list.

(C) The list required in paragraph (b)(4)(i)(A) of this section must contain at least the following information:

(1) the name, address, and telephone number of the funeral provider's place of business;

(2) a caption describing the list as a "general price list"; and

(3) the effective date for the price list;

(ii) Include on the price list, in any order, the retail prices (expressed either as the flat fee, or as the price per hour, mile or other unit of computation) and the other information specified below for at least each of the following items, if offered for sale:

(A) Forwarding of remains to another funeral home, together with a list of the services provided for any quoted price;

(B) Receiving remains from another funeral home, together with a list of the services provided for any quoted price;

(C) The price range for the direct cremations offered by the funeral provider, together with:

(1) A separate price for a direct cremation where the purchaser provides the container;

(2) separate prices for each direct cremation offered including an unfinished wood box or alternative container; and

(3) a description of the services and container (where applicable), included in each price;

(D) The price range for the immediate burials offered by the funeral provider, together with:

(1) A separate price for an immediate burial where the purchaser provides the casket;

(2) separate prices for each immediate burial offered including a casket or alternative container; and

(3) a description of the services and container (where applicable) included in that price;

(E) Transfer of remains to funeral home;

(F) Embalming;

(G) Other preparation of the body;

(H) Use of facilities and staff for viewing;

(I) Use of facilities and staff for funeral ceremony;

(J) Use of facilities and staff for memorial service;

(K) Use of equipment and staff for grave-side service;

(L) Hearse; and

(M) Limousine.

(iii) Include on the price list, in any order, the following information:

(A) Either of the following:

(1) the price range for the caskets offered by the funeral provider, together with the statement: "A complete price list will be provided at the funeral home."; or

(2) the prices of individual caskets, disclosed in the manner specified by paragraph (b)(2)(i) of this section; and

(B) Either of the following:

(1) the price range for the outer burial containers offered by the funeral provider, together with the statement: "A complete price list will be provided at the funeral home."; or

(2) the prices of individual outer burial containers, disclosed in the manner specified by paragraph (b)(3)(i) of this section; and

(C) Either of the following:

(1) the price for the basic services of funeral director and staff, together with a list of the principal basic services provided for any quoted price and, if the charge cannot be declined by the purchaser, the statement: "This fee for our basic services will be added to the total cost of the funeral arrangements you select. (This fee is already included in our charges for direct cremations, immediate burials, and forwarding or receiving remains.)". If the charge cannot be declined by the purchaser, the quoted price shall include all charges for the recovery of unallocated funeral provider overhead, and funeral providers may include in the required disclosure the phrase "and overhead" after the word "services"; or

(2) the following statement: "Please note that a fee of *(specify dollar amount)* for the use of our basic services is included in the price of our caskets. This same fee shall added to the total cost of your funeral arrangements if you provide the casket. Our services include (specify)." The fee shall include all charges for the recovery of unallocated funeral provider overhead, and the funeral providers may include in the required disclosure the phrase "and overhead" after the word "services." The statement must be placed on the general price list together with casket price range, required by paragraph (b)(4)(iii)(A)(1) of this section, or together with the prices of individual caskets, required by (b)(4)(iii)(A)(2) of this section.

(iv) The services fee permitted by § 453.2(b)(4)(iii)(C)(1) or (C)(2) is the only funeral provider fee for services, facilities or unallocated overhead permitted by this part to be non-declinable, unless otherwise required by law.

(5) *Statement of funeral goods and services selected.* (i) Give an itemized written statement for retention to each person who arranges a funeral or other disposition of human remains, at the conclusion of the discussion of arrangements. The statement must list at least the following information:

> **(A)** The funeral goods and funeral services selected by that person and the prices to be paid for each of them;
>
> **(B)** Specifically itemized cash advance items. (These prices must be given to the extent then known or reasonably ascertainable. If the prices are not known or reasonably ascertainable, a good faith estimate shall be given and a written statement of the actual charges shall be provided before the final bill is paid.); and
>
> **(C)** The total cost of the goods and services selected.

(ii) The information required by this paragraph (b)(5) of this section may be included on any contract, statement, or other document which the funeral provider would otherwise provide at the conclusion of discussion of arrangements.

(6) *Other pricing methods.* Funeral providers may give persons any other price information, in any other format, in addition to that required by paragraphs (b)(2), (3), and (4) of this section so long as the statement required by § 453.2(b)(5) is given when required by the rule.

16 C.F.R. § 453.3   Misrepresentations.

(a) Embalming Provisions—

(1) *Deceptive acts or practices.* In selling or offering to sell funeral goods or funeral services to the public, it is a deceptive act or practice for a funeral provider to:

> **(i)** Represent that State or local law requires that a deceased person be embalmed when such is not the case;
>
> **(ii)** Fail to disclose that embalming is not required by law except in certain special cases.

(2) *Preventive requirements.* To prevent these deceptive acts or practices, as well as the unfair or deceptive acts or practices defined in §§ 453.4(b)(1) and 453.5(2), funeral providers must:

> **(i)** Not represent that a deceased person is required to be embalmed for:
>
> > **(A)** Direct cremation;
> >
> > **(B)** Immediate burial; or
> >
> > **(C)** A closed casket funeral without viewing or visitation when refrigeration is available and when State or local law does not require embalming; and
>
> **(ii)** Place the following disclosure on the general price list, required by § 453.2(b)(4), in immediate conjunction with the price shown for embalming: "Except in certain special cases, embalming is not required by law. Embalming may be necessary, however, if you select certain funeral arrangements, such as a funeral with viewing. If you do not want embalming, you usually have the right to choose an arrangement that does not require you to pay for it, such as direct cremation or immediate burial." The phrase "except in certain special cases" need not be included in this disclosure if State or local law in the area(s) where the provider does business does not require embalming under any circumstances.

(b) Casket for cremation provisions.—

(1) *Deceptive acts or practices.* In selling or offering to sell funeral goods or funeral services to the public, it is a deceptive act or practice for a funeral provider to:

> **(i)** Represent that State or local law requires a casket for direct cremations;
>
> **(ii)** Represent that a casket is required for direct cremations.

(2) *Preventive requirements.* To prevent these deceptive acts or practices, as well as the unfair or deceptive acts or practices defined in § 453.4(a)(1), funeral providers must place the following disclosure in immediate conjunction with the price range shown for direct cremations: "If you want to arrange a direct cremation, you can use an alternative container. Alternative containers encase the body and can be made of materials like fiberboard or composition materials (with or without an outside covering). The containers we provide are (specify containers)." This disclosure only has to be placed on the general price list if the funeral provider arranges direct cremations.

(c) Outer burial container provisions—

(1) *Deceptive acts or practices.* In selling or offering to sell funeral goods and funeral services to the public, it is a deceptive act or practice for a funeral provider to:

> **(i)** Represent that State or local laws or regulations, or particular cemeteries, require outer burial containers when such is not the case;
>
> **(ii)** Fail to disclose to persons arranging funerals that State law does not require the purchase of an outer burial container.

(2) *Preventive requirement.* To prevent these deceptive acts or practices, funeral providers must place the following disclosure on the outer burial container price list, required by § 453.2(b)(3)(i), or, if the prices of outer burial containers are listed on the general price list, required by § 453.2(b)(4), in immediate conjunction with those prices: "In most areas of the country, State or local law does not require that you buy a container to surround the casket in the grave. However, many cemeteries ask that you have such a container so that the grave will not sink in. Either a grave liner or a burial vault will satisfy these requirements." The phrase "in most areas of the country" need not be included in this disclosure if State or local law in the area(s) where the provider does business does not require a container to surround the casket in the grave.

(d) General provisions on legal and cemetery requirements—

(1) *Deceptive acts or practices.* In selling or offering to sell funeral goods or funeral services to the public, it is a deceptive act or practice for funeral providers to represent that federal, state, or local laws, or particular cemeteries or crematories, require the purchase of any funeral goods or funeral services when such is not the case.

(2) *Preventive requirements.* To prevent these deceptive acts or practices, as well as the deceptive acts or practices identified in §§ 453.3(a)(1), 453.3(b)(1), and 453.3(c)(1), funeral providers must identify and briefly describe in writing on the statement of funeral goods and services selected (required by § 453.2(b)(5)) any legal, cemetery, or crematory requirement which the funeral provider represents to persons as compelling the purchase of funeral goods or funeral services for the funeral which that person is arranging.

(e) Provisions on preservative and protective value claims. In selling or offering to sell funeral goods or funeral services to the public, it is a deceptive act or practice for a funeral provider to:

(1) Represent that funeral goods or funeral services will delay the natural decomposition of human remains for a long-term or indefinite time;

(2) Represent that funeral goods have protective features or will protect the body from grave site substances, when such is not the case.

(f) Cash advance provisions—

(1) *Deceptive acts or practices.* In selling or offering to sell funeral goods or funeral services to the public, it is a deceptive act or practice for a funeral provider to:

(i) Represent that the price charged for a cash advance item is the same as the cost to the funeral provider for the item when such is not the case;

(ii) Fail to disclose to persons arranging funerals that the price being charged for a cash advance item is not the same as the cost to the funeral provider for the item when such is the case.

(2) *Preventive requirements.* To prevent these deceptive acts or practices, funeral providers must place the following sentence in the itemized statement of funeral goods and services selected, in immediate conjunction with the list of itemized cash advance items required by § 453.2(b)(5)(i)(B): "We charge you for our services in obtaining (specify cash advance items)," if the funeral provider makes a charge upon, or receives and retains a rebate, commission or trade or volume discount upon a cash advance item.

16 C.F.R. § 453.4   Required purchase of funeral goods or funeral services.

(a) Casket for cremation provisions—

(1) *Unfair or deceptive acts or practices.* In selling or offering to sell funeral goods or funeral services to the public, it is an unfair or deceptive act or practice for a funeral provider, or a crematory, to require that a casket be purchased for direct cremation.

(2) *Preventive requirement.* To prevent this unfair or deceptive act or practice, funeral providers must make an alternative container available for direct cremations, if they arrange direct cremations.

(b) Other required purchases of funeral goods or funeral services—

(1) *Unfair or deceptive acts or practices.* In selling or offering to sell funeral goods or funeral services, it is an unfair or deceptive act or practice for a funeral provider to:

(i) Condition the furnishing of any funeral good or funeral service to a person arranging a funeral upon the purchase of any other funeral good or funeral service, except as required by law or as otherwise permitted by this part;

(ii) Charge any fee as a condition to furnishing any funeral goods or funeral services to a person arranging a funeral, other than the fees for: (1) Services of funeral director and staff, permitted by § 453.2(b)(4)(iii)(C); (2) other funeral services and funeral goods selected by the purchaser; and (3) other funeral goods or services required to be purchased, as explained on the itemized statement in accordance with § 453.3(d)(2).

(2) *Preventive requirements.*

(i) To prevent these unfair or deceptive acts or practices, funeral providers must:

(A) Place the following disclosure in the general price list, immediately above the prices required by § 453.2(b)(4)(ii) and (iii): "The goods and services shown below are those we can provide to our customers. You may choose only the items you desire. If legal or other requirements mean you must buy any items you did not specifically ask for, we will explain the reason in writing on the statement we provide describing the funeral goods and services you selected." *Provided, however,* that if the charge for "services of funeral director and staff" cannot be declined by the purchaser, the statement shall include the sentence: "However, any funeral arrangements you select will include a charge for our basic services" between the second and third sentences of the statement specified above herein. The statement may include the phrase "and overhead" after the word "services" if the fee includes a charge for the recovery of unallocated funeral provider overhead;

(B) Place the following disclosure on the statement of funeral goods and services selected, required by § 453.2(b)(5)(i): "Charges are only for those items that you selected or that are required. If we are required by law or by a cemetery or

crematory to use any items, we will explain the reasons in writing below."

(ii) A funeral provider shall not violate this section by failing to comply with a request for a combination of goods or services which would be impossible, impractical, or excessively burdensome to provide.

16 C.F.R. § 453.5   Services provided without prior approval.

(a) Unfair or deceptive acts or practices. In selling or offering to sell funeral goods or funeral services to the public, it is an unfair or deceptive act or practice for any provider to embalm a deceased human body for a fee unless:

(1) State or local law or regulation requires embalming in the particular circumstances regardless of any funeral choice which the family might make; or

(2) Prior approval for embalming (expressly so described) has been obtained from a family member or other authorized person; or

(3) The funeral provider is unable to contact a family member or other authorized person after exercising due diligence, has no reason to believe the family does not want embalming performed, and obtains subsequent approval for embalming already performed (expressly so described). In seeking approval, the funeral provider must disclose that a fee will be charged if the family selects a funeral which requires embalming, such as a funeral with viewing, and that no fee will be charged if the family selects a service which does not require embalming, such as direct cremation or immediate burial.

(b) Preventive requirement. To prevent these unfair or deceptive acts or practices, funeral providers must include on the itemized statement of funeral goods and services selected, required by § 435.2(b)(5) the statement: "If you selected a funeral that may require embalming, such as a funeral with viewing, you may have to pay for embalming. You do not have to pay for embalming you did not approve if you selected arrangements such as a direct cremation or immediate burial. If we charged for embalming, we will explain why below."

16 C.F.R. § 453.6   Retention of documents.

To prevent the unfair or deceptive acts or practices specified in § 453.2 and § 453.3 of this rule, funeral providers must retain and make available for inspection by Commission officials true and accurate copies of the price lists specified in §§ 453.2(b)(2) through (4), as applicable, for at least one year after the date of their last distribution to customers, and a copy of each statement of funeral goods and services selected, as required by § 453.2(b)(5) for at least one year from the date of the arrangements conference.

16 C.F.R. § 453.7   Comprehension of disclosures.

To prevent the unfair or deceptive acts or practices specified in § 453.2 through § 453.5, funeral providers must make all disclosures required by those sections in a clear and conspicuous manner. Providers shall not include in the casket, outer burial container, and general price lists, required by §§ 453.2(b)(2)–(4), any statement or information that alters or contradicts the information required by this part to be included in those lists.

16 C.F.R. § 453.8   Declaration of intent.

(a) Except as otherwise provided in § 453.2(a), it is a violation of this rule to engage in any unfair or deceptive acts or practices specified in this rule, or to fail to comply with any of the preventive requirements specified in this rule;

(b) The provisions of this rule are separate and severable from one another. If any provision is determined to be invalid, it is the Commission's intention that the remaining provisions shall continue in effect.

(c) This rule shall not apply to the business of insurance or to acts in the conduct thereof.

16 C.F.R. § 453.9   State exemptions.

If, upon application to the Commission by an appropriate State agency, the Commission determines that:

(a) There is a State requirement in effect which applies to any transaction to which this rule applies; and

(b) That State requirement affords an overall level of protection to consumers which is as great as, or greater than, the protection afforded by this rule;

then the Commission's rule will not be in effect in that state to the extent specified by the Commission in its determination, for as long as the state administers and enforces effectively the state requirement.

A.11   FTC Used Car Rule

16 C.F.R.
§ 455.1   General duties of a used vehicle dealer; definitions.
§ 455.2   Consumer sales—window form.
§ 455.3   Window form.
§ 455.4   Contrary statements.
§ 455.5   Spanish language sales.
§ 455.6   State exemptions.
§ 455.7   Severability.

SOURCE: 49 Fed. Reg. 45,725 (Nov. 19, 1984), unless otherwise noted.

AUTHORITY: 15 U.S.C. § 2309; 15 U.S.C. §§ 41–58.

16 C.F.R. § 455.1   General duties of a used vehicle dealer; definitions.

(a) It is a deceptive act or practice for any used vehicle dealer, when that dealer sells or offers for sale a used vehicle in or affecting commerce as *commerce* is defined in the Federal Trade Commission Act:

   (1) To misrepresent the mechanical condition of a used vehicle;

   (2) To misrepresent the terms of any warranty offered in connection with the sale of a used vehicle; and

   (3) To represent that a used vehicle is sold with a warranty when the vehicle is sold without any warranty.

(b) It is an unfair act or practice for any used vehicle dealer, when that dealer sells or offers for sale a used vehicle in or affecting commerce as *commerce* is defined in the Federal Trade Commission Act:

   (1) To fail to disclose, prior to sale, that a used vehicle is sold without any warranty; and

   (2) To fail to make available, prior to sale, the terms of any written warranty offered in connection with the sale of a used vehicle.

(c) The Commission has adopted this Rule in order to prevent the unfair and deceptive acts or practices defined in paragraphs (a) and (b). It is a violation of this Rule for any used vehicle dealer to fail to comply with the requirements set forth in §§ 455.2 through 455.5 of this part. If a used vehicle dealer complies with the requirements of §§ 455.2 through 455.5 of this part, the dealer does not violate this Rule.

(d) The following definitions shall apply for purposes of this part:

   (1) *Vehicle* means any motorized vehicle, other than a motorcycle, with a gross vehicle weight rating (GVWR) of less than 8500 lbs., a curb weight of less than 6,000 lbs., and a frontal area of less than 46 sq. ft.

   (2) *Used vehicle* means any vehicle driven more than the limited use necessary in moving or road testing a new vehicle prior to delivery to a consumer, but does not include any vehicle sold only for scrap or parts (title documents surrendered to the state and a salvage certificate issued).

   (3) *Dealer* means any person or business which sells or offers for sale a used vehicle after selling or offering for sale five (5) or more used vehicles in the previous twelve months, but does not include a bank or financial institution, a business selling a used vehicle to an employee of that business, or a lessor selling a leased vehicle by or to that vehicle's lessee or to an employee of the lessee.

   (4) *Consumer* means any person who is not a used vehicle dealer.

   (5) *Warranty* means any undertaking in writing, in connection with the sale by a dealer of a used vehicle, to refund, repair, replace, maintain or take other action with respect to such used vehicle and provided at no extra charge beyond the price of the used vehicle.

   (6) *Implied warranty* means an implied warranty arising under state law (as modified by the Magnuson-Moss Act) in connection with the sale by a dealer of a used vehicle.

   (7) *Service contract* means a contract in writing for any period of time or any specific mileage to refund, repair, replace, or maintain a used vehicle and provided at an extra charge beyond the price of the used vehicle, provided that such contract is not regulated in your state as the business of insurance.

   (8) *You* means any dealer, or any agent or employee of a dealer, except where the term appears on the window form required by § 455.2(a).

16 C.F.R. § 455.2   Consumer sales—window form.

(a) General duty. Before you offer a used vehicle for sale to a consumer, you must prepare, fill in as applicable and display on that vehicle a "Buyers Guide" as required by this Rule.

   (1) The Buyers Guide shall be displayed prominently and conspicuously in any location on a vehicle and in such a fashion that both sides are readily readable. You may remove the form temporarily from the vehicle during any test drive, but you must return it as soon as the test drive is over.

   (2) The capitalization, punctuation and wording of all items, headings, and text on the form must be exactly as required by this Rule. The entire form must be printed in 100% black ink on a white stock no smaller than 11 inches high by 7 1/4 inches wide in the type styles, sizes and format indicated.

BUYERS GUIDE

28 pt Triumvirate Bold caps

2 pt Rule

IMPORTANT: Spoken promises are difficult to enforce. Ask the dealer to put all promises in writing. Keep this form.

10/12 Triumvirate Bold c & lc
flush left ragged right
maximum line 42 picas

_____   _____   _____   _____

VEHICLE MAKE   MODEL   YEAR   VIN NUMBER

10 pt Baseline Rule
6 pt Triumvirate Bold caps

_____

DEALER STOCK NUMBER (Optional)

10 pt Baseline Rule
6 pt Triumvirate Bold caps

WARRANTIES FOR THIS VEHICLE:

10 pt Triumvirate Bold caps

2 pt Rule

☐ **AS IS - NO WARRANTY**

54 pt Box
42 Pt Triumvirate Bold caps

YOU WILL PAY ALL COSTS FOR ANY REPAIRS. The dealer assumes no responsibility for any repairs regardless of any oral statements about the vehicle.

10/10 Triumvirate Bold c & lc
flush left ragged right
maximum line 42 picas

1 pt Rule

☐ **WARRANTY**

54 pt Box
42 pt Triumvirate Bold caps

☐ **FULL** ☐ **LIMITED WARRANTY. The dealer will pay _____% of the labor and _____% of the parts for the covered systems that fail during the warranty period. Ask the dealer for a copy of the warranty document for a full explanation of warranty coverage, exclusions, and the dealer's repair obligations. Under state law, "implied warranties" may give you even more rights.**

10/10 Triumvirate Bold c & lc
4½ picas indent on 2nd
line

SYSTEMS COVERED: **DURATION:**

10 pt Triumvirate Bold caps

10 pt Baseline Rile

_____   _____
_____   _____
_____   _____
_____   _____
_____   _____
_____   _____
_____   _____
_____   _____
_____   _____
_____   _____

☐ **SERVICE CONTRACT. A service contract is available at an extra charge on this vehicle. Ask for details as to coverage, deductable, price, and exclusions. If you buy a service contract within 90 days of the time of sale, state law "implied warranties" may give you additional rights.**

10/10 Triumvirate Bold c & lc
maximum line 42 picas

PRE PURCHASE INSPECTION: ASK THE DEALER IF YOU MAY HAVE THIS VEHICLE INSPECTED BY YOUR MECHANIC EITHER ON OR OFF THE LOT.

10/10 Triumvirate Bold caps
flush left ragged right
maximum line 42 picas

SEE THE BACK OF THIS FORM for important additional information, including a list of some major defects that may occur in used motor vehicles.

10/10 Triumvirate Bold c & lc
flush left ragged right
maximum line 42 picas

Below is a list of some major defects that may occur in used motor vehicles.

12 pt Triumvirate Bold lc
flush left ragged right
maximum line 42 pixas

2 pt Rule

8/9 Triumvirate Bold c & lc
flush left ragged right
maximum line 20 picas
1 em indent on 2nd line

Frame & Body
Frame-cracks, corrective welds, or rusted through
Dogtracks—bent or twisted frame

Engine
Oil leakage excluding normal seepage
Cracked block or head
Belts missing or inoperable
Knocks or misses related to camshaft lifters and
  push rods
Abnormal exhaust discharge

Transmission & Drive Shaft
Improper fluid level or leakage, excluding normal
  seepage
Cracked or damaged case which is visible
Abnormal noise or vibration caused by faulty
  transmission or drive shaft
Improper shifting or functioning in any gear
Manual clutch slips or chatters

Differential
Improper fluid level or leakage excluding normal
  seepage
Cracked or damaged housing which is visible
Abnormal noise of vibration caused by faulty
  differential

Cooling System
Leakage including radiator
Improperly functioning water pump

Electrical System
Battery leakage
Improperly functioning alternator, generator,
  battery, or starter

Fuel System
Visible leakage

Inoperable Accessories
Gauges or warning devices
Air conditioner
Heater & Defroster

Brake System
Failure warning light broken
Pedal not firm under pressure (DOT spec.)
Not enough pedal reserve (DOT spec.)
Does not stop vehicle in straight (DOT spec.)
Hoses damaged
Drum or rotor too thin (Mfgr Specs.)
Lining or pad thickness less than 1/32 inch
Power unit not operating or leaking
Structural or mechanical pans damaged

Steering System
Too much free play at steering wheel (DOT specs.)
Free play in linkage more than 1/4 inch
Steering gear binds or jams
Front wheels aligned improperly (DOT specs.)
Power unit belts cracked or slipping
Power unit fluid level improper

Suspension System
Ball joint seals damaged
Structural parts bent or damaged
Stabilizer bar disconnected
Spring broken
Shock absorber mounting loose
Rubber bushings damaged or missing
Radius rod damaged or missing
Shock absorber leaking or functioning improperly

Tires
Tread depth less than 2/32 inch
Sizes mismatched
Visible damage

Wheels
Visible cracks, damage, or repairs
Mounting bolts loose or missing

Exhaust System
Leakage

2 pt Rule

10 pt Baseline Rule
6 pt Triumvirate Bold caps

DEALER

ADDRESS

SEE FOR COMPLAINTS

2 pt Rule

10/12 Triumvirate Bold c & lc
maximum line 42 picas

IMPORTANT: The information on this form is part of any contract to buy this vehicle. Removal of this label before consumer purchase (except for purpose of test-driving) is a violation of federal law (16 C.F.R. 455).

When filling out the form, follow the directions in (b) through (e) of this section and § 455.4 of this part.

(b) Warranties—

(1) *No Implied Warranty—"As Is"/No Warranty.*

(i) If you offer the vehicle without any implied warranty, *i.e.,* "as is," mark the box provided. If you offer the vehicle with implied warranties only, substitute the disclosure specified below, and mark the box provided. If you first offer the vehicle "as is" or with implied warranties only but then sell it with a warranty, cross out the "As Is—No Warranty" or "Implied Warranties Only" disclosure, and fill in the warranty terms in accordance with paragraph (b)(2) of this section.

(ii) If your state law limits or prohibits "as is" sales of vehicles, that state law overrides this part and this rule does not give you the right to sell "as is." In such states, the heading "As Is—No Warranty" and the paragraph immediately accompanying that phrase must be deleted from the form, and the following heading and paragraph must be substituted. If you sell vehicles in states that permit "as is" sales, but you choose to offer implied warranties only, you must also use the following disclosure instead of "As Is—No Warranty":[29]

IMPLIED WARRANTIES ONLY

This means that the dealer does not make any specific promises to fix things that need repair when you buy the vehicle or after the time of sale. But, state law "implied warranties" may give you some rights to have the dealer take care of serious problems that were not apparent when you bought the vehicle.

(2) *Full/Limited Warranty.* If you offer the vehicle with a warranty, briefly describe the warranty terms in the space provided. This description must include the following warranty information:

(i) Whether the warranty offered is "Full" or "Limited."[30] Mark the box next to the appropriate designation.

(ii) Which of the specific systems are covered (for example, "engine, transmission, differential"). You cannot use shorthand, such as "drive train" or "power train" for covered systems.

(iii) The duration (for example, "30 days or 1,000 miles, whichever occurs first").

(iv) The percentage of the repair cost paid by you (for example, "The dealer will pay 100% of the labor and 100% of the parts.")

(v) If the vehicle is still under the manufacturer's original warranty, you may add the following paragraph below the "Full/ Limited Warranty" disclosure: MANUFACTURER'S WARRANTY STILL APPLIES. The manufacturer's original warranty has not expired on the vehicle. Consult the manufacturer's warranty booklet for details as to warranty coverage, service location, etc.

If, following negotiations, you and the buyer agree to changes in the warranty coverage, mark the changes on the form, as appropriate. If you first offer the vehicle with a warranty, but then sell it without one, cross out the offered warranty and mark either the "As Is—No Warranty" box or the "Implied Warranties Only" box, as appropriate.

(3) *Service contracts.* If you make a service contract (other than a contract that is regulated in your state as the business of insurance) available on the vehicle, you must add the following heading and paragraph below the "Full/Limited Warranty" disclosure and mark the box provided.[31]

[ ] Service Contract

---

29 See § 455.5 n.4 for the Spanish version of this disclosure.

30 A "Full" warranty is defined by the Federal Minimum Standards for Warranty set forth in 104 of the Magnuson-Moss Warranty Act, 15 U.S.C. 2304 (1975). The Magnuson-Moss Warranty Act does not apply to vehicles manufactured before July 4, 1975. Therefore, if you choose not to designate "Full" or "Limited" for such cars, cross out both designations, leaving only "Warranty".

31 See § 455.5 n.4 for the Spanish version of this disclosure.

A service contract is available at an extra charge on this vehicle. If you buy a service contract within 90 days of the time of sale, state law "implied warranties" may give you additional rights.

(c) Name and Address. Put the name and address of your dealership in the space provided. If you do not have a dealership, use the name and address of your place of business (for example, your service station) or your own name and home address.

(d) Make, Model, Model Year, VIN. Put the vehicle's make (for example, "Chevrolet"), model (for example, "Corvette"), model year, and Vehicle Identification Number (VIN) in the spaces provided. You may write the dealer stock number in the space provided or you may leave this space blank.

(e) Complaints. In the space provided, put the name and telephone number of the person who should be contacted if any complaints arise after sale.

(f) Optional Signature Line. In the space provided for the name of the individual to be contacted in the event of complaints after sale, you may include a signature line for a buyer's signature. If you opt to include a signature line, you must include a disclosure in immediate proximity to the signature line stating: "I hereby acknowledge receipt of the Buyers Guide at the closing of this sale." You may pre-print this language on the form if you choose.

[49 Fed. Reg. 45,725 (Nov. 19, 1984), *as amended at* 60 Fed. Reg. 62,205 (Dec. 5, 1995); 77 Fed. Reg. 73,912 (Dec. 12, 2012)]

16 C.F.R. § 455.3   Window form.

(a) Form given to buyer. Give the buyer of a used vehicle sold by you the window form displayed under § 455.2 containing all of the disclosures required by the Rule and reflecting the warranty coverage agreed upon. If you prefer, you may give the buyer a copy of the original, so long as that copy accurately reflects all of the disclosures required by the Rule and the warranty coverage agreed upon.

(b) Incorporated into contract. The information on the final version of the window form is incorporated into the contract of sale for each used vehicle you sell to a consumer. Information on the window form overrides any contrary provisions in the contract of sale. To inform the consumer of these facts, include the following language conspicuously in each consumer contract of sale:

The information you see on the window form for this vehicle is part of this contract. Information on the window form overrides any contrary provisions in the contract of sale.

16 C.F.R. § 455.4   Contrary statements.

You may not make any statements, oral or written, or take other actions which alter or contradict the disclosures required by §§ 455.2 and 455.3. You may negotiate over warranty coverage, as provided in § 455.2(b) of this part, as long as the final warranty terms are identified in the contract of sale and summarized on the copy of the window form you give to the buyer.

16 C.F.R. § 455.5   Spanish language sales.

If you conduct a sale in Spanish, the window form required by § 455.2 and the contract disclosures required by § 455.3 must be in that language. You may display on a vehicle both an English language window form and a Spanish language translation of that form. Use the following translation and layout for Spanish language sales:[32]

---

32 Use the following language for the "Implied Warranties Only" disclosure when required by § 455.2(b)(1):

Garantias implicitas solamente

Este termino significa que el concesionario no hace promesas especificas de arreglar lo que requiera reparacion cuando usted compra el vehiculo o despues del momento de la venta. Pero, las "garantias implicitas" de la ley estatal

GUÍA DEL COMPRADOR

IMPORTANTE: Las promesas verbales son difíciles de hacer cumplir. Solicite al concesionario que ponga todas las promesas por escrito. Conserve este formulario.

MARCA DEL VEHÍCULO   MODELO   AÑO   NÚMERO DE IDENTIFICACIÓN

NÚMERO DE ABASTO DEL DISTRIBUIDOR (Opcional)

GARANTÍAS PARA ESTE VEHÍCULO:

☐ COMO ESTÁ—SIN GARANTÍA

USTED PAGARÁ TODOS LOS GASTOS DE CUALQUIER REPARACIÓN QUE SEA NECESARIA. El concesionario no asume ninguna responsabilidad por cualquier reparación, independientemente de las declaraciones verbales que haya hecho acerca del vehículo.

☐ GARANTÍA

☐ **COMPLETA**   ☐ **LIMITADA.** El concesionario pagara el ___% de la mano de obra y ___% de los repuestos de los sistemas cubiertos que dejen de funcionar durante el período de garantía. Pida al concesionario una copia del documento de garantía donde se explican detalladamente la cobertura de la garantía, exclusiones y las obligaciones que tiene el concesionario de realizar reparaciones. Conforme a la ley estatal, las "garantías implícitas" pueden darle a usted incluso más derechos.

SISTEMAS CUBIERTOS POR LA GARANTÍA: **DURACIÓN:**

CONTRATO DE SERVICIO. Este vehículo tiene disponible un contrato de servicio a un precio adicional. Pida los detalles en cuanto a cobertura, deducible, precio y exclusiones. Si adquiere usted un contrato de servicio dentro de los 90 días del momento de la venta, las "garantías implícitas" de acuerdo a la ley del estado pueden concederle derechos adicionales.

INSPECCIÓN PREVIA A LA COMPRA: PREGUNTE AL CONCESIONARIO SI PUEDE USTED TRAER UN MECÁNICO PARA QUE INSPECCIONE EL AUTOMÓVIL O LLEVAR EL AUTOMÓVIL PARA QUE ESTE LO INSPECCIONE EN SU TALLER.

VÉASE EL DORSO DE ESTE FORMULARIO donde se proporciona información adicional importante, incluyendo una lista de algunos de los principales defectos que pueden ocurrir en vehículos usados.

GUÍA DEL COMPRADOR

IMPORTANTE: Las promesas verbales son difíciles de hacer cumplir. Solicite al concesionario que ponga todas las promesas por escrito. Conserve este formulario.

MARCA DEL VEHÍCULO   MODELO   AÑO   NÚMERO DE IDENTIFICACIÓN

NÚMERO DE ABASTO DEL DISTRIBUIDOR (Opcional)

GARANTÍAS PARA ESTE VEHÍCULO:

☐ GARANTÍAS IMPLÍCITAS SOLAMENTE

Este término significa que el concesionario no hace promesas específicas de arreglar lo que requiera reparación cuando usted compra el vehículo o después del momento de la venta. Pero, las "garantías implícitas" de la ley estatal pueden darle a usted algunos derechos y hacer que el concesionario resuelva problemas graves que no fueron evidentes cuando usted compró el vehículo.

☐ GARANTÍA

☐ COMPLETA   ☐ LIMITADA. El concesionario pagara el ___% de la mano de obra y ___% de los repuestos de los sistemas cubiertos que dejen de funcionar durante el período de garantía. Pida al concesionario una copia del documento de garantía donde se explican detalladamente la cobertura de la garantía, exclusiones y las obligaciones que tiene el concesionario de realizar reparaciones. Conforme a la ley estatal, las "garantías implícitas" pueden darle a usted incluso más derechos.

SISTEMAS CUBIERTOS POR LA GARANTÍA: DURACIÓN:

CONTRATO DE SERVICIO. Este vehículo tiene disponible un contrato de servicio a un precio adicional. Pida los detalles en cuanto a cobertura, deducible, precio y exclusiones. Si adquiere usted un contrato de servicio dentro de los 90 días del momento de la venta, las "garantías implícitas" de acuerdo a la ley del estado pueden concederle derechos adicionales.

INSPECCIÓN PREVIA A LA COMPRA: PREGUNTE AL CONCESIONARIO SI PUEDE USTED TRAER UN MECÁNICO PARA QUE INSPECCIONE EL AUTOMÓVIL O LLEVAR EL AUTOMÓVIL PARA QUE ESTE LO INSPECCIONE EN SU TALLER.

VÉASE EL DORSO DE ESTE FORMULARIO donde se proporciona información adicional importante, incluyendo una lista de algunos de los principales defectos que pueden ocurrir en vehículos usados.

A continuación presentamos una lista de algunos de los principales defectos que pueden ocurrir en vehículos usados.

Chasis y carrocería
Grietas en el chasis, soldaduras correctivas u oxidadas
Chasis doblado o torcido

Motor
Fuga de aceite, excluyendo el escape normal
Bloque o tapa de recámara agrietados
Correas que faltan o no funcionan
Fallo o pistoneo
Emisión excesiva de humo por el sistema de escape

Transmisión y eje de cardán
Nivel de líquido inadecuado o fuga, excluyendo filtración normal
Cubierta agrietada o visiblemente dañada
Vibración o ruido anormal ocasionado por una transmisión o eje de cardán defectuoso
Cambio de marchas o funcionamiento inadecuado en cualquier marcha
Embrague manual patina o vibra

Diferencial
Nivel de líquido inadecuado o fuga excluyendo filtración normal
Cubierta agrietada o visiblemente dañada
Ruido o vibración anormal ocasionado por diferencial defectuoso

Sistema de enfriamiento
Fuga, incluído el radiador
Bomba de agua defectuosa

Sistema eléctrico
Fuga en las baterías
Alternador, generador, batería, o motor de arranque defectuosos

Sistema de combustible
Escape visible de combustible

Accesorios averiados
Indicadores o medidores del cuadro de instrumentos
Aire acondicionado
Calefactor y Desempañador

Sistema de frenos
Luz de advertencia de falla dañada
Pedal no firme bajo presión (Especif. del Dpto. de Transp.)
Distancia insuficiente del pedal (Especif. del Dpto. de Transp.)
No detiene el vehículo en línea recta (Especif. del Dpto. de Transp.)
Conductos dañados
Tambor o disco muy delgados (Especif. del fabricante)
Grosor de las bandas de los frenos menor de 1/32 de pulgada
Sistema de servofreno dañado o con escape
Partes estructurales o mecánicas dañadas

Sistema de dirección
Juego excesivo en el volante (Especif. del Dpto. de Transp.)
Juego en el varillaje en exceso de 1/4 pulgada
Engranaje del volante de dirección se agarrota
Ruedas delanteras mal alineadas (Especif. del Dpto. de Transp.)
Correas del sistema de servodirección agrietadas o flojas
Nivel del líquido del sistema de servodirección inadecuado

Sistema de suspensión
Sellos de conexión de rodamientos defectuosos
Piezas estructurales dobladas o dañadas
Barra de estabilización desconectada
Resorte roto
Montura del amortiguador floja
Bujes de goma dañadas o ausentes
Estabilizador para curvas dañadas o ausente
Amortiguador tiene fuga o funciona defectuosamente

Llantas
Profundidad de la banda de rodamiento menor de 2/32 de pulgada
Diferentes tamaños de llanta
Daños visibles

Ruedas
Grietas visibles, daños o reparaciones
Pernos de montaje sueltos o ausentes

Sistema de Escape
Fuga

CONCESIONARIO

DIRECCIÓN

VÉASE PARA RECLAMACIONES

IMPORTANTE: La información contenida en este formulario forma parte de todo contrato de compra de este vehículo. Constituye una contravención de la ley federal (16 C.F.R. 455) quitar este rótulo antes de la compra del vehículo por el consumidor (salvo para conducir el automóvil en calidad de prueba).

[*Editor's note*: For the version of the Spanish language Buyer's Guide that includes the type size and font specification requirements for each line, please see the version published in the *Federal Register* at 77 Fed. Reg. 73,914, 73,915 (Dec. 12, 2012). This version is also available online as companion material to this treatise.]

16 C.F.R. § 455.6   State exemptions.

(a) If, upon application to the Commission by an appropriate state agency, the Commission determines, that—

> pueden darle a usted algunos derechos y hacer que el vendedor resuelva problemas graves que no fueron evidentes cuando usted compro el vehiculo.

Use the following language for the "Service Contract" disclosure required by § 455.2(b)(3):

> CONTRATO DE SERVICIO. Este vehiculo tiene disponible un contrato de servicio a un precio adicional. Pida los detalles en cuanto a cobertura, deducible, precio y exclusiones. Si adquiere usted un contrato de servicio dentro de los 90 dias del momento de la venta, las "garantias implicitas" de acuerdo a la ley del estado pueden concederle derechos adicionales.

(1) There is a state requirement in effect which applies to any transaction to which this rule applies; and

(2) That state requirement affords an overall level of protection to consumers which is as great as, or greater than, the protection afforded by this Rule; then the Commission's Rule will not be in effect in that state to the extent specified by the Commission in its determination, for as long as the State administers and enforces effectively the state requirement.

(b) Applications for exemption under Subsection (a) should be directed to the Secretary of the Commission. When appropriate, proceedings will be commenced in order to make a determination described in paragraph (a) of this section, and will be conducted in accordance with Subpart C of Part 1 of the Commission's Rules of Practice.

16 C.F.R. § 455.7   Severability.

The provisions of this part are separate and severable from one another. If any provision is determined to be invalid, it is the Commission's intention that the remaining provisions shall continue in effect.

Appendix B   Selected Consumer Financial Protection Act Provisions

This appendix includes statutory material relevant to the rule-writing authority of the Consumer Financial Protection Bureau (CFPB) regarding consumer financial services, focusing on three new types of rules that the CFPB may issue: rules prohibiting unfair, deceptive, or abusive acts or practices (discussed at § 3.2, *supra*); rules requiring certain disclosures (discussed at § 3.5, *supra*); and rules providing for consumers' right to obtain certain information (discussed at § 3.6, *supra*). As of late 2015, the CFPB has not issued any rules in these three areas. This appendix will include such rules when enacted.

As of July 21, 2011, rulemaking authority over many existing regulations has been transferred to the CFPB from the Federal Reserve Board, the Department of Housing and Urban Development, and other federal agencies, interpreting what are called the "enumerated statutes." Most of these rules interpreting enumerated statutes already are analyzed in other NCLC treatises (for example, Regulation Z is detailed in NCLC's *Truth in Lending*), and these rules are not discussed in this treatise or reprinted in this appendix. CFPB rules under the enumerated statutes are listed at § 3.1.2, *supra*, and found at 12 C.F.R. § 1002–1090.

The online version of this treatise under Primary Sources includes other material related to the CFPB. This material can be searched and also downloaded, printed, or even emailed.

12 U.S.C.

* * *

§ 5481   Definitions

* * *

§ 5512   Rulemaking authority

* * *

§ 5514   Supervision of nondepository covered persons
§ 5515   Supervision of very large banks, savings associations, and credit unions
§ 5516   Other banks, savings associations, and credit unions
§ 5517   Limitations on authorities of the Bureau; preservation of authorities

* * *

§ 5519   Exclusion for auto dealers

* * *

§ 5531   Prohibiting unfair, deceptive, or abusive acts or practices
§ 5532   Disclosures
§ 5533   Consumer rights to access information

* * *

§ 5551   Relation to State law
§ 5552   Preservation of enforcement powers of States

* * *

12 U.S.C. § 5481.   Definitions

Except as otherwise provided in this title, for purposes of this title, the following definitions shall apply:

* * *

(5) Consumer financial product or service

The term "consumer financial product or service" means any financial product or service that is described in one or more categories under—

> **(A)** paragraph (15) and is offered or provided for use by consumers primarily for personal, family, or household purposes; or
> **(B)** clause (i), (iii), (ix), or (x) of paragraph (15)(A), and is delivered, offered, or provided in connection with a consumer financial product or service referred to in subparagraph (A).

(6) Covered person

The term "covered person" means—

> **(A)** any person that engages in offering or providing a consumer financial product or service; and
> **(B)** any affiliate of a person described in subparagraph (A) if such affiliate acts as a service provider to such person.

(7) Credit

The term "credit" means the right granted by a person to a consumer to defer payment of a debt, incur debt and defer its payment, or purchase property or services and defer payment for such purchase.

* * *

(12) Enumerated consumer laws

Except as otherwise specifically provided in section 5519 of this title, subtitle G or subtitle H, the term "enumerated consumer laws" means—

> **(A)** the Alternative Mortgage Transaction Parity Act of 1982 (12 U.S.C. 3801 *et seq.*);
> **(B)** the Consumer Leasing Act of 1976 (15 U.S.C. 1667 *et seq.*);
> **(C)** the Electronic Fund Transfer Act (15 U.S.C. 1693 *et seq.*), except with respect to section 920 of that Act [15 U.S.C. 1693*o*–2];
> **(D)** the Equal Credit Opportunity Act (15 U.S.C. 1691 *et seq.*);
> **(E)** the Fair Credit Billing Act (15 U.S.C. 1666 *et seq.*);
> **(F)** the Fair Credit Reporting Act (15 U.S.C. 1681 *et seq.*), except with respect to sections 615(e) and 628 of that Act (15 U.S.C. 1681m(e), 1681w);
> **(G)** the Home Owners[1] Protection Act of 1998 (12 U.S.C. 4901 *et seq.*);
> **(H)** the Fair Debt Collection Practices Act (15 U.S.C. 1692 *et seq.*);
> **(I)** subsections (b) through (f) of section 43 of the Federal Deposit Insurance Act (12 U.S.C. 1831t(c)[(b)]–(f));
> **(J)** sections 502 through 509 of the Gramm-Leach-Bliley Act (15 U.S.C. 6802–6809) except for section 505 [15 U.S.C. 6805] as it applies to section 501(b) [15 U.S.C. 6801(b)];
> **(K)** the Home Mortgage Disclosure Act of 1975 (12 U.S.C. 2801 *et seq.*);
> **(L)** the Home Ownership and Equity Protection Act of 1994 (15 U.S.C. 1601 note);
> **(M)** the Real Estate Settlement Procedures Act of 1974 (12 U.S.C. 2601 *et seq.*);
> **(N)** the S.A.F.E. Mortgage Licensing Act of 2008 (12 U.S.C. 5101 *et seq.*);
> **(O)** the Truth in Lending Act (15 U.S.C. 1601 *et seq.*);
> **(P)** the Truth in Savings Act (12 U.S.C. 4301 *et seq.*);
> **(Q)** section 626 of the Omnibus Appropriations Act, 2009 (Public Law 111–8) [12 U.S.C. 5538]; and
> **(R)** the Interstate Land Sales Full Disclosure Act (15 U.S.C. 1701).

---

1   *Editor's note:* So in original. Probably should be "Homeowners".

* * *

(15) Financial product or service

(A) In general

The term "financial product or service" means—

(i) extending credit and servicing loans, including acquiring, purchasing, selling, brokering, or other extensions of credit (other than solely extending commercial credit to a person who originates consumer credit transactions);

(ii) extending or brokering leases of personal or real property that are the functional equivalent of purchase finance arrangements, if—

(I) the lease is on a non-operating basis;

(II) the initial term of the lease is at least 90 days; and

(III) in the case of a lease involving real property, at the inception of the initial lease, the transaction is intended to result in ownership of the leased property to be transferred to the lessee, subject to standards prescribed by the Bureau;

(iii) providing real estate settlement services, except such services excluded under subparagraph (C), or performing appraisals of real estate or personal property;

(iv) engaging in deposit-taking activities, transmitting or exchanging funds, or otherwise acting as a custodian of funds or any financial instrument for use by or on behalf of a consumer;

(v) selling, providing, or issuing stored value or payment instruments, except that, in the case of a sale of, or transaction to reload, stored value, only if the seller exercises substantial control over the terms or conditions of the stored value provided to the consumer where, for purposes of this clause—

(I) a seller shall not be found to exercise substantial control over the terms or conditions of the stored value if the seller is not a party to the contract with the consumer for the stored value product, and another person is principally responsible for establishing the terms or conditions of the stored value; and

(II) advertising the nonfinancial goods or services of the seller on the stored value card or device is not in itself an exercise of substantial control over the terms or conditions;

(vi) providing check cashing, check collection, or check guaranty services;

(vii) providing payments or other financial data processing products or services to a consumer by any technological means, including processing or storing financial or banking data for any payment instrument, or through any payments systems or network used for processing payments data, including payments made through an online banking system or mobile telecommunications network, except that a person shall not be deemed to be a covered person with respect to financial data processing solely because the person—

(I) is a merchant, retailer, or seller of any nonfinancial good or service who engages in financial data processing by transmitting or storing payments data about a consumer exclusively for purpose of initiating payments instructions by the consumer to pay such person for the purchase of, or to complete a commercial transaction for, such nonfinancial good or service sold directly by such person to the consumer; or

(II) provides access to a host server to a person for purposes of enabling that person to establish and maintain a website;

(viii) providing financial advisory services (other than services relating to securities provided by a person regulated by the Commission or a person regulated by a State securities Commission, but only to the extent that such person acts in a regulated capacity) to consumers on individual financial matters or relating to proprietary financial products or services (other than by publishing any bona fide newspaper, news magazine, or business or financial publication of general and regular circulation, including publishing market data, news, or data analytics or investment information or recommendations that are not tailored to the individual needs of a particular consumer), including—

(I) providing credit counseling to any consumer; and

(II) providing services to assist a consumer with debt management or debt settlement, modifying the terms of any extension of credit, or avoiding foreclosure;

(ix) collecting, analyzing, maintaining, or providing consumer report information or other account information, including information relating to the credit history of consumers, used or expected to be used in connection with any decision regarding the offering or provision of a consumer financial product or service, except to the extent that—

(I) a person—

(aa) collects, analyzes, or maintains information that relates solely to the transactions between a consumer and such person;

(bb) provides the information described in item (aa) to an affiliate of such person; or

(cc) provides information that is used or expected to be used solely in any decision regarding the offering or provision of a product or service that is not a consumer financial product or service, including a decision for employment, government licensing, or a residential lease or tenancy involving a consumer; and

(II) the information described in subclause (I)(aa) is not used by such person or affiliate in connection with any decision regarding the offering or provision of a consumer financial product or service to the consumer, other than credit described in section 5517(a)(2)(A) of this title;

(x) collecting debt related to any consumer financial product or service; and

(xi) such other financial product or service as may be defined by the Bureau, by regulation, for purposes of this title, if the Bureau finds that such financial product or service is—

(I) entered into or conducted as a subterfuge or with a purpose to evade any Federal consumer financial law; or

(II) permissible for a bank or for a financial holding company to offer or to provide under any provision of a Federal law or regulation applicable to a bank or a financial holding company, and has, or likely will have, a material impact on consumers.

(B) Rule of construction

(i) In general

For purposes of subparagraph (A)(xi)(II), and subject to clause (ii) of this subparagraph, the following activities provided to a covered person shall not, for purposes of this title, be considered incidental or complementary to a financial activity permissible for a financial holding company to engage in under any provision of a Federal law or regulation applicable to a financial holding company:

(I) Providing information products or services to a covered person for identity authentication.

(II) Providing information products or services for fraud or identify theft detection, prevention, or investigation.

(III) Providing document retrieval or delivery services.

(IV) Providing public records information retrieval.

(V) Providing information products or services for anti-money laundering activities.

(ii) Limitation

Nothing in clause (i) may be construed as modifying or limiting the authority of the Bureau to exercise any—

(I) examination or enforcement powers authority under this title with respect to a covered person or service provider engaging in an activity described in subparagraph (A)(ix); or

(II) powers authorized by this title to prescribe rules, issue orders, or take other actions under any enumerated consumer law or law for which the authorities are transferred under subtitle F or H.

(C) Exclusions
The term "financial product or service" does not include—
    (i) the business of insurance; or
    (ii) electronic conduit services.

* * *

(26) Service provider
    (A) In general
    The term "service provider" means any person that provides a material service to a covered person in connection with the offering or provision by such covered person of a consumer financial product or service, including a person that—
        (i) participates in designing, operating, or maintaining the consumer financial product or service; or
        (ii) processes transactions relating to the consumer financial product or service (other than unknowingly or incidentally transmitting or processing financial data in a manner that such data is undifferentiated from other types of data of the same form as the person transmits or processes).
    (B) Exceptions
    The term "service provider" does not include a person solely by virtue of such person offering or providing to a covered person—
        (i) a support service of a type provided to businesses generally or a similar ministerial service; or
        (ii) time or space for an advertisement for a consumer financial product or service through print, newspaper, or electronic media.
    (C) Rule of construction
    A person that is a service provider shall be deemed to be a covered person to the extent that such person engages in the offering or provision of its own consumer financial product or service.

* * *

[Pub. L. No. 111–203, tit. X, § 1002, 124 Stat. 1955 (July 21, 2010).]

* * *

12 U.S.C. § 5512.   Rulemaking authority

(a) In general
The Bureau is authorized to exercise its authorities under Federal consumer financial law to administer, enforce, and otherwise implement the provisions of Federal consumer financial law.

(b) Rulemaking, orders, and guidance
    (1) General authority
    The Director may prescribe rules and issue orders and guidance, as may be necessary or appropriate to enable the Bureau to administer and carry out the purposes and objectives of the Federal consumer financial laws, and to prevent evasions thereof.
    (2) Standards for rulemaking
    In prescribing a rule under the Federal consumer financial laws—
        (A) the Bureau shall consider—
            (i) the potential benefits and costs to consumers and covered persons, including the potential reduction of access by consumers to consumer financial products or services resulting from such rule; and
            (ii) the impact of proposed rules on covered persons, as described in section 5516 of this title, and the impact on consumers in rural areas;
        (B) the Bureau shall consult with the appropriate prudential regulators or other Federal agencies prior to proposing a rule and during the comment process regarding consistency with prudential, market, or systemic objectives administered by such agencies; and
        (C) if, during the consultation process described in subparagraph (B), a prudential regulator provides the Bureau with a written objection to the proposed rule of the Bureau or a portion thereof, the Bureau shall include in the adopting release a description of the objection and the basis for the Bureau decision, if any, regarding such objection, except that nothing in this clause shall be construed as altering or limiting the procedures under section 5513 of this title that may apply to any rule prescribed by the Bureau.
    (3) Exemptions
        (A) In general
        The Bureau, by rule, may conditionally or unconditionally exempt any class of covered persons, service providers, or consumer financial products or services, from any provision of this title, or from any rule issued under this title, as the Bureau determines necessary or appropriate to carry out the purposes and objectives of this title, taking into consideration the factors in subparagraph (B).
        (B) Factors
        In issuing an exemption, as permitted under subparagraph (A), the Bureau shall, as appropriate, take into consideration—
            (i) the total assets of the class of covered persons;
            (ii) the volume of transactions involving consumer financial products or services in which the class of covered persons engages; and
            (iii) existing provisions of law which are applicable to the consumer financial product or service and the extent to which such provisions provide consumers with adequate protections.
    (4) Exclusive rulemaking authority
        (A) In general
        Notwithstanding any other provisions of Federal law and except as provided in section 5581(b)(5) of this title, to the extent that a provision of Federal consumer financial law authorizes the Bureau and another Federal agency to issue regulations under that provision of law for purposes of assuring compliance with Federal consumer financial law and any regulations thereunder, the Bureau shall have the exclusive authority to prescribe rules subject to those provisions of law.
        (B) Deference
        Notwithstanding any power granted to any Federal agency or to the Council under this title, and subject to section 5581(b)(5)(E) of this title, the deference that a court affords to the Bureau with respect to a determination by the Bureau regarding the meaning or interpretation of any provision of a Federal consumer financial law shall be applied as if the Bureau were the only agency authorized to apply, enforce, interpret, or administer the provisions of such Federal consumer financial law.

(c) Monitoring
    (1) In general
    In order to support its rulemaking and other functions, the Bureau shall monitor for risks to consumers in the offering or provision of consumer financial products or services, including developments in markets for such products or services.
    (2) Considerations
    In allocating its resources to perform the monitoring required by this section, the Bureau may consider, among other factors—
        (A) likely risks and costs to consumers associated with buying or using a type of consumer financial product or service;
        (B) understanding by consumers of the risks of a type of consumer financial product or service;
        (C) the legal protections applicable to the offering or provision of a consumer financial product or service, including the extent to which the law is likely to adequately protect consumers;
        (D) rates of growth in the offering or provision of a consumer financial product or service;
        (E) the extent, if any, to which the risks of a consumer financial product or service may disproportionately affect traditionally underserved consumers; or
        (F) the types, number, and other pertinent characteristics of covered persons that offer or provide the consumer financial product or service.

(3) Significant findings
(A) In general
The Bureau shall publish not fewer than 1 report of significant findings of its monitoring required by this subsection in each calendar year, beginning with the first calendar year that begins at least 1 year after the designated transfer date.
(B) Confidential information
The Bureau may make public such information obtained by the Bureau under this section as is in the public interest, through aggregated reports or other appropriate formats designed to protect confidential information in accordance with paragraphs (4), (6), (8), and (9).
(4) Collection of information
(A) In general
In conducting any monitoring or assessment required by this section, the Bureau shall have the authority to gather information from time to time regarding the organization, business conduct, markets, and activities of covered persons and service providers.
(B) Methodology
In order to gather information described in subparagraph (A), the Bureau may—
(i) gather and compile information from a variety of sources, including examination reports concerning covered persons or service providers, consumer complaints, voluntary surveys and voluntary interviews of consumers, surveys and interviews with covered persons and service providers, and review of available databases; and
(ii) require covered persons and service providers participating in consumer financial services markets to file with the Bureau, under oath or otherwise, in such form and within such reasonable period of time as the Bureau may prescribe by rule or order, annual or special reports, or answers in writing to specific questions, furnishing information described in paragraph (4), as necessary for the Bureau to fulfill the monitoring, assessment, and reporting responsibilities imposed by Congress.
(C) Limitation
The Bureau may not use its authorities under this paragraph to obtain records from covered persons and service providers participating in consumer financial services markets for purposes of gathering or analyzing the personally identifiable financial information of consumers.
(5) Limited information gathering
In order to assess whether a nondepository is a covered person, as defined in section 5481 of this title, the Bureau may require such nondepository to file with the Bureau, under oath or otherwise, in such form and within such reasonable period of time as the Bureau may prescribe by rule or order, annual or special reports, or answers in writing to specific questions.
(6) Confidentiality rules
(A) Rulemaking
The Bureau shall prescribe rules regarding the confidential treatment of information obtained from persons in connection with the exercise of its authorities under Federal consumer financial law.
(B) Access by the Bureau to reports of other regulators
(i) Examination and financial condition reports
Upon providing reasonable assurances of confidentiality, the Bureau shall have access to any report of examination or financial condition made by a prudential regulator or other Federal agency having jurisdiction over a covered person or service provider, and to all revisions made to any such report.
(ii) Provision of other reports to the Bureau
In addition to the reports described in clause (i), a prudential regulator or other Federal agency having jurisdiction over a covered person or service provider may, in its discretion, furnish to the Bureau any other report or other confidential supervisory information concerning any insured depository institution, credit union, or other entity examined by such agency under authority of any provision of Federal law.
(C) Access by other regulators to reports of the Bureau
(i) Examination reports
Upon providing reasonable assurances of confidentiality, a prudential regulator, a State regulator, or any other Federal agency having jurisdiction over a covered person or service provider shall have access to any report of examination made by the Bureau with respect to such person, and to all revisions made to any such report.
(ii) Provision of other reports to other regulators
In addition to the reports described in clause (i), the Bureau may, in its discretion, furnish to a prudential regulator or other agency having jurisdiction over a covered person or service provider any other report or other confidential supervisory information concerning such person examined by the Bureau under the authority of any other provision of Federal law.
(7) Registration
(A) In general
The Bureau may prescribe rules regarding registration requirements applicable to a covered person, other than an insured depository institution, insured credit union, or related person.
(B) Registration information
Subject to rules prescribed by the Bureau, the Bureau may publicly disclose registration information to facilitate the ability of consumers to identify covered persons that are registered with the Bureau.
(C) Consultation with State agencies
In developing and implementing registration requirements under this paragraph, the Bureau shall consult with State agencies regarding requirements or systems (including coordinated or combined systems for registration), where appropriate.
(8) Privacy considerations
In collecting information from any person, publicly releasing information held by the Bureau, or requiring covered persons to publicly report information, the Bureau shall take steps to ensure that proprietary, personal, or confidential consumer information that is protected from public disclosure under section 552(b) or 552a of title 5 or any other provision of law, is not made public under this title.
(9) Consumer privacy
(A) In general
The Bureau may not obtain from a covered person or service provider any personally identifiable financial information about a consumer from the financial records of the covered person or service provider, except—
(i) if the financial records are reasonably described in a request by the Bureau and the consumer provides written permission for the disclosure of such information by the covered person or service provider to the Bureau; or
(ii) as may be specifically permitted or required under other applicable provisions of law and in accordance with the Right to Financial Privacy Act of 1978 (12 U.S.C. 3401 *et seq.*).
(B) Treatment of covered person or service provider
With respect to the application of any provision of the Right to Financial Privacy Act of 1978,[2] to a disclosure by a covered person or service provider subject to this subsection, the covered person or service provider shall be treated as if it were a "financial institution", as defined in section 1101 of that Act (12 U.S.C. 3401).
(d) Assessment of significant rules
(1) In general
The Bureau shall conduct an assessment of each significant rule or order adopted by the Bureau under Federal consumer financial law. The assessment shall address, among other relevant factors, the effectiveness of the rule or order in meeting the purposes and objectives of this title and the specific goals stated by the Bureau. The assessment

---

2 *Editor's note:* So in original. The comma probably should not appear.

shall reflect available evidence and any data that the Bureau reasonably may collect.

(2) Reports

The Bureau shall publish a report of its assessment under this subsection not later than 5 years after the effective date of the subject rule or order.

(3) Before publishing a report of its assessment, the Bureau shall invite public comment on recommendations for modifying, expanding, or eliminating the newly adopted significant rule or order.

[Pub. L. No. 111–203, tit. X, § 1022, 124 Stat. 1980 (July 21, 2010)]

* * *

12 U.S.C. § 5514.   Supervision of nondepository covered persons

(a) Scope of coverage

(1) Applicability

Notwithstanding any other provision of this title, and except as provided in paragraph (3), this section shall apply to any covered person who—

(A) offers or provides origination, brokerage, or servicing of loans secured by real estate for use by consumers primarily for personal, family, or household purposes, or loan modification or foreclosure relief services in connection with such loans;

(B) is a larger participant of a market for other consumer financial products or services, as defined by rule in accordance with paragraph (2);

(C) the Bureau has reasonable cause to determine, by order, after notice to the covered person and a reasonable opportunity for such covered person to respond, based on complaints collected through the system under section 5493(b)(3) of this title or information from other sources, that such covered person is engaging, or has engaged, in conduct that poses risks to consumers with regard to the offering or provision of consumer financial products or services;

(D) offers or provides to a consumer any private education loan, as defined in section 1650 of title 15, notwithstanding section 5517(a)(2)(A) of this title and subject to section 5517(a)(2)(C) of this title; or

(E) offers or provides to a consumer a payday loan.

(2) Rulemaking to define covered persons subject to this section

The Bureau shall consult with the Federal Trade Commission prior to issuing a rule, in accordance with paragraph (1)(B), to define covered persons subject to this section. The Bureau shall issue its initial rule not later than 1 year after the designated transfer date.

(3) Rules of construction

(A) Certain persons excluded

This section shall not apply to persons described in section 5515(a) or 5516(a) of this title.

(B) Activity levels

For purposes of computing activity levels under paragraph (1) or rules issued thereunder, activities of affiliated companies (other than insured depository institutions or insured credit unions) shall be aggregated.

(b) Supervision

(1) In general

The Bureau shall require reports and conduct examinations on a periodic basis of persons described in subsection (a)(1) for purposes of—

(A) assessing compliance with the requirements of Federal consumer financial law;

(B) obtaining information about the activities and compliance systems or procedures of such person; and

(C) detecting and assessing risks to consumers and to markets for consumer financial products and services.

(2) Risk-based supervision program

The Bureau shall exercise its authority under paragraph (1) in a manner designed to ensure that such exercise, with respect to persons described in subsection (a)(1), is based on the assessment by the Bureau of the risks posed to consumers in the relevant product markets and geographic markets, and taking into consideration, as applicable—

(A) the asset size of the covered person;

(B) the volume of transactions involving consumer financial products or services in which the covered person engages;

(C) the risks to consumers created by the provision of such consumer financial products or services;

(D) the extent to which such institutions are subject to oversight by State authorities for consumer protection; and

(E) any other factors that the Bureau determines to be relevant to a class of covered persons.

(3) Coordination

To minimize regulatory burden, the Bureau shall coordinate its supervisory activities with the supervisory activities conducted by prudential regulators, the State bank regulatory authorities, and the State agencies that licence, supervise, or examine the offering of consumer financial products or services, including establishing their respective schedules for examining persons described in subsection (a)(1) and requirements regarding reports to be submitted by such persons. The sharing of information with such regulators, authorities, and agencies shall not be construed as waiving, destroying, or otherwise affecting any privilege or confidentiality such person may claim with respect to such information under Federal or State law as to any person or entity other than such Bureau, agency, supervisor, or authority.

(4) Use of existing reports

The Bureau shall, to the fullest extent possible, use—

(A) reports pertaining to persons described in subsection (a)(1) that have been provided or required to have been provided to a Federal or State agency; and

(B) information that has been reported publicly.

(5) Preservation of authority

Nothing in this title may be construed as limiting the authority of the Director to require reports from persons described in subsection (a)(1), as permitted under paragraph (1), regarding information owned or under the control of such person, regardless of whether such information is maintained, stored, or processed by another person.

(6) Reports of tax law noncompliance

The Bureau shall provide the Commissioner of Internal Revenue with any report of examination or related information identifying possible tax law noncompliance.

(7) Registration, recordkeeping and other requirements for certain persons

(A) In general

The Bureau shall prescribe rules to facilitate supervision of persons described in subsection (a)(1) and assessment and detection of risks to consumers.

(B) Recordkeeping

The Bureau may require a person described in subsection (a)(1), to generate, provide, or retain records for the purposes of facilitating supervision of such persons and assessing and detecting risks to consumers.

(C) Requirements concerning obligations

The Bureau may prescribe rules regarding a person described in subsection (a)(1), to ensure that such persons are legitimate entities and are able to perform their obligations to consumers. Such requirements may include background checks for principals, officers, directors, or key personnel and bonding or other appropriate financial requirements.

(D) Consultation with State agencies

In developing and implementing requirements under this paragraph, the Bureau shall consult with State agencies regarding requirements or systems (including coordinated or combined systems for registration), where appropriate.

(c) Enforcement authority

(1) The Bureau to have enforcement authority

Except as provided in paragraph (3) and section 5581 of this title, with respect to any person described in subsection (a)(1), to the extent that Federal law authorizes the Bureau and another Federal agency to enforce Federal consumer financial law, the Bureau shall have exclusive authority to enforce that Federal consumer financial law.

(2) Referral

Any Federal agency authorized to enforce a Federal consumer financial law described in paragraph (1) may recommend in writing to the Bureau that the Bureau initiate an enforcement proceeding, as the Bureau is authorized by that Federal law or by this title.

(3) Coordination with the Federal Trade Commission

(A) In general

The Bureau and the Federal Trade Commission shall negotiate an agreement for coordinating with respect to enforcement actions by each agency regarding the offering or provision of consumer financial products or services by any covered person that is described in subsection (a)(1), or service providers thereto. The agreement shall include procedures for notice to the other agency, where feasible, prior to initiating a civil action to enforce any Federal law regarding the offering or provision of consumer financial products or services.

(B) Civil actions

Whenever a civil action has been filed by, or on behalf of, the Bureau or the Federal Trade Commission for any violation of any provision of Federal law described in subparagraph (A), or any regulation prescribed under such provision of law—

(i) the other agency may not, during the pendency of that action, institute a civil action under such provision of law against any defendant named in the complaint in such pending action for any violation alleged in the complaint; and

(ii) the Bureau or the Federal Trade Commission may intervene as a party in any such action brought by the other agency, and, upon intervening—

(I) be heard on all matters arising in such enforcement action; and

(II) file petitions for appeal in such actions.

(C) Agreement terms

The terms of any agreement negotiated under subparagraph (A) may modify or supersede the provisions of subparagraph (B).

(D) Deadline

The agencies shall reach the agreement required under subparagraph (A) not later than 6 months after the designated transfer date.

(d) Exclusive rulemaking and examination authority

Notwithstanding any other provision of Federal law and except as provided in section 5581 of this title, to the extent that Federal law authorizes the Bureau and another Federal agency to issue regulations or guidance, conduct examinations, or require reports from a person described in subsection (a)(1) under such law for purposes of assuring compliance with Federal consumer financial law and any regulations thereunder, the Bureau shall have the exclusive authority to prescribe rules, issue guidance, conduct examinations, require reports, or issue exemptions with regard to a person described in subsection (a)(1), subject to those provisions of law.

(e) Service providers

A service provider to a person described in subsection (a)(1) shall be subject to the authority of the Bureau under this section, to the same extent as if such service provider were engaged in a service relationship with a bank, and the Bureau were an appropriate Federal banking agency under section 1867(c) of this title. In conducting any examination or requiring any report from a service provider subject to this subsection, the Bureau shall coordinate with the appropriate prudential regulator, as applicable.

(f) Preservation of Farm Credit Administration authority

No provision of this title may be construed as modifying, limiting, or otherwise affecting the authority of the Farm Credit Administration.

[Pub. L. No. 111–203, tit. X, § 1024, 124 Stat. 1987 (July 21, 2010); Pub. L. No. 113-173, 128-Stat. 1899 (Sept. 26, 2014)]

12 U.S.C. § 5515.   Supervision of very large banks, savings associations, and credit unions

(a) Scope of coverage

This section shall apply to any covered person that is—

(1) an insured depository institution with total assets of more than $10,000,000,000 and any affiliate thereof; or

(2) an insured credit union with total assets of more than $10,000,000,000 and any affiliate thereof.

* * *

(c) Primary enforcement authority

(1) The Bureau to have primary enforcement authority

To the extent that the Bureau and another Federal agency are authorized to enforce a Federal consumer financial law, the Bureau shall have primary authority to enforce that Federal consumer financial law with respect to any person described in subsection (a).

(2) Referral

Any Federal agency, other than the Federal Trade Commission, that is authorized to enforce a Federal consumer financial law may recommend, in writing, to the Bureau that the Bureau initiate an enforcement proceeding with respect to a person described in subsection (a), as the Bureau is authorized to do by that Federal consumer financial law.

(3) Backup enforcement authority of other Federal agency

If the Bureau does not, before the end of the 120-day period beginning on the date on which the Bureau receives a recommendation under paragraph (2), initiate an enforcement proceeding, the other agency referred to in paragraph (2) may initiate an enforcement proceeding, including performing follow up supervisory and support functions incidental thereto, to assure compliance with such proceeding.

* * *

[Pub. L. No. 111–203, tit. X, § 1025, 124 Stat. 1990 (July 21, 2010)]

12 U.S.C. § 5516.   Other banks, savings associations, and credit unions

(a) Scope of coverage

This section shall apply to any covered person that is—

(1) an insured depository institution with total assets of $10,000,000,000 or less; or

(2) an insured credit union with total assets of $10,000,000,000 or less.

(b) Reports

The Director may require reports from a person described in subsection (a), as necessary to support the role of the Bureau in implementing Federal consumer financial law, to support its examination activities under subsection (c), and to assess and detect risks to consumers and consumer financial markets.

(1) Use of existing reports

The Bureau shall, to the fullest extent possible, use—

(A) reports pertaining to a person described in subsection (a) that have been provided or required to have been provided to a Federal or State agency; and

(B) information that has been reported publicly.

(2) Preservation of authority

Nothing in this subsection may be construed as limiting the authority of the Director from requiring from a person described in subsection (a), as permitted under paragraph (1), information owned or under the control of such person, regardless of whether such information is maintained, stored, or processed by another person.

(3) Reports of tax law noncompliance

The Bureau shall provide the Commissioner of Internal Revenue with any report of examination or related information identifying possible tax law noncompliance.

(c) Examinations

(1) In general

The Bureau may, at its discretion, include examiners on a sampling basis of the examinations performed by the prudential regulator to assess compliance with the requirements of Federal consumer financial law of persons described in subsection (a).

(2) Agency coordination

The prudential regulator shall—

(A) provide all reports, records, and documentation related to the examination process for any institution included in the sample referred to in paragraph (1) to the Bureau on a timely and continual basis;

(B) involve such Bureau examiner in the entire examination process for such person; and

(C) consider input of the Bureau concerning the scope of an examination, conduct of the examination, the contents of the examination report, the designation of matters requiring attention, and examination ratings.

(d) Enforcement

(1) In general

Except for requiring reports under subsection (b), the prudential regulator is authorized to enforce the requirements of Federal consumer financial laws and, with respect to a covered person described in subsection (a), shall have exclusive authority (relative to the Bureau) to enforce such laws.

(2) Coordination with prudential regulator

(A) Referral

When the Bureau has reason to believe that a person described in subsection (a) has engaged in a material violation of a Federal consumer financial law, the Bureau shall notify the prudential regulator in writing and recommend appropriate action to respond.

(B) Response

Upon receiving a recommendation under subparagraph (A), the prudential regulator shall provide a written response to the Bureau not later than 60 days thereafter.

(e) Service providers

A service provider to a substantial number of persons described in subsection (a) shall be subject to the authority of the Bureau under section 5515 of this title to the same extent as if the Bureau were an appropriate Federal bank agency under section 1867(c) of this title. When conducting any examination or requiring any report from a service provider subject to this subsection, the Bureau shall coordinate with the appropriate prudential regulator.

[Pub. L. No. 111–203, tit. X, § 1026, 124 Stat. 1993 (July 21, 2010)]

12 U.S.C. § 5517.   Limitations on authorities of the Bureau; preservation of authorities

(a) Exclusion for merchants, retailers, and other sellers of nonfinancial goods or services

(1) Sale or brokerage of nonfinancial good or service

The Bureau may not exercise any rulemaking, supervisory, enforcement or other authority under this title with respect to a person who is a merchant, retailer, or seller of any nonfinancial good or service and is engaged in the sale or brokerage of such nonfinancial good or service, except to the extent that such person is engaged in offering or providing any consumer financial product or service, or is otherwise subject to any enumerated consumer law or any law for which authorities are transferred under subtitle F or H.

(2) Offering or provision of certain consumer financial products or services in connection with the sale or brokerage of nonfinancial good or service

(A) In general

Except as provided in subparagraph (B), and subject to subparagraph (C), the Bureau may not exercise any rulemaking, supervisory, enforcement, or other authority under this title with respect to a merchant, retailer, or seller of nonfinancial goods or services, but only to the extent that such person—

(i) extends credit directly to a consumer, in a case in which the good or service being provided is not itself a consumer financial product or service (other than credit described in this subparagraph), exclusively for the purpose of enabling that consumer to purchase such nonfinancial good or service directly from the merchant, retailer, or seller;

(ii) directly, or through an agreement with another person, collects debt arising from credit extended as described in clause (i); or

(iii) sells or conveys debt described in clause (i) that is delinquent or otherwise in default.

(B) Applicability

Subparagraph (A) does not apply to any credit transaction or collection of debt, other than as described in subparagraph (C)(i), arising from a transaction described in subparagraph (A)—

(i) in which the merchant, retailer, or seller of nonfinancial goods or services assigns, sells or otherwise conveys to another person such debt owed by the consumer (except for a sale of debt that is delinquent or otherwise in default, as described in subparagraph (A)(iii));

(ii) in which the credit extended significantly exceeds the market value of the nonfinancial good or service provided, or the Bureau otherwise finds that the sale of the nonfinancial good or service is done as a subterfuge, so as to evade or circumvent the provisions of this title; or

(iii) in which the merchant, retailer, or seller of nonfinancial goods or services regularly extends credit and the credit is subject to a finance charge.

(C) Limitations

(i) In general

Notwithstanding subparagraph (B), subparagraph (A) shall apply with respect to a merchant, retailer, or seller of nonfinancial goods or services that is not engaged significantly in offering or providing consumer financial products or services.

(ii) Exception

Subparagraph (A) and clause (i) of this subparagraph do not apply to any merchant, retailer, or seller of nonfinancial goods or services—

(I) if such merchant, retailer, or seller of nonfinancial goods or services is engaged in a transaction described in subparagraph (B)(i) or (B)(ii); or

(II) to the extent that such merchant, retailer, or seller is subject to any enumerated consumer law or any law for which authorities are transferred under subtitle F or H, but the Bureau may exercise such authority only with respect to that law.

(D) Rules

(i) Authority of other agencies

No provision of this title shall be construed as modifying, limiting, or superseding the supervisory or enforcement authority of the Federal Trade Commission or any other agency (other than the Bureau) with respect to credit extended, or the collection of debt arising from such extension, directly by a merchant or retailer to a consumer exclusively for the purpose of enabling that consumer to purchase nonfinancial goods or services directly from the merchant or retailer.

(ii) Small businesses

A merchant, retailer, or seller of nonfinancial goods or services that would otherwise be subject to the authority of the Bureau solely by virtue of the application of subparagraph (B)(iii) shall be deemed not to be engaged significantly in offering or providing consumer financial products or services under subparagraph (C)(i), if such person—

(I) only extends credit for the sale of nonfinancial goods or services, as described in subparagraph (A)(i);

(II) retains such credit on its own accounts (except to sell or convey such debt that is delinquent or otherwise in default); and

(III) meets the relevant industry size threshold to be a small business concern, based on annual receipts, pursuant to section 3 of the Small Business Act (15 U.S.C. 632) and the implementing rules thereunder.

(iii) Initial year

A merchant, retailer, or seller of nonfinancial goods or services shall be deemed to meet the relevant industry size threshold described in clause (ii)(III) during the first year of operations of that business concern if, during that year, the receipts of that business concern reasonably are expected to meet that size threshold.

(iv) Other standards for small business

With respect to a merchant, retailer, or seller of nonfinancial goods or services that is a classified on a basis other than annual receipts for the purposes of section 3 of the Small Business Act (15 U.S.C. 632) and the implementing rules thereunder, such merchant, retailer, or seller shall be deemed to meet the relevant industry size threshold described in clause (ii)(III) if such merchant, retailer, or seller meets the relevant industry size threshold to be a small business concern based on the number of employees, or other such applicable measure, established under that Act [15 U.S.C. 631 *et seq.*].

(E) Exception from State enforcement

To the extent that the Bureau may not exercise authority under this subsection with respect to a merchant, retailer, or seller of nonfinancial goods or services, no action by a State attorney general or State regulator with respect to a claim made under this title may be brought under subsection 5552(a) of this title, with respect to an activity described in any of clauses (i) through (iii) of subparagraph (A) by such merchant, retailer, or seller of nonfinancial goods or services.

(b) Exclusion for real estate brokerage activities

(1) Real estate brokerage activities excluded

Without limiting subsection (a), and except as permitted in paragraph (2), the Bureau may not exercise any rulemaking, supervisory, enforcement, or other authority under this title with respect to a person that is licensed or registered as a real estate broker or real estate agent, in accordance with State law, to the extent that such person—

(A) acts as a real estate agent or broker for a buyer, seller, lessor, or lessee of real property;

(B) brings together parties interested in the sale, purchase, lease, rental, or exchange of real property;

(C) negotiates, on behalf of any party, any portion of a contract relating to the sale, purchase, lease, rental, or exchange of real property (other than in connection with the provision of financing with respect to any such transaction); or

(D) offers to engage in any activity, or act in any capacity, described in subparagraph (A), (B), or (C).

(2) Description of activities

The Bureau may exercise rulemaking, supervisory, enforcement, or other authority under this title with respect to a person described in paragraph (1) when such person is—

(A) engaged in an activity of offering or providing any consumer financial product or service, except that the Bureau may exercise such authority only with respect to that activity; or

(B) otherwise subject to any enumerated consumer law or any law for which authorities are transferred under subtitle F or H, but the Bureau may exercise such authority only with respect to that law.

(c) Exclusion for manufactured home retailers and modular home retailers

(1) In general

The Director may not exercise any rulemaking, supervisory, enforcement, or other authority over a person to the extent that—

(A) such person is not described in paragraph (2); and

(B) such person—

(i) acts as an agent or broker for a buyer or seller of a manufactured home or a modular home;

(ii) facilitates the purchase by a consumer of a manufactured home or modular home, by negotiating the purchase price or terms of the sales contract (other than providing financing with respect to such transaction); or

(iii) offers to engage in any activity described in clause (i) or (ii).

(2) Description of activities

A person is described in this paragraph to the extent that such person is engaged in the offering or provision of any consumer financial product or service or is otherwise subject to any enumerated consumer law or any law for which authorities are transferred under subtitle F or H.

(3) Definitions

For purposes of this subsection, the following definitions shall apply:

(A) Manufactured home

The term "manufactured home" has the same meaning as in section 5402 of title 42.

(B) Modular home

The term "modular home" means a house built in a factory in 2 or more modules that meet the State or local building codes where the house will be located, and where such modules are transported to the building site, installed on foundations, and completed.

(d) Exclusion for accountants and tax preparers

(1) In general

Except as permitted in paragraph (2), the Bureau may not exercise any rulemaking, supervisory, enforcement, or other authority over—

(A) any person that is a certified public accountant, permitted to practice as a certified public accounting firm, or certified or licensed for such purpose by a State, or any individual who is employed by or holds an ownership interest with respect to a person described in this subparagraph, when such person is performing or offering to perform—

(i) customary and usual accounting activities, including the provision of accounting, tax, advisory, or other services that are subject to the regulatory authority of a State board of accountancy or a Federal authority; or

(ii) other services that are incidental to such customary and usual accounting activities, to the extent that such incidental services are not offered or provided—

(I) by the person separate and apart from such customary and usual accounting activities; or

(II) to consumers who are not receiving such customary and usual accounting activities; or

(B) any person, other than a person described in subparagraph (A)[3] that performs income tax preparation activities for consumers.

(2) Description of activities

(A) In general

Paragraph (1) shall not apply to any person described in paragraph (1)(A) or (1)(B) to the extent that such person is engaged in any activity which is not a customary and usual accounting

---

3   *Editor's note:* So in original. Probably should be followed by a comma.

activity described in paragraph (1)(A) or incidental thereto but which is the offering or provision of any consumer financial product or service, except to the extent that a person described in paragraph (1)(A) is engaged in an activity which is a customary and usual accounting activity described in paragraph (1)(A), or incidental thereto.

(B) Not a customary and usual accounting activity

For purposes of this subsection, extending or brokering credit is not a customary and usual accounting activity, or incidental thereto.

(C) Rule of construction

For purposes of subparagraphs (A) and (B), a person described in paragraph (1)(A) shall not be deemed to be extending credit, if such person is only extending credit directly to a consumer, exclusively for the purpose of enabling such consumer to purchase services described in clause (i) or (ii) of paragraph (1)(A) directly from such person, and such credit is—

   (i) not subject to a finance charge; and

   (ii) not payable by written agreement in more than 4 installments.

(D) Other limitations

Paragraph (1) does not apply to any person described in paragraph (1)(A) or (1)(B) that is otherwise subject to any enumerated consumer law or any law for which authorities are transferred under subtitle F or H.

(e) Exclusion for practice of law

(1) In general

Except as provided under paragraph (2), the Bureau may not exercise any supervisory or enforcement authority with respect to an activity engaged in by an attorney as part of the practice of law under the laws of a State in which the attorney is licensed to practice law.

(2) Rule of construction

Paragraph (1) shall not be construed so as to limit the exercise by the Bureau of any supervisory, enforcement, or other authority regarding the offering or provision of a consumer financial product or service described in any subparagraph of section 5481(5) of this title—

   (A) that is not offered or provided as part of, or incidental to, the practice of law, occurring exclusively within the scope of the attorney-client relationship; or

   (B) that is otherwise offered or provided by the attorney in question with respect to any consumer who is not receiving legal advice or services from the attorney in connection with such financial product or service.

(3) Existing authority

Paragraph (1) shall not be construed so as to limit the authority of the Bureau with respect to any attorney, to the extent that such attorney is otherwise subject to any of the enumerated consumer laws or the authorities transferred under subtitle F or H.

(f) Exclusion for persons regulated by a State insurance regulator

(1) In general

No provision of this title shall be construed as altering, amending, or affecting the authority of any State insurance regulator to adopt rules, initiate enforcement proceedings, or take any other action with respect to a person regulated by a State insurance regulator. Except as provided in paragraph (2), the Bureau shall have no authority to exercise any power to enforce this title with respect to a person regulated by a State insurance regulator.

(2) Description of activities

Paragraph (1) does not apply to any person described in such paragraph to the extent that such person is engaged in the offering or provision of any consumer financial product or service or is otherwise subject to any enumerated consumer law or any law for which authorities are transferred under subtitle F or H.

(3) State insurance authority under Gramm-Leach-Bliley

Notwithstanding paragraph (2), the Bureau shall not exercise any authorities that are granted a State insurance authority under section 6805(a)(6) of title 15 with respect to a person regulated by a State insurance authority.

(g) Exclusion for employee benefit and compensation plans and certain other arrangements under title 26

(1) Preservation of authority of other agencies

No provision of this title shall be construed as altering, amending, or affecting the authority of the Secretary of the Treasury, the Secretary of Labor, or the Commissioner of Internal Revenue to adopt regulations, initiate enforcement proceedings, or take any actions with respect to any specified plan or arrangement.

(2) Activities not constituting the offering or provision of any consumer financial product or service

For purposes of this title, a person shall not be treated as having engaged in the offering or provision of any consumer financial product or service solely because such person is—

   (A) a specified plan or arrangement;

   (B) engaged in the activity of establishing or maintaining, for the benefit of employees of such person (or for members of an employee organization), any specified plan or arrangement; or

   (C) engaged in the activity of establishing or maintaining a qualified tuition program under section 529(b)(1) of title 26 offered by a State or other prepaid tuition program offered by a State.

(3) Limitation on Bureau authority

(A) In general

Except as provided under subparagraphs (B) and (C), the Bureau may not exercise any rulemaking or enforcement authority with respect to products or services that relate to any specified plan or arrangement.

(B) Bureau action pursuant to agency request

   (i) Agency request

The Secretary and the Secretary of Labor may jointly issue a written request to the Bureau regarding implementation of appropriate consumer protection standards under this title with respect to the provision of services relating to any specified plan or arrangement.

   (ii) Agency response

In response to a request by the Bureau, the Secretary and the Secretary of Labor shall jointly issue a written response, not later than 90 days after receipt of such request, to grant or deny the request of the Bureau regarding implementation of appropriate consumer protection standards under this title with respect to the provision of services relating to any specified plan or arrangement.

   (iii) Scope of Bureau action

Subject to a request or response pursuant to clause (i) or clause (ii) by the agencies made under this subparagraph, the Bureau may exercise rulemaking authority, and may act to enforce a rule prescribed pursuant to such request or response, in accordance with the provisions of this title. A request or response made by the Secretary and the Secretary of Labor under this subparagraph shall describe the basis for, and scope of, appropriate consumer protection standards to be implemented under this title with respect to the provision of services relating to any specified plan or arrangement.

(C) Description of products or services

To the extent that a person engaged in providing products or services relating to any specified plan or arrangement is subject to any enumerated consumer law or any law for which authorities are transferred under subtitle F or H, subparagraph (A) shall not apply with respect to that law.

(4) Specified plan or arrangement

For purposes of this subsection, the term "specified plan or arrangement" means any plan, account, or arrangement described in section 220, 223, 401(a), 403(a), 403(b), 408, 408A, 529, 529A, or 530 of title 26, or any employee benefit or compensation plan or arrangement, including a plan that is subject to title I of the Employee Retirement Income Security Act of 1974 [29 U.S.C. 1001 *et seq.*], or any prepaid tuition program offered by a State.

(h) Persons regulated by a State securities commission
(1) In general
No provision of this title shall be construed as altering, amending, or affecting the authority of any securities commission (or any agency or office performing like functions) of any State to adopt rules, initiate enforcement proceedings, or take any other action with respect to a person regulated by any securities commission (or any agency or office performing like functions) of any State. Except as permitted in paragraph (2) and subsection (f), the Bureau shall have no authority to exercise any power to enforce this title with respect to a person regulated by any securities commission (or any agency or office performing like functions) of any State, but only to the extent that the person acts in such regulated capacity.

(2) Description of activities
Paragraph (1) shall not apply to any person to the extent such person is engaged in the offering or provision of any consumer financial product or service, or is otherwise subject to any enumerated consumer law or any law for which authorities are transferred under subtitle F or H.

(i) Exclusion for persons regulated by the Commission
(1) In general
No provision of this title may be construed as altering, amending, or affecting the authority of the Commission to adopt rules, initiate enforcement proceedings, or take any other action with respect to a person regulated by the Commission. The Bureau shall have no authority to exercise any power to enforce this title with respect to a person regulated by the Commission.

(2) Consultation and coordination
Notwithstanding paragraph (1), the Commission shall consult and coordinate, where feasible, with the Bureau with respect to any rule (including any advance notice of proposed rulemaking) regarding an investment product or service that is the same type of product as, or that competes directly with, a consumer financial product or service that is subject to the jurisdiction of the Bureau under this title or under any other law. In carrying out this paragraph, the agencies shall negotiate an agreement to establish procedures for such coordination, including procedures for providing advance notice to the Bureau when the Commission is initiating a rulemaking.

(j) Exclusion for persons regulated by the Commodity Futures Trading Commission
(1) In general
No provision of this title shall be construed as altering, amending, or affecting the authority of the Commodity Futures Trading Commission to adopt rules, initiate enforcement proceedings, or take any other action with respect to a person regulated by the Commodity Futures Trading Commission. The Bureau shall have no authority to exercise any power to enforce this title with respect to a person regulated by the Commodity Futures Trading Commission.

(2) Consultation and coordination
Notwithstanding paragraph (1), the Commodity Futures Trading Commission shall consult and coordinate with the Bureau with respect to any rule (including any advance notice of proposed rulemaking) regarding a product or service that is the same type of product as, or that competes directly with, a consumer financial product or service that is subject to the jurisdiction of the Bureau under this title or under any other law.

(k) Exclusion for persons regulated by the Farm Credit Administration
(1) In general
No provision of this title shall be construed as altering, amending, or affecting the authority of the Farm Credit Administration to adopt rules, initiate enforcement proceedings, or take any other action with respect to a person regulated by the Farm Credit Administration. The Bureau shall have no authority to exercise any power to enforce this title with respect to a person regulated by the Farm Credit Administration.

(2) Definition
For purposes of this subsection, the term "person regulated by the Farm Credit Administration" means any Farm Credit System institution that is chartered and subject to the provisions of the Farm Credit Act of 1971 (12 U.S.C. 2001 *et seq.*).

(*l*) Exclusion for activities relating to charitable contributions
(1) In general
The Director and the Bureau may not exercise any rulemaking, supervisory, enforcement, or other authority, including authority to order penalties, over any activities related to the solicitation or making of voluntary contributions to a tax-exempt organization as recognized by the Internal Revenue Service, by any agent, volunteer, or representative of such organizations to the extent the organization, agent, volunteer, or representative thereof is soliciting or providing advice, information, education, or instruction to any donor or potential donor relating to a contribution to the organization.

(2) Limitation
The exclusion in paragraph (1) does not apply to other activities not described in paragraph (1) that are the offering or provision of any consumer financial product or service, or are otherwise subject to any enumerated consumer law or any law for which authorities are transferred under subtitle F or H.

(m) Insurance
The Bureau may not define as a financial product or service, by regulation or otherwise, engaging in the business of insurance.

(n) Limited authority of the Bureau
Notwithstanding subsections (a) through (h) and (*l*), a person subject to or described in one or more of such provisions—
(1) may be a service provider; and
(2) may be subject to requests from, or requirements imposed by, the Bureau regarding information in order to carry out the responsibilities and functions of the Bureau and in accordance with section 5512, 5562, or 5563 of this title.

(o) No authority to impose usury limit
No provision of this title shall be construed as conferring authority on the Bureau to establish a usury limit applicable to an extension of credit offered or made by a covered person to a consumer, unless explicitly authorized by law.

(p) Attorney General
No provision of this title, including section 5514(c)(1) of this title, shall affect the authorities of the Attorney General under otherwise applicable provisions of law.

(q) Secretary of the Treasury
No provision of this title shall affect the authorities of the Secretary, including with respect to prescribing rules, initiating enforcement proceedings, or taking other actions with respect to a person that performs income tax preparation activities for consumers.

(r) Deposit insurance and share insurance
Nothing in this title shall affect the authority of the Corporation under the Federal Deposit Insurance Act [12 U.S.C. 1811 *et seq.*] or the National Credit Union Administration Board under the Federal Credit Union Act [12 U.S.C. 1751 *et seq.*] as to matters related to deposit insurance and share insurance, respectively.

(s) Fair Housing Act
No provision of this title shall be construed as affecting any authority arising under the Fair Housing Act [42 U.S.C. 3601 *et seq.*].

[Pub. L. No. 111–203, tit. X, § 1027, 124 Stat. 1995 (July 21, 2010); Pub. L. No. 113-295, 128-Stat. 4062 (Dec. 19, 2014)]

* * *

12 U.S.C. § 5519.   Exclusion for auto dealers

(a) Sale, servicing, and leasing of motor vehicles excluded
Except as permitted in subsection (b), the Bureau may not exercise any rulemaking, supervisory, enforcement or any other authority, including

any authority to order assessments, over a motor vehicle dealer that is predominantly engaged in the sale and servicing of motor vehicles, the leasing and servicing of motor vehicles, or both.

(b) Certain functions excepted

Subsection (a) shall not apply to any person, to the extent that such person—

(1) provides consumers with any services related to residential or commercial mortgages or self-financing transactions involving real property;

(2) operates a line of business—

(A) that involves the extension of retail credit or retail leases involving motor vehicles; and

(B) in which—

(i) the extension of retail credit or retail leases are provided directly to consumers; and

(ii) the contract governing such extension of retail credit or retail leases is not routinely assigned to an unaffiliated third party finance or leasing source; or

(3) offers or provides a consumer financial product or service not involving or related to the sale, financing, leasing, rental, repair, refurbishment, maintenance, or other servicing of motor vehicles, motor vehicle parts, or any related or ancillary product or service.

(c) Preservation of authorities of other agencies

Except as provided in subsections (b) and (d), nothing in this title, including subtitle F, shall be construed as modifying, limiting, or superseding the operation of any provision of Federal law, or otherwise affecting the authority of the Board of Governors, the Federal Trade Commission, or any other Federal agency, with respect to a person described in subsection (a).

(d) Federal Trade Commission authority

Notwithstanding section 57a of title 15, the Federal Trade Commission is authorized to prescribe rules under sections 45 and 57a(a)(1)(B) of title 15.[4] in accordance with section 553 of title 5, with respect to a person described in subsection (a).

(e) Coordination with Office of Service Member Affairs

The Board of Governors and the Federal Trade Commission shall coordinate with the Office of Service Member Affairs, to ensure that—

(1) service members and their families are educated and empowered to make better informed decisions regarding consumer financial products and services offered by motor vehicle dealers, with a focus on motor vehicle dealers in the proximity of military installations; and

(2) complaints by service members and their families concerning such motor vehicle dealers are effectively monitored and responded to, and where appropriate, enforcement action is pursued by the authorized agencies.

(f) Definitions

For purposes of this section, the following definitions shall apply:

(1) Motor vehicle

The term "motor vehicle" means—

(A) any self-propelled vehicle designed for transporting persons or property on a street, highway, or other road;

(B) recreational boats and marine equipment;

(C) motorcycles;

(D) motor homes, recreational vehicle trailers, and slide-in campers, as those terms are defined in sections 571.3 and 575.103 (d) of title 49, Code of Federal Regulations, or any successor thereto; and

(E) other vehicles that are titled and sold through dealers.

(2) Motor vehicle dealer

The term "motor vehicle dealer" means any person or resident in the United States, or any territory of the United States, who—

(A) is licensed by a State, a territory of the United States, or the District of Columbia to engage in the sale of motor vehicles; and

(B) takes title to, holds an ownership in, or takes physical custody of motor vehicles.

[Pub. L. No. 111–203, tit. X, § 1029, 124 Stat. 2004 (July 21, 2010)]

12 U.S.C. § 5531.   Prohibiting unfair, deceptive, or abusive acts or practices

(a) In general

The Bureau may take any action authorized under part E to prevent a covered person or service provider from committing or engaging in an unfair, deceptive, or abusive act or practice under Federal law in connection with any transaction with a consumer for a consumer financial product or service, or the offering of a consumer financial product or service.

(b) Rulemaking

The Bureau may prescribe rules applicable to a covered person or service provider identifying as unlawful unfair, deceptive, or abusive acts or practices in connection with any transaction with a consumer for a consumer financial product or service, or the offering of a consumer financial product or service. Rules under this section may include requirements for the purpose of preventing such acts or practices.

(c) Unfairness

(1) In general

The Bureau shall have no authority under this section to declare an act or practice in connection with a transaction with a consumer for a consumer financial product or service, or the offering of a consumer financial product or service, to be unlawful on the grounds that such act or practice is unfair, unless the Bureau has a reasonable basis to conclude that—

(A) the act or practice causes or is likely to cause substantial injury to consumers which is not reasonably avoidable by consumers; and

(B) such substantial injury is not outweighed by countervailing benefits to consumers or to competition.

(2) Consideration of public policies

In determining whether an act or practice is unfair, the Bureau may consider established public policies as evidence to be considered with all other evidence. Such public policy considerations may not serve as a primary basis for such determination.

(d) Abusive

The Bureau shall have no authority under this section to declare an act or practice abusive in connection with the provision of a consumer financial product or service, unless the act or practice—

(1) materially interferes with the ability of a consumer to understand a term or condition of a consumer financial product or service; or

(2) takes unreasonable advantage of—

(A) a lack of understanding on the part of the consumer of the material risks, costs, or conditions of the product or service;

(B) the inability of the consumer to protect the interests of the consumer in selecting or using a consumer financial product or service; or

(C) the reasonable reliance by the consumer on a covered person to act in the interests of the consumer.

(e) Consultation

In prescribing rules under this section, the Bureau shall consult with the Federal banking agencies, or other Federal agencies, as appropriate, concerning the consistency of the proposed rule with prudential, market, or systemic objectives administered by such agencies.

(f) Consideration of seasonal income

The rules of the Bureau under this section shall provide, with respect to an extension of credit secured by residential real estate or a dwelling, if documented income of the borrower, including income from a small business, is a repayment source for an extension of credit secured by residential real estate or a dwelling, the creditor may consider the seasonality

---

4   *Editor's note:* So in original. The period probably should be a comma.

and irregularity of such income in the underwriting of and scheduling of payments for such credit.

[Pub. L. No. 111–203, tit. X, § 1031, 124 Stat. 2005 (July 21, 2010)]

12 U.S.C. § 5532.   Disclosures

(a) In general

The Bureau may prescribe rules to ensure that the features of any consumer financial product or service, both initially and over the term of the product or service, are fully, accurately, and effectively disclosed to consumers in a manner that permits consumers to understand the costs, benefits, and risks associated with the product or service, in light of the facts and circumstances.

(b) Model disclosures

(1) In general

Any final rule prescribed by the Bureau under this section requiring disclosures may include a model form that may be used at the option of the covered person for provision of the required disclosures.

(2) Format

A model form issued pursuant to paragraph (1) shall contain a clear and conspicuous disclosure that, at a minimum—

(A) uses plain language comprehensible to consumers;

(B) contains a clear format and design, such as an easily readable type font; and

(C) succinctly explains the information that must be communicated to the consumer.

(3) Consumer testing

Any model form issued pursuant to this subsection shall be validated through consumer testing.

(c) Basis for rulemaking

In prescribing rules under this section, the Bureau shall consider available evidence about consumer awareness, understanding of, and responses to disclosures or communications about the risks, costs, and benefits of consumer financial products or services.

(d) Safe harbor

Any covered person that uses a model form included with a rule issued under this section shall be deemed to be in compliance with the disclosure requirements of this section with respect to such model form.

(e) Trial disclosure programs

(1) In general

The Bureau may permit a covered person to conduct a trial program that is limited in time and scope, subject to specified standards and procedures, for the purpose of providing trial disclosures to consumers that are designed to improve upon any model form issued pursuant to subsection (b)(1), or any other model form issued to implement an enumerated statute, as applicable.

(2) Safe harbor

The standards and procedures issued by the Bureau shall be designed to encourage covered persons to conduct trial disclosure programs. For the purposes of administering this subsection, the Bureau may establish a limited period during which a covered person conducting a trial disclosure program shall be deemed to be in compliance with, or may be exempted from, a requirement of a rule or an enumerated consumer law.

(3) Public disclosure

The rules of the Bureau shall provide for public disclosure of trial disclosure programs, which public disclosure may be limited, to the extent necessary to encourage covered persons to conduct effective trials.

(f) Combined mortgage loan disclosure

Not later than 1 year after the designated transfer date, the Bureau shall propose for public comment rules and model disclosures that combine the disclosures required under the Truth in Lending Act [15 U.S.C. 1601 *et seq.*] and sections 2603 and 2604 of this title, into a single, integrated disclosure for mortgage loan transactions covered by those laws, unless the Bureau

determines that any proposal issued by the Board of Governors and the Secretary of Housing and Urban Development carries out the same purpose.

[Pub. L. No. 111–203, tit. X, § 1032, 124 Stat. 2006 (July 21, 2010)]

12 U.S.C. § 5533.   Consumer rights to access information

(a) In general

Subject to rules prescribed by the Bureau, a covered person shall make available to a consumer, upon request, information in the control or possession of the covered person concerning the consumer financial product or service that the consumer obtained from such covered person, including information relating to any transaction, series of transactions, or to the account including costs, charges and usage data. The information shall be made available in an electronic form usable by consumers.

(b) Exceptions

A covered person may not be required by this section to make available to the consumer—

(1) any confidential commercial information, including an algorithm used to derive credit scores or other risk scores or predictors;

(2) any information collected by the covered person for the purpose of preventing fraud or money laundering, or detecting, or making any report regarding other unlawful or potentially unlawful conduct;

(3) any information required to be kept confidential by any other provision of law; or

(4) any information that the covered person cannot retrieve in the ordinary course of its business with respect to that information.

(c) No duty to maintain records

Nothing in this section shall be construed to impose any duty on a covered person to maintain or keep any information about a consumer.

(d) Standardized formats for data

The Bureau, by rule, shall prescribe standards applicable to covered persons to promote the development and use of standardized formats for information, including through the use of machine readable files, to be made available to consumers under this section.

(e) Consultation

The Bureau shall, when prescribing any rule under this section, consult with the Federal banking agencies and the Federal Trade Commission to ensure, to the extent appropriate, that the rules—

(1) impose substantively similar requirements on covered persons;

(2) take into account conditions under which covered persons do business both in the United States and in other countries; and

(3) do not require or promote the use of any particular technology in order to develop systems for compliance.

[Pub. L. No. 111-203, tit. X, § 1033, 124 Stat. 2008 (July 21, 2010)]

* * *

12 U.S.C. § 5536.   Prohibited acts

(a) In general

It shall be unlawful for—

(1) any covered person or service provider—

(A) to offer or provide to a consumer any financial product or service not in conformity with Federal consumer financial law, or otherwise commit any act or omission in violation of a Federal consumer financial law; or

(B) to engage in any unfair, deceptive, or abusive act or practice;

(2) any covered person or service provider to fail or refuse, as required by Federal consumer financial law, or any rule or order issued by the Bureau thereunder—

(A) to permit access to or copying of records;

(B) to establish or maintain records; or

(C) to make reports or provide information to the Bureau; or

(3) any person to knowingly or recklessly provide substantial assistance to a covered person or service provider in violation of the provisions of section 5531 of this title, or any rule or order issued thereunder, and notwithstanding any provision of this title, the provider of such substantial assistance shall be deemed to be in violation of that section to the same extent as the person to whom such assistance is provided.

(b) Exception

No person shall be held to have violated subsection (a)(1) solely by virtue of providing or selling time or space to a covered person or service provider placing an advertisement.

[Pub. L. No. No. 111-203, tit. X, § 1036, 124 Stat. 2010 (July 21, 2010)]

* * *

12 U.S.C. § 5551.   Relation to State law

(a) In general

(1) Rule of construction

This title, other than sections 1044 through 1048, may not be construed as annulling, altering, or affecting, or exempting any person subject to the provisions of this title from complying with, the statutes, regulations, orders, or interpretations in effect in any State, except to the extent that any such provision of law is inconsistent with the provisions of this title, and then only to the extent of the inconsistency.

(2) Greater protection under State law

For purposes of this subsection, a statute, regulation, order, or interpretation in effect in any State is not inconsistent with the provisions of this title if the protection that such statute, regulation, order, or interpretation affords to consumers is greater than the protection provided under this title. A determination regarding whether a statute, regulation, order, or interpretation in effect in any State is inconsistent with the provisions of this title may be made by the Bureau on its own motion or in response to a nonfrivolous petition initiated by any interested person.

(b) Relation to other provisions of enumerated consumer laws that relate to State law

No provision of this title, except as provided in section 1083, shall be construed as modifying, limiting, or superseding the operation of any provision of an enumerated consumer law that relates to the application of a law in effect in any State with respect to such Federal law.

(c) Additional consumer protection regulations in response to State action

(1) Notice of proposed rule required

The Bureau shall issue a notice of proposed rulemaking whenever a majority of the States has enacted a resolution in support of the establishment or modification of a consumer protection regulation by the Bureau.

(2) Bureau considerations required for issuance of final regulation

Before prescribing a final regulation based upon a notice issued pursuant to paragraph (1), the Bureau shall take into account whether—

(A) the proposed regulation would afford greater protection to consumers than any existing regulation;

(B) the intended benefits of the proposed regulation for consumers would outweigh any increased costs or inconveniences for consumers, and would not discriminate unfairly against any category or class of consumers; and

(C) a Federal banking agency has advised that the proposed regulation is likely to present an unacceptable safety and soundness risk to insured depository institutions.

(3) Explanation of considerations

The Bureau—

(A) shall include a discussion of the considerations required in paragraph (2) in the Federal Register notice of a final regulation prescribed pursuant to this subsection; and

(B) whenever the Bureau determines not to prescribe a final regulation, shall publish an explanation of such determination in the Federal Register, and provide a copy of such explanation to each State that enacted a resolution in support of the proposed regulation, the Committee on Banking, Housing, and Urban Affairs of the Senate, and the Committee on Financial Services of the House of Representatives.

(4) Reservation of authority

No provision of this subsection shall be construed as limiting or restricting the authority of the Bureau to enhance consumer protection standards established pursuant to this title in response to its own motion or in response to a request by any other interested person.

(5) Rule of construction

No provision of this subsection shall be construed as exempting the Bureau from complying with subchapter II of chapter 5 of title 5.

(6) Definition

For purposes of this subsection, the term "consumer protection regulation" means a regulation that the Bureau is authorized to prescribe under the Federal consumer financial laws.

[Pub. L. No. 111–203, tit. X, § 1041, 124 Stat. 2011 (July 21, 2010)]

12 U.S.C. § 5552.   Preservation of enforcement powers of States

(a) In general

(1) Action by State

Except as provided in paragraph (2), the attorney general (or the equivalent thereof) of any State may bring a civil action in the name of such State in any district court of the United States in that State or in State court that is located in that State and that has jurisdiction over the defendant, to enforce provisions of this title or regulations issued under this title, and to secure remedies under provisions of this title or remedies otherwise provided under other law. A State regulator may bring a civil action or other appropriate proceeding to enforce the provisions of this title or regulations issued under this title with respect to any entity that is State-chartered, incorporated, licensed, or otherwise authorized to do business under State law (except as provided in paragraph (2)), and to secure remedies under provisions of this title or remedies otherwise provided under other provisions of law with respect to such an entity.

(2) Action by State against national bank or Federal savings association to enforce rules

(A) In general

Except as permitted under subparagraph (B), the attorney general (or equivalent thereof) of any State may not bring a civil action in the name of such State against a national bank or Federal savings association to enforce a provision of this title.

(B) Enforcement of rules permitted

The attorney general (or the equivalent thereof) of any State may bring a civil action in the name of such State against a national bank or Federal savings association in any district court of the United States in the State or in State court that is located in that State and that has jurisdiction over the defendant to enforce a regulation prescribed by the Bureau under a provision of this title and to secure remedies under provisions of this title or remedies otherwise provided under other law.

(3) Rule of construction

No provision of this title shall be construed as modifying, limiting, or superseding the operation of any provision of an enumerated consumer law that relates to the authority of a State attorney general or State regulator to enforce such Federal law.

(b) Consultation required

(1) Notice

(A) In general

Before initiating any action in a court or other administrative or regulatory proceeding against any covered person as authorized by subsection (a) to enforce any provision of this title, including any regulation prescribed by the Bureau under this title, a State attorney general or State regulator shall timely provide a copy of the complete complaint to be filed and written notice describing such action or proceeding to the Bureau and the prudential regulator, if any, or the designee thereof.

(B) Emergency action

If prior notice is not practicable, the State attorney general or State regulator shall provide a copy of the complete complaint and the notice to the Bureau and the prudential regulator, if any, immediately upon instituting the action or proceeding.

(C) Contents of notice

The notification required under this paragraph shall, at a minimum, describe—

> **(i)** the identity of the parties;
>
> **(ii)** the alleged facts underlying the proceeding; and
>
> **(iii)** whether there may be a need to coordinate the prosecution of the proceeding so as not to interfere with any action, including any rulemaking, undertaken by the Bureau, a prudential regulator, or another Federal agency.

(2) Bureau response

In any action described in paragraph (1), the Bureau may—

> **(A)** intervene in the action as a party;
>
> **(B)** upon intervening—
>
>> **(i)** remove the action to the appropriate United States district court, if the action was not originally brought there; and
>>
>> **(ii)** be heard on all matters arising in the action; and
>
> **(C)** appeal any order or judgment, to the same extent as any other party in the proceeding may.

(c) Regulations

The Bureau shall prescribe regulations to implement the requirements of this section and, from time to time, provide guidance in order to further coordinate actions with the State attorneys general and other regulators.

(d) Preservation of State authority

(1) State claims

No provision of this section shall be construed as altering, limiting, or affecting the authority of a State attorney general or any other regulatory or enforcement agency or authority to bring an action or other regulatory proceeding arising solely under the law in effect in that State.

(2) State securities regulators

No provision of this title shall be construed as altering, limiting, or affecting the authority of a State securities commission (or any agency or office performing like functions) under State law to adopt rules, initiate enforcement proceedings, or take any other action with respect to a person regulated by such commission or authority.

(3) State insurance regulators

No provision of this title shall be construed as altering, limiting, or affecting the authority of a State insurance commission or State insurance regulator under State law to adopt rules, initiate enforcement proceedings, or take any other action with respect to a person regulated by such commission or regulator.

[Pub. L. No. No. 111–203, tit. X, § 1042, 124 Stat. 2012 (July 21, 2010)]

* * *

Appendix C   Federal Regulation of Telemarketing, Junk Faxes, and Spam

C.1   Telemarketing Fraud

C.1.1   *Telemarketing and Consumer Fraud and Abuse Prevention Act*

15 U.S.C.

15 U.S.C. § 6101.   Findings

The Congress makes the following findings:

(1) Telemarketing differs from other sales activities in that it can be carried out by sellers across State lines without direct contact with the consumer. Telemarketers also can be very mobile, easily moving from State to State.

(2) Interstate telemarketing fraud has become a problem of such magnitude that the resources of the Federal Trade Commission are not sufficient to ensure adequate consumer protection from such fraud.

(3) Consumers and others are estimated to lose $40 billion a year in telemarketing fraud.

(4) Consumers are victimized by other forms of telemarketing deception and abuse.

(5) Consequently, Congress should enact legislation that will offer consumers necessary protection from telemarketing deception and abuse.

[Pub. L. No. 103-297, § 2, 108 Stat. 1545 (Aug. 16, 1994)]

15 U.S.C. § 6102.   Telemarketing rules

(a) In general

(1) The Commission shall prescribe rules prohibiting deceptive telemarketing acts or practices and other abusive telemarketing acts or practices.

(2) The Commission shall include in such rules respecting deceptive telemarketing acts or practices a definition of deceptive telemarketing acts or practices which may include acts or practices which shall include fraudulent charitable solicitations, and of entities or individuals that assist or facilitate deceptive telemarketing, including credit card laundering.

(3) The Commission shall include in such rules respecting other abusive telemarketing acts or practices—

  (A) a requirement that telemarketers may not undertake a pattern of unsolicited telephone calls which the reasonable consumer would consider coercive or abusive of such consumer's right to privacy,

  (B) restrictions on the hours of the day and night when unsolicited telephone calls can be made to consumers,

  (C) a requirement that any person engaged in telemarketing for the sale of goods or services shall promptly and clearly disclose to the person receiving the call that the purpose of the call is to sell goods or services and make such other disclosures as the Commission deems appropriate, including the nature and price of the goods and services;

  (D) a requirement that any person engaged in telemarketing for the solicitation of charitable contributions, donations, or gifts of money or any other thing of value, shall promptly and clearly disclose to the person receiving the call that the purpose of the call is to solicit charitable contributions, donations, or gifts, and make such other disclosures as the Commission considers appropriate, including the name and mailing address of the charitable organization on behalf of which the solicitation is made.

In prescribing the rules described in this paragraph, the Commission shall also consider recordkeeping requirements.

(b) Rulemaking authority

The Commission shall have authority to prescribe rules under subsection (a), in accordance with section 553 of Title 5. In prescribing a rule under this section that relates to the provision of a consumer financial product or service that is subject to the Consumer Financial Protection Act of 2010, including any enumerated consumer law thereunder, the Commission shall consult with the Bureau of Consumer Financial Protection regarding the consistency of a proposed rule with standards, purposes, or objectives administered by the Bureau of Consumer Financial Protection.

(c) Violations

Any violation of any rule prescribed under subsection (a)

  (1) shall be treated as a violation of a rule under section 57a of this title regarding unfair or deceptive acts or practices; and

  (2) that is committed by a person subject to the Consumer Financial Protection Act of 2010 shall be treated as a violation of a rule under section 1031 of that Act regarding unfair, deceptive, or abusive acts or practices.

(d) Securities and Exchange Commission rules

  (1) Promulgation

  (A) In general. Except as provided in subparagraph (B), not later than 6 months after the effective date of rules promulgated by the Federal Trade Commission under subsection (a) of this section, the Securities and Exchange Commission shall promulgate, or require any national securities exchange or registered securities association to promulgate, rules substantially similar to such rules to prohibit deceptive and other abusive telemarketing acts or practices by persons described in paragraph (2).

  (B) Exception. The Securities and Exchange Commission is not required to promulgate a rule under subparagraph (A) if it determines that—

    (i) Federal securities laws or rules adopted by the Securities and Exchange Commission thereunder provide protection from deceptive and other abusive telemarketing by persons described in paragraph (2) substantially similar to that provided by rules promulgated by the Federal Trade Commission under subsection (a) of this section; or

    (ii) such a rule promulgated by the Securities and Exchange Commission is not necessary or appropriate in the public interest, or for the protection of investors, or would be inconsistent with the maintenance of fair and orderly markets.

If the Securities and Exchange Commission determines that an exception described in clause (i) or (ii) applies, the Securities and Exchange Commission shall publish in the Federal Register its determination with the reasons for it.

  (2) Application

  (A) In general. The rules promulgated by the Securities and Exchange Commission under paragraph (1)(A) shall apply to a broker, dealer, transfer agent, municipal securities dealer, municipal securities broker, government securities broker, government securities dealer, investment adviser or investment company, or any individual associated with a broker, dealer, transfer agent, municipal securities dealer, municipal securities broker, government securities broker, government securities dealer, investment adviser or investment company. The rules promulgated by the Federal Trade Commission under subsection (a) of this section shall not apply to persons described in the preceding sentence.

    (B) Definitions. For purposes of subparagraph (A)—

        (i) the terms "broker", "dealer", "transfer agent", "municipal securities dealer", "municipal securities broker", "government securities broker", and "government securities dealer" have the meanings given such terms by paragraphs (4), (5), (25), (30), (31), (43), and (44) of section 78c(a) of this title;

        (ii) the term "investment adviser" has the meaning given such term by section 80b-2(a)(11) of this title; and

        (iii) the term "investment company" has the meaning given such term by section 80a-3(a) of this title.

(e) Commodity Futures Trading Commission rules

    (1) Application. The rules promulgated by the Federal Trade Commission under subsection (a) of this section shall not apply to persons described in section 9b(1) of Title 7.

    (2) Omitted

[Pub. L. No. 103-297, § 3, 108 Stat. 1545 (Aug. 16, 1994); Pub. L. No. 107-56, tit. X, § 1011(b)(1), (2), 115 Stat. 396 (Oct. 26, 2001); Pub. L. No. 111-203, tit. X, §§ 1100C(a), 1100H, 124 Stat. 2110, 2113 (July 21, 2010)]

15 U.S.C. § 6103.   Actions by States

(a) In general

Whenever an attorney general of any State has reason to believe that the interests of the residents of that State have been or are being threatened or adversely affected because any person has engaged or is engaging in a pattern or practice of telemarketing which violates any rule of the Commission under section 6102 of this title, the State, as parens patriae, may bring a civil action on behalf of its residents in an appropriate district court of the United States to enjoin such telemarketing, to enforce compliance with such rule of the Commission, to obtain damages, restitution, or other compensation on behalf of residents of such State, or to obtain such further and other relief as the court may deem appropriate.

(b) Notice

The State shall serve prior written notice of any civil action under subsection (a) or (f)(2) of this section upon the Commission and provide the Commission with a copy of its complaint, except that if it is not feasible for the State to provide such prior notice, the State shall serve such notice immediately upon instituting such action. Upon receiving a notice respecting a civil action, the Commission shall have the right (1) to intervene in such action, (2) upon so intervening, to be heard on all matters arising therein, and (3) to file petitions for appeal.

(c) Construction

For purposes of bringing any civil action under subsection (a) of this section, nothing in this chapter shall prevent an attorney general from exercising the powers conferred on the attorney general by the laws of such State to conduct investigations or to administer oaths or affirmations or to compel the attendance of witnesses or the production of documentary and other evidence.

(d) Actions by the Commission or the Bureau of Consumer Financial Protection

Whenever a civil action has been instituted by or on behalf of the Commission or the Bureau of Consumer Financial Protection for violation of any rule prescribed under section 6102 of this title, no State may, during the pendency of such action instituted by or on behalf of the Commission or the Bureau of Consumer Financial Protection, institute a civil action under subsection (a) or (f)(2) of this section against any defendant named in the complaint in such action for violation of any rule as alleged in such complaint.

(e) Venue; service of process

Any civil action brought under subsection (a) of this section in a district court of the United States may be brought in the district in which

the defendant is found, is an inhabitant, or transacts business or wherever venue is proper under section 1391 of Title 28. Process in such an action may be served in any district in which the defendant is an inhabitant or in which the defendant may be found.

(f) Actions by other State officials

    (1) Nothing contained in this section shall prohibit an authorized State official from proceeding in State court on the basis of an alleged violation of any civil or criminal statute of such State.

    (2) In addition to actions brought by an attorney general of a State under subsection (a) of this section, such an action may be brought by officers of such State who are authorized by the State to bring actions in such State on behalf of its residents.

[Pub. L. No. 103-297, § 4, 108 Stat. 1548 (Aug. 16, 1994); Pub. L. No. 111-203, tit. X, §§ 1100C(b), 1100H, 124 Stat. 2111, 2113 (July 21, 2010)]

15 U.S.C. § 6104.   Actions by private persons

(a) In general

Any person adversely affected by any pattern or practice of telemarketing which violates any rule of the Commission under section 6102 of this title, or an authorized person acting on such person's behalf, may, within 3 years after discovery of the violation, bring a civil action in an appropriate district court of the United States against a person who has engaged or is engaging in such pattern or practice of telemarketing if the amount in controversy exceeds the sum or value of $50,000 in actual damages for each person adversely affected by such telemarketing. Such an action may be brought to enjoin such telemarketing, to enforce compliance with any rule of the Commission under section 6102 of this title, to obtain damages, or to obtain such further and other relief as the court may deem appropriate.

(b) Notice

The plaintiff shall serve prior written notice of the action upon the Commission and provide the Commission with a copy of its complaint, except in any case where such prior notice is not feasible, in which case the person shall serve such notice immediately upon instituting such action. The Commission shall have the right (A) to intervene in the action, (B) upon so intervening, to be heard on all matters arising therein, and (C) to file petitions for appeal.

(c) Action by the Commission or the Bureau of Consumer Financial Protection

Whenever a civil action has been instituted by or on behalf of the Commission or the Bureau of Consumer Financial Protection for violation of any rule prescribed under section 6102 of this title, no person may, during the pendency of such action instituted by or on behalf of the Commission or the Bureau of Consumer Financial Protection, institute a civil action against any defendant named in the complaint in such action for violation of any rule as alleged in such complaint.

(d) Cost and fees

The court, in issuing any final order in any action brought under subsection (a) of this section, may award costs of suit and reasonable fees for attorneys and expert witnesses to the prevailing party.

(e) Construction

Nothing in this section shall restrict any right which any person may have under any statute or common law.

(f) Venue; service of process

Any civil action brought under subsection (a) of this section in a district court of the United States may be brought in the district in which the defendant is found, is an inhabitant, or transacts business or wherever venue is proper under section 1391 of Title 28. Process in such an action may be served in any district in which the defendant is an inhabitant or in which the defendant may be found.

[Pub. L. No. 103-297, § 5, 108 Stat. 1549 (Aug. 16, 1994); Pub. L. No. 111-203, tit. X, §§ 1100C(c), 1100H, 124 Stat. 2111, 2113 (July 21, 2010)]

15 U.S.C. § 6105.   Administration and applicability of chapter

(a) In general

Except as otherwise provided in sections 6102(d), 6102(e), 6103, and 6104 of this title, this chapter shall be enforced by the Commission under the Federal Trade Commission Act [15 U.S.C. § 41 *et seq.*]. Consequently, no activity which is outside the jurisdiction of that Act shall be affected by this chapter.

(b) Actions by the Commission

The Commission shall prevent any person from violating a rule of the Commission under section 6102 of this title in the same manner, by the same means, and with the same jurisdiction, powers, and duties as though all applicable terms and provisions of the Federal Trade Commission Act [15 U.S.C. § 41 *et seq.*] were incorporated into and made a part of this chapter. Any person who violates such rule shall be subject to the penalties and entitled to the privileges and immunities provided in the Federal Trade Commission Act [15 U.S.C.A. § 41 *et seq.*] in the same manner, by the same means, and with the same jurisdiction, power, and duties as though all applicable terms and provisions of the Federal Trade Commission Act [15 U.S.C.A. § 41 *et seq.*] were incorporated into and made a part of this chapter.

(c) Effect on other laws

Nothing contained in this chapter shall be construed to limit the authority of the Commission under any other provision of law.

(d) Enforcement by Bureau of Consumer Financial Protection

Except as otherwise provided in sections 6102(d), 6102(e), 6103, and 6104 of this title, and subject to subtitle B of the Consumer Financial Protection Act of 2010, this chapter shall be enforced by the Bureau of Consumer Financial Protection under subtitle E of the Consumer Financial Protection Act of 2010, with respect to the offering or provision of a consumer financial product or service subject to that Act.

[Pub. L. No. 103-297, § 6, 108 Stat. 1549 (Aug. 16, 1994); Pub. L. No. 111-203, tit. X, §§ 1100C(d), 1100H, 124 Stat. 2111, 2113 (July 21, 2010)]

15 U.S.C. § 6106.   Definitions

For purposes of this chapter:

(1) The term "attorney general" means the chief legal officer of a State.

(2) The term "Commission" means the Federal Trade Commission.

(3) The term "State" means any State of the United States, the District of Columbia, Puerto Rico, the Northern Mariana Islands, and any territory or possession of the United States.

(4) The term "telemarketing" means a plan, program, or campaign which is conducted to induce purchases of goods or services, or a charitable contribution, donation, or gift of money or any other thing of value, by use of one or more telephones and which involves more than one interstate telephone call. The term does not include the solicitation of sales through the mailing of a catalog which—

> **(A)** contains a written description, or illustration of the goods or services offered for sale,
>
> **(B)** includes the business address of the seller,
>
> **(C)** includes multiple pages of written material or illustrations, and
>
> **(D)** has been issued not less frequently than once a year,

where the person making the solicitation does not solicit customers by telephone but only receives calls initiated by customers in response to the catalog and during those calls takes orders only without further solicitation.

[Pub. L. No. 103-297, § 7, 108 Stat. 1550 (Aug. 16, 1994); Pub. L. No. 107-56, tit. X, § 1011(b)(3), 115 Stat. 396 (Oct. 26, 2001)]

15 U.S.C. § 6107.   Enforcement of orders

(a) General authority

Subject to subsections (b) and (c) of this section, the Federal Trade Commission may bring a criminal contempt action for violations of orders of the Commission obtained in cases brought under section 53(b) of this title.

(b) Appointment

An action authorized by subsection (a) of this section may be brought by the Federal Trade Commission only after, and pursuant to, the appointment by the Attorney General of an attorney employed by the Commission, as a special assistant United States Attorney.

(c) Request for appointment

(1) Appointment upon request or motion

A special assistant United States Attorney may be appointed under subsection (b) of this section upon the request of the Federal Trade Commission or the court which has entered the order for which contempt is sought or upon the Attorney General's own motion.

(2) Timing

The Attorney General shall act upon any request made under paragraph (1) within 45 days of the receipt of the request.

(d) Termination of authority

The authority of the Federal Trade Commission to bring a criminal contempt action under subsection (a) of this section expires 2 years after the date of the first promulgation of rules under section 6102 of this title. The expiration of such authority shall have no effect on an action brought before the expiration date.

[Pub. L. No. 103-297, § 9, 108 Stat. 1550 (Aug. 16, 1994)]

15 U.S.C. § 6108.   Review

Upon the expiration of 5 years following the date of the first promulgation of rules under section 6102 of this title, the Commission shall review the implementation of this chapter and its effect on deceptive telemarketing acts or practices and report the results of the review to the Congress.

[Pub. L. No. 103-297, § 10, 108 Stat. 1551 (Aug. 16, 1994)]

C.1.2   FTC Telemarketing Sales Rule

16 C.F.R.

§ 310.1 Scope of regulations in this part.
§ 310.2 Definitions.
§ 310.3 Deceptive telemarketing acts or practices.
§ 310.4 Abusive telemarketing acts or practices.
§ 310.5 Recordkeeping requirements.
§ 310.6 Exemptions.
§ 310.7 Actions by states and private persons.
§ 310.8 Fee for access to the National Do Not Call Registry.
§ 310.9 Severability.

SOURCE: 68 Fed. Reg. 4669 (Jan. 29, 2003), unless otherwise noted.

AUTHORITY: 15 U.S.C. §§ 6101–6108, 6151–6155.

16 C.F.R. § 310.1   Scope of regulations in this part.

This part implements the Telemarketing and Consumer Fraud and Abuse Prevention Act, 15 U.S.C. 6101–6108, as amended.

[75 Fed. Reg. 48,458 (Aug. 10, 2010)]

16 C.F.R. § 310.2   Definitions.

(a) *Acquirer* means a business organization, financial institution, or an agent of a business organization or financial institution that has authority from an organization that operates or licenses a credit card system to authorize merchants to accept, transmit, or process payment by credit card through the credit card system for money, goods or services, or anything else of value.

(b) *Attorney General* means the chief legal officer of a state.

(c) *Billing information* means any data that enables any person to access a customer's or donor's account, such as a credit card, checking, savings, share or similar account, utility bill, mortgage loan account, or debit card.

(d) *Caller identification service* means a service that allows a telephone subscriber to have the telephone number, and, where available, name of the calling party transmitted contemporaneously with the telephone call, and displayed on a device in or connected to the subscriber's telephone.

(e) *Cardholder* means a person to whom a credit card is issued or who is authorized to use a credit card on behalf of or in addition to the person to whom the credit card is issued.

(f) *Charitable contribution* means any donation or gift of money or any other thing of value.

(g) *Commission* means the Federal Trade Commission.

(h) *Credit* means the right granted by a creditor to a debtor to defer payment of debt or to incur debt and defer its payment.

(i) *Credit card* means any card, plate, coupon book, or other credit device existing for the purpose of obtaining money, property, labor, or services on credit.

(j) *Credit card sales draft* means any record or evidence of a credit card transaction.

(k) *Credit card system* means any method or procedure used to process credit card transactions involving credit cards issued or licensed by the operator of that system.

(l) *Customer* means any person who is or may be required to pay for goods or services offered through telemarketing.

(m) *Debt relief service* means any program or service represented, directly or by implication, to renegotiate, settle, or in any way alter the terms of payment or other terms of the debt between a person and one or more unsecured creditors or debt collectors, including, but not limited to, a reduction in the balance, interest rate, or fees owed by a person to an unsecured creditor or debt collector.

(n) *Donor* means any person solicited to make a charitable contribution.

(o) *Established business relationship* means a relationship between a seller and a consumer based on:

(1) the consumer's purchase, rental, or lease of the seller's goods or services or a financial transaction between the consumer and seller, within the eighteen (18) months immediately preceding the date of a telemarketing call; or

(2) the consumer's inquiry or application regarding a product or service offered by the seller, within the three (3) months immediately preceding the date of a telemarketing call.

(p) *Free-to-pay conversion* means, in an offer or agreement to sell or provide any goods or services, a provision under which a customer receives a product or service for free for an initial period and will incur an obligation to pay for the product or service if he or she does not take affirmative action to cancel before the end of that period.

(q) *Investment opportunity* means anything, tangible or intangible, that is offered, offered for sale, sold, or traded based wholly or in part on representations, either express or implied, about past, present, or future income, profit, or appreciation.

(r) *Material* means likely to affect a person's choice of, or conduct regarding, goods or services or a charitable contribution.

(s) *Merchant* means a person who is authorized under a written contract with an acquirer to honor or accept credit cards, or to transmit or process for payment credit card payments, for the purchase of goods or services or a charitable contribution.

(t) *Merchant agreement* means a written contract between a merchant and an acquirer to honor or accept credit cards, or to transmit or process for payment credit card payments, for the purchase of goods or services or a charitable contribution.

(u) *Negative option feature* means, in an offer or agreement to sell or provide any goods or services, a provision under which the customer's silence or failure to take an affirmative action to reject goods or services or to cancel the agreement is interpreted by the seller as acceptance of the offer.

(v) *Outbound telephone* call means a telephone call initiated by a telemarketer to induce the purchase of goods or services or to solicit a charitable contribution.

(w) *Person* means any individual, group, unincorporated association, limited or general partnership, corporation, or other business entity.

(x) *Preacquired account information* means any information that enables a seller or telemarketer to cause a charge to be placed against a customer's or donor's account without obtaining the account number directly from the customer or donor during the telemarketing transaction pursuant to which the account will be charged.

(y) *Prize* means anything offered, or purportedly offered, and given, or purportedly given, to a person by chance. For purposes of this definition, chance exists if a person is guaranteed to receive an item and, at the time of the offer or purported offer, the telemarketer does not identify the specific item that the person will receive.

(z) *Prize promotion* means:

(1) A sweepstakes or other game of chance; or

(2) An oral or written express or implied representation that a person has won, has been selected to receive, or may be eligible to receive a prize or purported prize.

(aa) *Seller* means any person who, in connection with a telemarketing transaction, provides, offers to provide, or arranges for others to provide goods or services to the customer in exchange for consideration.

(bb) *State* means any state of the United States, the District of Columbia, Puerto Rico, the Northern Mariana Islands, and any territory or possession of the United States.

(cc) *Telemarketer* means any person who, in connection with telemarketing, initiates or receives telephone calls to or from a customer or donor.

(dd) *Telemarketing* means a plan, program, or campaign which is conducted to induce the purchase of goods or services or a charitable contribution, by use of one or more telephones and which involves more than one interstate telephone call. The term does not include the solicitation of sales through the mailing of a catalog which: contains a written description or illustration of the goods or services offered for sale; includes the business address of the seller; includes multiple pages of written material or illustrations; and has been issued not less frequently than once a year, when the person making the solicitation does not solicit customers by telephone but only receives calls initiated by customers in response to the catalog and during those calls takes orders only without further solicitation. For purposes of the previous sentence, the term "further solicitation" does not include providing the customer with information about, or attempting to sell, any other item included in the same catalog which prompted the customer's call or in a substantially similar catalog.

(ee) *Upselling* means soliciting the purchase of goods or services following an initial transaction during a single telephone call. The upsell is a separate telemarketing transaction, not a continuation of the initial transaction. An "external upsell" is a solicitation made by or on behalf of a seller different from the seller in the initial transaction, regardless of whether the initial transaction and the subsequent solicitation are made by the same telemarketer. An "internal upsell" is a solicitation made by or on behalf of the same seller as in the initial transaction, regardless of whether the initial transaction and subsequent solicitation are made by the same telemarketer.

[75 Fed. Reg. 48,458 (Aug. 10, 2010)]

16 C.F.R. § 310.3   Deceptive telemarketing acts or practices.

(a) Prohibited deceptive telemarketing acts or practices. It is a deceptive telemarketing act or practice and a violation of this Rule for any seller or telemarketer to engage in the following conduct:

(1) Before a customer consents to pay[1] for goods or services offered, failing to disclose truthfully, in a clear and conspicuous manner, the following material information:

(i) The total costs to purchase, receive, or use, and the quantity of, any goods or services that are the subject of the sales offer;[2]

(ii) All material restrictions, limitations, or conditions to purchase, receive, or use the goods or services that are the subject of the sales offer;

(iii) If the seller has a policy of not making refunds, cancellations, exchanges, or repurchases, a statement informing the customer that this is the seller's policy; or, if the seller or telemarketer makes a representation about a refund, cancellation, exchange, or repurchase policy, a statement of all material terms and conditions of such policy;

(iv) In any prize promotion, the odds of being able to receive the prize, and, if the odds are not calculable in advance, the factors used in calculating the odds; that no purchase or payment is required to win a prize or to participate in a prize promotion and that any purchase or payment will not increase the person's chances of winning; and the no-purchase/no-payment method of participating in the prize promotion with either instructions on how to participate or an address or local or toll-free telephone number to which customers may write or call for information on how to participate;

(v) All material costs or conditions to receive or redeem a prize that is the subject of the prize promotion;

(vi) In the sale of any goods or services represented to protect, insure, or otherwise limit a customer's liability in the event of unauthorized use of the customer's credit card, the limits on a cardholder's liability for unauthorized use of a credit card pursuant to 15 U.S.C. 1643;

(vii) If the offer includes a negative option feature, all material terms and conditions of the negative option feature, including, but not limited to, the fact that the customer's account will be charged unless the customer takes an affirmative action to avoid the charge(s), the date(s) the charge(s) will be submitted for payment, and the specific steps the customer must take to avoid the charge(s); and

(viii) In the sale of any debt relief service:

(A) the amount of time necessary to achieve the represented results, and to the extent that the service may include a settlement offer to any of the customer's creditors or debt collectors, the time by which the debt relief service provider will make a bona fide settlement offer to each of them;

(B) to the extent that the service may include a settlement offer to any of the customer's creditors or debt collectors, the amount of money or the percentage of each outstanding debt that the customer must accumulate before the debt relief service provider will make a bona fide settlement offer to each of them;

(C) to the extent that any aspect of the debt relief service relies upon or results in the customer's failure to make timely payments to creditors or debt collectors, that the use of the debt relief service will likely adversely affect the customer's creditworthiness, may result in the customer being subject to collections or sued by creditors or debt collectors, and may increase the amount of money the customer owes due to the accrual of fees and interest; and

(D) to the extent that the debt relief service requests or requires the customer to place funds in an account at an insured financial institution, that the customer owns the funds held in the account, the customer may withdraw from the debt relief service at any time without penalty, and, if the customer withdraws, the customer must receive all funds in the account, other than funds earned by the debt relief service in compliance with § 310.4(a)(5)(i)(A) through (C).

(2) Misrepresenting, directly or by implication, in the sale of goods or services any of the following material information:

(i) The total costs to purchase, receive, or use, and the quantity of, any goods or services that are the subject of a sales offer;

(ii) Any material restriction, limitation, or condition to purchase, receive, or use goods or services that are the subject of a sales offer;

(iii) Any material aspect of the performance, efficacy, nature, or central characteristics of goods or services that are the subject of a sales offer;

(iv) Any material aspect of the nature or terms of the seller's refund, cancellation, exchange, or repurchase policies;

(v) Any material aspect of a prize promotion including, but not limited to, the odds of being able to receive a prize, the nature or value of a prize, or that a purchase or payment is required to win a prize or to participate in a prize promotion;

(vi) Any material aspect of an investment opportunity including, but not limited to, risk, liquidity, earnings potential, or profitability;

(vii) A seller's or telemarketer's affiliation with, or endorsement or sponsorship by, any person or government entity;

(viii) That any customer needs offered goods or services to provide protections a customer already has pursuant to 15 U.S.C. 1643;

(ix) Any material aspect of a negative option feature including, but not limited to, the fact that the customer's account will be charged unless the customer takes an affirmative action to avoid the charge(s), the date(s) the charge(s) will be submitted for payment, and the specific steps the customer must take to avoid the charge(s); or

(x) Any material aspect of any debt relief service, including, but not limited to, the amount of money or the percentage of the debt amount that a customer may save by using such service; the amount of time necessary to achieve the represented results; the amount of money or the percentage of each outstanding debt that the customer must accumulate before the provider of the debt relief service will initiate attempts with the customer's creditors or debt collectors or make a bona fide offer to negotiate, settle, or modify the terms of the customer's debt; the effect of the service on a customer's creditworthiness; the effect of the service on collection efforts of the customer's creditors or debt collectors; the percentage or number of customers who attain the represented results; and whether a debt relief service is offered or provided by a non-profit entity.

(3) Causing billing information to be submitted for payment, or collecting or attempting to collect payment for goods or services or a charitable contribution, directly or indirectly, without the customer's or donor's express verifiable authorization, except when the method of payment used is a credit card subject to protections of the Truth

---

1   When a seller or telemarketer uses, or directs a customer to use, a courier to transport payment, the seller or telemarketer must make the disclosures required by § 310.3(a)(1) before sending a courier to pick up payment or authorization for payment, or directing a customer to have a courier pick up payment or authorization for payment. In the case of debt relief services, the seller or telemarketer must make the disclosures required by § 310.3(a)(1) before the consumer enrolls in an offered program.

2   For offers of consumer credit products subject to the Truth in Lending Act, 15 U.S.C. 1601 *et seq.*, and Regulation Z, 12 CFR 226, compliance with the disclosure requirements under the Truth in Lending Act and Regulation Z shall constitute compliance with § 310.3(a)(1)(i) of this Rule.

in Lending Act and Regulation Z,[3] or a debit card subject to the protections of the Electronic Fund Transfer Act and Regulation E.[4] Such authorization shall be deemed verifiable if any of the following means is employed:

(i) Express written authorization by the customer or donor, which includes the customer's or donor's signature;[5]

(ii) Express oral authorization which is audio-recorded and made available upon request to the customer or donor, and the customer's or donor's bank or other billing entity, and which evidences clearly both the customer's or donor's authorization of payment for the goods or services or charitable contribution that are the subject of the telemarketing transaction and the customer's or donor's receipt of all of the following information:

(A) The number of debits, charges, or payments (if more than one);

(B) The date(s) the debit(s), charge(s), or payment(s) will be submitted for payment;

(C) The amount(s) of the debit(s), charge(s), or payment(s);

(D) The customer's or donor's name;

(E) The customer's or donor's billing information, identified with sufficient specificity such that the customer or donor understands what account will be used to collect payment for the goods or services or charitable contribution that are the subject of the telemarketing transaction;

(F) A telephone number for customer or donor inquiry that is answered during normal business hours; and

(G) The date of the customer's or donor's oral authorization; or

(iii) Written confirmation of the transaction, identified in a clear and conspicuous manner as such on the outside of the envelope, sent to the customer or donor via first class mail prior to the submission for payment of the customer's or donor's billing information, and that includes all of the information contained in §§ 310.3(a)(3)(ii)(A)–(G) and a clear and conspicuous statement of the procedures by which the customer or donor can obtain a refund from the seller or telemarketer or charitable organization in the event the confirmation is inaccurate; provided, however, that this means of authorization shall not be deemed verifiable in instances in which goods or services are offered in a transaction involving a free-to-pay conversion and preacquired account information.

(4) Making a false or misleading statement to induce any person to pay for goods or services or to induce a charitable contribution.

(b) Assisting and facilitating. It is a deceptive telemarketing act or practice and a violation of this Rule for a person to provide substantial assistance or support to any seller or telemarketer when that person knows or consciously avoids knowing that the seller or telemarketer is engaged in any act or practice that violates §§ 310.3(a), (c) or (d), or § 310.4 of this Rule.

(c) Credit card laundering. Except as expressly permitted by the applicable credit card system, it is a deceptive telemarketing act or practice and a violation of this Rule for:

(1) A merchant to present to or deposit into, or cause another to present to or deposit into, the credit card system for payment, a credit card sales draft generated by a telemarketing transaction that is not the result of a telemarketing credit card transaction between the cardholder and the merchant;

(2) Any person to employ, solicit, or otherwise cause a merchant, or an employee, representative, or agent of the merchant, to present to or deposit into the credit card system for payment, a credit card sales

draft generated by a telemarketing transaction that is not the result of a telemarketing credit card transaction between the cardholder and the merchant; or

(3) Any person to obtain access to the credit card system through the use of a business relationship or an affiliation with a merchant, when such access is not authorized by the merchant agreement or the applicable credit card system.

(d) Prohibited deceptive acts or practices in the solicitation of charitable contributions. It is a fraudulent charitable solicitation, a deceptive telemarketing act or practice, and a violation of this Rule for any telemarketer soliciting charitable contributions to misrepresent, directly or by implication, any of the following material information:

(1) The nature, purpose, or mission of any entity on behalf of which a charitable contribution is being requested;

(2) That any charitable contribution is tax deductible in whole or in part;

(3) The purpose for which any charitable contribution will be used;

(4) The percentage or amount of any charitable contribution that will go to a charitable organization or to any particular charitable program;

(5) Any material aspect of a prize promotion including, but not limited to: the odds of being able to receive a prize; the nature or value of a prize; or that a charitable contribution is required to win a prize or to participate in a prize promotion; or

(6) A charitable organization's or telemarketer's affiliation with, or endorsement or sponsorship by, any person or government entity.

[75 Fed. Reg. 48,458 (Aug. 10, 2010)]

16 C.F.R. § 310.4 Abusive telemarketing acts or practices.

(a) Abusive conduct generally. It is an abusive telemarketing act or practice and a violation of this Rule for any seller or telemarketer to engage in the following conduct:

(1) Threats, intimidation, or the use of profane or obscene language;

(2) Requesting or receiving payment of any fee or consideration for goods or services represented to remove derogatory information from, or improve, a person's credit history, credit record, or credit rating until:

(i) The time frame in which the seller has represented all of the goods or services will be provided to that person has expired; and

(ii) The seller has provided the person with documentation in the form of a consumer report from a consumer reporting agency demonstrating that the promised results have been achieved, such report having been issued more than six months after the results were achieved. Nothing in this Rule should be construed to affect the requirement in the Fair Credit Reporting Act, 15 U.S.C. 1681, that a consumer report may only be obtained for a specified permissible purpose;

(3) Requesting or receiving payment of any fee or consideration from a person for goods or services represented to recover or otherwise assist in the return of money or any other item of value paid for by, or promised to, that person in a previous telemarketing transaction, until seven (7) business days after such money or other item is delivered to that person. This provision shall not apply to goods or services provided to a person by a licensed attorney;

(4) Requesting or receiving payment of any fee or consideration in advance of obtaining a loan or other extension of credit when the seller or telemarketer has guaranteed or represented a high likelihood of success in obtaining or arranging a loan or other extension of credit for a person;

(5)(i) Requesting or receiving payment of any fee or consideration for any debt relief service until and unless:

(A) the seller or telemarketer has renegotiated, settled, reduced, or otherwise altered the terms of at least one debt pursuant to a settlement agreement, debt management plan,

---

3   Truth in Lending Act, 15 U.S.C. 1601 *et seq.*, and Regulation Z, 12 CFR part 226.

4   Electronic Fund Transfer Act, 15 U.S.C. 1693 *et seq.*, and Regulation E, 12 CFR part 205.

5   For purposes of this Rule, the term "signature" shall include an electronic or digital form of signature, to the extent that such form of signature is recognized as a valid signature under applicable federal law or state contract law.

or other such valid contractual agreement executed by the customer;

(B) the customer has made at least one payment pursuant to that settlement agreement, debt management plan, or other valid contractual agreement between the customer and the creditor or debt collector; and

(C) to the extent that debts enrolled in a service are renegotiated, settled, reduced, or otherwise altered individually, the fee or consideration either:

(1) bears the same proportional relationship to the total fee for renegotiating, settling, reducing, or altering the terms of the entire debt balance as the individual debt amount bears to the entire debt amount. The individual debt amount and the entire debt amount are those owed at the time the debt was enrolled in the service; or

(2) is a percentage of the amount saved as a result of the renegotiation, settlement, reduction, or alteration. The percentage charged cannot change from one individual debt to another. The amount saved is the difference between the amount owed at the time the debt was enrolled in the service and the amount actually paid to satisfy the debt.

(ii) Nothing in § 310.4(a)(5)(i) prohibits requesting or requiring the customer to place funds in an account to be used for the debt relief provider's fees and for payments to creditors or debt collectors in connection with the renegotiation, settlement, reduction, or other alteration of the terms of payment or other terms of a debt, provided that:

(A) the funds are held in an account at an insured financial institution;

(B) the customer owns the funds held in the account and is paid accrued interest on the account, if any;

(C) the entity administering the account is not owned or controlled by, or in any way affiliated with, the debt relief service;

(D) the entity administering the account does not give or accept any money or other compensation in exchange for referrals of business involving the debt relief service; and

(E) the customer may withdraw from the debt relief service at any time without penalty, and must receive all funds in the account, other than funds earned by the debt relief service in compliance with § 310.4(a)(5)(i)(A) through (C), within seven (7) business days of the customer's request.

(6) Disclosing or receiving, for consideration, unencrypted consumer account numbers for use in telemarketing; provided, however, that this paragraph shall not apply to the disclosure or receipt of a customer's or donor's billing information to process a payment for goods or services or a charitable contribution pursuant to a transaction;

(7) Causing billing information to be submitted for payment, directly or indirectly, without the express informed consent of the customer or donor. In any telemarketing transaction, the seller or telemarketer must obtain the express informed consent of the customer or donor to be charged for the goods or services or charitable contribution and to be charged using the identified account. In any telemarketing transaction involving preacquired account information, the requirements in paragraphs (a)(7)(i) through (ii) of this section must be met to evidence express informed consent.

(i) In any telemarketing transaction involving preacquired account information and a free-to-pay conversion feature, the seller or telemarketer must:

(A) obtain from the customer, at a minimum, the last four (4) digits of the account number to be charged;

(B) obtain from the customer his or her express agreement to be charged for the goods or services and to be charged using the account number pursuant to paragraph (a)(7)(i)(A) of this section; and,

(C) make and maintain an audio recording of the entire telemarketing transaction.

(ii) In any other telemarketing transaction involving preacquired account information not described in paragraph (a)(6)(i) of this section, the seller or telemarketer must:

(A) at a minimum, identify the account to be charged with sufficient specificity for the customer or donor to understand what account will be charged; and

(B) obtain from the customer or donor his or her express agreement to be charged for the goods or services and to be charged using the account number identified pursuant to paragraph (a)(7)(ii)(A) of this section; or

(8) Failing to transmit or cause to be transmitted the telephone number, and, when made available by the telemarketer's carrier, the name of the telemarketer, to any caller identification service in use by a recipient of a telemarketing call; provided that it shall not be a violation to substitute (for the name and phone number used in, or billed for, making the call) the name of the seller or charitable organization on behalf of which a telemarketing call is placed, and the seller's or charitable organization's customer or donor service telephone number, which is answered during regular business hours.

(b) Pattern of calls.

(1) It is an abusive telemarketing act or practice and a violation of this Rule for a telemarketer to engage in, or for a seller to cause a telemarketer to engage in, the following conduct:

(i) Causing any telephone to ring, or engaging any person in telephone conversation, repeatedly or continuously with intent to annoy, abuse, or harass any person at the called number;

(ii) Denying or interfering in any way, directly or indirectly, with a person's right to be placed on any registry of names and/or telephone numbers of persons who do not wish to receive outbound telephone calls established to comply with § 310.4(b)(1)(iii);

(iii) Initiating any outbound telephone call to a person when:

(A) that person previously has stated that he or she does not wish to receive an outbound telephone call made by or on behalf of the seller whose goods or services are being offered or made on behalf of the charitable organization for which a charitable contribution is being solicited; or

(B) that person's telephone number is on the "do-not-call" registry, maintained by the Commission, of persons who do not wish to receive outbound telephone calls to induce the purchase of goods or services unless the seller

(*i*) has obtained the express agreement, in writing, of such person to place calls to that person. Such written agreement shall clearly evidence such person's authorization that calls made by or on behalf of a specific party may be placed to that person, and shall include the telephone number to which the calls may be placed and the signature[6] of that person; or

(*ii*) as an established business relationship with such person, and that person has not stated that he or she does not wish to receive outbound telephone calls under paragraph (b)(1)(iii)(A) of this section; or

(iv) Abandoning any outbound telephone call. An outbound telephone call is "abandoned" under this section if a person answers it and the telemarketer does not connect the call to a sales representative within two (2) seconds of the person's completed greeting.

(v) Initiating any outbound telephone call that delivers a prerecorded message, other than a prerecorded message permitted for compliance with the call abandonment safe harbor in § 310.4(b)(4)(iii), unless:

---

6   For purposes of this Rule, the term "signature" shall include an electronic or digital form of signature, to the extent that such form of signature is recognized as a valid signature under applicable federal law or state contract law.

(A) in any such call to induce the purchase of any good or service, the seller has obtained from the recipient of the call an express agreement, in writing, that:

(i) The seller obtained only after a clear and conspicuous disclosure that the purpose of the agreement is to authorize the seller to place prerecorded calls to such person;

(ii) The seller obtained without requiring, directly or indirectly, that the agreement be executed as a condition of purchasing any good or service;

(iii) Evidences the willingness of the recipient of the call to receive calls that deliver prerecorded messages by or on behalf of a specific seller; and

(iv) Includes such person's telephone number and signature;[7] and

(B) In any such call to induce the purchase of any good or service, or to induce a charitable contribution from a member of, or previous donor to, a non-profit charitable organization on whose behalf the call is made, the seller or telemarketer:

(i) Allows the telephone to ring for at least fifteen (15) seconds or four (4) rings before disconnecting an unanswered call; and

(ii) Within two (2) seconds after the completed greeting of the person called, plays a prerecorded message that promptly provides the disclosures required by § 310.4(d) or (e), followed immediately by a disclosure of one or both of the following:

(A) In the case of a call that could be answered in person by a consumer, that the person called can use an automated interactive voice and/or keypress-activated opt-out mechanism to assert a Do Not Call request pursuant to § 310.4(b)(1)(iii)(A) at any time during the message. The mechanism must:

(1) Automatically add the number called to the seller's entity-specific Do Not Call list;

(2) Once invoked, immediately disconnect the call; and

(3) Be available for use at any time during the message; and

(B) In the case of a call that could be answered by an answering machine or voicemail service, that the person called can use a toll-free telephone number to assert a Do Not Call request pursuant to § 310.4(b)(1)(iii)(A). The number provided must connect directly to an automated interactive voice or keypress-activated opt-out mechanism that:

(1) Automatically adds the number called to the seller's entity-specific Do Not Call list;

(2) Immediately thereafter disconnects the call; and

(3) Is accessible at any time throughout the duration of the telemarketing campaign; and

(iii) Complies with all other requirements of this part and other applicable federal and state laws.

(C) Any call that complies with all applicable requirements of this paragraph (v) shall not be deemed to violate § 310.4(b)(1)(iv) of this part.

(D) This paragraph (v) shall not apply to any outbound telephone call that delivers a prerecorded healthcare message made by, or on behalf of, a covered entity or its business associate, as those terms are defined in the HIPAA Privacy Rule, 45 CFR 160.103.

(2) It is an abusive telemarketing act or practice and a violation of this Rule for any person to sell, rent, lease, purchase, or use any list established to comply with § 310.4(b)(1)(iii)(A), or maintained by the Commission pursuant to § 310.4(b)(1)(iii)(B), for any purpose except compliance with the provisions of this Rule or otherwise to prevent telephone calls to telephone numbers on such lists.

(3) A seller or telemarketer will not be liable for violating § 310.4(b)(1) (ii) and (iii) if it can demonstrate that, as part of the seller's or telemarketer's routine business practice:

(i) It has established and implemented written procedures to comply with § 310.4(b)(1)(ii) and (iii);

(ii) It has trained its personnel, and any entity assisting in its compliance, in the procedures established pursuant to § 310.4(b)(3)(i);

(iii) The seller, or a telemarketer or another person acting on behalf of the seller or charitable organization, has maintained and recorded a list of telephone numbers the seller or charitable organization may not contact, in compliance with § 310.4(b)(1)(iii)(A);

(iv) The seller or a telemarketer uses a process to prevent telemarketing to any telephone number on any list established pursuant to § 310.4(b)(3)(iii) or 310.4(b)(1)(iii)(B), employing a version of the "do-not-call" registry obtained from the Commission no more than thirty-one (31) days prior to the date any call is made, and maintains records documenting this process;

(v) The seller or a telemarketer or another person acting on behalf of the seller or charitable organization, monitors and enforces compliance with the procedures established pursuant to § 310.4(b)(3)(i); and

(vi) Any subsequent call otherwise violating § 310.4(b)(1)(ii) or (iii) is the result of error.

(4) A seller or telemarketer will not be liable for violating § 310.4(b)(1)(iv) if:

(i) The seller or telemarketer employs technology that ensures abandonment of no more than three (3) percent of all calls answered by a person, measured over the duration of a single calling campaign, if less than 30 days, or separately over each successive 30-day period or portion thereof that the campaign continues.

(ii) The seller or telemarketer, for each telemarketing call placed, allows the telephone to ring for at least fifteen (15) seconds or four (4) rings before disconnecting an unanswered call;

(iii) Whenever a sales representative is not available to speak with the person answering the call within two (2) seconds after the person's completed greeting, the seller or telemarketer promptly plays a recorded message that states the name and telephone number of the seller on whose behalf the call was placed[8]; and

(iv) The seller or telemarketer, in accordance with § 310.5(b)-(d), retains records establishing compliance with § 310.4(b)(4)(i)-(iii).

(c) Calling time restrictions. Without the prior consent of a person, it is an abusive telemarketing act or practice and a violation of this Rule for a telemarketer to engage in outbound telephone calls to a person's residence at any time other than between 8:00 a.m. and 9:00 p.m. local time at the called person's location.

(d) Required oral disclosures in the sale of goods or services. It is an abusive telemarketing act or practice and a violation of this Rule for a telemarketer in an outbound telephone call or internal or external upsell to induce the purchase of goods or services to fail to disclose truthfully, promptly, and in a clear and conspicuous manner to the person receiving the call, the following information:

(1) The identity of the seller;

(2) That the purpose of the call is to sell goods or services;

(3) The nature of the goods or services; and

(4) That no purchase or payment is necessary to be able to win a prize or participate in a prize promotion if a prize promotion is offered and that any purchase or payment will not increase the person's chances of winning. This disclosure must be made before or in conjunction with the description of the prize to the person called. If requested by that person, the telemarketer must disclose the no-purchase/no-payment

---

7 For purposes of this Rule, the term "signature" shall include an electronic or digital form of signature, to the extent that such form of signature is recognized as a valid signature under applicable federal law or state contract law.

8 This provision does not affect any seller's or telemarketer's obligation to comply with relevant state and federal laws, including but not limited to the TCPA, 47 U.S.C. 227, and 47 CFR part 64.1200.

entry method for the prize promotion; provided, however, that, in any internal upsell for the sale of goods or services, the seller or telemarketer must provide the disclosures listed in this section only to the extent that the information in the upsell differs from the disclosures provided in the initial telemarketing transaction.

(e) Required oral disclosures in charitable solicitations. It is an abusive telemarketing act or practice and a violation of this Rule for a telemarketer, in an outbound telephone call to induce a charitable contribution, to fail to disclose truthfully, promptly, and in a clear and conspicuous manner to the person receiving the call, the following information:

(1) The identity of the charitable organization on behalf of which the request is being made; and

(2) That the purpose of the call is to solicit a charitable contribution.

[75 Fed. Reg. 48,458 (Aug. 10, 2010); 76 Fed. Reg. 58,716 (Sept. 22, 2011)]

16 C.F.R. § 310.5   Recordkeeping requirements.

(a) Any seller or telemarketer shall keep, for a period of 24 months from the date the record is produced, the following records relating to its telemarketing activities:

(1) All substantially different advertising, brochures, telemarketing scripts, and promotional materials;

(2) The name and last known address of each prize recipient and the prize awarded for prizes that are represented, directly or by implication, to have a value of $25.00 or more;

(3) The name and last known address of each customer, the goods or services purchased, the date such goods or services were shipped or provided, and the amount paid by the customer for the goods or services;[9]

(4) The name, any fictitious name used, the last known home address and telephone number, and the job title(s) for all current and former employees directly involved in telephone sales or solicitations; provided, however, that if the seller or telemarketer permits fictitious names to be used by employees, each fictitious name must be traceable to only one specific employee; and

(5) All verifiable authorizations or records of express informed consent or express agreement required to be provided or received under this Rule.

(b) A seller or telemarketer may keep the records required by § 310.5(a) in any form, and in the same manner, format, or place as they keep such records in the ordinary course of business. Failure to keep all records required by § 310.5(a) shall be a violation of this Rule.

(c) The seller and the telemarketer calling on behalf of the seller may, by written agreement, allocate responsibility between themselves for the recordkeeping required by this Section. When a seller and telemarketer have entered into such an agreement, the terms of that agreement shall govern, and the seller or telemarketer, as the case may be, need not keep records that duplicate those of the other. If the agreement is unclear as to who must maintain any required record(s), or if no such agreement exists, the seller shall be responsible for complying with §§ 310.5(a)(1)–(3) and (5); the telemarketer shall be responsible for complying with § 310.5(a)(4).

(d) In the event of any dissolution or termination of the seller's or telemarketer's business, the principal of that seller or telemarketer shall maintain all records as required under this section. In the event of any sale, assignment, or other change in ownership of the seller's or telemarketer's business, the successor business shall maintain all records required under this section.

[75 Fed. Reg. 48,458 (Aug. 10, 2010)]

9　For offers of consumer credit products subject to the Truth in Lending Act, 15 U.S.C. 1601 et seq., and Regulation Z, 12 CFR 226, compliance with the recordkeeping requirements under the Truth in Lending Act, and Regulation Z, shall constitute compliance with § 310.5(a)(3) of this Rule.

16 C.F.R. § 310.6   Exemptions.

(a) Solicitations to induce charitable contributions via outbound telephone calls are not covered by § 310.4(b)(1)(iii)(B) of this Rule.

(b) The following acts or practices are exempt from this Rule:

(1) The sale of pay-per-call services subject to the Commission's Rule entitled "Trade Regulation Rule Pursuant to the Telephone Disclosure and Dispute Resolution Act of 1992," 16 CFR Part 308, provided, however, that this exemption does not apply to the requirements of §§ 310.4(a)(1), (a)(7), (b), and (c);

(2) The sale of franchises subject to the Commission's Rule entitled "Disclosure Requirements and Prohibitions Concerning Franchising," ("Franchise Rule") 16 CFR Part 436, and the sale of business opportunities subject to the Commission's Rule entitled "Disclosure Requirements and Prohibitions Concerning Business Opportunities," ("Business Opportunity Rule") 16 CFR Part 437, provided, however, that this exemption does not apply to the requirements of §§ 310.4(a)(1), (a)(7), (b), and (c);

(3) Telephone calls in which the sale of goods or services or charitable solicitation is not completed, and payment or authorization of payment is not required, until after a face-to-face sales or donation presentation by the seller or charitable organization, provided, however, that this exemption does not apply to the requirements of §§ 310.4(a)(1), (a)(7), (b), and (c);

(4) Telephone calls initiated by a customer or donor that are not the result of any solicitation by a seller, charitable organization, or telemarketer, provided, however, that this exemption does not apply to any instances of upselling included in such telephone calls;

(5) Telephone calls initiated by a customer or donor in response to an advertisement through any medium, other than direct mail solicitation, provided, however, that this exemption does not apply to calls initiated by a customer or donor in response to an advertisement relating to investment opportunities, debt relief services, business opportunities other than business arrangements covered by the Franchise Rule or Business Opportunity Rule, or advertisements involving goods or services described in §§ 310.3(a)(1)(vi) or 310.4(a)(2)–(4); or to any instances of upselling included in such telephone calls;

(6) Telephone calls initiated by a customer or donor in response to a direct mail solicitation, including solicitations via the U.S. Postal Service, facsimile transmission, electronic mail, and other similar methods of delivery in which a solicitation is directed to specific address(es) or person(s), that clearly, conspicuously, and truthfully discloses all material information listed in § 310.3(a)(1) of this Rule, for any goods or services offered in the direct mail solicitation, and that contains no material misrepresentation regarding any item contained in § 310.3(d) of this Rule for any requested charitable contribution; provided, however, that this exemption does not apply to calls initiated by a customer in response to a direct mail solicitation relating to prize promotions, investment opportunities, debt relief services, business opportunities other than business arrangements covered by the Franchise Rule or Business Opportunity Rule, or goods or services described in §§ 310.3(a)(1)(vi) or 310.4(a)(2)–(4); or to any instances of upselling included in such telephone calls; and

(7) Telephone calls between a telemarketer and any business, except calls to induce the retail sale of nondurable office or cleaning supplies; provided, however, that § 310.4(b)(1)(iii)(B) and § 310.5 of this Rule shall not apply to sellers or telemarketers of nondurable office or cleaning supplies.

[75 Fed. Reg. 48,458 (Aug. 10, 2010)]

16 C.F.R. § 310.7   Actions by states and private persons.

(a) Any attorney general or other officer of a state authorized by the state to bring an action under the Telemarketing and Consumer Fraud and

Abuse Prevention Act, and any private person who brings an action under that Act, shall serve written notice of its action on the Commission, if feasible, prior to its initiating an action under this Rule. The notice shall be sent to the Office of the Director, Bureau of Consumer Protection, Federal Trade Commission, Washington, D.C. 20580, and shall include a copy of the state's or private person's complaint and any other pleadings to be filed with the court. If prior notice is not feasible, the state or private person shall serve the Commission with the required notice immediately upon instituting its action.

(b) Nothing contained in this Section shall prohibit any attorney general or other authorized state official from proceeding in state court on the basis of an alleged violation of any civil or criminal statute of such state.

[75 Fed. Reg. 48,458 (Aug. 10, 2010)]

16 C.F.R. § 310.8   Fee for access to the National Do Not Call Registry.

(a) It is a violation of this Rule for any seller to initiate, or cause any telemarketer to initiate, an outbound telephone call to any person whose telephone number is within a given area code unless such seller, either directly or through another person, first has paid the annual fee, required by § 310.8(c), for access to telephone numbers within that area code that are included in the National Do Not Call Registry maintained by the Commission under § 310.4(b)(1)(iii)(B); provided, however, that such payment is not necessary if the seller initiates, or causes a telemarketer to initiate, calls solely to persons pursuant to §§ 310.4(b)(1)(iii)(B)(i) or (ii), and the seller does not access the National Do Not Call Registry for any other purpose.

(b) It is a violation of this Rule for any telemarketer, on behalf of any seller, to initiate an outbound telephone call to any person whose telephone number is within a given area code unless that seller, either directly or through another person, first has paid the annual fee, required by § 310.8(c), for access to the telephone numbers within that area code that are included in the National Do Not Call Registry; provided, however, that such payment is not necessary if the seller initiates, or causes a telemarketer to initiate, calls solely to persons pursuant to §§ 310.4(b)(1)(iii)(B)(i) or (ii), and the seller does not access the National Do Not Call Registry for any other purpose.

(c) The annual fee, which must be paid by any person prior to obtaining access to the National Do Not Call Registry, is $60 for each area code of data accessed, up to a maximum of $16,482; provided, however, that there shall be no charge to any person for accessing the first five area codes of data, and provided further, that there shall be no charge to any person engaging in or causing others to engage in outbound telephone calls to consumers and who is accessing area codes of data in the National Do Not Call Registry if the person is permitted to access, but is not required to access, the National Do Not Call Registry under this Rule, 47 CFR 64.1200, or any other Federal regulation or law. Any person accessing the National Do Not Call Registry may not participate in any arrangement to share the cost of accessing the registry, including any arrangement with any telemarketer or service provider to divide the costs to access the registry among various clients of that telemarketer or service provider.

(d) Each person who pays, either directly or through another person, the annual fee set forth in § 310.8(c), each person excepted under § 310.8(c) from paying the annual fee, and each person excepted from paying an annual fee under § 310.4(b)(1)(iii)(B), will be provided a unique account number that will allow that person to access the registry data for the selected area codes at any time for the twelve month period beginning on the first day of the month in which the person paid the fee ("the annual period"). To obtain access to additional area codes of data during the first six months of the annual period, each person required to pay the fee under § 310.8(c) must first pay $60 for each additional area code of data not

initially selected. To obtain access to additional area codes of data during the second six months of the annual period, each person required to pay the fee under § 310.8(c) must first pay $30 for each additional area code of data not initially selected. The payment of the additional fee will permit the person to access the additional area codes of data for the remainder of the annual period.

(e) Access to the National Do Not Call Registry is limited to telemarketers, sellers, others engaged in or causing others to engage in telephone calls to consumers, service providers acting on behalf of such persons, and any government agency that has law enforcement authority. Prior to accessing the National Do Not Call Registry, a person must provide the identifying information required by the operator of the registry to collect the fee, and must certify, under penalty of law, that the person is accessing the registry solely to comply with the provisions of this Rule or to otherwise prevent telephone calls to telephone numbers on the registry. If the person is accessing the registry on behalf of sellers, that person also must identify each of the sellers on whose behalf it is accessing the registry, must provide each seller's unique account number for access to the national registry, and must certify, under penalty of law, that the sellers will be using the information gathered from the registry solely to comply with the provisions of this Rule or otherwise to prevent telephone calls to telephone numbers on the registry.

[75 Fed. Reg. 48,458 (Aug. 10, 2010); 75 Fed. Reg. 51,934 (Aug. 24, 2010); 76 Fed. Reg. 53,636 (Aug. 29, 2011); 77 Fed. Reg. 51,697 (Aug. 27, 2012); 78 Fed. Reg. 53,642 (Aug. 30, 2013); Fed. Reg. 51,477 (Aug. 29. 2014)]

16 C.F.R. § 310.9   Severability.

The provisions of this Rule are separate and severable from one another. If any provision is stayed or determined to be invalid, it is the Commission's intention that the remaining provisions shall continue in effect.

[75 Fed. Reg. 48,458 (Aug. 10, 2010)]

C.2   Telephone and Fax Solicitations

C.2.1   Telephone Consumer Protection Act

C.2.1.1   Introduction

Appendix C.2.1 reprints the Telephone Consumer Protection Act as amended through Pub. L. No. 114-74 (Nov. 2, 2015), including some uncodified Congressional findings found in the 1991 Act. The 2015 amendments are shown in redline. The public law includes this uncodified amendment at its section 301(b):

> DEADLINE FOR REGULATIONS.—Not later than 9 months after the date of enactment of this Act, the Federal Communications Commission, in consultation with the Department of Treasury, shall prescribe regulations to implement the amendments made by this section.

Online updates to this treatise will address the effective date of these amendments, their scope, and substance.

C.2.1.2   Telephone Consumer Protection Act— Selected Provisions

Uncodified Congressional Findings of the TCPA of 1991

An Act to amend the Communications Act of 1934 to prohibit certain practices involving the use of telephone equipment.

Be it enacted by the Senate and House of Representatives of the United States of America in Congress assembled,

<< 47 USCA §§ 227 nt, 609 NOTE >>

SECTION 1. SHORT TITLE.

This Act may be cited as the "Telephone Consumer Protection Act of 1991".

<< 47 USCA § 227 NOTE >>

SEC. 2. FINDINGS.

The Congress finds that:

(1) The use of the telephone to market goods and services to the home and other businesses is now pervasive due to the increased use of cost-effective telemarketing techniques.

(2) Over 30,000 businesses actively telemarket goods and services to business and residential customers.

(3) More than 300,000 solicitors call more than 18,000,000 Americans every day.

(4) Total United States sales generated through telemarketing amounted to $435,000,000,000 in 1990, a more than four-fold increase since 1984.

(5) Unrestricted telemarketing, however, can be an intrusive invasion of privacy and, when an emergency or medical assistance telephone line is seized, a risk to public safety.

(6) Many consumers are outraged over the proliferation of intrusive, nuisance calls to their homes from telemarketers.

(7) Over half the States now have statutes restricting various uses of the telephone for marketing, but telemarketers can evade their prohibitions through interstate operations; therefore, Federal law is needed to control residential telemarketing practices.

(8) The Constitution does not prohibit restrictions on commercial telemarketing solicitations.

(9) Individuals' privacy rights, public safety interests, and commercial freedoms of speech and trade must be balanced in a way that protects the privacy of individuals and permits legitimate telemarketing practices.

(10) Evidence compiled by the Congress indicates that residential telephone subscribers consider automated or prerecorded telephone calls, regardless of the content or the initiator of the message, to be a nuisance and an invasion of privacy.

(11) Technologies that might allow consumers to avoid receiving such calls are not universally available, are costly, are unlikely to be enforced, or place an inordinate burden on the consumer.

(12) Banning such automated or prerecorded telephone calls to the home, except when the receiving party consents to receiving the call or when such calls are necessary in an emergency situation affecting the health and safety of the consumer, is the only effective means of protecting telephone consumers from this nuisance and privacy invasion.

(13) While the evidence presented to the Congress indicates that automated or prerecorded calls are a nuisance and an invasion of privacy, regardless of the type of call, the Federal Communications Commission should have the flexibility to design different rules for those types of automated or prerecorded calls that it finds are not considered a nuisance or invasion of privacy, or for noncommercial calls, consistent with the free speech protections embodied in the First Amendment of the Constitution.

(14) Businesses also have complained to the Congress and the Federal Communications Commission that automated or prerecorded telephone calls are a nuisance, are an invasion of privacy, and interfere with interstate commerce.

(15) The Federal Communications Commission should consider adopting reasonable restrictions on automated or prerecorded calls to businesses as well as to the home, consistent with the constitutional protections of free speech.

[Pub. L. No. 102-243 (Dec. 20, 1991)]

* * *

47 U.S.C. § 227. Restrictions on the use of telephone equipment

(a) Definitions

As used in this section—

(1) The term "automatic telephone dialing system" means equipment which has the capacity—

    (A) to store or produce telephone numbers to be called, using a random or sequential number generator; and

    (B) to dial such numbers.

(2) The term "established business relationship," for purposes only of subsection (b)(1)(C)(i), shall have the meaning given the term in section 64.1200 of title 47, Code of Federal Regulations, as in effect on January 1, 2003, except that—

    (A) such term shall include a relationship between a person or entity and a business subscriber subject to the same terms applicable under such section to a relationship between a person or entity and a residential subscriber; and

    (B) an established business relationship shall be subject to any time limitation established pursuant to paragraph (2)(G)).

(3) The term "telephone facsimile machine" means equipment which has the capacity (A) to transcribe text or images, or both, from paper into an electronic signal and to transmit that signal over a regular telephone line, or (B) to transcribe text or images (or both) from an electronic signal received over a regular telephone line onto paper.

(4) The term "telephone solicitation" means the initiation of a telephone call or message for the purpose of encouraging the purchase or rental of, or investment in, property, goods, or services, which is transmitted to any person, but such term does not include a call or message (A) to any person with that person's prior express invitation or permission, (B) to any person with whom the caller has an established business relationship, or (C) by a tax exempt nonprofit organization.

(5) The term "unsolicited advertisement" means any material advertising the commercial availability or quality of any property, goods, or services which is transmitted to any person without that person's prior express invitation or permission, in writing or otherwise.

(b) Restrictions on the use of automated telephone equipment

(1) Prohibitions

It shall be unlawful for any person within the United States, or any person outside the United States if the recipient is within the United States—

    (A) to make any call (other than a call made for emergency purposes or made with the prior express consent of the called party) using any automatic telephone dialing system or an artificial or prerecorded voice—

        (i) to any emergency telephone line (including any "911" line and any emergency line of a hospital, medical physician or service office, health care facility, poison control center, or fire protection or law enforcement agency);

        (ii) to the telephone line of any guest room or patient room of a hospital, health care facility, elderly home, or similar establishment; or

        (iii) to any telephone number assigned to a paging service, cellular telephone service, specialized mobile radio service, or other radio common carrier service, or any service for which the called party is charged for the call unless such call is made solely to collect a debt owed to or guaranteed by the United States;

    (B) to initiate any telephone call to any residential telephone line using an artificial or prerecorded voice to deliver a message without the prior express consent of the called party, unless the call is initiated for emergency purposes, is made solely pursuant to the collection of a debt owed to or guaranteed by the United States, or is exempted by rule or order by the Commission under paragraph (2)(B);

(C) to use any telephone facsimile machine, computer, or other device to send, to a telephone facsimile machine, an unsolicited advertisement, unless—

(i) the unsolicited advertisement is from a sender with an established business relationship with the recipient;

(ii) the sender obtained the number of the telephone facsimile machine through—

(I) the voluntary communication of such number, within the context of such established business relationship, from the recipient of the unsolicited advertisement, or

(II) a directory, advertisement, or site on the Internet to which the recipient voluntarily agreed to make available its facsimile number for public distribution, except that this clause shall not apply in the case of an unsolicited advertisement that is sent based on an established business relationship with the recipient that was in existence before the date of enactment of the Junk Fax Prevention Act of 2005 if the sender possessed the facsimile machine number of the recipient before such date of enactment; and

(iii) the unsolicited advertisement contains a notice meeting the requirements under paragraph (2)(D), except that the exception under clauses (i) and (ii) shall not apply with respect to an unsolicited advertisement sent to a telephone facsimile machine by a sender to whom a request has been made not to send future unsolicited advertisements to such telephone facsimile machine that complies with the requirements under paragraph (2)(E); or

(D) to use an automatic telephone dialing system in such a way that two or more telephone lines of a multi-line business are engaged simultaneously.

(2) Regulations; exemptions and other provisions

The Commission shall prescribe regulations to implement the requirements of this subsection. In implementing the requirements of this subsection, the Commission—

(A) shall consider prescribing regulations to allow businesses to avoid receiving calls made using an artificial or prerecorded voice to which they have not given their prior express consent;

(B) may, by rule or order, exempt from the requirements of paragraph (1)(B) of this subsection, subject to such conditions as the Commission may prescribe—

(i) calls that are not made for a commercial purpose; and

(ii) such classes or categories of calls made for commercial purposes as the Commission determines—

(I) will not adversely affect the privacy rights that this section is intended to protect; and

(II) do not include the transmission of any unsolicited advertisement;

(C) may, by rule or order, exempt from the requirements of paragraph (1)(A)(iii) of this subsection calls to a telephone number assigned to a cellular telephone service that are not charged to the called party, subject to such conditions as the Commission may prescribe as necessary in the interest of the privacy rights this section is intended to protect;

(D) shall provide that a notice contained in an unsolicited advertisement complies with the requirements under this subparagraph only if—

(i) the notice is clear and conspicuous and on the first page of the unsolicited advertisement;

(ii) the notice states that the recipient may make a request to the sender of the unsolicited advertisement not to send any future unsolicited advertisements to a telephone facsimile machine or machines and that failure to comply, within the shortest reasonable time, as determined by the Commission, with such a request meeting the requirements under subparagraph (E) is unlawful;

(iii) the notice sets forth the requirements for a request under subparagraph (E);

(iv) the notice includes—

(I) a domestic contact telephone and facsimile machine number for the recipient to transmit such a request to the sender; and

(II) a cost-free mechanism for a recipient to transmit a request pursuant to such notice to the sender of the unsolicited advertisement; the Commission shall by rule require the sender to provide such a mechanism and may, in the discretion of the Commission and subject to such conditions as the Commission may prescribe, exempt certain classes of small business senders, but only if the Commission determines that the costs to such class are unduly burdensome given the revenues generated by such small businesses;

(v) the telephone and facsimile machine numbers and the cost-free mechanism set forth pursuant to clause (iv) permit an individual or business to make such a request at any time on any day of the week; and

(vi) the notice complies with the requirements of subsection (d);

(E) shall provide, by rule, that a request not to send future unsolicited advertisements to a telephone facsimile machine complies with the requirements under this subparagraph only if—

(i) the request identifies the telephone number or numbers of the telephone facsimile machine or machines to which the request relates;

(ii) the request is made to the telephone or facsimile number of the sender of such an unsolicited advertisement provided pursuant to subparagraph (D)(iv) or by any other method of communication as determined by the Commission; and

(iii) the person making the request has not, subsequent to such request, provided express invitation or permission to the sender, in writing or otherwise, to send such advertisements to such person at such telephone facsimile machine;

(F) may, in the discretion of the Commission and subject to such conditions as the Commission may prescribe, allow professional or trade associations that are tax-exempt nonprofit organizations to send unsolicited advertisements to their members in furtherance of the association's tax-exempt purpose that do not contain the notice required by paragraph (1)(C)(iii), except that the Commission may take action under this subparagraph only—

(i) by regulation issued after public notice and opportunity for public comment; and

(ii) if the Commission determines that such notice required by paragraph (1)(C)(iii) is not necessary to protect the ability of the members of such associations to stop such associations from sending any future unsolicited advertisements; and

(G) (i) may, consistent with clause (ii), limit the duration of the existence of an established business relationship, however, before establishing any such limits, the Commission shall—

(I) determine whether the existence of the exception under paragraph (1)(C) relating to an established business relationship has resulted in a significant number of complaints to the Commission regarding the sending of unsolicited advertisements to telephone facsimile machines;

(II) determine whether a significant number of any such complaints involve unsolicited advertisements that were sent on the basis of an established business relationship that was longer in duration than the Commission believes is consistent with the reasonable expectations of consumers;

(III) evaluate the costs to senders of demonstrating the existence of an established business relationship within a specified period of time and the benefits to recipients of establishing a limitation on such established business relationship; and

(IV) determine whether with respect to small businesses, the costs would not be unduly burdensome; and

(ii) may not commence a proceeding to determine whether to limit the duration of the existence of an established business relationship before the expiration of the 3-month period that begins on the date of the enactment of the Junk Fax Prevention Act of 2005-; and

(H) may restrict or limit the number and duration of calls made to a telephone number assigned to a cellular telephone service to collect a debt owed to or guaranteed by the United States.

(3) Private right of action

A person or entity may, if otherwise permitted by the laws or rules of court of a State, bring in an appropriate court of that State—

(A) an action based on a violation of this subsection or the regulations prescribed under this subsection to enjoin such violation,

(B) an action to recover for actual monetary loss from such a violation, or to receive $500 in damages for each such violation, whichever is greater, or

(C) both such actions.

If the court finds that the defendant willfully or knowingly violated this subsection or the regulations prescribed under this subsection, the court may, in its discretion, increase the amount of the award to an amount equal to not more than 3 times the amount available under subparagraph (B) of this paragraph.

(c) Protection of subscriber privacy rights

(1) Rulemaking proceeding required

Within 120 days after December 20, 1991, the Commission shall initiate a rulemaking proceeding concerning the need to protect residential telephone subscribers' privacy rights to avoid receiving telephone solicitations to which they object. The proceeding shall—

(A) compare and evaluate alternative methods and procedures (including the use of electronic databases, telephone network technologies, special directory markings, industry-based or company-specific "do not call" systems, and any other alternatives, individually or in combination) for their effectiveness in protecting such privacy rights, and in terms of their cost and other advantages and disadvantages;

(B) evaluate the categories of public and private entities that would have the capacity to establish and administer such methods and procedures;

(C) consider whether different methods and procedures may apply for local telephone solicitations, such as local telephone solicitations of small businesses or holders of second class mail permits;

(D) consider whether there is a need for additional Commission authority to further restrict telephone solicitations, including those calls exempted under subsection (a)(3) of this section, and, if such a finding is made and supported by the record, propose specific restrictions to the Congress; and

(E) develop proposed regulations to implement the methods and procedures that the Commission determines are most effective and efficient to accomplish the purposes of this section.

(2) Regulations

Not later than 9 months after December 20, 1991, the Commission shall conclude the rulemaking proceeding initiated under paragraph (1) and shall prescribe regulations to implement methods and procedures for protecting the privacy rights described in such paragraph in an efficient, effective, and economic manner and without the imposition of any additional charge to telephone subscribers.

(3) Use of database permitted

The regulations required by paragraph (2) may require the establishment and operation of a single national database to compile a list of telephone numbers of residential subscribers who object to receiving telephone solicitations, and to make that compiled list and parts thereof available for purchase. If the Commission determines to require such a database, such regulations shall—

(A) specify a method by which the Commission will select an entity to administer such database;

(B) require each common carrier providing telephone exchange service, in accordance with regulations prescribed by the Commission, to inform subscribers for telephone exchange service of the opportunity to provide notification, in accordance with regulations established under this paragraph, that such subscriber objects to receiving telephone solicitations;

(C) specify the methods by which each telephone subscriber shall be informed, by the common carrier that provides local exchange service to that subscriber, of (i) the subscriber's right to give or revoke a notification of an objection under subparagraph (A), and (ii) the methods by which such right may be exercised by the subscriber;

(D) specify the methods by which such objections shall be collected and added to the database;

(E) prohibit any residential subscriber from being charged for giving or revoking such notification or for being included in a database compiled under this section;

(F) prohibit any person from making or transmitting a telephone solicitation to the telephone number of any subscriber included in such database;

(G) specify (i) the methods by which any person desiring to make or transmit telephone solicitations will obtain access to the database, by area code or local exchange prefix, as required to avoid calling the telephone numbers of subscribers included in such database; and (ii) the costs to be recovered from such persons;

(H) specify the methods for recovering, from persons accessing such database, the costs involved in identifying, collecting, updating, disseminating, and selling, and other activities relating to, the operations of the database that are incurred by the entities carrying out those activities;

(I) specify the frequency with which such database will be updated and specify the method by which such updating will take effect for purposes of compliance with the regulations prescribed under this subsection;

(J) be designed to enable States to use the database mechanism selected by the Commission for purposes of administering or enforcing State law;

(K) prohibit the use of such database for any purpose other than compliance with the requirements of this section and any such State law and specify methods for protection of the privacy rights of persons whose numbers are included in such database; and

(L) require each common carrier providing services to any person for the purpose of making telephone solicitations to notify such person of the requirements of this section and the regulations thereunder.

(4) Considerations required for use of database method

If the Commission determines to require the database mechanism described in paragraph (3), the Commission shall—

(A) in developing procedures for gaining access to the database, consider the different needs of telemarketers conducting business on a national, regional, State, or local level;

(B) develop a fee schedule or price structure for recouping the cost of such database that recognizes such differences and—

(i) reflect the relative costs of providing a national, regional, State, or local list of phone numbers of subscribers who object to receiving telephone solicitations;

(ii) reflect the relative costs of providing such lists on paper or electronic media; and

(iii) not place an unreasonable financial burden on small businesses; and

(C) consider (i) whether the needs of telemarketers operating on a local basis could be met through special markings of area white pages directories, and (ii) if such directories are needed as an adjunct to database lists prepared by area code and local exchange prefix.

(5) Private right of action

A person who has received more than one telephone call within any 12-month period by or on behalf of the same entity in violation of the regulations prescribed under this subsection may, if otherwise permitted by the laws or rules of court of a State bring in an appropriate court of that State—

(A) an action based on a violation of the regulations prescribed under this subsection to enjoin such violation,

(B) an action to recover for actual monetary loss from such a violation, or to receive up to $500 in damages for each such violation, whichever is greater, or

(C) both such actions.

It shall be an affirmative defense in any action brought under this paragraph that the defendant has established and implemented, with due care, reasonable practices and procedures to effectively prevent telephone solicitations in violation of the regulations prescribed under this subsection. If the court finds that the defendant willfully or knowingly violated the regulations prescribed under this subsection, the court may, in its discretion, increase the amount of the award to an amount equal to not more than 3 times the amount available under subparagraph (B) of this paragraph.

(6) Relation to subsection (b)

The provisions of this subsection shall not be construed to permit a communication prohibited by subsection (b) of this section.

(d) Technical and procedural standards

(1) Prohibition

It shall be unlawful for any person within the United States—

(A) to initiate any communication using a telephone facsimile machine, or to make any telephone call using any automatic telephone dialing system, that does not comply with the technical and procedural standards prescribed under this subsection, or to use any telephone facsimile machine or automatic telephone dialing system in a manner that does not comply with such standards; or

(B) to use a computer or other electronic device to send any message via a telephone facsimile machine unless such person clearly marks, in a margin at the top or bottom of each transmitted page of the message or on the first page of the transmission, the date and time it is sent and an identification of the business, other entity, or individual sending the message and the telephone number of the sending machine or of such business, other entity, or individual.

(2) Telephone facsimile machines

The Commission shall revise the regulations setting technical and procedural standards for telephone facsimile machines to require that any such machine which is manufactured after one year after December 20, 1991, clearly marks, in a margin at the top or bottom of each transmitted page or on the first page of each transmission, the date and time sent, an identification of the business, other entity, or individual sending the message, and the telephone number of the sending machine or of such business, other entity, or individual.

(3) Artificial or prerecorded voice systems

The Commission shall prescribe technical and procedural standards for systems that are used to transmit any artificial or prerecorded voice message via telephone. Such standards shall require that—

(A) all artificial or prerecorded telephone messages (i) shall, at the beginning of the message, state clearly the identity of the business, individual, or other entity initiating the call, and (ii) shall, during or after the message, state clearly the telephone number or address of such business, other entity, or individual; and

(B) any such system will automatically release the called party's line within 5 seconds of the time notification is transmitted to the system that the called party has hung up, to allow the called party's line to be used to make or receive other calls.

(e) Prohibition on provision of inaccurate caller identification information

(1) In general

It shall be unlawful for any person within the United States, in connection with any telecommunications service or IP—enabled voice service, to cause any caller identification service to knowingly transmit misleading or inaccurate caller identification information with the intent to defraud, cause harm, or wrongfully obtain anything of value, unless such transmission is exempted pursuant to paragraph (3)(B).

(2) Protection for blocking caller identification information

Nothing in this subsection may be construed to prevent or restrict any person from blocking the capability of any caller identification service to transmit caller identification information.

(3) Regulations

(A) In general

Not later than 6 months after the date of enactment of the Truth in Caller ID Act of 2009, the Commission shall prescribe regulations to implement this subsection.

(B) Content of regulations

(i) In general

The regulations required under subparagraph (A) shall include such exemptions from the prohibition under paragraph (1) as the Commission determines is appropriate.

(ii) Specific exemption for law enforcement agencies or court orders

The regulations required under subparagraph (A) shall exempt from the prohibition under paragraph (1) transmissions in connection with—

(I) any authorized activity of a law enforcement agency; or

(II) a court order that specifically authorizes the use of caller identification manipulation.

(4) Report

Not later than 6 months after the enactment of the Truth in Caller ID Act of 2009, the Commission shall report to Congress whether additional legislation is necessary to prohibit the provision of inaccurate caller identification information in technologies that are successor or replacement technologies to telecommunications service or IP-enabled voice service.

(5) Penalties

(A) Civil forfeiture

(i) In general

Any person that is determined by the Commission, in accordance with paragraphs (3) and (4) of section 503(b), to have violated this subsection shall be liable to the United States for a forfeiture penalty. A forfeiture penalty under this paragraph shall be in addition to any other penalty provided for by this Act. The amount of the forfeiture penalty determined under this paragraph shall not exceed $10,000 for each violation, or 3 times that amount for each day of a continuing violation, except that the amount assessed for any continuing violation shall not exceed a total of $1,000,000 for any single act or failure to act.

(ii) Recovery

Any forfeiture penalty determined under clause (i) shall be recoverable pursuant to section 504(a).

(iii) Procedure

No forfeiture liability shall be determined under clause (i) against any person unless such person receives the notice required by section 503(b)(3) or section 503(b)(4).

(iv) 2-Year statute of limitations

No forfeiture penalty shall be determined or imposed against any person under clause (i) if the violation charged occurred more than 2 years prior to the date of issuance of the required notice or notice or apparent liability.

(B) Criminal fine

Any person who willfully and knowingly violates this subsection shall upon conviction thereof be fined not more than $10,000 for each violation, or 3 times that amount for each day of a continuing violation, in lieu of the fine provided by section 501 for such a violation. This subparagraph does not supersede the provisions of section 501 relating to imprisonment or the imposition of a penalty of both fine and imprisonment.

(6) Enforcement by states

(A) In general

The chief legal officer of a State, or any other State officer authorized by law to bring actions on behalf of the residents of a State, may bring a civil action, as parens patriae, on behalf of the residents of that State in an appropriate district court of the United States to enforce this subsection or to impose the civil penalties for violation of this subsection, whenever the chief legal officer or other State officer has reason to believe that the interests of the residents of the State have been or are being threatened or adversely affected by a violation of this subsection or a regulation under this subsection.

(B) Notice

The chief legal officer or other State officer shall serve written notice on the Commission of any civil action under subparagraph (A) prior to initiating such civil action. The notice shall include a copy of the complaint to be filed to initiate such civil action, except that if it is not feasible for the State to provide such prior notice, the State shall provide such notice immediately upon instituting such civil action.

(C) Authority to intervene

Upon receiving the notice required by subparagraph (B), the Commission shall have the right

(i) to intervene in the action;

(ii) upon so intervening, to be heard on all matters arising therein; and

(iii) to file petitions for appeal.

(D) Construction

For purposes of bringing any civil action under subparagraph (A), nothing in this paragraph shall prevent the chief legal officer or other State officer from exercising the powers conferred on that officer by the laws of such State to conduct investigations or to administer oaths or affirmations or to compel the attendance of witnesses or the production of documentary and other evidence.

(E) Venue; service or process

(i) Venue

An action brought under subparagraph (A) shall be brought in a district court of the United States that meets applicable requirements relating to venue under section 1391 of title 28, United States Code.

(ii) Service of process

In an action brought under subparagraph (A)

(I) process may be served without regard to the territorial limits of the district or of the State in which the action is instituted; and

(II) a person who participated in an alleged violation that is being litigated in the civil action may be joined in the civil action without regard to the residence of the person.

(7) Effect on other laws

This subsection does not prohibit any lawfully authorized investigative, protective, or intelligence activity of a law enforcement agency of the United States, a State, or a political subdivision of a State, or of an intelligence agency of the United States.

(8) Definitions

For purposes of this subsection:

(A) Caller identification information

The term "caller identification information" means information provided by a caller identification service regarding the telephone number of, or other information regarding the origination of, a call made using a telecommunications service or IP-enabled voice service.

(B) Caller identification service

The term "caller identification service" means any service or device designed to provide the user of the service or device with the telephone number of, or other information regarding the origination of, a call made using a telecommunications service or IP-enabled voice service. Such term includes automatic number identification services.

(C) IP-Enabled voice service

The term "IP-enabled voice service" has the meaning given that term by section 9.3 of the Commission's regulations (47 C.F.R. 9.3), as those regulations may be amended by the Commission from time to time.

(9) Limitation

Notwithstanding any other provision of this section, subsection (f) shall not apply to this subsection or to the regulations under this subsection.

(f) Effect on State law

(1) State law not preempted

Except for the standards prescribed under subsection (d) of this section and subject to paragraph (2) of this subsection, nothing in this section or in the regulations prescribed under this section shall preempt any State law that imposes more restrictive intrastate requirements or regulations on, or which prohibits—

(A) the use of telephone facsimile machines or other electronic devices to send unsolicited advertisements;

(B) the use of automatic telephone dialing systems;

(C) the use of artificial or prerecorded voice messages; or

(D) the making of telephone solicitations.

(2) State use of databases

If, pursuant to subsection (c)(3) of this section, the Commission requires the establishment of a single national database of telephone numbers of subscribers who object to receiving telephone solicitations, a State or local authority may not, in its regulation of telephone solicitations, require the use of any database, list, or listing system that does not include the part of such single national database that relates to such State.

(g) Actions by States

(1) Authority of States

Whenever the attorney general of a State, or an official or agency designated by a State, has reason to believe that any person has engaged or is engaging in a pattern or practice of telephone calls or other transmissions to residents of that State in violation of this section or the regulations prescribed under this section, the State may bring a civil action on behalf of its residents to enjoin such calls, an action to recover for actual monetary loss or receive $500 in damages for each violation, or both such actions. If the court finds the defendant willfully or knowingly violated such regulations, the court may, in its discretion, increase the amount of the award to an amount equal to not more than 3 times the amount available under the preceding sentence.

(2) Exclusive jurisdiction of Federal courts

The district courts of the United States, the United States courts of any territory, and the District Court of the United States for the District of Columbia shall have exclusive jurisdiction over all civil actions brought under this subsection. Upon proper application, such courts shall also have jurisdiction to issue writs of mandamus, or orders affording like relief, commanding the defendant to comply with the provisions of this section or regulations prescribed under this section, including the requirement that the defendant take such action as is necessary to remove the danger of such violation. Upon a proper showing, a permanent or temporary injunction or restraining order shall be granted without bond.

(3) Rights of Commission

The State shall serve prior written notice of any such civil action upon the Commission and provide the Commission with a copy of its complaint, except in any case where such prior notice is not feasible, in which case the State shall serve such notice immediately upon instituting such action. The Commission shall have the right (A) to intervene in the action, (B) upon so intervening, to be heard on all matters arising therein, and (C) to file petitions for appeal.

(4) Venue; service of process

Any civil action brought under this subsection in a district court of the United States may be brought in the district wherein the defendant is found or is an inhabitant or transacts business or wherein the violation occurred or is occurring, and process in such cases may be served in any district in which the defendant is an inhabitant or where the defendant may be found.

(5) Investigatory powers

For purposes of bringing any civil action under this subsection, nothing in this section shall prevent the attorney general of a State, or an official or agency designated by a State, from exercising the powers conferred on the attorney general or such official by the laws of such State to conduct investigations or to administer oaths or affirmations or to compel the attendance of witnesses or the production of documentary and other evidence.

(6) Effect on State court proceedings

Nothing contained in this subsection shall be construed to prohibit an authorized State official from proceeding in State court on the basis of an alleged violation of any general civil or criminal statute of such State.

(7) Limitation

Whenever the Commission has instituted a civil action for violation of regulations prescribed under this section, no State may, during the pendency of such action instituted by the Commission, subsequently institute a civil action against any defendant named in the Commission's complaint for any violation as alleged in the Commission's complaint.

(8) Definition

As used in this subsection, the term "attorney general" means the chief legal officer of a State.

(h) Junk Fax Enforcement Report.

The Commission shall submit an annual report to Congress regarding the enforcement during the past year of the provisions of this section relating to sending of unsolicited advertisements to telephone facsimile machines, which report shall include—

(1) the number of complaints received by the Commission during such year alleging that a consumer received an unsolicited advertisement via telephone facsimile machine in violation of the Commission's rules;

(2) the number of citations issued by the Commission pursuant to section 503 during the year to enforce any law, regulation, or policy relating to sending of unsolicited advertisements to telephone facsimile machines;

(3) the number of notices of apparent liability issued by the Commission pursuant to section 503 during the year to enforce any law, regulation, or policy relating to sending of unsolicited advertisements to telephone facsimile machines;

(4) for each notice referred to in paragraph (3)—

    (A) the amount of the proposed forfeiture penalty involved;

    (B) the person to whom the notice was issued;

    (C) the length of time between the date on which the complaint was filed and the date on which the notice was issued; and

    (D) the status of the proceeding;

(5) the number of final orders imposing forfeiture penalties issued pursuant to section 503 during the year to enforce any law, regulation, or policy relating to sending of unsolicited advertisements to telephone facsimile machines;

(6) for each forfeiture order referred to in paragraph (5)—

    (A) the amount of the penalty imposed by the order;

    (B) the person to whom the order was issued;

    (C) whether the forfeiture penalty has been paid; and

    (D) the amount paid;

(7) for each case in which a person has failed to pay a forfeiture penalty imposed by such a final order, whether the Commission referred such matter for recovery of the penalty; and

(8) for each case in which the Commission referred such an order for recovery—

(A) the number of days from the date the Commission issued such order to the date of such referral;

(B) whether an action has been commenced to recover the penalty, and if so, the number of days from the date the Commission referred such order for recovery to the date of such commencement; and

(C) whether the recovery action resulted in collection of any amount, and if so, the amount collected.

[June 19, 1934, ch. 652, tit. II, § 227, *as added,* Dec. 20, 1991, Pub. L. No. 102-243, § 3(a), 105 Stat. 2395, *and amended,* Pub. L. No. 102-556, tit. IV, § 402, 106 Stat. 4194 (Oct. 28, 1992); Pub. L. No. 103-414, tit. III, § 303(a) (11), (12), 108 Stat. 4294 (Oct. 25, 1994); Pub. L. No. 108-187, § 12, 117 Stat. 2717 (Dec. 16, 2003); Pub. L. No. 109-21, §§ 2(a)–(g), 3, 199 Stat. 360 (July 9, 2005); Pub. L. No. 111-331, § 2, 124 Stat. 3572 (Dec. 22, 2010)]

* * *

C.2.2 FCC Rule on Telemarketing and Junk Faxes

AUTHORITY: 47 U.S.C. 154, 254(k); 403(b)(2)(B), (c), Pub. L. No. 104-104, 110 Stat. 56. Interpret or apply 47 U.S.C. 201, 218, 222, 225, 226, 227, 228, 254(k), 616, and 620 unless otherwise noted.

47 C.F.R. § 64.1200   Delivery restrictions.

(a) No person or entity may:

(1) Except as provided in paragraph (a)(2) of this section, initiate any telephone call (other than a call made for emergency purposes or is made with the prior express consent of the called party) using an automatic telephone dialing system or an artificial or prerecorded voice;

    (i) To any emergency telephone line, including any 911 line and any emergency line of a hospital, medical physician or service office, health care facility, poison control center, or fire protection or law enforcement agency;

    (ii) To the telephone line of any guest room or patient room of a hospital, health care facility, elderly home, or similar establishment; or

    (iii) To any telephone number assigned to a paging service, cellular telephone service, specialized mobile radio service, or other radio common carrier service, or any service for which the called party is charged for the call.

    (iv) A person will not be liable for violating the prohibition in paragraph (a)(1)(iii) of this section when the call is placed to a wireless number that has been ported from wireline service and such call is a voice call; not knowingly made to a wireless number; and made within 15 days of the porting of the number from wireline to wireless service, provided the number is not already on the national do-not-call registry or caller's company-specific do-not-call list.

(2) Initiate, or cause to be initiated, any telephone call that includes or introduces an advertisement or constitutes telemarketing, using an automatic telephone dialing system or an artificial or prerecorded voice, to any of the lines or telephone numbers described in paragraphs (a)(1)(i) through (iii) of this section, other than a call made with the prior express written consent of the called party or the prior express consent of the called party when the call is made by or on behalf of a tax-exempt nonprofit organization, or a call that delivers a "health care" message made by, or on behalf of, a "covered entity" or its "business associate," as those terms are defined in the HIPAA Privacy Rule, 45 CFR 160.103.

(3) Initiate any telephone call to any residential line using an artificial or prerecorded voice to deliver a message without the prior express written consent of the called party, unless the call;

    (i) Is made for emergency purposes;

    (ii) Is not made for a commercial purpose;

(iii) Is made for a commercial purpose but does not include or introduce an advertisement or constitute telemarketing;

(iv) Is made by or on behalf of a tax-exempt nonprofit organization; or

(v) Delivers a "health care" message made by, or on behalf of, a "covered entity" or its "business associate," as those terms are defined in the HIPAA Privacy Rule, 45 CFR 160.103.

(4) Use a telephone facsimile machine, computer, or other device to send an unsolicited advertisement to a telephone facsimile machine, unless—

(i) The unsolicited advertisement is from a sender with an established business relationship, as defined in paragraph (f)(6) of this section, with the recipient; and

(ii) The sender obtained the number of the telephone facsimile machine through—

(A) The voluntary communication of such number by the recipient directly to the sender, within the context of such established business relationship; or

(B) A directory, advertisement, or site on the Internet to which the recipient voluntarily agreed to make available its facsimile number for public distribution. If a sender obtains the facsimile number from the recipient's own directory, advertisement, or Internet site, it will be presumed that the number was voluntarily made available for public distribution, unless such materials explicitly note that unsolicited advertisements are not accepted at the specified facsimile number. If a sender obtains the facsimile number from other sources, the sender must take reasonable steps to verify that the recipient agreed to make the number available for public distribution.

(C) This clause shall not apply in the case of an unsolicited advertisement that is sent based on an established business relationship with the recipient that was in existence before July 9, 2005 if the sender also possessed the facsimile machine number of the recipient before July 9, 2005. There shall be a rebuttable presumption that if a valid established business relationship was formed prior to July 9, 2005, the sender possessed the facsimile number prior to such date as well; and

(iii) The advertisement contains a notice that informs the recipient of the ability and means to avoid future unsolicited advertisements. A notice contained in an advertisement complies with the requirements under this paragraph only if—

(A) The notice is clear and conspicuous and on the first page of the advertisement;

(B) The notice states that the recipient may make a request to the sender of the advertisement not to send any future advertisements to a telephone facsimile machine or machines and that failure to comply, within 30 days, with such a request meeting the requirements under paragraph (a)(4)(v) of this section is unlawful;

(C) The notice sets forth the requirements for an opt-out request under paragraph (a)(4)(v) of this section;

(D) The notice includes—

(1) A domestic contact telephone number and facsimile machine number for the recipient to transmit such a request to the sender; and

(2) If neither the required telephone number nor facsimile machine number is a toll-free number, a separate cost-free mechanism including a Web site address or email address, for a recipient to transmit a request pursuant to such notice to the sender of the advertisement. A local telephone number also shall constitute a cost-free mechanism so long as recipients are local and will not incur any long distance or other separate charges for calls made to such number; and

(E) The telephone and facsimile numbers and cost-free mechanism identified in the notice must permit an individual or

business to make an opt-out request 24 hours a day, 7 days a week.

(iv) A facsimile advertisement that is sent to a recipient that has provided prior express invitation or permission to the sender must include an opt-out notice that complies with the requirements in paragraph (a)(4)(iii) of this section.

(v) A request not to send future unsolicited advertisements to a telephone facsimile machine complies with the requirements under this subparagraph only if—

(A) The request identifies the telephone number or numbers of the telephone facsimile machine or machines to which the request relates;

(B) The request is made to the telephone number, facsimile number, Web site address or email address identified in the sender's facsimile advertisement; and

(C) The person making the request has not, subsequent to such request, provided express invitation or permission to the sender, in writing or otherwise, to send such advertisements to such person at such telephone facsimile machine.

(vi) A sender that receives a request not to send future unsolicited advertisements that complies with paragraph (a)(4)(v) of this section must honor that request within the shortest reasonable time from the date of such request, not to exceed 30 days, and is prohibited from sending unsolicited advertisements to the recipient unless the recipient subsequently provides prior express invitation or permission to the sender. The recipient's opt-out request terminates the established business relationship exemption for purposes of sending future unsolicited advertisements. If such requests are recorded or maintained by a party other than the sender on whose behalf the unsolicited advertisement is sent, the sender will be liable for any failures to honor the opt-out request.

(vii) A facsimile broadcaster will be liable for violations of paragraph (a)(4) of this section, including the inclusion of opt-out notices on unsolicited advertisements, if it demonstrates a high degree of involvement in, or actual notice of, the unlawful activity and fails to take steps to prevent such facsimile transmissions.

(5) Use an automatic telephone dialing system in such a way that two or more telephone lines of a multi-line business are engaged simultaneously.

(6) Disconnect an unanswered telemarketing call prior to at least 15 seconds or four (4) rings.

(7) Abandon more than three percent of all telemarketing calls that are answered live by a person, as measured over a 30-day period for a single calling campaign. If a single calling campaign exceeds a 30-day period, the abandonment rate shall be calculated separately for each successive 30-day period or portion thereof that such calling campaign continues. A call is "abandoned" if it is not connected to a live sales representative within two (2) seconds of the called person's completed greeting.

(i) Whenever a live sales representative is not available to speak with the person answering the call, within two (2) seconds after the called person's completed greeting, the telemarketer or the seller must provide:

(A) A prerecorded identification and opt-out message that is limited to disclosing that the call was for "telemarketing purposes" and states the name of the business, entity, or individual on whose behalf the call was placed, and a telephone number for such business, entity, or individual that permits the called person to make a do-not-call request during regular business hours for the duration of the telemarketing campaign; provided, that, such telephone number may not be a 900 number or any other number for which charges exceed local or long distance transmission charges, and

(B) An automated, interactive voice- and/or key press-activated opt-out mechanism that enables the called person to make a do-not-call request prior to terminating the call, including brief explanatory instructions on how to use such mechanism. When the called person elects to opt-out using such mechanism, the mechanism must automatically record the called person's number to the seller's do-not-call list and immediately terminate the call.

(ii) A call for telemarketing purposes that delivers an artificial or prerecorded voice message to a residential telephone line or to any of the lines or telephone numbers described in paragraphs (a)(1)(i) through (iii) of this section after the subscriber to such line has granted prior express written consent for the call to be made shall not be considered an abandoned call if the message begins within two (2) seconds of the called person's completed greeting.

(iii) The seller or telemarketer must maintain records establishing compliance with paragraph (a)(7) of this section.

(iv) Calls made by or on behalf of tax-exempt nonprofit organizations are not covered by this paragraph (a)(7).

(8) Use any technology to dial any telephone number for the purpose of determining whether the line is a facsimile or voice line.

(b) All artificial or prerecorded voice telephone messages shall:

(1) At the beginning of the message, state clearly the identity of the business, individual, or other entity that is responsible for initiating the call. If a business is responsible for initiating the call, the name under which the entity is registered to conduct business with the State Corporation Commission (or comparable regulatory authority) must be stated;

(2) During or after the message, state clearly the telephone number (other than that of the autodialer or prerecorded message player that placed the call) of such business, other entity, or individual. The telephone number provided may not be a 900 number or any other number for which charges exceed local or long distance transmission charges. For telemarketing messages to residential telephone subscribers, such telephone number must permit any individual to make a do-not-call request during regular business hours for the duration of the telemarketing campaign; and

(3) In every case where the artificial or prerecorded voice telephone message includes or introduces an advertisement or constitutes telemarketing and is delivered to a residential telephone line or any of the lines or telephone numbers described in paragraphs (a)(1)(i) through (iii), provide an automated, interactive voice- and/or key press-activated opt-out mechanism for the called person to make a do-not-call request, including brief explanatory instructions on how to use such mechanism, within two (2) seconds of providing the identification information required in paragraph (b)(1) of this section. When the called person elects to opt out using such mechanism, the mechanism, must automatically record the called person's number to the seller's do-not-call list and immediately terminate the call. When the artificial or prerecorded voice telephone message is left on an answering machine or a voice mail service, such message must also provide a toll free number that enables the called person to call back at a later time and connect directly to the automated, interactive voice- and/or key press-activated opt-out mechanism and automatically record the called person's number to the seller's do-not-call list.

(c) No person or entity shall initiate any telephone solicitation to:

(1) Any residential telephone subscriber before the hour of 8 a.m. or after 9 p.m. (local time at the called party's location), or

(2) A residential telephone subscriber who has registered his or her telephone number on the national do-not-call registry of persons who do not wish to receive telephone solicitations that is maintained by the Federal Government. Such do-not-call registrations must be honored indefinitely, or until the registration is cancelled by the consumer or the telephone number is removed by the database administrator. Any person or entity making telephone solicitations (or on whose behalf telephone solicitations are made) will not be liable for violating this requirement if:

(i) It can demonstrate that the violation is the result of error and that as part of its routine business practice, it meets the following standards:

(A) **Written procedures.** It has established and implemented written procedures to comply with the national do-not-call rules;

(B) **Training of personnel.** It has trained its personnel, and any entity assisting in its compliance, in procedures established pursuant to the national do-not-call rules;

(C) **Recording.** It has maintained and recorded a list of telephone numbers that the seller may not contact;

(D) **Accessing the national do-not-call database.** It uses a process to prevent telephone solicitations to any telephone number on any list established pursuant to the do-not-call rules, employing a version of the national do-not-call registry obtained from the administrator of the registry no more than 31 days prior to the date any call is made, and maintains records documenting this process.

Note to paragraph (c)(2)(i)(D): The requirement in paragraph 64.1200(c)(2)(i)(D) for persons or entities to employ a version of the national do-not-call registry obtained from the administrator no more than 31 days prior to the date any call is made is effective January 1, 2005. Until January 1, 2005, persons or entities must continue to employ a version of the registry obtained from the administrator of the registry no more than three months prior to the date any call is made.

(E) **Purchasing the national do-not-call database.** It uses a process to ensure that it does not sell, rent, lease, purchase or use the national do-not-call database, or any part thereof, for any purpose except compliance with this section and any such state or federal law to prevent telephone solicitations to telephone numbers registered on the national database. It purchases access to the relevant do-not-call data from the administrator of the national database and does not participate in any arrangement to share the cost of accessing the national database, including any arrangement with telemarketers who may not divide the costs to access the national database among various client sellers; or

(ii) It has obtained the subscriber's prior express invitation or permission. Such permission must be evidenced by a signed, written agreement between the consumer and seller which states that the consumer agrees to be contacted by this seller and includes the telephone number to which the calls may be placed; or

(iii) The telemarketer making the call has a personal relationship with the recipient of the call.

(d) No person or entity shall initiate any call for telemarketing purposes to a residential telephone subscriber unless such person or entity has instituted procedures for maintaining a list of persons who request not to receive telemarketing calls made by or on behalf of that person or entity. The procedures instituted must meet the following minimum standards:

(1) **Written policy.** Persons or entities making calls for telemarketing purposes must have a written policy, available upon demand, for maintaining a do-not-call list.

(2) **Training of personnel engaged in telemarketing.** Personnel engaged in any aspect of telemarketing must be informed and trained in the existence and use of the do-not-call list.

(3) **Recording, disclosure of do-not-call requests.** If a person or entity making a call for telemarketing purposes (or on whose behalf such a call is made) receives a request from a residential telephone subscriber not to receive calls from that person or entity, the person or entity must record the request and place the subscriber's name, if provided, and telephone number on the do-not-call list at the time the request is made. Persons or entities making calls for telemarketing purposes (or on whose behalf such calls are made) must honor a residential subscriber's do-not-call request within a reasonable time from the date such request is made. This period may not exceed thirty days from the date of such request. If such requests are recorded or maintained by a party other than the person or entity on whose behalf the telemarketing call is made, the person or entity on whose behalf the telemarketing call is made will be liable for any failures to honor the

do-not-call request. A person or entity making a call for telemarketing purposes must obtain a consumer's prior express permission to share or forward the consumer's request not to be called to a party other than the person or entity on whose behalf a telemarketing call is made or an affiliated entity.

(4) Identification of sellers and telemarketers. A person or entity making a call for telemarketing purposes must provide the called party with the name of the individual caller, the name of the person or entity on whose behalf the call is being made, and a telephone number or address at which the person or entity may be contacted. The telephone number provided may not be a 900 number or any other number for which charges exceed local or long distance transmission charges.

(5) Affiliated persons or entities. In the absence of a specific request by the subscriber to the contrary, a residential subscriber's do-not-call request shall apply to the particular business entity making the call (or on whose behalf a call is made), and will not apply to affiliated entities unless the consumer reasonably would expect them to be included given the identification of the caller and the product being advertised.

(6) Maintenance of do-not-call lists. A person or entity making calls for telemarketing purposes must maintain a record of a consumer's request not to receive further telemarketing calls. A do-not-call request must be honored for 5 years from the time the request is made.

(7) Tax-exempt nonprofit organizations are not required to comply with 64.1200(d).

(e) The rules set forth in paragraph (c) and (d) of this section are applicable to any person or entity making telephone solicitations or telemarketing calls to wireless telephone numbers to the extent described in the Commission's Report and Order, CG Docket No. 02-278, FCC 03-153, "Rules and Regulations Implementing the Telephone Consumer Protection Act of 1991."

(f) As used in this section:

(1) The term *advertisement* means any material advertising the commercial availability or quality of any property, goods, or services.

(2) The terms *automatic telephone dialing system* and *autodialer* mean equipment which has the capacity to store or produce telephone numbers to be called using a random or sequential number generator and to dial such numbers.

(3) The term *clear and conspicuous* means a notice that would be apparent to the reasonable consumer, separate and distinguishable from the advertising copy or other disclosures. With respect to facsimiles and for purposes of paragraph (a)(4)(iii)(A) of this section, the notice must be placed at either the top or bottom of the facsimile.

(4) The term *emergency purposes* means calls made necessary in any situation affecting the health and safety of consumers.

(5) The term *established business relationship for purposes of telephone solicitations* means a prior or existing relationship formed by a voluntary two-way communication between a person or entity and a residential subscriber with or without an exchange of consideration, on the basis of the subscriber's purchase or transaction with the entity within the eighteen (18) months immediately preceding the date of the telephone call or on the basis of the subscriber's inquiry or application regarding products or services offered by the entity within the three months immediately preceding the date of the call, which relationship has not been previously terminated by either party.

(i) The subscriber's seller-specific do-not-call request, as set forth in paragraph (d)(3) of this section, terminates an established business relationship for purposes of telemarketing and telephone solicitation even if the subscriber continues to do business with the seller.

(ii) The subscriber's established business relationship with a particular business entity does not extend to affiliated entities unless the subscriber would reasonably expect them to be included given the nature and type of goods or services offered by the affiliate and the identity of the affiliate.

(6) The term *established business relationship* for purposes of paragraph (a)(4) of this section on the sending of facsimile advertisements means a prior or existing relationship formed by a voluntary two-way communication between a person or entity and a business or residential subscriber with or without an exchange of consideration, on the basis of an inquiry, application, purchase or transaction by the business or residential subscriber regarding products or services offered by such person or entity, which relationship has not been previously terminated by either party.

(7) The term *facsimile broadcaster* means a person or entity that transmits messages to telephone facsimile machines on behalf of another person or entity for a fee.

(8) The term *prior express written consent* means an agreement, in writing, bearing the signature of the person called that clearly authorizes the seller to deliver or cause to be delivered to the person called advertisements or telemarketing messages using an automatic telephone dialing system or an artificial or prerecorded voice, and the telephone number to which the signatory authorizes such advertisements or telemarketing messages to be delivered.

(i) The written agreement shall include a clear and conspicuous disclosure informing the person signing that:

(A) By executing the agreement, such person authorizes the seller to deliver or cause to be delivered to the signatory telemarketing calls using an automatic telephone dialing system or an artificial or prerecorded voice; and

(B) The person is not required to sign the agreement (directly or indirectly), or agree to enter into such an agreement as a condition of purchasing any property, goods, or services.

(ii) The term "signature" shall include an electronic or digital form of signature, to the extent that such form of signature is recognized as a valid signature under applicable federal law or state contract law.

(9) The term *seller* means the person or entity on whose behalf a telephone call or message is initiated for the purpose of encouraging the purchase or rental of, or investment in, property, goods, or services, which is transmitted to any person.

(10) The term *sender* for purposes of paragraph (a)(4) of this section means the person or entity on whose behalf a facsimile unsolicited advertisement is sent or whose goods or services are advertised or promoted in the unsolicited advertisement.

(11) The term *telemarketer* means the person or entity that initiates a telephone call or message for the purpose of encouraging the purchase or rental of, or investment in, property, goods, or services, which is transmitted to any person.

(12) The term *telemarketing* means the initiation of a telephone call or message for the purpose of encouraging the purchase or rental of, or investment in, property, goods, or services, which is transmitted to any person.

(13) The term *telephone facsimile machine* means equipment which has the capacity to transcribe text or images, or both, from paper into an electronic signal and to transmit that signal over a regular telephone line, or to transcribe text or images (or both) from an electronic signal received over a regular telephone line onto paper.

(14) The term *telephone solicitation* means the initiation of a telephone call or message for the purpose of encouraging the purchase or rental of, or investment in, property, goods, or services, which is transmitted to any person, but such term does not include a call or message:

(i) To any person with that person's prior express invitation or permission;

(ii) To any person with whom the caller has an established business relationship; or

(iii) By or on behalf of a tax-exempt nonprofit organization.

(15) The term *unsolicited advertisement* means any material advertising the commercial availability or quality of any property, goods, or services which is transmitted to any person without that person's prior express invitation or permission, in writing or otherwise.

(16) The term *personal relationship* means any family member, friend, or acquaintance of the telemarketer making the call.

(g) Beginning January 1, 2004, common carriers shall:

(1) When providing local exchange service, provide an annual notice, via an insert in the subscriber's bill, of the right to give or revoke a notification of an objection to receiving telephone solicitations pursuant to the national do-not-call database maintained by the federal government and the methods by which such rights may be exercised by the subscriber. The notice must be clear and conspicuous and include, at a minimum, the Internet address and toll-free number that residential telephone subscribers may use to register on the national database.

(2) When providing service to any person or entity for the purpose of making telephone solicitations, make a one-time notification to such person or entity of the national do-not-call requirements, including, at a minimum, citation to 47 CFR 64.1200 and 16 CFR 310. Failure to receive such notification will not serve as a defense to any person or entity making telephone solicitations from violations of this section.

(h) The administrator of the national do-not-call registry that is maintained by the federal government shall make the telephone numbers in the database available to the States so that a State may use the telephone numbers that relate to such State as part of any database, list or listing system maintained by such State for the regulation of telephone solicitations.

[68 Fed. Reg. 44,177 (July 25, 2003), *as amended at* 68 Fed. Reg. 59,131 (Oct. 14, 2003); 69 Fed. Reg. 60,316 (Oct. 8, 2004); 70 Fed. Reg. 19,337 (Apr. 13, 2005); 70 Fed. Reg. 37,705 (June 30, 2005); 70 Fed. Reg. 75,070 (Dec. 19, 2005); 71 Fed. Reg. 25,977 (May 3, 2006); 71 Fed. Reg. 42,297 (July 26, 2006); 71 Fed. Reg. 56,893 (Sept. 28, 2006); 71 Fed. Reg. 75,122 (Dec. 14, 2006); 73 Fed. Reg. 40,186 (July 14, 2008); 73 Fed. Reg. 67,419 (Nov. 14, 2008); 77 Fed. Reg. 34233-01, (June 11, 2012); 77 Fed. Reg. 66,935 (Nov. 8, 2012)]

[**Effective Date Note:** The amendments to 47 C.F.R. §§ 64.1200(a)(2) and 64.1200(a)(3), published at 77 Fed. Reg. 34,233 (June 11, 2012), are effective October 16, 2013. 47 C.F.R. § 64.1200(a)(7), except § 64.1200(a)(7)(i)(B), published at 77 Fed. Reg. 34,233 (June 11, 2012), is effective November 15, 2012. 47 C.F.R. § 64.1200(a)(7)(i)(B), published at 77 Fed. Reg. 34,233 (June 11, 2012), is effective January 14, 2013. 47 C.F.R. § 64.1200(b)(3), published at 77 Fed. Reg. 34,233 (June 11, 2012), is effective January 14, 2013.]

* * *

C.3   Spam E-Mail

C.3.1   CAN-SPAM Act

15 U.S.C.

15 U.S.C. § 7701.   Congressional findings and policy

(a) Findings

The Congress finds the following:

(1) Electronic mail has become an extremely important and popular means of communication, relied on by millions of Americans on a daily basis for personal and commercial purposes. Its low cost and global reach make it extremely convenient and efficient, and offer unique opportunities for the development and growth of frictionless commerce.

(2) The convenience and efficiency of electronic mail are threatened by the extremely rapid growth in the volume of unsolicited commercial electronic mail. Unsolicited commercial electronic mail is currently estimated to account for over half of all electronic mail traffic, up from an estimated 7 percent in 2001, and the volume continues to rise. Most of these messages are fraudulent or deceptive in one or more respects.

(3) The receipt of unsolicited commercial electronic mail may result in costs to recipients who cannot refuse to accept such mail and who incur costs for the storage of such mail, or for the time spent accessing, reviewing, and discarding such mail, or for both.

(4) The receipt of a large number of unwanted messages also decreases the convenience of electronic mail and creates a risk that wanted electronic mail messages, both commercial and noncommercial, will be lost, overlooked, or discarded amidst the larger volume of unwanted messages, thus reducing the reliability and usefulness of electronic mail to the recipient.

(5) Some commercial electronic mail contains material that many recipients may consider vulgar or pornographic in nature.

(6) The growth in unsolicited commercial electronic mail imposes significant monetary costs on providers of Internet access services, businesses, and educational and nonprofit institutions that carry and receive such mail, as there is a finite volume of mail that such providers, businesses, and institutions can handle without further investment in infrastructure.

(7) Many senders of unsolicited commercial electronic mail purposefully disguise the source of such mail.

(8) Many senders of unsolicited commercial electronic mail purposefully include misleading information in the messages' subject lines in order to induce the recipients to view the messages.

(9) While some senders of commercial electronic mail messages provide simple and reliable ways for recipients to reject (or "opt-out" of) receipt of commercial electronic mail from such senders in the future, other senders provide no such "opt-out" mechanism, or refuse to honor the requests of recipients not to receive electronic mail from such senders in the future, or both.

(10) Many senders of bulk unsolicited commercial electronic mail use computer programs to gather large numbers of electronic mail addresses on an automated basis from Internet websites or online services where users must post their addresses in order to make full use of the website or service.

(11) Many States have enacted legislation intended to regulate or reduce unsolicited commercial electronic mail, but these statutes impose different standards and requirements. As a result, they do not appear to have been successful in addressing the problems associated with unsolicited commercial electronic mail, in part because, since an electronic mail address does not specify a geographic location, it can be extremely difficult for law-abiding businesses to know with which of these disparate statutes they are required to comply.

(12) The problems associated with the rapid growth and abuse of unsolicited commercial electronic mail cannot be solved by Federal legislation alone. The development and adoption of technological approaches and the pursuit of cooperative efforts with other countries will be necessary as well.

(b) Congressional determination of public policy

On the basis of the findings in subsection (a) of this section, the Congress determines that—

(1) there is a substantial government interest in regulation of commercial electronic mail on a nationwide basis;

(2) senders of commercial electronic mail should not mislead recipients as to the source or content of such mail; and

(3) recipients of commercial electronic mail have a right to decline to receive additional commercial electronic mail from the same source.

[Pub. L. No. 108-187, § 2, 117 Stat. 2699 (Dec. 16, 2003)]

15 U.S.C. § 7702.   Definitions

In this chapter:

(1) Affirmative consent

The term "affirmative consent", when used with respect to a commercial electronic mail message, means that—

    (A) the recipient expressly consented to receive the message, either in response to a clear and conspicuous request for such consent or at the recipient's own initiative; and

    (B) if the message is from a party other than the party to which the recipient communicated such consent, the recipient was given clear and conspicuous notice at the time the consent was communicated that the recipient's electronic mail address could be transferred to such other party for the purpose of initiating commercial electronic mail messages.

(2) Commercial electronic mail message

    (A) In general

The term "commercial electronic mail message" means any electronic mail message the primary purpose of which is the commercial advertisement or promotion of a commercial product or service (including content on an Internet website operated for a commercial purpose).

    (B) Transactional or relationship messages

The term "commercial electronic mail message" does not include a transactional or relationship message.

    (C) Regulations regarding primary purpose

Not later than 12 months after December 16, 2003, the Commission shall issue regulations pursuant to section 7711 of this title defining the relevant criteria to facilitate the determination of the primary purpose of an electronic mail message.

    (D) Reference to company or website

The inclusion of a reference to a commercial entity or a link to the website of a commercial entity in an electronic mail message does not, by itself, cause such message to be treated as a commercial electronic mail message for purposes of this chapter if the contents or circumstances of the message indicate a primary purpose other than commercial advertisement or promotion of a commercial product or service.

(3) Commission

The term "Commission" means the Federal Trade Commission.

(4) Domain name

The term "domain name" means any alphanumeric designation which is registered with or assigned by any domain name registrar, domain name registry, or other domain name registration authority as part of an electronic address on the Internet.

(5) Electronic mail address

The term "electronic mail address" means a destination, commonly expressed as a string of characters, consisting of a unique user name or mailbox (commonly referred to as the "local part") and a reference to an Internet domain (commonly referred to as the "domain part"), whether or not displayed, to which an electronic mail message can be sent or delivered.

(6) Electronic mail message

The term "electronic mail message" means a message sent to a unique electronic mail address.

(7) FTC Act

The term "FTC Act" means the Federal Trade Commission Act (15 U.S.C. 41 *et seq.*).

(8) Header information

The term "header information" means the source, destination, and routing information attached to an electronic mail message, including the originating domain name and originating electronic mail address, and any other information that appears in the line identifying, or purporting to identify, a person initiating the message.

(9) Initiate

The term "initiate", when used with respect to a commercial electronic mail message, means to originate or transmit such message or to procure the origination or transmission of such message, but shall not include actions that constitute routine conveyance of such message. For purposes of this paragraph, more than one person may be considered to have initiated a message.

(10) Internet

The term "Internet" has the meaning given that term in the Internet Tax Freedom Act (47 U.S.C. 151 nt).

(11) Internet access service

The term "Internet access service" has the meaning given that term in section 231(e)(4) of Title 47.

(12) Procure

The term "procure", when used with respect to the initiation of a commercial electronic mail message, means intentionally to pay or provide other consideration to, or induce, another person to initiate such a message on one's behalf.

(13) Protected computer

The term "protected computer" has the meaning given that term in section 1030(e)(2)(B) of Title 18.

(14) Recipient

The term "recipient", when used with respect to a commercial electronic mail message, means an authorized user of the electronic mail address to which the message was sent or delivered. If a recipient of a commercial electronic mail message has one or more electronic mail addresses in addition to the address to which the message was sent or delivered, the recipient shall be treated as a separate recipient with respect to each such address. If an electronic mail address is reassigned to a new user, the new user shall not be treated as a recipient of any commercial electronic mail message sent or delivered to that address before it was reassigned.

(15) Routine conveyance

The term "routine conveyance" means the transmission, routing, relaying, handling, or storing, through an automatic technical process, of an electronic mail message for which another person has identified the recipients or provided the recipient addresses.

(16) Sender

    (A) In general

Except as provided in subparagraph (B), the term "sender", when used with respect to a commercial electronic mail message, means a person who initiates such a message and whose product, service, or Internet web site is advertised or promoted by the message.

    (B) Separate lines of business or divisions

If an entity operates through separate lines of business or divisions and holds itself out to the recipient throughout the message as that particular line of business or division rather than as the entity of which such line of business or division is a part, then the line of business or the division shall be treated as the sender of such message for purposes of this chapter.

(17) Transactional or relationship message

    (A) In general

The term "transactional or relationship message" means an electronic mail message the primary purpose of which is—

        (i) to facilitate, complete, or confirm a commercial transaction that the recipient has previously agreed to enter into with the sender;

        (ii) to provide warranty information, product recall information, or safety or security information with respect to a commercial product or service used or purchased by the recipient;

        (iii) to provide—

(I) notification concerning a change in the terms or features of;

(II) notification of a change in the recipient's standing or status with respect to; or

(III) at regular periodic intervals, account balance information or other type of account statement with respect to, a subscription, membership, account, loan, or comparable ongoing commercial relationship involving the ongoing purchase or use by the recipient of products or services offered by the sender;

(iv) to provide information directly related to an employment relationship or related benefit plan in which the recipient is currently involved, participating, or enrolled; or

(v) to deliver goods or services, including product updates or upgrades, that the recipient is entitled to receive under the terms of a transaction that the recipient has previously agreed to enter into with the sender.

(B) Modification of definition

The Commission by regulation pursuant to section 7711 of this title may modify the definition in subparagraph (A) to expand or contract the categories of messages that are treated as transactional or relationship messages for purposes of this chapter to the extent that such modification is necessary to accommodate changes in electronic mail technology or practices and accomplish the purposes of this chapter.

[Pub. L. No. 108-187, § 3, 117 Stat. 2700 (Dec. 16, 2003)]

15 U.S.C. § 7703. Prohibition against predatory and abusive commercial e-mail

(a) Omitted

(b) United States Sentencing Commission

(1) Directive

Pursuant to its authority under section 994(p) of Title 28 and in accordance with this section, the United States Sentencing Commission shall review and, as appropriate, amend the sentencing guidelines and policy statements to provide appropriate penalties for violations of section 1037 of Title 18, as added by this section, and other offenses that may be facilitated by the sending of large quantities of unsolicited electronic mail.

(2) Requirements

In carrying out this subsection, the Sentencing Commission shall consider providing sentencing enhancements for—

(A) those convicted under section 1037 of Title 18 who—

(i) obtained electronic mail addresses through improper means, including—

(I) harvesting electronic mail addresses of the users of a website, proprietary service, or other online public forum operated by another person, without the authorization of such person; and

(II) randomly generating electronic mail addresses by computer; or

(ii) knew that the commercial electronic mail messages involved in the offense contained or advertised an Internet domain for which the registrant of the domain had provided false registration information; and

(B) those convicted of other offenses, including offenses involving fraud, identity theft, obscenity, child pornography, and the sexual exploitation of children, if such offenses involved the sending of large quantities of electronic mail.

(c) Sense of Congress

It is the sense of Congress that—

(1) Spam has become the method of choice for those who distribute pornography, perpetrate fraudulent schemes, and introduce viruses, worms, and Trojan horses into personal and business computer systems; and

(2) the Department of Justice should use all existing law enforcement tools to investigate and prosecute those who send bulk commercial e-mail to facilitate the commission of Federal crimes, including the tools contained in chapters 47 and 63 of Title 18 (relating to fraud and false statements); chapter 71 of Title 18 (relating to obscenity); chapter 110 of Title 18 (relating to the sexual exploitation of children); and chapter 95 of Title 18 (relating to racketeering), as appropriate.

[Pub. L. No. 108-187, § 4, 117 Stat. 2703 (Dec. 16, 2003)]

15 U.S.C. § 7704. Other protections for users of commercial electronic mail

(a) Requirements for transmission of messages

(1) Prohibition of false or misleading transmission information

It is unlawful for any person to initiate the transmission, to a protected computer, of a commercial electronic mail message, or a transactional or relationship message, that contains, or is accompanied by, header information that is materially false or materially misleading. For purposes of this paragraph—

(A) header information that is technically accurate but includes an originating electronic mail address, domain name, or Internet Protocol address the access to which for purposes of initiating the message was obtained by means of false or fraudulent pretenses or representations shall be considered materially misleading;

(B) a "from" line (the line identifying or purporting to identify a person initiating the message) that accurately identifies any person who initiated the message shall not be considered materially false or materially misleading; and

(C) header information shall be considered materially misleading if it fails to identify accurately a protected computer used to initiate the message because the person initiating the message knowingly uses another protected computer to relay or retransmit the message for purposes of disguising its origin.

(2) Prohibition of deceptive subject headings

It is unlawful for any person to initiate the transmission to a protected computer of a commercial electronic mail message if such person has actual knowledge, or knowledge fairly implied on the basis of objective circumstances, that a subject heading of the message would be likely to mislead a recipient, acting reasonably under the circumstances, about a material fact regarding the contents or subject matter of the message (consistent with the criteria used in enforcement of section 45 of this title).

(3) Inclusion of return address or comparable mechanism in commercial electronic mail—

(A) In general

It is unlawful for any person to initiate the transmission to a protected computer of a commercial electronic mail message that does not contain a functioning return electronic mail address or other Internet-based mechanism, clearly and conspicuously displayed, that—

(i) a recipient may use to submit, in a manner specified in the message, a reply electronic mail message or other form of Internet-based communication requesting not to receive future commercial electronic mail messages from that sender at the electronic mail address where the message was received; and

(ii) remains capable of receiving such messages or communications for no less than 30 days after the transmission of the original message.

(B) More detailed options possible

The person initiating a commercial electronic mail message may comply with subparagraph (A)(i) by providing the recipient a list or menu from which the recipient may choose the specific types of commercial electronic mail messages the recipient wants to receive or does not want to receive from the sender, if the list or menu includes an option under which the recipient may choose not to receive any commercial electronic mail messages from the sender.

(C) Temporary inability to receive messages or process requests

A return electronic mail address or other mechanism does not fail to satisfy the requirements of subparagraph (A) if it is unexpectedly and temporarily unable to receive messages or process requests due to a technical problem beyond the control of the sender if the problem is corrected within a reasonable time period.

(4) Prohibition of transmission of commercial electronic mail after objection

(A) In general

If a recipient makes a request using a mechanism provided pursuant to paragraph (3) not to receive some or any commercial electronic mail messages from such sender, then it is unlawful—

(i) for the sender to initiate the transmission to the recipient, more than 10 business days after the receipt of such request, of a commercial electronic mail message that falls within the scope of the request;

(ii) for any person acting on behalf of the sender to initiate the transmission to the recipient, more than 10 business days after the receipt of such request, of a commercial electronic mail message with actual knowledge, or knowledge fairly implied on the basis of objective circumstances, that such message falls within the scope of the request;

(iii) for any person acting on behalf of the sender to assist in initiating the transmission to the recipient, through the provision or selection of addresses to which the message will be sent, of a commercial electronic mail message with actual knowledge, or knowledge fairly implied on the basis of objective circumstances, that such message would violate clause (i) or (ii); or

(iv) for the sender, or any other person who knows that the recipient has made such a request, to sell, lease, exchange, or otherwise transfer or release the electronic mail address of the recipient (including through any transaction or other transfer involving mailing lists bearing the electronic mail address of the recipient) for any purpose other than compliance with this chapter or other provision of law.

(B) Subsequent affirmative consent

A prohibition in subparagraph (A) does not apply if there is affirmative consent by the recipient subsequent to the request under subparagraph (A).

(5) Inclusion of identifier, opt-out, and physical address in commercial electronic mail

(A) It is unlawful for any person to initiate the transmission of any commercial electronic mail message to a protected computer unless the message provides—

(i) clear and conspicuous identification that the message is an advertisement or solicitation;

(ii) clear and conspicuous notice of the opportunity under paragraph (3) to decline to receive further commercial electronic mail messages from the sender; and

(iii) a valid physical postal address of the sender.

(B) Subparagraph (A)(i) does not apply to the transmission of a commercial electronic mail message if the recipient has given prior affirmative consent to receipt of the message.

(6) Materially

For purposes of paragraph (1), the term "materially", when used with respect to false or misleading header information, includes the alteration or concealment of header information in a manner that would impair the ability of an Internet access service processing the message on behalf of a recipient, a person alleging a violation of this section, or a law enforcement agency to identify, locate, or respond to a person who initiated the electronic mail message or to investigate the alleged violation, or the ability of a recipient of the message to respond to a person who initiated the electronic message.

(b) Aggravated violations relating to commercial electronic mail

(1) Address harvesting and dictionary attacks—

(A) In general

It is unlawful for any person to initiate the transmission, to a protected computer, of a commercial electronic mail message that is unlawful under subsection (a) of this section, or to assist in the origination of such message through the provision or selection of addresses to which the message will be transmitted, if such person had actual knowledge, or knowledge fairly implied on the basis of objective circumstances, that—

(i) the electronic mail address of the recipient was obtained using an automated means from an Internet website or proprietary online service operated by another person, and such website or online service included, at the time the address was obtained, a notice stating that the operator of such website or online service will not give, sell, or otherwise transfer addresses maintained by such website or online service to any other party for the purposes of initiating, or enabling others to initiate, electronic mail messages; or

(ii) the electronic mail address of the recipient was obtained using an automated means that generates possible electronic mail addresses by combining names, letters, or numbers into numerous permutations.

(B) Disclaimer

Nothing in this paragraph creates an ownership or proprietary interest in such electronic mail addresses.

(2) Automated creation of multiple electronic mail accounts

It is unlawful for any person to use scripts or other automated means to register for multiple electronic mail accounts or online user accounts from which to transmit to a protected computer, or enable another person to transmit to a protected computer, a commercial electronic mail message that is unlawful under subsection (a) of this section.

(3) Relay or retransmission through unauthorized access

It is unlawful for any person knowingly to relay or retransmit a commercial electronic mail message that is unlawful under subsection (a) of this section from a protected computer or computer network that such person has accessed without authorization.

(c) Supplementary rulemaking authority

The Commission shall by regulation, pursuant to section 7711 of this title—

(1) modify the 10-business-day period under subsection (a)(4)(A) or subsection (a)(4)(B) of this section, or both, if the Commission determines that a different period would be more reasonable after taking into account—

(A) the purposes of subsection (a) of this section;

(B) the interests of recipients of commercial electronic mail; and

(C) the burdens imposed on senders of lawful commercial electronic mail; and

(2) specify additional activities or practices to which subsection (b) of this section applies if the Commission determines that those activities or practices are contributing substantially to the proliferation of commercial electronic mail messages that are unlawful under subsection (a) of this section.

(d) Requirement to place warning labels on commercial electronic mail containing sexually oriented material

(1) In general

No person may initiate in or affecting interstate commerce the transmission, to a protected computer, of any commercial electronic mail message that includes sexually oriented material and—

(A) fail to include in subject heading for the electronic mail message the marks or notices prescribed by the Commission under this subsection; or

(B) fail to provide that the matter in the message that is initially viewable to the recipient, when the message is opened by any recipient and absent any further actions by the recipient, includes only—

(i) to the extent required or authorized pursuant to paragraph (2), any such marks or notices;

(ii) the information required to be included in the message pursuant to subsection (a)(5) of this section; and

(iii) instructions on how to access, or a mechanism to access, the sexually oriented material.

(2) Prior affirmative consent

Paragraph (1) does not apply to the transmission of an electronic mail message if the recipient has given prior affirmative consent to receipt of the message.

(3) Prescription of marks and notices

Not later than 120 days after December 16, 2003, the Commission in consultation with the Attorney General shall prescribe clearly identifiable marks or notices to be included in or associated with commercial electronic mail that contains sexually oriented material, in order to inform the recipient of that fact and to facilitate filtering of such electronic mail. The Commission shall publish in the Federal Register and provide notice to the public of the marks or notices prescribed under this paragraph.

(4) Definition

In this subsection, the term "sexually oriented material" means any material that depicts sexually explicit conduct (as that term is defined in section 2256 of Title 18), unless the depiction constitutes a small and insignificant part of the whole, the remainder of which is not primarily devoted to sexual matters.

(5) Penalty

Whoever knowingly violates paragraph (1) shall be fined under Title 18 or imprisoned not more than 5 years, or both.

[Pub. L. No. 108-187, § 5, 117 Stat. 2706 (Dec. 16, 2003)]

15 U.S.C. § 7705. Businesses knowingly promoted by electronic mail with false or misleading transmission information

(a) In general

It is unlawful for a person to promote, or allow the promotion of, that person's trade or business, or goods, products, property, or services sold, offered for sale, leased or offered for lease, or otherwise made available through that trade or business, in a commercial electronic mail message the transmission of which is in violation of section 7704(a)(1) of this title if that person—

(1) knows, or should have known in the ordinary course of that person's trade or business, that the goods, products, property, or services sold, offered for sale, leased or offered for lease, or otherwise made available through that trade or business were being promoted in such a message;

(2) received or expected to receive an economic benefit from such promotion; and

(3) took no reasonable action—

(A) to prevent the transmission; or

(B) to detect the transmission and report it to the Commission.

(b) Limited enforcement against third parties

(1) In general

Except as provided in paragraph (2), a person (hereinafter referred to as the "third party") that provides goods, products, property, or services to another person that violates subsection (a) of this section shall not be held liable for such violation.

(2) Exception

Liability for a violation of subsection (a) of this section shall be imputed to a third party that provides goods, products, property, or services to another person that violates subsection (a) of this section if that third party—

(A) owns, or has a greater than 50 percent ownership or economic interest in, the trade or business of the person that violated subsection (a) of this section; or

(B)

(i) has actual knowledge that goods, products, property, or services are promoted in a commercial electronic mail message the transmission of which is in violation of section 7704(a)(1) of this title; and

(ii) receives, or expects to receive, an economic benefit from such promotion.

(c) Exclusive enforcement by FTC

Subsections (f) and (g) of section 7706 of this title do not apply to violations of this section.

(d) Savings provision

Except as provided in section 7706(f)(8) of this title, nothing in this section may be construed to limit or prevent any action that may be taken under this chapter with respect to any violation of any other section of this chapter.

[Pub. L. No. 108-187, § 6, 117 Stat. 2710 (Dec. 16, 2003)]

15 U.S.C. § 7706. Enforcement generally

(a) Violation is unfair or deceptive act or practice

Except as provided in subsection (b) of this section, this chapter shall be enforced by the Commission as if the violation of this chapter were an unfair or deceptive act or practice proscribed under section 57a(a)(1)(B) of this title.

(b) Enforcement by certain other agencies

Compliance with this chapter shall be enforced—

(1) under section 1818 of Title 12, in the case of—

(A) national banks, and Federal branches and Federal agencies of foreign banks, by the Office of the Comptroller of the Currency;

(B) member banks of the Federal Reserve System (other than national banks), branches and agencies of foreign banks (other than Federal branches, Federal agencies, and insured State branches of foreign banks), commercial lending companies owned or controlled by foreign banks, organizations operating under section 25 or 25A of the Federal Reserve Act (12 U.S.C. 601 and 611), and bank holding companies, by the Board;

(C) banks insured by the Federal Deposit Insurance Corporation (other than members of the Federal Reserve System) and insured State branches of foreign banks, by the Board of Directors of the Federal Deposit Insurance Corporation; and

(D) savings associations the deposits of which are insured by the Federal Deposit Insurance Corporation, by the Director of the Office of Thrift Supervision;

(2) under the Federal Credit Union Act (12 U.S.C. 1751 *et seq.*) by the Board of the National Credit Union Administration with respect to any Federally insured credit union;

(3) under the Securities Exchange Act of 1934 (15 U.S.C. 78a *et seq.*) by the Securities and Exchange Commission with respect to any broker or dealer;

(4) under the Investment Company Act of 1940 (15 U.S.C. 80a-1 *et seq.*) by the Securities and Exchange Commission with respect to investment companies;

(5) under the Investment Advisers Act of 1940 (15 U.S.C. 80b-1 *et seq.*) by the Securities and Exchange Commission with respect to investment advisers registered under that Act;

(6) under State insurance law in the case of any person engaged in providing insurance, by the applicable State insurance authority of the State in which the person is domiciled, subject to section 6701 of this title, except that in any State in which the State insurance authority elects not to exercise this power, the enforcement authority pursuant to this chapter shall be exercised by the Commission in accordance with subsection (a) of this section;

(7) under part A of subtitle VII of Title 49 by the Secretary of Transportation with respect to any air carrier or foreign air carrier subject to that part;

(8) under the Packers and Stockyards Act, 1921 (7 U.S.C. 181 *et seq.*) (except as provided in section 406 of that Act (7 U.S.C. 226, 227)), by the Secretary of Agriculture with respect to any activities subject to that Act;

(9) under the Farm Credit Act of 1971 (12 U.S.C. 2001 *et seq.*) by the Farm Credit Administration with respect to any Federal land bank, Federal land bank association, Federal intermediate credit bank, or production credit association; and

(10) under the Communications Act of 1934 (47 U.S.C. 151 *et seq.*) by the Federal Communications Commission with respect to any person subject to the provisions of that Act.

(c) Exercise of certain powers

For the purpose of the exercise by any agency referred to in subsection (b) of this section of its powers under any Act referred to in that subsection, a violation of this chapter is deemed to be a violation of a Federal Trade Commission trade regulation rule. In addition to its powers under any provision of law specifically referred to in subsection (b) of this section, each of the agencies referred to in that subsection may exercise, for the purpose of enforcing compliance with any requirement imposed under this chapter, any other authority conferred on it by law.

(d) Actions by the Commission

The Commission shall prevent any person from violating this chapter in the same manner, by the same means, and with the same jurisdiction, powers, and duties as though all applicable terms and provisions of the Federal Trade Commission Act (15 U.S.C. 41 *et seq.*) were incorporated into and made a part of this chapter. Any entity that violates any provision of that subtitle is subject to the penalties and entitled to the privileges and immunities provided in the Federal Trade Commission Act in the same manner, by the same means, and with the same jurisdiction, power, and duties as though all applicable terms and provisions of the Federal Trade Commission Act were incorporated into and made a part of that subtitle.[10]

(e) Availability of cease-and-desist orders and injunctive relief without showing of knowledge

Notwithstanding any other provision of this chapter, in any proceeding or action pursuant to subsection (a), (b), (c), or (d) of this section to enforce compliance, through an order to cease and desist or an injunction, with section 7704(a)(1)(C) of this title, section 7704(a)(2) of this title, clause (ii), (iii), or (iv) of section 7704(a)(4)(A) of this title, section 7704(b)(1)(A) of this title, or section 7704(b)(3) of this title, neither the Commission nor the Federal Communications Commission shall be required to allege or prove the state of mind required by such section or subparagraph.

(f) Enforcement by States

(1) Civil action

In any case in which the attorney general of a State, or an official or agency of a State, has reason to believe that an interest of the residents of that State has been or is threatened or adversely affected by any person who violates paragraph (1) or (2) of section 7704(a) of this title, who violates section 7704(d) of this title, or who engages in a pattern or practice that violates paragraph (3), (4), or (5) of section 7704(a) of this title, the attorney general, official, or agency of the State, as parens patriae, may bring a civil action on behalf of the residents of the State in a district court of the United States of appropriate jurisdiction—

(A) to enjoin further violation of section 7704 of this title by the defendant; or

(B) to obtain damages on behalf of residents of the State, in an amount equal to the greater of—

(i) the actual monetary loss suffered by such residents; or

(ii) the amount determined under paragraph (3).

(2) Availability of injunctive relief without showing of knowledge

Notwithstanding any other provision of this chapter, in a civil action under paragraph (1)(A) of this subsection, the attorney general, official, or agency of the State shall not be required to allege or prove the state of mind required by section 7704(a)(1)(C) of this title, section 7704(a)(2) of this title, clause (ii), (iii), or (iv) of section 7704(a)(4)(A) of this title, section 7704(b)(1)(A) of this title, or section 7704(b)(3) of this title.

(3) Statutory damages

(A) In general

For purposes of paragraph (1)(B)(ii), the amount determined under this paragraph is the amount calculated by multiplying the number of violations (with each separately addressed unlawful message received by or addressed to such residents treated as a separate violation) by up to $250.

(B) Limitation

For any violation of section 7704 of this title (other than section 7704(a)(1) of this title), the amount determined under subparagraph (A) may not exceed $2,000,000.

(C) Aggravated damages

The court may increase a damage award to an amount equal to not more than three times the amount otherwise available under this paragraph if—

(i) the court determines that the defendant committed the violation willfully and knowingly; or

(ii) the defendant's unlawful activity included one or more of the aggravating violations set forth in section 7704(b) of this title.

(D) Reduction of damages

In assessing damages under subparagraph (A), the court may consider whether—

(i) the defendant has established and implemented, with due care, commercially reasonable practices and procedures designed to effectively prevent such violations; or

(ii) the violation occurred despite commercially reasonable efforts to maintain compliance the practices and procedures to which reference is made in clause (i).

(4) Attorney fees

In the case of any successful action under paragraph (1), the court, in its discretion, may award the costs of the action and reasonable attorney fees to the State.

(5) Rights of Federal regulators

The State shall serve prior written notice of any action under paragraph (1) upon the Federal Trade Commission or the appropriate Federal regulator determined under subsection (b) of this section and provide the Commission or appropriate Federal regulator with a copy of its complaint, except in any case in which such prior notice is not feasible, in which case the State shall serve such notice immediately upon instituting such action. The Federal Trade Commission or appropriate Federal regulator shall have the right—

(A) to intervene in the action;

(B) upon so intervening, to be heard on all matters arising therein;

(C) to remove the action to the appropriate United States district court; and

(D) to file petitions for appeal.

(6) Construction

For purposes of bringing any civil action under paragraph (1), nothing in this chapter shall be construed to prevent an attorney general of a State from exercising the powers conferred on the attorney general by the laws of that State to—

(A) conduct investigations;

(B) administer oaths or affirmations; or

(C) compel the attendance of witnesses or the production of documentary and other evidence.

(7) Venue; service of process

(A) Venue

Any action brought under paragraph (1) may be brought in the district court of the United States that meets applicable requirements relating to venue under section 1391 of Title 28.

---

10 *Editor's note:* So in original.

(B) Service of process

In an action brought under paragraph (1), process may be served in any district in which the defendant—

    (i) is an inhabitant; or

    (ii) maintains a physical place of business.

(8) Limitation on State action while Federal action is pending

If the Commission, or other appropriate Federal agency under subsection (b) of this section, has instituted a civil action or an administrative action for violation of this chapter, no State attorney general, or official or agency of a State, may bring an action under this subsection during the pendency of that action against any defendant named in the complaint of the Commission or the other agency for any violation of this chapter alleged in the complaint.

(9) Requisite scienter for certain civil actions

Except as provided in section 7704(a)(1)(C) of this title, section 7704(a)(2) of this title, clause (ii), (iii), or (iv) of section 7704(a)(4)(A) of this title, section 7704(b)(1)(A) of this title, or section 7704(b)(3) of this title, in a civil action brought by a State attorney general, or an official or agency of a State, to recover monetary damages for a violation of this chapter, the court shall not grant the relief sought unless the attorney general, official, or agency establishes that the defendant acted with actual knowledge, or knowledge fairly implied on the basis of objective circumstances, of the act or omission that constitutes the violation.

(g) Action by provider of Internet access service

(1) Action authorized

A provider of Internet access service adversely affected by a violation of section 7704(a)(1) of this title, 7704(b) of this title, or 7704(d) of this title, or a pattern or practice that violates paragraph (2), (3), (4), or (5) of section 7704(a) of this title, may bring a civil action in any district court of the United States with jurisdiction over the defendant—

    (A) to enjoin further violation by the defendant; or

    (B) to recover damages in an amount equal to the greater of—

        (i) actual monetary loss incurred by the provider of Internet access service as a result of such violation; or

        (ii) the amount determined under paragraph (3).

(2) Special definition of "procure"

In any action brought under paragraph (1), this chapter shall be applied as if the definition of the term "procure" in section 7702(12) of this title contained, after "behalf" the words "with actual knowledge, or by consciously avoiding knowing, whether such person is engaging, or will engage, in a pattern or practice that violates this chapter".

(3) Statutory damages

(A) In general

For purposes of paragraph (1)(B)(ii), the amount determined under this paragraph is the amount calculated by multiplying the number of violations (with each separately addressed unlawful message that is transmitted or attempted to be transmitted over the facilities of the provider of Internet access service, or that is transmitted or attempted to be transmitted to an electronic mail address obtained from the provider of Internet access service in violation of section 7704(b)(1)(A)(i) of this title, treated as a separate violation) by—

    (i) up to $100, in the case of a violation of section 7704(a)(1) of this title; or

    (ii) up to $25, in the case of any other violation of section 7704 of this title.

(B) Limitation

For any violation of section 7704 of this title (other than section 7704(a)(1) of this title), the amount determined under subparagraph (A) may not exceed $1,000,000.

(C) Aggravated damages

The court may increase a damage award to an amount equal to not more than three times the amount otherwise available under this paragraph if—

    (i) the court determines that the defendant committed the violation willfully and knowingly; or

    (ii) the defendant's unlawful activity included one or more of the aggravated violations set forth in section 7704(b) of this title.

(D) Reduction of damages

In assessing damages under subparagraph (A), the court may consider whether—

    (i) the defendant has established and implemented, with due care, commercially reasonable practices and procedures designed to effectively prevent such violations; or

    (ii) the violation occurred despite commercially reasonable efforts to maintain compliance with the practices and procedures to which reference is made in clause (i).

(4) Attorney fees

In any action brought pursuant to paragraph (1), the court may, in its discretion, require an undertaking for the payment of the costs of such action, and assess reasonable costs, including reasonable attorneys' fees, against any party.

[Pub. L. No. 108-187, § 7, 117 Stat. 2711 (Dec. 16, 2003)]

15 U.S.C. § 7707.   Effect on other laws

(a) Federal law

(1) Nothing in this chapter shall be construed to impair the enforcement of section 223 or 231 of Title 47, chapter 71 (relating to obscenity) or 110 (relating to sexual exploitation of children) of Title 18, or any other Federal criminal statute.

(2) Nothing in this chapter shall be construed to affect in any way the Commission's authority to bring enforcement actions under FTC Act for materially false or deceptive representations or unfair practices in commercial electronic mail messages.

(b) State law

(1) In general

This chapter supersedes any statute, regulation, or rule of a State or political subdivision of a State that expressly regulates the use of electronic mail to send commercial messages, except to the extent that any such statute, regulation, or rule prohibits falsity or deception in any portion of a commercial electronic mail message or information attached thereto.

(2) State law not specific to electronic mail

This chapter shall not be construed to preempt the applicability of—

    (A) State laws that are not specific to electronic mail, including State trespass, contract, or tort law; or

    (B) other State laws to the extent that those laws relate to acts of fraud or computer crime.

(c) No effect on policies of providers of Internet access service

Nothing in this chapter shall be construed to have any effect on the lawfulness or unlawfulness, under any other provision of law, of the adoption, implementation, or enforcement by a provider of Internet access service of a policy of declining to transmit, route, relay, handle, or store certain types of electronic mail messages.

[Pub. L. No. 108-187, § 8, 117 Stat. 2716 (Dec. 16, 2003)]

15 U.S.C. § 7708.   Do-Not-E-Mail registry

(a) In general

Not later than 6 months after December 16, 2003, the Commission shall transmit to the Senate Committee on Commerce, Science, and Transportation and the House of Representatives Committee on Energy and Commerce a report that—

(1) sets forth a plan and timetable for establishing a nationwide marketing Do-Not-E-Mail registry;

(2) includes an explanation of any practical, technical, security, privacy, enforceability, or other concerns that the Commission has regarding such a registry; and

(3) includes an explanation of how the registry would be applied with respect to children with e-mail accounts.

(b) Authorization to implement

The Commission may establish and implement the plan, but not earlier than 9 months after December 16, 2003.

[Pub. L. No. 108-187, § 9, 117 Stat. 2716 (Dec. 16, 2003)]

15 U.S.C. § 7709. Study of effects of commercial electronic mail

(a) In general

Not later than 24 months after December 16, 2003, the Commission, in consultation with the Department of Justice and other appropriate agencies, shall submit a report to the Congress that provides a detailed analysis of the effectiveness and enforcement of the provisions of this chapter and the need (if any) for the Congress to modify such provisions.

(b) Required analysis

The Commission shall include in the report required by subsection (a) of this section—

(1) an analysis of the extent to which technological and marketplace developments, including changes in the nature of the devices through which consumers access their electronic mail messages, may affect the practicality and effectiveness of the provisions of this chapter;

(2) analysis and recommendations concerning how to address commercial electronic mail that originates in or is transmitted through or to facilities or computers in other nations, including initiatives or policy positions that the Federal Government could pursue through international negotiations, fora, organizations, or institutions; and

(3) analysis and recommendations concerning options for protecting consumers, including children, from the receipt and viewing of commercial electronic mail that is obscene or pornographic.

[Pub. L. No. 108-187, § 10, 117 Stat. 2716 (Dec. 16, 2003)]

15 U.S.C. § 7710. Improving enforcement by providing rewards for information about violations; labeling

The Commission shall transmit to the Senate Committee on Commerce, Science, and Transportation and the House of Representatives Committee on Energy and Commerce—

(1) a report, within 9 months after December 16, 2003, that sets forth a system for rewarding those who supply information about violations of this chapter, including—

(A) procedures for the Commission to grant a reward of not less than 20 percent of the total civil penalty collected for a violation of this chapter to the first person that—

(i) identifies the person in violation of this chapter; and

(ii) supplies information that leads to the successful collection of a civil penalty by the Commission; and

(B) procedures to minimize the burden of submitting a complaint to the Commission concerning violations of this chapter, including procedures to allow the electronic submission of complaints to the Commission; and

(2) a report, within 18 months after December 16, 2003, that sets forth a plan for requiring commercial electronic mail to be identifiable from its subject line, by means of compliance with Internet Engineering Task Force Standards, the use of the characters "ADV" in the subject line, or other comparable identifier, or an explanation of any concerns the Commission has that cause the Commission to recommend against the plan.

[Pub. L. No. 108-187, § 11, 117 Stat. 2717 (Dec. 16, 2003)]

15 U.S.C. § 7711. Regulations

(a) In general

The Commission may issue regulations to implement the provisions of this Act (not including the amendments made by sections 4 and 12). Any such regulations shall be issued in accordance with section 553 of Title 5.

(b) Limitation

Subsection (a) of this section may not be construed to authorize the Commission to establish a requirement pursuant to section 7704(a)(5)(A) of this title to include any specific words, characters, marks, or labels in a commercial electronic mail message, or to include the identification required by section 7704(a)(5)(A) of this title in any particular part of such a mail message (such as the subject line or body).

[Pub. L. No. 108-187, § 13, 117 Stat. 2717 (Dec. 16, 2003)]

15 U.S.C. § 7712. Application to wireless

(a) Effect on other law

Nothing in this chapter shall be interpreted to preclude or override the applicability of section 227 of Title 47 or the rules prescribed under section 6102 of this title.

(b) FCC rulemaking

The Federal Communications Commission, in consultation with the Federal Trade Commission, shall promulgate rules within 270 days to protect consumers from unwanted mobile service commercial messages. The Federal Communications Commission, in promulgating the rules, shall, to the extent consistent with subsection (c) of this section—

(1) provide subscribers to commercial mobile services the ability to avoid receiving mobile service commercial messages unless the subscriber has provided express prior authorization to the sender, except as provided in paragraph (3);

(2) allow recipients of mobile service commercial messages to indicate electronically a desire not to receive future mobile service commercial messages from the sender;

(3) take into consideration, in determining whether to subject providers of commercial mobile services to paragraph (1), the relationship that exists between providers of such services and their subscribers, but if the Commission determines that such providers should not be subject to paragraph (1), the rules shall require such providers, in addition to complying with the other provisions of this chapter, to allow subscribers to indicate a desire not to receive future mobile service commercial messages from the provider—

(A) at the time of subscribing to such service; and

(B) in any billing mechanism; and

(4) determine how a sender of mobile service commercial messages may comply with the provisions of this chapter, considering the unique technical aspects, including the functional and character limitations, of devices that receive such messages.

(c) Other factors considered

The Federal Communications Commission shall consider the ability of a sender of a commercial electronic mail message to reasonably determine that the message is a mobile service commercial message.

(d) Mobile service commercial message defined

In this section, the term "mobile service commercial message" means a commercial electronic mail message that is transmitted directly to a wireless device that is utilized by a subscriber of commercial mobile service (as such term is defined in section 332(d) of Title 47) in connection with such service.

[Pub. L. No. 108-187, § 14, 117 Stat. 2718 (Dec. 16, 2003)]

15 U.S.C. § 7713. Separability

If any provision of this chapter or the application thereof to any person or circumstance is held invalid, the remainder of this chapter and the application of such provision to other persons or circumstances shall not be affected.

[Pub. L. No. 108-187, § 15, 117 Stat. 2718 (Dec. 16, 2003)]

C.3.2   FTC CAN-SPAM Rule

TITLE 16. COMMERCIAL PRACTICES
CHAPTER I. FEDERAL TRADE COMMISSION
SUBCHAPTER C. REGULATIONS UNDER SPECIFIC ACTS OF CONGRESS
PART 316. CAN–SPAM RULE

16 C.F.R.
§ 316.1   Scope.
§ 316.2   Definitions.
§ 316.3   Primary purpose.
§ 316.4   Requirement to place warning labels on commercial electronic mail that contains sexually oriented material.
§ 316.5   Prohibition on charging a fee or imposing other requirements on recipients who wish to opt out.
§ 316.6   Severability.

SOURCE: 73 Fed. Reg. 29,677 (May 21, 2008), unless otherwise noted.

AUTHORITY: 15 U.S.C. §§ 7701-7713.

16 C.F.R. § 316.1   Scope.

This part implements the Controlling the Assault of Non-Solicited Pornography and Marketing Act of 2003 ("CAN-SPAM Act"), 15 U.S.C. 7701-7713.

16 C.F.R. § 316.2   Definitions.

(a) The definition of the term "affirmative consent" is the same as the definition of that term in the CAN-SPAM Act, 15 U.S.C. 7702(1).

(b) "Character" means an element of the American Standard Code for Information Interchange ("ASCII") character set.

(c) The definition of the term "commercial electronic mail message" is the same as the definition of that term in the CAN-SPAM Act, 15 U.S.C. 7702(2).

(d) The definition of the term "electronic mail address" is the same as the definition of that term in the CAN-SPAM Act, 15 U.S.C. 7702(5).

(e) The definition of the term "electronic mail message" is the same as the definition of that term in the CAN-SPAM Act, 15 U.S.C. 7702(6).

(f) The definition of the term "initiate" is the same as the definition of that term in the CAN-SPAM Act, 15 U.S.C. 7702(9).

(g) The definition of the term "Internet" is the same as the definition of that term in the CAN-SPAM Act, 15 U.S.C. 7702(10).

(h) "Person" means any individual, group, unincorporated association, limited or general partnership, corporation, or other business entity.

(*i*) The definition of the term "procure" is the same as the definition of that term in the CAN-SPAM Act, 15 U.S.C. 7702(12).

(j) The definition of the term "protected computer" is the same as the definition of that term in the CAN-SPAM Act, 15 U.S.C. 7702(13).

(k) The definition of the term "recipient" is the same as the definition of that term in the CAN-SPAM Act, 15 U.S.C. 7702(14).

(*l*) The definition of the term "routine conveyance" is the same as the definition of that term in the CAN-SPAM Act, 15 U.S.C. 7702(15).

(m) The definition of the term "sender" is the same as the definition of that term in the CAN-SPAM Act, 15 U.S.C. 7702(16), *provided that*, when more than one person's products, services, or Internet website are advertised or promoted in a single electronic mail message, each such person who is within the Act's definition will be deemed to be a "sender," except that, only one person will be deemed to be the "sender" of that message if such person: (A) is within the Act's definition of "sender"; (B) is identified in the "from" line as the sole sender of the message; and (C) is in compliance with 15 U.S.C. 7704(a)(1), 15 U.S.C. 7704(a)(2), 15 U.S.C. 7704(a)(3)(A)(i), 15 U.S.C. 7704(a)(5)(A), and 16 CFR 316.4.

(n) The definition of the term "sexually oriented material" is the same as the definition of that term in the CAN-SPAM Act, 15 U.S.C. 7704(d)(4).

(o) The definition of the term "transactional or relationship messages" is the same as the definition of that term in the CAN-SPAM Act, 15 U.S.C. 7702(17).

(p) "Valid physical postal address" means the sender's current street address, a Post Office box the sender has accurately registered with the United States Postal Service, or a private mailbox the sender has accurately registered with a commercial mail receiving agency that is established pursuant to United States Postal Service regulations.

16 C.F.R. § 316.3   Primary purpose.

(a) In applying the term "commercial electronic mail message" defined in the CAN-SPAM Act, 15 U.S.C. 7702(2), the "primary purpose" of an electronic mail message shall be deemed to be commercial based on the criteria in paragraphs (a)(1) through (3) and (b) of this section:[11]

(1) If an electronic mail message consists exclusively of the commercial advertisement or promotion of a commercial product or service, then the "primary purpose" of the message shall be deemed to be commercial.

(2) If an electronic mail message contains both the commercial advertisement or promotion of a commercial product or service as well as transactional or relationship content as set forth in paragraph (c) of this section, then the "primary purpose" of the message shall be deemed to be commercial if:

(i) A recipient reasonably interpreting the subject line of the electronic mail message would likely conclude that the message contains the commercial advertisement or promotion of a commercial product or service; or

(ii) The electronic mail message's transactional or relationship content as set forth in paragraph (c) of this section does *not* appear, in whole or in substantial part, at the beginning of the body of the message.

(3) If an electronic mail message contains both the commercial advertisement or promotion of a commercial product or service as well as other content that is not transactional or relationship content as set forth in paragraph (c) of this section, then the "primary purpose" of the message shall be deemed to be commercial if:

(i) A recipient reasonably interpreting the subject line of the electronic mail message would likely conclude that the message contains the commercial advertisement or promotion of a commercial product or service; or

(ii) A recipient reasonably interpreting the body of the message would likely conclude that the primary purpose of the message is the commercial advertisement or promotion of a commercial product or service. Factors illustrative of those relevant to this interpretation include the placement of content that is the commercial advertisement or promotion of a commercial product or service, in whole or in substantial part, at the beginning of the body of the message; the proportion of the message dedicated to such content; and how color, graphics, type size, and style are used to highlight commercial content.

(b) In applying the term "transactional or relationship message" defined in the CAN-SPAM Act, 15 U.S.C. 7702(17), the "primary purpose" of an electronic mail message shall be deemed to be transactional or relationship

---

11   The Commission does not intend for these criteria to treat as a "commercial electronic mail message" anything that is not commercial speech.

if the electronic mail message consists exclusively of transactional or relationship content as set forth in paragraph (c) of this section.

(c) Transactional or relationship content of email messages under the CAN-SPAM Act is content:

(1) To facilitate, complete, or confirm a commercial transaction that the recipient has previously agreed to enter into with the sender;

(2) To provide warranty information, product recall information, or safety or security information with respect to a commercial product or service used or purchased by the recipient;

(3) With respect to a subscription, membership, account, loan, or comparable ongoing commercial relationship involving the ongoing purchase or use by the recipient of products or services offered by the sender, to provide—

(i) Notification concerning a change in the terms or features;

(ii) Notification of a change in the recipient's standing or status; or

(iii) At regular periodic intervals, account balance information or other type of account statement;

(4) To provide information directly related to an employment relationship or related benefit plan in which the recipient is currently involved, participating, or enrolled; or

(5) To deliver goods or services, including product updates or upgrades, that the recipient is entitled to receive under the terms of a transaction that the recipient has previously agreed to enter into with the sender.

16 C.F.R. § 316.4 Requirement to place warning labels on commercial electronic mail that contains sexually oriented material.

(a) Any person who initiates, to a protected computer, the transmission of a commercial electronic mail message that includes sexually oriented material must:

(1) Exclude sexually oriented materials from the subject heading for the electronic mail message and include in the subject heading the phrase "SEXUALLY-EXPLICIT: "in capital letters as the first nineteen (19) characters at the beginning of the subject line;[12]

(2) Provide that the content of the message that is initially viewable by the recipient, when the message is opened by any recipient and absent any further actions by the recipient, include only the following information:

(i) The phrase "SEXUALLY-EXPLICIT": in a clear and conspicuous manner;[13]

---

12 The phrase "SEXUALLY-EXPLICIT" comprises 17 characters, including the dash between the two words. The colon (:) and the space following the phrase are the 18th and 19th characters.

13 This phrase consists of nineteen (19) characters and is identical to the phrase required in 316.5(a)(1) of this Rule.

(ii) Clear and conspicuous identification that the message is an advertisement or solicitation;

(iii) Clear and conspicuous notice of the opportunity of a recipient to decline to receive further commercial electronic mail messages from the sender;

(iv) A functioning return electronic mail address or other Internet-based mechanism, clearly and conspicuously displayed, that

(A) A recipient may use to submit, in a manner specified in the message, a reply electronic mail message or other form of Internet-based communication requesting not to receive future commercial electronic mail messages from that sender at the electronic mail address where the message was received; and

(B) Remains capable of receiving such messages or communications for no less than 30 days after the transmission of the original message;

(v) Clear and conspicuous display of a valid physical postal address of the sender; and

(vi) Any needed instructions on how to access, or activate a mechanism to access, the sexually oriented material, preceded by a clear and conspicuous statement that to avoid viewing the sexually oriented material, a recipient should delete the email message without following such instructions.

(b) Prior affirmative consent. Paragraph (a) does not apply to the transmission of an electronic mail message if the recipient has given prior affirmative consent to receipt of the message.

16 C.F.R. § 316.5 Prohibition on charging a fee or imposing other requirements on recipients who wish to opt out.

Neither a sender nor any person acting on behalf of a sender may require that any recipient pay any fee, provide any information other than the recipient's electronic mail address and opt-out preferences, or take any other steps except sending a reply electronic mail message or visiting a single Internet Web page, in order to:

(a) Use a return electronic mail address or other Internet-based mechanism, required by 15 U.S.C. 7704(a)(3), to submit a request not to receive future commercial electronic mail messages from a sender; or

(b) Have such a request honored as required by 15 U.S.C. 7704(a)(3)(B) and (a)(4).

16 C.F.R. § 316.6 Severability.

The provisions of this Part are separate and severable from one another. If any provision is stayed or determined to be invalid, it is the Commission's intention that the remaining provisions shall continue in effect.

Appendix D   State Telemarketing Statutes Summarized

This appendix summarizes the main features of state telemarketing laws. These summaries should only be used as a general guide. Advocates should consult the statutes themselves for details and precise statutory language.

These summaries include only state statutes that are clearly directed, at least in part, toward telemarketing. Some states have home solicitation sales statutes that do not specifically mention telephone sales but might be interpreted to cover such sales. If a state does not have a telemarketing statute listed in this appendix, the advocate should consult the state's home solicitation sales law to see if it might apply to the transaction. These summaries also do not include free-standing state statutes regarding auto-dialing, artificial voice messages, and junk faxes.

These summaries do not describe attorney general enforcement authority that is derived from the state UDAP statute, but mention attorney general enforcement authority only where the telemarketing statute itself specifically provides for the role that the attorney general is to play. Similarly, the summaries only list penalties that are specifically provided by the telemarketing statute, and do not describe UDAP penalties that may be incorporated by reference into the telemarketing statute.

ALABAMA

Telemarketing Statute: **Ala. Code §§ 8-19A-1 to 8-19A-24 (Telemarketing); Ala. Code §§ 8-19C-1 to 8-19C–12 (do-not-call list).**
Scope: Defines telemarketing broadly but lists 25 exceptions, such as persons calling for charitable donations or other non-commercial purposes, sales by established businesses, sales that involve face-to-face contact, and sales of securities, insurance, cable television, newspapers or magazines. Do-not-call provisions apply to persons or entities making telephone solicitations, as defined in §§ 8-19A-3 and 8-19A-4, above, to residential subscribers in Alabama. Local or long distance telephone companies and providers of Caller ID service may not be held liable for violations committed by other persons or entities.
Registration Requirements: Telephone solicitors must obtain a license, pay an annual fee, maintain a surety bond, and submit to the state agency a copy of the script, if any, provided to salespersons, copies of information provided to salespersons or prospective customers, and information about prizes.
Substantive Law: Solicitors must identify themselves, their company and the goods being sold, inform the consumer of cancellation rights, and reduce all sales transactions to a written contract. Solicitor must identify self, and may not block Caller ID. May not call residential subscribers who register on do-not-call list, which is to be coordinated with nation-wide list.
Private Right of Action: Yes. A violation is a UDAP violation. The statute also provides a private cause of action for actual damages, court costs, and attorney fees. Statute also gives the attorney general specific enforcement powers. Individual who receives more than one telephone solicitation within twelve months from, or on behalf of, same individual in violation of do-not-call statute, may sue for the greater of actual monetary loss or $2000 per knowing violation, and for a cease and desist order. (Bona fide error defense available.) Remedies are in addition to any other causes of action, penalties and remedies provided by law.
Special Penalties: Civil penalty of up to $10,000 for each violation, and violations may also be a Class C felony. For violation of do-not-call statute, Public Service Commission may seek civil penalties of up to $2000 per violation, and cease and desist orders.

ALASKA

Telemarketing Statute: **Alaska Stat. §§ 45.50.475, 45.63.010 to 45.63.100.**
Scope: Defines telemarketing broadly but lists 19 exceptions, such as sales made by licensed real estate brokers, funeral directors and insurance agents, and the sale of items "made by hand."
Registration Requirements: Telephone solicitors must register with the Department of Law.
Substantive Law: Solicitors must receive a signed written contract from the consumer before they collect payment and provide a refund if consumer returns the goods and makes written request within seven days after receiving property, or if services have not been provided and consumer makes written request within seven days after payment; may not state or imply that they are licensed by the state unless asked by the consumer; waiver prohibited. State regulations at 9 Alaska Admin. Code Ch. 14 require specific disclosures for certain types of sales, including prize or gift promotions, sales of metals, stones, minerals, oil wells, gas wells, some office supply sales, and sales of yellow pages advertising. Alaska Stat. § 45.50.475 also makes it a UDAP violation use recorded messages in telephonic solicitations or engage in telephonic solicitations to cellular or mobile telephone customers or residential customers who have told the company not to call or are on state or federal do-not-call list.
Private Right of Action: Violation is a UDAP violation.
Special Penalties: Certain violations are a Class C felony, certain others are a Class A misdemeanor.

ARIZONA

Telemarketing Statute: **Ariz. Rev. Stat. Ann. §§ 44-1271 to 44-1282.**
Scope: Covers "sellers," broadly defined as persons who, directly or through solicitors, initiate telephone calls to provide or arrange to provide goods or services to consumers in return for payment. Also covers solicitations in response to inquiries by consumers generated by certain advertisements, direct mail solicitations, and other solicitations. Partial exemptions for certain catalog sellers, some sellers with established retail locations, some business-to-business solicitations, sales in which seller provides descriptive literature before consumer pays (some exceptions), calls that are followed up by face-to-face meeting, and solicitors for certain businesses, except all are required to comply with § 1278, which prohibits unlawful practices.
Registration Requirements: Telephone sellers must register with secretary of state, and provide detailed information, including scripts, and details about prize promotions.
Substantive Law: Three-day right to cancel. Seller must identify self and company, state sales purpose of call, and disclose all charges. May not block Caller ID; may not call any person on national do-not-call list also forbidden); may not make unsolicited call to mobile phone or paging device; may not deliver pre-recorded message to residential number except by prior consent or for certain emergency purposes; may not use automatic dialing device unless it is able to exclude emergency numbers (fire, police, etc.), patient rooms at a hospital, nursing home, or similar facility, any number at which called party must pay for call, and numbers on seller's do-not-call list. Seller offering a recovery service may not charge or receive any consideration before full and complete performance of the service.
Private Right of Action: A violation is a UDAP violation, which carries an implied private cause of action. Purchaser may also rescind a sale by an unregistered seller and recover financial damages and attorney fees. Statute also gives attorney general specific enforcement powers. Consumer also recovers costs.
Special Penalties: Failure to register is a Class 5 felony.

ARKANSAS

Telemarketing Statute: **Ark. Code Ann. §§ 4-99-101 to 4-99-408.**

Scope: Defines specific types of telemarketing that are covered, and excludes persons selling securities, insurance, newspapers, magazines or memberships in book or record clubs, sales to previous customers, sales that involve face-to-face contact, and sales made by supervised financial institutions or burial associations, or public utilities.

Registration Requirements: Telephone solicitors must register with the Consumer Protection Division, pay a fee, and maintain a surety bond. Must provide information, including sales scripts and detailed information about any gift or prizes. Additional bond required for person offering prize promotion.

Substantive Law: Any solicitor who implies the consumer has won a prize must provide the consumer with certain information, including the location of the seller, the odds of winning, any rules or regulations, and the number of consumers who have won the prize in the past. Use of couriers is prohibited, and the consumer's express written authorization is required before telemarketer may submit check, draft, or other negotiable instrument to consumer's bank. Telemarketers may not block Caller ID or transmit fictitious or misleading Caller ID information. Establishes state do-not-call list and prohibits violation of FTC do-not-call rule. Solicitors must identify themselves and their company and the goods being sold. Telemarketers are prohibited from calling people who have listed themselves on a statewide database as not wanting to receive telephone solicitations. Telemarketers must quit providing information or attempting to sell immediately upon notice that the called party is not interested. A separate statute, Ark. Code Ann. § 4-28-401, requires registration of charitable organizations and professional telemarketers who solicit funds for charities. Certain willful violations are a Class D felony.

Private Right of Action: A violation is a UDAP violation. The statute gives attorney general specific enforcement powers.

Special Penalties: A knowing and willful violation is a Class A misdemeanor; enhanced penalty for targeting older or disabled persons based on five identified factors. Knowing and willful requirement does not apply to disclosure violations. Certain willful violations are Class D felonies.

CALIFORNIA

Telemarketing Statute: **Cal. Bus. & Prof. Code §§ 17511 to 17514 (West); Cal. Bus. & Prof. Code §§ 17591 to 17594 (West).**

Scope: Defines specific types of telemarketing that are covered, and lists 22 exceptions such as the sale of securities, sales made to previous customers, and sales that involve face-to-face contact. Exception for solicitations by certain tax exempt organizations.

Registration Requirements: Solicitors must register, pay a fee, and maintain a bond. Must provide detailed information, including sales scripts and information about gifts or prizes.

Substantive Law: Solicitors must provide consumers with certain information, including the solicitor's address and oral and written notification of the consumer's cancellation rights, and detailed information about gifts or prizes. Non-attorneys are prohibited from requesting or receiving payment for recovery of money or item of value paid for by, or promised to, the consumer in a previous telemarketing transaction, until 7 business days after that money or other item is delivered to the consumer. Third-party collections are prohibited unless goods are delivered before or at the same time the purchaser's payment is obtained. May not call consumer listed on FTC's do-not-call list. Mail solicitations that seek consent to provide information by telephone must include disclosures about the do-not-call rule.

Private Right of Action: For violation of do-not-call list provisions, recipient of prohibited call may bring action in small claims court for injunction; violation of injunction carries civil penalty of up to $1000, payable to the person who sought the injunction.

Special Penalties: Fine up to $10,000 and/or imprisonment up to one year, for each willful violation.

COLORADO

Telemarketing Statute: **Colo. Rev. Stat. §§ 6-1-301 to 6-1-305; Colo. Rev. Stat. §§ 6-1-901 to 6-1-908; 4 Colo. Code Regs. § 723-2.**

Scope: Defines telemarketing broadly but lists 20 exceptions, such as the sale of securities, newspapers or insurance, sales involving face-to-face contact, sales made by supervised financial institutions, and catalog sales.

Registration Requirements: Solicitors must register with the attorney general and file an application.

Substantive Law: Consumers may cancel transactions within 3 days, solicitors must refund payment to the consumers within 30 days of cancellation, and solicitors must disclose to consumers their cancellation rights. May not block Caller ID May not call person on Colorado do-not-call list. (Charitable and political organizations, which are exempt for free speech reasons, are encouraged to comply voluntarily.) Cell phone numbers may not be listed in commercial directories without consent. Telemarketer may not use electronic means to identify cell phone number and make commercial telephone solicitation.

Private Right of Action: Yes. A violation is a UDAP violation.

Special Penalties: Violations are Class 1 misdemeanors.

CONNECTICUT

Telemarketing Statute: **Conn. Gen. Stat. §§ 42-284 to 42-289.**

Scope: Initiating a sale, lease or rental of consumer goods or offering gifts or prizes with intent to sell, lease, or rent consumer goods by telephonic means, or by other advertising which invites but that does not disclose price or description of goods or services, consumer to telephone seller. Excludes sales involving prior negotiations at seller's place of business, prior business relationship, sale of newspapers by publisher, certain banking transactions, certain catalog sales, sales in which seller allows cancellation and full refund, certain sales regulated under other statutes, including utilities and securities, sales by business which sells same goods from fixed location and telemarketing sales are less than 50% of its total sales.

Registration Requirements: None specified.

Substantive Law: Written contract required, which discloses all terms of the sale. Telemarketer may not accept payment nor charge consumer's credit card until telemarketer receives signed copy of contract. May not block Caller ID. May not call person on do-not-call list (Conn. Gen. Stat. § 42-288a). Compilers or sellers of lists for telephone solicitation must delete names found on do-not-call list (does not apply to telephone directories). Explicitly bans unsolicited text or media messages (except for e-mail) sent to certain mobile phones or mobile electronic devices; certain unsolicited faxes and recorded messages.

Private Right of Action: Violation is a UDAP violation.

Special Penalties: Up to $11,000 in fines per each violation in addition to applicable UDAP penalties.

DISTRICT OF COLUMBIA

Telemarketing Statute: **D.C. Code §§ 22-3226.01 to 22-3226.15.**

Scope: Telemarketing is broadly defined, with exceptions for one-time or infrequent calls; information calls during which payment is not accepted; calls leading to face-to-face presentation; calls requested by consumer; servicing existing accounts; religious, political, charitable, educational or other non-profits; sales of newspapers; various sales regulated under other law, including securities, cable television, insurance, travel; sales if seller offers 7-day inspection and full refund.

Registration Requirements: Must register with mayor, and post bond for $50,000.

Substantive Law: Within first 30 seconds of call must identify self and company, and nature of goods being sold. Must disclose true name of solicitor, and total cost of goods or services. Forbids operating without a license, using name of charity without permission, knowing misrepresentations, false pretenses, charging a customer's account without express written authorization, using a courier to pick up payment before goods delivered with opportunity to inspect, causing a phone to ring more than 15 times, contacting a consumer who has expressly stated that he or she does not wish to receive calls from seller, calling between 9 p.m. and 8 a.m.

Private Right of Action: Yes, for actual and punitive damages, attorney fees and costs, declaratory judgment or injunction and any other equitable relief the court deems proper. This section is in addition to any other rights or remedies to which consumer may be entitled. Statute of limitations 3 years from date of call.

Special Penalties: Civil penalties of up to $1000 per violation; may be trebled for knowingly targeting older or disabled persons. Criminal penalties.

DELAWARE

Telemarketing Statute: **Del. Code Ann. tit. 6, §§ 2501A to 2509A.**

Scope: Defines telemarketing broadly, and lists 10 exemptions such as sales involving a face-to-face pre-sale presentation, customer-initiated calls that are not a result of a telemarketing solicitation, business-to-business transactions, solicitations by charities and non-profits, insurance, securities, certain catalog sales, calls by supervised financial institutions, and goods or services regulated by PUC or FCC.

Registration Requirements: With certain exceptions, any person transacting business with a customer located in Delaware through telemarketing as a seller or a telemarketing business must register and post $50,000 bond.

Substantive Law: At beginning of call, telemarketer must disclose name, name of seller, purpose of call, and nature of product; must make additional disclosures prior to payment or conclusion of call, including price, basic characteristics of the product, restrictions and limitations, refund policy, and information about prize promotions. Buyer has right to cancel within 7 days after receiving written confirmation of the order unless seller offers full money-back guarantee. Telemarketer must obtain buyer's express verifiable authorization before obtaining or submitting check, draft, or other negotiable paper. Telemarketers must discontinue calls for 10 years after request. Statute prohibits advance payment for recovery services; provision of substantial assistance to telemarketer violating statute; use of courier to pick up payment before merchandise is delivered with an opportunity to inspect it; and various deceptive acts.

Private Right of Action: Yes, for actual and punitive damages, attorney fees, court costs, and any other remedies provided by law, including equitable relief.

Special Penalties: None stated.

FLORIDA

Telemarketing Statute: **Fla. Stat. § 501.059; Fla. Stat. §§ 501.601 to 501.626 (Florida Telemarketing Act).**

Scope: Defines telemarketing broadly. Numerous exemptions including single transaction, charitable or political, calls leading to face-to-face transaction, securities, newspapers, certain book or recording clubs, insurance, cable television, certain business-to-business transactions, certain catalog sales, periodicals.

Registration Requirements: Sellers and salespersons must be licensed. Sellers must post bond or other acceptable security.

Substantive Law: Telephone solicitors must identify themselves and their companies, within the first 30 seconds of the call, must advise consumer of cancellation rights: cancellation by written notice within three business days of contract confirmation; refund, credit or replacement if goods returned within 7 business days after receipt. Certain provisions of this section do not apply if sellers offer full refund within 30 days if goods returned within 7 days of receipt. May not call consumers who place themselves on a "no-call" list, and must receive a signed written contract from the consumer before they collect payment. If a gift or premium is offered, caller must disclose value of item, odds if ascertainable, and any restrictions or conditions on the offer. May not directly or indirectly accept "novelty payment," defined as payment method that does not provide systematic monitoring to detect and deter fraud, including but not limited to remotely created checks and payment orders that do not bear account-holder's signature; certain cash-to-cash money transfers; certain

cash reload mechanisms for prepaid cards. All oral disclosures must be clear and intelligible. May not call between 9 p.m. and 8 a.m.; may not block Caller ID.

Private Right of Action: Any person injured by violation may bring civil action for actual and/or punitive damages, costs and attorney fees. Contract made pursuant to telemarketing call is unenforceable unless it complies with statutory requirements, and the prevailing party in any civil litigation under this section (§ 501.059) is entitled to costs and attorney fees. Statute also gives attorney general specific enforcement powers.

Special Penalties: Civil penalty in Class III category, pursuant to Fla. Stat. § 570.971 (currently up to $10,000 for each violation) and attorney fees and costs. Certain violations are third degree felonies. Enforcing authority may petition for appointment of receiver or sequestration of assets.

GEORGIA

Telemarketing Statute: **Ga. Code Ann. §§ 10-5B-1 to 105B-8, §§ 10-1-393.5, 10-1-393.6, 10-1 393.13.**

Scope: Defines telemarketing broadly.

Registration Requirements: None specified.

Substantive Law: Caller must identify company and provide a telephone number or address at which it can be contacted before beginning sales solicitation, and may not block consumer's Caller ID. Secretary of state is authorized to promulgate rules concerning telemarketing. Note that a separate statute, Ga. Code Ann. §§ 10-1-393.5 and 10-1-393.6, makes it a UDAP violation to engage in fraud or deceit or commit a theft offense while engaged in telemarketing or use a courier to pick up payment before goods delivered with opportunity to inspect; that prohibition adopts the FTC rule's definition of telemarketing, but includes intrastate as well as interstate calls, and explicitly includes Internet transactions and imposes an enhanced penalty for deliberate targeting of older or disabled persons. Unlawful to demand advance payment for removing derogatory information from consumer's credit record, improving consumer's credit rating, or recovering money or goods lost in previous telemarketing transaction (except for services of licensed attorney). Another separate statute, Ga. Code Ann. § 10-393.13, requires telemarketers to identify themselves and prohibits them from blocking their caller IDs.

Private Right of Action: Private right of action under § 10-1-399. A violation of Ga. Code Ann. § 10-1-393.5 is a UDAP violation. A violation of Ga. Code Ann. § 10-393.13 is remedied by the greater of actual damages or $10 per violation, and the action can proceed on a class-wide basis.

Special Penalties: Willful violation is a felony; double applicable civil and criminal penalties for intentional targeting of older or disabled persons.

HAWAII

Telemarketing Statute: **Haw. Rev. Stat. §§ 481P-1 to 481P-8.**

Scope: Telemarketing broadly defined, including investment opportunities and recovery services. Exemptions include polling, political or charitable calls, certain catalog sales, certain businesses regulated under other laws, i.e., securities, real estate, insurance.

Registration Requirements: None specified.

Substantive Law: Telemarketers must not call numbers listed on nationwide do-not-call registry. Within the first minute of the call, and before any sales solicitation, caller must disclose own name and that of company, and sales purpose of call. Must disclose full cost of goods, any restrictions or limitations, seller's cancellation or refund policy. No payment required until express verifiable contract confirmation received. Must allow 7 days after receipt of goods to review goods and return for cancellation if desired. Detailed recordkeeping requirements, including scripts, contracts and training materials, extensive information about prize promotions, and evidence to substantiate claims for health, nutrition or diet-related goods and services. May not use a courier to pick up immediate payment. Abusive practices explicitly prohibited. May not demand advance payment for credit repair, recovery services, or obtaining a loan. May not call before 8 a.m. or after 9 p.m., or cause telephone to ring more than 10 times. May not call a consumer who has requested not to be called; bona fide error a

defense, must keep do-not-call list. Noncomplying contracts are voidable; debt resulting from these contracts may not be reported to credit bureau.
Private Right of Action: Violation is a UDAP violation.
Special Penalties: See Haw. Rev. Stat. § 708-835.6. It is a Class B Felony to misrepresent, with intent to defraud, that person contacted will or is about to receive anything of value, or may be able to recover any losses suffered in connection with a prize promotion.

IDAHO

Telemarketing Statute: **Idaho Code Ann. §§ 48-1001 to 48-1108.**
Scope: Defines telemarketing broadly, but lists 10 exemptions, including isolated transactions, sales to previous customers, sales involving face-to-face contact, the sale of newspapers, magazines or periodicals, sales by licensed businesses or businesses that conduct 90% of their sales on location, and catalog sales.
Registration Requirements: Solicitors must register with the attorney general and pay a fee.
Substantive Law: Consumers can cancel purchases within 3 days and minors can cancel within a reasonable time; solicitors must also orally inform consumers of their right to cancel, disclose their street address and number, hang up immediately if requested, and send a written confirmation which includes the consumer's right to cancel. Solicitors cannot use devices that block consumers' Caller ID capacity. Various misrepresentations also prohibited. Abuse and intimidation explicitly prohibited. May not send unsolicited advertisement to fax machine. May not call persons on do-not-call list (home, mobile or pager numbers only). Nationwide do-not-call list may serve as Idaho's. Local exchange telephone companies must inform consumers of the provisions of this statute, either by annual bill stuffer or by information in phone directory. Written or tape-recorded verification required before telemarketer may charge a consumer's previously obtained account number.
Private Right of Action: Yes. A violation is a UDAP violation. Action must be brought within 2 years after party knows violation occurred. Noncomplying contracts are also null, void, and unenforceable.
Special Penalties: For calling persons on do-not-call list, penalties ranging from up to $500 for a first offense to up to $5000 for repeat violations.

ILLINOIS

Telemarketing Statute: **815 Ill. Comp. Stat. §§ 413/1 to 413/25; 815 Ill. Comp. Stat. §§ 402/1 to 402/99 (Restricted Call Registry, i.e., do-not-call list); 815 Ill. Comp. Stat. § 505/2P.1.**
Scope: Defines telemarketing broadly, with exceptions for calls made by autodialers, registered securities dealers, registered investment advisers, registered sellers of securities, or licensed insurance agents. Also exceptions for banks and credit unions.
Registration Requirements: None specified.
Substantive Law: Prohibits calls to emergency telephone numbers, and prohibits callers from continuing with a solicitation without the consumer's consent. Solicitors must identify themselves and their companies, and are prohibited from calling consumers who place themselves on a "no-call" list (45 or more days after obtaining copy of list containing consumer's name). National do-not-call registry will serve as Illinois do-not-call list. May not call between 9 p.m. and 8 a.m. May not block Caller ID. Express written consent required before presenting check, draft, etc. on consumer's account. Requires seller to send invoice with cancellation option at end of any free trial period.
Private Right of Action: Yes, for treble damages, costs and attorney fees. A violation is a UDAP violation.
Special Penalties: For calls to persons on no-call list, civil fines of up to $1000 first offense to $2500 subsequent offense.

INDIANA

Telemarketing Statute: **Ind. Code §§ 24-5-12-1 to 24-5-12-25.**
Scope: Solicitors who sell precious metals, precious stones, minerals, mineral rights or, in some circumstances, office equipment or supplies; who make false representations about prizes or identity of solicitor, manufacturer, or supplier; or who offer vacations at a reduced price that are contingent on attending certain time-share or membership campground sales presentations.
Registration Requirements: Solicitors must register and pay a fee to the attorney general.
Substantive Law: Contracts are voidable if the solicitor fails to properly register, if the solicitor uses misleading or deceptive statements or if the solicitor fails to deliver an ordered item within 4 weeks. Requires disclosures about gift or prize promotions. Prohibits solicitors from knowingly or intentionally blocking or attempting to block the display of their telephone number or identity by a Caller ID service.
Private Right of Action: Yes, for actual damages, court costs and attorney fees. Contract is also voidable in case of deception or failure to deliver within four weeks.
Special Penalties: Failure to register is a Class D felony; attorney general may seek UDAP penalties. Caller ID blocking violation is a misdemeanor.

Telemarketing Statute: **Ind. Code §§ 24-4.7-1-1 to 24-4.7-5-6.**
Scope: Defines "telephone sales call" and "telephone solicitor" broadly, but excludes calls regarding existing debts or contracts, sales of insurance or newspapers, calls by licensed real estate brokers and salespersons, certain calls on behalf of charitable organizations, and calls in response to a request. Texts, and certain other media messages explicitly covered. Explicitly covers those who provide substantial assistance or support to telemarketer, knowing or consciously avoiding knowing, that telemarketer has violated this act. (This provision does not apply to communications services providers who only transport, handle, or retransmit communications.)
Registration Requirements: None specified.
Substantive Law: Telemarketers must disclose their true names and the name of the business on whose behalf they are calling at the outset of the call. Contract that results from sales call (except certain sales in which consumer is allowed to return goods without payment, or for full refund) must be reduced to writing and signed, must include name, address and phone number of seller, price and description of goods, and notice that consumer is not obligated to pay unless he or she signs contract and returns it to seller. Contract may not exclude from its terms any written or oral representation made by telephone solicitor in connection with the transaction. Merchant may not charge consumer's credit card or cause any electronic transfer until signed contract is received. (Exemption for certain catalog sales.) May not call number on do-not-call list maintained by consumer protection division of attorney general's office. Telephone solicitor or other who collects consumer information (except for telephone directory) must omit telephone numbers of listed consumers. Regulations are found at 11 Ind. Admin. Code 1-1-1 through 2-82.
Private Right of Action: Contracts that violate this statute are voidable.
Special Penalties: Civil penalties of up to $10,000 for first violation; $25,000 for second and subsequent violations; repayment of all funds obtained by the violation; costs of the investigation and the action and state's reasonable attorney fees. Court may void contracts made in violation of this chapter, and order restitution to consumers.

IOWA

Telemarketing Statute: **Iowa Code § 714.8(15).**
Scope: Applies to persons who obtain or attempt to obtain another's property by deception through telephone communications involving direct or implied claims that the other person has won, or is about to win, a prize or may be able to recover losses suffered in connection with a prize promotion.
Registration Requirements: None specified.
Substantive Law: Criminalizes deceptive telemarketing prize promotions and recovery room operations.
Private Right of Action: None specified, but Iowa recognizes a private cause of action for violation of a criminal statute.
Special Penalties: Criminal penalties.

KANSAS

Telemarketing Statute: **Kan. Stat. Ann. §§ 50-670 to 50-679a.**

Scope: Defines telemarketing broadly, but excludes nonprofit organizations, newspaper publishers, calls made pursuant to prior negotiations or an existing business relationship unless the consumer has objected to these calls and asked that they cease, some sales in response to advertisements or catalogs, and sales in which the consumer may obtain a full refund.

Registration Requirements: None specified.

Substantive Law: Solicitors must follow up all sales transactions with a written confirmation, containing specific information, including the name and address of the solicitor; solicitors cannot charge the consumer until they receive an original copy of the confirmation signed by the consumer. Other prohibitions, which apply more broadly, require callers to identify themselves and the purpose of the call, and terminate the call immediately if the consumer expresses disinterest. May not send unsolicited fax after consumer requests orally or in writing that such transmissions cease; may not use courier to pick up payment before goods delivered, with opportunity to inspect; may not block Caller ID (grace period until 2005 for technical obstacles). Prohibits solicitors from blocking display of telephone number by a Caller ID service when the solicitor's service or equipment is capable of allowing the display of such number. Telephone solicitors may not call consumers on do-not-call list. Attorney general may designate nationwide do-not-call list as Kansas list.

Private Right of Action: Yes. A violation is a UDAP violation. Bona fide error defense available for violations of no-call list violations.

Special Penalties: Older or disabled consumers may recover punitive damages.

KENTUCKY

Telemarketing Statute: **Ky. Rev. Stat. Ann. §§ 367.461 to 367.46999 (West).**

Scope: Covers telephone solicitations, defined as live or recorded communication sent by telephone, or message sent by fax, to a residential, mobile or telephone paging device telephone number, for purpose of: a sale of goods or services, offering an investment, business, or employment opportunity, or offering a consumer loan; obtaining information for these purposes; or offering a prize, gift, etc., if any payment or attendance at a sales presentation will be required. Definition also includes certain calls in response to consumers inquiries generated by mass mailings or other notifications that state that the consumer has been specially selected, offer the consumer a prize or gift, or offer a free or discounted item if the consumer makes a purchase. Excludes most calls in response to the consumer's express request; debt collection calls; calls to persons with whom telemarketer or seller has prior or existing business relationship; merchant-to-merchant calls; and calls to out-of-state consumers.

Registration Requirements: Solicitors must obtain a permit from the attorney general. Merchant must post bond. Additional bond required for promotions which offer premium.

Substantive Law: Solicitors must immediately identify themselves, the goods being sold, and terminate the call if the consumer is disinterested; solicitors cannot request or accept payment until they receive a signed copy of a written contract from the consumer, unless consumer is given a notice of a 14-day right to cancel; also, several prohibitions apply to solicitors using automated messages. Harassment specifically forbidden, including causing phone to ring for more than 30 seconds, calling between 9 p.m. and 10 a.m., or calling consumers on do-not-call list. May not seek payment in advance for credit repair, finding a loan, or recovering funds lost to previous telemarketer. Detailed disclosure requirements for gifts and prizes, and business opportunities. May not: charge consumer's bank account without express written authorization, or charge credit card or make electronic funds transfer except in conformity with Ky. Rev. Stat. § 367.46963 (West); use courier to obtain payment before goods delivered with opportunity for inspection; solicit person under 18 (must ask age, but may accept answer); block Caller ID; contact credit card issuer seeking consumer's credit card number, (and issuer may not provide number to telemarketer); call persons listed on the FTC's nationwide do-not-call list; make calls before 10:00 a.m. or after 9:00 p.m.; sell information revealed during telephone solicitation without consumer's express written consent; make calls with artificial or prerecorded voice except for school emergency calls or with called party's express consent; engage in any unfair, false, misleading or deceptive practice or act. Automatic dialing device message must be preceded with live message, or message which allows consumer to respond with use of keypad, to determine if consumer wishes to hear message; must disconnect within ten seconds if consumer declines; may not call unlisted numbers, or hospital, nursing home or emergency numbers; may not use device between 9 p.m. and 8 a.m. (exceptions for certain calls to which consumer has consented, calls regarding previously ordered goods or pre-existing debt, calls regarding school attendance). May not use automatic dialing device to solicit persons to call a pay-per-call number. Phone company must discontinue pay-per-call line if it learns that automatic device is being used to solicit calls (§ 367.465).

Private Right of Action: Yes. Violation is UDAP violation (Ky. Rev. Stat. § 367.170 (West)). Actual damages recoverable, plus court costs and attorney fees. Bona fide error defense for no-call-list violations.

Special Penalties: Criminal penalties.

LOUISIANA

Telemarketing Statute: **La. Rev. Stat. Ann. §§ 45:821 to 45:833.**

Scope: Defines specific types of telemarketing that are covered and lists 20 exceptions, such as sales to previous customers, sales involving face-to-face contact, sales made by supervised financial institutions, and the sale of newspapers and securities.

Registration Requirements: Solicitors must register and maintain a bond.

Substantive Law: Solicitors must provide consumers with their street location and other information depending on the nature of the solicitation; consumers can cancel within 3 days of the sale; and contracts must be written, signed by the consumer, and contain specific information including the consumers right to cancel.

Private Right of Action: Violation is a UDAP violation.

Special Penalties: Up to $10,000 fine and 1 year in jail for specified violations.

Telemarketing Statute: **La. Rev. Stat. §§ 45:844.11 to 45:844.17 (Telephone Solicitation Relief Act).**

Scope: Unsolicited voice or data communications to residential telephone subscribers. Exceptions for existing debt or contract, existing or recent prior (within 6 months) business relationship, polling, certain charitable solicitations, political activity, periodic healthcare reminders from physician, dentist, optometrist, chiropractor or veterinarian.

Registration Requirements: Telemarketers register with Public Service Commission and pay fee for use of do-not-call database.

Substantive Law: May not call person listed on do-not-call database. Compiler or seller of lists of names for telephone solicitation (except telephone directories) must delete names of those listed on do-not-call database. Bona fide error defense available.

Private Right of Action: None specified.

Special Penalties: Administrative penalty of up to $1500 per violation, $3000 if called party is age 65 or over.

MAINE

Telemarketing Statute: **Me. Rev. Stat. Ann. tit. 10, §§ 1498, 1499-A, 1499-B.**

Scope: Section 1498 governs automated telephone solicitation in which a recorded message is played. Sections 1499-A and 1499-B govern all other telephone solicitation, broadly defined.

Registration Requirements: Solicitors using automated messages must register with the secretary of state (§ 1498).

Substantive Law: Solicitors using automated calling devices must identify themselves within the first minute of the call, and are prohibited from calling outside the hours of 9 a.m. to 5 p.m., may not call emergency numbers, cell phones, pagers, unlisted or unpublished numbers, or make more than one call to the same number during any one eight-hour period. Must assure that call disconnects within 5 seconds after consumer hangs up. Exceptions for calls giving information about ordered goods; responses to telephone inquiries; and governmental calls (§ 1498). Telemarketers are prohibited from blocking Caller ID or making calls to numbers on FTC's nationwide do-not-call list, and must disclose true name and name of business immediately when consumer answers. *See also* Me. Rev. Stat. Ann. tit. 32, § 14716 (violation of FTC's Telemarketing Rule by a transient seller of consumer goods also violates this subchapter (regulating sales by personal or telephone contact by seller who does not have a permanent place of business in Maine). Transient seller may not use courier to pick up payment before goods delivered, with opportunity to inspect.).

Private Right of Action: Violations are UDAP violations.

Special Penalties: Violation of § 1498 (prerecorded messages) is a UDAP violation.

MARYLAND

Telemarketing Statute: **Md. Code Ann., Com. Law §§ 14-2201 to 14-2205 (West) (Maryland Telephone Solicitations Act); Md. Code Ann., Com. Law §§ 14-3201 to 14-3202 (West) (Maryland Telephone Consumer Protection Act); Md. Code Ann., Pub. Util. Law §§ 8-204, 8-205 (West).**

Scope: The Maryland Telephone Solicitations Act applies to telephone solicitations, broadly defined, with exceptions including prior business relationship, catalog sales, sales in which seller offers refunds, and bona fide charitable organizations. The Maryland Telephone Consumer Protection Act incorporates the federal TCPA and the FTC telemarketing rule, and makes violations actionable under state law. Public utility statute covers use of automatic dialing device, and telephone solicitation, broadly defined to include pollsters.

Registration Requirements: None specified.

Substantive Law: Contracts must be reduced to writing, signed by the consumer, and contain the name and address of the solicitor. Merchant may not submit charge to consumer's account before receiving signed contract that complies with this section. Public utility law forbids use of automated dialing to solicit the purchase, lease or rental of goods or services; offer a gift or prize; conduct a poll; or request information that will be used to solicit the purchase, lease, or rental of goods or services. Exception for pre-existing business relationship. Caller must disconnect within 5 seconds after termination of the call by either party. Telephone solicitor may not block Caller ID. Section 14-3201 prohibits violation of (1) federal Telemarketing Consumer Fraud and Abuse Prevention Act as implemented by the FTC, or (2) federal Telephone Consumer Protection Act.

Private Right of Action: Violation of telemarketing statute is UDAP violation. Non-complying contracts are also unenforceable. Special private cause of action for actual damages or $500, whichever is greater, plus attorney fees, for each violation of federal laws incorporated by § 14-3201.

Special Penalties: Caller ID blocking by telephone solicitors or misuse of automatic dialing device is a misdemeanor.

MASSACHUSETTS

Telemarketing Statute: **Mass. Gen. Laws ch. 159, § 19E.**

Scope: Statute covers all sales of goods or services made by telephone to the consumer's residence.

Registration Requirements: None specified.

Substantive Law: Solicitors must immediately disclose their identity, the trade name of the person they represent, and the kinds of goods or services being offered for sale. Solicitors are prohibited from using a plan or scheme which misrepresents their true purpose.

Private Right of Action: None specified.

Special Penalties: None specified.

Telemarketing Statute: **Mass. Gen. Laws ch. 159C, §§ 1 to 14 (Telemarketing Solicitation).**

Scope: Unsolicited sales calls from a location in Massachusetts, or to a consumer in Massachusetts, for consumer goods and services, including stocks, bonds and mutual funds. Exceptions for calls requested by consumer; calls regarding existing contract or debt (performance not complete at time of call); calls to an existing customer, unless customer has requested no further calls; calls that lead to face-to-face meeting before sale is consummated; calls by non-profits; polls and surveys for non-commercial purposes.

Registration Requirements: None specified.

Substantive Law: Must disclose at beginning of call the sales purpose of the call, the name of the telemarketer and the prospective seller, and an accurate description of the goods. Before requesting payment, must disclose the cost of goods, including taxes, shipping and handling, any restrictions or limitations on an offer, the seller's return, refund and cancellation policy, and all "material aspects" of an investment opportunity. May not call between 8 p.m. and 8 a.m., send unsolicited faxes, use a recorded message device, block Caller ID, or call consumer listed on do-not-call list, maintained by Office of Consumer Affairs and Business Regulation and coordinated with nationwide list. Compilers and sellers of mailing lists for telephone sales must remove names of consumers on do-not-call list.

Private Right of Action: Consumer who receives more than one sales call in 12 months from same telemarketer in violation of this chapter has private right of action for the greater of actual monetary damages or $5000, and for injunctive relief. Bona fide error defense available. Prevailing party entitled to costs and reasonable attorney fees. Remedy is not exclusive, but is in addition to other remedies including chapter 93A.

Special Penalties: Attorney general may seek civil penalties of up to $5000 per violation ($1500 minimum for knowing violation involving consumer age 65 or over).

MICHIGAN

Telemarketing Statute: **Mich. Comp. Laws §§ 445.111 to 445.111e.** *See also* **Mich. Comp. Laws §§ 445.113, 445.116.**

Scope: Telemarketing is covered by the state's home solicitation sales law. "Home solicitation sale" does not include: (1) sales for less than $25; (2) sales pursuant to a preexisting revolving charge account agreement; (3) sales made at or pursuant to prior negotiations at a business establishment; (4) sales made pursuant to a general circulation printed advertisement; (5) sales by licensed insurance agents or licensed real estate professionals; (6) sales of agricultural equipment; (7) loans or extensions of credit that are regulated under other specified statutes; or (8) certain charitable or public safety solicitations covered by other statutes. Telephone solicitor code of conduct and do-not-call provisions apply to a "telephone solicitation," even when made by licensed insurance or real estate professional. Prescribed notice of cancellation language does not apply to telephone solicitation by telecommunications provider, if these comply with Telecommunications Act, Mich. Comp. Laws §§ 484.2505 through 484.2507.

Registration Requirements: None specified.

Substantive Law: Sales may not be made by telephone solicitations that use recorded messages. All agreements must be reduced to writing, be signed by the consumer and include a prescribed notice of cancellation; the consumer can cancel the transaction within 3 days of signing the agreement; and the solicitor must return payment to the consumer within 10 days of cancellation. At beginning of call, solicitor must identify self and company. On request, must provide a company phone number that will be answered by a natural person. May not block Caller ID. May not call person on the do-not-call list maintained by the Public Service Commission. Federal do-not-call list serves as state list. Before receipt of payment, seller must disclose total price of goods; any conditions or limitations on offers; seller's refund and cancellation policy; costs or conditions of winning a prize, including the odds; that no purchase is required to enter contest, and the no-purchase method of entry; any "material aspect" of a business opportunity; consumer's cancellation rights. May not accept payment, or charge consumer's bank account or credit card without "verifiable authorization" as defined. May not offer prize promotion for which purchase is necessary. May not use courier to pick up payment during period when consumer is entitled to cancel.

Private Right of Action: Violation is a UDAP violation. Person damaged by violation may sue for larger of actual damages or $250, and reasonable attorney fees.

Special Penalties: Knowing violation of certain provisions is a misdemeanor.

MINNESOTA

Telemarketing Statute: **Minn. Stat. §§ 325E.26 to 325E.31, 325E.395 (Automatic Dialing-Announcing Devices).**

Scope: Automatic dialing and announcing devices. Exemptions for prior business relationship, messages from school districts and messages advising employees of work schedules.

Registration Requirements: None specified.

Substantive Law: Automatic dialing and announcing devices may not be used without consent or between 9 p.m. and 9 a.m.; there must be a live operator, who discloses the name of the company, the sales purpose of the call, the identity of the goods or services offered and, if applicable, that the message solicits payment or commitment of funds; calling system must disconnect within ten seconds when the customer hangs up. Unsolicited advertising faxes include a toll-free number and a mailing address which the recipient may use to request that no more faxes be sent.

Private Right of Action: A violation is actionable under Minn. Stat. § 8.31.

Special Penalties: None specified.

Telemarketing Statute: **Minn. Stat. §§ 325G.12 to 325G.14 (Personal Solicitation of Sales).**

Scope: Sellers who regularly engage in transactions of the kind at issue and who use personal or telephone contact at place other than seller's place of business to sell personal, family, or household goods or services. Buyer-initiated calls, calls to buyers where the parties already know each other, and sales of newspapers by minors who also deliver papers are excluded.

Registration Requirements: None specified.

Substantive Law: Requires initial disclosure of seller's name, business name, type of goods or services being sold, and purpose of contact.

Private Right of Action: A violation is actionable under Minn. Stat. § 8.31.

Special Penalties: None specified.

MISSISSIPPI

Telemarketing Statute: **Miss. Code Ann. §§ 77-3-601 to 77-3-619.**

Scope: Defines telemarketing broadly, but excludes isolated transactions, supervised financial institutions, non-commercial calls, sales that involve face-to-face contact, sales of securities, food, newspapers, magazines, memberships in book or record clubs, non-profits, certain catalog sales, sales resulting from prior negotiations, and several other enumerated exceptions. Statute covers some sales resulting from call by buyer in response to flyer, notice, or postcard delivered to home.

Registration Requirements: Telephone solicitors must register with the attorney general and post a surety bond or other acceptable security.

Substantive Law: Solicitors may call only between the hours of 8:00 a.m. and 9:00 p.m. (no Sunday calls), must identify themselves, terminate the call if the consumer expresses disinterest, and provide the consumer with a written contract pursuant to the telephone call. Merchant may not submit charge to consumer's account until it receives signed contract.

Private Right of Action: None specified, but the language of the statute suggests there is a private right of action. Noncomplying contracts are unenforceable. Statute also gives attorney general specific enforcement powers.

Special Penalties: Civil penalty of up to $10,000 for each violation.

Telemarketing Statute: **Miss. Code Ann. §§ 77-3-701 to 77-3-737 (Mississippi Telephone Solicitation Act).** *Note: This statute is scheduled to sunset on July 1, 2017.*

Scope: Telephone solicitation broadly defined to include calls regarding the sale of any consumer goods or services, an extension of credit

for consumer goods or services, or the purchase, rental, or investment in property, with exemptions for pre-existing business relationship; religious, charitable or bona fide non-profit solicitations; sales calls leading to face-to-face presentation, calls which do not make the "major sales presentation," sales of newspapers, various businesses regulated under law including real estate, insurance, motor vehicles, financial institutions.

Registration Requirement: Telephone solicitors must register with Public Service Commission, and pay fee for access to do-not-call database unless otherwise allowed by the Commission.

Substantive Law: May not call consumers listed on no-call database established by Public Service Commission and coordinated with federal do-not-call list. Telephone solicitors must begin calls by identifying self and company, and disclosing purpose of call. May not call on a Sunday. May call only between 8 a.m. and 8 p.m. May not block Caller ID. May not used automated dialing system to deliver prerecorded message except in context of established business relationship.

Private Right of Action: None specified.

Special Penalties: Administrative penalty of up to $5000 per violation. Bona fide error defense available.

Telemarketing Statute: **Miss. Code Ann. §§ 77-3-451 to 77-3-459 (Automatic Dialing and Announcing Devices).**

Scope: Any automatic dialing and announcing device connected to telephone line.

Registration Requirements: None specified.

Substantive Law: Forbids use of autodialer with prerecorded message for sales purposes, except with prior permission of person called or pursuant to established business relationship. Must be operated by person who states identity of caller and purpose of message, and disconnects if recipient declines. Forbids prerecorded message that will be received between 9 p.m. and 9 a.m. local time.

Private Right of Action: None specified.

Special Penalties: Fine of up to $500 per violation, and disconnection for period specified by Public Service Commission.

Telemarketing Statute: **Miss. Code Ann. §§ 77-3-801 through 77-3-809 (Caller ID Anti-Spoofing Act).** *Note: This statute was held preempted by the federal Truth in Caller ID Act by Teltech Systems, Inc. v. Bryant, 702 F.3d 322 (5th Cir. 2012).*

Scope: Any call with an ability to access users on the public switched telephone network or a successor network. Does not apply to federal, state, county, or municipal government law enforcement agencies, intermediary service providers between the caller and the recipient, and blocking of caller identification.

Registration Requirements: None specified.

Substantive Law: A person cannot enter or cause to be entered false information into a caller identification system with the intent to defraud or mislead the recipient of the call. Such violation is an unlawful trade practice under § 75-24-5.

Private Right of Action: Violation is a UDAP violation.

Special Penalties: Misdemeanor and fine of up to $1000 and/or imprisonment for up to one year.

MISSOURI

Telemarketing Statute: **Mo. Rev. Stat. §§ 407.1070 to 407.1090 (Telemarketing Practices); Mo. Rev. Stat. §§ 407.1095 to 407.1110 (Telemarketing No-Call List).**

Scope: Telemarketing defined as plan, program or campaign, conducted to induce purchase or lease of merchandise, by use of one or more telephones, which involves more than one telephone call. Statute also covers investment opportunities. Exemptions for calls that will be followed by face-to-face negotiation before completion of sale; certain consumer-initiated calls; calls where consumer may return merchandise within 14 days for full refund; certain catalog sales, calls to consumer with established business relationship, certain calls by sellers who are regulated by other state or federal agency, business-to-business calls—but no exemption for sale of nondurable office supplies or cleaning supplies. Provider of telephone services not liable for violations of act by another.

Registration Requirements: None specified.

Substantive Law: Telemarketer must promptly disclose sales purpose of call, identity of telemarketer and seller, nature of merchandise or investment opportunity being sold, and, if a prize is being offered, that no purchase or payment is necessary to win. If call is by recorded or electronically generated voice, must disclose this at beginning. Before requesting payment, caller must disclose address or phone number where seller may be contacted, the cost and quantity of the merchandise, any material limitations or restrictions, material information about cancellation and other policies, material information about an investment opportunity, or a prize promotion (including the odds). Misrepresentations forbidden. Intimidation, harassment, night calls (9 p.m. to 8 a.m.) forbidden. May not request advance payment for credit repair, or for recovery of property lost to prior telemarketing scam. Verifiable authorization and confirmation required before payment by check, draft, or other means of access to consumer's account. May not use courier to obtain payment before goods or investment opportunity delivered, with opportunity to inspect. May not block consumer's Caller ID. Detailed record keeping requirements: advertising materials, verifiable authorizations, statistics on prizes, information about current and former employees, names and addresses of customers, and dates when goods shipped. Calls to persons on do-not-call list forbidden.

Private Right of Action: Violation is UDAP violation. Consumer also has right of action for actual and punitive damages, reasonable attorney fees, court costs and "any other remedy permitted by law." Consumer who receives two or more calls within a year from same seller in violation of no-call statute may bring action for injunction and the greater of actual monetary loss or $5000 per violation.

Special Penalties: Violations are Class A misdemeanors or Class D felonies. Attorney general may seek injunction or civil penalties (up to $5000 per violation) for calls to persons on no-call list.

MONTANA

Montana has two applicable statutes. The provisions of one statute do not apply to a claim brought under the other.

Telemarketing Statute: Mont. Code Ann. §§ 30-14-1401 to 30-14-1606.
Scope: Defines telemarketing broadly, but exempts calls initiated by a consumer without prior solicitation by telemarketer and calls in which a sale is not completed until after a face-to-face sales presentation. Also lists 18 exemptions from registration and bonding requirements, including: nonprofit organizations; business-to-business sales; licensed realtors, insurers, and securities dealers; solicitations for magazines, newspapers, satellite or cable television systems; businesses that publish certain types of catalogs; retail businesses that make most of their sales at their retail sites; food transactions of less than $100 per address; book, video or record clubs.

Registration Requirements: Telephone solicitors must register with the Department of Administration and maintain a bond.

Substantive Law: Telemarketers must promptly disclose their identity, purpose of call, nature of goods or services and inform consumer that purchases are not required to win a prize. A telemarketer may not block the called party's Caller ID. Prior to requesting any payment, telemarketers must disclose the total cost and any material restrictions, limitations or conditions pertaining to the purchase. Unless exception applies, sales are not final until purchaser receives notice of cancellation provisions. Repeated calls and other abusive practices are prohibited. Special restrictions on credit repair services, recovery of funds or property lost in prior telemarketing scams, use of telechecks, and use of couriers to pick up payments. Records must be kept for two years. Unsolicited advertising faxes prohibited. May not call consumer on do-not-call list, established by Department of Administration and coordinated with national list. (Exceptions for existing business relationship, non-profits, certain regulated entities, and licensed tradespeople or professionals setting up appointments.)

Private Right of Action: Yes, for actual damages or $500, whichever is greater, plus attorney fees. A violation is also a UDAP violation. Sales by

unlicensed telemarketers are void. For violations of no-call list statute, consumer who receives more than one forbidden call within 12 months has right of action for greater of actual damages or $5000 for each knowing violation. Bona fide error defense available.

Special Penalties: Criminal penalties.

Telemarketing Statute: Mont. Code Ann. §§ 30-14-501 to 30-14-508 (Personal Solicitation Sales).
Scope: Telemarketing is covered. The statute excludes sales where the consumer personally knows the seller, sales where the consumer initiates contact with the seller, the sale of insurance and newspaper subscriptions, and sales involving less than $25.

Registration Requirements: None specified.

Substantive Law: Solicitors must identify themselves, their company, and the goods being sold at the time of initial contact; consumers may cancel transactions within 3 days of signing a contract; solicitors must provide consumers with a notice of their right to cancel; and solicitors must return payment to the consumer within 10 days of cancellation.

Private Right of Action: Yes. A violation is a UDAP violation. If seller fails to comply with requirement to return down payment, seller is liable for entire down payment and if buyer prevails in court action for recovery, $500 plus costs and reasonable attorney fees.

Special Penalties: Civil fine of up to $1000 for failure to make required initial disclosures.

NEBRASKA

Telemarketing Statute: Neb. Rev. Stat. §§ 86-212 to 86-235 (Telemarketing and Prize Promotions).
Scope: Covers seller-initiated calls soliciting the sale, lease or rental of consumer goods or services, or extension of consumer credit, or seeking information to be used to directly solicit consumer sales or extensions of credit, or offering gifts or prizes with intent to solicit consumer sale. Also covers prize promotions in which consumer is notified by mail to call seller. Excludes calls in response to express request of called party, calls regarding existing contract or debt, clearly established business relationship, sales of periodicals by publisher. Telecommunications company offering services subject to the verification provisions of the Telephone Consumer Slamming Prevention Act.

Registration Requirements: None specified.

Substantive Law: Seller may not debit consumer's bank account without verifiable (written or tape recorded) authorization from consumer. Written confirmation must be sent to consumer, including terms of sale and procedure for obtaining a refund if confirmation is inaccurate. Five-day cooling-off period, measured from receipt of written notice. Cancellation rights must be disclosed orally during phone call, and in writing with any advertising or with delivery of the product. Must refund within 30 days after cancellation. Use of courier to pick up payment forbidden, unless goods delivered at same time. Advance payment for recovery service prohibited (except for services of attorney). Detailed disclosure requirements for prize promotion, including odds, value of prizes, and no-purchase option for entry. Seller in prize promotion may not misrepresent value of prize, or falsely state that consumer has already won, or request any payment from consumer prior to delivery of written disclosures. Recordkeeping requirements same as 16 C.F.R. § 310.5.

Private Right of Action: For actual damages, costs and attorney fees.

Special Penalties: Violation is a Class 1 misdemeanor. Certain violations in prize promotion punishable by civil penalty of up to $2000.

Telemarketing Statute: Neb. Rev. Stat. §§ 86-236 to 86-257 (Automatic Dialing and Announcing Device Act).
Scope: Statute covers solicitations using an automatic dialing-announcing device in which a recorded message is played; excludes calls made with consumer's prior invitation or permission; calls where there is an established business relationship between the consumer and the solicitor; tax-exempt nonprofit organizations; calls not made for commercial purposes, or made for commercial purposes but which do not include the transmission of an unsolicited advertisement.

Registration Requirements: Solicitors using automatic dialing-announcing devices must obtain permit from the Public Service Commission and pay $500 fee for each device.

Substantive Law: Requires disclosure of caller's identity at beginning of message; caller's telephone number (other than that of the device which made the call) or address must be disclosed during or after message. Calls may be made only between the hours of 8 a.m. and 9 p.m. Solicitors may not call consumers who place themselves on a "no-call" list. May not call any emergency number, pager, cell phone, guest or patient room at hospital or nursing home. May not engage two or more lines of business with multilane system. Must disconnect within five seconds after called party hangs up. Unsolicited advertising faxes prohibited.

Private Right of Action: None specified.

Special Penalties: Public Service Commission may administratively fine violator up to $1000 per violation after notice and hearing. Violations are Class II misdemeanors.

NEVADA

Telemarketing Statute: **Nev. Rev. Stat. §§ 228.500 to 228.640, 597.814 to 597.818**

Scope: Section 597.814 applies to "any person", with exceptions for political communication, certain public safety announcements, and certain communications with existing customers. § 598.0918 applies to any person during a solicitation by telephone or sales presentation. Other provisions apply to "telephone solicitors," broadly defined, with exceptions for delinquent debt, established business relationship, calls on behalf of tax-exempt charitable organizations, religious organizations, and political organizations.

Registration Requirements: None specified.

Substantive Law: Section 597.814 requires autodialed pre-recorded messages to include initial disclosures and prohibits calls between 8:00 p.m. and 9:00 a.m. and call-backs to people who terminate the first call. Section 598.0918 prohibits threatening, intimidating, profane, obscene language; harassment by repeat calls; calls between 8:00 p.m. and 9:00 a.m.; Caller ID blocking. Remaining provisions establish do-not-call rule and allow attorney general to use FTC's national do-not-call registry or establish state registry; requires telephone solicitors to maintain company-specific do-not-call lists. §§ 225 *et seq.* provide for the establishment of a do-not-call list and forbids telephone solicitation of numbers on the list, with exceptions for charitable, religious, and political organizations and for established business relationship.

Private Right of Action: Violation of do-not-call rule is UDAP violation.

Special Penalties: For violations of § 597.814, the telephone service to which the device was connected may be suspended for a period to be determined by the court.

Telemarketing Statute: **Nev. Rev. Stat. §§ 599B.005 to 599B.300.**

Scope: Defines specific types of telemarketing that are covered, including prize promotions, the sale of information relating to sporting events, and recovery services (solicitors that promise, for a fee, to recover goods that the consumer never received from a different solicitor). There are 26 exceptions, such as sales made by licensed broadcasters, insurance brokers, the sale of newspapers and magazines, and some charitable solicitations.

Registration Requirements: In 2009, the statute's registration requirements were temporarily repealed. The repeal was originally scheduled to sunset in 2011 but has been extended until June 30, 2017. Although registration requirements are repealed, sellers and salespersons must still appoint Secretary of State as their agent for service of process.

Substantive Law: Telemarketer must disclose true name, identity of seller, purpose of call, all charges, and all restrictions and conditions; specific restrictions on prize promotions and chance promotions; consumer has 30-day right to refund; delivery of goods or services must be accompanied by a prescribed form; Salesperson may not be associated with more than one seller at the same time. Sellers and salespersons must submit copies of scripts, etc., to attorney general and submit any new or revised material. All these provisions will sunset on June 30, 2017. Recovery service

solicitors cannot receive payment until their services are performed; solicitors cannot disclose the name or address of any consumer.

Private Right of Action: Older or disabled consumer can sue for actual damages, punitive damages, and attorney fees. Statute also gives attorney general specific enforcement powers.

Special Penalties: Criminal penalties. Enhanced penalty for deceptive practices directed towards older or disabled persons.

NEW HAMPSHIRE

Telemarketing Statute: **N.H. Rev. Stat. Ann. §§ 359-E:1 to 359-E:11 (Telemarketing).**

Scope: Applies to telemarketing, broadly defined, with exceptions for calls in response to requests, in connection with established business relationship, or on behalf of a non-profit charity, and political calls other than those using autodialers, plus a partial temporary exception for calls by newspapers. Also applies to use of automatic dialing system to place unsolicited recorded message calls to residential subscribers, seeking to give, sell, or lease goods or services, or obtain pledges, contributions, or information.

Exceptions: Pre-existing relationship.

Registration Requirements: Anyone wishing to use automatic dialing device for solicitation must register and pay a $20 per year fee.

Substantive Law: Requires compliance with FCC and FTC do-not-call list and FTC Telemarketing Rule. May not call emergency lines (911 or seven-digit police, fire or ambulance numbers designated as emergency numbers). Must immediately disclose identity of caller and purpose of call. Must disconnect within 30 seconds after called party hangs up. May not block Caller ID, and number displayed on Caller ID must be one at which solicitor receives phone calls. Note that N.H. Rev. Stat. Ann. § 361-B:2-a also requires some telephone sellers to disclose a legal name, a street address from which the business is actually conducted, and a telephone number for inquiries and complaints.

Private Right of Action: Violation is a UDAP violation. Any person injured by violation of telemarketing provisions has private cause of action for actual damages or $1000, which may be doubled or trebled if willful or knowing, plus attorney fees; may also seek injunctive relief; good faith error defense.

Special Penalties: Civil penalty of up to $5000. Bona fide error defense available.

NEW JERSEY

Telemarketing Statute: **N.J. Stat. Ann. §§ 56:8-119 to 56:8-135 (West).** *See also* **N.J. Stat. Ann. § 48:17-25 (West).**

Scope: Telemarketing broadly defined with exceptions for customer-requested call, established business relationship.

Registration Requirements: Telemarketer must register with Consumer Affairs Division of Department of Law and Public Safety, pay a fee, and post bond for $25,000.

Substantive Law: Telemarketer must identify self, company, and purpose of call within first thirty seconds. May not call between 9 p.m. and 8 a.m., block Caller ID, call commercial mobile phones, or call person on do-not-call list established by Consumer Affairs Division. *See also* N.J. Admin. Code §§ 13:45D-1.1 through 13:45D-5.2. These regulations will sunset on August 13, 2016.

Private Right of Action: Violation is a UDAP violation. Bona fide error defense available. Also no liability for isolated (i.e., only one within 12 months) call.

Special Penalties: None specified.

Telemarketing Regulations: **N.J. Admin. Code § 13:45A-1.1.** *Note: These regulations will sunset on December 14, 2018.*

Scope: Merchandise ordered by telephone from a person conducting a "mail order or catalog business."

Exceptions: Merchandise ordered pursuant to an open-end credit plan opened prior to the sale in question; merchandise such as quarterly magazines that cannot be produced until a future date; merchandise such as magazines that are ordered for serial delivery.

Registration Requirements: None specified.

Substantive Law: Seller cannot accept money through the mail or any electronic transfer medium and then allow six weeks to pass without delivering or mailing the merchandise, making a refund, sending the consumer a notice with specified content, or sending merchandise of similar or superior quality with a refund offer. Does not apply if seller discloses specific longer delivery period and complies with other requirements.

Private Right of Action: Violation is UDAP violation.

Special Penalties: None specified.

NEW MEXICO

Telemarketing Statute: **N.M. Stat. §§ 57-12-22 to 57-12-24.**

Scope: Defines telemarketing broadly. Faxes explicitly included. Exceptions for established business relationship; expression of political opinions; licensed real estate brokers.

Registration Requirements: None specified.

Substantive Law: Solicitors must promptly disclose the purpose of their call, fully disclose all costs associated with their goods, and may call only between the hours of 9:00 a.m. and 9:00 p.m.; they may not ask for credit card numbers unless the consumer has committed to making a purchase and expressed a desire to pay with a credit card, nor can solicitors use a pre-recorded message unless there is an existing business relationship and the consumer consents to hear the message. Prohibits misrepresenting call as courtesy call, survey, etc.; restricts abandoned calls; prohibits calls to residential subscribers who have registered on national do-not-call list; prohibits Caller ID blocking. Unsolicited fax or e-mail advertisements must conspicuously include a toll-free number which recipient may use to forbid further contacts.

Private Right of Action: Yes. Violation is UDAP violation. For fax or e-mail sent to person who has requested removal from mailing list, private right of action for greater of actual damages (including lost profits), $25 per fax or e-mail, or $5000 per day of violation, plus costs and reasonable attorney fees.

Special Penalties: None specified.

NEW YORK

Telemarketing Statute: **N.Y. Gen. Bus. Law §§ 399-p, 399-pp, 399-z (McKinney); N.Y. Pers. Prop. Law §§ 440 to 448 (McKinney) (Telephone Sales Protection Act).** *See also* **N.Y. Pub. Serv. Law § 92-d (McKinney).**

Scope: Telephone Sales Act: Seller's solicitation by telephone of sales of merchandise or certain travel services, paid for by credit card authorization. *Telemarketing Act:* "Telemarketing" means any plan, program or campaign which is conducted to induce payment or the exchange of any other consideration for any goods or services that involves more than one telephone call by a telemarketer in which the customer is located within the state at the time of the call.

Exceptions: Telephone Sales Act: Sales under $25, sale or rental of real property, regulated sales of insurance, securities, or commodities, certain catalog sales, prior relationship; solicitation of sales through media other than telephone calls; calls to implement or complete a transaction to which the consumer has previously consented. *Telemarketing Act:* Debt collection in compliance with FDCPA, calls leading to face-to-face negotiation, buyer initiated calls which do not result from any solicitation by seller, certain calls to for-profit businesses, calls pursuant to prior contractual relationship; businesses licensed under other law; non-profits; certain calls made in effort to develop new business.

Registration Requirements: Telephone Sales Act: None specified. *Telemarketing Act:* Must register with secretary of state (detailed information requirements), pay $500 fee, and post $25,000 bond or other acceptable form of security (letter of credit, CD, etc.).

Substantive Law: Telephone Sales Act: Written notice required, must be in same language as sales presentation, and disclose right to cancel; 3-day cooling-off period, begins to run when buyer receives written notice of right to cancel; upon cancellation, seller must recredit consumer's credit card for down payment and return any trade-ins; buyer must make goods available at buyer's residence; if seller does not collect them within a reasonable time, buyer owns goods without obligation. Seller may not assign obligation until five days after notice of right to cancel. *Telemarketing Act:* At beginning of call, must disclose name of company, purpose of call, cost of goods offered; additional disclosure requirements for prize promotions; abuse and harassment prohibited; may call residence only between 8 a.m. and 9 p.m.; may not call consumer who has requested not to be called; may not request advance fee for credit repair or recovery services (except services of licensed attorney), must obtain written authorization for any draw on buyer's bank account; detailed recordkeeping requirements; waivers forbidden; may not block Caller ID; may not call number on do-not-call list; automatic dialing device that disseminates prerecorded message must announce purpose of call and disconnect promptly if call terminated, and may not use a random or sequential number generator, or make calls to certain emergency numbers, hospitals, nursing homes, etc. Prohibits telemarketers and sellers from calling customers whose numbers are listed on FTC's nationwide do-not-call list. Prohibits calls that deliver prerecorded messages without consumer's express written agreement and requires that they include an automated opt-out mechanism.

Private Right of Action: Telephone Sales Act: If seller fails to refund payments upon cancellation, buyer may sue for the amount of payment, plus $100; reasonable costs and attorney fees within the discretion of the court; or consumer may recover against seller's bond. *Telemarketing Act:* Violation is a UDAP violation; private right of action for greater of actual damages or $50 per violation; may increase treble damages, up to $1000, in court's discretion, if violation is knowing or willful; attorney fees at court's discretion.

Special Penalties: Telephone Sales Act: Attorney general may seek injunction or civil penalty of up to $500 per violation. *Telemarketing Act:* Civil penalties of $1000 to $2000; denial or termination of registration; certain knowing violations are Class A or Class B misdemeanors; bona fide error defense available for violations of no-call list statute.

NORTH CAROLINA

Telemarketing Statute: **N.C. Gen. Stat. §§ 66-260 to 66-266.**

Scope: Applies to telephone sellers who attempt to convince the consumer to buy goods or services, enter a contest, or contribute to a charity, with over twenty-five explicit exemptions, including non-profits, various businesses licensed under other law, certain catalog sales, certain book, record or video clubs, calls leading to face-to-face presentation.

Registration Requirements: Annual registration and filing of basic information required.

Substantive Law: All promoted gifts and prizes must be awarded, seller must provide evidence of that fact, and must take out a bond in the amount of the value of the promoted gifts and prizes. Seller must determine if the consumer contacted is under 18 years of age and discontinue the call if the consumer is under that age. Seller cannot require consumer to make payment or call 900 number to obtain prize.

Private Right of Action: Violation is a state UDAP violation.

Special Penalties: State can seek up to $25,000 penalty for each violation where consumer is over 65 years of age.

Telemarketing Statute: **N.C. Gen. Stat. §§ 75-100 to 75-105 (Telephone Solicitations).**

Scope: Telephone solicitation broadly defined, with exceptions for small businesses averaging no more than 10 telephone solicitations per week; telephone solicitation for sole purpose of arranging face-to-face meeting; newspaper subscription sales; non-profits.

Registration Requirements: None specified.

Substantive Law: Prohibits calls to numbers registered on FTC's do-not-call list; allows state attorney general to create state do-not-call list if FTC's list ceases to operate; requires company-specific do-not-call lists; requires telemarketers to give identifying information at outset of call; requires compliance with most provisions of FTC telemarketing rule;

prohibits calls before 8:00 a.m. or after 9:00 p.m.; prohibits calls to telephone subscribers under age 18; prohibits threats, profanity, etc.; prohibits Caller ID blocking; prohibits autodialing to play recorded message with exceptions for non-profit, political organization or candidate, or poll-taker (if caller identifies self and purpose of call, and no solicitation is made).

Private Right of Action: Telephone subscriber may sue for injunction, statutory damages of $500 for first violation, $1000 for second, $5000 for third or additional violation within two years; attorney fees to prevailing plaintiff if defendant acted willfully, to defendant if plaintiff knew or should have known that action was malicious and frivolous. Contract is invalid, and no money is due thereunder, if contract or sales representations were deceptive or abusive as defined by FTC Telemarketing Rule, or violated other state or federal law. Statute also authorizes suit in state courts under Telephone Consumer Protection Act.

Special Penalties: Attorney general may seek civil penalties in same amounts as telephone subscriber, but amount is reduced to $100 if solicitor shows mistake and meets certain other conditions.

NORTH DAKOTA

Telemarketing Statute: **N.D. Cent. Code §§ 51-18-01 to 51-18-09.**

Scope: Statute governs home solicitation sales and telemarketing. Defines telemarketing broadly, but excludes nonprofit and charitable organizations, the sale of insurance, cable television and newspapers, sales of less than $25, sales by licensed broadcasters, and sales by telecommunications companies. Some restrictions apply only to "telepromoters," defined more narrowly.

Registration Requirements: None specified.

Substantive Law: Consumers have the right to cancel transactions within 3 days, or 15 days if they are 65 or older; solicitors must inform consumers of their right to cancel; all agreements must be reduced to writing, conform with specific font-size requirements, contain certain information regarding the goods and the solicitor, and be signed by the consumer; solicitors must return payment to consumers within 10 days of cancellation.

Private Right of Action: None specified. Noncomplying contracts are unenforceable.

Special Penalties: Violations are Class B misdemeanors.

Telemarketing Statute: **N.D. Cent. Code §§ 51-28-01 to 51-28-22.**

Scope: Telephone solicitation, broadly defined, for the purpose of encouraging charitable contributions or the purchase or rental of, or investment in, property, goods, services, or merchandise, with exceptions for calls in response to prior express written requests, established personal or business relationships, some solicitations by tax exempt charities, polls and political calls unless communication is a text message, and calls (other than text messages) in which sales presentation is completed only at a later face-to-face meeting.

Registration Requirements: None specified.

Substantive Law: No calls before 8:00 a.m. or after 9:00 p.m. Requires compliance with state or national do-not-call list. Attorney general establishes state do-not-call list, but may designate federal list as state list. At beginning of call, telephone solicitors must identify themselves and the business on whose behalf they are calling. Prohibits Caller ID blocking. Prerecorded messages prohibited unless called party consents, with some exceptions; must be preceded by live operator who discloses name of company and purpose of message; must disconnect within 10 seconds after subscriber hangs up; and must exclude emergency numbers, cell phones, pagers, or other calls for which called party must pay, guest or patient rooms at healthcare facilities, numbers on do-not-call list.

Private Right of Action: Any person who receives telephone solicitation or message in violation of this chapter may sue for injunction or damages or both. Court may award actual damages or up to $2000 for each violation, whichever is greater, plus costs, expenses, and attorney fees.

Special Penalties: Attorney general may impose civil penalties up to $2000 per violation.

OHIO

Telemarketing Statute: **Ohio Rev. Code Ann. §§ 4719.01 to 4719.99 (West).**

Scope: Defines telemarketing broadly, but lists 28 exceptions, such as solicitations by charitable organizations, one-time or infrequent solicitations, solicitations that involve face-to-face contact, numerous businesses licensed under other law, certain catalog sales, certain book, record and video clubs.

Registration Requirements: Solicitors must register and pay a fee with the attorney general, and also obtain a $50,000 surety bond.

Substantive Law: Within the first 60 seconds of the call, solicitors must identify themselves and the goods being sold, along with certain other information; transactions are not valid unless the solicitor receives a signed, written contract from the consumer. Contract must include notice of cancellation rights (7-day cooling-off period). Specific disclosure requirements for gift and prize promotions. Prohibits solicitor from intentionally blocking disclosure of telephone number from which call is made.

Private Right of Action: Yes. A violation is a UDAP violation. Statute also authorizes private suit for damages and/or injunction, plus costs and attorney fees; punitive damages are authorized for knowing violations; two-year statute of limitations. Statute also gives attorney general specific enforcement powers.

Special Penalties: Violations are 5th degree felonies.

OKLAHOMA

Telemarketing Statute: **Okla. Stat. tit. 15, §§ 775A.1 to 775A.5.**

Scope: Defines telemarketing broadly but lists 21 exceptions, such as the sale of securities, newspapers, magazines, food, memberships in book or record clubs, and sales that involve face-to-face contact. Specifically includes text messages.

Registration Requirements: Telephone solicitors must register with the attorney general and post $10,000 bond.

Substantive Law: Solicitors must allow the consumer to cancel any sales transaction within three business days after receipt of goods, refund payments upon purchaser's cancellation, and disclose cancellation rights, and cannot misrepresent that the consumer won a contest or will receive "free" goods. May not block Caller ID. May not use an automatic dialing system that results in abandoned calls that are more than 5% of the answered calls. May not engage in any other deceptive trade practice, as defined in § 752 of this title.

Private Right of Action: Yes. A violation is a UDAP violation.

Special Penalties: None specified.

Telemarketing Statute: **Okla. Stat. tit. 15, §§ 775B.1 to 775B.7 (Telemarketer Restriction Act).**

Scope: Solicitations for the sale of goods or services. Does not include solicitation for religious, charitable or political purposes, or for any nonprofit organization. Exceptions for established business relationship or for calls that will lead to face-to-face negotiations.

Registration Requirements: None specified.

Substantive Law: May not call numbers on do-not-call list established by attorney general.

Private Right of Action: Willful violation is UDAP violation.

Special Penalties: For inadvertent violation, attorney general may assess an administrative fine. Bona fide error defense available.

OREGON

Telemarketing Statute: **Or. Rev. Stat. §§ 646.551 to 646.578.**

Scope: Defines specific types of telemarketing that are covered, and excludes the sale of securities, burial services, newspapers or cable television, sales by supervised financial institutions, sales that involve face-to-face contact, sales to previous customers, and several other exceptions.

Registration Requirements: Telephone solicitors must register with the Department of Justice and pay a fee.

Substantive Law: Solicitors must disclose certain information to consumers if they are selling oil, gas, stone or metal, or if they represent to consumers that they have won a prize. May not call number listed on do-not-call list, or person who has requested telemarketer not to call.
Private Right of Action: Violation is UDAP violation.
Special Penalties: None specified.

PENNSYLVANIA

Telemarketing Statute: 73 Pa. Stat. Ann. §§ 2241 to 2249 (West).
Scope: Defines telemarketing broadly, but lists 12 exceptions, including catalog sales, newspaper and magazine sales, sales of food, and book, video and record club sales that meet certain criteria; most sales that involve a face-to-face contact; some business-to-business sales; sales by businesses that are licensed by, certified by, or registered with the federal or state government; solicitations by some nonprofit organizations; some sales to existing customers; some sales by established businesses that make most of their sales at a retail outlet in the state; some securities transactions; existing debt, contract payment or performance. The state's home solicitation sales law, 73 Pa. Stat. Ann. § 201-7 (West), also applies to telemarketing, broadly defined.
Registration Requirements: Telemarketers must register with attorney general, pay a fee, and post a bond.
Substantive Law: Calls between 9:00 p.m. and 8:00 a.m. prohibited; telemarketer must disclose purpose of call and identity of caller and seller; must terminate call upon consumer's request; cannot make repeat calls if consumer requests; signed written contract or opportunity to cancel required in most cases; safeguards against unauthorized submission of demand drafts; special disclosures and no-purchase entry option required for prize promotions; advance payment for recovery rooms prohibited. May not block Caller ID; may not call residential or wireless numbers listed on Bureau of Consumer Protection do-not-call list. (Bona fide error defense available.) Solicitation using auto-dialer or pre-recorded message player may not include 900- or other pay-per-call number. Prohibits violation of FTC telemarketing rule. State home solicitation sales law, 73 Pa. Stat. Ann. § 201-7 (West), also provides a right to cancel telemarketing sales, and state UDAP statute, 73 Pa. Stat. Ann. § 201-2(4)(xvii) and (xix) (West) also requires disclosures and prompt delivery in telemarketing sales.
Private Right of Action: Violation is UDAP violation.
Special Penalties: Attorney general may seek revocation of telemarketer's registration after second violation. Failure to register is a misdemeanor.

RHODE ISLAND

Telemarketing Statute: R.I. Gen. Laws §§ 5-61-1 to 5-61-6.
Scope: Defines specific types of telemarketing that are covered, and exempts persons selling securities, farm products, telephone answering services, cable television, newspapers, magazines or memberships in book or record clubs, sales to previous customers, sales involving face-to-face contact, and sales by supervised financial institutions.
Registration Requirements: Telephone solicitors must register and pay a fee and post a $30,000 bond or other acceptable form of security.
Substantive Law: Telephone solicitor must identify self, company, and product being sold. If consumer wishes to buy, solicitor must inform consumer of cancellation rights, seller's and salesperson's registration numbers, and company's street address. Oral disclosures must be clear and intelligible. Use of automatic dialing-announcing devices prohibited (except from employers about work schedules and from school districts) unless consumer has given consent or live operator obtains consent, and must disconnect within five seconds after consumer hangs up. Sellers must maintain do-not-call lists. Sellers may call only between 9 a.m. and 6 p.m. on weekdays, 10 a.m. and 5 p.m. on Saturdays. Also restricts text message advertisements sent to cell phones or pagers.
Private Right of Action: Private right of action for treble damages, costs and reasonable attorney fees, or for injunction.
Special Penalties: Violations can entail a fine of up to $10,000 and a year imprisonment.

SOUTH CAROLINA

Telemarketing Statute: S.C. Code Ann. §§ 16-17-445, 16-17-446. *The provisions regarding auto-dialed political calls were held unconstitutional by Cahaly v. LaRosa, 796 F.3d 399 (4th Cir. 2015), aff'g 25 F. Supp. 3d 817 (D.S.C. 2014).*
Scope: Unsolicited calls by telephone solicitor seeking to sell consumer goods or services or an extension of consumer credit. Excludes calls in response to request by called party, calls regarding existing debt or contract, preexisting business relationship, services sold by institutions licensed and regulated under title 38. Telephone companies are not responsible for enforcing this section.
Registration Requirements: None specified.
Substantive Law: Seller must promptly and clearly disclose the seller's identity, the sales purpose of the call and the nature of the goods or services offered, the cost, payment plan, and any extra charges (shipping, handling, taxes). Must remove consumer's name from list if consumer asks not to be called, and maintain system to prevent calls to consumers who ask not to be called. May not call between 9 p.m. and 8 a.m. For prize promotion, must disclose that no purchase or payment is necessary to win and, if requested, the no-payment method of entry. Autodialed prerecorded messages prohibited except for existing debt or contract, or existing or previous business relationship; may not be made between 7 p.m. and 8 a.m.; must disconnect within 5 seconds after called party hangs up; may not ring hospitals, police stations, fire departments, nursing homes, hotels, or vacation rental units. *See also* S.C. Code Ann. §§ 15-75-50 and 15-75-51 (forbids use of fax machine to send unsolicited advertising. Exceptions for existing business relationship, follow-up on prior contact.).
Private Right of Action: None specified, except for unsolicited fax advertising statute, which gives private remedy for injunction and actual damages, costs and attorney fees, or $200, applicable only after sender has been notified not to transmit to recipient.
Special Penalties: Civil penalties of up to $100 for first violation, $200 for second, $1000 for third and subsequent. Violation is a misdemeanor.

SOUTH DAKOTA

Telemarketing Statute: S.D. Codified Laws §§ 37-30A-1 to 37-30A-17; S.D. Codified Laws §§ 49-31-101 to 49-31-108 (Do-Not-Call Register).
Scope: Unsolicited calls by telephone solicitor or telemarketer to South Dakota consumer soliciting sale, lease or rental of consumer goods or extension of consumer credit, or to obtain information used to solicit consumer sale or extension of credit. Excludes calls made in response to request by consumer, prior business relationship, pre-existing debt or contract, sale of newspaper by publisher, calls by merchant with fixed location from which goods are sold, sales made after consumer has examined catalog or other advertising which discloses price and description of goods and terms of sale, and certain transactions in which consumer has right to return goods for a refund.
Registration Requirements: Telephone solicitor must register with Public Service Commission and pay $500 fee.
Substantive Law: Caller must immediately identify self and company, and sales purpose of call, and ask within 30 seconds if consumer is interested in listening. Must hang up if consumer says no, or at any time if consumer expresses disinterest. May not call between 9 p.m. and 9 a.m., or engage in unfair, deceptive or harassing conduct. Verbal agreements not binding until confirmed by written agreement which discloses all terms of sale and is signed by consumer. Telemarketer may not debit consumer's bank account or credit card until written and signed confirmation received. Goods sent without this written confirmation are unordered merchandise, for which consumer is not obligated to pay. Consumer who makes payment without written confirmation may cancel by giving written notice and returning goods. Seller must then return any payments and trade-ins and cancel any evidence of indebtedness. Ten-day cooling-off period, during which consumer may cancel by giving notice and returning the goods. Seller must provide refund and return payments within 30 days and terminate any indication of indebtedness. May not call consumer

listed on do-not-call list, to be maintained by Public Service Commission and coordinated with or replaced by national list.

Private Right of Action: For willful act or practice, action for greater of $500 or double damages, plus costs and attorney fees. Willful violation is UDAP violation.

Special Penalties: Willful and knowing violation with intent to defraud a consumer is a misdemeanor. Administrative fine of up to $5000 per violation of do-not-call statute.

TENNESSEE

Telemarketing Statute: **Tenn. Code Ann. §§ 47-18-1501 to 47-18-1527.**
Scope: Covers telephonic sales calls, broadly defined.

Registration Requirements: Autodialers that provide pre-recorded messages must obtain permit from Tennessee Regulatory Authority and post $10,000 bond or letter of credit.

Substantive Law: Prohibits solicitors from calling unlisted numbers and blocking Caller ID function on consumer's telephone equipment. Prohibits solicitors from making unsolicited calls unless they maintain a "no-call" list. Unsolicited calls exclude calls made in response to consumer's express request, calls made in connection with an existing debt or contract, and calls where there is a prior or existing business relationship. With certain exceptions, autodialers that provide pre-recorded messages may not be used between 9 p.m. and 8 a.m.; may not operate unattended, nor use random nor sequential dialing; must hang up within 10 seconds after called party hangs up or declines to hear message; must state name and telephone number of caller within first 25 seconds and again at the end of the call, and the telephone number must be answered during business hours by live operator; may not call unlisted numbers, hospitals, nursing homes, law enforcement or fire protection agencies; may not call without consent, but consent may be given in response to live operator; may not use to solicit pay-per-call call. Special provisions for credit card companies making telephone offers of services to cardholders: must prove that services were authorized, and if cardholder claims lack of authorization within three months after charges appear on bill, credit card company must refund amount equal to three months charges if it cannot prove authorization.

Private Right of Action: Individual or group that receives pre-recorded calls in violation of this section may seek injunction.

Special Penalties: Civil penalty of up to $1000 per call (both pre-recorded and general sales call provisions), waivable if violator has made restitution to consumers. Violation of prohibitions against Caller ID blocking and calling unlisted numbers is Class A misdemeanor. Other violations are punishable by civil penalty up to $1000.

Telemarketing Statute: **Tenn. Code Ann. §§ 65-4-401 to 65-4-408 (Telephone Solicitation).**
Scope: Sales calls to residential subscribers, except calls with subscriber's permission, calls to existing customers, certain charitable solicitations, and occasional calls (not more than three per week, and not part of a telemarketing plan) to specific persons whom the business reasonably believes to be interested in purchasing.
Registration Requirements: None specified.
Substantive Law: At beginning of call, must disclose identity of telemarketer and company. May not call between 9 p.m. and 8 a.m. May not block Caller ID. (Provider of Caller ID service not liable for violations of this part by others.) May not call numbers in do-not-call database maintained by the Tennessee Regulatory Authority.
Private Right of Action: See Consumer Telemarketing Act. The provisions of this act are in addition to that act and any other causes of action, remedies and penalties provided by law.
Special Penalties: Civil penalties of up to $2000 per knowing violation. Authority may issue cease and desist orders. Attorney general may seek injunction. Bona fide error defense available if defendant has established and implemented with due care reasonable practices and procedures to prevent violations.

TEXAS

Telemarketing Statute: **Bus. & Comm. Code Ann. §§ 302.001 through 302.304 (West) (Regulation of Telephone Solicitation).**
Scope: Telephone calls initiated to purchase, rent, claim, or receive a property or service. Includes those made by purchaser in response to solicitation by mail or other means. Numerous exemptions, including educational and non-profit corporations, sale of media subscriptions, catalog sellers, sales to a business for resale or recycling, sale of food, persons regulated by other law (securities, insurance, regulated financial institutions, etc.), solicitations for maintenance or repair or previously sold items, presentations that will lead to a face-to-face sales presentation, isolated transactions.
Registration Requirements: Registration required to make telephone presentations from a location in Texas or to a recipient in Texas. Must post $10,000 bond. Must provide description of items sold and copies of all scripts and sales literature. Additional requirements for prize promotions.
Substantive Law: Seller must make available a copy of the registration statement at its business location. Seller must disclose address. If a prize or premium is offered, must disclose the total number of individuals who received, within the last 12 months, the item with the highest value and the item with the lowest value. Additional requirements for sale of oil, gas, or mineral interests. If an item is represented as being offered at less than the usual price, must disclose the name of the manufacturer. May not make reference to compliance with this chapter. May not request a credit card or checking account number after offering a "free" item.
Private Right of Action: Violation is a UDAP. Person injured by seller's violation may bring action against the bond.
Special Penalties: Violation of certain provisions is a Class A misdemeanor. Civil penalties of up to $5000 per violation. Attorney general may seek an injunction and costs of investigation and prosecution. Penalties of up to $25,000 for violation of the injunction; $50,000 total for multiple violations.

Telemarketing Statute: **Tex. Util. Code Ann. §§ 55.121 to 55.138 (West) (Automatic Dialing and Announcing Devices).** *See also* **16 Tex. Admin. Code Ann. § 26.125 (West).**
Scope: Use of autodialers for pre-recorded messages, except certain emergency, public service, and school uses.
Registration Requirement: Users must obtain permit from Public Service Commission, and pay a fee.
Substantive Law: User must notify every telecommunications utility over whose system the device is to be used. May not use device to dial random or sequential numbers; may be used only between 9 a.m. and 9 p.m. weekdays and Saturdays and between noon and 9 p.m. on Sundays. May not make collection call at hours forbidden by FDCPA. Must either disconnect within five seconds after termination of call, or be introduced by live operator who secures called party's permission before beginning the recorded message. First 30 seconds of message must include nature of call, identity of person making call, and the telephone number from which the call is made. Special requirements for cross-promotion of pay per call. Automatic dialing and announcing device may not be used to deliver message of more than 30 seconds unless it is capable of recognizing a telephone answering device and disconnecting within 30 seconds. Regulations also ban automatic dialing and announcing devices calls to emergency numbers, patient or guest rooms at hospitals or nursing homes, and cell phones, pagers or other numbers where called party is charged for the call.
Private Right of Action: None specified.
Special Penalties: Administrative penalties of up to $1000 per day. Court or commission may require utility to disconnect service to user who violates this chapter. Willful violation is Class A misdemeanor.

UTAH

Telemarketing Statute: **Utah Code Ann. §§ 13-25a-101 to 13-25a-111 (West) (Telephone and Facsimile Solicitation Act).**
Scope: Telephone solicitation, broadly defined to include call encouraging the purchase, lease, rental or investment in property, goods or services, an extension of credit or certain charitable donations. Exceptions for established business relationship, call requested by consumer, existing debt or

contract, call required by law for medical purpose. Certain sections do not apply to charities or to various businesses regulated under other law.

Registration Requirements: None specified.

Substantive Law: Telephone solicitations: Caller must promptly identify self, and company, state purpose of call, discontinue call if requested, disconnect within 25 seconds of termination of call. No telephone solicitation between 9 p.m. and 8 a.m. or anytime on Sunday or legal holiday. May send faxes only to person with established business relationship, or who has given prior written permission. May not call Utah number included in federal do-not-call database. May not block Caller ID. May not use automatic dialing device to deliver pre-recorded message, except for calls requested by recipient, existing debt or contract, existing business relationship, or certain emergency notifications.

Private Right of Action: For greater of actual damages or $500, injunctive relief, costs and reasonable attorney fees. For faxes that violate this section, sent after recipient advised sender of objection to previous fax, for greater of $500 or actual pecuniary loss, plus costs and attorney fees.

Special Penalties: Administrative fines of $100 to $1000 per violation. Intentional violation, after having been notified by enforcing authority that conduct violates this statute, is Class A misdemeanor. Attorney general may sue for injunction, consumer restitution or enforcement of fines.

Telemarketing Statute: Utah Code Ann. §§ 13-26-1 to 13-26-11.

Scope: Telemarketing is defined broadly, but there are several exemptions from the registration requirement, including sales by nonprofit organizations, sales by licensed brokers, or certain other businesses licensed under other law, newspapers, catalog sales, isolated transactions, solicitation of present or former customers. Excludes sales or solicitations that occur solely through an Internet website without the use of a telephone call.

Registration Requirements: Solicitors must register with the attorney general and maintain a bond or other satisfactory security, in amounts ranging from $25,000 to $75,000, depending on size of business and whether it or any affiliated person have violated this chapter within the past 3 years.

Substantive Law: Consumers can cancel within 3 days of the sale or longer, depending on whether the solicitor disclosed their cancellation rights; use of fictitious names, false statements, failure to disclose material facts, and failure to refund payment within 30 days after cancellation are prohibited. May not use inmates in telephone soliciting operations if inmates would have access to personal data about an individual sufficient to physically locate or contact that individual.

Private Right of Action: None specified.

Special Penalties: Violation is either a Class A or B misdemeanor, or a third degree felony; also, civil penalty of up to $2500 for each unlawful transaction.

VERMONT

Telemarketing Statute: Vt. Stat. Ann. tit. 9, §§ 2464 to 2464d (Telemarketing Transactions).

Scope: "Telemarketer" means any person who initiates telephone calls to, or who receives telephone calls from, a consumer in connection with a plan, program or campaign to market goods and services.

Exceptions: Section 2464: Banks, when obtaining or submitting for payment checks, drafts, etc.; certain credit card transactions; debt collection calls; companies registered with and regulated by public service board; other exemptions as attorney general may provide by rule. Sections 2464a through 2464d: calls in response to inquiry by customer, established business relationship, calls by organization that has applied for non-profit status, and calls by person not regularly engaged in telephone solicitation. Certain licensed or registered telephone solicitors are also excluded from these prohibitions.

Registration Requirements: Telemarketers must register with secretary of state.

Substantive Law: May not use services of courier to pick up consumer's payment unless courier delivers goods at time of payment; may not obtain or submit for payment a check, draft or other form of negotiable instrument drawn on a person's checking, savings, share or other depository account without consumer's express written authorization.

Courier service or telemarketer's financial institution may not knowingly (includes willful blindness) assist telemarketer to violate this section. Party other than federally-insured depository institution may not process a telemarketing transaction for payment without obtaining proof of consumer's prior authorization. Prohibits electronic fund transfers from consumer's account unless consumer has given express oral authorization and has initiated the call, signed a written agreement, or purchased goods or services from the telemarketer within the previous two years. Entities other than federally-insured financial institutions may not process payments in violation of these restrictions. May not call numbers on federal do-not-call list.

Private Right of Action: Section 2464: Violation is UDAP violation. Sections 2464a to 2464d: For greater of actual damages or $500 per call (first offense), $1000 (repeat offense), costs and attorney fees, with punitive damages if violation willful.

Special Penalties: None specified. Failing to register is a crime.

VIRGINIA

Telemarketing Statute: Va. Code Ann. §§ 59.1-21.1 to 59.1-21.7:1.

Scope: Telemarketing, broadly defined, is covered by the state's home solicitation sales law, which excludes sales of less than $25, sales pursuant to a preexisting charge account or prior negotiations, and sale or lease of farm equipment.

Registration Requirements: None specified.

Substantive Law: Consumer has right to cancel the transaction within 3 days after the sale, or 30 days after the sale if solicitor misrepresents nature of transaction, except in certain emergencies complying with specified safeguards.

Private Right of Action: Yes. Violation is UDAP violation.

Special Penalties: None specified.

Telemarketing Statute: Va. Code Ann. §§ 59.1-510 to 59.1-518.

Scope: Calls to natural person's home, or any wireless telephone with a Virginia area code, offering or advertising any property, goods or services for sale, lease, license or investment, including an extension of credit. Exempts calls requested by consumer, or established business relationship.

Registration Requirements: None specified.

Substantive Law: Must promptly identify self and company. May not call between 9 p.m. and 8 a.m. May not block Caller ID. The number disclosed must enable the called party, during business hours, to request that no further calls be made. If a live sales representative is not available to speak to the customer within 2 seconds after the greeting, a message must be played with the identity of the caller and a phone number which recipient may call to request no further contact. May not call consumer who has requested not to be called; telemarketer must keep record of requests for 10 years. May not call number listed on federal do-not-call registry. (Bona fide error defense available.) Restrictions on auto-dialed artificial voice calls.

Private Right of Action: Private right of action for $500 per violation (up to $1500 if courts finds violation to be knowing), costs and reasonable attorney fees, and injunctive relief. Does not limit rights under other law. Violation of restrictions on auto-dialed artificial voice calls is a UDAP violation.

Special Penalties: Attorney general may sue for civil penalties of $500 per violation ($1000 if knowing), plus costs of investigation and action, and attorney fees.

WASHINGTON

Telemarketing Statute: Wash. Rev. Code §§ 19.158.010 to 19.158.901.

Scope: Defines telemarketing broadly, but lists 20 exceptions, such as isolated transactions, sales by supervised financial institutions, persons calling for charitable, political or other non-commercial purposes, sales that involve face-to-face contact, sales to prior customers, and sales of newspapers, magazines, or memberships in book or record clubs.

Registration Requirements: Telephone solicitors must register with the department of licensing.

Substantive Law: Solicitors must call between the hours of 8:00 a.m. and 9:00 p.m., identify themselves and the goods being sold, terminate the call if the consumer is disinterested, and follow up sales transactions with a written confirmation (allowing the purchaser to cancel), and cannot require that payment be made by credit card. Harassment explicitly forbidden.

Private Right of Action: Violation is UDAP violation. Statute also provides a private cause of action for actual damages, court costs and attorney fees. Statute also gives attorney general specific enforcement powers.

Special Penalties: $500 to $2000 civil penalty for each violation; criminal penalties.

WEST VIRGINIA

Telemarketing Statute: **W. Va. Code §§ 46A-6F-101 to 46A-6F-703 (Telemarketing).**

Scope: Unsolicited call from telemarketer to consumer, or telemarketer's invitation to call telemarketer with intent to sell or attempt to sell goods or services. Exceptions for sales to be completed at later face-to-face meeting (which may be regulated under home solicitation sales act)—this exemption does not apply to courier sent to collect payment; certain catalog sales; business-to-business sales; maintenance or repair contracts for goods previously purchased from seller; cable television; certain book and record clubs; newspapers and magazines; certain small scale sales of food; regulated sales of securities, investments, commodities, insurance, utilities, real estate; sales by businesses who do more than 50% of their sales at permanent place of business. Registration and bonding requirements do not apply to charitable organizations.

Registration Requirements: Telemarketers must register, pay a fee and post bond.

Substantive Law: Must disclose identity of company and sales purpose of call, cost of goods, restrictions and limitations. Additional disclosures for prize promotions or investment opportunities. Must provide for cancellation and refund for 7 days after goods received. Recordkeeping requirements (including copies of brochures, scripts, and advertising). Additional requirements for prize promotions. May not demand advance payment for credit repair. Verifiable authorization (written or tape recorded) required before debiting consumer's bank account. Use of courier forbidden unless requested by consumer, and unless consumer can inspect goods before paying courier. Abuse and harassment forbidden. May not call consumer who requests not to be called. May call only between 8 a.m. and 9 p.m.

Private Right of Action: Violation is UDAP violation. Actual damages. Non-complying contract is void.

Special Penalties: Civil penalties of $100 to $3000. Operation of fraudulent recovery service is a felony. Civil penalty of up to $5000 for failure to register.

WISCONSIN

Telemarketing Statute: **Wis. Stat. §§ 423.201 to 423.205, 100.52.**

Scope: Consumer transactions initiated by mail or telephone or text message solicitation directed at particular customer or by face-to-face meeting away from merchant's place of business, if offer or agreement to purchase is made at a place other than merchant's place of business; applies to all persons who make or solicit consumer approval transactions, directly collect payments or enforce debts arising from consumer approval transactions, or act as credit services organizations. Exceptions for cash transaction under $25, sale, lease or listing of real estate, auction sale, certain catalog sales, loan conducted and consummated entirely by mail, bona fide emergency (separate writing required). Do-not-call list statute does not apply to nonprofit organizations, consumer-requested calls, and certain calls to current clients.

Registration Requirements: Telephone solicitors must register and pay a fee.

Substantive Law: 3-day cooling-off period; do-not-call list; no pre-recorded messages without consent of called party.

Private Right of Action: None specified, but note that these provisions are part of the Wisconsin Consumer Act.

Special Penalties: For violation of do-not-call statute, $100 per violation.

Telemarketing Regulation: **Wis. Admin. Code ATCP §§ 127.02 to 127.20.**

Scope: Telemarketing, broadly defined as solicitation made by seller to consumer through any interactive electronic voice communication.

Exceptions: None specified.

Registration Requirements: None specified.

Substantive Law: Calls between 9:00 p.m. and 8:00 a.m. prohibited; telemarketers must inform consumers of their right to cancel within 3 days of their receiving required, written cancellation rights; telemarketers must promptly disclose their name, the company for which they are selling, that they are offering or promoting goods or services and the nature of those goods or services; prior to accepting payment, the telemarketer must inform the consumer of the nature and quantity of goods or services involved, the total cost, all material terms and conditions, and either the seller's mailing address or a phone number at which the consumer may contact the seller during business hours to obtain the seller's address. (Salesperson may use a fictitious name, if it is unique to that person and the employer keeps records of its salesepersons' fictitious names.) If sales presentation is in a language other than English, then required disclosures must be made in that language. (Contract must be in both English and other language.) Express verifiable authorization (defined) required before presenting check, draft or other negotiable instrument. Misrepresentation and harassment explicitly forbidden. Assisting others to commit violations (including credit card laundering) forbidden. Prize promotions are regulated by Wis. Admin. Code ATCP § 127.08. Violation of that statute by a telemarketer is a violation of telemarketing statute. Caller ID blocking prohibited. May not seek advance payment for arranging or seeking to arrange loan or extension of credit. May not contact consumer who has expressed a desire not to be called. (Bona fide error defense available).

Private Right of Action: None specified.

Special Penalties: None specified.

WYOMING

Telemarketing Statute: **Wyo. Stat. Ann. §§ 40-12-301 to 40-12-305 (Telephone Solicitation).**

Scope: Unsolicited call to consumer, to solicit sale of consumer goods or services (broadly defined), extension of credit for consumer goods or services, or information to be used in soliciting these things. Applies to calls made to both residential and mobile telephone numbers. Exceptions for calls at consumers request; existing debt or contract; existing business relationship; caller who makes fewer than 225 unsolicited calls per year.

Registration Requirements: Solicitors and merchants must register with attorney general.

Substantive Law: Must promptly identify self and company with contact information, disclose sales purpose of call, and nature of goods or services being offered. May not block Caller ID. May not call number on national do-not-call list, specifically defined as the list maintained by the Direct Marketing Association or successor organization. Automatic dialing devices banned, except for automatic dialing with live messages, calls or messages made solely in response to recipient's initiated calls, calls where numbers have been screened to exclude national do-no-call list and unlisted numbers, or where caller and recipient have an established business relationship. No calls before 8:00 a.m. or after 8:00 p.m.

Private Right of Action: None specified.

Special Penalties: Enforcing authority may seek civil penalty up to $500 for first violation, $2500 for second, $5000 for third and each subsequent violation, waivable if telemarketer makes full restitution to injured consumers. Attorney fees to prevailing party. Good faith error defense available.

Telemarketing Statute: **Wyo. Stat. Ann. §§ 40-14-251 to 40-14-255 (Home Solicitation Sales).**

Scope: Consumer credit sale of goods or services, with price of $25 or more (single or multiple contracts) if seller or seller's representative solicits buyer either face to face or by telephone, at a place other than seller's place of business and agreement or offer to purchase is made at place other than seller's place of business.

Exceptions: Buyer initiated transactions which take place entirely by mail or phone, preexisting charge account, prior negotiations at seller's place of business, bona fide emergency (writing required).

Registration Requirements: None specified.

Substantive Law: Written agreement required, in same language as sales presentation, including date of transaction and conspicuous notice of cancellation rights; 3-day cooling-off period.

Private Right of Action: None specified.

Special Penalties: None specified.

Appendix E   Federal RICO Statute

This appendix reprints the federal Racketeer Influenced and Corrupt Organizations (RICO) statute at Appendix E.1, *infra*. Federal statutes delineating two common predicate acts under the RICO statute, mail fraud and wire fraud, are reprinted at Appendix E.2, *infra*. State RICO statutes are summarized at Appendix F, *infra*.

E.1   The Federal RICO Statute

RACKETEER INFLUENCED AND CORRUPT ORGANIZATIONS

18 U.S.C.

§ 1961.   Definitions.
§ 1962.   Prohibited racketeering activities.
§ 1963.   Criminal penalties.
§ 1964.   Civil remedies.
§ 1965.   Venue and process.
§ 1966.   Expedition of actions.
§ 1967.   Evidence.
§ 1968.   Civil investigative demand.

18 U.S.C. § 1961.   Definitions

As used in this chapter—
(1) "racketeering activity" means

(A) any act or threat involving murder, kidnapping, gambling, arson, robbery, bribery, extortion, dealing in obscene matter, or dealing in a controlled substance or listed chemical (as defined in section 102 of the Controlled Substances Act), which is chargeable under State law and punishable by imprisonment for more than one year,

(B) any act which is indictable under any of the following provisions of title 18, United States Code: Section 201 (relating to bribery), section 224 (relating to sports bribery), sections 471, 472, and 473 (relating to counterfeiting), section 659 (relating to theft from interstate shipment) if the act indictable under section 659 is felonious, section 664 (relating to embezzlement from pension and welfare funds), section 1028 (relating to fraud and related activity in connection with identification documents), sections 891–894 (relating to extortionate credit transactions), section 1029 (relating to fraud and related activity in connection with access devices), section 1084 (relating to the transmission of gambling information), section 1341 (relating to mail fraud), section 1343 (relating to wire fraud), section 1344 (relating to financial institution fraud), section 1351 (relating to fraud in foreign labor contracting), section 1425 (relating to the procurement of citizenship or nationalization unlawfully), section 1426 (relating to the reproduction of naturalization or citizenship papers), section 1427 (relating to the sale of naturalization or citizenship papers), sections 1461–1465 (relating to obscene matter), section 1503 (relating to obstruction of justice), section 1510 (relating to obstruction of criminal investigations), section 1511 (relating to the obstruction of State or local law enforcement), section 1512 (relating to tampering with a witness, victim, or an informant), section 1513 (relating to retaliating against a witness, victim, or an informant), section 1542 (relating to false statement in application and use of passport), section 1543 (relating to forgery or false use of passport), section 1544 (relating to misuse of passport), section 1546 (relating to fraud and misuse of visas, permits, and other documents), sections 1581–1592 (relating to peonage and slavery, and trafficking in persons), section 1951 (relating to interference with commerce, robbery, or extortion), section 1952 (relating to racketeering), section 1953 (relating to interstate transportation of wagering paraphernalia), section 1954

(relating to unlawful welfare fund payments), section 1955 (relating to the prohibition of illegal gambling businesses), section 1956 (relating to the laundering of monetary instruments), section 1957 (relating to engaging in monetary transactions in property derived from specified unlawful activity), section 1958 (relating to use of interstate commerce facilities in the commission of murder-for-hire), section 1960 (relating to illegal money transmitters), sections 2251, 2251A, 2252, 2260 (relating to sexual exploitation of children), sections 2312 and 2313 (relating to interstate transportation of stolen motor vehicles), sections 2314 and 2315 (relating to interstate transportation of stolen property), section 2318 (relating to trafficking in counterfeit labels for phonorecords, computer programs or computer program documentation or packaging and copies of motion pictures or other audiovisual works), section 2319 (relating to criminal infringement of a copyright), section 2319A (relating to unauthorized fixation of and trafficking in sound recordings and music videos of live musical performances), section 2320 (relating to trafficking in goods or services bearing counterfeit marks), section 2321 (relating to trafficking in certain motor vehicles or motor vehicle parts), sections 2341–2346 (relating to trafficking in contraband cigarettes), sections 2421–24 (relating to white slave traffic), sections 175–178 (relating to biological weapons), sections 229–229F (relating to chemical weapons), section 831 (relating to nuclear materials),

(C) any act which is indictable under title 29, United States Code, section 186 (dealing with restrictions on payments and loans to labor organizations) or section 501(c) (relating to embezzlement from union funds),

(D) any offense involving fraud connected with a case under title 11 (except a case under section 157 of this title), fraud in the sale of securities, or the felonious manufacture, importation, receiving, concealment, buying, selling, or otherwise dealing in controlled substance or listed chemical (as defined in section 102 of the Controlled Substances Act), punishable under any law of the United States, or

(E) any act which is indictable under the Currency and Foreign Transactions Reporting Act,

(F) any act which is indictable under the Immigration and Nationality Act, section 278 (relating to importation of alien for immoral purpose) if the act indictable under such section of such Act was committed for the purpose of financial gain, or

(G) any act that is indictable under any provision listed in section 2332b(g)(5)(B);

(2) "State" means any State of the United States, the District of Columbia, the Commonwealth of Puerto Rico, any territory or possession of the United States, any political subdivision, or any department, agency, or instrumentality thereof;

(3) "person" includes any individual or entity capable of holding a legal or beneficial interest in property;

(4) "enterprise" includes any individual, partnership, corporation, association, or other legal entity, and any union or group of individuals associated in fact although not a legal entity;

(5) "pattern of racketeering activity" requires at least two acts of racketeering activity, one of which occurred after the effective date of this chapter and the last of which occurred within ten years (excluding any period of imprisonment) after the commission of a prior act of racketeering activity;

(6) "unlawful debt" means a debt

(A) incurred or contracted in gambling activity which was in violation of the law of the United States, a State or political subdivision thereof, or which is unenforceable under State or Federal law in whole or in part as to principal or interest because of the laws relating to usury, and

(B) which was incurred in connection with the business of gambling in violation of the law of the United States, a State or political subdivision thereof, or the business of lending money or a thing of value at a rate usurious under State or Federal law, where the usurious rate is at least twice the enforceable rate;

(7) "racketeering investigator" means any attorney or investigator so designated by the Attorney General and charged with the duty of enforcing or carrying into effect this chapter;

(8) "racketeering investigation" means any inquiry conducted by any racketeering investigator for the purpose of ascertaining whether any person has been involved in any violation of this chapter or of any final order, judgment, or decree of any court of the United States, duly entered in any case or proceeding arising under this chapter;

(9) "documentary material" includes any book, paper, document, record, recording, or other material; and

(10) "Attorney General" includes the Attorney General of the United States, the Deputy Attorney General of the United States, the Associate Attorney General of the United States, any Assistant Attorney General of the United States, or any employee of the Department of Justice or any employee of any department or agency of the United States so designated by the Attorney General to carry out the powers conferred on the Attorney General by this chapter. Any department or agency so designated may use in investigations authorized by this chapter either the investigative provisions of this chapter or the investigative power of such department or agency otherwise conferred by law.

[*Added by* Pub. L. No. 91-452, tit. IX, § 901(a), 84 Stat. 941 (Oct. 15, 1970), *and amended by* Pub. L. No. 95-575, § 3(c),92 Stat. 2465 (Nov. 2, 1978); Pub. L. No. 95-598, tit. III, § 314(g), 92 Stat. 2677 (Nov. 6, 1978); Pub. L. No. 98-473, tit. II, §§ 901(g), 1020, 98 Stat. 2136, 2143 (Oct. 12, 1984); Pub. L. No. 98-547, tit. II, § 205, 98 Stat. 2770 (Oct. 25, 1984); Pub. L. No. 99-570, tit. XIII, § 1365(b), 100 Stat. 3207–3235 (Oct. 27, 1986); Pub. L. No. 99-646, § 50(a), 100 Stat. 3605 (Nov. 10, 1986); Pub. L. No. 100-690, tit. VII, §§ 7013, 7020(c), 7032, 7054, 7514, 102 Stat. 4395, 4396, 4398, 4402, 4489 (Nov. 18, 1988); Pub. L. No. 101-73, tit. IX, § 968, 103 Stat. 506 (Aug. 9, 1989); Pub. L. No. 101-647, tit. XXXV, § 3560, 104 Stat. 4927 (Nov. 29, 1990); Pub. L. No. 103-322, tit. IX, § 90104, tit. XVI, § 160001(f), tit. XXXIII, § 330021(1), 108 Stat. 1987, 2037, 2150 (Sept. 13, 1994); Pub. L. No. 103-394, tit. III, § 312(b), 108 Stat. 4140 (Oct. 22, 1994); Pub. L. No. 104-132, tit. IV, § 433, 110 Stat. 1274 (Apr. 24, 1996); Pub. L. No. 104-153, § 3, 110 Stat. 1386 (July 2, 1996); Pub. L. No. 104-208, div. C, tit. II, § 202, 110 Stat. 3009–3565 (Sept. 30, 1996); Pub. L. No. 104-294, tit. VI, §§ 601(b)(3), (i)(3), 604(b)(6), 110 Stat. 3499, 3501, 3506 (Oct. 11, 1996); Pub. L. No. 107-56, tit. VIII, § 813, 115 Stat. 382 (Oct. 26, 2001); Pub. L. No. 107-273, div. B, tit. IV, § 4005(f)(1), 116 Stat. 1813 (Nov. 2, 2002); Pub. L. No. 108-193, § 5(b), 117 Stat. 2879 (Dec. 19, 2003); Pub. L. No. 108-458, 118 Stat. 3767 (Dec. 17, 2004); Pub. L. No. 109-164, tit. I, § 103(c), 119 Stat. 3563 (Jan. 10, 2006); Pub. L. No. 109-177, tit. IV, § 403(a), 120 Stat. 243 (Mar. 9, 2006); Pub. L. No. 113-4, 127 Stat. 54 (Mar. 7, 2013)]

18 U.S.C. § 1962.   Prohibited activities

(a) It shall be unlawful for any person who has received any income derived, directly or indirectly, from a pattern of racketeering activity or through collection of an unlawful debt in which such person has participated as a principal within the meaning of section 2, title 18, United States Code, to use or invest, directly or indirectly, any part of such income, or the proceeds of such income, in acquisition of any interest in, or the establishment or operation of, any enterprise which is engaged in, or the activities of which affect, interstate or foreign commerce. A purchase of securities on the open market for purposes of investment, and without the intention of controlling or participating in the control of the issuer, or of assisting another to do so, shall not be unlawful under this subsection if the securities of the issuer held by the purchaser, the members of his immediate family, and his or their accomplices in any pattern or racketeering activity or the collection of an unlawful debt after such purchase

do not amount in the aggregate to one percent of the outstanding securities of any one class, and do not confer, either in law or in fact, the power to elect one or more directors of the issuer.

(b) It shall be unlawful for any person through a pattern of racketeering activity or through collection of an unlawful debt to acquire or maintain, directly or indirectly, any interest in or control of any enterprise which is engaged in, or the activities of which affect, interstate or foreign commerce.

(c) It shall be unlawful for any person employed by or associated with any enterprise engaged in, or the activities of which affect, interstate or foreign commerce, to conduct or participate, directly or indirectly, in the conduct of such enterprise's affairs through a pattern of racketeering activity or collection of unlawful debt.

(d) It shall be unlawful for any person to conspire to violate any of the provisions of subsection (a), (b), or (c) of this section.

[*Added by* Pub. L. No. 91-452, tit. IX, § 901(a), 84 Stat. 942 (Oct. 15, 1970), *and amended by* Pub. L. No. 100-690, tit. VII, § 7033, 102 Stat. 4398 (Nov. 18, 1988)]

18 U.S.C. § 1963.   Criminal penalties

(a) Whoever violates any provision of section 1962 of this chapter shall be fined under this title or imprisoned not more than 20 years (or for life if the violation is based on a racketeering activity for which the maximum penalty includes life imprisonment), or both, and shall forfeit to the United States, irrespective of any provision of State law—

> **(1)** any interest the person has acquired or maintained in violation of section 1962;
>
> **(2)** any—
>
> > **(A)** interest in;
> >
> > **(B)** security of;
> >
> > **(C)** claim against; or
> >
> > **(D)** property or contractual right of any kind affording a source of influence over;
> >
> > any enterprise which the person has established, operated, controlled, conducted, or participated in the conduct of, in violation of section 1962; and
>
> **(3)** any property constituting, or derived from, any proceeds which the person obtained, directly or indirectly, from racketeering activity or unlawful debt collection in violation of section 1962.

The court, in imposing sentence on such person shall order, in addition to any other sentence imposed pursuant to this section, that the person forfeit to the United States all property described in this subsection. In lieu of a fine otherwise authorized by this section, a defendant who derives profits or other proceeds from an offense may be fined not more than twice the gross profits or other proceeds.

(b) Property subject to criminal forfeiture under this section includes—

> **(1)** real property, including things growing on, affixed to, and found in land; and
>
> **(2)** tangible and intangible personal property, including rights, privileges, interests, claims, and securities.

(c) All right, title, and interest in property described in subsection (a) vests in the United States upon the commission of the act giving rise to forfeiture under this section. Any such property that is subsequently transferred to a person other than the defendant may be the subject of a special verdict of forfeiture and thereafter shall be ordered forfeited to the United States, unless the transferee establishes in a hearing pursuant to subsection (l) that he is a bona fide purchaser for value of such property who at the time of purchase was reasonably without cause to believe that the property was subject to forfeiture under this section.

(d)

> **(1)** Upon application of the United States, the court may enter a restraining order or injunction, require the execution of a satisfactory performance bond, or take any other action to preserve the

availability of property described in subsection (a) for forfeiture under this section—

(A) upon the filing of an indictment or information charging a violation of section 1962 of this chapter and alleging that the property with respect to which the order is sought would, in the event of conviction, be subject to forfeiture under this section; or

(B) prior to the filing of such an indictment or information, if, after notice to persons appearing to have an interest in the property and opportunity for a hearing, the court determines that—

(i) there is a substantial probability that the United States will prevail on the issue of forfeiture and that failure to enter the order will result in the property being destroyed, removed from the jurisdiction of the court, or otherwise made unavailable for forfeiture; and

(ii) the need to preserve the availability of the property through the entry of the requested order outweighs the hardship on any party against whom the order is to be entered:

Provided, however, that an order entered pursuant to subparagraph (B) shall be effective for not more than ninety days, unless extended by the court for good cause shown or unless an indictment or information described in subparagraph (A) has been filed.

(2) A temporary restraining order under this subsection may be entered upon application of the United States without notice or opportunity for a hearing when an information or indictment has not yet been filed with respect to the property, if the United States demonstrates that there is probable cause to believe that the property with respect to which the order is sought would, in the event of conviction, be subject to forfeiture under this section and that provision of notice will jeopardize the availability of the property for forfeiture. Such a temporary order shall expire not more than fourteen days after the date on which it is entered, unless extended for good cause shown or unless the party against whom it is entered consents to an extension for a longer period. A hearing requested concerning an order entered under this paragraph shall be held at the earliest possible time, and prior to the expiration of the temporary order.

(3) The court may receive and consider, at a hearing held pursuant to this subsection, evidence and information that would be inadmissible under the Federal Rules of Evidence.

(e) Upon conviction of a person under this section, the court shall enter a judgment of forfeiture of the property to the United States and shall also authorize the Attorney General to seize all property ordered forfeited upon such terms and conditions as the court shall deem proper. Following the entry of an order declaring the property forfeited, the court may, upon application of the United States, enter such appropriate restraining orders or injunctions, require the execution of satisfactory performance bonds, appoint receivers, conservators, appraisers, accountants, or trustees, or take any other action to protect the interest of the United States in the property ordered forfeited. Any income accruing to, or derived from, an enterprise or an interest in an enterprise which has been ordered forfeited under this section may be used to offset ordinary and necessary expenses to the enterprise which are required by law, or which are necessary to protect the interests of the United States or third parties.

(f) Following the seizure of property ordered forfeited under this section, the Attorney General shall direct the disposition of the property by sale or any other commercially feasible means, making due provision for the rights of any innocent persons. Any property right or interest not exercisable by, or transferable for value to, the United States shall expire and shall not revert to the defendant, nor shall the defendant or any person acting in concert with or on behalf of the defendant be eligible to purchase forfeited property at any sale held by the United States. Upon application of a person, other than the defendant or a person acting in concert with or on behalf of the defendant, the court may restrain or stay the sale or disposition of the property pending the conclusion of any appeal of the criminal case giving rise to the forfeiture, if the applicant demonstrates that proceeding with the sale or disposition of the property will result in irreparable injury, harm or loss to him. Notwithstanding 31

U.S.C. 3302(b), the proceeds of any sale or other disposition of property forfeited under this section and any moneys forfeited shall be used to pay all proper expenses for the forfeiture and the sale, including expenses of seizure, maintenance and custody of the property pending its disposition, advertising and court costs. The Attorney General shall deposit in the Treasury any amounts of such proceeds or moneys remaining after the payment of such expenses.

(g) With respect to property ordered forfeited under this section, the Attorney General is authorized to—

(1) grant petitions for mitigation or remission of forfeiture, restore forfeited property to victims of a violation of this chapter, or take any other action to protect the rights of innocent persons which is in the interest of justice and which is not inconsistent with the provisions of this chapter;

(2) compromise claims arising under this section;

(3) award compensation to persons providing information resulting in a forfeiture under this section;

(4) direct the disposition by the United States of all property ordered forfeited under this section by public sale or any other commercially feasible means, making due provision for the rights of innocent persons; and

(5) take appropriate measures necessary to safeguard and maintain property ordered forfeited under this section pending its disposition.

(h) The Attorney General may promulgate regulations with respect to—

(1) making reasonable efforts to provide notice to persons who may have an interest in property ordered forfeited under this section;

(2) granting petitions for remission or mitigation of forfeiture;

(3) the restitution of property to victims of an offense petitioning for remission or mitigation of forfeiture under this chapter;

(4) the disposition by the United States of forfeited property by public sale or other commercially feasible means;

(5) the maintenance and safekeeping of any property forfeited under this section pending its disposition; and

(6) the compromise of claims arising under this chapter.

Pending the promulgation of such regulations, all provisions of law relating to the disposition of property, or the proceeds from the sale thereof, or the remission or mitigation of forfeitures for violation of the customs laws, and the compromise of claims and the award of compensation to informers in respect of such forfeitures shall apply to forfeitures incurred, or alleged to have been incurred, under the provisions of this section, insofar as applicable and not inconsistent with the provisions hereof. Such duties as are imposed upon the Customs Service or any person with respect to the disposition of property under the customs law shall be performed under this chapter by the Attorney General.

(i) Except as provided in subsection (l), no party claiming an interest in property subject to forfeiture under this section may—

(1) intervene in a trial or appeal of a criminal case involving the forfeiture of such property under this section; or

(2) commence an action at law or equity against the United States concerning the validity of his alleged interest in the property subsequent to the filing of an indictment or information alleging that the property is subject to forfeiture under this section.

(j) The district courts of the United States shall have jurisdiction to enter orders as provided in this section without regard to the location of any property which may be subject to forfeiture under this section or which has been ordered forfeited under this section.

(k) In order to facilitate the identification or location of property declared forfeited and to facilitate the disposition of petitions for remission or mitigation of forfeiture, after the entry of an order declaring property forfeited to the United States the court may, upon application of the United States, order that the testimony of any witness relating to the property forfeited be taken by deposition and that any designated book, paper, document, record, recording, or other material not privileged be produced at the same time and place, in the same manner as provided for the taking of depositions under Rule 15 of the Federal Rules of Criminal Procedure.

(*l*)

(1) Following the entry of an order of forfeiture under this section, the United States shall publish notice of the order and of its intent to dispose of the property in such manner as the Attorney General may direct. The Government may also, to the extent practicable, provide direct written notice to any person known to have alleged an interest in the property that is the subject of the order of forfeiture as a substitute for published notice as to those persons so notified.

(2) Any person, other than the defendant, asserting a legal interest in property which has been ordered forfeited to the United States pursuant to this section may, within thirty days of the final publication of notice or his receipt of notice under paragraph (1), whichever is earlier, petition the court for a hearing to adjudicate the validity of his alleged interest in the property. The hearing shall be held before the court alone, without a jury.

(3) The petition shall be signed by the petitioner under penalty of perjury and shall set forth the nature and extent of the petitioner's right, title, or interest in the property, the time and circumstances of the petitioner's acquisition of the right, title, or interest in the property, any additional facts supporting the petitioner's claim, and the relief sought.

(4) The hearing on the petition shall, to the extent practicable and consistent with the interests of justice, be held within thirty days of the filing of the petition. The court may consolidate the hearing on the petition with a hearing on any other petition filed by a person other than the defendant under this subsection.

(5) At the hearing, the petitioner may testify and present evidence and witnesses on his own behalf, and cross-examine witnesses who appear at the hearing. The United States may present evidence and witnesses in rebuttal and in defense of its claim to the property and cross-examine witnesses who appear at the hearing. In addition to testimony and evidence presented at the hearing, the court shall consider the relevant portions of the record of the criminal case which resulted in the order of forfeiture.

(6) If, after the hearing, the court determines that the petitioner has established by a preponderance of the evidence that—

(A) the petitioner has a legal right, title, or interest in the property, and such right, title, or interest renders the order of forfeiture invalid in whole or in part because the right, title, or interest was vested in the petitioner rather than the defendant or was superior to any right, title, or interest of the defendant at the time of the commission of the acts which gave rise to the forfeiture of the property under this section; or

(B) the petitioner is a bona fide purchaser for value of the right, title, or interest in the property and was at the time of purchase reasonably without cause to believe that the property was subject to forfeiture under this section;

the court shall amend the order of forfeiture in accordance with its determination.

(7) Following the court's disposition of all petitions filed under this subsection, or if no such petitions are filed following the expiration of the period provided in paragraph (2) for the filing of such petitions, the United States shall have clear title to property that is the subject of the order of forfeiture and may warrant good title to any subsequent purchaser or transferee.

(m) If any of the property described in subsection (a), as a result of any act or omission of the defendant—

(1) cannot be located upon the exercise of due diligence;

(2) has been transferred or sold to, or deposited with, a third party;

(3) has been placed beyond the jurisdiction of the court;

(4) has been substantially diminished in value; or

(5) has been commingled with other property which cannot be divided without difficulty;

the court shall order the forfeiture of any other property of the defendant up to the value of any property described in paragraphs (1) through (5).

[*Added by* Pub. L. No. 91-452, tit. IX, § 901(a), 84 Stat. 943 (Oct. 15, 1970), *and amended by* Pub. L. No. 98-473, tit. II, §§ 302, 2301(a)–(c), 98 Stat.

2040, 2192 (Oct. 12, 1984); Pub. L. No. 99-570, tit. XI, § 1153(a), 100 Stat. 3207–3213 (Oct. 27, 1986); Pub. L. No. 99-646, § 23, 100 Stat. 3597 (Nov. 10, 1986); Pub. L. No. 100-690, tit. VII, §§ 7034, 7058(d), 102 Stat. 4398, 4403 (Nov. 18, 1988); Pub. L. No. 101-647, tit. XXXV, § 3561, 104 Stat. 4927 (Nov. 29, 1990); Pub. L. No. 111-16, § 3, 123 Stat. 1607 (May 7, 2009)]

18 U.S.C. § 1964.   Civil remedies

(a) The district courts of the United States shall have jurisdiction to prevent and restrain violations of section 1962 of this chapter by issuing appropriate orders, including, but not limited to: ordering any person to divest himself of any interest, direct or indirect, in any enterprise; imposing reasonable restrictions on the future activities or investments of any person, including, but not limited to, prohibiting any person from engaging in the same type of endeavor as the enterprise engaged in, the activities of which affect interstate or foreign commerce; or ordering dissolution or reorganization of any enterprise, making due provision for the rights of innocent persons.

(b) The Attorney General may institute proceedings under this section. Pending final determination thereof, the court may at any time enter such restraining orders or prohibitions, or take such other actions, including the acceptance of satisfactory performance bonds, as it shall deem proper.

(c) Any person injured in his business or property by reason of a violation of section 1962 of this chapter may sue therefor in any appropriate United States district court and shall recover threefold the damages he sustains and the cost of the suit, including a reasonable attorney's fee, except that no person may rely upon any conduct that would have been actionable as fraud in the purchase or sale of securities to establish a violation of section 1962. The exception contained in the preceding sentence does not apply to an action against any person that is criminally convicted in connection with the fraud, in which case the statute of limitations shall start to run on the date on which the conviction becomes final.

(d) A final judgment or decree rendered in favor of the United States in any criminal proceeding brought by the United States under this chapter shall estop the defendant from denying the essential allegations of the criminal offense in any subsequent civil proceeding brought by the United States.

[*Added* Pub. L. No. 91-452, tit. IX, § 901(a), 84 Stat. 943 (Oct. 15, 1970), *and amended* Pub. L. No. 98-620, tit. IV, § 402(24)(A), 98 Stat. 3359 (Nov. 8, 1984); Pub. L. No. 104-67, tit. I, § 107, 109 Stat. 758 (Dec. 22, 1995)]

18 U.S.C. § 1965.   Venue and process

(a) Any civil action or proceeding under this chapter against any person may be instituted in the district court of the United States for any district in which such person resides, is found, has an agent, or transacts his affairs.

(b) In any action under section 1964 of this chapter in any district court of the United States in which it is shown that the ends of justice require that other parties residing in any other district be brought before the court, the court may cause such parties to be summoned, and process for that purpose may be served in any judicial district of the United States by the marshal thereof.

(c) In any civil or criminal action or proceeding instituted by the United States under this chapter in the district court of the United States for any judicial district, subpoenas issued by such court to compel the attendance of witnesses may be served in any other judicial district, except that in any civil action or proceeding no such subpena shall be issued for service upon any individual who resides in another district at a place more than one hundred miles from the place at which such court is held without approval given by a judge of such court upon a showing of good cause.

(d) All other process in any action or proceeding under this chapter may be served on any person in any judicial district in which such person resides, is found, has an agent, or transacts his affairs.

[*Added by* Pub. L. No. 91-452, tit. IX, § 901(a), 84 Stat. 944 (Oct. 15, 1970)]

18 U.S.C. § 1966. Expedition of actions

In any civil action instituted under this chapter by the United States in any district court of the United States, the Attorney General may file with the clerk of such court a certificate stating that in his opinion the case is of general public importance. A copy of that certificate shall be furnished immediately by such clerk to the chief judge or in his absence to the presiding district judge of the district in which such action is pending. Upon receipt of such copy, such judge shall designate immediately a judge of that district to hear and determine action.

[*Added by* Pub. L. No. 91-452, tit. IX, § 901(a), 84 Stat. 944 (Oct. 15, 1970), *and amended by* Pub. L. No. 98-620, tit. IV, § 402(24)(B), 98 Stat. 3359 (Nov. 8, 1984)]

18 U.S.C. § 1967. Evidence

In any proceeding ancillary to or in any civil action instituted by the United States under this chapter the proceedings may be open or closed to the public at the discretion of the court after consideration of the rights of affected persons.

[*Added by* Pub. L. No. 91-452, tit. IX, § 901(a), 84 Stat. 944 (Oct. 15, 1970)]

18 U.S.C. § 1968. Civil investigative demand

(a) Whenever the Attorney General has reason to believe that any person or enterprise may be in possession, custody, or control of any documentary materials relevant to a racketeering investigation, he may, prior to the institution of a civil or criminal proceeding thereon, issue in writing, and cause to be served upon such person, a civil investigative demand requiring such person to produce such material for examination.

(b) Each such demand shall—

(1) state the nature of the conduct constituting the alleged racketeering violation which is under investigation and the provision of law applicable thereto;

(2) describe the class or classes of documentary material produced thereunder with such definiteness and certainty as to permit such material to be fairly identified;

(3) state that the demand is returnable forthwith or prescribe a return date which will provide a reasonable period of time within which the material so demanded may be assembled and made available for inspection and copying or reproduction; and

(4) identify the custodian to whom such material shall be made available.

(c) No such demand shall—

(1) contain any requirement which would be held to be unreasonable if contained in a subpena duces tecum issued by a court of the United States in aid of a grand jury investigation of such alleged racketeering violation; or

(2) require the production of any documentary evidence which would be privileged from disclosure if demanded by a subpena duces tecum issued by a court of the United States in aid of a grand jury investigation of such alleged racketeering violation.

(d) Service of any such demand or any petition filed under this section may be made upon a person by—

(1) delivering a duly executed copy thereof to any partner, executive officer, managing agent, or general agent thereof, or to any agent thereof authorized by appointment or by law to receive service of process on behalf of such person, or upon any individual person;

(2) delivering a duly executed copy thereof to the principal office or place of business of the person to be served; or

(3) depositing such copy in the United States mail, by registered or certified mail duly addressed to such person at its principal office or place of business.

(e) A verified return by the individual serving any such demand or petition setting forth the manner of such service shall be prima facie proof of such service. In the case of service by registered or certified mail, such return shall be accompanied by the return post office receipt of delivery of such demand.

(f)

(1) The Attorney General shall designate a racketeering investigator to serve as racketeer document custodian, and such additional racketeering investigators as he shall determine from time to time to be necessary to serve as deputies to such officer.

(2) Any person upon whom any demand issued under this section has been duly served shall make such material available for inspection and copying or reproduction to the custodian designated therein at the principal place of business of such person, or at such other place as such custodian and such person thereafter may agree and prescribe in writing or as the court may direct, pursuant to this section on the return date specified in such demand, or on such later date as such custodian may prescribe in writing. Such person may upon written agreement between such person and the custodian substitute for copies of all or any part of such material originals thereof.

(3) The custodian to whom any documentary material is so delivered shall take physical possession thereof, and shall be responsible for the use made thereof and for the return thereof pursuant to this chapter. The custodian may cause the preparation of such copies of such documentary material as may be required for official use under regulations which shall be promulgated by the Attorney General. While in the possession of the custodian, no material so produced shall be available for examination, without the consent of the person who produced such material, by any individual other than the Attorney General. Under such reasonable terms and conditions as the Attorney General shall prescribe, documentary material while in the possession of the custodian shall be available for examination by the person who produced such material or any duly authorized representatives of such person.

(4) Whenever any attorney has been designated to appear on behalf of the United States before any court or grand jury in any case or proceeding involving any alleged violation of this chapter, the custodian may deliver to such attorney such documentary material in the possession of the custodian as such attorney determines to be required for use in the presentation of such case or proceeding on behalf of the United States. Upon the conclusion of any such case or proceeding, such attorney shall return to the custodian any documentary material so withdrawn which has not passed into the control of such court or grand jury through the introduction thereof into the record of such case or proceeding.

(5) Upon the completion of—

(i) the racketeering investigation for which any documentary material was produced under this chapter, and

(ii) any case or proceeding arising from such investigation, the custodian shall return to the person who produced such material all such material other than copies thereof made by the Attorney General pursuant to this subsection which has not passed into the control of any court or grand jury through the introduction thereof into the record of such case or proceeding.

(6) When any documentary material has been produced by any person under this section for use in any racketeering investigation, and no such case or proceeding arising therefrom has been instituted within a reasonable time after completion of the examination and analysis of all evidence assembled in the course of such investigation, such person shall be entitled, upon written demand made upon the Attorney General, to the return of all documentary material other than copies thereof made pursuant to this subsection so produced by such person.

(7) In the event of the death, disability, or separation from service of the custodian of any documentary material produced under any demand issued under this section or the official relief of such custodian from responsibility for the custody and control of such material, the Attorney General shall promptly—

(i) designate another racketeering investigator to serve as custodian thereof, and

(ii) transmit notice in writing to the person who produced such material as to the identity and address of the successor so designated. Any successor so designated shall have with regard to such materials all duties and responsibilities imposed by this section upon his predecessor in office with regard thereto, except that he shall not be held responsible for any default or dereliction which occurred before his designation as custodian.

(g) Whenever any person fails to comply with any civil investigative demand duly served upon him under this section or whenever satisfactory copying or reproduction of any such material cannot be done and such person refuses to surrender such material, the Attorney General may file, in the district court of the United States for any judicial district in which such person resides, is found, or transacts business, and serve upon such person a petition for an order of such court for the enforcement of this section, except that if such person transacts business in more than one such district such petition shall be filed in the district in which such person maintains his principal place of business, or in such other district in which such person transacts business as may be agreed upon by the parties to such petition.

(h) Within twenty days after the service of any such demand upon any person, or at any time before the return date specified in the demand, whichever period is shorter, such person may file, in the district court of the United States for the judicial district within which such person resides, is found, or transacts business, and serve upon such custodian a petition for an order of such court modifying or setting aside such demand. The time allowed for compliance with the demand in whole or in part as deemed proper and ordered by the court shall not run during the pendency of such petition in the court. Such petition shall specify each ground upon which the petitioner relies in seeking such relief, and may be based upon any failure of such demand to comply with the provisions of this section or upon any constitutional or other legal right or privilege of such person.

(i) At any time during which any custodian is in custody or control of any documentary material delivered by any person in compliance with any such demand, such person may file, in the district court of the United States for the judicial district within which the office of such custodian is situated, and serve upon such custodian a petition for an order of such court requiring the performance by such custodian of any duty imposed upon him by this section.

(j) Whenever any petition is filed in any district court of the United States under this section, such court shall have jurisdiction to hear and determine the matter so presented, and to enter such order or orders as may be required to carry into effect the provisions of this section.

[*Added by* Pub. L. No. 91-452, tit. IX, § 901(a), 84 Stat. 944 (Oct. 15, 1970)]

E.2   Federal Wire and Mail Fraud Statutes

18 U.S.C. § 1341.   Frauds and swindles

Whoever, having devised or intending to devise any scheme or artifice to defraud, or for obtaining money or property by means of false or fraudulent pretenses, representations, or promises, or to sell, dispose of, loan, exchange, alter, give away, distribute, supply, or furnish or procure for unlawful use any counterfeit or spurious coin, obligation,

security, or other article, or anything represented to be or intimated or held out to be such counterfeit or spurious article, for the purpose of executing such scheme or artifice or attempting so to do, places in any post office or authorized depository for mail matter, any matter or thing whatever to be sent or delivered by the Postal Service, or deposits or causes to be deposited any matter or thing whatever to be sent or delivered by any private or commercial interstate carrier, or takes or receives therefrom, any such matter or thing, or knowingly causes to be delivered by mail or such carrier according to the direction thereon, or at the place at which it is directed to be delivered by the person to whom it is addressed, any such matter or thing, shall be fined under this title or imprisoned not more than 20 years, or both. If the violation occurs in relation to, or involving any benefit authorized, transported, transmitted, transferred, disbursed, or paid in connection with, a presidentially declared major disaster or emergency (as those terms are defined in section 102 of the Robert T. Stafford Disaster Relief and Emergency Assistance Act (42 U.S.C. 5122)), or affects a financial institution, such person shall be fined not more than $1,000,000 or imprisoned not more than 30 years, or both.

[June 25, 1948, ch. 645, 62 Stat. 763; May 24, 1949, ch. 139, § 34, 63 Stat. 94; Pub. L. No. 91-375, § (6)(j)(11), 84 Stat. 778 (Aug. 12, 1970); Pub. L. No. 101-73, tit. IX, § 961(i), 103 Stat. 500 (Aug. 9, 1989); Pub. L. No. 101-647, tit. XXV, § 2504(h), 104 Stat. 4861 (Nov. 29, 1990); Pub. L. No. 103-322, tit. XXV, § 250006, tit. XXXIII, § 330016(1)(H), 108 Stat. 2087, 2147 (Sept. 13, 1994); Pub. L. No. 107-204, 116 Stat. 745 (July 30, 2002); Pub. L. No. 107-204, 116 Stat. 745 (July 30, 2002); Pub. L. No. 110-179, § 4, 121 Stat. 2557 (Jan. 7, 2008)]

* * *

18 U.S.C. § 1343.   Fraud by wire, radio, or television

Whoever, having devised or intending to devise any scheme or artifice to defraud, or for obtaining money or property by means of false or fraudulent pretenses, representations, or promises, transmits or causes to be transmitted by means of wire, radio, or television communication in interstate or foreign commerce, any writings, signs, signals, pictures, or sounds for the purpose of executing such scheme or artifice, shall be fined under this title or imprisoned not more than 20 years, or both. If the violation occurs in relation to, or involving any benefit authorized, transported, transmitted, transferred, disbursed, or paid in connection with, a presidentially declared major disaster or emergency (as those terms are defined in section 102 of the Robert T. Stafford Disaster Relief and Emergency Assistance Act (42 U.S.C. 5122)), or affects a financial institution, such person shall be fined not more than $1,000,000 or imprisoned not more than 30 years, or both.

[*Added by* July 16, 1952, ch. 879, § 18(a), 66 Stat. 722; *amended by* July 11, 1956, ch. 561, 70 Stat. 523; Pub. L. No. 101-73, tit. IX, § 961(j), 103 Stat. 500 (Aug. 9, 1989); Pub. L. No. 101-647, tit. XXV, § 2504(i), 104 Stat. 4861 (Nov. 29, 1990); Pub. L. No. 103-322, tit. XXXIII, § 330016(1)(H), 108 Stat. 2147 (Sept. 13, 1994); Pub. L. No. 107-204, 116 Stat. 745 (July 30, 2002); Pub. L. No. 110-179, § 3, 121 Stat. 2557 (Jan. 7, 2008)]

* * *

Appendix F   State RICO Statutes Summarized

This appendix summarizes the main features of state "RICO" statutes—state statutes that parallel the federal Racketeer Influenced and Corrupt Organizations (RICO) statute, which is reprinted in Appendix E.1, *supra*, and discussed in Chapter 7, *supra*. The state statutes are examined in Chapter 8, *supra*.

These summaries of state RICO statutes should only be used as a general guide. Advocates should consult the statutes themselves for details and precise statutory language.

ARIZONA

Ariz. Rev. Stat. Ann. §§ 13-2301 to 13-2323

Predicate Offenses: List of state offenses, including usury, extortionate extensions of credit, fraud (specifically including certain fraudulent conduct in marketing and sale of real property), restraint of trade, computer tampering, unlawful possession of access device, some securities offenses; manufacture, sale, or distribution of misbranded (falsely or inadequately labelled) drugs; and trafficking of persons for forced labor or services. A new section on residential mortgage fraud was added in 2007.
Pattern: Although only one offense is needed for the statutory definition of racketeering, or for a state criminal RICO conviction, a pattern is required for a civil RICO cause of action. A pattern requires either two or more related acts of racketeering within five years of each other, which were continuous or exhibit a threat of being continuous, or one single predicate act, if it is one of certain listed serious felonies (murder, kidnapping, drug offenses, etc.).
Does statute explicitly provide for private cause of action? Yes, for treble damages plus costs and attorney fees. No punitive damages or damages for emotional distress unless there is bodily injury. Most of the substantive provisions for which a civil action is allowed do not have any enterprise requirement.
Statute of limitations: Three years after actual discovery of violation, or ten years after events giving rise to cause of action, whichever comes first.
Special procedural provisions: Preponderance of the evidence required for civil cases. The extensive 1993 revisions of the private RICO statute added a long list of protections against abuse, including sanctions for frivolous or oppressive actions and requirements that complaints be verified, that fraud be pleaded with particularity, and that the words "racketeer" or "racketeering activity" not be used unless one of the predicate acts is a crime of violence.

CALIFORNIA

Cal. Penal Code §§ 186.1 to 186.8 (West)

Predicate Offenses: List of state offenses, including securities offenses and identity theft, certain computer crimes, and human trafficking (defined to include deprivation of liberty, or labor compelled, by fraud or deceit).
Pattern: Two or more interrelated predicate offenses that are committed as a criminal activity of organized crime. Most recent act must be within ten years, excluding periods of imprisonment, of prior act, and one offense must have occurred after enactment of the state RICO law.
Does statute explicitly provide for private cause of action? No.

COLORADO

Colo. Rev. Stat. §§ 18-17-101 to 18-17-109

Predicate Offenses: List of state offenses, including some securities offenses, telecommunications offenses, felony charitable fraud, making, financing or collecting an extortionate extension of credit, and usury, plus those listed in federal RICO, defrauding a secured creditor, gathering identity information by deception and possession of identity theft tools, criminal possession of an identification document; coercion of involuntary servitude (which includes coercion by "abusing or threatening abuse of the legal process," Colo. Rev. Stat. § 18-3-503).
Pattern: Two predicate offenses related to the conduct of the enterprise. The last offense must have occurred no more than ten years, excluding periods of imprisonment, after a prior act, and one offense must have occurred after enactment of the statute.
Does statute explicitly provide for private cause of action? Yes, for treble damages plus costs and attorney fees. Enterprise requirements are less strict in federal RICO.
Statute of limitations: Not specified.
Special procedural provisions: Standard of proof is clear and convincing evidence. Jury trial is available. Civil action may be brought by prosecutor or any aggrieved person.

CONNECTICUT

Conn. Gen. Stat. Ann. §§ 53-393 to 53-403

Predicate Offenses: List of state offenses, including extortionate credit transactions and securities offenses; also collection of unlawful debt.
Pattern: Two or more interrelated offenses. Last offense must have occurred within five years of a prior offense and at least one offense must have occurred after October 1, 1982.
Does statute explicitly provide for private cause of action? No. Forfeiture can be ordered by the court upon conviction of defendant. Court can direct transfer of assets to innocent persons or entities.
Statute of limitations: Five years after termination of unlawful conduct.

DELAWARE

Del. Code Ann. tit. 11, §§ 1501 to 1511

Predicate Offenses: List of state offenses, including all felonies and certain misdemeanors, plus those listed in federal RICO; also collection of unlawful debt; human trafficking, including debt bondage.
Pattern: Two or more interrelated predicate offenses; must not be so closely related as to constitute a single event. The last offense must occur within ten years of the prior incident and at least one must occur after July 9, 1986.
Does statute explicitly provide for private cause of action? Yes, for treble damages plus costs and attorney fees; punitive damages are recoverable "when appropriate." Private action is allowed only against a defendant who has been convicted of a racketeering offense. Injured person can also intervene in an action to claim property that is forfeited. Enterprise requirements are less strict than in federal RICO.
Statute of limitations: Private civil action must be brought within one year of defendant's conviction of a racketeering activity; must also be brought within five years of the unlawful activity itself, but this limitation is tolled during any attorney general proceeding and for two years after its termination.

FLORIDA

Fla. Stat. §§ 895.01 to 895.09

Predicate Offenses: List of state offenses, including usury, securities offenses, telemarketing offenses, time-share escrow offenses, extortion, fraud, exploitation of elderly or disabled person, and telemarketing offenses (as of October 1, 1996), plus those listed in federal RICO; also collection of unlawful debt.
Pattern: Two or more related predicate offenses. Last predicate offense must have occurred within five years of a prior offense and at least one must have occurred after statute's effective date.

Does statute explicitly provide for private cause of action? Yes, but only for equitable relief. (*But see* Fla. Stat. §§ 772.101 through 772.190, *infra*.) Plaintiff has claim to forfeited property superior to right or claim of state. Enterprise requirements are less strict than in federal RICO. Equitable relief is available without showing of special or irreparable damage. State and governmental subdivisions may sue for treble damages.

Statute of limitations: Five years, but suspended during prosecution for underlying offense and for two years thereafter.

Special procedural provisions: Standard of proof is clear and convincing evidence. Jury trial available.

Fla. Stat. §§ 772.101 to 772.19

Predicate Offenses: List of state offenses, including securities offenses, telemarketing offenses, usury, fraud, extortion, exploitation of an elderly person, and time share escrow offenses, plus most offenses listed in federal RICO, human trafficking, defined to include forced labor obtained by fraud, extortionate extensions of credit, loan sharking, or misuse of lending or other credit methods to establish a debt, which will be paid back by services.

Pattern: Two related predicate offenses. Last act must be no more than five years after a prior act. Acts of fraud arising out of the same contract are treated as one offense.

Does statute explicitly provide for private cause of action? Yes, for treble damages, with a minimum of $200, plus costs and attorney fees. Punitive damages are not allowed. Enterprise requirements are less strict than in federal RICO. A victim of human trafficking may, in the alternative, claim three times the amount gained from the human trafficking, plus costs and attorney fees.

Statute of limitations: Five years, but suspended during prosecution for underlying offense and for two years thereafter.

Special procedural provisions: Civil action can be pursued whether or not defendant is convicted of a predicate offense. Proof must be by clear and convincing evidence.

GEORGIA

Ga. Code Ann. §§ 16-14-1 to 16-14-12

Predicate Offenses: List of state offenses, including identity fraud, deceptive commercial e-mail, residential mortgage fraud, and, plus those listed in federal RICO, plus certain crimes which carry a sentence of at least one year imprisonment according to U.S. or any state's laws (must involve extortion, theft, securities fraud, or various kinds of violence or illegal drugs) plus violation of payday lending law, certain felonies involving motor vehicle titles and identification numbers of motor vehicles or parts; violations of computer systems protection act.

Pattern: Two similar or interrelated predicate offenses required. Last offense must have occurred within four years, excluding periods of imprisonment, of a prior act, and one offense must have occurred after July 1, 1980. The statute states that the legislative intent is to include only an interrelated pattern of criminal activity, the motive or effect of which is to derive pecuniary gain.

Does statute explicitly provide for private cause of action? Yes, for treble damages plus costs and attorney fees; punitive damages allowed, where appropriate. Enterprise requirements are less strict than in federal RICO. Injured person may also sue for injunctive relief and divestiture, without need to show irreparable harm. Injured person also can claim forfeited property, but must intervene in forfeiture proceeding.

Statute of limitations: Five years, suspended during pendency of related criminal prosecution or civil action and for two years thereafter.

Special procedural provisions: Jury trial available.

HAWAII

Haw. Rev. Stat. §§ 842-1 to 842-12

Predicate Offenses: List of offenses, including extortion, loan sharking, and labor trafficking, defined to include requiring labor to be performed to retire, repay, or service real or purported debt, if labor is the only

acceptable means of repayment; must be punishable by at least one year in jail. Also collection of unlawful debt.

Pattern: Statute silent.

Does statute explicitly provide for private cause of action? Yes, any person injured in business or property by a violation may seek actual damages, costs, and attorney fees. Enterprise requirements are less strict than in federal RICO.

Statute of limitations: Statute silent.

IDAHO

Idaho Code Ann. §§ 18-7801 to 18-7805

Predicate Offenses: List of state offenses, including fraud and usury; equivalent offenses under other states' laws.

Pattern: Two or more similar or related offenses. Last offense must have occurred within five years of a prior offense, and at least one offense must have occurred after July 1, 1981.

Does statute explicitly provide for private cause of action? Yes, for treble damages, plus costs and attorney fees. Enterprise requirements are less strict than in federal RICO.

Statute of limitations: Statute silent.

INDIANA

Ind. Code §§ 34-24-2-1 to 34-24-2-8 and 35-45-6-1 to 35-45-6-2

Predicate Offenses: List of state offenses, including fraud; human trafficking; unauthorized practice of law.

Pattern: Two similar or interrelated incidents. The last must be within five years of a prior incident, and one must have occurred after August 31, 1980. *See Kollar v. State*, 556 N.E.2d 936 (Ind. Ct. App. 1990) for detail re elements of proof of pattern.

Does statute explicitly provide for private cause of action? Yes, for treble damages, plus costs and attorney fees. Punitive damages allowed. Enterprise requirements are less strict than in federal RICO. Victim also may sue for injunctive relief, and need not show special or irreparable damage. Victim also may make a claim to forfeited property.

Statute of limitations: Statute silent.

Special procedural provisions: Jury trial available. Burden of proof is preponderance of the evidence.

IOWA

Iowa Code §§ 706A.1 to 706A.5

Predicate Offenses: "Specified unlawful activity" defined as any act, committed for financial gain on a continuing basis that is punishable as an indictable offense under the laws of the state in which it occurred and under the laws of Iowa.

Pattern: Statute silent.

Does statute explicitly provide for private cause of action? Yes, for treble damages plus costs and attorney fees. No recovery for pain and suffering. Aggrieved person may sue for injunction and divestiture.

Statute of limitations: Statute silent.

Special procedural provisions: Upon filing pleading, aggrieved person must notify the state attorney general. No need to show special injury to obtain an injunction. Standard of proof is preponderance of evidence. Criminal conviction or indictment not necessary. Pleadings must be verified. Fraud, coercion, and vicarious liability must be pled with particularity. Double damages plus attorney fees as sanction for frivolous pleading.

LOUISIANA

La. Rev. Stat. Ann. §§ 15:1351 to 15:1356

Predicate Offenses: List of state offenses, focusing on crimes of violence and drug offenses, but also including theft and extortion, identity theft, certain securities offenses; human trafficking.

Pattern: Two or more similar or related offenses. Last offense must have occurred within five years of a prior offense, and at least one offense must have occurred after August 21, 1992.

Does statute explicitly provide for private cause of action? Yes, for treble damages or $10,000, whichever is greater, plus costs and attorney fees. Enterprise requirements are less strict than in federal RICO. Injured person also has *in rem* claim to forfeited property.

Statute of limitations: Five years, suspended during pendency of related civil or criminal action and for two years thereafter.

MICHIGAN

Mich. Comp. Laws §§ 750.159f to 750.159x

Predicate Offenses: List of state offenses, including securities fraud, extortion, false pretenses, certain internet or computer crimes, certain offenses involving credit cards or financial transaction devices, identity theft, human trafficking (defined to include labor or services coerced by abusing or threatening to abuse legal process, or causing or threatening to cause financial harm), federal RICO offenses, and similar offenses in other states.

Pattern: Two similar or interrelated incidents which pose a threat of continued criminal activity. The last must have occurred within 10 years, excluding periods of imprisonment, after a prior incident, and one must have been committed within the state after April 1, 1996.

Does statute explicitly provide for private cause of action? No. Statute explicitly states that it does not create a private cause of action. Forfeited property can be used to pay claims of victims.

Statute of limitations: Six years.

MINNESOTA

Minn. Stat. §§ 609.901 to 609.912

Predicate Offenses: List of state felonies, including identity theft.

Pattern: Three or more related predicate offenses, two of which must be felonies other than conspiracy; offenses must not be so closely related as to constitute a single offense. Offenses must have been committed within ten years of commencement of criminal proceedings.

Does statute explicitly provide for private cause of action? No. But courts have discretion to grant forfeited property or fines to victims.

Statute of limitations: Ten years from commencement of criminal activity.

MISSISSIPPI

Miss. Code Ann. §§ 97-43-1 to 97-43-11

Predicate Offenses: List of state offenses, including securities offenses. Also collection of unlawful debt; human trafficking; conducting, organizing or managing an organized theft enterprise for the purpose of, inter alia, computer fraud or identity theft.

Pattern: Two or more similar or related predicate offenses. Last offense must have occurred within five years of a prior act, and at least one offense must have occurred after the effective date of the statute.

Does statute explicitly provide for private cause of action? Yes, injured person has cause of action for treble damages plus costs and attorney fees against person or enterprise convicted of violation. Enterprise requirements are less strict than in federal RICO. Injured person can also seek injunction and divestiture; a showing of immediate or irreparable injury is not required for an injunction. Aggrieved person can also claim forfeited property.

Statute of limitations: Five years, suspended during pendency of related criminal prosecution or civil action and for two years thereafter.

Special procedural provisions: Jury trial available.

NEVADA

Nev. Rev. Stat. §§ 207.350 to 207.520

Predicate Offenses: List of state offenses, including extortion, extortionate collection of debt, obtaining money or property by false pretenses, some securities offenses; and involuntary servitude and trafficking in persons. A 2009 revision added a new fraud offense: in the course of an enterprise or occupation, two or more similar or interrelated acts of fraud or deceit [defined] within four years, with a loss or intended loss of more than $250.

Pattern: Two or more similar or interrelated predicate offenses. Last offense must occur within five years of a prior act, and at least one offense must occur after July 1, 1983.

Does statute explicitly provide for private cause of action? Yes, for treble damages plus costs and attorney fees. Enterprise requirements are different than federal RICO. Injured person may also claim forfeited property.

Statute of limitations: Five years, suspended during pendency of related criminal prosecution or civil action and for two years thereafter.

Special procedural provisions: Jury trial available. Judicial decisions hold that predicate acts must be pleaded with same degree of specificity as in criminal indictment and that criminal conviction of the defendant is not a prerequisite to a civil action.

NEW JERSEY

N.J. Stat. Ann. §§ 2C:41-1 to 2C:41-6.2 (West)

Predicate Offenses: List of state offenses, including extortion, usury, and fraudulent practices, plus most of those listed in federal RICO, human trafficking, defined to include labor compelled by abuse or threatened abuse of the law or legal process. Also collection of unlawful debt.

Pattern: Two or more interrelated predicate offenses. Last act must have occurred within ten years (excluding periods of imprisonment) of a prior act. One offense must have occurred after effective date of statute.

Does statute explicitly provide for private cause of action? Yes, for treble damages plus costs and attorney fees.

Statute of limitations: Statute is silent, but judicial decisions say four years.

NEW MEXICO

N.M. Stat. §§ 30-42-1 to 30-42-6

Predicate Offenses: List of state offenses punishable by at least one year imprisonment, including fraud, extortion, securities offenses, and loan sharking, altering serial numbers, engine numbers, etc. on motor vehicles.

Pattern: Two or more predicate offenses. Last offense must be within five years of a prior act and at least one offense must have occurred after the statute's effective date.

Does statute explicitly provide for private cause of action? Yes, for treble damages plus costs and attorney fees. Enterprise requirements are different than in federal RICO.

Statute of limitations: Statute silent.

NEW YORK

N.Y. Penal Law §§ 460.00 to 460.80 (McKinney)

Predicate Offenses: List of state offenses, including false statements, criminal usury, schemes to defraud, and certain securities offenses, labor trafficking, defined to include "requiring that the labor be performed to retire, repay or service a real or purported debt that the actor has caused by a systematic or ongoing course of conduct with intent to defraud such person," residential mortgage fraud.

Pattern: Three or more related predicate offenses, but not so closely related as to constitute a single offense; at least two offenses must be felonies other than conspiracy; one felony within 5 years of commencement of action, and each act within 3 years of a prior act; many other requirements.

Does statute explicitly provide for private cause of action? No.

Statute of limitations: Ten years.

NORTH CAROLINA

N.C. Gen. Stat. §§ 75D-1 to 75D-14

Predicate Offenses: Most state offenses if chargeable by indictment, plus those listed in federal RICO. To maintain a civil RICO action, at least one offense must be other than federal mail fraud, federal wire fraud, or a securities offense.

Pattern: Two or more similar or interrelated offenses. One offense must have occurred no more than four years after a prior offense, excluding any period of imprisonment, and one offense must have occurred after October 1, 1986.

Does statute explicitly provide for private cause of action? Yes, for treble damages plus costs and attorney fees. Enterprise requirements are less strict than in federal RICO. Victim can also claim forfeited assets but must intervene in forfeiture proceeding.

Statute of limitations: Five years, suspended during pendency of civil action by state and for two years thereafter.

Special procedural provisions: Jury trial available. Plaintiff must notify attorney general of filing of suit, and attorney general can seek a stay of the action.

NORTH DAKOTA

N.D. Cent. Code §§ 12.1-06.1-01 to 12.1-06.1-08

Predicate Offenses: List of offenses including usury, extortion, fraud, certain computer crimes including hijacking and hacking, and securities violations. If offense occurred in another state, it must be punishable by imprisonment for more than one year. Offenses must have been committed for financial gain. Human trafficking, which specifically includes services coerced by "debt bondage" [defined] or abuse or threat to abuse the legal system.

Pattern: Two or more predicate offenses. Last offense must have occurred within 10 years, excluding periods of imprisonment, of a prior offense, and one offense must have occurred after July 8, 1987.

Does statute explicitly provide for private cause of action? Yes, for treble damages plus costs and attorney fees. Enterprise requirements may be entirely avoidable.

Statute of limitations: Seven years from discovery of violation.

Special procedural provisions: Plaintiff must notify attorney general of filing of suit. Burden of proof is preponderance of the evidence.

OHIO

Ohio Rev. Code Ann. §§ 2923.31 to 2923.36 (West)

Predicate Offenses: List of state offenses, including extortion, usury, credit repair clinic registration law, and mortgage broker registration law, plus those listed in federal RICO.

Pattern: Two or more related predicate offenses, but not so closely related as to constitute a single event. For civil suit, at least one offense must be other than federal mail fraud, federal wire fraud, or a securities offense. Unless one of the incidents was murder, last offense must be within six years, not including periods of imprisonment, of a prior offense. One offense must have occurred after January 1, 1986.

Does statute explicitly provide for private cause of action? Yes, for treble damages plus costs and attorney fees. Enterprise requirements are less strict than in federal RICO. Victim can also sue for equitable relief including injunction and divestiture. Victims also have right to forfeited property, if civil action is brought within 180 days after entry of sentence of forfeiture. The right to forfeited property is limited to the amount of treble damages, civil penalties, costs and attorney fees awarded in the civil action. If more than one victim makes a claim, and the amount of forfeited property is not sufficient to satisfy all claims, each victim shall receive a pro rata share.

Statute of limitations: Five years after conduct terminated or cause of action accrued, or any longer statute which may be applicable. Suspended during pendency of civil or criminal proceedings and for two years thereafter.

Special procedural provisions: Proof by clear and convincing evidence required for treble damages. Special or irreparable injury need not be shown to get injunctive relief. Statute explicitly states that it is not necessary that defendant have been convicted of the predicate offenses.

OKLAHOMA

Okla. Stat. tit. 22, §§ 1401 to 1419

Predicate Offenses: List of felonies, including extortion, fraud, human trafficking (defined to include debt bondage, or labor coerced by abuse of the law or legal process), securities offense; exploitation of elderly persons or disabled adults; and certain computer crimes.

OREGON

Or. Rev. Stat. §§ 166.715 to 166.735

Predicate Offenses: List of state offenses, including securities offenses and usury, offenses involving real estate and escrow, outfitters and guides, mortgage bankers and mortgage brokers, business and commercial offenses, communications crimes, identity theft, plus some offenses listed in federal RICO; also, collection of unlawful debt; involuntary servitude in the second degree, defined to include compelling labor by "abusing or threatening to abuse the law or legal process" or "threatening to collect an unlawful debt"; violations of the statute governing labor contractors.

Pattern: Two or more similar or interrelated predicate offenses. Last offense must have occurred within five years of a prior offense and at least one must have occurred after November 1, 1981.

Does statute explicitly provide for private cause of action? Yes, for treble damages plus costs and attorney fees; punitive damages allowed when appropriate. Criminal conviction of defendant is necessary in some cases. Enterprise requirements are less strict than in federal RICO. Victim may also sue for injunction and divestiture. Victim has claim to forfeited property.

Statute of limitations: Five years, suspended during pendency of a related civil action or criminal prosecution.

Special procedural provisions: No need to show special or irreparable injury to get injunction. Jury trial available.

PENNSYLVANIA

18 Pa. Cons. Stat. § 911

Predicate Offenses: List of state offenses, including charging more than 25% APR for debt unless otherwise authorized by law; human trafficking, defined to include labor coerced by debt coercion and threats of certain financial harm, including violations of usury law.

Pattern: Two or more predicate offenses, one after effective date of statute.

Does statute explicitly provide for private cause of action? No. Attorney general may seek divestiture.

Statute of limitations: Statute silent.

PUERTO RICO

P.R. Laws Ann. tit. 25, §§ 971 to 971s

Predicate Offenses: List of state offense, including extortion; also, collection of illegal debt.

Pattern: Two acts of organized criminal activity within a ten year period, excluding any period of imprisonment, at least one of which occurred after June 19, 1987.

Does statute explicitly provide for private cause of action? Yes, for treble damages, costs and attorney fees.

Statute of limitations: Ten years, except where other statute establishes longer limitations period.

RHODE ISLAND

R.I. Gen. Laws §§ 7-15-1 to 7-15-11

Predicate Offenses: List of state offenses, including extortion; also, collection of unlawful debt.

Pattern: None required.

Does statute explicitly provide for private cause of action? Yes, for treble damages plus costs and attorney fees. Victim may also intervene in

forfeiture proceeding and seek escrow of forfeited assets. Statute explicitly states that criminal conviction of defendant is unnecessary.
Statute of limitations: Statute silent.

UTAH

Utah Code Ann. §§ 76-10-1601 to 76-10-1609 (West)
Predicate Offenses: List of state offenses, including theft by deception, theft by extortion, usury, securities offenses, violations of Land Sales Practices Act, defrauding creditors, making false credit report, mortgage fraud, confidence game, false statements, deceptive business practices, identity fraud, plus most offenses listed in federal RICO, human trafficking.
Pattern: Three or more similar or interrelated offenses, demonstrating continuing unlawful conduct. Last offense must have occurred within five years of a prior offense and at least one offense must have occurred after July 31, 1981.
Does statute explicitly provide for private cause of action? Yes, for double damages plus costs and attorney fees. Victim may also request injunctive relief. A principal is liable for actual damages for an agent's actions within the scope of his or her employment. A principal is liable for double damages if the agent's misconduct was authorized or "recklessly tolerated" by the principal's board of directors or a "high managerial agent."
Statute of limitations: Three years.
Special procedural provisions: Statute explicitly states that criminal conviction of defendant is unnecessary. Fraud cases are subject to arbitration. Proof must be by clear and convincing evidence. If a case pursuant to this statute is dismissed or disposed of on summary judgment, or if defendant is found not liable, prevailing party shall recover costs, including reasonable attorney fees.

VIRGIN ISLANDS

V.I. Code Ann. tit. 14, §§ 600 to 614
Predicate Offenses: List of state offenses, including statutes regulating loans, disclosure of finance charges, extortion, fraud and false statements.
Pattern: Two or more offenses, not isolated, related to the conduct of the enterprise, at least one of which occurred after November 9, 1990.
Does statute explicitly provide for private cause of action? Yes, for treble damages (not including pain and suffering), costs and reasonable attorney fees. Victim has a claim to forfeited property.
Statute of limitations: Five years, excluding any period of imprisonment, unless a longer statute applies.

Special procedural provisions: Fraud, coercion or conspiracy must be pleaded with particularity. Showing of special or irreparable injury not required for injunction. Pleadings must be verified and signed by plaintiff's attorney, if any.

WASHINGTON

Wash. Rev. Code §§ 9A.82.010 to 9A.82.904
Predicate Offenses: List of state offenses, including extortion, collection of unlawful debt, collection of extortionate extension of credit, telephone solicitation violations, securities fraud, pursuing a pattern of skimming homeowners' equity, identity theft, and unlicensed practice of profession or business. Securities fraud may be a predicate offense only if defendant has been convicted criminally.
Pattern: Three or more similar or interrelated offenses. The last must have occurred within five years, excluding periods of imprisonment, of the earliest, and one must have occurred after July 1, 1985.
Does statute explicitly provide for private cause of action? Yes, for actual damages, which may, in the court's discretion, be trebled, plus costs and attorney fees. Enterprise requirements may be entirely avoidable. Victim also has a claim on forfeited property.
Statute of limitations: Three years from discovery, or from when discovery reasonably should have occurred.
Special procedural provisions: Standard of proof is preponderance of evidence. Plaintiff must serve notice of suit on attorney general.

WISCONSIN

Wis. Stat. §§ 946.80 to 946.93
Predicate Offenses: List of state offenses, including securities offenses, franchise law violations, loan sharking, identity theft and some frauds, plus offenses listed in federal RICO, certain types of welfare fraud.
Pattern: Three or more similar or related predicate offenses, the motive of which is to derive pecuniary gain. Last offense must have occurred within seven years of the first, and at least one must have occurred after April 27, 1982.
Does statute explicitly provide for private cause of action? Yes, for double damages plus costs and attorney fees; punitive damages allowed when appropriate. Enterprise requirements are less strict than in federal RICO. Victim may also claim assets in forfeiture proceeding.
Statute of limitations: Six years, but suspended during pendency of related criminal or civil case and for two years thereafter.
Special procedural provisions: Jury trial is available.

Appendix G   Federal False Claims Act

31 U.S.C.

* * *

* * *

31 U.S.C. § 3729.   False claims

(a) Liability for certain acts.—

(1) In general.—Subject to paragraph (2), any person who—

(A) knowingly presents, or causes to be presented, a false or fraudulent claim for payment or approval;

(B) knowingly makes, uses, or causes to be made or used, a false record or statement material to a false or fraudulent claim;

(C) conspires to commit a violation of subparagraph (A), (B), (D), (E), (F), or (G);

(D) has possession, custody, or control of property or money used, or to be used, by the Government and knowingly delivers, or causes to be delivered, less than all of that money or property;

(E) is authorized to make or deliver a document certifying receipt of property used, or to be used, by the Government and, intending to defraud the Government, makes or delivers the receipt without completely knowing that the information on the receipt is true;

(F) knowingly buys, or receives as a pledge of an obligation or debt, public property from an officer or employee of the Government, or a member of the Armed Forces, who lawfully may not sell or pledge property; or

(G) knowingly makes, uses, or causes to be made or used, a false record or statement material to an obligation to pay or transmit money or property to the Government, or knowingly conceals or knowingly and improperly avoids or decreases an obligation to pay or transmit money or property to the Government,

is liable to the United States Government for a civil penalty of not less than $5,000 and not more than $10,000, as adjusted by the Federal Civil Penalties Inflation Adjustment Act of 1990 (28 U.S.C. 2461 note; Public Law 104-410[1], plus 3 times the amount of damages which the Government sustains because of the act of that person.

(2) Reduced damages.—If the court finds that—

(A) the person committing the violation of this subsection furnished officials of the United States responsible for investigating false claims violations with all information known to such person about the violation within 30 days after the date on which the defendant first obtained the information;

(B) such person fully cooperated with any Government investigation of such violation; and

(C) at the time such person furnished the United States with the information about the violation, no criminal prosecution, civil action, or administrative action had commenced under this title with respect to such violation, and the person did not have actual knowledge of the existence of an investigation into such violation,

the court may assess not less than 2 times the amount of damages which the Government sustains because of the act of that person.

(3) Costs of civil actions.—A person violating this subsection shall also be liable to the United States Government for the costs of a civil action brought to recover any such penalty or damages.

(b) Definitions.—For purposes of this section—

(1) the terms "knowing" and "knowingly" —

(A) mean that a person, with respect to information—

(i) has actual knowledge of the information;

(ii) acts in deliberate ignorance of the truth or falsity of the information; or

(iii) acts in reckless disregard of the truth or falsity of the information; and

(B) require no proof of specific intent to defraud;

(2) the term "claim"—

(A) means any request or demand, whether under a contract or otherwise, for money or property and whether or not the United States has title to the money or property, that—

(i) is presented to an officer, employee, or agent of the United States; or

(ii) is made to a contractor, grantee, or other recipient, if the money or property is to be spent or used on the Government's behalf or to advance a Government program or interest, and if the United States Government—

(I) provides or has provided any portion of the money or property requested or demanded; or

(II) will reimburse such contractor, grantee, or other recipient for any portion of the money or property which is requested or demanded; and

(B) does not include requests or demands for money or property that the Government has paid to an individual as compensation for Federal employment or as an income subsidy with no restrictions on that individual's use of the money or property;

(3) the term "obligation" means an established duty, whether or not fixed, arising from an express or implied contractual, grantor-grantee, or licensor-licensee relationship, from a fee-based or similar relationship, from statute or regulation, or from the retention of any overpayment; and

(4) the term "material" means having a natural tendency to influence, or be capable of influencing, the payment or receipt of money or property.

(c) Exemption from disclosure.—Any information furnished pursuant to subsection (a)(2) shall be exempt from disclosure under section 552 of title 5.

(d) Exclusion.—This section does not apply to claims, records, or statements made under the Internal Revenue Code of 1986.

[(e) Redesignated (d)]

[Pub. L. No. 97-258, 96 Stat. 978 (Sept. 13, 1982); Pub. L. No. 99-562, § 2, 100 Stat. 3153 (Oct. 27, 1986); Pub. L. No. 103-272, § 4(f)(1)(O), 108 Stat. 1362 (July 5, 1994); Pub. L. No. 111-21, § 4(a), 123 Stat. 1621 (May 20, 2009)]

31 U.S.C. § 3730.   Civil actions for false claims

<For constitutionality of provisions of Pub. L. No. 111-148, see National Federation of Independent Business v. Sebelius, Secretary of Health and Human Services, 2012 WL 2427810.>

(a) Responsibilities of the Attorney General.—The Attorney General diligently shall investigate a violation under section 3729. If the Attorney General finds that a person has violated or is violating section 3729, the

---

1   *Editor's note:* So in original. Probably should read "Public Law 101-410."

Attorney General may bring a civil action under this section against the person.

(b) Actions by private persons.—

(1) A person may bring a civil action for a violation of section 3729 for the person and for the United States Government. The action shall be brought in the name of the Government. The action may be dismissed only if the court and the Attorney General give written consent to the dismissal and their reasons for consenting.

(2) A copy of the complaint and written disclosure of substantially all material evidence and information the person possesses shall be served on the Government pursuant to Rule 4(d)(4) of the Federal Rules of Civil Procedure.[2] The complaint shall be filed in camera, shall remain under seal for at least 60 days, and shall not be served on the defendant until the court so orders. The Government may elect to intervene and proceed with the action within 60 days after it receives both the complaint and the material evidence and information.

(3) The Government may, for good cause shown, move the court for extensions of the time during which the complaint remains under seal under paragraph (2). Any such motions may be supported by affidavits or other submissions in camera. The defendant shall not be required to respond to any complaint filed under this section until 20 days after the complaint is unsealed and served upon the defendant pursuant to Rule 4 of the Federal Rules of Civil Procedure.

(4) Before the expiration of the 60-day period or any extensions obtained under paragraph (3), the Government shall—

(A) proceed with the action, in which case the action shall be conducted by the Government; or

(B) notify the court that it declines to take over the action, in which case the person bringing the action shall have the right to conduct the action.

(5) When a person brings an action under this subsection, no person other than the Government may intervene or bring a related action based on the facts underlying the pending action.

(c) Rights of the parties to *qui tam* actions.—

(1) If the Government proceeds with the action, it shall have the primary responsibility for prosecuting the action, and shall not be bound by an act of the person bringing the action. Such person shall have the right to continue as a party to the action, subject to the limitations set forth in paragraph (2).

(2)

(A) The Government may dismiss the action notwithstanding the objections of the person initiating the action if the person has been notified by the Government of the filing of the motion and the court has provided the person with an opportunity for a hearing on the motion.

(B) The Government may settle the action with the defendant notwithstanding the objections of the person initiating the action if the court determines, after a hearing, that the proposed settlement is fair, adequate, and reasonable under all the circumstances. Upon a showing of good cause, such hearing may be held in camera.

(C) Upon a showing by the Government that unrestricted participation during the course of the litigation by the person initiating the action would interfere with or unduly delay the Government's prosecution of the case, or would be repetitious, irrelevant, or for purposes of harassment, the court may, in its discretion, impose limitations on the person's participation, such as—

(i) limiting the number of witnesses the person may call;

(ii) limiting the length of the testimony of such witnesses;

(iii) limiting the person's cross-examination of witnesses; or

(iv) otherwise limiting the participation by the person in the litigation.

(D) Upon a showing by the defendant that unrestricted participation during the course of the litigation by the person initiating the action would be for purposes of harassment or would cause the

defendant undue burden or unnecessary expense, the court may limit the participation by the person in the litigation.

(3) If the Government elects not to proceed with the action, the person who initiated the action shall have the right to conduct the action. If the Government so requests, it shall be served with copies of all pleadings filed in the action and shall be supplied with copies of all deposition transcripts (at the Government's expense). When a person proceeds with the action, the court, without limiting the status and rights of the person initiating the action, may nevertheless permit the Government to intervene at a later date upon a showing of good cause.

(4) Whether or not the Government proceeds with the action, upon a showing by the Government that certain actions of discovery by the person initiating the action would interfere with the Government's investigation or prosecution of a criminal or civil matter arising out of the same facts, the court may stay such discovery for a period of not more than 60 days. Such a showing shall be conducted in camera. The court may extend the 60-day period upon a further showing in camera that the Government has pursued the criminal or civil investigation or proceedings with reasonable diligence and any proposed discovery in the civil action will interfere with the ongoing criminal or civil investigation or proceedings.

(5) Notwithstanding subsection (b), the Government may elect to pursue its claim through any alternate remedy available to the Government, including any administrative proceeding to determine a civil money penalty. If any such alternate remedy is pursued in another proceeding, the person initiating the action shall have the same rights in such proceeding as such person would have had if the action had continued under this section. Any finding of fact or conclusion of law made in such other proceeding that has become final shall be conclusive on all parties to an action under this section. For purposes of the preceding sentence, a finding or conclusion is final if it has been finally determined on appeal to the appropriate court of the United States, if all time for filing such an appeal with respect to the finding or conclusion has expired, or if the finding or conclusion is not subject to judicial review.

(d) Award to *qui tam* plaintiff.—

(1) If the Government proceeds with an action brought by a person under subsection (b), such person shall, subject to the second sentence of this paragraph, receive at least 15 percent but not more than 25 percent of the proceeds of the action or settlement of the claim, depending upon the extent to which the person substantially contributed to the prosecution of the action. Where the action is one which the court finds to be based primarily on disclosures of specific information (other than information provided by the person bringing the action) relating to allegations or transactions in a criminal, civil, or administrative hearing, in a congressional, administrative, or Government[3] Accounting Office report, hearing, audit, or investigation, or from the news media, the court may award such sums as it considers appropriate, but in no case more than 10 percent of the proceeds, taking into account the significance of the information and the role of the person bringing the action in advancing the case to litigation. Any payment to a person under the first or second sentence of this paragraph shall be made from the proceeds. Any such person shall also receive an amount for reasonable expenses which the court finds to have been necessarily incurred, plus reasonable attorneys' fees and costs. All such expenses, fees, and costs shall be awarded against the defendant.

(2) If the Government does not proceed with an action under this section, the person bringing the action or settling the claim shall receive an amount which the court decides is reasonable for collecting the civil penalty and damages. The amount shall be not less than 25 percent and not more than 30 percent of the proceeds of the action or settlement and shall be paid out of such proceeds. Such person shall also receive an amount for reasonable expenses which the court finds to have been

---

2   *Editor's note:* See, now, Rule 4(i) of the Federal Rules of Civil Procedure.

3   *Editor's note:* So in original. Probably should be "General".

necessarily incurred, plus reasonable attorneys' fees and costs. All such expenses, fees, and costs shall be awarded against the defendant.

(3) Whether or not the Government proceeds with the action, if the court finds that the action was brought by a person who planned and initiated the violation of section 3729 upon which the action was brought, then the court may, to the extent the court considers appropriate, reduce the share of the proceeds of the action which the person would otherwise receive under paragraph (1) or (2) of this subsection, taking into account the role of that person in advancing the case to litigation and any relevant circumstances pertaining to the violation. If the person bringing the action is convicted of criminal conduct arising from his or her role in the violation of section 3729, that person shall be dismissed from the civil action and shall not receive any share of the proceeds of the action. Such dismissal shall not prejudice the right of the United States to continue the action, represented by the Department of Justice.

(4) If the Government does not proceed with the action and the person bringing the action conducts the action, the court may award to the defendant its reasonable attorneys' fees and expenses if the defendant prevails in the action and the court finds that the claim of the person bringing the action was clearly frivolous, clearly vexatious, or brought primarily for purposes of harassment.

(e) Certain actions barred.—

(1) No court shall have jurisdiction over an action brought by a former or present member of the armed forces under subsection (b) of this section against a member of the armed forces arising out of such person's service in the armed forces.

(2)

(A) No court shall have jurisdiction over an action brought under subsection (b) against a Member of Congress, a member of the judiciary, or a senior executive branch official if the action is based on evidence or information known to the Government when the action was brought.

(B) For purposes of this paragraph, "senior executive branch official" means any officer or employee listed in paragraphs (1) through (8) of section 101(f) of the Ethics in Government Act of 1978 (5 U.S.C. App.).

(3) In no event may a person bring an action under subsection (b) which is based upon allegations or transactions which are the subject of a civil suit or an administrative civil money penalty proceeding in which the Government is already a party.

(4)

(A) The court shall dismiss an action or claim under this section, unless opposed by the Government, if substantially the same allegations or transactions as alleged in the action or claim were publicly disclosed—

(i) in a Federal criminal, civil, or administrative hearing in which the Government or its agent is a party;

(ii) in a congressional, Government[4] Accountability Office, or other Federal report, hearing, audit, or investigation; or

(iii) from the news media,

unless the action is brought by the Attorney General or the person bringing the action is an original source of the information.

(B) For purposes of this paragraph, "original source" means an individual who either (i) prior to a public disclosure under subsection (e)(4)(a), has voluntarily disclosed to the Government the information on which allegations or transactions in a claim are based, or (2) who has knowledge that is independent of and materially adds to the publicly disclosed allegations or transactions, and who has voluntarily provided the information to the Government before filing an action under this section.

(f) Government not liable for certain expenses.—The Government is not liable for expenses which a person incurs in bringing an action under this section.

---

4 *Editor's note:* So in original. Probably should be "General".

(g) Fees and expenses to prevailing defendant.—In civil actions brought under this section by the United States, the provisions of section 2412(d) of title 28 shall apply.

(h) Relief from retaliatory actions.—

(1) In general.—Any employee, contractor, or agent shall be entitled to all relief necessary to make that employee, contractor, or agent whole, if that employee, contractor, or agent is discharged, demoted, suspended, threatened, harassed, or in any other manner discriminated against in the terms and conditions of employment because of lawful acts done by the employee, contractor, agent or associated others in furtherance of an action under this section or other efforts to stop 1 or more violations of this subchapter.

(2) Relief.—Relief under paragraph (1) shall include reinstatement with the same seniority status that employee, contractor, or agent would have had but for the discrimination, 2 times the amount of back pay, interest on the back pay, and compensation for any special damages sustained as a result of the discrimination, including litigation costs and reasonable attorneys' fees. An action under this subsection may be brought in the appropriate district court of the United States for the relief provided in this subsection.

(3) Limitation on bringing civil action.—A civil action under this subsection may not be brought more than 3 years after the date when the retaliation occurred.

[Pub. L. No. 97-258, 96 Stat. 978 (Sept. 13, 1982); Pub. L. No. 99-562, §§ 3, 4, 100 Stat. 3154, 3157 (Oct. 27, 1986); Pub. L. No. 100-700, § 9, 102 Stat. 4638 (Nov. 19, 1988); Pub. L. No. 101-280, § 10(a), 104 Stat. 162 (May 4, 1990); Pub. L. No. 103-272, § 4(f)(1)(P), 108 Stat. 1362 (July 5, 1994); Pub. L. No. 111-21, § 4(d), 123 Stat. 1624 (May 20, 2009); Pub. L. No. 111-148, Title X, § 10104(j)(2), 124 Stat. 901 (Mar. 23, 2010); Pub. L. No. 111-203, Title X, § 1079A(c), 124 Stat. 2079 (July 21, 2010)]

31 U.S.C. § 3731.   False claims procedure

(a) A subpoena requiring the attendance of a witness at a trial or hearing conducted under section 3730 of this title may be served at any place in the United States.

(b) A civil action under section 3730 may not be brought—

(1) more than 6 years after the date on which the violation of section 3729 is committed, or

(2) more than 3 years after the date when facts material to the right of action are known or reasonably should have been known by the official of the United States charged with responsibility to act in the circumstances, but in no event more than 10 years after the date on which the violation is committed,

whichever occurs last.

(c) If the Government elects to intervene and proceed with an action brought under 3730(b), the Government may file its own complaint or amend the complaint of a person who has brought an action under section 3730(b) to clarify or add detail to the claims in which the Government is intervening and to add any additional claims with respect to which the Government contends it is entitled to relief. For statute of limitations purposes, any such Government pleading shall relate back to the filing date of the complaint of the person who originally brought the action, to the extent that the claim of the Government arises out of the conduct, transactions, or occurrences set forth, or attempted to be set forth, in the prior complaint of that person.

(d) In any action brought under section 3730, the United States shall be required to prove all essential elements of the cause of action, including damages, by a preponderance of the evidence.

(e) Notwithstanding any other provision of law, the Federal Rules of Criminal Procedure, or the Federal Rules of Evidence, a final judgment rendered in favor of the United States in any criminal proceeding charging fraud or false statements, whether upon a verdict after trial or upon a plea of guilty or nolo contendere, shall estop the defendant from denying the essential elements of the offense in any action which involves the same transaction as in the criminal proceeding and which is brought under subsection (a) or (b) of section 3730.

[Pub. L. No. 97-258, 96 Stat. 979 (Sept. 13, 1982); Pub. L. No. 99-562, § 5, 100 Stat. 3158 (Oct. 27, 1986); Pub. L. No. 111-21, § 4(b), 123 Stat. 1623 (May 20, 2009)]

31 U.S.C. § 3732.   False claims jurisdiction

(a) Actions under section 3730.—Any action under section 3730 may be brought in any judicial district in which the defendant or, in the case of multiple defendants, any one defendant can be found, resides, transacts business, or in which any act proscribed by section 3729 occurred. A summons as required by the Federal Rules of Civil Procedure shall be issued by the appropriate district court and served at any place within or outside the United States.

(b) Claims under state law.—The district courts shall have jurisdiction over any action brought under the laws of any State for the recovery of funds paid by a State or local government if the action arises from the same transaction or occurrence as an action brought under section 3730.

(c) Service on State or local authorities.—With respect to any State or local government that is named as a co-plaintiff with the United States in an action brought under subsection (b), a seal on the action ordered by the court under section 3730(b) shall not preclude the Government or the person bringing the action from serving the complaint, any other pleadings, or the written disclosure of substantially all material evidence and information possessed by the person bringing the action on the law enforcement authorities that are authorized under the law of that State or local government to investigate and prosecute such actions on behalf of such governments, except that such seal applies to the law enforcement authorities so served to the same extent as the seal applies to other parties in the action.

[*Added by* Pub. L. No. 99-562, § 6(a), 100 Stat. 3158 (Oct. 27, 1986), *and amended by* Pub. L. No. 111-21, § 4(e), 123 Stat. 1625 (May 20, 2009)]

31 U.S.C. § 3733.   Civil investigative demands

(a) In general.—

(1) **Issuance and service.**—Whenever the Attorney General, or a designee (for purposes of this section), has reason to believe that any person may be in possession, custody, or control of any documentary material or information relevant to a false claims law investigation, the Attorney General, or a designee, may, before commencing a civil proceeding under section 3730(a) or other false claims law, or making an election under section 3730(b), issue in writing and cause to be served upon such person, a civil investigative demand requiring such person—

(A) to produce such documentary material for inspection and copying,

(B) to answer in writing written interrogatories with respect to such documentary material or information,

(C) to give oral testimony concerning such documentary material or information, or

(D) to furnish any combination of such material, answers, or testimony.

The Attorney General may delegate the authority to issue civil investigative demands under this subsection. Whenever a civil investigative demand is an express demand for any product of discovery, the Attorney General, the Deputy Attorney General, or an Assistant Attorney General shall cause to be served, in any manner authorized by this section, a copy of such demand upon the person from whom the discovery was obtained and shall notify the person to whom such demand is issued of the date on which such copy was served. Any information obtained by the Attorney General or a designee of the Attorney General under this section may be shared with any *qui tam* relator if the

Attorney General or designee determine it is necessary as part of any false claims act investigation.

(2) **Contents and deadlines.**—

(A) Each civil investigative demand issued under paragraph (1) shall state the nature of the conduct constituting the alleged violation of a false claims law which is under investigation, and the applicable provision of law alleged to be violated.

(B) If such demand is for the production of documentary material, the demand shall—

(i) describe each class of documentary material to be produced with such definiteness and certainty as to permit such material to be fairly identified;

(ii) prescribe a return date for each such class which will provide a reasonable period of time within which the material so demanded may be assembled and made available for inspection and copying; and

(iii) identify the false claims law investigator to whom such material shall be made available.

(C) If such demand is for answers to written interrogatories, the demand shall—

(i) set forth with specificity the written interrogatories to be answered;

(ii) prescribe dates at which time answers to written interrogatories shall be submitted; and

(iii) identify the false claims law investigator to whom such answers shall be submitted.

(D) If such demand is for the giving of oral testimony, the demand shall—

(i) prescribe a date, time, and place at which oral testimony shall be commenced;

(ii) identify a false claims law investigator who shall conduct the examination and the custodian to whom the transcript of such examination shall be submitted;

(iii) specify that such attendance and testimony are necessary to the conduct of the investigation;

(iv) notify the person receiving the demand of the right to be accompanied by an attorney and any other representative; and

(v) describe the general purpose for which the demand is being issued and the general nature of the testimony, including the primary areas of inquiry, which will be taken pursuant to the demand.

(E) Any civil investigative demand issued under this section which is an express demand for any product of discovery shall not be returned or returnable until 20 days after a copy of such demand has been served upon the person from whom the discovery was obtained.

(F) The date prescribed for the commencement of oral testimony pursuant to a civil investigative demand issued under this section shall be a date which is not less than seven days after the date on which demand is received, unless the Attorney General or an Assistant Attorney General designated by the Attorney General determines that exceptional circumstances are present which warrant the commencement of such testimony within a lesser period of time.

(G) The Attorney General shall not authorize the issuance under this section of more than one civil investigative demand for oral testimony by the same person unless the person requests otherwise or unless the Attorney General, after investigation, notifies that person in writing that an additional demand for oral testimony is necessary.

(b) Protected material or information.—

(1) **In general.**—A civil investigative demand issued under subsection (a) may not require the production of any documentary material, the submission of any answers to written interrogatories, or the giving of any oral testimony if such material, answers, or testimony would be protected from disclosure under—

(A) the standards applicable to subpoenas or subpoenas duces tecum issued by a court of the United States to aid in a grand jury investigation; or

(B) the standards applicable to discovery requests under the Federal Rules of Civil Procedure, to the extent that the application of such standards to any such demand is appropriate and consistent with the provisions and purposes of this section.

(2) Effect on other orders, rules, and laws.—Any such demand which is an express demand for any product of discovery supersedes any inconsistent order, rule, or provision of law (other than this section) preventing or restraining disclosure of such product of discovery to any person. Disclosure of any product of discovery pursuant to any such express demand does not constitute a waiver of any right or privilege which the person making such disclosure may be entitled to invoke to resist discovery of trial preparation materials.

(c) Service; jurisdiction.—

(1) By whom served.—Any civil investigative demand issued under subsection (a) may be served by a false claims law investigator, or by a United States marshal or a deputy marshal, at any place within the territorial jurisdiction of any court of the United States.

(2) Service in foreign countries.—Any such demand or any petition filed under subsection (j) may be served upon any person who is not found within the territorial jurisdiction of any court of the United States in such manner as the Federal Rules of Civil Procedure prescribe for service in a foreign country. To the extent that the courts of the United States can assert jurisdiction over any such person consistent with due process, the United States District Court for the District of Columbia shall have the same jurisdiction to take any action respecting compliance with this section by any such person that such court would have if such person were personally within the jurisdiction of such court.

(d) Service upon legal entities and natural persons.—

(1) Legal entities.—Service of any civil investigative demand issued under subsection (a) or of any petition filed under subsection (j) may be made upon a partnership, corporation, association, or other legal entity by—

(A) delivering an executed copy of such demand or petition to any partner, executive officer, managing agent, or general agent of the partnership, corporation, association, or entity, or to any agent authorized by appointment or by law to receive service of process on behalf of such partnership, corporation, association, or entity;

(B) delivering an executed copy of such demand or petition to the principal office or place of business of the partnership, corporation, association, or entity; or

(C) depositing an executed copy of such demand or petition in the United States mails by registered or certified mail, with a return receipt requested, addressed to such partnership, corporation, association, or entity at its principal office or place of business.

(2) Natural persons.—Service of any such demand or petition may be made upon any natural person by—

(A) delivering an executed copy of such demand or petition to the person; or

(B) depositing an executed copy of such demand or petition in the United States mails by registered or certified mail, with a return receipt requested, addressed to the person at the person's residence or principal office or place of business.

(e) Proof of service.—A verified return by the individual serving any civil investigative demand issued under subsection (a) or any petition filed under subsection (j) setting forth the manner of such service shall be proof of such service. In the case of service by registered or certified mail, such return shall be accompanied by the return post office receipt of delivery of such demand.

(f) Documentary material.—

(1) Sworn certificates.—The production of documentary material in response to a civil investigative demand served under this section

shall be made under a sworn certificate, in such form as the demand designates, by—

(A) in the case of a natural person, the person to whom the demand is directed, or

(B) in the case of a person other than a natural person, a person having knowledge of the facts and circumstances relating to such production and authorized to act on behalf of such person.

The certificate shall state that all of the documentary material required by the demand and in the possession, custody, or control of the person to whom the demand is directed has been produced and made available to the false claims law investigator identified in the demand.

(2) Production of materials.—Any person upon whom any civil investigative demand for the production of documentary material has been served under this section shall make such material available for inspection and copying to the false claims law investigator identified in such demand at the principal place of business of such person, or at such other place as the false claims law investigator and the person thereafter may agree and prescribe in writing, or as the court may direct under subsection (j)(1). Such material shall be made so available on the return date specified in such demand, or on such later date as the false claims law investigator may prescribe in writing. Such person may, upon written agreement between the person and the false claims law investigator, substitute copies for originals of all or any part of such material.

(g) Interrogatories.—Each interrogatory in a civil investigative demand served under this section shall be answered separately and fully in writing under oath and shall be submitted under a sworn certificate, in such form as the demand designates, by—

(1) in the case of a natural person, the person to whom the demand is directed, or

(2) in the case of a person other than a natural person, the person or persons responsible for answering each interrogatory.

If any interrogatory is objected to, the reasons for the objection shall be stated in the certificate instead of an answer. The certificate shall state that all information required by the demand and in the possession, custody, control, or knowledge of the person to whom the demand is directed has been submitted. To the extent that any information is not furnished, the information shall be identified and reasons set forth with particularity regarding the reasons why the information was not furnished.

(h) Oral examinations.—

(1) Procedures.—The examination of any person pursuant to a civil investigative demand for oral testimony served under this section shall be taken before an officer authorized to administer oaths and affirmations by the laws of the United States or of the place where the examination is held. The officer before whom the testimony is to be taken shall put the witness on oath or affirmation and shall, personally or by someone acting under the direction of the officer and in the officer's presence, record the testimony of the witness. The testimony shall be taken stenographically and shall be transcribed. When the testimony is fully transcribed, the officer before whom the testimony is taken shall promptly transmit a copy of the transcript of the testimony to the custodian. This subsection shall not preclude the taking of testimony by any means authorized by, and in a manner consistent with, the Federal Rules of Civil Procedure.

(2) Persons present.—The false claims law investigator conducting the examination shall exclude from the place where the examination is held all persons except the person giving the testimony, the attorney for and any other representative of the person giving the testimony, the attorney for the Government, any person who may be agreed upon by the attorney for the Government and the person giving the testimony, the officer before whom the testimony is to be taken, and any stenographer taking such testimony.

(3) Where testimony taken.—The oral testimony of any person taken pursuant to a civil investigative demand served under this section shall be taken in the judicial district of the United States within which such person resides, is found, or transacts business, or in such other place as may be agreed upon by the false claims law investigator conducting the examination and such person.

(4) Transcript of testimony.—When the testimony is fully transcribed, the false claims law investigator or the officer before whom the testimony is taken shall afford the witness, who may be accompanied by counsel, a reasonable opportunity to examine and read the transcript, unless such examination and reading are waived by the witness. Any changes in form or substance which the witness desires to make shall be entered and identified upon the transcript by the officer or the false claims law investigator, with a statement of the reasons given by the witness for making such changes. The transcript shall then be signed by the witness, unless the witness in writing waives the signing, is ill, cannot be found, or refuses to sign. If the transcript is not signed by the witness within 30 days after being afforded a reasonable opportunity to examine it, the officer or the false claims law investigator shall sign it and state on the record the fact of the waiver, illness, absence of the witness, or the refusal to sign, together with the reasons, if any, given therefor.

(5) Certification and delivery to custodian.—The officer before whom the testimony is taken shall certify on the transcript that the witness was sworn by the officer and that the transcript is a true record of the testimony given by the witness, and the officer or false claims law investigator shall promptly deliver the transcript, or send the transcript by registered or certified mail, to the custodian.

(6) Furnishing or inspection of transcript by witness.—Upon payment of reasonable charges therefor, the false claims law investigator shall furnish a copy of the transcript to the witness only, except that the Attorney General, the Deputy Attorney General, or an Assistant Attorney General may, for good cause, limit such witness to inspection of the official transcript of the witness' testimony.

(7) Conduct of oral testimony.—

(A) Any person compelled to appear for oral testimony under a civil investigative demand issued under subsection (a) may be accompanied, represented, and advised by counsel. Counsel may advise such person, in confidence, with respect to any question asked of such person. Such person or counsel may object on the record to any question, in whole or in part, and shall briefly state for the record the reason for the objection. An objection may be made, received, and entered upon the record when it is claimed that such person is entitled to refuse to answer the question on the grounds of any constitutional or other legal right or privilege, including the privilege against self-incrimination. Such person may not otherwise object to or refuse to answer any question, and may not directly or through counsel otherwise interrupt the oral examination. If such person refuses to answer any question, a petition may be filed in the district court of the United States under subsection (j)(1) for an order compelling such person to answer such question.

(B) If such person refuses to answer any question on the grounds of the privilege against self-incrimination, the testimony of such person may be compelled in accordance with the provisions of part V of title 18.

(8) Witness fees and allowances.—Any person appearing for oral testimony under a civil investigative demand issued under subsection (a) shall be entitled to the same fees and allowances which are paid to witnesses in the district courts of the United States.

(*i*) Custodians of documents, answers, and transcripts.—

(1) Designation.—The Attorney General shall designate a false claims law investigator to serve as custodian of documentary material, answers to interrogatories, and transcripts of oral testimony received under this section, and shall designate such additional false claims law investigators as the Attorney General determines from time to time to be necessary to serve as deputies to the custodian.

(2) Responsibility for materials; disclosure.—

(A) A false claims law investigator who receives any documentary material, answers to interrogatories, or transcripts of oral testimony under this section shall transmit them to the custodian. The custodian shall take physical possession of such material, answers,

or transcripts and shall be responsible for the use made of them and for the return of documentary material under paragraph (4).

(B) The custodian may cause the preparation of such copies of such documentary material, answers to interrogatories, or transcripts of oral testimony as may be required for official use by any false claims law investigator, or other officer or employee of the Department of Justice. Such material, answers, and transcripts may be used by any such authorized false claims law investigator or other officer or employee in connection with the taking of oral testimony under this section.

(C) Except as otherwise provided in this subsection, no documentary material, answers to interrogatories, or transcripts of oral testimony, or copies thereof, while in the possession of the custodian, shall be available for examination by any individual other than a false claims law investigator or other officer or employee of the Department of Justice authorized under subparagraph (B). The prohibition in the preceding sentence on the availability of material, answers, or transcripts shall not apply if consent is given by the person who produced such material, answers, or transcripts, or, in the case of any product of discovery produced pursuant to an express demand for such material, consent is given by the person from whom the discovery was obtained. Nothing in this subparagraph is intended to prevent disclosure to the Congress, including any committee or subcommittee of the Congress, or to any other agency of the United States for use by such agency in furtherance of its statutory responsibilities.

(D) While in the possession of the custodian and under such reasonable terms and conditions as the Attorney General shall prescribe—

(i) documentary material and answers to interrogatories shall be available for examination by the person who produced such material or answers, or by a representative of that person authorized by that person to examine such material and answers; and

(ii) transcripts of oral testimony shall be available for examination by the person who produced such testimony, or by a representative of that person authorized by that person to examine such transcripts.

(3) Use of material, answers, or transcripts in other proceedings.—Whenever any attorney of the Department of Justice has been designated to appear before any court, grand jury, or Federal agency in any case or proceeding, the custodian of any documentary material, answers to interrogatories, or transcripts of oral testimony received under this section may deliver to such attorney such material, answers, or transcripts for official use in connection with any such case or proceeding as such attorney determines to be required. Upon the completion of any such case or proceeding, such attorney shall return to the custodian any such material, answers, or transcripts so delivered which have not passed into the control of such court, grand jury, or agency through introduction into the record of such case or proceeding.

(4) Conditions for return of material.—If any documentary material has been produced by any person in the course of any false claims law investigation pursuant to a civil investigative demand under this section, and—

(A) any case or proceeding before the court or grand jury arising out of such investigation, or any proceeding before any Federal agency involving such material, has been completed, or

(B) no case or proceeding in which such material may be used has been commenced within a reasonable time after completion of the examination and analysis of all documentary material and other information assembled in the course of such investigation,

the custodian shall, upon written request of the person who produced such material, return to such person any such material (other than copies furnished to the false claims law investigator under subsection (f)(2) or made for the Department of Justice under paragraph (2)(B)) which has not passed into the control of any court, grand jury, or agency through introduction into the record of such case or proceeding.

(5) Appointment of successor custodians.—In the event of the death, disability, or separation from service in the Department of Justice of the custodian of any documentary material, answers to interrogatories, or transcripts of oral testimony produced pursuant to a civil investigative demand under this section, or in the event of the official relief of such custodian from responsibility for the custody and control of such material, answers, or transcripts, the Attorney General shall promptly—

    (A) designate another false claims law investigator to serve as custodian of such material, answers, or transcripts, and

    (B) transmit in writing to the person who produced such material, answers, or testimony notice of the identity and address of the successor so designated.

Any person who is designated to be a successor under this paragraph shall have, with regard to such material, answers, or transcripts, the same duties and responsibilities as were imposed by this section upon that person's predecessor in office, except that the successor shall not be held responsible for any default or dereliction which occurred before that designation.

(j) Judicial proceedings.—

    (1) Petition for enforcement.—Whenever any person fails to comply with any civil investigative demand issued under subsection (a), or whenever satisfactory copying or reproduction of any material requested in such demand cannot be done and such person refuses to surrender such material, the Attorney General may file, in the district court of the United States for any judicial district in which such person resides, is found, or transacts business, and serve upon such person a petition for an order of such court for the enforcement of the civil investigative demand.

    (2) Petition to modify or set aside demand.—

      (A) Any person who has received a civil investigative demand issued under subsection (a) may file, in the district court of the United States for the judicial district within which such person resides, is found, or transacts business, and serve upon the false claims law investigator identified in such demand a petition for an order of the court to modify or set aside such demand. In the case of a petition addressed to an express demand for any product of discovery, a petition to modify or set aside such demand may be brought only in the district court of the United States for the judicial district in which the proceeding in which such discovery was obtained is or was last pending. Any petition under this subparagraph must be filed—

        (i) within 20 days after the date of service of the civil investigative demand, or at any time before the return date specified in the demand, whichever date is earlier, or

        (ii) within such longer period as may be prescribed in writing by any false claims law investigator identified in the demand.

      (B) The petition shall specify each ground upon which the petitioner relies in seeking relief under subparagraph (A), and may be based upon any failure of the demand to comply with the provisions of this section or upon any constitutional or other legal right or privilege of such person. During the pendency of the petition in the court, the court may stay, as it deems proper, the running of the time allowed for compliance with the demand, in whole or in part, except that the person filing the petition shall comply with any portions of the demand not sought to be modified or set aside.

    (3) Petition to modify or set aside demand for product of discovery.—

      (A) In the case of any civil investigative demand issued under subsection (a) which is an express demand for any product of discovery, the person from whom such discovery was obtained may file, in the district court of the United States for the judicial district in which the proceeding in which such discovery was obtained is or was last pending, and serve upon any false claims law investigator identified in the demand and upon the recipient of the demand, a petition for an order of such court to modify or set aside those

portions of the demand requiring production of any such product of discovery. Any petition under this subparagraph must be filed—

        (i) within 20 days after the date of service of the civil investigative demand, or at any time before the return date specified in the demand, whichever date is earlier, or

        (ii) within such longer period as may be prescribed in writing by any false claims law investigator identified in the demand.

      (B) The petition shall specify each ground upon which the petitioner relies in seeking relief under subparagraph (A), and may be based upon any failure of the portions of the demand from which relief is sought to comply with the provisions of this section, or upon any constitutional or other legal right or privilege of the petitioner. During the pendency of the petition, the court may stay, as it deems proper, compliance with the demand and the running of the time allowed for compliance with the demand.

    (4) Petition to require performance by custodian of duties.—At any time during which any custodian is in custody or control of any documentary material or answers to interrogatories produced, or transcripts of oral testimony given, by any person in compliance with any civil investigative demand issued under subsection (a), such person, and in the case of an express demand for any product of discovery, the person from whom such discovery was obtained, may file, in the district court of the United States for the judicial district within which the office of such custodian is situated, and serve upon such custodian, a petition for an order of such court to require the performance by the custodian of any duty imposed upon the custodian by this section.

    (5) Jurisdiction.—Whenever any petition is filed in any district court of the United States under this subsection, such court shall have jurisdiction to hear and determine the matter so presented, and to enter such order or orders as may be required to carry out the provisions of this section. Any final order so entered shall be subject to appeal under section 1291 of title 28. Any disobedience of any final order entered under this section by any court shall be punished as a contempt of the court.

    (6) Applicability of federal rules of civil procedure.—The Federal Rules of Civil Procedure shall apply to any petition under this subsection, to the extent that such rules are not inconsistent with the provisions of this section.

(k) Disclosure exemption.—Any documentary material, answers to written interrogatories, or oral testimony provided under any civil investigative demand issued under subsection (a) shall be exempt from disclosure under section 552 of title 5.

(*l*) Definitions.—For purposes of this section—

    (1) the term "false claims law" means—

      (A) this section and sections 3729 through 3732; and

      (B) any Act of Congress enacted after the date of the enactment of this section which prohibits, or makes available to the United States in any court of the United States any civil remedy with respect to, any false claim against, bribery of, or corruption of any officer or employee of the United States;

    (2) the term "false claims law investigation" means any inquiry conducted by any false claims law investigator for the purpose of ascertaining whether any person is or has been engaged in any violation of a false claims law;

    (3) the term "false claims law investigator" means any attorney or investigator employed by the Department of Justice who is charged with the duty of enforcing or carrying into effect any false claims law, or any officer or employee of the United States acting under the direction and supervision of such attorney or investigator in connection with a false claims law investigation;

    (4) the term "person" means any natural person, partnership, corporation, association, or other legal entity, including any State or political subdivision of a State;

    (5) the term "documentary material" includes the original or any copy of any book, record, report, memorandum, paper, communication, tabulation, chart, or other document, or data compilations stored in or accessible through computer or other information retrieval systems, together with instructions and all other materials necessary to use or interpret such data compilations, and any product of discovery;

(6) the term "custodian" means the custodian, or any deputy custodian, designated by the Attorney General under subsection (i)(1);

(7) the term "product of discovery" includes—

(A) the original or duplicate of any deposition, interrogatory, document, thing, result of the inspection of land or other property, examination, or admission, which is obtained by any method of discovery in any judicial or administrative proceeding of an adversarial nature;

(B) any digest, analysis, selection, compilation, or derivation of any item listed in subparagraph (A); and

(C) any index or other manner of access to any item listed in subparagraph (A); and

(8) the term "official use" means any use that is consistent with the law, and the regulations and policies of the Department of Justice, including use in connection with internal Department of Justice memoranda and reports; communications between the Department of Justice and a Federal, State, or local government agency, or a contractor of a Federal, State, or local government agency, undertaken in furtherance of a Department of Justice investigation or prosecution of a case; interviews of any *qui tam* relator or other witness; oral examinations; depositions; preparation for and response to civil discovery requests; introduction into the record of a case or proceeding; applications, motions, memoranda and briefs submitted to a court or other tribunal; and communications with Government investigators, auditors, consultants and experts, the counsel of other parties, arbitrators and mediators, concerning an investigation, case or proceeding.

[*Added by* Pub. L. No. 99-562, § 6(a), 100 Stat. 3159 (Oct. 27, 1986), *and amended by* Pub. L. No. 111-21, § 4(c), 123 Stat. 1623 (May 20, 2009)]

Appendix H State False Claims Act Statutes Summarized

CALIFORNIA

Cal. Gov't Code §§ 12650 to 12656 (West) (False Claims Act)

Claims covered by the statute: Include knowingly false statements regarding a claim for payment presented to a state or political subdivision or the state's grantee or contractor, conspiracy to commit such a violation, failure to return public property or money, and inadvertently submitting a false claim and failing to disclose the false claim after discovery. § 12651(a).

Exemptions: Requests or demands for money, property, or services that state or political subdivision has paid to an individual as compensation for employment with state or political subdivision or as an income subsidy with no restrictions on the individual's use of the money, property, or services. § 12650(b)(2). Statute does not apply to any controversy involving an amount of less than $500 in value. Also does not apply to claims, records, or statements made regarding workers' compensation claims; claims, records, or statements made under Revenue and Taxation Code; or claims, records, or statements for a person's assets that have been transferred to the Commissioner of Insurance pursuant to § 1011 of the Insurance Code. § 12651. No action by qui tam plaintiff that is based upon allegations or transactions that are the subject of a civil suit or an administrative civil money penalty proceeding in which the state or political subdivision is already a party. § 12652(d)(2).

Who may initiate action as a private plaintiff?: Qui tam plaintiff must be an "original source" of the information if the fraudulent allegations or transactions have already been publicly disclosed. § 12652(d)(3)(B).

Procedure for initiating action and state intervention: Qui tam plaintiff files complaint, which may remain under seal for up to 60 days. § 12652(c)(2). Within 60 days after receiving a complaint alleging violations that involve state funds but not political subdivision funds, attorney general may elect to intervene. § 12652(c)(2). Before the 60-day period expires, attorney general shall notify the court that it intends to intervene or decline, in which case the plaintiff has the right to conduct the action. § 12652(c)(6). Within 15 days after receiving a complaint alleging violations that *exclusively* involve political subdivision funds, attorney general must forward copies of the complaint and written disclosure of material evidence and information to the appropriate prosecuting authority for disposition, and must notify the qui tam plaintiff of the transfer. Within 45 days after attorney general forwards the complaint and written disclosure, the prosecuting authority may intervene. § 12652(c)(7)(A), (B). Prior to expiration of 45-day period, the prosecuting authority must either intervene, or decline, in which case the qui tam plaintiff has the right to proceed. § 12652(c)(7)(D).

Elements of proof: The state, political subdivision, or qui tam plaintiff must prove all essential elements of the cause of action, including damages, by a preponderance of the evidence. § 12654(c). Knowing violation does not require proof of specific intent to defraud. § 12650(b)(3).

Remedies and attorney fees for state: Treble damages and civil penalty of between $5,500 and $11,000 per violation, plus costs of action. § 12651(b). However, court may assess between two and three times the amount of damages and no civil penalty if violator provided officials with all known information within 30 days after date first obtained and fully cooperated with the investigation, and when violator provided the information no criminal prosecution, civil action, or administrative action had commenced, and violator did not have actual knowledge of the investigation's existence. § 12651(b). If attorney general's office or office of the prosecuting authority of the political subdivision conducts the action, it shall receive a fixed 33% of the proceeds of the action or settlement of the claim. When both attorney general and a prosecuting authority are involved in a qui tam action, the court may award the prosecuting authority a portion of the attorney general's fixed 33% of the recovery, taking into account the

prosecuting authority's contribution to investigating and conducting the action. § 12652(g)(2).

Awards to plaintiffs bringing action: If state or political subdivision intervenes: between 15 and 33 % of the proceeds of the action or settlement, depending upon the extent to which the qui tam plaintiff substantially contributed to the prosecution of the action. § 12652(g)(2). If state or political subdivision does not intervene: between 25 and 50% of the proceeds. § 12652(g)(3). If action is brought by present or former employee of the state or political subdivision: no minimum guaranteed recovery, but court may award deemed appropriate but in no case more than 33 % of the proceeds if the state or political subdivision goes forth with the action or 50% if it declines. § 12652(g)(4). Whether or not the state or political subdivision intervenes, if qui tam plaintiff planned and initiated the violation, then court may reduce share, but shall not award the plaintiff more than 33% of the proceeds if the state or political subdivision goes forth with the action or 50% if it declines. § 12652(g)(5). If state, political subdivision, or qui tam plaintiff prevails in or settles any action, the qui tam plaintiff shall receive reasonable expenses necessarily incurred, plus reasonable attorney fees and costs. § 12652(g)(8).

Anti-retaliation provision: Employee, contractor or agent is entitled to all make-whole relief if discharged, demoted, suspended, threatened, harassed, or in any other manner discriminated against in the terms and conditions of employment because of lawful acts done in furtherance of an action under the statute or other efforts to stop a violation. Remedies include reinstatement with appropriate seniority, twice the amount of back pay, interest on back pay, and special damages, plus reasonable attorney fees and costs. Punitive damages available where appropriate. § 12653.

Statute of limitations and other defenses: Six years after date violation is committed or three years after date when material facts are or reasonably should have been known by the attorney general or prosecuting authority, but in no event more than ten years after the date the violation is committed, whichever occurs last. § 12654(a).

COLORADO

Colo. Rev. Stat. §§ 25.5-4-303.5 to 25.5-4-310 (Medicaid False Claims Act)

Claims covered by the statute: Include knowingly false statements regarding a claim for payment under the "Colorado Medical Assistance Act" presented to a state or state's grantee or contractor, failure to return public property or money, knowing purchase of public property from state officer or employee in connection with the "Colorado Medical Assistance Act" who lawfully may not sell the property, and conspiracy to commit a violation. § 25.5-4-305(1)(a)-(g).

Exemptions: Request or demand for money or property that the state has paid to an individual as compensation for employment by the state or as an income subsidy with no restriction on that individual's use of the money or property. § 25.5-4-304(1)(b). No action brought under the Act against a member of the general assembly, member of the state judiciary, or elected official in the state's executive branch if action is based upon evidence or information known to the state when the action was brought. No action by relator that is based upon allegations or transactions that are the subject of a civil suit or an administrative civil money penalty proceeding in which the state is already a party. § 25.5-4-306(5).

Who may initiate action as a private plaintiff?: Relator must be an "original source" of the information if allegations or transactions have already been publicly disclosed. § 25.5-4-306(5)(c).

Procedure for initiating action and state intervention: Relator files complaint in camera, which remains under seal for at least 60 days. § 25.5-4-306(2)(b). Prior to expiration of 60-day period, the state must intervene or decline, in which case relator has the right to conduct the action.

§ 25.5-4-306(2)(d). State may intervene at a later date upon a showing of good cause. § 25.5-4-306(3)(c).

Elements of proof: State or relator must prove all essential elements of cause of action, including damages, by a preponderance of the evidence. § 25.5-4-307(3). Knowing violation does not require proof of specific intent to defraud. § 25.5-4-304(3)(b).

Remedies and attorney fees for state: Treble damages and civil penalty of between $5,500 and $11,000. § 25.5-4-305(1). However, court may assess not less than twice the amount of damages if violator provided state officials responsible for investigating violations with all known information within 30 days after date first obtained and fully cooperated with investigation, and when violator provided information a criminal prosecution, civil action, or administrative action had not commenced and violator did not have actual knowledge of the investigation's existence§ 25.5-4-305(2). Violator is also liable to the state for the costs of the action. § 25.5-4-305(3).

Awards to plaintiffs bringing action: If state intervenes: between 15 and 25 % of the proceeds of the action or settlement of the claim, depending upon the extent to which the relator substantially contributed to the prosecution of the action. If such an action is based primarily on disclosures of information other than that provided by the relator, relating to allegations or transactions in a criminal, civil, or administrative hearing, in a legislative, administrative, or state auditor's report, hearing, audit, or investigation, or from the news media: an award deemed appropriate, but in no case more than 10% of the proceeds. Relator shall also receive an amount for reasonable expenses necessarily incurred, plus reasonable attorney fees and costs. If state does not intervene: an amount that the court decides is reasonable for collecting the civil penalty and damages; between 25 and 30% of the proceeds of the action or settlement, plus reasonable expenses necessarily incurred, reasonable attorney fees and costs. § 25.5-4-306(4). Whether or not state intervenes, court may reduce award if relator planned and initiated the fraud, or if the action is largely based on disclosures in the media or public hearings. § 25.5-4-306(4)(c).

Anti-retaliation provision: Employee, contractor or agent is entitled to all make-whole relief if discharged, demoted, suspended, threatened, harassed, or in any other manner discriminated against in the terms and conditions of employment by the defendant or any other person because of lawful acts done in furtherance of an action or an effort to stop a violation. Relief includes reinstatement with appropriate seniority, twice the amount of back pay, interest on back pay, and special damages, including reasonable attorney fees and costs. Private action authorized. § 25.5-4-306(7).

Statute of limitations and other defenses: Six years after date violation is committed or three years after date when material facts are or reasonably should have been known by the state official with responsibility to act, but in no event more than ten years after date violation is committed. § 25.5-4-307(1).

CONNECTICUT

Conn. Gen. Stat. §§ 4-274 to 4-289 (False Claims and Other Prohibited Acts Under State-Administered Health or Human Services Programs)

Claims covered by the statute: Include knowingly false or fraudulent claim for payment or approval under state-administered health or human services program, conspiracy to commit a violation, failure to return public property or money, knowing purchase of public property from a state officer or employee related to a state-administered health or human services program who lawfully may not sell the property, and knowing concealment or avoidance of obligation to pay or transmit money or property to the state under a state-administered health or human services program. § 4-275(a).

Exemptions: Request or demand for money or property that the state has paid to an individual as compensation for state employment or as an income subsidy with no restrictions on that individual's use of the money or property. § 4-274(2). No action brought by qui tam plaintiff against a member of the General Assembly or judiciary, an elected officer, or department head of the state if the action is based on evidence or information known to the state when the action was brought, or that is based upon

allegations or transactions that are the subject of a civil suit or an administrative civil penalty proceeding in which the state is already a party. § 4-282(a).

Who can initiate action as private plaintiff?: Individual bringing action must be an "original source" of the information if the fraudulent allegations or transactions have already been publicly disclosed. § 4-282.

Procedure for initiating action and state intervention: Civil action in the superior court for the judicial district of Hartford against any violator shall be brought in the name of the state. Complaint shall be filed in camera and remain under seal for at least 60 days. Prior to expiration of 60-day period, attorney general must either intervene or decline, in which case the individual has the right to proceed. If individual brings the action, no person other than the state may intervene or bring a related action based upon the same facts. § 4-277.

Elements of proof: Attorney general or person initiating the action must prove all essential elements of the cause of action, including damages, by a preponderance of the evidence. § 4-286. Knowing violation does not require proof of intent to defraud. § 4-274. Defendant may not deny essential elements of the offense that involves the same transaction as in a criminal proceeding where there was a verdict after trial or upon a plea of guilty or nolo contendere. § 4-287.

Remedies and attorney fees for state: Treble damages and civil penalty of between $5,500 and $11,000, plus costs of investigation and prosecution. § 4-275(b). However, court may assess not less than twice the amount of damages sustained if violator provided state officials responsible for investigating false claims violations with all known information not later than 30 days after date first obtained and fully cooperated with investigation, and when information was provided no criminal prosecution, civil action or administrative action had commenced and violator did not have actual knowledge of investigation's existence. § 4-275(c).

Awards to plaintiffs bringing action: If state intervenes: between 15% and 25% of proceeds of action or settlement, based upon the extent to which individual substantially contributed to the prosecution of the action, plus amount for reasonable expenses necessarily incurred, reasonable attorney fees and costs. § 4-278(e). If such action is based primarily on disclosures of information that was not provided by the individual bringing the action relating to allegations or transactions in a criminal, civil or administrative hearing, in a report, hearing, audit or investigation conducted by the General Assembly, a committee of the General Assembly, the Auditors of Public Accounts, a state agency or quasi-public agency, or from the news media: an amount deemed appropriate, but not more than 10% of the proceeds. § 4-278(f). If state does not intervene: between 25 and 30% of the proceeds of the action or settlement, plus reasonable expenses necessarily incurred, reasonable attorney fees and costs. § 4-279(b). Whether or not state intervenes, court may reduce award if complaint is based primarily upon publicly disclosed information or if individual planned and initiated the violation. § 4-281.

Anti-retaliation provision: Employee, contractor or agent is entitled to all make-whole relief if discharged, demoted, suspended, threatened, harassed, or in any other manner discriminated against in the terms and conditions of employment because of lawful acts done in furtherance of an action under the Act or other efforts to stop a violation. Relief includes reinstatement with appropriate seniority, twice the amount of back pay, interest on back pay, and special damages, including reasonable attorney fees and costs. Private action authorized. § 4-284.

Statute of limitations and other defenses: Six years after date violation is committed, or three years after date when material facts are or reasonably should have been known by the state official with responsibility to act in the circumstances, but in no event more than ten years after date violation is committed, whichever occurs last. § 4-285.

DELAWARE

Del. Code Ann. tit. 6, §§ 1201 to 1211 (False Claims and Reporting Act)

Claims covered by the statute: Include knowingly false statements regarding a claim for payment presented to the state or state's grantee or contractor, conspiracy to commit such a violation, failure to return public property or money, and knowing concealment or avoidance of an obligation to pay or transmit property to the state. § 1201(a).

Exemptions: Request or demand for money or property that the government has paid to an individual as compensation for employment with the government or as an income subsidy with no restrictions on that individual's use of the money or property. § 1202(1). Actions based upon allegations or transactions that are the subject of a civil suit or an administrative proceeding in which the government is already a party. § 1206(a).

Who can initiate action as private plaintiff?: Any person or labor organization as defined by tit. 19, § 1107A(d). § 1203(b)(1). Party bringing action must be an "original source" of the information if fraudulent allegations or transactions have already been publicly disclosed. § 1206(b).

Procedure for initiating action and state intervention: Action shall be brought in the name of the government. § 1203(b)(1). Complaint must be served on the Department of Justice, filed in camera, and must remain under seal for at least 60 days. Within 60-day period, or within 20 days of being notified by the court that the seal has expired, Department of Justice shall either intervene or decline, in which case the private party bringing the action has the right to proceed. § 1203(b)(4). When a private party brings an action, no party other than the Department of Justice may intervene or bring a related action based upon the same facts. § 1203(b)(5). Department of Justice may intervene at a later date upon a showing of good cause. § 1204(d).

Elements of proof: Department of Justice or private party shall be required to prove all essential elements of the cause of action, including damages, by a preponderance of the evidence. § 1209(b). Knowing violation does not require specific proof of intent to defraud. § 1202(3).

Remedies and attorney fees for state: Treble damages and civil penalty of between $5,500 and $11,000 for each violation. However, court may assess not less than twice the amount of damages sustained if violator provided officials with all known information within 30 days after date first obtained and fully cooperated with investigation, and when information was provided no criminal prosecution, civil action, investigation or administrative action had commenced and violator did not have actual knowledge of the investigation's existence. reasonable attorney fees and costs authorized. § 1201(b).

Awards to plaintiffs bringing action: If Department of Justice intervenes: between 15 and 25% of proceeds of action or settlement, based upon extent to which party substantially contributed to the prosecution of the action. If such action is based primarily on disclosures of information that was not provided by the individual bringing the action relating to allegations or transactions in a criminal, civil or administrative hearing, in a report, hearing, audit or investigation conducted by the General Assembly, a committee of the General Assembly, the Auditors of Public Accounts, a state agency or a quasi-public agency, or from the news media: an amount deemed appropriate, but in no case more than 10% of the proceeds. Shall also receive an amount for reasonable expenses necessarily incurred, plus reasonable attorney fees and costs. § 1205(a). If Department of Justice does not intervene: between 25 and 30% of proceeds, plus reasonable expenses necessarily incurred, attorney fees and costs. § 1205(b). Whether or not Department of Justice intervenes, court may reduce award if individual planned and initiated the violation. § 1205(c).

Anti-retaliation provision: Employee, contractor or agent entitled to all make-whole relief if discharged, demoted, suspended, threatened, harassed, or in any other manner discriminated against in the terms and conditions of employment because of lawful acts done in furtherance of an action under the Act or to stop a violation. Relief includes reinstatement with appropriate seniority, twice the amount of back pay, interest on the back pay, and special damages, including reasonable attorney fees and costs. § 1208.

Statute of limitations and other defenses: Six years after date violation is committed or three years after date when material facts are or reasonably should have been known by the official with responsibility to act, but in no event more than ten years after date violation is committed, whichever occurs last. § 1209(a).

DISTRICT OF COLUMBIA

D.C. Code §§ 2-381.01 to 2-381.10 (Procurement Related Claims)

Claims covered by the statute: Include knowingly false statements regarding a claim for payment presented to the District or District's grantee or contractor, failure to return public property or money, knowing purchase of public property from a District officer or employee who lawfully may not sell the property, conspiracy to commit a violation, inadvertently submitting a false claim and failing to disclose the false claim after discovery, and knowing concealment or knowing and improper avoidance of an obligation to pay or transmit property to the District. § 2-381.02(a).

Exemptions: Request or demand for money or property that the District has paid to an individual as compensation for District employment or as an income subsidy with no restrictions on that individual's use of the money or property. § 2-381.01(1)(B). No claims, records, or statements made pursuant to those portions of title 47 that refer or relate to taxation. § 2-381.02(d).

Who can initiate action as private plaintiff?: Qui tam plaintiff must be an "original source" of the information if the fraudulent allegations or transactions have already been publicly disclosed. § 2-381.03(c)(2).

Procedure for initiating action and state intervention: Action shall be brought in the name of the District. § 2-381.03(b)(1). Complaint must be filed in camera and may remain under seal for up to 180 days. Prior to expiration of 180-day period, the attorney general for the District of Columbia must either intervene or decline, in which case the qui tam plaintiff has the right to proceed. When a qui tam plaintiff brings an action, no person other than the District may intervene or bring a related action based upon the same facts. § 2-381.03(b). District may intervene at a later date upon a showing of good cause. § 2-381.03(e)(2).

Elements of proof: District or qui tam plaintiff is required to prove all essential elements of the cause of action, including damages, by a preponderance of the evidence. § 2-381.05(c). Knowing violation does not require specific proof of intent to defraud. § 2-381.01(7)(B). Defendant may not deny essential elements of the offense that involves the same transaction as in a criminal proceeding where there was a verdict after trial or upon a plea of guilty or nolo contendere. § 2-381.05(d).

Remedies and attorney fees for state: Treble damages, a civil penalty of between $5,500 and $11,000 for each false or fraudulent claim, and reasonable attorney fees and costs. § 2-381.02(a). However, court may assess not less than twice the amount of damages sustained if violator provided District officials with all known information within 30 days after date first obtained and fully cooperated with investigation, and when violator furnished District with information no criminal prosecution, civil action, investigation or administrative action had commenced, and violator did not have actual knowledge of the investigation's existence. § 2-381.02(b). Person who knowingly makes or presents false, fictitious, or fraudulent claim upon or against the District of Columbia, or any department or agency, shall be imprisoned not more than one year and assessed a fine of not more than $100,000 for each violation. § 2-381.09.

Awards to plaintiffs bringing action: If District intervenes: between 15 and 25% of proceeds of action or settlement, depending upon the extent to which the qui tam plaintiff substantially contributed to the prosecution of the action. § 2-381.03(f)(1)(A). If such action is based primarily on disclosures of information that was not provided by the individual bringing the action relating to allegations or transactions in a criminal, civil, or administrative hearing, in a report, hearing, audit, or investigation conducted by a District agency, or from the news media: an amount deemed appropriate, but in no case more than 10% of proceeds. § 2-381.03(f)(1)(B). Reasonable expenses necessarily incurred, reasonable attorney fees and costs authorized. § 2-381.03(f)(1)(C). If District does not intervene: between 25 and 30% of proceeds of action or settlement, plus reasonable expenses necessarily incurred, reasonable attorney fees and costs. § 2-381.03(f)(2). Whether or not District intervenes, court may reduce award if qui tam plaintiff planned and initiated the violation. § 2-381.03(4)(A).

Anti-retaliation provision: Employee, contractor or agent is entitled to all make-whole relief if discharged, demoted, suspended, threatened, harassed, or in any other manner discriminated against in the terms and conditions of employment because of lawful acts done in furtherance of an action under the Act or other efforts to stop a violation. Relief includes reinstatement with appropriate seniority, twice the amount of back pay, interest on back pay, and special damages, including reasonable attorney fees and costs. § 2-381.04.

Statute of limitations and other defenses: Six years after date violation is committed or three years after date when material facts are or reasonably should have been known by the District official charged with the responsibility to act, but in no event more than ten years after date violation is committed, whichever occurs last. § 2-381.05(a).

FLORIDA

Fla. Stat. §§ 68.081 to 68.092 (False Claims Act)

Claims covered by the statute: Include knowingly false statements regarding a claim for payment presented to the state or state's grantee or contractor, failure to return public property or money, knowing purchase of public property from a state officer or employee who lawfully may not sell the property, conspiracy to commit a violation, and knowing concealment or knowing and improper avoidance of an obligation to pay or transmit property to the state. § 68.082(2).

Exemptions: No action against a member of the legislature or judiciary or a senior executive branch official if action is based on evidence or information known to the state government when the action was brought. § 68.087(1). No action brought by qui tam plaintiff based upon allegations or transactions that are the subject of a civil action or an administrative proceeding in which the state is already a party. § 68.087(2). No action brought under the Act against any county or municipality. § 68.087(6).

Who can initiate action as private plaintiff?: Qui tam plaintiff must be an "original source" of the information if fraudulent allegations or transactions have already been publicly disclosed. May not be acting as an attorney for the state government or an employee or former employee of the state government, and the action is based upon information obtained in the course or scope of government employment. May not have obtained the information from an employee or former employee of the state government who was not acting in the course or scope of government employment. § 68.087.

Procedure for initiating action and state intervention: Complaint shall be identified on its face as a qui tam action and filed in the circuit court of the Second Judicial Circuit, in and for Leon County. While complaint is under seal for 60-day period, action may be voluntarily dismissed by the qui tam plaintiff only if the Department of Financial Services gives written consent and reasons for consent. Prior to expiration of 60-day period, Department may intervene or decline, in which case the qui tam plaintiff has the right to proceed. No person other than the Department may intervene or bring a related action based upon the same facts. § 68.083. State may intervene at a later date upon a showing of good cause. § 68.084(3).

Elements of proof: Department or qui tam plaintiff is required to prove all essential elements of the cause of action, including damages, by a preponderance of the evidence. § 68.09(1). Defendant may not deny essential elements of the offense that involves the same transaction as in a criminal proceeding where there was a verdict after trial or upon a plea of guilty or nolo contendere. § 68.09(2). For knowing violation, no proof of specific intent to defraud is required. Innocent mistake is a defense to an action under the Act. § 68.082(c).

Remedies and attorney fees for state: Treble damages and civil penalty of between $5,500 and $11,000. However, court may assess not less than twice the amount of damages sustained if violator provided state officials responsible for investigating false claims violations with all known information not later than 30 days after date first obtained and fully cooperated with investigation, and when information was provided no criminal prosecution, civil action or administrative action had commenced and violator did not have actual knowledge of investigation's existence. § 68.082(2), (3). Reasonable attorney fees, expenses and costs are authorized. § 68.086(1). The state entity injured by the false or claim shall be awarded compensatory damages. If the action was based on a claim of funds from the state Medicaid program, 10% of any remaining proceeds shall be deposited

into the Operating Trust Fund to fund rewards for persons who report and provide information relating to Medicaid fraud pursuant to § 409.9203. § 68.085(3).

Awards to plaintiffs bringing action: If Department intervenes: between 15 and 25% of proceeds of action or settlement, depending upon the extent to which the qui tam plaintiff substantially contributed to the prosecution of the action. If such action is based primarily on disclosures of information that was not provided by the individual bringing the action relating to allegations or transactions in a criminal, civil, or administrative hearing, in a report, hearing, audit, or investigation, or from the news media: an amount deemed appropriate, but in no case more than 10% of proceeds. Shall also receive an amount for reasonable expenses necessarily incurred, plus reasonable attorney fees and costs. § 68.085(1). If Department does not intervene: between 25 and 30% of proceeds of action or settlement, plus reasonable expenses necessarily incurred, reasonable attorney fees and costs. § 68.085(2). Whether or not Department intervenes, court may reduce award if qui tam plaintiff planned and initiated the violation. § 68.085(4).

Anti-retaliation provision: Employee who is discharged, demoted, suspended, threatened, harassed, or in any other manner discriminated against in the terms and conditions of employment by his or her employer because of lawful acts done by or on behalf of the employee or others in furtherance of an action under the Act shall have a cause of action under § 112.3187 ("Whistle-blower's Act"). § 68.088.

Statute of limitations and other defenses: Six years after date violation is committed or three years after date when material facts are or reasonably should have been known by the official charged with the responsibility to act, but in no event more than ten years after date violation is committed, whichever occurs last. § 68.089. Innocent mistake is a defense to an action under the Act. § 68.082(1)(c).

GEORGIA

Ga. Code Ann. §§ 23-3-120 to 23-3-127 (False or Fraudulent Claims)

Claims covered by the statute: Include knowingly false statements regarding a claim for payment presented to the state or local government or government's grantee or contractor, failure to return public property or money, knowing purchase of public property from an officer or employee who lawfully may not sell the property, conspiracy to commit a violation, and knowing concealment or knowing and improper avoidance of an obligation to pay or transmit property to the state or local government. § 23-3-121(a).

Exemptions: Request or demand for money or property that the state or local government has paid to an individual as compensation for state or local government employment or as an income subsidy with no restrictions on that individual's use of the money or property. § 23-3-120(1). Act does not apply to claims, records, or statements made concerning taxes under the state's revenue laws. § 23-3-121(e). action brought by individual against a member of the General Assembly or member of the judiciary if the action is based upon evidence or information known to the state when the action was brought. No action brought by individual based upon allegations or transactions that are the subject of a civil or administrative proceeding to which the state is already a party. § 23-3-122(j).

Who can initiate action as private plaintiff?: Action may be brought by a private person upon written approval by the attorney general. § 23-3-122(b1). Plaintiff must be an "original source" of the information if the allegations or transactions have already been publicly disclosed. § 23-3-122(j)(3).

Procedure for initiating action and state intervention: Action must be brought in the name of the state or local government, as applicable. § 23-3-122(b1). Complaint must be filed in camera and under seal, and shall remain under seal for at least 60 days. § 23-3-122(b)(2). Prior to expiration of 60-day period, state or local government must either intervene or decline, in which case the person bringing the action has the right to proceed. § 23-3-122(b)(4). When a person brings action, no person other than the state or, if delegated the authority by the attorney general, the local government may intervene or bring a related civil action based upon the same facts. § 23-3-122(b)(5). State or local government may intervene at a later date upon a showing of good cause. § 23-3-122(e).

Elements of proof: Qui tam plaintiff is required to prove all essential elements of the cause of action, including damages, by a preponderance of the evidence. § 23-3-123(e). Knowing violation does not require specific proof of intent to defraud. § 23-2-120 (2). Qui tam plaintiff is not required to identify specific claims that result from an alleged course of misconduct or any specific records or statements used if the facts alleged in the complaint would provide a reasonable indication that one or more violations are likely to have occurred and if the allegations in the pleading provide adequate notice of the specific nature of the misconduct to permit the state or a local government to investigate effectively and defendants to defend fairly the allegations made. § 23-3-123(c). Defendant may not deny essential elements of the offense that involves the same transaction as in a criminal proceeding where there was a verdict after trial or upon a plea of guilty or nolo contendere. § 23-3-123(f).

Remedies and attorney fees for state: Treble damages and civil penalty of between $5,500 and $11,000. However, court may assess not less than twice the amount of damages sustained if violator provided state or local officials responsible for investigating false claims violations with all known information within 30 days after date first obtained and fully cooperated with investigation, and when information was provided no criminal prosecution, civil action or administrative action had commenced and violator did not have actual knowledge of investigation's existence. § 23-3-121(b). Costs, reasonable expenses, and reasonable attorney fees authorized. § 23-3-121(c).

Awards to plaintiffs bringing action: If state or local government intervenes: between 15 and 25% of proceeds of action or settlement, depending upon the extent to which the individual substantially contributed to the prosecution of the action. If such action is based primarily on disclosures of information that was not provided by the individual bringing the action relating to allegations or transactions in a criminal, civil, or administrative hearing, in a legislative, administrative, or State Accounting Office report, hearing, audit, or investigation, or from the news media: an amount deemed appropriate, but in no case more than 10% of proceeds. Plaintiff shall also receive an amount for reasonable expenses necessarily incurred, plus reasonable attorney fees and costs. If state or local government does not intervene: between 25 and 30% of proceeds of action or settlement, plus reasonable expenses necessarily incurred, reasonable attorney fees and costs. Whether or not government intervenes, court may reduce award if plaintiff planned and initiated the violation. § 23-3-122(h).

Anti-retaliation provision: Employee, contractor or agent entitled to all make-whole relief if discharged, demoted, suspended, threatened, harassed, or in any other manner discriminated against in the terms and conditions of employment because of lawful acts done in furtherance of an action under the Act or other efforts to stop a violation. Relief includes reinstatement with appropriate seniority, twice the amount of back pay, interest on back pay, and special damages, including reasonable attorney fees and costs. Private action authorized. § 23-3-122(l).

Statute of limitations and other defenses: Six years after date violation is committed or three years after date when material facts are or reasonably should have been known by the state or local government official with responsibility to act, but in no event more than ten years after date violation is committed, whichever occurs last. § 23-3-123(a).

Ga. Code Ann. §§ 168 to 168.6 (False Medicaid Claims Act)

Claims covered by the statute: Include knowingly false statements regarding a claim for payment presented to the state Medicaid program or program's grantee or contractor, failure to return public property or money, knowing purchase of public property from an officer or employee of the Medicaid program who lawfully may not sell the property, conspiracy to commit a violation, and knowing concealment or knowing and improper avoidance of an obligation to pay or transmit property to the Medicaid program. § 49-4-168.1(a).

Exemptions: No action based upon allegations or transactions that are the subject of a civil or administrative proceeding to which the state is already a party. No action with respect to any claim relating to assessment, payment, nonpayment, refund, or collection of taxes. § 49-4-168.2(j), (k).

Who can initiate action as private plaintiff?: Plaintiff must be an "original source" of the information if allegations or transactions have already been publicly disclosed. § 49-4-168.2(l).

Procedure for initiating action and state intervention: Private person may bring action in the name of the state. Complaint must be filed in camera and remain under seal for at least 60 days. Prior to expiration of 60-day period, attorney general must either intervene or decline, in which case the person bringing the action has the right to proceed. When a person brings action, no person other than the attorney general may intervene or bring a related civil action based upon the same facts. § 49-4-168.2.

Elements of proof: The state or person bringing the action is required to prove all essential elements, including damages, by a preponderance of the evidence. § 49-4-168.3(a). Knowing violation requires no proof of specific intent to defraud. § 49-4-168.

Remedies and attorney fees for state: Treble damages and civil penalty of between $5,500 and $11,000. However, court may assess not less than twice the amount of damages sustained if violator provided Medicaid program officials responsible for investigating false claims violations with all known information within 30 days after date first obtained and fully cooperated with investigation, and when information was provided no criminal prosecution, civil action, investigation or administrative action had commenced and violator did not have actual knowledge of the investigation's existence. § 49-4-168.1(b). Recovery of all costs of any civil action authorized. § 49-4-168.1(c).

Awards to plaintiffs bringing action: If attorney general intervenes: between 15 and 25% of proceeds of action or settlement, depending upon the extent to which the individual substantially contributed to the prosecution of the action. If such action is based primarily on disclosures of information that was not provided by the individual bringing the action relating to allegations or transactions in a criminal, civil, or administrative hearing, in a legislative, administrative, or attorney general hearing, audit, or investigation, or from the news media: an amount deemed appropriate, but in no case more than 10% of proceeds. Plaintiff shall also receive an amount for reasonable expenses necessarily incurred, plus reasonable attorney fees and costs. If attorney general does not intervene: between 25 and 30% of proceeds of action or settlement, plus reasonable expenses necessarily incurred, reasonable attorney fees and costs. Whether or not government intervenes, court may reduce award if plaintiff planned and initiated the violation. § 49-4-168.2(i).

Anti-retaliation provision: Employee, contractor or agent entitled to all make-whole relief if discharged, demoted, suspended, threatened, harassed, or in any other manner discriminated against in the terms and conditions of employment because of lawful acts done in furtherance of an action under the Act or other efforts to stop a violation. Relief includes reinstatement with appropriate seniority, twice the amount of back pay, interest on back pay, and special damages, including reasonable attorney fees and costs. Private action authorized. § 49-4-168.4.

Statute of limitations and other defenses: Six years after date violation was committed, or four years after date when material facts are or reasonably should have been known by the state official charged with the responsibility to act, whichever occurs last. In no event more than ten years after date violation was committed. § 49-4-168.5.

HAWAII

Haw. Rev. Stat. §§ 46-171 to 46-181 (Qui Tam Actions or Recovery of False Claims to the Counties)

Claims covered by the statute: Include knowingly false statements regarding a claim for payment presented to the county or county's grantee or contractor, failure to return public property or money, knowing purchase of public property from a county officer or employee who lawfully may not sell the property, conspiracy to commit a violation, knowing concealment or knowing and improper avoidance of an obligation to pay or transmit property to the county, and inadvertently submitting a false claim and failing to disclose the false claim after discovery. § 46-171(a).

Exemptions: Request or demand for money or property that a county has paid to an individual as compensation for employment or as an income subsidy with no restrictions on that individual's use of the money or property. § 46-171(e). Act does not apply to any controversy involving an amount of less than $500 in value. § 46-171(d). No action by private person against any elected official of the county if action is based upon evidence or information known to the county. No action by private person that is based upon allegations or transactions that are the subject of a civil suit or an administrative civil money penalty proceeding in which the county is already a party. § 46-177(f).

Who can initiate action as private plaintiff?: Plaintiff must be an "original source" of the information if the allegations or transactions have already been publicly disclosed. § 46-181(b).

Procedure for initiating action and state intervention: Action shall be brought in the name of the county. Complaint must be filed in camera and remain under seal for at least 60 days. Prior to expiration of 60-day period, the county shall either intervene or decline, in which case the person bringing the action has the right to proceed. When a person brings an action, no person other than the county may intervene or bring a related action based upon the same facts. § 46-175.

Elements of proof: A determination that a person has violated the Act shall be based on a preponderance of the evidence. § 46-173. Proof of specific intent to defraud is not required. § 46-171(d).

Remedies and attorney fees for state: Treble damages and civil penalty of between $5,500 and $11,000, plus attorney fees and costs. However, court may assess not less than twice the amount of damages sustained if violator provided county officials responsible for investigating false claims violations with all known information within 30 days after date first obtained and fully cooperated with investigation, and when information was provided no criminal prosecution, civil action, investigation or administrative action had commenced, and violator did not have actual knowledge of investigation's existence. § 46-171(a), (b).

Awards to plaintiffs bringing action: If county intervenes: between 15 and 25% of proceeds of action or settlement, depending upon the extent to which the individual substantially contributed to the prosecution of the action. If such action is based primarily on disclosures of information that was not provided by the individual bringing the action relating to allegations or transactions in a criminal, civil, or administrative hearing, in a legislative or administrative report, hearing, audit, or investigation, or from the news media: an amount deemed appropriate, but in no case more than 10% of proceeds. Plaintiff shall also receive an amount for reasonable expenses necessarily incurred, plus reasonable attorney fees and costs. If county does not intervene: between 25 and 30% of proceeds, plus reasonable expenses necessarily incurred, reasonable attorney fees and costs. Whether or not county intervenes, court may reduce award if plaintiff planned and initiated the violation. § 46-177

Anti-retaliation provision: Employee, contractor or agent entitled to all make-whole relief necessary if discharged, demoted, suspended, threatened, harassed, or in any other manner discriminated against in the terms and conditions of employment, contract, or agency relationship because of lawful acts done in furtherance of an action or other efforts to stop or address any conduct described in the Act. Relief includes reinstatement with appropriate seniority, twice the amount of back pay, interest on back pay, and special damages, including reasonable attorney fees and costs. Private action authorized. § 46-180.

Statute of limitations and other defenses: Six years after false claim is discovered or by exercise of reasonable diligence should have been discovered and, in any event, no more than ten years after date violation is committed. § 46-174.

Haw. Rev. Stat. §§ 661-21 to 661-31 (Qui Tam Actions or Recovery of False Claims to the State)

Claims covered by the statute: Include knowingly false statements regarding a claim for payment presented to the state or state's grantee or contractor, failure to return public property or money, knowing purchase of public property from a state officer or employee who lawfully may not sell the property, conspiracy to commit a violation, knowing concealment or knowing and improper avoidance of an obligation to pay or transmit property to the state, and inadvertently submitting a false claim and failing to disclose the false claim after discovery. § 661-21(a).

Exemptions: Request or demand for money or property that the state has paid to an individual as compensation for employment or as an income subsidy with no restrictions on that individual's use of the money or property. § 661-21(e). Act does not apply to any controversy involving an amount of less than $500 in value. § 661-21(d). No action by private person against a member of the state senate or house of representatives, member of the judiciary, or elected official in the executive branch if the action is based on evidence or information known to the state or that is based upon allegations or transactions that are the subject of a civil suit or an administrative civil money penalty proceeding in which the state is already a party. § 661-27(f).

Who can initiate action as private plaintiff?: Plaintiff must be an "original source" of the information if the allegations or transactions have already been publicly disclosed. § 661-31.

Procedure for initiating action and state intervention: Action shall be brought in the name of the state. Complaint must be filed in camera and remain under seal for at least 60 days. Prior to expiration of 60-day period, the state must either intervene or decline, in which case the person bringing the action has the right to proceed. When a person brings an action, no person other than the state may intervene or bring a related action based upon the same facts. § 661-25.

Elements of proof: A determination that a person has violated the Act shall be based on a preponderance of the evidence. § 661-23. Proof of specific intent to defraud is not required. § 661-21(d).

Remedies and attorney fees for state: Treble damages and civil penalty of between $5,500 and $11,000, plus attorney fees and costs. However, court may assess not less than twice the amount of damages sustained if violator provided state officials responsible for investigating false claims violations with all known information not later than 30 days after date first obtained and fully cooperated with investigation, and when information was provided no criminal prosecution, civil action or administrative action had commenced and violator did not have actual knowledge of investigation's existence. § 661-21(a), (b).

Awards to plaintiffs bringing action: If state intervenes: between 15 and 25% of proceeds of action or settlement, depending upon the extent to which the individual substantially contributed to the prosecution of the action. If such action is based primarily on disclosures of information that was not provided by the individual bringing the action relating to allegations or transactions in a criminal, civil, or administrative hearing, in a legislative or administrative report, hearing, audit, or investigation, or from the news media: an amount deemed appropriate, but in no case more than 10% of proceeds. Plaintiff shall also receive an amount for reasonable expenses necessarily incurred, plus reasonable attorney fees and costs. If state does not intervene: between 25 and 30% of proceeds of action or settlement, plus reasonable expenses necessarily incurred, reasonable attorney fees and costs. Whether or not county intervenes, court may reduce award if plaintiff planned and initiated the violation. § 661-27.

Anti-retaliation provision: Employee, contractor or agent entitled to all make-whole relief necessary if discharged, demoted, suspended, threatened, harassed, or in any other manner discriminated against in the terms and conditions of employment, contract, or agency relationship because of lawful acts done in furtherance of an action or other efforts to stop or address any conduct described in the Act. Relief includes reinstatement with appropriate seniority, twice the amount of back pay, interest on back pay, and special damages, including reasonable attorney fees and costs. Private action authorized. § 661-30.

Statute of limitations and other defenses: Six years after false claim is discovered or by exercise of reasonable diligence should have been discovered and, in any event, no more than ten years after date violation is committed. § 661-24.

ILLINOIS

740 Ill. Comp. Stat. §§ 175/1 to 175/8 (False Claims Act)

Claims covered by the statute: Include knowingly false statements regarding a claim for payment presented to the state or state's grantee or contractor, failure to return public property or money, knowing purchase of public property from a state officer or employee or member of the state National Guard who lawfully may not sell the property, conspiracy to commit a violation, and knowing concealment or knowing and improper avoidance of an obligation to pay or transmit property to the state. § 175/3(a).

Exemptions: Request or demand for money or property that the state has paid to an individual as compensation for state employment or as an income subsidy with no restrictions on that individual's use of the money or property. § 175/3(b)(2)(B). Act does not apply to claims, records, or statements made under the state Income Tax Act. § 175/3(c). No action brought against a member of the General Assembly, member of the judiciary, or exempt official if the action is based upon evidence or information known to the state when the action was brought. No action based upon allegations or transactions that are the subject of a civil suit or an administrative civil money penalty proceeding in which the state is already a party. § 175/4(e).

Who can initiate action as private plaintiff?: Plaintiff must be an "original source" of the information if the allegations or transactions have already been publicly disclosed. § 175/4(e)(4). No action brought by a former or present member of the state National Guard against a member of the Guard arising out of such person's service. § 175/4(e).

Procedure for initiating action and state intervention: Action shall be brought in the name of the state. Complaint shall be filed in camera and remain under seal for at least 60 days. Prior to expiration of 60-day period, the state must either intervene or decline, in which case the person bringing the action has the right to proceed. When a person brings an action, no person other than the state may intervene or bring a related action based upon the same facts. § 175/4(b).

Elements of proof: The state is required to prove all essential elements of the cause of action, including damages, by a preponderance of the evidence. § 175/5(d). Defendant may not deny essential elements of the offense that involves the same transaction as in a criminal proceeding where there was a verdict after trial or a plea of guilty or nolo contendere. § 175/5(e). Knowing violation requires no proof of specific intent to defraud. § 175/3(b).

Remedies and attorney fees for state: Treble damages and civil penalty of between $5,500 and $11,000, plus costs of action. Penalties are intended to be remedial rather than punitive, and do not preclude criminal prosecution for the same conduct. § 175/3(a). Reasonable expenses necessarily incurred, including reasonable attorney fees and costs. § 175/4(a).

Awards to plaintiffs bringing action: If state intervenes: between 15 and 25% of proceeds of action or settlement, depending upon the extent to which the individual substantially contributed to the prosecution of the action. If such action is based primarily on disclosures of information that was not provided by the individual bringing the action relating to allegations or transactions in a criminal, civil, or administrative hearing, in a legislative, administrative or Auditor General's report, hearing, audit, or investigation, or from the news media: an amount deemed appropriate, but in no case more than 10% of proceeds. Plaintiff shall also receive an amount for reasonable expenses necessarily incurred, plus reasonable attorney fees and costs. If state does not intervene: between 25 and 30% of proceeds of action or settlement, plus reasonable expenses necessarily incurred, reasonable attorney fees and costs. Whether or not county intervenes, court may reduce award if plaintiff planned and initiated the violation. § 175/4(d).

Anti-retaliation provision: Employee, contractor or agent entitled to all make-whole relief if discharged, demoted, suspended, threatened, harassed, or otherwise discriminated against in the terms and conditions of employment because of lawful acts done in furtherance of an action under the Act or to stop a violation. Relief includes reinstatement with appropriate seniority, twice the amount of back pay, interest on back pay, and special damages, including reasonable attorney fees and costs. Private action authorized. § 175/4(g).

Statute of limitations and other defenses: Six years after date violation was committed or four years after date when material facts are or reasonably should have been known by state official charged with the responsibility to act, whichever occurs last. In no event more than ten years after date violation was committed. § 175/5(b).

INDIANA

Ind. Code §§ 5-11-5.5-1 to 5-11-5.5-18 (False Claims and Whistleblower Protection)

Claims covered by the statute: Include knowingly false statements regarding a claim for payment presented to the state or state's grantee or contractor, failure to return public property or money, knowing purchase of public property from an employee who lawfully may not sell the property, conspiracy to commit a violation, and avoidance of an obligation to pay or transmit property to the state. § 5-11-5.5-2(b).

Exemptions: Act does not apply to a claim, record, or statement concerning income tax, or a claim, request, demand, statement, record, act, or omission made or submitted after June 30, 2014 in relation to the Medicaid program. § 5-11-5.5-2(a). No action brought by individual against the state, a state officer, judge, justice, member of the general assembly, state employee, or employee of a political subdivision that is based upon information known to the state at the time the action was brought. § 5-11-5.5-7(d). No action by individual that is based upon an act that is the subject of a civil suit, criminal prosecution, or administrative proceeding in which the state is a party. § 5-11-5.5-7(e).

Who can initiate action as private plaintiff?: No action based on information discovered by a present or former state employee in the course of the employee's employment, unless the employee, acting in good faith, has exhausted existing internal procedures for reporting and recovering the amount owed the state, and the state has failed to act on the information within a reasonable amount of time. § 5-11-5.5-7(b). No action may be brought by an incarcerated offender, including an offender incarcerated in another jurisdiction. § 5-11-5.5-7(c). Plaintiff must have "direct and independent knowledge" of the information if the allegations or transactions have already been publicly disclosed and must have voluntarily provided the information to the state. § 5-11-5.5-7(f).

Procedure for initiating action and state intervention: Action must be brought in the name of the state, and may be filed in a circuit or superior court in the county in which the person resides, the county in which a defendant resides, or Marion County. Complaint must be filed under seal and remain under seal for at least 120 days. Prior to end of 120-day period, attorney general must either intervene or decline, in which case person who filed complaint has the right to proceed. After a person has filed a complaint, no person other than attorney general or inspector general may intervene or bring another action based upon the same facts. § 5-11-5.5-4. Upon a showing of good cause, attorney general or inspector general may intervene at a later time. § 5-11-5.5-5.

Elements of proof: The state is required to establish the essential elements of the offense and damages by a preponderance of the evidence. Defendant may not deny essential elements of the offense that involves the same transaction as in a criminal proceeding where there was a verdict after trial or a plea of guilty or nolo contendere. § 5-11-5.5-9(c).

Remedies and attorney fees for state: Treble damages and a civil penalty of at least $5,000, plus costs of action. However, court may assess not less than twice the amount of damages sustained if violator provided state officials responsible for investigating false claims violations with all known information not later than 30 days after date first obtained and fully cooperated with investigation, and when information was provided no criminal prosecution, civil action or administrative action had commenced and violator did not have actual knowledge of investigation's existence. § 5-11-5.5-2(b), (c).

Awards to plaintiffs bringing action: If state intervenes: between 15 and 25% of proceeds of action or settlement, plus reasonable attorney fees, expenses and costs. If such action is based primarily on disclosures of information contained in transcript of criminal, civil, or administrative hearing, in a legislative, administrative, or other public report, hearing, audit, or investigation, or a news media report: an amount deemed appropriate, but in no case more than 10% of proceeds. If state does not intervene: between 25 and 30% of proceeds, plus reasonable attorney fees, expenses and costs. Person who planned and initiated the violation is not entitled to any amount. § 5-11-5.5-6.

Anti-retaliation provision: Employee who has been discharged, demoted, suspended, threatened, harassed, or otherwise discriminated against in the terms and conditions of employment by employer because the employee objected to an act or omission described in the Act or initiated, testified, assisted, or participated in an investigation, action, or hearing is entitled to all make-whole relief. Relief includes reinstatement with appropriate seniority, twice the amount of back pay, interest on back pay, and special damages, including reasonable attorney fees and costs. Private action authorized. § 5-11-5.5-8.

Statute of limitations and other defenses: Six years after the date on which the violation is committed or three years after the date when material facts are or reasonably should have been discovered by a state officer or employee responsible for addressing the false claim, but in no case later than ten years after date violation is committed. § 5-11-5.5-9(b).

Ind. Code §§ 5-11-5.7-1 to 5-11-5.7-18 (Medicaid False Claims and Whistleblower Protection)

Claims covered by the statute: Include knowingly false statements regarding a claim for payment presented to the state or state's grantee or contractor, failure to return public property or money, knowing purchase of public property from an employee who lawfully may not sell the property, conspiracy to commit a violation, and avoidance of an obligation to pay or transmit property to the state. § 5-11-5.7-2(a).

Exemptions: Act applies only to claims, requests, demands, statements, records, acts, and omissions made or submitted in relation to the Medicaid program. § 5-11-5.7-1(a). No action brought by individual against the state, a state officer, judge, justice, member of the general assembly, state employee, or employee of a political subdivision if action is based upon information known to the state when action was brought. § 5-11-5.7-7(c). No action by individual that is based upon an act that is the subject of a civil suit, criminal prosecution, or administrative proceeding in which the state is a party. § 5-11-5.7-7(d).

Who can initiate action as private plaintiff?: If plaintiff planned and initiated the violation or has been convicted of a crime related to the person's violation, the court must dismiss the person as plaintiff upon motion of the attorney general or inspector general. § 5-11-5.7-4(h). No action may be brought by an incarcerated offender, including an offender incarcerated in another jurisdiction. § 5-11-5.7-7(b). Plaintiff must voluntarily disclose to the state the information on which publicly disclosed allegations or transactions in a claim are based, or have knowledge that is "independent of and materially adds to the publicly disclosed allegations or transactions" and voluntarily provide this information to the state before an action is filed. § 5-11-5.7-7(e).

Procedure for initiating action and state intervention: Action must be brought in name of the state and may be filed in any court with jurisdiction. § 5-11-5.7-4(a)1). Complaint must be filed under seal and remain under seal for at least 60 days. Prior to end of 60-day period, attorney general or inspector general must either intervene or decline, in which case person who filed complaint has the right to proceed. After a person has filed a complaint, no person other than the attorney general or the inspector general may intervene or bring another action based upon the same facts. § 5-11-5.7-4. Upon a showing of good cause, attorney general or inspector general may intervene at a later time. § 5-11-5.7-5(f).

Elements of proof: The state is required to establish the essential elements of the offense and damages by a preponderance of the evidence. Defendant may not deny essential elements of the offense that involves the same transaction as in a criminal proceeding where there was a verdict after trial or a plea of guilty or nolo contendere. § 5-11-5.7-9(c), (d). Knowing violation does not require specific proof of intent to defraud. § 5-11-5.7-1(b)(4).

Remedies and attorney fees for state: Treble damages and civil penalty of between $5,500 and $11,000, plus costs of bringing action. § 5-11-5.7-2(a). However, court may assess not less than twice the amount of damages sustained if violator provided state officials responsible for investigating false claims violations with all known information not later than 30 days after date first obtained and fully cooperated with investigation, and when information was provided no criminal prosecution, civil action or

administrative action had commenced and violator did not have actual knowledge of investigation's existence. § 5-11-5.7-2(b).

Awards to plaintiffs bringing action: If state intervenes: between 15 and 25% of proceeds of action or settlement, plus reasonable attorney fees, expenses and costs. If such action is based primarily on disclosures of information contained in transcript of criminal, civil, or administrative hearing, in a legislative, administrative, or other public state report, hearing, audit, or investigation, or a news media report: an amount deemed appropriate, but in no case more than 10% of proceeds. If state does not intervene: between 25 and 30% of proceeds, plus reasonable attorney fees, expenses and costs. Person who planned and initiated the violation is not entitled to any amount. § 5-11-5.7-6.

Anti-retaliation provision: Employee, contractor or agent who has been discharged, demoted, suspended, threatened, harassed, or otherwise discriminated against in the terms and conditions of employment because of lawful acts done to object to or otherwise stop an act or omission or initiate, testify, assist, or participate in an investigation, action, or hearing is entitled to all make-whole relief. Relief includes reinstatement with appropriate seniority, twice the amount of back pay, interest on back pay, and special damages, including reasonable attorney fees and costs. Private action authorized. § 5-11-5.7-8.

Statute of limitations and other defenses: Six years after date violation is committed or three years after date when material facts are or reasonably should have been known by a state officer or employee responsible for addressing the false claim, but in no case later than ten years after date violation is committed, whichever occurs later. § 5-11-5.7-9(b).

IOWA

Iowa Code §§ 685.1 to 685.7 (False Claims Law)

Claims covered by the statute: Include knowingly false statements regarding a claim for payment presented to the state or state's grantee or contractor, failure to return public property or money, knowing purchase of public property from a state officer or employee or member of the state national guard who lawfully may not sell the property, conspiracy to commit a violation, and knowing concealment or knowing and improper avoidance of an obligation to pay or transmit property to the state. § 685.2(1).

Exemptions: Request or demand for money or property that the state has paid to an individual as compensation for state employment or as an income subsidy with no restrictions on that individual's use of the money or property. § 685.1(a). Act does not apply to claims, records, or statements made relating to state revenue and taxation. § 685.2(5). No action by qui tam plaintiff based upon allegations or transactions that are the subject of a civil suit or an administrative civil penalty proceeding in which the state is already a party. § 685.3(5).

Who can initiate action as private plaintiff?: Plaintiff must be an "original source" of the information if the allegations or transactions have already been publicly disclosed. § 685.3(5). No action brought by a former or present member of the state national guard against a member of the state national guard arising out of such person's services in the national guard. § 685.3(5).

Procedure for initiating action and state intervention: Qui tam plaintiff may bring action in the name of the state. Complaint must be filed in camera and remain under seal for at least 60 days. Prior to expiration of 60-day period, state must either intervene or decline, in which case qui tam plaintiff has the right to proceed. When qui tam plaintiff brings an action, no person other than the state may intervene or bring a related action based upon the same facts. State may intervene at a later date upon a showing of good cause. § 685.3.

Elements of proof: The state must prove all essential elements of the cause of action, including damages, by a preponderance of the evidence. § 685.4(4). Defendant may not deny essential elements of the offense that involves the same transaction as in a criminal proceeding where there was a verdict after trial or a plea of guilty or nolo contendere. § 685.4(5). Knowing violation does not require proof of specific intent to defraud. § 685.1(7)(b).

Remedies and attorney fees for state: Treble damages and civil penalty allowed under federal False Claims Act, plus costs of bringing action. However, court may assess not less than twice the amount of damages sustained if violator provided state officials responsible for investigating false claims violations with all known information not later than 30 days after date first obtained and fully cooperated with investigation, and when information was provided no criminal prosecution, civil action or administrative action had commenced and violator did not have actual knowledge of investigation's existence. § 685.2.

Awards to plaintiffs bringing action: If state intervenes: between 15 and 25% of proceeds of action or settlement, based upon extent to which qui tam plaintiff substantially contributed to the prosecution of the action, plus reasonable attorney fees, expenses and costs. If such action is based primarily on disclosures of information contained in transcript of criminal, civil, or administrative hearing, or in a legislative, administrative, or state auditor report, hearing, audit, or investigation, or from the news media: an amount deemed appropriate, but in no case more than 10% of proceeds. If state does not intervene: between 25 and 30% of proceeds, plus reasonable attorney fees, expenses and costs. Court may reduce share if qui tam plaintiff planned and initiated the violation. § 685.3.

Anti-retaliation provision: Employee, contractor or agent is entitled to all make-whole relief if discharged, demoted, suspended, threatened, harassed, or in any other manner discriminated against in the terms and conditions of employment because of lawful acts done in furtherance of an action or other efforts to stop a violation. Relief includes reinstatement with appropriate seniority, twice the amount of back pay, interest on back pay, and special damages, including reasonable attorney fees and costs. Private action authorized. § 685.3(6).

Statute of limitations and other defenses: Six years after date violation is committed, or three years after date when material facts are or reasonably should have been known by the state official with responsibility to act, but in no event more than ten years after date violation is committed, whichever occurs last. § 685.4.

LOUISIANA

La. Rev. Stat. Ann. §§ 46:437.1 to 46:440.3 (Medical Assistance Programs Integrity Act)

Claims covered by the statute: Include knowingly false statements regarding a claim for payment from medical assistance programs, conspiracy to defraud, and knowing submission of a claim for goods, services, or supplies that were medically unnecessary or of substandard quality or quantity. § 46:438.3. Also includes "illegal remuneration" claims that a person has paid or received bribes in exchange for medical referrals reimbursed by Medicaid. § 46:438.2.

Exemptions: Certain "safe harbor" exceptions to illegal remuneration claims are listed in the Act. § 46:438(D). No false claims action unless the amount of alleged actual damages is $1,000 or more. § 46:438.3(G).

Who can initiate action as private plaintiff?: Plaintiff must be an "original source" of the information if the allegations or transactions have already been publicly disclosed. § 46:439.1(D).

Procedure for initiating action and state intervention: Complaint shall be captioned: "Medical Assistance Programs Ex Rel.: [insert name of qui tam plaintiff(s)] v. [insert name of defendant(s)]" and be filed with the appropriate state or federal district court. Complaint must be filed under seal and remain under seal for at least 90 days. If secretary or attorney general does not intervene, the qui tam plaintiff has the right to proceed with the action unless the secretary or attorney general shows that proceeding would adversely affect the prosecution of any pending criminal actions or criminal investigations into the activities of the defendant. Such a showing shall be made to the court in camera and neither the qui tam plaintiff nor the defendant will be informed of the information revealed in camera. In such a case, the qui tam action shall be stayed for no more than one year. § 46:439.2(4)(a). When a qui tam plaintiff proceeds with the action, court may permit secretary or attorney general to intervene at a later date upon a showing of good cause. § 46:439.2(4)(b).

Elements of proof: Prior to forfeiture of property, a contradictory hearing shall be held during which the secretary or the attorney general shall prove, by clear and convincing evidence, that the property in question is subject to forfeiture. No such hearing is required if the owner of the property in question agrees to the forfeiture. § 46:437.7(B). In case brought by state: the burden of proof is on the medical assistance programs and by a preponderance of the evidence, except that the defendant has the burden of proving that goods, services, or supplies were actually provided to an eligible recipient in the quantity and quality submitted on a claim. § 46:438.8(A). Proof by a preponderance of the evidence of a false or fraudulent claim or illegal remuneration shall be deemed if the defendant has pled guilty to, been convicted of, or entered a nolo contendere plea to a criminal charge in any federal or state court to charges arising out of the same circumstances, or if an order has been rendered against a defendant for a violation of the Act. § 46:438.8(B). In case brought by qui tam plaintiff: the burden of proof is the same as for the state. § 46:439.1(C).

Remedies and attorney fees for state: Court may order health care provider or other person to forfeit property that constitutes or was derived directly or indirectly from gross proceeds traceable to the violation. § 46:437.7(A). Action to recover costs, expenses, and attorney fees is ancillary to the action brought to seek recovery for a violation of the Act. § 46:438.1. State may recover actual damages (the difference between what the medical assistance programs paid, or would have paid, and the amount that should have been paid, plus interest at the maximum rate of legal interest from the date the damage occurred to the date of repayment), a civil fine not to exceed $10,000 per violation, or an amount equal to three times the value of the illegal remuneration, whichever is greater, and a civil penalty of between $5,500 and $11,000 plus interest, as well as costs, expenses, fees, and attorney fees. § 46:438.6. If requested by the secretary or the attorney general, the court may reduce to not less than twice the actual damages if violator provided all information known about the specific allegation to the secretary or attorney general no later than 30 days after first obtained and fully with all federal or state investigations concerning the specific allegation, and when information was provided no criminal, civil, or departmental investigation or proceeding had commenced. § 46:438.7.

Awards to plaintiffs bringing action: If state intervenes: between 15 and 25% of recovery, based upon extent to which qui tam plaintiff substantially contributed to the prosecution of the action. If such action is based primarily on disclosures of specific information, other than information provided by the qui tam plaintiff, relating to allegations or transactions in criminal, civil, or administrative hearings, or from the news media: an amount deemed appropriate, but in no case more than 10% of proceeds. § 46:439.4(A). If state does not intervene: between 25 and 30% of the recovery. Plaintiff also entitled to reasonable attorney fees, expenses and costs. § 46:439.4(B). Whether or not state intervenes, court may reduce award if plaintiff planned and initiated the violation. § 46:439.4(D). Percentage of qui tam plaintiff's share shall be determined using the total amount of the award or settlement. § 46:439.4(G).

Anti-retaliation provision: Employee, contractor or agent entitled to all make-whole relief if discharged, demoted, suspended, threatened, harassed, or in any other manner discriminated against in the terms and conditions of employment because of lawful acts done in furtherance of an action under the Act or other efforts to stop a violation. Relief includes reinstatement with appropriate seniority, twice the amount of back pay, interest on back pay, and special damages, including reasonable attorney fees and costs. Private action authorized. § 46:439.1(E). No employee shall be discharged, demoted, suspended, threatened, harassed, or discriminated against in any manner in the terms and conditions of his employment because of any lawful act engaged in by the employee or on behalf of the employee in furtherance of any action taken in regard to a health care provider or other person from whom recovery is or could be sought. Employee may seek relief under state or federal law. Exemplary damages authorized. § 440.3(A). No individual shall be threatened, harassed, or discriminated against in any manner by a health care provider or other person because of any lawful act engaged in by the individual or on behalf of the individual in furtherance of any action taken in regard to a health care provider or other person from whom recovery is or could be sought, except that a health care provider may arrange for a recipient to receive goods, services, or supplies from another health care provider if the recipient agrees and the arrangement is approved by the secretary. Individual may seek relief under state or federal law. Exemplary damages authorized. § 440.3(B).

Statute of limitations and other defenses: Six years after date violation is committed or three years after date material facts are or reasonably should have been known by the state official charged with the responsibility to act in the circumstances, but no more than ten years after date violation is committed, whichever occurs last. § 46:439.1(B).

MARYLAND

Md. Code Ann., Gen. Prov. §§ 8-101 to 8-111 (West) (False Claims Act)

Claims covered by the statute: Include knowingly false statements regarding a claim for payment from a governmental entity or entity's contractor or grantee, conspiracy to commit a violation, failure to return public property or money, knowing purchase of public property from an officer, employee or agent of governmental entity who lawfully may not sell the property, and knowing concealment or knowing and improper avoidance of an obligation to pay or transmit property to the governmental entity, including misrepresenting the time at which a trade was made to make the transaction appear less favorable. § 8-102(b).

Exemptions: Request or demand for money or other property that a governmental entity has paid to an individual as compensation for employment or as an income subsidy with no restrictions on that individual's use of the money or other property. § 8-101(b)(2). Act does not apply to claims, records, or statements related to state or local taxes. § 8-102(a). No action by individual against any member of the legislative branch or state judiciary, any member of the Governor's Executive Council, the Attorney General, the Comptroller, or the State Treasurer if the action is based upon evidence or information known to the state when the action was filed. § 8-106(a). No action by individual that is based upon allegations or transactions that are the subject of a civil suit or an administrative civil money penalty proceeding in which the state is already a party. § 8-106(c).

Who can initiate action as private plaintiff?: If the person initiating a civil is convicted of criminal conduct arising from participation in the violation prior to a final determination of the action, the person shall be dismissed from the action and may not receive any share of proceeds. § 8-105(b)(3). Person must have "direct and independent knowledge of the information on which the allegations are based" and have voluntarily disclosed information to state before filing action if allegations or transactions have been publicly disclosed. § 8-106(d). No action by current or former public employee or public official if the allegations of the action are based substantially on allegations of wrongdoing or misconduct that the person had a duty or obligation to report or investigate within the scope of public employment or office, or information or records to which the person had access as a result of public employment or office. § 8-106(b). A person who is or was employed by the state, a local government, or any other political subdivision of the state as an auditor, investigator, attorney, a financial officer, or a contracting officer may not bring an action that is based upon allegations or transactions that the person discovered or learned of while acting in the particular employment capacity. § 8-106(f).

Procedure for initiating action and state intervention: Action shall be brought in the name of the governmental entity. Complaint shall be filed in camera and remain under seal for at least 60 days. Prior to expiration of 60-day period, governmental entity must either intervene or decline. If governmental entity does not intervene, before unsealing the complaint the court shall dismiss the action. If a person initiates an action, no person other than the governmental entity may intervene in the action or initiate a related action based on the facts underlying the pending action. § 8-104.

Elements of proof: All essential elements of the cause of action, including damages, shall be proven by a preponderance of the evidence. § 8-108(d). Defendant may not deny essential elements of the offense that involves the same transaction as in a criminal proceeding where there was a verdict

after trial or upon a plea of guilty or nolo contendere. § 8-108(e). Knowing violation does not require proof of specific intent to defraud. § 8-101(f)(1).

Remedies and attorney fees for state: Treble damages and civil penalty of not more than $10,000 for each violation. The total amount owed may not be less than the amount of the actual damages incurred as a result of the violation. § 8-102(c). Court must consider a number of specified factors in determining appropriate amount of fines and damages. § 8-102(d).

Awards to plaintiffs bringing action: Between 15 and 25% of the proceeds of the action or settlement of the claim, proportional to the amount of time and effort that the person substantially contributed to the action's final resolution, plus reasonable expenses, attorney fees and costs. If such action is based primarily on disclosures of specific information relating to allegations or transactions in criminal, civil, or administrative hearings, in a legislative or administrative report, hearing, audit, or investigation, or from the news media: an amount deemed appropriate, but in no case more than 10% of proceeds. Court may reduce share if action if plaintiff planned and initiated or otherwise deliberately participated in the violation. § 8-105.

Anti-retaliation provision: No retaliatory action against an employee, contractor, or grantee who acts lawfully in furtherance of an action filed under the Act, discloses or threatens to disclose to a supervisor or to a public body an activity, policy, or practice reasonably believed to be in violation the Act, provides information to or testifies before a public body conducting an investigation, hearing, or inquiry into a violation, or objects or refuses to participate in any activity, policy, or practice reasonably believed to be a violation. Relief includes injunction, reinstatement with appropriate seniority, twice the amount of lost wages, benefits, and other remuneration, including interest, reasonable attorney fees and costs, punitive damages, and a civil penalty of up to $1,000 for the first violation and $5,000 for each subsequent violation. Private action authorized against a person other than a supervisor in state government, an appointing authority in state government, or the head of a principal unit in state government. § 8-107.

Statute of limitations and other defenses: Six years after date violation occurred or three years after date when material facts are or reasonably should have been known by the relator or the governmental entity official with responsibility for acting, but in no event more than ten years after date violation is committed. § 8-108(a).

Md. Code Ann., Health-General §§ 2-601 to 2-611 (West) (False Claims Against State Health Plans and State Health Programs)

Claims covered by the statute: Include knowingly false statements regarding a claim for payment from a state health plan or program or contractor/grantee, conspiracy to commit a violation, failure to return public property or money, knowing purchase of public property from an officer or employee of state health plan or program who lawfully may not sell the property, and knowing concealment or knowing and improper avoidance of an obligation to pay or transmit property to the state. § 2-602(a).

Exemptions: Request or demand for money or other property that the state, through a state health plan or state health program, has paid to an individual as compensation for state employment or as an income subsidy with no restrictions on that individual's use of the money or other property. § 2-601(b)(2). No action by individual against any member of the legislative branch or the state judiciary, any member of the Governor's Executive Council, the Attorney General, the Comptroller, or the State Treasurer if the action is based on evidence or information known to the state when the action was filed. § 2-606(a). No action by individual that is based upon allegations or transactions that are the subject of a civil suit or an administrative civil money penalty proceeding in which the state is already a party. § 2-606(c).

Who can initiate action as private plaintiff?: If the person initiating a civil is convicted of criminal conduct arising from participation in the violation prior to a final determination of the action, the person shall be dismissed from the action and may not receive any share of proceeds. § 2-605(b)(3). Person must have "direct and independent knowledge of the information on which the allegations are based" and have voluntarily disclosed information to state before filing action if allegations or transactions have been publicly disclosed. § 2-606(d). No action by former or current public employee or public official if the allegations of the action are based substantially upon allegations of wrongdoing or misconduct that the person had a duty or obligation to report or investigate within the scope of public employment or office, or information or records to which the person had access as a result of public employment or office. § 2-606(b). Act does not apply to an employee as defined under the Health Care Worker Whistleblower Protection Act. § 2-607(c).

Procedure for initiating action and state intervention: Action must be brought in the name of the state. Complaint must be filed in camera and remain under seal for at least 60 days. Prior to expiration of 60-day period, state must either intervene or decline. If state does not intervene, before unsealing the complaint the court shall dismiss the action. If a person initiates an action, no person other than the state may intervene in the action or initiate a related action based on the facts underlying the pending action. § 2-604.

Elements of proof: All essential elements of the cause of action, including damages, shall be proven by a preponderance of the evidence. § 2-609(e). Defendant may not deny essential elements of the offense that involves the same transaction as in a criminal proceeding where there was a verdict after trial or upon a plea of guilty or nolo contendere. § 2-609(f).

Remedies and attorney fees for state: Treble damages and civil penalty of not more than $10,000 for each violation. The total amount owed may not be less than the amount of the actual damages incurred as a result of the violation. § 2-602(b). Court must consider a number of specified factors in determining appropriate amount of fines and damages. § 2-602(c). Attorney fees and costs authorized. § 2-603(b).

Awards to plaintiffs bringing action: Between 15 and 25% of the proceeds of the action or settlement of the claim, proportional to the amount of time and effort that the person substantially contributed to the action's final resolution, plus reasonable expenses, attorney fees and costs. If such action is based primarily on disclosures of specific information relating to allegations or transactions in criminal, civil, or administrative hearings, in a legislative or administrative report, hearing, audit, or investigation, or from the news media: an amount deemed appropriate, but in no case more than 10% of proceeds. Court may reduce plaintiff's share if action if plaintiff planned and initiated or otherwise deliberately participated in the violation. § 2-605.

Anti-retaliation provision: No retaliatory action against an employee, contractor, or grantee who acts lawfully in furtherance of an action filed under the Act, discloses or threatens to disclose to a supervisor or to a public body an activity, policy, or practice reasonably believed to be in violation the Act, provides information to or testifies before a public body conducting an investigation, hearing, or inquiry into a violation, or objects or refuses to participate in any activity, policy, or practice reasonably believed to be a violation. Relief includes injunction, reinstatement with appropriate seniority, twice the amount of lost wages, benefits, and other remuneration, including interest, reasonable attorney fees and costs, punitive damages, and a civil penalty of up to $1,000 for the first violation and $5,000 for each subsequent violation. Private action authorized against a person other than a supervisor in state government, an appointing authority in state government, or the head of a principal unit in state government. § 2-607.

Statute of limitations and other defenses: Six years after date violation occurred or three years after date when material facts are or reasonably should have been known by the relator, the state's Inspector General, or the Director of the State's Medicaid Fraud Control Unit, but in no event more than ten years after date violation is committed. § 2-609(a).

MASSACHUSETTS

Mass. Gen. Laws ch. 12, §§ 5A to 5O (False Claims)

Claims covered by the statute: Include knowingly false statements regarding a claim for payment from commonwealth, conspiracy to commit a violation, knowing presentation of a claim that includes items or services resulting from a violation of section 1128B of the Social Security Act, failure to return public property or money, knowing purchase of public property from officer or employee of commonwealth or political subdivision

who lawfully may not sell the property, knowing concealment or knowing and improper avoidance of an obligation to pay or transmit property to commonwealth or political subdivision, and inadvertently submitting a false claim and failing to disclose the false claim after discovery by the later of 60 days after the date on which the false claim or receipt of overpayment was identified or the date any corresponding cost report is due, if applicable. § 5B(a).

Exemptions: Request or demand for money or property that the commonwealth or a political subdivision has paid to an individual as compensation for employment with the commonwealth or political subdivision thereof or as an income subsidy with no restrictions on that individual's use of the money or property. § 5A. Act does not apply to claims, records or statements made or presented to establish, limit, reduce or evade liability for paying taxes to the commonwealth or other governmental authority. § 5A(d). No action brought against governor, lieutenant governor, attorney general, treasurer, secretary of state, auditor, a member of the general court, the inspector general or a member of the judiciary if the action is based on evidence or information known to the commonwealth when the action was brought. § 5G(a). No action based upon allegations or transactions that are the subject of a civil suit or an administrative proceeding in which the commonwealth or any political subdivision is already a party. § 5G(b). Attorney fees and costs authorized. § 5I(1).

Who can initiate action as private plaintiff?: Relator must be an "original source" of the information if the allegations or transactions have already been publicly disclosed. § 5G(c).

Procedure for initiating action and state intervention: Relator may bring action in superior court on behalf of and in the name of the relator or the commonwealth or any political subdivision. § 5C(2). Complaint shall be filed under seal and remain under seal for 120 days after service upon the attorney general. § 5C(3). Prior to expiration of 120-day period, attorney general must either intervene or decline, in which case the relator shall have the right to proceed. § 5C(4). If relator brings an action, no person other than the attorney general may intervene or bring a related action based upon the same facts. § 5C(5).

Elements of proof: Knowing violation requires no proof of specific intent to defraud. § 5A. Party bringing action is required to prove all essential elements of the cause of action, including damages, by a preponderance of the evidence. § 5L. Defendant may not deny essential elements of the offense that involves the same transaction as in a criminal proceeding where there was a verdict after trial or a plea of guilty or nolo contendere. § 5K(3).

Remedies and attorney fees for state: Treble damages and civil penalty of between $5,500 and $11,000 per violation, plus reasonable attorney fees, reasonable expert fees and costs. Costs include costs of any review or investigation undertaken by the attorney general, or by the state auditor or the inspector general in cooperation with the attorney general. § 5B(a). However, the court may assess not less than twice the amount of damages, including consequential damages, if violator provided state officials responsible for investigating false claims violations with all known information not later than 30 days after date first obtained and fully cooperated with investigation, and when information was provided no criminal prosecution, civil action or administrative action had commenced and violator did not have actual knowledge of investigation's existence. § 5B(b).

Awards to plaintiffs bringing action: If attorney general intervenes: between 15 and 25% of the proceeds in the action or settlement, based upon the extent to which the relator substantially contributed to the prosecution of the action, plus reasonable expenses necessarily incurred, including reasonable attorney fees and costs. If such action is based primarily on disclosures of information relating to allegations or transactions in criminal, civil, or administrative hearing, in a legislative, administrative, auditor or inspector general hearing, audit, or investigation, or from the news media: an amount deemed appropriate, but in no case more than 10% of proceeds. If state does not intervene: between 25 and 30% of proceeds, plus reasonable attorney fees, expenses and costs. Whether or not attorney general intervenes, court may reduce or eliminate share if relator planned and initiated the violation. § 5F.

Anti-retaliation provision: No employer shall make, adopt or enforce any rule, regulation or policy preventing an employee, contractor or agent from disclosing information to a government or law enforcement agency or from acting to further efforts to stop a violation of the Act. No employer shall require as a condition of employment, during the term of employment or at the termination of employment that any employee, contractor or agent agree to, accept or sign an agreement that limits or denies the rights to bring an action or provide information to a government or law enforcement agency pursuant to the Act. Any such agreement shall be void. § 5J(1). Employee, contractor or agent is entitled to all make-whole relief if discharged, demoted, suspended, threatened, harassed or in any other manner discriminated against in the terms and conditions of employment because of lawful acts done in furtherance of an action under the Act, or other efforts to stop a violation. § 5J(2). Relief includes reinstatement with appropriate seniority, twice the amount of back pay, interest on back pay, and special damages. Reasonable attorney fees and costs authorized. § 5J(3). Private action authorized. § 5J(4).

Statute of limitations and other defenses: Six years after date violation occurred or three years after date when material facts are or reasonably should have been known by the official at the attorney general's office with responsibility to act, but in no event more than ten years after date violation is committed, whichever occurs last. § 5K(1).

MICHIGAN

Mich. Comp. Laws §§ 400.601 to 400.615 (Medicaid False Claim Act)

Claims covered by the statute: Include knowing statements or false representations of a material fact in an application for Medicaid benefits, knowing statements or false representations of a material fact for use in determining rights to a Medicaid benefit, and concealment or failure to disclose event affecting eligibility with intent to obtain a benefit or in an amount greater than that to which a person is entitled. § 400.603. Also include kickbacks or bribes in connection with the furnishing of goods or services for which payment is or may be made in whole or in part pursuant to a program established under the Social Welfare Act. § 400.604. Also include knowing and willful making of a false statement or false representation of a material fact with respect to the conditions or operation of an institution or facility so that the institution or facility may qualify, upon initial certification or upon recertification, as a hospital, skilled nursing facility, intermediate care facility, or home health agency. § 400.605. Also include entering into an agreement, combination, or conspiracy to defraud the state by obtaining or aiding another to obtain the payment or allowance of a false claim under the Social Welfare Act. § 400.606. Also include knowingly false claims made or presented to a state employee or officer under the Social Welfare Act, claims that falsely represent that the goods or services involved were medically necessary in accordance with professionally accepted standards, and knowing concealment or avoidance of an obligation to pay or transmit money or property to the state pertaining to a claim presented under the Social Welfare Act. § 400.607.

Exemptions: No action by individual that is based upon allegations or transactions that are the subject of a civil suit or an administrative civil money penalty proceeding to which the state or federal government is already a party. § 400.610a(12).

Who can initiate action as private plaintiff?: Individual bringing the action must be an "original source" of the information if the allegations or transactions have already been publicly disclosed. § 400.610a(13). A person who is convicted of criminal conduct arising from a violation of the Act shall not initiate or remain a party and is not entitled to share in monetary proceeds resulting from action or settlement. § 400.610a(11).

Procedure for initiating action and state intervention: Any person may bring action in the name of the state. Complaint filed under seal and remains so for 90 days. Prior to 90-day expiration period, attorney general must either intervene or decline, in which case the person bringing the action has the right to proceed. In action brought by individual, a person other than the attorney general shall not intervene in the action or bring another action on behalf of the state based upon the same facts. § 400.610.

Elements of proof: Person bringing action is required to prove all essential elements of the cause of action, including damages, by a preponderance of the evidence. § 400.615. Knowing violation does not require proof of specific intent to defraud. § 400.602(f). Not necessary to show that person had knowledge of similar acts having been performed in the past by a person acting on his or her behalf, nor to show that person had actual notice that the acts by the persons acting on his or her behalf occurred in order to establish the fact that a false statement or representation was knowingly made. § 400.608. A criminal action need not be brought against a person in order for that person to be civilly liable under the Act. § 400.612.

Remedies and attorney fees for state: Person who violates provision regarding false statements or representations in applications is guilty of a felony, punishable by imprisonment of up to four years, or a fine of not more than $50,000, or both. § 400.603. Person who engages in kickbacks or bribes is guilty of a felony, punishable by imprisonment for up to four years, or by a fine of not more than $30,000, or both. § 400.604. Person who violates provision regarding false statements or representations with respect to conditions or operation of institution or facility is guilty of a felony, punishable by imprisonment for up to four years, or by a fine of not more than $30,000, or both. § 400.605. Person who violates provision regarding agreements to defraud state by means of a false claim is guilty of a felony, punishable by imprisonment for up to ten years, or by a fine of not more than $50,000, or both. § 400.606. Person who violates provision regarding the making or presentation of false records or statements to conceal or avoid an obligation to transmit money or property to the state is guilty of a felony punishable by imprisonment for not more than four years or a fine of not more than $50,000, or both. § 400.607. Attorney general may recover all costs incurred in the litigation and recovery of Medicaid restitution, including the cost of investigation and attorney fees. § 400.610b. A person who receives a benefit that the person is not entitled to receive by reason of fraud or making a fraudulent statement or knowingly concealing a material fact, or who engages in any conduct prohibited by the Act, must forfeit and pay to the state the full amount received, plus a civil penalty of between $5,000 and $10,000 per claim, plus treble damages. § 400.612.

Awards to plaintiffs bringing action: If attorney general intervenes: between 15 and 25% of proceeds resulting from the action or any settlement based on the amount of effort involved, plus necessary expenses, costs and reasonable attorney fees. If such action is based primarily on disclosure of specific information from a criminal, civil, or administrative hearing in a state or federal department or agency, a legislative report, hearing, audit, or investigation, or the news media: up to 10% of proceeds. If attorney general does not intervene: between 25 and 30% of proceeds, plus necessary expenses, reasonable attorney fees and costs. Whether or not attorney general intervenes, court may reduce or eliminate share if person bringing the action planned and initiated the violation. § 400.610a.

Anti-retaliation provision: Employer shall not discharge, demote, suspend, threaten, harass, or in any other manner discriminate against an employee in the terms and conditions of employment because of lawful acts in furtherance of an action under the Act or because the employee cooperates with or assists in an investigation under the Act. Relief includes reinstatement without loss of seniority, twice the amount of lost back pay, interest on back pay and special damages. § 400.610c.

Statute of limitations and other defenses: Six years after date violation was committed or three years after date when material facts are or reasonably should have been known by the state official with responsibility to act, but in no event more than ten years after date violation was committed. § 400.614.

MINNESOTA

Minn. Stat. §§ 15C.01 to 15C.16 (False Claims Against the State)

Claims covered by the statute: Include knowingly false statements regarding a claim for payment presented to the state or state's grantee or contractor, failure to return public property or money, knowing purchase of public property from a state officer or employee who lawfully may not sell the property, conspiracy to commit a violation, and knowing concealment or knowing and improper avoidance of an obligation to pay or transmit property to the state. § 15C.02. Act does not apply to claims, records, or statements relating to taxation. § 15C.03.

Exemptions: Request or demand for money or property that the state or a political subdivision has paid to an individual as compensation for state or political subdivision employment, or as an income subsidy with no restrictions on that individual's use of the money or property. § 15C-01. No action by an individual against the state, legislature, judiciary, executive branch, or political subdivision, or respective officers, members, or employees if the action is based on evidence or information known to the state or political subdivision when the action was brought. No action by an individual that is based upon allegations or transactions that are the subject of a civil action or an administrative proceeding for a monetary penalty to which the state or a political subdivision is already a party. § 15C.05(c).

Who can initiate action as private plaintiff?: Individual bringing the action must be an "original source" of the information if the allegations or transactions have already been publicly disclosed. § 15C.05(f).

Procedure for initiating action and state intervention: A person may maintain an action on the person's own account and that of the state, the person's own account and that of a political subdivision, or on the person's own account and that of both the state and a political subdivision. Complaint must be filed in camera and remain under seal for at least 60 days. If action is brought by an individual, no person may bring another action based upon the same facts. § 15C.05. Within 60 days after receiving complaint, prosecuting attorney must intervene or decline, in which case the individual has the right to proceed. §§ 15C.06, 15C.07.

Elements of proof: State or political subdivision or individual plaintiff must prove the essential elements of the cause of action, including damages, by a preponderance of the evidence. A finding of guilt in a criminal proceeding charging a false statement or fraud, whether upon a verdict of guilty or a plea of guilty or nolo contendere, stops the person found guilty from denying an essential element of that offense in an action based upon the same transaction as the criminal proceeding. § 15C.11. No proof of specific intent to defraud is required for knowing violation, "but in no case is a person who acts merely negligently, inadvertently, or mistakenly with respect to information deemed to have acted knowingly." § 15C-01.

Remedies and attorney fees for state: Treble damages and civil penalty of between $5,500 and $11,000 per claim, plus costs of action (reasonable costs, reasonable attorney fees, and the reasonable fees of expert consultants and expert witnesses). However, court may assess not less than twice the amount of damages sustained if violator provided state officials responsible for investigating false claims violations with all known information not later than 30 days after date first obtained and fully cooperated with investigation, and when information was provided no criminal prosecution, civil action or administrative action had commenced and violator did not have actual knowledge of investigation's existence. § 15C.02.

Awards to plaintiffs bringing action: If state intervenes at the outset: between 15 and 25% of any recovery of the civil penalty and damages or settlement, depending upon the extent to which the person substantially contributed to the conduct of the action. If state does not intervene at all: between 25 and 30%, as the court determines is reasonable. If state does not intervene at the outset but subsequently intervenes: between 15 and 30%, depending up on the extent to which the person substantially contributed to the prosecution of the action. § 15C.13. Statute authorizes reasonable costs, reasonable attorney fees, and reasonable fees of expert consultants and expert witnesses. § 15C.12.

Anti-retaliation provision: Employee, contractor or agent is entitled to all make-whole relief if discharged, demoted, suspended, threatened, harassed, or in any other manner discriminated against in the terms and conditions of employment because of lawful acts done in furtherance of an action or other efforts to stop a violations. Relief includes reinstatement with appropriate seniority, twice the amount of back pay, interest on back pay, and special damages sustained, including reasonable attorney fees and costs. Private action authorized. § 15C.145.

Statute of limitations and other defenses: Three years after the date of discovery of the fraudulent activity by the prosecuting attorney or six years after the fraudulent activity occurred, whichever occurs later, but in no event more than ten years after date violation is committed. § 15C.11. No liability for mere negligence, inadvertence, or mistake with respect to activities involving a false or fraudulent claim. § 15C.02(d).

MONTANA

Mont. Code Ann. §§ 17-8-401 to 17-8-416 (False Claims Act)

Claims covered by the statute: Include knowingly false statements regarding a claim for payment presented to a governmental entity or entity's grantee or contractor, failure to return public property or money, knowing purchase of public property of governmental entity from person who lawfully may not sell the property, conspiracy to commit a violation, knowing concealment or knowing and improper avoidance of an obligation to pay or transmit property to a governmental entity, and inadvertently submitting a false claim and failing to disclose the false claim after discovery. § 17-8-403(1).

Exemptions: Act does not apply to claims, records, or statements made in relation to claims filed with the state compensation insurance fund or to claims, records, payments, or statements made under the tax laws or made to the department of natural resources and conservation under title 77. § 17-8-403(5). No action by individual against the state or an officer or employee of the state arising from conduct within the scope of the officer's or employee's duties to the state unless the officer or employee has a financial interest in the conduct upon which the complaint or action arises. § 17-8-403(7).

Who can initiate action as private plaintiff?: Individual bringing the action must be an "original source" of the information if the allegations or transactions have already been publicly disclosed. § 17-8-403(6). If the person bringing the action is convicted of criminal conduct arising from the person's role in the violation, the person must be dismissed from the action and may not receive any share of proceeds. § 17-8-410(5).

Procedure for initiating action and state intervention: Action must be brought in the name of the governmental entity. Complaint must be filed under seal and remain under seal for at least 60 days. Within 60 days after receiving complaint, the government attorney may intervene or decline, in which case the person bringing the action has the right to proceed. When a person files action, no person other than the government attorney may intervene or bring a related action based upon the same facts. § 17-8-406.

Elements of proof: The plaintiff must prove each essential element of the cause of action, including damages, by a preponderance of the evidence. A person convicted of or who pleaded guilty or nolo contendere to a criminal offense may not deny the essential elements of the offense in an action under the Act that involves the same event or events as the criminal proceeding. § 17-8-409. Knowing violation does not require a specific intent to defraud. § 17-8-402(4).

Remedies and attorney fees for state: Treble damages and civil penalty of between $5,500 and $11,000 per violation, plus expenses, attorney fees and costs. § 17-8-403(1). However, court may assess between two and three times the amount of damages sustained if violator provided officials responsible for investigating false claims violations with all known information not later than 30 days after date first obtained and fully cooperated with investigation, and when information was provided no criminal prosecution, civil action or administrative action had commenced and violator did not have actual knowledge of investigation's existence. § 17-8-403.

Awards to plaintiffs bringing action: If government entity intervenes: between 15 and 25% of the proceeds in the action or settlement, based upon the extent to which the relator substantially contributed to the prosecution of the action, plus reasonable expenses necessarily incurred, including reasonable attorney fees and costs. If such action is based primarily on disclosures of information relating to allegations or transactions in criminal, civil, or administrative hearing, in a legislative, administrative, auditor or inspector general report, hearing, or investigation, or from the news media: an amount deemed appropriate, but in no case more than 10% of proceeds. If state does not intervene: between 25 and 30% of proceeds, plus reasonable attorney fees, expenses and costs. Whether or not attorney general intervenes, court may reduce or eliminate share if person bringing the action planned and initiated the violation. § 17-8-410.

Anti-retaliation provision: Governmental entity, private entity, or person may not adopt or enforce a rule, regulation, or policy preventing an employee, agent, or contractor from disclosing information to a government or law enforcement agency regarding acts in furtherance of an investigation of a violation or an action under the Act. Governmental entity, private entity, or person may not discharge, demote, suspend, threaten, harass, or deny promotion to or in any other manner discriminate against an employee, agent, or contractor because of the disclosure of information to a government or law enforcement agency pertaining to a violation of the Act. Employee, contractor or agent is entitled to all make-whole relief if discharged, demoted, suspended, threatened, harassed, or in any other manner discriminated against in the terms and conditions of employment because of lawful acts done in furtherance of an action or efforts to stop a violations. Relief includes reinstatement with appropriate seniority, twice the amount of back pay, interest on back pay, and special damages, including reasonable attorney fees and costs. Private action authorized. § 17-8-412.

Statute of limitations and other defenses: Six years after date violation was committed or three years after date when material facts are or reasonably should have been known by the governmental entity official with responsibility to act, but in no event more than ten years after date violation was committed. § 17-8-404.

NEVADA

Nev. Rev. Stat. §§ 357.010 to 357.250 (Submission of False Claims to State or Local Government)

Claims covered by the statute: Include knowingly false statements regarding a claim for payment presented to a state or political subdivision or entity's grantee or contractor, failure to return public property or money, knowing purchase of public property from person who lawfully may not sell the property, conspiracy to commit a violation, knowing concealment or knowing and improper avoidance of an obligation to pay or transmit property to state or political subdivision, and inadvertently submitting a false claim and failing to disclose the false claim after discovery. § 357.040(1).

Exemptions: Request or demand for money or property that the state or political subdivision has paid or provided to a natural person as compensation for employment or an income subsidy with no restriction on the person's use of the money or property. § 357.020(2). No action by individual against a member of the legislature or judiciary, an elected officer of the executive department of the state government, or a member of the governing body of a political subdivision if the action is based upon evidence or information known to the state or political subdivision at the time the action was brought. No action by individual that is based upon allegations or transactions that are the subject of a civil action or administrative proceeding for a monetary penalty to which the state or political subdivision is already a party. § 357.080(3).

Who can initiate action as private plaintiff?: Individual bringing the action must be an "original source" of the information if the allegations or transactions have already been publicly disclosed. § 357.100. If individual is convicted of criminal conduct arising from role in the violation, such individual must be dismissed from the action and must not receive any share of recovery. § 357.210(3).

Procedure for initiating action and state intervention: Action must be brought in the name of the state or political subdivision, or both. Action may be brought in any judicial district in the state in which the defendant can be found, resides, transacts business or in which any of the alleged fraudulent activities occurred. Complaint must remain under seal for at least 60 days or until the attorney general has elected whether to intervene. § 357.080. Within 60 days after receiving complaint, attorney general may intervene or decline, in which case the private plaintiff has the right to proceed. § 357.110. Upon showing of good cause, attorney general may intervene at a later date if the interest of the state or a political subdivision is not being adequately represented by the private plaintiff. If this occurs, the private plaintiff retains primary responsibility for conducting the action and any recovery must be apportioned as if the attorney general had not intervened. § 357.130.

Elements of proof: The standard of proof is a preponderance of the evidence. A finding of guilty or guilty but mentally ill in a criminal proceeding charging false statement or fraud, whether upon a verdict or plea of guilty or guilty but mentally ill or nolo contendere estops the person found guilty or guilty but mentally ill from denying an essential element of that offense in an action based upon the same transaction as the criminal proceeding. § 357.170(2). Proof of specific intent to defraud is not required. § 357.040(1).

Remedies and attorney fees for state: Treble damages and civil penalty of between $5,500 and $11,000. § 357.040(2). However, court may give judgment for between two and three times the amount of damages sustained and no civil penalty if violator provided state officials responsible for investigating false claims violations with all known information not later than 30 days after date first obtained and fully cooperated with investigation, and when information was provided no criminal prosecution, civil action or administrative action had commenced and violator did not have actual knowledge of investigation's existence. § 357.050. Statute authorizes reasonable costs, attorney fees and the fees of expert consultants and expert witnesses. § 357.180(1).

Awards to plaintiffs bringing action: If attorney general intervenes: between 15 and 33% of any recovery, according to the extent of the private plaintiff's contribution to the conduct of the action. If attorney general does not intervene: between 25 and 50% of recovery. Whether or not attorney general intervenes, court may reduce or eliminate share if person bringing the action planned and initiated the violation. § 357.210. Statute authorizes reasonable costs, attorney fees and the fees of expert consultants and expert witnesses. § 357.180(1). In action brought by an original source, court may award not more than 10% of the recovery to the original source, with consideration given to the role of the original source in advancing the claim to litigation. § 357.225.

Anti-retaliation provision: Employee, contractor or agent who is discharged, demoted, suspended, threatened, harassed or discriminated against in the terms and conditions of employment as a result of any lawful act in furtherance of an action under the act is entitled to all make-whole relief including limitation, reinstatement with appropriate seniority or damages in lieu of reinstatement if appropriate, twice the amount of lost compensation, interest on the lost compensation, any special damage sustained, and punitive damages if appropriate. May also receive attorney fees and costs. § 357.250.

Statute of limitations and other defenses: Three years after attorney general discovers or reasonably should have discovered the fraudulent activity, or six years after the fraudulent activity occurred, but in no event more than ten years after fraudulent activity occurred. § 357.170(1).

NEW HAMPSHIRE

N.H. Rev. Stat. Ann. §§ 167:61-b to 167:61-e (Medicaid Fraud and False Claims)

Claims covered by the statute: Include false statements regarding a claim for payment presented to department officer, employee, grantee or contractor, conspiracy to commit a violation, failure to return public property or money, knowing concealment or knowing and improper avoidance of an obligation to pay or transmit property to state or political subdivision, and inadvertently submitting a false claim and failing to disclose the false claim after discovery. § 167:61-b.

Exemptions: Act does not apply to any controversy involving damages to the department of less than $5,000 in value. § 167:61-b(IV). No action against any department official or any division, board, bureau, commission or agency within the department. § 167:61-b(III).

Who can initiate action as private plaintiff?: Relator must be an "original source" of the information if the allegations or transactions have already been publicly disclosed. If relator is convicted of criminal conduct arising from role in the violation, relator shall be dismissed from the action and shall not receive any share of proceeds. No action where relator is a present or former employee of the state and the action is based upon information discovered by the employee during the course of employment, unless the employee first, in good faith, exhausted any existing internal procedures for reporting and seeking recovery of the falsely claimed sums through official channels and the state failed to act on the information provided within a reasonable period of time. § 167:61-e.

Procedure for initiating action and state intervention: Action must be brought in the name of the state against a defendant that (1) has its principal place of business within the state or (2) during the 12-month period immediately preceding the date the action is filed, received reimbursement from the state's Medicaid program, equal to 10% or more of the defendant's aggregate reimbursement from all state medical assistance programs governed by title XIX of the Social Security Act. Complaint must be filed in camera and remain under seal for at least 60 days. Prior to expiration of 60-day period, state must either intervene or decline, in which case relator has the right to proceed. When relator brings an action, no person other than the state may intervene or bring a related action based on the facts underlying the pending action. State may intervene at a later date upon a showing of good cause. § 167:61-c.

Elements of proof: The state is required to prove all essential elements of the cause of action, including damages, by a preponderance of the evidence. § 167:61-b(VI). Knowing violation does not require proof of specific intent to defraud. § 167:61-b(V)(b)(2).

Remedies and attorney fees for state: Treble damages and civil penalty of between $5,000 and $10,000, plus attorney fees and costs. However, court may assess between two and three times the amount of damages sustained and no civil penalty if violator provided state officials responsible for investigating false claims violations with all known information not later than 30 days after date first obtained and fully cooperated with investigation, and when information was provided no criminal prosecution, civil action or administrative action had commenced and violator did not have actual knowledge of investigation's existence. § 167:61-b.

Awards to plaintiffs bringing action: If government entity intervenes: between 15 and 25% of the proceeds in the action or settlement, based upon the extent to which the relator substantially contributed to the prosecution of the action, plus reasonable expenses necessarily incurred, including reasonable attorney fees and costs. If such action is based primarily on disclosures of information relating to allegations or transactions in criminal, civil, or administrative hearing, in a legislative or administrative report, hearing, or investigation, or from the news media: an amount deemed appropriate, but in no case more than 10% of proceeds. If state does not intervene: between 25 and 30% of proceeds, plus necessary expenses, costs and reasonable attorney fees. Whether or not attorney general intervenes, court may reduce share of proceeds if person bringing the action planned and initiated the violation. § 167:61-e.

Anti-retaliation provision: Employee who is discharged, demoted, suspended, threatened, harassed, or in any other manner discriminated against in the terms and conditions of employment because of lawful acts done in furtherance of an action under the Act, including investigation for, initiation of, testimony for, or assistance in an action, is entitled to all make-whole relief. Relief includes reinstatement with appropriate seniority, twice the amount of back pay, interest on back pay, and special damages, including reasonable attorney fees and costs. Private action authorized. § 167:61-c(IV).

Statute of limitations and other defenses: Six years after date violation is committed or three years after date when material facts are or reasonably should have been known by the official in the attorney general's office with responsibility to act, but in no event more than ten years after date violation is committed, whichever occurs last. § 167:61-b(VII).

NEW JERSEY

N.J. Stat. Ann. §§ 2A:32C-1 to 2A:32C-18 (West) (False Claims Act)

Claims covered by the statute: Include false statements regarding a claim for payment presented to state or to grantee, contractor or other recipient of state funds, conspiracy to commit a violation, failure to return public property or money, knowing purchase of public property from person who lawfully may not sell the property, and knowing concealment or avoidance of an obligation to pay or transmit property to state. § 2A:32C-3.

Exemptions: Act does not apply to claims, records, or statements made in connection with state tax laws. § 2A:32C-2. No member of the legislature or judiciary, senior executive branch official, or member of a county or municipal governing body may be civilly liable if the action is based upon evidence or information known to the state when the action was brought. No action by individual based upon allegations or transactions that are the subject of a pending action or administrative proceeding to which the state is already a party. § 2A:32C-9.

Who can initiate action as private plaintiff?: Individual must be an "original source" of the information if the allegations or transactions have already been publicly disclosed. No action where individual is a present or former employee or agent of the state and the action is based upon information discovered by the employee in any civil, criminal or administrative investigation or audit within the scope of the employee's or agent's duties or job description. § 2A:32C-9. If the person bringing the action is convicted of criminal conduct arising from role in violation of this act, person shall be dismissed from the action and shall not receive any share of proceeds. § 2A:32C-7(g).

Procedure for initiating action and state intervention: Action must be brought in the name of the state. Complaint shall remain under seal for at least 60 days. Prior to expiration of 60-day period, state must either intervene or decline, in which case individual has the right to proceed. When individual brings an action, no person other than the state may intervene or bring a related action based upon the same facts. § 2A:32C-5. State may intervene at a later date upon a showing of good cause. § 2A:32C-6(f).

Elements of proof: The state or the person bringing the action shall be required to prove all essential elements of the cause of action, including damages, by a preponderance of the evidence. § 2A:32C-12. Knowing violation does not require proof of specific intent to defraud. Acts occurring by innocent mistake or as a result of mere negligence are a defense. § 2A:32C-2.

Remedies and attorney fees for state: Treble damages and civil penalty allowed under federal False Claims Act for each claim. § 2A:32C-3. However, court may assess not less than twice the amount of damages if violator provided state officials responsible for investigating false claims violations with all known information not later than 30 days after date first obtained and fully cooperated with investigation, and when information was provided no criminal prosecution, civil action or administrative action had commenced and violator did not have actual knowledge of investigation's existence. § 2A:32C-4. The state entity injured by the false claim shall be awarded an amount not to exceed its compensatory damages, and any remaining proceeds, including civil penalties, shall be deposited in the General Fund. The attorney general shall receive a fixed 10% of the proceeds in any action or settlement of the claim that it brings, which shall be deposited in the "False Claims Prosecution Fund." § 2A:32C-7. Statute authorizes reasonable attorney fees, expenses and costs. § 2A:32C-8.

Awards to plaintiffs bringing action: If attorney general intervenes: between 15 and 25% of the proceeds in the action or settlement, based upon the extent to which the individual substantially contributed to the prosecution of the action. If such action is based primarily on disclosures of information relating to allegations or transactions in criminal, civil, or administrative hearing, in a legislative, administrative, or inspector general report, hearing, audit, or investigation, or from the news media: an amount deemed appropriate. If state does not intervene: between 25 and 30% of proceeds. Whether or not attorney general intervenes, court may reduce share of proceeds if person bringing the action planned and initiated the violation. § 2A:32C-7. Statute authorizes reasonable attorney fees, expenses and costs. § 2A:32C-8.

Anti-retaliation provision: No employer shall make, adopt, or enforce any rule, regulation, or policy preventing an employee from disclosing information to a state or law enforcement agency or from acting to further a false claims action. Employer that discharges, demotes, suspends, threatens, harasses, denies promotion to, or in any other manner discriminates against an employee in the terms and conditions of employment because of lawful acts done by in disclosing information to a state or law enforcement agency or in furthering a false claims action is liable for all make-whole relief, including reinstatement with appropriate seniority status, twice the amount of back pay, interest on the back pay, special damage, reasonable attorney fees and costs, and, where appropriate, punitive damages. Private action authorized. § 2A:32C-10.

Statute of limitations and other defenses: Six years after date violation is committed or three years after date when material facts are or reasonably should have been known by the state official with responsibility to act, but in no event more than ten years after date violation is committed, whichever occurs last. § 2A:32C-11. Acts occurring by innocent mistake or as a result of mere negligence are a defense. § 2A:32C-2.

NEW MEXICO

N.M. Stat. §§ 27-14-1 to 27-14-15 (Medicaid False Claims Act)

Claims covered by the statute: Include knowingly false claims for payment under the Medicaid program, claims for which person receiving a Medicaid benefit or payment is not authorized or eligible, conspiracy to commit a violation, knowing concealment or avoidance of an obligation to pay or transmit money or property to the state relative to the Medicaid program, knowing receipt of benefit or payment on behalf of another person under the Medicaid program and conversion of that benefit or payment to own personal use, knowingly false statements concerning conditions or operation of a health care facility so that facility may qualify for Medicaid certification or recertification, and claims under Medicaid program for a service or product that was not provided. § 27-14-4.

Exemptions: No action brought against a department official that is substantially based on evidence or information known to the department when the action was brought. No action by qui tam plaintiff that is substantially based upon allegations or transactions that are the subject of a civil suit or an administrative proceeding in which the department is already a party. § 27-14-10.

Who can initiate action as private plaintiff?: Private action may be brought by an affected person on behalf of the person bringing suit and for the state. § 27-14-7. Qui tam plaintiff must be an "original source" of the information if the allegations or transactions have already been publicly disclosed. § 27-14-10(C). If person bringing the action is convicted of criminal conduct arising from role in the violation, that person shall be dismissed from the action and shall not receive any share of proceeds. § 27-14-9(C).

Procedure for initiating action and state intervention: Action shall be brought in the name of the state. Complaint shall be filed in writing and remain under seal for at least 60 days. Within 60 days, department must investigate, and upon determination that there is not substantial evidence that a violation has occurred, complaint shall be dismissed. Prior to expiration of 60-day period, department must either intervene or decline, in which case the person bringing the action has the right to proceed if the department determined that there is substantial evidence that a violation occurred. § 27-14-7. Department may intervene at a later date upon a showing of good cause. § 27-14-8.

Elements of proof: Department or qui tam plaintiff is be required to prove all essential elements of the cause of action, including damages, by a preponderance of the evidence. Defendant may not deny the essential elements of the offense in any action that involves the same transaction as a criminal proceeding that charged the defendant with fraud or false statements in which there was a final judgment rendered, whether upon a verdict after trial or a plea of guilty. § 27-14-13.

Remedies and attorney fees for state: Treble damages. § 27-14-4. Civil penalty of up to $10,000 for each false claim, plus attorney fees and costs of investigation and enforcement of civil remedies. § 30-44-8.

Awards to plaintiffs bringing action: If department intervenes: between 15 and 25% of the proceeds in the action or settlement, based upon the extent to which the qui tam plaintiff substantially contributed to the prosecution of the action, plus reasonable expenses necessarily incurred, including reasonable attorney fees and costs. If such action is based primarily on disclosures of information relating to allegations or transactions in criminal, civil, or administrative hearing, in a legislative, administrative, auditor or inspector general report, hearing, or investigation, or from the news media: an amount deemed appropriate, but in no case more than 10% of proceeds. If state does not intervene: between 25 and 30% of proceeds, plus reasonable attorney fees, expenses and costs. Whether or not

attorney general intervenes, court may reduce share if person bringing the action planned and initiated the violation. § 27-14-9.

Anti-retaliation provision: Employee who is discharged, demoted, suspended, threatened, harassed or otherwise discriminated against in the terms and conditions of employment because of lawful acts done in disclosing information to the department or in furthering a false claims action is entitled to all make-whole relief. Relief includes reinstatement with appropriate seniority, twice the amount of back pay, interest on back pay, and special damages, including reasonable attorney fees and costs. Private action authorized. § 27-14-12.

Statute of limitations and other defenses: Four years limitations period. §§ 71-14-13, 37-1-4.

N.M. Stat. §§ 44-9-1 to 44-9-14 (Fraud Against Taxpayers Act)

Claims covered by the statute: Include knowingly false statements regarding a claim for payment presented to a state or state's grantee or contractor, failure to return public property or money, knowing purchase of public property from person who lawfully may not sell the property, conspiracy to commit a violation, knowing concealment or avoidance of an obligation to pay or transmit property to state, and inadvertently submitting a false claim and failing to disclose the false claim within a reasonable time after discovery. § 44-9-3(A).

Exemptions: No action by qui tam plaintiff against an elected or appointed state official, a member of the state legislature or a member of the judiciary if the action is based on evidence or information known to the state agency to which the false claim was made or to the attorney general when the action was filed. No action by qui tam plaintiff that is based upon allegations or transactions that are the subject of a criminal, civil or administrative proceeding in which the state or political subdivision is a party unless it is determined and certified in writing that the action is in the interest of the state or political subdivision. Upon motion of the attorney general or political subdivision, a court may, in its discretion, dismiss an action brought by a qui tam plaintiff if the elements of the alleged false claim have been publicly disclosed at the time the complaint is filed. § 44-9-9.

Who can initiate action as private plaintiff?: If person bringing the action is convicted of criminal conduct arising from role in the violation, that person shall be dismissed from the action and shall not receive any share of proceeds. § 44-9-7(C)(2). No action by a present or former employee of the state or political subdivision unless the employee, during employment and in good faith, exhausted existing internal procedures for reporting false claims and the state or political subdivision failed to act on the information provided within a reasonable period of time. § 44-9-9.

Procedure for initiating action and state intervention: Action shall be brought in the name of the state or political subdivision. Complaint must be filed in camera in district court and remain under seal for at least 60 days. Prior to expiration of 60-day period, attorney general or political subdivision must either intervene or decline, in which case qui tam plaintiff has the right to proceed. When qui tam plaintiff brings an action, no person other than the attorney general or a political subdivision may intervene or bring a related action based upon the same facts. § 44-9-5. Attorney general or political subdivision may intervene at a later date upon a showing of good cause. § 44-9-6.

Elements of proof: Proof of specific intent to defraud is not required. § 44-9-3(B). The state or political subdivision or qui tam plaintiff is required to prove all essential elements of the cause of action, including damages, by a preponderance of the evidence. Defendant may not deny the essential elements of the offense in any action that involves the same transaction as a criminal proceeding in which there was a final judgment rendered, whether upon a verdict after trial or a plea of guilty. § 44-9-12.

Remedies and attorney fees for state: Treble damages and civil penalty of between $5,000 and $10,000, plus costs and reasonable attorney fees, including fees of attorney general, state agency or political subdivision counsel. However, court may assess no less than twice the amount of damages if violator provided state officials responsible for investigating false claims violations with all known information not later than 30 days after date first obtained and fully cooperated with investigation, and when information was provided no criminal prosecution, civil action or administrative action had commenced and violator did not have actual knowledge of investigation's existence. § 44-9-3.

Awards to plaintiffs bringing action: If attorney general or political subdivision intervenes: between 15 and 25% of proceeds of action or settlement, based upon extent to which qui tam plaintiff substantially contributed to the prosecution of the action, plus reasonable attorney fees and expenses. If such action is based primarily on disclosures of information relating to allegations or transactions in criminal, civil, or administrative hearing, in a legislative, administrative, auditor or inspector general report, hearing, or investigation, or from the news media: no more than 10% of proceeds unless attorney general or political subdivision determines and certifies in writing that the qui tam plaintiff provided a significant contribution in advancing the matter, in which case the plaintiff receives between 15 and 25%. If state or political subdivision does not intervene: between 25 and 30% of proceeds, plus reasonable attorney fees and expenses. Whether or not attorney general or political subdivision intervenes, court may reduce share if person bringing the action planned and initiated the violation. § 44-9-7.

Anti-retaliation provision: Employer shall not make, adopt or enforce a rule, regulation or policy preventing an employee from disclosing information to a government or law enforcement agency or from acting in furtherance of an action. Employee who is discharged, demoted, suspended, threatened, harassed, denied promotion or in any other manner discriminate against an employee in the terms and conditions of employment because of the lawful acts done in disclosing information to a government or law enforcement agency or in furthering an action is entitled to all make-whole relief. Relief includes reinstatement with appropriate seniority, twice the amount of back pay, interest on back pay, special damages, reasonable attorney fees and costs, and, if appropriate, punitive damages. Private action authorized. § 44-9-11.

Statute of limitations and other defenses: "A civil action pursuant to the Fraud Against Taxpayers Act may be brought at any time." § 44-9-12.

NEW YORK

New York State Fin. Law §§ 187 to 194 (McKinney) (False Claims Act)

Claims covered by the statute: Include false statements regarding a claim for payment presented to state or to state's grantee or contractor, conspiracy to commit a violation, failure to return public property or money, knowing purchase of public property from officer or employee of state or local government who lawfully may not sell the property, and knowing concealment or knowing and improper avoidance of an obligation to pay or transmit property to state or local government. § 189(1). The Act applies to claims, records, or statements made under the tax law only if (i) the net income or sales of the person against whom the action is brought equals or exceeds $1,000,000 for any taxable year subject to any action brought; (ii) the damages pleaded in such action exceed $350,000; and (iii) the person is alleged to have violated § 189(1)(a), (b), (c), (d), (e), (f) or (g). § 189(4).

Exemptions: Request or demand for money or property that state or a local government has already paid to an individual as compensation for government employment or as an income subsidy with no restrictions on that individual's use of the money or property. § 188(1). No action against the federal government, the state or a local government, or any officer or employee thereof acting in his or her official capacity. § 190(1), (2). If qui tam plaintiff is convicted of criminal conduct arising from role in the violation, that person shall be dismissed from the qui tam action and shall not receive any share of proceeds. § 190(8). No qui tam action that is based upon allegations or transactions that are the subject of a pending civil action or an administrative action in which the state or a local government is already a party. No qui tam action if the state or local government has reached a binding settlement or other agreement with the violator resolving the matter and such agreement has been approved in writing by the attorney general or applicable local government attorney. No qui tam action against a member of the legislature, member of the judiciary, or senior executive branch official if the action is based upon evidence or information known to the state when the action was brought. § 190(9).

Who can initiate action as private plaintiff?: Qui tam plaintiff must be an "original source" of the information if the allegations or transactions have already been publicly disclosed. § 190(9).

Procedure for initiating action and state intervention: Complaint must be filed in supreme court in camera and remain under seal for at least 60 days. Prior to expiration of 60-day period, state must either intervene, intervene "as of right, so as to aid and assist the plaintiff in the action," or decline, in which case the qui tam plaintiff has the right to proceed. When person brings a qui tam action, no person other than the attorney general or a local government attorney may intervene or bring a related civil action based upon the same facts. The attorney general has the right to intervene at a later date upon a showing of good cause. § 190. The attorney general shall consult with the commissioner of the department of taxation and finance prior to filing or intervening in any action based upon the filing of false claims, records or statements made under the tax law. If the state declines to participate or to authorize participation by a local government, the qui tam plaintiff must obtain approval from the attorney general before making any motion to compel the department of taxation and finance to disclose tax records. § 189(4).

Elements of proof: In pleading an action, qui tam plaintiff shall not be required to identify specific claims that result from an alleged course of misconduct, or any specific records or statements used, if the facts alleged, if ultimately proven true, would provide a reasonable indication that one or more violations are likely to have occurred, and if the allegations provide adequate notice of the specific nature of the alleged misconduct to permit the state or a local government effectively to investigate and defendants fairly to defend the allegations made. § 192(1-a). The state, local government or qui tam plaintiff is required to prove all essential elements of the cause of action, including damages, by a preponderance of the evidence. § 192(2). Knowing violation requires no proof of specific intent to defraud. Acts occurring by mistake or as a result of mere negligence are not covered by the law. § 188(3)(b).

Remedies and attorney fees for state: Treble damages and civil penalty of between $6,000 and $12,000, plus consequential damages, attorney fees and costs. However, court may assess not more than twice the amount of damages sustained if violator provided officials responsible for investigating false claims violations with all known information within 30 days after date first obtained and fully cooperated with any government investigation, and when information was provided no criminal prosecution, civil action, or administrative action had commenced and violator did not have actual knowledge of the investigation's existence. § 189.

Awards to plaintiffs bringing action: If attorney general or local government intervenes: between 15 and 25% of proceeds of action or settlement, based upon extent to which qui tam plaintiff substantially contributed to the prosecution of the action, plus reasonable expenses necessarily incurred, attorney fees and expenses. If such action is based primarily on disclosures of information relating to allegations or transactions in criminal, civil, or administrative hearing, in a legislative or administrative report, hearing, audit or investigation, or from the news media: no more than 10% of proceeds. If attorney general or local government does not intervene: between 25 and 30% of proceeds, plus reasonable expenses necessarily incurred, attorney fees and costs. Court may reduce share if qui tam plaintiff planned and initiated the violation. § 190.

Anti-retaliation provision: Current or former employee, contractor or agent of any private or public employer who is discharged, demoted, suspended, threatened, harassed or in any other manner discriminated against in the terms and conditions of employment, or otherwise harmed or penalized by an employer or prospective employer because of lawful acts done in furtherance of an action or other efforts to stop a violation is entitled to all make-whole relief. Relief includes an injunction to restrain continued discrimination; hiring, contracting or reinstatement to the position person would have had but for the discrimination or to an equivalent position; reinstatement of full fringe benefits and seniority rights; twice the amount of back pay, plus interest; and special damages, including reasonable attorney fees and costs. § 191.

Statute of limitations and other defenses: Limitations period of ten years. § 192. Acts occurring by mistake or as a result of mere negligence are not covered by the law. § 188(3)(b).

NORTH CAROLINA

N.C. Gen. Stat. §§ 1-605 to 1-618 (False Claims Act)

Claims covered by the statute: Include knowingly false statements regarding a claim for payment presented to the state or state's grantee or contractor, failure to return public property or money, knowing purchase of public property from a state officer or employee who lawfully may not sell the property, conspiracy to commit a violation, and knowing concealment or knowing and improper avoidance of an obligation to pay or transmit property to the state. § 1-607(a).

Exemptions: Requests or demands for money or property that the state has paid to an individual as compensation for state employment or as an income subsidy with no restrictions on that individual's use of the money or property. § 1-606(2). Act does not apply to claims, records, or statements made under chapter 105 (governing levy of taxes). § 1-607(c). No qui tam action against a member of the General Assembly, member of the judiciary, or senior executive branch official acting in one's official capacity if the action is based on evidence or information known to the state when the action was brought. No qui tam action that is based upon allegations or transactions that are the subject of a civil suit or an administrative civil money penalty proceeding in which the state is already a party. § 1-611.

Who can initiate action as private plaintiff?: Qui tam plaintiff must be an "original source" of the information if the allegations or transactions have already been publicly disclosed. § 1-611(d). If qui tam plaintiff is convicted of criminal conduct arising from role in violation, qui tam plaintiff shall be dismissed from the action and shall not receive any share of proceeds. § 1-610(f). No action by former of current public employee or public official if the allegations of such action are based substantially upon allegations of wrongdoing or misconduct which such person had a duty or obligation to report or investigate within the scope of his or her public employment or office, or information or records to which the person had access as a result of his or her public employment or office. § 1-611(c).

Procedure for initiating action and state intervention: Action shall be brought in the name of the state. Complaint must be filed in camera and remain under seal for at least 120 days. Prior to expiration of 120-day period, the state must either intervene or decline, in which case the qui tam plaintiff has the right to proceed. In a quit tam action, no person other than the state may intervene or bring a related action based upon the same facts. § 1-608. State may intervene at a later date upon a showing of good cause. § 1-609.

Elements of proof: State or qui tam plaintiff is required to prove all essential elements of the cause of action, including damages, by a preponderance of the evidence. § 1-615(c). Defendant may not deny the essential elements of the offense in any action that involves the same transaction as a criminal proceeding that charged the defendant with fraud or false statements in which there was a final judgment rendered, whether upon a verdict after trial or a plea of guilty or *nolo contendre.* § 1-615(d). Knowing violation requires no proof of specific intent to defraud. § 1-606(4).

Remedies and attorney fees for state: Treble damages and civil penalty of between $5,500 and $11,000, plus costs of action. However, court may assess not more than twice the amount of damages sustained and no civil penalty if violator provided state officials responsible for investigating false claims violations with all known information not later than 30 days after date first obtained and fully cooperated with investigation, and when information was provided no criminal prosecution, civil action or administrative action had commenced and violator did not have actual knowledge of investigation's existence. § 1-607.

Awards to plaintiffs bringing action: If state intervenes: between 15 and 25% of proceeds of action or settlement, based upon extent to which qui tam plaintiff substantially contributed to the prosecution of the action, plus reasonable expenses necessarily incurred, attorney fees and expenses. If such action is based primarily on disclosures of information relating to allegations or transactions in a criminal, civil, or administrative hearing at the state or federal level, in a congressional, legislative, administrative, General Accounting Office or State Auditor's report, hearing, audit, or investigation, or from the news media: no more than 10% of proceeds. If state does not intervene: between 25 and 30% of proceeds, plus reasonable expenses necessarily incurred, attorney fees and costs. Whether or not state intervenes, court may reduce share if qui tam plaintiff planned and initiated the violation. § 1-610.

Anti-retaliation provision: Employee, contractor or agent who is discharged, demoted, suspended, threatened, harassed, or in any other manner discriminated against in the terms and conditions of employment because of lawful acts done in furtherance of an action under the Act shall be entitled to all make-whole relief. Relief includes reinstatement with appropriate seniority, twice the amount of back pay, interest on back pay, and special damages, including reasonable attorney fees and costs. Private action authorized. § 1-613.

Statute of limitations and other defenses: Six years after date violation was committed or three years after date when material facts are or reasonably should have been known by the state official with responsibility to act, but in no event more than ten years after date violation is committed, whichever occurs last. § 1-615(a).

OKLAHOMA

Okla. Stat. tit. 63, §§ 5053 to 5053.7 (Medicaid False Claims Act)

Claims covered by the statute: Include knowingly false statements regarding a claim for payment presented to the state or state's grantee or contractor, failure to return public property or money, knowing purchase of public property from a state officer or employee who lawfully may not sell the property, conspiracy to commit a violation, and knowing concealment or avoidance of an obligation to pay or transmit property to the state. § 5053.1(B).

Exemptions: Act does not apply to claims, records or statements under the state Tax Code. § 5053.1(E). No action brought by an individual that is based upon allegations or transactions that are the subject of a civil suit or an administrative civil money penalty proceeding in which the state is already a party. § 5053.5(A).

Who can initiate action as private plaintiff?: Individual bringing the action must be an "original source" of the information if the allegations or transactions have already been publicly disclosed. § 5053.5(B). If individual bringing the action is convicted of criminal conduct arising from his or her role in the violation of the Act, that individual shall be dismissed from the action and shall not receive any share of proceeds. § 5053.4(C).

Procedure for initiating action and state intervention: Action shall be brought in the name of the state. Complaint shall be filed in camera and remain under seal for at least 60 days. Prior to expiration of 60-day period, state must either intervene or decline, in which case individual has the right to proceed. When an individual brings an action under this Act, under the federal False Claims Act, or under any similar provision of the law of any other state, no person other than the state may intervene or bring a related action based upon the same facts. § 5053.2.

Elements of proof: For knowing violation, no proof of specific intent to defraud is required. § 5053.1(A)(1). The state is required to prove all essential elements of the cause of action, including damages, by a preponderance of the evidence. Defendant may not deny the essential elements of the offense in any action that involves the same transaction as a criminal proceeding that charged the defendant with fraud or false statements in which there was a final judgment rendered, whether upon a verdict after trial or upon a plea of guilty or nolo contendre. § 5053.6.

Remedies and attorney fees for state: Treble damages and civil penalty of between $5,000 and $10,000, plus costs of civil action to recover penalty and damages. However, court may assess not less than twice the amount of damages if violator provided state officials responsible for investigating false claims violations with all known information not later than 30 days after date first obtained and fully cooperated with investigation, and when information was provided no criminal prosecution, civil action or administrative action had commenced and violator did not have actual knowledge of investigation's existence. § 5053.1(B), (C).

Awards to plaintiffs bringing action: If state intervenes: between 15 and 25% of proceeds of action or settlement, based upon extent to which individual substantially contributed to the prosecution of the action, plus reasonable expenses necessarily incurred, attorney fees and expenses. If such action is based primarily on disclosures of information relating to allegations or transactions in criminal, civil, or administrative hearing, in a Congressional, legislative, administrative or State Auditor and Inspector report, hearing, audit or investigation, or from the news media: no more than 10% of proceeds. If state does not intervene: between 25 and 30% of proceeds, plus reasonable expenses necessarily incurred, attorney fees and costs. Whether or not state intervenes, court may reduce share if individual planned and initiated the violation. § 5053.4.

Anti-retaliation provision: Employee who is discharged, demoted, suspended, threatened, harassed, or in any other manner discriminated against in the terms and conditions of employment by employer because of lawful acts done in furtherance of an action under the Act is entitled to all make-whole relief. Relief includes reinstatement with appropriate seniority, twice the amount of back pay, interest on back pay, and special damages, including reasonable attorney fees and costs. Private action authorized. § 5053.5(E).

Statute of limitations and other defenses: Six years after date violation is committed or three years after date when material facts are or reasonably should have been known by the state official with responsibility to act, but in no event more than ten years after date violation is committed, whichever occurs last. § 5053.6(B).

RHODE ISLAND

R.I. Gen. Laws §§ 9-1.1-1 to 9-1.1-9 (False Claims Act)

Claims covered by the statute: Include knowingly false statements regarding a claim for payment presented to the state or to contractor or grantee, failure to return public property or money, knowing purchase of public property from a state officer or employee or member of the state National Guard who lawfully may not sell the property, conspiracy to commit a violation, and knowing concealment or knowing and improper avoidance of an obligation to pay or transmit property to the state. § 9-1.1-3(a).

Exemptions: Request or demand for money or property that the state has paid to an individual as compensation for state employment or as an income subsidy with no restrictions on that individual's use of the money or property. Act does not apply to claims, records, or statements made under state personal income tax law. § 9-1.1-3. No action brought by private person against the governor, lieutenant governor, attorney general, members of the general assembly, member of the judiciary, treasurer, secretary of state, auditor general, any director of a state agency, and any other individual appointed by the governor if the action is based upon evidence or information known to the state when the action was brought. No action brought by private person that is based upon allegations or transactions that are the subject of a civil suit or an administrative civil money penalty proceeding in which the state is already a party. § 9-1.1-4(e).

Who can initiate action as private plaintiff?: Individual bringing the action must be an "original source" of the information if the allegations or transactions have already been publicly disclosed. § 9-1.1-4(e)(4). If person bringing the action is convicted of criminal conduct arising from his or her role in the violation, that person shall be dismissed from the action and shall not receive any share of proceeds. § 9-1.1-4(d)(3). No action brought by a former or present member of the state National Guard against a member of the Guard arising out of such person's service in the Guard. § 9-1.1-4(e).

Procedure for initiating action and state intervention: Action shall be brought in the name of the state. Complaint shall be served on the state upon the attorney general, and filed in camera. Complainant must remain under seal for at least 60 days. Prior to expiration of 60-day period, state must either intervene or decline, in which case qui tam plaintiff has the right to proceed. State may intervene at a later date upon a showing of good cause. § 9-1.1-4.

Elements of proof: For knowing violation, no proof of specific intent to defraud is required. § 9-1.1-3(b). The state is required to prove all essential elements of the cause of action, including damages, by a preponderance of the evidence. Defendant may not deny the essential elements of the offense in any action that involves the same transaction as a criminal proceeding that charged the defendant with fraud or false statements in which there was a final judgment rendered, whether upon a verdict after trial or a plea of guilty or nolo contendre. § 9-1.1-5(d), (e).

Remedies and attorney fees for state: Treble damages and civil penalty of between $5,500 and $11,000, plus costs of action. § 9-1.1-3(a).

Awards to plaintiffs bringing action: If state intervenes: between 15 and 25% of proceeds of action or settlement, based upon extent to which individual substantially contributed to the prosecution of the action, plus reasonable expenses necessarily incurred, attorney fees and expenses. If such action is based primarily on disclosures of information relating to allegations or transactions in criminal, civil, or administrative hearing, in a legislative, administrative or Auditor General's report, hearing, audit or investigation, or from the news media: no more than 10% of proceeds. If state does not intervene: between 25 and 30% of proceeds, plus reasonable expenses necessarily incurred, attorney fees and costs. Whether or not state intervenes, court may reduce share if individual planned and initiated the violation. § 9-1.1-4.

Anti-retaliation provision: Employee, contractor or agent who is discharged, demoted, suspended, threatened, harassed, or in any other manner discriminated against in the terms and conditions of employment because of lawful acts done in furtherance of an action under the Act or other efforts to stop a violation is entitled to all make-whole relief. Relief includes reinstatement with appropriate seniority, twice the amount of back pay, interest on back pay, and special damages, including reasonable attorney fees and costs. Private action authorized. § 9-1.1-4(g).

Statute of limitations and other defenses: Six years after date violation is committed or three years after date when material facts are or reasonably should have been known by the state official with responsibility to act, but in no event more than ten years after date violation is committed, whichever occurs last. § 9-1.1-5(b).

TENNESSEE

Tenn. Code Ann. §§ 4-18-101 to 4-18-108 (False Claims Act)

Claims covered by the statute: Include knowingly false statements regarding a claim for payment presented to the state or to political subdivision, failure to return public property or money, knowing purchase of public property from any person who lawfully may not sell the property, conspiracy to defraud the state or political subdivision, knowing concealment or avoidance of an obligation to pay or transmit property to the state or political subdivision, and knowingly false or fraudulent conduct, representation, or practice in order to procure anything of value directly or indirectly from the state or political subdivision. § 4-18-103.

Exemptions: Act does not apply to any controversy involving an amount of less than $500 in value, unless the controversy arose from a violation of chapter 58 of title 4 (Eligibility Verification for Entitlements Act). Act does not apply to claims, records, or statements regarding workers' compensation claims, and also does not apply to claims, records, or statements made under any statute applicable to any tax administered by the department of revenue. § 4-18-103. No action brought by qui tam plaintiff against a member of the general assembly, member of the state judiciary, elected official in the state's executive branch, or a member of the governing body or other elected official of any political subdivision if the action is based on evidence or information known to the state or political subdivision when the action was brought. No action brought by qui tam plaintiff that is based upon allegations or transactions that are the subject of a civil suit or an administrative proceeding in which the state or political subdivision is already a party. § 4-18-104(d). Act does not apply to claims covered by the Medicaid False Claims Act, including without limitation, claims arising out of funds paid to or by TennCare managed care organizations. § 4-18-108.

Who can initiate action as private plaintiff?: Qui tam plaintiff must be an "original source" of the information if the allegations or transactions have already been publicly disclosed. No action brought by qui tam plaintiff that is based upon information discovered by a present or former employee of the state or political subdivision during the course of such person's employment unless that employee first, in good faith, exhausted existing internal procedures for reporting and seeking recovery of the falsely claimed sums through official channels and unless the state or political subdivision failed to act on the information within a reasonable period of time. § 4-18-104(d).

Procedure for initiating action and state intervention: A person may bring a civil action for a violation for the person and for the state in the name of the state if any state funds are involved, or for a political subdivision in the name of the political subdivision if political subdivision funds are involved, or for both the state and political subdivision if state and political subdivision funds are involved. Complaint must be filed in circuit or chancery court in camera and may remain under seal for up to 60 days. Prior to expiration of 60-day period, attorney general must either intervene or decline, in which case qui tam plaintiff shall has the right to proceed. Within 15 days after receiving a complaint alleging violations that exclusively involve political subdivision funds, attorney general shall forward copies of the complaint and written disclosure of material evidence and information to the appropriate prosecuting authority for disposition, and shall notify the qui tam plaintiff of the transfer. Within 45 days after the complaint is forwarded, the prosecuting authority may elect to intervene. Prior to expiration of 45-day period, the prosecuting authority must either intervene or decline, in which case qui tam plaintiff has the right to proceed. Within 15 days after receiving a complaint alleging violations that involve both state and political subdivision funds, the attorney general shall forward copies of the complaint and written disclosure to the appropriate prosecuting authority, and shall coordinate its review and investigation with those of the prosecuting authority. Within 60 days after receiving a complaint alleging violations that involve both state and political subdivision funds, the attorney general or the prosecuting authority, or both, may elect to intervene. Prior to expiration of 60-day period, the attorney general must either intervene, notify the court that that the prosecuting authority elects to intervene, or decline, in which case qui tam plaintiff has the right to proceed. When a person brings an action, no other person may bring a related action based upon the same facts. 4-18-104.

Elements of proof: For knowing violation, no proof of specific intent to defraud is required. § 4-18-102(2)(B). The state, political subdivision, or qui tam plaintiff is required to prove all essential elements of the cause of action, including damages, by a preponderance of the evidence. Defendant may not deny the essential elements of the offense in any action that involves the same transaction as a criminal proceeding that charged the defendant with fraud or false statements in which there was a guilty verdict rendered, whether upon a plea of guilty or nolo contendere, except for a plea of nolo contendere made prior to July 1, 2001. § 4-18-106.

Remedies and attorney fees for state: Treble damages and civil penalty of between $2,500 and $10,000 for each false claim, plus costs of civil action to recover penalties or damages. § 4-18-103(a). However, court may assess between two and three times the amount of damages and no civil penalty if violator provided state officials responsible for investigating false claims violations with all known information not later than 30 days after date first obtained and fully cooperated with investigation, and when information was provided no criminal prosecution, civil action or administrative action had commenced and violator did not have actual knowledge of investigation's existence. § 4-18-103(b).

Awards to plaintiffs bringing action: If state or political subdivision intervenes: between 25 and 33% of the proceeds of the action or settlement of the claim, depending upon the extent to which the qui tam plaintiff substantially contributed to the prosecution of the action, plus reasonable expenses necessarily incurred, attorney fees and costs. If state or political subdivision does not intervene: between 35 and 50% of the proceeds, plus reasonable expenses necessarily incurred, attorney fees and costs. If the action is based primarily on information from a present or former employee who actively participated in the fraudulent activity, the employee is not entitled to any minimum guaranteed recovery, but the court may award the qui tam plaintiff any sums it considers appropriate: up to 33% of the proceeds if the state or political subdivision intervenes, or up to 50% if it does not intervene. The court must take into account the significance of the information, the role of the qui tam plaintiff in advancing the case to litigation, the scope of the present or past employee's

involvement in the fraudulent activity, and the employee's attempts to avoid or resist the activity. § 4-18-104(g).

Anti-retaliation provision: No employer shall make, adopt, or enforce any rule, regulation, or policy preventing an employee from disclosing information to a government or law enforcement agency or from acting in furtherance of an action. No employer shall discharge, demote, suspend, threaten, harass, deny promotion to, or in any other manner discriminate against an employee in the terms and conditions of employment because of lawful acts done in disclosing information to a government or law enforcement agency or in furthering a false claims action. Employer who violates anti-retaliation provision is liable for all make-whole relief, including reinstatement with appropriate seniority, twice the amount of back pay, interest on back pay, special damages, reasonable attorney fees and costs, and, where appropriate, punitive damages. Employee may bring an action in the appropriate chancery court of the state. An employee who is retaliated against due to participation in conduct that directly or indirectly resulted in the submission of a false claim to the state or a political subdivision is entitled to remedies if, and only if: (1) the employee voluntarily disclosed information to a government or law enforcement agency or acted in furtherance of a false claims action, including investigation for, initiation of, testimony for, or assistance in an action filed or to be filed; and (2) the employee had been harassed, threatened with termination or demotion, or otherwise coerced by the employer or its management into engaging in the fraudulent activity in the first place. § 4-18-105.

Statute of limitations and other defenses: Three years after the date of discovery by the official of the state or political subdivision with responsibility to act or, in any event, no more than ten years after date violation was committed. § 4-18-106(a).

Tenn. Code Ann. §§ 71-5-181 to 71-5-185 (Medicaid False Claims Act)

Claims covered by the statute: Include knowingly presentation of a false or fraudulent claim for payment or approval under the Medicaid program, knowingly false record or statement material to a false or fraudulent claim under the Medicaid program, conspiracy to commit a violation, and knowing concealment or knowingly and improper avoidance of an obligation to pay or transmit money or property to the state relative to the Medicaid program. § 71-5-182.

Exemptions: No action brought by individual that is based upon allegations or transactions that are the subject of a civil suit or an administrative civil monetary penalty proceeding in which the state is already a party. § 71-5-183(e)(1).

Who can initiate action as private plaintiff?: Individual must be an "original source" of the information if the allegations or transactions have already been publicly disclosed.

If person bringing the action is convicted of criminal conduct arising from role in violation, that person shall be dismissed from the action and shall not receive any share of proceeds. § 71-5-183.

Procedure for initiating action and state intervention: Action shall be brought in the name of the state. Complaint must be filed in camera and remain under seal for at least 60 days. Prior to expiration of 60-day period, state must either intervene or decline, in which case person bringing the action has the right to proceed. § 71-5-183.

Elements of proof: For knowing violation, no proof of specific intent to defraud is required. § 71-5-182(a)(3). The state is required to prove all essential elements of the cause of action, including damages, by a preponderance of the evidence. Defendant may not deny the essential elements of the offense in any action that involves the same transaction as a criminal proceeding that charged the defendant with fraud or false statements in which there was a final judgment rendered, whether upon a verdict after trial or a plea of guilty or nolo contendre. § 71-5-184.

Remedies and attorney fees for state: Treble damages and civil penalty of between $5,000 and $25,000, plus costs of a civil action brought to recover penalty or damages. However, court may assess not less than twice the amount of damages if violator provided state officials responsible for investigating false claims violations with all known information not later than 30 days after date first obtained and fully cooperated with investigation, and when information was provided no criminal prosecution, civil action or administrative action had commenced and violator did not have actual knowledge of investigation's existence. § 71-5-182.

Awards to plaintiffs bringing action: If state intervenes: between 15 and 25% of the proceeds of the action or settlement, depending upon the extent to which the person substantially contributed to the prosecution of the action, plus reasonable expenses necessarily incurred, attorney fees and costs. If such action is based primarily on disclosures of information relating to allegations or transactions in criminal, civil, or administrative hearing, report, audit or investigation, or from the news media: no more than 10% of proceeds. If state does not intervene: between 25 and 30% of proceeds, plus reasonable expenses necessarily incurred, attorney fees and costs. Whether or not state intervenes, court may reduce share if individual planned and initiated the violation. § 71-5-183.

Anti-retaliation provision: Employee, contractor or agent is entitled to all make-whole relief if discharged, demoted, suspended, threatened, harassed, or in any other manner discriminated against in the terms and conditions of employment because of lawful acts done in furtherance of an action under the Act or other efforts to stop a violation. Relief includes reinstatement with appropriate seniority, twice the amount of back pay, interest on back pay, and special damages, including reasonable attorney fees and costs. § 71-5-183(g).

Statute of limitations and other defenses: Six years after date violation is committed or three years after material facts are or reasonably should have been known by the state official with responsibility to act, but in no event more than ten years after violation is committed, whichever occurs last. § 71-5-184(b).

TEXAS

Tex. Hum. Res. Code Ann. §§ 36.001 to 36.117 (West) (Medicaid Fraud Prevention Act). *See also* **Tex. Hum. Res. Code Ann. § 32.039 (West)**

Claims covered by the statute: Include knowingly false statements that permit a person to receive an unauthorized benefit or payment under the Medicaid program, knowing concealment of information regarding Medicaid benefits, knowingly false statements concerning certification or recertification of facilities required by the Medicaid program, paying or receiving bribes in exchange for referrals or ordering of supplies, knowing presentation of claims for unapproved or unlicensed products or services, conspiracy to commit a violation, knowing obstruction of an investigation by the attorney general of an alleged unlawful act, knowing concealment or knowingly and improper avoidance of an obligation to pay or transmit money or property to the under the Medicaid program, and knowing engagement in conduct that constitutes a violation under § 32.039(b) (Medical Assistance Program, Damages and Penalties). § 36.002.

Exemptions: No action that is based on allegations or transactions that are the subject of a civil suit or an administrative penalty proceeding in which the state is already a party. § 36.113(a).

Who can initiate action as private plaintiff?: Individual must be an "original source" of the information if the allegations or transactions have already been publicly disclosed. § 36.113. If the person bringing the action is convicted of criminal conduct arising from the person's role in the violation of the court shall dismiss the person from the action and the person may not receive any share of the proceeds. § 36.111(b).

Procedure for initiating action and state intervention: Action shall be brought in the name of the person and of the state. § 36.101. Petition must be filed in camera and remain under seal until at least 180 days. Prior to expiration of 180-day period, attorney general must either intervene or decline, in which case person bringing the action has the right to proceed. § 36.102. State may intervene at a later date upon a showing of good cause. § 36.104(b-1). A person other than the state may not intervene or bring a related action based upon the same facts. § 36.106.

Elements of proof: Proof of person's specific intent to commit an unlawful act under the Act is not required in a civil or administrative proceeding to show that a person acted "knowingly." § 36.0011. The state or person bringing the action must establish each element of the action, including damages, by a preponderance of the evidence. § 36.1021.

Remedies and attorney fees for state: Violator is liable for treble damages, plus prejudgment interest. Violator is also liable for civil penalty of between $5,500 and $11,000, or between $5,500 and $15,000 per violation for any unlawful act resulting in harm to an elderly person, a person with a disability, or a minor. However, trier of fact may assess a total of not more than twice the amount of damages if violator gave attorney general all known information not later than 30 days after date first obtained and when violator furnished information, the attorney general had not yet begun an investigation. § 36.052. Attorney general may recover fees, expenses, and costs reasonably incurred in obtaining injunctive relief or civil remedies or in conducting investigations, including court costs, reasonable attorney fees, witness fees and deposition fees. § 36.007.

Awards to plaintiffs bringing action: If state intervenes: between 15 and 25% of the proceeds, depending on the extent to which the person substantially contributed to the prosecution of the action. If state does not intervene: between 25 and 30% of the proceeds. Entitlement to proceeds is not affected if state intervenes at a later date. If action is based primarily on disclosures of specific information relating to allegations or transactions in a state or federal criminal or civil hearing, in a state or federal legislative or administrative report, hearing, audit, or investigation, or from the news media: an amount deemed appropriate, but not more than 10% of the proceeds. Statute authorizes recovery of reasonable expenses, reasonable attorney fees, and costs necessarily incurred. § 36.110. If action was brought by a person who planned and initiated the violation, court may reduce the share of the proceeds. § 36.111.

Anti-retaliation provision: Employee, contractor or agent who is discharged, demoted, suspended, threatened, harassed, or in any other manner discriminated against in the terms and conditions of employment because of a lawful act taken in furtherance of an action under the Act or other efforts to stop a violation is entitled to reinstatement with appropriate seniority, twice the amount of back pay, interest on back pay, and special damages, including reasonable attorney fees and costs. Private action authorized. § 36.115.

Statute of limitations and other defenses: Person may recover for an unlawful act for a period of up to six years before the date the lawsuit was filed, or for a period beginning when the unlawful act occurred until up to three years from the date the state knows or reasonably should have known material facts, whichever period is longer, regardless of whether the unlawful act occurred more than six years before the date the lawsuit was filed. In no event shall a person recover for an unlawful act that occurred more than ten years before the date the lawsuit was filed. § 36.104(b).

VERMONT

Vt. Stat. Ann. tit. 32, §§ 630 to 642 (False Claims Act)

Claims covered by the statute: Include knowingly false statements regarding a claim for payment presented to state state's grantee or contractor, knowing presentation of claim that includes items or services resulting from a violation of state chapter on Bribery or section 1128B of the Social Security Act, knowing presentation of claim that includes items or services for which the state could not receive payment from the federal government due to the operation of the Medicaid program because the claim includes designated health services furnished to an individual on the basis of a referral that would result in the denial of payment under the Medicare program, failure to return public property or money, knowing purchase of public property from a state officer or employee who lawfully may not sell the property, conspiracy to commit a violation, knowing concealment or knowing and improper avoidance of an obligation to pay or transmit property to the state, and inadvertently submitting a false claim and failing to disclose by the later of 120 days after the date on which the false claim was identified or the date any corresponding cost report is due, if applicable. § 631(a).

Exemptions: Request or demand for money or property that the state has paid to an individual as compensation for state employment or as an income subsidy with no restrictions on that individual's use of the money or property. § 630(1). Act does not apply to claims, records, or statements made or presented to establish, limit, reduce, or evade liability for the payment of tax to the state. § 631(d). No action by an individual against a member of the state legislative branch, the attorney general, a member of the judiciary, or a senior executive branch official if the action is based on evidence or information known to the state when the action was brought. No action by an individual that is based upon allegations or transactions that are the subject of a civil suit or an administrative civil money penalty proceeding in which the state is already a party. § 636.

Who can initiate action as private plaintiff?: If relator is convicted of criminal conduct arising from his or her role in the violation, relator shall be dismissed from the action and shall not receive any share of the proceeds. § 635. Relator must be an "original source" of the information if the allegations or transactions have already been publicly disclosed. § 636(c).

Procedure for initiating action and state intervention: Relator may bring a civil action in the Civil Division of the Superior Court in Washington County or in any county where an act prohibited by the statute occurred. Action shall be brought in the name of the state. Complainant must be filed in camera and must remain under seal for at least 60 days. Prior to expiration of 60-day period, attorney general must either intervene or decline, in which case relator has the right to proceed. When relator brings an action, no person other than attorney general may intervene or bring a related action based upon the same facts. § 632

Elements of proof: Knowing violation required no proof of specific intent to defraud. § 630(2). The party bringing the action is required to prove all essential elements of the cause of action, including damages, by a preponderance of the evidence. § 640. Defendant may not deny the essential elements of the offense in any action that involves the same transaction as a criminal proceeding that charged the defendant with fraud or false statements in which there was a final judgment rendered, whether upon a verdict after trial or a plea of guilty or nolo contendre. § 639(d).

Remedies and attorney fees for state: Treble damages and civil penalty of between $5,500 and $11,000, plus costs. However, court may enter judgment for not less than twice the amount of damages and no civil penalty if violator provided state officials responsible for investigating false claims violations with all known information not later than 30 days after date first obtained and fully cooperated with investigation, and when information was provided no criminal prosecution, civil action or administrative action had commenced and violator did not have actual knowledge of investigation's existence. § 631(c).

Awards to plaintiffs bringing action: If attorney general intervenes: between 15 and 25% of proceeds recovered and collected in action or settlement of the claim, depending upon the extent to which the relator substantially contributed to the prosecution of the action, plus expenses reasonably incurred, attorney fees and costs. If such action is based primarily on disclosures of specific information relating to allegations or transactions in a criminal, civil, or administrative hearing, in a legislative, administrative, or state auditor hearing, audit, investigation, or report, or from the news media: amount deemed appropriate, but in no case more than 10% of proceeds. If attorney general does not intervene: between 25 and 30% of proceeds, plus expenses reasonably incurred, attorney fees and costs. Whether or not attorney general intervenes, court may reduce or eliminate share of proceeds if relator planned or initiated the violation. § 635.

Anti-retaliation provision: Employee, contractor or agent is entitled to all make-whole relief if discharged, demoted, suspended, threatened, harassed, or in any other manner discriminated against in the terms and conditions of employment because of lawful acts done in furtherance of an action under the Act or other efforts to stop a violation. Relief includes reinstatement with appropriate seniority, twice the amount of back pay, interest on back pay, and special damages, including reasonable attorney fees and costs. Private action authorized. No employer shall make, adopt, or enforce any rule, regulation, or policy preventing an employee, contractor, or agent from disclosing information to a government or law enforcement agency or from acting to further efforts to stop a violation. No employer shall require as a condition of employment, during the term of employment or at the termination of employment, that any employee, contractor or agent agree to an agreement that limits or denies the right to bring an action or provide information to a government or law enforcement agency pursuant to the Act. Any such agreement shall be void. § 638.

Statute of limitations and other defenses: Six years after date violation was committed or three years after date when material facts are or reasonably should have been known by the official in the attorney general's office with responsibility to act, but in no event more than ten years after date violation is committed, whichever occurs last. § 639(a).

VIRGINIA

Va. Code Ann. §§ 8.01-216.1 to 8.01-216.9 (Fraud Against Taxpayers Act)

Claims covered by the statute: Include knowingly false statements regarding a claim for payment presented to the commonwealth or commonwealth's grantee or contractor, conspiracy to commit such a violation, failure to return public property or money, knowing purchase of public property from officer or employee of commonwealth who lawfully may not sell the property, and knowing concealment or avoidance of an obligation to pay or transmit property to the commonwealth. § 8.01-216.3(A).

Exemptions: Requests or demands for money or property that the commonwealth has paid to an individual as compensation for employment with the commonwealth or as income subsidy with no restriction on that individual's use of the money or property. § 8.01-216.2. Act does not apply to claims, records or statements relating to state or local taxes. § 8.01-216.3(D). No action brought against any department, authority, board, bureau, commission, or agency or political subdivision of the commonwealth, a member of the General Assembly or the judiciary, or an exempt official if the action is based on evidence or information known to the commonwealth when the action was brought. No action by an individual based upon allegations or transactions that are the subject of a civil suit or an administrative proceeding in which the commonwealth is already a party. § 8.01-216.8.

Who can initiate action as private plaintiff?: Individual must be an "original source" of the information if the allegations or transactions have already been publicly disclosed. § 8.01-216.8. If action is brought by a person who planned and initiated the violation or if person is convicted of criminal conduct arising from his role in the violation, that person shall be dismissed from the action and shall not receive any share of the proceeds. § 8.01-216.7(C). No action by an incarcerated inmate of a state or local correctional facility. § 8.01-216.8.

Procedure for initiating action and state intervention: Action shall be brought in the name of the commonwealth. Complaint shall be served on the commonwealth, filed in camera, and shall remain under seal for at least 120 days. Prior to expiration of 120-day period, the commonwealth must either intervene or decline, in which case the person bringing the action has the right to proceed. When a person brings an action under this section, no person other than the commonwealth may intervene or bring a related action based upon the same facts. § 8.01-216.5.

Elements of proof: Knowing violation does not require proof of specific intent to defraud. § 8.01-216.3(C). The commonwealth is required to prove all essential elements of the cause of action, including damages, by a preponderance of the evidence. Defendant may not deny the essential elements of the offense in any action that involves the same transaction as a criminal proceeding that charged the defendant with fraud or false statements in which there was a final judgment rendered, whether upon a verdict after trial or a plea of guilty or nolo contendre. § 8.01-216.9.

Remedies and attorney fees for state: Treble damages and civil penalty of between $5,500 and $11,000, plus reasonable attorney fees and costs. However, court may assess not less than twice the amount of damages that the Commonwealth sustains if violator provided state officials responsible for investigating false claims violations with all known information not later than 30 days after date first obtained and fully cooperated with investigation, and when information was provided no criminal prosecution, civil action or administrative action had commenced and violator did not have actual knowledge of investigation's existence. Violator is liable for costs of action to recover penalty or damages. § 8.01-216.3(A), (B).

Awards to plaintiffs bringing action: If commonwealth intervenes: between 15 and 25% of the proceeds of the action or settlement of the claim, depending upon the extent to which the person substantially contributed to the prosecution of the action, plus reasonable expenses necessarily incurred, reasonable attorney fees and costs. If such action is based primarily on disclosures of specific information relating to allegations or transactions in a criminal, civil, or administrative hearing, in a legislative, administrative, or Auditor of Public Accounts' report, hearing, audit, or investigation, or from the news media: an amount deemed appropriate, but in no case more than 10% of proceeds. If Commonwealth does not intervene: between 25 and 30% of proceeds, plus reasonable expenses necessarily incurred, reasonable attorney fees and costs. § 8.01-216.7.

Anti-retaliation provision: Employee, contractor or agent is entitled to all make-whole relief necessary if discharged, demoted, suspended, threatened, harassed, or in any other manner discriminated against in the terms and conditions of employment because of lawful acts done in furtherance of an action under the Act or other efforts to stop a violation. Relief includes reinstatement with appropriate seniority, twice the amount of back pay, interest on back pay, and special damages, including reasonable attorney fees and costs. Relief will be reduced by any amount awarded to the employee through a state or local grievance process. Private action authorized. Provision constitutes a waiver of sovereign immunity and creates a cause of action if the commonwealth is the employer responsible for the adverse employment action. § 8.01-216.8.

Statute of limitations and other defenses: Six years after date violation is committed or three years after date when material facts are or reasonably should have been known by the official charged with responsibility to act, but in that event no more than ten years after date violation is committed, whichever occurs last. 8.01-216.9.

WASHINGTON

Wash. Rev. Code §§ 74.66.005 to 74.66.130 (Medicaid Fraud False Claims Act)

Claims covered by the statute: Include knowingly false statements regarding a claim for payment presented to the government entity or entity's grantee or contractor, failure to return public property or money, knowing purchase of public property from a government entity officer or employee who lawfully may not sell the property, conspiracy to commit a violation, and knowing concealment or knowing and improper avoidance of an obligation to pay or transmit property to the government. § 74.66.020.

Exemptions: No qui tam action based upon allegations or transactions that are the subject of a civil suit or an administrative civil money penalty proceeding in which the state is already a party. § 74.66.080(1).

Who can initiate action as private plaintiff?: If person bringing the action is convicted of criminal conduct arising from his or her role in the violation, that person must be dismissed from the action and may not receive any share of proceeds. § 74.66.070(3). Qui tam plaintiff must be an "original source" of the information if the allegations or transactions have already been publicly disclosed. § 74.66.080(2).

Procedure for initiating action and state intervention: Action must be brought in the name of the government entity. Relator must serve a copy of the complaint and written disclosure of substantially all material evidence and information on the attorney general in electronic format. Complaint must be filed in camera and remain under seal for at least 60 days, Prior to expiration of 60-day period, attorney general must either intervene or decline, in which case relator has the right to proceed. When a relator brings an action, no person other than the attorney general may intervene or bring a related action based upon the same facts. § 74.66.050.

Elements of proof: Knowing violation does not require proof of specific intent to defraud. § 74.66.010(7)(b). The attorney general is required to prove all essential elements of the cause of action, including damages, by a preponderance of the evidence. Defendant may not deny the essential elements of the offense in any action that involves the same transaction as a criminal proceeding that charged the defendant with fraud or false statements in which there was a final judgment rendered, whether upon a verdict after trial or a plea of guilty or nolo contendre. § 74.66.100.

Remedies and attorney fees for state: Treble damages and civil penalty of between $5,500 and $11,000 plus costs. However, court may assess not less than twice the amount of damages if violator provided state officials

responsible for investigating false claims violations with all known information not later than 30 days after date first obtained and fully cooperated with investigation, and when information was provided no criminal prosecution, civil action or administrative action had commenced and violator did not have actual knowledge of investigation's existence. § 74.66.020.

Awards to plaintiffs bringing action: If attorney general intervenes: between 15 and 25% of the proceeds of the action or settlement, depending upon the extent to which the relator substantially contributed to the prosecution of the action, plus expenses, fees, and costs. If such action is based primarily on disclosures of specific information relating to allegations or transactions in a criminal, civil, or administrative hearing, in a legislative or administrative report, hearing, audit, or investigation, or from the news media: an amount deemed appropriate, but in no case more than 10% of proceeds. If attorney general does not intervene: between 25 and 30% of proceeds, plus expenses, fees, and costs. Whether or not attorney general intervenes, court may reduce share of proceeds to extent deemed appropriate if person bringing the action planned or initiated the violation. § 74.66.070.

Anti-retaliation provision: Employee, contractor or agent is entitled to all make-whole relief if discharged, demoted, suspended, threatened, harassed, or in any other manner discriminated against in the terms and conditions of employment because of lawful acts done in furtherance of an action under the Act or other efforts to stop a violation. Relief includes reinstatement with appropriate seniority, twice the amount of back pay, interest on back pay, and special damages sustained, including reasonable attorney fees and costs. Private action authorized. § 74.66.090.

Statute of limitations and other defenses: A civil action may be brought "at any time, without limitation" after the date the violation is committed. § 74.66.100(2).

WISCONSIN

Wis. Stat. § 20.931 (False Claims for Medical Assistance)

Claims covered by the statute: Include knowing presentation of false claims for medical assistance, knowingly false records or statements to obtain approval or payment of a false claim for medical assistance, conspiracy to defraud the state by obtaining payment of a false claim for medical assistance knowing concealment or avoidance of an obligation to pay or transmit money or property to the medical assistance program, and failing to disclose a false claim after discovery.

Exemptions: No action brought by a private person against a state public official if the action is based upon information known to the attorney general at the time that the action is brought. No action brought by a private person that is based upon allegations or transactions that are the subject of a civil action or an administrative proceeding to assess a civil forfeiture in which the state is a party if that action or proceeding was commenced prior to the date that the action is filed.

Who can initiate action as private plaintiff?: If the person bringing the action is convicted of criminal conduct arising from his or her role in a violation, the court shall dismiss the person as a party and the person shall not receive any share of proceeds or any expenses, costs and fees.

Procedure for initiating action and state intervention: Must bring action in the name of the state. Complaint must be filed in camera and remain under seal for at least 60 days. Prior to expiration of 60-day period, attorney general must either intervene or decline, in which case the person bringing the action may proceed. If a person brings a valid action under the Act, no person other than the state may intervene or bring a related action while the original action is pending based upon the same facts. State may intervene at a later date upon a showing of good cause.

Elements of proof: "Knowingly" as used in provision does not mean specifically intending to defraud. The plaintiff is required to prove all essential elements of the cause of action or complaint, including damages, by a preponderance of the evidence. Defendant may not deny the essential elements of the offense in any action that involves the same transaction as the criminal action that charged the defendant with fraud or false statements if a judgment of guilty has been entered.

Remedies and attorney fees for state: Treble damages and civil penalty of between $5,000 and $10,000 for each violation. However, court may assess between two and three times the amount of damages and no penalty if violator provided state officials responsible for investigating false claims violations with all known information not later than 30 days after date first obtained and fully cooperated with investigation, and when information was provided no criminal prosecution, civil action or administrative action had commenced and violator did not have actual knowledge of investigation's existence.

Awards to plaintiffs bringing action: If state intervenes: between 15 and 25% of the proceeds of the action or settlement, depending upon the extent to which the person contributed to the prosecution of the action or claim. If such action is based primarily upon disclosures of specific information relating to allegations or transactions specifically in a criminal, civil, or administrative hearing, or in a legislative or administrative report, hearing, audit, or investigation, or report made by the news media: no more than 10% of proceeds. Provision also authorizes recovery of reasonable expenses necessarily incurred, reasonable attorney fees and costs. If state does not intervene: between 25 and 30% of proceeds, plus expenses, fees and costs. Whether or not state intervenes, court may reduce share of proceeds if person bringing the action planned or initiated the violation.

Anti-retaliation provision: Employee who is discharged, demoted, suspended, threatened, harassed, or in any other manner discriminated against because of lawful actions taken in furtherance of an action or claim filed under the Act is entitled to all make-whole relief. Relief includes reinstatement with appropriate seniority, twice the amount of back pay, interest on back pay at the legal rate, and special damages, including reasonable actual attorney fees and costs. Private action authorized.

Statute of limitations and other defenses: Action must be brought within ten years.

Appendix I   State Debt Relief Statutes Summarized

I.1   Introduction

This appendix summarizes state debt relief statutes, and in particular state statutes that regulate debt-management plans, debt settlement, debt adjusting, debt pooling, and similar services. Appx. I.2, *infra*, summarizes the Uniform Debt-Management Services Act, a model act adopted in seven states. Appx. I.3, *infra*, then summarizes debt relief statutes enacted in the fifty states.

For those seven states adopting the model act, Appx. I.3 merely references that fact and does not repeat the summary of the model act found in Appx. I.2, *infra*, but only describes any differences in how each state implemented the Uniform Act. The Uniform Debt-Management Services Act is summarized in Appx. I.2 because it has taken on some independent significance concerning debt relief regulation. The regulation of debt relief services also is discussed in Chapter 10, *supra*.

I.2   The Uniform Debt-Management Services Act

I.2.1   Introduction

The Uniform Law Commission (also known as the National Conference of Commissioners on Uniform State Laws) first adopted the Uniform Debt-Management Services Act in 2005. The Act addresses primarily debt-management plans (described in § 10.2.1, *supra*) and debt settlement (described in § 10.2.2, *supra*). Other services may, however, fall within its scope. This model act was revised in 2008 and also in 2011.[1]

The 2008 amendments added a new category of "certified debt specialist" (who deals with debt settlement plans) and strengthened the provision addressing whether an entity can call itself tax-exempt. Among the most important changes made in 2011 were:

- Making the professional services (attorney, CPA, financial planner) exemptions more specific in an apparent attempt to prevent the "fronting" of professional licenses;
- Banning up-front fees for debt settlement; and
- Adding a definition of lead generators and some restrictions on their activities.

No state has adopted the 2005 original version. The 2008 version with some variations is now law in Colorado, Delaware, Nevada, North Dakota, Rhode Island, and Tennessee.[2] Only Utah has adopted the 2011 version.[3] This appendix summarizes the 2011 version and indicates where that version varies from the 2008 version.

I.2.2   The Uniform Debt-Management Services Act (2011)

Scope & Key Definitions: Services as an intermediary between an individual and one or more creditors of the individual for the purpose of obtaining concessions, defined as assent to repayment of a debt on terms more favorable to the individual than the terms of the contract between the individual and the creditor. § 2.

---

1   The complete text of each version is available from the Commission's website at www.uniformlaws.org.

2   Unif. Law Comm'n, Map of Uniform Debt-Management Services Act (2008) Enactments, *available at* http://uniformlaws.org.

3   Unif. Law Comm'n, Acts, Debt-Management Services (2011), *available at* www.uniformlaws.org.

Exceptions: Legal services provided in an attorney client relationship, if provided by an attorney authorized to practice in the state, who provides legal services in representing the individual in the individual's relationship with the creditor, and there is no intermediary between the individual and the creditor except the attorney or a person under the direct supervision of the attorney. Accounting services provided in an accountant client relationship, if provided by a CPA authorized to practice in the state, who provides accounting services in representing the individual in the individual's relationship with the creditor, and there is no intermediary between the accountant and the creditor except the accountant or a person under the direct supervision of the accountant. Financial planning services provided in a planner client relationship if the administrator determines by rule that financial planners are licensed by the state, subject to a disciplinary mechanism, subject to a code of professional responsibility and a continuing education requirement. Providing services to an individual who the provider has no reason to know resides in this state at the time of the agreement. (Act is limited to providers that enter agreements with persons residing in the state.) Provider who receives no compensation from, or on behalf of, the individuals to whom it provides services or from their creditors. The following persons acting in the regular scope of their employment: judicial officer or person acting under the orders of a court or administrative agency or an assignee for the benefit of creditors; a bank or its affiliate (defined); a title insurer, escrow company or other entity that provides bill-paying services if the debt management is incidental to the bill-paying. §§ 2, 3.

2011 changes from earlier versions re exceptions: The professional services (attorney, CPA, financial planner) exemptions are made more specific, in an apparent attempt to prevent the "fronting" of professional licenses.

Registration/Licensing: Registration, $50,000 bond (or irrevocable letter of credit or certain government bonds), and insurance ($250,000—to be adjusted for inflation) required. Applicant must provide a copy of its three most commonly used education programs, a description of its financial analysis method, and budget plan, copies of form agreements, and a fee schedule. Providers must be accredited and counselors must be certified, or become certified within twelve months of hiring. §§ 4, 5, 13, 14.

Disclosures: Before providing debt-management services, provide individual with a clear and conspicuous list, in a form the individual may keep, of the goods and services to be provided and the price. Must disclose in its advertising, and in a separate notice to prospective clients, that the debt-management plans are not suitable for everybody, that there are alternatives, that a plan may result in a decreased credit rating, that forgiveness of debt may have tax consequences, and whether the provider receives compensation from creditors. All documents and disclosures must be in English, but a provider who negotiates in a language other than English must translate all documents and disclosures into that language. Special requirements for electronic disclosures and websites. §§ 17, 18, 21, 30.

Pre-Agreement Services: Must provide the individual, through the services of a certified counselor, with education in personal financial management, with a financial analysis, and a detailed plan. Must provide a copy of the plan, and a list of creditors expected to participate in the plan and grant concessions, participate in the plan but not grant concessions, or not participate in the plan. §§ 17, 18, 21.

2011 changes from earlier versions re pre-agreement services: § 17 requirement for financial analysis was expanded to specify items to be considered: assets, income, debt and other liabilities.

Contract Terms: An agreement must include an itemized list of services to be provided, and the cost or the method of determining the cost; a schedule of the dates and amounts of payments by or on behalf of the individual, with an estimated date for the final payment; termination and cancellation rights; contact information for complaints to the administrator. If a plan contemplates regular payments to creditors: a schedule of dates and amounts of payments to each creditor and expected concessions; a list of creditors not expected to participate, to whom payments will not be made. If a plan contemplates settlement for less than the amount of principal: the expected duration of the plan; the time when an individual may expect a settlement offer; the amount of savings that must accrue before a settlement offer can be made, expressed as both a dollar amount and a percentage of accrued debt. The provider must notify the individual within five days if a creditor rejects or withdraws from a plan. A plan may authorize the provider to settle for up to 50% of the principal; larger settlements require the assent of the individual, given after the creditor assents. §§ 18, 19, 21.

2011 changes from earlier versions re contract terms: The 2011 act added the disclosure requirements for debt settlement plans: "the expected duration [. . .] percentage of accrued debt."

Cancellation/Termination/Refund Rights: An individual may terminate a plan at will, upon notice, at which time provider must refund all unexpended funds, less authorized fees. A provider may terminate an agreement for sixty days' non-payment or other good cause, or if it becomes clear that a plan has failed, and must then return any funds not disbursed to creditors, less authorized fees. §§ 19, 20, 22.

2011 changes from earlier versions re cancellations and refunds: Replaces the three-day right to cancel with right to cancel at any time without penalty or obligation. And eliminates the three-day cooling off period during which services may not be provided. Provider may terminate for sixty days non-payment. Requires refund within seven days after cancellation. Requires more detailed disclosure of cancellation rights.

Handling of Funds: Money paid to the provider must be deposited, within two business days of receipt, in a trust account in an insured financial institution, separate from the provider's own funds. For debt settlement plan, entity that administers the account must not be an affiliate of provider, may not give or receive payment for referrals, must refund all money upon cancellation (except funds owed to provider.). Provider must reconcile accounts at least once a month and must provide an accounting to the individual once a month, within five days after a request (only one request per calendar month), and upon termination or cancellation of agreement. Must disburse funds to creditors by the due dates established by the creditors; correct any missed or misdirected payments that result from provider error and reimburse the individual for any charges imposed by creditors as a result of the error. For plans that contemplate settlement for less than the amount of principal, the individual is allowed to deposit money in in insured bank account, owned by the individual. §§ 22, 27.

2011 changes from earlier versions re handling of funds: Imposed additional requirements for trust accounts for debt settlement.

Other Customer Service Requirements: Provider must act in good faith (UCC definition); maintain a toll-free communication system staffed a level that will enable an individual to speak to a debt counselor or customer relations person during ordinary business hours. §§ 15, 16.

Limits on Fees: Provider may not impose a charge for debt-management services before an agreement is signed. Dollar amounts are adjusted for inflation. For a plan that contemplates reduction of finance charges: set-up fee of $50; monthly maintenance fee of the lesser of $50 or $10 times the number of accounts remaining in the plan. For a plan that contemplates settlement for less than the amount of principal: 30% of the amount of savings, which may be paid in installments if the debt is being settled by installment payments. These installments must be paid at the same time as the installment payments to the creditor and may not be a greater percentage of provider's total fee than the amount paid to the creditor is of the total settlement amount. For counseling and education provided to an individual who does not assent to an agreement, $100. A greater amount may be authorized by the administrator if the extent of the education and counseling warrant the greater amount. The counseling fee must be refunded if, within ninety days after completion of counseling, the individual assents to a plan. Returned check fee: the lesser of $25 or the amount allowed by other law. A provider may not solicit voluntary contributions from or on behalf of an individual. It may accept contributions, but only if, for thirty days after the termination of the agreement, the aggregate amount received does not exceed the amount of permitted fees. §§ 23, 24.

2011 changes from earlier versions re limits on fees: Eliminated up-front fees for debt settlement; limited the amount of fees to be taken form installments.

Prohibited Practices: Agreements may not authorize the application of the law of any jurisdiction except the United States or the state; except as permitted by the Federal Arbitration Act, limit available forums or procedural rights; limit or release the liability of any person for violating agreement of this act; indemnify any person for liability for arising under an agreement or this act. Including a secured debt in the plan, with certain exceptions; misappropriating funds held in trust; settling a debt for more than 50% of the amount of principal without consent of the debtor, given after the creditor assents; taking a power of attorney that allows settlement for more than 50% of the debt; trying to exercise a power of attorney after termination of an agreement; transferring money from a bank account except to pay creditors as permitted by agreement, return money to the individual, or pay a fee; offering a gift, bonus or other compensation to an individual for making an agreement; compensating its employees based on the number of customers referred; structuring a plan to result in negative amortization, unless the creditor agrees to refund or waive the finance charge upon repayment; settling, or telling the individual it has settled a debt, without receiving a certificate from the creditor that the debt is settled; misrepresenting the benefits of the plan; misrepresenting its non-profit or tax exempt status or ability to provide legal services; taking a confession of judgment; using any unfair, deceptive or unconscionable practice; taking a promissory note, post-dated check or mortgage; lending money (except by deferring a fee at no additional expense). §§ 19, 24, 28.

2011 changes from earlier versions re prohibited practices: Added the prohibition on including secured debt; added lead generators to list of persons to whom bonuses may not be offered if they have financial interest in the plan; forbade offer of bonuses to those who compensate their employees based on number of referrals. Added restriction to tax-entities use of that term—must be operating as such under law of the state.

Public Remedies: The administrator [the agency chosen by the state to administer this statute, suggestions are the attorney general or the agency that enforces the UDAP statute] may enforce the act by issuing cease and desist orders (including for restitution); imposing penalties of up to $20K; bringing a civil action to enforce an order or obtain restitution; intervene in an individual's action (see below). §§ 32, 33, 35

2011 changes from earlier versions re public remedies: Adds lead generators and others who provide services to providers to list of those who may be subject to cease and desist orders and penalties.

Private Remedies: If a provider is unlicensed at the time the agreement is signed, the agreement is voidable at the option of the individual, who may recover all fees, charges, and payments made to the provider, except sums already disbursed to creditors, plus punitive damages, costs and reasonable attorney fees. If provider takes impermissible fees, the agreement is voidable, and the individual may recover three times the amount of fees charges and payments made to the provider, plus costs and reasonable attorney fees.

Private right of action for the greater of $5000 or compensatory damages for injury, including non-economic injury; punitive damages, costs and attorney fees. Class actions permitted. Bona fide error defense available. If an act violates both this statute and the UDAP statute, double recovery is not permitted. A provider that delegates any of its obligations under an agreement or this act to a third person, including an independent contractor, is liable for that person's violations. §§ 25, 31, 35, 36

Statute of Limitations: Actions by administrator: 4 years after conduct giving rise to complaint. Private actions: 2 years after the latest of individual's last transmission of money to a provider; individual's last transmission of money to a creditor at the direction of the provider; provider's last disbursement to a creditor; provider's last accounting to individual; termination of administrator's proceedings resulting from violation; the date when individual discovered or reasonably discovered facts giving rise to the claim. Period pursuant to discovery rule tolled during time when provider or defendant (if different) materially and willfully misrepresented information required by this act to be disclosed, if the information was material to establishing liability of the defendant under this act. § 37.

I.3 State-by-State Analysis of Debt Relief Legislation

Arizona

Citation: Ariz. Rev. Stat. Ann. §§ 6-701 through 6-716.

Administrator: Department of Financial Institutions. § 6-101.

Scope & Key Definitions: Debt-management Companies: entities that, for compensation, engage in the business of receiving money or evidences thereof, in this state or from a resident of this state, as an agent of a debtor for the purpose of distribution to his creditors in payment or partial payment of his obligations. § 6-701.

Exceptions: Attorneys whose principal activities are other than debt management; banks, savings and loan associations, and financing or lending institutions licensed under federal or Arizona law; judicial officers or anyone acting under court order. Certain nonprofits: fraternal, religious, or cooperative organizations whose principal activity is not debt management, that offer services only to their members and do not directly or indirectly collect compensation from debtors; nonprofits that provide services to the public and do not directly or indirectly collect any compensation from the debtors. Transactions in which funds are paid to a joint control agent, to be disbursed in payments for construction or improvement of real property; Escrow agents, mortgage brokers, mortgage bankers and loan originators, who are regulated under other sections of Arizona law. Bill-paying services that do not accept past-due accounts, negotiate with creditors, provide counseling, or take control of funds except for agreed-upon fees. §§ 6-701, 6-702.

Registration/Licensing: Licensing required. Both licensees and exempt nonprofits must post bond, in sums depending on the amount of funds disbursed in the prior year. The superintendent may also require bonding of individual officers or employees who have access to client funds. Applicant must furnish copy of standard contract used between licensee and debtor, and advise agency of changes and amendments to this contract. §§ 6-703, 6-704.

Disclosures: Must provide debtor with a written contract, listing the creditors with whom debt-management company intends to negotiate. § 6-709.

Pre-Agreement Services: Provide a budget analysis. Licensee may accept an account only if analysis shows to be it reasonably likely that debtor can make payments sufficient to cover agreed payments and fees. §§ 6-710.

Contract Terms: Not specified.

Cancellation/Termination/Refund Rights: Contract must be terminable at will upon five days' notice. § 6-709.

Handling of Funds: Funds received from debtor must be kept in a trustee checking account, and remitted to creditors within seven days of receipt, unless reasonable payment of one or more obligations requires that funds be held to accumulate a certain sum. If a compromise is arranged, licensee must "allow debtor the full benefit of that compromise." Upon request, must provide debtor with a written accounting each month, or a verbal accounting at any time during business hours. Licensees and exempt nonprofits must file annual reports with the superintendent. § 6-709.

Customer Service Requirements: Record-keeping and record retention requirements. § 6-709.

Limits on Fees: Non-refundable retainer of $39; monthly fees of the lesser of $50 or three quarters of one percent of the total amount of the debt (which may not include a mortgage or rent payment); unusual out-of-pocket expenses, if agreed to in advance by the debtor and the superintendent. Licensee may not charge any fee until it has given notice to all creditors listed in the contract. §§ 6-709.

Prohibited Practices: Licensee may not alter the amount of any payment without debtor's consent; purchase from creditor any obligation of the debtor; operate as a collection agency and as a licensee on the same debtor's account; execute a contract with blanks not filled in; execute a promissory note or a mortgage of real or personal property for any fee; pay or receive a bonus for referrals; use false, misleading or deceptive advertising in any form. The superintendent is authorized to promulgate rules for advertising. § 6-710.

Public Remedies: Not specified in this statute.

Private Remedies: Person who suffers loss or damage as a result of neglect or default, breach of contract or violation of this statute by licensee has a right of action on the bond. § 6-704.

Statute of Limitations: Two years for action on bond. § 6-704.

Arkansas

Citation: Ark. Code Ann. §§ 5-63-301 to 5-63-305.

Administrator: Violations of this criminal statute may be prosecuted by attorney general or district attorney.

Scope & Key Definitions: Offering or contracting, for consideration, to receive money from debtor for distribution to creditors or act as an intermediary between debtor and creditors to negotiate settlement or alteration of terms of payment of debt. § 5-63-301.

Exceptions: Nonprofits, if fees or charges do not exceed actual cost of offering debt-management service. Attorneys, banks, fiduciaries, title insurer or abstract company doing escrow business, employer adjusting debts for its employees, judicial officer or other person acting pursuant to court order, association adjusting debts for its members. § 5-63-301, 5-63-305.

Registration/Licensing: No.

Disclosures: Not specified.

Pre-Agreement Services: Not specified.

Contract Terms: Not specified.

Cancellation/Termination/Refund Rights: Not specified.

Handling of Funds: Not specified.

Customer Service Requirements: Not specified.

Limits on Fees: Nonprofits' fees may not exceed actual expenses of providing services. § 5-63-305.

Prohibited Practices: Debt adjusting by persons not exempt pursuant to § 5-63-305. §5-63-302.

Public Remedies: District attorney or attorney general may sue to enjoin unlawful debt adjusting, and court may appoint a receiver to supervise return of funds to debtors. Unlawful debt adjusting is a misdemeanor. §§ 5-63-303, 5-63-604.

Private Remedies: Not specified.

Statute of Limitations: Not specified in this statute.

California

Citation: Cal. Fin. Code §§ 12000 through 12404 (West).

Administrator: Commissioner of Business Oversight.

Scope & Key Definitions: Proraters, defined as persons who for compensation, engage in whole or in part in the business of receiving money or evidences thereof, for the purpose of distributing it among creditors in payment or partial payment of the obligations of the debtor. § 12002.1. Certain accredited nonprofits that provide education, debt settlement and debt-management plans are exempt from licensing, but subject to detailed requirements as to fees, services, disclosure, advertising, etc. § 12104.

Exceptions: Banks and other financial institutions, title companies, escrow agents and finance lenders licensed under other provisions of state or federal law; attorneys or certified public accountants in the regular course of their practice; joint control agents who disburse funds for construction or improvement of real property; merchant-owned or member-owned credit reporting agencies; and licensed real estate professionals. Burden of proof for proving any exemption is on the person claiming the exemption. §§ 12100, 12101.5.

Registration/Licensing: Proraters must be licensed and post bond of $25,000. §§ 12205, 12206.

Exempt nonprofits need not be licensed but must post $25,000 bond and have professional liability insurance. Nonprofits must be accredited by independent accrediting agency, and counselors must be certified. § 12104.

Disclosures: Exempt nonprofits must disclose the following: contact information for complaints to the Department of Corporations, a copy of their best practices code (upon request), the percentage of their funding that comes from creditors, that debt-management plans are not for everyone, that alternatives to debt management are available, what services will be provided, and what fees charged. § 12104. Licensees must conspicuously post a fee schedule in their place of business.

Pre-Agreement Services: Exempt Nonprofits: provide debtors with a copy of the debt-management plan, in prescribed form, at the inception date of the plan. § 12104

Contract Terms: Licensees: Contracts must list all debts to be prorated, each creditor's name, and the total amount to be pro-rated. Contracts must provide payments reasonably within debtor's ability to pay, disclose the rate and amount of charges, the approximate number of installments required, the name and address of the prorater, and other information required by the Commissioner. §§ 12315.1, 12319.

Cancellation/Termination/Refund Rights: Licensee may not charge a cancellation or termination fee. §§ 12314.1.

Handling of Funds: Exempt nonprofits: Funds must be deposited in a trust account in a federally insured financial institution; must provide debtor with an accounting every three months or upon request. Funds must be disbursed within 15 days of receipt or on a scheduled disbursement date, using electronic processing where available. § 12104. Licensees must deposit funds in a trust account, designated by name that makes clear that the funds are not those of the licensee or its officers or employees. At least once a month, pro-rater must pay not less than 70% of the funds received to debtor's creditors. Pro-rater must also provide a receipt within five days after receipt of funds (unless paid by check or money order) and provide a detailed accounting every six months, or within seven days upon demand. §§ 12300.5, 12321, 12322.

Customer Service Requirements: Exempt nonprofits: Must respond to complaints within five days; provide access to management plan services regardless of consumer's ability to pay fees, lack of creditor participation, or amount of debt. § 12104. *Licensees:* Must provide a copy of contract to debtor immediately after execution. § 12320. Within five days of the effective date of a contract, must notify all listed creditors of the proposed monthly payment. § 12315.1. Must observe reasonable precautions against theft, alteration of documents, burglary or hold-up. § 12300.1. Must have at least one person with a minimum of five years' experience in consumer credit extension or credit collection activity. One such qualified person must be on duty at each business location whenever it is open for business. § 12331.

Limits on Fees: Exempt nonprofits: one-time $50 fee for education and counseling; for debt-management plans, a monthly fee of the lesser of $35 or 8% of the sum disbursed monthly; for debt settlement plans, not more than 15% of the amount forgiven. For debt-settlement plans, payment may be required only after debt has been successfully settled. § 12104. *Licensees:* 12% of the first $3000 disbursed, 11% of the next $2000 at 10% of remaining disbursements, not counting "recurring obligations" defined as most current bills (rent, utility, alimony, insurance) and mortgage payments; origination fee, $50, which must be refunded if debtor completes 12 months of payments without default; $4 per disbursement for mortgage, $1 for other recurring obligations. No cancellation or termination fee. § 12314.1. Pro-rater may not charge fee before it has consent of at least 51% of the indebtedness and of the number of creditors listed in pro-rater's contract with debtor, or that number of creditors have accepted payment. §§ 12314, 12315.

Prohibited Practices: Exempt nonprofits: Referral fees or compensation of counselors based on outcomes; the purchase of debt or making of loans. § 12104. *Licensees:* May not engage in business outside the state of California; use any form of false, misleading or deceptive advertising; purchase debtors' obligations from creditor; execute a contract with blanks not filled in; take any negotiable instrument, wage assignment, chattel or real estate mortgage, confession of judgment or power of attorney for provider's charges; lend money or credit; offer any reward for referral of customers; receive compensation from anyone other than the debtor for activities as prorater; solicit or require debtor to purchase insurance; engage in unauthorized practice of law (detailed definition); disclose a list of creditors to any individual or firm for the purpose of soliciting the accounts; advertise in violation of Commissioner's rules; operate a collection agency in the same premises as a pro-rater. Pro-rater's license may not be issued to collection agency. §§ 12200.3, 12311, 12317, 12318, 12323, 12324, 12325, 12327 through 12330.

Public Remedies: Willful and knowing violations are punishable by fine and imprisonment. Commissioner of Business Oversight may impose cease and desist orders. Commissioner may bring civil action for injunction, restitution or disgorgement, or may impose civil penalties of up to $2500 per violation, or $10,000 if violation is willful. §§ 12102, 12105, 12107, 12200.

Private Remedies: Licensees Remedies: If a pro-rater takes an excessive charge the contract is void, and pro-rater must return all charges received from debtor. Bona fide error defense available. § 12316.

Statute of Limitations: For actions on the bond, two years after the default complained of. § 12212.

Colorado

This statute is based upon the 2008 version of the Uniform Debt-Management Services Act, summarized at Appx. I.2, supra, with variations as noted below.

Citation: Colo. Rev. Stat. §§ 12-14.5-201 through 12-14.5-242. This statute will sunset on September 1, 2024.

Administrator: Assistant Attorney General, designated by Attorney General to administer this statute. § 12-14.5-202.

Scope & Key Definitions: Substantially similar to 2005 uniform act. § 12-14.5-202.

Exceptions: Substantially similar to uniform act, but also exempts entities subject to the Foreclosure Prevention Act. Professional services exemption explicitly excludes persons who provide services on behalf of an attorney or accountant who are not employees of the attorney or accountant. §§ 12-14.5-202, 12-14.5-203.

Registration/Licensing: Substantially similar to uniform act but without requirements for accreditation or certification. Note that a 2011 amendment deleted the definitions of certified debt counselor and certified debt specialist as well as the requirement to provide evidence of accreditation. But other sections still require certain services to be provided by a "debt counselor" or "debt specialist". §§ 12-14.5-204, 12-14.5-206, 12-14.5-213.

Disclosures: Substantially similar to uniform act. §§ 12-14.5-217, 12-14.5-218, 12-14.5-230.

Pre-Agreement Services: Substantially similar to uniform act. § 12-14.5-217.

Contract Terms: Substantially similar to uniform act. §§ 12-14.5-219, 12-14.5-221.

Cancellation/Termination/Refund Rights: Three-day cancellation right, extended to 30 days if provider did not comply with notice requirements. Agreement must be accompanied by a cancellation form. Three-day right may be waived if a personal financial emergency requires earlier dispersal of funds. Waiver must include a statement in consumer's own words describing the emergency. Form waivers not valid. § 12-14.5-220. Provider may terminate if consumer fails to make payment for 60 days. If an agreement is terminated, either by provider or by debtor, provider must return to debtor all funds held in trust. § 12-14.5-226.

Handling of Funds: Substantially similar to uniform act. § 12-14.5-222, 12-14.5-227.

Customer Service Requirements: Substantially similar to uniform act. §§ 12-14.5-215, 12-14.5-216.

Limits on Fees: Provider may not charge fees until the provider and the individual have signed a contract that meets statutory standards. Debt-management plans: Substantially similar to uniform act, except that fees not adjusted for inflation. For debt settlement plans: may not seek payment until after at least one creditor has settled, and debtor has made one payment. The fee may be a percentage of the amount saved or bear the same proportional relationship to the total fee for settling the entire debt balance as the debt settled bears to the entire debt amount. A provider may not solicit a voluntary contribution. §§ 12-14.5-223, 12-14.5-224.

Prohibited Practices: Substantially similar to uniform act. §§ 12-14.5-219, 12-14.5-228.

Public Remedies: Substantially similar to uniform act. §§ 12-14.5-202, 12-14.5-233.

Private Remedies: Substantially similar to uniform act. §§ 12-14.5-225, 12-14.5-231, 12-14.5-235, 12-14.5-236.

Statute of Limitations: Substantially similar to uniform act. § 12-14.5-237.

Connecticut

Connecticut has two statutes.

Citation: Conn. Gen. Stat. §§ 36a-655 through 36a-670. Note that this statute has been found unconstitutional to the extent that it permits the Banking Commissioner to regulate the practice of law.[4]

Administrator: Banking Commissioner. § 36a-2.

Scope & Key Definitions: Debt adjusters. Debt adjustment is defined as, for or with the expectation of a fee, receiving as agent for a consumer debtor, money or evidences thereof, for the purpose of distribution among creditors in full or partial payment of debtor's obligations. § 36a-655.

Exceptions: Attorneys who engage in debt negotiation as an ancillary matter to representing a client; banks, or fiduciary, financial or lending institutions that perform debt adjustment in the course of their regular business; title insurance or abstract companies while doing an escrow business; any person acting pursuant to law or a court order. § 36a-663.

Registration/Licensing: License required (reduced fee for bona fide non-profit organizations). Bonding required, the greater of $40,000, or twice the amount of the average daily amount received from debtors in a twelve-month period. §§ 36a-656, 36a-664.

Disclosures: Not specified.

Pre-Agreement Services: Before entering into a contract, licensee must provide individualized credit counseling and budget assistance without charge; and determine that plan is suitable for debtor, and that debtor is able to make payments. § 36a-660.

Contract Terms: Licensee must provide debtor with a written agreement setting forth services to be provided and fees. § 36a-660.

Cancellation/Termination/Refund Rights: Not specified.

Handling of Funds: License must maintain a separate bank account for payments received from debtors for the benefit of creditors; make payments to creditors within a reasonable time; provide a written accounting to debtor at least quarterly and a verbal accounting at debtor's request any time during business hours. §§ 36a-659, 36a-660.

Customer Service Requirements: Licensee must contact creditors to determine whether they will accept payments and keep complete and adequate records. § 36a-660.

Limits on Fees: Not specified.

Prohibited Practices: Licensee may not purchase any obligation of the debtor; operate as collection agency and licensee on the same debtor's account; execute any contract with blanks not filled in; directly or indirectly require the purchase of other services or materials as a condition of

entering into an agreement; pay a bonus for referring debtor to licensee, or accept a bonus for referring debtor to another entity; use any false, misleading or deceptive advertising. § 36a-661.

Public Remedies: Fine and imprisonment for unlicensed practice or certain other violations. § 36a-665.

Private Remedies: If debt adjuster is not licensed, or takes any fee not specified in the contract, the contract is voidable. § 36a-661a.

Statute of Limitations: Not specified.

Citation: Conn. Gen. Stat. §§ 36a-671 through 36a-671e.

Administrator: Banking Commissioner. § 36a-2.

Scope & Key Definitions: Debt negotiators. Debt negotiation is defined as, for or in expectation of a fee, assisting a consumer debtor in negotiating or attempting to negotiate with one or more creditors or mortgagees; foreclosure rescue services explicitly included. § 36a-671.

Exceptions: Attorneys performing debt negotiation services ancillary to representation of a client; banks and credit unions (but not certain subsidiaries); licensed debt adjuster (see above) performing debt adjustment services; bona fide tax-exempt nonprofits. § 36a-671c.

Registration/Licensing: License required. Bonding required: $50,000 (higher for negotiators of certain large mortgage loans). Additional mortgage loan originator license required to negotiate residential mortgage loans. §§ 36a-671, 36a-671d, 36a-671e.

Disclosures: Not specified.

Pre-Agreement Services: The licensee must provide a detailed list of services, costs, and results to be achieved; a statement certifying that the licensee has reviewed the consumer's debt, and an individual evaluation of whether the plan can reduce the consumer's debt or, where applicable, prevent foreclosure. § 361-671b.

Contract Terms: see cancellation rights, below.

Cancellation/Termination/Refund Rights: Right to cancel for three business days after signing contract. The contract must clearly disclose this right. § 36a-671b.

Handling of Funds: Not specified.

Customer Service Requirements: Not specified.

Limits on Fees: The Banking Commissioner may establish a schedule of maximum fees for specific services. § 36a-671b.

Prohibited Practices: May not charge a fee for any service before the service is fully performed, but may receive periodic payments for services, as the services are rendered, if these payments are clearly stated in the contract. § 36a-671b.

Public Remedies: Not specified.

Private Remedies: A contract that does not conform to the statute is voidable by the consumer. § 36a-671b.

Statute of Limitations: Not specified.

Delaware

This statute is based upon the 2008 version of the Uniform Debt-Management Services Act, summarized at Appx. I.2, supra, with variations as noted below.

Citation: Del. Code Ann. tit. 6, §§ 2401A to 2439A.

Administrator: Attorney General.

Scope & Key Definitions: Substantially similar to uniform act. § 2402A.

Exceptions: Substantially similar to 2005 act. §§ 2402A, 2403A.

Registration/Licensing: Substantially similar to uniform act. §§ 2404A, 2405A, 2406A, 2013A, 2014A.

Disclosures: Substantially similar to uniform act. Requires additional warnings as to consequences of non-payment pursuant to debt settlement plan. §§ 2417A, 2418A, 2421A, 2430A.

Pre-Agreement Services: Substantially similar to uniform act. § 2417A.

Contract Terms: Substantially similar to uniform act. § 2419A.

Cancellation/Termination/Refund Rights: Substantially similar to uniform act. Includes both three-day cooling-off period, with right to full refund, and right to cancel at any time, with right to limited refund. §§ 2419A, 2420A, 2422A, 2426A.

---

4   Persels & Associates, L.L.C. v. Banking Com'r, ___ A.3d ___, 318 Conn. 652 (2015).

Handling of Funds: Substantially similar to uniform act. §§ 2402A, 2422A, 2427A,

Customer Service Requirements: Substantially similar to uniform act. §§ 2402A, 2415A, 2416A.

Limits on Fees: Substantially similar to 2005 act. Allows a setup fee for debt settlement plans. Amounts adjusted for inflation. § 2423A, 2324A, 2432(f).

Prohibited Practices: Substantially similar to uniform act. Some additional restrictions on sale of goods unrelated to debt management. Requirements for use of term nonprofit. § 2428A.

Public Remedies: Substantially similar to uniform act. Civil penalties up to $50,000. $75,000 for knowing and willful violation. § 2433.

Private Remedies: Substantially similar to uniform act. §§ 2425A, 2431A, 2435A, 2436A.

Statute of Limitations: Substantially similar to uniform act, except provides 3 year statute of limitations for private actions. §2437A.

Florida

Citation: Fla. Stat. §§ 817.801 through 817.806.

Administrator: Not specified (criminal statute).

Scope & Key Definitions: Credit counseling: confidential money management, debt reduction or financial education services. Debt management: for a fee, seeking to effect the adjustment, compromise or discharge of unsecured debt, or receiving from debtor money or things of value for disbursement to creditors. § 817.801.

Exceptions: Debt adjustment in the practice of law; Fannie Mae, Freddie Mac and the Florida Housing Corporation; regulated financial institutions, consumer reporting agencies. § 817.803.

Registration/Licensing: $100,000 insurance. § 817.804.

Disclosures: Not specified.

Pre-Agreement Services: Not specified.

Contract Terms: Not specified.

Cancellation/Termination/Refund Rights: Not specified.

Handling of Funds: Provider must maintain a separate trust account for funds received from debtors, and disburse to creditors within thirty days of receipt all funds received, less authorized fees. § 817.805.

Customer Service Requirements: Not specified.

Limits on Fees: $50 setup or consultation fee. Thereafter $120/year for additional consultations; or for debt management the greater of 7.5% of monthly payment or $35/month. Insufficient funds fees permitted. § 817.802.

Prohibited Practices: Not specified.

Public Remedies: Violation is a third-degree felony. § 817.806.

Private Remedies: Violation is a UDAP. Consumer has private right of action for actual damages, which are not less than the amount paid to the provider, plus reasonable costs and attorney fees. § 817.806.

Statute of Limitations: Not specified in this statute.

Georgia

Citation: Ga. Code Ann. §§ 18-5-1 through 18-5-4.

Administrator: Attorney General.

Scope & Key Definitions: Debt adjusting. For a fee, seeking to effect adjustment, compromise or discharge of a debt, or receiving funds from debtor for distribution to creditors. § 18-5-1.

Exceptions: Debt adjusting in the practice of law. Fannie Mae or Freddie Mac; regulated financial institutions. § 18-5-3.

Registration/Licensing: Insurance: greater of $100,000 or 10% of the monthly average amount of deposits made by debtors. § 18-5-3.1.

Disclosures: Not specified.

Pre-Agreement Services: Not specified.

Contract Terms: Not specified.

Cancellation/Termination/Refund Rights: Not specified.

Handling of Funds: Funds received from debtors must be placed in separate trust account. Funds, less authorized fees, must be disbursed to creditors within 30 days of receipt. § 18-5-3.2.

Customer Service Requirements: Not specified.

Limits on Fees: 7.5% of the amount paid monthly. Insufficient funds fees permitted. § 18-5-2.

Prohibited Practices: Not specified.

Public Remedies: Violation is a misdemeanor. District attorney or attorney general may seek civil fines of up to $50,000. § 18-5-4.

Private Remedies: Violation is a UDAP. Debtor has private right of action for all fees, charges and contributions paid to provider, plus $5000, § 18-5-4.

Statute of Limitations: Not specified in this statute.

Idaho

The debt-management provisions are part of a statute regulating collection agencies, debt counselors, credit counselors, and credit repair organizations.

Citation: Idaho Code Ann. §§ 26-2221 through 26-2251.

Administrator: Department of Finance.

Scope & Key Definitions: Debt counselors and credit counselors. Persons who engage, or attempt to engage, in Idaho, in the business of receiving money from debtors for payment to or prorating of a debt owed to creditors; provide counseling or other services to debtors in the management of their debts, or contract with debtors to effect the adjustment, compromise or discharge of debts. §§ 26-2222, 26-2223.

Exceptions: Attorneys performing services incidental to the practice of law and not engaged in a separate business to perform services authorized by this act; regulated lenders or financial institutions; government agencies or instrumentalities; licensed real estate professionals acting within the scope of their licenses; escrow companies. § 26-2239.

Registration/Licensing: Licensing required. Applicants must provide copies of all contracts, forms, form letters, and advertisements they plan to use. Bonding required. §§ 26-2223, 26-2224, 26-2232A.

Disclosures: Not specified.

Pre-Agreement Services: Not specified.

Contract Terms: Not specified.

Cancellation/Termination/Refund Rights: Not specified.

Handling of Funds: Funds received from debtors must be kept in a trust account, in an insured financial institution, separate from licensee's business funds. § 26-2233.

Customer Service Requirements: Licensees must deal fairly, openly, honestly and without deception. § 26-2229.

Limits on Fees: Debt counselors who receive funds from debtors may not take more than 15% of the amount received at any time; may not charge any other fees. Debt counselors who do not hold funds may not charge more than 20% of the principal amount of debtor's unsecured debt at the time of contracting. In case of cancellation, counselor must refund 50% of any collected fees associated with the amount of debt remaining unsettled at the time of the termination of the contract. § 26-2229.

Prohibited Practices: False or misleading statements that a debt or extension of credit can be eliminated, reduced or substituted (including statements made without sufficient information on which to base a reasonable belief.); any other false or misleading statements; misappropriation of funds; misrepresentation of government affiliation; unauthorized practice of law. § 26-2226, 26-2229A, 26-2243.

Public Remedies: Unlicensed practice and mishandling of trust funds are felonies. Director of the Department of Finance may issue cease and desist orders, order restitution, or impose civil penalties of up to $5000 per violation, or bring a civil action for injunction, restitution, or other appropriate remedies, or refer a matter to the Attorney General for criminal prosecution. §§ 26-2226, 26-2227, 26-2238, 26-2244, 26-2245, 26-2247.

Private Remedies: Not specified.

Statute of Limitations: Not specified in the statute.

Illinois

Illinois has two statutes, one for credit counselling and debt management, and one for debt settlement.

Citation: 205 Ill. Comp. Stat. §§ 665/2 through 665/22 (credit counseling and debt management).

Administrator: Secretary of Financial and Professional Regulation.

Scope & Key Definitions: Credit Counselors: Entities that are not debt-management services that provide guidance, educational programs or advice addressing budgeting, personal finance, financial literacy, saving and spending practices, and the sound use of consumer credit or offers counseling to families with financial problems.

Debt Management Service: Planning and management of debtor's financial affairs including, for a fee, receiving funds for distribution to debtor's creditors in payment or partial payment of debts, or soliciting financial contributions by creditors. Does not include debt settlement service, covered by a separate statute (see below). § 665/2.

Exceptions: Attorneys engaged in the practice of law; banks and other financial institutions; title insurers and others while doing escrow business; judicial officers and persons acting pursuant to court order; employers for their employees; bill payment services [defined]. § 665/2.

Registration/Licensing: License and $25,000 bond required for debt-management service. §§ 665/3, 665/4.

Disclosures: Not specified.

Pre-Agreement Services: Debt management service must provide debtor with written contract, setting forth charges agreed upon for services. § 665/11. Must prepare and retain a written analysis of debtor's income and expenses, to substantiate that the plan is feasible and practical. § 665/11.

Contract Terms: Not specified.

Cancellation/Termination/Refund Rights: Not specified.

Handling of Funds: Provider must issue a receipt for all payments. Funds received from debtors must be placed in a trust fund, separate from provider's funds, and disbursed within 30 days of first receipt of funds, 15 days for other funds, unless the debtor's obligations require that the funds be held to accumulate a sum certain. Must render an accounting at least quarterly, or within seven days of a request by debtor (not more than three requests per six month period), showing amounts received and disbursed. §§ 665/11, 665/14.

Customer Service Requirements: Not specified.

Limits on Fees: Debt management service may charge initial counseling fee of up to $50. After completion of counseling, monthly fees of up to $50. § 665/12.

Prohibited Practices: May not use false, deceptive or misleading advertising; require debtor to purchase any insurance, stock, or other property; give or accept any payment for referrals; make loans, issue credit cards or act as an agent for obtaining credit cards; act as a loan broker; operate any other business at the licensed location. § 665/13.

Public Remedies: Unlicensed practice is a felony. Civil penalty for unlicensed practice is the greater of $1000 or four times the amount of consumer debt enrolled. The Secretary of Financial and Professional Regulation may issue cease and desist orders, and may order restitution to a consumer harmed by violation of this statute, up to the amount of consumer's actual loss. Civil penalties are paid into the Debt Management Services Consumer Protection Fund, which may be used to provide restitution to injured consumers. The Secretary may also sue to enjoin unlicensed practice. §§ 665/2, 665/16, 665/16.5, 665/17, 665/20.

Private Remedies: Contract made by unlicensed entity is void. §665/16.

Statute of Limitations: Not specified in statute.

Citation: 225 Ill. Comp. Stat. §§ 429/1 through 429/999 (debt settlement).

Administrator: Secretary of Financial and Professional Regulation.

Scope & Key Definitions: Debt Settlement. Any person or entity that offers, for a fee, to serve as an intermediary between a consumer and creditors, to attempt to settle the debt for less than the full amount of the principal or the amount outstanding; advising or encouraging consumer to accumulate funds for the purpose of seeking or obtaining settlement of debt. § 429/10.

Exceptions: Debt management (see above); tax-exempt entities covered by the debt-management act; attorneys engaged in the practice of law; escrow agents, accountants, broker dealers or investment advisers in securities, acting in the practice of their professions through the entity used in the ordinary practice of their professions; banks and other financial institutions and lenders, in the ordinary practice of their businesses; collection agencies collecting debt; public officers acting in their official capacity and others acting pursuant to court order; persons performing services incidental to winding up a business enterprise; licensed real estate professionals in the ordinary course of their profession, and not holding themselves out as debt settlement providers. § 429/10.

Registration/Licensing: License and $100,000 bond required. §§ 429/15, 429/20.

Disclosures: Advertising must disclose that debt settlement services are not appropriate for everyone; failure to pay monthly bills on time will result in increased balances and harm credit rating; and not all creditors will agree to participate and some may pursue collection, including lawsuits. § 429/105. Numerous pre-contract disclosures are required, including right to cancel at any time. A model disclosure form is included in the statute. The consumer must sign and date an acknowledgement of having received this form. (Electronic signatures permitted.) § 429/115.

Pre-Agreement Services: Before entering into a contract, must provide an individual analysis of consumer's income, expenses and debts, and a good faith estimate of the time it will require to complete the program, the total owed to each creditor, the amount of savings needed to complete the program, and the monthly savings amount. § 429/110. Must provide debtor with a written contract setting forth charges for agreed-upon services. § 429/55. Must prepare and retain a written analysis of debtor's income and expenses to substantiate that plan is feasible and practical. § 429/55.

Contract Terms: Contract must be in writing, signed, and dated. Must include name and contact information of provider; a list of debts covered by the program, including name of creditor and amount owed; description of services to be provided and a good faith estimate of the time frame; itemized list of fees; estimate of total fees; statement of proposed saving goals, including the amount consumer must save each month, and the amount that must be accumulated before provider will make an offer on each debt; the individualized financial analysis; statutorily required disclosures (see above); cancellation form. If provider communicates with consumer in a language other than English, all documents and disclosures must be translated into that language. § 429/120.

Cancellation/Termination/Refund Rights: Consumer may cancel at any time and receive a full refund of sums not disbursed to creditor and all unearned fees. Contract must include a form notifying consumer of these rights. Refunds must be made within 5 business days after cancellation. Provider must notify creditors of cancellation. § 429/115, 429/135.

Handling of Funds: Must provide receipts for all payments, maintain records enabling debtor to ascertain at any reasonable time fees paid, amount held in trust, settlement offers made and accepted. Must furnish debtor, within seven days of request with an accounting showing total amount received and total disbursements to creditors. Funds received from debtors for disbursement to creditors must be kept in a trust account, separate from provider's own funds. The funds in the account remain property of the debtor until disbursed to creditor. At least once per month, or within seven days of request, must provide debtor with an accounting showing total amount received, total amount paid to each creditor, charges deducted, amount held in reserve, and the status of each of debtor's accounts. §§ 429/55, 429/65 429/130.

Customer Service Requirements: Provider must act in good faith. § 429/140.

Limits on Fees: $50 enrollment fee. Settlement fee up to 15% of the savings, to be collected only after creditor agrees to accept specific sum in full satisfaction of the debt, and funds are paid either by the provider or by the consumer pursuant to a settlement negotiated by the provider. No settlement fee may be collected if the settlement amount is greater than the principal amount of the debt. § 429/125.

Prohibited Practices: In advertising, may not make unsubstantiated claims about the results or outcomes of its services, or make any other deceptive representations (including omission of material facts.) May not enter into a contract without determining that the consumer can meet the requirements, including fees and estimated periodic savings, and that the plan is suitable for the consumer. Provider may not be named on consumer's bank account, take a power of attorney or create a demand draft on, or otherwise exercise control over a bank account held by or on behalf of consumer. May not advise consumers to stop paying or communicating with creditors; change the address on any of consumer's accounts; make loans or solicit any mortgage, note or any negotiable instrument other than a check dated no later than one day after the date of signature; take a confession of judgment or power of attorney to confess judgment; take any release or waiver of any right of the consumer; give or receive any bonus for referrals; disclose confidential information, except to consumer or to creditor for purpose of providing settlement services; violate any do not call statute; purchase debts or engage in the practice of debt collection; include any secured debt in a debt settlement agreement; prohibit or limit consumer's communication with creditors; require the purchase of ancillary goods and services by consumer or imply that this purchase is required. §§ 429/130, 429/145.

Public Remedies: Unlicensed practice is a felony. The Secretary may issue cease and desist orders; impose civil penalties of up to $10,000 per violation of this statute; seek injunctions; authorize restitution, up to the amount of consumer's actual loss, to be paid out of the Debt Settlement Consumer Protection Fund. §§ 429/80, 429/83 429/85, 429/95.

Private Remedies: Contract that does not comply with the statute is void. Violation of this statute is a UDAP. §§ 429/120, 429/150. 429/155.

Statute of Limitations: Not specified in this statute.

Indiana

Indiana has two statutes, one covering budget counseling and debt management, and one covering debt settlement.

Citation: Ind. Code §§ 28-1-29-0.5 through 28-1-29-18 (budget counseling and debt management).

Administrator: Department of Financial Institutions.

Scope & Key Definitions: Budget counseling, credit counseling, debt management and debt pooling for consumer debtors. Does not cover debt settlement, regulated by § 24-5-15-2.5. License may not be granted to anyone who is an employee or owner of, or affiliated with, a collection agency or process serving business. (Persons licensed before 1981 are grandfathered.) § 28-1-29-1, 28-1-29-4.5.

Exceptions: Attorneys, and persons under the direct supervision of attorneys, to the extent that the attorney's debt-management services are incidental to the practice of law; depository financial institutions; bill paying services with which consumer contracts for the convenience of paying bills, and retains full control over all funds, provided that the company's actions are not an attempt, as determined by the director of financial institutions, to circumvent the limitations under this chapter. § 28-1-29-0.5.

Registration/Licensing: License and bond required. Bond amount $50,000 to $100,000, depending on the amount held in trust for Indiana residents. §§ 28-1-29-3, 28-1-29-6.

Disclosures: Must disclose in writing, in prescribed form, that plans are not for everyone, that alternatives are available, and whether licensee will receive compensation from creditors. Electronic disclosures must be on a screen containing no other information, which the debtor must see before proceeding to assent to the forming of an agreement. Disclosures and documents must be in English, but a licensee who communicates with a debtor in a language other than English must provide a translation. §§ 28-1-29-7.7, 28-1-29-15, 28-1-29-16.

Pre-Agreement Services: Licensee must provide debtor with a budget analysis; a list of creditors whom licensee expects to participate in the plan and grant concessions, participate and not grant concessions, and refuse to participate. If debtor is to make periodic payments, provider must determine that plan is suitable for debtor, and that debtor will be able to make payments, and must reasonably believe that listed creditors will accept the payments. Income must be verified; monthly expense figures must be reasonable for family size and location; amount of debts to be paid outside the plan must be verified with a credit report. § 28-1-29-7.7, 28-1-29-8.

Contract Terms: Written contract must include services to be provided; amount or method of determining fees; detailed schedule of payments; list of creditors and amount of payments to each; creditors expected not to participate; debtor's cancellation rights; that provider may cancel for cause; contact information for the Department; authority to establish a trust account. Term of plan may not exceed sixty months. § 28-1-19-8.

Cancellation/Termination/Refund Rights: Debtor may terminate the agreement at will, by giving written or electronic notice to licensee. If debtor terminates, or it becomes clear that the plan has failed, licensee must refund any unexpended funds, within fifteen days, less the $100 close-out fee. Contract is considered terminated if debtor fails to make payment for 90 days, but statute provides a procedure for "letter of continuation" in which debtor may explain the reasons for non-payment, and the agreement continued or modified. § 28-1-29-8, 28-1-29-8.3, 28-1-29-8.8.

Handling of Funds: Must provide a receipt for any payment not made by check, money-order, or pre-authorized withdrawal. Money collected for disbursement to creditors must be held in trust account. May not commingle trust funds and licensee's own funds. Must make remittances with thirty days, unless debtor's obligations require funds to be held until a sum certain is accumulated; promptly correct misdirected or missed payments, and reimburse debtor for any costs or fees imposed by creditor as a result of the mistake. Must reconcile bank statements every thirty days. If licensee suspects misappropriation, must report to the department within five days, describing the remedial action taken or to be taken. Must provide itemized accounting to debtor every month, or within seven days of debtor's request. At termination must provide debtor with list showing which creditors are paid in full and which remain unpaid. § 28-1-29-8, 28-1-29.8.8, 28-1-29-9.

Customer Service Requirements: If a creditor agrees to debt reduction, provider must notify debtor in writing of the concession, and that it may result in taxable income, even though debtor receives no money. Licensee must notify debtor within 5 days if creditor rejects or withdraws from the plan, and advise debtor that he or she has a right to terminate or modify the agreement. Licensee must act in good faith. Must maintain a communication system, staffed at a sufficient level to enable debtor to speak to a counselor or customer service person during normal business hours. §§ 28-1-29-7.7, 28-1-29-8.

Limits on Fees: Fee may be charged only after a plan is set up and the first payment to a creditor made. Setup fee, $50. Monthly fee of the lesser of $75 or 15% of the amount licensee receives for payment of creditors, but not less than $5. Upon cancellation by the debtor, or non-payment, the licensee may withhold $100 as a closeout fee. Licensee may charge only one setup and one close-out fee, unless debtor leaves the services of the licensee for more than six months. Returned check fee, $25. §§ 28-1-29-8.3.

Prohibited Practices: May not misappropriate funds; seek to exercise a power of attorney after termination of agreement; debit money from debtor's account for any purpose except return to debtor, agreed payment to creditor, or authorized fee; provide a gift or reward to debtor for entering into a plan; give or receive a bonus for referrals; structure a plan so as to result in negative amortization, unless creditor agrees to refund or waive finance charges upon payment of principal; compensate employees based on the number of consumers who enter into plans; settle a debt or lead consumer to believe a debt is settled, without receiving certification from creditor that debt is paid in full; make misrepresentations about the plan or licensee's services, licensee's authority to practice law, licensee's nonprofit or tax-exempt status; take a confession of judgment or power of attorney to confess judgment; use any other unfair, unconscionable or deceptive act or practice, including withholding of material information; purchase debtor's obligations; take a promissory note, post-dated check, mortgage or other security interest; lend money or provide credit; charge or provide credit for insurance, club membership, goods, services, Internet access or any other goods or services not directly related to the provision of debt management; engage in the unauthorized practice of law; solicit voluntary contributions from debtor. May not use deceptive advertising; specifically may not state that "no financial problem is too great for licensee to solve" or that licensee will use its own funds to pay debtor's bills. May not solicit or accept voluntary contributions from debtor. §§ 28-1-29-9.5, 28-1-29-9.7, 28-1-29-17.

Public Remedies: Some violations of this chapter are misdemeanors. Department may issue cease and desist orders, order restitution, or pursue a civil action to enforce an order, and/or obtain restitution or injunction. Department may impose civil penalty of up to $10,000 ($20,000 for willful violation of order). § 28-1-29-13.

Private Remedies: If a person knowingly violates this chapter, all its debt-management agreements are void; the debtor, or the department on behalf of the debtor, may recover any payments made to the violator. Licensees are liable for violations by lead generators or other persons to whom they delegate duties. Lead generators or other persons who provide services to licensees and violate this chapter commit a deceptive act, actionable under the UDAP statute. § 28-1-29-3, 28-1-29-18.

Statute of Limitations: Not specified in this statute.

Citation: Ind. Code §§ 24-5-15-1 through 24-5-15-11 (debt settlement, included in statute regulating credit services organizations).

Administrator: Attorney general.

Scope & Key Definitions: Debt settlement, defined as renegotiation or settlement of debt or alteration of terms of payment, including reduction in balance, interest rate, or fees. §§ 24-5-15-2.5.

Exceptions: Lenders regulated under other state or Federal law; FDIC insured financial institutions; credit unions; tax-exempt nonprofit organizations; attorneys licensed in Indiana, acting within the scope of practice as an attorney; licensed real estate brokers or stock broker-dealers acting within the scope of their licenses; loan servicers; debt-management providers (see above). § 24-5-15-2.

Registration/Licensing: $25,000 bond, or irrevocable letter of credit required, if provider will take fees before complete performance of services. § 25-5-15-8.

Disclosures: Must provide a written statement including a list of services to be performed and fees; an explanation of buyer's right to make claims against the bond; a description of consumer's rights to review credit report, pursuant to FCRA; information about the availability of nonprofit credit counseling. § 24-5-15-6.

Pre-Agreement Services: Not specified.

Contract Terms: Must state terms and conditions of payment, including total amounts of payments; a detailed description of services to be performed and results to be achieved; contact information for the licensee. Must include cancellation forms. §24-5-15-7.

Cancellation/Termination/Refund Rights: Right to cancel within 3 business days must be disclosed in proximity to the space reserved for buyer's signature, and a cancellation form, in prescribed format provided. § 24-5-15-7.

Handling of Funds: Not specified.

Customer Service Requirements: Not specified.

Limits on Fees: Not specified.

Prohibited Practices: Making false or misleading statements; taking a power of attorney for any purpose other than inspecting documents; requiring consumer to waive any right provided by state or federal law. § 24-5-15-5.

Public Remedies: Violation is a UDAP, actionable by the Attorney General. § 24-5-15-11.

Private Remedies: A person damaged by a credit service organization's violation of this statute may bring a civil action for the greater of $1000 or twice actual damages, and attorney fees or may bring an action against the bond or letter of credit for actual damages. § 24-5-15-9.

Statute of Limitations: Not specified in this statute.

Iowa

Citation: Iowa Code §§ 533A.1 through 533A.17.
Administrator: Superintendent of Banking.
Scope & Key Definitions:

Debt Management: For a fee, arranging or attempting to arrange or negotiate the amount or terms of a debt; receiving money from a debtor for distribution to creditors for payment or partial payment of a debt; serving as an intermediary for the purpose of obtaining concessions from creditors.

Debt Settlement: Seeking to settle the amount of debtor's debt for less than the amount owed. § 533A.1.

Exceptions: Nonprofit religious, fraternal or co-operative organizations, offering to debtors gratuitous debt-management services; attorneys, acting "solely as an incident to the practice of law"; banks and other financial institutions and lenders, licensed under other provisions of law, while acting in the course of their regular business or performing an escrow function; abstract companies performing an escrow function; licensees' employees while performing services for licensed employer; judicial officers or others acting under court order; certain providers of money transmission or currency exchange. § 522A.2.

Registration/Licensing: License and $25,000 bond required. Applicant must provide a description of the services it proposes to offer and copies of form contracts and disclosure forms. Superintendent of Banking may authorize applicants to be licensed through a nationwide licensing system. § 533A.2.

Disclosures: Licensee must explain it program to each potential client so that potential client can make an informed decision as to its suitability. Before entering into contract, licensee must disclose: the total fee that debtor will pay during the term of the contract; that results cannot be guaranteed; the tax consequences of obtaining concessions from creditor; for a program in which licensee does not distribute funds to creditors, debtor must still pay, and creditors can continue collection efforts; for a debt settlement program, that credit score may be harmed, and that failure to make payments may result in collection action, including litigation. § 533A.8.

Pre-Agreement Services: Licensee must make a comprehensive review of debtor's debts and budget, to determine if program is an appropriate option. § 533A.8.

Contract Terms: Contract must be in writing, and include: total charges, and when and how they must be paid; description of services to be performed; beginning and expiration date of contract. Contract for debt settlement must include a comprehensive list of creditors and the estimated amount needed to fund settlements. § 533A.8.

Cancellation/Termination/Refund Rights: Debtor may cancel at any time. Upon cancellation, no further installments are due. If debtor cancels during first year, licensee may keep only 50% of the installments received. § 533A.9.

Handling of Funds: Funds for distribution to creditors must be kept in a trust account, and remitted to creditors within forty-five days of first payment, thirty days of subsequent payments unless funds must be accumulated to a sum certain. Must provide an itemized written accounting once a month, and a verbal accounting upon request during business hours. § 533A.8.

Customer Service Requirements: Licensee must inform debtor if creditor refuses to participate in the plan. If a compromise is arranged, debtor shall have full benefit of the compromise. § 533A.8.

Limits on Fees: Fees must be agreed upon in advance and listed in the contract. $50 one-time initiation fee. An additional fee may only be charged after 50% of the listed creditors have agreed to the plan or accepted a first payment. If the licensee will receive money from the debtor and pass it along to creditors the maximum additional fee is 15% of the amount paid to creditors. Otherwise, the maximum additional fee is 18% of the total amount of the debts enrolled in the licensee's program, collected in one of two ways: the "total of debt method" or the "percent of savings method." Both methods call for the fee to be paid in monthly installments, subject to additional terms specified in the statute.

Donations may not be charged to a debtor or a creditor, deducted from a payment to a creditor, nor from a debtor's account, nor from payments made pursuant to the contract. If licensee asks for a donation, it must make clear that the donation is voluntary, and not a condition for receiving services. § 533A.9, § 533A.9A.

Prohibited Practices: Entering into a plan without determining that plan is appropriate and debtor can meet the requirements determined by the budget analysis; entering into a contract for a period of more than 60 months; charging debtor services provided by third party; require donations from debtor, or deduct donations from a debtor's account or from payments made to creditor; purchase obligations of debtor; operate as a collection agency on debtor's account with disclosing this fact to both debtor and creditor; take any promissory note, chattel or real property mortgage, wage assignment or other security; pay or receive any bonus for referrals; advertise unlawfully; make statements in advertising that are inconsistent with the statutorily required disclosures; make or encourage debtor to make any false or misleading claims about creditor's right to collect; dispute or cause debtor to dispute a debt without good faith belief that debt is not valid; dispute a debt without written consent of debtor; engage in unauthorized practice of law; attempt to induce debtor to waive rights provided by this section.

For debt settlement programs: advise a debtor to stop making payments to creditors; to represent that debt is settled without receiving written certification from creditor that debt is settled or is part of a payment plan in full settlement of the debt; misrepresent that licensee will pay bills, that program will stop creditor's collection efforts, that program will not harm credit rating, that licensee is competent to give legal advice, or that participation in program can eliminate the need for bankruptcy. § 533A.11, 533A.17.

Public Remedies: Unlicensed practice is a misdemeanor. Superintendent of banking may issue cease and desist order against unlicensed practitioner, require restitution, impose a civil penalty of up to $5000 or bring a civil action for injunction.§§ 533A.13, 533A.16.

Private Remedies: None specified.

Statute of Limitations: Not specified in this statute.

Kansas

Kansas has two statutes, a credit services organizations statute and a criminal statute forbidding debt adjusting by anyone except licensed CSOs and attorneys.

Citation: Kan. Stat. Ann. 21-6502 (criminal statute).

Administrator: Not specified.

Scope & Key Definitions: Criminal statute, which forbids debt adjusting: for consideration, receiving funds from debtor and making distributions among specified creditors.

Exceptions: Attorneys, if debt adjusting is incidental to the ordinary practice of law. Credit services organizations, registered pursuant to Kan. Stat. §§ 50-1116 through 50-1135. See below.

Registration/Licensing: No.

Disclosures: Not specified.

Pre-Agreement Services: Not specified.

Contract Terms: Not specified.

Cancellation/Termination/Refund Rights: Not specified.

Handling of Funds: Not specified.

Customer Service Requirements: Not specified.

Limits on Fees: Not specified.

Prohibited Practices: Not specified.

Public Remedies: Unlicensed debt adjusting is a misdemeanor.

Private Remedies: Not specified.

Statute of Limitations: Not specified in this statute.

Citation: Kan. Stat. Ann. §§ 50-1116 through 50-1135 (credit services organizations).

Administrator: Bank Commissioner. § 50-1117.

Scope & Key Definitions: Debt management services undertaken for compensation. Receiving funds for distribution to consumer's creditors, offering to improve consumer's credit record, or negotiating or offering to negotiate deferral or reduction of consumer's obligations. § 50-1117.

Exceptions: Attorneys, licensed to practice in Kansas, and their law firms [defined], acting in the scope of their practice. §§ 50-1116 and 50-1117.

Registration/Licensing: Registration and $25,000 bond required. (Bond requirement may be increased up to $1,000,000 by rules adopted by Commissioner of Banking.) Application must include a description of the applicant's consumer education program. §§ 50-1118, 50-1119.

Disclosures: Not specified.

Pre-Agreement Services: Registrant must provide consumer with education designed to improve financial literacy; prepare a written budget analysis and plan and determine whether consumer can reasonably meet the plan requirements; make a list of creditors expected to participate in the plan and creditors not expected to participate. § 50-1120.

Contract Terms: Contracts must be written, in at least 12-point type, and include: a description of services to be provided and an itemized list of fees; notice that consumer may cancel at any time; schedule of amounts an due dates of payments; for creditors expected to participate, the amount owed, amount and date of each payment, and expected payoff date; disclosure if registrant may receive compensation from creditors; disclosure that registrant may not require consumer to buy other products or services, or make voluntary contributions; authorization to disclose financial information to the Commissioner of Banks in the course of investigation or examination; contact information for the Commissioner of Banks, for questions and complaints. § 50-1120.

Cancellation/Termination/Refund Rights: Consumer may cancel at any time; notice of this right must be included in contracts. Cancellation fees explicitly forbidden. §§ 50-1120, 50-1126.

Handling of Funds: Within four days of receipt, must deposit funds in a trust account in an insured financial institution, separate from registrant's funds. Must disburse funds to creditors within ten days; correct any misdirected payments and reimburse consumer for any charges imposed by creditor for the mistake; return funds to consumer within ten days if consumer rescinds the agreement. Must provide an accounting every three months showing total amounts received from consumer to date, paid to each creditor to date, paid as fees to registrant, and left in the account, and the amount that each creditor has agreed to accept as payment in full. Annual reports to commissioner required. §§ 50-1117, 50-1122 through 50-1124.

Customer Service Requirements: Not specified.

Limits on Fees: May charge fees only after registrant and consumer have executed a contract. One-time setup fee $50. (Cost of a credit report must be paid from this fee.) Monthly fee the lesser of $20 or $5/creditor/month. May not charge additional fees for budget analysis, counseling, etc. May not impose cancellation fee. Voluntary contributions may be requested, only if they do not exceed the amount of the permitted setup and monthly fee. $50 for a counseling session if consumer does not enter into a contract. May accept payments from creditors, provided that creditor does not assess the fee to the consumer. § 50-1126.

Prohibited Practices: Delaying payment for the purpose of increasing charges due from consumer; false or misleading statements or fraudulent or deceptive acts; advising consumer to make false statements to creditors or CRAs; receiving compensation for debt-management services if the person has acted as a creditor of the consumer; operating a collection agency; lending money, providing credit, or taking a promissory note, or a security interest in real or personal property; giving or receiving a bonus for referrals; structuring an agreement to provide negative amortization; charging for or providing credit insurance; simulating process, or giving false appearance of government authorization; attempting to cause consumer to waive rights. Registrant or its owners or officers may not be owner or officer of any creditor that will receive payment on behalf of a debt-management client. § 50-1121.

Public Remedies: Violation of this act, or rules and regulations promulgated by Commissioner, is a misdemeanor. Commissioner of Banks may issue cease and desist orders and impose penalties of up to $10,000 per incident of unlawful act or practice, or bring a civil action for an injunction. § 50-1129, 50-1131, 50-1134.

Private Remedies: If registrant charges unauthorized fees, the contract is void and registrant must return the amount of the unauthorized fees. A consumer injured by a violation of this act has a private right of action for not less than the amount paid by the consumer to the credit services

organization plus costs and reasonable attorney fees. Punitive damages are available. Violation of this act is a UDAP. Remedies provided by this act are in addition to UDAP remedies. §§ 50-1126, 50-1132, 50-1133.
Statute of Limitations: Not specified in this statute.

Kentucky

Citation: Ky. Rev. Stat. Ann. §§ 380.010 through 380.990 (West).
Administrator: Attorney General.
Scope & Key Definitions: Debt adjusting, budget counseling, debt management, debt modification or settlement, debt pooling, offering for a fee to serve as an intermediary between debtor and creditors, receive money to disburse to creditors, or seek adjustment, compromise, settlement, modification or discharge of debt. Foreclosure prevention explicitly included. § 380.010
Exceptions: Tax-exempt religious, charitable or educational organization, that is not in the business of debt adjusting; attorneys rendering services in the course of their practice, and not principally engaged in the business of debt adjusting; employees of a debtor; persons acting under court order or pursuant to state or federal law; creditor or creditor's agent whose services in debt adjustment are rendered without cost to the debtor; person who makes a loan and disburses the proceeds to creditors, without charging debtor for debt adjustment services. § 380.030.
Registration/Licensing: Registration, bonding ($25,000; $50,000 if registrant deals with residential mortgages) and insurance ($100,000 to $250,000, depending on the volume of registrant's business; $250,000 if registrant deals with residential mortgages). §§ 380.040.
Disclosures: Before receiving any personal information from debtor, debt adjuster must provide disclosure of its policies and practices as to personal information. § 380.090.
Pre-Agreement Services: Not specified.
Contract Terms: Contract must be in writing and show services to be performed and an itemization of the amount or method of determining fees; the schedule and dates of payments, and date of final payment; if a plan calls for payments to creditors, then a list of creditors, payments to be made, and expected concessions; list of creditors expected not to participate, that adjuster may terminate for cause, upon return of unexpended funds to debtor; contact information for the Attorney General for consumer complaints; that participation in the plan may not stop collection efforts, including litigation; the earliest date by which adjuster will contact creditors or the amount that must be accumulated before negotiations will begin; that debtor has the right to cancel at any time. The contract must clearly disclose debtor's fourteen-day right of cancellation, and include a cancellation form. §§ 380.060, 380.100.
Cancellation/Termination/Refund Rights: Fourteen day right to cancel, which must be disclosed, in prescribed form, in the contract. Debtor may also cancel at any time, and debt adjuster must refund any unexpended funds. §§ 380.060, 380.100.
Handling of Funds: Must keep funds for distribution to creditors in a trust account, and disburse them within 30 days of receipt. Registrants' accounts must be audited annually by an independent CPA. § 380.040.
Customer Service Requirements: Debt adjuster must take reasonable precautions to protect debtors' personal information [defined]. The statute prescribes standards for debt adjusters' information security programs. The debt adjuster must notify debtor within five days if a creditor rejects or withdraws from the plan. A debt adjuster may obtain a power of attorney to settle a debt if the amount owed after settlement is not more than 50% of the amount owed before. Debtor's assent must be obtained for any other settlement. §§ 380.070, 380.100.
Limits on Fees: Initial setup fee, $75. Consultation fee, $50/calendar year. Monthly fee of the greater of $30 or 8.5% of the amount paid by the debtor that month. May not accept any other fee in advance of complete performance of all services in connection with a mortgage or other consensual lien on residential real property. Bad check charge, the greater of $20 or the amount of the fee imposed by registrant's bank. Amounts adjusted for inflation. §§ 380.040.

Prohibited Practices: May not settle a debt for more than 50% of the amount owed without debtor's consent, given after creditor agrees; take a power of attorney permitting such settlement or permitting any settlement of a debt secured by residential real property; exercise a power of attorney after debtor has terminated an agreement; take money from debtor's account except for return to the debtor or payment of authorized disbursement or fee; structure debt to result in negative amortization, unless the creditor agrees to refund or waive finance charges upon payment of the principal; settle debt or inform debtor that debt is settled without receiving written certification that the debt is settled or part of a plan that upon completion will result in full settlement; misrepresent the benefits of the plan; misrepresent its authority to give legal advice; take a confession of judgment, promissory note post-dated check, mortgage or security interest; lend money or provide credit, except the deferral of a fee at no cost to debtor; charge for any insurance, club membership, or other product or service not directly related to debt adjusting or educational services; any other false, misleading, deceptive or unconscionable act. May not sell or transfer personal information without authorization from debtor. Agreements may not provide for the application of another state's law; restrict debtor's remedies under this chapter or other law; limit or release liability for violating this chapter or failing to perform an agreement. Waiver of rights is void and unenforceable. §§ 380.040, 380.080, 380.100, 380.120.
Public Remedies: Violation of this chapter is a misdemeanor. Attorney general may sue for civil penalties up to $5000 per violation. The court may also order restitution or appoint a receiver. § 380.990.
Private Remedies: Consumer who enters into debt adjusting agreement and suffers ascertainable loss of money or property as a result of violation of this chapter has a private right of action for actual damages or such equitable relief as the court deems proper. Nothing in this section limits a person's rights to seek punitive damages where appropriate. Reasonable costs and attorney fees in the discretion of the court. Violation of this statute is a UDAP. § 380.110.
Statute of Limitations: For private right of action, later of two years after the violation, or one year after termination of Attorney General's action. § 381.110.

Louisiana

Louisiana has two statutes, a credit services act and a criminal statute forbidding unlicensed for-profit debt adjusting.

Citation: La. Rev. Stat. Ann. § 14:331 (criminal statute).
Administrator: Not specified.
Scope & Key Definitions: Criminal statute forbidding for-profit debt adjusting. For a fee, taking funds for disbursement to debtor's creditors, or seeking to effect the adjustment, compromise or discharge of debt.
Exceptions: Nonprofit or charitable corporations engaged in debt adjusting; debt adjusting incidental to the practice of law; banks and fiduciaries in the regular course of their business; title insurers and abstract companies doing escrow business; judicial officers or others acting pursuant to court order; debt adjusting incident to the practice of a certified public accountant; bona fide trade or mercantile associations arranging adjustment of debts with business establishments; employers for their employees; lender that, with authorization of debtor, disburses loan funds to creditors, without compensation for debt adjustment services.
Registration/Licensing: See Financial Planning and Management Statute, below.
Disclosures: Not specified.
Pre-Agreement Services: Not specified.
Contract Terms: Not specified.
Cancellation/Termination/Refund Rights: Not specified.
Handling of Funds: Not specified.
Customer Service Requirements: Not specified.
Limits on Fees: Not specified.
Prohibited Practices: Not specified.
Public Remedies: Practice of debt adjustment in violation of this section is a misdemeanor.

Private Remedies: Not specified.

Statute of Limitations: Not specified in this statute.

Citation: La. Rev. Stat. Ann. §§ 37:2581 through 37:2600 (credit services act).

Scope & Key Definitions: Financial Planning and Management Services. Planning and management of the financial affairs of an individual, and the distribution of money to the individual's creditors or acting as agent in the distribution of money to creditors, whether or not the planner receives a fee. § 37:2582.

Administrator: Division of Occupational Standards.

Exceptions: Nonprofit organizations providing debt-management services; attorneys, banks, fiduciaries, or other financing and lending institutions, in the regular course of their business; title insurers and abstract companies doing an escrow business; licensees' employees; judicial officers or others acting under court order; employers for their employees; associations for their members. § 37:2582.

Registration/Licensing: License required. $10,500 bond. (Cash deposit may be substituted). § 37:2584.

Disclosures: Not specified.

Pre-Agreement Services: Licensee must prepare a written analysis of debtor's income and expenses, to substantiate that the plan is feasible and practical. § 37:2591.

Contract Terms: Licensee must provide debtor with a written contract setting forth all charges and services. § 37:2591.

Cancellation/Termination/Refund Rights: Debtor may cancel upon 30 days written notice. §§ 37:2591.

Handling of Funds: Licensee must provide a receipt for each payment. Licensee must provide debtor, within seven days of request, an statement showing the total amount received and the amount disbursed to each creditor. Must promptly remit funds to creditors. § 37:2591, 37:2594.

Customer Service Requirements: Not specified.

Limits on Fees: Reasonable fee of up to 12% of the amount of listed debts. $25 setup fee, which is included in the 12% cap. Cancellation or default fee, for contracts in effect for less than 90 days, of the lesser of $25 or 9% of the remaining indebtedness; for contracts in force more than 90 days, $50. § 37:2592.

Prohibited Practices: Taking a promissory note, mortgage, security interest, or other promise to pay any fee or charge; use false, misleading, or deceptive advertising. § 37:2593.

Public Remedies: Violation is a misdemeanor. Director of the Division of Occupational Standards may ask Attorney General to bring action to enjoin violations. § 37:2596, 37:2597.

Private Remedies: Contract made by unlicensed person is void. § 37:2596.

Statute of Limitations: Not specified in this statute.

Maine

Maine has two statutes, a debt-management services statute, and criminal statute forbidding unregistered debt management.

Citation: Me. Rev. Stat. Ann. tit. 17, §§ 701 through 703 (criminal statute).

Administrator: Not specified.

Scope & Key Definitions: Criminal statute, forbidding budget planning, making a contract with debtor pursuant to which debtor makes periodic payments to planner, who distributes the funds among specified creditors. § 702.

Exceptions: Registered debt-management providers (see below); attorneys, provided that budget planning is not the "exclusive business" of the attorney; supervised financial institutions and supervised lenders, which are regulated under other statutes. § 701.

Registration/Licensing: See Debt Management Providers, below.

Disclosures: Not specified.

Pre-Agreement Services: Not specified.

Contract Terms: Not specified.

Cancellation/Termination/Refund Rights: Not specified.

Handling of Funds: Not specified.

Customer Service Requirements: Not specified.

Limits on Fees: Not specified.

Prohibited Practices: Not specified.

Public Remedies: Violations are crimes punishable by fine and jail. § 703.

Private Remedies: Not specified.

Statute of Limitations: Not specified in this statute.

Citation: Maine Rev. Stat. Ann. tit. 32, §§ 6172 through 6183 (debt-management services).

Administrator: Superintendent of Consumer Credit Protection (within the Department of Professional and Financial Regulation). § 6172.

Scope & Key Definitions: Debt Management Services Providers. For a fee or other consideration, receiving funds from a consumer for distribution to creditors, or arranging for a consumer to distribute funds, in full or partial payment of consumer's obligations or acting or offering to act as an intermediary between consumer and creditors, for the purpose of adjusting, settling, discharging, compromising or otherwise altering the terms of payment. § 6172.

Exceptions: Attorneys, if debt management is not their "exclusive activity"; supervised lenders and supervised financial organizations (defined), regulated under other specified statutes. § 6172.

Registration/Licensing: Registration and $50,000 bond required. Counselors must be certified. Special training requirements if debt management includes a residential mortgage. Consumer education programs must be submitted to the Superintendent of Consumer Credit Protection for approval. §§ 6173, 6174, 6174-B.

Disclosures: Not specified.

Pre-Agreement Services: Debt management providers must offer consumer education programs. § 6174-B.

Contract Terms: Contracts must be in writing and must itemize the services provided and charges; provide contact information for the Bureau of Consumer Credit Protection and disclose the existence of the bond; identify the financial institution in which trust funds are held; disclose that either party may cancel the contract by giving written notice; include a complete list of creditors and obligations covered by the contract, and whether the obligations are individual or those of consumer and a spouse or other household member; the amount to be disbursed to each creditor; authorization to disclose financial information to the administrator; notice that consumer must be given a copy of the contract. If the services include a transfer of real property, provider must provide consumer with contact information for HUD-approved housing counselors, and must advise consumer whether or not a deficiency will be owed. §§ 6176, 6183.

Cancellation/Termination/Refund Rights: Either party may cancel by giving written notice. § 6176.

Handling of Funds: Funds for distribution to creditors must be deposited, within two business days of receipt, in a trust account in a supervised financial institution, separate from the operating accounts of the provider. Provider must remit funds to creditors within fifteen business days of receipt, correct any misdirected payments, and reimburse consumer for any charges imposed by creditor because of the misdirection. Must provide a written accounting at least quarterly, showing funds received and the disbursements to each creditor. §§ 6175, 6177.

Customer Service Requirements: Not specified.

Limits on Fees: Only one fee per household. $75 initial setup fee. For plans that distribute monthly payments, monthly fee of $40. For plans that negotiate settlement, reasonable fee of not more than 15% of the amount by which debt is reduced by each settlement. $50 for consumer education program. §§ 6174-A, 6174-B.

Prohibited Practices: May not purchase consumer's debts; lend money or provide credit; take a mortgage or other security interest; operate as a debt collector; structure a debt that would result, at the conclusion of the projected term for the agreement, in negative amortization; use false or misleading advertising. The prohibitions on purchase of debt, lending money and taking a mortgage do not apply to certain debt-management services involving the sale or transfer of real property. §§ 6179, 6180, 6183.

Public Remedies: Superintendent of Consumer Credit Protection may issue cease and desist orders, order forfeiture of the bond, or bring civil action for penalties of up to $5000. § 6181.

Private Remedies: Private right of action for actual damages plus costs and reasonable attorney fees for violations of statute or rule, or unfair, unconscionable or deceptive practices that cause actual damage to a consumer. If the services involved the transfer of real property, consequential damages may be recovered. § 6181, 6183.

Statute of Limitations: Not specified in this statute.

Maryland

Maryland has two statutes, debt management and debt settlement.

Citation: Md. Code Ann., Fin. Inst. §§ 12-901 through 12-931 (West) (debt management).

Administrator: Commissioner of Financial Regulation in the Department of Labor, Licensing and Regulation. § 1-101.

Scope & Key Definitions: Debt Management. Receiving funds from a consumer for distribution to creditors in full or partial payment of debts. § 12-901(g).

Exceptions: Attorneys, escrow agents and certified public accountants in the regular practice of their professions; banks, credit unions and savings and loans; bill payment services that do not provide counseling or negotiate compromises or new payment schedules with individual creditors; providers of accelerated mortgage payment services (defined in § 12-401 of this title); title insurers or abstract companies; judicial officers or persons acting under court orders; persons performing services incidental to the dissolution or liquidation of a business entity; trade or mercantile association arranging the adjustment of debts with a business enterprise; licensed mortgage lenders who do not receive funds for the purpose of distribution among creditors. Debt settlement providers (see below) that comply with the debt settlement subtitle, negotiate reductions in payments, make no more than six settlement payments on any debt, and establish a dedicated account separate from any debt-management accounts. § 12-902.

Registration/Licensing: License, bonding ($10,000 to $1,000,000 as determined by the commissioner) and insurance required. Counselors must be comprehensively trained. Application must include descriptions of applicant's consumer education plan, financial analysis method and initial budget plan, a copy of applicant's debt-management agreement, applicant's plan to ensure that counselors are certified within six months of hiring, and a copy of contract or fee-for-service agreements between applicant and anyone who provides services related to the debt-management business. §§ 12-904, 12-906, 12-907, 12-908, 12-914.

Disclosures: Advertisements must include licensee's license number. § 12-925.

Pre-Agreement Services: Must provide a list of services offered and prices. Licensee, through a certified counselor, must provide consumer education program and a written summary of available options. Must advise consumer of the requirement for pre-bankruptcy counseling, and whether the licensee is authorized to provide this counseling, and how to obtain a list of approved pre-bankruptcy counselors; must provide a financial analysis and initial budget plan; a list showing which creditors are expected to participate and which are expected not to participate in the plan; a written contract showing services to be provided, and costs, with a schedule of payments and itemization of fees; the name of the financial institution where trust funds are held; disclosure of the existence of the required bond; notice that either party may rescind the agreement upon written notice; disclosure if the licensee may receive compensation from creditors; disclosure that licensee may not require voluntary contributions or the purchase of other services or supplies; authorization to reveal financial information to the Commissioner; warning that entering into the plan may harm consumer's credit rating and credit score; contact information for complaints to the Commissioner. Licensee must have a reasonable expectation, based on past experience, that the listed creditors will accept the agreed-upon payments, and must determine that the plan is suitable for the consumer and that the consumer will be able to make the payments. The required information may be provided via the Internet if consumer is advised of the availability of counseling and given the opportunity to discuss the financial analysis and plan with a counselor at any time. §§ 12-916, 12-918.

Contract Terms: Contract must be in writing and include contact information for the licensee and the financial institution holding the trust account, notice of rescission rights, description of services to be provided, schedule of payments, itemization of fees, list of participating creditors and schedule of payments to each, list of creditors expected not to participate, disclosure if licensee receives compensation from creditors, disclosure that licensee may not require the purchase of other goods and services, warning that plan may harm consumer's credit rating and credit scores, contact information for Commissioner of Financial Regulation. § 12-916.

Cancellation/Termination/Refund Rights: Either party may rescind at any time by giving written notice; this right must be disclosed in contract. In addition to any other cancellation right, may cancel or modify agreement if a creditor withdraws. Debtor who rescinds is entitled to a refund of all unexpended funds. §§ 12-916, 12-918.

Handling of Funds: Funds for disbursement to creditors must be deposited, within two days of receipt, in a trust account in an insured financial institution, separate from licensee's operating funds. Must disburse funds within eight days of receipt; correct any misdirected payments and reimburse consumer for any charges imposed by creditor as a result of the misdirection. Licensee must provide an accounting showing funds received and the date and amount of disbursements, at least quarterly and upon termination of the agreement. §§ 12-901(o), 12-917, 12-919.

Customer Service Requirements: Must notify debtor if creditor withdraws from or refuses to participate in plan, and advise consumer of right to rescind or modify contract. § 12-918.

Limits on Fees: $50 consultation fee (from which cost of obtaining a credit report must be paid) No other fees may be imposed until after consumer and licensee have executed a debt-management agreement. Monthly fee of the lesser of $40 or $8 per creditor. May not solicit voluntary contributions, but may accept contributions if the total amount does not exceed the permitted fees. Licensee may charge a fee for counseling or education to consumer who does not enter into debt-management program. Bad check fees as permitted by Comm. Law § 15-802. § 12-918.

Prohibited Practices: May not purchase debt or obligation of consumer; lend money or provide credit; take a mortgage or other security interest; operate as a collection agency; structure an agreement to result in negative amortization of any debt; use any false, misleading or deceptive representations in the offer, sale, or performance of any service; offer a bonus for referrals; offer consumer any gift or reward for executing an agreement; charge for or provide credit insurance; compromise a debt without obtaining the consumer's consent and determining that the compromise benefits the consumer; use false, deceptive or misleading advertising; pay an incentive to employees for enrolling consumers; violate any law governing debt-management and related services. May not directly or indirectly receive any fee for referring consumer to a lender or other provider of consumer service if the licensee or any owner, officer, director, principal or employee of the licensee is an owner, partner, officer, director, principal or employee of the service provider. (Referrals permitted if no fee is directly or indirectly collected, and the consumer is advised of the relationship.) § 12-920.

Public Remedies: Willful violation of the statute is a felony. The Commissioner may issue cease and desist orders, impose civil penalties of up to $1000 per violation, and petition the court to enforce orders. §§ 12-928, 12-929.

Private Remedies: Contract with unlicensed person is void; consumer may recover all fees, along with reasonable attorney fees. If a licensee imposes an unauthorized fee or charge, the agreement is void and the licensee must return the amount of the unauthorized payment. A consumer has a private right of action for damages caused by violations, including costs and reasonable attorney fees. §§ 12-916, 12-918, 12-930.

Statute of Limitations: Not specified in this statute.

Citation: Md. Code Ann., Fin. Inst. §§ 12-1001 through 12-1017 (West) (debt settlement). This statute is scheduled to sunset on June 30, 2016.

Administrator: Commissioner of Financial Regulation in the Department of Labor, Licensing and Regulation. § 1-101.

Scope & Key Definitions: Debt Settlement. A program represented directly or by implication to renegotiate, settle, reduce or otherwise alter the terms of payment between a consumer and a creditor. § 12-1001.

Exceptions: Debt management (see above); attorneys providing services in the course of an attorney-client relationship; escrow agents, certified public accountants, and banking institutions in the regular course of their businesses; bill payment services that do not negotiate with creditors or provide counseling; providers of accelerated mortgage payment services (defined by § 12-401 of this title); title insurers, title insurance agencies and abstract companies; persons performing services incidental to the dissolution or winding-up of a business enterprise; trade or mercantile associations arranging the adjustment of debts with a business enterprise; mortgage lenders in the course of their business; collection agencies while engaged in their business.§§ 12-1001 through 12-1003.

Registration/Licensing: Registration required. $50,000 bond required if provider establishes dedicated accounts. §§ 12-1004, 12-1014.

Disclosures: Advertisements must disclose that, if plan results in failure to make timely payments, this may reduce consumer's creditworthiness, result in collection action, including litigation, and increase the amount the consumer owes. § 12-1013.

Pre-Agreement Services: None specified.

Contract Terms: Contract must specify services to be provided and fees; list of creditors and the amount owed to each; total amount of debt included in the agreement; a good faith estimate of the time needed to complete the plan; the time by which provider will make a settlement offer, or the amount of funds or percentage of the debt that must be accumulated before provider will make an offer; notice that the consumer may withdraw at any time, at which time provider may not charge a penalty but may collect any settlement fees it has earned; explanation that consumer owns the dedicated account; warning that consumer may have to pay taxes on the amount by which debt is reduced. § 12-1012.

Cancellation/Termination/Refund Rights: Consumer may withdraw at any time. If consumer requests withdrawal, funds in the dedicated account, including interest, less settlement fees earned by registrant, must be refunded to consumer within 7 days of the request. Cancellation fees forbidden. § 12-1010.

Handling of Funds: Consumer may be required to deposit funds in an account in an insured financial institution, provided that fund, including accrued interest remain property of the consumer; the financial institution or entity administering the account is not owned, controlled or in any way affiliated with the registrant, and does not pay or accept fees for referrals involving the registrant, although it may charge account-related fees. § 12-1010.

Customer Service Requirements: None specified.

Limits on Fees: No fee may be charged until provider and consumer have entered into an agreement, provider has renegotiated at least one debt, and consumer has made at least one payment. Provider may, however, require consumer to deposit funds into a bank account owned and controlled by consumer, to be used for debt settlement fees and payments. Debt settlement fee must bear the same proportionate relationship to the total fee as the amount of the settled debt bears to the total amount of debt, or settlement fee may be calculated as a percentage of the sum by which the amount of the debt exceeds the settlement. (Must be same percentage for all debts). No cancellation fee permitted, but provider may collect fees earned in compliance with this section. §§ 12-1010.

Prohibited Practices: May not misrepresent any material aspect of debt settlement service. § 12-1011.

Public Remedies: Violations of this subtitle are UDAPs. § 12-1016.

Private Remedies: Violations of this subtitle are UDAPs. § 12-1016.

Statute of Limitations: Not specified in this statute.

Massachusetts

Citation: Mass. Gen. Laws Ann. ch. 180, § 4A.

Administrator: Attorney General. Mass. Gen. Laws Ann. Ch. 12, Sec. 8F.

Scope & Key Definitions: Credit counseling services may be performed only by licensed attorneys or by nonprofit charitable corporations that are regulated by Mass. Gen. Laws. Ch. 12. Credit counseling services: (a) the providing of financial and budgetary advice and judgment to individuals in connection with the creation of a budgetary plan; or (b) the creation of a plan whereby an individual turns over an agreed amount of his income to a nonprofit credit counseling corporation that distributes it to his creditors in accordance with a plan that they have approved and that may provide for smaller payments or a longer term than the original contract; or (c) the providing of educational services relating to the use of credit; or (d) any combination of these.

Exceptions: Not specified.

Registration/Licensing: Charitable corporations must file annual reports with Attorney General. Mass. Gen. Laws Ann. Ch. 12, Sec. 8F.

Disclosures: Not specified.

Pre-Agreement Services: Not specified.

Contract Terms: Not specified.

Cancellation/Termination/Refund Rights: Not specified.

Handling of Funds: Nonprofits are subject to detailed reporting and record-keeping requirements, to assure honesty and transparency in handling of donors' funds. Mass. Gen. Laws Ann. Ch. 12, Sec. 8F.

Customer Service Requirements: Not specified.

Limits on Fees: Not specified.

Prohibited Practices: Not specified.

Public Remedies: Not specified.

Private Remedies: Not specified.

Statute of Limitations: Not specified.

Michigan

Citation: Mich. Comp. Laws §§ 451.411 through 451.437.

Administrator: Department of Insurance and Financial Services. 451.412.

Scope & Key Definitions: Debt Management: planning and management of debtor's financial affairs and receipt of money from debtor for distribution in payment or partial payment of debts. § 451.412.

Exceptions: Attorneys or certified public accountants, providing debt management incidental to their practices; banks, credit unions, fiduciaries and lenders in the regular scope of their businesses; title insurers or abstract companies doing an escrow business; licensees' employees in the course of their employment; judicial officers or persons acting under court order. Persons performing debt-management services and being compensated primarily from government organizations, governmentally sponsored organizations, charitable trusts, or tax exempt foundations may be exempted from any provision of the act, upon a showing of safeguards in the handling of debtors' funds, if the exemption is found to be in the public interest. §§ 451.413, 451.414.

Registration/Licensing: License and bond ($25,000 to $100,000 as determined by the department) required. Individual applicant must present evidence that he or she is a certified counselor; business entity must show that the counselors it employs will become certified within 180 days of employment. §§ 451.413, 451.414, 451.415, 451.416.

Disclosures: Copies of advertising and sales literature must be provided to the department at least 10 days before use, and may not be used if the department finds them to be misleading. § 451.430.

Pre-Agreement Services: Before entering into a contract, licensee must provide debtor with a written budget analysis and determine that the debtor can reasonably meet the requirements of a debt-management plan. § 451.422.

Contract Terms: Contracts must set forth a list of creditors and the amount owed to each; the total amount of licensee's charges; the beginning and ending dates of the contract; the number of months and the amount of principal and interest needed to liquidate all listed debts except mortgage and land contract interest payments; notice of three-day right to cancel. Licensee must provide debtor with a copy of the contract. § 451.424.

Cancellation/Termination/Refund Rights: Right to cancel, without cost, within 3 days of signing contract. If a debtor fails to make a payment within 60 days after it is due, creditor may, in its discretion cancel the contract if it concludes that plan is no longer suitable for debtor, if debtor fails to affirmatively communicate debtor's desire to continue the plan, or if creditors refuse to go on accepting payments. §§ 451.424, 451.428.

Handling of Funds: All funds received must be distributed to creditors monthly, except for the amounts due for monthly fees and closeout fee. Funds for distribution to creditors must be deposited, within two days of receipt, in a trust account in an insured financial institution. Accounts must be reconciled at least once a month, and must have a balance equal to or greater than the sum of the escrow balances in each debtor's account. If the balance falls below this amount, licensee must report to the director, describing the remedial action to be taken. If funds are kept in an out-of-state account, licensee must post bond in the amount of 100% of the average amount of the deposits held in the account from month to month. Licensee must give a receipt for cash payments immediately, and for non-cash payments within three business days of receipt; provide debtor an accounting at least monthly, and within five days of request; provide a more detailed accounting every 90 days; conduct an audit of all files and procedures at least once a year. Wage assignments by debtor to licensee are permitted, if otherwise in accordance with state law. §§ 451.424, 451.425, 451.426, 451.431.

Customer Service Requirements: None specified.

Limits on Fees: Upon establishing a plan, $25. This fee must be refunded and the account closed unless, within forty-five days, 51% in number and dollar amount of the creditors consent to the program. Total fees (including the up-front fee) may not exceed 15% of the debt to be liquidated. $25 cancellation fee if plan is not successfully completed. (This fee may not be collected if debtor exercises the three-day right to cancel.) Provider may offer the debtor the opportunity to purchase educational materials or credit reports. Fees for these items are not subject to the 15% cap. §§ 451.412, 451.423, 451.428.

Prohibited Practices: Licensee may not purchase any obligation of the debtor; execute a contract with blanks not filled in; lend money or extend credit except pursuant to a plan approved by the department; take a confession of judgment, or power of attorney to confess judgment, or appear as the debtor in a judicial proceeding; take a promissory note, mortgage, or security interest as security for a fee; give or receive a bonus for referrals; take a release of any obligation to be performed by the licensee; disclose the debtors who have contracted with licensee to anyone other than the director, or disclose the creditors to anyone other than the debtor, the director, or other creditors if necessary to secure cooperation in a plan; use any false, misleading, or deceptive advertising; fail to give debtor the full benefit of any compromise; employ any scheme or artifice to defraud; make untrue statements (including the omission of material fact). The prohibition on paying or receiving bonuses does not apply to payment to participate in a locator service, or receipt of funds from a fair share or similar program [defined]. § 451.429.

Public Remedies: The Department of Financial and Insurance Services may issue cease and desist orders, or bring an action for injunction. Willful violation of the act is a felony; willful violation of a cease and desist order or injunction is criminal contempt. §§ 451.433, 451.434.

Private Remedies: If a licensee collects an unauthorized charge (except in case of bona fide clerical or computer error), the contract is void and licensee must return all payments, less the amount distributed to creditors, plus a penalty equal to the amount of the unauthorized charge. §§ 451.414, 451.428.

Statute of Limitations: Six years from accrual of claim. (Different statutes for actions involving real property.) § 451.435.

Minnesota

Minnesota has two statutes: debt management and debt settlement.

Citation: Minn. Stat. §§ 332A.02 through 332A.19 (debt management).

Administrator: Commissioner of Commerce.

Scope & Key Definitions: Debt Management: Whether or not a fee is charged, managing the financial affairs of a debtor by receiving funds from the debtor and directing periodic payments to creditors with the primary purpose to effect the full payment of consumer debts. § 332A.02.

Exceptions: Attorneys, authorized to practice in Minnesota, whose exclusive or principal practice does not involve debt-management services and who do not have a business relationship with a debt-management services provider that involves provision of debt-management services. Escrow agents, accountants, broker-dealers in securities; banks, other financial and lending institutions, title insurers, and insurance companies; persons performing credit services for their employer, who is not in the business of debt management; the state, its political subdivisions, public agencies and their employees; collection agencies providing services to a creditor; "qualified organizations" serving as representative payees for Social Security or SSI recipients; accredited mortgage payment providers (defined); trustees, guardians and conservators; debt settlement services providers (see below). § 332A.02.

Registration/Licensing: Registration and $5000 bond required. Accreditation required. Application must include copy of standard debt-management agreement and proof of accreditation. §§ 332A.03, 332A.04.

Disclosures: Not specified.

Pre-Agreement Services: Before entering into a debt-management agreement, registrant must provide individualized counseling, provide a financial analysis, disclose that debt-management plans are not suitable for everyone and that there are alternatives, determine that the debtor is able to meet the requirements of the plan and will receive a net tangible benefit, and disclose the registrant's registration number. § 332A.10.

Contract Terms: Contracts must contain an itemization of fees and the total amount of fees reasonably anticipated to be paid over the term of the agreement; disclosure that the term of the agreement may be extended and charges increased if debts are increased by interest, late or over limit or other fees imposed by creditor; explanation of debtor's cancellation rights; registrant's refund policy; detailed description of services to be provided. § 332A.10.

Cancellation/Termination/Refund Rights: Debtor may cancel the agreement at any time, upon ten days' notice, and registrant may cancel upon 30 days' notice. Cancellation rights must be clearly disclosed in the debt-management agreement. The agreement is automatically terminated if debts are paid in full. Upon cancellation or termination, registrant must return all unexpended funds to debtor. Registrant must notify debtor if creditor withdraws from or refuses to participate in plan, and inform debtor of right to withdraw form plan. §§ 332A.11, 332A.13.

Handling of Funds: Funds for payment of creditors must be held in a separate trust account and disbursed to creditors within 42 days of receipt, unless earlier disbursement is required to comply with due dates, or where obligation requires funds to be accumulated to reach a sum certain, or if debtor's payment is returned for insufficient funds or some reason makes the withholding of funds in the interest of debtor.

Registrant must provide debtor with an accounting at least monthly, and upon termination or cancellation of contract. Registrant must notify debtor if creditor withdraws from or refuses to participate in plan, and inform debtor of right to withdraw form plan. §§ 332A.12, 332A.13.

Customer Service Requirements: Registrant must actively seek the consent of creditors and promptly notify debtor if creditor rejects or withdraws from the plan. § 332A.13.

Limits on Fees: $50 origination fee. Reasonable monthly fee not to exceed the lesser of $75 or 15% of the monthly payment amount. No fee may be charged for recurring payments (such as rent or mortgage, utilities, insurance, child support, etc.). New or additional agreements permitted if no new origination fee is charged. Modifications to agreements must be signed and in writing, except if debtor requests the addition or deletion of a creditor, or chooses to voluntarily increase the payments; or the payments are increased by not more than $19 per creditor or $20 total as a result of incorrect information given by the debtor. §§ 332A.10, 332A.13.

Prohibited Practices: Contracts may not include a hold harmless clause; a confession of judgment, power of attorney to confess judgment, or permission to appear as debtor in any judicial proceeding; waiver of right to jury trial in any action by or against debtor; assignment of or order for payment of wages or other compensation for service; an agreement not to assert any claim or defense; waiver of any provisions of this chapter or release of any obligations required to be performed by debt-management service; mandatory arbitration clause or any clause selecting law other than that of Minnesota. Registrant may not purchase any obligation of debtor; use or threaten to use any legal process against a debtor while the debt-management agreement remains executor; advise debtor to stop paying a creditor or in any indicate that this is beneficial to the debtor; require the purchase of stock, insurance, or any goods or services as a condition of performing a debt-management agreement; compromise any debt without debtor's consent, or if compromise does not inure solely to the benefit of debtor; receive as security for a fee a promissory note, mortgage or security interest; lend money or provide credit; receive any benefit in return for referring debtor to a lender or debt-management provider; structure an agreement to result in negative amortization of any debt; offer a benefit to employees or other persons, for referring debtors or enrolling them in the program; contract with a debtor without a thorough written budget analysis showing that debtor is reasonably able to meet the requirements of the plan, and will be benefited; charge for or provide credit insurance; operate a collection agency or process serving business, or employ any person who is an employee or owner of such a business; solicit an voluntary contribution from debtor; commit any unfair, deceptive or unconscionable act. Deceptive advertising, including misleading statements or omissions about rates, terms and conditions; misrepresentation of nonprofit status; misrepresentation of government affiliation. §§ 332A.10, 332A.14, 332A.16.

Public Remedies: The Attorney General enforces this statute. § 332A.18.
Private Remedies: If a registrant violates this chapter, debtor has a right to rescind the agreement; all fees not paid to creditors must be refunded to debtor within ten days of rescission. Violation of this chapter is a UDAP. Private right of action for actual, incidental and consequential damages, plus up to $1000 statutory damages, and for injunction. Class actions permitted. The remedies are cumulative and not exclusive. §§ 332A.17, 332A.18.
Statute of Limitations: Not specified in this statute.

Citation: Minn. Stat. §§ 332B.02 through 332B.14 (debt settlement).
Administrator: Commissioner of Commerce
Scope & Key Definitions: Debt Settlement. A person who does either of the following is engaged in the provision of debt settlement services whether or not a fee is charged: acting or offering to act as an intermediary between consumer and creditors, for the purpose of negotiating settlement for less than the full amount of the debt; or advising consumers to accumulate funds for future payment of a reduced amount of a debt. § 332B.02.
Exceptions: Attorneys, authorized to practice in Minnesota, whose exclusive or principal practice does not involve debt settlement services and who do not have a business relationship with a debt settlement services provider that involves provision of debt settlement services. §§ 332B.02.
Registration/Licensing: Registration and $5000 bond required. Application must include copy of standard debt settlement plan, and if applicant intends to provide credit counseling, proof of accreditation. §§ 332B.03, 332B.04.
Disclosures: Not specified.
Pre-Agreement Services: Before entering into a contract, registrant must inform the debtor that debt settlement is not suitable for everyone, and that alternatives include credit counseling, debt management, and bankruptcy; prepare an individualized financial analysis and conclude that debtor can meet the requirements of a plan and receive a net benefit; provide an itemized list of services and fees; make a determination, upon a sufficient basis, which listed creditors are likely to participate in a plan and which are not; if not all creditors are likely to participate, registrant must obtain debtor's permission to proceed without them; must provide a conspicuous warning that successful reduction or elimination of debt cannot be guaranteed; that if debtor stops paying creditors, collection action, including litigation may result, and debt will be increased by interest and other charges; that forgiveness of debt may result in tax liability; and that debtor's credit rating may be worsened. These warnings must be in prescribed form. § 332B.06.
Contract Terms: Before performing any services, registrant must enter into, and provide debtor with a copy of a written contract, which discloses

registrant's registration number; is written in debtor's primary language, if registrant negotiated in that language; a conspicuous disclosure of the total amount of fees and itemization of fees; detailed description of services; debtor's cancellation rights; registrant's refund policy; registrant's contact information; list of creditors and amount owed to each. Any modification of the agreement must be in writing. § 332B.06.
Cancellation/Termination/Refund Rights: Consumer may cancel upon ten days written notice. Provider must refund all fees except those permitted by § 332B.09. Return of fees is not required if provider obtained a settlement offer that debtor refused, or if debtor entered into a settlement offer with creditor for an amount equal to or lower the settlement offer. Right to cancel must be conspicuously disclosed in the contract. Agreement terminates automatically upon the payment of all settled debts and fees, at which point provider must return any remaining funds to debtor. Provider may cancel on thirty days' notice. If a creditor withdraws from the program, provider must notify debtor of right to modify the plan. If 50% or more of the creditors withdraw, provider must notify debtor of right to cancel. §§ 332B.07, 332B.10.
Handling of Funds: Debtor funds must be held in trust and disbursed within 42 days. Must provide a detailed accounting to debtor every month and upon cancellation or termination. §§ 332B.06, 332B.08.
Customer Service Requirements: Registrant must inform debtor within 24 hours of any settlement offer. If a creditor withdraws, registrant must inform debtor within 15 days and advise debtor of right to modify the agreement. If more than 50% of creditors withdraw, registrant must advise debtor of right to cancel. § 332B.09.
Limits on Fees: Fees may be calculated on a percentage of debt or a percentage of savings basis. *Percentage of debt:* 15% of total. Provider may charge a nonrefundable origination fee of $200 for aggregate debt less than $20,000 or $400 for aggregate debt of $20,000 or more, plus a monthly fee of $50 for debt less than $40,000 or $60 for debt of $40,000 or more, plus a settlement fee for the remaining permitted amount. Collection of monthly fees must cease when the amount collected reaches 40% of the permitted fee. *Percentage of savings:* 30% of the savings actually negotiated. No other fees may be charged. § 332B.09.
Prohibited Practices: Agreement may not contain any provision forbidden by the Debt Management Act (see above). All practices forbidden by the Debt Management Act (see above). May not promise or guarantee that any debt will be settled; misrepresent the timing of negotiations; misrepresent that charges will not continue to accrue or that debtor will not be subject to collection efforts and legal action; misrepresent tax consequences of settlement; exercise or attempt to exercise a power of attorney after debtor has terminated an agreement; misrepresent that entering into agreement will not harm credit rating; challenge a debt without debtor's consent; make any false or misleading claim as to creditor's right to collect; misrepresent that registrant can negotiate a better settlement than debtor alone; engage in unauthorized practice of law, or misrepresent its authority to give legal advice; settle a debt or lead debtor to believe it is settled without receiving written certification from creditor that payment is in full settlement.

Advertising: any false, deceptive, or misleading statement about its services; misrepresent nonprofit status; misrepresent government affiliation; claim or imply that secured debts can be settled. Lead generators must make clear that they provide only referrals, may not represent that any service is guaranteed, and may not misrepresent the benefits of debt settlement services. §§ 332B.06, 332B.09, 332B.10, 332B.11.
Public Remedies: The Attorney General enforces this statute. § 332B.12.
Private Remedies: If a registrant commits a material violation of the terms of this chapter, debtor may rescind the agreement, and registrant must refund, within ten days, all fees not paid to creditors. Violation of this chapter is a UDAP. Debtor has a private right of action against a registrant or lead generator who violates this chapter for actual, incidental and consequential damages, plus up to $5000 statutory damages and reasonable attorney fees, and for injunction. Class actions permitted. These remedies are cumulative and not exclusive. §§ 332B.12, 332B.12.
Statute of Limitations: Not specified in this statute.

Mississippi

Citation: Miss. Code Ann. §§ 81-22-1 through 81-22-31. This statute is scheduled to sunset on July 1, 2017. § 8-11-31.

Administrator: Department of Banking and Consumer Finance.

Scope & Key Definitions: Debt Management Services Providers: For a fee or other consideration, receiving funds from a consumer for distribution to creditors in full or partial payment of debts; or arranging or assisting a consumer in arranging the distribution of funds among creditors in full or partial payment of debts; or exercising control over funds of a consumer for this purpose; or serving as an intermediary between consumer and creditors for purposes of compromising, negotiating, or otherwise deferring, reducing or altering terms of payment; or offering to improve a consumer's credit record, history, or rating. § 81-22-3.

Exceptions: Debt adjusting or credit record error correction incidental to the practice of law; attorneys in the regular practice of law; title insurers adjusting debts out of escrow funds in the regular course of business; judicial officers or others acting under court order; debt adjustment incidental to the practice of a certified public accountant; bona fide trade or mercantile associations arranging adjustment of debts with business establishments; employers who adjust debts for their employees; lender that, at debtor's request, disburses loan proceeds among creditors, without being compensated for this service; regulated financial institutions. § 81-22-3.

Registration/Licensing: License and $50,000 bond required. Bonding also required for third-party payment processors. §§ 81-22-5, 81-22-7, 81-22-28.

Disclosures: Not specified.

Pre-Agreement Services: Not specified.

Contract Terms: Debt management agreement must be in writing and include an itemization of services to be performed and charges; notice of the existence of the bond and contact information Department of Banking and Consumer Finance; notice of consumer's cancellation rights; the identification of the financial institution where trust funds are kept; a list of creditors and an itemization of the amount to be paid by consumer and remitted to each creditor; consumer's consent to financial institution's disclosure of confidential information to the Department during examination of the provider. § 81-22-11.

Cancellation/Termination/Refund Rights: Either party may cancel by giving written notice. Right to cancel must be disclosed in contract. § 81-22-11.

Handling of Funds: Funds received from consumers must be deposited, within two days of receipt, in a federally insured escrow account, separate from licensee's operating accounts, in a supervised financial institution. Licensee must remit funds to creditors within fifteen days of receipt, must correct any misdirected funds resulting from licensee's error, and reimburse consumer for any charges imposed by creditor as a result of the misdirection. Must provide a written accounting to consumer at least quarterly. Additional requirements for accounting for Fair Share contributions from creditors. §§ 81-22-9, 81-22-15.

Customer Service Requirements: Not specified.

Limits on Fees: Initial consultation must be free. Provider may then charge a one-time setup fee of up to $75, a monthly maintenance fee of up to $30, $15 for obtaining an individual credit report, $25 for a joint report. May charge up to $50 for optional education course and materials—but must inform consumer that this is not required. Nonprofit counseling agencies approved by the U.S. Trustee may charge a bankruptcy consultation fee of up to $50. § 81-22-13.

Prohibited Practices: Licensee my not purchase consumer's debt; lend money or provide credit; take a mortgage or security interest; operate as a debt collector; structure an agreement to result in negative amortization. May not use false or deceptive advertising. §§ 81-22-19, 81-22-21.

Public Remedies: The Commissioner of Banking and Consumer Finance may impose cease and desist orders, penalties of up to $500 per violation, and may sue for injunction. §§ 81-22-3, 81-22-23.

Private Remedies: If provider violates this chapter, or a rule adopted by the commissioner, or engages in an unfair, deceptive or unconscionable practice, resulting in actual damage to a consumer, the consumer has a private right of action for actual damages in an amount determined by the court, plus costs and reasonable attorney fees. § 81-22-23.

Statute of Limitations: Not specified in this statute.

Missouri

Citation: Mo. Rev. Stat. §§ 425.010 through 425.043.

Scope & Key Definitions: For consideration, providing debt relief services seeing to renegotiate, settle, or otherwise alter the terms of debt. § 425.010.

Exceptions: Attorneys, persons acting pursuant to law or court order; creditors who do not charge for debt adjustment; person who disburses loan proceeds at direction of debtor, without charging for this service. Nothing in the statute forbids an individual or organization from administering a debt-management or debt settlement plan free of charge. §§ 425.025, 425.040.

Registration/Licensing: License and bond required: $50,000 if provider does not handle consumer funds; $100,000 if it does. § 425.027.

Disclosures: Before contracting, providers must clearly and conspicuously disclose the amount of time needed to obtain the represented results; if debt settlement is contemplated, the time by which provider will make bona fide settlement offers to each creditor or collector, and the amount that debtor must accumulate before settlement offers can be made; that if plan involves failure to make timely payments, this will result in damage to creditworthiness, possible collection actions by creditors, and an increase in debt due to interest and late fees; if debtor will deposit funds in an account, debtors cancellation and refund rights. § 425.043.

Pre-Agreement Services: Not specified.

Contract Terms: Not specified.

Cancellation/Termination/Refund Rights: Debtor may withdraw from plan at any time without penalty. If debtor withdraws from an agreement, provider must refund all sums in trust account, less any fees earned by provider, within seven days after withdrawal. § 425.043.

Handling of Funds: Funds received from debtor must be placed in a trust account, in an insured financial institution. Funds in the trust account, and any accrued interest, are owned by debtor. If provider does not administer the account, the entity administering the account may not be owned, controlled or affiliated with provider; may not give or receive any consideration for referrals. § 425.043.

Customer Service Requirements: Not specified.

Limits on Fees: $50 setup fee; monthly fees the greater of $35 or 8% of the amount distributed to creditors. May not receive any fee for debt settlement before provider has renegotiated or settled at least one debt, and debtor has made a payment. Settlement fee must either bear the same proportionate relationship to total fee as settled debt does to total amount of debt owed, or be a percentage of the amount saved.§ 425.010, 425.043.

Prohibited Practices: Debt adjusting without a debt-management plan or debt settlement plan. Misrepresenting any aspect of debt relief services, § 425.020, 425.043.

Public Remedies: Attorney general may sue to enjoin unlawful debt adjustment; court may appoint a receiver to supervise return of funds to debtors. § 425.030.

Private Remedies: Not specified.

Statute of Limitations: Not specified in this statute.

Montana

Montana has two statutes: debt management and debt settlement.

Citation: Mont. Code Ann. §§ 30-14-2001 through 30-14-2015 (debt management).

Administrator: Department of Justice.

Scope & Key Definitions: Credit counseling services: For a fee, providing debt-management services to consumers. Debt management services are the receipt of money from consumers, pursuant to a written agreement, for distribution to creditors in full or partial payment of debts. §§ 30-14-2002, § 30-14-2003.

Exceptions: Banking institutions, building and loan associations, credit unions, escrow businesses or title companies; attorneys or certified public accountants who provide credit counseling incidental to and not as a principal business of their practice; debt collectors that do not hold themselves out as credit counselors. § 30-14-2002.

Registration/Licensing: License and $50,000 bond required. Providers must be accredited and counselors certified. § 30-14-2004.

Disclosures: Not specified.

Pre-Agreement Services: Not specified.

Contract Terms: Written agreement must include description of services to be provided and a clear statement of costs; notice of consumer's right to cancel upon ten days' notice; a list of all debts subject to the agreement; indication of how disputes will be resolved; a statement that the credit counseling service "has a duty to advocate the interests of the consumer who is a party to the debt-management plan and not promote the interests of any third party that is in conflict with the primary obligation of advocating the interests of the consumer." § 30-14-2010.

Cancellation/Termination/Refund Rights: Right to cancel upon ten days' notice must be disclosed in contract. § 30-14-2010.

Handling of Funds: Consumers' funds for the payment of creditors must be deposited in a trust account in an insured financial institution in an account used only for these funds. Must provide the consumer, at least quarterly, with a report of funds received and disbursed. §§ 20-14-2003, 30-14-2010.

Customer Service Requirements: Not specified.

Limits on Fees: May not charge any fee before a written and dated debt-management agreement has been signed by consumer. The Department of Justice will make rules, setting the maximum setup fee and monthly fee. The provider may not require consumer to purchase counseling or materials as a condition of entering into a debt-management plan. § 30-14-2010.

Prohibited Practices: A contract may not include a hold harmless clause, confession of judgment, or waiver of jury trial. Provider may not purchase consumer's obligation; lend money or provide credit; take a mortgage or other security interest; operate as a collection agency; structure a plan in a way that any of the debts subject to the plan are not fully amortized at the plan's conclusion; charge for or provide credit insurance; cause or seek to cause consumer to waive any rights or benefits provided by this part; make a false promise or misrepresent any material fact to induce a consumer to enter into a plan. §§ 30-14-2010, 30-14-2013.

Public Remedies: The department, the Attorney General, or a county attorney may sue on behalf of state residents who have suffered a loss as a result of violation of this statute. Fines of up to $5000 for unlicensed practice, or failure to maintain trust account or required records. § 30-14-2015.

Private Remedies: If a provider imposes any unauthorized fee, the contract is void and provider must return all fees received from or on behalf of the consumer. Violation of this part is a UDAP. A person harmed by a violation has a cause of action for the greater of $500 or actual and consequential damages, plus costs and attorney fees; may also sue for injunctive or other appropriate equitable relief. Class actions permitted. The remedies of this section are not exclusive. §§ 30-14-2010, 30-14-2015.

Statute of Limitations: Not specified in this statute.

Citation: Mont. Code Ann. §§ 30-14-2101 through 30-14-2104 (debt settlement).

Scope & Key Definitions: Debt Settlement: negotiation, adjustment or settlement of consumer's debt, without holding, receiving or disbursing consumer's funds. § 30-14-2101.

Administrator: Attorney General.

Exceptions: Attorneys, escrow agents, accountants, broker-dealers in securities, or investment advisers in securities, when acting in the ordinary practice of their professions; banks and various other financial institutions authorized to make loans; persons who perform credit services for an employer that is not a debt settlement service; public officers in their official capacities or others acting under court order; persons performing services incidental to the dissolution or winding up of a business enterprise; debt-management services subject to the debt-management act (see above). § 30-14-2101.

Registration/Licensing: Annual filing required; insurance of at least $100,000 required. § 30-14-2102.

Disclosures: Before entering into an agreement, provider must disclose, in writing in at least 12 point type, the type and amount of all fees; that debt settlement may have an impact on debtor's credit history, and may have tax consequences; that creditors' collection activity may continue while provider seeks to settle debt; that any settlement amount is an estimate, and is not guaranteed to be accepted by the creditor; that creditors are not required to accept settlement offers; that debtor must meet certain savings goals; that provider does not provide legal, accounting, tax or bankruptcy advice or assistance; that payments made to settlement provider will not be used to make payments to creditor; that debt settlement may not be the only option. § 30-14-2102.

Pre-Agreement Services: Not specified.

Contract Terms: Contract must be in writing, and include a schedule of fees. § 30-14-2103.

Cancellation/Termination/Refund Rights: If debtor cancels, provider must return 50% collected service fees, on a pro rata basis for those accounts that have not received a settlement offer at the time of cancellation. § 30-14-2103.

Handling of Funds: Not applicable.

Customer Service Requirements: Not specified.

Limits on Fees: Aggregate fees of not more than 20% of the principal amount of the debt; not more than 5% of the principal amount for a setup fee. May not collect any fees before executing a debt settlement services contract, that itemizes the amount and timing of all fees to be charged. Setup fee is nonrefundable. § 30-14-2103.

Prohibited Practices: May not provide services without a written contract; make loans or offer credit; take any confession of judgment or power of attorney to confess judgment, or appear as or on behalf of the debtor in any judicial proceeding; take a release of any obligation of debt settlement provider; use false, misleading or deceptive advertising; receive any compensation from anyone other than the debtor or a person on debtor's behalf for performing services for debtor; disclose debtor's name or personal information to anyone order than debtor's creditors, or providers agents affiliates or contractors; disclose creditor's name to anyone other than debtor, a company acting on behalf of debtor or the settlement provider, or another creditor (to the extent necessary to secure that creditor's cooperation in a plan); advertise before filing the required financial statement; misrepresent facts or make false promises to induce debtor to enter into a contract; violate any provisions of the state or federal do-not-call registry. § 30-14-2103.

Public Remedies: Attorney general or county attorney may sue for injunction, restitution, attorney fees and costs. May accept assurances of discontinuance. Court may award penalties of up to $10,000 for violation of an assurance of discontinuance. § 30-14-2104.

Private Remedies: Violation is a UDAP. § 30-14-2104.

Statute of Limitations: Not specified in this statute.

Nebraska

Citation: Neb. Rev. Stat. §§ 69-1201 through 69-1217.

Administrator: Secretary of State.

Scope & Key Definitions: Debt Management: For a fee, the planning and management of financial affairs of a debtor who is a wage earner whose principal income is derived from wages, salary or commission, by receiving money from debtor for disbursement to creditors in full or partial payment of debts. § 69-1201.

Exceptions: Any of the following when engaged in the regular practice of their professions: attorneys; banks, fiduciaries and lending institutions; title insurers and abstract companies doing an escrow business; employees of licensees; judicial officers or others acting under court order. § 69-1202.

Registration/Licensing: License and $10,000 bond required. Applicant must provide Secretary of State with a copy of its form contract, and advise Secretary of any changes or amendments within thirty days. §§ 69-1203, 69-1204.

Disclosures: Not specified.

Pre-Agreement Services: Before contracting, licensee must provide a budget analysis and conclude that debtor is reasonably able to meet the payments. § 69-1213.

Contract Terms: Contract must be in writing, and include a complete list of obligations to be adjusted and creditors; total charges and the beginning and expiration date of the contract, and cancellation rights. No contract may be for more than 36 months. §§ 69-1209, 96-1212.

Cancellation/Termination/Refund Rights: If a contract is cancelled, licensee is entitled to receive 25% of the remaining unamortized fee. § 69-1212.

Handling of Funds: Licensee must maintain a separate bank account for funds received from debtors for disbursement to creditors. Funds must be remitted to creditor within fifteen days (seven if in the form of cash) unless reasonable payment requires that funds be held to accumulate a sum certain. In no case may licensee retain funds more than 35 days after receipt. Must provide debtor with a written accounting every 90 days, and a verbal accounting upon request during business hours. If a compromise is arranged, debtor must have full benefit of the compromise. §§ 69-1210, 69-1213.

Customer Service Requirements: Not specified.

Limits on Fees: Fee must be agreed upon and disclosed in contract. No fee may be charged until the debt-management program is arranged and approved by debtor. The total fee may not exceed 15% of the amount to be paid out, and shall be amortized over the period of the contract. An initial fee of $25 must be credited towards the total. §§ 69-1212, 69-2013.

Prohibited Practices: License may be revoked for "a continuous course of unfair conduct." Licensee may not purchase any obligation of debtor; act as collection agency and licensee on the same debtor's account; execute a contract with blanks not filled in; take a promissory note, mortgage or security interest as security for any fee; pay or receive any bonus for referrals; use false, misleading or deceptive advertising. §§ 69-1207, 69-1214.

Public Remedies: Unlicensed practice is a misdemeanor. § 69-1215.

Private Remedies: Not specified in statute.

Statute of Limitations: Two years after accrual of cause of action. § 69-1216.

Nevada

This statute is based upon the 2008 version of the Uniform Debt-Management Services Act, summarized at Appx. I.2, supra, with variations as noted below.

Citation: Nev. Rev. Stat. §§ 676A.010 through 676A.780.

Administrator: Commissioner of Financial Institutions.

Scope & Key Definitions: Credit counseling, debt management, and debt settlement. Credit counseling: education and assistance concerning debts, which may include development of a debt-management or debt settlement plan. Debt management: A plan contemplating regular payments to a creditor, in which creditor will reduce finance charges or late or delinquency charges, but not the principal amount of the debt. Debt settlement: A plan contemplating regular payments into a bank account owned by the debtor and not controlled by the provider, from which individual will make payments to the provider for authorized fees, and to creditors to settle debts for less than the amount of the principal. §§ 676A.020, 676A.110, 676A.130, 676A.140, 676A.150.

Exceptions: Substantially similar to uniform act. § 676A.140, 676A.270.

Registration/Licensing: Substantially similar to uniform act. §§ 676A.300, 676A.310, 676A.320, 676A.390, 676A.400.

Disclosures: Substantially similar to uniform act. §§ 676A.520, 676A.530, 676A.560, 676A.600.

Pre-Agreement Services: Substantially similar to uniform act. § 676A.520.

Contract Terms: Substantially similar to uniform act. § 676A.540.

Cancellation/Termination/Refund Rights: Substantially similar to uniform act. Includes three-day cancellation right. §§ 676A.540, 676A.550, 676A.570, 676A.620, 676A.720.

Handling of Funds: Substantially similar to uniform act. § 676A.260, 676A.500, 676A.570, 676A.630.

Customer Service Requirements: Substantially similar to uniform act. §§ 676A.170, 676A.510, 676A.540.

Limits on Fees: Substantially similar to uniform act. Forbids upfront setup fees for debt settlement plans. Dollar amounts in this section are adjusted for inflation. §§ 676A.230, 676A.580, 676A.590.

Prohibited Practices: Substantially similar to uniform act. §§ 676A.540, 676A.700.

Public Remedies: Substantially similar to uniform act. Penalty amounts adjusted for inflation. §§ 676A.730, 676A.740.

Private Remedies: Substantially similar to uniform act. Statutory damage amount adjusted for inflation. §§ 676A.610, 676A.760, 676A.770.

Statute of Limitations: Substantially similar to uniform act. § 676A.780.

New Hampshire

Citation: N.H. Rev. Stat. Ann. §§ 399-D:1 through 399-D:28.

Administrator: Bank Commissioner.

Scope & Key Definitions: Debt Adjustment. For direct or indirect compensation: providing debt-management advice or counseling; creating debt-management plans; negotiating with creditors on behalf of debtor; receiving funds from debtor for disbursement to creditors in full or partial payment of debts; serving as an intermediary between consumer and creditor for purpose of obtaining concessions. § 399-D:2.

Exceptions: Attorneys in the practice of law; banks and certain other fiduciary and lending institutions that perform debt adjustment in the regular course of their business; title insurance or abstract company doing escrow business; any person acting pursuant to court order or federal or New Hampshire law; licensees' employees; licensed mortgage banker, broker, originator or servicer, if such person conducts no other activity that would require a license. § 399-D:4.

Registration/Licensing: License and $25,000 bond required. Applicant must file a copy of its form contract with its application. If debt adjuster engages in mortgage loan modification activity, it must obtain a mortgage license. §§ 399-D:3, 399-D:5, 399-D:6.

Disclosures: Before execution of the contract, licensee must disclose in writing any direct or indirect compensation it will receive for debt adjustment services from persons other than the consumer. § 399-D:14.

Pre-Agreement Services: Licensee must make a thorough budget analysis to determine whether debtor can meet the requirements of a plan. The plan should be for no longer than is reasonable and consistent with the budget analysis, unless debtor makes a written request for a longer plan, with lower payments and a higher fee. § 399-D:15.

Contract Terms: Contract must include a complete list of debts to be adjusted, and of creditors; total charges; beginning and expiration date. May not enter into contract in which debts will not be discharged within 60 months, exclusive of contractual debts which exceed the 60-month period. § 399-D:20.

Cancellation/Termination/Refund Rights: Provisions for settlement in case of cancellation or pre-payment must be clearly stated in the contract. In case of prepayment of the debts, cancellation by the debtor upon 30 days' notice, or cancellation by licensee after 30 days' willful default by debtor, licensee who has complied with all terms of the contract may charge a cancellation fee of the lesser of $50 or 5% of the service charge due for the unexpired term of the contract. After cancellation, licensee must notify all creditors within ten days. §§ 399-D:14, 399-D:15.

Handling of Funds: Funds received from debtors must be deposited in a separate bank account within 24 hours of receipt. Licensee must provide a written accounting every 90 days and at termination, and a verbal accounting whenever requested by debtor during business hours. If a compromise is arranged with one or more creditors, debtor shall have the full benefit of the compromise. Licensee must remit funds to creditors, less authorized fees, within ten days of receipt, unless consumer's obligation requires that funds be accumulated to reach a sum certain. After cancellation, licensee must notify all creditors within ten days. §§ 399-D:15, 399-D:21.

Customer Service Requirements: Not specified.

Limits on Fees: Fees must be clearly stated in the contract, including provision for settlement in case of cancellation of prepayment. No fee may be collected before the contract has been in force for thirty days, and the licensee has written consent from creditors who hold obligations representing 25% of the amount of the debt and 25% of the number of creditors, or that number of creditors have accepted payment. Thereafter, fees must be amortized equally each month over the life of the contract. The provider may require a $25 payment upon signing, which will be held in escrow, and returned to debtor if debtor fulfills the conditions of the contract, or retained if debtor fails to make a required payment in excess of sixty days. Monthly payments may not exceed 10% of the amount owed for a plan period of 10 months or less; 12.5% for a plan period of more than ten but less than 18 months; 15% for a plan period of 18 months or more. § 399-D:14.

Prohibited Practices: May not use any false, deceptive or misleading advertising (banking department may review licensees' advertising); employ any device, scheme, or artifice to defraud; to make untrue statements or omit material facts; purchase any obligation of a debtor; act as licensee and collection agency on the same debtor's account; execute any contract with blanks not filled in; take a promissory note, wage assignment, mortgage or security interest; pay or receive any bonus for referrals; practice law, associate with an attorney, take a power of attorney authorizing licensee to employ or terminate an attorney, refer debtor to a specific attorney, borrow money from or pledge assets to an attorney; enter into a contract in which debtor's obligations will not be discharged within sixty months, exclusive of contractual debts which exceed the sixty month period; use any word or phrase stating or implying it is bonded or approved by the state. Any waiver of compliance with this chapter, or any rule or order under this chapter, is void. §§ 399-D:11, 399-D:13-a, 399-D:16, 399-D:17, 399-D:26.

Public Remedies: Banking department may issue cease and desist orders. Attorney general may sue to enforce these orders; court may award civil penalty of up to $10,000 for violation of cease and desist order. Violation is a misdemeanor if committed by a natural person, a felony if committed by any other person. Willful violation of a cease and desist order, or certain provisions of the statute is a felony. Administrative fines of $2500 for knowing or $1500 for negligent violation of this chapter. §§ 399-D:23, 399-D:24, 399-D:24-a.

Private Remedies: Not specified.

Statute of Limitations: Not specified in this statute.

New Jersey

New Jersey has two statutes, a criminal statute forbidding unlicensed debt adjustment, and a statute allowing debt adjusting and credit counseling by certain nonprofits.

Citation: N.J. Stat. Ann. § 2C:21-19(f) (West) (criminal statute).

Administrator: Not specified.

Scope & Key Definitions: Debt adjusting as defined in chapter 17:16G. (see below).

Exceptions: See below.

Registration/Licensing: Not specified.

Disclosures: Not specified.

Pre-Agreement Services: Not specified.

Contract Terms: Not specified.

Cancellation/Termination/Refund Rights: Not specified.

Handling of Funds: Not specified.

Customer Service Requirements: Not specified.

Limits on Fees: Not specified.

Prohibited Practices: Unlicensed practice.

Public Remedies: Non-exempt person who engages in debt adjustment without a license is guilty of a crime of the fourth degree. (See below for exemptions.)

Private Remedies: Not specified.

Statute of Limitations: Not specified in this statute.

Citation: N.J. Stat. Ann. §§ 17:16G-1 through 17:16G-9 (West) (statute regulating debt adjusting and credit counseling by non-profits).

Administrator: Commissioner of the Department of Banking

Scope & Key Definitions: Debt adjustment and credit counseling. Nonprofit social service agencies and nonprofit credit counseling agencies only. Debt adjustment: acting or offering to act as an intermediary between debtor and creditors for the purpose of settling or otherwise altering the terms of payment, or receives money from the debtor for distribution among debtor's creditors. §§ 17:16G-1, 17:16G-2.

Exceptions: Attorney not principally engaged in debt adjustment; employees of debtor; person acting pursuant to court order or authority conferred by federal or New Jersey law; creditor or its agent, whose services are performed without receiving compensation from debtor; lender who, at debtor's request, disburses loan funds to creditors, without being paid for debt adjustment services; HUD-certified housing counselor participating in counseling program approved by the N.J. Housing and Mortgage Finance Agency that does not hold or disburse debtor's funds. § 17:16G-1.

Registration/Licensing: License and bond required. Amount of bond to be set by Commissioner of the Department of Banking. § 17:16G-2, 17:16G-5.

Disclosures: Not specified.

Pre-Agreement Services: Not specified.

Contract Terms: Not specified.

Cancellation/Termination/Refund Rights: Not specified.

Handling of Funds: Funds received from debtors must be deposited in separate bank account, in the name of the debt adjuster for the benefit of the debtors. Debt adjuster must disburse funds received from debtor, less authorized fee, to creditors within ten days of receipt. § 17:16G-9.

Customer Service Requirements: Not specified.

Limits on Fees: Licensee may charge a fee to cover the cost of providing debt adjustment and credit counseling services. Debt adjustment fee may not exceed 1% of debtor's monthly income. In no case may it exceed $15 per month. Commissioner will establish the maximum fee for credit counseling. § 17:16G-6.

Prohibited Practices: Not specified.

Public Remedies: Civil penalties of up to $1000 first offense, $5000 second or subsequent offense. The commissioner may sue to enjoin violations. § 17:16G-8.

Private Remedies: Any debtor injured by a violation has a private right of action for recovery of damages. § 17:16G-8.

Statute of Limitations: Not specified in this statute.

New York

New York has two statutes: a criminal statute generally forbidding budget planning, and a statute allowing budget planning by licensed nonprofits.

Citation: N.Y. Gen. Bus. Law §§ 455–457 (McKinney) (criminal statute).

Administrator: Not specified.

Scope & Key Definitions: Budget planning forbidden: For compensation, accepting funds from debtor for distribution to creditors. § 455

Exceptions: Charitable corporation, as defined in the not-for-profit-corporation law, or incorporated in another state with similar not-for-profit status, licensed pursuant to Banking Law (see below); attorneys and law firms who negotiate directly with creditors on behalf of a client, deposit funds received from client in client account, pay creditors from that account, and offer budget planning services through the same legal entity that the attorney uses to practice law. § 455.

Registration/Licensing: Not specified.

Disclosures: Not specified.

Pre-Agreement Services: Not specified.

Contract Terms: Not specified.

Cancellation/Termination/Refund Rights: Not specified.

Handling of Funds: Not specified.

Customer Service Requirements: Not specified.

Limits on Fees: Not specified.

Prohibited Practices: Unlicensed budget planning. § 465.

Public Remedies: Unlicensed budget planning is a misdemeanor. § 457.

Private Remedies: Not specified.
Statute of Limitations: Not specified in this statute.

Citation: N.Y. Banking Law §§ 579–587 (McKinney) (allowing budget planning by certain entities).
Administrator: Superintendent of Financial Services § 2.
Scope & Key Definitions: Budget planners. Defined in General Business Law (see above). Only charitable corporations, as defined in § 102(a) of the not-for-profit-corporation law, may be licensed to practice budget planning. § 579.
Exceptions: See above.
Registration/Licensing: License and $250,000 bond required. (Superintendent has authority to increase or decrease amount of bond). Licensees must submit to the department a copy of their form contract. § 580, 584-a.
Disclosures: Not specified.
Pre-Agreement Services: Licensee must provide, directly or indirectly, budgeting, educational and counseling services to the debtors for whom it provides budget planning. § 581.
Contract Terms: Contracts must include a complete list of obligations to be adjusted and creditors; total fees for such services, including any adjustments for estimated available rebates from creditors (but licensee is not required to share rebates with clients); statement of the fees expressed as a percentage of the total amount to be adjusted; beginning and ending date of contract; settlement terms in case of prepayment or cancellation; notice of debtor's three-day cancellation right; terms under which payments are made by debtor. § 584-a.
Cancellation/Termination/Refund Rights: Right to cancel for three days after signing must be disclosed in contract. § 584-a.
Handling of Funds: Licensee may not commingle money received from debtors with operating funds of licensee or any other business. Must make timely payments to creditors. § 584-b.
Customer Service Requirements: Not specified.
Limits on Fees: Superintendent of financial services has authority to order licensee to reduce fees that superintendent determines to be unreasonable. § 585.
Prohibited Practices: False or deceptive advertising. Unlicensed person may not describe self as "budget planner", "licensed budget planner" or use the term "budget planning" in advertisement, business card or letterhead. Licensee may not purchase any obligation of debtor; seek payment of obligations of creditors not receiving payments pursuant to contract; execute a contract with any blanks not filled in; pay or receive a bonus for referrals; disclose or threaten to disclose information about a debt, or any other conduct, that could coerce payment of a debt by a debtor with whom it has a contract; simulate legal or judicial process or give a false appearance that a communication is authorized, approved or issued by a government entity or an attorney. No licensee, or director, manager or officer of a licensee, may be a director, manager, officer, owner or controlling party of a creditor or subsidiary of a creditor, that is receiving or will receive payments from the licensee on behalf of a debtor. Licensee may not disclose identifying information of debtor, except in response to subpoena or other process, or to a creditor in order to establish an account. § 584-b.
Public Remedies: Unlicensed practice is a misdemeanor. See General Business Law above.
Private Remedies: Not specified.
Statute of Limitations: Not specified in this statute.

North Carolina

Citation: N.C. Gen. Stat. §§ 14-423 through 14-426.
Administrator: Commissioner of Banks.
Scope & Key Definitions: Debt adjusting: for consideration, acting as an intermediary between debtor and creditors, for purpose of holding and distributing funds to creditors, or negotiating settlement of debts. Foreclosure assistance explicitly included. § 14-423.
Exceptions: Employee of debtor adjusting employer's debts; persons acting pursuant to court order or authority conferred by law; creditors who adjust debts without charge to the debtor; lender who, at debtor's request

disburses loan proceeds to creditors without charging debtor for this service; intermittent or casual debt adjustment by one not in the business of debt adjustment; attorney licensed to practice in North Carolina who is not employed by debt adjuster; organization involved in credit counseling, education and debt-management services that complies with all the requirements below. § 14-426.
Registration/Licensing: Provider must be accredited by independent accrediting organization acceptable to the Commissioner of Banks. § 14-426.
Disclosures: Not specified.
Pre-Agreement Services: Must provide individual counseling and budget assistance without charge, before entering into a plan; determine that debtor has financial ability to complete plan, and that plan is suitable for debtor. § 14-426.
Contract Terms: Contract must disclose the amount of fees. § 14-426.
Cancellation/Termination/Refund Rights: Not specified.
Handling of Funds: Must provide individual accounting, at least quarterly. § 14-426.
Customer Service Requirements: Not specified.
Limits on Fees: Nominal consideration only, to cover the cost of administering the plan: setup fee of up to $40 and monthly payments of lesser of $40 or 10% of amount distributed. §§ 14-423, 14-427.
Prohibited Practices: May not require purchase of other services or materials as condition of entering into plan. May not receive any benefit for referring debtor to a provider of services. § 14-426.
Public Remedies: Debt adjusting is a misdemeanor. Attorney general or district attorney may sue to enjoin unlawful debt adjusting, and seek appointment of receiver to return funds to consumers. §§ 14-424, 14-425.
Private Remedies: Not specified.
Statute of Limitations: Not specified in this statute.

North Dakota

North Dakota has two statutes: consumer credit counseling and debt settlement. The debt settlement statute is based upon the 2008 version of the Uniform Debt-Management Services Act, summarized at Appx. I.2, supra, with variations as noted below.

Citation: N.D. Cent. Code §§ 13-07-01 through 13-07-07 (consumer credit counseling).
Administrator: Attorney General.
Scope & Key Definitions: Consumer credit counseling. Making agreements contemplating that debtor will liquidate debts by structured settlements or that creditor will reduce fees for late payments, default or delinquency. § 13-07-01.
Exceptions: Not specified.
Registration/Licensing: Bond required, for the greater of $5000 or the highest amount accrued in provider's trust account during the previous year. § 13-07-03.
Disclosures: Not specified.
Pre-Agreement Services: Must perform a thorough, written budget analysis, and conclude that debtor can reasonably meet the requirements of the plan, and that debtor will be benefited by the plan. § 13-07-02.
Contract Terms: Contract must be in writing, and include amount to be retained by provider; cancellation rights; itemized list of debts with names of creditors and amounts owed. § 13-07-02.
Cancellation/Termination/Refund Rights: Either party may cancel upon 30 days' notice. Upon cancellation, provider must notify creditors within 30 days. § 13-07-06.
Handling of Funds: Funds received from debtors must be deposited, within one business day of receipt, in a trust account in an insured financial institution, and not commingled with provider's funds. Interest shall be credited to debt-management education programs. Must maintain weekly statements of account, and furnish statement to debtor upon request. § 13-07-04, 13-07-05.
Customer Service Requirements: Not specified.

Limits on Fees: $50 origination fee. Additional fee of up to 15% of the amount paid by consumer. The rest of consumer's payments must be forwarded to creditors within 45 days of deposit. § 13-07-06.

Prohibited Practices: May not take confession of judgment, or power of attorney to confess judgment, or appear as debtor in any judicial proceeding. § 13-07-07.

Public Remedies: Attorney general may seek injunction, or civil penalty of up to $5000. § 13-07-07.

Private Remedies: Not specified.

Statute of Limitations: Not specified in this statute.

Citation: N.D. Cent. Code §§ 13-11-01 through 13-11-30 (debt settlement).

Administrator: Commissioner of the Department of Financial Institutions. § 13-11-01.

Scope & Key Definitions: Debt settlement services: for any fee or compensation, offering to provide advice or services as an intermediary between debtor and creditors to obtain settlement or adjustment of debt for less than the current balance; offering or providing services to encourage or assist consumer to accumulate funds for the purpose of seeking to obtain a settlement; offering to act, or acting as an intermediary between individual and state of federal government for the purpose of obtaining a settlement of a tax debt. § 13-11-01.

Exceptions: Substantially similar to uniform act, plus consumer credit counselors licensed pursuant to chapter 13-07 (see above). § 13-11-01.

Registration/Licensing: License and $50,000 bond required. §§ 13-11-02, 13-11-04.

Disclosures: Advertising and marketing materials must disclose that debt settlement services are not appropriate for everyone; failure to timely pay monthly bills will result in increased balances and harm to credit rating; not all creditors will agree to reduce the principal balance, and they may pursue collection, including lawsuits. Statements in advertising as to results or outcomes must be substantiated. § 13-11-12.

Pre-Agreement Services: Before entering into a contract, provider must disclose that debt settlement is not suitable for all customers; debt settlement will likely harm consumer's credit rating; use of settlement service will not stop creditor's collection activity, including garnishment and lawsuits; not all creditors will accept settlement offers; consumer should consider other alternatives including nonprofit credit counseling and bankruptcy; the consumer remains obligated to make scheduled payments to creditors, and provider will not make such payments; the consequences of non-payment; the amount of time necessary to receive the represented results; the sum of money or percentage of the debt that must be accumulated before settlement offers can be made; contact information for the Department of Financial Institutions. Consumer must sign and date an acknowledgement of having received these warnings. (Model form included in statute.) Must prepare an individualized financial analysis, including a good faith estimate of time required to settle debts, total savings required, and the amount debtor must save each month. Must determine that the consumer can reasonably meet the savings goals, and the plan is suitable for the consumer. Provider must prepare and retain a written analysis of debtor's income and expenses, to substantiate that the plan is feasible and practical. §§ 13-11-13, 13-11-17, 13-11-18.

Contract Terms: Substantially similar to uniform act. Must include detailed savings plan for the consumer, and individual analysis and notice form (see pre-agreement services, above). §§ 13-11-12, 13-11-19.

Cancellation/Termination/Refund Rights: Consumer may cancel at any time before provider has fully performed, and receive refund of unearned fees and funds not paid to creditors. Refunds must be made within seven days after cancellation. Provider must notify creditors of cancellation. Cancellation rights must be included in pre-contract disclosures. §§ 13-11-17, 13-11-19, 13-11-20.

Handling of Funds: Must issue receipts for all payments; maintain records so that debtor may, at any reasonable time, ascertain the status of the account, including fees paid, sum held in trust, settlement offers made and received, and legally enforceable settlements; provide debtor with an account statement, within seven days of request, showing total amount received and total disbursements. Debtor's funds must be deposited, by the end of the business day following receipt, in a trust account separate

from provider's own funds. Once a month, and within seven days after written demand, must provide itemized accounting. (Not more than three written demands per six month period). Trust account not required if only funds received are for earned settlement fees. §§ 13-11-13, 13-11-14.

Customer Service Requirements: Substantially similar to uniform act. § 13-11-15.

Limits on Fees: Up-front and maintenance fees forbidden. Settlement fee of up to 30% of savings may be imposed after provider negotiates a legally enforceable settlement, for less than the principal amount of the debt, and the settlement amount is paid. Provider may not solicit voluntary contributions from debtor or affiliate of debtor. §§ 13-11-21, 13-11-22.

Prohibited Practices: Substantially similar to uniform act, but does not include choice of law provisions or limits on available forums. § 13-11-23.

Public Remedies: Violation is a Class C felony. Commissioner may issue cease and desist orders, and impose civil penalties of up to $5000. Attorney general may enforce this chapter. Violation is a UDAP. §§ 13-11-26, 13-11-27

Private Remedies: Contract that violates the provisions of this statute is voidable. Violation is a UDAP. Provider is liable for violations by persons, including independent contractors, to whom it delegates its duties. Aggrieved person has right of action for the greater of $2000 or actual restitution, plus costs, expenses, and reasonable attorney fees. Remedy is cumulative and not exclusive. §§ 13-11-25, 13-11-28, 13-11-29.

Statute of Limitations: Not specified in statute.

Ohio

Citation: Ohio Rev. Code Ann. §§ 4710.01 through 4710.99 (West).

Administrator: Attorney General.

Scope & Key Definitions: Debt adjusting, budget counseling, debt management or debt pooling. Effecting the compromise of debts, or receiving from debtor funds for distribution to creditors. § 4710.01.

Exceptions: Fannie Mae, Freddie Mac, regulated financial institutions; debt adjusting in the practice of law; "incidental" debt adjusting by creditor; certain registered mortgage professionals. § 4710.03.

Registration/Licensing: Insurance coverage of not less than $100,000. § 4710.02.

Disclosures: Not specified.

Pre-Agreement Services: Not specified.

Contract Terms: Not specified.

Cancellation/Termination/Refund Rights: Not specified.

Handling of Funds: Must disburse funds, less authorized contributions, to creditors within thirty days of receipt; maintain a separate trust account. § 4710.02.

Customer Service Requirements: Not specified.

Limits on Fees: Reasonable fees of up to $75 initial fee; monthly fee of greater of $30 or 8.5% of debtor's monthly payments; yearly fee of $100; reasonable insufficient funds fee. Must have procedure to waive or discontinue fees if debtor is unable to pay them. § 4710.02.

Prohibited Practices: Not specified.

Public Remedies: Violations are a UDAP. Violations of insurance and audit requirements are punishable by fine of up to $10,000. Violations are a misdemeanor. §§ 4710.04, 4710.99.

Private Remedies: Violations are a UDAP. § 4710.04.

Statute of Limitations: Not specified in this statute.

Oregon

Citation: Ore. Rev. Stat. §§ 697.602 through 697.842.

Administrator: Department of Consumer and Business Services.

Scope & Key Definitions: Debt management. For valuable consideration, receiving funds from consumer for distribution among consumer's creditors, or offering to improve consumer's credit history or credit rating, or modifying or offering to modify terms of an existing loan, serving as an intermediary with consumers creditors seeking to obtain concessions, providing advice or instruction concerning debt management, or providing consumer's identifying information to a debt-management provider for the purpose of arranging debt management. A nonprofit budget and credit counseling agency, approved pursuant to the Bankruptcy Code, may negotiate for an alternative payment schedule or the reduction of a claim. § 697.602.

Exceptions: Nonprofit budget and credit counseling agency, approved pursuant to the Bankruptcy Code, that provides individual or group bankruptcy counseling and does not receive or offer to receive funds for distribution among creditors; nonprofits that provide advice, assistance, instructional services or materials for a fee reasonably calculated to cover the cost of services and materials; HUD-certified housing counselors. Attorneys providing debt management incidentally to the practice of law; financial institutions, trust companies, consumer finance agencies; escrow agents, acting to close an escrow, provided they are not assisting unregistered and non-exempt provider of debt-management services; mortgage bankers, brokers and loan originators; registered broker-dealers in securities or commodities, acting in accordance with regulations of the SEC or the CFTC; consumer reporting agencies; public bodies; persons acting pursuant to court order; accredited educational institutions, performing the service as part of a class or duty that the institution provides regularly, without receiving consideration for the debt management. Employees of registrant do not need to register individually. Persons claiming an exemption have the burden of proof as to entitlement. §697.612,

Registration/Licensing: Registration and $10,000 bond required. The director of the Department of Consumer and Business Services may vary by rule the amount of the bond. §§ 697.612, 697.632, 697.642.

Disclosures: Must disclose tax consequences of debt settlement, and recommend consultation with a tax professional. Provider that does not hold funds must disclose that results are not guaranteed and creditor is not required to accept a settlement; that creditor's collection efforts will continue, and consumer's credit score will be damaged. §§ 697.652, 697.707.

Pre-Agreement Services: Before signing a contract, registrant must provide debtor with a budget analysis, separate from the contract, that evaluates whether debt management will be advantageous to the consumer. § 697.652.

Contract Terms: A debt-management contract must provide contact information for the provider; a list of creditors and debts covered; the amount the consumer can reasonably pay, if the plan includes holding funds for distribution to creditors; an itemization of services to be provided and fees, including the method of calculating the fees; a schedule of the time and amount of installments, and the allocation of payments, and the estimated time necessary to complete the contract; notice of right to accounting, and of cancellation rights. § 697.652.

Cancellation/Termination/Refund Rights: Consumer may cancel within three days of contracting, and provider must return all payments. May cancel at any time upon ten days' notice, and provider must return all unexpended funds. Provider may cancel if consumer fails to make a required payment within sixty days. Cancellation and termination rights must be disclosed in contract. § 697.652.

Handling of Funds: Client funds must be kept in a trust account in an insured financial institution, separate from provider's operating funds. Provider must allow consumer to examine accounts during business hours. Provider may not deposit more than $250,000 in a trust account for one consumer's funds. Must provide a written accounting every ninety days. Upon consumer's request, must provide an electronic accounting within two business days, a written accounting within seven business days. Upon consumer's cancellation must refund all funds not already distributed to creditors. Right to accounting, and cancellation rights must be disclosed in contract. §§ 697.652, 697.682.

Customer Service Requirements: Not specified.

Limits on Fees: Up to $50 to recover the costs of an initial counseling session or educational class. Monthly fee of the lesser or $65 or 15% of the funds received from consumer for payment to creditors, if provider receives funds for distribution. If provider does not hold consumer's funds, a fee of the lesser of $65 per month or 15% of the amount of debt. Settlement fee of 7.5% of the difference between the amount of the debt and the amount consumer paid, exclusive of authorized fees. Must

refund all fees if consumer exercises three day right to cancel. §§ 697.652, 697.692.

Prohibited Practices: May not induce or attempt to induce consumer to waive rights provided by this chapter. Waivers of rights pursuant to this chapter are void and unenforceable. May not make, or advise consumer to make, a statement that registrant knows, or in the exercise of reasonable care should know, is untrue or misleading; misrepresent its authority to provide debt management, tax, accounting, bankruptcy, or legal advice; charge for referrals if the person to whom consumer is referred will extend credit to consumer on the same terms it provides to its other customers; perform services without a reasonable good faith belief, based on budget analysis, that service will be advantageous and consumer can and will comply; sign a contract, promise to pay or other instrument, with blanks not filled in; take payment or security for an unauthorized amount; take a wage assignment, mortgage, or security interest to secure an amount larger than the statutorily permitted fees; take a confession of judgment, power of attorney to confess judgment or to appear for consumer in a judicial proceeding; contract for later charges or reserves for liquidated damages; release any obligation that provider is required to perform; cancel an agreement except for non-payment; use any false or misleading advertising, including misrepresentation of government affiliation or approval, the provider's qualification, or the benefits consumer can expect to receive from the services. §§ 697.652, 697.662.

Public Remedies: Civil penalties of up to $5000 per violation. Director may issue cease and desist orders; sue to enjoin violations or appoint a receiver, and for damages on behalf of injured persons. §§ 697.652, 697.762, 697.832.

Private Remedies: Private right of action by a consumer who suffers an ascertainable loss of money or property in connection with a violation of this statute. Reasonable attorney fees in the discretion of the court. Remedy is not exclusive and does not limit statutory or common law rights of action. §§ 697.718, 697.822, 697.832.

Statute of Limitations: Greater of three years after violation, or two years after the facts on which the action is based should have been discovered, but not more than five years after violation. § 697.718.

Pennsylvania

Pennsylvania has three statutes, a criminal law forbidding "debt pooling," and statutes regulating debt management and debt settlement.

Citation: 63 Pa. Stat. Ann. §§ 2401 through 2449 (West) (debt management). Parts of this act were found unconstitutional by *U.S. Organization for Bankruptcy Alternatives, Inc. v. Department of Banking.*[5] Effective November 2, 2012, parts were replaced by 63 Pa. Cons. Stat. §§ 2501–2593 (discussed in the next summary).

Administrator: Department of Banking. § 2402.

Scope & Key Definitions: Debt Management: periodically receiving funds from a consumer for distribution to creditors in full or partial payment of personal debts. § 2402.

Exceptions: Regulated banking institutions; judicial officers and persons acting pursuant to court order; state local or government agencies; attorneys who provide legal services in an attorney-client relationship, if debt management or debt settlement is incidental to legal practice. Employees of licensees or exempt persons are not required to obtain individual licenses. The following are exempt from licensing, but must comply with the provisions of the act if they offer debt management or debt settlement: certified public accountants, providing services within an accountant-client relationship; licensed title insurance companies; licensed mortgage lenders, brokers or loan correspondents. § 2404.

Registration/Licensing: License and bond (greater than the amount of Pennsylvania consumer funds licensee will hold directly or in trust) required for debt management. Reduced license fee for certain nonprofits. Agencies must be accredited and counselors must be certified, or become certified within six months after issuance of the license. Applicant must

---

5 991 A.2d 370 (Pa. Commw. Ct. 2010).

provide a description of its education program and a copy of its standard contract. License may not be issued to applicant that offers payday loans. §§ 2403, 2405, 2406, 2407, 2410.1.

Disclosures: Not specified.

Pre-Agreement Services: Licensee must provide educational services at no cost; must prepare a financial analysis and budget, and determine whether consumer will benefit from licensee's services. Before consumer enters into a contract, certified counselor must orally (i.e., not electronically) review the analysis, budget and services agreement with the consumer. § 2414.

Contract Terms: Agreement must include contact information for provider; a description of services provided and fees; the location of the trust account; a list of creditors expected to participate, with amount owed and schedule of payments; a list of creditors expected not to participate; dates and amounts of payments; amount of fees to be retained from each payment; bold print notice that plan may negatively affect consumer's credit; notice of termination rights; disclosure if licensee may receive compensation from creditor; explanation of dispute resolution mechanism; explanation of applicable privacy laws. If a licensee communicates in a language other than English, it must provide an agreement and other required documents and disclosures in that language. § 2414.

Cancellation/Termination/Refund Rights: Either party may terminate upon ten days' notice. Upon termination, provider must promptly refund any sums that have not been distributed to creditors. Termination rights must be clearly disclosed in contract. § 2414.

Handling of Funds: Funds for distribution to creditors must be deposited, within two business days of receipt, a trust account in an insured financial institution. Licensee must promptly disburse funds to creditors; correct any missed misdirected payments that result from licensee's error, and compensate consumer for any charges imposed by creditor as a result of the error; reconcile the account at least once a month, and provide accounting at least quarterly. Licensee may not transfer funds to or from consumer's account except for refund to consumer, or authorized payments to creditors or authorized fees. In case of termination, licensee must promptly refund any payments not made to creditors. § 2414.

Customer Service Requirements: Licensee must have written policy to prevent conflict of interest. Licensee must have a toll-free number, disclosed in its advertising, and maintain a communications system that allows clients or inquiring persons to individually speak with a counselor or consumer representative during business hours. § 2414.

Limits on Fees: Setup fee $50. Monthly maintenance fee of the lesser of $50 or $10 times the number of accounts initially included. Actual cost of obtaining a credit report. Insufficient funds fee, not to exceed the fee permitted by Pennsylvania bad check law. Licensee may not solicit voluntary contributions. All fees adjusted for inflation. § 2415.

Prohibited Practices: Licensee may not offer payday loans; conduct business under a name or at a location different from the one listed on the license; engage in any business other than debt management without thirty days' notice to the department; hold Pennsylvania consumer funds in an amount exceeding the amount of its bond. Licensee or certain related persons may not purchase an obligation of consumer; lend money or extend credit to consumer; offer or provide credit insurance to consumer; take a mortgage or security interest from consumer; give or receive a bonus for referrals. Licensee may not operate a collection agency; structure an agreement that results in negative amortization of any debt; compromise any debt without written consent of the consumer; disseminate false, misleading or deceptive information; disclose consumer's identifying information, except to the department, or to a creditor as needed to secure creditor's cooperation and administer an agreement; delegate any of its duties to an unlicensed person; compensate its employees on the basis of the number of agreements made or the total amount of debt covered by the agreements. §§ 2410.1, 2414.

Public Remedies: Department may issue cease and desist orders; order restitution; impose civil penalties of up to $10,000 per violation; bring action for injunction. §§ 2416, 2417.

Private Remedies: Violations are UDAPs. § 2416.

Statute of Limitations: Not specified in this statute.

Citation: 63 Pa. Con. St. §§ 2501 through 2593 (debt settlement).

Administrator: Banking and Securities Commission.

Scope & Key Definitions: Debt settlement. Acting as an intermediary between an individual and one or more unsecured creditors, for the purpose of obtaining reduction in the principal of a consumer debt. § 2502.

Exceptions: Legal services performed in an attorney-client relationship by an attorney authorized to practice in Pennsylvania; accounting services performed in an accountant-client relationship by a CPA authorized to practice in Pennsylvania; financial planning services performed in a planner-client relationship by a licensed financial planner. § 2505. Judicial officers, persons acting under orders of court or administrative agency, assignees for benefit of creditors; chartered financial institutions; title insurers, escrow agents, and bill-payers, if the debt settlement is incidental to the bill-paying; licensed debt-management providers (see above) if the debt settlement is incidental to the debt-management; attorneys not holding selves out as debt settlement providers, who settle debts in the normal course of legal practice, providing attorneys are not compensated by a debt settlement provider. §§ 2502, 2503.

Registration/Licensing: License, $25,000 bond, and insurance required. Applicant must provide a copy of its standard debt settlement agreement. Reduced license fee for certain nonprofits. § 2521, 2523, 2524, 2525.

Disclosures: Before consumer agrees to pay for goods or services, provider must disclose in a clear and conspicuous manner, in writing: the amount of time necessary to obtain the represented results; if services include negotiating settlement offers, the time by which provider will make a settlement offer to each creditor; the cost for debt settlement services or the method of calculating the fee for settling each debt, and the total estimated program costs; if service will result in failure to make timely payments, warning that damage to credit will result, and individual may be subjected to collection action, and that the amount owed will increase due to fees and interest; if program requires individual to place funds in bank account, that individual owns the funds, can terminate the plan at any time, and withdraw the funds (other than funds already earned by the provider) within seven days; that cancelled or forgiven debt may be considered income for tax purposes. § 2552.

Pre-Agreement Services: Not specified.

Contract Terms: Not specified.

Cancellation/Termination/Refund Rights: Debtor may cancel at any time on three days' notice; may withdraw funds from account (less any amount already earned by provider) after seven days. These rights must be disclosed in pre-agreement disclosures. § 2552.

Handling of Funds: Provider may require individual to accumulate funds in a bank account, which must be in the name of the individual and the funds must be owned by the individual. If account is not administered by provider, the entity administering the account must not be owned or controlled by, or affiliated with the provider, and may not give or receive any compensation for referrals by the provider. § 2552.

Customer Service Requirements: Provider must act in good faith (UCC definition) §§ 2502, 2551.

Limits on Fees: Provider may not collect fee until it has settled, negotiated or altered the terms of at least one debt, and individual has made at least one payment. The fee must either bear the same proportional relationship to the total fee as the settled fee does to the total amount of debt (calculated as of the time of enrollment) or be a percentage of the amount saved, which must be the same for all debts. § 2552.

Prohibited Practices: Licensee may not conduct business at an address or under a name other than that given in its license application; conduct any business other than debt settlement without giving the department notice 30 days before beginning the business. May not misrepresent any aspect of debt settlement services, including expected amount of savings, time needed to achieve results, the sum that must be accumulated before settlement offers will be made, the effect of the service on creditworthiness, the effect on creditors' collection efforts; the number or percentage of individual who attain the expected results; provider's nonprofit status; estimated costs. §§ 2533, 2552.

Public Remedies: Department may order restitution, or issue cease and desist orders, sue for injunctions, and impose civil penalties of up to $10,000. Violation of this statute is a UDAP. §§ 2571, 2572, 2574.

Private Remedies: Agreement made by unlicensed provider is voidable. Violation of this statute is a UDAP. §§ 2552, 2574.

Statute of Limitations: Not specified in this statute.

Citation: 18 Pa. Con. Stat. § 7312 (criminal statute).

Administrator: Not specified.

Scope & Key Definitions: Debt pooling. For consideration, making a contract whereby person receives funds from debtors, to be distributed among creditors according to a plan.

Exceptions: Attorneys, partnerships or professional corporations all members of which are attorneys; Better Business Bureaus, legal services corporations, and welfare agencies that act without compensation or profit on behalf of debtors; tax-exempt nonprofits.

Registration/Licensing: Not specified.

Disclosures: Not specified.

Pre-Agreement Services: Not specified.

Contract Terms: Not specified.

Cancellation/Termination/Refund Rights: Not specified.

Handling of Funds: Not specified.

Customer Service Requirements: Not specified.

Limits on Fees: Not specified.

Prohibited Practices: Not specified.

Remedies:

Public Remedies: Unlicensed debt pooling is a misdemeanor. (See licensing statutes, above.)

Private Remedies: Not specified.

Statute of Limitations: Not specified in this statute.

Rhode Island

This statute is based upon the 2008 version of the Uniform Debt-Management Services Act, summarized at Appx. I.2, supra, with variations as noted below.

Citation: R.I. Gen. Laws §§ 19-14.8-1 through 19-14.8-43.

Administrator: Department of Business Regulation.

Scope & Key Definitions: Substantially similar to uniform act. § 19-14.8-2.

Exceptions: Substantially similar to uniform act. §§ 19-14.8-2, 19-14.8-3.

Registration/Licensing: Substantially similar to uniform act. §§ 19-14.8-4, 19-14.8-5, 19-14.8-6, 19-14.8-13, 19-14.8-14. *See also* § 19-14-2 (list of financial professions for which licensing is required).

Disclosures: Substantially similar to uniform act. §§ 19-14.8-17, 19-14.8-18, 19=14.8-21, 19-14.8-30.

Pre-Agreement Services: Substantially similar to uniform act. § 19-14.8-17.

Contract Terms: Substantially similar to uniform act. §§ 19-14.8-19, 19-14.8-21.

Cancellation/Termination/Refund Rights: Substantially similar to uniform act. (Includes both 3-day cancellation right, and right to cancel at any time) §§ 19-14.8-19, 19-14.8-20, 19-14.6-26.

Handling of Funds: Substantially similar to uniform act. §§ 19-14.8-2, 19-14.8-22, 19-14.8-27.

Customer Service Requirements: Substantially similar to uniform act. §§ 19-14.8-2, 19-14.8-15, 19-14.1-16, § 19-14.8-19.

Limits on Fees: Substantially similar to uniform act. §§ 19-14.8-23, 19-14.8-24.

Prohibited Practices: Substantially similar to uniform act. §§ 19-14.8-19, 19-14.8-28.

Public Remedies: Substantially similar to uniform act. § 19-14.8-33.

Private Remedies: Substantially similar to uniform act. §§ 19-14.8-25, 19-14.8-31, 19-14.8-35, 19-14.8-36.

Statute of Limitations: Substantially similar to uniform act. § 19-14.8-37.

South Carolina

South Carolina has two statutes, one regulating debt management and debt settlement, and one (found in the subchapter regulating the practice of law) generally forbidding debt pooling by non-lawyers.

Citation: S.C. Code Ann. §§ 37-7-101 through 37-7-122 (debt management and settlement).

Administrator: Department of Consumer Affairs.

Scope & Key Definitions: Consumer Credit Counseling: Receiving or offering to receive funds for the purpose of distribution among consumer's creditors in full or partial payment of consumer's debts; improving or offering to improve consumer's credit rating. Debt settlement: negotiating or offering to negotiate to reduce or defer consumer's obligations with respect to credit extended by others. § 37-7-101.

Exceptions: Faith-based nonprofit organizations; attorneys; banks, fiduciaries, credit unions, savings and loan associations and savings banks; certified public accountants providing credit counseling advice pursuant to an accounting practice; judicial officers or others acting pursuant to court-order; housing counselors certified by the South Carolina Housing Authority engaged in counseling pursuant to the High Cost and Consumer Home Loans statute; licensed mortgage brokers, real estate brokers, salesmen and property managers; credit reporting agencies or certain affiliates or subsidiaries that obtain reports to resell to the consumer, or to monitor on behalf of the consumer. § 37-7-101.

Registration/Licensing: License and bond (the greater of $25,000 or the amount of South Carolina consumers' funds in providers account at the time of application or renewal) required. Application must include copies of the applicant's consumer education program and standard debt-management plan. Continuing professional education requirements. §§ 37-7-102, 37-7-103, 37-7-104, 37-7-105.

Disclosures: Must disclose in a separate writing, that debt-management plans are not suitable for everyone, and that provider does not offer plans for secured debt. § 37-7-108.

Pre-Agreement Services: Licensee must provide individualized credit counseling and education session, and a thorough written budget analysis, and may not offer a debt-management plan unless it concludes, based on this analysis, that the plan is suitable and consumer is reasonably likely to meet the requirements. §§ 37-7-108, 37-7-113.

Contract Terms: Contracts must include a reasonable estimate of the total payments and fees; a schedule dates and amounts of payments; disclosure of terms applicable to late payment or default; detailed description of services to be performed, and an estimate of the time required (five-year maximum contract term); list of creditors expected to accept payments, with total amount due, schedule and amount of payments, and anticipated payoff date; a list of creditors expected not to participate in the plan; consumer's right to cancel on ten days' notice and receive refund of sums not distributed to creditors; disclosure if licensee may receive funds from creditors for providing education to consumer; notice that licensee may not require voluntary contributions, or the purchase of other goods and services during the plan; and the phone number of the Department of Consumer Affairs. § 37-7-110.

Cancellation/Termination/Refund Rights: Consumer may cancel upon ten days' notice and receive refund of sums not distributed to creditors. This right must be conspicuously disclosed in contract, near the signature line. § 37-7-110.

Handling of Funds: Consumers' funds for distribution to creditors must be deposited in a trust account, separate from licensee's funds, within one business day of receipt, and disbursed to creditors within five days of receipt. The account must be reconciled once a month, and provide consumer with an itemized accounting every ninety days, or within seven days of request (no more than 3 requests per 6 month period). Licensee must provide receipts for payments, or provide a means for debtor to view the status of the account electronically. Licensee must correct misdirected payments resulting from licensee's error. If consumer cancels contract, licensee must refund all unexpended funds. § 37-7-111.

Customer Service Requirements: Licensee must keep a record of creditors' consent to a plan. § 37-7-109.

Limits on Fees: No fee may be collected before contract is signed. Amount of setup fee determined by Department of Consumer Affairs; if within forty-five days of establishment of the plan, lack of consent by creditors makes plan unsuitable, the fee must be refunded. Other fees also set by Department regulation. §§ 37-7-109, 37-7-112.

Prohibited Practices: Licensee may not: require the purchase of any other goods or services as a condition for entering into a debt-management plan; solicit the sale of other goods or services during the term of the plan; require voluntary contributions from consumer; obtain an agreement from consumer waiving any rights provided by this chapter; charge a fee to rescind a debt-management contract; use false, misleading or deceptive advertising; give or receive a bonus for referrals; unreasonably disclose information about consumer's accounts; use unconscionable means to obtain a contract or collect a debt; engage in other unfair or deceptive acts or practices; collect a payment from consumer before it is due; operate another business at the licensed location without the consent of the Department; execute a contract with blanks not filled in; make loans to debtors; issue credit cards or act as an agent to procure customers for a credit card company or financial institution; purchase any obligation of consumer; take a promissory note or other negotiable instrument except a check or draft; misrepresent its authority to provide legal services or advice; or compensate its employees based on the number of contracts sold. §§ 37-7-110, 37-7-116.

Public Remedies: Violation of this chapter is a misdemeanor. The Department of Consumer Affairs may issue cease and desist orders, and impose civil penalties of $1000 to $2500 for violation of orders. §§ 37-7-117, 37-7-118, 37-7-119.

Private Remedies: Contracts made in violation of § 37-7-116 (prohibited practices) are void. A consumer injured by a violation of this chapter has a private right of action for actual damages, punitive damages, costs and reasonable attorney fees. Violation of this chapter is a UDAP. UDAP remedies are cumulative and in addition to those provided by this chapter. §§ 37-7-116, 37-7-117, 37-7-118.

Statute of Limitations: Three years following the latest of: individual's last transmission of money to provider, individual's last transmission of money to creditor at direction of provider, date when individual discovered or reasonably should have discovered facts giving rise to the claim, or termination of proceedings by director with respect to violation. § 37-7-117.

Citation: S.C. Code Ann. § 40-5-370 (debt pooling).
Scope & Key Definitions: Debt pooling: for compensation, services in connection with a plan in which debtor deposits fund for distribution among debtor's creditors, are the practice of law.
Exceptions: Not specified.
Registration/Licensing: Not specified.
Disclosures: Not specified.
Pre-Agreement Services: Not specified.
Contract Terms: Not specified.
Cancellation/Termination/Refund Rights: Not specified.
Handling of Funds: Not specified.
Customer Service Requirements: Not specified.
Limits on Fees: Not specified.
Prohibited Practices: Debt pooling for compensation by non-attorneys.
Public Remedies: Violation is a misdemeanor.
Private Remedies: Not specified.
Statute of Limitations: Not specified in this statute.

South Dakota

Citation: S.D. Codified Laws §§ 37-34-1 through 37-34-3.
Scope & Key Definitions: Debt adjusting: For consideration, contracting with debtor to receive periodic payments for distributions to creditors according to a plan, or to effect the adjustment, compromise or discharge of indebtedness. § 37-34-1.
Exceptions: Debt adjusting incident to the lawful practice of law; banks and fiduciaries in the regular course of their business; title insurers and abstract companies while doing an escrow business; judicial officers or others acting under court order; nonprofit or charitable corporations; employers for their employees; bona fide trade or mercantile associations arranging adjustments of debts with business establishments; lender who, at debtor's request, adjusts debts when disbursing loan proceeds, without being compensated for this service; mediators pursuant to chapter 54-13. § 37-34-3.
Registration/Licensing: $50,000 bond. § 37-34-3.
Disclosures: None specified.
Pre-Agreement Services: None specified.
Contract Terms: None specified.
Cancellation/Termination/Refund Rights: None specified.
Handling of Funds: Not specified.
Customer Service Requirements: Not specified.
Limits on Fees: Not specified.
Prohibited Practices: Debt adjustment by person who is neither exempt nor bonded. §§ 37-7-2.
Public Remedies: Debt adjusting without filing a bond is a misdemeanor. § 37-7-2.
Private Remedies: Not specified.
Statute of Limitations: Not specified in this statute.

Tennessee

This statute is based upon the 2008 version of the Uniform Debt-Management Services Act, summarized at Appx. I.2, supra, with variations as noted below.

Citation: Tenn. Code Ann. §§ 47-18-5501 through 47-18-5541.
Administrator: Commissioner of Commerce and Insurance.
Scope & Key Definitions: Substantially similar to uniform act. § 47-18-5502.
Exceptions: Substantially similar to uniform act, plus registered credit services businesses that do not engage in debt counseling, debt management, or debt settlement. §§ 47-18-5502, 47-18-5503.
Registration/Licensing: Substantially similar to uniform act. Counselors and debt specialists must be certified. §§ 47-18-5504, 47-18-5506, 47-18-5513, 47-18-5514.
Disclosures: Substantially similar to uniform act. §§ 47-18-5517, 47-18-5518, 47-18-21, 47-18-5530.
Pre-Agreement Services: Substantially similar to uniform act. § 47-18-5517.
Contract Terms: Substantially similar to uniform act. § 47-18-5519, 47-18-5521.
Cancellation/Termination/Refund Rights: Provider may terminate for sixty days' non-payment. Individual may cancel within three days of signing, using a form provided in the agreement, or at will upon notice, and provider will refund: for a debt-management plan, all funds not paid to creditors, less authorized fees; for a debt settlement plan, 65% of the portion of the setup fee[6] that has not been credited against settlement fees. The three-day cancellation right may be waived if a personal financial emergency requires disbursement of funds within three days. §§ 47-18-5519, 47-18-5520, 47-18-5523, 47-18-5526
Handling of Funds: Substantially similar to uniform act. §§ 47-18-5522, 47-18-5527.
Customer Service Requirements: Substantially similar to uniform act. §§ 47-18-5502, 47-18-5515, 47-18-5516.

---

6   The authorization for 65% appears in § 47-18-5526(b)(2), which states: "Sixty-five percent (65%) of any portion of the set-up fee received pursuant to § 47-18-5523(d)(2) that has not been credited against settlement fees." But the cross-referenced paragraph has been repealed. It is not clear what impact this has on § 47-18-5526(b)(2). But the legislative history of the amendment indicates that the intent was to prevent service providers from charging any setup fee. *See* Summary of Tenn. Senate S.B. 1446 (Apr. 14, 2014), *available at* http://wapp.capitol.tn.gov. Therefore the reference to setup fees in § 47-18-5526(b)(2) was probably overlooked and was intended to be repealed too.

Limits on Fees: Substantially similar to uniform act. Forbids upfront fees for debt settlement service. §§ 47-18-5523, 47-18-5524.

Prohibited Practices: Substantially similar to uniform act. §§ 47-18-5519, 47-18-5528.

Public Remedies: Substantially similar to uniform act. § 47-18-5533.

Private Remedies: Substantially similar to uniform act. §§ 47-18-5525, 47-18-5531, 47-18-35, 47-18-36.

Statute of Limitations: Substantially similar to uniform act. § 47-18-5537.

Texas

Citation: Tex. Fin. Code Ann. §§ 394.201 through 394.215 (West).

Administrator: Consumer Credit Commissioner.

Scope & Key Definitions: Consumer debt-management services: acting as an intermediary between a consumer and his or her creditors, for the purpose of obtaining or seeking to obtain concessions from one or more creditors. § 394.202.

Exceptions: Attorneys (so long as they do not work for providers or hold themselves out as providers of debt-management services); title insurer, abstract company or others engaged in escrow business; a judicial officer or other person acting under court order; a consumer's representative payee authorized by federal or state law while paying bills for the consumer; one who pays bills for a consumer with the consumer's funds, without negotiating with creditors, arranging a new payment schedule, or otherwise changing the terms of a debt; financial institutions. The following transactions are not debt-management: extensions of credit, including refinances or debt consolidation loans; bankruptcy services provided by a licensed attorney. § 394.203.

Registration/Licensing: Registration and bond or insurance required. Bond of not less than $25,000 or more than $100,000, equal to the average daily balance in the trust account for Texas consumers over the preceding twelve months. Insurance of $100,000. The finance commission may, by rule, permit other forms of security. Applicant must provide copies of its standard agreements and disclosure forms. Counselors must be certified, or become certified within 12 months of starting employment with licensee. §§ 394.202, 394.204, 394.205, 394.206.

Disclosures: Must disclose in a separate written document that debt-management plans are not suitable for everyone, and that alternatives exist; that if provider is not a nonprofit tax-exempt organization, it cannot require donations; whether some of its funding comes from contributions from creditors. § 394.208.

Pre-Agreement Services: Before enrolling consumer in a plan, provide counseling and education by a certified counselor; prepare an individualized financial analysis with recommendations for the consumer; conclude based on that analysis that consumer is reasonably able to meet the requirements of the plan; reasonably expects that creditors will accept the plan payments. § 394.208.

Contract Terms: Agreements must itemize the services to be provided and the fees; include a list of creditors, with amount owed and a schedule of the date and amount of payments to each creditor; disclose the existence of provider's security bond or insurance for consumer claims; state that the existence of a plan may impact consumer's credit rating; disclose that either party may terminate on ten days' notice, and that consumer who cancels is entitled to a refund of unexpended funds. An agreement may include a voluntary arbitration or mediation provision. If a provider negotiates with consumer in a language other than English, it must provide an agreement in that language. § 394.209.

Cancellation/Termination/Refund Rights: A consumer may cancel an agreement on ten days' notice. The provider may continue making scheduled payments to creditors during these ten days. After cancellation provider must return all funds in the trust fund and, for a debt settlement plan, 65% of the amount of the setup fee that has not been credited against setup fees. §§ 394.208, 394.2095.

Handling of Funds: Funds received for distribution to creditors must be kept in a trust account in a federally insured financial institution, separate from the provider's operating funds. The provider must provide consumer with a detailed accounting once per calendar quarter, and upon ten days after a request by consumer. After cancellation provider must return all funds in the trust fund and, for a debt settlement plan, 65% of the amount of the setup fee that has not been credited against settlement fees. §§ 394.202, 394.208, 394.211, 394.213.

Customer Service Requirements: All providers, including those that do business on the Internet, must maintain a telephone system that enables consumers to speak with a counselor during ordinary business hours. § 394.208.

Limits on Fees: If a consumer does not enter into a debt-management agreement, provider may charge a $100 fee for counseling and education. The commissioner may authorize a greater fee if the nature of the program warrants. The counseling fee must be refunded if consumer signs a debt-management agreement within 90 days after the completion of counseling. For a plan that contemplates reduction of finance or late charges, provider may charge: $100 for consultation and setup, and a monthly fee the lesser of $50 or $10 times the number of accounts remaining in the plan when the fee is assessed. For plans that contemplate settlement for less than the amount of principal: consultation and setup fee of the lesser of $400 or 4% of the amount of outstanding debt at the time the plan is established; monthly fee of the lesser of $50 or $10 times the number of accounts remaining in the plan; and a settlement fee based on either a flat fee, such that this fee plus the setup and maintenance fees do not exceed 17% of the amount of principal included in the plan, or a percentage of savings, such that the settlement fee and setup and monthly fees do not exceed 30% of the amount saved. The flat fee may be assessed in monthly payments. The fee based on savings may be assessed only after settlement of a debt, and the total fees may not exceed 20% of the principal. The fee limitations for debt settlement for less than the principal amount do not apply if fees do not become due before a settlement agreement is reached and one payment towards settlement, in which case reasonable fees may be charged. In this case, a flat fee must bear the same relationship to the total fee as the principal amount of the debt settled bears to the total debt, or a percentage of savings fee must be the same percentage for all debts. Returned check charge of the lesser of $25 or the amount permitted by other law. The amount of fees and charges is adjusted for inflation. §§ 394.210, 394.2101.

Prohibited Practices: Providers may not use false or deceptive advertising; purchase any obligation of consumer; take a promissory note, mortgage, or security interest; lend money or provide credit to consumer; offer a bonus for referrals; misrepresent its authority to provide legal advice or services; use unconscionable means to obtain a contract with consumer; engage in unfair, deceptive or unconscionable acts or practices; require or attempt to require a voluntary contribution. Agreements may not include a confession of judgment; waiver of jury trial; assignment of wages or other compensation for services; waiver of any provisions of this subchapter. §§ 394.207, 394.212.

Public Remedies: The commissioner may issue cease and desist orders; order corrective action, including restitution; impose administrative penalties of up to $1000 per violation; or, upon relation of the attorney general, bring an action for injunction. § 394.214.

Private Remedies: If a provider is unregistered at the time of contracting, the contract is void and consumer may recover all fees paid under the void agreement, plus costs and reasonable attorney fees. A consumer aggrieved by violation of this chapter, a rule adopted by the finance commission pursuant to this chapter, or an unconscionable, unfair or deceptive act or practice has a private right of action for actual damages; punitive damages for acts pursuant to a void agreement; costs and reasonable attorney fees; injunction or other equitable relief to prevent violations. These remedies are not exclusive, and consumer is not required to exhaust administrative remedies. § 394.215.

Statute of Limitations: Not specified in this statute.

Utah

Utah has two statutes, one covering debt-management services, and one covering consumer credit services, which broadly covers credit counseling and credit repair, as well as debt management. The first statute is based upon the 2011 version of the Uniform Debt-Management Services Act, summarized at Appx. I.2, supra, with variations as noted below.

Citation: Utah Code Ann. §§ 13-42-101 through 13-42-141 (West) (debt-management services).

Administrator: Division of Consumer Protection.

Scope & Key Definitions: Substantially similar to uniform act. § 13-42-102.

Exceptions: Substantially similar to uniform act. Note the definitions of attorney, accountant and financial planner exceptions that are based on the 2011 version of the uniform act. §§ 13-42-102, 13-42-103.

Registration/Licensing: Substantially similar to uniform act, except bond amount is $100,000 (to be adjusted for inflation). §§ 13-42-104, 13-42-105, 13-42-106, 13-42-113, 13-42-114.

Disclosures: Substantially similar to uniform act. §§ 13-42-117, 13-42-118, 13-42-130.

Pre-Agreement Services: Substantially similar to uniform act. § 13-42-117.

Contract Terms: Substantially similar to uniform act. §§ 13-42-118, 13-42-119, 13-42-121.

Cancellation/Termination/Refund Rights: Substantially similar to uniform act. §§ 12-42-19, 12-42-120.

Handling of Funds: Substantially similar to uniform act. §§ 13-42-102, 13-42-122, 13-42-127.

Customer Service Requirements: Substantially similar to uniform act. §§ 13-42-115, 34-42-116.

Limits on Fees: Substantially similar to uniform act, except does not impose 30% limit of fees based on percentage of savings. §§ 13-42-123, 13-42-124.

Prohibited Practices: Substantially similar to uniform act. §§ 13-42-118, 13-42-119, 13-42-128 13-42-131.

Public Remedies: Substantially similar to uniform act. § 13-42-133.

Private Remedies: Substantially similar to uniform act. §§ 13-42-119, 13-42-125, 13-42-131, 13-42-135, 13-42-136.

Statute of Limitations: Substantially similar to uniform act. § 13-42-137.

Citation: Utah Code Ann. §§ 13-21-1 through 13-21-9 (West) (credit services organizations statute).

Administrator: Department of Commerce, Consumer Protection Division. § 13-2-1.

Scope & Key Definitions: Credit repair, credit counseling, or debt reduction or debt-management plans. § 13-21-2.

Exceptions: Regulated lender that derives at least 35% of its income from making loans or extensions of credit; depository institution regulated by the FDIC or the NCUA; licensed real estate broker acting within the scope of the license; attorney providing services in the course of law practice, if credit services are incidental to the law practice; licensed securities broker-dealer acting within the scope of the license; credit reporting agency, if the credit services are incidental to its credit reporting; persons licensed under the debt-management act (see above). The burden of proof as to an exemption is on the party claiming the exemption. §§ 13-21-2, 13-21-8.

Registration/Licensing: Registration and $100,000 bond (or letter of credit or CD) required. Applicant must provide copies of form agreements, sales literature and other relevant documents. §§ 13-21-3, 13-21-3.5

Disclosures: Before an agreement is signed, credit services organization must provide a written statement disclosing consumer's FCRA right to review his or her credit report and dispute any inaccurate items; a detailed description of the services to be provided by the credit services organization and the prices; the existence of the organization's bond, and the procedure for making claims. §§ 13-21-5, 13-21-6.

Pre-Agreement Services: Not specified.

Contract Terms: Contract must be in writing, and must conspicuously disclose consumer's five-day right to cancel (and include a cancellation form); the terms and conditions, and total amount, of payments; a description of the services to be performed, estimated time for performing them, and organization's refund policy; contact information for the organization's agent who is authorized to receive service of process. § 13-21-7.

Cancellation/Termination/Refund Rights: Five-day right to cancel after contracting. Notice of this right must be included in contract, and a cancellation form attached. Upon cancellation, all payments made pursuant to the contract must be refunded within ten days after receipt of notice. Contract must also disclose provider's refund policy. § 13-21-7.

Handling of Funds: Not specified.

Customer Service Requirements: Not specified.

Limits on Fees: May not charge any fee before complete performance of agreed services. § 13-21-3.

Prohibited Practices: May not challenge, or advise a consumer to challenge, a statement in a credit report without a good faith belief that the statement is inaccurate, outdated or unverifiable; charge for referral to a lender who will provide credit on the same terms it would provide to the general public; make or advise a consumer to make any false statement to a credit reporting agency, creditor, or prospective lender; make false or misleading statements, or engage in any act or practice that would result in fraud or deception in the provision of credit services. § 13-21-3.

Public Remedies: Violation is a misdemeanor. The director of the Consumer Protection Division may issue cease and desist orders; impose administrative penalties of up to $2500 per violation; bring a civil action for damages or injunction. §§ 13-21-8, 13-21-9.

Private Remedies: A buyer injured by a violation of this chapter has a private right of action for the greater of the amount paid by the buyer to the credit services organization or actual damages; costs and reasonable attorney fees. Punitive damages may be awarded. The remedies of this chapter are in addition to those provided by other law. § 13-21-9.

Statute of Limitations: Not specified in this statute.

Vermont

Citation: Vt. Stat. Ann. tit. 8, §§ 2751–2768.

Administrator: Commissioner of Financial Regulation.

Scope & Key Definitions: Debt Adjustment: Serving as an intermediary between debtor and creditor for the purpose of obtaining concessions, or distributing funds among creditors in full or partial payment of debtor's debts. § 2751.

Exceptions: Bona fide nonprofit religious, fraternal or cooperative organization, offering services only to its members; attorneys engaged in the practice of law; financial institutions or licensed lenders that perform debt adjustment in the course of their principal business; certified public accountants offering services in the course of accounting practice; any person acting pursuant to law or court order. § 2763.

Registration/Licensing: License and $50,000 bond required. Applicant must provide copy of all advertising materials, and a copy of its form contract. §§ 2752, 2753, 2755.

Disclosures: Not specified.

Pre-Agreement Services: Not specified.

Contract Terms: Contract must itemize services to be provided and fees; disclose that debt-management services are not suitable for all debtors, and a list of debts included and the interest rate on each; disclose the three-day rescission right and include a cancellation form; disclose, if applicable, that creditors may compensate the licensee and that secured debt is not covered by the contract. If a contract is negotiated in a language other than English, all required disclosures must be in that language. §§ 2759, 2759a.

Cancellation/Termination/Refund Rights: Right to cancel within three business days after contracting. This right must be disclosed in the contract, and a cancellation form provided. If debtor exercises this right, provider must give refund within ten days after receipt of cancellation notice.

Debtor may also cancel at any time without cancellation premium or penalty. §§ 2759a, 2759b.

Handling of Funds: Funds for distribution to creditors must be kept in a trust account in an insured financial institution, separate from licensee's own funds, and disbursed to creditors in a timely manner, at least once every thirty days. Licensee must provide debtor with an itemized accounting at least quarterly. If a contract is rescinded pursuant to the three-day cancellation right, licensee must return all funds. §§ 2759a, 2759c, 2760, 2760a.

Customer Service Requirements: Licensee must comply with Vermont law protecting financial privacy. § 2760c.

Limits on Fees: Licensee may not take any fee before entering into a contract. Fees must be agreed upon in advance. $50 setup fee, plus 10% of payments received for distribution to creditors. Cancellation fees prohibited. §§ 2759b, 2762.

Prohibited Practices: Misrepresenting that one is licensed; using false or deceptive advertising, of failing to include licensee's name and address; structuring an agreement to result in negative amortization of any debt; purchasing any obligation of debtor; lending money or providing credit to any debtor; taking a mortgage or security interest; seeking to collect from debtor for creditors not receiving payment pursuant to a debt-management plan; signing a contract with blanks not filled in; giving or receiving a bonus for referrals; disclosing or threatening to disclose confidential information to coerce payment of a debt; using simulated process or any documents that gives a false appearance of being approved or issued by government, a government agency, or an attorney; no licensee or various affiliates may be an owner or controlling party of any creditor that is receiving payments from licensee on behalf of debtor, without express written consent from the commissioner. § 2760b.

Public Remedies: Criminal penalties of up to two years imprisonment or $1500 fine. Commissioner may order restitution or impose civil penalty of up to $1500 per violation. § 2764.

Private Remedies: Consumer has private right of action for restitution against licensee or person who should have been licensed who violates this chapter. § 2764.

Statute of Limitations: Not specified in this statute.

Virgin Islands

Citation: V.I. Code Ann. tit. 12A §§ 401 through 441. *This is a version of the 2005 uniform act.*

Administrator: Lieutenant governor.

Scope & Key Definitions: Substantially similar to uniform act. § 402.

Exceptions: Substantially similar to 2005 act. §§ 402, 403.

Registration/Licensing: Substantially similar to uniform act. §§ 404, 405, 413, 414.

Disclosures: Substantially similar to uniform act. §§ 417, 418, 421, 430.

Pre-Agreement Services: Substantially similar to uniform act. § 417.

Contract Terms: Substantially similar to uniform act. §§ 417, 419, 421.

Cancellation/Termination/Refund Rights: Substantially similar to 2005 act. Includes both 3-day cancellation right and cancellation at will; permits provider to withhold 35% of setup fee for debt settlement if debtor exercises right to cancel after expiration of three-day cancellation right. §§ 420, 426.

Handling of Funds: Substantially similar to uniform act. §§ 402, 422, 427.

Customer Service Requirements: Substantially similar to uniform act. 402, 415, 416.

Limits on Fees: Substantially similar to 2005 act. Allows setup fee for debt settlement plans. §§ 423, 424.

Prohibited Practices: Substantially similar to uniform act. §§ 419, 428.

Public Remedies: Substantially similar to uniform act. § 433.

Private Remedies: Substantially similar to uniform act. §§ 425, 431, 435, 436.

Statute of Limitations: Substantially similar to uniform act. § 437.

Virginia

Citation: Va. Code Ann. §§ 6.2-2000 to 6.2025.

Administrator: Commissioner of Financial Institutions.

Scope & Key Definitions: Debt Management Plans. Debt pooling and distribution service: an arrangement in which a consumer gives money or control of funds to a person for distribution to the consumer's creditors. Debt settlement: action taken to obtain debt forgiveness or a reduction of payments, charges or fees. § 6.2-2000.

Exceptions: Attorneys licensed to practice in Virginia. Definition of credit counselor excludes CPA's in the ordinary practice of their profession. §§ 6.2-2000, 6.2-2001.

Registration/Licensing: License and bond ($25,000 to $350,000 amount to be determined by the Commissioner of Financial Institutions) required. Applicant must have an acceptable procedure to avoid conflicts of interest. Applicant must provide a copy of its standard debt-management plan. Licensees must be accredited and counselors must be certified. No license may be issued to a collection agency, creditor, association of creditors, credit-granting organization or association of such organizations. §§ 6.2-2001, 6.2-2002, 6.2-2003, 6.2-2005.

Disclosures: Not specified.

Pre-Agreement Services: At the time of executing a plan, licensee must believe in good faith that the listed creditors will participate in the plan, and must promptly advise consumer of any changes by a creditor. § 6.2-2014.

Contract Terms: Debt management plans must include a list of services provided and a clear explanation of costs; notice of consumer's right to terminate at will and to receive a refund (see below); an explanation of the method of dispute resolution; an explanation of consumer's and licensee's obligations under the agreement; notice of privacy rights; warning that participation in the plan may harm consumer's credit rating. § 6.2-2014

Cancellation/Termination/Refund Rights: If consumer terminates the contract, licensee must return all payments not already distributed to creditors. In addition, if consumer terminates contract within five days after signing, licensee must refund all fees; if terminated within five to thirty-one days, must refund all fees except the setup fee. § 6.2-2014.

Handling of Funds: Funds for disbursement to creditors must be kept in a trust account in an insured financial institution, separate from licensee's own funds. Licensee must provide written receipts, or a means by which consumer can view the status of the account electronically. Licensee must provide an itemized accounting to consumer at least quarterly. Funds should be disbursed to creditors within eight days of receipt; and must explain in writing any exceptions to the eight-day rule. § 6.2-2014.

Customer Service Requirements: Licensees must maintain safeguards against conflict of interest. § 6.2-2014.

Limits on Fees: Setup fee: $75. Monthly maintenance fee, the lesser of $60 or 15% of the amount disbursed. May also charge the actual cost of obtaining a credit report, and any bank charges for any automatic debiting. §§ 6.2-2000, 6.2-2015, 6.2-2016.

Prohibited Practices: Licensee may not purchase any obligation of the consumer; lend money or provide credit to a consumer; operate as a debt collector; take a mortgage or security interest in the property of the consumer; structure plan in a way that would result in negative amortization of any debt at the conclusion of the plan; give legal advice or perform legal services for a consumer; employ any person who is employed at the same time by a creditor or collection agency; take a power of attorney authorizing a confession of judgment; make an agreement authorizing the licensee or a third person to sue consumer in a court outside Virginia, or waiving any right provided by this chapter. False or misleading advertising, including calling the licensee by any name other than the one on the license. §§ 6.2-2014, 6.2-2017.

Public Remedies: Violation of this chapter is a misdemeanor. The Commissioner may issue cease and desist orders; impose civil penalties of up to $1000; refer violations to the Attorney General. The Attorney General may sue to enforce this chapter, and for damages, injunction or restitution. §§ 6.2-2019, 6.2-2021, 6.2-2022, 6.2-2024.

Private Remedies: Violation of this chapter is a UDAP and subject to all the enforcement provisions of the UDAP act. Any person who suffers loss by reason of violation of any provision of this chapter has a private right of action to enforce the provision, and if successful may recover reasonable attorney fees, expert witness fees, and court costs. §§ 6.2-2023, 6.2-2025.
Statute of Limitations: Not specified in this statute.

Washington

Washington has two statutes, one regulating debt adjusters, and one regulating third parties administering bank accounts for, among others, debt adjusters.

Citation: Wash. Rev. Code. §§ 18.28.0001 through 18.28.910 (debt adjusters).
Administrator: Department of Financial Institutions.
Scope & Key Definitions: Managing, settling, adjusting, prorating, or liquidating the indebtedness of a debtor, or receiving funds for the purpose or distributing those funds among creditors in partial payment of the obligations of a debtor. Wash. Rev. Code. § 18.28.010.
Exceptions: Attorneys, escrow agents, accountants, broker-dealers in securities, performing services incidental to the practice of their respective professions. Financial institutions, crop credit associations, development credit corporations, industrial development corporations, title insurance companies, insurance companies. Third-party account administrators, defined as an independent entity that holds and administers a dedicated bank account for fees and payments to creditors, debt collectors, debt adjusters, or debt adjusting agencies, in connection with the renegotiation, settlement, reduction or other alteration of terms of payment or other terms of a debt. Employees performing debt adjustment services for employer who is not in business of debt adjustment. Public officers in their official capacities, or any person acting under court order. Persons performing services incidental to the winding up or dissolution of a partnership, corporation or other business enterprise. Nonprofits that deal exclusively with debts owed by commercial enterprises to business organizations. Nonprofits that do not assess a service against the debtor of more than $15/month, but note that these nonprofits are required to file detailed reports with the Wash. Rev. Code. §§ 18.28.0001, 18.28.010.
Registration/Licensing: No.
Disclosures: Not specified.
Pre-Agreement Services: Not specified.
Contract Terms: Contract must have a list of creditors and debts included and the approximate total; precise payment terms, within the debtor's ability to pay; the rate and amount of adjuster's charges; the approximate number and amount of installments necessary to pay in full; requirement for adjuster to notify debtor within five days if creditor refuses to accept payment; clear notice of the three-day cancellation right. Adjuster must provide debtor with a copy of the contract immediately after signing, and a receipt for payments, within five days after payment, unless made by check or money order. Wash. Rev. Code §§ 18.28.100, 18.28.110.
Cancellation/Termination/Refund Rights: Right to cancel within three days after contract signing must be clearly disclosed in contract. In case of cancellation or default, the lesser of $25 or 6% of the remaining indebtedness. §§ 18.28.100, 18.28.080.
Handling of Funds: Must make a permanent record of all payments and disbursements. Distribute to creditors, within forty days after receipt of payment, at least 85% of the payment. Render an account to debtor once a month, or within ten days after written demand. Funds received from debtor must be kept in a separate trust account, not commingled with funds of adjuster. If debtor cancels or defaults, adjuster may take from the account fees authorized by this chapter, and must return the balance to the debtor by the earlier of five days after debtor's demand or thirty days after the cancellation or default. Wash. Rev. Code §§ 18.28.110, 18.28.150.
Customer Service Requirements: Not specified.
Limits on Fees: Initial fee of not more than $25. Total fee, including the initial fee and any fees charged by financial institution or third party administrator, may not exceed 15% of the debt. May retain up to 15% of

any payment (not counting fair share payments), but total fees retained may not exceed 15% of payments received to date. No fee whatsoever may be applied against payments for rent and utility payments for housing. In case of cancellation or default, the lesser of $25 or 6% of the remaining indebtedness. Before retaining any fee, adjuster must notify all listed creditors that the debtor has engaged the debt adjuster. Wash. Rev. Code §§ 18.28.080.
Prohibited Practices: Taking a contract with blank spaces when signed by debtor. Receiving or charging a fee in the form of a promissory note or other promise to pay, or accepting a mortgage or other security, on real or personal property. Lending money or extending credit. Taking a confession of judgment or power of attorney to confess judgment. False or misleading advertising. Offering or providing compensation for referrals to debt adjuster. Accepting payment from anyone except debtor or person acting on debtor's behalf, except for fair share payments to nonprofit. Disclosing identity of debtors who had contracted with debt adjuster, or disclosing debts to anyone except another creditor of debtor as necessary to secure creditor's cooperation in debt adjustment plan. Providing legal services or legal advice; misrepresenting adjuster's authority to perform legal services; communicating in the name of an attorney or on attorney's stationary; assuming authority or taking a power of attorney to hire, discharge, or arrange the terms and compensation of an attorney. Wash. Rev. Code §§ 18.28.120, 18.28.130.
Public Remedies: Violations of this chapter are misdemeanors. Attorney general may seek injunction to restrain or prevent violations. Civil penalty of up to $1000 for violation of injunction. Wash. Rev. Code §§ 18.28.190, 18.28.200.
Private Remedies: If debt adjuster contracts for or receives a fee in excess of that permitted by this chapter, except as a result of accidental and bona fide error, the contract is void, and adjuster must return all payments received and not yet distributed to creditors. Violation of this chapter is an unfair and deceptive act under Chapter 19.86 of the Revised Code of Washington. Wash. Rev. Code §§ 18.28.090, 18.28.185.
Statute of Limitations: Not specified in this statute.

Citation: Wash. Rev. Code §§ 19.230.350 and 19.230.360 (third party administrators, based on part of the uniform money services act).
Administrator: Director of Financial Institutions. § 19.230.010.
Scope & Key Definitions: Third-party account administrators: independent entities that hold and administer dedicated bank accounts for fees and payments to creditors, debt collectors, debt adjusters, or debt adjusting agencies, in connection with the renegotiation, settlement, reduction or other alteration of terms of payment or other terms of a debt. Wash. Rev. Stat. § 19.230.350.
Exceptions: Financial institutions. Attorneys, insurance companies, and title insurers, if services are ancillary to the practice of their respective professions. Wash. Rev. Code § 19.230.020.
Registration/Licensing: Third-party administrator must be licensed as a money transmitter. Must post bond of not less than $10,000 or more than $550,000, as determined by the director of financial institutions, based on licensee's prior year's business. Wash. Rev. Code §§ 19.230.050, 19.230.350.
Disclosures: Not specified.
Pre-Agreement Services: Not specified.
Contract Terms: Contract must disclose the rate and amount of all fees. Statutory 15% limit on fees must be disclosed on the front of the contract in at least 12-point type. Wash. Rev. Code § 19.230.350.
Cancellation/Termination/Refund Rights: Debtor may withdraw from the service at any time, and must receive all funds in the account, except funds earned by the debt adjuster (see debt adjustment statute, above), within seven business days of debtor's request. Wash. Rev. Code § 19.230.350.
Handling of Funds: Debtor's funds must be held in an account at an insured financial institution. The debtor owns the funds and must be paid any accrued interest. Wash. Rev. Code § 19.230.350.
Customer Service Requirements: Not specified.
Limits on Fees: Aggregate of fees charged by debt adjuster and third-party administrator may not exceed 15% of the debt. Wash. Rev. Code § 19.230.350.

Prohibited Practices: Deceptive advertising, unfair and deceptive acts, scheme or artifice to defraud. Giving or accepting any form of compensation for referrals of business involving a debt adjuster. Wash. Rev. Code. §§ 19.230.340, 19.230.350.

Public Remedies: Director of financial institutions may assess civil penalties up to $100/day. Wash. Rev. Code. § 19.230.290

Private Remedies: Violation is an unfair and deceptive act under Chapter 19.86 of the Revised Code of Washington. Wash. Rev. Code. § 19.230.350.

Statute of Limitations: Not specified in this statute.

West Virginia

Citation: W.Va. Code § 61-10-23.

Scope & Key Definitions: Debt pooling: charging for providing advice or a plan by which debtor deposits funds with debt pooler for distribution to creditors.

Exceptions: Licensed attorneys.

Registration/Licensing: No.

Disclosures: Not specified.

Pre-Agreement Services: Not specified.

Contract Terms: Not specified.

Cancellation/Termination/Refund Rights: Not specified.

Handling of Funds: Not specified.

Customer Service Requirements: Not specified.

Limits on Fees: Not more than 2% of funds actually deposited. Nonprofits may impose an additional fee of up to 5%, to defray the actual cost of counseling services.

Prohibited Practices: Not specified.

Public Remedies: Violation is a misdemeanor.

Private Remedies: Not specified.

Statute of Limitations: Not specified in this statute.

Wisconsin

Citation: Wis. Stat. § 218.02.

Administrator: Division of Banking.

Scope & Key Definitions: Adjustment Service Companies: engaging the business, for a surcharge or other consideration, of pro-rating debtor's income to creditors or purchasing debtor's debts. § 218.02(1)(a).

Exceptions: Not specified.

Registration/Licensing: License required. The Division of Banking may require licensees to obtain a bond in the sum of not more than $5000. §§ 218.02(2).

Disclosures: Not specified.

Pre-Agreement Services: Not specified.

Contract Terms: Not specified.

Cancellation/Termination/Refund Rights: Not specified.

Handling of Funds: Not specified.

Customer Service Requirements: If a licensee settles or reduces a debt, it must provide debtor with a verified statement showing the amount due creditors by the terms of the settlement or reduction. § 218.02(8).

Limits on Fees: Not specified.

Prohibited Practices: Not specified.

Public Remedies: Violation of this section is punishable by $500 fine and/or ninety days' imprisonment. § 218.02(10).

Private Remedies: Not specified.

Statute of Limitations: Not specified in this statute.

Wyoming

Citation: Wyo. Stat. §§ 33-14-101 through 33-14-103.

Scope & Key Definitions: Debt adjustment, budget counseling, debt management or debt pooling: for a fee, offer or provide services to effect the adjustment, compromise or discharge of any debt, or receive from debtor and disburse to creditors money or anything of value. § 33-13-101.

Exceptions: Tax-exempt nonprofit counseling services; attorneys authorized to practice in Wyoming, and partnerships or professional corporations all members of which are attorneys. § 33-14-101, 33-14-102.

Registration/Licensing: Not specified.

Disclosures: Not specified.

Pre-Agreement Services: Not specified.

Contract Terms: Not specified.

Cancellation/Termination/Refund Rights: Not specified.

Handling of Funds: Not specified.

Customer Service Requirements: Not specified.

Limits on Fees: Not specified.

Prohibited Practices: Debt adjustment by persons other than nonprofits or attorneys forbidden.

Public Remedies: Violation is a misdemeanor. § 33-14-103.

Private Remedies: None specified.

Statute of Limitations: Not specified in this statute.

Appendix J   Mailing of Unordered Merchandise

* * *

39 U.S.C. § 3009.   Mailing of unordered merchandise

(a) Except for (1) free samples clearly and conspicuously marked as such, and (2) merchandise mailed by a charitable organization soliciting contributions, the mailing of unordered merchandise or of communications prohibited by subsection (c) of this section constitutes an unfair method of competition and an unfair trade practice in violation of section 45(a)(1) of title 15.

(b) Any merchandise mailed in violation of subsection (a) of this section, or within the exceptions contained therein, may be treated as a gift by the recipient, who shall have the right to retain, use, discard, or dispose of it in any manner he sees fit without any obligation whatsoever to the sender.

All such merchandise shall have attached to it a clear and conspicuous statement informing the recipient that he may treat the merchandise as a gift to him and has the right to retain, use, discard, or dispose of it in any manner he sees fit without any obligation whatsoever to the sender.

(c) No mailer of any merchandise mailed in violation of subsection (a) of this section, or within the exceptions contained therein, shall mail to any recipient of such merchandise a bill for such merchandise or any dunning communications.

(d) For the purposes of this section, "unordered merchandise" means merchandise mailed without the prior expressed request or consent of the recipient.

[Pub. L. No. 91-375, 84 Stat. 749 (Aug. 12, 1970)]

* * *

Appendix K   Restore Online Shoppers' Confidence Act

15 U.S.C. § 8401.   Findings; declaration of policy

The Congress finds the following:

(1) The Internet has become an important channel of commerce in the United States, accounting for billions of dollars in retail sales every year. Over half of all American adults have now either made an online purchase or an online travel reservation.

(2) Consumer confidence is essential to the growth of online commerce. To continue its development as a marketplace, the Internet must provide consumers with clear, accurate information and give sellers an opportunity to fairly compete with one another for consumers' business.

(3) An investigation by the Senate Committee on Commerce, Science, and Transportation found abundant evidence that the aggressive sales tactics many companies use against their online customers have undermined consumer confidence in the Internet and thereby harmed the American economy.

(4) The Committee showed that, in exchange for "bounties" and other payments, hundreds of reputable online retailers and websites shared their customers' billing information, including credit card and debit card numbers, with third party sellers through a process known as "data pass". These third party sellers in turn used aggressive, misleading sales tactics to charge millions of American consumers for membership clubs the consumers did not want.

(5) Third party sellers offered membership clubs to consumers as they were in the process of completing their initial transactions on hundreds of websites. These third party "post-transaction" offers were designed to make consumers think the offers were part of the initial purchase, rather than a new transaction with a new seller.

(6) Third party sellers charged millions of consumers for membership clubs without ever obtaining consumers' billing information, including their credit or debit card information, directly from the consumers. Because third party sellers acquired consumers' billing information from the initial merchant through "data pass", millions of consumers were unaware they had been enrolled in membership clubs.

(7) The use of a "data pass" process defied consumers' expectations that they could only be charged for a good or a service if they submitted their billing information, including their complete credit or debit card numbers.

(8) Third party sellers used a free trial period to enroll members, after which they periodically charged consumers until consumers affirmatively canceled the memberships. This use of "free-to-pay conversion" and "negative option" sales took advantage of consumers' expectations that they would have an opportunity to accept or reject the membership club offer at the end of the trial period.

[Pub. L. No. 111-345, § 2, 124 Stat. 3618 (Dec. 29, 2010)]

15 U.S.C. § 8402.   Prohibitions against certain unfair and deceptive internet sales practices

(a) Requirements for certain internet-based sales

It shall be unlawful for any post-transaction third party seller to charge or attempt to charge any consumer's credit card, debit card, bank account, or other financial account for any good or service sold in a transaction effected on the Internet, unless—

(1) before obtaining the consumer's billing information, the post-transaction third party seller has clearly and conspicuously disclosed to the consumer all material terms of the transaction, including—

(A) a description of the goods or services being offered;

(B) the fact that the post-transaction third party seller is not affiliated with the initial merchant, which may include disclosure of the name of the post-transaction third party in a manner that clearly differentiates the post-transaction third party seller from the initial merchant; and

(C) the cost of such goods or services; and

(2) the post-transaction third party seller has received the express informed consent for the charge from the consumer whose credit card, debit card, bank account, or other financial account will be charged by—

(A) obtaining from the consumer—

(i) the full account number of the account to be charged; and

(ii) the consumer's name and address and a means to contact the consumer; and

(B) requiring the consumer to perform an additional affirmative action, such as clicking on a confirmation button or checking a box that indicates the consumer's consent to be charged the amount disclosed.

(b) Prohibition on data-pass used to facilitate certain deceptive Internet sales transactions

It shall be unlawful for an initial merchant to disclose a credit card, debit card, bank account, or other financial account number, or to disclose other billing information that is used to charge a customer of the initial merchant, to any post-transaction third party seller for use in an Internet-based sale of any goods or services from that post-transaction third party seller.

(c) Application with other law

Nothing in this chapter shall be construed to supersede, modify, or otherwise affect the requirements of the Electronic Funds Transfer Act (15 U.S.C. 1693 *et seq.*) or any regulation promulgated thereunder.

(d) Definitions

In this section:

(1) Initial merchant

The term "initial merchant" means a person that has obtained a consumer's billing information directly from the consumer through an Internet transaction initiated by the consumer.

(2) Post-transaction third party seller

The term "post-transaction third party seller" means a person that—

(A) sells, or offers for sale, any good or service on the Internet;

(B) solicits the purchase of such goods or services on the Internet through an initial merchant after the consumer has initiated a transaction with the initial merchant; and

(C) is not—

(i) the initial merchant;

(ii) a subsidiary or corporate affiliate of the initial merchant; or

(iii) a successor of an entity described in clause (i) or (ii).

[Pub. L. No. 111-345, § 3, 124 Stat. 3619 (Dec. 29, 2010)]

15 U.S.C. § 8403.   Negative option marketing on the internet

It shall be unlawful for any person to charge or attempt to charge any consumer for any goods or services sold in a transaction effected on the Internet through a negative option feature (as defined in the Federal Trade Commission's Telemarketing Sales Rule in part 310 of title 16, Code of Federal Regulations), unless the person—

(1) provides text that clearly and conspicuously discloses all material terms of the transaction before obtaining the consumer's billing information;

(2) obtains a consumer's express informed consent before charging the consumer's credit card, debit card, bank account, or other financial account for products or services through such transaction; and

(3) provides simple mechanisms for a consumer to stop recurring charges from being placed on the consumer's credit card, debit card, bank account, or other financial account.

[Pub. L. No. 111-345, § 4, 124 Stat. 3620 (Dec. 29, 2010)]

15 U.S.C. § 8404.   Enforcement by Federal Trade Commission

(a) In general

Violation of this chapter or any regulation prescribed under this chapter shall be treated as a violation of a rule under section 18 of the Federal Trade Commission Act (15 U.S.C. 57a) regarding unfair or deceptive acts or practices. The Federal Trade Commission shall enforce this chapter in the same manner, by the same means, and with the same jurisdiction, powers, and duties as though all applicable terms and provisions of the Federal Trade Commission Act (15 U.S.C. 41 *et seq.*) were incorporated into and made a part of this chapter.

(b) Penalties

Any person who violates this chapter or any regulation prescribed under this chapter shall be subject to the penalties and entitled to the privileges and immunities provided in the Federal Trade Commission Act as though all applicable terms and provisions of the Federal Trade Commission Act were incorporated in and made part of this chapter.

(c) Authority preserved

Nothing in this section shall be construed to limit the authority of the Commission under any other provision of law.

[Pub. L. No. 111-345, § 5, 124 Stat. 3620 (Dec. 29, 2010)]

15 U.S.C. § 8405.   Enforcement by State attorneys general

(a) Right of action

Except as provided in subsection (e), the attorney general of a State, or other authorized State officer, alleging a violation of this chapter or any regulation issued under this chapter that affects or may affect such State or its residents may bring an action on behalf of the residents of the State in any United States district court for the district in which the defendant is found, resides, or transacts business, or wherever venue is proper under section 1391 of Title 28, to obtain appropriate injunctive relief.

(b) Notice to Commission required

A State shall provide prior written notice to the Federal Trade Commission of any civil action under subsection (a) together with a copy of its complaint, except that if it is not feasible for the State to provide such prior notice, the State shall provide such notice immediately upon instituting such action.

(c) Intervention by the Commission

The Commission may intervene in such civil action and upon intervening—

(1) be heard on all matters arising in such civil action; and

(2) file petitions for appeal of a decision in such civil action.

(d) Construction

Nothing in this section shall be construed—

(1) to prevent the attorney general of a State, or other authorized State officer, from exercising the powers conferred on the attorney general, or other authorized State officer, by the laws of such State; or

(2) to prohibit the attorney general of a State, or other authorized State officer, from proceeding in State or Federal court on the basis of an alleged violation of any civil or criminal statute of that State.

(e) Limitation

No separate suit shall be brought under this section if, at the time the suit is brought, the same alleged violation is the subject of a pending action by the Federal Trade Commission or the United States under this chapter.

[Pub. L. No. 111-345, § 5, 124 Stat. 3620 (Dec. 29, 2010)]

Appendix L   Federal Computer Fraud Abuse Act

* * *

18 U.S.C. § 1030.   Fraud and related activity in connection with computers

(a) Whoever—

(1) having knowingly accessed a computer without authorization or exceeding authorized access, and by means of such conduct having obtained information that has been determined by the United States Government pursuant to an Executive order or statute to require protection against unauthorized disclosure for reasons of national defense or foreign relations, or any restricted data, as defined in paragraph y. of section 11 of the Atomic Energy Act of 1954, with reason to believe that such information so obtained could be used to the injury of the United States, or to the advantage of any foreign nation willfully communicates, delivers, transmits, or causes to be communicated, delivered, or transmitted, or attempts to communicate, deliver, transmit or cause to be communicated, delivered, or transmitted the same to any person not entitled to receive it, or willfully retains the same and fails to deliver it to the officer or employee of the United States entitled to receive it;

(2) intentionally accesses a computer without authorization or exceeds authorized access, and thereby obtains—

(A) information contained in a financial record of a financial institution, or of a card issuer as defined in section 1602(n) of title 15, or contained in a file of a consumer reporting agency on a consumer, as such terms are defined in the Fair Credit Reporting Act (15 U.S.C. 1681 *et seq.*);

(B) information from any department or agency of the United States; or

(C) information from any protected computer;

(3) intentionally, without authorization to access any nonpublic computer of a department or agency of the United States, accesses such a computer of that department or agency that is exclusively for the use of the Government of the United States or, in the case of a computer not exclusively for such use, is used by or for the Government of the United States and such conduct affects that use by or for the Government of the United States;

(4) knowingly and with intent to defraud, accesses a protected computer without authorization, or exceeds authorized access, and by means of such conduct furthers the intended fraud and obtains anything of value, unless the object of the fraud and the thing obtained consists only of the use of the computer and the value of such use is not more than $5,000 in any 1-year period;

(5)

(A) knowingly causes the transmission of a program, information, code, or command, and as a result of such conduct, intentionally causes damage without authorization, to a protected computer;

(B) intentionally accesses a protected computer without authorization, and as a result of such conduct, recklessly causes damage; or

(C) intentionally accesses a protected computer without authorization, and as a result of such conduct, causes damage and loss.

(6) knowingly and with intent to defraud traffics (as defined in section 1029) in any password or similar information through which a computer may be accessed without authorization, if—

(A) such trafficking affects interstate or foreign commerce; or

(B) such computer is used by or for the Government of the United States;[1]

_____
1   *Editor's note:* So in original. Probably should be followed by "or".

(7) with intent to extort from any person any money or other thing of value, transmits in interstate or foreign commerce any communication containing any—

(A) threat to cause damage to a protected computer;

(B) threat to obtain information from a protected computer without authorization or in excess of authorization or to impair the confidentiality of information obtained from a protected computer without authorization or by exceeding authorized access; or

(C) demand or request for money or other thing of value in relation to damage to a protected computer, where such damage was caused to facilitate the extortion;

shall be punished as provided in subsection (c) of this section.

(b) Whoever conspires to commit or attempts to commit an offense under subsection (a) of this section shall be punished as provided in subsection (c) of this section.

(c) The punishment for an offense under subsection (a) or (b) of this section is—

(1)

(A) a fine under this title or imprisonment for not more than ten years, or both, in the case of an offense under subsection (a)(1) of this section which does not occur after a conviction for another offense under this section, or an attempt to commit an offense punishable under this subparagraph; and

(B) a fine under this title or imprisonment for not more than twenty years, or both, in the case of an offense under subsection (a)(1) of this section which occurs after a conviction for another offense under this section, or an attempt to commit an offense punishable under this subparagraph;

(2)

(A) except as provided in subparagraph (B), a fine under this title or imprisonment for not more than one year, or both, in the case of an offense under subsection (a)(2), (a)(3), or (a)(6) of this section which does not occur after a conviction for another offense under this section, or an attempt to commit an offense punishable under this subparagraph;

(B) a fine under this title or imprisonment for not more than 5 years, or both, in the case of an offense under subsection (a)(2), or an attempt to commit an offense punishable under this subparagraph, if—

(i) the offense was committed for purposes of commercial advantage or private financial gain;

(ii) the offense was committed in furtherance of any criminal or tortious act in violation of the Constitution or laws of the United States or of any State; or

(iii) the value of the information obtained exceeds $5,000; and

(C) a fine under this title or imprisonment for not more than ten years, or both, in the case of an offense under subsection (a)(2), (a)(3) or (a)(6) of this section which occurs after a conviction for another offense under this section, or an attempt to commit an offense punishable under this subparagraph;

(3)

(A) a fine under this title or imprisonment for not more than five years, or both, in the case of an offense under subsection (a)(4) or (a)(7) of this section which does not occur after a conviction for another offense under this section, or an attempt to commit an offense punishable under this subparagraph; and

(B) a fine under this title or imprisonment for not more than ten years, or both, in the case of an offense under subsection (a)(4) or (a)(7) of this section which occurs after a conviction for another offense under this section, or an attempt to commit an offense punishable under this subparagraph;

(4)

(A) except as provided in subparagraphs (E) and (F), a fine under this title, imprisonment for not more than 5 years, or both, in the case of—

(i) an offense under subsection (a)(5)(B), which does not occur after a conviction for another offense under this section, if the offense caused (or, in the case of an attempted offense, would, if completed, have caused)—

(I) loss to 1 or more persons during any 1-year period (and, for purposes of an investigation, prosecution, or other proceeding brought by the United States only, loss resulting from a related course of conduct affecting 1 or more other protected computers) aggregating at least $5,000 in value;

(II) the modification or impairment, or potential modification or impairment, of the medical examination, diagnosis, treatment, or care of 1 or more individuals;

(III) physical injury to any person;

(IV) a threat to public health or safety;

(V) damage affecting a computer used by or for an entity of the United States Government in furtherance of the administration of justice, national defense, or national security; or

(VI) damage affecting 10 or more protected computers during any 1-year period; or

(ii) an attempt to commit an offense punishable under this subparagraph;

(B) except as provided in subparagraphs (E) and (F), a fine under this title, imprisonment for not more than 10 years, or both, in the case of—

(i) an offense under subsection (a)(5)(A), which does not occur after a conviction for another offense under this section, if the offense caused (or, in the case of an attempted offense, would, if completed, have caused) a harm provided in subclauses (I) through (VI) of subparagraph (A)(i); or

(ii) an attempt to commit an offense punishable under this subparagraph;

(C) except as provided in subparagraphs (E) and (F), a fine under this title, imprisonment for not more than 20 years, or both, in the case of—

(i) an offense or an attempt to commit an offense under subparagraphs (A) or (B) of subsection (a)(5) that occurs after a conviction for another offense under this section; or

(ii) an attempt to commit an offense punishable under this subparagraph;

(D) a fine under this title, imprisonment for not more than 10 years, or both, in the case of—

(i) an offense or an attempt to commit an offense under subsection (a)(5)(C) that occurs after a conviction for another offense under this section; or

(ii) an attempt to commit an offense punishable under this subparagraph;

(E) if the offender attempts to cause or knowingly or recklessly causes serious bodily injury from conduct in violation of subsection (a)(5)(A), a fine under this title, imprisonment for not more than 20 years, or both;

(F) if the offender attempts to cause or knowingly or recklessly causes death from conduct in violation of subsection (a)(5)(A), a fine under this title, imprisonment for any term of years or for life, or both; or

(G) a fine under this title, imprisonment for not more than 1 year, or both, for—

(i) any other offense under subsection (a)(5); or

(ii) an attempt to commit an offense punishable under this subparagraph.

[**(5)** Repealed. Pub. L. 110-326, Title II, § 204(a)(2)(D), Sept. 26, 2008, 122 Stat. 3562]

(d)

(1) The United States Secret Service shall, in addition to any other agency having such authority, have the authority to investigate offenses under this section.

(2) The Federal Bureau of Investigation shall have primary authority to investigate offenses under subsection (a)(1) for any cases involving espionage, foreign counterintelligence, information protected against unauthorized disclosure for reasons of national defense or foreign relations, or Restricted Data (as that term is defined in section 11y of the Atomic Energy Act of 1954 (42 U.S.C. 2014(y)), except for offenses affecting the duties of the United States Secret Service pursuant to section 3056(a) of this title.

(3) Such authority shall be exercised in accordance with an agreement which shall be entered into by the Secretary of the Treasury and the Attorney General.

(e) As used in this section—

(1) the term "computer" means an electronic, magnetic, optical, electrochemical, or other high speed data processing device performing logical, arithmetic, or storage functions, and includes any data storage facility or communications facility directly related to or operating in conjunction with such device, but such term does not include an automated typewriter or typesetter, a portable hand held calculator, or other similar device;

(2) the term "protected computer" means a computer—

(A) exclusively for the use of a financial institution or the United States Government, or, in the case of a computer not exclusively for such use, used by or for a financial institution or the United States Government and the conduct constituting the offense affects that use by or for the financial institution or the Government; or

(B) which is used in or affecting interstate or foreign commerce or communication, including a computer located outside the United States that is used in a manner that affects interstate or foreign commerce or communication of the United States;

(3) the term "State" includes the District of Columbia, the Commonwealth of Puerto Rico, and any other commonwealth, possession or territory of the United States;

(4) the term "financial institution" means—

(A) an institution,[2] with deposits insured by the Federal Deposit Insurance Corporation;

(B) the Federal Reserve or a member of the Federal Reserve including any Federal Reserve Bank;

(C) a credit union with accounts insured by the National Credit Union Administration;

(D) a member of the Federal home loan bank system and any home loan bank;

(E) any institution of the Farm Credit System under the Farm Credit Act of 1971;

(F) a broker-dealer registered with the Securities and Exchange Commission pursuant to section 15 of the Securities Exchange Act of 1934;

(G) the Securities Investor Protection Corporation;

(H) a branch or agency of a foreign bank (as such terms are defined in paragraphs (1) and (3) of section 1(b) of the International Banking Act of 1978); and

(I) an organization operating under section 25 or section 25(a) of the Federal Reserve Act;

(5) the term "financial record" means information derived from any record held by a financial institution pertaining to a customer's relationship with the financial institution;

(6) the term "exceeds authorized access" means to access a computer with authorization and to use such access to obtain or alter information in the computer that the accesser is not entitled so to obtain or alter;

---

2   *Editor's note:* So in original. The comma probably should not appear.

(7) the term "department of the United States" means the legislative or judicial branch of the Government or one of the executive departments enumerated in section 101 of title 5;

(8) the term "damage" means any impairment to the integrity or availability of data, a program, a system, or information;

(9) the term "government entity" includes the Government of the United States, any State or political subdivision of the United States, any foreign country, and any state, province, municipality, or other political subdivision of a foreign country;

(10) the term "conviction" shall include a conviction under the law of any State for a crime punishable by imprisonment for more than 1 year, an element of which is unauthorized access, or exceeding authorized access, to a computer;

(11) the term "loss" means any reasonable cost to any victim, including the cost of responding to an offense, conducting a damage assessment, and restoring the data, program, system, or information to its condition prior to the offense, and any revenue lost, cost incurred, or other consequential damages incurred because of interruption of service; and

(12) the term "person" means any individual, firm, corporation, educational institution, financial institution, governmental entity, or legal or other entity.

(f) This section does not prohibit any lawfully authorized investigative, protective, or intelligence activity of a law enforcement agency of the United States, a State, or a political subdivision of a State, or of an intelligence agency of the United States.

(g) Any person who suffers damage or loss by reason of a violation of this section may maintain a civil action against the violator to obtain compensatory damages and injunctive relief or other equitable relief. A civil action for a violation of this section may be brought only if the conduct involves 1 of the factors set forth in subclauses (I), (II), (III), (IV), or (V) of subsection (c)(4)(A)(i). Damages for a violation involving only conduct described in subsection (c)(4)(A)(i)(I) are limited to economic damages. No action may be brought under this subsection unless such action is begun within 2 years of the date of the act complained of or the date of the discovery of the damage. No action may be brought under this subsection for the negligent design or manufacture of computer hardware, computer software, or firmware.

(h) The Attorney General and the Secretary of the Treasury shall report to the Congress annually, during the first 3 years following the date of the enactment of this subsection, concerning investigations and prosecutions under subsection (a)(5).

(i)

(1) The court, in imposing sentence on any person convicted of a violation of this section, or convicted of conspiracy to violate this section, shall order, in addition to any other sentence imposed and irrespective of any provision of State law, that such person forfeit to the United States—

    (A) such person's interest in any personal property that was used or intended to be used to commit or to facilitate the commission of such violation; and

    (B) any property, real or personal, constituting or derived from, any proceeds that such person obtained, directly or indirectly, as a result of such violation.

(2) The criminal forfeiture of property under this subsection, any seizure and disposition thereof, and any judicial proceeding in relation thereto, shall be governed by the provisions of section 413 of the Comprehensive Drug Abuse Prevention and Control Act of 1970 (21 U.S.C. 853), except subsection (d) of that section.

(j) For purposes of subsection (*i*), the following shall be subject to forfeiture to the United States and no property right shall exist in them:

(1) Any personal property used or intended to be used to commit or to facilitate the commission of any violation of this section, or a conspiracy to violate this section.

(2) Any property, real or personal, which constitutes or is derived from proceeds traceable to any violation of this section, or a conspiracy to violate this section[3]

[*Added by* Pub. L. No. 98-473, tit. II, § 2102(a), 98 Stat. 2190 (Oct. 12, 1984), *and amended by* Pub. L. No. 99-474, § 2, 100 Stat. 1213 (Oct. 16, 1986); Pub. L. No. 100-690, tit. VII, § 7065, 102 Stat. 4404 (Nov. 18, 1988); Pub. L. No. 101-73, tit. IX, § 962(a)(5), 103 Stat. 502 (Aug. 9, 1989); Pub. L. No. 101-647, tit. XII, § 1205(e), tit. XXV, § 2597(j), tit. XXXV, § 3533, 104 Stat. 4831, 4910, 4925 (Nov. 29, 1990); Pub. L. No. 103-322, tit. XXIX, § 290001(b) to (f), 108 Stat. 2097–2099 (Sept. 13, 1994); Pub. L. No. 104-294, tit. II, § 201, tit. VI, § 604(b)(36), 110 Stat. 3491, 3508 (Oct. 11, 1996); Pub. L. No. 107-56, tit. V, § 506(a), tit. VIII, § 814, 115 Stat. 366, 382 (Oct. 26, 2001); Pub. L. No. 107-273, tit. IV, §§ 4002(b)(1), (12), 4005(a)(3), (d)(3), 116 Stat. 1807, 1808, 1812, 1813 (Nov. 2, 2002); Pub. L. No. 107-296, tit. II, § 225(g), 116 Stat. 2158 (Nov. 25, 2002); Pub. L. No. 110-326, tit. II, §§ 203, 204(a), 205–208, 122 Stat. 3561, 3563 (Sept. 26, 2008)]

* * *

---

3 *Editor's note:* So in original. A period probably should appear.

Index